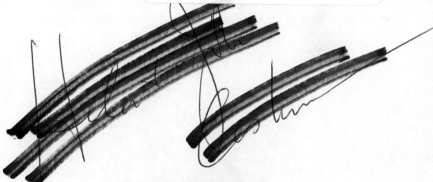

An Anthology
of Devotional
Literature

An Anthology of Devotional Literature

Thomas S. Kepler, Compiler

BAKER BOOK HOUSE
Grand Rapids, Michigan

PHOTOLITHOPRINTED BY CUSHING - MALLOY, INC.
ANN ARBOR, MICHIGAN, UNITED STATES OF AMERICA
1977

To

J. T. K.
E. L. T.

In
Memory of

R. W. T.
O. L. K.

PREFACE

There is only one sorrow, not to be a saint," said Léon Bloy. After several years of concentrated study of the classical devotional writings of the Christian centuries I agree with him. Among the contributors to the devotional life of the Church I have discovered anew the "fellowship of the saints." I have met afresh Thomas à Kempis, Francis of Assisi, Brother Lawrence; have made a closer friendship with Dionysius the Areopagite, Lancelot Andrewes, Blessed Henry Suso; have admired more deeply Teresa of Avila, William Law, John of the Cross; have discovered new spiritual friends in John Comenius, Isaac of Nineveh, Rulman Merswin, Elizabeth Rowe; have found spiritual vitality in the contemporary devotional writings of Thomas Kelly, Rufus Jones, Muriel Lester, Gerald Heard.

Although these men and women are of different backgrounds, come from diverse countries, live in various centuries, and face dissimilar problems, they speak a common language, the language of the Spirit, by which they have learned how to "practice the presence of God." This "fellowship of the saints" has taught me a lesson not to be forgotten: either these "saints" were under an illusion—and I do not believe they were—or else many of us are missing the "feast of the Kingdom" which they have enjoyed so thoroughly! Do we not too often satisfy our spiritual hunger with crumbs from the table of God, when we might, like the saints, richly participate in the banquet which God so freely offers us?

The term "saint" is used by different people with diverse connotations. Some mean by "saints" those men and women who have become canonized for their holiness; they are now in an exalted place in heaven and entitled to a place of veneration on earth. Others use the term "saint" for people who have attained a high state of holy living; usually they refer to these spiritual geniuses as "saintly" rather than labeling them "saints." In using the term I have reserved three general qualifications for "canonizing" men and women in this anthology: (1) Their interests must have concentrated on the life of prayer and devotion. (2) They must have left among their writings significant interpretations of the spiritual life. (3) They must have written in prose rather than in poetry—an anthology of poet-mystics is a study by itself.

Two writers especially, Baron von Hügel and Douglas Steere, have helped me to appreciate the standards by which a "saint" should be judged. Baron von Hügel once told Rufus Jones that saints fulfill four conditions of life:

He, or as is more often the case, *she*, must have been throughout life loyal to the Faith of the Church. . . . The person must have been heroic. . . . The person who is to rank as a saint must have been the recipient of powers beyond his ordinary capacities. . . . He must, she must, have been radiant. . . . [The saints] may possibly be wrong about those first three conditions, but they are gloriously right about that fourth condition —a saint must be *radiant*.[1]

Douglas Steere speaks about "The Authority of the Saint" in these words:

What is an "apostle," or if you like, a "saint"? Either term is so alien to our ordinary habits of thought that it needs definition and clarification and illustration. If a "saint" or an "apostle" were defined as a religious genius, the modern mind would be better able to understand it. . . . [However] the apostle or saint, as apostle or saint, is not a genius. . . . He is an apostle only as whatever capacities he possesses are wholly open to use for the purposes of God. He is an apostle by reason of the totality of his abandonment to God. He is an apostle because the supernatural world that impinges

[1] Rufus Jones, *The Radiant Life* (New York: The Macmillan Co., 1944), pp. 4-5.

7

upon the natural has become real enough to reckon on in every calculation of life. An apostle is "just a human being released from the love of self and enslaved by the love of God," and he rejoices in it. The life of an apostle is one where "God and His eternal order have more and more their undivided sway." The only difference between an apostle [or saint] and ourselves is that he has faced and accepted without condition the quiet demand, "Who chooseth me must give and hazard all he hath," and we have not. . . . In an apostle we see exemplified the profound truth of the old maxim that if you want to be good, you must be heroically good.[2]

My appreciation of this "fellowship of the saints" has given me the belief that our age can become God's Kingdom to the degree that men and women can become saints; on the saints must the spiritual leadership of civilization rest. The saints as the "saving remnant" of our era are not necessarily geniuses; rather they are ordinary men and women with spiritual capacities whose divine spark has been fanned into its highest purpose. The life of each Christian saint is conditioned in the following ten ways:

1. His life is saturated with an intense love of the Christian religion as a way of adjusting himself to himself, to his fellow men, to God. He is a "religion-intoxicated" person!

2. He lives with a joyous, radiant, lighthearted freedom, because his life is totally dependent on God. "A saint is a person who has quit worrying about himself," because his life is centered in God.

3. He emulates Christ in everything he does. Each day at dawn he offers a prayer: "May the image of Christ radiate through me this day in every life situation."

4. He freely opens his life to God's agape—redemptive, free-giving love—and as the recipient of God's agape he desires to help the needy, the lost, the unfortunate, the unhappy. He volunteers to bear the burdens of his fellow men

[2] Douglas Steere, On Beginning from Within (2nd ed.; New York: Harper & Bros., 1943), pp. 33-36.

and thus fulfills the spiritual laws of God.

5. He looks upon Christianity as not merely a theoretical ideal; for him it is a practical way of living with individuals in an unchristian society. It is more than an "interim ethic." Like St. Francis, the saint loves "not . . . humanity, but men."

6. He believes that the Kingdom of God can come into history. But it must continue in him as it began in Christ. With Jacques Maritain he concurs that he must "purify the springs of history within his own heart."

7. He has a continuous humility. Like Katherine Mansfield, looking at her writings shortly before her death and saying with beautiful humility, "Not one of these dare I show to God," he feels that his best is always minute as compared with God's majestic and holy perfection.

8. He looks wistfully into the eyes of every person, regardless of race, color, creed, or nation, as a brother in whom lie the potentialities of a Christian saint.

9. He is not one desirous of escaping the world through the art of devotion. Rather he is one who becomes stimulated to use the results of worship to better the world: he knows how to practice the "process of alternation" between worship and social activity. He is a person who can live heroically "in the world" because he has contact with the Source of Life which is about him, yet which is not always clearly evident in the lives of ordinary men and women. Through his intimacy with God's Spirit he has found an energy and a wisdom which teach him to transcend the world. No saint has better expressed this type of experience than Cyprian in a letter to his friend Donatus. Writing seventeen centuries ago from Carthage, North Africa, he has characterized the saint in every age—including the present:

This seems a cheerful world, Donatus, when I view it from this fair garden under the shadow of these vines. But if I climbed some great mountain and looked out over the wide lands, you know very well what I would see. Brigands on the high roads, pirates on the seas, in the amphitheatres men murdered to please applauding crowds, under all roofs misery and selfishness. It is really a bad world, Donatus, an incredibly bad world. Yet in the midst of it I have found a quiet and holy people. They have discovered a joy which is a thousand times better than any pleasure of this sinful life. They are despised and persecuted, but they care not. They have overcome the world. These people, Donatus, are the Christians—and I am one of them.

10. He is, in the words of a child who loved . cathedral windows, "a man the light shines through."

Through the saints in this anthology the light sends its rays in every direction. They are men and women who transmit the light of one who was the Light of the World!

The writings of 137 saints are included in this book. All of the most notable devotional classics which have stood the test of the centuries are, I believe, characterized by representative excerpts—though it is hardly to be hoped that every reader will find all his favorite passages. For the other saints there has been the necessity of selection; even in so large a volume the restriction of space has caused the exclusion of numbers of men and women whose lives and writings make them worthy of this fellowship. Other factors being equal, I have tried to choose excerpts representative of significant periods or schools of religious thought. Particularly in the case of contemporary writings the choice has not been easy; only the long glance back a century from now will tell us which ones have "lived." Nevertheless, the choice was necessary if the anthology was to be complete. Though arbitrary to some extent, it has been made within certain norms. I have tried to choose outstanding representatives of various schools and from these representatives select excerpts which best touch various areas of life. These contemporary writings do at least give one a "feel" of the current religious idiom in its many phases of devotional thought; they also show how the saints of the last nineteen centuries have left their influence upon present-day interpreters.

Selections from the twenty-seven books of the New Testament are not included since those writings by themselves compose an anthology owned by most people.

I admit a utilitarian purpose in bringing these writings together—namely, to help men and women of the twentieth century attain to sainthood. Each selection in the book is the result of a real life situation; thus each one has suggestive value for us today. To make the selections more understandable, I have given for each author a brief biographical sketch revealing something of the situation out of which he wrote. As a further aid to understanding the situation of each, the Appendix carries a chronological list of the saints paralleled with the important events of church history. Those who wish to read further will find in the Chronology the major devotional writings of each contributor; they may also make use of the Bibliography, which lists books of four types: (1) books dealing with the lives and experiences of the saints; (2) books interpreting prayer and worship; (3) books of practical psychological-religious suggestions for the attaining of "sainthood"; (4) devotional aids for developing the life of a saint.

Acknowledgment is due the authors and publishers who have granted permission to reprint copyright material, which includes not only the writings of contemporary and recent authors but also the work of contemporary and recent translators of older writings. Identification of these is included in the introductions to the individual excerpts Titles which I have supplied are enclosed in brackets.

THOMAS S. KEPLER

CONTENTS

THE PATRISTIC PERIOD
THE MARTYRS AND SAINTS CREATE HOLY PLACES

THE DARK AGES
THE SAINTS KEEP CHRISTIANITY ALIVE

THE GOLDEN AGE OF MYSTICISM
AFTER THE DARK AGES THE FELLOWSHIP OF THE SAINTS BEGINS AFRESH

THE SIXTEENTH CENTURY
PROTESTANT SAINTS JOIN THE FELLOWSHIP

THE SEVENTEENTH CENTURY
THE QUIETISTIC TREND LEAVES ITS IMPRESS ON THE SAINTS

THE NINETEENTH CENTURY UNTIL THE CLOSE OF WORLD WAR I

THE FELLOWSHIP INCLUDES MEN OF EVERY HIGH RELIGIOUS INTEREST

CONTENTS

SAINTS IN THE TWENTIETH CENTURY: AFTER WORLD WAR I UNTIL NOW

UPON THE SHOULDERS OF THE SAINTS THE COMING OF THE KINGDOM DEPENDS

APPENDIX

THE PATRISTIC PERIOD

THE MARTYRS AND THE SAINTS CREATE HOLY PLACES

Clement of Rome

(40?-97?)

CLEMENT is described by several early writers as leader of the church at Rome in the later years of the first century, but the accounts differ, and little is definitely known of him. Origen and others since have wished to connect him with the co-worker of Paul mentioned in Phil. 4:3, but his youth at the time makes the identification unlikely. Similarities of his letter to those of Paul may be explained by familiarity with the Pauline writings after they were circulating among the churches.

The First Epistle of Clement to the Corinthians is his only known writing, the so-called "Second Epistle" and other "Clementines" being long ago recognized as from later periods. Written in Greek to the church at Corinth on behalf of the church at Rome about A.D. 96, the letter soon was passed among all the churches, and for three centuries was so highly esteemed that it vied for a place in the New Testament. The letter is an attempt to restore order in the Corinthian church, where some were revolting against the authority of their officers. Clement urges that the Corinthians put away strife and emulate Christ and the saints. Of the sixty-five brief chapters four are reproduced here. The translation is that of Alexander Roberts and James Donaldson in *The Ante-Nicene Fathers* (New York, 1885).

[INSIGHTS INTO CHRISTIAN LOVE]

From *The First Epistle to the Corinthians*

38. LET THE MEMBERS OF THE CHURCH SUBMIT THEMSELVES, AND NO ONE EXALT HIMSELF ABOVE ANOTHER

Let our whole body, then, be preserved in Christ Jesus; and let every one be subject to his neighbour, according to the special gift bestowed upon him. Let the strong not despise the weak, and let the weak show respect unto the strong. Let the rich man provide for the wants of the poor; and let the poor man bless God, because He hath given him one by whom his need may be supplied. Let the wise man display his wisdom, not by [mere] words, but through good deeds. Let the humble not bear testimony to himself, but leave witness to be borne to him by another. Let him that is pure in the flesh not grow proud of it, and boast, knowing that it was another who bestowed on him the gift of continence. Let us consider, then, brethren, of what matter we were made,—who and what manner of beings we came into the world, as it were out of a sepulchre, and from utter darkness. He who made us and fashioned us, having prepared His bountiful gifts for us before we were born, introduced us into His world. Since, therefore, we receive all these things from Him, we ought for everything to give Him thanks; to whom be glory for ever and ever. Amen.

39. THERE IS NO REASON FOR SELF-CONCEIT

Foolish and inconsiderate men, who have neither wisdom nor instruction, mock and deride us, being eager to exalt themselves in their own conceits. For what can a mortal man do? or what strength is there in one made out of the dust? For it is written, "There was no shape before mine eyes, only I heard a sound, and a voice [saying], What then? Shall a man be pure before the Lord? or shall such an one be [counted] blameless in his deeds, seeing He does not confide in His servants, and has charged even His angels with perversity? The heaven is not clean in His sight: how much less they that dwell in houses of clay, of which also we ourselves were made! He smote them as a moth; and from morning even until evening they endure not. Because they could furnish no assistance to themselves, they perished. He breathed upon them, and they died, because they had no wisdom. But call now, if any one will answer thee, or if thou wilt look to any of the holy angels; for wrath destroys the foolish man, and envy killeth him that is in error. I have seen the foolish taking root, but their habitation was presently consumed. Let their sons be far from safety; let them be despised before the gates of those less than themselves, and there shall be none to deliver. For what was prepared for them, the righteous shall eat; and they shall not be delivered from evil.

49. The Praise of Love

Let him who has love in Christ keep the commandments of Christ. Who can describe the [blessed] bond of the love of God? What man is able to tell the excellence of its beauty, as it ought to be told? The height to which love exalts is unspeakable. Love unites us to God. Love covers a multitude of sins. Love beareth all things, is long-suffering in all things. There is nothing base, nothing arrogant in love. Love admits of no schisms: love gives rise to no seditions: love does all things in harmony. By love have all the elect of God been made perfect; without love nothing is well-pleasing to God. In love has the Lord taken us to Himself. On account of the Love he 'bore us, Jesus Christ our Lord gave His blood for us by the will of God; His flesh for our flesh, and His soul for our souls.

56. Let Us Admonish and Correct One Another

Let us then also pray for those who have fallen into any sin, that meekness and humility may be given to them, so that they may submit, not unto us, but to the will of God. For in this way they shall secure a fruitful and perfect remembrance from us, with sympathy for them, both in our prayers to God, and our mention of them to the saints. Let us receive correction, beloved, on account of which no one should feel displeased. Those exhortations by which we admonish one another are both good [in themselves] and highly profitable, for they tend to unite us to the will of God. For thus saith the holy Word: "The Lord hath severely chastened me, yet hath not given me over to death." "For whom the Lord loveth He chasteneth, and scourgeth every son whom He receiveth." "The righteous," saith it, "shall chasten me in mercy, and reprove me; but let not the oil of sinners make fat my head." And again he saith, "Blessed is the man whom the Lord reproveth, and reject not thou the warning of the Almighty. For He causes sorrow, and again restores [to gladness]; He woundeth, and His hands make whole. He shall deliver thee in six troubles, yea, in the seventh no evil shall touch thee. In famine He shall rescue thee from death, and in war He shall free thee from the power of the sword. From the scourge of the tongue will He hide thee, and thou shalt not fear when evil cometh. Thou shalt laugh at the unrighteous and the wicked, and shalt not be afraid of the beasts of the field. For the wild beasts shall be at peace with thee: then shalt thou know that thy house shall be in peace, and the habitation of thy tabernacle shall not fail. Thou shalt know also that thy seed shall be great, and thy children like the grass of the field. And thou shalt come to the grave like ripened corn which is reaped in its season, or like a heap of the threshing-floor which is gathered together at the proper time." Ye see, beloved, that protection is afforded to those that are chastened of the Lord; for since God is good, He corrects us, that we may be admonished by His holy chastisement.

Justin Martyr

(110?-165?)

"STRAIGHTWAY a flame was kindled in my soul; and a love of the prophets, and of those men who are friends of Christ, possessed me; . . . I found this philosophy alone to be safe and profitable." In these words lie the basis of Justin's religious experience, a conviction that Christianity is the most true and divine of all philosophies.

Justin was born in Samaria, was reared in a wealthy Roman family, and was well educated. In his extensive travels he was able to come into contact with various types of religious and philosophic thought. After following for a time the ideas of Socrates and Plato, he found his final answer to life's problems in Christ. He was active in Ephesus, then settled at Rome, where he became a Christian teacher. In Rome adherents of certain schools of philosophers, especially the Cynics, conspired against him and brought about his martyrdom. He was one of the most heroic apologists of the Christian faith against Roman hostilities.

On the Sole Government of God, presented here in its entirety, was apparently written amid Justin's difficulties at Rome. In it he draws upon a number of non-Christian writers to prove the unity of God and the falsity of other "deities." The translation from the Greek is that of G. Reith in The Ante-Nicene Fathers (New York, 1885).

ON THE SOLE GOVERNMENT OF GOD

I. OBJECT OF THE AUTHOR

Although human nature at first received a union of intelligence and safety to discern the truth, and the worship due to the one Lord of all, yet envy, insinuating the excellence of human greatness, turned men away to the making of idols; and this superstitious custom, after continuing for a long period, is handed down to the majority as if it were natural and true. It is the part of a lover of man, or rather of a lover of God, to remind men who have neglected it of that which they ought to know. For the truth is of itself sufficient to show forth, by means of those things which are contained under the pole of heaven, the order [instituted by] Him who has created them. But forgetfulness having taken possession of the minds of men, through the long-suffering of God, has acted recklessly in transferring to mortals the name which is applicable to the only true God; and from the few the infection of sin spread to the many, who were blinded by popular usage to the knowledge of that which was lasting and unchangeable. For the men of former generations, who instituted private and public rites in honour of such as were more powerful, caused forgetfulness of the Catholic faith to take possession of their posterity; but I, as I have just stated, along with a God-loving mind, shall employ the speech of one who loves man, and set it before those who have intelligence, which all ought to have who are privileged to observe the administration of the universe, so that they should worship unchangeably Him who knows all things. This I shall do, not by mere display of words, but by altogether using demonstration drawn from the old poetry in Greek literature, and from writings very common amongst all. For from these the famous men who have handed down idol-worship as law to the multitudes, shall be taught and convicted by their own poets and literature of great ignorance.

II. Testimonies to the Unity of God

First, then, Aeschylus, in expounding the arrangement of his work, expressed himself also as follows respecting the only God:

> Afar from mortals place the holy God,
> Nor ever think that He, like to thyself,
> In fleshly robes is clad; for all unknown
> Is the great God to such a worm as thou.
> Divers similitudes He bears; at times
> He seems as a consuming fire that burns
> Unsated; now like water, then again
> In sable folds of darkness shrouds Himself.
> Nay, even the very beasts of earth reflect
> His sacred image; whilst the wind, clouds, rain,
> The roll of thunder and the lightning flash,
> Reveal to men their great and sovereign Lord.
> Before Him sea and rocks, with every fount,
> And all the water floods, in reverence bend;
> And as they gaze upon His awful face,
> Mountains and earth, with the profoundest depths
> Of ocean, and the highest peaks of hills,
> Tremble: for He is Lord Omnipotent;
> And this the glory is of God Most High.

But he was not the only man initiated in the knowledge of God; for Sophocles also thus describes the nature of the only Creator of all things, the One God:

> There is one God, in truth there is but one,
> Who made the heavens and the broad earth beneath,
> The glancing waves of ocean, and the winds;
> But many of us mortals err in heart,
> And set up, for a solace in our woes,
> Images of the gods in stone and brass,
> Or figures carved in gold or ivory;
> And, furnishing for these, our handiworks,

> Both sacrifice and rite magnificent,
> We think that thus we do a pious work.

And Philemon also, who published many explanations of ancient customs, shares in the knowledge of the truth; and thus he writes:

> Tell me what thoughts of God we should conceive?
> One, all things seeing, yet Himself unseen.

Even Orpheus, too, who introduces three hundred and sixty gods, will bear testimony in my favour from the tract called *Diathecae*, in which he appears to repent of his error by writing the following:

> I'll speak to those who lawfully may hear;
> All others, ye profane, now close the doors!
> And, O Musaeus, hearken thou to me,
> Who offspring art of the light-bringing moon.
> The words I tell thee now are true indeed,
> And if thou former thoughts of mine hast seen,
> Let them not rob thee of the blessed life;
> But rather turn the depths of thine own heart
> Unto that place where light and knowledge dwell.
> Take thou the word divine to guide thy steps;
> And walking well in the straight certain path,
> Look to the one and universal King,
> One, self-begotten, and the only One
> Of whom all things, and we ourselves, are sprung.
> All things are open to His piercing gaze,
> While He Himself is still invisible;
> Present in all His works, though still unseen,
> He gives to mortals evil out of good,
> Sending both chilling wars and tearful griefs;
> And other than the Great King there is none.
> The clouds for ever settle round His throne;
> And mortal eyeballs in mere mortal eyes
> Are weak to see Jove, reigning over all.
> He sits established in the brazen heavens

Upon His throne; and underneath His
feet
He treads the earth, and stretches His
right hand
To all the ends of ocean, and around
Tremble the mountain ranges, and the
streams,
The depths, too, of the blue and hoary
sea.

He speaks indeed as if he had been an
eye-witness of God's greatness. And
Pythagoras agrees with him when he
writes:

Should one in boldness say, Lo, I am
God!
Besides the One—Eternal—Infinite,
Then let him from the throne he has
usurped
Put forth his power and form another
globe,
Such as we dwell in, saying, This is
mine.
Nor only so, but in this new domain
For ever let him dwell. If this he can,
Then verily he is a god proclaimed.

III. TESTIMONIES TO A FUTURE JUDGMENT

Then further concerning Him, that
He alone is powerful, both to institute
judgment on the deeds performed in life,
and on the ignorance of the Deity [dis-
played by men], I can adduce witnesses
from your own ranks; and first Sophocles, who speaks as follows:

That time of times shall come, shall
surely come,
When from the golden ether down
shall fall
Fire's teeming treasure, and in burning
flames
All things of earth and heaven shall be
consumed;
And then, when all creation is dissolved,
The sea's last wave shall die upon the
shore,
The bald earth stript of trees, the burning air
No winged thing upon its breast shall
bear.
There are two roads to Hades, well we
know;
By this the righteous, and by that the
bad,
On to their separate fates shall tend;
and He,

Who all things had destroyed, shall all
things save.

And Philemon again:

Think'st thou, Nicostratus, the dead, who
here
Enjoyed whate'er of good life offers
man,
Escape the notice of Divinity,
As if they might forgotten be of Him?
Nay, there's an eye of Justice watching
all;
For if the good and bad find the same
end,
Then go thou, rob, steal, plunder, at
thy will,
Do all the evil that to thee seems good.
Yet be not thou deceived; for under-
neath
There is a throne and place of judgment
set,
Which God the Lord of all shall oc-
cupy;
Whose name is terrible, nor shall I dare
To breathe it forth in feeble human
speech.

And Euripides:

Not grudgingly he gives a lease of life,
That we the holders may be fairly
judged;
And if a mortal man doth think to hide
His daily guilt from the keen eye of
God,
It is an evil thought; so if perchance
He meets with leisure-taking Justice,
she
Demands him as her lawful prisoner:
But many of you hastily commit
A twofold sin, and say there is no God.
But, ah! there is; there is. Then see that
he
Who, being wicked, prospers, may re-
deem
The time so precious, else hereafter
waits
For him the due reward of punish-
ment.

IV. GOD DESIRES NOT SACRIFICES, BUT
RIGHTEOUSNESS

And that God is not appeased by the
libations and incense of evil-doers, but
awards vengeance in righteousness to
each one, Philemon again shall bear testimony to me:

If any one should dream, O Pamphilus,
By sacrifice of bulls or goats—nay, then,

By Jupiter—of any such like things;
Or by presenting gold or purple robes,
Or images of ivory and gems;
If thus he thinks he may propitiate God,
He errs, and shows himself a silly one.
But let him rather useful be, and good,
Committing neither theft nor lustful
    deeds,
Nor murder foul, for earthly riches'
    sake.
Let him of no man covet wife or child,
His splendid house, his wide-spread
    property,
His maiden, or his slave born in his
    house,
His horses, or his cattle, or his beeves.
Nay, covet not a pin, O Pamphilus,
For God, close by you, sees whate'er
    you do.
He ever with the wicked man is wroth,
But in the righteous takes a pleasure
    still,
Permitting him to reap fruit of his toil,
And to enjoy the bread his sweat has
    won.
But being righteous, see thou pay thy
    vows,
And unto God the giver offer gifts.
Place thy adorning not in outward
    shows,
But in an inward purity of heart;
Hearing the thunder then, thou shalt
    not fear,
Nor shalt thou flee, O master, at its
    voice,
For thou art conscious of no evil deed,
And God, close by you, sees whate'er
    you do.

Again, Plato, in *Timaeus*, says: "But if any one on consideration should actually institute a rigid inquiry, he would be ignorant of the distinction between the human and the divine nature; because God mingles many things up into one, [and again is able to dissolve one into many things,] seeing that He is endued with knowledge and power; but no man either is, or ever shall be, able to perform any of these."

V. The Vain Pretensions of False Gods

But concerning those who think that they shall share the holy and perfect name, which some have received by a vain tradition as if they were gods, Menander in the *Auriga* says:

If there exists a god who walketh out
With an old woman, or who enters in
By stealth to houses through the fold-
    ing-doors,
He ne'er can please me; nay, but only he
Who stays at home, a just and righteous
    God,
To give salvation to His worshippers.

The same Menander, in the *Sacerdos*, says:

There is no God, O woman, that can
    save
One man by another; if indeed a man,
With sound of tinkling cymbals, charm
    a god
Where'er he listeth, then assuredly
He who doth so is much the greater
    god.
But these, O Rhode, are but the cun-
    ning schemes
Which daring men of intrigue, un-
    abashed,
Invent to earn themselves a livelihood,
And yield a laughing-stock unto the
    age.

Again, the same Menander, stating his opinion about those who are received as gods, proving rather that they are not so, says:

Yea, if I this beheld, I then should wish
That back to me again my soul re-
    turned.
For tell me where, O Getas, in the
    world
'Tis possible to find out righteous gods?

And in the *Depositum*:

There's an unrighteous judgment, as it
    seems,
Even with the gods.

And Euripides the tragedian, in *Orestes*, says:

Apollo having caused by his command
The murder of the mother, knoweth not
What honesty and justice signify.
We serve the gods, whoever they may
    be;
But from the central regions of the earth
You see Apollo plainly gives response
To mortals, and whate'er he says we do.
I him obeyed, when she that bore me fell
Slain by my hand: *he* is the wicked man.
Then slay him, for 'twas he that sinned,
    not I.
What could I do? Think you not that
    the god

Should free me from the blame which I
do bear?

The same also in *Hippolytus*:

But on these points the gods do not
judge right.

And in *Ion*:

But in the daughter of Erechtheus
What interest have I? for that pertains
Not unto such as me. But when I come
With golden vessels for libations, I
The dew shall sprinkle, and yet needs
must warn
Apollo of his deeds; for when he weds
Maidens by force, the children secretly
Begotten he betrays, and then neglects
When dying. Thus not you; but while
you may
Always pursue the virtues, for the gods
Will surely punish men of wickedness.
How is it right that you, who have pre-
scribed
Laws for men's guidance, live unright-
eously?
But ye being absent, I shall freely speak,
And ye to men shall satisfaction give
For marriage forced, thou Neptune,
Jupiter,
Who over heaven presides. The temples
ye
Have emptied, while injustice ye repay.
And though ye laud the prudent to the
skies,
Yet have ye filled your hands with
wickedness.
No longer is it right to call men ill
If they do imitate the sins of gods;
Nay, evil let their teachers rather be.

And in *Archelaus*:

Full oft, my son, do gods mankind per-
plex.

And in *Bellerophon*:

They are no gods, who do not what is
right.

And again in the same:

Gods reign in heaven most certainly,
says one;
But it is false,—yea, false: and let not
him
Who speaks thus, be so foolish as to use
Ancient tradition, or to pay regard
Unto my words: but with unclouded
eye
Behold the matter in its clearest light.

Power absolute, I say, robs men of life
And property; transgresses plighted
faith;
Nor spares even cities, but with cruel
hand
Despoils and devastates them ruthlessly.
But they that do these things have more
success
Than those who live a gentle pious life;
And cities small, I know, which rever-
ence gods,
Submissive bend before the many spears
Of larger impious ones; yea, and me-
thinks
If any man lounge idly, and abstain
From working with his hands for suste-
nance,
Yet pray the gods; he very soon will
know
If they from his misfortunes will avert.

And Menander in *Diphilus*:

Therefore ascribe we praise and honour
great
To Him who Father is, and Lord of all;
Sole maker and preserver of mankind,
And who with all good thinks our earth
has stored.

The same also in the *Piscatores*:

For I deem that which nourishes my life
Is God; but he whose custom 'tis to meet
The wants of men,—He needs not at our
hands
Renewed supplies, Himself being all in
all.

The same in the *Fratres*:

God ever is intelligence to those
Who righteous are: so wisest men have
thought.

And in the *Tibicinae*:

Good reason finds a temple in all things
Wherein to worship; for what is the
mind,
But just the voice of God within us
placed?

And the tragedian in *Phrixus*:

But if the pious and the impious
Share the same lot, how could we think
it just,
If Jove, the best, judges not uprightly?

In *Philoctetes*:

You see how honourable gain is deemed
Even to the gods; and how he is admired

Whose shrine is laden most with yellow
 gold.
What, then, doth hinder thee, since it
 is good
To be like gods, from thus accepting
 gain?

In *Hecuba*:

O Jupiter! whoever thou mayest be,
Of whom except in word all knowledge fails;

and:

Jupiter, whether thou art indeed
A great necessity, or the mind of man,
I worship thee!

VI. We Should Acknowledge One Only God

Here, then, is a proof of virtue, and of
a mind loving prudence, to recur to the
communion of the unity, and to attach
one's self to prudence for salvation, and
make choice of the better things according to the free-will placed in man; and
not to think that those who are possessed
of human passions are lords of all, when
they shall not appear to have even equal
power with men. For in Homer, Demodocus says he is self-taught—

God inspired me with strains—

though he is a mortal. Aesculapius and
Apollo are taught to heal by Chiron the
Centaur,—a very novel thing indeed, for
gods to be taught by a man. What need
I speak of Bacchus, who the poet says is
mad? or of Hercules, who he says is unhappy? What need to speak of Mars and
Venus, the leaders of adultery; and by
means of all these to establish the proof
which has been undertaken? For if some
one, in ignorance, should imitate the
deeds which are said to be divine, he
would be reckoned among impure men,
and a stranger to life and humanity; and
if any one does so knowingly, he will
have a plausible excuse for escaping
vengeance, by showing that imitation of
godlike deeds of audacity is no sin. But
if any one should blame these deeds, he
will take away their well-known names,
and not cover them up with specious and
plausible words. It is necessary, then, to
accept the true and invariable Name, not
proclaimed by my words only, but by
the words of those who have introduced
us to the elements of learning, in order
that we may not, by living idly in this
present state of existence, not only as
those who are ignorant of the heavenly
glory, but also as having proved ourselves ungrateful, render our account to
the Judge.

Clement of Alexandria

(150?-220?)

AMONG the Christian Gnostics of Alexandria, "the second Athens," who attempted to wed philosophy to Christianity and made the city for a time the intellectual center of Christendom, Clement stands next to his distinguished pupil Origen. Little is known of his life, but one may guess that he was born in Athens into a family wealthy enough to give him the best available education in Greek literature and philosophy. After his conversion he was able to travel in Greece, Egypt, Italy, and Palestine in his eagerness to learn from the most eminent Christian teachers. Of these he chose to remain with Pantaenus, whom he succeeded about 190 as head of the catechetical school in Alexandria. After thirteen years he was forced to flee during Severus' persecution, and the rest of his life was spent in obscurity, probably in Palestine and Syria.

Of Clement's several writings, all in Greek, the *Miscellanies* (*Stromateis*) is the most important. Written in eight books at intervals during the last years of his career in Alexandria, it consists of discussions of a variety of subjects well deserving the title, but generally bearing on the theme that the highest unity with God is through knowledge. The following excerpt includes chapters xix and xx from Book I and chapter ii from Book II in the translation by Wilson from *The Ante-Nicene Fathers* (New York, 1885).

[THE PHILOSOPHIC APPROACH TO DIVINE TRUTH]

From *Miscellanies*

THAT THE PHILOSOPHERS HAVE ATTAINED TO SOME PORTION OF TRUTH

Since, then, the Greeks are testified to have laid down some true opinions, we may from this point take a glance at the testimonies. Paul, in the Acts of the Apostles, is recorded to have said to the Areopagites, "I perceive that ye are more than ordinarily religious. For as I passed by, and beheld your devotions, I found an altar with the inscription, To The Unknown God. Whom therefore ye ignorantly worship, Him declare I unto you. God, that made the world and all things therein, seeing that He is Lord of heaven and earth, dwelleth not in temples made with hands; neither is worshipped with men's hands, as though He needed anything, seeing He giveth to all life, and breath, and all things; and hath made of one blood all nations of men to dwell on all the face of the earth, and hath determined the times before appointed, and the bounds of their habitation; that they should seek God, if haply they might feel after Him, and find Him; though He be not far from every one of us: for in Him we live, and move, and have our being; as certain also of your own poets have said, For we also are His offspring." Whence it is evident that the apostle, by availing himself of poetical examples from the *Phenomena* of Aratus, approves of what had been well spoken by the Greeks; and intimates that, by the unknown God, God the Creator was in a roundabout way worshipped by the Greeks; but that it was necessary by positive knowledge to apprehend and learn Him by the Son. "Wherefore, then, I send thee to the Gentiles," it is said, "to open their eyes, and to turn them from darkness to light, and from the power of Satan unto God; that they may receive forgiveness of sins, and inheritance among them that are sanctified by faith which is in Me." Such, then, are the eyes of the blind which are opened. The knowledge of the Father by the Son is the comprehension of the "Greek circumlocution;" and to turn from the power of Satan is to change from sin, through which bondage was produced. We do not, indeed, receive absolutely all philosophy, but that of which Socrates speaks in Plato. "For there are (as they say) in the mysteries many bearers of the thyrsus, but few bacchanals;" meaning, "that many are called, but few chosen." He accordingly plainly adds: "These, in my opinion, are none else than those who have philosophized right; to belong to whose number, I myself have left nothing undone in life, as far as I could, but have endeavoured in every way. Whether we have endeavoured rightly and achieved aught, we shall know when we have gone there, if God will, a little afterwards." Does he not then seem to declare from the Hebrew Scriptures the righteous man's hope, through faith, after death? And in *Demodocus* (if that is really the work of Plato): "And do not imagine that I call it philosophizing to spend life pottering about the arts, or learning many things, but something different; since I, at least, would consider this a disgrace." For he knew, I reckon, "that the knowledge of many things does not educate the mind," according to Heraclitus. And in the fifth book of the *Republic*, he says, " 'Shall we then call all these, and the others which study such things, and those who apply themselves to the meaner arts, philosophers?' 'By no means,' I said, 'but like philosophers.' 'And whom,' said he, 'do you call true?' 'Those,' said I, 'who delight in the contemplation of truth. For philosophy is not in geometry, with its postulates and hypotheses; nor in music, which is conjectural; nor in astronomy, crammed full of physical, fluid, and probable causes. But the knowledge of the good and truth itself are requisite,—what is good being one thing, and the ways to the good another.' " So that he does not allow that the curriculum of training

suffices for the good, but co-operates in rousing and training the soul to intellectual objects. Whether, then, they say that the Greeks gave forth some utterances of the true philosophy by accident, it is the accident of a divine administration (for no one will, for the sake of the present argument with us, deify chance); or by good fortune, good fortune is not unforeseen. Or were one, on the other hand, to say that the Greeks possessed a natural conception of these things, we know the one Creator of nature; just as we also call righteousness natural; or that they had a common intellect, let us reflect who is its father, and what righteousness is in the mental economy. For were one to name "prediction," and assign as its cause "combined utterance," he specifies forms of prophecy. Further, others will have it that some truths were uttered by the philosophers, in appearance.

The divine apostle writes accordingly respecting us: "For now we see as through a glass;" knowing ourselves in it by reflection, and simultaneously contemplating, as we can, the efficient cause, from that, which, in us, is divine. For it is said, "Having seen thy brother, thou hast seen thy God:" methinks that now the Saviour God is declared to us. But after the laying aside of the flesh, "face to face,"—then definitely and comprehensively, when the heart becomes pure. And by reflection and direct vision, those among the Greeks who have philosophized accurately, see God. For such, through our weakness, are our true views, as images are seen in the water, and as we see things through pellucid and transparent bodies. Excellently therefore Solomon says: "He who soweth righteousness, worketh faith." "And there are those who, sowing their own, make increase." And again: "Take care of the verdure on the plain, and thou shalt cut grass and gather ripe hay, that thou mayest have sheep for clothing." You see how care must be taken for external clothing and for keeping. "And thou shalt intelligently know the souls of thy flock." "For when the Gentiles, which have not the law, do by nature the things contained in the law, these, having not the law, are a law unto themselves; uncircumcision observing the precepts of the law," according to the apostle, both before the law and before the advent. As if making comparison of those addicted to philosophy with those called heretics, the Word most clearly says: "Better is a friend that is near, than a brother that dwelleth afar off." "And he who relies on falsehoods, feeds on the winds, and pursues winged birds." I do not think that philosophy directly declares the Word, although in many instances philosophy attempts and persuasively teaches us probable arguments, but it assails the sects. Accordingly it is added: "For he hath forsaken the ways of his own vineyard, and wandered in the tracks of his own husbandry." Such are the sects which deserted the primitive Church. Now he who has fallen into heresy passes through an arid wilderness, abandoning the only true God, destitute of God, seeking waterless water, reaching an uninhabited and thirsty land, collecting sterility with his hands. And those destitute of prudence, that is, those involved in heresies, "I enjoin," remarks Wisdom, saying, "Touch sweetly stolen bread and the sweet water of theft;" the Scripture manifestly applying the terms bread and water to nothing else but to those heresies, which employ bread and water in the oblation, not according to the canon of the Church. For there are those who celebrate the Eucharist with mere water. "But begone, stay not in her place:" *place* is the synagogue, not the Church. He calls it by the equivocal name, *place*. Then He subjoins: "For so shalt thou pass through the water of another;" reckoning heretical baptism not proper and true water. "And thou shalt pass over another's river," that rushes along and sweeps down to the sea; into which he is cast who, having diverged from the stability which is according to truth, rushes back into the heathenish and tumultous waves of life.

IN WHAT RESPECT PHILOSOPHY CONTRIBUTES TO THE COMPREHENSION OF DIVINE TRUTH

As many men drawing down the ship, cannot be called many causes, but one cause consisting of many;—for each individual by himself is not the cause of the ship being drawn, but along with the rest;—so also philosophy, being the search for truth, contributes to the comprehension of truth; not as being the cause of comprehension, but a cause along with other things, and co-operator; perhaps also a joint cause. And as the several virtues are causes of the happiness of one individual; and as both the sun, and the fire, and the bath, and clothing are of one getting warm: so while truth is one, many things contribute to its investigation. But its discovery is by the Son. If then we consider, virtue is, in power, one. But it is the case, that when exhibited in some things, it is called prudence, in others temperance, and in others manliness or righteousness. By the same analogy, while truth is one, in geometry there is the truth of geometry; in music, that of music; and in the right philosophy, there will be Hellenic truth. But that is the only authentic truth, unassailable, in which we are instructed by the Son of God. In the same way we say, that the drachma being one and the same, when given to the shipmaster, is called the fare; to the tax-gatherer, tax; to the landlord, rent; to the teacher, fees; to the seller, an earnest. And each, whether it be virtue or truth, called by the same name, is the cause of its own peculiar effect alone; and from the blending of them arises a happy life. For we are not made happy by names alone, when we say that a good life is happiness, and that the man who is adorned in his soul with virtue is happy. But if philosophy contributes remotely to the discovery of truth, by reaching, by diverse essays, after the knowledge which touches close on the truth, the knowledge possessed by us, it aids him who aims at grasping it, in accordance with the Word, to apprehend knowledge. But the Hellenic truth is distinct from that held by us (although it has got the same name), both in respect of extent of knowledge, certainly of demonstration, divine power, and the like. For we are taught of God, being instructed in the truly "sacred letters" by the Son of God. Whence those, to whom we refer, influence souls not in the way we do, but by different teaching. And if, for the sake of those who are fond of fault-finding, we must draw a distinction, by saying that philosophy is a concurrent and co-operating cause of true apprehension, being the search for truth, then we shall avow it to be a preparatory training for the enlightened man; not assigning as the cause that which is but the joint-cause; nor as the upholding cause, what is merely co-operative; nor giving to philosophy the place of a *sine qua non*. Since almost all of us, without training in arts and sciences, and the Hellenic philosophy, and some even without learning at all, through the influence of a philosophy divine and barbarous, and by power, have through faith received the word concerning God, trained by self-operating wisdom. But that which acts in conjunction with something else, being of itself incapable of operating by itself, we describe as co-operating and concausing, and say that it becomes a cause only in virtue of its being a joint-cause, and receives the name of cause only in respect of its concurring with something else, but that it cannot by itself produce the right effect.

Although at one time philosophy justified the Greeks, not conducting them to that entire righteousness to which it is ascertained to co-operate, as the first and second flight of steps help you in your ascent to the upper room, and the grammarian helps the philosopher. Not as if by its abstraction, the perfect Word would be rendered incomplete, or truth perish; since also sight, and hearing, and the voice contribute to truth, but it is the mind which is the appropriate faculty for knowing it. But of those things which co-operate, some contribute a greater amount of power; some, a less. Perspicuity accordingly aids in the communication of truth, and logic in preventing us from falling under the heresies by which we are assailed. But the teaching, which is according to the Saviour, is complete in itself and without defect, being "the power and wisdom of God;" and the Hellenic philosophy does not, by its approach, make the truth more powerful; but rendering powerless the assault of sophistry against it, and frustrating the treacherous plots laid against the truth, is said to be the proper "fence and wall of the vineyard." And the truth which is according to faith is as necessary for life as bread; while the preparatory discipline is like sauce and sweetmeats. "At the end of the dinner, the dessert is pleasant," according to the Theban Pindar. And the Scripture has expressly said, "The innocent will become wiser by understanding, and the wise will receive knowledge." "And he that speaketh of himself," saith the Lord, "seeketh his own glory; but He that seeketh His glory that sent Him is true, and there is no unrighteousness in Him." On the other hand, therefore, he who appropriates what belongs to the barbarians, and vaunts it is his own, does wrong, increasing his own glory and falsifying the truth. It is such an one that is by Scripture called a "thief." It is therefore said, "Son, be not a liar; for falsehood leads to theft." Nevertheless the thief possesses really, what he has possessed himself of dishonestly, whether it be gold, or silver, or speech, or dogma. The ideas, then, which they have stolen, and which are partially true, they know by conjecture and necessary logical deduction: on becoming disciples, therefore, they will know them with intelligent apprehension.

THE KNOWLEDGE OF GOD CAN BE ATTAINED ONLY THROUGH FAITH

"Be not elated on account of thy wisdom," say the Proverbs. "In all thy ways acknowledge her, that she may direct thy ways, and that thy foot may not stumble." By these remarks he means to show that our deeds ought to be conformable to reason, and to manifest further that we ought to select and possess what is useful out of all culture. Now the ways of wisdom are various that lead right to the way of truth. Faith is the way. "Thy foot shall not stumble" is said with reference to some who seem to oppose the one divine administration of Providence. Whence it is added, "Be not wise in thine own eyes," according to the impious ideas which revolt against the administration of God. "But fear God," who alone is powerful. Whence it follows as a consequence that we are not to oppose God. The sequel especially teaches clearly, that "the fear of God is departure from evil;" for it is said, "and depart from all evil." Such is the discipline of wisdom ("for whom the Lord loveth He chastens"), causing pain in order to produce understanding, and restoring to peace and immortality. Accordingly, the Barbarian philosophy, which we follow, is in reality perfect and true. And so it is said in the book of Wisdom: "For He hath given me the unerring knowledge of things that exist, to know the constitution of the word," and so forth, down to "and the virtues of roots." Among all these he comprehends natural science, which treats of all the phenomena in the world of sense. And in continuation, he alludes also to intellectual objects in what he subjoins: "And what is hidden or manifest I know; for Wisdom, the artificer of all things, taught me." You have, in brief, the professed aim of our philosophy; and the learning of these branches, when pursued with right course of conduct, leads through Wisdom, the artificer of all things, to the Ruler of all,—a Being difficult to grasp and apprehend, ever receding and withdrawing from him who pursues. But He who is far off has—oh ineffable marvel!—come very near. "I am a God that draws near," says the Lord. He is in essence remote; "for how is it that what is begotten can have approached the Unbegotten?" But He is

very near in virtue of that power which holds all things in its embrace. "Shall one do aught in secret, and I see him not?" For the power of God is always present, in contact with us, in the exercise of inspection, of beneficence, of instruction. Whence Moses, persuaded that God is not to be known by human wisdom, said, "Show me Thy glory;" and into the thick darkness where God's voice was, pressed to enter—that is, into the inaccessible and invisible ideas respecting Existence. For God is not in darkness or in place, but above both space and time, and qualities of objects. Wherefore neither is He at any time in a part, either as containing or as contained, either by limitation or by section. "For what house will ye build to Me?" saith the Lord. Nay, He has not even built one for Himself, since He cannot be contained. And though heaven be called His throne, not even thus is He contained, but He rests delighted in the creation.

It is clear, then, that the truth has been hidden from us; and if that has been already shown by one example, we shall establish it a little after by several more. How entirely worthy of approbation are they who are both willing to learn, and able, according to Solomon, "to know wisdom and instruction, and to perceive the words of wisdom, to receive knotty words, and to perceive true righteousness," there being another [righteousness as well], not according to the truth, taught by the Greek laws, and by the rest of the philosophers. "And to direct judgments," it is said—not those of the bench, but he means that we must preserve sound and free of error the judicial faculty which is within us—"That I may give subtlety to the simple, to the young man sense and understanding." "For the wise man," who has been persuaded to obey the commandments, "having heard these things, will become wiser" by knowledge; and "the intelligent man will acquire rule, and will understand a parable and a dark word, the sayings and enigmas of the wise." For it is not spurious words which those inspired by God and those who are gained over by them adduce, nor is it snares in which the most of the sophists entangle the young, spending their time on nought true. But those who possess the Holy Spirit "search the deep things of God,"—that is, grasp the secret that is in the prophecies. "To impart of holy things to the dogs" is forbidden, so long as they remain beasts. For never ought those who are envious and perturbed, and still infidel in conduct, shameless in barking at investigation, to dip in the divine and clear stream of the living water. "Let not the waters of thy fountain overflow, and let thy waters spread over thine own streets." For it is not many who understand such things as they fall in with; or know them even after learning them, though they think they do, according to the worthy Heraclitus. Does not even he seem to thee to censure those who believe not? "Now my just one shall live by faith," the prophet said. And another prophet also says, "Except ye believe, neither shall ye understand." For how ever could the soul admit the transcendental contemplation of such themes, while unbelief respecting what was to be learned struggled within? But faith, which the Greeks disparage, deeming it futile and barbarous, is a voluntary preconception, the assent of piety—"the subject of things hoped for, the evidence of things not seen," according to the divine apostle. "For hereby," pre-eminently, "the elders obtained a good report. But without faith it is impossible to please God." Others have defined faith to be a uniting assent to an unseen object, as certainly the proof of an unknown thing is an evident assent. If then it be choice, being desirous of something, the desire is in this instance intellectual. And since choice is the beginning of action, faith is discovered to be the beginning of action, being the foundation of rational choice in the case of any one who exhibits to himself the previous demonstration through faith. Voluntarily to follow what is useful, is the first principle of understanding. Unswerving choice, then, gives considerable momentum in the direction of knowledge. The exercise of faith directly becomes knowledge, reposing on a sure foundation. Knowledge, accordingly, is defined by the sons of the philosophers as a habit, which cannot be overthrown by reason. Is there any other true condition such as this, except piety, of which alone the Word is teacher? I think not. Theophrastus says that sensation is the root of faith. For from it the rudimentary principles extend to the reason that is in us, and the understanding. He who believeth then the divine Scriptures with sure judgment, receives in the voice of God, who bestowed the Scripture, a demonstration that cannot be impugned. Faith, then, is not established by demonstration. "Blessed therefore those who, not having seen, yet have believed." The Siren's songs, exhibiting a power above human, fascinated those that came near, conciliating them, almost against their will, to the reception of what was said.

Tertullian

(160?–230?)

As THE first notable Christian writer to use Latin, Tertullian has been called "the father of Latin theology." He was not so much an original thinker as one who gave order and precision to existing theology. Born in Carthage, son of a proconsular centurion, he was educated for the law at Rome and probably practiced for a few years until, not long after his conversion, he was ordained a presbyter. During his ministry in Carthage and Rome he devoted his brilliant talents to writings defending the faith against critics both outside and inside the church. His most important work is his devastating attack on the Gnostic heresy in the five books *Against Marcion*. However, he himself adhered to the Montanist heresy, with its legalistic asceticism and primitive view of the end of the world, and about 207 broke with the orthodox church and became leader of a Montanist group in Carthage.

On the Testimony of the Soul is a brief work which, like many of his writings, cannot be definitely dated before or after the schism, though the content suggests it is an early work. In scintillating fashion it portrays the mental stature of the early Christians and frames a background for understanding a type of their religious experience. It is presented here complete in the translation of S. Thelwall from *The Ante-Nicene Fathers* (New York, 1885).

ON THE TESTIMONY OF THE SOUL

*I*f, with the object of convicting the rivals and persecutors of Christian truth, from their own authorities, of the crime of at once being untrue to themselves and doing injustice to us, one is bent on gathering testimonies in its favour from the writings of the philosophers, or the poets, or other masters of this world's learning and wisdom, he has need of a most inquisitive spirit, and a still greater memory to carry out the research. Indeed, some of our people, who still continued their inquisitive labours in ancient literature, and still occupied memory with it, have published works we have in our hands of this very sort; works in which they relate and attest the nature and origin of their traditions, and the grounds on which opinions rest, and from which it may be seen at once that we have embraced nothing new or monstrous—nothing for which we cannot claim the support of ordinary and well-known writings, whether in ejecting error from our creed, or admitting truth into it. But the unbelieving hardness of the human heart leads them to slight even their own teachers, otherwise approved and in high renown, whenever they touch upon arguments which are used in defence of Christianity. Then the poets are fools, when they describe the gods with human passions and stories; then the philosophers are without reason, when they knock at the gates of truth. He will thus far be reckoned a wise and sagacious man who has gone the length of uttering sentiments that are almost Christian; while if, in a mere affectation of judgment and wisdom, he sets himself to reject their ceremonies, or to convicting the world of its sin, he is sure to be branded as a Christian. We will have nothing, then, to do with the literature and the teaching, perverted in its best results, which is believed in its errors rather than its truth. We shall lay no stress on it, if some of their authors have declared that there is one God, and one God only. Nay, let it be granted that there is nothing in heathen writers which a Christian approves, that it may be put out of his power to utter a single word of reproach. For all are not familiar with their teachings; and those who are, have no assurance in regard to their truth. Far less do men assent to our writings, to which no one comes for guidance unless he is already a Christian. I call in a new testimony, yea, one which is better known than all literature, more discussed than all doctrine, more public than all publications, greater than the whole man—I mean all which is man's. Stand forth, O soul, whether thou art a divine and eternal substance, as most philosophers believe—if it is so, thou wilt be the less likely to lie,—or whether thou art the very opposite of divine, because indeed a mortal thing, as Epicurus alone thinks—in that case there will be the less temptation for thee to speak falsely in this case: whether thou art received from heaven, or sprung from earth; whether thou art formed of numbers, or of atoms; whether thine existence begins with that of the body, or thou art put into it at a later stage; from whatever source, and in whatever way, thou makest man a rational being, in the highest degree capable of thought and knowledge,—stand forth and give thy witness. But I call thee not as when, fashioned in schools, trained in libraries, fed in Attic academies and porticoes, thou belchest wisdom. I address thee simple, rude, uncultured and untaught, such as they have thee who have thee only; that very thing of the road, the street, the work-shop, wholly. I want thine inexperience, since in thy small experience no one feels any confidence. I demand of thee the things thou bringest with thee into man, which thou knowest either from thyself, or from thine author, whoever he may be. Thou art not, as I well know, Christian; for a man becomes a Christian, he is not born one. Yet Christians earnestly press thee for a testimony; they press thee, though an alien, to bear witness against thy friends, that they may be put to shame before thee, for hating and mocking us on account of things which convict thee as an accessory.

II. We give offence by proclaiming that there is one God, to whom the name of God alone belongs, from whom all things come, and who is Lord of the whole universe. Bear thy testimony, if thou knowest this to be the truth; for openly and with a perfect liberty, such as we do not possess, we hear thee both in private and in public exclaim, "Which may God grant," and, "If God so will." By expressions such as these thou declarest that there is one who is distinctively God, and thou confessest that all power belongs to Him to whose will, as Sovereign, thou dost look. At the same time, too, thou deniest any others to be truly gods, in calling them by their own names of Saturn, Jupiter, Mars, Minerva; for thou affirmest Him to be God alone to whom thou givest no other name than God; and though thou sometimes callest these other gods, thou plainly usest the designation as one which does not really belong to them, but is, so to speak, a borrowed one. Nor is the nature of the God we declare unknown to thee: "God is good, God does good," thou art wont to say; plainly suggesting further, "But man is evil." In asserting an antithetic proposition, thou, in a sort of indirect and figurative way, reproachest man with his wickedness in departing from a God so good. So, again, as among us, as belonging to the God of benignity and goodness, "Blessing" is a most sacred act in our religion and our life, thou too sayest as readily as a Christian needs, "God bless thee;" and when thou turnest the blessing of God into a curse, in like manner thy very words confess with us that His power over us is absolute and entire. There are some who, though they do not deny the existence of God, hold withal that He is neither Searcher, nor Ruler, nor Judge; treating with especial disdain those of us who go over to Christ out of fear of a coming judgment, as they think, honouring God in freeing Him from the cares of keeping watch, and the trouble of taking note,—not even regarding Him as capable of anger. For if God, they say, gets angry, then He is susceptible of corruption and passion; but that of which passion and corruption can be affirmed may also perish, which God cannot do. But these very persons elsewhere, confessing that the soul is divine, and bestowed on us by God, stumble against a testimony of the soul itself, which affords an answer to these views. For if either divine or God-given, it doubtless knows its giver; and if it knows Him, it undoubtedly fears Him too, and especially as having been by Him endowed so amply. Has it no fear of Him whose favour it is so desirous to possess, and whose anger it is so anxious to avoid? Whence, then, the soul's natural fear of God, if God cannot be angry? How is there any dread of Him whom nothing offends? What is feared but anger? Whence comes anger, but from observing what is done? What leads to watchful oversight, but judgment in prospect? Whence is judgment, but from power? To whom does supreme authority and power belong, but to God alone? So thou art always ready, O soul, from thine own knowledge, nobody casting scorn upon thee, and no one preventing, to exclaim, "God sees all," and "I commend thee to God," and "May God repay," and "God shall judge between us." How happens this, since thou art not Christian? How is it that, even with the garland of Ceres on the brow, wrapped in the purple cloak of Saturn, wearing the white robe of the goddess Isis, thou invokest God as judge? Standing under the statue of Aesculapius, adorning the brazen image of Juno, arraying the helmet of Minerva with dusky figures, thou never thinkest of appealing to any of these deities. In thine own forum thou appealest to a God who is elsewhere; thou permittest honour to be rendered in thy temples to a foreign god. Oh, striking testimony to truth, which in the very midst of demons obtains a witness for us Christians!

III. But when we say that there are demons—as though, in the simple fact that we alone expel them from the men's bodies, we did not also prove their existence—some disciple of Chrysippus begins to curl the lip. Yet thy curses suffi-

ciently attest that there are such beings, and that they are objects of thy strong dislike. As what comes to thee as a fit expression of thy strong hatred of him, thou callest the man a dæmon who annoys thee with his filthiness, or malice, or insolence, or any other vice which we ascribe to evil spirits. In expressing vexation, contempt, or abhorrence, thou hast Satan constantly upon thy lips; the very same we hold to be the angel of evil, the source of error, the corrupter of the whole world, by whom in the beginning man was entrapped into breaking the commandment of God. And (the man) being given over to death on account of his sin, the entire human race, tainted in their descent from him, were made a channel for transmitting his condemnation. Thou seest, then, thy destroyer; and though he is fully known only to Christians, or to whatever sect confesses the Lord, yet, even thou hast some acquaintance with him yet thou abhorrest him.

IV. Even now, as the matter refers to thy opinion on a point the more closely belonging to thee, in so far as it bears on thy personal well-being, we maintain that after life has passed away thou still remainest in existence, and lookest forward to a day of judgment, and according to thy deserts art assigned to misery or bliss, in either way of it for ever; that, to be capable of this, thy former substance must needs return to thee, the matter and the memory of the very same human being: for neither good nor evil couldst thou feel if thou wert not endowed again with that sensitive bodily organization, and there would be no grounds for judgment without the presentation of the very person to whom the sufferings of judgment were due. That Christian view, though much nobler than the Pythagorean, as it does not transfer thee into beasts; though more complete than the Platonic, since it endows thee again with a body; though more worthy of honour than the Epicurean, as it preserves thee from annihilation,—yet, because of the name connected with it, it is held to be nothing but vanity and folly, and, as it is called, a mere presumption. But we are not ashamed of ourselves if our presumption is found to have thy support. Well, in the first place, when thou speakest of one who is dead, thou sayest of him, "Poor man" —poor, surely, not because he has been taken from the good of life, but because he has been given over to punishment and condemnation. But at another time thou speakest of the dead as free from trouble; thou professest to think life a burden, and death a blessing. Thou art wont, too, to speak of the dead as in repose, when, returning to their graves beyond the city gates with food and dainties, thou art wont to present offerings to thyself rather than to them; or when, coming from the graves again, thou art staggering under the effects of wine. But I want thy sober opinion. Thou callest the dead poor when thou speakest thine own thoughts, when thou art at a distance from them. For at their feast, where in a sense they are present and recline along with thee, it would never do to cast reproach upon their lot. Thou canst not but adulate those for whose sake thou art feasting it so sumptuously. Dost thou then speak of him as *poor* who feels not? How happens it that thou cursest, as one capable of suffering from thy curse, the man whose memory comes back on thee with the sting in it of some old injury? It is thine imprecation that "the earth may lie heavy on him," and that there may be trouble "to his ashes in the realm of the dead." In like manner, in thy kindly feeling to him to whom thou art indebted for favours, thou entreatest "repose to his bones and ashes," and thy desire is that among the dead he may "have pleasant rest." If thou hast no power of suffering after death, if no feeling remains,—if, in a word, severance from the body is the annihilation of thee, what makes thee lie against thyself, as if thou couldst suffer in another state? Nay, why dost thou fear death at all? There is nothing after death to be feared,

if there is nothing to be felt. For though it may be said that death is dreadful not for anything it threatens afterwards, but because it deprives us of the good of life; yet, on the other hand, as it puts an end to life's discomforts, which are far more numerous, death's terrors are mitigated by a gain that more than outweighs the loss. And there is no occasion to be troubled about a loss of good things, which is amply made up for by so great a blessing as relief from every trouble. There is nothing dreadful in that which delivers from all that is to be dreaded. If thou shrinkest from giving up life because thy experience of it has been sweet, at any rate there is no need to be in any alarm about death if thou hast no knowledge that it is evil. Thy dread of it is the proof that thou art aware of its evil. Thou wouldst never think it evil—thou wouldst have no fear of it at all—if thou wert not sure that after it there is something to make it evil, and so a thing of terror. Let us leave unnoticed at this time that natural way of fearing death. It is a poor thing for any one to fear what is inevitable. I take up the other side, and argue on the ground of a joyful hope beyond our term of earthly life; for desire of posthumous fame is with almost every class an inborn thing. I have not time to speak of the Curtii, and the Reguli, or the brave men of Greece, who afford us innumerable cases of death despised for after renown. Who at this day is without the desire that he may be often remembered when he is dead? Who does not give all endeavour to preserve his name by works of literature, or by the simple glory of his virtues, or by the splendour even of his tomb? How is it the nature of the soul to have these posthumous ambitions, and with such amazing effort to prepare the things it can only use after decease? It would care nothing about the future, if the future were quite unknown to it. But perhaps thou thinkest thyself surer, after thy exit from the body, of continuing still to feel, than of any future resurrection, which is a doctrine laid at our door as one of our presumptuous suppositions. But it is also the doctrine of the soul; for if any one inquires about a person lately dead as though he were alive, it occurs at once to say, "He has gone." He is expected to return, then.

V. These testimonies of the soul are simple as true, commonplace as simple, universal as commonplace, natural as universal, divine as natural. I don't think they can appear frivolous or feeble to anyone, if he reflect on the majesty of nature, from which the soul derives its authority. If you acknowledge the authority of the mistress, you will own it also in the disciple. Well, nature is the mistress here, and her disciple is the soul. But everything the one has taught or the other learned, has come from God —the Teacher of the teacher. And what the soul may know from the teachings of its chief instructor, thou canst judge from that which is within thee. Think of that which enables thee to think; reflect on that which in forebodings is the prophet, the augur in omens, the foreseer of coming events. Is it a wonderful thing, if, being the gift of God to man, it knows how to divine? Is it anything very strange, if it knows the God by whom it was bestowed? Even fallen as it is, the victim of the great adversary's machinations, it does not forget its Creator, His goodness and law, and the final end both of itself and of its foe. Is it singular then, if, divine in its origin, its revelations agree with the knowledge God has given to His own people? But he who does not regard those outbursts of the soul as the teaching of a congenital nature and the secret deposit of an inborn knowledge, will say that the habit and, so to say, the vice of speaking in this way has been acquired and confirmed from the opinions of published books widely spread among men. Unquestionably the soul existed before letters, and speech before books, and ideas before the writing of them, and man himself before the poet and philosopher. Is it then to be believed, that before lit-

erature and its publication no utterances of the sort we have pointed out came from the lips of men? Did nobody speak of God and His goodness, nobody of death, nobody of the dead? Speech went a-begging, I suppose; nay, (the subjects being still awanting, without which it cannot even exist at this day, when it is so much more copious, and rich, and wise), it could not exist at all if the things which are now so easily suggested, that cling to us so constantly, that are so very near to us, that are somehow born on our very lips, had no existence in ancient times, before letters had any existence in the world—before there was a Mercury, I think, at all. And whence was it, I pray, that letters themselves came to know, and to disseminate for the use of speech, what no mind had ever conceived, or tongue put forth, or ear taken in? But, clearly, since the Scriptures of God, whether belonging to Christians or to Jews, into whose olive tree we have been grafted—are much more ancient than any secular literature, (or, let us only say, are of a somewhat earlier date, as we have shown in its proper place when proving their trustworthiness); if the soul have taken these utterances from writings at all, we must believe it has taken them from ours, and not from yours, its instruction coming more naturally from the earlier than the later works. Which latter indeed waited for their own instruction from the former; and though we grant that light has come from you, still it has flowed from the first fountainhead originally; and we claim as entirely ours, all you may have taken from us and handed down. Since it is thus, it matters little whether the soul's knowledge was put into it by God or by His book. Why, then, O man, wilt thou maintain a view so groundless, as that those testimonies of the soul have gone forth from the mere human speculations of your literature, and got hardening of common use?

VI. Believe, then, your own books, and as to our Scriptures so much the more believe writings which are divine, but in the witness of the soul itself give like confidence to Nature. Choose the one of these you observe to be the most faithful friend of truth. If your own writings are distrusted, neither God nor Nature lie. And if you would have faith in God and Nature, have faith in the soul; thus you will believe yourself. Certainly you value the soul as giving you your true greatness,—that to which you belong; which is all things to you, without which you can neither live nor die; on whose account you even put God away from you. Since, then, you fear to become a Christian, call the soul before you, and put her to the question. Why does she worship another? why name the name of God? Why does she speak of demons, when she means to denote spirits to be held accursed? Why does she make her protestations towards the heavens, and pronounce her ordinary execrations earthwards? Why does she render service in one place, in another invoke the Avenger? Why does she pass judgments on the dead? What Christian phrases are those she has got, though Christians she neither desires to see nor hear? Why has she either bestowed them on us, or received them from us? Why has she either taught us them, or learned them as our scholar? Regard with suspicion this accordance in words, while there is such difference in practice. It is utter folly—denying a universal na-ture—to ascribe this exclusively to our language and the Greek, which are regarded among us as so near akin. The soul is not a boon from heaven to Latins and Greeks alone. Man is the one name belonging to every nation upon earth: there is one soul and many tongues, one spirit and various sounds; every country has its own speech, but the subjects of speech are common to all. God is everywhere, and the goodness of God is everywhere; demons are everywhere, and the cursing of them is everywhere; the invocation of divine judgment is everywhere, death is everywhere, and the sense of death is everywhere, and all the world over is found the witness of the soul. There is not a soul of man that does not, from the light that is in itself, proclaim the very things we are not permitted to speak above our breath. Most justly, then, every soul is a culprit as well as a witness: in the measure that it testifies for truth, the guilt of error lies on it; and on the day of judgment it will stand before the courts of God, without a word to say. Thou proclaimedst God, O soul, but thou didst not seek to know Him: evil spirits were detested by thee, and yet they were the objects of thy adoration; the punishments of hell were foreseen by thee, but no care was taken to avoid them; thou hadst a savour of Christianity, and withal wert the persecutor of Christians.

Origen

(185?-254?)

THE first thinker to give Christian truth scientific standing, as conforming to the science of that time, Origen stands as one of the greatest comprehensive minds of the Christian tradition. No person of finer spirit or higher aims ornaments the history of the early church. He was born in Alexandria of Christian parents and was educated by his father, a teacher of rhetoric, and by Clement of Alexandria. When his father was martyred and Clement fled in the persecution of Severus, he was appointed by Bishop Demetrius, though he was only eighteen, to succeed Clement as head of the catechetical school. For twenty-eight years he brought honor to the school and the city by the increasing reputation of his writings, until in 231 Demetrius, apparently from jealousy, engineered his official expulsion from the church. In Caesarea, where he had spent some time years before during the persecution of Carcalla, the banished scholar was welcomed and aided in establishing a school; and there he stayed for most of his later years.

Origen was probably the most prolific of early Christian writers—particularly during the period 218-28 when his wealthy friend Ambrose supplied him with a staff of copyists—but only a few of his writings are extant in the original Greek. Of his doctrinal works all of importance have been lost except the four books of *On the Fundamental Doctrines* (*De principiis*), preserved in a Latin translation by Rufinus (345?-410), who took liberties with the text. From this the opening chapter is presented here in the translation of Frederick Crombie from *The Ante-Nicene Fathers* (New York, 1885).

ON GOD

From *On the Fundamental Doctrines*

I know that some will attempt to say that, even according to the declarations of our own Scriptures, God is a body, because in the writings of Moses they find it said, that "our God is a consuming fire;" and in the Gospel according to John, that "God is a Spirit, and they who worship Him must worship Him in spirit and in truth." Fire and spirit, according to them, are to be regarded as nothing else than a body. Now, I should like to ask these persons what they have to say respecting that passage where it is declared that God is light; as John writes in his Epistle, "God is light, and in Him there is no darkness at all." Truly He is that light which illuminates the whole understanding of those who are capable of receiving truth, as is said in the thirty-sixth Psalm, "In Thy light we shall see light." For what other light of God can be named, "in which any one

sees light," save an influence of God, by which a man, being enlightened, either thoroughly sees the truth of all things, or comes to know God Himself, who is called the truth? Such is the meaning of the expression, "In Thy light shall we see light;" i.e., in Thy word and wisdom, which is Thy Son, in Himself we shall see Thee the Father. Because He is called light, shall He be supposed to have any resemblance to the light of the sun? Or how should there be the slightest ground for imagining, that from that corporeal light any one could derive the cause of knowledge, and come to the understanding of the truth?

2. If, then, they acquiesce in our assertion, which reason itself has demonstrated, regarding the nature of light, and acknowledge that God cannot be understood to be a body in the sense that light is, similar reasoning will hold

true of the expression "a consuming fire." For what will God consume in respect of His being fire? Shall He be thought to consume material substance, as wood, or hay, or stubble? And what in this view can be called worthy of the glory of God, if He be a fire, consuming materials of that kind? But let us reflect that God does indeed consume and utterly destroy; that He consumes evil thoughts, wicked actions, and sinful desires, when they find their way into the minds of believers; and that, inhabiting along with His Son those souls which are rendered capable of receiving His word and wisdom, according to his own declaration, "I and the Father shall come, and We shall make our abode with him," He makes them, after all their vices and passions have been consumed, a holy temple, worthy of Himself. Those, moreover, who, on account of the expression "God is a Spirit," think that He is a body, are to be answered, I think, in the following manner. It is the custom of sacred Scripture, when it wishes to designate anything opposed to this gross and solid body, to call it spirit, as in the expression, "The letter killeth, but the spirit giveth life," where there can be no doubt that by "letter" are meant bodily things, and by "spirit" intellectual things, which we also term "spiritual." The apostle, moreover, says, "Even unto this day, when Moses is read, the veil is upon their heart: nevertheless, when it shall turn to the Lord, the veil shall be taken away: and where the Spirit of the Lord is, there is liberty." For so long as any one is not converted to a spiritual understanding, a veil is placed over his heart, with which veil, i.e., a gross understanding, Scripture itself is said or thought to be covered: and this is the meaning of the statement that a veil was placed over the countenance of Moses when he spoke to the people, i.e., when the law was publicly read aloud. But if we turn to the Lord, where also is the word of God, and where the Holy Spirit reveals spiritual knowledge, then the veil is taken away,

and with unveiled face we shall behold the glory of the Lord in the holy Scriptures.

3. And since many saints participate in the Holy Spirit, He cannot therefore be understood to be a body, which being divided into corporeal parts, is partaken of by each one of the saints; but He is manifestly a sanctifying power, in which all are said to have a share who have deserved to be sanctified by His grace. And in order that what we say may be more easily understood, let us take an illustration from things very dissimilar. There are many persons who take a part in the science or art of medicine: are we therefore to suppose that those who do so take to themselves the particles of some body called medicine, which is placed before them, and in this way participate in the same? Or must we not rather understand that all who with quick and trained minds come to understand the art and discipline itself, may be said to be partakers of the art of healing. But these are not to be deemed altogether parallel instances in a comparison of medicine to the Holy Spirit, as they have been adduced only to establish that that is not necessarily to be considered a body, a share in which is possessed by many individuals. For the Holy Spirit differs widely from the method or science of medicine, in respect that the Holy Spirit is an intellectual existence, and subsists and exists in a peculiar manner, whereas medicine is not at all of that nature.

4. But we must pass on to the language of the Gospel itself, in which it is declared that "God is a Spirit," and where we have to show how that is to be understood agreeably to what we have stated. For let us inquire on what occasion these words were spoken by the Saviour, before whom He uttered them, and what was the subject of investigation. We find, without any doubt, that He spoke these words to the Samaritan woman, saying to her, who thought, agreeably to the Samaritan view, that God ought to be worshipped on Mount Gerizim, that

"God is a Spirit." For the Samaritan woman, believing Him to be a Jew, was inquiring of Him whether God ought to be worshipped in Jerusalem or on this mountain; and her words were, "All our fathers worshipped on this mountain, and ye say that in Jerusalem is the place where we ought to worship." To this opinion of the Samaritan woman, therefore, who imagined that God was less rightly or duly worshipped, according to the privileges of the different localities, either by the Jews in Jerusalem or by the Samaritans on Mount Gerizim, the Saviour answered that he who would follow the Lord must lay aside all preference for particular places, and thus expressed Himself: "The hour is coming when neither in Jerusalem nor on this mountain shall the true worshippers worship the Father. God is a Spirit, and they who worship Him must worship Him in spirit and in truth." And observe how logically He has joined together the spirit and the truth: He called God a Spirit, that He might distinguish Him from bodies; and He named Him the truth, to distinguish Him from a shadow or an image. For they who worshipped in Jerusalem worshipped God neither in truth nor in spirit, being in subjection to the shadow or image of heavenly things; and such also was the case with those who worshipped on Mount Gerizim.

5. Having refuted, then, as well as we could, every notion which might suggest that we were to think of God as in any degree corporeal, we go on to say that, according to strict truth, God is incomprehensible, and incapable of being measured. For whatever be the knowledge which we are able to obtain of God, either by perception or reflection, we must of necessity believe that He is by many degrees far better than what we perceive Him to be. For, as if we were to see any one unable to bear a spark of light, or the flame of a very small lamp, and were desirous to acquaint such a one, whose vision could not admit a greater degree of light than what we have stated, with the brightness and splendour of the sun, would it not be necessary to tell him that the splendour of the sun was unspeakably and incalculably better and more glorious than all this light which he saw? So our understanding, when shut in by the fetters of flesh and blood, and rendered, on account of its participation in such material substances, duller and more obtuse, although, in comparison with our bodily nature, it is esteemed to be far superior, yet, in its efforts to examine and behold incorporeal things, scarcely holds the place of a spark or lamp. But among all intelligent, that is, incorporeal beings, what is so superior to all others—so unspeakably and incalculably superior—as God, whose nature cannot be grasped or seen by the power of any human understanding, even the purest and brightest?

6. But it will not appear absurd if we employ another similitude to make the matter clearer. Our eyes frequently cannot look upon the nature of the light itself—that is, upon the substance of the sun; but when we behold his splendour or his rays pouring in, perhaps, through windows or some small openings to admit the light, we can reflect how great is the supply and source of the light of the body. So, in like manner, the works of Divine Providence and the plan of this whole world are a sort of rays, as it were, of the nature of God, in comparison with His real substance and being. As, therefore, our understanding is unable of itself to behold God Himself as He is, it knows the Father of the world from the beauty of His works and the comeliness of His creatures. God, therefore, is not to be thought of as being either a body or as existing in a body, but as an uncompounded intellectual nature, admitting within Himself no addition of any kind; so that He cannot be believed to have within him a greater and a less, but is such that He is in all parts Μονάς, and, so to speak, Ἑνάς, and is the mind and source from which all intellectual nature or mind takes its beginning. But mind, for its movements or

operations, needs no physical space, nor sensible magnitude, nor bodily shape, nor colour, nor any other of those adjuncts which are the properties of body or matter. Wherefore that simple and wholly intellectual nature can admit of no delay or hesitation in its movements or operations, lest the simplicity of the divine nature should appear to be circumscribed or in some degree hampered by such adjuncts, and lest that which is the beginning of all things should be found composite and differing, and that which ought to be free from all bodily intermixture, in virtue of being the one sole species of Deity, so to speak, should prove, instead of being one, to consist of many things. That mind, moreover, does not require space in order to carry on its movements agreeably to its nature, is certain from observation of our own mind. For if the mind abide within its own limits, and sustain no injury from any cause, it will never, from diversity of situation, be retarded in the discharge of its functions; nor, on the other hand, does it gain any addition or increase of mobility from the nature of particular places. And here, if any one were to object, for example, that among those who are at sea, and tossed by its waves, the mind is considerably less vigorous than it is wont to be on land, we are to believe that it is in this state, not from diversity of situation, but from the commotion or disturbance of the body to which the mind is joined or attached. For it seems to be contrary to nature, as it were, for a human body to live at sea; and for that reason it appears, by a sort of inequality of its own, to enter upon its mental operations in a slovenly and irregular manner, and to perform the acts of the intellect with a duller sense, in as great degree as those who on land are prostrated with fever; with respect to whom it is certain, that if the mind do not discharge its functions as well as before, in consequence of the attack of disease, the blame is to be laid not upon the place, but upon the bodily malady, by which the body, being disturbed and disordered, renders

to the mind its customary services under by no means the well-known and natural conditions: for we human beings are animals composed of a union of body and soul, and in this way (only) was it possible for us to live upon the earth. But God, who is the beginning of all things, is not to be regarded as a composite being, lest perchance there should be found to exist elements prior to the beginning itself, out of which everything is composed, whatever that be which is called composite. Neither does the mind require bodily magnitude in order to perform any act or movement; as when the eye by gazing upon bodies of larger size is dilated, but is compressed and contracted in order to see smaller objects. The mind, indeed, requires magnitude of an intellectual kind, because it grows, not after the fashion of a body, but after that of intelligence. For the mind is not enlarged, together with the body, by means of corporeal additions, up to the twentieth or thirtieth year of life; but the intellect is sharpened by exercises of learning, and the powers implanted within it for intelligent purposes are called forth; and it is rendered capable of greater intellectual efforts, not being increased by bodily additions, but carefully polished by learned exercises. But these it cannot receive immediately from boyhood, or from birth, because the framework of limbs which the mind employs as organs for exercising itself is weak and feeble; and it is unable to bear the weight of its own operations, or to exhibit a capacity for receiving training.

7. If there are any now who think that the mind itself and the soul is a body, I wish they would tell me by way of answer how it receives reasons and assertions on subjects of such importance —of such difficulty and such subtlety? Whence does it derive the power of memory? and whence comes the contemplation of invisible things? How does the body possess the faculty of understanding incorporeal existences? How does a bodily nature investigate the processes of the various arts, and contemplate

the reasons of things? How, also, is it able to perceive and understand divine truths, which are manifestly incorporeal? Unless, indeed, some should happen to be of opinion, that as the very bodily shape and form of the ears or eyes contributes something to hearing and to sight, and as the individual members, formed by God, have some adaptation, even from the very quality of their form, to the end for which they were naturally appointed; so also he may think that the shape of the soul or mind is to be understood as if created purposely and designedly for perceiving and understanding individual things, and for being set in motion by vital movements. I do not perceive, however, who shall be able to describe or state what is the colour of the mind, in respect of its being mind, and acting as an intelligent existence. Moreover, in confirmation and explanation of what we have already advanced regarding the mind or soul—to the effect that it is better than the whole bodily nature—the following remarks may be added. There underlies every bodily sense a certain peculiar sensible substance, on which the bodily sense exerts itself. For example, colours, form, size, underlie vision; voices and sound, the sense of hearing; odours, good or bad, that of smell; savours, that of taste; heat or cold, hardness or softness, roughness or smoothness, that of touch. Now, of those senses enumerated above, it is manifest to all that the sense of mind is much the best. How, then, should it not appear absurd, that under those senses which are inferior, substances should have been placed on which to exert their powers, but that under this power, which is far better than any other, i.e., the sense of mind, nothing at all of the nature of a substance should be placed, but that a power of an intellectual nature should be an accident, or consequent upon bodies? Those who assert this, doubtless do so to the disparagement of that better substance which is within them; nay, by so doing, they even do wrong to God Himself, when they imagine He may be understood by means of a bodily nature, so that according to their view He is a body, and that which may be understood or perceived by means of a body; and they are unwilling to have it understood that the mind bears a certain relationship to God, of whom the mind itself is an intellectual image, and that by means of this it may come to some knowledge of the nature of divinity, especially if it be purified and separated from bodily matter.

8. But perhaps these declarations may seem to have less weight with those who wish to be instructed in divine things out of the holy Scriptures, and who seek to have it proved to them from that source how the nature of God surpasses the nature of bodies. See, therefore, if the apostle does not say the same thing, when, speaking of Christ, he declares, that "He is the image of the invisible God, the first-born of every creature." Not, as some suppose, that the nature of God is visible to some and invisible to others: for the apostle does not say "the image of God invisible" to men or "invisible" to sinners, but with unvarying constancy pronounces on the nature of God in these words: "the image of the invisible God." Moreover, John, in his Gospel, when asserting that "no one hath seen God at any time," manifestly declares to all who are capable of understanding, that there is no nature to which God is visible: not as if He were a being who was visible by nature, and merely escaped or baffled the view of a frailer creature, but because by the *nature* of His being it is impossible for Him to be seen. And if you should ask of me what is my opinion regarding the Only-begotten Himself, whether the nature of God, which is naturally invisible, be not visible even to Him, let not such a question appear to you at once to be either absurd or impious, because we shall give you a logical reason. It is one thing to see, and another to know: to see and to be seen is a property of bodies; to know and to be known, an attribute of intellectual being. Whatever, therefore, is a

property of bodies, cannot be predicated either of the Father or of the Son; but what belongs to the nature of deity is common to the Father and the Son. Finally, even He Himself, in the Gospel, did not say that no one has *seen* the Father, save the Son, nor any one the Son, save the Father; but His words are: "No one *knoweth* the Son, save the Father; nor any one the Father, save the Son." By which it is clearly shown, that whatever among bodily natures is called seeing and being seen, is termed, between the Father and the Son, a knowing and being known, by means of the power of knowledge, not by the frailness of the sense of sight. Because, then, neither seeing nor being seen can be properly applied to an incorporeal and invisible nature, neither is the Father, in the Gospel, said to be seen by the Son, nor the Son by the Father, but the one is said to be known by the other.

9. Here, if any one lay before us the passage where it is said, "Blessed are the pure in heart, for they shall see God," from that very passage, in my opinion, will our position derive additional strength; for what else is seeing God in heart, but, according to our exposition as above, understanding and knowing Him with the mind? For the names of the organs of sense are frequently ap-plied to the soul, so that it may be said to see with the eyes of the heart, i.e., to perform an intellectual act by means of the power of intelligence. So also it is said to hear with the ears when it per-ceives the deeper meaning of a statement. So also we say that it makes use of teeth, when it chews and eats the bread of life which cometh down from heaven. In like manner, also, it is said to employ the services of other members, which are transferred from their bodily appella-tions, and applied to the powers of the soul, according to the words of Solomon, "You will find a divine sense." For he knew that there were within us two kinds of senses: the one mortal, corruptible, human; the other immortal and intellec-tual, which he now termed divine. By this divine sense, therefore, not of the eyes, but of a pure heart, which is the mind, God may be seen by those who are worthy. For you will certainly find in all the Scriptures, both old and new, the term "heart" repeatedly used instead of "mind," i.e., intellectual power. In this manner, therefore, although far be-low the dignity of the subject, have we spoken of the nature of God, as those who understand it under the limitation of the human understanding. In the next place, let us see what is meant by the name of Christ.

Cyprian

(200?-258)

CONVERSION, ordination, and elevation to the place of bishop of Carthage within only two years, followed by martyrdom after ten more years—such is the outline of Cyprian's swift career. At the time of his conversion in 246 he seems to have been a Carthaginian of some affluence and considerable learning. He has been called the spiritual son of Tertullian, whose writings he is said to have studied daily. Scarcely had he discovered his episcopal responsibilities when the first universal persecution of Christians was begun under Decius, and the rest of his life was lived under threat of the martyrdom that at last overtook him.

Cyprian's writings consist of eighty-odd letters and a dozen treatises, in which the most significant ideas are concerned with the church. Concepts such as "Outside the church there is no salvation" and "Where the bishop is, there is the church" come from his writings, yet his emphasis on the unity of the bishops as the foundation of the church was not authoritarian so much as ecumenical. The treatise *On the Advantage of Patience*, here presented complete, has an authority few can equal, for it was written from no ivory tower but amid the stern realities of travail and persecution. The translation from the original Latin is by Ernest Wallis in *The Ante-Nicene Fathers* (New York, 1886).

ON THE ADVANTAGE OF PATIENCE

As I am about to speak, beloved brethren, of patience, and to declare its advantages and benefits, from what point should I rather begin than this, that I see that even at this time, for your audience of me, patience is needful, as you cannot even discharge this duty of hearing and learning without patience? For wholesome discourse and reasoning are then effectually learnt, if what is said be patiently heard. Nor do I find, beloved brethren, among the rest of the ways of heavenly discipline wherein the path of our hope and faith is directed to the attainment of the divine rewards, anything of more advantage, either as more useful for life or more helpful to glory, than that we who are labouring in the precepts of the Lord with the obedience of fear and devotion, should especially, with our whole watchfulness, be careful of patience.

2. Philosophers also profess that they pursue this virtue; but in their case the patience is as false as their wisdom also is. For whence can he be either wise or patient, who has neither known the wisdom nor the patience of God? since He Himself warns us, and says of those who seem to themselves to be wise in this world, "I will destroy the wisdom of the wise, and I will reprove the understanding of the prudent." Moreover, the blessed Apostle Paul, filled with the Holy Spirit, and sent forth for the calling and training of the heathen, bears witness and instructs us, saying, "See that no man despoil you through philosophy and vain deceit, after the tradition of men, after the elements of the world, and not after Christ, because in Him dwelleth all the fulness of divinity." And in another place he says: "Let no man deceive himself; if any man among you thinketh himself to be wise, let him become a fool to this world, that he may become wise. For the wisdom of this world is foolishness with God. For it is written, I will rebuke the wise in their own craftiness." And again: "The Lord knoweth the thoughts of the wise, that they are foolish." Wherefore if the wisdom among them be not true, the patience also cannot be true. For if he is wise who is

lowly and meek—but we do not see that philosophers are either lowly or meek, but greatly pleasing themselves, and for the very reason that they please themselves, displeasing God—it is evident that the patience is not real among them where there is the insolent audacity of an affected liberty, and the immodest boastfulness of an exposed and half-naked bosom.

3. But for us, beloved brethren, who are philosophers, not in words, but in deeds, and do not put forward our wisdom in our garb, but in truth—who are better acquainted with the consciousness, than with the boast, of virtues—who do not speak great things, but live them,—let us, as servants and worshippers of God, show, in our spiritual obedience, the patience which we learn from heavenly teachings. For we have this virtue in common with God. From Him patience begins; from Him its glory and its dignity take their rise. The origin and greatness of patience proceed from God as its author. Man ought to love the thing which is dear to God; the good which the Divine Majesty loves, it commends. If God is our Lord and Father, let us imitate the patience of our Lord as well as our Father; because it behoves servants to be obedient, no less than it becomes sons not to be degenerate.

4. But what and how great is the patience in God, that, most patiently enduring the profane temples and the images of earth, and the sacrilegious rites instituted by men, in contempt of His majesty and honour, He makes the day to begin and the light of the sun to arise alike upon the good and the evil; and while He waters the earth with showers, no one is excluded from His benefits, but upon the righteous equally with the unrighteous He bestows His undiscriminating rains. We see that with undistinguishing equality of patience, at God's behest, the seasons minister to the guilty and the guiltless, the religious and the impious—those who give thanks and the unthankful; that the elements wait on them; the winds blow, the fountains

flow, the abundance of the harvests increases, the fruits of the vineyards ripen, the trees are loaded with apples, the groves put on their leaves, the meadows their verdure; and while God is provoked with frequent, yea, with continual offences, He softens His indignation, and in patience waits for the day of retribution, once for all determined; and although He has revenge in His power, He prefers to keep patience for a long while, bearing, that is to say, mercifully, and putting off, so that, if it might be possible, the long protracted mischief may at some time be changed, and man, involved in the contagion of errors and crimes, may even though late be converted to God, as He Himself warns and says, "I do not will the death of him that dieth, so much as that he may return and live." And again, "Return unto me, saith the Lord." And again: "Return to the Lord your God; for He is merciful, and gracious, and patient, and of great pity, and who inclines His judgment towards the evils inflicted." Which, moreover, the blessed apostle referring to, and recalling the sinner to repentance, sets forward, and says: "Or despisest thou the riches of His goodness, and forbearance, and long-suffering, not knowing that the patience and goodness of God leadeth thee to repentance? But after thy hardness and impenitent heart thou treasurest up unto thyself wrath in the day of wrath and of revelation of the righteous judgment of God, who shall render to every one according to his works." He says that God's judgment is just, because it is tardy, because it is long and greatly deferred, so that by the long patience of God man may be benefited for life eternal. Punishment is then executed on the impious and the sinner, when repentance for the sin can no longer avail.

5. And that we may more fully understand, beloved brethren, that patience is a thing of God, and that whoever is gentle, and patient, and meek, is an imitator of God the Father; when the Lord in His Gospel was giving precepts for

salvation, and, bringing forth divine warnings, was instructing His disciples to perfection, He laid it down, and said, "Ye have heard that it is said, Thou shalt love thy neighbour, and have thine enemy in hatred. But I say unto you, Love your enemies, and pray for them which persecute you; that ye may be the children of your Father which is in heaven, who maketh His sun to rise on the good and on the evil, and raineth upon the just and on the unjust. For if ye love them which love you, what reward shall ye have? do not even the publicans the same? And if ye shall salute your brethren only, what do ye more (than others)? do not even the heathens the same thing? Be ye therefore perfect, even as your Father in heaven is perfect." He said that the children of God would thus become perfect. He showed that they were thus completed, and taught that they were restored by a heavenly birth, if the patience of God our Father dwell in us—if the divine likeness, which Adam had lost by sin, be manifested and shine in our actions. What a glory is it to become like to God! what and how great a felicity, to possess among our virtues, that which may be placed on the level of divine praises!

6. Nor, beloved brethren, did Jesus Christ, our God and Lord, teach this in words only; but He fulfilled it also in deeds. And because He had said that He had come down for this purpose, that He might do the will of His Father; among the other marvels of His virtues, whereby He showed forth the marks of a divine majesty, He also maintained the patience of His Father in the constancy of His endurance. Finally, all His actions, even from His very advent, are characterized by patience as their associate; in that, first of all, coming down from that heavenly sublimity to earthly things, the Son of God did not scorn to put on the flesh of man, and although He Himself was not a sinner, to bear the sins of others. His immortality being in the meantime laid aside, He suffers Himself to become mortal, so that the guiltless may be put to death for the salvation of the guilty. The Lord is baptized by the servant; and He who is about to bestow remission of sins, does not Himself disdain to wash His body in the laver of regeneration. For forty days He fasts, by whom others are feasted. He is hungry, and suffers famine, that they who had been in hunger of the word and of grace may be satisfied with heavenly bread. He wrestles with the devil tempting Him; and, content only to have overcome the enemy, He strives no further than by words. He ruled over His disciples not as servants in the power of a master; but, kind and gentle, He loved them with a brotherly love. He deigned even to wash the apostles' feet, that since the Lord is such among His servants, He might teach, by His example, what a fellow-servant ought to be among his peers and equals. Nor is it to be wondered at, that among the obedient He showed Himself such, since He could bear Judas even to the last with a long patience—could take meat with His enemy—could know the household foe, and not openly point him out, nor refuse the kiss of the traitor. Moreover, in bearing with the Jews, how great equanimity and how great patience, in turning the unbelieving to the faith by persuasion, in soothing the unthankful by concession, in answering gently to the contradictors, in bearing the proud with clemency, in yielding with humility to the persecutors, in wishing to gather together the slayers of the prophets, and those who were always rebellious against God, even to the very hour of His cross and passion!

7. And moreover, in His very passion and cross, before they had reached the cruelty of death and the effusion of blood, what infamies of reproach were patiently heard, what mockings of contumely were suffered, so that *He* received the spittings of insulters, who with His spittle had a little before made eyes for a blind man; and He in whose name the devil and his angels is now scourged by His servants, Himself suffered scourgings! He was crowned with

thorns, who crowns martyrs with eternal flowers. He was smitten on the face with palms, who gives the true palms to those who overcome. He was despoiled of His earthly garment, who clothes others in the vesture of immortality. He was fed with gall, who gave heavenly food. He was given to drink of vinegar, who appointed the cup of salvation. That guiltless, that just One,—nay, He who is innocency itself and justice itself,—is counted among transgressors, and truth is oppressed with false witnesses. He who shall judge is judged; and the Word of God is led silently to the slaughter. And when at the cross of the Lord the stars are confounded, the elements are disturbed, the earth quakes, night shuts out the day, the sun, that he may not be compelled to look on the crime of the Jews, withdraws both his rays and his eyes, He speaks not, nor is moved, nor declares His majesty even in His very passion itself. Even to the end, all things are borne perseveringly and constantly, in order that in Christ a full and perfect patience may be consummated.

8. And after all these things, He still receives His murderers, if they will be converted and come to Him; and with a saving patience, He who is benignant to preserve, closes His Church to none. Those adversaries, those blasphemers, those who were always enemies to His name, if they repent of their sin, if they acknowledge the crime committed, He receives, not only to the pardon of their sin, but to the reward of the heavenly kingdom. What can be said more patient, what more merciful? Even he is made alive by Christ's blood who has shed Christ's blood. Such and so great is the patience of Christ; and had it not been such and so great, the Church would never have possessed Paul as an apostle.

9. But if we also, beloved brethren, are in Christ; if we put Him on, if He is the way of our salvation, who follow Christ in the footsteps of salvation, let us walk by the example of Christ, as the Apostle John instructs us, saying, "He who saith he abideth in Christ, ought himself also to walk even as He walked." Peter also, upon whom by the Lord's condescension the Church was founded, lays it down in his epistle, and says, "Christ suffered for us, leaving you an example, that ye should follow His steps, who did no sin, neither was deceit found in His mouth; who, when He was reviled, reviled not again; when He suffered, threatened not, but gave Himself up to him that judged Him unjustly."

10. Finally, we find that both patriarchs and prophets, and all the righteous men who in their preceding likeness wore the figure of Christ, in the praise of their virtues were watchful over nothing more than that they should preserve patience with a strong and stedfast equanimity. Thus Abel, who first initiated and consecrated the origin of martyrdom, and the passion of the righteous man, makes no resistance nor struggles against his fratricidal brother, but with lowliness and meekness he is patiently slain. Thus Abraham, believing God, and first of all instituting the root and foundation of faith, when tried in respect of his son, does not hesitate nor delay, but obeys the commands of God with all the patience of devotion. And Isaac, prefigured as the likeness of the Lord's victim, when he is presented by his father for immolation, is found patient. And Jacob, driven forth by his brother from his country, departs with patience; and afterwards with greater patience, he suppliantly brings him back to concord with peaceful gifts, when he is even more impious and persecuting. Joseph, sold by his brethren and sent away, not only with patience pardons them, but even bountifully and mercifully bestows gratuitous supplies of corn on them when they come to him. Moses is frequently condemned by an ungrateful and faithless people, and almost stoned; and yet with gentleness and patience he entreats the Lord for those people. But in David, from whom, according to the flesh, the nativity of Christ springs, how great and marvellous and Christian is the patience, that he often had it in his power to be able to kill king Saul, who was persecuting him and desiring to slay him;

and yet, chose rather to save him when placed in his hand, and delivered up to him, not repaying his enemy in turn, but rather, on the contrary, even avenging him when slain! In fine, so many prophets were slain, so many martyrs were honoured with glorious deaths, who all have attained to the heavenly crowns by the praise of patience. For the crown of sorrows and sufferings cannot be received unless patience in sorrow and suffering precede it.

11. But that it may be more manifestly and fully known how useful and necessary patience is, beloved brethren; let the judgment of God be pondered, which even in the beginning of the world and of the human race, Adam, forgetful of the commandment, and a transgressor of the given law, received. Then we shall know how patient in this life we ought to be who are born in such a state, that we labour here with afflictions and contests. "Because," says He, "thou hast hearkened to the voice of thy wife, and hast eaten of the tree of which alone I had charged thee that thou shouldest not eat, cursed shall be the ground in all thy works: in sorrow and in groaning shalt thou eat of it all the days of thy life. Thorns and thistles shall it give forth to thee, and thou shalt eat the food of the field. In the sweat of thy face shalt thou eat thy bread, till thou return into the ground from which thou wast taken: for dust thou art, and to dust shalt thou go." We are all tied and bound with the chain of this sentence, until, death being expunged, we depart from this life. In sorrow and groaning we must of necessity be all the days of our life: it is necessary that we eat our bread with sweat and labour.

12. Whence every one of us, when he is born and received in the inn of this world, takes his beginning from tears; and, although still unconscious and ignorant of all things, he knows nothing else in that very earliest birth except to weep. By a natural foresight, the untrained soul laments the anxieties and labours of the mortal life, and even in the beginning bears witness by its wails

and groans to the storms of the world which it is entering. For the sweat of the brow and labour is the condition of life so long as it lasts. Nor can there be supplied any consolations to those that sweat and toil other than patience; which consolations, while in this world they are fit and necessary for all men, are especially so for us who are more shaken by the siege of the devil who daily standing in the battle-field, are wearied with the wrestlings of the inveterate and skilful enemy; for us who, besides the various and continual battles of temptations, must also in the contest of persecutions forsake our patrimonies, undergo imprisonment, bear chains, spend our lives, endure the sword, the wild beasts, fires, crucifixions—in fine, all kinds of torments and penalties, to be endured in the faith and courage of patience; as the Lord Himself instructs us, and says, "These things have I spoken unto you, that in me ye might have peace. But in the world ye shall have tribulation; yet be confident, for I have overcome the world." And if we who have renounced the devil and the world, suffer the tribulations and mischiefs of the devil and the world with more frequency and violence, how much more ought we to keep patience, wherewith as our helper and ally, we may bear all mischievous things!

13. It is the wholesome precept of our Lord and Master: "He that endureth," saith He, "unto the end, the same shall be saved;" and again, "If ye continue," saith He, "in my word ye shall be truly my disciples; and ye shall know the truth, and the truth shall make you free." We must endure and persevere, beloved brethren, in order that, being admitted to the hope of truth and liberty, we may attain to the truth and liberty itself; for that very fact that we are Christians is the substance of faith and hope. But that hope and faith may attain to their result, there is need of patience. For we are not following after present glory, but future, according to what Paul the apostle also warns us, and says, "We are saved by hope; but hope that is seen is not hope:

for what a man seeth, why doth he hope for? But if we hope for that which we see not, then do we by patience wait for it." Therefore, waiting and patience are needful, that we may fulfil that which we have begun to be, and may receive that which we believe and hope for, according to God's own showing. Moreover, in another place, the same apostle instructs the righteous and the doers of good works, and them who lay up for themselves treasures in heaven with the increase of the divine usury, that they also should be patient; and teaches them, saying, "Therefore, while we have time, let us labour in that which is good unto all men, but especially to them who are of the household of faith. But let us not faint in well-doing, for in its season we shall reap." He admonishes that no man should impatiently faint in his labour, that none should be either called off or overcome by temptations and desist in the midst of the praise and in the way of glory; and the things that are past perish, while those which have begun cease to be perfect; as it is written, "The righteousness of the righteous shall not deliver him in whatever day he shall transgress;" and again, "Hold that which thou hast, that another take not thy crown." Which word exhorts us to persevere with patience and courage, so that he who strives towards the crown with the praise now near at hand, may be crowned by the continuance of patience.

14. But patience, beloved brethren, not only keeps watch over what is good, but it also repels what is evil. In harmony with the Holy Spirit, and associated with what is heavenly and divine, it struggles with the defence of its strength against the deeds of the flesh and the body, wherewith the soul is assaulted and taken. Let us look briefly into a few things out of many, that from a few the rest also may be understood. Adultery, fraud, manslaughter, are mortal crimes. Let patience be strong and stedfast in the heart; and neither is the sanctified body and temple of God polluted by adultery, nor is the innocence dedicated to righteousness stained with the contagion of fraud; nor, after the Eucharist carried in it, is the hand spotted with the sword and blood.

15. Charity is the bond of brotherhood, the foundation of peace, the holdfast and security of unity, which is greater than both hope and faith, which excels both good works and martyrdoms, which will abide with us always, eternal with God in the kingdom of heaven. Take from it patience; and deprived of it, it does not endure. Take from it the substance of bearing and of enduring, and it continues with no roots nor strength. The apostle, finally, when he would speak of charity, joined to it endurance and patience. "Charity," he says, "is large-souled; charity is kind; charity envieth not; is not puffed up, is not provoked, thinketh not evil; loveth all things, believeth all things, hopeth all things, beareth all things." Thence he shows that it can tenaciously persevere, because it knows how to endure all things. And in another place: "Forbearing one another," he says, "in love, using every effort to keep the unity of the spirit in the bond of peace." He proved that neither unity nor peace could be kept unless brethren should cherish one another with mutual toleration, and should keep the bond of concord by the intervention of patience.

16. What beyond;—that you should not swear nor curse; that you should not seek again your goods when taken from you; that, when you receive a buffet, you should give your other cheek to the smiter; that you should forgive a brother who sins against you, not only seven times, but seventy times seven times, but, moreover, all his sins altogether; that you should love your enemies; that you should offer prayer for your adversaries and persecutors? Can you accomplish these things unless you maintain the stedfastness of patience and endurance? And this we see done in the case of Stephen, who, when he was slain by the Jews with violence and stoning, did not ask for vengeance for himself, but for pardon for his murderers, saying, "Lord, lay not this sin to their charge." It be-

hoved the first martyr of Christ thus to be, who, forerunning the martyrs that should follow him in a glorious death, was not only the preacher of the Lord's passion, but also the imitator of His most patient gentleness. What shall I say of anger, of discord, of strife, which things ought not to be found in a Christian? Let there be patience in the breast, and these things cannot have place there; or should they try to enter they are quickly excluded and depart, that a peaceful abode may continue in the heart, where it delights the God of peace to dwell. Finally, the apostle warns us, and teaches, saying: "Grieve not the Holy Spirit of God, in whom ye are sealed unto the day of redemption. Let all bitterness, and anger, and wrath, and clamour, and blasphemy, be put away from you." For if the Christian have departed from rage and carnal contention as if from the hurricanes of the sea, and have already begun to be tranquil and meek in the harbour of Christ, he ought to admit neither anger nor discord within his breast, since he must neither return evil for evil, nor bear hatred.

17. And moreover, also, for the varied ills of the flesh, and the frequent and severe torments of the body, wherewith the human race is daily wearied and harassed, patience is necessary. For since in that first transgression of the commandment strength of body departed with immortality, and weakness came on with death—and strength cannot be received unless when immortality also has been received—it behoves us, in this bodily frailty and weakness, always to struggle and to fight. And this struggle and encounter cannot be sustained but by the strength of patience. But as we are to be examined and searched out, diverse sufferings are introduced; and a manifold kind of temptations is inflicted by the losses of property, by the heats of fevers, by the torments of wounds, by the loss of those dear to us. Nor does anything distinguish between the unrighteous and the righteous more, than that in affliction the unrighteous man impatiently complains and blasphemes, while the right-

eous is proved by his patience, as it is written: "In pain endure, and in thy low estate have patience; for gold and silver are tried in the fire."

18. Thus Job was searched out and proved, and was raised up to the very highest pinnacle of praise by the virtue of patience What darts of the devil were sent forth against him! What tortures were put in use! The loss of his estate is inflicted, the privation of a numerous offspring is ordained for him. The master, rich in estate, and the father, richer in children, is on a sudden neither master nor father! The wasting of wounds is added; and, moreover, an eating pest of worms consumes his festering and wasting limbs. And that nothing at all should remain that Job did not experience in his trials, the devil arms his wife also, making use of that old device of his wickedness, as if he could deceive and mislead all by women, even as he did in the beginning of the world. And yet Job is not broken down by his severe and repeated conflicts, nor the blessing of God withheld from being declared in the midst of those difficulties and trials of his, by the victory of patience. Tobias also, who, after the sublime works of his justice and mercy, was tried with the loss of his eyes, in proportion as he patiently endured his blindness, in that proportion deserved greatly of God by the praise of patience.

19. And, beloved brethren, that the benefit of patience may still more shine forth, let us consider, on the contrary, what mischief impatience may cause. For as patience is the benefit of Christ, so, on the other hand, impatience is the mischief of the devil; and as one in whom Christ dwells and abides is found patient, so he appears always impatient whose mind the wickedness of the devil possesses. Briefly let us look at the very beginnings. The devil suffered with impatience that man was made in the image of God. Hence he was the first to perish and to ruin others. Adam, contrary to the heavenly command with respect to the deadly food, by impatience fell into death; nor did he keep the grace received

from God under the guardianship of patience. And in order that Cain should put his brother to death, he was impatient of his sacrifice and gift; and in that Esau descended from the rights of the first-born to those of the younger, he lost his priority by impatience for the pottage. Why was the Jewish people faithless and ungrateful in respect of the divine benefits? Was it not the crime of impatience, that they first departed from God? Not being able to bear the delays of Moses conferring with God, they dared to ask for profane gods, that they might call the head of an ox and an earthen image leaders of their march; nor did they ever desist from their impatience, until, impatient always of docility and of divine admonition, they put to death their prophets and all the righteous men, and plunged even into the crime of the crucifixion and bloodshedding of the Lord. Moreover, impatience makes heretics in the Church, and, after the likeness of the Jews, drives them in opposition to the peace and charity of Christ as rebels, to hostile and raging hatred. And, not at length to enumerate single cases, absolutely everything which patience, by its works, builds up to glory, impatience casts down into ruin.

20. Wherefore, beloved brethren, having diligently pondered both the benefits of patience and the evils of impatience, let us hold fast with full watchfulness the patience whereby we abide in Christ, that with Christ we may attain to God; which patience, copious and manifold, is not restrained by narrow limits, nor confined by strait boundaries. The virtue of patience is widely manifest, and its fertility and liberality proceed indeed from a source of one name, but are diffused by overflowing streams through many ways of glory; nor can anything in our actions avail for the perfection of praise, unless from this it receives the substance of its perfection. It is patience which both commends and keeps us to God. It is patience, too, which assuages anger, which bridles the tongue, governs the mind, guards peace, rules discipline, breaks the force of lust, represses the violence of pride, extinguishes the fire of enmity, checks the power of the rich, soothes the want of the poor, protects a blessed integrity in virgins, a careful purity in widows, in those who are united and married a single affection. It makes men humble in prosperity, brave in adversity, gentle towards wrongs and contempts. It teaches us quickly to pardon those who wrong us; and if you yourself do wrong, to entreat long and earnestly. It resists temptations, suffers persecutions, perfects passions and martyrdoms. It is patience which firmly fortifies the foundations of our faith. It is this which lifts up on high the increase of our hope. It is this which directs our doing, that we may hold fast the way of Christ while we walk by His patience. It is this that makes us to persevere as sons of God, while we imitate our Father's patience.

21. But since I know, beloved brethren, that very many are eager, either on account of the burden or the pain of smarting wrongs, to be quickly avenged of those who act harshly and rage against them, we must not withhold the fact in the furthest particular, that placed as we are in the midst of these storms of a jarring world, and, moreover, the persecutions both of Jews or Gentiles, and heretics, we may patiently wait for the day of (God's) vengeance, and not hurry to revenge our suffering with a querulous haste, since it is written, "Wait ye upon me, saith the Lord, in the day of my rising up for a testimony; for my judgment is to the congregations of the nations, that I may take hold on the kings, and pour out upon them my fury." The Lord commands us to wait, and to bear with brave patience the day of future vengeance; and He also speaks in the Apocalypse, saying, "Seal not the sayings of the prophecy of this book: for now the time is at hand for them that persevere in injuring to injure, and for him that is filthy to be filthy still; but for him that is righteous to do things still more righteous, and likewise for him that is holy to do things still more holy. Behold, I come quickly; and my reward is with me, to render to every man ac-

cording to his deeds." Whence also the martyrs crying out and hastening with grief breaking forth to their revenge, are bidden still to wait, and to give patience for the times to be fulfilled and the martyrs to be completed. "And when He had opened," says he, "the fifth seal, I saw under the altar of God the souls of them that were slain for the word of God, and for their testimony; and they cried with a loud voice, saying, How long, O Lord, holy and true, dost Thou not judge and avenge our blood on them that dwell on the earth? And there were given to them each white robes; and it was said unto them that they should rest yet for a little season, until the number of their fellow-servants and brethren is fulfilled, who afterwards shall be slain after their example."

22. But when shall come the divine vengeance for the righteous blood, the Holy Spirit declares by Malachi the prophet, saying, "Behold, the day of the Lord cometh, burning as an oven; and all the aliens and all the wicked shall be stubble; and the day that cometh shall burn them up, saith the Lord." And this we read also in the Psalms, where the approach of God the Judge is announced as worthy to be reverenced for the majesty of His judgment: "God shall come manifest, our God, and shall not keep silence; a fire shall burn before Him, and round about Him a great tempest. He shall call the heaven above, and the earth beneath, that He may separate His people. Gather His saints together unto Him, who establish His covenant in sacrifices; and the heavens shall declare His righteousness, for God is the Judge." And Isaiah foretells the same things, saying: "For, behold, the Lord shall come like a fire, and His chariot as a storm, to render vengeance in anger; for in the fire of the Lord they shall be judged, and with His sword shall they be wounded." And again: "The Lord God of hosts shall go forth, and shall crumble the war to pieces; He shall stir up the battle, and shall cry out against His enemies with strength, I have held my peace; shall I always hold my peace?"

23. But who is this that says that he has held his peace before, and will not hold his peace for ever? Surely it is He who was led as a sheep to the slaughter; and as a lamb before its shearer is without voice, so He opened not His mouth. Surely it is He who did not cry, nor was His voice heard in the streets. Surely He who was not rebellious, neither contradicted, when He offered His back to stripes, and His cheeks to the palms of the hands; neither turned away His face from the foulness of spitting. Surely it is He who, when He was accused by the priests and elders, answered nothing, and, to the wonder of Pilate, kept a most patient silence. This is He who, although He was silent in His passion, yet by and by will not be silent in His vengeance. This is our God, that is, not the God of all, but of the faithful and believing; and He, when He shall come manifest in His second advent, will not be silent. For although He came first shrouded in humility, yet He shall come manifest in power.

24. Let us wait for Him, beloved brethren, our Judge and Avenger, who shall equally avenge with Himself the congregation of His Church, and the number of all the righteous from the beginning of the world. Let him who hurries, and is too impatient for his revenge, consider that even He Himself is not yet avenged who is the Avenger. God the Father ordained His Son to be adored; and the Apostle Paul, mindful of the divine command, lays it down, and says: "God hath exalted Him, and given Him a name which is above every name, that in the name of Jesus every knee should bow, of things heavenly, and things earthly, and things beneath." And in the Apocalypse the angel withstands John, who wishes to worship him, and says: "See thou do it not; for I am thy fellow-servant, and of thy brethren. Worship Jesus the Lord." How great is the Lord Jesus, and how great is His patience, that He who is adored in heaven is not yet avenged on earth! Let us, beloved brethren, consider His patience in our persecutions and sufferings; let us

give an obedience full of expectation to His advent; and let us not hasten, servants as we are, to be defended before our Lord with irreligious and immodest eagerness. Let us rather press onward and labour, and, watching with our whole heart, and stedfast to all endur-ance, let us keep the Lord's precepts; so that when that day of anger and vengeance shall come, we may not be punished with the impious and sinners, but may be honoured with the righteous and those that fear God.

Ephraem Syrus

(306?-373?)

SYRIAN Christianity is animated by the spirit of Ephraem Syrus, whose hymns have become the molding pattern of Christian thought in that part of the world. He is called "the father of Syrian Christian hymnody." Born at Nisibis, Mesopotamia, the son of a priest of the deity Abizal (or Abnil), he was converted by Bishop Jacob of Nisibis and ordained a deacon. Declining ecclesiastical advancement, he devoted himself to writing and teaching and to relieving suffering in the long war with the Persians, during which the city was besieged four times over a quarter century. When the city at last surrendered in 363, he fled with other Christians to Edessa, where he spent the remainder of his life.

The remnants of Ephraem's voluminous commentaries and doctrinal works are of merely historical interest, but his hymns have lived in the worship of Syriac-speaking peoples, especially the collection of seventy-two called *Nisibene Hymns*. Of these the first twenty were written amid the suffering of the last years in Nisibis, the rest in Edessa. Three of the earlier hymns are presented here in the translation of J. T. Sarsfield Stopford from *The Nicene and Post-Nicene Fathers* (New York, 1889).

[PRAYERS OF A SUFFERING CITY]

From *Nisibene Hymns*

IV

My God, without ceasing I will tread the threshold of Thy house; I who have rejected all grace, I will ask with boldness, that I may receive with confidence.

RESPONSE: *Our hope, be thou our Wall!*

2. For if, O Lord, the earth enriches manifold a single grain of wheat, how then shall my prayers be enriched by Thy grace!

3. Because of the voices of my children, their sighs and their groans, open to me the door of Thy mercy! Make glad for their voices the mourning of their sackcloth!

4. O firstborn that wast a weaned *child*, and wast familiar with the children, the accurst sons of Nazareth, hearken to my lambs that have seen the wolves, for lo! they cry.

5. For a flock, O my Lord, in the field, if so be it has seen the wolves, flees to the shepherd, and takes refuge under his staff, and he drives away them that would devour it.

6. Thy flock has seen the wolves, and lo! it cries loudly. Behold how terrified it is! Let thy Cross be a staff, to drive out them that would swallow it up!

7. Accept the cry of my little ones that are altogether pure. It was He, the Infant of days, that could appease, O Lord, the Ancient of days.

8. The day when the Babe came down in the midst of the stall, the Watchers descended and proclaimed peace—may that *peace* be in all my streets for all my offspring.

9. Seventy and two old men, the elders of that people, sufficed not for its breaches. The Babe it was, the Son of

Mary, that gave peace on every side.

10. Have mercy, O Lord, on my children! In my children call to mind Thy childhood, Thou who wast a child! Let them that are like Thy childhood be saved by Thy grace!

11. Mingled in the midst of the flock are the cry of innocents and the voice of the sheep, that call on the Shepherd of all to deliver them from all. . . .

13. There is a joy that is affliction, misery is hidden in it; there is a misery that is profit, it is a fountain of joys in that new world.

14. The happiness that my persecutor has gained, woes are hidden in it; therefore I rejoice. The wretchedness that I have gained from him, happiness is concealed for me in it.

15. Who will not give praise to Him that has begotten us, and can beget again, from the midst of evil rumours, the voices of glad tidings!

16. Thou, Healer of all, hast visited me in my sicknesses! Payment for Thy medicines I cannot give Thee, for they are priceless.

17. Thy mercies in richness surpass Thy medicines: they cannot be bought, they are given freely, it is for tears they are bartered.

18. How, O my Master, can a desolate city, whose king is far off and her enemy nigh, stand firm without *aid* of mercy?

19. A harbour and refuge art Thou at all times. When the seas covered me, Thy mercy descended and drew me out. Again let Thy help lay hold on me!

20. Apply to my afflictions the medicine of Thy salvation and the passion of Thy help! Thy sign can become a medicine to heal all.

21. I am greatly opprest, and I hasten to complain against him that troubles me. Let Thy mercy, my Lord, take the bitterness from the cup that my sins have mixed.

22. I look on all sides, and weep that I am desolate. Very many though be my chiefs and my deliverers, one is He that has delivered me.

23. My young men have fled, O Lord, and gone forth, and are like chickens which an eagle pursues; lo! they hide in a secret place: may Thy peace bring them back!

24. The sound of my grape-gatherers, lo! my ears miss it, for their voices fail. Let it resound with the glad tidings, O Blessed One, of Thy salvation!

25. A voice of terror I have heard on my towers, as my defenders cry while they guard my walls. Still Thou it with the voice of peace!

26. The noise of my husbandmen shall speak peace without my walls; the shouting of my dwellers shall speak peace within my walls, that I may give peace without and within.

27. Make an end, O Lord, of the mourning of this Thy pure altar, and of Thy chaste priest who stands clothed in mourning, covered over with sackcloth!

28. The Church and her ministers shall give praise for Thy salvation; the city and its dwellers. Be the voice of peace, O Lord, the reward of their voices!

V

1. Cause to be heard in Thy grace the tidings of Thy salvation: for an hearing has been made, a path of passage; our minds have been downtrodden by messages of terror.

RESPONSE: *Praises to Thy victory! Glory to Thy Dominion.*

2. Comfort Thou with profits, *though* small and scanty, those that have had harvest of hurt by their labour; at a time of profit they have gained *but* loss.

3. It is manifest that He has stood, portioning wrath upon earth: loss and profit in anger He divided. There are whom He has cast down of a sudden, and there are whom He has puffed up of a sudden.

4. To teach *us* that He can chastise in all ways; when He saw the persecutors were terrible before mine eyes, He laid me out before my children, and they my beloved chastised me.

5. Lo! He taught me to fear Himself and not man; for when there was none to smite us, His wrath gave command of a sudden, and every man stretched himself out and chastised himself.

6. In like manner that Babylonian who struck down all kings when he was confident and hoped that there was none to smite him, God caused that by his own hands he should strike himself down.

7. His majesty and his mind of a sudden became mad together: he rent and cast off his garments; he went forth and wandered in the desert; he drove himself out first, and then his servants drove him out.

8. He showed to all kings whom he had led captive and brought down that not by his own power could he have overcome: the power that struck him down was that which punished them.

9. I have stood and borne, O my Lord, the blows of my deliverers. Thou art able in Thy grace to make me profit by the smiters: Thou art able in Thy justice to punish me by *my* helpers.

10. The day when the host was bold to come up against Samaria; their plenty and their pleasure, their treasures and their possessions, they cast away and forsook and fled. He crowned her by her persecutors.

11. My beloved ones crowned me, and my deliverers healed me. Through the guilt of my dwellers my helpers chastised me; give me drink from Thy vines, of the cup of consolation!

12. The corn and the vine preserve, O my Lord, by Thy grace! Be the husbandman cheered by the vine of the grape-gatherer; be the vinedresser glad in the corn of the husbandman!

13. They are joined each to each, the corn and the grape. In the field the reapers wine can make cheerful, in the vineyard the dressers bread strengthens in turn.

14. These two things have power to comfort my troubles: the Trinity has power to comfort more exceedingly; whom I will praise because of a sudden I was delivered through grace.

15. But the man whose life is preserved through grace, if he goes away to murmur at the loss of his goods, he is thankless for the grace of Him who had pity on him.

16. Of His own will He destroys one thing instead of another. He destroys possession and spares the possessor; He destroys our plants instead of our lives.

17. Let us fear to murmur, lest His own wrath be roused, and He spare the possessions and smite the possessor; that we may learn in the end His mercy in the beginning.

18. Let us learn against whom it is meet for us to murmur. Learn thou to murmur, not against the Chastener, but against thine own will, that made thee sin and thou wast punished.

19. Let us put away murmuring and turn unto prayer; for if the possessor dies, his possessions also cease for him; but while he survives, he seeks to recover his losses.

20. Let consolations be multiplied in mercy to my dwellers: let the remainder and residue console *us* in the midst of wrath; and cause Thou us to forget in the residue the mourning of our devastation!

21. Heal and increase, O my Lord, the fruits Thy wrath has left! They seem to me like sick ones that have escaped in pestilence. Make me to forget in these weak ones the suffering of the many!

22. While I speak, O my Lord, I call to mind that this too is the month when the blossom pined and dropped off in blight; may it return to soundness, to be a consolation!

23. For these escaped the pestilence that carried off their brethren. The vines, *though* voiceless, wept when before them a multitude was cut down and felled of trees that they loved.

24. The company of plants, lo! the earth misses! The roots for the husbandmen weep and cause them to weep. Their beauty had spread and gave shade, and it was torn away in one hour.

25. The axe came nigh and struck, and struck the husbandman; the blow *was* on the trees, and it caused the husbandman to suffer; every axe that smote, he bore the pain of it.

VI

1. I will run in my affections to Him who heals freely. He who healed my

sorrows, the first and the second, *He who cured the third*, He will heal the fourth.

RESPONSES: *Heal me, Thou Son the First Born!*

2. My sons, O my Lord, drank and were drunken of the tidings which wrath had mixed; and they rushed on my adornments, and spoiled and cast away my ornaments; they rent and spared not my garments and my crowns. . . .

8. Restrain him that he come not, and wag at me his head, and stamp on me his heel, and rejoice that the voice of his fame thus troubles the world; and be uplifted yet a little!

9. My sons, O my Lord, have seen my nakedness, yea have uncovered me and wept. Uncover Thou me before my children, who are pained by my pain, and let not those mock at me, the accursed that *have* no pity!

10. My lands had brought forth fruits and pleasant things; good things in the vineyard, abundance in the fields. But as I rested secure, of a sudden wrath overtook *me*.

11. The husbandmen *were* plundered, the spoilers heaped *the grain;* what thou had borrowed and sown these destroyed. With one's debt his hunger haply will also remain unsatisfied, for his bread *is* snatched from him.

12. The husbandman, O my Lord, *is* plundered, for he lent to the earth; she has received the deposit and given it to a stranger; she has borrowed it of the husbandman and paid it to the spoiler.

13. Be jealous over me who am Thine, and to Thee, O my Lord, am I betrothed! The Apostle who betrothed me to Thee told me that Thou art jealous. For *as* a wall to *chaste* wives is the jealously of their husbands.

14. Samson stirred up seas because he was mightily jealous over his wife, *though* she was greatly defiled and was divided against him. Keep Thy Church, for no other has she beside Thee!

15. Whoso is not jealous over his spouse despises her. Jealousy it is that can make known the love that is within.

Thou art called jealous, that Thou mayest show me Thy love.

16. The nature of woman is this; it is weak and rash: it is jealousy keeps it under fear every hour. Thou hast been named among the jealous, that Thou mightest make known Thy solicitude.

17. Every man has been master of something that *was* not his own; every man has gone forth gathering something that he scattered not. The day of confusion I have prepared for myself by my crimes.

18. How shall they bear the suffering, the labourers and tillers? In the face of the vinedresser they have cut down the vines, and driven away the flocks of the husbandman; his sowing they have reaped and carried off.

19. They had yoked cattle, sown, and harrowed, they had ploughed, planted, nurtured. They stood afar and wept; and they went away bereft of all. The labour *was* for the toilers, the increase for the spoilers.

20. The rulers, O my Lord, maintained not order in the midst of *Thy* wrath. If they had willed *it* they might have kept order, but our iniquity suffered it not. *Though* wrath had greatly abated, wrath compelled *them* to spoil.

21. To whom on any side shall I look for comfort, for my plantations that are laid low, and my possessions that are laid waste? Let the message of the voice of peace drive away my sadness from me!

22. Give me not over; lest it be thought that Thou hast given me a writing of divorce, and sent me away and driven me out! Let them not call me, O my Lord, the forsaken and the disgraced!

23. I have not anything to call to mind before Thine eyes, for I am wholly despised. Call Thou to mind for me, O my God, this only, that none other have I set before me beside Thee!

24. Who would not weep for me, with voice and wailing? for before the days of full *moon* I was chaste and crowned, and after the days of full moon I was uncovered and made bare.

25. My chaste daughters of the cham-

bers wander in the fields; for the wrath that makes all drunken has caused my honourable women to be despised. Let Thy mercy, which gives peace to all, restore these beloved ones to honour!

26. My elder *daughters* and my younger, lo! they cry before Thee; the damsels with their voices, they that are aged with their tears; my virgins with their fasts, my chaste ones with their sackcloth!

27. Mine eyes to all the streets I lift up, and lo! they are deserted. There are left of a hundred ten, and a thousand of ten thousand. Give Thou peace and fill my streets with the tumult of my dwellers!

28. Bring back them that are without, and make them glad that are within! Mighty is Thy grace, that Thou extendest it within and without. Let the wings of thy grace gather my chickens together!

29. Let the prayer of my just men save my fugitives! The unbelievers have plundered me, and the believers have sustained me. In them that believe put Thou to shame them that believe not!

30. There came together on one day two festivals as one: the Feast of Thine Ascension and the Feast of Thy Champions; the feast that wove Thy Crown, and the memorial of the crowning of Thy servants.

31. Have Thou mercy because there were doubled for us *these* feasts on one day; and there were doubled for us instead of them, *even* the two feasts in one, suffering from the voice of *ill* tidings, and mourning from desolation!

32. Give peace to my festivals! for both my feasts have ceased; and instead of rejoicing, *of* my remnants in festivals, tremblings and desolations meet me in every place.

33. Bring home mine that are far off, make glad mine that are nigh; and in the midst of our land shall be preached good tidings of joy; and I shall render in return for peace praise from every mouth!

Gregory of Nyssa
(331?-396?)

IN THE list of Nicene Fathers there is no more reverenced name than that of Gregory of Nyssa. One of the four great Fathers of the Greek Church, he is acclaimed as one of the notable orators, writers, and theologians of the Eastern Church. One critic calls him "the Father of Fathers."

Gregory was born into a wealthy Christian home, the son of a rhetorician who died early. The boy was reared under the pious influence of his mother Emmelia, his grandmother Macrina, his older brother Basil, and his sister Macrina. Because of delicate health he was educated at home. Shy and retiring, he avoided baptism for years, and finally sought monastic life at Pontus. In 370 when his brother Basil became bishop of Eusebius, Gregory reluctantly became bishop of Nyssa, a small town in west Cappadocia. As bishop he suffered many persecutions from the more liberal Arians and Sabellians. The later years of his life are obscure; the last known event about him is his attendance in 394 at a synod in Constantinople.

From his pen come a number of devotional and ascetic tracts, conservative in theology and of extreme mystical tone, such as is later found in Dionysius the Areopagite. *On Pilgrimages* pictures the saintly view that God is to be found where we are, especially by men and women of modesty. It contains a deep note of asceticism. It is translated by William Moore and Henry Austin Wilson in *The Nicene and Post-Nicene Fathers* (New York, 1889).

ON PILGRIMAGES

Since, my friend, you ask me a question in your letter, I think that it is incumbent upon me to answer you in their proper order upon all the points connected with it. It is, then, my opinion that it is a good thing for those who have dedicated themselves once for all to the higher life to fix their attention continually upon the utterances in the Gospel, and, just as those who correct their work in any given material by a rule, and by means of the straightness of that rule bring the crookedness which their hands detect to straightness, so it is right that we should apply to these questions a strict and flawless measure as it were, —I mean, of course, the Gospel rule of life,—and in accordance with that, direct ourselves in the sight of God. Now there are some amongst those who have entered upon the monastic and hermit life, who have made it a part of their devotion to behold those spots at Jerusalem, where the memorials of our Lord's life in the flesh are on view; it would be well, then, to look to this Rule, and if the finger of its precepts points to observance of such things, to perform the work, as the actual injunction of our Lord; but if they lie quite outside the commandment of the Master, I do not see what there is to command any one who has become a law of duty to himself to be zealous in performing any of them. When the Lord invites the blest to their inheritance in the kingdom of heaven, He does not include a pilgrimage to Jerusalem amongst their good deeds; when He announces the Beatitudes, He does not name amongst them that sort of devotion. But as to that which neither makes us blessed nor sets us in the path to the kingdom, for what reason it should be run after, let him that is wise consider. Even if there were some profit in what they do, yet even so, those who are perfect would do best not to be eager in practising it; but since this matter, when closely looked into, is found to inflict upon those who have begun to lead the stricter life a moral mischief, it is so far from being worth an earnest pursuit, that it actually requires the greatest caution to prevent him who has devoted himself to God from being penetrated by any of its hurtful influences. What is it, then, that is hurtful in it? The Holy Life is open to all, men and women alike. Of that contemplative Life the peculiar mark is Modesty. But Modesty is preserved in societies that live distinct and separate, so that there should be no meeting and mixing up of persons of opposite sex; men are not to rush to keep the rules of Modesty in the company of women, nor women to do so in the company of men. But the necessities of a journey are continually apt to reduce this scrupulousness to a very indifferent observance of such rules. For instance, it is impossible for a woman to accomplish so long a journey without a conductor; on account of her natural weakness she has to be put upon her horse and to be lifted down again; she has to be supported in difficult situations. Whichever we suppose, that she has an acquaintance to do this yeoman's service, or a hired attendant to perform it, either way the proceeding cannot escape being reprehensible; whether she leans on the help of a stranger, or on that of her own servant, she fails to keep the law of correct conduct; and as the inns and hostelries and cities of the East present many examples of licence and of indifference to vice, how will it be possible for one passing through such smoke to escape without smarting eyes? Where the ear and the eye is defiled, and the heart too, by receiving all those foulnesses through eye and ear, how will it be possible to thread without infection such seats of contagion? What advantage, moreover, is reaped by him who reaches those celebrated spots themselves? He cannot imagine that our Lord is living, in the body, there at the present day, but has gone away from us foreigners; or that the Holy Spirit is in abundance at Jerusalem, but unable to travel as far as us. Whereas, if it is really possible to infer God's presence from visible symbols, one might more justly consider that He dwelt in the Cappadocian nation than in any of the spots outside it. For how many Altars there are there, on which the name of our Lord is glorified! One could hardly count so many in all the rest of the world. Again, if the Divine grace was more abundant about Jerusalem than elsewhere, sin would not be so much the fashion amongst those that live there; but as it is, there is no form of uncleanness that is not perpetrated amongst them; rascality, adultery, theft, idolatry, poisoning, quarrelling, murder, are rife; and the last kind of evil is so excessively prevalent, that nowhere in the world are people so ready to kill each other as there; where kinsmen attack each other like wild beasts, and spill each other's blood, merely for the sake of lifeless plunder. Well, in a place where such things go on, what proof, I ask, have you of the abundance of Divine grace? But I know what many will retort to all that I have said; they will say, "Why did you not lay down this rule for yourself as well? If there is no gain for the godly pilgrim in return for having been there, for what reason did you undergo the toil of so long a journey?" Let them hear from me my plea for this. By the necessities of that office in which I have been placed by the Dispenser of my life to live, it was my duty, for the purpose of the correction which the Holy Council had resolved upon, to visit the places where the Church in Arabia is; secondly, as Arabia is on the confines of the Jerusalem district, I had promised that I would confer also with the Heads of the Holy Jerusalem Churches, because matters with them were in confusion, and needed an arbiter; thirdly, our most religious Emperor had granted us facilities for the journey, by postal conveyance, so that we had to endure none of those inconveniences which in the case of others we have noticed; our waggon was, in fact, as good as a church or monastery to us, for all of us were singing psalms and fasting in the Lord during the whole journey. Let our own case

therefore cause difficulty to none; rather let our advice be all the more listened to, because we are giving it upon matters which came actually before our eyes. We confessed that the Christ Who was manifested is very God, as much before as after our sojourn at Jerusalem; our faith in Him was not increased afterwards any more than it was diminished. Before we saw Bethlehem we knew His being made man by means of the Virgin; before we saw His Grave we believed in His Resurrection from the dead; apart from seeing the Mount of Olives, we confessed that His Ascension into heaven was real. We derived only thus much of profit from our travelling thither, namely that we came to know by being able to compare them, that our own places are far holier than those abroad. Wherefore, O ye who fear the Lord, praise Him in the places where ye now are. Change of place does not effect any drawing nearer unto God, but wherever thou mayest be, God will come to thee, if the chambers of thy soul be found of such a sort that He can dwell in thee and walk in thee. But if thou keepest thine inner man full of wicked thoughts, even if thou wast on Golgotha, even if thou wast on the Mount of Olives, even if thou stoodest on the memorial-rock of the Resurrection, thou wilt be as far away from receiving Christ into thyself, as one who has not even begun to confess Him. Therefore, my beloved friend, counsel the brethren to be absent from the body to go to our Lord, rather than to be absent from Cappadocia to go to Palestine; and if any one should adduce the command spoken by our Lord to His disciples that they should not quit Jerusalem, let him be made to understand its true meaning. Inasmuch as the gift and the distribution of the Holy Spirit had not yet passed upon the Apostles, our Lord commanded them to remain in the same place, until they should have been endued with power from on high. Now, if that which happened at the beginning, when the Holy Spirit was dispensing each of His gifts under the appearance of a flame, continued until now, it would be right for all to remain in that place where that dispensing took place; but if the Spirit "bloweth" where He "listeth," those, too, who have become believers here are made partakers of that gift; and that according to the proportion of their faith, not in consequence of their pilgrimage to Jerusalem.

Chrysostom

(345?-407)

AFTER a severe life as an ascetic John "the Golden-Mouthed" became the ablest preacher of the Eastern Church. Born of a rich patrician family, he became at twenty a pupil of Libanius the rhetorician at Antioch. At first he intended to practice law but decided against that profession because of its worldliness. He then studied the Scriptures and was baptized by Bishop Meletus of Antioch in 368. Imbued with asceticism, he went into solitude with an old Syrian monk for four years in a mountain near Antioch. When he was forced to return to Antioch in 380 because of his health, he tempered his ascetic practices. In 386 he was ordained priest, and in 398 he became patriarch of Constantinople.

In Constantinople his friendliness to Origen's thought and his criticism of the lax clergy brought him enmity and trouble. When he was exiled by Empress Eudoxia to Cucusus near Armenia, his influence on his friends by letters was tremendous. Out of his deep knowledge of God Chrysostom knows in his troubled days that *None Can Harm Him Who Does Not Injure Himself*. Of his friends he asks, "Let us endure all painful things bravely that we may obtain those everlasting and pure blessings in Christ Jesus!" This treatise is presented, with some abridgment, from the translation by W. R. W. Stephens in *The Nicene and Post-Nicene Fathers* (New York, 1889).

NONE CAN HARM HIM WHO DOES NOT INJURE HIMSELF

I know well that to coarse-minded persons, who are greedy in the pursuit of present things, and are nailed to earth, and enslaved to physical pleasure, and have no strong hold upon spiritual ideas, this treatise will be of a strange and paradoxical kind: and they will laugh immoderately, and condemn me for uttering incredible things from the very outset of my theme. Nevertheless, I shall not on this account desist from my promise, but for this very reason shall proceed with great earnestness to the proof of what I have undertaken. For if those who take that view of my subject will please not to make a clamour and disturbance, but wait to the end of my discourse, I am sure that they will take my side, and condemn themselves, finding that they have been deceived hitherto, and will make a recantation, and apology, and crave pardon for the mistaken opinion which they held concerning these matters, and will express great gratitude to me, as patients do to physicians, when they have been relieved from the disorders which lay seige to their body. . . .

Now in the place of an orator we have the common assumption of mankind which in the course of ages has taken deep root in the minds of the multitude, and declaims to the following effect throughout the world. "All things" it says "have been turned upside down, the human race is full of much confusion and many are they who every day are being wronged, insulted, subjected to violence and injury, the weak by the strong, the poor by the rich: and as it is impossible to number the waves of the sea, so is it impossible to reckon the multitude of those who are the victims of intrigue, insult, and suffering; and neither the correction of law, nor the fear of being brought to trial, nor anything else can arrest this pestilence and disorder, but the evil is increasing every day, and the groans, and lamentations, and weeping of the sufferers are universal; and the judges who are appointed to reform such evils, themselves intensify the tempest, and inflame the disorder, and hence many of the more senseless and despicable kind, seized with a new kind of frenzy, accuse the providence of God, and when they see the forbearing man often violently seized, racked, and oppressed, and the audacious, impetuous, low and low-born man waxing rich, and invested with authority, and becoming formidable to many, and inflicting countless troubles upon the more moderate, and this perpetrated both in town and country, and desert, on sea and land. This discourse of ours of necessity comes in by way of direct opposition to what has been alleged, maintaining a contention which is new, as I said at the beginning, and contrary to opinion, yet useful and true, and profitable to those who will give heed to it and be persuaded by it; for what I undertake is to prove (only make no commotion) that no one of those who are wronged is wronged by another, but experiences this injury at his own hands.

2. But in order to make my argument plainer, let us first of all enquire what injustice is, and of what kind of things the material of it is wont to be composed; also what human virtue is, and what it is which ruins it; and further what it is which seems to ruin it but really does not. For instance (for I must complete my argument by means of examples) each thing is subject to one evil which ruins it; iron to rust, wool to moth, flocks of sheep to wolves. The virtue of wine is injured when it ferments and turns sour: of honey when it loses its natural sweetness, and is reduced to a bitter juice. Ears of corn are ruined by mildew and drought, and the fruit, and leaves, and branches of vines by the mischievous host of locusts, other trees by the caterpillar, and irrational creatures by diseases of various kinds: and not to lengthen the list by going through all possible examples, our own flesh is subject to fevers, and palsies, and a crowd of other maladies. As then each one of these things is liable to that which ruins its virtue, let us now consider what it is which injures the human race, and what it is which ruins the virtue of a human being. Most men think that there are divers things which have this effect; for I must mention the erroneous opinions on the subject, and, after confuting them, proceed to exhibit that which really does ruin our virtue: and to demonstrate clearly that no one could inflict this injury or bring this ruin upon us unless we betrayed ourselves. The multitude then having erroneous opinions imagine that there are many different things which ruin our virtue: some say it is poverty, others bodily disease, others loss of property, others calumny, others death, and they are perpetually bewailing and lamenting these things: and whilst they are commiserating the sufferers and shedding tears they excitedly exclaim to one another, "What a calamity has befallen such and such a man! he has been deprived of all his fortune at a blow." Of another again one will say: "such and such a man has been attacked by severe sickness and is despaired of by the physicians in attendance." Some bewail and lament the inmates of the prison, some those who have been expelled from their country and transported to the land of exile, others those who have been deprived of their freedom, others those who have been seized and made captives by enemies, others those who have been drowned, or burnt, or buried by the fall of a house, but no one mourns those who are living in wickedness: on the contrary, which is worse than all, they often congratulate them, a practice which is the cause of all manner of evils. Come then (only, as I exhorted you at the outset, do not make a commotion), let me prove that none of the things which have been mentioned injure the man who lives soberly, nor can ruin his virtue. For tell

me if a man has lost his all either at the hands of calumniators or of robbers, or has been stripped of his goods by knavish servants, what harm has the loss done to the virtue of the man?

But if it seems well let me rather indicate in the first place what is the virtue of a man, beginning by dealing with the subject in the case of existences of another kind so as to make it more intelligible and plain to the majority of readers.

3. What then is the virtue of a horse? is it to have a bridle studded with gold and girths to match, and a band of silken threads to fasten the housing, and clothes wrought in divers colours and gold tissue, and head gear studded with jewels, and locks of hair plaited with gold cord? or is it to be swift and strong in its legs, and even in its paces, and to have hoofs suitable to a well bred horse, and courage fitted for long journies and warfare, and to be able to behave with calmness in the battle field, and if a rout takes place to save its rider? Is it not manifest that these are the things which constitute the virtue of the horse, not the others? Again, what should you say was the virtue of asses and mules? is it not the power of carrying burdens with contentment, and accomplishing journies with ease, and having hoofs like rock? Shall we say that their outside trappings contribute anything to their own proper virtue? By no means. And what kind of vine shall we admire? one which abounds in leaves and branches, or one which is laden with fruit? or what kind of virtue do we predicate of an olive? is it to have large boughs, and great luxuriance of leaves, or to exhibit an abundance of its proper fruit dispersed over all parts of the tree? Well, let us act in the same way in the case of human beings also: let us determine what is the virtue of man, and let us regard that alone as an injury, which is destructive to it. What then is the virtue of man? not riches that thou shouldest fear poverty: nor health of body that thou shouldest dread sickness, nor the opinion of the public, that thou shouldest view an evil reputation with alarm, nor life simply for its own sake, that death should be terrible to thee: nor liberty that thou shouldest avoid servitude: but carefulness in holding true doctrine, and rectitude in life. Of these things not even the devil himself will be able to rob a man, if he who possesses them guards them with the needful carefulness: and that most malicious and ferocious demon is aware of this. For this cause also he robbed Job of his substance, not to make him poor, but that he might force him into uttering some blasphemous speech; and he tortured his body, not to subject him to infirmity, but to upset the virtue of his soul. But nevertheless when he had set all his devices in motion, and turned him from a rich man into a poor one (that calamity which seems to us the most terrible of all), and had made him childless who was once surrounded by many children, and had scarified his whole body more cruelly than the executioners do in the public tribunals (for their nails do not lacerate the sides of those who fall into their hands so severely as the gnawing of the worms lacerated his body), and when he had fastened a bad reputation upon him (for Job's friends who were present with him said "thou hast not received the chastisement which thy sins deserve," and directed many words of accusation against him), and after he had not merely expelled him from city and home and transferred him to another city, but had actually made the dunghill serve as his home and city; after all this, he not only did him no damage but rendered him more glorious by the designs which he formed against him. And he not only failed to rob him of any of his possessions although he had robbed him of so many things, but he even increased the wealth of his virtue. For after these things he enjoyed greater confidence inasmuch as he had contended in a more severe contest. Now if he who underwent such sufferings, and this not at the hand of man, but at the hand of the devil who is more wicked than all men, sustained no injury, which of those persons who say such and such a man in-

jured and damaged me will have any defence to make in future? For if the devil who is full of such great malice, after having set all his instruments in motion, and discharged all his weapons, and poured out all the evils incident to man, in a superlative degree upon the family and the person of that righteous man nevertheless did him no injury, but as I was saying rather profited him: how shall certain be able to accuse such and such a man alleging that they have suffered injury at their hands, not at their own? . . .

5. When then neither loss of money, nor slander, nor railing, nor banishment, nor diseases, nor tortures, nor that which seems more formidable than all, namely death, harms those who suffer them, but rather adds to their profit, whence can you prove to me that any one is injured when he is not injured at all from any of these things? For I will endeavour to prove the reverse, showing that they who are most injured and insulted, and suffer the most incurable evils are the persons who do these things. For what could be more miserable than the condition of Cain, who dealt with his brother in this fashion? what more pitiable than that of Phillip's wife who beheaded John? or the brethren of Joseph who sold him away, and transported him into the land of exile? or the devil who tortured Job with such great calamities? For not only on account of his other iniquities, but at the same time also for this assault he will pay no trifling penalty. Dost thou see how here the argument has proved even more than was proposed, shewing that those who are insulted not only sustain no harm from these assaults, but that the whole mischief recoils on the head of those who contrive them? For since neither wealth nor freedom, nor life in our native land nor the other things which I have mentioned, but only right actions of the soul, constitute the virtue of man, naturally when the harm is directed against these things, human virtue itself is no wise harmed. . . . And what shall I say of Paul? Did he not suffer so many distresses that even to make a list of them is no easy matter? He was put in prison, loaded with chains, dragged hither and thither, scourged by the Jews, stoned, lacerated on the back not only by thongs, but also by rods, he was immersed in the sea, oftentimes beset by robbers, involved in strife with his own countrymen, continually assailed both by foes and by acquaintance, subjected to countless intrigues, struggling with hunger and nakedness, undergoing other frequent and lasting mischances and afflictions: and why need I mention the greater part of them? he was dying every day: but yet, although subjected to so many and such grievous sufferings, he not only uttered no blasphemous word, but rejoiced over these things and gloried in them: and one time he says "I rejoice in my sufferings," and then again "not only this but we also glory in afflictions." If then he rejoiced and gloried when suffering such great troubles what excuse will you have, and what defence will you make if you blaspheme when you do not undergo the smallest fraction of them.

6. But I am injured in other ways, one will say, and even if I do not blaspheme, yet when I am robbed of my money I am disabled from giving alms. This is a mere pretext and pretence. For if you grieve on this account know certainly that poverty is no bar to almsgiving. For even if you are infinitely poor you are not poorer than the woman who possessed only a handful of meal, and the one who had only two mites, each of whom having spent all her substance upon those who were in need was an object of surpassing admiration: and such great poverty was no hindrance to such great lovingkindness, but the alms bestowed from the two mites was so abundant and generous as to eclipse all who had riches, and in wealth of intention and superabundance of zeal to surpass those who cast in much coin. Wherefore even in this matter thou art not injured but rather benefited, receiving by means of a small contribution rewards more glorious than they who put down large

sums. But since, if I were to say these things for ever, sensuous characters which delight to grovel in worldly things, and revel in present things would not readily endure parting from the fading flowers (for such are the pleasant things of this life) or letting go its shadows: but the better sort of men indeed cling to both the one and the other, while the more pitiable and abject cling more strongly to the former than to the latter, come let us strip off the pleasant and showy masks which hide the base and ugly countenance of these things, and let us expose the foul deformity of the harlot. For such is the character of a life of this kind which is devoted to luxury, and wealth and power: it is foul and ugly and full of much abomination, disagreeable and burdensome, and charged with bitterness. For this indeed is the special feature in this life which deprives those who are captivated by it of every excuse, that although it is the aim of their longings and endeavours, yet it is filled with much annoyance and bitterness, and teems with innumerable evils, dangers, bloodshed, precipices, crags, murders, fears and tremblings, envy and ill-will, and intrigue, perpetual anxiety and care, and derives no profit, and produces no fruit from these great evils save punishment and revenge, and incessant torment. But although this is its character it seems to be to most men an object of ambition, and eager contention, which is a sign of the folly of those who are captivated by it, not of the blessedness of the thing itself. Little children indeed are eager and excited about toys and cannot take notice of the things which become full grown men. There is an excuse for them on account of their immaturity: but these others are debarred from the right of defence, because, although of full age they are childish in disposition, and more foolish than children in their manner of life.

Now tell me why is wealth an object of ambitions? For it is necessary to start from this point, because to the majority of those who are afflicted with this grievous malady it seems to be more precious than health and life, and public reputation, and good opinion, and country, and household, and friends, and kindred and everything else. Moreover the flame has ascended to the very clouds: and this fierce heat has taken possession of land and sea. Nor is there any one to quench this fire: but all people are engaged in stirring it up, both those who have been already caught by it, and those who have not yet been caught, in order that they may be captured. And you may see everyone, husband and wife, household slave, and freeman, rich and poor, each according to his ability carrying loads which supply much fuel to this fire by day and night: loads not of wood of faggots (for the fire is not of that kind), but loads of souls and bodies, of unrighteousness and iniquity. For such is the material of which a fire of this kind is wont to be kindled. For those who have riches place no limit anywhere to this monstrous passion, even if they compass the whole world: and the poor press on to get in advance of them, and a kind of incurable craze, and unrestrainable frenzy and irremediable disease possesses the souls of all. And this affection has conquered every other kind and thrust it away expelling it from the soul: neither friends nor kindred are taken into account: and why do I speak of friends and kindred? not even wife and children are regarded, and what can be dearer to man than these? but all things are dashed to the ground and trampled underfoot, when this savage and inhuman mistress has laid hold of the souls of all who are taken captive by her. For as an inhuman mistress, and harsh tyrant, and savage barbarian, and public and expensive prostitute she debases and exhausts and punishes with innumerable dangers and torments those who have chosen to be in bondage to her; and yet although she is terrible and harsh, and fierce and cruel, and has the face of a barbarian, or rather of a wild beast, fiercer than a wolf or a lion, she seems to those who have been taken captive by her gentle and loveable, and sweeter than honey. And although she forges swords and weapons against them every day, and digs pitfalls and leads them to precipices and crags and weaves endless snares of punishment for them, yet is she supposed to make these things objects of ambition to those who have been made captive, and those who are desiring to be captured. And just as a sow delights and revels in wallowing in the ditch and mire, and beetles delight in perpetually crawling over dung; even so they who are captivated by the love of money are more miserable than these creatures. For the abomination is greater in this case, and the mire more offensive: for they who are addicted to this passion imagine that much pleasure is derived from it: which does not arise from the nature of the thing, but of the understanding which is afflicted with such an irrational taste. And this taste is worse in their case than in that of brutes: for as with the mire and the dung the cause of pleasure is not in them, but in the irrational nature of the creatures who plunge into it; even so count it to be in the case of human beings.

7. And how might we cure those who are thus disposed? It would be possible if they would open their ears to us, and unfold their heart, and receive our words. For it is impossible to turn and divert the irrational animals from their unclean habit; for they are destitute of reason: but this the gentlest of all tribes, honoured by reason and speech, I mean human nature, might, if it chose, readily and easily be released from the mire and the stench, and the dung hill and its abomination. For wherefore, O man, do riches seem to thee worthy such diligent pursuit? Is it on account of the pleasure which no doubt is derived from the table? or on account of the honour and the escort of those who pay court to thee, because of thy wealth? is it because thou art able to defend thyself against those who annoy thee, and to be an object of fear to all? For you cannot name any other reasons, save pleasure and flattery, and fear, and the power of taking revenge; for wealth is not generally wont to make any one wiser, or more self-controlled, or more gentle, or more intelli-

gent, or kind, or benevolent, or superior to anger, or gluttony or pleasure: it does not train any one to be moderate, or teach him how to be humble, nor introduce and implant any other piece of virtue in the soul. Neither could you say for which of these things it deserves to be so diligently sought and desired. For not only is it ignorant how to plant and cultivate any good thing, but even if it finds a store of them it mars and stunts and blights them; and some of them it even uproots, and introduces their opposites, unmeasured licentiousness, unseasonable wrath, unrighteous anger, pride, arrogance, foolishness. But let me not speak of these; for they who have been seized by this malady will not endure to hear about virtue and vice, being entirely abandoned to pleasure and therefore enslaved to it. Come then let us forego for the time being the consideration of these points, and let us bring forward the others which remain, and see whether wealth has any pleasure, or any honour: for in my eyes the case is quite the reverse. And first of all, if you please, let us investigate the meals of rich and poor, and ask the guests which they are who enjoy the purest and most genuine pleasure; is it they who recline for a full day on couches, and join breakfast and dinner together, and distend their stomach, and blunt their senses, and sink the vessel by an overladen cargo of food, and waterlog the ship, and drench it as in some shipwreck of the body, and devise fetters and manacles, and gags, and bind their whole body with the band of drunkenness and surfeit more grievous than an iron chain, and enjoy no sound pure sleep undisturbed by frightful dreams, and are more miserable than madmen and introduce a kind of self-imposed demon into the soul and display themselves as a laughing stock to the gaze of their servants, or rather to the kinder sort amongst them as a tragical spectacle eliciting tears, and cannot recognize any of those who are present, and are incapable of speaking or hearing but have to be carried away from their couches to their bed;—or is it they who are sober and vigilant, and limit their eating by their need, and sail with a favourable breeze, and find hunger and thirst the best relish in their food and drink? For nothing is so conducive to enjoyment and health as to be hungry and thirsty when one attacks the viands, and to identify satiety with simple necessity of food, never overstepping the limits of this, nor imposing a load upon the body too great for its strength.

8. But if you disbelieve my statement study the physical condition, and the soul of each class. Are not the bodies vigorous of those who live thus moderately (for do not tell me of that which rarely happens, although some may be weak from some other circumstance, but form your judgment from those instances which are of constant occurrence), I say are they not vigorous, and their senses clear, fulfilling their proper function with much ease? whereas the bodies of the others are flaccid and softer than wax, and beset with a crowd of maladies? For gout soon fastens upon them, and untimely palsy, and premature old age, and headache, and flatulence, and feebleness of digestion, and loss of appetite, and they require constant attendance of physicians, and perpetual doseing, and daily care. Are these things pleasurable? tell me. Who of those that know what pleasure really is would say so? For pleasure is produced when desire leads the way, and fruition follows: now if there is fruition, but desire is nowhere to be found, the conditions of pleasure fail and vanish. On this account also invalids, although the most charming food is set before them, partake of it with a feeling of disgust and sense of oppression: because there is no desire which gives a keen relish to the enjoyment of it. For it is not the nature of the food, or of the drink but the appetite of the eaters which is wont to produce the desire, and is capable of causing pleasure. Therefore also a certain wise man who had an accurate knowledge of all that concerned pleasure, and understood how to moralize about these things said "the full soul mocketh at honeycombs:"

showing that the conditions of pleasure consist not in the nature of the meal, but in the disposition of the eaters. Therefore also the prophet recounting the wonders in Egypt and in the desert mentioned this in connection with the others "He satisfied them with honey out of the rock." And yet nowhere does it appear that honey actually sprang forth for them out of the rock: what then is the meaning of the expression? Because the people being exhausted by much toil and long travelling, and distressed by great thirst rushed to the cool spring, their craving for drink serving as a relish, the writer wishing to describe the pleasures which they received from those fountains called the water honey, not meaning that the element was converted into honey, but that the pleasure received from the water rivalled the sweetness of honey, inasmuch as those who partook of it rushed to it in their eagerness to drink.

Since then these things are so and no one can deny it, however stupid he may be: is it not perfectly plain that pure, undiluted, and lively pleasure is to be found at the tables of the poor? whereas at the tables of the rich there is discomfort, and disgust and defilement? as that wise man has said "even sweet things seem to be a vexation."

9. But riches some one will say procure honour for those who possess them, and enable them to take vengeance on their enemies with ease. And is this a reason, pray, why riches seem to you desirable and worth contending for;—that they nourish the most dangerous passion in our nature, leading on anger into action, swelling the empty bubbles of ambition, and stimulating and urging men to arrogance? Why these are just the very reasons why we ought resolutely to turn our backs upon riches, because they introduce certain fierce and dangerous wild beasts into our heart depriving us of the real honour which we might receive from all, and introducing to deluded men another which is the opposite of this, only painted over with its colours, and persuading them to fancy that

it is the same, when by nature it is not so, but only seems to be so to the eye. For as the beauty of courtesans, made up as it is of dyes and pigments, is destitute of real beauty, yet makes a foul and ugly face appear fair and beautiful to those who are deluded by it when it is not so in reality: even so also riches force flattery to look like honour. For I beg you not to consider the praises which are openly bestowed through fear and fawning: for these are only tints and pigments; but unfold the conscience of each of those who flatter you in this fashion, and inside it you will see countless accusers declaring against you, and loathing and detesting you more than your bitterest adversaries and foes. And if ever a change of circumstances should occur which would remove and expose this mask which fear has manufactured, just as the sun when it emits a hotter ray than usual discloses the real countenances of those women whom I mentioned, then you will see clearly that all through the former time you were held in the greatest contempt by those who paid court to you, and you fancied you were enjoying honour from those who thoroughly hated you, and in their heart poured infinite abuse upon you, and longed to see you involved in extreme calamities. For there is nothing like virtue to produce honour,—honour neither forced nor feigned, nor hidden under a mask of deceit, but real and genuine, and able to stand the test of hard times.

10. But do you wish to take vengeance on those who have annoyed you? This, as I was saying just now, is the very reason why wealth ought specially to be avoided. For it prepares thee to thrust the sword against thyself, and renders thee liable to a heavier account in the future day of reckoning, and makes thy punishment intolerable. For revenge is so great an evil that it actually revokes the mercy of God, and cancels the forgiveness of countless sins which has been already bestowed. For he who received remission of the debt of ten thousand talents, and after having obtained so great a boon by merely asking for it then made a demand of one hundred pence from his fellow servant, a demand, that is, for satisfaction for his transgression against himself, in his severity towards his fellow servant recorded his own condemnation; and for this reason and no other he was delivered to the tormentors, and racked, and required to pay back the ten thousand talents; and he was not allowed the benefit of any excuse or defence, but suffered the most extreme penalty, having been commanded to deposit the whole debt which the lovingkindness of God had formerly remitted. Is this then the reason, pray, why wealth is so earnestly pursued by thee, because it so easily conducts thee into sin of this kind? Nay verily, this is why you ought to abhor it as a foe and an adversary teeming with countless murders. But poverty, some one will say, disposes men to be discontented and often also to utter profane words, and condescend to mean actions. It is not poverty which does this, but littleness of soul: for Lazarus also was poor, aye! very poor: and besides poverty he suffered from infirmity, a bitterer trial than any form of poverty, and one which makes poverty more severely felt; and in addition to infirmity there was a total absence of protectors, and difficulty in finding any to supply his wants, which increased the bitterness of poverty and infirmity. For each of these things is painful in itself, but when there are none to minister to the sufferer's wants, the suffering becomes greater, the flame more painful, the distress more bitter, the tempest fiercer, the billows stronger, the furnace hotter. And if one examines the case thoroughly there was yet a fourth trial besides these—the unconcern and luxury of the rich man who dwelt hard by. And if you would find a fifth thing, serving as fuel to the flame, you will see quite clearly that he was beset by it. For not only was that rich man living luxuriously, but twice, and thrice, or rather indeed several times in the day he saw the poor man: for he had been laid at his gate, being a grievous spectacle of pitiable distress, and the bare sight of

him was sufficient to soften even a heart of stone: and yet even this did not induce that unmerciful man to assist this case of poverty: but he had his luxurious table spread, and goblets wreathed with flowers, and pure wine plentifully poured forth, and grand armies of cooks, and parasites, and flatterers from early dawn, and troops of singers, cupbearers, and jesters; and he spent all his time in devising every species of dissipation, and drunkenness, and surfeiting, and in revelling in dress and feasting and many other things. But although he saw that poor man every day distressed by grievous hunger and the bitterest infirmity, and the oppression of his many sores, and by destitution, and the ills which result from these things, he never even gave him a thought: yet the parasites and the flatterers were pampered even beyond their need; but the poor man, and he so very poor, and encompassed with so many miseries, was not even vouchsafed the crumbs which fell from that table, although he greatly desired them: and yet none of these things injured him, he did not give vent to a bitter word, he did not utter a profane speech; but like a piece of gold which shines all the more brilliantly when it is purified by excessive heat, even so he, although oppressed by these sufferings, was superior to all of them, and to the agitation which in many cases is produced by them. For if generally speaking poor men, when they see rich men, are consumed with envy and racked by malicious ill-will, and deem life not worth living, and this even when they are well supplied with necessary food, and have persons to minister to their wants; what would the condition of this poor man have been had he not been very wise and noble hearted, seeing that he was poor beyond all other poor men, and not only poor, but also infirm, and without any one to protect or cheer him, and lay in the midst of the city as if in a remote desert, and wasted away with bitter hunger, and saw all good things being poured upon the rich man as out of a fountain, and had not the benefit of any human consolation,

but lay exposed as a perpetual meal for the tongues of the dogs, for he was so enfeebled and broken down in body that he could not scare them away? Dost thou perceive that he who does not injure himself suffers no evil? for I will again take up the same argument.

11. For what harm was done to this hero by his bodily infirmity? or by the absence of protectors? or by the coming of the dogs? or the evil proximity of the rich man? or by the great luxury, haughtiness and arrogance of the latter? Did it enervate him for the contest on behalf of virtue? Did it ruin his fortitude? Nowhere was he harmed at all, but the multitude of sufferings, and the cruelty of the rich man, rather increased his strength, and became the pledge for him of infinite crowns of victory, a means of adding to his rewards, and augmentation of his recompense, and a promise of an increased requital. For he was crowned not merely on account of his poverty, or of his hunger or of his sores, or of the dogs licking them: but because, having such a neighbour as the rich man, and being seen by him every day, and perpetually overlooked he endured this trial bravely and with much fortitude, a trial which added no small flame but in fact a very strong one to the fire of poverty, and infirmity and loneliness.

And, tell me, what was the case of the blessed Paul? for there is nothing to prevent my making mention of him again. Did he not experience innumerable storms of trial? And in what respect was he injured by them? Was he not crowned with victory all the more in consequence,—because he suffered hunger, because he was consumed with cold and nakedness, because he was often tortured with the scourge, because he was stoned, because he was cast into the sea? But then some one says he was Paul, and called by Christ. Yet Judas also was one of the twelve, and he too was called of Christ; but neither his being of the twelve nor his call profited him, because he had not a mind disposed to virtue. But Paul although struggling with hunger, and at a loss to procure necessary food, and daily undergoing such great sufferings, pursued with great zeal the road which leads to heaven: whereas Judas although he had been called before him, and enjoyed the same advantages as he did, and was initiated in the highest form of Christian life, and partook of the holy table and that most awful of sacred feasts, and received such grace as to be able to raise the dead, and cleanse the lepers, and cast out devils, and often heard discourses concerning poverty, and spent so long a time in the company of Christ Himself, and was entrusted with the money of the poor, so that his passion might be soothed thereby (for he was a thief) even then did not become any better, although he had been favoured with such great condescension. For since Christ knew that he was covetous, and destined to perish on account of his love of money he not only did not demand punishment of him for this at that time, but with a view to softening down his passion he was entrusted with the money of the poor, that having some means of appeasing his greed he might be saved from falling into that appalling gulf of sin, checking the greater evil beforehand by a lesser one.

12. Thus in no case will any one be able to injure a man who does not choose to injure himself: but if a man is not willing to be temperate, and to aid himself from his own resources no one will ever be able to profit him. Therefore also that wonderful history of the Holy Scriptures, as in some lofty, large, and broad picture, has portrayed the lives of the men of old time, extending the narrative from Adam to the coming of Christ: and it exhibits to you both those who are upset, and those who are crowned with victory in the contest, in order that it may instruct you by means of all examples that no one will be able to injure one who is not injured by himself, even if all the world were to kindle a fierce war against him. For it is not stress of circumstances, nor variation of seasons, nor insults of men in power, nor intrigues besetting thee like snow storms, nor a crowd of calamities, nor a promiscuous collection of all the ills to which mankind is subject, which can disturb even slightly the man who is brave, and temperate, and watchful; just as on the contrary the indolent and supine man who is his own betrayer cannot be made better, even with the aid of innumerable ministrations. . . .

13. Would you like me to illustrate this argument in the case of whole nations? What great forethought was bestowed upon the Jewish nation! was not the whole visible creation arranged with a view to their service? was not a new and strange method of life introduced amongst them? For they had not to send down to a market, and so they had the benefit of things which are sold for money without paying any price for them: neither did they cleave furrows nor drag a plough, nor harrow the ground, nor cast in seed, nor had they need of rain and wind, and annual seasons, nor sunshine, nor phases of the moon, nor climate, nor anything of that kind; they prepared no threshing floor, they threshed no grain, they used no winnowing fan for separating the grain from the chaff, they turned no millstone, they built no oven, they brought neither wood nor fire into the house, they needed no baker's art, they handled no spade, they sharpened no sickle, they required no other art, I mean of weaving or building or supplying shoes: but the word of God was everything to them. And they had a table prepared off hand, free of all toil and labour. For such was the nature of the manna; it was new and fresh, nowhere costing them any trouble, nor straining them by labour. And their clothes, and shoes, and even their physical frame forgot their natural infirmity: for the former did not wear out in the course of so long a time nor did their feet swell although they made such long marches. Of physicians, and medicine, and all other concern about that kind of art, there was no mention at all amongst them; so completely banished was infirmity of every kind: for it is said "He brought them out with silver and gold; and there was not one

feeble person among their tribes." But like men who had quitted this world, and were transplanted to another and a better one, even so did they eat and drink, neither did the sun's ray when it waxed hot smite their heads; for the cloud parted them from the fiery beam, hovering all round them, and serving like a portable shelter for the whole body of the people. Neither at night did they need a torch to disperse the darkness, but they had the pillar of fire, a source of unspeakable light, supplying two wants, one by its shining, the other by directing the course of their journey; for it was not only luminous, but also conducted that countless host along the wilderness with more certainty than any human guide. And they journeyed not only upon land but also upon sea as if it had been dry land; and they made an audacious experiment upon the laws of nature by treading upon that angry sea, marching through it as if it had been the hard and resisting surface of a rock; and indeed when they placed their feet upon it the element became like solid earth, and gently sloping plains and fields; but when it received their enemies it wrought after the nature of sea; and to the Israelites indeed it served as a chariot, but to their enemies it became a grave; conveying the former across with ease, but drowning the latter with great violence. And the disorderly flood of water displayed the good order and subordination which marks reasonable and highly intelligent men, fulfilling the part at one time of a guardian, at another of an executioner, and exhibiting these opposites together on one day. What shall one say of the rocks which gave forth streams of water? what of the clouds of birds which covered the whole face of the earth by the number of their carcases? what of the wonders in Egypt? what of the marvels in the wilderness? what of the triumphs and bloodless victories? for they subdued those who opposed them like men keeping holiday rather than making war. And they vanquished their own masters without the use of arms; and overcame those who fought with them after they left Egypt by means of singing and music; and what they did was a festival rather than a campaign, a religious ceremony rather than a battle. For all these wonders took place not merely for the purpose of supplying their need, but also that the people might preserve more accurately the doctrine which Moses inculcated of the knowledge of God; and voices proclaiming the presence of their Master were uttered on all sides of them. For the sea loudly declared this, by becoming a road for them to march upon, and then turning into sea again: and the waters of the Nile uttered this voice when they were converted into the nature of blood; and the frogs, and the great army of locusts, and the caterpillar and blight declared the same thing to all the people; and the wonders in the desert, the manna, the pillar of fire, the cloud, the quails, and all the other incidents served them as a book, and writing which could never be effaced, echoing daily in their memory and resounding in their mind. Nevertheless after such great and remarkable providence, after all those unspeakable benefits, after such mighty miracles, after care indescribable, after continual teaching, after instruction by means of speech, and admonition by means of deeds, after glorious victories, after extraordinary triumphs, after abundant supply of food, after the plentiful production of water, after the ineffable glory with which they were invested in the eyes of the human race, being ungrateful and senseless they worshipped a calf, and paid reverence to the head of a bull, even when the memorials of God's benefits in Egypt were fresh in their minds, and they were still in actual enjoyment of many more. . . .

15. Again, I ask, was the virtue of the "three children" corrupted by the troubles which beset them? Whilst they were still young, mere youths, of immature age, did they not undergo that grievous affliction of captivity? had they not to make a long journey from home, and when they had arrived in the foreign country were they not cut off from fa-

therland and home and temple, and altar and sacrifices, and offerings, and drink offerings, and even the singing of psalms? For not only were they debarred from their home, but as a consequence from many forms of worship also. Were they not given up into the hands of barbarians, wolves rather than men? and, most painful calamity of all, when they had been banished into so distant and barbarous a country, and were suffering such a grievous captivity were they not without teacher, without prophets, without ruler? "for," it is written, "there is no ruler, nor prophet, nor governor, nor place for offering before Thee and finding mercy." Yea moreover they were cast into the royal palace, as upon some cliff and crag, and a sea full of rocks and reefs, being compelled to sail over that angry sea without a pilot, or signal man, or crew, or sails; and they were cooped up in the royal court as in a prison. For inasmuch as they knew spiritual wisdom, and were superior to worldly things, and despised all human pride and made the wings of their soul soar upwards, they counted their sojourn there as an aggravation of their trouble. For had they been outside the court, and dwelling in a private house they would have enjoyed more independence: but having been cast into that prison (for they deemed the splendour of the palace no better than a prison, no safer than a place of rocks and crags) they were straightway subjected to cruel embarrassment. For the king commanded them to be partakers of his own table, a luxurious, unclean and profane table, a thing which was forbidden them, and seemed more terrible than death; and they were lonely men hemmed in like lambs amongst so many wolves. And they were constrained to choose between being consumed by famine or rather led off to execution, and tasting of forbidden meats. What then did these youths do, forlorn as they were, captives, strangers, slaves of those who commanded these things. They did not consider that this strait or the absolute power of him who possessed the state sufficed to justify their compliance; but they employed every device and expedient to enable them to avoid the sin, although they were abandoned on every side. For they could not influence men by money: how should they, being captives? nor by friendship and social intercourse? how should they being strangers? nor could they get the better of them by any exertion of power: how was it possible being slaves? nor master them by force of numbers: how could they being only three? Therefore they approached the eunuch who possessed the necessary authority, and persuaded him by their arguments. For when they saw him fearful and trembling, and in an agony of alarm concerning his own safety, and the dread of death which agitated his soul was intolerable: "for I fear" said he "my lord the king, lest he should see your countenances sadder than the children which are of your sort and so shall ye endanger my head to the king," having released him from this fear they persuaded him to grant them the favour. And inasmuch as they brought to the work all the strength which they had, God also henceforth contributed his strength to it. For it was not God's doing only that they achieved those things for the sake of which they were to receive a reward, but the beginning and starting point was from their own purpose, and having manifested that to be noble and brave, they won for themselves the help of God, and so accomplished their aim.

16. Dost thou then perceive that if a man does not injure himself, no one else will be able to harm him? Behold at least youthfulness, and captivity and destitution, and removal into a foreign land, and loneliness, and dearth of protectors, and a stern command, and great fear of death assailing the mind of the eunuch, and poverty, and feebleness of numbers, and dwelling in the midst of barbarians, and having enemies for masters, and surrender into the hands of the king himself, and separation from all their kindred, and removal from priests and prophets, and from all others who cared

for them, and the cessation of drink offerings and sacrifices, and loss of the temple and psalmody, and yet none of these things harmed them; but they had more renown then than when they enjoyed these things in their native land. And after they had accomplished this task first and had wreathed their brows with the glorious garland of victory, and had kept the law even in a foreign land, and trampled under foot the tyrant's command, and overcome fear of the avenger, and yet received no harm from any quarter, as if they had been quietly living at home and enjoying the benefit of all those things which I mentioned, after they had thus fearlessly accomplished their work they were again summoned to other contests. And again they were the same men; and they were subjected to a more severe trial than the former one, and a furnace was kindled, and they were confronted by the barbarian army in company with the king: and the whole Persian force was set in motion and everything was devised which tended to put deceit or constraint upon them: divers kinds of music, and various forms of punishment, and threats, and what they saw on every side of them was alarming, and the words which they heard were more alarming than what they saw; nevertheless inasmuch as they did not betray themselves, but made the most of their own strength, they never sustained any kind of damage: but even won for themselves more glorious crowns of victory than before. For Nabuchadonosor bound them and cast them into the furnace, yet he burnt them not, but rather benefited them, and rendered them more illustrious. And although they were deprived of temple (for I will repeat my former remarks) and altar, and fatherland, and priests and prophets, although they were in a foreign and barbarous country, in the very midst of the furnace, surrounded by all that mighty host, the king himself who wrought this looking on, they set up a glorious trophy, and won a notable victory, having sung that admirable and extraordinary hymn which from that day

to this has been sung throughout the world and will continue to be sung to future generations.

Thus then when a man does not injure himself, he cannot possibly be hurt by another: for I will not cease harping constantly upon this saying. For if captivity, and bondage, and loneliness and loss of country and all kindred and death, and burning, and a great army and a savage tyrant could not do any damage to the innate virtue of the three children captives, bondmen, strangers though they were in a foreign land, but the enemy's assault became to them rather the occasion of greater confidence: what shall be able to harm the temperate man? There is nothing, even should he have the whole world in arms against him. But, some one may say, in their case God stood beside them, and plucked them out of the flame. Certainly He did; and if thou wilt play thy part to the best of thy power, the help which God supplies will assuredly follow.

17. Nevertheless the reason why I admire those youths, and pronounce them blessed, and enviable, is not because they trampled on the flame, and vanquished the force of the fire: but because they were bound, and cast into the furnace, and delivered to the fire for the sake of true doctrine. For this it was which constituted the completeness of their triumph, and the wreath of victory was placed on their brows as soon as they were cast into the furnace and before the issue of events it began to be weaved for them from the moment that they uttered those words which they spoke with much boldness and freedom of speech to the king when they were brought into his presence. "We have no need to answer thee concerning this thing: for our God in Heaven whom we serve is able to rescue us out of the burning fiery furnace: and He will deliver us out of thy hands, O King. But if not, be it known unto thee, O King, that we will not serve thy Gods nor worship the golden image which thou hast set up." After the utterance of these words I proclaimed them conquerors;

after these words having grasped the prize of victory, they hastened on to the glorious crown of martyrdom, following up the confession which they made through their words with the confession made through their deeds. But if when they had been cast into it, the fire had respect for their bodies, and undid their bonds, and suffered them to go down into it without fear, and forgot its natural force, so that the furnace of fire became as a fountain of cool water, this marvel was the effect of God's grace and of the divine wonder-working power. Yet the heroes themselves even before these things took place, as soon as they set foot in the flames had erected their trophy, and won their victory, and put on their crown, and had been proclaimed conquerors both in Heaven and on earth, and so far as they were concerned nothing was wanting for their renown. What then wouldst thou have to say to these things? Hast thou been driven into exile, and expelled from thy country? Behold so also were they. Hast thou suffered captivity, and become the servant of barbarian masters. Well! this also thou wilt find befell these men. But thou hast no one present there to regulate thy state nor to advise or instruct thee? Well! of attention of this kind these men were destitute. Or thou hast been bound, burned, put to death? for thou canst not tell me of anything more painful than these things. Yet lo! these men having gone through them all, were made more glorious by each one of them, yea more exceedingly illustrious, and increased the store of their treasures in Heaven. And the Jews indeed who had both temple, and altar, and ark and cherubim, and mercy-seat, and veil, and an infinite multitude of priests, and daily services, and morning and evening sacrifices, and continually heard the voices of the prophets, both living and departed, sounding in their ears, and carried about with them the recollection of the wonders which were done in Egypt, and in the wilderness, and all the rest, and turned the story of these things over in their hands, and had them inscribed upon their door posts and enjoyed the benefit at that time of much supernatural power and every other kind of help were yet no wise profited, but rather damaged, having set up idols in the temple itself, and having sacrificed their sons and daughters under trees, and in almost every part of the country in Palestine having offered those unlawful and accursed sacrifices, and perpetrated countless other deeds yet more monstrous. But these men although in the midst of a barbarous and hostile land, having their occupation in a tyrant's house, deprived of all that care of which I have been speaking, led away to execution, and subjected to burning, not only suffered no harm there from small or great, but became the more illustrious. Knowing then these things, and collecting instances of the like kind from the inspired divine Scriptures (for it is possible to find many such examples in the case of various other persons) we deem that neither a difficulty arising from seasons or events, nor compulsion and force, nor the arbitrary authority of potentates furnish a sufficient excuse for us when we transgress. I will now conclude my discourse by repeating what I said at the beginning, that if any one be harmed and injured he certainly suffers this at his own hands, not at the hands of others even if there be countless multitudes injuring and insulting him: so that if he does not suffer this at his own hands, not all the creatures who inhabit the whole earth and sea if they combined to attack him would be able to hurt one who is vigilant and sober in the Lord. Let us then, I beseech you, be sober and vigilant at all times, and let us endure all painful things bravely that we may obtain those everlasting and pure blessings in Christ Jesus our Lord, to whom be glory and power, now and ever throughout all ages. Amen.

Augustine

(354-430)

Two of the great devotional classics of Christendom come from Augustine. Living at a time when the Roman Empire was beginning to fall, he envisions the church as *The City of God*. And out of his own life, torn between licentiousness and intellectual pursuits until his conversion, comes the fabric for one of the classic spiritual autobiographies of all literature, *The Confessions*.

Augustine was born at Tagaste, North Africa. His father Patricius became a Christian only toward the end of his life, but his mother Monica was a lifelong Christian who had great influence on her son. At nineteen, in reading Cicero's *Hortensius*, Augustine was moved to the search for religious truth. His attention was then drawn to Manicheism with its dualistic system which saw evil caused by a force of darkness in the universe. Later he turned to Neo-Platonism, which saw God as the source of all good, and evil as a mere illusion. Finally, guided by Bishop Ambrose, Augustine found his answer to salvation in Paul's letter to the Romans, and was baptized in Milan during the Easter season of 387. He was made bishop of Hippo, North Africa, in 395 and held this post the remainder of his life.

The following selections from *The Confessions* (*ca.* 397) were translated by E. B. Pusey; those from *The City of God* (*ca.* 413-26) by John Healey.

[REFLECTIONS ON THE MAJESTY AND MERCY OF GOD]

From *The Confessions*

FROM BOOK I

. . . *And* how shall I call upon my God, my God and Lord, since, when I call for Him, I shall be calling Him to myself? and what room is there within me, whither my God can come into me? Whither can God come into me, God who made heaven and earth? Is there, indeed, O Lord my God, aught in me that can contain Thee? Do then heaven and earth, which Thou hast made, and wherein Thou hast made me, contain Thee? or, because nothing which exists could exist without Thee, doth therefore whatever exists contain Thee? Since, then, I too exist, why do I seek that Thou shouldest enter into me, who were not, wert Thou not in me? Why? Because I am not gone down in hell, and yet Thou art there also. For *if I go down into hell, Thou art there*. I could not be then, O my God, could not be at all, wert Thou not in me; or, rather, unless I were in Thee, *of whom are all things, by whom are all things, in whom are all things?* Even so, Lord, even so. Whither do I call Thee, since I am in Thee? or whence canst Thou enter into me? For whither can I go beyond heaven and earth, that thence my God should come into me, who hath said, *I fill the heaven and the earth?*

3. Do the heaven and earth then contain Thee, since Thou fillest them? or dost Thou fill them and yet overflow, since they do not contain Thee? And whither, when the heaven and the earth are filled, pourest Thou forth the remainder of Thyself? Or hast Thou no need that aught contain Thee, who containest all things, since what Thou fillest Thou fillest by containing it? For the vessels which Thou fillest uphold Thee not, since, though they were broken, Thou wert not poured out. And when Thou art *poured out* on us, Thou art not cast down, but Thou upliftest us; Thou

are not dissipated, but Thou gatherest us. But Thou who fillest all things, fillest Thou them with Thy whole self? or, since all things cannot contain Thee wholly, do they contain part of Thee? and all at once the same part? or each its own part, the greater more, the smaller less? And is, then, one part of Thee greater, another less? or, art Thou wholly every where, while nothing contains Thee wholly?

4. What art Thou then, my God? What, but the Lord God? *For who is Lord but the Lord? or who is God save our God?* Most highest, most good, most potent, most omnipotent; most merciful, yet most just; most hidden, yet most present; most beautiful, yet most strong; stable, yet incomprehensible; unchangeable, yet all-changing; never new, never old; all-renewing, and *bringing age upon the proud, and they know it not;* ever working, ever at rest; still gathering, yet nothing lacking; supporting, filling, and overspreading; creating, nourishing, and maturing; seeking, yet having all things. Thou lovest, without passion; art jealous, without anxiety; repentest, yet grievest not; art angry, yet serene; changest Thy works, Thy purpose unchanged; receivest again what Thou findest, yet didst never lose; never in need, yet rejoicing in gains; never covetous, yet exacting usury. Thou receivest over and above, that Thou mayest owe; and who hath aught that is not Thine? Thou payest debts, owing nothing; remittest debts, losing nothing. And what have I now said, my God, my life, my holy joy? or what saith any man when he speaks of Thee? Yet woe to him that speaketh not, since mute are even the most eloquent.

5. Oh! that I might repose on Thee! Oh! that Thou wouldest enter into my heart, and inebriate it, that I may forget my ills, and embrace Thee, my sole good? What art Thou to me? In Thy pity, teach me to utter it. Or what am I to Thee that Thou demandest my love, and, if I give it not, art wroth with me, and threatenest me with grievous woes? Is it then a slight woe to love Thee not?

Oh! for Thy mercies' sake, tell me, O Lord my God, what Thou art unto me. *Say unto my soul, I am thy salvation.* So speak, that I may hear. Behold, Lord, my heart is before Thee; open Thou the ears thereof, and *say unto my soul, I am thy salvation.* After this voice let me haste, and take hold on Thee. Hide not Thy face from me. Let me die—lest I die—only let me see Thy face.

6. Narrow is the mansion of my soul; enlarge Thou it, that Thou mayest enter in. It is ruinous; repair Thou it. It has that within which must offend Thine eyes; I confess and know it. But who shall cleanse it? or to whom should I cry, save Thee? *Lord, cleanse me from my secret faults, and spare Thy servant from the power of the enemy. I believe, and therefore do I speak.* Lord, Thou knowest. *Have I not confessed against myself my transgressions unto Thee, and Thou, my God, hast forgiven the iniquity of my heart? I contend not in judgment with Thee,* who art the truth; I fear to deceive myself; *lest mine iniquity lie unto itself.* Therefore I contend not in judgment with Thee; *for if Thou, Lord, shouldest mark iniquities, O Lord, who shall abide it?*

7. Yet suffer me to speak unto Thy mercy, me, *dust and ashes.* Yet suffer me to speak, since I speak to Thy mercy, and not to scornful man. Thou too, perhaps, despisest me, yet wilt Thou *return and have compassion* upon me. For what would I say, O Lord my God, but that I know not whence I came into this dying life (shall I call it?) or living death. Then immediately did the comforts of Thy compassion take me up, as I heard (for I remember it not) from the parents of my flesh, out of whose substance Thou didst sometime fashion me. Thus there received me the comforts of woman's milk. For neither my mother nor my nurses stored their own breasts for me; but Thou didst bestow the food of my infancy through them, according to Thine ordinance, whereby Thou distributest Thy riches through the hidden springs of all things. Thou also gavest me to desire no more than Thou gavest;

and to my nurses willingly to give me what Thou gavest them. For they, with an heaven-taught affection, willingly gave me, what they abounded with from Thee. For this my good from them, was good for them. Nor, indeed, from them was it, but through them; for from Thee, O God, are all good things, and *from my God is all my health*. This I since learned, Thou, through these Thy gifts, within me and without, proclaiming Thyself unto me. For then I knew but to suck; to repose in what pleased, and cry at what offended my flesh; nothing more. . . .

24. Hear, Lord, my prayer; let not my soul faint under Thy discipline, nor let me faint in confessing unto Thee all Thy mercies, whereby Thou hast drawn me out of all my most evil ways, that Thou mightest become a delight to me above all the allurements which I once pursued; that I may most entirely love Thee, and clasp Thy hand with all my affections, and Thou mayest yet rescue me from every temptation, even unto the end. For, lo, O Lord, my King and my God, for Thy service be whatever useful thing my childhood learned; for Thy service, that I speak—write—read—reckon. For Thou didst grant me Thy discipline, while I was learning vanities; and my sin of delighting in those vanities Thou hast forgiven. In them, indeed, I learnt many a useful word, but these may as well be learned in things not vain; and that is the safe path for the steps of youth. . . .

31. Yet, Lord, to Thee, the Creator and Governor of the universe, most excellent and most good, thanks were due to Thee our God, even hadst Thou destined for me boyhood only. For even then I was, I lived, and felt; and had an implanted providence over my own well-being,—a trace of that mysterious Unity, whence I was derived;—I guarded by the inward sense the entireness of my senses, and in these minute pursuits, and in my thoughts on things minute, I learnt to delight in truth, I hated to be deceived, had a vigorous memory, was gifted with speech, was soothed by friendship, avoided pain, baseness, ignorance. In so small a creature, what was not wonderful, not admirable? But all are gifts of my God; it was not I, who gave them me; and good these are, and these together are myself. Good, then, is He that made me, and He is my good; and before Him will I exult for every good which of a boy I had. For it was my sin, that not in Him, but in His creatures—myself and others—I sought for pleasures, sublimities, truths, and so fell headlong into sorrows, confusions, errors. Thanks be to Thee, my joy and my glory and my confidence, my God, thanks be to Thee for Thy gifts; but do Thou preserve them to me. For so wilt Thou preserve me, and those things shall be enlarged and perfected, which Thou hast given me, and I myself shall be with Thee, since even to be Thou hast given me.

FROM BOOK II

13. For so doth pride imitate exaltedness; whereas Thou Alone art God exalted over all. Ambition, what seeks it, but honours and glory? whereas Thou Alone art to be honoured above all, and glorious for evermore. The cruelty of the great would fain be feared; but who is to be feared but God alone, out of whose power what can be wrested or withdrawn? when, or where, or whither, or by whom? The tendernesses of the wanton would fain be counted love: yet is nothing more tender than Thy charity; nor is aught loved more healthfully than Thy truth, bright and beautiful above all. Curiosity makes semblance of a desire of knowledge; whereas Thou supremely knowest all. Yea, ignorance and foolishness itself is cloked under the name of simplicity and uninjuriousness; because nothing is found more single than Thee: and what less injurious, since they are his own works, which injure the sinner? Yea, sloth would fain be at rest; but what stable rest besides the Lord? Luxury affects to be called plenty and abundance; but Thou art the fulness and never-failing plenteousness of incorruptible pleasures. Prodigality presents a shadow of liberality: but Thou art the most over-

flowing Giver of all good. Covetousness would possess many things: and Thou possessest all things. Envy disputes for excellency: what more excellent than Thou? Anger seeks revenge: who revenges more justly than Thou? Fear startles at things unwonted and sudden, which endanger things beloved, and takes forethought for their safety; but to Thee what unwonted or sudden, or who separateth from Thee what Thou lovest? Or where but with Thee is unshaken safety? Grief pines away for things lost, the delight of its desires; because it would have nothing taken from it, as nothing can from Thee.

From Book IV

12. O madness, which knowest not how to love men, like men! O foolish man that I then was, enduring impatiently the lot of man! I fretted then, sighed, wept, was distracted; had neither rest nor counsel. For I bore about a shattered and bleeding soul, impatient of being borne by me, yet where to repose it, I found not. Not in calm groves, not in games and music, nor in fragrant spots, nor in curious banquettings, nor in the pleasures of the bed and the couch; nor (finally) in books or poesy, found it repose. All things looked ghastly, yea, the very light; whatsoever was not what he was, was revolting and hateful, except groaning and tears. For in those alone found I a little refreshment. But when my soul was withdrawn from them, a huge load of misery weighed me down. To Thee, O Lord, it ought to have been raised, for Thee to lighten; I knew it; but neither could or would; the more, since, when I thought of Thee, Thou wert not to me any solid or substantial thing. For Thou wert not Thyself, but a mere phantom, and my error was my God. If I offered to discharge my load thereon, that it might rest, it glided through the void, and came rushing down again on me; and I had remained to myself a hapless spot, where I could neither be, nor be from thence. For whither should my heart flee from my heart? Whither should I flee from myself? Whither not follow myself?

From Book VII

16. And being thence admonished to return to myself, I entered even into my inward self, Thou being my Guide: and able I was, for Thou wert become my Helper. And I entered and beheld with the eye of my soul, (such as it was,) above the same eye of my soul, above my mind, the Light Unchangeable. Not this ordinary light, which all flesh may look upon, nor as it were a greater of the same kind, as though the brightness of this should be manifold brighter, and with its greatness take up all space. Not such was this light, but other, yea, far other from all these. Nor was it above my soul, as oil is above water, nor yet as heaven above earth: but above to my soul, because It made me; and I below It, because I was made by It. He that knows the Truth, knows what that Light is; and he that knows It, knows eternity. Love knoweth it. O Truth Who art Eternity! and Love Who art Truth! and Eternity Who art Love! Thou art my God, to Thee do I sigh night and day. Thee when I first knew, Thou liftedst me up, that I might see there was what I might see, and that I was not yet such as to see. And Thou didst beat back the weakness of my sight, streaming forth Thy beams of light upon me most strongly, and I trembled with love and awe: and I perceived myself to be far off from Thee. . . . And I said, "Is Truth therefore nothing because it is not diffused through space finite or infinite?" And Thou criedst to me from afar; "Yea verily, *I AM that I AM*." . . .

21. And I looked back on other things; and I saw that they owed their being to Thee; and were all bounded in Thee: but in a different way; not as being in space; but because Thou containest all things in Thine hand in Thy Truth; and all things are true so far as they be; nor is there any falsehood, unless when that is thought to be, which is not. And I saw that all things did harmonize, not with their places only, but with their seasons.

And that Thou, who only art Eternal, didst not begin to work after innumerable spaces of times spent; for that all spaces of times, both which have passed, and which shall pass, neither go nor come, but through Thee, working, and abiding.

22. And·I perceived and found it nothing strange, that bread which is pleasant to a healthy palate, is loathsome to one distempered: and to sore eyes light is offensive, which to the sound is delightful. And Thy righteousness displeaseth the wicked; much more the viper and reptiles, which Thou hast created good, fitting in with the inferior portions of Thy Creation, with which the very wicked also fit in; and that the more, by how much they be unlike Thee; but with the superior creatures, by how much they become more like to Thee. And I enquired what iniquity was, and found it to be no substance, but the perversion of the will, turned aside from Thee, O God, the Supreme, towards these lower things, and *casting out its bowels*, and puffed up outwardly. . . .

24. Then I sought a way of obtaining strength, sufficient to enjoy Thee; and found it not, until I embraced *that Mediator betwixt God and men, the Man Christ Jesus, who is over all, God blessed for evermore*, calling unto me, and saying, *I am the way, the truth, and the life*, and mingling that food which I was unable to receive, with our flesh. *For the Word was made flesh*, that Thy wisdom, whereby Thou createdst all things, might provide milk for our infant state. For I did not hold to my Lord Jesus Christ, I humbled to the humble; nor knew I yet whereto His infirmity would guide us. For Thy Word, the Eternal Truth, far above the· higher parts of Thy Creation, raises up the subdued unto Itself: but in this lower world built for Itself a lowly habitation of our clay, whereby to abase from themselves such as would be subdued, and bring them over to Himself; allaying their swelling, and fomenting their love; to the end they might go on no further in self-confidence, but rather consent to become weak, seeing before their feet the Divinity weak by taking our *coats of skin;* and wearied, might cast themselves down upon It, and It rising, might lift them up. . . .

FROM BOOK IX

1. *O Lord, I am Thy servant; I am Thy servant, and the son of Thy handmaid: Thou hast broken my bonds in sunder. I will offer to Thee the sacrifice of praise.* Let my heart and my tongue praise Thee; yea let *all my bones say, O Lord, who is like unto Thee?* Let them say, and answer Thou me, and *say unto my soul, I am thy salvation.* Who am I, and what am I? What evil have not been either my deeds, or if not my deeds, my words, or if not my words, my will? But Thou, O Lord, art good and merciful, and Thy right hand had respect unto the depth of my death, and from the bottom of my heart emptied that abyss of corruption. And this Thy whole gift was, to nill what I willed, and to will what Thou willedst. But where through all those years, and out of what low and deep recess was my free-will called forth in a moment, whereby to submit my neck to Thy *easy yoke*, and my shoulders unto Thy *light burthen, O Christ Jesus, my Helper and my Redeemer?* How sweet did it at once become to me, to want the sweetnesses of those toys! and what I feared to be parted from, was now a joy to part with. For Thou didst cast them forth from me, Thou true and highest sweetness. . . . Now was my soul free from the biting cares of canvassing and getting, and weltering in filth, and scratching off the itch of lust. And my infant tongue spake freely to Thee, my brightness, and my riches, and my health, the Lord my God.

FROM BOOK X

1. Let me know Thee, O Lord, who knowest me: *let me know Thee as I am known.* Power of my soul, enter into it, and fit it for Thee, that Thou mayest have and hold it *without spot or wrinkle.* This is my hope, *therefore do I speak;* and in this hope do I rejoice, when I rejoice healthfully. Other things of this

life are the less to be sorrowed for, the more they are sorrowed for; and the more to be sorrowed for, the less men sorrow for them. For behold, Thou *lovest the truth*, and *he that doth it, cometh to the light*. This would I do in my heart before Thee in confession: and in my writing, before many witnesses.

2. And from Thee, O Lord, *unto whose eyes* the abyss of man's conscience is naked, what could be hidden in me though I would not confess it? For I should hide Thee from me, not me from Thee. But now, for that my groaning is witness, that I am displeased with myself, Thou shinest out, and art pleasing, and beloved, and longed for; that I may be ashamed of myself, and renounce myself, and choose Thee, and neither please Thee, nor myself, but in Thee. To Thee therefore, O Lord, am I open, whatever I am; and with what fruit I confess unto Thee, I have said. Nor do I it with words and sounds of the flesh, but with the words of my soul, and the cry of the thought which Thy ear knoweth. For when I am evil, then to confess to Thee, is nothing else than to be displeased with myself; but when holy, nothing else than not to ascribe it to myself: because Thou, O Lord, *blessest the godly*, but first Thou *justifieth him when ungodly*. My confession then, O my God, in Thy sight, is made silently, and not silently. For in sound, it is silent; in affection, it cries aloud. For neither do I utter any thing right unto men, which Thou hast not before heard from me; nor dost Thou hear any such thing from me, which Thou hast not first said unto me. . . .

8. Not with doubting, but with assured consciousness, do I love Thee, Lord. Thou hast stricken my heart with Thy word, and I loved Thee. Yea also *heaven, and earth, and all that therein is*, behold, on every side they bid me love Thee; nor cease to say so unto all, *that they may be without excuse*. But more deeply *wilt Thou have mercy on whom Thou wilt have mercy, and wilt have compassion on whom Thou hast had compassion*: else in deaf ears do the heaven and the earth speak Thy praises. But what do I love, when I love Thee? not beauty of bodies, nor the fair harmony of time, nor the brightness of the light, so gladsome to our eyes, nor sweet melodies of varied songs, nor the fragrant smell of flowers, and ointments, and spices, not manna and honey, not limbs acceptable to embracements of flesh. None of these I love, when I love my God; and yet I love a kind of light, and melody, and fragrance, and meat, and embracement, when I love my God, the light, melody, fragrance, meat, embracement of my inner man: where there shineth unto my soul, what space cannot contain, and there soundeth, what time beareth not away, and there smelleth, what breathing disperseth not, and there tasteth, what eating diminisheth not, and there clingeth, what satiety divorceth not. This is it which I love, when I love my God. . . .

26. Great is the power of memory, a fearful thing, O my God, a deep and boundless manifoldness; and this thing is the mind, and this am I myself. What am I then, O my God? What nature am I? . . . So great is the force of memory, so great the force of life, even in the mortal life of man. What shall I do then, O Thou my true life, my God? I will pass even beyond this power of mine which is called memory: yea, I will pass beyond it, that I may approach unto Thee, O sweet Light. What sayest Thou to me? See, I am mounting up through my mind towards Thee who abidest above me. Yea I now will pass beyond this power of mine which is called memory, desirous to arrive at Thee, whence Thou mayest be arrived at; and to cleave unto Thee, whence one may cleave unto Thee. For even beasts and birds have memory; else could they not return to their dens and nests, nor many other things they are used unto: nor indeed could they be used to any thing, but by memory. I will pass then beyond memory also, that I may arrive at Him who hath separated me from the four-footed beasts and made me wiser than the fowls of the air, I will pass beyond memory

also, and where shall I find Thee, Thou truly good and certain sweetness? And where shall I find Thee? If I find Thee without my memory, then do I not retain Thee in my memory. And how shall I find Thee, if I remember Thee not? . . .

37. Where then did I find Thee, that I might learn Thee? For in my memory Thou wert not, before I learned Thee. Where then did I find Thee, that I might learn Thee, but in Thee above me? Place there is none; *we go backward and forward*, and there is no place. Every where, O Truth, dost Thou give audience to all who ask counsel of Thee, and at once answerest all, though on manifold matters they ask Thy counsel. Clearly dost Thou answer, though all do not clearly hear. All consult Thee on what they will, though they hear not always what they will. He is thy best servant, who looks not so much to hear that from Thee, which himself willeth; as rather to will that, which from Thee he heareth.

38. Too late loved I Thee, O Thou Beauty of ancient days, yet ever new! too late I loved Thee! And behold, Thou wert within, and I abroad, and there I searched for Thee; deformed I, plunging amid those fair forms, which Thou hadst made. Thou wert with me, but I was not with Thee. Things held me far from Thee, which, unless they were in Thee, were not at all. Thou calledst, and shoutedst, and burstest, my deafness. Thou flashedst, shonest, and scatteredst my blindness. Thou breathed odours, and *I drew in breath* and *pant for Thee*. I tasted and *hunger and thirst*. Thou touchedst me, and I burned for Thy peace. . . .

FROM BOOK XI

3. O Lord my God, give ear unto my prayer, and let Thy mercy hearken unto my desire: because it is anxious not for myself alone, but would serve brotherly charity; and Thou seest my heart, that so it is. I would sacrifice to Thee the service of my thought and tongue; do Thou give me, what I may offer Thee.

For *I am poor and needy, Thou rich to all that call upon Thee;* Who, inaccessible to care, carest for us. *Circumcise* from all rashness and all lying both *my* inward and outward *lips*: let Thy Scriptures be my pure delights: let me not be deceived in them, nor deceive out of them. Lord, hearken and pity, O Lord my God, Light of the blind, and Strength of the weak; yea also Light of those that see, and Strength of the strong; hearken unto my soul, and hear it *crying out of the depths*. For if thine ears be not with us in the depths also, whither shall we go? whither cry? *The day is Thine, and the night is Thine;* at Thy beck the moments flee by. Grant thereof a space for our meditations in the *hidden things of Thy law,* and close it not against us who *knock.* For not in vain wouldest Thou have the darksome secrets of so many pages written; nor are those forests without their harts which retire therein and range and walk; feed, lie down, and ruminate. *Perfect* me, O Lord, and *reveal* them *unto* me. Behold, Thy voice is my joy; Thy voice exceedeth the abundance of pleasures. Give what I love: for I do love; and this hast Thou given: forsake not Thy own gifts, nor despise Thy green herb that thirsteth. Let me confess unto Thee whatsoever I shall find in Thy books, and *hear the voice of praise,* and drink-in Thee, and meditate on the *wonderful things out of Thy law;* even from the *beginning,* wherein *Thou madest the heaven and the earth,* unto the everlasting reigning of Thy holy city with Thee.

4. *Lord, have mercy on me, and hear my desire.* For it is not, I deem, of the earth, not of gold and silver, and precious stones, or gorgeous apparel, or honours and offices, or the pleasures of the flesh, or necessaries for the body and for this life of our pilgrimage: *all which shall be added unto those that seek Thy kingdom and Thy righteousness.* Behold, O Lord my God, wherein is my desire. *The wicked have told me of delights, but not such as Thy law, O Lord.* Behold, wherein is my desire. Behold, Father, behold, and see and approve; and be it

pleasing in the sight of Thy mercy, that I may find grace before Thee, that the inward parts of Thy words be *opened* to me *knocking.* I beseech by our Lord Jesus Christ Thy Son, *the Man of Thy right hand, the Son of man, whom Thou hast established for Thyself,* as Thy Mediator and ours, through Whom Thou soughtest us, not seeking Thee, but soughtest us, that we might seek Thee,—Thy *Word, through Whom Thou madest all things,* and among them, me also;—Thy Only-Begotten, through Whom Thou calledst to adoption the believing people, and therein me also;—I beseech Thee by Him, who *sitteth at Thy right hand, and intercedeth with Thee for us, in Whom are hidden all the treasures of wisdom and knowledge.* These do I seek in Thy books. *Of Him did Moses write;* this saith Himself; this saith the Truth. . . .

41. O Lord my God, what a depth is that recess of Thy mysteries, and how far from it have the consequences of my transgressions cast me! Heal mine eyes, that I may share the joy of Thy light. Certainly, if there be a mind gifted with such vast knowledge and foreknowledge, as to know all things past and to come, as I know one well-known Psalm, truly that mind is passing wonderful, and fearfully amazing; in that nothing past, noth-

ing to come in after-ages, is any more hidden from him, than when I sung that Psalm, was hidden from me what, and how much of it had passed away from the beginning, what, and how much there remained unto the end. But far be it that Thou the Creator of the Universe, the Creator of souls and bodies, far be it, that Thou shouldest in such wise know all things past and to come. Far, far more wonderfully, and far more mysteriously, dost Thou know them. For not, as the feelings of one who singeth what he knoweth, or heareth some well-known song, are through expectation of the words to come, and the remembering of those that are past, varied, and his senses divided,—not so doth any thing happen unto Thee, unchangeably eternal, that is, the eternal Creator of minds. Like then as Thou *in the Beginning* knewest *the heaven and the earth,* without any variety of Thy knowledge, so *madest* Thou *in the Beginning* heaven *and earth,* without any distraction of Thy action. Whoso understandeth, let him confess unto Thee; and whoso understandeth not, let him confess unto Thee. Oh how high art Thou, and yet the humble in heart are Thy dwelling-place; for Thou *raisest up those that are bowed down,* and they fall not, whose elevation Thou art.

[ON ATTAINING THE CITY OF GOD]

From *The City of God*

FROM BOOK I

That most glorious society and celestial city of God's faithful, which is partly seated in the course of these declining times, wherein "he that liveth by faith," is a pilgrim amongst the wicked; and partly in that solid estate of eternity, which as yet the other part doth patiently expect, until "righteousness be turned into judgment," being then by the proper excellence to obtain the last victory, and be crowned in perfection of peace; have I undertaken to defend in this work: which I intend unto you (my

dearest Marcelline) as being your due by my promise, and exhibit it against all those that prefer their false gods before this city's founder: the work is great and difficult, but God the Master of all difficulties is our helper. For I know well what strong arguments are required to make the proud know the virtue of humility, by which (not being enhanced by human glory, but endowed with divine grace) it surmounts all earthly loftiness, which totters through the one transitory instability. For the King, the builder of this city, whereof we are now to discourse, hath opened his mind to His people, in the divine law, thus: "God resisteth the proud, and giveth grace to the humble." . . .

7. Yea but (will some say) why doth God suffer His mercy to be extended unto the graceless and thankless? Oh! why should we judge, but because it is His work "that maketh the sun to shine daily both on good and bad, and the rain to fall both on the just and the unjust"? For what though some by meditating upon this, take occasion to reform their enormities with repentance? and other some (as the apostle saith) despising the richness of God's goodness, and long suffering, in their hardness of heart and impenitency "do lay up unto themselves wrath against the day of wrath, and the revelations of God's just judgment, who will reward each man according to his works"? Nevertheless God's patience still inviteth the wicked unto repentance as this scourge doth instruct the good unto patience. The mercy of God embraceth the good with love, as His severity doth correct the bad with pains. For it seemed good to the almighty Providence to prepare such goods, in the world to come, as the just only should enjoy and not the unjust: and such evils as the wicked only should feel, and not the godly. But as for these temporal goods of this world, He hath left them to the common use of both good and bad; that the good of this world should not be too much desired, because even the wicked do also partake them: and that the evils of this world should not be too cowardly avoided, wherewith the good are sometimes affected. But there is great difference in the use both of that estate in this world, which is called prosperous, and that which is called adverse. For neither do these temporal goods extol a good man, nor do the evil deject him. But the evil man must needs be subject to the punishment of this earthly unhappiness, because he is first corrupted by this earthly happiness: yet in the distributing of these temporal blessings God showeth His provident operation. For if all sin were presently punished, there

should be nothing to do at the last judgment: and again, if no sin were here openly punished, the divine providence would not be believed. And so in prosperity, if God should not give competency of worldly and apparent blessings to some that ask them, we would say He hath nothing to do with them: and should He give them to all that ask them, we should think He were not to be served but for them, and so His service should not make us godly, but rather greedy. This being thus, whatever affliction good men and bad do suffer together in this life, it doth not prove the persons undistinct, because so they both do jointly endure like pains; for as in one fire, gold shineth and chaff smoketh, and as under one flail the straw is bruised, and the ear cleansed; nor is the lees and the oil confused because they are both pressed in one press, so likewise one and the same violence of affliction, proveth, purifieth, and melteth the good, and condemneth, wasteth, and casteth out the bad. And thus in one and the same distress do the wicked offend God by detestation and blasphemy, and the good do glorify Him by praise and prayer. So great is the difference wherein we ponder not what, but how a man suffers his affects. For one and the same motion maketh the mud smell filthily, and the unguent smell most fragrantly.

From Book V

2. Wherefore the great and mighty God with His Word and His Holy Spirit (which three are one), God only omnipotent, Maker and Creator of every soul, and of everybody, in participation of whom, all such are happy that follow His truth and reject vanities: He that made man a reasonable creature of soul and body, and He that did neither let him pass unpunished for his sin, nor yet excluded him from mercy: He that gave both unto good and bad essence with the stones, power of production with the trees, senses with the beasts of the field, and understanding with the angels; He, from whom is all being, beauty, form and order, number, weight and measure;

He, from whom all nature, mean and excellent, all seeds of form, all forms of seed, all motion, both of forms and seeds derive and have being: He that gave flesh the original, beauty, strength, propagation, form and shape, health and symmetry: He that gave the unreasonable besides these, phantasy, understanding, and will: He (I say) having left neither heaven, nor earth, nor angel, nor man, no nor the most base and contemptible creature, neither the bird's feather, nor the herb's flower, nor the tree's leaf, without the true harmony of their parts, and peaceful concord of composition; it is no way credible, that He would leave the kingdoms of men, and their bondages and freedoms loose and uncomprised in the laws of His eternal providence.

FROM BOOK IX

4. To Him we owe that Greek *latria*, or service, both in ourselves and sacrifices, for we are all His temple, and each one His temples, He vouchsafing to inhabit us all in some and each in particular, being no more in all than in one: for He is neither multiplied nor diminished, our hearts elevated to Him are His altars: His only Son is the Priest by whom we please Him: we offer Him bloody sacrifices when we shed our blood for His truth: and incense when we burn in zeal to Him, the gifts He giveth us, we do in vows return Him: His benefits we consecrate unto Him in set solemnities, lest the body of time should bring them into ungrateful oblivion: we offer Him the sacrifices of humility and praises on the altar of our heart in the fire of fervent love: for by the sight of Him (as we may see Him), and to be joined with Him, are we purged from our guilty and filthy affects and consecrated in His name: He is our blessed founder, and our desires' accomplishment. Him we elect, or rather re-elect, for by our neglect we lost Him. Him, therefore, we re-elect (whence religion is derived), and to Him we do hasten with the wings of love to attain rest in him: being to be blessed by attainment of that final perfection, for our good (whose end the

philosophers jangled about) is nothing but to adhere unto Him, and by His intellectual and incorporeal embrace, our soul grows great with all virtue and true perfection. This good are we taught to love with all our heart, with all our soul, and all our strength. To this good we ought to be led by those that love us, and to lead those we love. So are the two commandments fulfilled, wherein consist all the law and the prophets. "Thou shalt love the Lord thy God with all thine heart, with all thy soul, and with all thy mind; and thou shalt love thy neighbour as thyself." For to teach a man how to love himself, was this end appointed, whereunto refer all his works for beatitude, for he that loves himself desires but to be blessed. And the end of this is, coherence with God. So then the command of loving his neighbour, being given to him that knows how to love himself, what does it but command and commend the love of God unto him? Thus God's true worship, true piety, true religion, and due service to God only, wherefore what immortal power soever (virtuous or otherwise) that loves itself, it desires we should but be His servants for beatitude, of whence it has beatitude by serving Him. If it worship not God, it is wretched, as wanting God: if it do, then will not it be worshipped for God. It rather holds, and loves to hold, as the Holy Scripture writes, "He that sacrifices to any gods but the one God, shall be rooted out," for to be silent in other points of religion there is none dare say a sacrifice is due but unto God alone. But much is taken from divine worship and thrust into human honours, either by excessive humility or pestilent flattery: yet still with a reserved notice that they are men, held worthy indeed of reverence and honour, or at most of adoration. But whoever sacrificed but to him whom he knew, or thought, or feigned to be a god: and how ancient a part of God's worship a sacrifice is, Cain and Abel do show full proof, God Almighty rejecting the elder brother's sacrifice, and accepting the younger's.

12. But all miracles (done by angels or whatever divine power), confirming the true adoration of one God unto us (in whom only we are blessed), we believe truly are done by God's power working in these immortals that love us in true piety. Hear not those that deny that the invisible God works visible miracles: is not the world a miracle? Yet visible, and of His making. Nay, all the miracles done in this world are less than the world itself, the heaven and earth and all therein, yet God made them all, and after a manner that man cannot conceive nor comprehend. For though these visible miracles of nature, be now no more admired, yet ponder them wisely, and they are more admirable than the strangest: for man is a greater miracle than all that He can work. Wherefore God that made heaven and earth (both miracles) scorns not as yet to work miracles in heaven and earth, to draw men's souls that yet affect visibilities, unto the worship of His invisible essence. But where and when He will do this, His unchangeable will only can declare: at whose disposing all time past has been, and to come, is. He moves all things in time, but time moves not Him, nor knows He future effects otherwise than present. Nor hears our prayers otherwise than He foresees them ere we pray: for when His angels hear them, He hears in them, as in His true temples (not made with hands) and so does He hold all things effected temporally in His saints, by His eternal disposition.

From Book X

1. We give the name of the city of God unto that society whereof that Scripture bears witness, which has got the most excellent authority and pre-eminence of all other works whatsoever, by the disposing of the divine providence, not the affectation of men's judgments. For there it is said: "Glorious things are spoken of thee, thou city of God:" and in another place, "Great is the Lord, and greatly to be praised, in the city of our God, even upon His holy mountain, increasing the joy of all the earth." And by and by in the same psalm: "As we have heard, so have we seen in the city of the Lord of Hosts, in the city of our God: God hath established it for ever." And in another: "The rivers' streams shall make glad the city of God, the most high has sanctified His tabernacle, God is in the midst of it unmoved." These testimonies, and thousands more, teach us that there is a city of God, whereof His inspired love makes us desire to be members. The earthly citizens prefer their gods before this heavenly city's holy founder, knowing not that He is the God of gods, not of those false, wicked, and proud ones (which wanting His light so universal and unchangeable, and being thereby cast into an extreme needy power, each one follows his own state, as it were, and begs peculiar honours of his servants), but of the godly and holy ones, who select their own submission to Him, rather than the world's to them, and love rather to worship Him, their God, than to be worshipped for gods themselves. . . .

2. It is a great and admirable thing for one to transcend all creatures, corporal or incorporal, frail and mutable, by speculation; and to attain to the deity itself, and learn of that, that it made all things that are not of the divine essence. For so does God teach a man, speaking not by any corporal creature unto him, nor reverberating the air between the ear and the speaker, nor by any spiritual creature, or apparition, as in dreams, or otherwise. For so He does speak as unto bodily ears, and as by a body, and by breach of air and distance. For visions are very like bodies. But He speaks by the truth, if the ears of the mind be ready, and not the body. For he speaks unto the best part of the whole man, and that wherein God only does excel him; and understand a man in the best fashion, you cannot then but say he is made after God's image, being nearer to God only by that part wherein he excels his others, which he has shared with him by beasts. But yet the mind itself, wherein reason and understanding are natural inherents, is weakened and darkened by the mist of inveterate error, and disenabled to enjoy

by inherence, nay, even to endure that immutable light, until it be gradually purified, cured, and made fit for such an happiness, therefore it must first be purged, and instructed by faith, to set it the surer; wherein truth itself, God's Son, and God, taking on our manhood without wasting of godhead, ordained that faith, to be a pass for man to God, by His mean that was both God and man, for by His manhood is He mediator, and by man He is our way. For if the way lie between him that goes and the place to which he goes, there is hope to attain it. But if one have no way, nor know which way to go, what boots it to know whither to go? And the only sure, plain, infallible high way is this mediator, God and man: God, our journey's end, and man, our way unto it.

FROM BOOK XII

13. . . . In humility therefore there is this to be admired, that it elevates the heart; and in pride this, that it dejects it. This seems strangely contrary, that elevation should be below, and dejection aloft. But godly humility subjects one to his superior: and God is above all; therefore humility exalts one, in making him God's subject. But pride the vice, refusing this subjection, falls from him that is above all; and so becomes more base by far (than those that stand) fulfilling this place of the Psalm: "Thou hast cast them down in their own exaltation." He says not when they were exalted, they were dejected afterwards: but, in their very exaltation were they cast down, their elevation was their ruin. And therefore in that humility is so approved in, and commended to the City of God that is yet pilgrim upon earth and so highly extolled by Christ the King thereof; and pride, the just contrary, shewn by Holy Scripture, to be so predominant in His adversaries the devil and his angels: in this very thing the great difference of the two cities, the godly and the ungodly, with both their angels accordingly, lies most apparent: God's love swaying in the one, and self-love in the other. So that the devil had not seduced mankind

to such a palpable transgression of God's express charge, but that evil will and self-love had got place in them before, for He delighted in that which was said, "Ye shall be as gods:" which they might sooner have been by obedience and coherence with their Creator than by proud opinion that they were their own beginners, for the created gods are not gods of themselves but by participation of the God that made them, but man desiring more, became less, and choosing to be sufficient in himself, fell from that all-sufficient God.

This then is the mischief, man liking himself as if he were his own light, which if he had pleased himself withal, he might have been like: this mischief (I say) was first in his soul, and thence was drawn on to the following mischievous act, for the scripture is true that says, "Pride goeth before destruction, and a haughty mind before the fall:" the fall which was in secret, foreruns the fall which was in public, the first being taken for no fall at all, for who takes exaltation to be ruin, though the defect proved in the place of height?

But who sees not that ruin lies in the express breach of God's precepts? For therefore did God forbid it, that being done, all excuse and avoidance of justice might be excluded. And therefore I dare say it is good that the proud should fall into some broad and disgraceful sin thereby to take a dislike of themselves, who fell by too much liking themselves; for Peter's sorrowful dislike of himself, when he wept, was more healthful to his soul than his unsound pleasure that he took in himself when he presumed. Therefore says the Psalmist: "Fill their faces with shame, that they may seek Thy name, O Lord:" that is, that they may delight in Thee and seek Thy name, who before, delighted in themselves, and sought their own.

FROM BOOK XV

19. . . . One may not be so given to contemplation, that he neglect the good of his neighbour: nor so far in love with action that he forget Divine speculation.

In contemplation one may not seek for idleness, but for truth: to benefit himself by the knowledge thereof, and not to grudge to impart it unto others. In action one may not aim at highness of honour, because "all under the sun is mere vanity:" but to perform the work of a superior unto the true end, that is, unto the benefit and salvation of the subject, as we said before, and this made the apostle say, "If any man desire the office of a bishop, he desireth a good work:" what this office was, he explains not; it is an office of labour, and not of honour. The Greek word signifies that he that is herein installed, is to watch over his people that are under him: Episcopus, a bishop, comes of ἐπὶ, which is, "over," and σκοπός, which is, "a watching," or "an attendance:" so that we may very well translate ἐπίσκοπος, "a superintendent," to shew that he is no true bishop, who desires rather to be lordly himself, than profitable unto others. No man therefore is forbidden to proceed in a laudable form of contemplation. But to affect sovereignty, though the people must be governed, and though the place be well discharged, yet notwithstanding is liable to be deemed unfitting. Wherefore the love of truth requires a holy retiredness: and the necessity of charity, a just employment, which if it be not imposed upon us, we ought not to seek it, but betake ourselves wholly to the holy search after truth: but if we be called forth unto a place, the law and need of charity binds us to undertake it. Yet may we not for all this, give over our first resolution, lest we lose the sweetness of that, and be surcharged with the weight of the other.

From Book XVII

16. But God's mercy is so great in the vessels whom He has prepared for glory, that even the first age of man, which is his infancy, where the flesh rules without control, and the second, his childhood, where his reason is so weak that it gives way to all enticements, and the mind is altogether incapable of religious precepts; if notwithstanding they be washed in the fountain of regeneration, and he die at this or that age, he is translated from the powers of darkness to the glories of Christ, and freed from all pains, eternal and purificatory. His regeneration only is sufficient to clear him from that after death which his carnal generation had contracted with death. But when he comes to years of discretion, and is capable of good counsel, then must he begin a fierce conflict with vice lest it allure him to damnation. Indeed the freshwater soldier is the more easily put to flight, his practice will make him valorous, and to pursue victory with all his endeavour, which he must evermore essay by a weapon called "the love of true righteousness," and this is kept in the faith of Christ, for if the command be present, and the assisting spirit absent, the very forbidding of the crime inflames the perverse flesh to run the sooner into it, sometimes producing open enormities, and sometimes secret ones, far worse than the other, in that pride, and ruinous self-conceit, persuades men that they are virtues.

Then therefore sin is quelled, when it is beaten down by the love of God, which none but He gives and He only, by Jesus Christ the Mediator of God and man, who made Himself mortal, that we might be made eternal: few are so happy to pass their youth without taint of some damnable sin or other, either in deed, opinion, or so; but let them, above all, seek to suppress by the fulness of spirit all such evil motions as shall be incited by the looseness of the flesh. Many, having betaken themselves to the law, becoming prevaricators thereof through sin, are afterwards fain to fly unto the law of grace assistant, which making them both truer penitents, and stouter opponents, subjects their spirits to God, and so they get the conquest of the flesh. He therefore that will escape hell fire, must be both baptised and justified in Christ, and this is the only way to pass from the devil unto Him. And let him assuredly believe that there is no purgatory pains except before that great and terrible judgment. Indeed, it is true that the fire of hell shall be more forcible against some than against others, according to the diversity of their deserts, whether it be adapted in nature to the quality of their merits, or remain one fire unto all, and yet be not felt alike of all.

Leo the Great
(390?-461)

BORN and reared in Tuscany, made a deacon in 431, and raised to bishop of Rome in 440, Leo may be called the first pope. In 445 he obtained from the Emperor Valentian III a decree which commanded all to obey the Roman bishop, basing his authority on Matthew 16:16-19 —"the primacy of Peter." Leo felt that other bishops were in charge of individual flocks, but the Roman bishop had charge of the whole church, other bishops being but his assistants. When the Council of Chalcedon in 451 placed Constantinople on equal footing with Rome, he protested vehemently.

Many sermons and letters of Leo have been preserved. Of his eight sermons on the Nativity, the sixth stresses the mystical note that "the birth of Christ is the birth of peace to the Church," where men "that are remodeled after one pattern must have a spirit like the model." It is given in its entirety in the translation from the Latin by Charles Lett Feltoe in *The Nicene and Post-Nicene Fathers* (New York, 1889).

ON THE FEAST OF THE NATIVITY, VI

I. CHRISTMAS MORNING IS THE MOST APPROPRIATE TIME FOR THOUGHTS ON THE NATIVITY

*O*n all days and at all times, dearly beloved, does the birth of our Lord and Saviour from the Virgin-mother occur to the thoughts of the faithful, who meditate on divine things, that the mind may be aroused to the acknowledgment of its Maker, and whether it be occupied in the groans of supplication, or in the shouting of praise, or in the offering of sacrifice, may employ its spiritual insight on nothing more frequently and more trustingly than on the fact that GOD the Son of GOD, begotten of the co-eternal Father, was also born by a human birth. But this Nativity which is to be adored in heaven and on earth is suggested to us by no day more than this when, with the early light still shedding its rays on nature, there is borne in upon our senses the brightness of this wondrous mystery. For the angel Gabriel's converse with the astonished Mary and her conception by the Holy Ghost, as wondrously promised as believed, seem to recur not only to the memory but to the very eyes. For to-day the Maker of the world was born of a Virgin's womb, and He, who made all natures, became Son of her, whom He created. To-day the Word of GOD appeared clothed in flesh, and that which had never been visible to human eyes began to be tangible to our hands as well. To-day the shepherds learnt from angels' voices that the Saviour was born in the substance of our flesh and soul; and to-day the form of the Gospel message was pre-arranged by the leaders of the LORD's flocks, so that we too may say with the army of the heavenly host: "Glory in the highest to GOD, and on earth peace to men of good will."

II. CHRISTIANS ARE ESSENTIALLY PARTICIPATORS IN THE NATIVITY OF CHRIST

Although, therefore, that infancy, which the majesty of GOD's Son did not disdain, reached mature manhood by the growth of years and, when the triumph of His passion and resurrection was completed, all the actions of humility which were undertaken for us ceased, yet to-day's festival renews for us the holy childhood of Jesus born of the Virgin Mary: and in adoring the birth of our Saviour, we find we are celebrating the commencement of our own life. For the birth of Christ is the source of life for Christian folk, and the birthday of the Head is the birthday of the body. Although every individual that is called has his own order, and all the sons of the Church are separated from one another by intervals of time, yet as the entire body of the faithful being born in the font of baptism is crucified with Christ in His passion, raised again in His resurrection, and placed at the Father's right hand in His ascension, so with Him are they born in this nativity. For any believer in whatever part of the world that is re-born in Christ, quits the old paths of his original nature and passes into a new man by being re-born; and no longer is he reckoned of his earthly father's stock but among the seed of the Saviour, who became the Son of man in order that we might have the power to be the sons of GOD. For unless He came down to us in this humiliation, no one would reach His presence by any merits of his own. Let not earthly wisdom shroud in darkness the hearts of the called on this point, and let not the frailty of earthly thoughts raise itself against the loftiness of GOD's grace, for it will soon return to the lowest dust. At the end of the ages is fulfilled that which was ordained from all eternity: and in the presence of realities, when signs and types have ceased, the Law and prophecy have become Truth: and so Abraham is found the father of all nations, and the promised blessing is given to the world in his seed: nor are they only Israelites whom blood and flesh begot, but the whole body of the adopted enter into possession of the heritage prepared for the sons of Faith. Be not disturbed by the cavils of silly questionings, and let not the effects of the Divine word be dissipated by human calculation; we with Abraham believe in GOD and "waver not through unbelief," but "know

most assuredly that what the LORD promised, He is able to perform."

III. PEACE WITH GOD IS HIS BEST GIFT TO MAN

The Saviour then, dearly beloved, is born not of fleshly seed but of the Holy Spirit, in such wise that the condemnation of the first transgression did not touch Him. And hence the very greatness of the boon conferred demands of us reverence worthy of its splendour. For, as the blessed Apostle teaches, "we have received not the spirit of this world but the Spirit which is of GOD, that we may know the things which are given us by GOD:" and that Spirit can in no other way be rightly worshipped, except by offering Him that which we received from Him. But in the treasures of the LORD's bounty what can we find so suitable to the honour of the present feast as the peace, which at the LORD's nativity was first proclaimed by the angel-choir? For that it is which brings forth the sons of GOD, the nurse of love and the mother of unity: the rest of the blessed and our eternal home; whose proper work and special office it is to join to GOD those whom it removes from the world. Whence the Apostle incites us to this good end, in saying, "being justified therefore by faith let us have peace towards God." In which brief sentence are summed up nearly all the commandments; for where true peace is, there can be no lack of virtue. But what is it, dearly beloved, to have peace towards GOD, except to wish what He bids, and not to wish what He forbids? For if human friendships seek out equality of soul and similarity of desires, and difference of habits can never attain to full harmony, how will he be partaker of divine peace, who is pleased with what displeases GOD and desires to get delight from what he knows to be offensive to GOD? That is not the spirit of the sons of GOD; such wisdom is not acceptable to the noble family of the adopted. That chosen and royal race must live up to the dignity of its regeneration, must love what the Father loves, and in nought disagree with its Maker, lest the LORD should again say: "I have begotten and raised up sons, but they have scorned Me: the ox knoweth his owner and the ass his master's crib: but Israel hath not known Me and My people hath not acknowledged me."

IV. WE MUST BE WORTHY OF OUR CALLING AS SONS AND FRIENDS OF GOD

The mystery of this boon is great, dearly beloved, and this gift exceeds all gifts that GOD should call man son, and man should name GOD Father: for by these terms we perceive and learn the love which reached so great a height. For if in natural progeny and earthly families those who are born of noble parents are lowered by the faults of evil intercourse, and unworthy offspring are put to shame by the very brilliance of their ancestry; to what end will they come who through love of the world do not fear to be outcast from the family of Christ? But if it gains the praise of men that the father's glory should shine again in their descendants, how much more glorious is it for those who are born of GOD to regain the brightness of their Maker's likeness and display in themselves Him who begat them, as saith the LORD: "Let your light so shine before men that they may see your good works and glorify your Father which is in heaven?" We know indeed, as the Apostle John says, that "the whole world lieth in the evil one," and that by the stratagems of the Devil and his angels numberless attempts are made either to frighten man in his struggle upwards by adversity or to spoil him by prosperity, but "greater is He that is in us, than he that is against us," and they who have peace with GOD and are always saying to the Father with their whole hearts "thy will be done" can be overcome in no battles, can be hurt by no assaults. For accusing ourselves in our confessions and refusing the spirit's consent to our fleshly lusts, we stir up against us the enmity of him who is the author of sin, but secure a peace with GOD that nothing can destroy, by accepting His gracious service, in order that we may not only surrender ourselves in obedience to our King but also be united to Him by our free-will. For if we are like-minded, if we wish what He wishes, and disapprove what He disapproves, He will finish all our wars for us, He who gave the will, will also give the power: so that we may be fellow-workers in His works, and with the exultation of Faith may utter that prophetic song: "the LORD is my light and my salvation: whom shall I fear? the LORD is the defender of my life: of whom shall I be afraid?"

V. THE BIRTH OF CHRIST IS THE BIRTH OF PEACE TO THE CHURCH

They then who "are born not of blood nor of the will of the flesh nor of the will of man but of GOD," must offer to the Father the unanimity of peace-loving sons, and all the members of adoption must meet in the First-begotten of the new creation, who came to do not His own Will but His that sent Him; inasmuch as the Father in His gracious favour has adopted as His heirs not those that are discordant nor those that are unlike Him, but those that are in feeling and affection one. They that are re-modelled after one pattern must have a spirit like the model. The birthday of the LORD is the birthday of peace: for thus says the Apostle, "He is our peace, who made both one;" since whether we be Jew or Gentile, "through Him we have access in one Spirit to the Father." And it was this in particular that He taught His disciples before the day of His passion which He had of His own free-will fore-ordained, saying, "My peace I give unto you, My peace I leave for you;" and lest under the general term the character of His peace should escape notice, He added, "not as the world give I unto you." The world, He says, has its friendships, and brings many that are apart into loving harmony. There are also minds which are equal in vices, and similarity of desires produces equality of affection. And if any are perchance to be found who are not pleased with what is mean and dishonourable, and who exclude from the terms of their connexion unlawful compacts, yet even such if they be either Jews, heretics or heathens, belong not to GOD's friendship but to this world's peace. But the peace of the spiritual and of catholics coming down from above and leading upwards refuses to hold communion with the lovers of the world, resists all obstacles and flies from pernicious pleasures to true joys, as the LORD says: "Where thy treasure is, there will thy heart be also:" that is, if what you love is below, you will descend to the lowest depth: if what you love is above, you will reach the topmost height: thither may the Spirit of peace lead and bring us, whose wishes and feeling are at one, and who are of one mind in faith and hope and in charity: since "as many as are led by the Spirit of GOD these are sons of GOD" who reigneth with the Son and Holy Spirit for ever and ever. Amen.

THE DARK AGES
THE SAINTS KEEP CHRISTIANITY ALIVE

Dionysius the Areopagite
(*ca.* 500)

THE original Dionysius the Areopagite is mentioned in Acts 17:34 as one of Paul's converts at Athens. Eusebius says he was the first bishop of Athens; another tradition says that he suffered martyrdom. His main importance is due to the mystical writings in Greek during the fifth and sixth centuries by a writer who assumed his name. From his pen came *On the Heavenly Hierarchy*, *On the Ecclesiastical Hierarchy*, *On the Names of God*, *On Mystical Theology*, and ten letters. He was first quoted as an authority at the Council of Constantinople (533) against the Council of Chalcedon (451).

Probably a Syrian monk, "Dionysius the Areopagite" may be called the first Christian writer who carefully delineated mystical awareness and the ecstatic way by which man climbs to a oneness with God. His language and figures of speech found particular repetition in the fourteenth century, when mysticism reached its zenith. In the Western Church he became a guide to mystical theology, and exerted a deep influence on Hugh of St. Victor, Albertus Magnus, Dionysius the Carthusian, and Thomas Aquinas.

On Mystical Theology depicts the way man climbs to fellowship with God. It is presented complete from the translation of Dionysius' works by John Parker (London, 1897).

ON MYSTICAL THEOLOGY

I. WHAT IS THE DIVINE GLOOM?

Triad supernal, both super-God and super-good, Guardian of the Theosophy of Christian men, direct us aright to the super-unknown and super-brilliant and highest summit of the mystic Oracles, where the simple and absolute and changeless mysteries of theology lie hidden within the super-luminous gloom of the silence, revealing hidden things, which in its deepest darkness shines above the most super-brilliant, and in the altogether impalpable and invisible, fills to overflowing the eyeless minds with glories of surpassing beauty. This then be my prayer; but thou, O dear Timothy, by the persistent commerce with the mystic visions, leave behind both sensible perceptions and intellectual efforts, and all objects of sense and intelligence, and all things not being and being, and be raised aloft unknowingly to the union, as far as attainable, with Him who is above every essence and knowledge. For by the resistless and absolute ecstasy in all purity, from thyself and all, thou wilt be carried on high, to the superessential ray of the Divine darkness, when thou hast cast away all, and become free from all.

II. But see that none of the uninitiated listen to these things—those I mean who are entangled in things being, and fancy there is nothing superessentially above things being, but imagine that they know, by their own knowledge, Him, who has placed darkness as His hiding-place. But, if the Divine initiations are above such, what would any one say respecting those still more uninitiated, such as both portray the Cause exalted above all, from the lowest of things created, and say that It in no wise excels the no-gods fashioned by themselves and of manifold shapes, it being our duty both to attribute and affirm all the attributes of things existing to It, as Cause of all, and more properly to deny them all to It, as being above all, and not to consider the negations to be in opposition to the affirmations, but far rather that It, which is above every abstraction and definition, is above the privations.

III. Thus, then, the divine Bartholomew says that Theology is much and least, and the Gospel broad and great, and on the other hand concise. He seems to me to have comprehended this supernaturally, that the good Cause of all is both of much utterance, and at the same time of briefest utterance and without utterance; as having neither utterance nor conception, because It is superessentially exalted above all, and manifested without veil and in truth, to those alone who pass through both all things consecrated and pure, and ascend above every ascent of all holy summits, and leave behind all divine lights and sounds, and heavenly words, and enter into the gloom, where really is, as the Oracles say, He who is beyond all. For even the divine Moses is himself strictly bidden to be first purified, and then to be separated from those who are not so, and after entire cleansing hears the many-voiced trumpets, and sees many lights, shedding pure and streaming rays; then he is separated from the multitude, and with the chosen priests goes first to the summit of the divine ascents, although even then he does not meet with Almighty God Himself, but views not Him (for He is viewless) but the place where He is. Now this I think signifies that the most Divine and Highest of the things seen and contemplated are a sort of suggestive expression of the things subject to Him who is above all, through which His wholly inconceivable Presence is shown, reaching to the highest spiritual summits of His Most holy places; and then he (Moses) is freed from them who are both seen and seeing, and enters into the gloom of the *Agnosia;* a gloom veritably mystic, within which he closes all perceptions of knowledge and enters into the altogether impalpable and unseen, being wholly of Him who is beyond all, and of none, neither himself nor other; and by inactivity of all knowledge, united in his better part to the altogether Unknown, and by knowing nothing, knowing above mind.

II. How We Ought both to Be United and Render Praise to the Cause of All and Above All

I. We pray to enter within the super-bright gloom, and through not seeing and not knowing, to see and to know that the not to see nor to know is itself the above sight and knowledge. For this is veritably to see and to know and to celebrate superessentially the Superessential, through the abstraction of all existing things, just as those who make a lifelike statue, by extracting all the encumbrances which have been placed upon the clear view of the concealed, and by bringing to light, by the mere cuttting away, the genuine beauty concealed in it. And, it is necessary, as I think, to celebrate the abstractions in an opposite way to the definitions. For, we used to place these latter by beginning from the foremost and descending through the middle to the lowest, but, in this case, by making the ascents from the lowest to the highest, we abstract everything, in order that, without veil, we may know that *Agnosia*, which is enshrouded under all the known, in all things that be, and may see that superessential gloom, which is hidden by all the light in existing things.

III. What Are the Affirmative Expressions Respecting God, and What the Negative

I. In the *Theological Outlines*, then, we celebrated the principal affirmative expressions respecting God—how the Divine and good Nature is spoken of as One—how as Threefold—what is that within it which is spoken of as Paternity and Sonship—what the Divine name of "the Spirit" is meant to signify, —how from the immaterial and indivisible Good the Lights dwelling in the heart of Goodness sprang forth, and remained, in their branching forth, without departing from the coeternal abiding in Himself and in Themselves and in each other,—how the superessential Jesus takes substance in veritable human nature—and whatever other things, made known by the Oracles, are celebrated throughout the *Theological Outlines;* and in the treatise concerning *Divine Names,* how He is named Good—how Being—how Life and Wisdom and Power—and whatever else belongs to the nomenclature of God. Further, in the *Symbolical Theology,* what are the Names transferred from objects of sense to things Divine—what are the Divine forms?—what the Divine appearances, and parts and organs?—what the Divine places and ornaments?—what the angers? —what the griefs?—and the Divine wrath?—what the carousals, and the ensuing sicknesses?—what the oaths,—and what the curses?—what the sleepings, and what the awakings?—and all the other Divinely formed representations, which belong to the description of God, through symbols. And I imagine that you have comprehended, how the lowest are expressed in somewhat more words than the first. For, it was necessary that the *Theological Outlines,* and the unfolding of the Divine Names should be expressed in fewer words than the *Symbolic Theology;* since, in proportion as we ascend to the higher, in such a degree the expressions are circumscribed by the contemplations of the things intelligible. As even now, when entering into the gloom which is above mind, we shall find, not a little speaking, but a complete absence of speech, and absence of conception. In the other case, the discourse, in descending from the above to the lowest, is widened according to the descent, to a proportionate extent; but now, in ascending from below to that which is above, in proportion to the ascent, it is contracted, and after a complete ascent, it will become wholly voiceless, and will be wholly united to the unutterable. But, for what reason in short, you say, having attributed the Divine attributes from the foremost, do we begin the Divine abstraction from things lowest? Because

it is necessary that they who place attributes on that which is above every attribute, should place the attributive affirmation from that which is more cognate to it; but that they who abstract, with regard to that which is above every abstraction, should make the abstraction from things which are further removed from it. Are not life and goodness more (cognate) than air and stone? and He is not given to debauch and to wrath, more (removed) than He is not expressed nor conceived.

IV. That the Pre-eminent Cause of Every Object of Sensible Perception Is None of the Objects of Sensible Perception

I. We say then that the Cause of all, which is above all, is neither without being, nor without life—nor without reason, nor without mind, nor is a body —nor has shape—nor form—nor quality, or quantity, or bulk—nor is in a place— nor is seen—nor has sensible contact— nor perceives, nor is perceived, by the senses—nor has disorder and confusion, as being vexed by earthly passions,—nor is powerless, as being subject to casualties of sense,—nor is in need of light;—neither is It, nor has It, change, or decay, or division, or deprivation, or flux,—or any other of the objects of sense.

V. That the Pre-eminent Cause of Every Object of Intelligible Perception Is None of the Objects of Intelligible Perception

I. On the other hand, ascending, we say, that It is neither soul, nor mind, nor has imagination, or opinion, or reason, or conception; neither is expressed, nor conceived; neither is number, nor order, nor greatness, nor littleness; nor equality, nor inequality; nor similarity, nor dissimilarity; neither is standing, nor moving; nor at rest; neither has power, nor is power, nor light; neither lives, nor is life; neither is essence nor eternity, nor time; neither is Its touch intelligible, neither is It science, nor truth; nor kingdom, nor wisdom; neither one, nor oneness; neither Deity, nor Goodness; nor is It Spirit according to our understanding; nor Sonship, nor Paternity; nor any other thing of those known to us, or to any other existing being; neither is It any of non-existing nor of existing things, nor do things existing know It, as It is; nor does It know existing things, *quâ* existing; neither is there expression of It, nor name, nor knowledge; neither is It darkness, nor light; nor error, nor truth; neither is there any definition at all of It, nor any abstraction. But when making the predications and abstractions of things after It, we neither predicate, nor abstract from It; since the all-perfect and uniform Cause of all is both above every definition and the pre-eminence of Him, who is absolutely freed from all, and beyond the whole, is also above every abstraction.

Benedict of Nursia

(480?-543?)

WHEN on October 28, 312 Constantine defeated Maxentius and, believing the Christian God had given him the victory, made Christianity the state religion, there began a secularizing of the church as its members became "worldly." In reaction many pious Christians sought in monasticism a way of "saving themselves from the world." But after a time the monasteries degenerated, and Benedict of Nursia arose as the great reformer. Born of good family in the Umbrian village of Nursia and educated in Rome, Benedict grew disgusted with the evils of the city and sought the life of a hermit in a cave of the mountains at Subiaco, forty miles away. Reports of his piety spread, and he became head of a monastic group near by. About 529 he founded a new monastery on the hill of Monte Cassino, halfway between Rome and Naples, and remained there until his death. This monastery became the ideal pattern, with its regulations laid down in the *Rule*, composed by Benedict soon after its establishment.

In the seventy-three chapters of his *Rule* Benedict gives sane, effective precepts for regulating monastic life, dealing with general principles, worship, work, study, and discipline. He reveals a sound knowledge of human nature, Roman genius for organization, and deep religious devotion. Reproduced here are the Prologue and first seven chapters, in the translation of Verheyen (1906), used by permission of St. Benedict's College, Atchison, Kansas.

[BASIC PRINCIPLES OF MONASTIC LIFE]

From the *Rule*

PROLOGUE

Listen, O my son, to the precepts of thy master, and incline the ear of thy heart, and cheerfully receive and faithfully execute the admonitions of thy loving Father, that by the toil of obedience thou mayest return to Him from whom by the sloth of disobedience thou hadst gone away.

To thee, therefore, my speech is now directed, who, giving up thine own will, takest up the strong and most excellent arms of obedience, to do battle for Christ the Lord, the true King.

In the first place, beg of Him by most earnest prayer, that He perfect whatever good thou dost begin, in order that He who now hath been pleased to count us in the number of His children, need never be grieved at our evil deeds. For we ought at all times so to serve Him with the good things which He hath given us, that He may not, like an angry father, disinherit His children, nor, like a dread lord, enraged at our evil deeds, hand us over to everlasting punishment as most wicked servants, who would not follow Him to glory.

Let us then rise at length, since the Scripture arouseth us, saying: "It is now the hour for us to rise from sleep;" and having opened our eyes to the deifying light, let us hear with awestruck ears what the divine voice, crying out daily, doth admonish us, saying: "To-day, if you shall hear his voice, harden not your hearts." And again: "He that hath ears to hear let him hear what the Spirit saith to the churches." And what doth He say?—"Come, children, hearken unto me, I will teach you the fear of the Lord." "Run whilst you have the light of life, that the darkness of death overtake you not."

And the Lord seeking his workman in the multitude of the people, to whom He proclaimeth these words, saith again: "Who is the man that desireth life and loveth to see good days?" If hearing this thou answerest, "I am he," God saith to thee: "If thou wilt have true and everlasting life, keep thy tongue from evil, and thy lips from speaking guile; turn away from evil and do good; seek after peace and pursue it." And when you shall have done these things, my eyes shall be upon you, and my ears unto your prayers. And before you shall call upon me I will say: "Behold, I am here."

What, dearest brethren, can be sweeter to us than this voice of the Lord inviting us? See, in His loving kindness, the Lord showeth us the way to life. Therefore, having our loins girt with faith and the performance of good works, let us walk His ways under the guidance of the Gospel, that we may be found worthy of seeing Him who hath called us to His kingdom. If we desire to dwell in the tabernacle of His kindgom, we cannot reach it in any way, unless we run thither by good works. But let us ask the Lord with the Prophet, saying to Him: "Lord, who shall dwell in Thy tabernacle, or who shall rest in Thy holy Hill?"

After this question, brethren, let us listen to the Lord answering and showing us the way to this tabernacle, saying: "He that walketh without blemish and worketh justice; he that speaketh truth in his heart; who hath not used deceit in his tongue, nor hath done evil to his neighbor, nor hath taken up a reproach against his neighbor," who hath brought to naught the foul demon tempting him, casting him out of his heart with his temptation, and hath taken his evil thoughts whilst they were yet weak and hath dashed them against Christ; who fearing the Lord are not puffed up by their goodness of life, but holding that the actual good which is in them cannot be done by themselves, but by the Lord, they praise the Lord working in them, saying with the Prophet: "Not to us, O Lord, not to us; but to Thy name give glory." Thus also the Apostle Paul hath not taken to himself any credit for his preaching, saying: "By the grace of God, I am what I am." And again he saith: "He that glorieth, let him glory in the Lord."

Hence, the Lord also saith in the Gospel: "He that heareth these my words and doeth them, shall be likened to a wise man who built his house upon a rock; the floods came, the winds blew, and they beat upon that house, and it fell not, for it was founded on a rock." The Lord fulfilling these words waiteth for us from day to day, that we respond to his holy admonitions by our works. Therefore, our days are lengthened to a truce for the amendment of the misdeeds of our present life; as the Apostle saith: "Knowest thou not that the patience of God leadeth thee to penance?" For the good Lord saith: "I will not the death of the sinner, but that he be converted and live."

Now, brethren, that we have asked the Lord who it is that shall dwell in His tabernacle, we have heard the conditions for dwelling there; and if we fulfil the duties of tenants, we shall be heirs of the kingdom of heaven. Our hearts and our bodies must, therefore, be ready to do battle under the biddings of holy obedience; and let us ask the Lord that He supply by the help of His grace what is impossible to us by nature. And if, flying from the pains of hell, we desire to reach life everlasting, then, while there is yet time, and we are still in the flesh, and are able during the present life to fulfill all these things, we must make haste to do now what will profit us forever.

We are, therefore, about to found a school of the Lord's service, in which we hope to introduce nothing harsh or burdensome. But even if, to correct vices or to preserve charity, sound reason dictateth anything that turneth out somewhat stringent, do not at once fly in dismay from the way of salvation, the beginning of which cannot but be narrow. But as we advance in the religious life and faith, we shall run the way of God's commandments with expanded hearts and unspeakable sweetness of love; so that never departing from His guidance and persevering in the monastery in His doctrine till death, we may by patience share in the sufferings of Christ, and be found worthy to be coheirs with Him of His kingdom.

I. Of the Kinds of the Life of Monks

It is well known that there are four kinds of monks. The first kind is that of Cenobites, that is, the monastic, who live under a rule and an abbot.

The second kind is that of Anchorites, or Hermits, that is, of those who, no longer in the first fervor of their conversion, but taught by long monastic practice and the help of many brethren, have already learned to fight against the devil; and going forth from the rank of their brethren well trained for single combat in the desert, they are able, with the help of God, to cope single-handed, without the help of others, against the vices of the flesh and evil thoughts.

But a third and most vile class of monks is that of Sarabaites, who have been tried by no rule under the hand of a master, as gold is tried in the fire; but, soft as lead, and still keeping faith with the world by their works, they are known to belie God by their tonsure. Living in two's and three's, or even singly, without a shepherd, enclosed, not in the Lord's sheepfold, but in their own, the gratification of their desires is law unto them; because what they choose to do they call holy, but what they dislike they hold to be unlawful.

But the fourth class of monks is that called Landlopers, who keep going their whole life long from one province to another, staying three or four days at a time in different cells as guests. Always roving and never settled, they indulge their passions and the cravings of their appetite, and are in every way worse than the Sarabaites. It is better to pass all these over in silence than to speak of their most wretched life.

Therefore, passing these over, let us go on with the help of God to lay down a rule for that most valiant kind of monks, the Cenobites.

II. What Kind of Man the Abbot Ought to Be

The Abbot who is worthy to be over a monastery, ought always to be mindful of what he is called, and make his works square with his name of superior. For he is supposed to hold the place of Christ in the monastery, when he is called by his name, according to the saying of the Apostle: "You have received the spirit of adoption of sons, whereby we cry *Abba* (Father)." Therefore, the Abbot should never teach, prescribe, or command (which God forbid) anything contrary to the laws of the Lord; but his commands and teaching should be instilled like a leaven of divine justice into the minds of his disciples.

Let the Abbot always bear in mind that he must give an account in the dread judgment of God of both his own teaching and of the obedience of his disciples. And let the Abbot know that whatever lack of profit the master of the house shall find in the sheep, will be laid to the blame of the shepherd. On the other hand, he will be held blameless, if he gave all a shepherd's care to his restless and unruly flock, and took all pains to correct their corrupt manners; so that their shepherd, acquitted at the Lord's judgment seat, may say to the Lord with the Prophet: "I have not hid Thy justice within my heart. I have declared Thy truth and Thy salvation. But they contemning have despised me."

Then at length eternal death will be the crushing doom of the rebellious sheep under his charge.

When, therefore, anyone taketh the name of Abbot he should govern his disciples by a twofold teaching; namely, he should show them all that is good and holy by his deeds more than by his words; explain the commandments of God to intelligent disciples by words, but show the divine precepts to the dull and simple by his works. And let him show by his actions, that whatever he teacheth his disciples as being contrary to the law of God must not be done, "lest perhaps when he hath preached to others, he himself should become a castaway," and he himself committing sin, God one day say to him: "Why dost thou declare My justices, and take My covenant in thy mouth? But thou hast hated discipline, and hast cast my words behind thee." And: "Thou who sawest the mote in thy brother's eye, hast not seen the beam in thine own."

Let him make no distinction of persons in the monastery. Let him not love one more than another, unless it be one whom he findeth more exemplary in good works and obedience. Let not a free-born be preferred to a freedman, unless there be some other reasonable cause. But if from a just reason the Abbot deemeth it proper to make such a distinction, he may do so in regard to the rank of anyone whomsoever; otherwise let everyone keep his own place; for "whether bond or free," we are all one in Christ, and we all bear an equal burden of servitude under one Lord, "for there is no respect of persons with God." We are distinguished with Him in this respect alone, if we are found to excel others in good works and in humility. Therefore, let him have equal charity for all, and impose a uniform discipline for all according to merit.

For in his teaching the Abbot should always observe that principle of the Apostle in which he saith: "Reprove, entreat, rebuke," that is, mingling gentleness with severity, as the occasion may call for, let him show the severity of the master and the loving affection of a father. He must sternly rebuke the undisciplined and restless; but he must exhort the obedient, meek, and patient to advance in virtue. But we charge him to rebuke and punish the negligent and haughty. Let him not shut his eyes to the sins of evil-doers; but on their first appearance let him do his utmost to cut them out from the root at once, mindful of the fate of Heli, the priest of Silo. The well-disposed and those of good understanding, let him correct at the first and second admonition only with words; but let him chastise the wicked and the hard of heart, and the proud and disobedient at the very first offense with stripes and other bodily punishments, knowing that it is written: "The fool is not corrected with words." And again: "Strike thy son with the rod, and thou shalt deliver his soul from death."

The Abbot ought always to remember what he is and what he is called, and to know that to whom much hath been entrusted, from him much will be required; and let him understand what a difficult and arduous task he assumeth in governing souls and accommodating himself to a variety of characters. Let him so adjust and adapt himself to everyone—to the one by gentleness of speech, to another by reproofs, and to still another by entreaties, to each one according to his bent and understanding, —that he not only suffer no loss in his flock, but may rejoice in the increase of a worthy fold.

Above all things, that the Abbot may not neglect or undervalue the welfare of the souls entrusted to him, let him not have too great a concern about fleeting, earthly, perishable things; but let him always consider that he hath undertaken the government of souls, of which he must give an account. And that he may not perhaps complain of the want of earthly means, let him remember what is written: "Seek ye first the kingdom of God and His justice, and all these things shall be added unto you." And again: "There is no want to them that fear

Him." And let him know that he who undertaketh the government of souls must prepare himself to give an account for them; and whatever the number of brethren he hath under his charge, let him be sure that on judgment day he will, without doubt, have to give an account to the Lord for all these souls, in addition to that of his own. And thus, whilst he is in constant fear of the Shepherd's future examination about the sheep entrusted to him, and is watchful of his account for others, he is made solicitous also on his own account; and whilst by his admonitions he had administered correction to others, he is freed from his own failings.

III. Of Calling the Brethren for Counsel

Whenever any weighty matters are to be transacted in the monastery, let the Abbot call together the whole community, and make known the matter which is to be considered. Having heard the brethren's views, let him weigh the matter with himself and do what he thinketh best. It is for this reason, however, we said that all should be called for counsel, because the Lord often revealeth to the younger what is best. Let the brethren, however, give their advice with humble submission, and let them not presume stubbornly to defend what seemeth right to them, for it must depend rather on the Abbot's will, so that all obey him in what he considereth best. But as it becometh disciples to obey their master, so also it becometh the master to dispose all things with prudence and justice. Therefore, let all follow the Rule as their guide in everything, and let no one rashly depart from it.

Let no one in the monastery follow the bent of his own heart, and let no one dare to dispute insolently with his Abbot, either inside or outside of the monastery. If any one dare to do so, let him be placed under the correction of the Rule. Let the Abbot himself, however, do everything in the fear of the Lord and out of reverence for the Rule, knowing that, beyond a doubt, he will have to give an account to God, the most just Judge, for all his rulings. If, however, matters of less importance, having to do with the welfare of the monastery, are to be treated of, let him use the counsel of the seniors only, as it is written: "Do all things with counsel, and thou shalt not repent when thou hast done."

IV. The Instruments of Good Works

(1) In the first place to love the Lord God with the whole heart, the whole soul, the whole strength.

(2) Then, one's neighbor as one's self.

(3) Then, not to kill.

(4) Not to commit adultery.

(5) Not to steal.

(6) Not to covet.

(7) Not to bear false witness.

(8) To honor all men.

(9) And what one would not have done to himself, not to do to another.

(10) To deny one's self in order to follow Christ.

(11) To chastise the body.

(12) Not to seek after pleasures.

(13) To love fasting.

(14) To relieve the poor.

(15) To clothe the naked.

(16) To visit the sick.

(17) To bury the dead.

(18) To help in trouble.

(19) To console the sorrowing.

(20) To hold one's self aloof from worldly ways.

(21) To prefer nothing to the love of Christ.

(22) Not to give way to anger.

(23) Not to foster a desire for revenge.

(24) Not to entertain deceit in the heart.

(25) Not to make a false peace.

(26) Not to forsake charity.

(27) Not to swear, lest perchance one swear falsely.

(28) To speak the truth with heart and tongue.

(29) Not to return evil for evil.

(30) To do no injury, yea, even patiently to bear the injury done us.

(31) To love one's enemies.

(32) Not to curse them that curse us, but rather to bless them.

(33) To bear persecution for justice's sake.

(34) Not to be proud.

(35) Not to be given to wine.

(36) Not to be a great eater.

(37) Not to be drowsy.

(38) Not to be slothful.

(39) Not to be a murmurer.

(40) Not to be a detractor.

(41) To put one's trust in God.

(42) To refer what good one sees in himself, not to self, but to God.

(43) But as to any evil in himself, let him be convinced that it is his own and charge it to himself.

(44) To fear the day of judgment.

(45) To be in dread of hell.

(46) To desire eternal life with all spiritual longing.

(47) To keep death before one's eyes daily.

(48) To keep a constant watch over the actions of our life.

(49) To hold as certain that God sees us everywhere.

(50) To dash at once against Christ the evil thoughts which rise in one's heart.

(51) And to disclose them to our spiritual father.

(52) To guard one's tongue against bad and wicked speech.

(53) Not to love much speaking.

(54) Not to speak useless words and such as provoke laughter.

(55) Not to love much or boisterous laughter.

(56) To listen willingly to holy reading.

(57) To apply one's self often to prayer.

(58) To confess one's past sins to God daily in prayer with sighs and tears, and to amend them for the future.

(59) Not to fulfil the desires of the flesh.

(60) To hate one's own will.

(61) To obey the commands of the Abbot in all things, even though he himself (which Heaven forbid) act otherwise, mindful of that precept of the Lord: "What they say, do ye; what they do, do ye not."

(62) Not to desire to be called holy before one is; but to be holy first, that one may be truly so called.

(63) To fulfil daily the commandments of God by works.

(64) To love chastity.

(65) To hate no one.

(66) Not to be jealous; not to entertain envy.

(67) Not to love strife.

(68) Not to love pride.

(69) To honor the aged.

(70) To love the younger.

(71) To pray for one's enemies in the love of Christ.

(72) To make peace with an adversary before the setting of the sun.

(73) And never to despair of God's mercy.

Behold, these are the instruments of the spiritual art, which, if they have been plied without ceasing day and night and approved on judgment day, will merit for us from the Lord that reward which He hath promised: "The eye hath not seen, nor the ear heard, neither hath it entered into the heart of man, what things God hath prepared for them that love Him." But the workshop in which we perform all these works with diligence is the enclosure of the monastery, and stability in the community.

V. Of Obedience

The first degree of humility is obedience without delay. This becometh those who, on account of the holy subjection which they have promised, or of the fear of hell, or the glory of life everlasting, hold nothing dearer than Christ. As soon as anything hath been commanded by the superior they permit no delay in the execution, as if the matter had been commanded by God Himself. Of these the Lord saith: "At the hearing of the ear he hath obeyed Me." And again He saith to the teachers: "He that heareth you heareth Me."

Such as these, therefore, instantly quitting their own work and giving up their own will, with hands disengaged, and leaving unfinished what they were doing, follow up, with the ready step of obedience, the word of command with deeds; and thus, as if in the same moment, both matters—the master's command and the disciple's finished work—are, in the swiftness of the fear of God, speedily finished together, whereunto the desire of advancing to eternal life urgeth them. They, therefore, seize upon the narrow way whereof the Lord saith: "Narrow is the way which leadeth to life," so that, not living according to their own desires and pleasures but walking according to the judgment and will of another, they live in monasteries, and desire an Abbot to be over them. Such as these truly live up to the maxim of the Lord in which He saith: "I came not to do My own will, but the will of Him that sent Me."

This obedience, however, will be acceptable to God and agreeable to men then only, if what is commanded is done without hesitation, delay, lukewarmness, grumbling, or complaint. Because the obedience which is rendered to superiors is rendered to God. For He Himself hath said: "He that heareth you heareth Me." And it must be rendered by the disciples with a good will, "For the Lord loveth a cheerful giver." For if the disciple obeyeth with an ill will, and murmureth, not only with his lips but also in his heart, even though he fulfil the command, yet it will not be acceptable to God, who regardeth the heart of the murmurer. And for such an action he acquireth no reward; rather he incurreth the penalty of murmurers, unless he maketh satisfactory amendment.

VI. Of Silence

Let us do what the Prophet saith: "I said, I will take heed to my ways, that I sin not with my tongue: I have set a guard to my mouth, I was dumb, and was humbled, and kept silence even from good things." Here the Prophet showeth that, if at times we ought to refrain from useful speech for the sake of silence, how much more ought we to abstain from evil words on account of the punishment due to sin.

Therefore, because of the importance of silence, let permission to speak be seldom given to perfect disciples even for good and holy and edifying discourse, for it is written: "In much talk thou shalt not escape sin." And elsewhere: "Death and life are in the power of the tongue." For it belongeth to the master to speak and to teach; it becometh the disciple to be silent and to listen. If, therefore, anything must be asked of the superior, let it be asked with all humility and respectful submission. But coarse jests, and idle words or speech provoking laughter, we condemn everywhere to eternal exclusion; and for such speech we do not permit the disciple to open his lips.

VII. Of Humility

Brethren, the Holy Scripture crieth to us saying: "Every one that exalteth himself shall be humbled; and he that humbleth himself shall be exalted." Since, therefore, it saith this, it showeth us that every exaltation is a kind of pride. The Prophet declareth that he guardeth himself against this, saying: "Lord, my heart is not puffed up; nor are my eyes haughty. Neither have I walked in great matters nor in wonderful things above me." What then? "If I was not humbly minded, but exalted my soul; as a child that is weaned is towards his mother so shalt Thou reward my soul."

Hence, brethren, if we wish to reach the greatest height of humility, and speedily to arrive at that heavenly exaltation to which ascent is made in the present life by humility, then, mounting by our actions, we must erect the ladder which appeared to Jacob in his dream, by means of which angels were shown to him ascending and descending. Without a doubt, we understand this ascending and descending. Without a doubt, we understand this ascending and descending to be nothing else but that we descend by pride and ascend by humility. The erected ladder, however, is our life in the present world, which, if the heart is humble, is by the Lord lifted up to heaven. For we say that our body and our soul are the two sides of this ladder; and into these sides the divine calling hath inserted various degrees of humility or discipline which we must mount.

The first degree of humility then, is, that a man always have the fear of God before his eyes, shunning all forgetfulness, and that he be ever mindful of all that God hath commanded, that he always considereth in his mind how those who despise God will burn in hell for their sins, and that life everlasting is prepared for those who fear God. And whilst he guardeth himself evermore against sin and vices of thought, word, deed, and self-will, let him also hasten to cut off the desires of the flesh.

Let a man consider that God always seeth him from Heaven, that the eye of God beholdeth his works everywhere, and that the angels report them to Him every hour. The Prophet telleth us this when he showeth God thus ever present in our thoughts, saying: "The searcher of hearts and reins is God." And again; "The Lord knoweth the thoughts of men." And he saith: "Thou hast understood my thoughts afar off." And: "The thoughts of man shall give praise to Thee." Therefore, in order that he may always be on his guard against evil thoughts, let the humble brother always say in his heart: "Then I shall be spotless before Him, if I shall keep myself from iniquity."

We are thus forbidden to do our own will, since the Scripture saith to us; "And turn away from thy evil will." And thus, too, we ask God in prayer that His will may be done in us. We are, therefore, rightly taught not to do our own will, when we guard against what Scripture saith: "There are ways that to men seem right, the end whereof plungeth into the depths of hell." And also when we are filled with dread at what is said of the negligent: "They are corrupted and become abominable in their pleasure." But as regards desires of the flesh, let us believe that God is thus ever present to us, since the Prophet saith to the Lord: "Before Thee is all my desire."

We must, therefore, guard thus against evil desires, because death hath his station near the entrance of pleasure. Whence the Scripture commandeth, saying: "Go not after thy lusts." If, therefore, the eyes of the Lord observe the good and the bad, and the Lord always looketh down from heaven on the children of men, to see whether there be anyone that understandeth or seeketh God; and if our actions are reported to the Lord day and night by the angels who are appointed to watch over us daily, we must ever be on our guard, brethren, as the Prophet saith in the psalm, that God may at no time see us "gone aside to evil and become unprofitable," and having spared us in the present time, because He is kind and waiteth for us to be changed for the better, say to us in the future: "These things thou hast done and I was silent."

The second degree of humility is, when a man loveth not his own will, nor is pleased to fulfil his own desires, but by his deeds carrieth out that word of the Lord which saith: "I came not to do My own will but the will of Him that sent Me." It is likewise said: "Self-will hath its punishment, but necessity winneth the crown."

The third degree of humility is, that for the love of God a man subject himself to a superior in all obedience, imitating the Lord, of whom the Apostle saith: "He became obedient unto death."

The fourth degree of humility is, that, if hard and distasteful things are commanded, nay, even though injuries are inflicted, he accept them with patience and even temper, and not grow weary or give up, but hold out, as the Scripture saith: "He that shall persevere unto the end shall be saved." And again: "Let thy heart take courage, and wait thou for the Lord." And showing that a faithful man ought even to bear every disagreeable thing for the Lord, it saith in the person of the suffering: "For Thy sake we suffer death all the day long; we are counted as sheep for the slaughter." And secure in the hope of the divine reward, they go on joyfully, saying: "But in all these things we overcome because of Him that hath loved us." And likewise in another place the Scripture saith: "Thou, O God, hast proved us; thou hast tried us by fire as silver is tried; Thou hast brought us into a net, Thou hast laid afflictions on our back." And to show us that we ought to be under a superior, it continueth, saying: "Thou hast set men over our heads." And fulfilling the command of the Lord by patience also in adversities and injuries, when struck on the one cheek they turn also the other; the despoiler of their coat they give their cloak also; and when forced to go one mile they go two; with the Apostle Paul they bear with false brethren and "bless those who curse them."

The fifth degree of humility is, when one hideth from his Abbot none of the evil thoughts which rise in his heart or the evils committed by him in secret, but humbly confesseth them. Concerning this the Scripture exhorts us, saying: "Reveal thy way to the Lord and trust in Him." And it saith further; "Confess to the Lord, for He is good, for His mercy endureth forever." And the Prophet likewise saith: "I have acknowledged my sin to Thee and my injustice I have not concealed. I said I will confess against myself my injustice to the Lord; and Thou hast forgiven the wickedness of my sins."

The sixth degree of humility is, when a monk is content with the meanest and worst of everything, and in all that is enjoined him holdeth himself as a bad and worthless workman, saying with the Prophet; "I am brought to nothing and I knew it not; I am become as a beast before Thee, and I am always with Thee."

The seventh degree of humility is, when, not only with his tongue he declareth, but also in his inmost soul believeth, that he is the lowest and vilest of men, humbling himself and saying with the Prophet: "But I am a worm and no man, the reproach of men and the outcast of the people." "I have been exalted and humbled and confounded." And also: "It is good for me that Thou hast humbled me, that I may learn Thy commandments."

The eighth degree of humility is, when a monk doeth nothing but what is sanctioned by the common rule of the monastery and the example of his elders.

The ninth degree of humility is, when a monk withholdeth his tongue from speaking, and keeping silence doth not speak until he is asked; for the Scripture showeth that "in the multitude of words there shall not want sin;" and that "a man full of tongue is not established in the earth."

The tenth degree of humility is, when a monk is not easily moved and quick for laughter, for it is written: "The fool exalteth his voice in laughter."

The eleventh degree of humility is, that, when a monk speaketh, he speak gently and without laughter, humbly and with gravity, with few and sensible words, and that he be not loud of voice, as it is written: "The wise man is known by the fewness of his words."

The twelfth degree of humility is, when a monk is not only humble of heart, but always letteth it appear also in his whole exterior to all that see him; namely, at the Work of God, in the garden, on a journey, in the field, or wherever he may be, sitting, walking, or standing, let him always have his head bowed down, his eyes fixed on the ground, ever holding himself guilty of his sins, thinking that he is already standing before the dread judgment seat of God, and always saying to himself in his heart what the publican in the Gospel said, with his eyes fixed on the ground: "Lord, I am a sinner and not worthy to lift up mine eyes to heaven;" and again with the Prophet: "I am bowed down and humbled exceedingly."

Having, therefore, ascended all these degrees of humility, the monk will presently arrive at that love of God, which being perfect, casteth out fear. In virtue of this love all things which at first he observed not without fear, he will now begin to keep without any effort, and as it were, naturally by force of habit, no longer from the fear of hell, but from the love of Christ, from the very habit of good and the pleasure in virtue. May the Lord be pleased to manifest all this by His Holy Spirit in His laborer now cleansed from vice and sin.

Gregory the Great
(540?-604)

GREGORY the Great, Ambrose, Augustine, and Jerome are the four great Doctors of the Latin Church. As a synthesizer of theology, an administrator, and a force behind the Christian missionary movement to Great Britain, Gregory had strong influence in the Middle Ages. He became the voice which was able to popularize Augustine's thought for the Western Church. He was born of a Roman senatorial Christian family and by 573 was made the governor, or prefect, of Rome. However, the next year he was attracted to the monastic life and gave his wealth for helping the poor and founding monasteries. He himself became a member of St. Andrew monastery, but found the life of a hermit too quiet for his active disposition. In 579 he was appointed papal ambassador to the court of Constantinople; in 586 he was made abbot of St. Andrew monastery; and in 590 he was chosen pope. Against the invasion of the Lombards he proved Rome's strongest leader, and was able to keep Rome free of invasion throughout his pontificate. A man of sane, balanced understanding, Gregory easily ranks as the most conspicuous leader of his time.

Gregory's writings include a biography of Benedict, whose discipline he tried to enforce on monasteries generally, and also letters, ethical treatises, and scriptural expositions—all following the thought of Augustine. *The Book of Pastoral Rule*, from which brief scattered excerpts are reproduced, shows the practical religious insight of this rugged saint. The translation is by James Barmby in *The Nicene and Post-Nicene Fathers* (New York, 1895).

[THE CONDUCT OF A PASTOR]
From *The Book of Pastoral Rule*

The conduct of a prelate ought so far to transcend the conduct of the people as the life of a shepherd is wont to exalt him above the flock. For one whose estimation is such that the people are called his flock is bound anxiously to consider what great necessity is laid upon him to maintain rectitude. It is necessary, then, that in thought he should be pure, in action chief; discreet in keeping silence, profitable in speech; a near neighbour to every one in sympathy, exalted above all in contemplation; a familiar friend of good livers through humility, unbending against the vices of evil-doers through zeal for righteousness; not relaxing in his care for what is inward from being occupied in outward things, nor neglecting to provide for outward things in his solicitude for what is inward. . . .

The ruler should always be pure in thought, inasmuch as no impurity ought to pollute him who has undertaken the office of wiping away the stains of pollution in the hearts of others also; for the hand that would cleanse from dirt must needs be clean, lest, being itself sordid with clinging mire, it soil whatever it touches all the more. . . .

The ruler should always be chief in action, that by his living he may point out the way of life to those that are put under him, and that the flock, which follows the voice and manners of the shepherd, may learn how to walk better through example than through words.

For he who is required by the necessity of his position to speak the highest things is compelled by the same necessity to exhibit the highest things. For that voice more readily penetrates the hearer's heart, which the speaker's life commends, since what he commands by speaking he helps the doing of by shewing. . . .

The ruler should be discreet in keeping silence, profitable in speech; lest he either utter what ought to be suppressed or suppress what he ought to utter. For, as incautious speaking leads into error, so indiscreet silence leaves in error those who might have been instructed. . . .

The ruler also ought to understand how commonly vices pass themselves off as virtues. For often niggardliness palliates itself under the name of frugality, and on the other hand prodigality hides itself under the appellation of liberality. Often inordinate laxity is believed to be loving-kindness, and unbridled wrath is accounted the virtue of spiritual zeal. Often precipitate action is taken for the efficacy of promptness, and tardiness for the deliberation of seriousness. Whence it is necessary for the ruler of souls to distinguish with vigilant care between virtues and vices, lest either niggardliness get possession of his heart while he exults in seeming frugal in expenditure; or, while anything is prodigally wasted, he glory in being as it were compassionately liberal; or in remitting what he ought to have smitten he draw on those that are under him to eternal punishment; or in mercilessly smiting an offence, he himself offend more grievously; or by immaturely anticipating mar what might have been done properly and gravely; or by putting off the merit of a good action change it to something worse. . . .

Since, then, we have shewn what manner of man the pastor ought to be, let us now set forth after what manner he should teach. For, as long before us Gregory Nazianzen of reverend memory has taught, one and the same exhortation does not suit all, inasmuch as neither are all not bound together by similarity of character. For the things that profit some often hurt others; seeing that also for the most part herbs which nourish some animals are fatal to others; and the gentle hissing that quiets horses incites whelps; and the medicine which abates one disease aggravates another; and the food which invigorates the life of the strong kills little children. Therefore according to the quality of the hearers ought the discourse of teachers to be fashioned, so as to suit all and each for their several needs, and yet never deviate from the art of common edification. For what are the intent minds of hearers but, so to speak, a kind of tight tensions of strings in a harp, which the skilful player, that he may produce a tune not at variance with itself, strikes variously? And for this reason the strings render back a consonant modulation, that they are struck indeed with one quill, but not with one kind of stroke. Whence every teacher also, that he may edify all in the one virtue of charity, ought to touch the hearts of his hearers out of one doctrine, but not with one and the same exhortation.

Differently to be admonished are these that follow:—

Men and women.

The poor and the rich.

The joyful and the sad.

Prelates and subordinates.

Servants and masters.

The wise of this world and the dull.

The impudent and the bashful.

The forward and the fainthearted.

The impatient and the patient.

The kindly disposed and the envious.

The simple and the insincere.

The whole and the sick.

Those who fear scourges, and therefore live innocently; and those who have grown so hard in iniquity as not to be corrected even by scourges.

The too silent, and those who spend time in much speaking.

The slothful and the hasty.

The meek and the passionate.

The humble and the haughty.

The obstinate and the fickle.

The gluttonous and the abstinent.

Those who mercifully give of their

own, and those who would fain seize what belongs to others.

Those who neither seize the things of others nor are bountiful with their own; and those who both give away the things they have, and yet cease not to seize the things of others.

Those that are at variance, and those that are at peace.

Lovers of strifes and peacemakers.

Those that understand not aright the words of sacred law; and those who understand them indeed aright, but speak them without humility.

Those who, though able to preach worthily, are afraid through excessive humility; and those whom imperfection or age debars from preaching, and yet rashness impels to it. . . .

(*Admonition* 7.) Differently to be admonished are the wise of this world and the dull. For the wise are to be admonished that they leave off knowing what they know: the dull also are to be admonished that they seek to know what they know not. In the former this thing first, that they think themselves wise, is to be thrown down; in the latter, whatsoever is already known of heavenly wisdom is to be built up; since, being in no wise proud, they have, as it were, prepared their hearts for supporting a building. With those we should labour that they become more wisely foolish, leave foolish wisdom, and learn the wise foolishness of God: to these we should preach that from what is accounted fool-

ishness they should pass, as from a nearer neighbourhood, to true wisdom. . . .

But in the midst of these things we are brought back by the earnest desire of charity to what we have already said above; that every preacher should give forth a sound more by his deeds than by his words, and rather by good living imprint footsteps for men to follow than by speaking shew them the way to walk in. For that cock, too, whom the Lord in his manner of speech takes to represent a good preacher, when he is now preparing to crow, first shakes his wings, and by smiting himself makes himself more awake; since it is surely necessary that those who give utterance to words of holy preaching should first be well awake in earnestness of good living, lest they arouse others with their voice while themselves torpid in performance; that they should first shake themselves up by lofty deeds, and then make others solicitous for good living; that they should first smite themselves with the wings of their thoughts; that whatsoever in themselves is unprofitably torpid they should discover by anxious investigation, and correct by strict animadversion, and then at length set in order the life of others by speaking; that they should take heed to punish their own faults by bewailings, and then denounce what calls for punishment in others; and that, before they give voice to words of exhortation, they should proclaim in their deeds all that they are about to speak.

Isaac of Nineveh

(seventh century?)

As Nestorian bishop of Nineveh, Isaac was known for his administrative ability. Oddly, he was also gifted as one of the greatest writers on the life of asceticism. Among the few devotional writers to come out of the Eastern Church after the first four centuries, he ranks high, even though his known works are few, the most important being *On the Contempt of the World*. Because of his disciplined habits of study, he died almost blind in the monastery of Rabbun Shabor. The following excerpts are both clear insights into the differences between contemplation and prayer. The translations from the Syrian are from A. S. Wensinck, *The Mystic Treatises of Isaac of Nineveh* (Amsterdam, 1923).

THE DEGREES OF PRAYER

Sometimes from prayer a certain contemplation is born which makes prayer vanish from the lips. And he to whom this contemplation happens becomes as a corpse without soul, in ecstasy. This we call sight during prayer and not an image or form forged by phantasy. . . . Also in this contemplation . . . there are degrees and differences in gifts. But till this point there is still prayer. For thought has not yet passed into the state where there is no prayer, but to a state superior to it. For the motions of the tongue and the heart during prayer are keys. What comes after them is the entering into the treasury. Here then all mouths and tongues are silent, and the heart, the treasurer of the thoughts, the mind, the governor of the senses, the daring spirit, that swift bird, and all their means and powers and the beseeching persuasions have to stand still there: for the master of the house has come.

For like as the whole force of the laws and commandments which God has laid down for mankind have their term in the purity of the heart, according to the words of the Fathers, so all kinds and habits of prayer with which mankind prays unto God, have their term in pure prayer. Lamentations and self-humiliations and beseechings and inner supplications and sweet tears and all other habits which prayer possesses—as I have said—have their boundary, and the domain within which they are set into motion is pure prayer.

As soon as the spirit has crossed the boundary of pure prayer and proceeded onwards, there is neither prayer, nor emotions, nor tears, nor authority, nor freedom, nor beseechings, nor desire, nor longing after any of those things which are hoped for in this world or in the world to be.

Therefore there is no prayer beyond pure prayer, and all its emotions and habits by their authority with freedom conduct the spirit thus far and there is struggle in it; but beyond this limit it passes into ecstasy and is no longer prayer. From here onwards the spirit desists from prayer; there is sight, but the spirit does not pray.

Every kind of prayer which exists is set into motion by the impulses of the soul. But when the mind has entered the emotions of spirituality, then it can no longer pray.

Prayer is different from contemplation during prayer, though they are caused by each other. One is the seed; the other the load of the harvest borne by the hands, while the reaper is astonished by the indescribable sight of how from the mean and bare grains of seed glorious ears suddenly grow up before him. And during sight he remains without motion.

Every prayer is demand and request, or praise or thanksgiving. But judge whether there exists any of these modes, or demand of anything, when the mind has passed into this domain and has entered into this place.

I ask this of those who know the truth. It is not given to every one to inquire into these distinctions, but only to those who have been personally witnesses and ministers of this matter or have been brought up in the presence of the spiritual authors of such experiences, and have received the truth from their mouth and have passed their days with such occupations, asking and answering concerning matters of truth. As among ten thousand men there is scarcely to be found a single one who has fulfilled the commandments and the laws to any extent and who has been deemed worthy of serenity of soul, so there is rarely to be found one among many who, on account of strenuous vigilance, has been deemed worthy of pure prayer, and who has made his way into this domain and been deemed worthy of this mystery. Not many are deemed worthy of pure prayer—only a few. But as to that mystery which lies beyond, there is scarcely to be found a single man in every generation who has drawn near to this knowledge of God's grace.

Prayer is a beseeching for, a caring for, a longing for something, either liberation from evil things here or in the world to come, or a desire for promised things, or a demand for something by which man wishes to be brought nearer unto God. In these emotions are included all habits of prayer. But its being pure or not depends upon the following circumstances: If, when the spirit is prepared to offer one of the emotions which I have enumerated, any foreign deliberation or distraction mingles itself with it, prayer is called non-pure, because it has brought upon the altar of the Lord an animal which it is not allowed to offer.

But when the spirit gives itself with longing to one of these emotions . . . at the time of the beseeching, and when on account of its alacrity the gaze of the emotion is directed by the eye of faith beyond the curtain of the heart, the entrances of the soul are closed thereby against the foreign deliberations which are called strangers whom the law does not allow to enter the tabernacle. This is called the accepted offering of the heart and pure prayer. Its boundaries are at this point. What lies beyond cannot be called prayer. . . .

But sometimes they (the Holy Fathers) designate by spiritual prayer that which they sometimes call contemplation; and sometimes knowledge; and sometimes revelations of intelligible things. Dost thou see how the Fathers change their designations of spiritual things? This is because accurate designations can only be established concerning earthly things. The things of the world-to-be do not possess a true name but only cognition which is exalted above all names and signs and forms and colours and habits and composite denominations. When, therefore, the knowledge of the soul exalts itself above this circle of visible things, the Fathers use concerning this knowledge any designations they like, though no one does know the real names in order that the psychic deliberations may be based on them. We use denominations and riddles, according to the word of the holy Dionysius who says: We use signs and syllables, conventional names and words in behalf of the senses. But when by spiritual working our soul is moved unto divine things, then the senses and their workings are superfluous to us, as also the spiritual forces of the soul are superfluous as soon as our soul becomes the image of the Godhead through unification with the incomprehensible and radiant rays of the sublime—by those impulses which are not for the eyes. . . .

As the saints in the world to come do not pray, there the mind being engulfed by the divine spirit, but they swell in ecstasy in that delightful glory, so the mind, when it has been made worthy of perceiving the future blessedness, will forget itself and all that is here, and it will not be moved any longer by the thought of anything. . . .

All excellence whatever and all orders of prayer whatever, in body or in spirit, are in the realm of free will, as well as the mind that dominates the senses. But when the influence of the spirit reigns over the mind that regulates the senses and the deliberations, freedom is taken away from nature which no longer governs but is governed. And how could there be prayer at that time, when nature does not possess power over its self, but is conducted by an outward force without knowing whither. Nature then does not direct the emotions of the spirit according to its will, but captivity reigns over nature in that hour and conducts it there where sensual apperception ceases; because nature even has no will at that time, even to this extent that it does not know whether it is in or without the body, as Scripture testifies. Has therefore such a one prayer who is a captive to this degree and who even does not know himself? . . .

When there is no prayer, can then this unspeakable gift be designated by the name of prayer? The cause, as we say, is therein, that at the time of prayer this gift is granted unto those who are worthy. And in prayer it has its starting-point because this glorious gift cannot be granted except at this time, according to the testimony of the Fathers. . . .

If any one asks: How is it that at this time only these great and unspeakable gifts are granted? we answer: Because at this time, more than in any other hour, man is concentrated and prepared to look unto God and to desire and to expect compassion from Him. In short, it is the time that the demand of him who is at the gate of the king and asks desiringly and beseechingly, is likely to be heard. And what time is there when man is so cautious and fit and prepared as the time when he prays? Or should it be becoming that he should be deemed worthy of this at the time when he sleeps or settles any affair or is distracted of mind? However, the saints do not even know a time of idleness, because at all times they are occupied by spiritual things, for when they are not standing in preparation for prayer, they often meditate upon some stories of the scriptures, or their mind meditates in contemplation of the created things, or with other things meditation of which is profitable.

At the time of prayer the gaze of the spirit is exclusively fixed on God, and the tendency of its emotion is wholly directed towards Him, and it offers to Him the beseechings of the heart with the necessary zeal, with fervour and ardour. Therefore it is becoming that at this time, when a single thought dominates the soul, divine mercy should well forth from Him. For we see also that when we offer the visible sacrifice, while every one is standing in prayer, supplicating and beseeching, the mind being concentrated upon God, the gift of the spirit descends upon the bread and wine which we lay on the altar. . . .

What time is so holy and fit for sanctification and the receiving of gifts as the time of prayer, in which man speaks with God? At this time man utters his desires unto God, beseeching Him and speaking with Him, and his whole emotion and thought are concentrated from all sides upon Him with compulsion: of God alone he thinks and Him alone he supplicates; his whole thought is absorbed in discourse with Him and his heart is full of Him. It is in this state, therefore, that the Holy Ghost joins with the things for which man prays some unattainable insights, which it stirs in him in accordance with his aptitude of being moved so that by these insights the emotion of prayer ceases, the mind is absorbed in ecstasy and the desired object of prayer is forgotten. The impulses are drowned in a heavy drunkenness and man is no longer in this world. Then there is no longer distinction of body or of soul, nor recollection of anything. . . .

Prayer namely is steadfastness of mind which is terminated only by the light of the Holy Trinity through ecstasy. Thou seest how prayer is terminated when those insights which are born in the spirit from prayer pass into ecstasy, as I have said in the beginning of this treatise and in several places further on. . . .

Steadfastness of mind is highness of intelligible apperceptions which resembles the colour of the sky over which rises, at the time of prayer, the light of the Holy Trinity. When is a man deemed worthy of the whole of this grace such that during prayer he is exalted unto this height? Euagrius says: When the mind puts off the old man and puts on the new one by grace, then it also sees its steadfastness at the time of prayer, resembling sapphire or the colour of heaven, as the place of God was called by the elders of Israel, to whom it appeared on the mountain.

So, as I have said, this gift is not to be called spiritual prayer, but what then? The fruit of pure prayer, which is engulfed in the spirit. The mind has ascended here above prayer. And having found what is more excellent, it desists from prayer. And further there is no longer prayer, but the gaze in ecstasy at the unattainable things which do not belong to the world of mortals, and peace without knowledge of any earthly thing. This is the well known ignorance concerning which Euagrius says: Blessed is he who has reached, during prayer, unconsciousness which is not to be surpassed.

HOW GOD OPERATES IN MAN

The first emotion that befalls a man by divine grace and draws the soul towards life, strikes the heart with the thought concerning the transitory character of this nature. This thought is naturally connected with contempt of the world. And then begin all the beautiful emotions which educate unto life. That divine power which accompanies man makes as it were a foundation in him which desires to reveal life in him. As to this emotion which I mentioned, if a man does not extinguish it by clinging to the things of this world and to idle intercourse, and if he makes this emotion increase in his soul by perpetual concentration and by gazing at himself, he will bring himself near to that which no tongue is able to tell.

This thought is greatly hated by Satan and he strives with all his power to eradicate it from man. And if he were able to give him the kingdom of the whole earth in order to efface by thought of it from his mind this deliberation, he would not do otherwise. For Satan knows that if this recollection remains with him, his mind will no longer stay in this world of error, and his means will not reach man.

This sight is clad with fiery emotions and he that has caught it will no longer contemplate the world nor remain with the body.

Verily, my beloved, if God should grant this veracious sight unto the children of man for a short time, the course of the world would stand still. It is a bond before which nature cannot stand upright. And he unto whom this intercourse with his soul is given—verily, it is a gift from God, stronger than all partial workings which in this middle state are presented unto those who with an upright heart desire repentance. It is especially given to him of whom God knows that he is worthy of the real transition from this world unto profitable life, because He finds good will in him. It will increase and remain with a man through his dwelling alone by himself. Let us ask this gift in prayer; and for the sake of this gift let us make long vigils. And as it is a gift without equal, let us keep watch with tears at the gate of our Lord, that He may give it to us. Further we need not weary ourselves with the trouble of this world. This is the beginning of the impulse of life, which will fully bring about in a man the perfection of righteousness.

On the second working upon man. When a man follows his discipline perfectly and when he has succeeded in rising above the degree of repentance, and when he is near to taste the contemplation of his service, when it is given him from above to taste the delight of spiritual knowledge, a second working, after the first, will take its origin here.

In the first place man is assured concerning God's care for him and illuminated concerning His love of the creatures—rational creatures—and His manifold care for the things which regard them. Then there arises in him that sweetness of God and the flame of His love which burns in the heart and kindles all the affections of body and soul. And this power he will perceive in all the species of the creation and all things which he meets. From time to time he will become drunk by it as by wine; his limbs will relax, his mind will stand still and his heart will follow God as a captive. And so he will be, as I have said, like a man drunk by wine. And according as his inner senses are strengthened, so this sight will be strengthened and according as he is careful about discipline and watchfulness and applies himself to recitation and prayer, so the power of sight will be founded and bound in him.

In truth, my brethren, he that reaches this from time to time will not remember that he is clad with a body, nor will he know that he is in the world. This is the beginning of spiritual sight in a man, and this is the principle of all intellectual revelations. By this the intellect will be educated unto hidden things and become mature, and by this he will be gradually elevated unto other things which are higher than human nature. In short, by this will be conducted unto man all divine visions and spiritual revelations which the saints receive in this world. Thus nature can become acquainted with the gifts of revelation that happen in this life.

This is the root of our apperception in our Creator. Blessed is he that has preserved this good seed when it fell in his soul, and has made it to increase without destroying it by idle things and by the distractions of that which is transitory.

William the Pious

(886-918)

BY THE tenth century the life of monasteries had begun to decline. Even those under the rules of Benedict were relaxed in moral discipline through the shallowness of their members. Benedictine monks, allowed to be freed from labor for study, spent their time instead in idleness and vice. Thus the "Cluniac movement," given stimulus by Duke William I of Aquitaine (southwest France), called "the Pious," was an attempt to remedy the laxity of monastic habits. The monastery of Cluny was established by William under the terms of his charter on September 11, 910. The charter is another example of weaving the tone of sincere worship into the fabric of total living. Although Duke William does not rank among the "saints," his charter exhibits the interest of laymen in piety and shows their interest in the life of asceticism as a reform of religious laxity. Cluny was to be free from secularization or invasion, under the regulation of Benedict's *Rule*, and given to a rigid asceticism. The translation into English is anonymous from the French in Martin Bouguet, *Recueil des historiens des Gaules et de la France* (Paris, 1874).

CHARTER OF THE CLUNY MONASTERY

To all who think wisely it is evident that the providence of God has made it possible for rich men, by using well their temporal possessions, to be able to merit eternal rewards. . . . I, William, count and duke, after diligent reflection, and desiring to provide for my own safety while there is still time, have decided that it is advisable, indeed absolutely necessary, that from the possessions which God has given me I should give some portion for the good of my soul. I do this, indeed, in order that I who have thus increased in wealth may not at the last be accused of having spent all in caring for my body, but rather may rejoice, when fate at length shall snatch all things away, in having preserved something for myself. I cannot do better than follow the precepts of Christ and make His poor my friends. That my gift may be durable and not transitory I will support at my own expense a congregation of monks. And I hope that I shall receive the reward of the righteous because I have received those whom I believe to be righteous and who despise the world, although I myself am not able to despise all things.

Therefore be it known to all who live in the unity of the faith and who await the mercy of Christ, and to those who shall succeed them and who shall continue to exist until the end of the world, that, for the love of God and of our Saviour Jesus Christ, I hand over from my own rule to the holy apostles, namely, Peter and Paul, the possessions over which I hold sway—the town of Cluny, with the court and demesne manor, and the church in honor of St. Mary, the mother of God, and of St. Peter, the prince of the apostles, together with all the things pertaining to it, the villas, the chapels, the serfs of both sexes, the vines, the fields, the meadows, the woods, the waters and their outlets, the mills, the incomes and revenues, what is cultivated and what is not, all without reserve. These things are situated in or about the county of Macon, each one marked off by definite bounds. I give, moreover, all these things to the aforesaid apostles —I, William, and my wife Ingelberga— first for the love of God; then for the soul of my lord King Odo, of my father and my mother; for myself and my wife, —for the salvation, namely, of our souls and bodies; and not least, for that of Ava, who left me these things in her will; for the souls also of our brothers and sisters and nephews, and of all our relatives of both sexes; for our faithful ones who adhere to our service; for the advancement, also, and integrity of the Catholic religion. Finally, since all of us Christians are held together by one bond of love and faith, let this donation be for all—for the orthodox, namely, of past, present, or future times.

I give these things, moreover, with this understanding, that in Cluny a monastery shall be constructed in honor of the holy apostles Peter and Paul, and that there the monks shall congregate and live according to the rule of St. Benedict, and that they shall possess and make use of these same things for all time. In such wise, however, that the venerable house of prayer which is there shall be faithfully frequented with vows and supplications, and that heavenly conversations shall be sought after with all desire and with the deepest ardor; and also that there shall be diligently directed to God prayers and exhortations, as well for me as for all, according to the order in which mention has been made of them above. And let the monks themselves, together with all aforesaid possessions, be under the power and dominion of the abbot Berno, who, as long as he shall live, shall preside over them regularly according to his knowledge and ability. But after his death, those same monks shall have power and permission to elect any one of their order whom they please as abbot and rector, following the will of God and the rule promulgated by St. Benedict—in such wise that neither by the intervention of our own or of any other power may they be impeded from making a purely canonical election. Every five years, moreover, the aforesaid monks shall pay to the church of the apostles at Rome ten shillings to supply them with lights; and they shall have the protection of those same apostles and the defense of the Roman pontiff; and those monks may, with their whole heart and soul, according to their ability and knowledge, build up the aforesaid place.

We will, further, that in our times and in those of our successors, according as the opportunities and possibilities of that place shall allow, there shall daily, with the greatest of zeal, be performed works of mercy towards the poor, the needy, strangers, and pilgrims. It has pleased us also to insert in this document that, from this day, those same monks there congregated shall be subject neither to our yoke, nor to that of our relatives, nor to the sway of the royal might, nor to that of any earthly power. And, through God and all His saints, and by the awful day of judgment, I warn and admonish that no one of the secular princes, no count, no bishop, not even the pontiff of the aforesaid Roman see, shall invade the property of these servants of God, or alienate it, or diminish it, or exchange it, or give it as a benefice to any one, or set up any prelate over them against their will.

THE GOLDEN AGE OF MYSTICISM
AFTER THE DARK AGES THE FELLOWSHIP OF THE SAINTS BEGINS AFRESH

Anselm of Canterbury
(1033-1109)

As FATHER of medieval scholasticism Anselm has been called "the second Augustine." From his birthplace at Aosta in north Italy he came to Normandy in 1060 to the famed school of his countryman Lanfranc at the abbey of Bec. In due time, after King William had called Lanfranc across the Channel to Canterbury, Anselm became abbot of Bec and for fifteen years made it the outstanding center of learning in Europe. In 1093 Anselm himself was made archbishop of Canterbury.

Anselm is best known for his intellectual pursuits, especially his stress on reason as a tool for clarifying as well as proving orthodox beliefs. While at Bec he wrote, among others, his two brief treatises undertaking a logical proof of God, *Monologion* (Soliloquy) and *Proslogion* (Discourse). His most famous work, written as archbishop, is *Cur Deus Homo* (Why God Became Man), which presents the satisfaction theory of the cross—the death of the sinless Christ as repayment to God of the debt of sinful humanity.

The following chapters from the beginning and conclusion of *Proslogion* show Anselm's ontological argument for God's existence—that thought of a perfect being could not exist unless such a being existed. This translation from the original Latin by J. S. Maginnis was first published in the quarterly *Bibliotheca Sacra*, July, 1851.

[THE EXISTENCE OF GOD]
From *Proslogion*

I. EXHORTATION TO THE CONTEMPLATION OF GOD

O vain man! flee now, for a little while from thine accustomed occupations; hide thyself for a brief moment from thy tumultous thought; cast aside thy cares; postpone thy toilsome engagements; devote thyself awhile to God; repose for a moment in him; enter into the sanctuary of thy soul, exclude thence all else but God, and whatever may aid thee in finding him; then, within the closed doors of thy retirement, inquire after thy God. Say now, O my whole heart; say now to thy God: I seek thy face; thy face O Lord do I seek. Therefore now, O Lord, my God, teach thou my heart where and how it may seek for thee; where and how

it may find thee. If thou art not here, O Lord, where, while thou art absent, shall I find thee? But if thou art everywhere, why do I not see thee present? Truly thou dwellest in light inaccessible! But where is this inaccessible light, or how can I approach to light inaccessible? Who will lead me and conduct me into it, that I may behold thee there? And then by what signs, or under what form shall I seek thee? I have never seen thee, O Lord my God; I know not thy face. What shall this thine exile do,—O Lord, thou most High, what shall he do, banished so far from thee? What shall thy servant do, cast far away from thy presence, and yet in anguish with love for thy perfections? He pants to see thee, but thy face is too far from him; he

113

desires to approach unto thee, but thy habitation is inaccessible; he longs to find thee, but knows not thine abode. He attempts to seek thee, but knows not thy face. O Lord, thou art my Lord and my God, yet I have never seen thee. Thou hast created and redeemed me, and hast conferred upon me all my goods, but as yet I know thee not. In fine, I was created that I might behold thee; but I have not yet attained to the end of my creation. O miserable lot of man, since he has lost that for which he was created! O hard and cruel misfortune! Alas! what has he lost and what has he found? What has departed and what remains? He has lost the blessedness for which he was created; he has found misery for which he was not created. That has departed, without which there is no happiness; that remains, which, in itself, is naught but misery. Then man was accustomed to eat the bread of angels, for which he now hungers; now he eats the bread of sorrows, of which he was then ignorant. Alas! the common affliction of man, the universal wailing of the sons of Adam! The father of our race was filled to satiety, we pine, from hunger; he abounded, we are in want; he possessed happiness, but miserably deserted it; we are destitute of happiness, and pitifully long for it; but alas! our desires are unsatisfied. Why, since he could easily have done it, did he not preserve for us that which we should so greatly need? Why did he thus exclude from us the light and surround us with darkness? Why has he deprived us of life and inflicted death? Miserable beings! Whence have we been expelled? Whither are we driven? From what heights have we been precipitated? Into what abyss are we plunged? From our native land into exile; from the presence of God into the darkness which now envelops us; from the sweets of immortality into the bitterness and horror of death. —Unhappy change!—from good so great to evil so enormous! O heavy loss! heavy grief! heavy all! But alas! wretch that I am, miserable son of Eve, estranged from God, at what did I aim? What have I accomplished? Whither did I direct my course? Where have I arrived? To what did I aspire? for what do I now sigh? I sought for good, but behold confusion and trouble! I attempted to go to God, but I only stumbled upon myself. In my retirement I sought for rest, but in the depths of my heart I found tribulation and anguish. I desired to laugh by reason of the joy of my mind, but I am compelled to roar by reason of the disquietude of my heart. I hoped for happiness, but behold! from this my sighs are multiplied. And thou, O Lord, how long? How long O Lord wilt thou forget us? How long wilt thou turn thy face from us? When wilt thou have respect unto us and hear us? When wilt thou enlighten our eyes and show us thy face? When wilt thou restore thyself unto us? Have respect unto us, O Lord hear us, enlighten us, show thyself to us. Restore thyself unto us, that it may be well with us; it is so ill with us without thee. Have pity upon our toils and our efforts after thee; we can do nothing without thee. Invite us; aid us. I beseech thee, O Lord, let me not despair in my longing; but let me be refreshed by hope. My heart is embittered in its own desolation; assuage thou its sorrows by thy consolations. O Lord, oppressed with hunger I have commenced to seek thee; let me not cease till I am filled from thy bounty; famished, I have approached unto thee; let me not depart unfed; poor, I have come to thy riches; miserable, to thy compassion; let me not return empty and despised. And if, before I partake of this divine food, I long for it; grant, after my desires are excited that I may have sufficient to satisfy them. O Lord I am bowed down and can look only towards the earth; raise thou me, that I may look upwards. Mine iniquities have gone over my head; they cover me over, and as a heavy burden they bear me down. Set me free; deliver me from mine iniquities, lest their pit shall close upon me its mouth. Let me behold thy light, whether from the depth or from the distance. Teach me to seek thee; and while I seek show thyself to me; because, unless thou teach, I cannot seek thee; unless thou show thyself, I cannot find thee; let me seek thee by desiring thee; let me desire thee by seeking thee. Let me find thee by loving thee; let me love thee in finding thee. I confess, O Lord, and render thee thanks that thou hast created in me this thine image, that I may be mindful of thee, that I may contemplate and love thee; but it is so injured by contact with vice, so darkened by the vapor of sin, that it cannot attain to that for which it was created, unless thou wilt renew and reform it. I attempt not to penetrate to thy height, for with this my feeble intelligence can bear no comparison; but I desire, in some degree, to understand thy truth which my heart believes and loves. For I seek not to understand in order that I may believe; but I believe in order that I may understand, for I believe for this reason that unless I believe I cannot understand.

II. That God Truly Exists, Although the Fool Hath Said in His Heart, There Is No God

Therefore, O Lord, thou who dost impart understanding to faith, grant, so far as thou seest this knowledge would be expedient for me, that I may know that thou art as we believe, and that thou art this which we believe. And, indeed, we believe that thou art something, than which nothing greater can be conceived. Shall we, therefore, conclude that there is no such Being, merely because the fool hath said in his heart, there is no God? But surely even this same fool, when he hears me announce that there is something than which nothing greater can be conceived, understands what he hears, and what he understands is in his conception, even if he does not know that it exists. For, it is one thing for an object to be in the conception, and another to know that it exists. For, when the painter conceives, beforehand, the picture which he is about to sketch, he has it, indeed, in his conception; but he knows that it does not yet exist, for he has not as yet executed it. But, after he has painted, he not only has in his conception what he has just produced, but he knows that it exists. Even the fool, therefore, is convinced that there exists in his conception, something than which nothing greater can be conceived; because, when he hears this mentioned, he understands it, or forms an idea of it, and whatever is understood, is in the intelligence. And surely that, than which a greater cannot be conceived, cannot exist in the intelligence alone. For, let it be supposed that it exists only in the intelligence; then something greater can be conceived; for it can be conceived to exist in reality also, which is greater. If, therefore, that than which a greater cannot be conceived, exists in the conception or intelligence alone, then that very thing, than which a greater cannot be conceived, is something than which a greater can be conceived, which is impossible. There exists, therefore, beyond doubt, both in the intelligence and in reality, something than which a greater cannot be conceived.

III. That God Cannot Be Conceived Not to Exist

Indeed, so truly does this exist, that it cannot be conceived not to exist. For it is possible to conceive of the existence of something which cannot be conceived not to exist; and this is greater than that which can be conceived not to exist. Wherefore, if that, than which a greater cannot be conceived, can be conceived not to exist, then this something, than which a greater cannot be conceived, is something than which a greater can be conceived; which is a contradiction. So truly, therefore, does something exist, than which a greater cannot be conceived, that it is impossible to conceive this not to exist. And this art thou, O Lord our God! So truly, therefore, dost thou exist, O Lord my God, that thou canst not be conceived not to exist. For this there is the highest reason. For, if any mind could conceive of anything better than thou art, then the creature could ascend above the Creator, and become his judge; which is supremely absurd. Everything else, indeed, which exists besides thee, can be conceived not to exist. Thou alone, therefore, of all things, hast being in the truest sense, and consequently in the highest degree; for everything else that is, exists not so truly, and has, consequently, being only in an inferior degree. Why, therefore, has the fool said in his heart, there is no God? since it is so manifest to an intelligent mind, that of all things thine existence is the highest reality. Why, unless because he is a fool, and destitute of reason?

XXII. That God Alone Is What He Is and Who He Is

Thou alone, O Lord, art what thou art and who thou art. For that which is one thing in its whole and another in its parts, and in which there is anything mutable, is not what it is, in an absolute sense. And that which begins from non-existence and can be conceived of as not existing, and which unless it subsist through something else, must return to non-existence; also whatever has a past which is now no longer, and a future, which is yet to come, this does not exist in proper and absolute sense. But thou art what thou art; because whatsoever thou art at any time or in any manner, thou art this at all times and absolutely. And thou art who thou art properly and simply; because thou hast neither a past nor a future, but only a present, neither canst thou be conceived of as not existing at any moment. But thou art life and light and wisdom and blessedness and eternity, and many things good of this nature, and yet thou art none other than the one supreme Good, absolutely self-sufficient, needing nothing, but whom all things else need in order to their existence and well-being.

XXIV. An Attempt to Conceive the Nature and Vastness of This Good

Now, O my soul, awake and arouse all thy powers; conceive, so far as thou canst, what and how great is thy good. For if all good things are pleasing, consider attentively how pleasing is that good which contains in itself the sweetness of all other things else that are good, and not such sweetness as we experienced in created things, but such as excels this as far as the Creator is superior to the creature. For if life created is good, how good is life creative? If salvation procured is pleasing, how pleasing is that healing power which has procured all salvation? If that wisdom is lovely which consists in a knowledge of things which are formed, how lovely is the wisdom which has formed all things from nothing? In fine, if things that are pleasing, afford great delight, what and how great the delight which he affords by whom these pleasing things themselves have been created?

XXV. What and How Great Are the Blessings of Those Who Enjoy This Good

O, who shall enjoy this good! What will he possess and what will he not possess? Surely he will have all that he desires, and nothing which he desires not. For here will be good for the body and for the mind, such as eye hath not seen nor ear heard, nor the heart of man conceived. Why, therefore, O vain man, dost thou rove through a variety of things in search of pleasures for thy body, and for thy mind? Fix thy love upon this One Good which comprehends all other good, and it is sufficient. Direct thy desires to this single good which constitutes every species of good, and it is enough. For what dost thou love, O my body? What dost thou desire, O my soul? There, there alone is found whatsoever thou lovest and whatsoever thou desirest. If beauty delights; *the righteous shall shine as the sun.* If velocity, or strength, or corporeal freedom, which nothing can oppose; *they shall be like the angels of God;* for the body is *sown an animal body and it is raised a spiritual body,* not indeed by nature, but by divine power. If a long and vigorous life; there is a healthful eternity, and eternal health; for *the righteous shall live forever;* and *the salvation of the righteous is of the Lord.* If complete satisfaction; they shall be satisfied *when the glory of God shall appear.* If satisfaction more than complete; *they shall be abundantly satisfied from the fatness of thy house.* If melody delights thee; there choirs of angels chant without cessation, their harmonious praises to God. If pleasure unmixed and free from all impurity; thou shalt cause them to drink of the river of thy pleasure, O God. If wisdom; there wisdom itself, even the wisdom of God presents itself to the contemplation of the righteous. If friendship; they love God more than themselves, and each other as themselves; and God loves them more than they love themselves; because they love him and themselves and each other through him, and he loves himself and them through himself. If concord; they have all one will, for they have no other than the will of God. If power; the will of the righteous will be as omnipotent as that of God. For as God will be able to do whatever he shall will through himself, so they will be able to do whatsoever they shall will through him; because as their will can differ nothing from his, so his will differ nothing from theirs; and whatsoever he shall will must of necessity come to pass. If honor and riches; God will make his good and faithful servants rulers over many things; nay, he will constitute them his children and they shall be called gods; and where his Son shall be, there shall they be; heirs indeed, of God and joint heirs with Christ. If true security; surely as the righteous will be certain that these good things, or rather that this one good will never, by any means fail them, so they will be certain that they will never of their own accord cast it away, that God who loves them will never deprive them of it against their will, and that there is nothing more powerful than God which can separate them from him against his will and their own. But what and how great is this joy, where such and great good is found? O heart of man, poor and needy heart, inured to trouble and overwhelmed by misery! how wouldst thou rejoice if thou could abound with all this? Ask thy most inward depths if they could contain the joy which would flow from blessedness so great. But surely if any other, whom thou lovest altogether as thyself, should possess the same blessedness, thy joy would be double; for thou wouldst rejoice not less for him than for thyself. But if two, three, or a still greater number should partake of the same, thou wouldst rejoice as much for each one as for thyself, if thou shouldst love each as thyself. Therefore in this perfected love of innumerable happy angels and men, where no one will love each other less than himself, each one will in like manner rejoice for the other as for himself. If, therefore, the heart of man can scarcely contain its own joy, arising from this great good, how will it find room for the aggregate of such joys? And, indeed, since the more any one loves another, the more he will rejoice in his good; and since in this state of perfect felicity each will love God incomparably more than himself, and all others with him, so he will rejoice more beyond conception, in the felicity of God than in that of himself and of all others with him. But if they shall love God with all the heart, with all the mind and all the soul, so that all the heart and all the mind and all the soul would, notwithstanding, be insufficient for the greatness of their love; surely they will so rejoice with all the heart, with all the mind and with all the soul that the whole heart and mind and soul would be insufficient for the fulness of their joy.

Hugh of St. Victor
(1096?-1141)

A NATIVE German, Hugh spent his adult life in the monstery of St. Victor, at Paris. He became head of the school and was highly respected for his learning, piety, and quiet modesty. Bernard of Clairvaux was one of his closest friends.

Hugh was deeply influenced by Neo-Platonism and by Dionysius the Areopagite, on whose *Heavenly Hierarchy* he wrote a commentary. He analyzed three stages by which man finally attains a mystical vision of God: (1) cogitation, in which sense precepts are formed; (2) meditation, wherein the concepts are intellectually investigated; and (3) contemplation, in which intuition is employed to search the inner meaning of the concepts. The excerpt below shows his conception of a high mystical fellowship in God. It is quoted from *The Graces of Interior Prayer* by Auguste Poulain and is used by permission of B. Herder Book Co. and Kegan, Paul, Trench, Trubner & Co.

THE EMBRACE

The Soul: What is that sweet thing that comes sometimes to touch me at the thought of God? It affects me with such vehemence and sweetness that I begin wholly to go out of myself and to be lifted up, whither I know not. Suddenly, I am renewed and changed; it is a state of inexpressible well-being. My consciousness rejoices. I lose the memory of my former trials, my soul rejoices, my mind becomes clearer, my heart is enflamed, my desires are satisfied. I feel myself transported into a new place, I know not where. I grasp something interiorly as if with the embraces of love. I do not know what it is, and yet I strive with all my strength to hold it and not to lose it. I struggle deliciously to prevent myself leaving this thing which I desire to embrace for ever, and I exult with ineffable intensity, as if I had at last found the goal of all my desires. I seek for nothing more. I wish for nothing more. All my aspiration is to continue at the point I have reached. Is it my Beloved? Tell me, I pray thee, if this be He, that when He return, I may conjure Him not to depart, and to establish in me His permanent dwelling-place?

The Man: Yes, it is truly the Beloved who visits thee. But He comes invisible, hidden, incomprehensible. He comes to touch thee, not to be seen; to intimate His presence to thee, not to be understood; to make thee taste of Him, not to pour Himself out in his entirety; to draw thy affection, not to satisfy thy desire; to bestow the first-fruits of His love, not to communicate it in its fulness. Behold in this the most certain pledge of thy future marriage: that thou art destined to see Him and to possess Him eternally, because He already gives himself to thee at times to taste; with what sweetness thou knowest. Therefore in the times of His absence thou shalt console thyself; and during His visits thou shalt renew thy courage which is ever in need of heartening. We have spoken at great length, O my soul. I ask thee to think of none but Him, love none but Him, listen to none but Him, to take hold of none but Him, possess none but Him.

The Soul: That indeed is what I desire, what I choose; that is what I long for from the depths of my heart.

Bernard of Clairvaux

(1090-1153)

KNOWN as one of the great orators of the church as well as one of the most "God-fearing and holy" monks, Bernard gave vital impetus to the monastic movement. He was reared near Dijon, France, by a knightly father and a deeply religious mother. At the age of twenty-two he and thirty companions became neophytes in the monastery at Cîteaux. Three years later he was sent out at the head of a group of his fellows to found a new monastery at Clairvaux. Though offered high ecclesiastical positions, he remained abbot there until his death. But his influence went far beyond Clairvaux—as an antagonist of Abelard's liberal views, as one who healed the papal schism in 1130, and as preacher of the Second Crusade.

Many of Bernard's writings were preserved, and they had a strong influence on Luther and Calvin. They include over five hundred personal letters, hymns which are still sung, doctrinal treatises, and sermons, of which eighty-six deal with the Song of Solomon as an allegory of divine-human love. The following chapters from *On the Love of God* give a careful insight into Bernard's deep mystical devotion. They are reprinted from the translation of Terence L. Connolly (New York, 1937) by permission of Spiritual Book Associates.

[DEGREES OF LOVE OF GOD]

From *On the Love of God*

I. WHY AND HOW GOD SHOULD BE LOVED

You wish, therefore, to hear from me why and how God should be loved? And I: the reason for loving God is God Himself; the way is to love Him beyond measure. Is this enough? It is, perchance, but only for one who is wise. But if to the unwise I am debtor, where enough has been said to the wise I must also, as usual, administer to the needs of others. And so out of consideration for those who are slower to understand, I shall consider it no burden to repeat what I have said, more fully rather than more profoundly. There is a twofold reason, I should say, why God should be loved for His own sake: because nothing can be more justly, nothing more profitably loved. Indeed when the question is asked why God should be loved it may have one of two meanings. For the question may arise from the fact that a person does not clearly see what particularly constitutes the basis of his inquiry: whether it is God's title to our love or our own advantage in loving Him. To be sure, I would give the same answer to both of these questions: I find no other worthy reason for loving Him except Himself. And first let us examine the question of God's title to our love. A very special title to it is His who gave Himself to us despite the fact that we were so undeserving. For, what better than Himself could even He have given? If, then, in asking the reason why we should love God we seek to know His title to our love, it is chiefly this: because He hath first loved us. He it is who is clearly deserving of being loved in return, especially if one considers who He is that loved, who they are whom He loved and how much He loved them. And who is He? Is He not the One to whom every spirit bears witness: Thou art my God, for Thou hast no need of my goods? And the true love of this Sovereign One lies in this, that it does not seek its own interests. But to whom is such unmixed love shown? When we were enemies, it is said, we were reconciled to God. God, therefore, has loved His enemies and that, gratis. But how much? As much as Saint

John says: God so loved the world as to give his only begotten Son. And Saint Paul adds: He spared not even His own Son, but delivered Him up for us all. That very Son says of Himself: Greater love than this no man hath, that a man lay down his life for his friends. Thus has the Just deserved from the ungodly, the Greatest from the least, the All-powerful from the weak. But some one may say: Yes, thus has He deserved of mankind, but of the Angels, not so. That is true, because the Angels had no need of it. Moreover, He who succored men in so great a necessity preserved the Angels from it, and He who by His love for men brought it about that they should no longer remain such as they were, The Same with equal love bestowed upon the Angels the grace of never becoming such as men once were.

VIII. The First Degree of Love

Love is a natural affection, one of four. They are well known; there is no need of mentioning them by name. (They are love, fear, joy and sorrow.) It would therefore be just that what is natural should serve its own Author before all others. Hence the first commandment is called the greatest: Thou shalt love the Lord thy God, etc. But since nature is rather weak and feeble, it is impelled at the bidding of necessity to serve itself first. And there is carnal love by which before all other things man loves himself for his own sake, as it is written: first . . . that which is natural; afterwards that which is spiritual. And it is not imposed by a command but implanted in nature; for who ever hated his own flesh? But truly if this love, as is its wont, begins to be too precipitate or too lavish and is not at all satisfied with the riverbed of necessity, overflowing rather widely it will be seen to invade the fields of pleasure. At once its overflow is held in check by the commandment that opposes itself to it: Thou shalt love thy neighbor as thyself. It happens, very justly indeed, that the sharer in nature should not be excluded from a part in grace as well, especially in that grace which is inborn in nature itself. If man finds it a burden, I do not say to relieve his brother in matters of necessity but to administer to his pleasures, let him restrain his own unless he wishes to be a transgressor of the law. Let him be as indulgent as he likes to himself, so long as he is mindful to show the same degree of indulgence to his neighbor. The bridle of temperance is put upon you, O man, out of the law of life and of discipline lest you should go after your concupiscences and perish; lest in the goods of nature you become a slave to your soul's enemy, that is, to lust. How much more justly and honorably do you give such things to your fellow-sharer, that is, your neighbor rather than to your enemy! And if indeed, according to the advice of the wise man, you turn away from your own pleasures, and according to the teaching of the Apostle, content with food and raiment, you find it no burden to withhold your love for a little while from carnal desires which war against the soul; surely, I think, what you take away from your soul's enemy you will find no burden to bestow upon the sharer of your nature. Your love will then be both temperate and just if what is taken from your own pleasures is not denied to your brother's needs. Thus carnal love is made to belong to our neighbor when it is extended to the common good.

But if, while you are sharing what you have with your neighbor, even the necessities of life should, perchance, be lacking to you, what will you do? What indeed, unless with all confidence you should ask of Him who giveth to all men abundantly, and upbraideth not; who openest thy hand, and fillest with blessing every living creature? There is no doubt, surely, that He who is not absent in the midst of plenty will gladly be present in the time of need. He says, at length: seek ye first the kingdom of God and His justice, and all these things shall be added to you. He promises that He will of His own accord give whatever is necessary to him who restricts himself in superfluities and loves his neighbor. This, surely, is to seek first the kingdom of God and to implore help against the tyranny of sin, that you prefer to bear the yoke of modesty and restraint rather than endure that sin should reign in your mortal body. But this, too, is part of the righteousness in question, not to possess the gift of nature independently of him whose common nature you share.

Nevertheless, in order that it may be perfect justice to love one's neighbor, it is imperative that it be referred to God as its cause. Otherwise how can he love his neighbor without alloy who does not love him in God? He surely cannot love in God who does not love God. God must be loved first, in order that one's neighbor, too, may be loved in God. God, therefore, who makes all else that is good, makes Himself to be loved. And He does it as follows. He who fashioned nature, it is He who shields it from harm as well. For it was so fashioned that it should have as a necessary Protector, Him whom it had as Maker, in order that what could not have come into being save through Him should not be able to subsist at all without Him. And lest the creature might not know this about itself and consequently (which God forbid) in its pride arrogate to itself the benefits it had received from its Creator, the same Maker, in His high and salutary counsel wills that man should be harassed with troubles; so that when man has failed and God has come to his assistance, while man is being delivered by God, God, as is fitting, may be honored by man. For this is what He says: call upon Me in the day of trouble: I will deliver thee, and thou shalt glorify Me. Thus it comes to pass in this wise that a man, an animal and carnal by nature, who knew how to love no one except himself may begin even for his own sake, to love God too, because in Him beyond a shadow of doubt, as he has often learned from experience, he can do all things—those, to be sure, which it is good to be able to do—and without Him he can do nothing.

IX. The Second and Third Degrees of Love

A man, therefore, loves God but still for a while for his own sake, not for Himself. It is, however, a sort of prudence to know what you are able to do by yourself, what with God's help, and to preserve yourself guiltless for Him who keeps you unharmed. But if tribulation assails you again and again, and on this account there occurs an oft-repeated turning towards God; and as often, there follows deliverance obtained from God, is it not true that even though the breast were of steel or the heart of stone in one so many times rescued, it must of necessity be softened at the grace of the Rescuer so that man might love God not merely for his own sake but for God Himself. From the occasion that arises from frequent needs it is necessary that man should frequently, in repeated intercourse, go to God who in such intercourse is tasted, and it is by tasting that it is proved how sweet is the Lord. Thus it happens that when once His sweetness has been tasted, it draws us to the pure love of God more than our need impels. Just as in the case of the Samaritans who said, speaking to the woman who had announced that the Lord was come: We now believe, not for thy saying: for we ourselves have heard Him, and know that this is indeed the Savior of the world, similarly I say, we too, following their example, speaking to our flesh may justly say: We now love God, not for your necessity; for we ourselves have tasted and know how sweet is the Lord. For it is true that a need of the flesh is a sort of speech, and the benefits which it knows from experience it proclaims in transports of joy. And so for one who feels thus, it will not now be hard to fulfil the commandment in regard to loving his neighbor. For he truly loves God and in this way also loves the things which are God's. He loves purely and it is no burden for the pure to be obedient to the command; rather purifying his heart, as it is written, in the obedience of charity. He loves justly and gladly embraces a just command. This love is deservedly acceptable because it is disinterested (i.e. not offered with a view to obtaining future favors). It is pure because it is paid neither by word or tongue, but by deed and truth. It is just, since it is paid back as it is received. For he who loves thus, to be sure, loves in no other wise than he is loved; seeking, in his turn, not the things that are his own but the things that are Jesus Christ's, just as He sought the things that are ours, or rather ourselves and not His own. It is thus he loves who says: Give praise to the Lord, for He is good. He who gives praise to the Lord not because He is good to him but because He is good, he truly loves God for God and not for his own sake. It is not thus that he loves of whom it is said: he will praise thee when thou shalt do well to him. This is the third degree of love by which God is now loved for His very self.

X. The Fourth Degree of Love

Happy is he who has deserved to attain as high as the fourth degree, where a man does not love even himself except for the sake of God. Thy justice, (O Lord), is as the mountains of God. This love is a mountain and the high mountain of God. In truth, a curdled mountain, a fat mountain. Who shall ascend into the mountain of the Lord? Who will give me wings like a dove, and I will fly and be at rest? This place is in peace: and this abode in Sion. Woe is me, that my sojourning is prolonged! Flesh and blood, vessel of clay, when will your earthly dwelling-place compass this? When will the mind experience such an affection as this so that inebriated with divine love, forgetful of self, and become in its own eyes like a vessel that is destroyed, the whole of it may continue on to God and being joined to God, become one spirit with Him, and say: For Thee my flesh and my heart hath fainted away: thou art the God of my heart, and the God that is my portion forever? Blessed and holy, I would say, is he to whom it has been given to experience such a thing in this mortal life at rare intervals or even once, and this suddenly and scarcely for the space of a single moment. In a certain manner to lose yourself as though you were not, and to be utterly unconscious of yourself and to be emptied of your-

self and, as it were, brought to nothing, this pertains to heavenly intercourse, not to human affection. And if indeed, any one among mortals is suddenly from time to time (as has been said) even for the space of a moment admitted to this, straightway the wicked world grows envious, the evil of the day throws everything into confusion, the body of death becomes a burden, the necessity of the flesh causes unrest, the fainting away of corruption offers no support, and what is more vehement than these, fraternal charity (i.e. obligations to one's neighbor) recalls one (from the state of contemplation). Alas! he is forced to return to himself, to fall back upon his own, and in his wretchedness to cry out: Lord, I suffer violence, answer Thou for me; and this: Unhappy man that I am, who shall deliver me from the body of this death?

Since, however, Scripture says God hath made all things for Himself, it will certainly come to pass that the creature will at one time or other conform itself to its Author and be of one mind with Him. We ought therefore be transformed into this same disposition of soul, so that as God has willed that everything should be for Himself, so we too may deliberately desire neither ourselves nor any other thing to have been in the past, or to be in the future, unless it be equally for His sake, to wit, for His sole will, not for our own pleasure. A need satisfied (calmed by satisfaction), or good fortune received will not delight us so much as that His will is seen perfectly fulfilled in us and by us; which, too, is what we daily ask in prayer when we say: Thy will be done on earth as it is in heaven. O love, holy and chaste! O sweet and pleasing affection! O pure and undefiled intention of the will! the more surely undefiled and purer, as there is mixed with it, now, nothing of its own; so much the sweeter and more pleasing, as its every feeling is wholly divine. To be thus affected is to become one with God. Just as a little drop of water mixed with a lot of wine seems entirely to lose its own identity, while it takes on the taste of wine and its color; just as iron, heated and glowing, looks very much like fire, having divested itself of its original and characteristic appearance; and just as air flooded with the light of the sun is transformed into the same splendor of light so that it appears not so much lighted up as to be light itself; so it will inevitably happen that in saints every human affection will then, in some ineffable manner, melt away from self and be entirely transfused into the will of God. Otherwise how will God—be all in all, if in man there is left anything at all of man himself. The substance, indeed, will remain, but in another form, another glory, and another power (i.e. a man's human nature and individual identity will remain, transfigured). When will this be? Who will see this? Who will possess it? When shall I come and appear before the face of God? O Lord, my God, my heart hath said to Thee: my face hath sought Thee: Thy face, O Lord, will I still seek. Will I, do you think, see Thy holy temple?

As for me, I think that it will not have come to pass with perfect fulfilment that: Thou shalt love the Lord thy God with thy whole heart, and with thy whole soul, and with thy whole strength, until the heart itself is no longer compelled to think about the body, and the soul ceases to have to attend to quickening the body and to providing it with sense-perception, and the body's strength freed from vexations is made strong in the power that is of God. For it is impossible wholly to concentrate all these (the heart, mind and virtue) upon God and to hold them fixed upon the Divine Countenance so long as it is necessary for them, absorbed and dissipated, to be subject to this frail and wretched body. And so, in a spiritual and immortal body, in a body perfect, calm and acceptable, and in all things subject to the spirit, let the soul hope to apprehend the fourth degree of love, or, rather, to be apprehended in it; for, in truth, it is within the power of God to give it to whomsoever He wishes, not for human diligence to procure by its own efforts. Then, I say, she will easily come into the possession of the highest

degree, when without the slightest delay, as she hastens most eagerly into the joy of her Lord, no allurement of the flesh will now retard her progress, no vexation destroy her peace. Do we think, however, that the holy martyrs actually attained to this grace, even in part, while still detained in those victorious bodies of theirs? Great power of love, certainly, had caught up their souls, within, and thus they had strength so to expose their bodies, without, and condemn their tortures. But, assuredly, the sense of most bitter pain could not but disturb their calm, although it had no power to destroy their peace.

XV. The Four Degrees of Love

Nevertheless, because we are carnal and are born of the concupiscence of the flesh, it follows as a necessary consequence that our desire for personal gratification, or our love should have its source in the flesh. But if it is directed according to the right order of things, advancing by its several degrees under the guidance of grace, it will at last be consummated by the spirit because: that was not first which is spiritual, but that which is natural; afterwards that which is spiritual. First, therefore, man loves himself for his own sake; for, he is flesh and he can have no taste for anything except in relation to himself. And when he sees that he cannot subsist of himself he begins to seek God through faith as something, as it were, necessary for him, and to love Him. Thus he loves God according to the second degree, but for his own sake, not for Himself. But when, in truth, on account of his own necessity he has begun to worship and come to Him again and again by meditating, by reading, by prayer and by being obedient, little by little God becomes known to him through experience, in a sort of familiarity, and consequently He grows sweet; and thus by tasting how sweet is the Lord he passes to the third degree so that he loves God now, not for his own sake but for Himself. Yes, in this degree he stands still for a very long time and I know not if the fourth degree is attained in its perfection by any man in this life so that forsooth, a man loves himself only for the sake of God. If there are any who have experience of this let them declare it; to me, I confess, it seems impossible. But it will be so, beyond a doubt, when the good and faithful servant has been brought into the joy of his Lord and inebriated with the plenty of God's house. For, forgetful of himself in a wonderful way, as it were, and as if entirely freed of self he will continue on, wholly, into God, and thereafter being joined to Him he will be one spirit with Him. I am of the opinion that this is what the prophet meant when he said: I will enter into the powers of the Lord: O Lord I will be mindful of Thy justice alone. He felt, certainly, that when he entered into the spiritual powers of the Lord he would have laid aside self in all that concerns the infirmities of the flesh, so that he would have to give no thought to the flesh, but his whole being would in the spirit, be mindful of the justice of the Lord alone.

Then, for certain, the several individual members of Christ will be able to say, every one concerning himself, what Paul said of the Head: And if we have known Christ according to the flesh; but now we know Him so no longer. No one, there, will know himself according to the flesh because flesh and blood shall not possess the kingdom of God. Not that the substance of flesh will not be there, but that every carnal necessity will be wanting and the love of the flesh will be absorbed in the love of the spirit, and human affections, weak as they now are, shall be changed into those which are divine. Then the net of charity which now, drawn through this great and vast sea does not cease to gather together fish of every kind, when brought at last to the shore, casting forth the bad, will retain only the good. Indeed in this life the net of charity includes fish of every kind within its vast folds, where, fashioning itself to suit all according to the time and taking over the good and evil fortunes of all and, in a sense, making them its own, it is wont not only to rejoice with them that rejoice, but also to weep with them that weep. But when it shall have reached the shore (eternity) casting away as bad fishes everything that it suffered in sadness, it will retain those only which can give it pleasure and be to it a source of gladness. For can it be that Paul, for instance, will then be weak with the weak or be on fire for those who are scandalized, where scandals and weakness will be far away? Or will he, surely, mourn for those who have not done penance, where it is certain there will be no one either sinning or doing penance? Far be it from us to think that he will lament and weep over those who are to be condemned to everlasting fire together with the devil and his angels, in that city (of God) which the stream of the river maketh—joyful, and whose gates the Lord loveth—above all the tabernacles of Jacob; because in the tabernacles although the joy of victory is sometimes felt, there is, nevertheless, the anxiety of combat and often danger to life itself, but in that native land no suffering or sadness will be allowed to enter in, even as it is sung thereof: The dwelling in thee is as it were of all rejoicing; and again: everlasting joy shall be unto them. Finally, how shall one be mindful of mercy where the justice of God alone will be remembered? Just so, where now there will be no place for misery or occasion for pity, surely there can be no feeling of compassion.

Hildegarde of Bingen

(1098-1179)

AMONG the women saints, Hildegarde ranks in stature with Catherine of Siena and Theresa of Avila. With her, it may be said, German mysticism began. She was born in Böckelheim on the Naab, possibly of a family related to the court. She was educated privately under Jutta, sister of Count Meginhard. Hildegarde was in time given the Benedictine habit, and eventually became abbess at Disibodenberg. She later moved to a new convent near Bingen, where she remained the rest of her life.

As a visionary and prophetic figure whose activities encompass political reform, the influence of her letters was felt beyond German borders. *A Vision* exemplifies her high tone of spiritual intuition based on patristic tradition and liturgy. The translation here is by Carol North Valhope in *The Soul Afire* (New York, 1944) and is reprinted by permission of Pantheon Books.

A VISION

I saw what seemed to be a great iron-coloured mountain. On it sat some one in such a glory of light that his radiance dazzled me. On either side a wing both broad and long was spread like a gentle shadow.

Before him, at the foot of the mountain, stood a shape covered over and over with eye upon eye, so that this multitude of eyes prevented me from seeing anything that resembled a human form. In front of this shape there was another, that seemed a boy in a pale garment and shod with white. Upon its head he (who sat on the mountain) shed such a flood of splendour that I could not see its face. He who sat on the mountain also bred sparks of living light and cast them about both shapes in a lovely stream. In the mountain there were many windows that framed the heads of men, white and wan.

Then suddenly, he upon the mountain called in a loud and penetrating voice:

"O frail man! dust of the dust of the earth, ash of ashes, cry out and tell of the coming of pure salvation, so that those may be instructed who see into the very marrow of the Scriptures and still will not proclaim or preach them because their blood is tepid and they are dulled to the cause of God. Open to them the house of secrets, for they are hesitant and hide it in remote fields and garner no fruit. Grow into a fountain of plenty, flow out in mystical teachings so that those who would hold you in contempt because of the fall of Eve be shaken by the tide of your waters. For it is not from man that you have this insight and this depth. You receive it from above, from that sacred Judge on High, where the serene intercourse between shining shapes will beam in the clearest light. Arise then, and speak, and give tiding of what has been revealed to you with the supreme strength and help of God! For He who governs all His creatures in goodness and might, He pervades all who fear Him and serve Him in love and delight and humility with the clarity of heaven, and guides the patient pilgrim on the right path to the joyful beholding of eternity."

The great iron-coloured mountain symbolises the power and the constancy of God's eternal kingdom that cannot be destroyed by the impact of unsteadfast mutability. And he, who is seated on the mountain, and dazzles your sight with his glory, reflects him in the realm of the Blessed, who rules the circle of earth, lifted in the rays of changeless serenity and intangible to the mind of man. The long and broad wings, like shadows on either side, symbolise protection, tender and mild, that curbs with warning and also with chastisement. They are the adequate symbols of the ineffable nature of unerring justice that weighs all in her scales.

At the foot of the mountain stands the shape covered over and over with eye upon eye. In deep humility and oblivious of self, it recognises the kingdom of God and, sheltered in the fear of the Lord, toils among men eagerly and persistently, with the clear gaze of a good and just purpose. It has such hosts of eyes that you cannot see anything resembling a human form. Thanks to this sight that pierces through all things, it has so utterly overcome that forgetfulness of what is right and Godly that sweeps over men so often when they are overwhelmed by the tedium of living, that its wakefulness can no longer be clouded by weak and earthly questioning.

Beside this shape is another, that of a boy in a pale garment and shod with white. For those who fear God, precede, and the poor in spirit follow. For who fears God with devotion is also informed with the bliss of the poor in spirit that does not ask for pride or a boastful heart, but loves simplicity and soberness. Inconspicuously clothed in devotion, as in a pale and insignificant garment, it ascribes its good works not to itself but to God, and joyfully follows in the candid footsteps of God's Son. He who is seated on the mountain sheds such splendour upon its head that you cannot see its face. For the serene visitation of Him who governs all creatures in a praiseworthy fashion pours forth strength and power in such abundance that a weak mortal cannot grasp such a lavishing of heavenly riches upon the poverty of man.

From Him who is seated on the mountain fly many sparks of live fire that flit about the shapes in utter loveliness. This means: God Almighty exhales various and strong forces that shine in divine clearness and, as surrounding helpers and protectors, caress and anoint with fiery touch those who truly fear God and submit with faithful love to poorness of spirit.

In the mountain many windows can be seen that frame the heads of men, white or wan. This means: at such a lofty height, the striving and the doing of men cannot be kept secret or hidden from the incomparably deep and sharp recognition of God. Often through themselves they reveal a pale coolness or a warm glow of their being, now men whose heart and hand is weary and who sink into ignominious sleep, and now men who are wakeful and honourably vigilant. Thus says Solomon in witness of my words: "He becometh poor that dealeth with a slack hand; but the hand of the diligent maketh rich." (Proverbs 10.4) This means: that man has made himself weak and poor who did not want to conquer his own sin, or to forgive the sins of others, who has never been filled with the miraculous works of beatitude. But he who has wrought at the great work of salvation, is a runner on the path of truth who reaches toward the fountain of glory that yields him the most precious treasures of heaven and earth. Whoever, then, has for his own the knowledge of the Holy Ghost and the plumed pinions of faith, let him not transgress my admonitions, but savour and absorb them in his soul.

Francis of Assisi

(1182-1226)

GIOVANNI Francesco Bernardone, who became famous as Francis of Assisi—"the troubadour of God"—began the history of Italian mysticism. A lad born of wealthy parents and given to revelry and worldly excitement, he in early years followed the life of a soldier. His conversion, which was a gradual change, came to its climax while he was on a pilgrimage to Rome. On returning to Assisi he manifested his new interest in Christianity by caring for lepers and rebuilding the church of St. Damian. In 1209 came his desire "to imitate Christ" by living a life of poverty and ministering to the poor. By 1216 he and his followers were known as the "Penitents of Assisi." He carried on this ministry, especially among the people of the cities, until his death in 1226.

As founder of the Franciscan order he became perhaps the outstanding saint of the Middle Ages, certainly the most beloved. Evelyn Underhill has aptly described Francis as one who "walked, literally, in an enchanted world; where every living thing was a theophany, and all values were transvaluated by love." Wedded to "Lady Poverty," he devoted himself to the needs of the poor and the sick.

Francis wrote little, but his friends wrote much about him, some regarding his "Acts" and some giving "Mirrors" of his perfection. Of all writings about Francis, *The Little Flowers* is the classic book. The excerpts given here are from a concluding section about Francis' disciple Friar Giles, but they undoubtedly mirror the beliefs and virtues of Francis himself. They are from Thomas Okey's translation in the "Everyman's Library" edition and are used by permission of the publisher, E. P. Dutton & Co.

[SOME BASIC VIRTUES OF A SAINT]

From *The Little Flowers of St. Francis*

III. CHAPTER OF HOLY HUMILITY

*N*o man can attain to any knowledge or understanding of God, save by the virtue of holy humility: for the straight way upward is the straight way downward. All the perils and the great falls that have come to pass in this world have come about for no cause save the lifting up of the head, to wit, of the mind, in pride; and this is proven by the fall of the devil, that was cast out of heaven; and by the fall of our first parent, Adam, that was driven out of paradise through the exaltation of the head, to wit, through disobedience; and again by the Pharisee, whereof Christ speaketh in the gospel, and by many other ensamples. And so contrariwise: for all the great and good things that have e'er come to pass in this world, have come to pass through the abasement of the head, to wit, through

the humility of the mind, even as is proven by the blessed and most humble Virgin Mary, and by the publican, and by the holy thief on the cross, and by many other ensamples in the scriptures. And, therefore, it were well if we could find some great and heavy weight that we might ever hang about our necks, in order that it might ever bear us down, to wit, that it might ever make us humble ourselves. A friar asked Friar Giles, "Tell me, father, how shall we flee from this sin of pride?" To whom Friar Giles answered, "My brother, be persuaded of this: never hope to be able to flee from pride, except thou first place thy mouth where thou hast set thy feet; but if thou wilt consider well the blessings of God, then shalt thou know that of thy duty thou art held to bow thy head. And, again, if thou wilt think much on thy faults and on thy manifold offences against God, most of all wilt thou have cause to humble thyself. But woe unto those that would be honoured for their wickedness! One degree in humility hath he risen that knoweth himself to be the enemy of his own good; another degree in humility is to render to others those things that are theirs, and not to appropriate them to ourselves, to wit, that every good thing and every virtue a man findeth in himself, he ought not to own it to himself, but to God alone, from whom proceedeth every grace and every virtue and every good thing; but all sin or passion of the soul, or whatsoever vice a man find in himself, this should he own to himself, since it proceedeth from himself and from his own wickedness, and not from others. Blessed is that man that knoweth himself, and deemeth himself vile in the sight of God, and even so in the sight of men. Blessed is he that ever judgeth himself and condemneth himself, and not others, for he shall not be judged at that dread and last judgment eternal. Blessed is he that shall bend diligently under the yoke of obedience and under the judgment of others, even as the holy apostles did before and after they received the Holy Spirit." Likewise said Friar Giles, "He that would gain and possess perfect peace and rest must needs account every man his superior; he must ever hold himself the subject and inferior of others. Blessed is that man who in his deeds and in his words desireth not to be seen or known, save only in that unalloyed being, and in that simple adornment which God created and adorned him with. Blessed is the man that knoweth how to treasure up and hide divine revelations and consolations, for there is nothing so hidden but that God shall reveal it, when it pleaseth Him. If a man were the most perfect and the holiest man in the world, and yet deemed and believed himself the most miserable of sinners and the vilest wretch on the earth—therein is true humility. Holy humility knoweth not how to prate, and the blessed fear of God knoweth not how to speak." Said Friar Giles, "Methinks humility is like unto a thunderbolt; for even as the bolt maketh a terrible crash, breaking, crushing, and burning all that it findeth in its path, and then naught of that bolt is found, so, in like manner, humility smiteth and scattereth and burneth and consumeth every wickedness and every vice and every sin; and yet is found to be naught in itself. The man that possesseth humility findeth grace in the sight of God, through that humility, and perfect peace with his neighbour."

IV. Chapter of the Holy Fear of God

He that feareth naught showeth that he hath naught to lose. The holy fear of God ordaineth, governeth, and ruleth the soul and maketh it to come to a state of grace. If any man possess any grace or divine virtue, holy fear is that which preserveth it. And he that hath not yet gained virtue or grace, holy fear maketh him to gain it. The holy fear of God is the bringer of divine graces, for it maketh the soul, wheresoever she abideth, to attain quickly to holy virtue and divine graces. All creatures that have fallen into sin would never have fallen if they had had the holy fear of God. But this holy gift of fear is given only to the perfect; for the more perfect a man is, the more god-fearing and humble he is. Blessed is he that knoweth he is in a dungeon in this world, and ever remembereth how grievously he hath offended his Lord. A man ought ever to fear pride with a great fear, lest it thrust against him and make him fall from the state of grace wherein he standeth; for a man can never stand secure being girt about with enemies; and our enemies are the seductions of this miserable world and our own flesh that, together with the devil, is ever the enemy of the soul. A man hath need of greater fear lest his own wickedness overcome him and beguile him than of any other of his enemies. It is impossible that a man can rise and ascend to any divine grace, or virtue, or persevere therein, without holy fear. He that feareth not God goeth in danger of perishing, and in yet greater peril of everlasting perdition. The fear of God maketh a man to obey humbly, and maketh him bow down his head under the yoke of obedience; and the greater the fear a man hath, the more fervently doth he worship. Not a little gift is prayer to whomsoever it is given. The virtuous words of men, however great they may appear to me, are not therefore accounted nor rewarded according to our measure, but according to the measure and good pleasure of God; for God regardeth not the sum of our toils, but the sum of our love and humility. Therefore, the better part for us is to love always, and fear with great humility, and never put trust in ourselves for any good thing; ever having suspicion of those thoughts that are begotten in the mind under the semblance of good.

V. CHAPTER OF HOLY PATIENCE

He that with steadfast humility and patience suffereth and endureth tribulation, through fervent love of God, soon shall attain to great grace and virtues, and shall be lord of this world, and shall have a foretaste of the next and glorious world. Everything that a man doeth, good or evil, he doeth it unto himself; therefore, be not offended with him that doeth thee an injury, for rather oughtest thou to have humble patience with him, and only grieve within thee for his sin, taking compassion on him and praying God earnestly for him. The stronger a man is to endure and suffer patiently injuries and tribulations, for love of God, the greater is he in the sight of God, and no more; and the weaker a man is to endure pain and adversity, for love of God, the less is he in the sight of God. If any man praise thee, speaking well of thee, render thou that praise to God alone; and if any man speak evil of thee, or revile thee, aid thou him, speaking evil of thyself, and worse. If thou wilt make good thine own cause, strive ever to make it appear ill, and uphold thy fellow's cause, ever imputing guilt to thyself, and ever praising and truly excusing thy neighbour. When any man would contend or have the law of thee, if thou wouldst win, lose; and then shalt thou win; but if thou wouldst go to law to win, when thou

thinkest to win, then shalt thou find thou hast lost heavily. Therefore, my brother, believe of a surety, the straight way of salvation is the way to perdition. But when we are not good bearers of tribulation, then we cannot be seekers after everlasting consolations. Much greater consolation and a more worthy thing it is to suffer injuries and revilings patiently, without murmuring, for love of God, than to feed a hundred poor folk and fast continually every day. But how shall it profit a man, or what shall it avail him, to despise himself and afflict his body with great fastings and vigils and scourgings, if he be unable to endure a small injury from his neighbour? For which thing, a man shall receive a much greater reward and greater merit than for all the afflictions a man can give to himself of his own will; because to endure the revilings and injuries of one's neighbour, with humble patience and without murmuring, purgeth sin away much more quickly than doth a fount of many tears. Blessed is the man that ever holdeth before the eyes of the mind the memory of his sins and the good gifts of God; for he will endure with patience every tribulation and adversity, whereby he looketh for great consolations. The truly humble man looketh for no reward nor merit from God, but striveth ever only how he can give satisfaction in all things, owning himself God's debtor: and every good thing he hath, that, he knoweth he hath through the goodness of God, and not through any merit of his own; and every adversity he endureth, he knoweth it to be truly because of his sins. A certain friar asked Friar Giles, saying, "If in our time any great adversity, or tribulation, should befall, what should we do in that case?" To whom Friar Giles answered, saying, "My brother, I would have thee know that if the Lord rained down stones and arrows from heaven, they could not injure nor do any hurt to us, if we were such men as we ought to be; for if a man were verily what he ought to be, he would transmute every evil and every tribulation into good; for we know what the apostle said, that all things work together for good to them that love God; even so all things work together for ill and to the condemnation of him that hath an evil will. If thou wilt save thyself and go to celestial glory, thou shalt desire no vengeance nor punishment of any creature; for the heritage of the saints is ever to do good and ever to suffer evil. If thou knewest in very truth how grievously thou hast offended thy Creator, thou wouldst know that it is a worthy and just thing that all creatures should persecute thee and give thee pain and tribulation, in order that these creatures might take vengeance for the offences thou hast done to their Creator. A high and great virtue it is for a man to overcome himself; for he that overcometh himself shall overcome all his enemies, and attain to all good. And yet a greater virtue would it be if a man suffered himself to be overcome by all men; for he would be lord over all his enemies, to wit, his vices, the devil, the world, and his own flesh. If thou wilt save thyself, renounce and despise all consolation that the things of this world and all mortal creatures can give thee; for greater and more frequent are the falls that come through prosperity and through consolation than are those that come through adversity and tribulation." Once on a time a religious was murmuring against his superior, in the presence of Friar Giles, by reason of a harsh obedience he had laid upon him; to whom Friar Giles said, "My dearest, the more thou murmurest the heavier is the weight of thy burden, and the harder shall it be to thee to bear; and the more humbly and devoutly thou shalt place thy neck under the yoke of holy obedience, the lighter and easier will that obedience be to bear. But methinks thou wouldst not be rebuked in this world, for love of Christ, and yet wouldst be with Christ in the next world; thou wouldst not be persecuted or cursed for Christ's sake in this world, and in the next, wouldst be blessed and received by Christ; thou wouldst not labour in this world, and in the next, wouldst rest and be at peace. I tell thee, friar, friar, thou are sorely beguiled; for

by the way of poverty and of shame and of reviling a man cometh to true celestial honour; and by enduring patiently mocking and cursing, for love of Christ, a man shall come to the glory of Christ. Therefore, well saith a worldly proverb,

He whose gifts cost him no woe,
Good gifts from others must forgoe.

How useful is the nature of the horse! for how swiftly soever the horse runneth, he yet letteth himself be ruled and guided, and leapeth hither and thither, and forward and backward, according to the will of his rider: and so, likewise, ought the servant of God to do, to wit, he should let himself be ruled, guided, turned aside, and bent, according to the will of his superior, or of any other man, for love of Christ. If thou wouldst be perfect, strive diligently to be full of grace and virtue, and fight valiantly against vice, enduring patiently every adversity for the love of thy Lord, that was mocked and afflicted and reviled and scourged and crucified and slain for love of thee, and not for His own sin, nor for His glory, nor for His profit, but only for thy salvation. And to do all this that I have told thee, above all things it is necessary that thou overcome thyself; for little shall it profit a man to lead and draw souls to God, if first he overcome not himself, and lead and draw himself to God."

VI. CHAPTER OF SLOTH

The slothful man loseth both this world and the next; for himself beareth no fruit and he profiteth not another. It is impossible for a man to gain virtue without diligence and great toil. When thou canst abide in a safe place stand not in a perilous place: he abideth in a safe place who striveth and suffereth and worketh and toileth through God, and for the Lord God; and not through fear of punishment, or for a price, but for love of God. The man that refuseth to suffer and labour for love of Christ, verily he refuseth the glory of Christ; and even as diligence is useful and profitable to us, so is negligence ever against us. Even as sloth is the way that leads to hell, so is holy diligence the way that leads to heaven. A man ought to be very diligent to gain and keep virtue and the grace of God, ever labouring faithfully with this grace and virtue; for many times it befalleth that the man who laboureth not faithfully loseth the fruit for the leaves, or the grain for the straw. To some God giveth of His grace good fruit with few leaves; to others He giveth fruit and leaves together; and there are others that have neither fruit nor leaves. Methinks 'tis a greater thing to know how to guard and keep well the good gifts and graces given to us by the Lord, than to know how to gain them. For albeit a man may know well how to gain, yet if he know not how to save and treasure up, he shall never be rich; but some there be that make their gains little by little, and are grown rich because they save well their gains and their treasure. Oh, how much water would the Tiber have stored up if it flowed not away to the sea! Man asketh of God an infinite gift, that is without measure and without bounds, and yet will not love God, save with measure and with bounds. He that would be loved of God and have infinite reward from Him, beyond all bounds and beyond all measure, let him love God beyond all bounds and beyond all measure, and ever serve Him infinitely. Blessed is he that loveth God with all his heart and with all his mind, and ever afflicteth his body and his mind for love of God, seeking no reward under heaven, but accounting himself only a debtor. If a man were in sore poverty and need, and another man said to him, "I will lend thee a very precious thing for the space of three days: know that if thou use well this thing within this term of three days thou shalt gain an infinite treasure, and be rich evermore," is it not a sure thing that this poor man would be very careful to use well and diligently this thing so precious, and would strive much to make it fruitful and profit him well: so do I say likewise that this thing lent unto us by the hand of God is our body, which the good God

hath lent us for three days; for all our times and years are but as three days in the sight of God. Therefore if thou wouldst be rich and enjoy the divine sweetness everlastingly, strive to labour well and make this thing, lent by the hand of God, bear good fruit; to wit, thy body, in this space of three days; to wit, in the brief time of thy life: for if thou are not careful of gain in this present life, while thou hast yet time, thou shalt not enjoy that everlasting riches nor find holy rest in that celestial peace everlastingly. But if all the possessions of the world were in the hands of one person that never turned them to account himself, nor put them out for others to use, what fruit or what profit would he have of those things? Of a surety, neither profit nor fruit would he have. But it might well be that a man, having few possessions and using them well, should have much profit and a great abundance of fruit for himself and for others. A worldly proverb saith, "Never set an empty pot on the fire hoping thy neighbour will come and fill it." And so likewise God willeth that no grace be left empty; for the good God never giveth a grace to any man that it be kept empty, rather doth he give it that a man may use it and bring forth fruit of good works; for goodwill sufficeth not except a man strive to pursue it and use it to a profit of holy words. On a time a wayfarer said to Friar Giles, "Father, I pray thee give me some consolation." Whereto Friar Giles answered, "My brother, strive to stand well with God and straightway shalt thou have the consolation thou needest; for if a man make not a pure dwelling-place ready in his soul, wherein God may abide and rest, never shall he find an abiding place nor rest nor true consolation in any creature. When a man would work evil he never asketh much counsel for the doing thereof; but, ere they do good, many folk seek much counsel and make long delay." Once Friar Giles said to his companions, "My brethren, methinks, in these days, one findeth no man that would do those things that he seeth are most profitable, and not only for the soul but also for the body. Believe me, my brethren, I can swear, of a truth, that the more a man flees and shuns the burden and the yoke of Christ the more grievous he maketh it to himself and the more heavily it weigheth upon him, and the greater is the burden; but the more ardently a man taketh up his burden, ever heaping up more weight of his own will, the lighter and the more pleasant he feeleth it to bear. Would to God that men would labour to win the good things of the body, since they would win also those of the soul; forasmuch as the body and the soul, without any doubt, must ever be joined together, either to suffer or to enjoy; to wit, either ever to suffer together in hell everlasting pains and boundless torments, or, through the merits of good works, to enjoy perpetual joys and ineffable consolations with the saints and angels in paradise. Because, if a man laboured well, or forgave well, yet lacked humility, his good deeds would be turned to evil; for many have there been that have wrought many works that seemed good and praiseworthy, but since they lacked humility they were discovered and known to be done through pride; and their deeds have shown this, for things done through humility are never corrupted." A friar said to Friar Giles, "Father, methinks we know not yet how to understand our own good." To whom Friar Giles answered, "My brother, of a surety each man worketh the art he hath learned, for no man can work well except he have first learned: wherefore I would have thee know, my brother, that the noblest art in this world is the art of working well; and who could know that art except first he learn it? Blessed is that man in whom no created thing can beget evil; but yet more blessed is he that receiveth in himself good edification from all things he sees or hears."

VII. CHAPTER OF THE CONTEMPT OF TEMPORAL THINGS

Many sorrows and many woes will the miserable man suffer that putteth his desire and his heart and his hope in earthly things, whereby he forsaketh and loseth heavenly things, and at last shall e'en lose also these earthly things. The eagle soareth very high, but if she had tied a weight to her wings she would not be able to fly very high: and even so for the weight of earthly things a man cannot fly on high, to wit, he cannot attain to perfection; but the wise man that bindeth the weight of the remembrance of death and judgment to the wings of his heart, could not for the great fear thereof go astray nor fly at the vanities nor riches of this world, which are a cause of damnation. Every day we see worldly men toil and moil much and encounter great bodily perils to gain these false riches; and after they have toiled and gained much, in a moment they die and leave behind all that they gained in their lives; therefore put not thy trust in this false world that beguileth every man that believeth therein, for it is a liar. But whoso desireth and would be great and truly rich, let him seek after and love everlasting riches, and good things that ever savour sweetly and never satiate and never grow less. If we would not go astray, let us take pattern from the beasts and the birds, for these, when they are fed, are content and seek not their living save from hour to hour when their need cometh: even so should a man be content with satisfying his needs temperately, and not seek after superfluities. Friar Giles said that the ant was not so pleasing to St. Francis as other living things because of the great diligence she hath in gathering together and storing up, in the time of summer, a treasure of grain for the winter; but he was wont to say that the birds pleased him much more, because they laid not up one day for the next. But yet the ant teacheth us that we ought not to be slothful in the summer of this present life, so that we be not found empty and barren in the winter of the last day and judgment.

X. CHAPTER OF HOLY PENITENCE

A man ought ever to afflict himself much and mortify his body, and suffer willingly every injury, tribulation, anguish, sorrow, shame, contempt, reproach, adversity, and persecution, for love of our good Lord and Master, Jesus Christ, who gave us the example in Himself; for from the first day of His glorious Nativity, until His most holy Passion, He ever endured anguish, tribulation, sorrow, contempt, pain, and persecution, solely for our salvation. Therefore, if we would attain to a state of grace, above all things it is necessary that we walk, as far as lieth in us, in the paths and in the footsteps of our good Master, Jesus Christ. A secular once asked of Friar Giles, saying, "Father, in what way can we men in the world attain to a state of grace?" Whereto Friar Giles answered, "My brother, a man ought first to grieve for his sins, with great contrition of heart, and then he should confess to the priest with bitterness and sorrow of heart, accusing himself sincerely, without concealment and without excuse: then he must fulfil the penance perfectly that is given and laid upon him by his confessor. Likewise, he must guard himself against every vice and every sin, and against every occasion of sin; and also he must exercise himself in good and virtuous works before God and towards his neighbour; and, doing these things, a man shall attain to a state of grace and of virtue. Blessed is that man that hath continual sorrow for his sins, bewailing them ever, day and night, in bitterness of heart, solely for the offences he hath done to God! Blessed is the man that hath ever before the eyes of his mind the afflictions and the pains and the sorrows of Jesus Christ, and that for love of Him neither desireth nor receiveth any temporal consolation in this bitter and stormy world, until he attain to that heavenly consolation of life eternal, where all his desires shall be fully satisfied with gladness."

XVII. Chapter of Holy Obedience

The more bound under the yoke of holy obedience the religious is, for love of God, the greater fruit of himself he will yield unto God; and the more he is subject to his superior, for God's honour, the more free and more cleansed shall he be from his sins. The truly obedient religious is like unto a knight well armed and well horsed that breaks fearlessly through the ranks of his enemies and scatters them, because none of them can do him hurt. But he that obeys with murmurings, and as one driven, is like unto an unarmed and ill-horsed knight, that when he joineth battle shall be dragged to the ground by his enemies and wounded and taken by them and sometimes cast into prison and slain. The religious that would live according to the determination of his own will, showeth that he would build a perpetual habitation in the abyss of hell. When the ox putteth his neck under the yoke, then he plougheth the earth well, so that it bringeth forth good fruit in due season; but when the ox goeth wandering around, the ground is left untilled and wild, and giveth not fruit in its season. Even so the religious that bendeth his neck under the yoke of obedience yieldeth much fruit to the Lord God in its time; but he that is not obedient with a good heart to his superior, is barren and wild and without any fruit from his vows. Wise and great-hearted men bend their necks readily, without fear and without doubt, under the yoke of holy obedience; but foolish and faint-hearted men strive to wrest their necks from under the yoke of holy obedience, and then would obey no creature. I deem it a greater perfection in the servant of God to obey his superior with a pure heart, for reverence and love of God, than it would be to obey God in person if He commanded him: for he that is obedient to the Lord's vicar would surely obey sooner the Lord Himself if He commanded him. Methinks also that if any man having the grace of speaking with angels had promised obedience to another, and it befell that while he was standing and discoursing with these angels this other man to whom he had promised obedience called him, I say, that straightway he ought to leave his converse with the angels and run to do that obedience, for honour of God. He that hath put his neck under the yoke of holy obedience, and then would draw back his neck from under that obedience, that he might follow a life of greater perfection, I say, that if he be not first perfect in the state of obedience, it is a sign of great pride that lieth hidden in his soul. Obedience is the way that leadeth to every good and every virtue, and disobedience is the way to every evil and every vice.

XVIII. Chapter of the Remembrance of Death

If a man had the remembrance of his death and of the last eternal judgment and of the pains and the torments of damned souls ever before the eyes of his mind, of a surety, nevermore would the desire come upon him to sin or to offend God. But if it were possible that any man had lived from the beginning of the world, even to the time that now is, and during all this time had endured every adversity, tribulation, pain, affliction, and sorrow, and if he were to die, and his soul should go to receive everlasting reward in heaven, what hurt would all that ill he had endured, in past times, do him? And so, likewise, if a man during all the aforesaid time had had every good thing and every joy and pleasure and consola-tion the world could give, and then when he died his soul should receive the everlasting pains of hell, what would all the good things he had received, during that past time, profit him? An unstable man said to Friar Giles, "I tell thee, fain would I live much time in this world and have great riches and abundance of all things, and I would be greatly honoured." Whereto Friar Giles answered, "My brother, but if thou wert lord of all the world, and shouldst live therein for a thousand years in every joy and delight and pleasure and temporal consolation, ah, tell me, what reward or what merit wouldst thou expect to have from this thy miserable flesh which thou hadst served and pleased so greatly! I say unto thee, that the man who liveth well in the sight of God, and guardeth him well from offending God, he shall surely receive from God the highest good and an infinite and everlasting reward, and great bounty and great riches, and great honour and long life eternal in that perpetual glory of heaven, whereunto may the good God, our Lord and King Jesus Christ, bring us, to the praise of Jesus Christ and of His poor little one, Francis."

Bonaventura

(1221-1274)

As a biographer of Francis of Assisi and a careful student of Dionysius the Areopagite, Bonaventura lent a strong influence to later mystical writers. He was born in Bagnorea; taught at the University of Paris; joined the Franciscan order about 1243, of which he became "minister-general" in 1257; was closely associated with Thomas Aquinas; and in 1273 was created a cardinal.

Influenced less by Aristotle than was his colleague Thomas Aquinas, and more a devotee of Augustine and Dionysius the Areopagite, Bonaventura stands as a transitional figure who links the Dionysian mysticism of the early sixth century with future saints of the Western Church. He had a fine intermingling of contemplative ability, intellectual acumen, and strong administrative faculties.

"The Speculation of the Poor Man in the Wilderness," translated from the Latin by Thomas Davidson, is from The Soul's Progress in God, from Selections from the World's Classics of Devotion by permission of Funk & Wagnalls. "Devotion," from Sabinus Mollitor's translation of The Virtues of a Religious Superior, by permission of B. Herder Book Co., is a writing in which Bonaventura describes a model superior. He closely followed this description in his own life.

THE SPECULATION OF THE POOR MAN IN THE WILDERNESS

ON THE DEGREES OF ASCENSION TO GOD, AND THE BEHOLDING OF HIM THROUGH HIS FOOTSTEPS IN THE UNIVERSE

From *The Soul's Progress in God*

Blessed is the man whose strength is in thee; in whose heart are the highways to Zion. Passing through the valley of weeping, they make it a place of spring" (Ps. 85:4-6). Since bliss is naught but the enjoyment of the supreme good, and the supreme good is above us, no one can become blest unless he ascend above himself, with ascension not of the body but of the heart. But we can not be lifted above ourselves, save through a higher power lifting us up. For however much our inward steps may be ordered, nothing is done unless divine aid accompany. But divine aid accompanies those who ask it from the heart, humbly and devoutly, and this is to sigh for it in this vale of tears—which is done by fervent prayer. Prayer, therefore, is the mother and source of uprising to God. Wherefore Dionysius, in his "Mystic Theology" wishing to instruct us in the way to attain mental transports, sets down prayer as the first step. Let us each, therefore, pray and say to our Lord God: "Lead me, O Lord, in thy way, and I will walk in thy truth. Let my heart rejoice to fear thee" (Ps. 86:11). In praying this prayer, we are illuminated to know the steps of ascension to God. For, inasmuch as in our present condition this universe of things is a stair whereby we may ascend to God; and since among these things some are his footprints, some his image, some corporeal, some spiritual, some temporal, some eternal; and hence some outside of us, and some inside; in order that we may attain to the consideration of the first principle, which is altogether spiritual, eternal, and above us, we must pass through the footsteps, which are corporeal, temporal and outside of us; and this is to be led in the way of God (John 14:6). We must also enter into our own minds, which are the image of God, eternal, spiritual, and within us; and this is

to enter into the truth of God. We must also rise aloft to the eternal, which is purely spiritual and above us, by looking at the First Principle; and this is to rejoice in the knowledge of God and in reverence for his majesty. This, then, is the three-days' journey in the wilderness. This is the threefold illumination of one day; the first is as the evening, the second as the morning, and the third as noonday. This has regard to the threefold existence of things; that is, in matter, in intelligence, and in the divine art, as it is written: "Let there be made; he made, and it was made" (Gen. 1:2, 3). This also has regard to the triple substance in Christ, who is our stair—that is, the corporeal, the spiritual, and the divine.

According to this triple progress, our minds have three principal outlooks. The first is toward corporeal things without, and with reference to this it is called animality or sensuality. The second is directed inward upon and into itself, and with reference to this it is called spirit. The third is directed upward above itself, and in reference to this it is called mind. With all these it must dispose itself to ascend to God, that it may love him with the whole mind, the whole heart, and the whole soul, in which consist at once perfect observance of the law and Christian wisdom.

But since every one of the aforesaid modes is doubled, according as we come to consider God as Alpha and as Omega, or according as we come to see God in each of the above modes through a glass and in a glass, or because each of these considerations has to be commingled with the other that is joined to it, and also to be considered in its purity, so it is necessary that these three grades should rise to the number of six; whence, as God finished the universal world in six days and rested on the seventh, so the smaller world is led in the most orderly way, by six successive grades of illumination, to the rest of contemplation. Typical of this are the six steps leading to the throne of Solomon (Kings 10:19); the six-winged seraphim which Isaiah saw (Isaiah 6:2); the six days after which God called Moses from the midst of the darkness (Ex. 24:16); the six days after which, as we read in Matthew, Christ led his disciples up into a mountain and was transfigured before them (Matt. 17:1).

Corresponding, therefore, to the six grades of ascension into God are the six grades of the powers of the soul, whereby we ascend from the lowest to the highest; from the external to the most internal; from the temporal to the eternal; namely, sense, imagination, reason, intellect, intelligence, and the apex of the mind, or the spark of synteresis. These grades are implanted in us by nature, deformed by sin, reformed by grace, to be purged by justice, exercised by knowledge, perfected by wisdom. For, according to the first institution of nature, man was created fit for the quiet contemplation; and, for this reason, God placed him in a paradise of delights; but, turning away from the true light to mutable good, he himself was made crooked through his own fault, and his whole race through original sin, which infected human nature in two ways—the mind with ignorance, and the flesh with concupiscence; so that man, blinded and bowed down, sits in darkness and sees not the light of heaven, unless he be aided by grace with justice against concupiscence, and by knowledge with wisdom against ignorance. All this is done through Jesus Christ, "who for us was made wisdom from God and justice and sanctification and redemption" (1 Cor. 1:30). He, being the power and wisdom of God, the Incarnate Word full of grace and truth, made grace and truth. To wit, he infused the grace of charity, which when it comes "of a pure heart, a good conscience, and faith unfeigned" (1 Tim. 1:5), rectifies the whole soul in its threefold outlook above mentioned. He also taught the knowledge of truth, accord-

ing to the three modes of theology—that is, symbolic, proper, and mystical—so that, through symbolic theology, we might rightly use sensible things; through theology proper, intelligible things; and through mystical theology, might be caught up into supermental ecstasies.

Whoever, therefore, would ascend to God must avoid deforming sin and exercise the above-named natural powers, with a view to reforming grace, and this by prayer; with a view to purifying justice, and this in conversation; with a view to illuminating science, and this in meditation; with a view to perfecting wisdom, and this in contemplation. Therefore, even as no one comes to wisdom save through grace, justice, and knowledge, so no one comes to contemplation save by clear meditation, holy conversation, and devout prayer. As grace, therefore, is the foundation of rightness of will and of the clear illumination of reason, so we must first pray, then live holily, and thirdly, attend to the manifestations of truth; and, so attending, we must gradually rise, till we reach the high mountain where the God of gods is seen in Zion.

And, since we must ascend Jacob's ladder before we descend, let us place the first step in the ascent at the bottom, holding up this whole sensible world before us as a mirror, through which we may rise to God, the supreme artificer, that we may be true Hebrews, passing forth from Egypt to the land promised to our fathers; also that we may be Christians, passing forth with Christ from this world to the Father; and that we may be lovers of wisdom, that calleth and saith: "Come unto me all ye that desire me, and be ye filled with mine offspring" (Eccles. 24:20). "For, from the greatness and beauty of created things, their Creator may be seen and known" (Wisd. of Sol. 13:5). The supreme power, wisdom, and benevolence of the Creator is reflected in all created things, as is reported in threefold fashion by the sense of the flesh to the interior sense. For the sense of the flesh lends itself to the intellect when it investigates with reason, believes with faith, or contemplates with intellect.

In contemplating, it considers the actual existence of things; in believing, their habitual course; in reasoning, their potential pre-excellence.

The first point of view, which is that of contemplation, considering things in themselves, sees in them weight, number, and measure; weight, which marks the point to which they tend; number, whereby they are distinguished; measure, whereby they are limited; and whereby it sees in them mode, species, order, as well as substance, virtue, and action, from which it may rise, as from footsteps, to understand the power, wisdom, and boundless goodness of the Creator.

The second point of view, which is that of faith, considering this world, attends to its origin, course, and termination. For by faith we believe that the ages were arranged by the word of life (Heb. 11:3); by faith we believe that the epochs of the three laws—the law of nature, the law of Scripture, and the law of grace—succeed each other and have elapsed in the most perfect order; by faith we believe that the world will be terminated by a final judgment. In the first we observe the power; in the second, the providence; in the third, the justice of the supreme principle.

The third point of view—that of reason—investigating, sees that some things are only, and some are and live only, whereas some are, live, and discern; and that the first are inferior; the second, middle; the third, superior. It sees, likewise, that some are only corporeal, and some partly corporeal, partly spiritual; whence it concludes that there are some purely spiritual, as better and worthier than either. It sees, moreover, that some are mutable and corruptible, as terrestrial things; others mutable and incorruptible, as supercelestial things. From these visible things therefore it rises to consider God's power, wisdom and goodness, as being, living, and intelligent, as purely spiritual, incorruptible, and intransmutable. This consideration, again, is extended according to the sevenfold condition of created things, which is the sevenfold witness of the divine power, wisdom, and goodness,

if we consider the origin, magnitude, multitude, beauty, plenitude, action and order of all things. For the origin of things, in respect to creation, distinction, and adornment, as far as the works of the six days are concerned, proclaims the divine power, producing all things from nothing; the divine wisdom, as clearly distinguishing all things; the divine goodness, as generously adorning all things. The magnitude of things—in respect to the bulk of length, breadth, and depth; in respect to the excellence of the power extending itself in length, breadth, and depth, as is manifest in the diffusion of light; in respect to the efficacy of action, intimate, continuous, and diffused as is manifested in the action of fire—clearly indicates the immensity of the power, wisdom, and goodness of the threefold God, who exists uncircumscribed in all created things, through power, presence, and essence. The multitude of things—in respect to their diversity, general, special, and individual, in substance, in form of figure, and in efficacy, beyond all human estimation—manifestly involves and displays the immensity of the three above-named conditions in God. The beauty of things—in respect to the variety of lights, figures, and colors, in bodies simple, mixed, and organized, as in the heavenly bodies and minerals, as in stones and metals, plants and animals—plainly proclaims the above three things. The plenitude of things—in that matter is full of forms, in respect to seminal reasons, form is full of virtue as to active power, and virtue is full of effects as to efficiency—manifestly declares this same thing. Action, manifold, according as it is natural, artificial, or moral by its most manifold variety, shows the immensity of that power, art, and goodness which indeed is to all things the cause of being, the ground of understanding, and the order of living. Order, in respect to the ration of duration, situation, and influence—that is, to sooner or later, higher or lower, nobler or baser—in the book of creation, clearly manifests the primacy, sublimity, and divinity of the first principle in regard to infinity of power, while the order of the divine laws, precepts, and judgments in the book of Scripture manifests the immensity of his wisdom; and the order of the divine sacraments, benefits, and retributions in the body of the Church manifests the immensity of his goodness, so that order itself most evidently leads us by the hand to that which is first and highest, mightiest, and wisest and best. He, therefore, who is not enlightened by all these splendors of created things is blind; he who is not waked by such callings is deaf; he who from all these effects does not praise God is dumb; he who after such intimation does not observe the first principle is foolish.

Open, therefore, thine eyes; draw near thy spiritual ears; unseal thy lips, and apply thy heart, that in all created things thou mayest see, hear, praise, love, magnify, and honor God, lest peradventure the universal frame of things should rise up against thee. Yea, for this the universe will fight against them that are without senses, whereas to them that have senses, it will be a matter of glory, who can say with the prophet: "Thou, Lord, hast made me glad through thy work; I will triumph in the works of thy hands" (Ps. 92:4). "O Lord, how manifold are thy works! In wisdom hast thou made them all. The earth is full of thy riches" (Ps. 104:24).

DEVOTION

From *The Virtues of a Religious Superior*

The sixth and last wing of the ecclesiastical Seraph, without which the others can accomplish nothing, and which is, therefore, the most necessary of all, is piety or devotion to God. It incites zeal for justice, infuses loving compassion, strengthens patience, sets up an edifying example and enlightens discretion. This is the "unction of the Spirit," teaching all things beneficial for salvation, as St. John says: "Let the unction which you have received from him, abide in you. And you have no need that any man teach you; but as his unction teacheth you of all things."

2. Piety enlightens the mind to know what is best. "He (the Holy Ghost) will teach you all things, and bring all things to your mind." It inflames the soul with a desire for what is good. "They that eat me, shall yet hunger; and they that drink me, shall yet thirst." It infuses strength for attaining perfection. "It is God who worketh in you, both to will and to accomplish." It engenders horror of sin. "I have hated and abhorred iniquity." It leads to the practice of virtue. "He brought me into the cellar of wine, he set in order charity in me." It regulates external conduct and expression. "Never have I joined myself with them that play; neither have I made myself partaker of them that walk in lightness." It renders knowledge of faith sweet. "For the wisdom of doctrine is according to her name," namely, delicious knowledge. It raises hope to confidence. "For the Spirit himself giveth testimony to our spirit, that we are sons of God." It kindles the love of God. "The charity of God is poured forth in our hearts, by the Holy Ghost, who is given to us." It places us on familiar terms with God. "The Lord spoke to Moses face to face, as a man is wont to speak to his friend." It instills confidence towards God. "We have confidence towards God. And whatsoever we shall ask, we shall receive of him." It enriches our prayers. "May the whole burnt-offering be made fat," and, "Make a fat offering." It produces devotion and fervor. "Sweet, beneficent, and gentle is the spirit of wisdom." It nourishes humility. "To whom shall I have respect, but to him that is poor and little." It extracts the oil of the spirit as in a hot cauldron. It bestows constancy in adversity. "The Lord is my light and my salvation, whom shall I fear?" St. Paul in his devotion says: "Who then shall separate us from the love of Christ?" It makes all good works delightful. "Her conversa-

tion has no bitterness, nor her company any tediousness, but joy and gladness." It raises the mind to heaven. "If he turns his heart to him, he shall draw his spirit and breath unto himself." It engenders disgust for the world. "I have seen all things that are done under the sun, and behold all is vanity and vexation of spirit." It arouses a desire for heavenly things. "I am straitened between two: having a desire to be dissolved and to be with Christ." It wipes out sin and the punishment of sin. "Many sins are forgiven her, because she hath loved much." It increases supernatural merit. "If riches be desired in life, what is richer than wisdom, which maketh all things." It greatly edifies our neighbor. "Offer sacrifice to God, incense and a good savour for a memorial." "We are a good odour of Christ." It drives away devils. "The smoke thereof driveth away all kinds of devils." It invites the Angels and Saints. "Princes went before joined with singers." "When thou didst pray with tears . . . I offered thy prayer to the Lord."

3. These and many other blessings are conferred by the grace of piety or devotion. Hence a superior who has to guide souls ought to make every effort to possess it, for by means of it he is always informed of what should be done, assisted in doing it, and safeguarded against neglect. He should not only pray for himself, but also for those that have been entrusted to his care and for those whom he is not able to preserve from evil without the help of God. "Unless the Lord build the house, they labor in vain that build it." The superior should be a mediator between God and his subjects, in order that, solicitous for the interests of God among them, while instructing, correcting and guiding them on the way to higher things, he may also faithfully promote their interests before God by conciliating Him, imploring His grace, and preserving the brethren from evil. Then he may say with Moses: "I was the mediator and stood between the Lord and you."

4. Devotion may be *general*, or *special*, or *continuous*. It is general in divine of-

fice; special, in prayers; continuous in the performing of all duties. In regard to the divine office, a superior must possess a threefold zeal; namely, to see that everything is done in an orderly manner and without mistakes. "Let all things be done decently, and according to order." David and the chief officers of the army separated for the ministry the sons of Asaph, of Ham and Idithun; to prophesy with harps, and with psalteries, and with cymbals according to their number serving in their appointed office." He should also see to it that the work of the Lord, namely, the divine Office, is performed assiduously. "Cursed be he that doeth the work of the Lord deceitfully." He should see to its devout, reverent, distinct, and attentive recitation, guarding against interruptions and disturbances, remembering that it is said: "With the whole heart and mouth praise ye Him and bless the name of the Lord."

5. The Holy Ghost has commanded the recitation of the divine Office in the Church for *five reasons*. The first is *to imitate the heavenly choirs*. The Saints and Angels are unceasingly engaged in the presence of God in singing His praises. "Blessed are they," says the Psalmist, "that dwell in thy house, O Lord, they shall praise thee for ever and ever." Christ, according to His promise, "Behold I am with you all days, even to the consummation of the world," deigns to be truly with us here sacramentally as well as spiritually, and hence it behooves us to the best of our ability to render Him honor and praise according to the example of the celestial Spirits, so that even though we do not praise Him continuously, as those heavenly chanters do, we sing at least from time to time His praises in spite of our frailty, imitating "that Jerusalem, which is above, . . . which is our mother."

6. The divine Office has been established, secondly, that we should *render thanks to God* at certain hours, mindful of His blessings, and praying for His grace from time to time turn to Him, who was born of the Virgin Mary at night, dragged before the council at early

morn, arose at daylight, was scourged at the third hour, and a little later sent the Holy Ghost upon the Apostles, was crucified at the sixth hour, died upon the cross at the ninth, and being at supper in the afternoon gave us the Sacraments, and was buried at Compline. The celebration of Holy Mass, however, not only reminds us of the mystery of His Passion, but also exhibits the grace of His Real Presence, and under the form of the Blessed Sacrament nourishes us in a spiritual manner with His Flesh and Blood. As it is right and proper, therefore, never to forget these things, so it is also proper always to recall them at stated hours. "I will remember," says the Prophet, "the tender mercies of the Lord, the praise of the Lord for all the things that the Lord hath bestowed on us."

7. In the third place the divine Office was established, in order that through it we may be continuously incited to devotion and kindled with the love of God, lest through indolence and the multitude of our occupations our Love grow lukewarm. In the Book of Leviticus the Lord says: "This is the perpetual fire which shall never go out on the altar. . . . The priest shall feed it, putting wood on it every day in the morning." This fire is the fervor of devotion, which ought always to burn on the altar of our heart, which the devout priest ought to nourish constantly by putting on it the fuel of divine praises, that it may never be extinguished. "I will bless the Lord at all times, His praises shall be always in my mouth."

8. The fourth reason for which the divine Office was instituted is that we may through it draw the faithful, who know how to set aside certain hours for prayer, to the practice of devotion, so that they may assemble in church at least when the offices of divine praise are performed therein, and be less easily distracted when they see the clerics celebrating the divine Office. "All the multitude of the people," says St. Luke, "was praying without, at the hour of incense." Most people would scarcely ever devote themselves to prayer if they were not called to church from worldly occupations at stated times to engage in divine service and listen to the word of God.

9. The fifth purpose of the divine Office is to exhibit *the beauty of the Christian religion.* Jews, Gentiles, and heretics from time to time assemble in their churches to celebrate their false rites. It is evidently far more proper and fitting for those who have the true and holy mysteries of the Sacraments to assemble often for the purpose of celebrating and venerating them and performing the solemn service of praise due to the Creator. For by this means they make themselves worthy of more grace, and of eternal life, and the laity are led to love and revere their holy religion. "To the festivals he added beauty, and set in order the solemn times, . . . that they should praise the holy name of the Lord."

Hence among all the external observances of religion the greatest attention ought to be given to the divine Office, so that, as has been said, it may be performed in an orderly, earnest and devout manner. At other times we labor for God, but during the time of divine service we assist at His throne, are ready to listen to and address Him, and He addresses us, and at the same time we implore His help in our necessities.

10. Special devotion consists in private prayers; in the customary *recitation of vocal prayers,* such as psalms, litanies, and others, which each one performs in secret and according to his personal inclinations. "Thus shall you pray," says Christ, "Our Father," etc. A second form of special prayer consists in *holy meditation,* when a person reflects upon his sins, misery, and future punishment, or recalls to mind the general and special favors he has received from God, the Passion of Christ, the sweet balm of His goodness and His promises of future reward, in order to derive from the consideration of these things sentiments of devotion, of fear and love of God, of desire, compunction and spiritual joy. "I meditated in the night with my own heart: and I was exercised and I swept my spirit." Special devotion manifests itself, thirdly,

in *pious aspirations,* tears and sighs, outbursts of love, and other internal and ineffable affections of the heart, in exaltations, ecstasies, raptures and absorption of the soul in God. Through these "he who is joined to the Lord is one spirit" with Him through the light of pure intelligence, through the knowledge of God, the ardor of His love, and a sweet and intimate union full of joy. "The spirit himself asketh for us with unspeakable groanings."

11. If a superior by the cares and distractions of his office is prevented from devoting himself to special devotions and prayers, he should, at least occasionally when it is possible, and as it were by stealth, engage in the practice of prayer, that he may not become entirely cold, neglect prayer, become a stranger to God, and the grace of God's mercy may not insensibly, as it were, be withdrawn from him. This was the reason why Moses, when harassed by the care of the people, frequently sought solace in the Tabernacle, entering into familiar intercourse with God and being thereby refreshed in mind and heart. Christ, after preaching to the multitudes during the day, spent the nights alone in prayer. Although a superior may have little time for prayer, still, because it is his duty to pray for others, he may sometimes for their sake be vouchsafed a greater measure of grace, in order that he may benefit also by praying those whom he benefits by his care and attention. But let him not neglect prayer, or refuse to improve the opportunity, when offered, lest he be deprived of the grace of prayer in punishment for his ingratitude.

12. Devotion should be *assiduous* or *continuous* in a superior, as in all that desire to advance in virtue. He should first, constantly think of God. "I set the Lord always in my sight, . . . my eyes are ever towards the Lord." Man ought to endeavor to find God everywhere and at every moment, as if He were really present in a visible manner. Elias and Eliseus were wont to say: "As the Lord liveth, in whose sight I stand." For as the Angels do not cease to contemplate God wherever they are sent, so a virtuous man, as far as he is able, should never lose the thought of God from his heart. Should this ever happen, let him do penance. St. Bernard says: "Consider every moment lost in which you do not think of God." Even if you cannot always concentrate your mind on Him in meditation, direct it to Him at least by calling to mind His presence, and when an opportunity occurs, turn recollection into meditation or prayer, as an artist carries the materials for drawing about him in order to sketch a picture when he has an opportunity.

13. Secondly, a superior should *continually endeavor to please God by every word and deed,* always act as if He were present, avoid whatever is apt to displease Him, be sorry if he has done anything displeasing to God, and eager to please Him more and more. "We labor, whether absent or present, to please him. For we must all be manifest before the judgment seat of Christ." A religious should always act as if he were about to appear before the tribunal of the Supreme Judge. "Be you then also ready; for at what hour you think not, the Son of Man will come." He sees whatever we do, and as He does not forget the good works that merit reward, even though a long time may elapse, so also does He not forget the sins that deserve punishment if they are not purged from the soul by penance. "Every man that passeth beyond his own bed, despising his soul, and saying: Who seeth me? . . . No man seeth me: whom do I fear? the Most High will not remember my sins. . . . And he knoweth not that the eyes of the Lord are far brighter than the sun, beholding round about all the ways of men."

14. The third form of assiduous or constant prayer consists in *doing everything devoutly* by directing at least the intention towards God, *strengthening oneself by prayer* for every eventuality, and *rendering thanks to and praising God* for every blessing. A superior should ask God to inspire him in the performance of his duties, to direct everything towards the attainment of salvation, to increase and preserve His blessings. As a sailor

who sees a storm coming, hastens to reach a safe harbor, so the religious should always fly to the harbor of prayer, in which he may escape every danger, and, in all that he does, should trust more to prayer than to his own labors and ex-ertions. "As we know not what to do, we can only turn our eyes to thee." "As the eyes of servants are on the hands of their masters, . . . so are our eyes unto the Lord our God."

Thomas Aquinas

(1225?-1274)

CALLED the "Angelic Doctor," Thomas Aquinas systematized thought and brought about the wedding of faith and reason, theology and philosophy, thus giving to the Western Church its basic synthesis. It can be said that he "saved" Christian thought for the intellectual people of his time. He made Aristotle the second standard for the church.

He was born near Aquino, Italy, of a noble family. In 1243 he entered the Dominican order, against the will of his parents, and studied at Cologne under Albertus Magnus. From the time of receiving his degree of bachelor of divinity in 1248 until his death, he was a teacher at Paris and in Italy. During these years he wrote in a prolific manner, his most important work being *Summa Theologica*, begun in 1265 and never fully completed. In 1879 Pope Leo XIII declared his writings to be the basis for theological instruction.

As a close friend of Bonaventura, Thomas gave greater stress to the rational side of religion, though he was a man of deep mystical piety. Bonaventura gave emphasis to the Dionysian mystical element in religion. Together they stand as "the two bright lights of medieval thought."

"Of the Contemplative Life" gives an accurate focus of religious experience—through the eyes of scholasticism—in which the passion of the soul was "the search for the truth involving the inner struggle for the knowledge of God." It is a selection from his ten-volume *Summa Theologica*, and as it appears here is from *Thomas Aquinas*, an arrangement of works selected and edited by M. C. D'Arcy and published by E. P. Dutton & Co. in the "Everyman's Library" series. It is used by permission.

OF THE CONTEMPLATIVE LIFE

From *Summa Theologica*

We must now consider the contemplative life, under which head there are eight points of inquiry: (1) Whether the contemplative life belongs to the intellect only, or also to the affections? (2) Whether the moral virtues pertain to the contemplative life? (3) Whether the contemplative life consists in one act or in several? (4) Whether the consideration of any and every truth pertains to the contemplative life? (5) Whether the contemplative life of man on this earth can arise to the vision of God? (6) Of the movements of contemplation assigned by Dionysius. (7) Of the pleasure of contemplation. (8) Of the duration of contemplation.

I. WHETHER THE CONTEMPLATIVE LIFE HAS NOTHING TO DO WITH THE AFFECTIONS, AND PERTAINS WHOLLY TO THE INTELLECT

We proceed thus to the First Article.

Objection 1. It would seem that the contemplative life has nothing to do with the affections and pertains wholly to the intellect. For Aristotle says that *the end of contemplation is truth.* Now truth pertains wholly to the intellect. Therefore it would seem that the contemplative life wholly regards the intellect.

Obj. 2. Further, Gregory says that *Rachel, which is interpreted "vision of the principle,"* signifies the contemplative life. Now the vision of a principle belongs properly to the intellect. Therefore the contemplative life belongs properly to the intellect.

Obj. 3. Further, Gregory says that it belongs to the contemplative life, *to rest from external action.* Now the affective or appetitive power inclines to external actions. Therefore it would seem that the contemplative life has nothing whatever to do with the appetitive faculty.

On the contrary, Gregory says that *the contemplative life is to cling with our whole mind to the love of God and our neighbour, and to desire nothing beside our Creator.* Now desire and love pertain to the affective or appetitive power, as stated above. Therefore the contemplative life has also something to do with the affective or appetitive power.

I answer that, as stated above, the life of those is called contemplative who are chiefly intent on the contemplation of truth. Now intention is an act of the will, as stated above, because intention is the seeking of an end which is the object of the will. Consequently the contemplative life, as regards the essence of the action, pertains to the intellect, but as regards the motive cause of the exercise of that action it belongs to the will, which moves all the other powers, even the intellect, to their actions, as stated above.

Now the appetitive power moves one to observe things either with the senses or with the intellect, sometimes for love of the thing seen because, as it is written, *where thy treasure is, there is thy heart also,* sometimes for love of the very knowledge that one acquires by observation. Wherefore Gregory makes the contemplative life to consist in the *love of God,* inasmuch as through loving God we are aflame to gaze on His beauty. And since every one rejoices when he obtains what he loves, it follows that the contemplative life terminates in delight, which is seated in the affective power, the result being that love also becomes more intense.

Reply Obj. 1. From the very fact that truth is the end of contemplation, truth can be regarded as an appetible good, both lovable and delightful, and in this respect it pertains to the appetitive power.

Reply Obj. 2. We are urged to the vision of the first principle, namely God, by the love thereof; wherefore Gregory says that *the contemplative life tramples on all cares and longs to see the face of its Creator.*

Reply Obj. 3. The appetitive power moves not only the bodily members to perform external actions, but also the intellect to practise the act of contemplation, as stated above.

II. Whether the Moral Virtues Pertain to the Contemplative Life

We proceed thus to the Second Article.

Objection 1. It would seem that the moral virtues pertain to the contemplative life. For Gregory says that *the contemplative life is to cling to the love of God and our neighbour with the whole mind.* Now all the moral virtues whose exercise is prescribed by the Commandments, are reducible to the love of God and of our neighbour, for *love . . . is the fulfilling of the Law.* Therefore it would seem that the moral virtues belong to the contemplative life.

Obj. 2. Further, the contemplative life is chiefly directed to the contemplation of God; for Gregory says that *the mind tramples on all cares and longs to gaze on the face of its Creator.* Now no one can accomplish this without cleanness of heart, which is a result of moral virtue. For it is written: *Blessed are the clean of heart, for they shall see God,* and, *Follow peace with all men, and holiness, without which no man shall see God.* Therefore it would seem that the moral virtues pertain to the contemplative life.

Obj. 3. Further, Gregory says that *the contemplative life gives beauty to the soul,* wherefore it is signified by Rachel, of whom it is said that she was *of a beautiful countenance.* Now the beauty of the soul consists in the moral virtues, especially temperance, as Ambrose says. Therefore it seems that the moral virtues pertain to the contemplative life.

On the contrary, the moral virtues are

directed to external actions. Now Gregory says that it belongs to the contemplative life *to rest from external action*. Therefore the moral virtues do not pertain to the contemplative life.

I answer that a thing may belong to the contemplative life in two ways, essentially or as a predisposition. The moral virtues do not belong to the contemplative life essentially, because the end of the contemplative life is the consideration of truth: and as Aristotle says, *knowledge*, which pertains to the consideration of truth, *has little influence on the moral virtues*: wherefore he declares that the moral virtues pertain to active but not to contemplative happiness.

On the other hand, the moral virtues belong to the contemplative life as a predisposition. For the act of contemplation, wherein the contemplative life essentially consists, is hindered both by the impetuosity of the passions which withdraw the soul's intention from intelligible to sensible things, and by outward disturbances. Now the moral virtues curb the impetuosity of the passions, and quell the disturbance of outward occupations. Hence moral virtues belong to the contemplative life as a predisposition.

Reply Obj. 1. As stated above, the contemplative life has its motive cause on the part of the affections, and in this respect the love of God and our neighbour is requisite to the contemplative life. Now motive causes do not enter into the essence of a thing, but dispose and perfect it. Wherefore it does not follow that the moral virtues belong essentially to the contemplative life.

Reply Obj. 2. Holiness or cleanness of heart is caused by the virtues that are concerned with the passions which hinder the purity of the reason; and peace is caused by justice which deals with human acts: *The work of justice shall be peace*, since he who refrains from wronging others lessens the occasions of quarrels and disturbances. Hence the moral virtues dispose one to the contemplative life by causing peace and cleanness of heart.

Reply Obj. 3. Beauty, as stated above, consists in a certain clarity and due proportion. Now each of these is found fundamentally in the reason; because both the light that makes beauty seen, and the establishing of due proportion among things, belong to reason. Hence, since the contemplative life consists in an act of the reason, there is beauty in it by its very nature and essence; wherefore it is written of the contemplation of wisdom: *I became a lover of her beauty*.

On the other hand, beauty is in the moral virtues by participation, in so far as they belong to the rational order; and especially is it in temperance, which restrains the concupiscences which especially darken the light of reason. Hence it is that the virtue of chastity most of all makes man apt for contemplation, since venereal pleasures most of all weigh the mind down to sensible objects, as Augustine says.

III. WHETHER THERE ARE VARIOUS ACTIONS PERTAINING TO THE CONTEMPLATIVE LIFE

We proceed thus to the Third Article.

Objection 1. It would seem that there are various actions pertaining to the contemplative life. For Richard of S. Victor distinguishes between *contemplation, meditation,* and *cogitation.* Yet all these apparently pertain to contemplation. Therefore it would seem that there are various actions pertaining to the contemplative life.

Obj. 2. Further, the apostle says: *But we . . . beholding* (speculantes) *the glory of the Lord with open face, are transformed into the same clarity.* Now this belongs to the contemplative life. Therefore in addition to the three aforesaid, vision (*speculatio*) belongs to the contemplative life.

Obj. 3. Further, Bernard says that *the first and greatest contemplation is admiration of the Majesty.* Now according to Damascene admiration is a kind of fear. Therefore it would seem that several acts are requisite for the contemplative life.

Obj. 4. Further, *prayer, reading,* and *meditation* are said to belong to the contemplative life. Again, *hearing* belongs to the contemplative life: since it is stated that Mary (by whom the contemplative life is signified) *sitting . . . at the Lord's feet, heard His word.* Therefore it would seem that several acts are requisite for the contemplative life.

On the contrary, "life" signifies here the operation on which a man is chiefly intent. Wherefore if there are several operations of the contemplative life, there will be, not one, but several contemplative lives.

I answer that we are now speaking of the contemplative life as applicable to man. Now according to Dionysius, between man and angel there is this difference, that an angel perceives the truth by simple apprehension, whereas man becomes acquainted with a simple truth by a process from manifold data. Accordingly, then, the contemplative life has one act wherein it is finally completed, namely the contemplation of truth, and from this act it derives its unity. Yet it has many acts whereby it arrives at this final act. Some of these pertain to the reception of principles, from which it proceeds to the contemplation of truth; others are concerned with the elaboration from these principles of the truth which is sought; and the last and crowning act is the contemplation itself of the truth.

Reply Obj. 1. According to Richard of S. Victor *cogitation* would seem to regard the consideration of the many things from which a person intends to gather one simple truth. Hence cogitation may comprise not only the perceptions of the senses in taking cognizance of certain effects, but also the data of the imagination and the discourse of reason concerning the various indications, or whatever they may be, that lead to the truth in view: although, according to Augustine, cogitation may signify any actual operation of the intellect.—*Meditation* would seem to be the process of reason from certain principles that lead to the contemplation of some truth: and *consideration* has the same meaning, according to Bernard, although, according to Aristotle, every operation of the intellect may be called *consideration.*—But *contemplation* regards the simple act of gaz-

ing on the truth; wherefore Richard says again that *contemplation is the soul's clear and free dwelling upon the object of its gaze; meditation is the survey of the mind while occupied in searching for the truth; and cogitation is the mind's glance which is prone to wander.*

Reply Obj. 2. According to a gloss of Augustine on this passage, *beholding* (*speculatio*) denotes *seeing in a mirror* (*speculo*), *not from a watch-tower* (*specula*). Now to see a thing in a mirror is to see a cause in its effect wherein its likeness is reflected. Hence *beholding* would seem to be reducible to meditation.

Reply Obj. 3. *Admiration* is a kind of fear resulting from the apprehension of a thing that surpasses our *faculties*: hence it results from the contemplation of the sublime truth. For it was stated above that contemplation terminates in the affections.

Reply Obj. 4. Man reaches the knowledge of truth in two ways. First, by means of things received from another. In this way, as regards the things he receives from God, he needs *prayer: I called upon God, and the spirit of wisdom came upon me*: while as regards the things he receives from man, he needs *hearing*, in so far as he receives from the spoken word, and *reading*, in so far as he draws upon documents committed to writing. Secondly, he needs to apply himself by his personal study, and thus he requires *meditation*.

IV. WHETHER THE CONTEMPLATIVE LIFE CONSISTS IN THE MERE CONTEMPLATION OF GOD, OR ALSO IN THE CONSIDERATION OF ANY AND EVERY TRUTH

We proceed thus to the Fourth Article.
Objection 1. It would seem that the contemplative life consists not only in the contemplation of God, but also in the consideration of any truth. For it is written: *Wonderful are Thy works, and my soul knoweth right well.* Now the knowledge of God's works is effected by any contemplation of the truth. Therefore it would seem that it pertains to the contemplative life to contemplate not

only the divine truth, but also any other.

Obj. 2. Further, Bernard says that *contemplation consists in admiration first of God's majesty, secondly of His judgments, thirdly of His benefits, fourthly of His promises.* Now of these four the first alone regards the divine truth, and the other three pertain to His effects. Therefore the contemplative life consists not only in the contemplation of the divine truth, but also in the consideration of truth regarding the effects of God's activity.

Obj. 3. Further, Richard of S. Victor distinguishes six species of contemplation. The first belongs to *the imagination alone,* and consists in thinking of corporeal things. The second is in *the imagination guided by reason,* and consists in considering the order and disposition of sensible objects. The third is in *the reason based on the imagination;* when, to wit, from the consideration of the visible we rise to the invisible. The fourth is in *the reason and conducted by the reason,* when the mind is intent on things invisible of which the imagination has no cognizance. The fifth is *above the reason,* but not contrary to reason, when by divine revelation we become cognizant of things that cannot be comprehended by the human reason. The sixth is *above reason and contrary to reason;* when, to wit, by the divine enlightening we know things that seem contrary to human reason, such as the doctrine of the mystery of the Trinity. Now only the last of these would seem to pertain to the divine truth. Therefore the contemplation of truth regards not only the divine truth, but also that which is considered in creatures.

Obj. 4. Further, in the contemplative life the contemplation of truth is sought as being the perfection of man. Now any truth is a perfection of the human intellect. Therefore the contemplative life consists in the contemplation of any truth.

On the contrary, Gregory says that *in contemplation we seek God, who is the first principle.*

I answer that, as stated above, a thing may belong to the contemplative life in two ways: principally, and secondarily or as a predisposition. That which belongs principally to the contemplative life is the contemplation of the divine truth, because this contemplation is the end of the whole human life. Hence Augustine says that *the contemplation of God is promised us as being the goal of all our actions and the everlasting perfection of our joys.* This contemplation will be perfect in the life to come, when we shall see God face to face, wherefore it will make us perfectly happy: whereas now the contemplation of the divine truth is competent to us imperfectly, namely *through a glass* and *in a dark manner.* Hence it bestows on us a certain inchoate beatitude, which begins now and will be continued in the life to come; wherefore Aristotle places man's ultimate happiness in the contemplation of what is best, i.e. of the intelligible.

Since, however, God's effects show us the way to the contemplation of God Himself: *The invisible things of God . . . are clearly seen, being understood by the things that are made,* it follows that the contemplation of the effects of God's activity also belongs to the contemplative life, inasmuch as man is guided thereby to the knowledge of God. Hence Augustine says that *in the study of creatures we must not exercise an empty and futile curiosity, but should make them the stepping-stones to things imperishable and everlasting.*

Accordingly it is clear from what has been said that four things pertain, in a certain order, to the contemplative life: first, the moral virtues; secondly, other acts exclusive of contemplation; thirdly, contemplation of the effects of God's activity; fourthly, the complement of all which is the contemplation of the divine truth itself.

Reply Obj. 1. David sought the knowledge of God's works, so that he might be led by them to God; wherefore he says elsewhere: *I meditated on all Thy works: I meditated upon the works of Thy hands: I stretched forth my hands to Thee.*

Reply Obj. 2. By considering the divine

judgments man is guided to the consideration of the divine justice; and by considering the divine benefits and promises, man is led to the knowledge of God's mercy or goodness, as by effects already manifested or yet to be vouchsafed.

Reply Obj. 3. These six denote the steps whereby we ascend by means of creatures to the contemplation of God. For the first step consists in the mere consideration of sensible objects; the second step consists in going forward from sensible to intelligible objects; the third step is to judge of sensible objects according to intelligible things; the fourth is the absolute consideration of the intelligible objects to which one has attained by means of sense-data; the fifth is the contemplation of those intelligible objects that are unattainable by way of sense-data, but which the reason is able to grasp; the sixth step is the consideration of such intelligible things as the reason can neither discover nor grasp, which pertain to the sublime contemplation of divine truth, wherein contemplation is ultimately perfected.

Reply Obj. 4. The ultimate perfection of the human intellect is the divine truth: and other truths perfect the intellect in relation to the divine truth.

V. Whether in the Present State of Life the Contemplative Life Can Reach to the Vision of the Divine Essence

We proceed thus to the Fifth Article.
Objection 1. It would seem that in the present state of life the contemplative life can reach to the vision of the divine essence. For, as stated, Jacob said: *I have seen God face to face, and my soul has been saved.* Now the vision of God's face is the vision of the divine essence. Therefore it would seem that in the present life one may come, by means of contemplation, to see God in His essence.

Obj. 2. Further, Gregory says that *contemplative men withdraw within themselves in order to explore spiritual things, nor do they ever carry with them the shadows of things corporeal, or if these follow them they prudently drive them away: but being desirous of seeing the incomprehensible light, they suppress all the images of their limited comprehension, and through longing to reach what is above them, they overcome that which they are.* Now man is not hindered from seeing the divine essence, which is the incomprehensible light, save by the necessity of turning to imagery drawn from bodily things. Therefore it would seem that the contemplation of the present life can extend to the vision of the incomprehensible light in its essence.

Obj. 3. Further, Gregory says: *All creatures are small to the soul that sees its Creator: wherefore when the man of God,* the blessed Benedict, to wit, *saw a fiery globe upon the tower and angels returning to heaven, without doubt he could only see such things by the light of God. . . .*

On the contrary, Gregory says: *As long as we live in this mortal flesh, no one reaches such a height of contemplation as to fix the eyes of his mind on the ray itself of incomprehensible light.*

I answer that, as Augustine says, *no one seeing God lives this mortal life wherein the bodily senses have their play: and unless in some way he depart this life, whether by going altogether out of his body, or by withdrawing from his carnal senses, he is not caught up into that vision.* This has been carefully discussed above where we spoke of rapture, and in the First Part where we treated of the vision of God.

Accordingly we must state that one may be in this life in two ways. First, in actual fact, that is to say, by actually making use of the bodily senses, and thus contemplation in the present life can nowise attain to the vision of God's essence. Secondly, one may be in this life potentially and not in actual fact, that is to say, when the soul is united to the mortal body as to its form, yet so as to make use neither of the bodily senses, nor even of the imagination, as happens in rapture; and in this way the contemplation of the present life can attain to the vision of the divine essence. Consequently the highest degree of contemplation in the present life is that which Paul had in rapture, whereby he was in a middle state between the present life and the life to come.

Reply Obj. 1. As Dionysius says, *if any one seeing God, understood what he saw, he saw not God himself, but something belonging to God.* And Gregory says: *By no means is God seen now in His glory; but the soul sees something of lower degree, and therefore it goes forward by the straight road and afterwards it attains to the glory of vision.* Accordingly the words of Jacob, *I saw God face to face,* do not imply that he saw God's essence, but that he saw some shape, imaginary, of course, wherein God spoke to him.—Or, *since we know a man by his face, by the face of God he signified his knowledge of Him,* according to a gloss of Gregory on the same passage.

Reply Obj. 2. In the present state of life human contemplation is impossible without sense-imagery, because it is connatural to man to see the intelligible species in the phantasms, as Aristotle says. Yet the intellect when gaining knowledge does not rest content with this sense-imagery, but contemplates therein the purity of the intelligible truth; and this not only in natural knowledge, but also in that which we obtain by revelation. For Dionysius says that *the divine glory shows us the angelic hierarchies under certain symbolic figures, and by its power we are brought back to the single ray of light,* i.e. to the simple knowledge of the intelligible truth. It is in this sense that we must understand the statement of Gregory that *contemplatives do not carry along with them the shadows of things corporeal,* since their contemplation is not fixed on them, but on the consideration of the intelligible truth.

Reply Obj. 3. By these words Gregory does not imply that the blessed Benedict, in that vision, saw God in His essence, but he wishes to show that because *all creatures are small to him that sees God,* it follows that all things can easily be seen through the enlightenment of the divine light. Wherefore he adds: *For however little he may see of the Creator's light, all created things become petty to him.*

VI. Whether the Operation of Contemplation Is Fittingly Divided into a Threefold Movement, Circular, Straight, and Oblique

We proceed thus to the Sixth Article.

Objection 1. It would seem that the operation of contemplation is unfittingly divided into a threefold movement, *circular, straight,* and *oblique.* For contemplation pertains exclusively to rest: *When I go into my house, I shall repose myself with her.* Now movement is opposed to rest. Therefore the operations of the contemplative life should not be described as movements.

Obj. 2. Further, the action of the contemplative life pertains to the intellect, whereby man is like the angels. Now Dionysius describes these movements as being different in the angels from what they are in the soul. For he says that the *circular* movement in the angel is *according to his enlightenment by the beautiful and the good.* On the other hand, he assigns the circular movement of the soul to several things: the first of which is the *withdrawal of the soul into itself from externals;* the second is *a certain concentration of its powers, whereby it is rendered free of error and of outward occupation;* and the third is *union with those things that are above it.*—Again, he describes differently their respective straight movements. For he says that the straight movement of the angel is that by which he proceeds to the care of those things that are beneath him. On the other hand, he describes the straight movement of the soul as being twofold: first, *its progress towards things that are near it;* secondly, *its uplifting from external things to simple contemplation.*—Further, he assigns a different oblique movement to each. For he assigns the oblique movement of the angels to the fact that *while providing for those who have less they remain unchanged in relation to God:* whereas he assigns the oblique movement of the soul to the fact that *the soul is enlightened in divine knowledge by reasoning and discoursing.*—Therefore it would seem that the operations of contemplation are unfittingly assigned according to the ways mentioned above.

Obj. 3. Further, Richard of S. Victor mentions many other different movements in likeness to the birds of the air. *For some of these rise at one time to a great height, at another swoop down to earth, and they do so repeatedly; others fly now to the right, now to the left again and again; others go forwards or lag behind many times; others fly in a circle now more now less extended; and others hover almost immovably in one place.* Therefore it would seem that there are only three movements of contemplation.

On the contrary, stands the authority of Dionysius.

I answer that, as stated above, the operation of the intellect, wherein contemplation essentially consists, is called a movement, in so far as movement is the act of a perfect thing, according to Aristotle. Since, however, it is through sensible objects that we come to the knowledge of intelligible things, and since sensible operations do not take place without movement, the result is that even intelligible operations are described as movements, and are differentiated in likeness to various movements. Now of bodily movements, local movements are the most perfect and come first, as proved; wherefore the foremost among intelligible operations are described by being likened to them. These movements are of three kinds; for there is the *circular* movement, by which a thing moves uniformly round one point as centre, another is the *straight* movement by which a thing goes from one point to another; the third is *oblique*, being composed as it were of both the others. Consequently, in intelligible operations, that which is simply uniform is compared to circular movement; the intelligible operation by which one proceeds from one point to another is compared to the straight movement; while the intelligible operation which unites something of uniformity with progress to various points is compared to the oblique movement.

Reply Obj. 1. External bodily ·movements are opposed to the quiet of contemplation, which consists in rest from outward occupations; but the movements of intellectual operations belong to the quiet or contemplation.

Reply Obj. 2. Man is like the angels in intellect generically, but the intellective power is much higher in the angel than in man. Consequently these movements must be ascribed to souls and angels in different ways, according as the two intellects differ in point of uniformity of knowledge. For the angelic intellect has uniform knowledge in two respects. First, because it does not acquire intelligible truth from the variety of composite objects; secondly, because it understands the truth of intelligible objects not discursively, but by simple intuition. On the other hand, the intellect of the soul acquires intelligible truth from sensible objects, and understands it by a certain discourse of the reason.

Wherefore Dionysius assigns the *circular* movement of the angels to the fact that their intuition of God is uniform and unceasing, having neither beginning nor end: even as a circular movement having neither beginning nor end is uniformly around the one same centre. But on the part of the soul, ere it arrive at this uniformity, its twofold lack of uniformity needs to be removed. First, that which arises from the variety of external things: this is removed by the soul withdrawing from externals, and so the first thing he mentions regarding the circular movement of the soul is *the soul's withdrawal into itself from external objects.* Secondly, another lack of uniformity requires to be removed from the soul, and this is owing to the discoursing of reason. This is done by directing all the soul's operations to the simple contemplation of the intelligible truth, and this is indicated by his saying in the second place that *the soul's intellectual powers must be uniformly concentrated,* in other words that discourse must be laid aside and the soul's gaze fixed in the contemplation of the one simple truth. In this operation of the soul there is no error, even as there is clearly no error in the understanding of first principles which we know by simple intuition. Afterwards, these two things being premised, he mentions thirdly the uniformity which is like that of the angels, for then all things being laid aside, the soul continues in the contemplation of God alone. This he expresses by saying: *Then being thus made uniform unitedly*, i.e. in harmony, *and with united powers, it is conducted to the good and the beautiful.* The *straight* movement of the angel cannot apply to his proceeding from one thing to another by considering them, but only to the order of his providence, namely to the fact that the higher angel enlightens the lower angels through the angels that are intermediate. He indicates this when he says: *The angel's movement takes a straight line when he proceeds to the care of things subject to him, taking in his course whatever things are direct*, i.e. in keeping with the dispositions of the direct order. Whereas he ascribes the *straight* movement in the soul to the soul's proceeding from exterior sensibles to the knowledge of intelligible objects. The *oblique* movement in the angels he describes as being composed of the straight and circular movements, inasmuch as their care for those beneath them is in accordance with their contemplation of God: while the *oblique* movement in the soul he also declares to be partly straight and partly circular, is so far as in reasoning it makes use of the light received from God.

Reply Obj. 3. These varieties of movement that are taken from the distinction between above and below, right and left, forwards and backwards, and between wider and sharper curves, are all comprised under either straight and oblique movement, because they all denote discursions of reason. For if the reason pass from the genus to the species, or from the part to the whole, it will be, as he explains, from above to below: if from one opposite to another, it will be from right to left; if from the cause to the effect, it will be backwards and forwards; if it be about accidents that surround a thing near at hand or far remote, there will be motion in a curve. The discoursing of

reason from sensible to intelligible objects, if it be according to the order of natural reason, belongs to the straight movement; but if it be according to the divine enlightenment, it will belong to the oblique movement as explained above. That alone which he describes as immobility belongs to the circular movement.

Wherefore it is evident that Dionysius describes the movement of contemplation with much greater fullness and depth.

VII. WHETHER THERE IS DELIGHT IN CONTEMPLATION

We proceed thus to the Seventh Article.

Objection 1. It would seem that there is no delight in contemplation. For delight belongs to the appetitive power; whereas contemplation resides chiefly in the intellect. Therefore it would seem that there is no delight in contemplation.

Obj. 2. Further, all strife and struggle is a hindrance to delight. Now there is strife and struggle in contemplation. For Gregory says that *when the soul strives to contemplate God, it is in a state of struggle; at one time it almost overcomes, because by understanding and feeling it tastes something of the incomprehensible light, and at another time it almost succumbs, because even while tasting it fails.* Therefore there is no delight in contemplation.

Obj. 3. Further, delight is the result of a perfect operation, as stated. Now the contemplation of men on earth is imperfect: *We see now through a glass in a dark manner.* Therefore seemingly there is no delight in the contemplative life.

Obj. 4. Further, a lesion of the body is an obstacle to delight. Now contemplation causes a lesion of the body; wherefore it is stated that after Jacob had said *"I have seen God face to face"* . . . *he halted on his foot . . . because he touched the sinew of his thigh and it shrank.* Therefore seemingly there is no delight in contemplation.

On the contrary, it is written of the contemplation of wisdom: *Her conversation hath no bitterness, nor her company*

any tediousness, but joy and gladness: and Gregory says that *the contemplative life is sweetness exceedingly lovable.*

I answer that there may be delight in any particular contemplation in two ways. First by reason of the operation itself, because each individual delights in the operation which befits him according to his own nature or habit. Now contemplation of the truth befits a man according to his nature as a rational animal: the result being that *all men naturally desire to know,* so that consequently they delight in the knowledge of truth. And more delightful still does this become to one who has the habit of wisdom and knowledge, the result of which is that he contemplates without difficulty. Secondly, contemplation may be delightful by reason of its object, in so far as one contemplates that which one loves; even as bodily vision gives pleasure, not only because to see is pleasurable in itself, but because one sees a person whom one loves. Since, then, the contemplative life consists chiefly in the contemplation of God, of which charity is the motive, as stated above, it follows that there is delight in the contemplative life, not only by reason of the contemplation itself, but also by reason of the divine love.

In both respects the delight thereof surpasses all human delight, both because spiritual delight is greater than carnal pleasure, as stated above, when we were treating of the passions, and because the love whereby God is loved out of charity surpasses all love. Hence it is written: *O taste and see that the Lord is sweet.*

Reply Obj. 1. Although the contemplative life consists chiefly in an act of the intellect, it has its beginning in the appetite, since it is through charity that one is urged to the contemplation of God. And since the end corresponds to the beginning, it follows that the term also and the end of the contemplative life is found in the appetite, since one delights in seeing the object loved, and the very delight in the object seen arouses a yet greater love. Wherefore Gregory says that *when we see one whom we love, we are so aflame as to love him more.* And this is the ulti-mate perfection of the contemplative life, namely that the divine truth be not only seen but also loved.

Reply Obj. 2. Strife or struggle arising from the disagreeable nature of an external thing, hinders delight in that thing. For a man delights not in a thing against which he strives. But in that for which he strives; when he has obtained it, other things being equal, he delights yet more: wherefore Augustine says that *the more peril there was in the battle, the greater the joy in the triumph.* But there is no strife or struggle in contemplation from the side of the truth which we contemplate, though there is on the part of our defective understanding and our corruptible body which drags us down to lower things: *The corruptible body is a load upon the soul, and the earthly habitation presseth down the mind that museth upon many things.* Hence it is that when man attains to the contemplation of truth, he loves it yet more, while he hates the more his own deficiency and the weight of his corruptible body, so as to say with the apostle: *Unhappy man that I am, who shall deliver me from the body of this death?* Wherefore Gregory says: *When God is once known by desire and understanding, He withers all carnal pleasure in us.*

Reply Obj. 3. The contemplation of God in this life is imperfect in comparison with the contemplation in heaven; and in like manner the delight of contemplation to men upon earth is imperfect as compared with the delight of contemplation in heaven, of which it is written: *Thou shalt make them drink of the torrent of Thy pleasure.* Yet, though the contemplation of divine things which is to be had by men upon earth is imperfect, it is more delightful than all other contemplation however perfect, on account of the excellence of that which is contemplated. Hence Aristotle says: *It is our lot to have less clear intuitions of those noble and god-like substances, . . . and though we establish contact with them even feebly, that knowledge owing to the sublime nature of its object gives us more pleasure than all that is round* about us; and Gregory says in the same sense: *The contemplative life is sweetness exceedingly lovable; for it carries the soul away above itself, it opens heaven and discovers the spiritual world to the eyes of the mind.*

Reply Obj. 4. After contemplation Jacob was lame of one foot, *because we need to grow weak in the love of the world ere we wax strong in the love of God*, as Gregory says: *Thus when we have known the sweetness of God, we have one foot sound while the other halts; since every one who halts on one foot leans only on that foot which is sound.*

VIII. WHETHER THE CONTEMPLATIVE LIFE IS CONTINUOUS

We proceed thus to the Eighth Article.
Objection 1. It would seem that the contemplative life is not continuous. For the contemplative life consists essentially in things pertaining to the intellect. Now all the intellectual perfections of this life will be made void: *Whether prophecies shall be made void, or tongues shall cease, or knowledge shall be destroyed.* Therefore the contemplative life is made void.

Obj. 2. Further, a man tastes the sweetness of contemplation by snatches and for a short time only: wherefore Augustine says: *Thou admittest me to a most unwonted affection in my inmost soul, to a strange sweetness, . . . yet through my grievous weight I sink down again.* Again, Gregory commenting on the words of Job: *When a spirit passed before me*, says: *The mind does not remain long at rest in the sweetness of inward contemplation, for it is recalled to itself and beaten back by the very immensity of the light.* Therefore the contemplative life is not continuous.

Obj. 3. Further, that which is not connatural to man cannot be continuous. Now the contemplative life, according to Aristotle, *is a life above human measure.* Therefore seemingly the contemplative life is not continuous.

On the contrary, our Lord said: *Mary hath chosen the best part, which shall not be taken away from her,* since, as Gregory says, *the contemplative life begins here so as it may be perfected in our heavenly home.*

I answer that a thing may be described as continuous in two ways: first, in its nature; secondly, in our practice of it. It is evident that in regard to itself contemplative life is continuous for two reasons: first, because it is about incorruptible and unchangeable things; secondly, because it has no contrary, for there is nothing contrary to the pleasure of contemplation, as stated. But even in our practice contemplative life is continuous, —both because it belongs to us in virtue of the activity of the incorruptible part of the soul, namely the intellect, wherefore it can endure after this life,—and because in the works of the contemplative life we work not with our bodies, so that we are the more able to persevere in the works thereof, as Aristotle remarks.

Reply Obj. 1. The manner of contemplation is not the same here as in heaven: yet the contemplative life is said to remain by reason of charity, wherein it has both its beginning and its end. Gregory speaks in this sense: *The contemplative life begins here, so as to be perfected in our heavenly home, because the fire of love which begins to burn here is aflame with a yet greater love when we see Him Whom we love.*

Reply Obj. 2. No action can last long at its highest pitch. Now the highest point of contemplation is to reach the uniformity of divine contemplation, according to Dionysius, and as we have stated above. Hence although contemplation cannot last long in this respect, it can be of long duration in the other contemplative acts.

Reply Obj. 3. Aristotle declares the contemplative life to be above man, because it befits us *so far as there is in us something divine,* namely the intellect, which is incorruptible and impassible in itself, wherefore its act can endure longer.

Anonymous

THE MIRROR OF SIMPLE SOULS

(*ca.* 1300)

THIS writing, composed under Franciscan influence, shows reflections of Dionysius, Richard of St. Victor, and Bonaventura. In the latter part of the fourteenth century it influenced another anonymous writing, *The Cloud of Unknowing*. Originally in French, this manuscript was translated in the late fourteenth century by an unknown English mystic. It represents an advanced type of devotional literature.

The Mirror of Simple Souls joins France and England, the thirteenth and fourteenth centuries in the mystical quest. The following selection is from an edition by Clare Kirchberger.

[THE SOUL AND LOVE]

From *The Mirror of Simple Souls*

A GREAT REBUKE THAT LOVE GIVETH TO THEM THAT REFUSE THE SENDING OF GOD, AND HOW THEY BE THEREFORE ENCUMBERED OF THEMSELVES ALL THEIR LIFETIME, AND HOW THEY MIGHT HAVE BEEN UNENCUMBERED AND BY WHAT MEANS AND FOR HOW LITTLE.

*N*ow understand, auditors of this book," saith Love, "the gloss of this book, for the thing is as much worth as it is appreciated. And all that men have need for, is needful, and no more. And when I desired (it)," saith Love, "and when it pleaseth me, and was necessary to you, I hold need (to be) this, that I desired it —ye refused me by as many messages as I sent you. But none knew it," saith Love, "but I alone. I sent you the Thrones for to answer you and to summon you, and the Cherubin to enlumine you and the Seraphin for to embrace or kiss you. By all these messengers I sent to you," saith Love, "that made you with my will of the Beings where I would have had you, and ye always refused it. And when I saw that," saith Love, "I left you in your waywardness to your (own) knowledge. But if ye had heard me," saith Love, "ye had been wholly another, by your own record. But ye should well wit, and all ye in life encumbered by your own spirit's

self, that never shall you be without some encumbering, and all for this," saith Love, "that ye would not obey my messengers and Virtues when I would it, I sent by many messengers to make you free both body and spirit. And for this," saith Love, "you would not when I sent to you by the sensitive Virtues and by mine angels. Therefore, I show you I may not by right give you the freedom that I have, for Right may not do it. And if you had," saith Love, "obeyed when I called you by the wills of Virtues that I sent you, you had had by rights the freedom that I have. Ah, soul!" saith Love, "how you are encumbered by your self!"

"Yea, soothly," saith this soul, "my body is in feebleness and my soul in dread, and often I have heaviness," saith she, "will I or nill I of these two natures, that the far-off freedom I may not have."

"Ah, soul, alas!" saith Love, "what evil ye have for this little gain! and all for this that you obeyed not the teachings of perfection, in which I urged you to disencumber yourself in the flower of your youth. And always you would not yet move yourself, nor nothing would you do, but always refused my messenger that I made you wit, by the noble messengers that ye have heard; and such folk," saith Love, "be encumbered of themselves unto their death day.

"Oh, without fail," saith Love, "and if they had willed, they had been delivered of that in which they are in right great servitude, at little profit, and they shall (continue) to be so as compared to the other. And if they had heard me, they had been delivered for right little; for so little," saith Love, "as (merely) to give themselves (up) there where I would have had then, (even) as I showed them, by the Virtues whose office this is. I say," saith Love, "they had been all free of soul and body, if they had done my counsel by the Virtues that said my will concerning what was necessary for them before I delighted myself in them, with all my freedom. And because they did it not, they all abide in this (state) that ye have heard 'with' themselves. Thus think the free naughted (souls) and arrayed with delights, that see by themselves, the servitude of the others; for the very sun shineth in the light of them, so they see the motes within the sunbeam, by the brightness of the sun and of the beam. And when this sun is in the soul and this beam and this brightness, the body hath no more feebleness, nor the soul dread, for the very Sun of Righteousness, when he did his miracles on earth, never healed soul without body; but he healed both body and soul; and right so he doeth yet, but he doeth it to none that hath no faith in the same."

Now see how worthy, and strong and right free is she, and of all things disencumbered, whom Faith and Love govern; but none may come to this unless Faith hallow him.

OF CERTAIN MEANS WHEREBY THEY THAT BE MARRED AND IN LIFE OF SPIRIT MAY COME OVER TO THE BEING THAT IS NEXT THE BEING OF THIS SOUL WHICH HATH ATTAINED THE HIGHEST BEING; AND IN WHAT CASE THE SOUL IS IN THE TIME OF THAT BEING.

"I have said," saith Love, "that they whom I have summoned by their own inwardness to obey the perfection of virtues, who ought to have done so, that they dwell unto the time of death encumbered of themselves, though they travail every day with themselves to fulfil the perfection of the apostles, by study of reason and of goodwill, they shall never be unencumbered of themselves, neither of body nor of soul. No soothly," saith Love, "since the running fancies of their inward arguments giveth it them not. It may not to them come, for all that ever is done of them, it is all encumbrances to them. This wit all they who undertake works of themselves without the fervour of the willing of their inwardness."

"For thus I say it," saith this free soul, "to all them that live in study of life of perfection, that they be on their guard and keep themselves that they refuse not the askings of the fervent desires of the will of the spirit, as clearly as they feel them, whereby they may have the better (life) after those lives that be called 'life marred' and 'life of spirit'; that they may come to this life that never worketh nor asketh: for the settled can (have) no better than this.

"I say," saith Love, "that they be on their guard, that is to say, that those which stand in the state of the twain first lives of perfection, that they follow duly and diligently all the good stirrings and fervours that the soul willeth and desireth, as much as they may, for it is needful for them to do so if they will have the better (life) afterwards; for the former lives be but maiden servants that array the house against the coming of the great Being, to lodge the state that is the freedom of not-willing, in which the soul is of all points freed. To this come they that give all, for all who give all, have all and not else. And thus much," saith this free soul, "I will say to them that be marred, that they keep the peace, and fulfil perfectly the will and the fervour of cutting desire of the work of their spirit, as I have said, in holding their wits so close, that they have nothing by work of deliberation beyond the will of the spirit, so that they may reach to these rightful works, that is most nigh the being that we have spoken of. Where the eldest born daughter of the high King is set, there faileth her nothing of gentleness. And this lady," saith Love, "hath this being attained, the which is most highest and most worthy and most noble. And I shall tell you how," saith Love, "there is not so much as the quantity of a point in her that is not fulfilled by me, so that nothing created may dwell in her thought. And she hath piety in her, but not of appearance, and nevertheless," saith Love, "piety and courtesy be not from this soul departed, when there is time of need."

"That is right," saith this soul, "no more is it from Jesus Christ by whom I have life. When that his precious soul was glorified, as soon as she was knit to the body of the manhood and to nature divine in the Person of the Son, there dwelled in him pity and courtesy. And he who is courteous loveth not but that thing that he ought to love. He loveth not the spiritual things, who loveth temporalities. Nor he loveth never divinely who loveth bodily. They that love the Deity feel little of the humanity—during the time of that usage. Never was a soul knit, nor oned, nor divinely fulfilled, that feeleth bodily things. Of what should the inwardness of these souls feel? for God does not move himself, nor does she move herself."

Now understand by nobleness of understanding the gloss of these words. The meaning of these words that the soul saith, that her inwardness feeleth not, she moveth not herself, it is meant for the time of ravishing in union. There be three manners of unions that devout souls feel, in sundry dispositions, but I mean of the highest, that is best; and that is the union where, through ravishing of love, the soul is knit and oned to God, so that God and the soul is one spirit. For St. Paul saith: it is not two spirits, God and the soul, that is thus oned to him, but it is all one spirit in time of this union. Of what, then, should her inwardness feel in the time of this union, or (how) should she herself move herself? Oh, she may not do it, for she is all molten in God for the time. Ah, this blessed oneness lasteth but a little while in any creature that is here

in deadly life, for the corruption of nature may not suffer it. But it may oft be had by the goodness of God, who is the worker of this work in souls where he vouchsafes (it). To him be offered all glory and praisings to everlasting laud.

Lo ye that study this book, thus ye must within yourselves gloss such dark words. And if ye cannot come soon to the understanding thereof, offer it meekly up to God, and by the custom of oft reading thereon, ye shall come thereto. A few words more I say in this book, to bring you into the way, notwithstanding that I was purposed before to have glossed no more. God grant us alway to do his pleasing and bring us to him when it is his will.

How these souls be never feeble nor encumbered of themselves.

"Ah God," saith Reason, "what these souls be! certainly through baptism be they never openly feeble," saith Reason, "nor encumbered of themselves."

"Oh," saith this soul, "no soothly no, love destroyeth not, but she keepeth and nourisheth and feedeth all those that trust in her. Sun and darkness and seas be fulfilled. I sing," saith this soul, "(at) one time, song, (at) other time, unsong, and all for them that yet shall be free; so that they may here, in this book, learn some point of freedom and what thing behoveth them before they come thereto."

How this soul hath perceived the coast of the country where she ought to be.

"This soul hath perceived by divine light the coasts of the country where she ought to be. She passeth the sea to gather the shoots of the high cedar; for none taketh nor attaineth to this cedar unless they pass the high sea, in naughting their wills unto the waves. Understand ye lovers what this is."

Of the debts of this soul, and how they be paid, and by whom, and who is his next neighbor.

"I have said," saith Love, "that this soul is fallen of me into naught, and less than naught without number. For right as God is not to be comprehended as to his might, so is this soul in infinite debt for but one hour in time without more, that she had will, against him. So that she oweth him, without default, the debt of that which his will willeth; and so many times as she hath willed to rob God of his will, she is in debt as much as his will is worth."

"Ah, visible and insufferable debt," saith this soul, "who shall pay this debt? Ah, Lord, certainly you; for your plenteous goodness, that is swimming and flowing full of courtesy, may not suffer but that I be quit by you, God of love, for you have my debts paid in a moment!"

"The right sweet Far Night hath supplied the last penny of my debt. And I say to him, 'as much care have ye for me as I for you, though I gave you as much as you have, for such is the largesse of your divine nature.' 'So willeth he,' so saith this gentle Far Night, that is my counsel. These two debts, the one and the other, be henceforward all one, for this is the counsel of my next neighbour, and thereto I consent."

"O clean, pure Lady Soul," saith Reason, "who is your next neighbour?"

"His Exalting Ravishing that uptaketh me and throweth me in the very midst of divine love, in which," saith this soul, "I am drowned. Then is it right that he sustain me of himself, for I am laid in him; I must stint," saith this soul, "for I may not tell it."

"No soothly," saith Love, "no more than the sun may stay or dwell, no more may this soul say of this life as compared to that which—truth to say—truly is."

How THIS SOUL IS A SPRING OF DIVINE LOVE, AND HOW SHE SEETH THAT SHE IS NAUGHT, AND HOW THIS NAUGHT GIVETH HER ALL.

"Ah, Lady Soul," saith Abashings, "ye be a continual spring of divine love, of the which spring of divine love waxeth the well of divine knowing, and the streams of divine laud."

"And of this spring of divine love, the well of divine knowing, and of the streams of divine lauding, I remain," saith this confirmed soul, "perfectly in his divine will."

"Now hath this soul," saith Love, "her right name of Naught, in which she moveth, for she seeth that she is naught, and that she hath not of aught, neither of her nor of her even-Christian, nor of God himself. For she is so little, that she may not herself find, and all thing wrought is so far from her, that she may not feel it, and God is so great that she may nothing of him comprehend. And because of this naught, she is fallen into certainty of naught-knowing and into certainty of naught-availing, and into certainty of naught-willing. And this naught, which we speak of," saith Love, "giveth her the all, and otherwise might she not have it."

OF TWO THINGS THAT THIS SOUL DOETH NOT, WHICH MAKETH HER TO HAVE PEACE; AND HOW SHE IS NO MORE ENCUMBERED OF THINGS THAT SHE DOETH WITHOUT HER, THAN IF SHE DID IT NOT; AND WHO BE PERFECTLY FREE.

"This soul," saith Love, "is imprisoned and fettered and holden in a country of entire peace, for she is there in full sufficiency. There she shippeth and saileth and floateth and swimmeth, and is filled of divine peace without the moving of her inwardness and without the work of her outward doing. For these twain aforesaid unmake this peace, if it may so befall; but not of this soul, for she is in sovereignty. Nothing may grieve her, nor nothing encumber. If she do anything by her outward wits, that is always *without* her; and if God do his work in her, (then) it is, of himself in her, *without* herself, *for* him. No more is this soul encumbered of anything that she doth, than is her angel of the keeping of her. For no more be the angels encumbered to keep us than if they kept us not; neither is this soul (encumbered) any more by what she doth, than if she did it not. For she hath naught of herself, she hath all given freely without any 'forwhy?' in him that is all. For she is lady beyond the thought of her youth, and Sun that shineth, heateth and nourisheth of life of being, discovereth her from her former being. This soul," saith Love, "hath not held doubt nor trust."

"Eh, what then, for God?" saith Reason.

"Certain confidence," saith Love, "and true agreement to will only (and wholly) the divine ordering; thus it is that she is perfectly free."

OF FOUR COSTS THAT THIS SOUL IS MADE FREE OF; HOW SHE HATH LOST HER NAME BY UNION OF LOVE AND IS TURNED ABOUT TO LOVE, AND HOW YET THERE IS MORE HIGH THAN THIS; HOW NONE MAY UNDERSTAND THIS BOOK BUT THEY THAT LOVE HATH MADE IT FOR.

Of four costs behoveth a bondman to have before he might be free and called a gentleman; and right thus it is in the understanding of this spiritual doing.

The first cost that this soul which is free hath, is this, that she hath no grudging of conscience, though she work not the work of virtues. Ah, for God! understand it, ye that hear this, if ye may! How might Love have this usage concerning all the works of virtues, since work ceaseth when love hath this usage?

The second cost is, that she hath nothing of will, no more than have the dead in graves, but only the divine will of God. This soul recketh not nor hath heart of righteousness, nor of mercy. She planteth all in the sole will of him that moveth her in him; this is the second cost by which the soul is made free.

The third cost is, that she holdeth this; that even as God could no more will aught but goodness, so she believeth that she could not will other than his divine will. Love hath arrayed her so with himself, that it maketh her thus to hold of herself. For he, of his bounty, hath turned her into this favour by goodness. Also of his love hath he, unto this love, by love, turned her. And of his will, hath her in his will, by divine will, purely turned. She is of him, in him, for him, thus led; and this holdeth she, otherwise she should not be free of all costs.

Understand the gloss, auditors of this book! Where the stream or the flood lieth that drowneth the thought. This is then when she is in being; in the which God maketh her to have (a) being; there hath she given her will, so that she may not will but the will of him that hath led her of himself, for him, unto his bounty. And she that is thus free of all costs, liveth in sovereignty, and there she loseth her name and is drowned, and in this drowning left of him, in him, for him, in himself. So loseth she her name, right as doth a water that cometh out of the sea, that is called Oise or Meuse, and when it entereth into the sea it loseth its name and its courses by which it ran in many countries in doing its work; and ceaseth in the sea. There it resteth itself and hath lost its labour; and right so soothly it is of this soul. In order to gloss the meaning ye have of this and for this, enough ensamples; how this soul cometh to the sea and doth her labour and how she stinteth in the sea, there hath she lost her name and her labour. She hath no name but the name of him, in whom she is perfectly moved, that is, in Love. That is the spouse of her Joy which hath drawn the thought wholly into him. She is, then, this that is. And that soundeth marvellous to her; then is she marvellous and Love is her pleasure, the which Love delighteth her.

Now is this soul without name, save the name of the very Union where Love moveth her. Right as the Water that we have spoken of, that hath the name of the sea—for it is sea as soon as it is entered into the sea—it is not drawn to anything contrary by any nature of the ground. Also, no matter maketh of it nor of the sea aught but one thing, not twain, but one; and right so it is of her of whom we speak. For Love hath drawn all her nature into him, that Love and this soul are all one thing; not twain, for that were discord, but only one, and therefore this is a good "accord." "It is right," saith Love, "that this soul that thus is free of these four costs, that she ascend afterwards to sovereignty."

"Ah, Love," saith Reason, "is there yet anything more high?"

"Yea," saith Love, "this that is her next neighbour. For when she is thus free of these four costs and noble by all the freedoms that of her be descended—for no churl is accepted in this marriage—this soul that is thus noble, falleth then," saith Love, "into dismay that is called naught, thinking of the far-off results of what is near; that is her most nigh neighbour. And then liveth this soul," saith Love, "not in the former life of grace, nor in the life of spirit, but gloriously and divinely; for God hath hallowed her in this point by himself, and nothing contrary to goodness may befall her."

Understand holily, all as it is; so may God give you always being without removing! This I say to the persons for whom Love hath made this book, to him for whom I have written it. But among you that have not been such, nor be, nor shall be, ye trouble yourselves in vain, if ye will understand it. He who is not this, tasteth not this. (For it is to be) in God without being, (for) in God's self is being. Understand the gloss! He that is lame of limbs may not well go, nor the feeble may not swim.

"Ah, without fail," saith Reason, "this is well said; (he who is) cumbered, encumbereth (others)."

OF THE RUDENESS OF THEM THAT BE GOVERNED BY REASON, AND HOW THIS SOUL WILL NO MORE FOLLOW THEIR COURSE.

Thus then speaketh this soul, abashed by naught-thinking, by this far night of night; who in peace delighteth herself. "Soothly," saith she, "they that be governed by reason, the rudeness nor the cumberings of them no man may say. By their teachings it appeareth; it is the work of an ass and not of a man, if any man would hear them. But God hath kept me well," saith this soul, "from such lore of Reason's disciples; they shall not hold me in their counsel, nor their doctrine will I no more hear; I have been long therein holden, sometime I thought it was good, it is not now my best; of that, they know nothing; for a little wit may not put a price (upon a) thing of worthy value, nor understand anything unless reason be master thereof; and if they did understand it any time, it is not often. And therefore, I say," saith this soul, "that their rudeness I will no more hear: let

them tell me nothing, for I can no more suffer it. I have neither ways nor means; to God this work pertaineth, who doth in me his works: I owe him no work since himself worketh. If I (put in) mine, I should unmake his, and for this cause the work and teaching of the disciples of Reason would harm me. If I believed them, in such dread I should abandon this work, by their counsel. They follow (after) to attain a thing that is impossible, but I excuse them for their intention.

HOW THIS SOUL IS FREE AND CONSUMED BY MORTALITY, AND BRENT IN THE BURNING FIRE OF CHARITY; AND HOW THIS SOUL SEEKETH NO MORE GOD BY OUTWARD WORKS. OF THE MARVEL THAT REASON HATH OF THIS, AND OF THE PEACE OF MARY AND THE TROUBLE OF MARTHA.

"This soul," saith Love, "is free and right free, surmounted free of tree, crop and root, and of all its branches. Her lot hath this of freedom, ended of every cost; there hath she her full purity. She answereth to none, nor oweth she to do so, unless he be of her lineage, this is to say, unless it be according to her disposition within herself. This soul findeth none that calleth her, nor none that she answereth to, nor her enemy hath no more answers from her."

"This is right," saith this soul, "since I draw God to me, it behoveth that he support me. God his bounty, he may not lose."

"This soul," saith Love, "is consumed by mortality, and brent in the burning fire of charity, and the powder of her not cast nor thrown, but given into the high sea by naught-willing of will. She is right gentle and noble in prosperities, and highly noble in adversities, and excellent noble in all places that she is in."

"She who is such," saith this soul, "she seeketh no more God by penances, nor by no sacraments of Holy Church, nor by thoughts nor by words, nor by works, nor by holy creatures, nor by creatures of above, nor by righteousness, nor by mercy, nor by glory, nor by divine knowing, nor by divine love, nor by divine praise and laud."

"Ah, Lord God," saith Reason, "what saith this creature at first? This is all deadly! What shall my disciples say? I know not what to say nor what to answer, to excuse this!"

"Oh, what marvel is it," saith this soul, "these folks of, thy nursing be on foot without going, and have hands without work, and mouths without speech, and eyes without sight, and ears without hearing, and reason without reason, and body without life, and heart without understanding, as long as they have this being, and therefore it is marvel upon marvel (to them)."

"Yea, soothly," saith Love, "this is to them right marvellous marvels; for they be full far from the country where these others have these usages of high worthiness. But they that be such as we speak of, that be in the country in which God liveth himself, they have not marvel thereof."

"No, forsooth," saith this soul that is free, "for it were a point of villeinage, and I shall tell you how. If a king give one of his servants that truly hath served him a great gift, by which the servant were rich all the days of his life after, and never (had) to do service more, why should a wise man marvel at this, or why should he blame the king for his gift, and the freedom of the gift?"

"Nay," saith Courtesy, "a wise man marvelleth not of the thing that is done, that pertaineth to be done, but alloweth it and praiseth it and loveth it; and if he marvel, he showeth in that, that he doeth that which he ought not do. But the servile hearts that be not wise, that know not for default of wit what honour and courtesy is, nor what the gifts be of a noble lord, they have thereof great wonder, and that is no marvel!"

"They have cause in themselves," saith Truth, "as ye have heard before."

"Ah, for God," saith Nobility-of-unity of the freed soul, "why should anyone marvel that hath any wit in him? If I say great things or mean these things, or though I have by all, of all, in all, my full sufficiency, my Beloved is great, who great gifts giveth and maketh it all at his will, He is fulfilled abundantly of all goodness of himself. And I am full enlumined and abundantly fulfilled of abundance of delights, by holding his divine bounty in me, without seeking him by the paps of his consolations, as this book deviseth," saith this soul. "He calleth me to peace, without fail."

"It is right," saith pure Courtesy. "It fitteth the Beloved since he is worthy, that he of his bounty call his lover to peace."

Martha is troubled, peace hath Mary. Praised is Martha, but more Mary. Mary hath but one intention in her, and that only one intent maketh her to have peace, and Martha in many intentions have ofttimes unrest. And therefore a free soul may only have one intention. She heareth oft, this soul, things that she heareth not, and is full ofttimes where this soul is not, and feeleth ofttimes that which she feeleth not. "I hold," saith she, "for this, mine (own which) I shall not let go; it is in my will, befall what may; for he is with me, then it were a default if I (let myself be) dismayed."

OF THE DEATH OF REASON BY THE STRONG SPEECH OF THIS SOUL; AND HOW LOVE ASKETH IN THE STEAD OF REASON "WHO IS MOTHER TO REASON AND TO OTHER VIRTUES?" AND HOW IT IS MEEKNESS AND WHICH MEEKNESS IT IS.

"This soul," saith Love, "is lady of virtues, daughter of deity, sister of wisdom, and the spouse of love."

"Soothly," saith this soul, "but this seemeth to Reason a marvellous language, and that is no wonder, for it shall not be long until he shall not be; but I was," saith this soul, "and am, and shall be without failing; for love hath neither beginning, nor comprehending, nor end; and I am (nothing) but love, how might I then have end? It may not be."

"Ah, God," saith Reason, "how dare any say this! I dare not hear it. I fall, Lady Soul; soothly my heart faileth me to hear you. I have no life."

"Alas, alas! Why had this death not been long ere this time," saith this soul, "for until this (death had been) I might not freely hold mine heritage. And this that is mine is that (whereby) I fell you with love and wound you to death. Now is Reason dead," saith this soul.

"Then shall I say," saith Love, "this which Reason should say if she were alive in you and which she would ask of you, our Beloved," saith Love to this soul, which is Love and none other thing than Love.

These sayings, then, that Love saith to this creature of divine bounty, have thrown Reason and the works of virtues under his feet, and to death brought (them), without recovering. "Now I say that (which) Reason should say. She should ask," saith Love, "who is mother of her, and of the other virtues that be of her germain."

"And these, be they mothers of none?" saith this soul.

"Yes," saith Love, "all the virtues be mothers."

"And of whom?" saith this soul.

"Of peace and of holiness," saith Love.

"Then be all the virtues that be germain to Reason mothers of holiness?" saith this soul.

"Sooth," saith Love, "of that holiness that Reason understandeth, but of none other."

"And who is then mother of virtues?" saith this soul.

"Meekness," saith Love, "but not that meekness that is meekness by works of virtue. She is germain sister of Reason. I say 'sister,' because it is a greater thing to be mother than child; this ye see well; and nearer is kin than stranger."

"Oh," saith this soul that speaketh in the person of Reason, "then is that meekness that is mother of these virtues but a daughter. Who is this, and of whence cometh she, that is mother of so great a lineage as be the virtues, and tutor to feelings, when virtues be mothers? Who is ancestor to this feeling? Can none tell whence this line cometh?"

"No," saith Love, "they that know cannot put it into speech."

"This is sooth," saith this soul, "but I shall add here to this what I shall say. This meekness that is tutor and mother is

daughter of divine majesty. She cometh of the divine deity, where the mother is ancestor of these branches, whose root is of such great fruitfulness. We still ourselves, speech overwhelmeth it. She hath given the stock and the fruit of her root and branches. Therefore near lieth the peace of the far night, which disencumbers her of work; speech and thought it maketh all shadow; for her far night disencumbereth her so that nothing shadoweth her."

How this soul is free of all, and how she hath so planted her will in the Trinity, that she may not sin unless she unplant it.

"This soul," saith Love, "is quit of services, for she liveth in freedom. Whoso serveth, he is not free; whoso feeleth he is not dead, whoso desireth he would (have), whoso would (have), he beggeth. And whoso beggeth, he hath a lack of divine sufficiency. But they that be truly always upholden and taken of love and naughted by love, and all overspread of love, they have no heart but on love, even though they should suffer evermore torments and endure them, though the torments were as great as God is great in bounty. Never loved the soul finely that doubteth that this be not true.

"This soul hath given all by freedom of nobility of the work of the Trinity. In the same Trinity this soul planteth so deeply her will, that she may not sin, unless she unplant it. For she hath nothing wherewith to sin, for without will may no creature sin. Now ye dare not reck of sin if she leave her will there where she hath planted it, that is, in him, who hath given it her freely, of his bounty; thence will she not take it, but there she planteth it all wholly, freely, without any 'for-why?' And not for her (sake), but for him, for two things. One is because it is good, and the second is, because he willeth it. Up to this time hath she no peace fully, steadfastly, nor peaceably, till she be of her will purely departed. These that such be resemble always a drunken (man), for the drunken man, he is no more afeared for anything that is coming to him, whatever adventure may befall him, than if it came not to him. And if he be (afeared), he is not all fully drunk.

"And also if this soul have anything wherewith to will, it is ill planted. She may yet fall if she be assailed with adversities or with prosperities. Then is she not whole, for she is not naked. No, since she hath wherewith to will or to unwill, or to withhold her will."

WHAT IT BEHOVETH THEM TO DO THAT BE IN LIFE OF SPIRIT, TO COME TO LORDSHIP AND SOVEREIGNTY.

"And yet I will thus much say," saith Love to all those that be in life of spirit, "that if it be asked of them, let them do the asking of the desire of their inwardness, in following the works of perfection by the study of reason, willing or not. For if they will, by this they may be and shall come to the being that we have spoken of, and shall yet be lords of themselves and of heaven and earth."

"And how, Lord?" saith Reason that to this cannot answer.

"By this way," saith this soul that is free; "if she holdeth all without care or without heart and all giveth without heart, and all taketh without heart, and all hath without heart; and if her heart feel it, this is she not."

"I have said," saith Love, "that they do the asking of their inwardness, if it be asked, for otherwise I commend it them not; and if they leave all the will of their outwardness for the inward life of spirit, they shall yet come to all lordship and sovereignty."

"Oh," saith the spirit that this same seeketh in life marred, "tell me how?"

"Forsooth," saith this soul that standeth in freedom, "none can see it but he only that *is* this thing in creatures, of his bounty for creature. But this I shall tell you," saith this free soul, "what behoveth a creature ere he come thereto. It behoveth him perfectly to do the contrary of his will in appeasing the virtues up to the throat, and hold this point without falling (away, namely, that) the spirit

have alway lordship without contrariosity."

"Ah God," saith Truth, "how sick is the body of the heart, where such a spirit is."

"Soothly I say," saith this free soul, "that it behoveth to have such inward working in life marred, this is to say, in life of spirit, so that it destroy the humours of all sickness, in a swift moment. Such physician hath Fervour-of-spirit."

"This is sooth," saith Love, "whoso that doubteth in this, if he had assayed, he should with the sooth."

HOW THEY THAT BE IN LIFE OF SPIRIT MUST ALWAY DO THE CONTRARY OF THEIR PLEASAUNCE IF THEY WILL HAVE PEACE, AND HOW THEY THAT BE FREE MUST DO ALL THAT PLEASETH THEM OR ELSE THEY SHALL LOSE PEACE. WHAT THING IT IS THAT GIVETH THIS SOUL AND IS MOST NOBLE BEING THAT MAY BE HAD IN THIS LIFE.

"Now I shall tell you," saith Love, "of the soul in freeness, and also of them of the life which we have spoken of, that we call life of spirit, it may have no peace unless the body do alway the contrary of its will. This is to be understood, that these folks do the contrary of that which delighteth them. For otherwise, else, they should fall into loss of this life, unless they do alway the contrary of their pleasure. And they that be free have to do all the contrary, for right as them behoveth in life of spirit to do all the contrary of their will, unless they will lose peace, (so) behoveth it in life that is free, to do all that pleaseth them, unless they will lose peace. If they be come into the state of freedom, that is, if they be fallen from virtues into Love, and from Love into Naught, they do nothing except it please them; and if they do (otherwise), they rob themselves of peace, freedom, noblesse. For until then is not the soul wholly refined, until she do that which pleaseth her and that she be grudging of doing the contrary of her pleasances. That is right," saith Love, "for her will is ours, she hath passed the Red Sea, and her enemies therein left. Her pleasing *is* our will, by the purity of unity of the will of the Deity, wherein we have enclosed her. Her will is ours, for she is moved from grace into perfection; from works of Virtues and from Virtues into Love; and from Love into Naught, and from Naught into clarifyings of God, who seeth with eyes of his majesty; who in this point hath enlightened her by himself, and (she) is so left in him, that she neither seeth him nor herself. If she saw herself in this divine bounty, she would be *for* herself; but he seeth this bounty in her who wist this of her before she was. When he gave her of his bounty then he made her lady. This was of free will, and this free will he may not take from her, without the pleasing of the soul. Now he hath it without any 'for-why?' right in such a way as he had it before she was lady thereover. Now naught is but he; no one (is) loved but he; for none *is* but he. This calleth her alone, this maketh her a lone soul, and the all, sole, alone (ness) of his own being giveth her that point, that is the most noble being that any creature may have, in this life of perfection. And under this there be five (beings) in which men must live according to the perfection of the call of every (man), before a soul may have this, which is the sixth, which is most profitable and best and the most noble and the most gentle of all the other five. And in paradise is the seventh, that is made perfect without any lack. And thus doeth God of his bounty in his creatures, his divine works. The Holy Ghost inspireth where he will and is marvellous in his creatures."

Meister Eckhart

(1260?-1328?)

MEISTER Eckhart was educated in Paris and taught at Cologne. Originally a German Dominican friar, Eckhart was in the latter years of his life tried for heresy. After his death a number of his teachings were condemned by a papal bull of John XXII because they savored of Neo-Platonism. He saw man as directly touched by the Spirit of God, with churchly rites of some value, but not of primary importance. To him the main import of religious experience was man's realization of union with God through mystical fellowship.

Eckhart combined vital intellectual ability with deep mystical insight. His commanding presence, his strange sensitivity for the supra-sensible, influenced and inspired those who knew him. As the greatest figure of the fourteenth century mystical movement, and also one of Christendom's greatest devotional figures, he is called the "Father of the Friends of God."

"About Disinterest" is a scholarly treatise, and the other two works are from his sermons. They are reprinted by permission of Harper & Brothers from *Meister Eckhart, A Modern Translation* by Raymond Bernard Blakney.

ABOUT DISINTEREST

I have read much of what has been written, both by heathen philosophers and sages and in the Old and New Testaments. I have sought earnestly and with great diligence that good and high virtue by which man may draw closest to God and through which one may best approximate the idea God had of him before he was created, when there was no separation between man and God; and having delved into all this writing, as far as my intelligence would permit, I find that [high virtue] to be pure disinterest, that is, detachment from creatures. Our Lord said to Martha: "*Unum est necessarium,*" which is to say: to be untroubled and pure, one thing is necessary and that is disinterest.

The teachers praise love, and highly too, as St. Paul did, when he said: "No matter what I do, if I have not love, I am nothing." Nevertheless, I put disinterest higher than love. My first reason is as follows. The best thing about love is that it makes me love God. Now, it is much more advantageous for me to move God toward myself than for me to move toward him, for my blessing in eternity depends on my being identified with God. He is more able to deal with me and join me than I am to join him. Disinterest brings God to me and I can demonstrate it this way: Everything likes its own habitat best; God's habitat is purity and unity, which are due to disinterest. Therefore God necessarily gives himself to the disinterested heart.

In the second place, I put disinterest above love because love compels me to suffer for God's sake, whereas disinterest makes me sensitive only to God. This ranks far above suffering for God or in God; for, when he suffers, man pays some attention to the creature from which his suffering comes, but being disinterested, he is quite detached from the creature. I demonstrate that, being disinterested, a man is sensitive only to God, in this way: Experience must always be an experience of something, but disinterest comes so close to zero that nothing but God is rarefied enough to get into it, to enter the disinterested heart. That is why a disinterested person is sensitive to nothing but God. Each person experiences things in his own way and thus every distinguishable thing is seen and understood according to the approach of the beholder and not, as it might be, from its own point of view.

The authorities also praise humility above other virtues, but I put disinterest above humility for the following reasons. There can be humility without disinterest but disinterest cannot be perfect without humility; perfect humility depends on self-denial; disinterest comes so near to zero that nothing may intervene. Thus, there cannot be disinterest without humility and, anyway, two virtues are better than one!

The second reason I put disinterest above humility is that in humility man abases himself before creatures, and in doing so pays some attention to the creatures themselves. Disinterest, however, stays within itself. No transference of attention [such as humility] can ever rank so high that being self-contained will not go higher. As the prophet puts it: "*Omnis gloria filiae regis ab intus*," which means, "the glory of the king's daughter comes from within her." Perfectly disinterested, a man has no regard for anything, no inclination to be above this or below that, no desire to be over or under; he remains what he is, neither loving nor hating, and desiring neither likeness to this or unlikeness to that. He desires only to be one and the same; for to want to be this or that is to want something; and the disinterested person wants nothing. Thus everything remains unaffected as far as he is concerned.

Someone may say: Surely our Lady had all the virtues and therefore she must have been perfectly disinterested. If then, disinterest ranks above virtue, why did the Lady glory in her humility rather than in disinterest? She said: "*Quia respexit Dominus humilitatem ancillae suae*." That means: "He hath regarded the low estate of his handmaiden."

I reply by saying that in God there is both disinterest and humility as well, to the extent that virtues may be attributed to God. You should know that it was loving humility that made God stoop to human nature, the same humility by which he created heaven and earth, as I shall later explain. And if our Lord, willing to become man, still remained unaffected in his disinterest, our Lady must have known that he desired this of her, too, and that therefore he would have regard to her humility rather than to her disinterest. Thus she continued, unmoved in her disinterestedness, and yet she gloried in humility.

If, however, she had said: "He hath regarded my disinterest," her disinterest would have been qualified by the thought and not perfect, for she would have departed from it. Any departure from disinterest, however small, disturbs it; and there you have the reason why our Lady gloried in humility rather than in disinterest. The prophet says: *"Audiam, qui loquatur in me Dominus Deus,"* which means "I will be silent and hear what God the Lord will utter within me"—as if to say, "If God the Lord wants to speak to me, let him come in, for I shall not go out." As Boethius puts it: "Ye people, why do you seek without for the blessing that is within you?"

I also put disinterest above mercy, for mercy is nothing but a man's going out to the want of a fellow and the heart is disturbed by it. Disinterest, however, is exempt from this, being self-contained and allowing nothing to disturb. To speak briefly: When I survey the virtues, I find none as flawless, as conductive to God as disinterest.

A philosopher named Avicenna said: "The rank of a disinterested mind is so high that what it sees is true, what it desires comes to pass, what it commands must be done." You may take this for the truth, that when a free mind is really disinterested, God is compelled to come into it; and if it could get along without contingent forms, it would then have all the properties of God himself. Of course, God cannot give his properties away and so he can do nothing for the disinterested mind except to give himself to it and it is then caught up into eternity, where transitory things no longer affect it. Then the man has no experiences of the physical order and is said to be dead to the world, since he has no appetite for any earthly thing. That is what St. Paul meant by saying: "I live; yet not I, but Christ liveth in me."

You may ask: "What is this disinterest, that it is so noble a matter?" Know, then, that a mind unmoved by any contingent affection or sorrow, or honor, or slander, or vice, is really disinterested—like a broad mountain that is not shaken by a gentle wind. Unmovable disinterest brings man into his closest resemblance to God. It gives God his status as God. His purity is derived from it, and then his simplicity and unchangeable character. If man is to be like God, to the extent that any creature may resemble him, the likeness will come through disinterest, and man proceeds from purity to simplicity and from simplicity to unchangeableness, and thus the likeness of God and man comes about. It is an achievement of the grace that allures man away from temporal things and purges him of the transitory. Keep this in mind: to be full of things is to be empty of God, while to be empty of things is to be full of God.

Bear in mind also that God has been immovably disinterested from the beginning and still is and that his creation of the heavens and the earth affected him as little as if he had not made a single creature. But I go further. All the prayers a man may offer and the good works he may do will affect the disinterested God as little as if there were neither prayers nor works, nor will God be any more compassionate or stoop down to man any more because of his prayers and works than if they were omitted.

Furthermore, I say that when the Son in the Godhead willed to be human and became so, suffering martyrdom, the immovable disinterest of God was affected as little as if the Son had never become human at all.

Perhaps, then, you will say: "I take it, therefore, that prayers and good works are so much lost motion; God pays no attention to them and will not be moved by them. And yet they say that God wants us to pray to him about everything."

Now pay close attention and understand what I mean, if you can. When God first looked out of eternity (if one may say that he ever *first* looked out), he saw everything as it would happen and at the same time he saw when and how he would create each thing. He foresaw the loving prayers and good deeds each person might do and knew which prayers and which devotions he would heed. He foresaw that tomorrow morning you will cry out to him in earnest prayer and that tomorrow morning he will not heed you because he had already heard your prayer in his eternity, before you became a person; and if your prayer is neither honest nor earnest, he will not deny it now, for it is already denied in eternity. In that first eternal vision, God looked on each thing-to-be and therefore he does what he now does without a reason. It was all worked out beforehand.

Still, even if God remains forever unmoved, disinterested, the prayers and good works of people are not lost on that account, for well-doing is never without its reward. Philippus says: "God the Creator holds things to the course and order he ordained for them in the beginning." To God there is neither past nor future and he loves the saints, having foreseen them before ever the world began. Then, when events, foreseen by God in eternity, come to pass in time, people think that God has taken a new departure, either to anger or toward some agreeable end; but it is we who change, while he remains unchanged. Sunshine hurts ailing eyes but is agreeable to sound ones, and yet it is the same sunshine in both cases. God does not see through time, nor does anything new happen in his sight.

Isidore makes the same point in his book on the highest good. He says: "Many people ask what God was doing before he created heaven and earth. Where did he get his new impulse to make creatures? This is the answer: There never was a departure in God, nor a change of intention, and if there ever was a time when creatures did not exist as they do now, still they existed forever in God, in the mind of God." God did not make heaven and earth as our time-bound speech describes creation; they came into being when He spoke the word out of eternity. Moses said to our Lord, "Lord, if Pharaoh asks who you are, what shall I tell him?" The Lord replied: "Tell him that *he-who-is* sent you." We might say: The unchanging One hath sent me!

Someone well may ask: had Christ this unmoved disinterest when he said: "My soul is sorrowful even unto death"? Or Mary, when she stood underneath the cross? Much has been made of her lamentations. How are such things compatible with unmoved disinterest?

On this point the authorities say that a person is not one, but two people. One is called the outward man—the sensual person. He is served by the five senses, which function by means of the soul's agents. The other is the inner man—the spiritual person. But notice this, that a man who loves God prefers not to use the agents of the soul in the outward man any more than necessary and then the inner man has recourse to the five senses only to the degree to which he can guide and lead them. He guards them against animal diversions—such as people choose when they live like animals without intelligence. Such people are more properly called animals than persons.

Whatever strength the soul possesses, beyond what it devotes to the five senses, it gives to the inner man. If this inner man is devoted to some high and noble enterprise, the soul recalls its agents and the person is said to be senseless or rapt because his enterprise or object is an unintelligible idea or is unintelligible without being an idea. Remember that God requires of every spiritual person a love which includes all the agents of the soul. Thus he said: "Love your God with all your heart."

There are people who squander the strength of their souls in the outward man. These are the people, all of whose desires and thoughts turn on transient goods, since they are unaware of the inner person. Sometimes a good man robs his outward person of all the soul's agents, in order to dispatch them on some higher enterprise; so, conversely, animal people rob the inner person of the soul's agents and assign them to the outward man. A man may be ever so active outwardly and still leave the inner man unmoved and passive.

Now both in Christ and our Lady, there was an outward man and an inner person and, while they taught about external matters, they were outwardly active but inwardly unmoved and disinterested. This is how it was when Christ said: "My soul is sorrowful even unto death." And whatever the lamentations and other speeches of our Lady, inwardly she was still unmoved and disinterested. Take an illustration. A door swings to and fro through an angle. I compare the breadth of the door to the outward man and the hinge to the inner person. When the door swings to and fro, the breadth of the door moves back and forth, but the hinge is still unmoved and unchanged. It is like this here.

Now I ask what the object of pure disinterest is. I reply that it is neither this nor that. Pure disinterest is empty nothingness, for it is on that high plane on which God gives effect to his will. It is not possible for God to do his will in every heart, for even though he is almighty, he cannot act except where he finds preparations made or he makes them himself. I say "or makes them" on account of St. Paul, for God did not find him ready; he prepared St. Paul by an infusion of grace. Otherwise, I say that God acts where he finds that preparations have been made.

God's activity is not the same in a man as in a stone; and there is a simile for that, too, in nature. If a bake oven is heated and lumps of dough are put into it, some of oatmeal, some of barley, some of rye, and some of wheat, then, even though there is only one heat for all in the oven, it will not act the same way on the various doughs; for one turns into a pretty loaf, another to a rough loaf, and others still rougher. That is not due to the heat but to the material, which differs. Similarly God does not work in all hearts alike but according to the preparation and sensitivity he finds in each. In a given heart, containing this or that, there may be an item which prevents God's highest activity. Therefore if a heart is to be ready for him, it must be emptied out to nothingness, the condition of its maximum capacity. So, too, a disinterested heart, reduced to nothingness, is the optimum, the condition of maximum sensitivity.

Take an illustration from nature. If I wish to write on a white tablet, then no matter how fine the matter already written on it, it will confuse me and prevent me from writing down [my thoughts]; so that, if I still wish to use the tablet, I must first erase all that is written on it, but it will never serve me as well for writing as when it is clean. Similarly, if God is to write his message about the highest matters on my heart, everything to be referred to as "this or that" must first come out and I must be disinterested. God is free to do his will on his own level when my heart, being disinterested, is bent on neither this nor that.

Then I ask: What is the prayer of the disinterested heart? I answer by saying that a disinterested man, pure in heart, has no prayer, for to pray is to want something from God, something added that one desires, or something that God is to take away. The disinterested person, however, wants nothing, and neither has he anything of which he would be rid. Therefore he has no prayer, or he prays only to be uniform with God. In this sense we may understand the comment of St. Dionysius on a text of St. Paul—"they which run in a race run all, but one receiveth the prize"—that is, all the soul's agents race for the prize but only the soul's essence receives it. Thus, Dionysius says: "This race is precisely the flight from creatures to union with the uncreated." When the soul achieves this, it loses its identity, it absorbs God and is reduced to nothing, as the dawn at the rising of the sun. Nothing helps toward this end like disinterest.

To this point we may quote a saying of St. Augustine: "There is a heavenly door for the soul into the divine nature— where somethings are reduced to nothings." On earth, this door is precisely disinterest, and when disinterest reaches its apex it will be unaware of its knowledge, it will not love its own love, and will be in the dark about its own light. Here, too, we may quote the comment of an authority: "Blessed are the pure in heart who leave everything to God now as they did before ever they existed." No one can do this without a pure, disinterested heart.

That God prefers a disinterested heart

for his habitation may be seen from the question: "What is God looking for in everything?" I reply with these words from the Book of Wisdom: "I seek peace in all things." There is, however, no peace except in disinterest. Therefore God prefers it to any other condition or virtue. Remember, too, that the more his heart is trained to be sensitive to divine influences, the happier man is; the further he pushes his preparation, the higher he ascends in the scale of happiness.

But no man can be sensitive to divine influence except by conforming to God, and in proportion to his conformity he is sensitive to divine influence. Conformity comes of submission to God. The more subject to creatures a man is, the less he conforms to God, but the pure, disinterested heart, being void of creatures, is constantly worshiping God and conforming to him, and is therefore sensitive to his influence. That is what St. Paul means by saying: "Put ye on the Lord Jesus Christ"—that is, conform to Christ! Remember that when Christ became man, he was not one man but took all human nature on himself. If you get out, therefore, and clear of creatures, what Christ took on himself will be left to you and you will have to put on Christ.

If any man will see the excellence and use of perfect disinterest, let him take seriously what Christ said to his disciples about his humanity: "It is expedient for you that I go away: for if I go not away, the Comforter will not come unto you" —as if he said: "You take too much pleasure in my visible form and therefore the perfect pleasure of the Holy Spirit cannot be yours." Therefore discard the form and be joined to the formless essence, for the spiritual comfort of God is very subtle and is not extended except to those who despise physical comforts.

Heed this, intelligent people: Life is good to the man who goes, on and on, disinterestedly. There is no physical or fleshly pleasure without some spiritual harm, for the desires of the flesh are contrary to those of the spirit, and the desires of the spirit are contrary to the flesh. That is why to sow the undisciplined love of the flesh is to be cut off by death, but to sow the disciplined love of the spirit is to reap of the spirit, life eternal. The less one pays attention to the creature things, the more the Creator pursues him.

Listen to this, man of intelligence: If the pleasure we take in the physical form of Christ diminishes our sensitivity to the Holy Spirit, how much more will the pleasure we take in the comfort of transitory things be a barrier against God? Disinterest is best of all, for by it the soul is unified, knowledge is made pure, the heart is kindled, the spirit wakened, the desires quickened, the virtues enhanced. Disinterest brings knowledge of God; cut off from the creature, the soul unites with God; for love apart from God is like water to a fire, while love with God is the honeycomb in the honey.

Hear this, every intelligent spirit: The steed swiftest to carry you to perfection is suffering, or none shall attain eternal life except he pass through great bitterness with Christ. Nothing pierces man like suffering and nothing is more honey sweet than to have suffered. The surest basis on which perfection rests is humility, and he whose nature kneels in deepest lowliness—his spirit shall rise up to the heights of divinity; for as love brings sorrow, sorrow also brings love. Human ways are various: one person lives thus and another so.

For him who wishes to attain the utmost in life in his time, I set down here several aphorisms, much abbreviated, and taken from many writings.

Among men, be aloof; do not engage yourself to any idea you get; free yourself from everything chance brings to you, things that accumulate and cumber you; set your mind in virtue to contemplation, in which the God you bear in your heart shall be your steady object, the object from which your attention never wavers; and whatever else your duty may be, whether it be fasting, watching, or praying, dedicate it all to this one end, doing each only as much as is necessary to your single end. Thus you shall come to the goal of perfection.

Someone may ask: "Who could long endure this unwavering contemplation of the divine object?" I reply: No one living in such times as these. I tell you privately about these things only to have you know what the highest is, so that you may desire it and aspire to it. And if this vision is withdrawn from you, if you are a good man, the withdrawal shall be to you as if the eternity of bliss were taken away, but you must return at once to the pursuit of it, so that it may return to you. Even so, set a perpetual watch over yourself and your thoughts and let your refuge be in this [vision], in which you abide as constantly as possible. Lord God, be thou praised forever! Amen.

[CHERISH IN YOURSELF THE BIRTH OF GOD]

W here is he that is born king of the Jews?" Now let us see where this birth takes place. It takes place, as I have so often said before, in the soul, exactly as it does in eternity and with no difference, for it is the same birth and occurs in the essence, the core of the soul.

This raises questions. Granted that God is Mind in all things and is more intimate to each than anything is to itself —and more natural—and granted that where God is, knowing himself, he acts by the utterance of his word: what special right has the soul to this act of God more than other creatures of reason, in which he also is? Let us study the distinction.

God in things is activity, reality, and power, but in the soul he is procreative. For creatures are only God's footprints, but by nature, the soul is patterned after God himself. This pattern must be adorned and fulfilled by divine conception and no other creature except the soul is adapted to such a function. In fact, whatever the perfection that may come to the soul, let it be divine light, or grace, or any other blessing, it cannot come except by birth. No other way is possible. Cherish in yourself the birth of God, and with it all goodness and comfort, all rapture, reality, and truth will be yours. Reject it and you reject all goodness and blessing; but given the birth of God, whatever comes your way will bring with it unsullied reality and stability. Whatever you try to get without it will come to nothing, try how you will. It alone gives blessing. All else corrupts. Moreover, in this birth you will have a part in the divine stream [that flows into life] and will share its benefits. But the creature in which God's idea is not to be found is not eligible [to these benefits]. It is the soul that is especially designed for the birth of God and so it occurs exclusively in the soul, where the Father's child is conceived in the core, the inmost recess, where no idea ever glowed or agent of the soul crept in.

The second question is this. Let us say that this act of conception takes place in the core or essence of the soul. It must then take place in the sinner as well as the saint. How, then, does it add grace or benefit me? For [saint or sinner], the cores of their beings are both alike. Indeed, even in hell, the aristocratic element in one's nature persists eternally. But we should notice that the divine birth has the distinctive property of being always accompanied by new light. To the soul it brings a great light, because it is the way of goodness to diffuse itself. In this birth God pours himself into the soul, and the light at the core of the soul grows so strong that it spills out, radiates through the soul's agents, even passing the outward man. This is what happened to Paul when God touched him with light on the road [to Damascus] and spoke to him. A semblance of this light appeared outwardly, so that his companies saw it enveloping Paul as it does with saints. The light in the soul's core overflows into the body, which becomes radiant with it. The sinner is not adapted to this, nor is he worthy of it when he is filled with sin or wickedness, which is a kind of darkness.

As he [John 1] says: "The darkness neither received nor comprehended the light." There is the obstacle! The avenue by which the light ought to get in is littered and barricaded by falseness and darkness, for light and darkness are incompatible, like God and creature. If God is to get in, the creature must get out. This light is well known to man. When one turns to God, a light at once begins to glimmer and shine within, instructing one in what to do and what not to do, and giving lots of intimations of good, of which, previously, one was ignorant and understood nothing.

"How do you know that?" For example, suppose you are moved to turn away from the world. How could such a thing happen without this enlightenment? It is so tender and so delightful that it makes you disdain anything but God or the divine. It coaxes you Godward and you become aware of many good impulses even though you are unaware of their origin. This inward constraint can by no means be due to creatures nor can it be instigated by them, for the effects of creatures and their suggestions come altogether from the outside. Nevertheless, the core of the soul is affected by creatures and the freer you keep yourself from them the more light, truth, and discernment you will have. Therefore, no one will err in anything unless first he loses track of this [inward light] and then puts too much emphasis on externalities.

St. Augustine says: "There are many people who have sought light and truth, but they look for it outside themselves, where it is not." Thus, at last, they get so far off the track that they cannot find their way back to the core of their souls and they never discover the truth, for truth is at the core of the soul and not outside the man. To be enlightened and discerning, cherish the birth of God's Son in the core of the soul and then the soul's agents will be illuminated, and the outward man as well.

When God touches the soul with truth, its light floods the soul's agents and that man knows more than anyone could ever teach him. Thus the prophet says: "I know more than I was ever taught." See! God's Son cannot be born in sinners because this light cannot shine in them. It is incompatible with the darkness of sin because it occurs in the essence of the soul and not in the agents.

Here, too, is another question. If God begets his Son only in the soul's essence, and not in the soul's agents, what have the agents to do with it all? Is their function to be voided by idleness? Of what use is the birth if it does not affect the soul's agents? The question is well put, but let us notice some distinctions.

Each creature works toward some end. That end comes first in its intentions and last in execution. So God, too, intends a blessed end in all his works, that is, in himself. It is the aim of all God does that the agents of the soul should be redirected inward, toward himself, by means of the birth of his Son. He waylays everything in the soul and invites it to his convocation or feast, but if the soul is scattered among its agents and spread out in externalities, the agent of sight in the eyes, of hearing in the ears, of taste in the tongue, then its inward action is feebler because scattered forces do not fulfill [their mission]. Therefore if the inward work of the soul is to be efficient, it must recall its agents and gather them in from their dispersion to one inward effort.

St. Augustine says: "There is more to the soul when it loves than there is when it give life to the body." An illustration: There was once a heathen scholar who was devoted to the study of mathematics and he was sitting by the embers [on his hearth] making the calculation his art required. Then someone came along who did not know that he was a scholar and, brandishing his sword, he said: "Tell me your name. Out with it! Or I'll kill you!" But the scholar was so absorbed that he did not hear what the enemy said, or notice what he threatened to do. And so the enemy shouted at him for some time until, getting no response, he struck off the scholar's head. Now, this was due to a secular pursuit.

How incomparably much more we

ought to be absorbed away from things and focus all our faculties on the contemplation, the knowing of the unique, immeasurable, uncreated, eternal truth! Focus all your intelligence and all your capacities to this end. Turn them on the core of the soul in which all this buried treasure lies, but know, if you wish to do this, that you must drop all other activities and achieve unself-consciousness, in which you will find it.

Another question still. Is it not better for each agent of the soul to continue with its own activity, neither of them hindering the other and none of them hindering God? Can there be not creature-knowledge in me, except it be a hindrance, just as God knows everything and his knowledge does not hinder him—for it is so with the saints. But notice this distinction. The saints see in God an idea, and in that idea all things are comprehended—and the same is true of God, who sees everything in himself. He does not need to turn from one thing to the other, as we do. If, during this life, we always had a mirror before us—a mirror in which we saw everything all at once, and seeing all, knew all, then neither activity nor knowledge would be a hindrance, but as it is, we have to turn from one thing to the other and therefore we cannot pay attention to one without depriving the other. Furthermore, the soul is so bound up with its agents, that where they go the soul must go too and be present when and where they function, overseeing their work, for otherwise nothing would come of what they do. If then the soul goes out to attend to external activities, it will necessarily be the weaker to its inward efforts and for this birth in the soul God will and must have a pure, free, and unencumbered soul, in which there is nothing but him alone, a soul that waits for nothing and nobody but him.

Thus Christ says: "Whosoever loves another more than me and is attached to father and mother and many other things, is not worthy of me. . . . I have not come into the world to bring peace, but the sword, so that I may cut off everything, and separate brother, child, mother and friend who are the real enemies." If your eye sees everything, your ear hears everything, and your heart remembers everything, then truly in all these things your soul is destroyed.

Thus, too, there is an authority who says; "To accomplish the inward act [of God] a person must withdraw all his soul's agents, as it were, into a corner of the soul, and conceal himself from all ideas and forms, and then he may do it." It must be done by means of forgetting and losing self-consciousness. It is in the stillness, in the silence, that the word of God is to be heard. There is no better avenue of approach to this Word than through stillness, through silence. It is to be heard there as it is—in that unself-consciousness, for when one is aware of nothing, that word is imparted to him and clearly revealed.

But you may be saying: "Sir, you make our salvation depend entirely on ignorance. That sounds wrong. God made man so that he could know, as the prophet says: 'Lord, make them to know!' Where there is ignorance there is error and vanity. The ignorant person is brutal. He is an ass and a fool, as long as he remains ignorant." And that is true. But one must achieve this unself-consciousness by means of transformed knowledge. *This* ignorance does not come from lack of knowledge but rather it is from knowledge that one may achieve this ignorance. Then we shall be informed by the divine unconsciousness and in that our ignorance will be ennobled and adorned with supernatural knowledge. It is by reason of this fact that we are made perfect by what happens to us rather than by what we do.

One authority says: "The power of hearing is better than the power of seeing, for one learns more wisdom by listening than by looking, and listening, he learns better to live by wisdom." It is said of a heathen scholar, who lay dying, that his disciples were discussing his great art when he died, and he raised his head and exclaimed: "O let me learn still more of this great art that I may practice it eternally." Hearing brings more into a man, but seeing he gives out more, even in the very act of looking. And therefore we shall all be blessed more in eternal life by our power to hear than by our power to see. For the power to hear the eternal word is within me and the power to see will leave me; for hearing I am passive, and seeing I am active.

Our blessedness doesˉnot depend on the deeds we do but rather on our passiveness to God. For as God is more exalted than creatures, so his work is higher than mine. Indeed, out of his unmeasurable love God has set our blessedness in passivity, in bearing rather than doing, and incomparably more in receiving than in giving. Each of his gifts only prepares us afresh to receive another, a new gift, and more and more gifts. Each divine gift only increases our sensitivity and desire to receive another, which is greater still. On this point, some of the authorities say that in this way the soul is made equal to God. For, just as there is no end to God's gifts, there is no end to the soul's power to receive them. As God is almighty in action, the soul also is boundless in its capacity to take, and thus it is transformed with God and in God. It is necessary that God should both be active and passive in order that he may know and love himself in the soul, and the soul may know as he knows and love as he loves. It is for this reason that the soul is more blessed by what is his than by what is its own, and for this reason its blessing depends more on what he does than on anything we can do.

St. Dionysius' disciples asked him how Timothy came to outstrip them all in perfection. Dionysius replied: "Timothy is a man who is passive to God. He who is skilled in this will outstrip all men." In this sense, your ignorance is not a fault but your chief virtue and your passivity is the chief of your actions. In view of this, you ought to put an end to all your efforts, silence all your faculties, and then you will really discover this birth [of God's Son] in yourself. If you will find him who is born king, pass by everything else you might find and leave it behind. That we *may* pass by and leave behind all that is not pleasing to this king, may he help us, who therefor became the child of man that we might become the children of God. Amen.

GOD ENTERS A FREE SOUL

I have read a text from the Gospel, first in Latin, which means in English: "Our Lord Jesus Christ went into a little castle and was received by a virgin who was a wife."

But notice this text with care! It must necessarily be that the person who received Jesus was a virgin. A virgin, in other words, is a person who is free of irrelevant ideas, as free as he was before he existed. Ye see—someone might ask: How can a person, once born and launched into rational life, be as devoid of ideas as if he did not exist? How can he be free?

Listen to the analysis I shall now make. If I were sufficiently intelligent to comprehend all the ideas ever conceived by man or God himself, and if I were detached from them, so that I did not regard them as mine to take or leave, in either past or future, and if I were free and empty of them in this Now-moment, the present, as it is the blessed will of God for me to be, and if I were perpetually doing God's will, then I would be a virgin in reality, as exempt from idea-handicaps as I was before I was born.

Nevertheless, I assert that being a virgin will not deprive a man of the results of his efforts. Rather, he will be virgin and detached from them and none of them will keep him back from the highest truth—if he, like Jesus, is free and pure and himself virgin. As the authorities say, "like to like" is the condition of unity, so that one must be innocent and virgin if he is to receive the innocent Jesus.

Now stop, look, and listen in earnest. To remain virgin forever is never to bear fruit. To be fruitful, it is necessary to be a wife. "Wife" is the optimum term that may be applied to the soul. It is even above "virgin." That within himself, a man should receive God is good; and receiving God, the man is still virgin. Nevertheless, it is better that God should be fruitful through him, for fruitfulness alone is real gratitude for God's gift and in fruitfulness the soul is a wife, with newborn gratitude, when it bears Jesus back again into the Father's heart.

Many good gifts, received in virginity, are not brought to birth in wifely fruitfulness by which God is gratefully pleased. The gifts decay and come to nothing, so that the man is never blessed or bettered by them. The virgin in him is useless when it does not ripen into the wife who is fruitful. Here is the mischief! It is against this that I have said: "Jesus entered a little castle and was received by a virgin who was a wife." This must needs be so, as I have shown.

Married people seldom bear fruit more than once a year, but now I shall speak of another kind of married persons—those who are married to prayers, fasts, vigils, and all sorts of external disciplines and chastisements. Any devotion to any practice that limits your freedom to wait upon God in this present moment and to follow him into the light, by which he may show you what to do and what not to do—how to be as new and free with each moment as if you had never had, or wanted, or could have another—any such commitment or premeditated practice that limits your freedom—I now call "married life." In it, your soul will bring forth no fruit other than the discipline to which you are so anxiously committed and you will trust neither God nor yourself, until you are finished with it. In other words, you will find no peace, for no one can be fruitful until he is done with his own work. I put this down as an interval [of effort] from which the yield is small, because it has to come out of self-designed bondage and not out of freedom. I call them married who live in this voluntary bondage. They seldom

bear fruit and before God there is little profit in them, as I have explained.

A virgin who is a wife, free and unfettered in affections, is equally near both to God and to self. She brings forth much fruit and is big withal, no less and no more than God himself is. This virgin who is a wife accomplishes this birth, bears fruit every day an hundred- or a thousandfold—yes, she gives birth times without number and bears fruit from the most fertile of soils. To speak plainly, she bears fruit out of the ground in which the Father begets his eternal Word. She is thus fruitful and parturient. For Jesus is the light and shine of the paternal heart (as St. Paul puts it, he is the glory and reflection of the Father's heart—the power shining through). This Jesus is united with her [the virgin soul] and she with him. She is illumined and radiates him as the One and only pure, clear light of the Father.

I have often said before that there is an agent in the soul, untouched by time and flesh, which proceeds out of the Spirit and which remains forever in the Spirit and is completely spiritual. In this agent, God is perpetually verdant and flowering with all the joy and glory that is in him. Here is joy so hearty, such inconceivably great joy that no one can ever fully tell it, for in this agent the eternal Father is ceaselessly begetting his eternal Son and the agent is parturient with God's offspring and is itself the Son, by the Father's unique power.

For this reason, if a person had a whole kingdom or all this world's goods and left it all solely for God's sake, to become the poorest man who ever lived on earth, and if then God gave him as much to suffer as he ever gave any man, and if this person suffered it out until he was dead, and if then, even for the space of a moment, God once let him see what he is in this agent of the soul, all his suffering and poverty would seem like a very little thing beside the joy of it, so great in that moment. Indeed, if afterwards God never gave him the Kingdom of Heaven at all, he would feel sufficiently repaid for all he had suffered, for God himself is in that agent of the soul in that eternal Now-movement.

If the spirit were only always united with God in this agent, a man could never grow old. For the Now-moment, in which God made the first man and the Now-moment in which the last man will disappear, and the Now-moment in which I am speaking are all one in God, in whom there is only one Now. Look! The person who lives in the light of God is conscious neither of time past nor of time to come but only of the one eternity. In fact, he is bereft of wonder, for all things are intrinsic in him. Therefore he gets, nothing new out of future events, nor from chance, for he lives in the Now-moment that is, unfailingly, "in verdure newly clad." Such is the divine glory of this agent in the soul.

There is, however, still another agent, which also is not incarnate but which proceeds out of the spirit, yet remains in it and is always only spiritual. In this second agent, God glows and burns without ceasing, in all his fullness, sweetness, and rapture. Truly, it holds joy so great and rapture so unmeasured that no one can tell it or reveal it. Yet I say that if there were one person who could look into it for a moment and still keep his right mind, all he had ever suffered or that God wished him to suffer would be a very little thing indeed, nothing at all. Nay—I go even further—suffering would be to him always a joy and pleasure.

If you wish to know rightly whether your suffering is yours or of God, you can tell in the following way. If you are suffering because of yourself, whatever the manner, that suffering hurts and is hard to bear. If you suffer for God's sake and for God alone, that suffering does not hurt and is not hard to bear, for God takes the burden of it. If an hundred-weight were loaded on my neck and then someone else took it at once on his neck, I had just as lief it were an hundred as one. It would not then be heavy to me and would not hurt me. To make a long story short, what one suffers through God and for God alone is made sweet and easy.

As I said in the first place, at the beginning of the sermon, "Jesus went into a little castle and was received by a virgin who was a wife." Why? It must needs be that she was a virgin and a wife and I have told you how he was received, but I have not yet told you what the little castle was and that I shall now do.

I have said that there is one agent alone in the soul that is free. Sometimes I have called it the tabernacle of the Spirit. Other times I have called it the Light of the Spirit and again, a spark. Now I say that it is neither this nor that. It is something higher than this or that, as the sky is higher than the earth and I shall call it by a more aristocratic name than I have ever used before, even though it disowns my adulation and my name, being far beyond both. It is free of all names and unconscious of any kind of forms. It is at once pure and free, as God himself is, and like him is perfect unity and uniformity, so that there is no possible way to spy it out.

God blossoms and is verdant in this agent of which I speak, with all the Godhead and spirit of God and there he begets his only begotten Son as truly as if it were in himself. For he lives really in this agent, the Spirit together with the Father giving birth to the Son and in that light, he is the Son and the Truth. If you can only see with my heart, you may well understand what I am saying, for it is true and the Truth itself bespeaks my word.

Look and see: this little castle in the soul is exalted so high above every road [of approach], with such simplicity and uniformity, that the aristocratic agent of which I have been telling you is not worthy to look into it, even once for a moment. No, nor are the other agents, of which I have also spoken, ever able to peek in to where God glows and burns like a fire with all his abundance and rapture. So altogether one and uniform is this little castle, so high above all ways and agencies, that none can ever lead to it—indeed—not even God himself.

It is the truth as God lives. God himself cannot even peek into it for a moment—

or steal into it—in so far as he has particular selfhood and the properties of a person. This is a good point to notice, for the onefold One has neither a manner nor properties. And therefore, if God is to steal into it [the little castle in the soul] it [the adventure] will cost him all his divine names and personlike properties; He would have to forgo all these if he is to gain entrance. Except as he is the onefold One, without ways or properties —neither the Father nor the Holy Spirit in this [personal] sense, yet something that is neither this nor that—See!—it is only as he is One and onefold that he may enter into that One which I have called the Little Castle of the soul. Otherwise he cannot get in by any means or be at home there, for in part the soul is like God—otherwise it would not be possible.

What I have been saying to you is true, as I call on Truth to bear witness and my soul to be the pledge. That we, too, may be castles into which Jesus may enter and be received and abide eternally with us in the manner I have described, may God help us! Amen.

Richard Rolle de Hampole

(1290?-1349)

WHILE a student at Oxford, Richard Rolle came under the influence of the writings of the Fathers of the Church. This was the stimulus which led to his conversion and to his becoming a hermit. At Hampole he became spiritual director of a Cistercian convent. Richard of St. Victor, Bernard, and Bonaventura left their influence on Richard Rolle, although his mysticism by its practical tone is individualistic. With a heart filled with love—similar to the experience of Francis of Assisi—his writings and preaching glorified God's love and saintly purity.

Richard's most famous work is *The Pricke of Conscience*, but "Song of Love" can well be called the theme of his mystical writings. To his friends he said, "Let us love burningly!" This short selection appears in *Richard Rolle, Selected Works*, edited and translated by George C. Heseltine. It is used by permission of Longmans, Green & Co.

SONG OF LOVE

My song is a sighing, my life is spent in longing for the sight of my King, so fair in His brightness.

So fair in Thy beauty! Lead me to Thy light, and feed me on Thy love! Make me to grow swiftly in love and be Thou Thyself my prize.

When wilt Thou come, Jesus my joy, to save me from care and give Thyself to me, that I may see Thee evermore?

Could I but come to Thee, all my desires were fulfilled. I seek nothing but Thee alone, who art all my desire.

Jesus my Saviour! My comforter! Flower of all beauty! My help and my succour! When may I see Thee in Thy majesty?

When wilt Thou call me? I languish for Thy presence, to see Thee above all things. Let not Thy love for me fail! In my heart I see the canopy that shall cover us both.

Now I grow pale and wan for love of my beloved Jesus both God and man. Thy love did teach me when I ran to Thee, wherefore now I know how to love Thee.

I sit and sing of the love-longing that is bred in my breast. Jesus! Jesus! Jesus! Why am I not led to Thee?

Full well I know Thou seest my state. My thought is fixed upon love. When I shall see Thee and dwell with Thee, then shall I be filled and fed.

Jesus, Thy love is constant and Thou knowest best how to love me. When shall my heart break forth to come to Thee, my rest?

Jesus, Jesus, Jesus! I mourn for Thee! When may I turn hence to Thee, my life and my living?

Jesus, my dear and my darling! My delight is to sing of Thee. Jesus my mirth and my melody! When wilt Thou come, my king?

Jesus, my salvation and my sweetness, my hope and my comfort! Jesus, I desire to die whenever it shall please Thee. The longing that my Love has sent to me overwhelms me.

All woe is gone from me, since my breast has been inflamed with the love of Christ so sweet, whom I will never leave, but do promise to love always.

For love can cure my evil and bring me to His bliss, and give me Him for whom I sigh, Jesus, my love, my sweeting.

A longing has come upon me that binds me day and night until I shall see His face so fair and bright.

Jesus, my hope, my salvation, my only joy! Let not Thy love cool, let me feel Thy love and dwell with Thee in safety.

Jesus, with Thee alone I am great. I would rather die than possess all this world and have power over it.

When wilt Thou pity me, Jesus, that I may be with Thee, to love Thee and look upon Thee?

Do Thou ordain for me my settle and sit me thereon, for then we can never part.

And I shall sing of Thy love, in the light of the brightness of Heaven for ever and ever. Amen.

Johannes Tauler

(1300?-1361)

ALTHOUGH lacking the intellectual virility of his teacher, Meister Eckhart, Johannes Tauler is considered the most staunch of the German mystics. Broad in his practical love of humanity and deep in his spiritual love of God, he was ready to criticize the corruption within the Church, but he did not sway from the orthodox beliefs of his time.

He was a Dominican monk, but in 1339 was driven from Strasbourg to Basel with other monks who suspended mass when the interdict of Pope John XXII involving the inquisition of the "spirituals" was enforced. During the bubonic plague, 1348-49, Tauler was a great source of help to the distressed.

In his sermons he attempted to make men aware of their transcendent spiritual heritage, which he taught lay mainly in their inner fellowship with God. As a well-balanced, practical man, without either the brilliance or the ecstasy common to other mystics, Tauler was a "Friend of God" who possessed something of the spirit of the Reformation before it occurred. The three sermons reprinted here are from *The Inner Way,* a translation by Arthur Wollaston Hutton of selected sermons by Tauler.

ON THE EXALTATION OF THE HOLY CROSS

THE FIRST SERMON

And I, if I be lifted up from the earth, will draw all things unto Myself."

To-day we celebrate the Festival of the Exaltation of the Holy Cross, on which hung, out of love, the Salvation of the World. We must be born again, through the Cross, into the true nobility which was ours in eternity. We must be born and revived there again by love for this Cross. Words cannot describe the merits of the Cross. Our Lord said: "I, if I be lifted up from the earth, will draw all things unto Me." By this He signifies that He wishes to draw to Himself our worldly hearts, and our love for and gratification in worldly things, which we had gladly possessed in the creature, and our haughty minds, which were well satisfied with ourselves, and with our worldly-mindedness and love, in the temporal gratification of our senses. All this He will draw unto Himself, that He may be thus exalted, and that He may become great in us and in our hearts; for to the man to whom God has ever been great, all creatures seem small, and fleeting pleasures are as nothing.

This health-giving Cross signifies the Noble Man, Christ, Who is exalted far above our imagination, above Saints and Angels, and above all the joy, bliss and blessedness that they enjoy together; and, as His true place is in the Highest, He desires to dwell also in our highest places, that is in our uppermost and innermost love and desires. He will draw up the lowest powers to the highest, and lead the lowest with the highest unto Himself. If we do this, He will draw us after Himself into His highest and most secret place. For thus it must needs be; if I am to come to Him, I must receive Him into myself. So much of mine, so much of His; it is an equal bargain.

Oh! How often this Holy Cross is quite forgotten, so that this ground and secret place is quite closed up and refused to God, while favour and love are shown to the creature; which, sad to say, in these dangerous times, reigns supreme both in worldly and religious people, so that their hearts are lost in the creature. This is the most grievous pity that man's heart and mind can conceive; and, if he only knew how it would end, he would wither up in terror of the vengeance of God. But it is as much unheeded as though it were all mockery. It has, also, become the custom, and men approve of it, and call it an honour, and it is all as though it were a play. The Saints, if they could, would cry aloud and weep tears of blood, and the Wounds of our Lord would be torn open again by this misery; that a heart, for which He gave His beautiful Life and His loving Holy Spirit, should be so shamelessly taken from Him, while He is driven forth. Children, do not think that these are my words only; all Scripture teaches you this: "No man can serve two masters. For he will hate the one and love the other." Jesus says: "If thine eye offend thee, pluck it out and cast it from thee;" and elsewhere: "Where thy treasure is, there is thy heart also." Now, find out how much God has of thy heart; whether He is thy Treasure. St. Augustine says: "Lovest thou the earth, thou art also of the earth; for the soul is more with that which she loveth, than where she gives life to the body." St. Paul says: "If I should deliver my body to be burned, and should speak with the tongues of men and of Angels, and should give all my goods to feed the poor, and yet not have charity, it profiteth me nothing."

Now, dear sisters, ye ought, with great and adoring thankfulness and active love, to accept the grace which God has given to your Order through the Sacrament of the Body of the Lord. I desire, also, with all my heart and soul, that this practice should not be allowed to grow slack nor fall asleep in these anxious times; for nature will not long endure; ye must cleave firmly to God, or ye will fall away. Mark, it was not thus in days gone by; therefore, these people ought to exercise great and powerful self-restraint, that they may be preserved from this dangerous state. Do not imagine that this only need be done to attain to a state of great perfection: "They that are in health need not a physician, but they that are ill." It is necessary, on account of man's human weakness, that he should be protected by God's help, and preserved from the sad state of things which prevails widely amongst religious people. Therefore, none should speak as though they had attained to great perfection or did great deeds. It is sufficient, if they keep the rules of their Order, as far as they can, and mean to do so, and that they have permission to leave undone that which they cannot do. No great powers of reason are necessary for this. It will suffice, if they desire to do willingly that which is right, and if their eyes are so far opened that they will be able to guard themselves against this grievous wrong, and if they keep their eyes open. For this reason, our young sisters should go often and willingly to receive the Lord's Body. I excuse and also answer for our dear elder sisters, for they went very reverently in days gone by, when the flesh was not so weak as now; and they kept their Order very strictly, and loved and obeyed the rules. They also readily kept up the good old custom of communicating every fortnight. Their great sanctity and perfection were sufficient; for in those days things were better than now, and less harmful to the fallen nature to be found in young people, whose inclinations are stronger now than they were then. Therefore much more help is needed now than then; and without great self-restraint it is impossible to endure in the highest state. Now everything sinks down to the level of animal pleasures, and the desires of the senses. Therefore, dear sisters, I require of you no great perfection and sanctity, only that ye should feel joy in and love for our Holy Order, and that ye should intend to keep the rules as far as ye can, and that ye should willingly keep silence in all places where it is ordained—at table and in the choir, and that ye should withdraw yourselves willingly from all human intimacies that estrange you from God. The old are impelled to do so by holiness, and the young by modesty. For if ye do this devoutly, God will reveal himself to you, while ye flee from all the causes that could bring this hurt to your souls. Learn, that intolerable sufferings have fallen upon some convents; and, if they had not exercised themselves very diligently in this discipline, they might have been brought to nought. If ye experience no sweetness, do not let this terrify you. If man does his part, and yet feels forsaken in his heart, it is far better for him, than any feelings or experiences would be that he could have. This bitter grief brings him nearer to the Source of Living Truth than any feelings. Our Lord said: "My God, my God, why hast Thou forsaken Me?" and on Mount Olivet; "Not as I will, but as Thou wilt."

Children, fear not, for our Lord says: "If any man will come after Me . . . let him take up his Cross and follow Me."

This Cross signifies the crucified Jesus, Who ought to be and must be born. St. Paul says: "They that are Christ's have crucified the flesh with all its lusts." These lusts must be tamed and restrained.

The second power is the power of anger, which man should be able to control in all things. He should always think that another is more likely to be right than he, and thus avoid strife. He must learn forbearance, and how to be quiet and kindly wherever he may be. One man may be sitting alone, or in an assembly, while others are sitting there, who are noisy and seldom silent. Ye must learn to be forbearing and to endure, and to commune with your own hearts. A man cannot work at a trade without having learnt it. If anyone wanted to be an umbrella-maker, and would not learn his trade, he might do great harm to the work if he tried to carry it on before he had learned it; thus it is in all adversities, we must learn how to struggle.

The two other powers, by which this noble Cross must be borne, are not so evident; they are the powers of reason, and of inwardly spiritual desires. Thus, in short, Christ must be born in us and of us, in the inner and outer man; and thus we shall be born again in Him, in the Fruit of His Spirit. As it is written: "Ye must be as new-born babes." Dear children, if ye live thus, every day will be consecrated; and all your sins will be forgiven you in this birth of the Holy Cross. Amen.

THE SECOND SERMON

"And I, if I be lifted up from the earth, will draw all things unto Myself."

To-day we celebrate the Exaltation of the Holy Cross, whose worth it is impossible to describe, and to which all the honour that we can conceive is due, because we give it to Him, Who died thereon. Therefore religious people take up the Cross, and begin to fast according to their rule; and this is a thing worth doing by all who have it in their power.

Now, we are told how a Christian king once took the Holy Cross to a Pagan king, with all the honour and dignity that his dominions could produce, in accordance with his rank, though not in accordance with the honour due to the Holy Cross; and he wanted to go to Jerusalem. When he arrived before the gates, they closed themselves by means of a strong, thick wall; and an Angel, who was standing on the wall, said: "Thou comest here with the Cross, riding in great pomp; and yet He, who died thereon, was driven forth in great sorrow and shame, barefoot, and carrying the Cross on His back." Then the king threw himself from his horse, tore off all his clothes, save his shirt, and bore the Holy Cross on his back. Then the gates opened of themselves, and he bore it into the city, where many wonderful signs were done, on the sick, the lame and the blind.

Our Lord said: "I, if I be lifted up . . . will draw all things unto Me." As St. Gregory says: "Man is all things, for he has a likeness with all things." Many men may be found, who find the Cross, and are drawn to it by manifold sufferings and much discipline, that God may thus draw them to Himself; but this suffering must be lifted up; as we to-day celebrate the Exaltation of the Holy Cross, so it must not only be found but also lifted up. If man would only examine himself, and commune with his own heart, he would find the Cross twenty times a day in many a painful suggestion and fall, whereby, were he alone, he would be crucified; but he does not lift it up, and thus he wrongs it. All the burdens of the Cross should be lifted up in God, and willingly accepted by man as his Cross, both without and within, in the body and in the spirit. Thus man should be drawn to God, Who desires to draw all things unto Himself, as He said when He was about to be lifted up.

Now, men may be found, who outwardly bear this Cross, disciplining themselves well externally, and bearing the burden of their Order. They sing, they read, they go to the choir, or to the refectory; and thus, with the outer man, carry on small services for our Lord. Do ye imagine that ye were created and made for that only by God? He desires also to have you for His especial Friends. Now such men bear the Cross externally, but they carefully protect themselves from its entrance into themselves, and seek distraction wherever they can. They do not carry the Cross with our Lord, but with Simon Rufus who was compelled to carry it. But even bearing it thus is very good; for it protects them indeed from many vices and from levity, and it saves them from the terrible fires of purgatory, and possibly from an eternity in hell.

Now, our dear Lord says that He "will draw all things unto Himself." He who desires to draw things must first collect them and then draw them. This our Lord does also; He first gathers up all man's wanderings, the dissipation of his senses, his powers, his words and works, and inwardly, all his thoughts and intentions, his imaginations, his desires and pleasures and his understanding. Then, when all are collected, God draws the man to Himself. For, first of all ye must cast off all to which ye cling externally and internally in your gratifications. This casting off is a weary Cross, and the heavier and stronger the clinging is, the heavier the Cross will also be. For all the pleasure and delight that ye have in the creature, however holy and divine it may appear to be, or is called, or as it may seem to thee—all must be cast off, if thou desirest to be truly lifted up and drawn to God. This is the first and lowest grade in the outer man.

If ye desire to raise the Cross in the inner man, it is necessary that all inner delights should be withdrawn from him, all clinging to spiritual pleasures, and even from those which arise out of virtue. The Schoolmen dispute as to whether man should make use of any virtue; it ought to be used fruitfully and only in God's service. These things cannot, indeed, exist without pleasure; but it should be without any addition of self. What do ye imagine that pleasure and satisfaction consist of? That a man willingly fasts, watches, prays and carries out the rules of his Order? This pleasure our Lord would have nothing to do with; He desired that I should act rightly towards my Order. Why do ye imagine that God seldom allows a day or a night to pass by like that which preceded it, and that what helped you in meditation yesterday, does not help you at all to-day or to-morrow, and that many imaginations and ideas come to you with no results? Take thy Cross from God and suffer, and then it will become a blissful Cross. How couldest thou otherwise carry it to God, and receive it from Him in true resignation, and thank God for it, and say with our dear Lady: "My soul doth magnify the Lord, and my spirit hath rejoiced in God my Saviour" for thou must thus praise and glorify God in everything.

Man must always have a Cross; it was necessary that Christ should suffer before He entered into His Glory. Whatever thou mayest encounter in thy inmost heart, either in seeing or tasting, let it alone, do not meddle with it, ask not what it is, but fall back upon thy nothingness. Our Lord said: "If any man will come after Me, . . . let him take up his Cross and follow Me." It is not in comfort, but with the Cross that we must follow God. The Holy Apostle, St. Andrew, said: "I welcome thee, thou much-to-be-desired Cross, for I have longed for thee with all my heart. Take me from amongst men, and give me again to my Master." This must not take place one day and not on the next; but it must go on at all times, unceasingly; thou must ever be examining thyself in all things. Yea, though the number of thy sins and transgressions be great; if thou fallest seventy times a day, yet turn and come again to God, and pass on so quickly to God that thy sin will escape thy memory, and when thou comest to confession thou wilt not be able to say what it was. This should not terrify thee; it did not come to pass for thy hurt, but to show thee thy nothingness, and to make thee feel contempt for thyself. Ye should do all calmly, and not dejectedly, if ye feel that in your hearts ye are ready and prepared to do the Will of God. Man is not sinless, as our dear Lady was, therefore he must

be content to bear all this suffering and this Cross. St. Paul says: "We know that to them that love God, all things work together unto good;" the gloss adds "and sin also." Hold thy peace, flee unto God, and look upon thy nothingness; stay at home, do not run at once to thy confessor. St. Matthew followed God at once, and leaving all his affairs unsettled; and, if thou findest that thou hast sinned, do not make thy Cross too heavy outwardly. Leave it to truth, and be faithful and at rest; for none will be condemned except those who wantonly turn to temporal things; while to those who delight in the love of God, and think only of Him, everything will prove a discipline.

Yet, I must warn you in all faithfulness that, if ye willingly allow yourselves to be possessed by the creature, and give it place, it will most assuredly cause your condemnation; and, even if God gives you true repentance, though this is uncertain, yet ye will have to suffer in the awful fires of purgatory. If ye realised it, ye might shrivel up in great fear and anxiety; and if ye went thus to receive the Lord's Body, ye would be acting just as if thou wert to take a young and tender child and tread it underfoot in a miry path. And yet this is done to the living Son of God, Who, out of love, has given Himself for us. Thus ye go to confessions, and do not guard yourselves against the cause of your sin. The Pope with all his Cardinals could not absolve you; for yours is no true repentance, and ye are guilty of the Holy Body of our Lord.

Our Lord said: "If any man will come after Me, let him deny himself and take up his Cross and follow Me." This self-denial and this Cross are held before many a Friend of God, who is driven towards it, so that we cannot say how a man ought to forget himself and deny himself in all the circumstances that may arise. That which costs nothing is worthless. "He who soweth sparingly, shall also reap sparingly" and "with what measure you mete, it shall be measured to you again," but no one should think of this, but solely of God. What will become of all those of whom ye might be told, who will not leave their old ways and customs, but who cleave externally to that which is real to their senses? Thou must forsake thyself and die utterly to thyself. He said: "Follow thou Me." The servant does not go before his master; he follows after him. Not according to the servant's will, but according to the will of the master. No other teaching is necessary for us, if we only take heed how little, in this world, servants can follow their own will; but how they must use all their diligence and all their strength in carrying out in all ways their master's will and service. A grain of wheat must die before it can bring forth fruit, and so must thou also die absolutely to thy own will. Man ought therefore to give up himself and his own will entirely to God; and, when he thus gives himself from his heart to God, he ought to be as though he possessed no will. A virgin stood in the choir and sang: and said: "Lord, this time is mine and Thine, but, if I commune with my own heart, my time is Thine not mine."

If man is to give himself to God, he must first of all give up his own will entirely, for man is just as though he were formed of three men: his animal nature, in which he is guided by his senses; his powers of reason; and his highest nature, which is in the Image and Likeness of God. In his highest and innermost nature man should turn and lie down in the fire of the Divine Abyss, and come out of himself, and allow himself to be taken prisoner. He should suppress and pass over the two lowest ways and natures, as St. Bernard says: "Man must draw away his animal nature, with the lusts of the flesh, from all the things that he possessed with delight." Ye know what a hard Cross that is, and how heavy it is! And he says, that it is no less hard for the outer man to enter into the inner man, and to pass, from things that are figurative and visible, to the invisible, that is to their very Source, as St. Augustine understands it. All the attacks and the crosses, that, coming to the two lower natures of man, seem to him as though they would draw him away and hinder him from entering, should be taken up by him as his Cross, while he commends all to God. Whether they come from the senses or from reason, he should leave them all alone, and commend them to the lower powers. And he should raise himself above them in the highest power with all his might; just as Abraham left the ass and the servant below, when he went up the mountain to offer his sacrifice unto God; he went up alone with his son into the mountain. Therefore, leave your animal nature which is indeed an ass, and your servant, which is natural reason, which is here surely a servant, for it has served, and guide man up the ascent of this mountain; for there he must stay. Leave the two below, and go up alone with the son, that is with thy mind, into the secret place, the Holy of Holies. Offer up thy sacrifice, and especially offer up thyself, and enter in, and hide there thy secret mind in the mystery of the Divine Abyss. As the prophet said in the Psalter: "Lord, Thou shall hide them in the secret of Thy Face." In that secret place the created spirit is brought back again to its uncreatedness, where it had been from everlasting before it was created, and where it recognised itself as God in God, and yet in itself as of the creature, and created. But in God all things are God, who rest on this foundation. Proclus says: "When man once enters here, whatever may befall the outer man, sorrow, poverty or whatever it may be, he heeds it not." As the Prophet says; "Thou shalt hide them . . . from the disturbance of men." These follow our Lord, as our Lord says elsewhere: "I am in the Father, and He is in Me, and I in you and ye in Me." That we may be drawn with all our hearts, as He desired to draw all things after Him, and that we may thus inherit the Cross, that by the Holy Cross we may enter into the true Source, may God help us. Amen.

THE THIRD SERMON

"I was exalted like a cedar in Libanus, and as a cypress-tree on Mount Sion."

We celebrate to-day the Exaltation of the Holy Cross; but it is impossible to say how it was raised up; neither can we fully describe or imagine its value. We can say of it that which we find written in the Book of Ecclesiasticus: "I was exalted like a cedar in Libanus, and as a cypress-tree on Mount Sion."

Frankincense grows on Mount Lebanon; it signifies a spiritual sacrifice, for it should at all times be the desire of our hearts to be a peculiar sacrifice unto God. The smoke of the cedar-tree drives away all the poison of the serpent. Still more the poison of the Devil and all his wicked cunning is chased away by the power of the Holy Cross; that is by the bitter Sorrow and sharp Suffering of our Lord Jesus Christ; for He says of Himself: "I was exalted like a cypress-tree on Mount Sion." The cypress is of such a nature, that if a man partakes of the wood, when unable to retain his food, it enables him to retain it. In the same way, the man who draws unto himself the Lord's Holy Cross, and embraces it, namely, His painful and bitter Suffering, will be enabled to retain that most precious and noble Food, the Holy Word of God. The holy Saints and Prophets have said that the Word of God only becomes fruitful in those men, who at all times draw it earnestly and diligently unto themselves, that all things may become fruitful unto them. The precious Sufferings of our Lord have also a sweet scent, tasting sweeter than any sweetness; for they draw man's heart to Him; as our Lord Himself has said: "And I, if I be lifted up . . . will draw all things to Myself." It is indeed true, that the man in whom the bitter Suffering of our Lord is always found, will at all times be drawn unto our Lord, in true humility, and patience, and with fervent and Divine Love. For in the same way that Christ suffered willingly, so must we also at all times, as far as lies in our power, follow after Him earnestly, in patience and suffering, that we may always be imprisoned, bound and condemned with Him in spirit.

Our Lord Jesus Christ, before He was nailed to the Holy Cross, was bereft of all His garments, so that not a thread was left on His Body; and lots were cast for His garments before His eyes. Now, know of a truth, that if thou desirest ever to come to true perfection, thou must be destitute of all that is not of God, so that thou hast not a thread left; and thou must see lots cast for thy things before thine eyes; while other men look upon it all, and esteem it as mockery, folly and heresy. Our Lord said: "If any man will come after Me, let him . . . take up his Cross, and follow Me." For it is written in the Apocalypse that great and unutterable plagues must come, which will be scarcely less terrible than the Judgment Day; though that will not come yet, for we are still living in historic time, days, years and hours. And when these plagues, which are prophesied, come upon us, those only will recover who bear the Cross. And because this was true, God gave the Angel leave to hurt and to destroy all that was upon the earth. Then God said to the Angel: "Thou shalt spare none, save those who have the banner, the mark, the sign on their foreheads," signifying the Holy Cross. Every man who has not the Cross of Jesus Christ in him and before him, undoubtedly, will not be spared. By the Cross we understand pain. God did not tell the Angel to spare men with great powers, nor the seers, nor those who worked in their own way, but only the suffering. He did not say: "He, who will follow Me, or come after Me, must follow Me, gazing at Me," but he said, "by leaving all and suffering."

Now I wish to say a few words about the Cross. Know, then, that every man who takes up the Cross will be made thereby the very best man to be found in these days; and no plagues can harm him. Neither can he ever enter into purgatory. But also there is no greater pain than daily and hourly carrying a Cross on our backs for the sake of God, in humble resignation. It is, alas! no longer the fashion to suffer for the sake of God, and to bear the Cross for Him; for the diligence and real earnestness, that perchance were found in man, have been extinguished and have grown cold; and now no one is willing any longer to suffer distress for the sake of God. Could we find out any way in which no one would have to suffer, that is what we should choose for our life. Alas! one and all think only of self, in all their works and ways.

It is not outward exercises, such as fasting, watching, lying on hard beds, and making long pilgrimages, that please God. All these things serve thereto; fasting, watching, prayer, and all the other things already mentioned; therefore, do all these things, as far as they will help thee to take up thy Cross truly. No one is too old, too ill and too deaf to take up the Cross, and to carry it after our Lord Jesus Christ.

Learn that the Holy Cross is made of four pieces of wood, one above, one below, and two in the middle. The upper part is divine, fervent love. The left arm, which is deep humility, is nailed on with the heedlessness of men, and all the things that may befall him then; it is more than scorn, for in that there is a tinge of pride; the other arm of the Cross must be real, true, inner purity, this must be nailed to the Cross with a willing lack of all, whatever it may be, that could defile its purity, either outwardly or inwardly. The feet signify true and perfect obedience; they are nailed on with true and willing resignation of all that thou and thine possess. Whatever it may be that thou possessest, leave all at once for the sake of God, however hard it may be, that thou mayest not possess thyself in any way, either in deed or in word. The four parts of the Cross were fastened together in the middle with *fiat voluntas tua*, which means that the pieces of wood were fitted into each other, signifying the true and perfect renunciation of thy free will, and a yielding up of all for the sake of God.

Now notice, first, the left hand, which signifies humility. By this we must understand, as St. Augustine says, that the man who walks in true humility will most certainly have to suffer. Know, that man must be brought to nought in his own esteem, and in the eyes of all men.

He must also be raised up, bare, and having no restingplace, and lots must be cast before his eyes for all that he has or is; as was done with the garments of our Lord Jesus Christ; that is, thou must be mocked, destroyed and spurned. Thy life also must be regarded as unworthy of notice, as folly, so that those who are with thee or pass thee by, will scorn and condemn thee, will estimate and judge thy life before thy face, as full of error and heresy; and hate thee and all thy works and ways. Now, when thou knowest and seest all this, thou must neither reject it, nor receive it unthankfully, so that thou speakest evil, or shouldest say of it: "Such a man as he is unfair to me." Dear friend, guard thyself both outwardly and inwardly against such opposition. Thou oughtest to think: "Alas! I, poor man, am unworthy that such a noble man should scorn and ignore me;" and then thou shouldest bow to it and look upon it as nothing. Thus thou wilt be bearing the Cross with our Lord. The right hand is true purity; it is nailed on with a willing lack of all things that are not of God, and that could stain that purity. The feet are true obedience, and signify that man should be obedient to his Superiors and the Holy Church. They are nailed on with true resignation, so that man will willingly in all things resign himself to the Will of God. The middle part is the free going out and giving up of thy will to the Will of God; which means, however great the suffering may be which is laid upon thee by God or man, thou wilt yet willingly suffer all for love of God, and rejoice, and bend willingly to the Cross of suffering, whether guilty or innocent. Now, thou mightest say: "Lord, I cannot do it, I am too weak." Learn then, that thou hast two wills, an upper and a lower will, as Christ also had two wills. The natural and lower will desires at all times to be freed from the Cross; but the higher says with Christ: "Not as I will but as Thou wilt in all things." The top of the Cross is the Love of God; it has no resting-place, for at all times it is a pure, bare going forth, forsaken of God and all creatures, so that thou canst truly say with Christ: "My God, My God, why hast Thou forsaken Me?" The Sacred Head of our Lord Jesus Christ had no resting-place; if a man experienced Divine Love and a sweet consciousness of God's Presence in his absolute resignation, what would it matter to him though the whole world were against him?

A good and holy man asked our Lord why He allowed His dear Friends to suffer so terribly. Then our Lord said: "Man is naturally inclined to the pleasures of the senses and harmful delights; therefore I hedge him in, in all his ways, so that I alone may be his delight." The Head of Divine, sweet Love hung inclined on the stem of the Holy Cross. Learn, children, it cannot be otherwise; though we try to turn it as we may, we must always bear a Cross, if we desire to be good men and to come to Eternal Life. We must suffer sharply and keenly, and bear a Cross of some kind, for, if we flee from one, another will fall upon us. No man has ever been born, who was such a good talker that he could prove that this was not true. Thou canst flee where thou wilt, and do what thou wilt, yet it must be borne. God may take it on His shoulder for a little while, and bear the burden over the most difficult places; and then man feels so light and free, that he cannot believe that he ever had anything to suffer, especially because he feels no suffering; but, as soon as God lays down the burden, the burden of suffering rests heavily on him again, in all its bitterness and insupportability. The Eternal Son of God, Jesus Christ, has borne all this before, in the heaviest way possible; and all those who have been His dearest Friends have borne it after Him. This Cross is the fiery chariot in which Elias went up to heaven.

There was a thoughtful daughter of our Order who had longed much and often to see our Lord as a Babe. Suddenly, during her devotions, our Lord appeared to her as a Babe, lying swathed in a bed of sharp thorns, so that she could not get to the Babe till she had laboured much, and had used force, in grasping the thorns. When she came to herself again she realised that those who truly desire Him must boldly face pain, sharpness and suffering.

Some men say: "Yea, and were I so pure and innocent, that I had not deserved it from God on account of my sins, still I would gladly and joyfully bear suffering for the Will of God, so that it might be useful and profitable to me." Now, know, that a guilty and sinful man may suffer, in such a way, that it may be more useful and profitable to him than to an innocent man. But how? In the same way, that a man, who wants to make a great jump, will go back that he may have a good run; for the further he goes back, the further he will jump. Every man should act in this way. He must always look upon himself as sinful and heedless, and must judge of himself as unworthy in the sight of God and of all creatures. Thus he will be drawn nearer and more powerfully to God, and by this means he will get closer to the Eternal Goodness of Divine Truth.

Children, the more thoroughly a man knows himself from the bottom of his heart, truly despising and condemning himself, not glossing over his sins, but deeming himself utterly unworthy, the nearer will he draw to God in truth, and the more perfect will be his converse with God.

That we may all draw this precious Cross of our Lord after us, in steadfast patience and with loving hearts, with happy countenances, cheerfully, joyfully and willingly suffering all things for God, giving up all things for Him, and accepting all things that are disagreeable to us as from the open, loving Hand of God and not from the creature; that we may be lifted up in our hearts in steadfast patience even unto the end, may He help us, Who for our sakes was lifted up upon the Cross that He might draw all things unto Himself. Amen.

Heinrich Suso

(1300?-1366)

AMANDUS VON BERG, deeply devoted to his saintly mother, took her maiden name, becoming Heinrich Suso. At thirteen he entered a Dominican monastery; at twenty-eight he came under the stimulus of Meister Eckhart; until forty he practiced rigid asceticism. With Eckhart and Tauler he became a leader of the "Friends of God" in fourteenth-century Germany. Evelyn Underhill, writing of him in *Mysticism*, says: "To Suso, subjective, romantic, deeply interested in his own soul and his personal relation with God, mysticism was not so much a doctrine to be imparted to other men, as an intimate personal adventure." These maxims, which are taken from his writings, are spiritual guideposts to show how the inner spirit directs the outer acts of man.

His last years were spent in a Dominican monastery at Ulm.

[SELECTED MAXIMS]

Let thy walk be an interior one, and be not given to break out either in words or in thy walk.

Act according to the truth in simplicity, and, whatever happens, be not helpful to thyself; for he who helps himself too much will not be helped by the truth.

When thou art with men pay no heed to what thou seest or hearest, and cleave to that alone which has shown itself to thee (i.e., remember God alone who has shown himself to thee under these outward things).

Be careful that in thy actions thy reason goes first; for when the sensual appetite gets the start, every evil comes of it.

God wishes not to deprive us of pleasure; but he wishes to give us pleasure in its totality; that is to say, all pleasure.

The more mightily thou humblest thyself, the higher thou shalt be exalted.

He who wishes to dwell in his inmost interior must rid himself of all multiplicity. We must habitually reject all that is not one thing.

Where the sensual appetite is the moving principle of a man's actions, there is toil, suffering, and mental darkness.

What greater pleasure is there than to find myself the one thing that I ought to be, and the whole thing that I ought to be? (i.e., one with God, who is one and all.)

A man should remain stedfast in his state of freedom from mental images, and of self-restraint. Herein lies the greatest delight.

In what does a truly detached man exercise himself? In annihilating himself.

When a man detaches himself from himself without allowing the sensual appetite to break out, he destroys self. If he acted otherwise, he would be helping himself by means of his sensual appetite.

When our love is given to a sensible image or person, it is accident, loving accident, and this we have no right to do; nevertheless I bear with myself in this until I get quit of it. It is, however, an interiorly simple act, when a man does not love the image which is present to him, but when all things are to him one, and that one is God.

Keep thy feelings within thee both in weal and wo; for a man who does this loves more in one year than one who lets his feelings break out, loves in three.

Some men are to be met with who have had an interior drawing from God, and have not followed it. The interior and exterior of these men are far apart, and it is in this that many fail.

Take heed not to break out exteriorly in a way unlike the (divine and interior) pattern.

A man should be on his guard against the inclination which leads him to catch at everything which may save him from having to yield to the invitations of the simple truth. If thou wilt not submit to be simple, thou wilt have to submit to be manifold.

Wilt thou be of use to all creatures, turn thyself away from all creatures.

Live as if there were no creature on earth but thee.

Nature loves nature and makes itself its aim. Some men's nature has not been sufficiently crusht, and when this happens, they continue exterior.

The power of refraining from things gives a man more power than would the possession of the things.

One deflection from the right course brings along with it another.

See that nature in thee is unburdened, and that thy outward man is conformable to thy inward man.

Look well to the inward man; for on this depends thy exterior and interior life.

It belongs to perfect detachment to keep nature at all times bridled.

A man should never lose sight of himself, lest nature should run away.

Thou lamentest that thou art still too active, undetached, and impatient. Nevertheless, despair not. The more keenly thou feelest this, the better.

Perishable love is a root of all vices, and a cloak of all truth.

The setting of the sensual nature is the rising of the truth. When the powers of the soul have ceased to work, and the elements have been purified, the powers remain fixt upon their eternal object, if they have been directed toward it according to their ability.

To be worsted is to gain the victory in the estimation of God's friends (Matt. 5:39).

There is nothing pleasurable save what is uniform with the most inmost depths of the divine nature.

Our nature in its present state is richly endowed. The more it goes out of itself, the further it is from God; and the more it turns inward the nearer to him it is.

He who has attained to the purification of the senses in God performs so much the better all the operations of the senses.

If a man subjects his nature, when it has been purified, to the truth, his nature is guided in such sort that it performs much more perfectly all exterior actions. Otherwise it wastes itself upon temporal matters, and can do nothing really well.

Purity, intelligence, and virtue give a feeling of wealth to those who possess them. When the sensible possession of these virtues is withdrawn from such persons by God, it sometimes happens that they die to all creatures. Those who profit by this withdrawal are brought nigher to God by it.

What is that which drives a man to pursue evil courses? It is the craving for something which may satisfy him. Yet we can only find this in abnegation, and not in evil courses.

The reason why some men so often fall into a faulty sadness is that they do not at all times keep an eye upon themselves to avoid in everything doing what deserves punishment.

If a man can not comprehend the matter, let him be passive, and the matter will comprehend him.

Abide within thyself. The plea of seeking things outside thee presents itself as a necessity; but it is only a way of helping self.

Remain stedfast in thyself until thou art drawn out of thyself without any act of thine.

We should not move until we have observed whether it be God or nature that is working in us.

Take care that nature works in thee its works from out itself without the concurrence of other causes.

A truly detached man should attend to four things. First, he should be very virtuous in his walk, that things may flow from him without him. Secondly, he should also be virtuous and quiet with regard to his senses, and not carry tales hither and thither, for this is calculated to fill his mind with images. Thus his interior senses will be able to act inactively. Thirdly, he should not be given to attach himself; and he should take care that there is nothing heterogeneous in him. Fourthly, he should not be contentious, but he should behave lovingly to those by whom God may be pleased to purify him.

All the powers have one object and one work, and this is to be conformed to the eternal truth.

It is bad to begin many things and to bring none to an end.

Observe whether the intimacy between good people arises from inclination or from simplicity. The first is far too common.

Offer not thyself too much to anyone. Those please least who offer most.

An interior humble walk beseems thee. When a thing acts in opposition to its nature, it is always unbecoming to it.

Happy the man whose words and ways are few. The more words and ways there are in any man, the more there is of what is accidental. Stay within thyself, and be not like such men, otherwise thou wilt suffer for it.

Some men act from their sensible feelings both in suffering and in joy; but a man should not look to himself in this.

Our eyes should not look outward, except to rid ourselves of interior images.

In the spiritual annihilation of self the final consummation is attained. When Christ had said "Into thy hands I commend my spirit," he added immediately, "It is consummated."

God and the devil are in man. He who guides himself and he who forsakes himself discover the difference (i.e., the self-willed find in themselves hell, and the detached heaven).

He who desires to have rest at all times must be on his guard against himself in this as in everything else (i.e., this desire is a species of self-seeking).

He who is interior amid exterior things is much more interior than he who is only interior when within himself.

It is good for a man to guide himself in nothing; and he is on the right road

who contemplates under the forms of things their eternal essences.

A detached man is always interiorly alike.

When a man still complains and is impatient, all this springs from imperfection. It must therefore be got rid of.

There are many more reasoning men than simple men. Those are called reasoning men in whom reason rules. But the simple man, through his inaction, is freed from the multiplicity of images which are generated by sensible objects, and he does not contemplate things as sensible, for simplicity has become his nature, and he is like a vessel (full of God) and like a child.

How happy is the man who abides stedfast against multiplicity. What a sensible entrance he has into familiar intercourse with heaven.

A good intention often impedes true union.

We should bear as regularly with that part of us which comes from Adam (i.e., the consequences of the fall) as with that by which we attain eternal bliss.

He who wishes to possess all things must become as nothing to himself and all things.

Wouldst thou be a detached man? Take care that, however God may act toward thee, whether directly by himself or indirectly by his creatures, thou abidest always the same, by a complete renunciation of what is thine.

All those who allow themselves a wrong liberty make themselves their own aim and object.

A detached man must be unformed from the forms and images of creatures; he must be formed upon Christ and transformed into the Godhead.

He who regards himself in Christ lets all things follow their rightful course.

When a man has died to self and begun to live in Christ, it is well with him.

When a man strives by turning inward to conform himself to the truth, it is clearly brought home to him that he had gone forth out of himself, and he observes that there is still something of the creature in him, on which the attraction acted. In this he bears with himself, and perceives that he has not yet ceased from all action. Now, thus to bear with self is to become simple. The going out of self produces a kind of weariness; but when he has turned away from creatures this weariness passes off.

What is truly detached man's object in all things? It is to die to himself; and when he dies to himself all things die to him.

What is the least obstacle? It is a thought. What is the greatest obstacle? It is when the soul abides in the obstinacy of its self-will.

A detached man should not let any moment pass away unmarked.

A detached man should not be always looking to see what he needs, but he should be always looking to see what he can do without.

If a detached man wishes to conform himself to the truth, he must in the first place be diligent in turning inward from things of sense, for God is a spirit. Secondly, he must take note whether he has attached himself to any obstacle (i.e., anything which stands between him and God). Thirdly, he must observe whether he is his own guide in anything, owing to the sensual appetite having got the start. Fourthly, he must, in the light which fills his soul, consider the presence of the all-penetrating divine essence in him, and that he is one of its vessels.

The more a man turns away from himself and all created things, the more perfect are the union and bliss to which he attains.

Rest on nothing which is not God.

Keep thy senses closed to every image which may present itself. Be empty of everything which the outward-gazing mind selects, which takes captive the will and brings earthly joy or delight into the heart.

If thou art where a sin or imperfection is committed, add not aught of thine to it, and have nothing to do with it.

He who always dwells with himself becomes possest of very ample means.

The recreation which a detached man grants to his nature should be confined to strict necessity, and it should be taken in harmless occupations, from which he can readily and without attachment turn away to God.

Gather together and draw in thy soul from the external senses, through which it has dissipated itself upon the multiplicity of outward things.

Be stedfast, and never rest content until thou hast obtained the now of eternity as thy present possession in this life, so far as this is possible to human infirmity.

It happened once to a half-detached man, that, on a certain occasion when he had been too self-conscious in suffering, it was said to him: Thou shouldst be so attentive to me and so forgetful of thyself that when thou knowest it is well with me thou shouldst care nothing how it fares with thee.

In the case of a detached man who draws his senses inward from external objects and establishes himself in the inner castle of his soul, the less he finds within to cling to, the more painful are his interior sufferings; and the more quickly he dies, the more swiftly he bursts through to God.

To give the senses a wide field withdraw the man from his interior.

See that thou undertakest nothing which will carry thee out of thyself.

If things come in search of thee, let them not find thee.

Be quick in turning inward into thyself.

A detached man should keep the powers of his soul under such restraint that, on looking within, this is apparent to him.

The more or less detachment a man has, the more or less will he be disturbed by transitory things.

Go in again, and return over and over again into unity, and enjoy God.

Establish thyself in absolute detachment; for an unbounded longing, even for what is divine when it is excessive, may become a secret obstacle.

A detached man remains always inactive as regards himself, just as if he were unconscious of himself; for in that object, which is God, all things are well and harmoniously ordered in him.

Give heed also to thy outward man that it be at one with thy inward man, by the subjection of all fleshly appetites.

To return again into God by detachment is often more pleasing to him than a self-satisfied stability.

Some persons find no hindrance in going out of themselves, but they want stedfastness in this state.

Natural life shows itself in movement and in the operations of the senses. He who detaches himself from himself in this, and dies to himself in stillness, begins a supernatural life.

Jan van Ruysbroeck
(1293-1381)

GREATEST of the Flemish saints, Ruysbroeck ranks near the top of all mystic figures. Rufus Jones says of him in *The Flowering of Mysticism*: "This man, who never loved a maid and knew little of romantic love, speaks with rare insight of the intrinsic nature of love." The last thirty-eight years of his life were spent as prior of a monastery at Groenendael. Like Francis of Assisi he was fond of birds, trees, and animals. He entered into the work of the monastery with simple joy, and found ecstasy in every experience. A saint in his own right, his influence was to radiate far in one of his pupils, Gerhard Groot, who wrote *The Imitation of Christ*. The selection below is from *The Adornment of the Spiritual Marriage*, and is reprinted from Jane T. Stoddart's translation of Maurice Maeterlinck's *Ruysbroeck and the Mystics*. The work portrays Ruysbroeck's mystic love for all things.

[MORAL LESSONS AND SPIRITUAL INSTRUCTIONS]

From *The Adornment of the Spiritual Marriage*

ON THE KINGDOM OF THE SOUL

*H*e who desires to obtain and to preserve virtue will adorn, occupy, and arrange his soul like to a kingdom. Free will is the king of the soul. He is free by nature, and yet more free through divine mercy. He will be crowned with a crown named charity. This crown and this kingdom we shall receive from the Emperor, who is the Lord, the Ruler and the King of kings, and we shall possess, rule, and maintain this kingdom in His name. The sovereign, free will, shall dwell in the highest town of the kingdom—that is to say, in the strong desires of the soul. And he will be adorned with a robe of two parts. The right side of the robe shall be a virtue which is called strength, so that he may be strong and powerful to conquer every obstacle, and to dwell at last in heaven in the palace of the great Emperor, bending his crowned head with love and passionate self-surrender before the supreme and sovereign King. This is the fitting work of charity. Through it we receive the crown. Through it we adorn the crown, and through it we maintain and possess the kingdom through all eternity. The left side of the robe shall be a cardinal virtue, which is called moral strength. Through its aid shall free will, the king, put down all immorality and fulfil all virtue, and shall have the power to maintain his kingdom unto death.

This king shall choose councillors in his country, the wisest to be found in the land. These will be two divine virtues, knowledge and discretion, enlightened by the grace of God. They will dwell near the king, in a palace which is called the soul's strength of reason; but they will be clothed and adorned with a moral virtue which is called temperance, so that the king may always act or refrain from acting according to their counsels. By knowledge we shall purge the conscience from all its faults and adorn it with every virtue; and by discretion we shall give and take, do and leave undone, speak and be silent, fast and eat, listen and reply; and in all things we shall act according to knowledge and discretion, clothed with their moral virtue, which is called temperance or moderation.

This king, free will, shall also set up in his kingdom a judge, who shall be called justice, a divine virtue when it springs from love; and it is one of the highest moral virtues. This judge shall dwell in the conscience, in the centre of the kingdom, in the strongest passions. And he will be adorned with moral virtue, which is called prudence. For justice cannot be perfect. This judge, justice, shall travel through the kingdom with the power and the force of the king, accompanied by wisdom of counsel and by his own prudence. He will promote and dismiss, judge and condemn, kill and keep alive, mutilate, blind and restore sight, lift, up and put down, organise, punish, and chastise every sin with perfect justice, and at last destroy all vices.

The people of this kingdom—that is, all the pure of soul—shall be established on humility and in the fear of God; they shall be subject unto God in all virtues, each according to his own capacity. He who has thus occupied, adorned, and regulated the kingdom of his soul, has gone forth in love and virtue towards God, himself, and his neighbour.

Christ the Sun of the Soul

The sun shines in the east, in the centre of the world, on the mountains; it hastens summer in that region, and creates good fruits and potent wines, filling the earth with joy. The same sun shines in the west, at the ends of the earth; there the country is colder, and the power of its heat is less, yet nevertheless it produces a great many excellent fruits; but few wines are found there.

Those men who dwell in the west of their own being, remain in the outward senses, and by their good intentions, their virtues, and their outward practices, through God's grace, they produce abundant harvests and virtues in various ways, but they seldom taste the wine of inward joy and of spiritual consolation.

The man who will feel the shining of the Eternal Sun, which is Christ Himself, will have clear vision, and will dwell on the mountains of the east, concentrating all his energies and raising his heart towards God, free and careless as regards joy, sorrow, and all creatures. There Christ the Sun of Righteousness shines on the free and uplifted heart; and these are the mountains which I have in mind. Christ, the glorious sun and the divine brightness, shines and illumines and enkindles by His inward coming, and the power of His Spirit, the free heart and all the powers of the soul.

When summer draws near, and the sun rises higher in the heavens, it draws the moisture of the soil through the roots and the trunk of the trees, until it reaches the branches, and hence come foliage, flowers, and fruits. So likewise, when Christ, the Eternal Sun, rises in our hearts, so that the summer reigns over their adornment of virtues, He sends His light and His fire into our will, and draws the heart from the multitude of earthly things, and creates unity and close fellowship, and makes the heart to grow and become green through inward love, and to bear the flowers of loving devotion and the fruits of gratitude and affection, and preserves these fruits in the sorrow and humility we feel because of our impotence.

The Lesson from the Bee

Observe the wise bee and make it your model. It dwells in a community in the midst of its companions, and it goes forth, not during the storm, but when the weather is calm and still and the sun is shining; and it flies towards all the flowers on which it can find sweetness. It does not rest on any flower, neither in its beauty nor in its sweetness, but it draws from each calix honey and wax—that is to say, the sweetness and the substance of its brightness—and it bears them back to the community in which all the bees are assembled, so that the honey and wax may profitably bear fruit.

The opened heart on which Christ, the Eternal Sun, is shining, grows and flourishes under His rays, and flows with all its inner powers into joy and sweetnesses.

Now the wise man will act like the bee, and he will fly out in order to settle with care, intelligence, and prudence on all the gifts and on all the sweetness which he has experienced, and on all the good which God has done to him; and through the rays of the sun and his own inward observation he will experience a multitude of consolations and blessings. And he will not rest on any flower of all these gifts, but, laden with gratitude and praise, he will fly back again toward the home in which he longs to dwell and rest for evermore with God.

The Dew of Mid-Day

Sometimes in these burning days there falls the honey-dew of some false sweetness, which soils the fruits or completely spoils them. It falls for the most part at noon, in bright sunshine, and its great drops can hardly be distinguished from rain. Even so there are some men who can be caught away from their outward senses by some brightness which is the gift of the enemy. And this brightness enwraps and envelops them, and at that moment they behold images, falsehoods, and many kinds of truths, and voices speak to them in different ways, and all this is seen and received with great joy. And here there fall at times the honey-drops of a false sweetness in which the man delights himself. He who values it highly receives a great quantity, and so the man is often injured, for if he holds for true such things as have no resemblance to truth, because they have been shown or taught him, he falls into error and the fruit of virtue is lost. But those who have climbed by the paths which I have pointed out above, although they may indeed be tempted by that spirit and by that brightness, will recognise them and receive no injury.

The Lesson from the Ant

I will give a brief parable to those who live in continual ebullitions of love, in order that they may endure this disposition nobly and becomingly, and may attain to a higher virtue.

There is a little insect which is called the ant; it is strong and wise, and very tenacious of life, and it lives with its fellows in warm and dry soils. The ant works during summer and collects food and grain for the winter, and it splits the grain so that it may not become rotten or spoiled, and may be eaten when there is nothing more to be found. And it does not make strange paths, but all follow the same path, and after waiting till the proper time they become able to fly.

So should these men do; they will be strong by waiting for the coming of Christ, wise against the appearance and the inspiration of the enemy. They will not choose death, but they will prefer God's glory alone and the winning of fresh virtues. They will dwell in the community of their heart and of their powers, and will follow the invitation and the constraint of divine unity. They will live in rich and warm soils, or, in other words, in the passionate heat of love, and in great impatience. And they will work during the summer of this life, and will gather in for eternity the fruits of virtue. These they will divide in two—one part means that they will always desire the supreme joy of eternity; the other, that by their reason they will always restrain themselves as much as possible, and wait the time that God has appointed for them, and so the fruit of virtue shall be preserved into eternity. They will not follow strange paths or curious methods, but through all storms they will follow the path of love, towards the place whither love shall guide them. And when the set time has come, and they have persevered in all the virtues, they shall be fit to behold God, and their wings shall bear them towards His mystery.

What Shall the Forsaken Do?

He shall humbly consider that he hath nothing of his own save his misery, and shall say with resignation and self-abandonment the same words which were spoken by holy Job: "The Lord gave, and the Lord hath taken away; blessed be the name of the Lord." And in all things he shall yield up his own will, saying and thinking in his heart, "Lord, I am as willing to be poor and without all those things of which Thou hast deprived me, as I should be ready to be rich, Lord, if Thy will were so, and if in that state I might further Thy glory. It is not my natural will which must be done, but Thy will and the will of my spirit. Lord, I am Thine, and I should be Thine as gladly in hell as in heaven, if in that way I could advance Thy glory. So then, O Lord, fulfil in me the good pleasure of Thy will." Out of all sufferings and all renunciations the man will draw for himself an inward joy; he will resign himself into the hands of God, and will rejoice to suffer in promoting God's glory. And if he perseveres in this course, he will enjoy secret pleasures never tasted before; for nothing so rejoices the lover of God as to feel that he belongs to his Beloved. And if he has truly risen to this height in the path of virtues, it is not necessary that he shall have passed through the different states which we have pointed out in previous chapters, for he feels in himself, in work, in humble obedience, and in patience and resignation, the source of every virtue. This method has therefore an everlasting certainty.

At this season the sun enters into the sign of Libra, for the day and night are equal, and light and darkness evenly balanced. Even so for the resigned soul Jesus Christ is in the sign of Libra; and whether He grants sweetness or bitterness, darkness or light, of whatever nature His gift may be, the man retains his balance, and all things are one to him, with the exception of sin, which has been driven out once for all. When all consolation ·has been withdrawn from these resigned ones, so that they believe they have lost all their virtues, and are forsaken of God and of every creature; then, if they know how to reap the various fruits, the corn and wine are ripe and ready.

THE SETTING OF THE ETERNAL SUN

When the time came for Christ to gather in and bear away to the eternal kingdom the fruits of all the virtues that ever were and ever shall be practised upon earth, then the Eternal Sun began to set; for He humbled Himself and gave up the life of His body into the hands of His enemies. And in His distress he was misunderstood and forsaken by His friends, and all consolation, from without and from within, was taken away from His human nature, and it was overwhelmed with misery and pain, with scorn and heaviness, and in it He paid all the debt that justice claimed for sin. He suffered these things with humble patience, and in this resignation He fulfilled the highest tasks of love, and so He received and redeemed our eternal heritage. Thus was adorned the lower part of His noble humanity, for in it He suffered this sorrow for our sins. And this is why He calls Himself the Saviour of the world; this is why He is now famous and glorified, exalted and seated at the right hand of His Father, where He reigns with power. And every creature on earth, in heaven, and in hell, bends continually the knee before His glorious name.

THE NATURE OF GOD

We must consider and examine the sublime nature of God: how it is simplicity and purity; height that cannot be scaled and depth that cannot be sounded; breadth without understanding and length without end; awful silence and the savage wilderness; rest of all saints in the union and in the common joy which He shares with His saints throughout eternity.

THE DIVINE GENEROSITY

The incomprehensible wealth and sublimity and the universality of the gifts which flow forth from the divine nature awake wonder in the heart of man, and above all he marvels at the universal presence of God and of His works, a presence which is above everything, for he beholds the inconceivable essence, which is the common joy of God and of all the saints.

And he sees that the Divine Persons send forth one common effluence in works, in grace, and in glory, in nature and above nature, in all states and in all times, in men and in the glorified saints, in heaven and on earth, in all reasonable creatures, and in those which are without reason or material, according to the merits, the needs, and the receptivity of each. And he sees the creation of the heaven and the earth, the sun and the moon, the four elements with all the creatures, and the course of the heavens, which is common to all. God, with all His gifts, is common to all, men and angels are a common gift, and the soul with all its faculties. . . .

When man thus considers the wealth and the marvellous sublimity of the divine nature, and all the manifold gifts which He grants and offers to His creatures, amazement is stirred up in his spirit at the sight of so manifold a wealth and majesty; at the sight of the immense faithfulness of God to all His creatures. This causes a strange joy of spirit, and a boundless trust in God, and this inward joy surrounds and penetrates all the forces of the souls in the secret places of the spirit.

CHRIST THE LOVER OF ALL MEN

Consider how Christ gave Himself to all in perfect faithfulness. His secret and sublime prayer flowed forth towards His Father, and was for the common good of all who desire salvation. Jesus Christ was all things to all men in His love, in His teaching, in His reproaches, in His consolations and sweetness, in His generous gifts, in His gracious forgiveness. His soul and His body, His life, His death, and His service were and are for the common good of all. His sacrament and His gifts are for all. Christ received neither food, nor drink, nor anything that was needful for His body, without thinking of the common good of all those who shall be saved even until the last day.

Christ had nothing of His own, but all was held in common, body and soul, mother and disciples, tunic and cloak. He ate and drank for us, He lived and toiled for us. His toil and grief and misery were indeed His own, but the blessings and the good which flowed from them were the common possession of all. And the glory of His merits shall be the possession of all throughout eternity.

HOW CHRIST GAVE HIMSELF TO US IN THE SACRAMENT

There is a special benefit which Christ, in the Holy Church, has left to all the good: namely, that supper of the great feast of Passover, which He instituted when the time had come for Him to leave His sorrow and go to the Father, after He had eaten of the paschal lamb with His disciples and the ancient law had been fulfilled. At the end of the meal and of the feast, He wished to give them a special food, which He had long desired to give. In this way He would make an end of the ancient law and bring in the new, and so He took bread in His sacred hands and consecrated His sacred body and afterwards His blood, and gave them to all His disciples, and left them as a common gift to all just men, for their eternal benefit.

This gift and this special food rejoice and adorn all great festivals and all banquets in heaven and on earth. In this gift Christ gives Himself to us in three ways: He gives us His flesh and His blood and His bodily life, glorified and full of joys and sorrows; and He gives us His Spirit, with its supreme faculties, full of glory and of gifts, of truth and justifying power; and He gives us His personality, with the divine light which raises His Spirit and the spirits of all enlightened beings into the sublime unity and joy of God.

Christ desires that we shall remember Him whenever we consecrate, offer, and receive His body. Consider now in what way we shall remember Him. We shall observe and examine how Christ inclines Himself towards us, by loving affection, by great desires, by a tender joy and warm influence passing into our bodily nature. For He gives us that which He received from our humanity, His flesh, His blood, and His bodily nature. We shall likewise observe and examine that precious body, tortured, furrowed, and wounded with love, because of His faithfulness towards us. So shall we be adorned and nourished in the lower part of our human nature. In this sublime gift of the Sacrament He also gives us His Spirit full of glory, and the richer gifts of virtues and unspeakable mercies of charity and goodness.

By these we are nourished and adorned and enlightened in the unity of our spirit and in our higher powers, because Christ with all His riches dwells within us.

In the sacrament of the altar He further bestows upon us His sublime personality and His incomprehensible light. Through this we are united and given up to the Father, and the Father receives His elect children at the same time as His only begotten Son, and so we reach our divine inheritance and our eternal felicity.

If a man has diligently considered these things, he will meet Christ in the same way in which Christ comes to him. He will rise to receive Christ with eager joy in his heart, his desires, his love, and all his powers. And it is thus that Christ Himself receives. This joy cannot possibly be too great, for our nature receives His nature, the glorified humanity of Christ, full of gladness and merit. Therefore I desire that in thus receiving man shall, as it were, dissolve and flow forth through his desires, his joys, and his pleasures, for he receives the most lovely, the most gracious, and the kindest of the children of men, and is made one with Him. In this union and this joy great delights often come to men, and many mysterious and secret marvels of divine treasures are manifested and revealed. When in so receiving a man meditates on the torment and the sufferings of this precious body of Christ of which he is partaking, there sometimes enters into him a devotion so loving and a compassion so keen that he desires to be nailed with Christ to the word of the Cross, and to shed his heart's blood in honour of Christ. And he presses into the wounds and into the open heart of Christ his Saviour. In such exercises revelations and great benefits have often come to men.

The Soul's Hunger For God

Here there begins an eternal hunger, which shall nevermore be satisfied. It is the yearning and the inward aspiration of our faculty of love, and of our created spirit towards an uncreated good. And as the spirit desires joy, and is invited and constrained by God to partake of it, it is always longing to realise joy. Behold then the beginning of an eternal aspiration and of eternal efforts, while our impotence is likewise eternal. These are the poorest of all men, for they are eager and greedy, and they can never be satisfied. Whatever they eat or drink, they can never have enough, for this hunger lasts continually. For a created vessel cannot contain an uncreated good, and hence that continual struggle of the hungry soul and its feebleness which is swallowed up in God. There are here great banquets of food and drink, which none knoweth saving he who partakes of them; but full satisfaction of joy is the food which is ever lacking, and so the hunger is perpetually renewed. Yet streams of honey flow within reach, full of all delights, for the spirit tastes these pleasures in every imaginable way, but always according to its creaturely nature and below God, and that is why the hunger and the impatience are without end. If God were to grant to this man all the gifts which are possessed by all the saints, and everything that He has to offer, but were to deny Himself, the open-mouthed eagerness of his spirit would be still hungry and unsatisfied. Emotion and the inward contact with God are the explanation of our hunger and our striving; for the Spirit of God gives chase to our spirit, and the closer the contact the greater the hunger and the striving. This is the life of love in its highest development, above reason and higher than all understanding; for in such love reason can neither give nor take away, for our love is in touch with the divine love. And I think that once this point is reached there will be no more separation from God. The contact of God with us, so long as we feel it, and our own loving efforts, are both created and of the nature of the creature, and so they may grow and increase all the days of our life.

The Labour and Rest of Love

In one single moment and at the same time, love labours and rests in its beloved. And the one is strengthened by the other; for the loftier the love, the greater is the rest, and the greater is the rest, the closer is the love; for the one lives in the other, and he who loves not rests not, neither does he who rests not know aught of love. There are, nevertheless, some righteous men who believe that they neither love nor rest in God. But this thought itself springs from love, and because their desire to love is greater than their ability, therefore it seems to them that they are powerless to love. And in this labour they taste of love and rest, for none except the resigned, passive, and enlightened man can understand how one may rest and also enjoy.

The Christian Life

He (the believer) is hungry and thirsty, for he sees the food of angels and the drink of heaven. He labours diligently in love, for he beholds his rest. He is a pilgrim, and he sees his fatherland. He strives in love for the victory, for he sees his crown. Consolation, peace, joy, beauty, and riches, and all that the heart can desire, are shown to the reason which is enlightened to see God in spiritual similitudes and without measure or limit. . . . Those who do not possess, at the same time, the power of rest and action, and are not exercised in both, have not received this righteousness of the just.

The Coming of the Bridegroom

What is this eternal coming of our Bridegroom? It is a new birth and a new illumination which are without interruption; for the source from which the brightness streams, and which is itself the brightness, is living and fertile; and so the manifestation of the eternal light is renewed without interruption, in the secret depths of the spirit. . . . And the coming of the Bridegroom is so swift that He is always coming, and that He dwells within us with His unfathomable riches, and that He returns ever anew in person, with such new brightness that it seems as if He had never come before. For His coming is comprised beyond all limit of time, in an eternal *Now;* and He is ever received with new desires and a new delight. Behold, the joys and the pleasures which this Bridegroom brings with Him at His coming are boundless and without limit, for they are Himself. And this is why the eyes of the spirit, by which the loving soul beholds its Bridegroom, are opened so wide that they will never shut again. For the contemplation and the fixed gaze of the spirit are eternal in the secret manifestation of God. And the comprehension of the spirit is so widely opened, as it waits for the appearance of the Bridegroom, that the spirit itself becomes vast as that which it comprehends. And so is God beheld and understood by God, in whom all our blessedness is found.

Rulman Merswin

(1307-1382)

DISILLUSIONED by worldly standards of success and deeply attracted to the preaching of Tauler, Rulman Merswin dedicated himself to religion at the age of forty. His wife shared his conversion, and with their wealth they devoted all their efforts to the cause of religion. In 1367 the Strasbourg banker and his wife purchased the Green Isle as a place where mystical piety could be practiced, and opened it to both laity and clergy who wished to pursue the devotional life. After his wife's death Merswin spent the remaining twelve years of his life on the island. Four days after he died his friends found a number of mystical treatises in a chest. Some were by Merswin and others were ascribed to "The Friend of God" from Oberland. Whether Merswin wrote all the treatises, scholars cannot agree; but they do agree that he was the author of many of them. Some hold that Merswin's "Friend of God" is his literary creation, just as in England about the same time William Langland created his figure of Piers Plowman. "A Letter Sent from Heaven" is representative of Merswin's mystical feeling. It is translated by Gottlob C. Cast from the Middle High German for this volume.

A LETTER SENT FROM HEAVEN

My dearly beloved and secret friends of God, all thirteen of you shall know that the Eternal and Almighty Heavenly Father was very much inclined to send upon the whole world a great plague so that only very few human beings would escape. Therefore it came to pass that the great and lofty queen of heaven and earth, the dear mother of God, came to speak to the Eternal Father on Christmas eve and pleaded with Him very fervently and implored Him to postpone the storm of this great plague for three years. Then the Heavenly Father said: "Dear Mary, lofty and all-highest queen, I cannot refuse your request. It shall be granted, but on condition that the secret friends of God who were together last year— thirteen of them—shall meet at some place and there be my captives for the three years; and after these three years their entire lives. And if it should come to pass that after the three years the Holy Spirit should admonish them, that they should continue to live thus in their seclusion or to journey through the world wherever each one of them might be impelled to go."

If now these thirteen dear friends will do this for the love of God and be steadfast, then the plague shall be postponed for three years, and the great storm shall be postponed. But in these same three years the Heavenly Father will not cease to urge and attack man in many ways, as He has done in past years, and will do it rather more than less, so that He may see whether the Christian people would become somewhat better in these three years. But if the world does not improve in spite of this, it will stand before God in fear and trembling. Now the Eternal Father desires that these thirteen secret friends shall be His captives for these three years and shall live in confinement, that they may keep their silence and speak with no one these three years. They shall desist from everything that may call to mind the world or cause trouble from outside, be it in whatever way it may. From all that they shall abstain and shall have nothing more to do than to wait and see what message may come to them from within, as the prophet said: "I sit here and wait what God will say within me."

Thus they shall be the Eternal Father's captives these three years and shall speak to no one except on Tuesday and also on Thursday after Ascension Day at noon. And they shall do this with the intention that, if it should come to pass that any one of them should be in sore need of something, he might ask for it; or, in case one of their fellow men who had completely surrendered to God and who would like to become altogether a spiritual man should be in need of something. Him they may hear on these two half days, but no more; and they may practice the six deeds of mercy on him. And the laymen who are among you shall go to the altar on Sunday and Wednesday and Friday, and shall receive the holy sacrament. And if it should happen that a high festival should fall on the following days, anyone who felt inclined to attend might go there. And if there is a layman among you who does not live with a priest, whoever that layman may be, let him see to it that he do not fail to come to some priest and live with him, but without talking to him except in making confession or in helping in the performing of mass.

Anonymous

THEOLOGIA GERMANICA

(Fourteenth Century)

FROM the society known as the "Friends of God" some unknown writer has brought forth that group's finest literary monument, *Theologia Germanica*. Written by a priest of the Teutonic order, the manuscript was found and published by Martin Luther in 1516. Because of its beauty of style, its deep simplicity, and its unfanatical interpretation of mysticism, this writing has clearly interpreted the pattern of devotional living for common men. Plato, Eckhart, Dionysius the Areopagite, and Tauler strongly influenced the writer. Its popularity is evidenced by the fact that in Germany it has gone through ninety editions. Of *Theologia Germanica* Luther said, "Next to the Bible and St. Augustine, no book hath ever come into my hands, whence I have learnt or would wish to learn more of what God, Christ, and man and all things are." The chapters here are representative of the entire work. It was translated from the German in the last century by Susanna Winkworth.

[ON LIVING A PERFECT LIFE]

From *Theologia Germanica*

V. HOW WE ARE TO TAKE THAT SAYING, THAT WE MUST COME TO BE WITHOUT WILL, WISDOM, LOVE, DESIRE, KNOWLEDGE, AND THE LIKE.

Certain men say that we ought to be without will, wisdom, love, desire, knowledge, and the like. Hereby is not to be understood that there is to be no knowledge in man, and that God is not to be loved by him, nor desired and longed for, nor praised and honoured; for that were a great loss, and man were like the beasts [and as the brutes that have no reason]. But it meaneth that man's knowledge should be so clear and perfect that he should acknowledge of a truth [that in himself he neither hath nor can do any good thing, and that none of his knowledge, wisdom and art, his will, love and good works do come from himself, nor are of man, nor of any creature, but] that all these are of the eternal God, from whom they all proceed. [As Christ himself saith, "Without me, ye can do nothing." St. Paul saith also, "What hast thou that thou hast not received?" As much as to say—nothing. "Now if thou didst receive it, why dost thou glory as if thou hadst not received it?" Again he saith, "Not that we are sufficient of ourselves to think anything as of ourselves, but our sufficiency is of God."] Now when a man duly perceiveth these things in himself, he and the creature fall behind, and he doth not call any thing his own, and the less he taketh this knowledge unto himself, the more perfect doth it become. So also is it with the will, and love and desire, and the like. For the less we call these things our own, the more perfect and noble and godlike do they become, and the more we think them our own, the baser and less pure and perfect do they become.

Behold on this sort must we cast all things from us, and strip ourselves of them; we must refrain from claiming anything for our own. When we do this, we shall have the best, fullest, clearest and noblest knowledge that a man can have, and also the noblest and purest love, will and desire; for then these will be all of God alone. It is much better that they should be God's than the creature's. Now that I ascribe anything good to myself, as if I were, or had done, or knew, or could perform any good thing, or that it were mine, this is all of sin and folly. For if the truth were rightly known by me, I should also know that I am not that good thing and that it is not mine, nor of me, and that I do not know it, and cannot do it, and the like. If this came to pass, I should needs cease to call anything my own.

It is better that God, or his works, should be known, as far as it be possible to us, and loved, praised and honoured, and the like, and even that man should but vainly imagine he loveth or praiseth God, than that God should be altogether unpraised, unloved, unhonoured, and unknown. For when the vain imagination and ignorance are turned into an understanding and knowledge of the truth the claiming anything for our own will cease

of itself. Then the man says: "Behold! I, poor fool that I was, imagined it was I, but behold! it is, and was, of a truth, God!"

VII. OF THE EYES OF THE SPIRIT WHEREWITH MAN LOOKETH INTO ETERNITY AND INTO TIME, AND HOW THE ONE IS HINDERED OF THE OTHER IN ITS WORKING.

Let us remember how it is written and said that the soul of Christ had two eyes, a right and a left eye. In the beginning, when the soul of Christ was created, she fixed her right eye upon eternity and the Godhead, and remained in the full intuition and enjoyment of the Divine Essence and Eternal Perfection; and continued thus unmoved and undisturbed by all the accidents and travail, suffering, torment and pain that ever befell the outward man. But with the left eye she beheld the creature and perceived all things therein, and took note of the difference between the creatures, which were better or worse, nobler or meaner; and thereafter was the outward man of Christ ordered.

Thus the inner man of Christ, according to the right eye of his soul, stood in the full exercise of his divine nature, in perfect blessedness, joy and eternal peace. But the outward man and the left eye of Christ's soul, stood with him in perfect suffering, in all tribulation, affliction and travail; and this in such sort that the inward and right eye remained unmoved, unhindered and untouched by all the travail, suffering, grief and anguish that ever befell the outward man. It hath been said that when Christ was bound to the pillar and scourged, and when he hung upon the cross, according to the outward man, yet his inner man, or soul according to the right eye, stood in as full possession of divine joy and blessedness as it did after his ascension, or as it doth now. In like manner his outward man, or soul with the left eye, was never hindered, disturbed or troubled by the inward eye in its contemplation of the outward things that belonged to it.

Now the created soul of man hath also two eyes. The one is the power of seeing into eternity, the other of seeing into time and the creatures, of perceiving how they differ from each other as aforesaid, of giving life and needful things to the body, and ordering and governing it for the best. But these two eyes of the soul of man cannot both perform their work at once; but if the soul shall see with the right eye into eternity, then the left eye must close itself and refrain from working, and be as though it were dead. For if the left eye be fulfilling its office toward outward things; that is, holding converse with time and the creatures; then must the right eye be hindered in its working; that is, in its contemplation. Therefore whosoever will have the one must let the other go; for "no man can serve two masters."

IX. How it is better and more profitable for a Man that he should perceive what God will do with him, or to what end He will make Use of him, than if he knew all that God had ever wrought, or would ever work through all the Creatures; and how Blessedness lieth alone in God, and not in the Creatures, or in any Works.

We should mark and know of a very truth that all manner of virtue and goodness, and even that Eternal Good which is God Himself, can never make a man virtuous, good, or happy, so long as it is outside the soul; [that is, so long as the man is holding converse with outward things through his senses and reason, and doth not withdraw into himself and learn to understand his own life, who and what he is.] The like is true of sin and evil. [For all manner of sin and wickedness can never make us evil, so long as it is outside of us; that is, so long as we do not commit it, or do not give consent to it.]

Therefore although it be good and profitable that we should ask, and learn and know, what good and holy men have wrought and suffered, and how God hath dealt with them, and what he hath wrought in and through them, yet it were a thousand times better that we should in ourselves learn and perceive and understand, who we are, how and what our own life is, what God is and is

doing in us, what he will have from us, and to what ends he will or will not make use of us. [For, of a truth, thoroughly to know oneself, is above all art, for it is the highest art. If thou knowest thyself well, thou art better and more praiseworthy before God, than if thou didst not know thyself, but didst understand the course of the heavens and of all the planets and stars, also the virtue of all herbs, and the structure and dispositions of all mankind, also the nature of all beasts, and, in such matters, hadst all the skill of all who are in heaven and on earth. For it is said, there came a voice from heaven, saying, "Man, know thyself."] Thus that proverb is still true, "going out were never so good, but staying at home were much better."

Further, ye should learn that eternal blessedness lieth in one thing alone, and in nought else. And if ever man or the soul is to be made blessed, that one thing alone must be in the soul. Now some might ask, "But what is that one thing?" I answer, it is Goodness, or that which hath been made good, and yet neither this good nor that, which we can name, or perceive or show; but it is all and above all good things.

Moreover, it needeth not to enter into the soul, for it is there already, only it is unperceived. When we say we should come unto it, we mean that we should seek it, feel it, and taste it. And now since it is One, unity and singleness is better than manifoldness. For blessedness lieth not in much and many, but in One and oneness. In one word, blessedness lieth not in any creature, or work of the creatures, but it lieth alone in God and in his works. Therefore I must wait only on God and his work, and leave on one side all creatures with their works, and first of all myself. In like manner all the great works and wonders that God has ever wrought or shall ever work in or through the creatures, or even God himself with all his goodness, so far as these things exist or are done outside of me, can never make me blessed, but only in so far as they exist and are done and loved, known, tasted and felt within me.

X. How the perfect Men have no other Desire than that they may be to the Eternal Goodness what his Hand is to a Man, and how they have lost the Fear of Hell, and Hope of Heaven.

Now let us mark: Where men are enlightened with the true light, they perceive that all which they might desire or choose, is nothing to that which all creatures, as creatures, ever desired or chose or knew. Therefore they renounce all desire and choice, and commit and commend themselves and all things to the Eternal Goodness. Nevertheless, there remaineth in them a desire to go forward and get nearer to the Eternal Goodness; that is, to come to a clearer knowledge, and warmer love, and more comfortable assurance, and perfect obedience and subjection; so that every enlightened man could say: "I would fain be to the Eternal Goodness, what his own hand is to a man." And he feareth always that he is not enough so, and longeth for the salvation of all men. And such men do not call this longing their own, nor take it unto themselves, for they know well that this desire is not of man, but of the Eternal Goodness; for whatsoever is good shall no one take unto himself as his own, seeing that it belongeth to the Eternal Goodness only.

Moreover, these men are in a state of freedom, because they have lost the fear of pain or hell, and the hope of reward or heaven, but are living in pure submission to the Eternal Goodness, in the perfect freedom of fervent love. This mind was in Christ in perfection, and is also in his followers, in some more, and in some less. But it is a sorrow and shame to think that the Eternal Goodness is ever most graciously guiding and drawing us, and we will not yield to it. What is better and nobler than true poorness in spirit? Yet when that is held up before us, we will have none of it, but are always seeking ourselves, and our own things. [We like to have our mouths always filled with good things,] that we may have in ourselves a lively taste of pleasure and sweetness. When this is so, we are well pleased, and think it standeth not amiss with us.

[But we are yet a long way off from a perfect life. For when God will draw us up to something higher, that is, to an utter loss and forsaking of our own things, spiritual and natural, and withdraweth his comfort and sweetness from us, we faint and are troubled, and can in no wise bring our minds to it; and we forget God and neglect holy exercises, and fancy we are lost for ever.] This is a great error and a bad sign. For a true lover of God, loveth him or the Eternal Goodness alike, in having and in not having, in sweetness and in bitterness, in good or evil report, and the like, for he seeketh alone the honour of God, and not his own, either in spiritual or natural things. And therefore he standeth alike unshaken in all things, at all seasons. [Hereby let every man prove himself, how he standeth towards God, his Creator and Lord.]

XIV. Of three Stages by which a Man is led upwards till he attaineth true Perfection.

Now be assured that no one can be enlightened unless he be first cleansed or purified and stripped. So also, no one can be united with God unless he be first enlightened. Thus there are three stages: first, the purification; secondly, the enlightening; thirdly, the union. [The purification concerneth those who are beginning or repenting, and is brought to pass in a threefold wise; by contrition and sorrow for sin, by full confession, by hearty amendment. The enlightening belongeth to such as are growing, and also taketh place in three ways: to wit, by the eschewal of sin, by the practice of virtue and good works, and by the willing endurance of all manner of temptation and trials. The union belongeth to such as are perfect, and also is brought to pass in three ways: to wit, by pureness and singleness of heart, by love, and by the contemplation of God, the Creator of all things.]

XXVI. Touching Poorness of Spirit and true Humility and whereby we may discern the true and lawful free Men whom the Truth hath made free.

But it is quite otherwise where there is poorness of spirit, and true humility;

and it is so because it is found and known of a truth that a man, of himself and his own power, is nothing, hath nothing, can do and is capable of nothing but only infirmity and evil. Hence followeth that the man findeth himself altogether unworthy of all that hath been or ever will be done for him, by God or the creatures, and that he is a debtor to God and also to all the creatures in God's stead, both to bear with, and to labour for, and to serve them. And therefore he doeth not in any wise stand up for his own rights, but from the humility of his heart he saith, "It is just and reasonable that God and all creatures should be against me, and have a right over me, and to me, and that I should not be against any one, nor have a right to any thing." Hence it followeth that the man doth not and will not crave or beg for any thing, either from God or the creatures, beyond mere needful things, and for those only with shamefacedness, as a favour and not as a right. And he will not minister unto or gratify his body or any of his natural desires, beyond what is needful, nor allow that any should help or serve him except in case of necessity, and then always in trembling; for he hath no right to any thing, and therefore he thinketh himself unworthy of any thing. So likewise all his own discourse, ways, words and works seem to this man a thing of nought and a folly. Therefore he speaketh little, and doth not take upon himself to admonish or rebuke any, unless he be constrained thereto by love or faithfulness towards God, and even then he doth it in fear, and so little as may be.

Moreover, when a man hath this poor and humble spirit, he cometh to see and understand aright, how that all men are bent upon themselves, and inclined to evil and sin, and that on this account it is needful and profitable that there be order, customs, law and precepts, to the end that the blindness and foolishness of men may be corrected, and that vice and wickedness may be kept under, and constrained to seemliness. For without ordinances, men would be much more mischievous and ungovernable than dogs and cattle. And few have come to the knowledge of the truth but what have begun with holy practices and ordinances, and exercised themselves therein so long as they knew nothing more nor better.

Therefore one who is poor in spirit and of a humble mind doth not despise or make light of law, order, precepts and holy customs, nor yet of those who observe and cleave wholly to them, but with loving pity and gentle sorrow, crieth: "Almighty Father, Thou Eternal Truth, I make my lament unto Thee, and it grieveth Thy Spirit too, that through man's blindness, infirmity, and sin, that is made needful and must be, which in deed and truth were neither needful nor right." [For those who are perfect are under no law.

So order, laws, precepts and the like are merely an admonition to men who understand nothing better and know and perceive not wherefore all law and order is ordained.] And the perfect accept the law along with such ignorant men as understand and know nothing better, and practise it with them, to the intent that they may be restrained thereby, and kept from evil ways, or if it be possible, brought to something higher.

Behold! all that we have said of poverty and humility is so of a truth, and we have the proof and witness thereof in the pure life of Christ, and in his words. For he both practised and fulfilled every work of true humility and all other virtues, as shineth forth in his holy life, and he saith also expressly: "Learn of me, for I am meek and lowly of heart: and ye shall find rest unto your souls." Moreover he did not despise and set at nought the law and the commandments, nor yet the men who are under the law. [He saith: "I am not come to destroy the law or the prophets but to fulfil."] But he saith further, that to keep them is not enough, we must press forward to what is higher and better, as is indeed true. [He saith: "Except your righteousness shall exceed the righteousness of the Scribes and Pharisees, ye shall in no case enter into the kingdom of Heaven." For the law forbiddeth evil works, but Christ condemneth also evil thoughts; the law alloweth us to take vengeance on our enemies, but Christ commandeth us to love them. The law forbiddeth not the good things of this world, but he counselleth us to despise them. And he hath set his seal upon all he said, with his own holy life; for he taught nothing that he did not fulfil in work, and he kept the law and was subject unto it to the end of his mortal life.] Likewise St. Paul saith: "Christ was made under the law to redeem them that were under the law." That is, that he might bring them to something higher and nearer to himself. He said again, "The Son of man came not to be ministered unto but to minister."

In a word: in Christ's life and words and works, we find nothing but true, pure humility and poverty such as we have set forth. And therefore where God dwelleth in a man, and the man is a true follower of Christ, it will be, and must be, and ought to be the same. But where there is pride, and a haughty spirit, and a light careless mind, Christ is not, nor any true follower of his.

Christ said: "My soul is troubled, even unto death." He meaneth his bodily death. [That is to say: from the time that he was born of Mary, until his death on the cross, he had not one joyful day, but only trouble, sorrow and contradiction.] Therefore it is just and reasonable that his servants should be even as their Master. Christ saith also: "Blessed are the poor in spirit," (that is, those who are truly humble,) "for theirs is the kingdom of Heaven." And thus we find it of a truth, where God is made man. For in Christ and in all his true followers, there must needs be thorough humility and poorness of spirit, a lowly retiring disposition, and a heart laden with a secret sorrow and mourning, so long as this mortal life lasteth. And he who dreameth otherwise is deceived, and deceiveth others with him as aforesaid. Therefore nature and Self always avoid this life, and cling to a life of false freedom and ease, as we have said.

Behold! now cometh an Adam or an Evil Spirit, wishing to justify himself and make excuse, and saith; "Thou wilt almost have it that Christ was bereft of self and the like, yet he spake often of himself, and glorified himself in this and that." Answer: when a man in whom the truth worketh, hath and ought to have a will towards any thing, his will and endeavour and works are for no end, but that the truth may be seen and manifested; and this will was in Christ, and to this end, words and works are needful. And what Christ did because it was the most profitable and best means thereunto, he no more took unto himself than any thing else that happened. Dost thou say now: "Then there was a Wherefore in Christ?" I answer, if thou wert to ask the sun, "Why shinest thou?" he would say: "I must shine, and cannot do otherwise, for it is my nature and property; but this my property, and the light I give, is not of myself, and I do not call it mine." So likewise is it with God and Christ and all who are godly and belong unto God. In them is no willing, nor working nor desiring but has for its end, goodness, as goodness, for the sake of goodness, and they have no other Wherefore than this.

XXVII. How we are to take Christ's Words when he bade us to forsake all Things; and wherein the Union with the Divine Will standeth.

Now, according to what hath been said, ye must observe that when we say, as Christ also saith, that we ought to resign and forsake all things, this is not to be taken in the sense that a man is neither to do nor to purpose any thing; for a man must always have something to do and to order so long as he liveth. But we are to understand by it that the union with God standeth not in any man's powers, in his working or abstaining, perceiving or knowing, nor in that of all the creatures taken together.

Now what is this union? It is that we should be of a truth purely, simply, and wholly at one with the One Eternal Will of God, or altogether without will, so that the created will should flow out into the Eternal Will, and be swallowed up and lost therein, so that the Eternal Will alone should do and leave undone in us. Now mark what may help or further us towards this end. Behold, neither exercises, nor words, nor works, nor any creature nor creature's work, can do this. In this wise therefore must we renounce and forsake all things, that we must not imagine or suppose that any words, works, or exercises, any skill or cunning or any created thing can help or serve us thereto. Therefore we must suffer these things to be what they are, and enter into the union with God. Yet outward things must be, and we must do and refrain so far as is necessary, especially we must sleep and wake, walk and stand still, speak and be silent, and much more of the like. These must go on so long as we live.

XXVIII. How, AFTER A UNION WITH THE DIVINE WILL, THE INWARD MAN STANDETH IMMOVEABLE, THE WHILE THE OUTWARD MAN IS MOVED HITHER AND THITHER.

Now, when this union truly cometh to pass and becometh established, the inward man standeth henceforward immoveable in this union; and God suffereth the outward man to be moved hither and thither, from this to that, of such things as are necessary and right. So that the outward man saith in sincerity, "I have no will to be or not to be, to live or die, to know or not to know, to do or to leave undone and the like; but I am ready for all that is to be, or ought to be, and obedient thereunto, whether I have to do or to suffer." And thus the outward man hath no Wherefore or purpose, but only to do his part to further the Eternal Will. For it is perceived of a truth, that the inward man shall stand immoveable, and that it is needful for the outward man to be moved. And if the inward man have any Wherefore in the actions of the outward man, he saith only that such things must be and ought to be, as are ordained by the Eternal Will. And where God Himself dwelleth in the man, it is thus; as we plainly see in Christ. Moreover, where there is this union, which is the offspring of a Divine light and dwelleth in its beams, there is no spiritual pride or irreverent spirit, but boundless humility, and a lowly broken heart; also an honest blameless walk, justice, peace, content, and all that is of virtue must needs be there. Where they are not, there is no right union, as we have said. For just as neither this thing nor that can bring about or further this union, so there is nothing which hath power to frustrate or hinder it, save the man himself with his self-will, that doeth him this great wrong. Of this be well assured.

XXXII. How GOD IS A TRUE, SIMPLE, PERFECT GOOD, AND HOW HE IS A LIGHT AND A REASON AND ALL VIRTUES, AND HOW WHAT IS HIGHEST AND BEST, THAT IS, GOD, OUGHT TO BE MOST LOVED BY US.

In short, I would have you to understand, that God (in so far as He is good) is goodness as goodness, and not this or that good. But here mark one thing. Behold! what is sometimes here and sometimes there is not everywhere, and above all things and places; so also, what is to-day, or to-morrow, is not always, at all times, and above all time; and what is some thing, this or that, is not all things and above all things. Now behold, if God were some thing, this or that, he would not be all in all, and above all, as He is; and so also, He would not be true Perfection. Therefore God is, and yet He is neither this nor that which the creature, as creature, can perceive, name, conceive or express. Therefore if God (in so far as He is good) were this or that good, He would not be all good, and therefore he would not be the One Perfect Good, which He is. Now God is also a Light and a Reason, the property of which is to give light and shine, and take knowledge; and inasmuch as God is Light and Reason, He must give light and perceive. And all this giving and perceiving of light existeth in God without the creature; not as a work fulfilled, but as a substance or well-spring. But for it to flow out into a work, something really done and accomplished, there must be creatures through whom this can come to pass. Look ye: where this Reason and Light is at work in a creature, it perceiveth and knoweth and teacheth what itself is; how that it is good in itself and neither this thing nor that thing. This Light and Reason knoweth and teacheth men, that it is a true, simple, perfect Good, which is neither this nor that special good, but comprehendeth every kind of good.

Now, having declared that this Light teacheth the One Good, what doth it teach concerning it? Give heed to this. Behold! even as God is the one Good and Light and Reason, so is He also Will and Love and Justice and Truth, and in short all virtues. But all these are in God one Substance, and none of them can be put in exercise and wrought out into deeds without the creature, for in God, without the creature, they are only as a Substance or well-spring, not as a work. But where the One, who is yet all these, layeth hold of a creature, and taketh possession of it, and directeth and maketh use of it, so that He may perceive in it somewhat of His own, behold, in so far as He is Will and Love, He is taught of Himself, seeing that He is also Light and Reason, and He willeth nothing but that One thing which He is.

Behold! in such a creature, there is no longer anything willed or loved but that which is good, because it is good, and for no other reason than that it is good, not because it is this or that, or pleaseth or displeaseth such a one, is pleasant or painful, bitter or sweet, or what not. All this is not asked about nor looked at. And such a creature doth nothing for its own sake, or in its own name, for it hath quitted all Self, and Me, and Mine, and We and Ours, and the like, and these are departed. It no longer saith, "I love myself, or this or that, or what not." And if you were to ask Love, "what lovest thou?" she would answer, "I love Goodness." "Wherefore?" "Because it is good, and for the sake of Goodness." So it is good and just and right to deem that if there were ought better than God, that must be loved better than God. And thus God loveth not Himself as Himself, but as Goodness. And if there were, and He knew, ought better than God, He would love that and not Himself. Thus the Self and the Me are wholly sundered from God, and belong to Him only in so far as they are necessary for Him to be a Person.

Behold! all that we have said must indeed come to pass in a godlike man, or one who is truly "made a partaker of the divine nature;" for else he would not be truly such.

XXXVII. How in God, as God, there can neither be Grief, Sorrow, Displeasure, nor the like, but how it is otherwise in a Man who is "made a Partaker of the Divine Nature"

In God, as God, neither sorrow nor grief nor displeasure can have place, and yet God is grieved on account of men's sins. Now since grief cannot befall God without the creature, this cometh to pass where He is made man, or when he dwelleth in a godlike man. And there, behold, sin is so hateful to God, and grieveth Him so sore, that he would willingly suffer agony and death, if one man's sins might be thereby washed out. And if He were asked whether he would rather live and that sin should remain, or die and destroy sin by His death, He would answer that he would a thousand times rather die. For to God one man's sin is more hateful, and grieveth him worse than His own agony and death. Now if one man's sin grieveth God so sore, what must the sins of all men do? Hereby ye may consider, how greatly man grieveth God with his sins.

And therefore where God is made man, or when He dwelleth in a truly godlike man, nothing is complained of but sin, and nothing else is hateful; for all that is, and is done, without sin, is as God will have it, and is His. But the mourning and sorrow of a truly godlike man on account of sin, must and ought to last until death, should he live till the Day of Judgment, or for ever. From this cause arose that hidden anguish of Christ, of which none can tell or knoweth ought save himself alone, and therefore it is called a mystery.

Moreover, this is an attribute of God,

which He will have, and is well pleased to see in a man; and it is indeed God's own, for it belongeth not unto the man, he cannot make sin to be so hateful to himself. And where God findeth this grief for sin, he loveth and esteemeth it more than ought else; because it is, of all things, the bitterest and saddest that man can endure.

All that is here written touching this divine attribute, which God will have man to possess, that it may be brought into exercise in a living soul, is taught us by that true Light, which also teacheth the man in whom this godlike sorrow worketh, not to take it unto himself, any more than if he were not there. For such a man feeleth in himself that he hath not made it to spring up in his heart, and that it is none of his, but belongeth to God alone.

Anonymous

THE CLOUD OF UNKNOWING

(Fourteenth Century)

IN this anonymous work the mystical theology of Dionysius the Areopagite first appears in English literature. No clues regarding the author's vocation or nationality can be discerned. We can merely say that he was scholarly; was affected by Dionysius, Augustine, Richard of St. Victor, and Bonaventura; was a psychologist of careful insight; was concerned with defining God as the "wholly other" who is sought by man, who "must pass above all clean and unclean being things, above all ascensions of all holy ends or terms set unto man or angels." Not a book always easy to read, it is nevertheless tremendously rewarding. The opening chapters are a good index of its style and contents. They are reprinted from the edition of Justin McCann by permission of Benziger Bros.

[PROGRESS TOWARD GOD]
From *The Cloud of Unknowing*

I. OF FOUR DEGREES OF CHRISTIAN MEN'S LIVING; AND OF THE COURSE OF HIS CALLING THAT THIS BOOK WAS MADE UNTO

*G*hostly friend in God, thou shalt well understand that I find, in my boisterous beholding, four degrees of Christian men's living, and they be these: *Common, Special, Singular,* and *Perfect.* Three of these may be begun and ended in this life; and the fourth may by grace be begun here, but it shall ever last without end in the bliss of heaven. And right as thou seest how they be set here in order, each after other, first *Common,* then *Special,* after *Singular,* and last *Perfect:* right so me thinketh that in the same order and in the same course hath our Lord of his great mercy called thee and led thee unto him by the desire of thine heart.

For first thou knowest well, that when thou wert living in the *common* degree of Christian men's living in company of thy worldly friends, it seemeth to me that the everlasting love of his Godhead through the which he made thee and wrought thee when thou wert nought, and then bought thee with the price of his precious blood when thou wert lost in Adam, might not suffer thee to be so far from him in form and degree of living. And therefore he kindled thy desire full graciously, and fastened by it a leash of a lovely longing, and led thee by it into a more *special* state and form of living, to be a servant of the special servants of his; where thou mightest learn to live more specially and more ghostly in his service than thou didst, or mightest do, in the common degree of living before.

And what more? Yet it seemeth that he would not leave thee thus lightly, for the love of his heart, the which he hath evermore had unto thee since thou wert aught. But what did he? Seest thou not how sweetly and how graciously he hath privily pulled thee to the third degree and manner of living, the which is called *singular*? In the which solitary form and manner of living thou mayest learn to lift up the foot of thy love, and to step towards that state and degree of living that is *perfect*, and the last state of all.

II. A SHORT STIRRING TO MEEKNESS AND TO THE WORKS OF THIS BOOK

Look up now, thou weak wretch, and see what thou art. What art thou, and how hast thou merited thus to be called by our Lord? What weary wretched heart and sleeping in sloth is that, the which is not wakened with the drawing of this love and the voice of his calling? Beware now in this while of thine enemy; and hold thyself never the holier nor the better, for the worthiness of this calling and for the singular form of living that thou art in; but the more wretched and cursed, unless thou do that in thee is goodly, by grace and by counsel, to live according to thy calling. And insomuch thou shouldest be more meek and loving to thy ghostly Spouse, in that he, that is the Almighty God, King of kings and Lord of lords, would meek himself so low unto thee, and, among all the flock of his sheep, so graciously would choose thee to be one of his specials, and then set thee in the place of pasture, where thou mayest be fed with the sweetness of his love, in earnest of thine heritage the kingdom of heaven.

Do on then fast, I pray thee. Look now forwards and let the backwards be. And see what thou lackest and not what thou hast; for that is the readiest getting and keeping of meekness. All thy life now must all ways stand in desire, if thou shalt advance in degree of perfection. This desire must all ways be wrought in thy will, by the hand of Almighty God and thy consent. But one thing I tell thee: he is a jealous lover and suffereth no fellowship, and he liketh not to work in thy will unless he be only with thee by himself. He asketh no help but only thyself. He wills thou do but look upon him and let him alone. And keep thou the windows and the door from flies and enemies assailing. And if thou be willing to do this, thou needest but meekly to set upon him with prayer, and soon will he help thee. Set on them: let me see how thou bearest thee. He is full ready, and doth but abide thee. But what shalt thou do, and how shalt thou set on?

III. HOW THE WORK OF THIS BOOK SHALL BE WROUGHT, AND OF THE WORTHINESS OF IT BEFORE ALL OTHER WORKS

Lift up thine heart unto God with a meek stirring of love; and mean himself and none of his goods. And thereto look that thou loathe to think on aught but himself, so that nought work in thy mind nor in thy will but only himself. And do that in thee is to forget all the creatures that ever God made and the works of them, so that thy thought or thy desire be not directed or stretched to any of them, neither in general nor in special. But let them be, with a seemly recklessness, and take no heed of them.

This is the work of the soul that most pleaseth God. All saints and angels have joy of this work and hasten them to help it with all their might. All fiends be mad when thou dost thus, and try for to defeat it in all that they can. All men living on earth be wonderfully helped by this work, thou knowest not how. Yea, the souls in purgatory are eased of their pains by virtue of this work. Thou thyself art cleansed and made virtuous by no work so much. And yet it is the lightest work of all, when a soul is helped with grace in sensible list; and soonest done. But else it is hard and wonderful for thee to do.

Cease not, therefore, but travail therein till thou feel list. For at the first time when thou dost it, thou findest but a darkness, and as it were a *cloud of unknowing*, thou knowest not what, saving that thou feelest in thy will a naked intent unto God. This darkness and this cloud, howsoever thou dost, is betwixt thee and thy God, and hindereth thee, so that thou mayest neither see him clearly by light of understanding in thy reason, nor feel him in sweetness of love in thine affection. And therefore shape thee to bide in this darkness as long as thou mayest, evermore crying after him whom thou lovest. For if ever thou shalt see him or feel him, as it may be here, it must always be in this cloud and in this darkness. And if thou wilt busily travail as I bid thee, I trust in his mercy that thou shalt come thereto.

IV. OF THE SHORTNESS OF THIS WORK, AND HOW IT MAY NOT BE COME TO BY NO CURIOSITY OF WIT, NOR BY IMAGINATION

But for this, that thou shalt not err in this working, and ween that it be otherwise than it is, I shall tell thee a little more thereof, as me thinketh.

This work asketh no long time ere it be once truly done, as some men ween; for it is the shortest work of all that man may imagine. It is neither longer nor shorter than is an atom; the which atom, by the definition of true philosophers in the science of astronomy, is the least part of time. And it is so little that, for the littleness of it, it is indivisible and nearly incomprehensible. This is that time of the which it is written: *All the time that is given to thee, it shall be asked of thee how thou hast spent it.* And a right thing it is that thou shouldst give account of it. For it is neither longer nor shorter, but exactly equal to one single stirring that is within in the principal working power of thy soul, the which is thy will. For even so many willings or desirings— no more nor no fewer—may be and are in one hour in thy will, as are atoms in one hour. And if thou wert reformed by grace to the first state of man's soul, as it was before sin, then shouldst thou evermore be lord of that stirring or of those stirrings. So that none should go amiss, but all should stretch unto the sovereign desirable, and unto the highest willable thing, the which is God.

For he is even meet to our soul by measuring of his Godhead; and our soul is even meet unto him by the worthiness of our creation to his image and likeness. And he by himself without more, and none but he, is sufficient to the full, and much more, to fulfill the will and the desire of our soul. And our soul, by virtue of this reforming grace, is made sufficient to the full to comprehend all him by love, the which is incomprehensible to all created knowing powers, as is angel or man's soul. He is incomprehensible, I mean, by their knowing and not by their loving. And therefore I call them in this case knowing powers.

But see. All reasonable creatures, angel and man, have in them, each one by himself, one principal working power, the which is called a knowing power, and another principal working power, the which is called a loving power. Of the which two powers, to the first, the which is a knowing power, God who is the maker of them is evermore incomprehensible; but to the second, the which is the loving power, he is, in every man diversely, all comprehensible to the full. Insomuch that one loving soul alone in itself, by virtue of love, may comprehend in itself him who is sufficient to the full —and much more, without comparison— to fill all the souls and angels that may be. And this is the endless marvellous miracle of love, the working of which shall never have end, for ever shall he do it, and never shall he cease for to do it. See, whoso by grace see many; for the feeling of this is endless bliss, and the contrary is endless pain.

And therefore whoso were reformed by grace thus to continue in heeding all the stirrings of his will, should never be in this life—as he may not be without these stirrings in nature—without some taste of the endless sweetness; nor in the bliss of heaven without the full food. And therefore have no wonder that I stir thee to this work. For this is the work, as thou shalt hear afterward, in the which man should have continued if he never had sinned. And to this working was man made, and all things for man, to help him and further him thereto. And by this working shall man be repaired again. And for want of this working a man falleth evermore deeper and deeper into sin, and further and further from God. And by heeding and continual working in this work alone, without more, a man riseth evermore higher and higher from sin, and nearer and nearer unto God.

And therefore take good heed unto time, how thou spendest it; for nothing is more precious than time. In one little time, as little as it is, may heaven be won and lost. A token it is that time is precious: for God, that is giver of time, giveth never two times together, but each one after other. And this he doth because he would not reverse the order or the appointed course in the causes of his creation. For time is made for man, and not man for time. And therefore God, who is the ruler of nature, would not in his giving of time go before the stirring of nature in man's soul; the which stirring is even according to one time only. So that man shall have no excuse against God in the Doom, and at the giving account of the spending of time, saying thus: "Thou givest two times at once, and I have but one stirring at once."

But sorrowfully thou sayest now: "How shall I do? And if it be true what thou sayest, how shall I give account of each time severally; I that unto this day, being now four-and-twenty years of age, have never taken heed of time? If I would now amend it, thou knowest well, by very reason of thy words written before, how it may not be according to the course of nature or of common grace, that I should be able to heed any more times, or make satisfaction for any more, than for those that be to come. Yea, and moreover well I know by very experience, that of those that be to come I shall in no wise, for abundance of frailty and slowness of spirit, be able to heed one in a hundred. So that I am verily confounded by these reasons. Help me now, for the love of Jesu!"

Right well hast thou said "for the love of Jesu." For in the love of Jesu there shall be thine help. Love is such a power that it maketh all things to be shared. Therefore love Jesu, and all thing that he hath it is thine. He by his Godhead is maker and giver of time. He by his Manhood is the true heeder of time. And he, by his Godhead and his Manhood together, is the truest judge and the asker of account of the spending of time. Knit thee therefore to him, by love and by belief; and then by virtue of that knot thou shalt be common partaker with him and with all that by love so be knitted unto him; that is to say, with our Lady Saint Mary, that full was of all grace in heeding of time, with all the angels of heaven that never may lose time, and with all the saints in heaven and on earth, that by the grace of Jesus heed time full justly in virtue of love.

Lo! here lieth comfort; understand thou wisely and pick thee some profit. But of one thing I warn thee beyond all other: I cannot see who may truly claim fellowship thus with Jesu and his just Mother, his high angels and also with his saints, unless he be such a one as doth that in him is, with the help of grace, in heeding of time. So that he be seen to be of profit on his part, so little as it is, unto the fellowship; as each one of them is on his.

And therefore take heed to this work and to the marvellous manner of it within in thy soul. For if it be truly conceived, it is but a sudden stirring, and as it were unadvised, speedily springing unto God as a sparkle from the coal. And it is marvellous to number the stirrings that may be in one hour wrought in a soul that is disposed to this work. And yet, in one stirring of all these, it may have suddenly and perfectly forgotten all created things. But fast after each stirring, through the corruption of the flesh, it falleth down again to some thought, or to some done or undone deed. But what matter? For fast after, it riseth again as suddenly as it did before.

And here may men shortly conceive the manner of this working, and clearly know that it is far from any fantasy, or any false imagination, or quaint opinion; the which be caused, not by such a devout and a meek blind stirring of love, but by a proud, curious and an imaginative wit. Such a proud, curious wit must always be borne down and stiffly trodden under foot, if this work shall truly be conceived in purity of spirit. For whoso heareth this work either read or spoken, and weeneth that it may or should be come to by travail in their wits, and therefore sit and seek in their wits how it may be: in this curiosity they travail their imagination peradventure against the course of nature, and they feign a manner of working the which is neither bodily nor ghostly. Truly this man, whatsoever he be, is perilously deceived. Insomuch, that unless God of his great goodness show his merciful miracle, and make him soon to leave work and meek him to the counsel of proved workers, he shall fall either into frenzies, or else into other great mischiefs of ghostly sins and devils' deceits; through the which he may lightly be lost, both life and soul, without any end. And therefore for God's love beware in this work, and travail not in thy wits nor in thy imagination in nowise: for I tell thee truly, it may not be come to by travail in them; and therefore leave them and work not with them.

And ween not, because I call it a darkness or a cloud, that it is any cloud congealed of the vapours that fly in the air, or any darkness such as in thine house on nights, when the candle is out. For such a darkness and such a cloud mayest thou imagine with curiosity of wit, for to bear before thine eyes in the lightest day of summer; and also contrariwise in the darkest night of winter thou mayest imagine a clear shining light. Let be such falsehoods; I mean not thus. For when I say darkness, I mean a lacking of knowing: as all thing that thou knowest not, or hast forgotten, is dark to thee; for thou seest it not with thy ghostly eye. And for this reason it is called, not a cloud of the air, but a *cloud of unknowing*; which is betwixt thee and thy God.

V. THAT IN THE TIME OF THIS WORK ALL THE CREATURES THAT EVER HAVE BEEN, BE NOW, OR EVER SHALL BE, AND ALL THE WORKS OF THE SAME CREATURES, SHOULD BE HID UNDER THE CLOUD OF FORGETTING

And if ever thou shalt come to this cloud and dwell and work therein as I bid thee, thou must, as this *cloud of un-*

knowing is above thee, betwixt thee and thy God, right so put a *cloud of forgetting* beneath thee, betwixt thee and all the creatures that ever be made. Thou thinkest, peradventure, that thou art full far from God, because this *cloud of unknowing* is betwixt thee and thy God; but surely, if it be well conceived, thou art full further from him when thou hast no *cloud of forgetting* betwixt thee and all the creatures that ever be made. As oft as I say "all the creatures that ever be made," so oft do I mean, not only the creatures themselves, but also the works and the conditions of the same creatures. I except not one creature, whether they be bodily creatures or ghostly; nor yet any condition or work of any creature, whether they be good or evil. But, to speak shortly, all should be hid under the *cloud of forgetting* in this case.

For although it be full profitable sometimes to think of certain conditions and deeds of some certain special creatures, nevertheless in this work it profiteth little or nought. Because mind or thinking of any creature that ever God made, or of any of their deeds either, is a manner of ghostly light; for the eye of thy soul is opened on it and close fixed thereupon, as the eye of a shooter is upon the prick that he shooteth to. And one thing I tell thee, that everything that thou thinkest upon is above thee for the time and betwixt thee and thy God. And insomuch thou art the further from God, that aught is in thy mind but only God.

Yea—and if it be courteous and seemly to say—in this work it profiteth little or nought to think of the kindness or the worthiness of God, nor on our Lady, nor on the saints or angels in heaven, nor yet on the joys of heaven: that is to say, with a special beholding to them, as though thou wouldst by that beholding feed and increase thy purpose. I trow that on nowise it should help in this case and in this work. For although it be good to think upon the kindness of God, and to love him and praise him for it: yet it is far better to think upon the naked being of him, and to love him and praise him for himself.

Catherine of Siena

(1347-1380)

CATHERINE and Francis of Assisi rank as the greatest of the Italian saints. In *Mysticism* Evelyn Underhill comprehensively describes Catherine in these words: "She was a great active and a great ecstatic; at once politician, teacher, and contemplative, holding a steady balance between the inner and the outer life. With little education she yet contrived, in a short career dogged by persistent ill-health, to change the course of history, rejuvenate religion, and compose, in her Divine Dialogue, one of the jewels of Italian religious literature." From the home of a Siena dyer Catherine rose to a place of staunch leadership, evidenced by her influence in having the papacy moved from Avignon back to Rome. A Dominican nun, she was canonized in 1461. The following selection concerns the yearning of the soul for oneness with God. It is taken from *The Dialogue of St. Catherine of Siena*, translated by Algar Thorold, and used by permission of The Newman Bookshop.

[A TREATISE ON TEARS]

From *The Dialogue*

HOW THIS DEVOUT SOUL SEEKS KNOWLEDGE FROM GOD CONCERNING THE STATE AND FRUIT OF TEARS

Then this soul, yearning with very great desire, and rising as one intoxicated both by the union which she had had with God, and by what she had heard and tasted of the Supreme and Sweet Truth, yearned with grief over the ignorance of creatures, in that they did not know their Benefactor, or the affection of the love of God. And nevertheless she had joy from the hope of the promise that the Truth of God had made to her, teaching her the way she was to direct her will (and the other servants of God as well as herself) in order that He should do mercy to the world. And, lifting up the eye of her intellect upon the sweet Truth, to whom she remained united, wishing to know somewhat of the aforesaid states of the soul of which God had spoken to her, and seeing that the soul passes through these states with tears, she wished to learn from the Truth concerning the different kinds of tears, and how they came to be, and whence they proceeded, and the fruit that resulted from weeping. Wishing then to know this from the Sweet, Supreme and First Truth, as to the manner of being and reason of the aforesaid tears, and inasmuch as the truth cannot be learnt from any other than from the Truth Himself, and nothing can be learnt in the Truth but what is seen by the eye of the intellect, she made her request of the Truth. For it is necessary for him who is lifted with desire to learn the Truth with the light of faith.

Wherefore, knowing that she had not forgotten the teaching which the Truth, that is, God, had given her, that in no other way could she learn about the different states and fruits of tears, she rose out of herself, exceeding every limit of her nature with the greatness of her desire. And, with the light of a lively faith, she opened the eye of her intellect upon the Eternal Truth, in whom she saw and knew the Truth, in the matter of her request, for God Himself manifested it to her, and condescending in His benignity to her burning desire, fulfilled her petition.

HOW THERE ARE FIVE KINDS OF TEARS

Then said the Supreme and Sweet Truth of God, "Oh, beloved and dearest daughter, thou beggest knowledge of the reasons and fruits of tears, and I have not despised thy desire. Open well the eye of thy intellect and I will show thee, among the aforesaid states of the soul, of which I have told thee, concerning the imperfect tears caused by fear; but first rather of the tears of wicked men of the world. These are the tears of damnation. The former are those of fear, and belong to men who abandon sin from fear of punishment, and weep for fear. The third are the tears of those who, having abandoned sin, are beginning to serve and taste Me, and weep for very sweetness; but since their love is imperfect, so also is their weeping, as I have told thee. The fourth are the tears of those who have arrived at the perfect love of their neighbour, loving Me without any regard whatsoever for themselves. These weep and their weeping is perfect. The fifth are joined to the fourth and are tears of sweetness let fall with great peace, as I will explain to thee. I will tell thee also of the tears of fire, without bodily tears of the eyes, which satisfy those who often would desire to weep and cannot. And I wish thee to know that all these various graces may exist in one soul, who, rising from fear and imperfect love, reaches perfect love in the unitive state. Now I will begin to tell thee of these tears in the following way."

OF THE DIFFERENCE OF THESE TEARS, ARISING
FROM THE EXPLANATION OF THE AFORESAID
STATE OF THE SOUL

"I wish thee to know that every tear proceeds from the heart, for there is no member of the body that will satisfy the heart so much as the eye. If the heart is in pain the eye manifests it. And if the pain be sensual the eye drops hearty tears which engender death, because proceeding from the heart, they are caused by a disordinate love distinct from the love of Me; for such love, being disordinate and an offence to Me, receives the meed of mortal pain and tears. It is true that their guilt and grief are more or less heavy, according to the measure of their disordinate love. And these form that first

class, who have the tears of death, of whom I have spoken to thee, and will speak again. Now, begin to consider the tears which give the commencement of life, the tears, that is, of those who, knowing their guilt, set to weeping for fear of the penalty they have incurred.

"These are both hearty and sensual tears, because the soul, not having yet arrived at perfect hatred of its guilt on account of the offence thereby done to Me, abandons it with a hearty grief for the penalty which follows the sin committed, while the eye weeps in order to satisfy the grief of the heart.

"But the soul, exercising herself in virtue, begins to lose her fear, knowing that fear alone is not sufficient to give her eternal life, as I have already told thee when speaking of the second stage of the soul. And so she proceeds, with love, to know herself and My goodness in her, and begins to take hope in My mercy in which her heart feels joy. Sorrow for her grief, mingled with the joy of her hope in My mercy, causes her eye to weep, which tears issue from the very fountain of her heart.

"But, inasmuch as she has not yet arrived at great perfection, she often drops sensual tears, and if thou askest Me why, I reply: Because the root of self-love is not sensual love, for that has already been removed, as has been said, but it is a spiritual love with which the soul desires spiritual consolations or loves some creature spiritually. (I have spoken to thee at length regarding the imperfections of such souls.) Wherefore, when such a soul is deprived of the thing she loves, that is, internal or external consolation, the internal being the consolation received from Me, the external being that which she had from the creature, and when temptations and the persecutions of men come on her, her heart is full of grief. And, as soon as the eye feels the grief and suffering of the heart, she begins to weep with a tender and compassionate sorrow, pitying herself with the spiritual compassion of self-love; for her self-will is not yet crushed and destroyed in everything, and in this way she lets fall sensual tears—tears, that is, of spiritual passion. But, growing, and exercising herself in the light of self-knowledge, she conceives displeasure at herself and finally perfect self-hatred. From this she draws true knowledge of My goodness with a fire of love, and she begins to unite herself to Me, and to conform her will to Mine and so to feel joy and compassion. Joy in herself through the affection of love, and compassion for her neighbour, as I told thee in speaking of the third stage. Immediately her eye, wishing to satisfy the heart, cries with hearty love for Me and for her neighbour, grieving solely for My offence and her neighbour's loss, and not for any penalty or loss due to herself; for she does not think of herself, but only of rendering glory and praise to My Name, and, in an ecstasy of desire, she joyfully takes the food prepared for her on the table of the Holy Cross, thus conforming herself to the humble, patient, and immaculate Lamb, My only-begotten Son, of whom I made a Bridge, as I have said. Having thus sweetly travelled by that Bridge, following the doctrine of My sweet Truth, enduring with true and sweet patience every pain and trouble which I have permitted to be inflicted upon her for her salvation, having manfully received them all, not choosing them according to her own tastes, but accepting them according to Mine, and not only, as I said, enduring them with patience, but sustaining them with joy, she counts it glory to be persecuted for My Name's sake in whatever she may have to suffer. Then the soul arrives at such delight and tranquillity of mind that no tongue can tell it. Having crossed the river by means of the Eternal Word, that is, by the doctrine of My only-begotten Son, and, having fixed the eye of her intellect on Me, the Sweet Supreme Truth, having seen the Truth, knows it; and knowing it, loves it. Drawing her affection after her intellect, she tastes My Eternal Deity, and she knows and sees the Divine nature united to your humanity.

"Then she reposes in Me, the Sea Pacific, and her heart is united to Me in love, as I told thee when speaking of the fourth and unitive state. When she thus feels Me, the Eternal Deity, her eyes let fall tears of sweetness, tears indeed of milk, nourishing the soul in true patience; an odoriferous ointment are these tears, shedding odours of great sweetness.

"Oh, best beloved daughter, how glorious is that soul who has indeed been able to pass from the stormy ocean to Me, the Sea Pacific, and in that Sea, which is Myself, the Supreme and Eternal Deity, to fill the pitcher of her heart. And her eye, the conduit of her heart, endeavours to satisfy her heart-pangs, and so sheds tears. This is the last stage in which the soul is blessed and sorrowful.

"Blessed she is through the union which she feels herself to have with Me, tasting the divine love; sorrowful through the offences which she sees done to My goodness and greatness, for she has seen and tasted the bitterness of this in her self-knowledge, by which self-knowledge, together with her knowledge of Me, she arrived at the final stage. Yet this sorrow is no impediment to the unitive state, which produces tears of great sweetness through self-knowledge, gained in love of the neighbour, in which exercise the soul discovers the plaint of My divine mercy, and grief at the offences caused to her neighbour, weeping with those who weep, and rejoicing with those who rejoice—that is, who live in My love. Over these the soul rejoices, seeing glory and praise rendered Me by My servants, so that the third kind of grief does not prevent the fourth, that is, the final grief belonging to the unitive state; they rather give savour to each other, for, had not this last grief (in which the soul finds such union with Me), developed from the grief belonging to the third state of neighbourly love, it would not be perfect. Therefore it is necessary that the one should flavour the other, else the soul would come to a state of presumption, induced by the subtle breeze of love of her own reputation, and would fall at once, vomited from the heights to the depths. Therefore it is necessary to bear with others and practise continually love to one's neighbour, together with true knowledge of oneself.

"In this way will she feel the fire of My love in herself, because love of her neighbour is developed out of love of Me—that is, out of that learning which the soul obtained by knowing herself and My goodness in her. When, therefore, she sees herself to be ineffably loved by Me, she loves every rational creature with the self-same love with which she sees herself to be loved. And, for this reason, the soul that knows Me immediately expands to the love of her neighbour, because she sees that I love that neighbour ineffably, and so, herself, loves the object which she sees Me to have loved still more. She further knows that she can be of no use to Me and can in no way repay Me that pure love with which she feels herself to be loved by Me, and therefore endeavours to repay it through the medium which I have given her, namely, her neighbour, who is the medium through which you can all serve Me. For, as I have said to thee, you can perform all virtues by means of your neighbour, I having given you all creatures, in general and in particular, according to the diverse graces each has received from Me, to be ministered unto by you; you should therefore love them with the same pure love with which I have loved you. That pure love cannot be returned directly to Me, because I have loved you without being Myself loved, and without any consideration of Myself whatsoever, for I loved you without being loved by you —before you existed; it was, indeed, love that moved Me to create you to My own image and similitude. This love you cannot repay to Me, but you can pay it to My rational creature, loving your neighbour without being loved by him and without consideration of your own advantage, whether spiritual or temporal, but loving him solely for the praise and glory of My Name, because he has been loved by Me.

"Thus will you fulfil the commandment of the law, to love Me above everything, and your neighbour as yourselves.

"True indeed is it that this height cannot be reached without passing through the second stage, namely the second stage of union which becomes the third (and final) stage. Nor can it be preserved when it has been reached if the soul abandon the affection from which it has been developed, the affection to which the second class of tears belongs. It is therefore impossible to fulfil the law given by Me, the Eternal God, without fulfilling that of your neighbour, for these two laws are the feet of your affection by which the precepts and counsels are observed, which were given you, as I have told thee, by My Truth, Christ crucified. These two states united nourish your soul in virtue, making her to grow in the perfection of virtue and in the unitive state. Not that the other state is changed because this further state has been reached for this further state does but increase the riches of grace in new and various gifts and admirable elevations of the mind, in the knowledge of the truth, as I said to thee, which, though it is mortal, appears immortal because the soul's perception of her own sensuality is mortified and her will is dead through the union which she has attained with Me.

"Oh, how sweet is the taste of this union to the soul, for, in tasting it, she sees My secrets! Wherefore she often receives the spirit of prophecy, knowing the things of the future. This is the effect of My Goodness, but the humble soul should despise such things, not indeed in so far as they are given her by My love, but in so far as she desires them by reason of her appetite for consolation, considering herself unworthy of peace and quiet of mind, in order to nourish virtue within her soul. In such a case let her not remain in the second stage, but return to the valley of self-knowledge. I give her this light, My grace permitting, so that she may ever grow in virtue. For the soul is never so perfect in this life that she cannot attain to a higher perfection of love. My only-begotten Son, your Captain, was the only One who could increase in no perfection, because He was one thing with Me, and I with Him, wherefore His soul was blessed through union with the Divine nature. But do ye, His pilgrim-members, be ever ready to grow in greater perfection, not indeed to another stage, for as I have said, ye have now reached the last, but to that further grade of perfection in the last stage, which may please you by means of My Grace."

How the Four Stages of the Soul, to Which Belong the Five Aforesaid State of Tears, Produce Tears of Infinite Value: and How God Wishes To Be Served As the Infinite, and Not As Anything Finite

"These five states are like five principal canals which are filled with abundant tears of infinite value, all of which give life if they are disciplined in virtue, as I have said to thee. Thou askest how their value can be infinite. I do not say that in this life your tears can become infinite, but I call them infinite, on account of the infinite desire of your soul from which they proceed. I have already told thee how tears come from the heart, and how the heart distributes them to the eye, having gathered them in its own fiery desire. As, when green wood is on the fire, the moisture it contains groans on account of the heat, because the wood is green, so does the heart, made green again by the renovation of grace drawn into itself among its self-love which dries up the soul, so that fiery desire and tears are united. And inasmuch as desire is never ended, it is never satisfied in this life, but the more the soul loves the less she seems to herself to love. Thus is holy desire, which is founded in love, exercised, and with this desire the eye weeps. But when the soul is separated from the body and has reached Me, her End, she does not on that account abandon desire, so as to no longer yearn for Me or love her neighbour, for love has entered into her like a woman bearing the fruits of all other virtues. It is true that suffering is over and ended, as I have said to thee, for the soul that desires Me possesses Me in very truth, without any fear of ever losing that which she has so long desired; but, in this way, hunger is kept up, be-cause those who are hungry are satisfied, and as soon as they are satisfied hunger again; in this way their satiety is without disgust, and their hunger without suffer-ing, for, in Me, no perfection is wanting.

"Thus is your desire infinite, otherwise it would be worth nothing, nor would any virtue of yours have any life if you served Me with anything finite. For I, who am the Infinite God, wish to be served by you with infinite service, and the only infinite thing you possess is the affection and desire of your souls. In this sense I said that there were tears of in-finite value, and this is true as regards their mode, of which I have spoken, namely, of the infinite desire which is united to the tears. When the soul leaves the body the tears remain behind, but the affection of love has drawn to itself the fruit of the tears, and consumed it, as happens in the case of the water in your furnace. The water has not really been taken out of the furnace, but the heat of the fire has consumed it and drawn it into itself. Thus the soul, having arrived at tasting the fire on My divine charity, and having passed from this life in a state of love towards Me and her neighbour, having further possessed that unitive love which caused her tears to fall, does not cease to offer Me her bless-ed desires, tearful indeed, though without pain or physical weeping, for physical tears have evaporated in the furnace, be-coming tears of fire of the Holy Spirit. Thou seest then how tears are infinite, how, as regards the tears shed in this life only, no tongue can tell what different sorrows may cause them. I have now told thee the difference between four of these states of tears."

Of the Fruit of Worldly Men's Tears

"It remains for Me to tell thee of the fruit produced by tears shed with desire, and received into the soul. But first will I speak to thee of that first class of men whom I mentioned at the beginning of this My discourse; those, that is, who live miserably in the world, making a god of created things and of their own sensual-ity, from which comes damage to their body and soul. I said to thee that every tear proceeded from the heart, and this is the truth, for the heart grieves in proportion to the love it feels. So worldly men weep when their heart feels pain, that is, when they are deprived of something which they loved.

"But many and diverse are their complainings. Dost thou know how many? There are as many as there exist different loves. And inasmuch as the root of self-love is corrupt, everything that grows from it is corrupt also. Self-love is a tree on which grow nothing but fruits of death, putrid flowers, stained leaves, branches bowed down, and struck by various winds. This is the tree of the soul. For ye are all trees of love, and without love ye cannot live, for ye have been made by Me for love. The soul who lives virtuously, places the root of her tree in the valley of true humility; but those who live thus miserably are planted on the mountain of pride, whence it follows that since the root of the tree is badly planted, the tree can bear no fruits of life but only of death. Their fruits are their actions, which are all poisoned by many and diverse kinds of sin, and if they should produce some good fruit among their actions, even it will be spoilt by the foulness of its root, for no good actions done by a soul in mortal sin are of value for eternal life, for they are not done in grace. Let not, however, such a soul abandon on this account its good works, for every good deed is rewarded, and every evil deed punished. A good action performed out of a state of grace is not sufficient to merit eternal life, as has been said, but My Justice, My Divine Goodness, grants an incomplete reward, imperfect as the action which obtains it. Often such a man is rewarded in temporal matters; sometimes I give him more time in which to repent, as I have already said to thee in another place. This also will I sometimes do, I grant him the life of grace by means of My servants who are pleasing and acceptable to Me. I acted in this way with My glorious apostle Paul, who abandoned his infidelity, and the persecutions he directed against the Christians, at the prayer of St. Stephen. See truly, therefore, that, in whatever state a man may be, he should never stop doing good.

"I said to thee that the flowers of this tree were putrid, and so in truth they are. Its flowers are the stinking thoughts of the heart, displeasing to Me, and full of hatred and unkindness towards their neighbour. So if a man be a thief, he robs Me of honour, and takes it himself. This flower stinks less than that of false judgment, which is of two kinds. The first with regard to Me, by which men judge My secret judgments, gauging falsely all My mysteries, that is, judging that which I did in love, to have been done in hatred; that which I did in truth to have been done in falsehood; that which I give them for life, to have been given them for death. They condemn and judge everything according to their weak intellect; for they have blinded the eye of their intellect with sensual self-love, and hidden the pupil of the most holy Faith, which they will not allow to see or know the Truth. The second kind of false judgment is directed against a man's neighbour, from which often come many evils, because the wretched man wishes to set himself up as the judge of the affections and heart of other rational creatures, when he does not yet know himself. And, for an action which he may see, or for a word he may hear, he will judge the affection of the heart. My servants always judge well, because they are founded on Me, the Supreme Good; but such as these always judge badly, for they are founded on evil. Such critics as these cause hatreds, murders, unhappinesses of all kinds to their neighbours, and remove themselves far away from the love of My servants' virtue.

"Truly these fruits follow the leaves, which are the words which issue from their mouth in insult to Me and the Blood of My only-begotten Son, and in hatred to their neighbours. And they think of nothing else but cursing and condemning My works, and blaspheming and saying evil of every rational creature, according as their judgment may suggest to them.

The unfortunate creatures do not remember that the tongue is made only to give honour to Me, and to confess sins, and to be used in love of virtue, and for the salvation of the neighbour. These are the stained leaves of that most miserable fault, because the heart from which they proceeded was not clean, but all spotted with duplicity and misery. How much danger, apart from the spiritual privation of grace to the soul, of temporal loss may not occur! For ye have all heard and seen how, through words alone, have come revolutions of states, and destructions of cities, and many homicides and other evils, a word having entered the heart of the listener, and having passed through a space not large enough for a knife.

"I say that this tree has seven branches drooping to the earth, on which grow the flowers and leaves in the way I have told you. These branches are the seven mortal sins which are full of many and diverse wickednesses, contained in the roots and trunk of self-love and of pride, which first made both branches and flowers of many thoughts, the leaves of words, and the fruits of wicked deeds. They stand drooping to the earth because the branches of mortal sin can turn no other way

than to the earth, the fragile disordinate substance of the world. Do not marvel, they can turn no way but that in which they can be fed by the earth; for their hunger is insatiable, and the earth is unable to satisfy them. They are insatiable and unbearable to themselves, and it is conformable to their state that they should always be unquiet, longing and desiring that thing which they have to satiety. This is the reason why such satiety cannot content them, because they (who are infinite in their being) are always desiring something finite; because their being will never end, though their life to grace ends when they commit mortal sin.

"Man is placed above all creatures, and not beneath them, and he cannot be satisfied or content except in something greater than himself. Greater than himself there is nothing but Myself, the Eternal God. Therefore I alone can satisfy him, and, because he is deprived of this satisfaction by his guilt, he remains in continual torment and pain. Weeping follows pain, and when he begins to weep the wind strikes the tree of self-love, which he has made the principle of all his being."

Walter Hilton

(d. 1396)

INFLUENCED especially by Dionysius and Richard of St. Victor, Walter Hilton left *The Scale of Perfection* as one of the most illuminating writings showing the steps to divine companionship. Through *reason* one emerges into *light;* through *light* one climbs the ascent to *love.* Hilton was a canon of Thurgarton in Nottinghamshire. Although broad in learning, he was more of a divine lover than a speculative metaphysician. In his accent on "the dark night" from which the soul must climb he prepares the way for John of the Cross. "Of the Contemplative Life" describes the ladder by which one climbs to perfection. It is from *The Scale of Perfection,* edited by Evelyn Underhill.

[THE CONTEMPLATIVE LIFE]
From *The Scale of Perfection*

III. OF CONTEMPLATIVE LIFE AND THE WORKS
THEREOF

*C*ontemplative life lieth in perfect love and charity felt inwardly by ghostly virtues, and by soothfast knowing and sight of God and ghostly things. This life belongeth specially to them which forsake for the love of God all worldly riches, worships and outward businesses and wholly give them body and soul up, their mights and their cunning, to service of God by ghostly occupation. Now then, since it is so that thy state asketh for to be contemplative, for that is the end and the intent of thine enclosing, that thou mightest more freely and entirely give thee to ghostly occupation: then behoveth thee for to be right busy night and day with travail of body and of spirit, for to come to that life as near as thou mightest, by such means as thou hopest were best unto thee.

Nevertheless, before I tell thee of the means, I shall tell thee first a little more of this life contemplative, that thou mightest somewhat see what it is, and then set it as a mark in the sight of thy soul whereto thou shalt draw in all thine occupation.

IV. Of the First Part of Contemplation

Contemplative life hath three parts. The first lieth in knowing of God and of ghostly things, gotten by reason, by teaching of man, and by study in Holy Writ; without ghostly affections and inly savour felt by the special gift of the Holy Ghost. This part have specially some lettered men, and great clerks which by long study and travail in Holy Writ come into this knowing, more or less, after the subtlety of kindly wit and continuance of study upon the general gift that God gives each man that hath use of reason. This knowing is good, and it may be called a part of contemplation in as mickle as it is a sight of soothfastness, and a knowing of ghostly things. Nevertheless it is but a figure and a shadow of very contemplation, for it hath not ghostly savour in God nor inwardly sweetness, which may no man feel, but he be in mickle charity. For that is the proper well of our Lord, to the which comes none alien. But this manner of knowing is common to good and to bad, for it may be had without charity. And therefore it is not very contemplation, as oftentimes heretics, hypocrites, and fleshly living men have more such knowing than many true Christian men; and yet have

these men no charity. Of this manner knowing speaketh Saint Paul thus: *Si habuero omnem scientiam et noverim mysteria omnia, caritatem autem non habuero, nihil sum.* If I had full knowing of all thing, yea! and knew all privities and I had no charity, I am right nought. Nevertheless, if they that have this knowing keep them in meekness and charity, and flee worldly and fleshly sins of their mights, it is to them a good way and a great disposing to very contemplation if they be true and pray devoutly after the grace of the Holy Ghost.

Other men that have this knowing and turn it into pride and vain glory of themselves, or into covetise and yearning of worldly states, worships and riches, not meekly taking it in praising of God, nor charitably spending it in the profit of their even-christians, some of them fall either into errors and heresies, or into other open sins by the which they scandalize themselves and all Holy Kirk. Of this knowing said Saint Paul thus: *Scientia inflat, caritas autem edificat.* Knowing alone lifteth up the heart into pride; but meddle it with charity and then turneth it into edification. This knowing alone, it is but water, unsavoury and cold; and therefore if they that have it would meekly offer it up to our Lord and pray Him of His grace, He should with His blessing turn the water into wine, as He did for the prayer of His mother at the feast of Architriclin. That is for to say, he should turn the unsavoury knowing into wisdom, and the cold naked reason into ghostly light and burning love, by the gift of the Holy Ghost.

V. Of the Second Part of Contemplation

The second part of contemplation lieth principally in affection, without light of understanding of ghostly things; and this is commonly of simple and unlettered men which give them wholly to devotion. And this is felt on this manner. When a man or a woman in meditation of God, by grace of the Holy Ghost feeleth fervour of love and ghostly sweetness, by the mind of His Passion or of any of His works in His manhood; or he feels a great trust in the goodness and the mercy of God, for the forgiveness of his sins and for His great gifts of grace, or else he feeleth a dread in his affection with great reverence of the privy dooms of God which he seeth not, and of His rightwiseness; or in prayer he feeleth the thought of his heart draw up from all earthly things, strained together with all the mights of it, upstying into our Lord by fervent desire and with ghostly delight; and nevertheless in that time he hath no open sight in understanding of ghostly things, nor of privities of Holy Writ in special, but only that him thinketh for the time nothing liketh him so mickle as for to pray or think as he doth for savour, delight, and confort, that he findeth therein; and yet can he nought tell what it is, but he feeleth it well, for out of it spring many sweet tears, burning desires, and still mournings, which scour and cleanse the heart from all the filth of sin, and maketh it melt into wonderful sweetness of Jhesu Christ, buxom, supple and ready for to fulfill all God's will. In so mickle that him thinketh he maketh no care what becomes of himself so that God's will were fulfilled, with such many stirrings more than I can or may say. This feeling may not be had without great grace; and who so hath it, for the time he is in charity. Which charity may not be lost, nor lessened, though the fervour of it pass away, but by a deadly sin; and that is comfortable. This may be called the second part of contemplation.

VI. Of the Lower Degree of the Second Part of Contemplation

Nevertheless this part hath two degrees. The lower degree of this feeling, men which are active may have by grace when they be visited on our Lord, as mightily and as fervently as they that give them wholly to contemplative life and have this gift. But this feeling in his fervour cometh not always when a man would nor it lasteth not well long. It cometh and goeth as he will that giveth it. And therefore who so have it, meek himself and thank God, and keep it privy, but

if it be to his confessor and hold it as long as he may with discretion. And when it is withdrawn dread not too mickle, but stand in faith and in a meek hope, with patient abiding till it come again. This is a little tasting of the sweetness of the love of God, of the which David saith thus in the psalter: *Gustate et videte quam suavis est Dominus.* Taste and see ye the sweetness of our Lord.

VII. Of the Higher Degree of the Second Part of Contemplation

But the higher degree of this part may not be had and holden, but of them which are in great rest of body and of soul; the which by grace of Jhesu Christ and long travail bodily and ghostly feel a rest of heart and cleanness in conscience, so that them liketh nothing so mickle for to do, as to sit still in rest of body and for to alway pray to God and think on our Lord; and for to think some time of the blessed name of Jhesu, which is comfortable and delectable to them, that they by the mind of it, feel them fed in their affection. And not only that name, but all other manner of prayers, as the Paternoster, or the Ave, or hymns or psalms and other devout sayings of Holy Kirk are turned as it were into a ghostly mirth and sweet song, by the which they are comforted and strengthened against all sins, and mickle relieved of bodily disease. Of this degree speaketh Saint Paul thus: *Nolite inebriari vino sed implemini Spiritu sancto, loquentes vobismetipsis in hymnis et psalmis, et conticis spiritualibus, cantantes et psallentes in cordibus vestris Domino.* Be ye not drunken with wine, but be ye fulfilled of the Holy Ghost, saying to thyself in hymns and psalms and ghostly songs, singing and psalming in your heart to our Lord. Whoso hath this grace, keep he himself in lowness, and look that he be aye desiring for to come to more knowing and feeling of God, in the third part of contemplation.

VIII. Of the Third Part of Contemplation

The third part of contemplation, which is perfect as it may be here, lieth both in cognition and in affection: that is for to say, in knowing and in perfect living of God. And that is when a man's soul first is reformed by fullhead of virtues to the image of Jhesu; and after when he is visited, is taken in from all earthly and fleshly affections, from vain thoughts and imaginings of all bodily creatures, and as it were mickle is ravished out of the bodily wits and then by the grace of the Holy Ghost is illumined for to see by understanding Soothfastness, which is God, and ghostly things, with a soft sweet burning love in Him, so perfectly that by ravishing of love the soul is oned for the time and conformed to the image of the Trinity. The beginning of this contemplation may be felt in this life, but the fullhead of it is kept until the bliss of heaven. Of this oning and conforming to our Lord speaketh Saint Paul, thus: *Qui adhaeret Deo unus spiritus est cum illo.* That is for to say who so by ravishing of love is fastened to God, then God and a soul are not two but both one. Not in flesh, but in one spirit. And soothly in this oning is the marriage made atwixt God and the soul, which shall never be broken.

IX. OF THE PARTING OF THE THIRD PART OF
CONTEMPLATION FROM THE SECOND,
AND OF PRAISING THEREOF

That other part may be called burning love in devotion; but this is burning love in contemplation. That is lower; this is the higher. That is the sweeter to the bodily feeling; this is the sweeter to the ghostly feeling, for it is more inward, more ghostly, more worthy and more wonderful. For this is verily a tasting, so little as it is, and an earnest of the sight of heavenly joy, not clearly, but half in murkness, which shall be fulfilled and openly cleared in the bliss of heaven; as Saint Paul saith: *Videmus nunc per speculum in aenigmate; tunc autem videbimus facie ad faciem.* We see now God by a mirror, as it were in a murkness, but in heaven shall we see openly face to face. This is the illumination of understanding in delights of loving, as David saith in

psalter: *Et nox mea illuminatio mea in deliciis meis.* My night is my light in my delight. The tother part is milk for children, this is whole meat for perfect men, which have assayed wits to choose good from evil; as Saint Paul saith: *Perfectorum est solidus cibus qui habent sensus exercitatos ad discretionem boni et mali.*

The working and the full use of this gift may no man have, but if he be first reformed to the likeness of Jhesu by fullhead of virtues. Nor there may no man living in flesh deadly have it continually in its fullhead and in the overpassing, but by times when he is visited. And also I conceive of the writing of holy men, it is a well short time; for soon after he falleth in a sobriety of bodily feeling. And all this work maketh charity. Thus, as I understand, saith Saint Paul of himself: *Sive excedimus, Deo, sive sobrii sumus, vobis; caritas Christi urget nos.* Whether we overpass our bodily wits to God in Contemplation, or we are more sober to you by bodily feeling, the charity of Christ stirreth us. Of this part of contemplation and of conforming to God, speaketh Saint Paul openly thus: *Nos autem revelata facie gloriam Domini speculantes, transformamur in eamdem imaginem, a claritate in claritatem tanquam a Domini Spiritu.* And this is thus mickle for to say, Saint Paul in the person of himself and of perfect men saith thus: We, first reformed by virtues, the face of our soul uncovered by opening of the ghostly eye, behold as in a mirror heavenly joy, full shapen and oned to the image of our Lord, from clarity of faith into clarity of understanding or else from clarity of desire to clarity of blessed love. And all this is wrought of the Spirit of our Lord in a man's soul, as Saint Paul saith. This part of Contemplation God gives where that He will; to learned and to lewd, men and women occupied in prelacy, and to solitary also; but it is special, not common. And also though a man which is active have the gift of it by a special grace, nevertheless the full use of it may no man have, but he be solitary and in life contemplative.

XIII. How and in What Things a Contemplative Man Should Be Occupied

In knowing and ghostly feeling of these should be the occupation of a contemplative man, for in these four may be understood the full knowing of ghostly things. This occupation is that ilk one thing which Saint Paul coveted, saying thus: *Unum vero, quae retro sunt obliviscens, in anteriora me extendam sequor si quo modo comprehendam supernum bravium.* Thus mickle is this for to say: One thing, as who saith, is lief to me for to covet, and that is that I might forget all things which are hindward or backward, and I shall stretch out mine heart aye forthward, for to feel and to grip the sovereign meed of the endless bliss. Hindward are all bodily things, forthward are ghostly things; and therefore Saint Paul would forget all bodily things and his own body also, with this that he might see ghostly things.

XIV. How in Reason and in Will Virtue Beginneth, and in Love and in Liking It Is Made Perfect

Now I have told thee a little of contemplation, what it should be; for this intent, that thou mightest know it and set it as a mark before the sight of thy soul, and for to desire all thy lifetime for to come to one part of it by the grace of our Lord Jhesu Christ. This is the conforming of a soul to God; which may not be had, but if he be first reformed by fullhead of virtues turned into affection. And that is when a man loveth virtue, for it is good in itself.

There is many man that hath virtue, as lowness, patience, charity to his evenchristian and such other, only in his reason and will, and hath no ghostly delight nor love in them. For ofttime he feeleth grouching, heaviness yet he doth them, by stirring of reason for dread of God. This man hath virtues in reason and in his will, not the love of them in affection; but when by the grace of Jhesu, and by ghostly and bodily exercise, reason is y-turned into light, and will into love, then hath he virtues in affection, for he hath so well gnawen upon the bitter bark of the nut that he hath broken it, and feedeth him with the kernel. That is for to say, the virtues which were first heavy for to do are now turned into very delight and savour, as a man when him liketh in meekness, in patience, in cleanness, in sobriety and in charity, as in any delices. Soothly until virtues be thus turned into affection he may have the second part of contemplation, but to the third soothfastly shall he not come. Now since virtues are disposing to contemplation, then behoves thee for to use certain means for to come to virtues.

Margery Kempe

(ca. 1400)

IN 1934 *The Book of Margery Kempe* was discovered in the English manor house of W. Butler-Bowdon. The book not only tells much about English personalities of the early fifteenth century, but it also portrays the marvelous manner in which God touched Margery Kempe's life.

She was born in Lynn, England, of a wealthy family. Her education was probably rather mediocre, as she seems to have been without knowledge of either Latin or French. She went on pilgrimages abroad, to Rome, Jerusalem, and the Baltic. Her visits and interviews with Philip Repington, bishop of Lincoln, and Thomas Arundel, archbishop of Canterbury, are recorded. She seems to have been dependent upon them for spiritual advice.

From her writings we infer that she was acquainted with the works of Walter Hilton, Juliana of Norwich, Bridget of Sweden, Catherine of Siena, Richard Rolle, Bonaventura, Heinrich Suso, and with *The Cloud of Unknowing*. Apparently a very sensitive and unpredictable person, she nevertheless ranks among the interesting figures of the mystical tradition. These selections from a modern version of her work by W. Butler-Bowdon are reprinted by permission of The Devin-Adair Co.

[CONTEMPLATIONS AND CONSOLATIONS]

From *The Book of Margery Kempe*

XIV. HER DESIRE FOR DEATH. OUR LORD CONSOLES HER AND PROMISES THAT SHE SHALL BE SAFE WHEREVER SHE GOES

This creature thought it was full merry to be reproved for God's love. It was to her great solace and comfort when she was chidden and scolded for the love of Jesus, for reproving sin, for speaking of virtue, and for conversing in Scripture which she had learnt in sermons and in communing with clerks. She imagined to herself what death she might die for Christ's sake. She thought she would like to be slain for God's love, but feared the point of death and therefore imagined for herself the most soft death, as she thought, for fear of impatience, which was to be bound head and foot to a post, and her head to be smitten off with a sharp axe, for God's love.

Then said Our Lord in her mind:—"I thank thee, daughter, that thou wouldst suffer death for My love, for, as often as thou thinkest so, thou shalt have the same reward in Heaven as if thou hadst suf-

fered the same death. And yet shall no man slay thee, nor fire burn thee, nor water drown thee, nor wind harm thee, for I may not forget how thou art written on My hands and My feet. It likes me well, the pains I have suffered for thee. I shall never be wroth with thee, but I shall love thee without end, though all the world be against thee. Dread thee not, for they have no understanding of thee. I swear to thy mind, that if it were possible for Me to suffer pain again as I have done before, I would rather suffer as much pain as ever I did for thy soul alone, rather than thou shouldst part from Me without end. Therefore, daughter, just as thou see-est the priest take the child at the font-stone and dip it in the water and wash it from original sin, right so shall I wash thee in My Precious Blood from all thy sin.

"And though I withdraw sometimes the feeling of grace from thee, either of speech or of weeping, dread thee not thereof, for I am a hidden God in thee, so that thou shouldst have no vainglory, and that thou shouldst know well thou mayest not have tears or such dalliance, except when God will send them to thee, for they are the free gifts of God without thy merit, and He may give them to whom He will, and do thee no wrong.

"Therefore take them meekly and thankfully, when I send them, and suffer patiently when I withdraw them, and seek busily till thou mayest get them, for tears of compunction, devotion, and compassion are the highest and surest gifts that I give on earth.

"And what should I do more for thee unless I took thy soul out of thy body and put it in Heaven, and that I will not do yet. Nevertheless wherever God is, Heaven is, and God is in thy soul, and many an angel is about thy soul, to keep it both night and day, for when thou go-est to church, I go with thee; when thou sittest at thy meat, I sit with thee; when thou go-est to bed, I go with thee: and when thou go-est out of town, I go with thee.

"Daughter, there was never a child so obedient to the father as I will be to thee, to help thee and keep thee. I fare sometimes with My grace to thee, as I do with the sun. Sometimes thou knowest well that the sun shineth all abroad, that many men may see it, and sometimes it is hid under a cloud, that men may not see it, and yet the sun is there, nevertheless, in his heat and in his brightness. And right so fare I with thee and with My chosen souls.

"Though it be that thou weep not always at thy list, My grace is nevertheless in thee. Therefore I prove that thou art a very daughter to me, and a mother also, a sister, a wife and a spouse, as witness the Gospel where Our Lord saith unto His disciples:—"He that doth the will of My Father in Heaven is both mother, brother and sister unto Me." When thou study-est to please Me, then thou art a very daughter. When thou weepest and mournest for My pain and My Passion, then art thou a very mother having compassion on her child. When thou weepest for other men's sins and adversities, then

art thou a very sister. And when thou sorrowest that thou art so long from the bliss of Heaven, then art thou a very spouse and a wife, for it belongeth to the wife to be with her husband, and to have no very joy till she cometh into his presence."

XXII. Our Lord Praises Her and Promises Her Eternal Life

As this creature lay in contemplation for weeping, in her spirit she said to Our Lord Jesus Christ:—

"Ah! Lord, maidens dance now merrily in Heaven. Shall not I do so? For, because I am no maiden, lack of maidenhood is to me now great sorrow; methinketh I would I had been slain when I was taken from the font-stone, so that I should never have displeased Thee, and then shouldst Thou, blessed Lord, have had my maidenhood without end. Ah! dear God, I have not loved Thee all the days of my life and that sore rueth me; I have run away from Thee, and Thou hast run after me; I would fall into despair, and Thou wouldst not suffer me."

"Ah! Daughter, how often have I told thee that thy sins are forgiven thee, and that we are united (in love) together without end. Thou art to Me a singular love, daughter, and therefore I promise thee thou shalt have a singular grace in Heaven, daughter, and I promise thee that I shall come to thine end at thy dying with My Blessed Mother, and My holy angels and twelve apostles, Saint Katherine, Saint Margaret, Saint Mary Magdalene and many other saints that are in Heaven, who give great worship to Me for the grace that I give to thee, thy God, thy Lord Jesus. Thou needst dread no grievous pains in thy dying, for thou shalt have thy desire, that is to have more mind of My Passion than of thine own pain. Thou shalt not dread the devil of Hell, for he hath no power in thee. He dreadeth thee more than thou dost him. He is wroth with thee because thou tormentest him more with thy weeping than doth all the fire in Hell; thou winnest many souls from him with thy weeping. And I have promised thee that thou shouldst have no other Purgatory than the slander and speech of the world, for I have chastised thee Myself as I would, by many great dreads and torments that thou hast had with evil spirits, both asleep and awake for many years. And therefore I shall preserve thee at thine end through My mercy, so that they shall have no power over thee either in body or in soul. It is a great grace and miracle that thou hast thy bodily wits, for the vexation thou hast had with them aforetime.

"I have also, daughter, chastised thee with the dread of My Godhead, and many times have I terrified thee with great tempests of winds, so that thou thoughtst vengeance would have fallen on thee for sin. I have proved thee by many tribulations, many great griefs, and many grievous sicknesses, insomuch that thou hast been anointed for death, and all, through My grace, hast thou escaped. Therefore dread thee naught, daughter, for with Mine own hands which were nailed to the Cross, I will take thy soul from thy body with great mirth and melody, with sweet smells and good odours, and offer it to My Father in Heaven, where thou shalt see Him face to face, living with Him without end.

"Daughter, thou shalt be right welcome to My Father, and My Mother, and to all My saints in Heaven, for thou hast given them drink full many times with the tears of thine eyes. All My holy saints shall rejoice at thy coming home. Thou shalt be full filled with all manner of love that thou covetest. Then shalt thou bless the time that thou wert wrought, and the Body that thee hath (dearly) bought. He shall have joy in thee and thou in Him without end.

"Daughter, I promise thee the same grace that I promised Saint Katherine, Saint Margaret, Saint Barbara, and Saint Paul, insomuch that what creature on earth unto the Day of Doom asketh thee any boon and believeth that God loveth thee, he shall have his boon or else a better thing. Therefore they that believe that God loveth thee, they shall be blessed without end. The souls in Purgatory shall rejoice in thy coming home, for they know well that God loveth thee specially. And men on earth shall rejoice in God for thee, for He shall work much grace for thee and make all the world to know that God loveth thee. Thou hast been despised for My love and therefore thou shalt be worshipped for My love.

"Daughter, when thou art in Heaven, thou shalt be able to ask what thou wilt, and I shall grant thee all thy desire. I have told thee beforetime that thou art a singular lover, and therefore thou shalt have a singular love in Heaven, a singular reward, and a singular worship. And, forasmuch as thou art a maiden in thy soul, I shall take thee by the one hand in Heaven, and My Mother by the other hand, and so shalt thou dance in Heaven with other holy maidens and virgins, for I may call thee dearly bought, and Mine own dearworthy darling. I shall say to thee, Mine own blessed spouse:—'Welcome to Me with all manner of joy and gladness, here to dwell with Me and never to depart from Me without end, but ever to dwell with Me in joy and bliss, which no eye may see, nor ear hear, nor tongue tell, nor heart think, that I have ordained for thee and all My servants who desire to love and please Me as thou dost.' "

LXV. Our Lord Again Consoles Her

Our Lord Jesus Christ said unto the said creature:—

"Daughter, thou shalt well see when thou art in Heaven with Me, that there is no man damned, but that he is well worthy to be damned, and thou shalt hold thyself well pleased with all, My works. And, therefore, daughter, thank Me highly for this great charity that I work in thy heart, for it is Myself, Almighty God, that maketh thee to weep every day for thine own sins, for the great compassion that I give thee for My bitter Passion, and for the sorrows that My Mother had here on earth, for the anguish that she suffered, and the tears that she wept. Also, daughter, for the holy martyrs in Heaven; when thou hearest of them, thou givest Me thanks with crying and weeping for the grace that

I have shewn to them. And when thou see-est any lepers, thou hast great compassion on them yielding Me thanks and praisings that I am more favourable to thee than I am to them. And also daughter, for the great sorrow that thou hast for all this world, that thou mightst help them as thou wouldst help thyself, both ghostly and bodily; and furthermore, or the sorrows that thou hast for the souls in Purgatory, that thou wouldst so gladly that they were out of their pain, that they might praise Me without end.

"And all this is Mine own goodness that I give to thee, wherefore thou art much bounden to thank Me. And, nevertheless, yet I thank thee for the great love thou hast for Me, and because thou hast such great will and such great desire that all men and women should love Me right well; for, as thou thinkest, all the world, holy and unholy, all of them would have money to live with, as is lawful to them, but all will not busy themselves to love Me, as they do to get themselves temporal goods. Also, daughter, I thank thee because thou thinkest that thou art so long out of My Blessed Presence. Furthermore, I thank thee specially, because thou canst suffer no man to break My commandments, nor to swear by Me, without it being a great pain to thee, and because thou art always ready to reprove them of their swearing for My love. And therefore thou hast suffered many a shrewd word and many a reproof, and thou shalt therefore have many a joy in Heaven.

"Daughter, I sent once Saint Paul unto thee, to strengthen thee and comfort thee, so that thou shouldst boldly speak in My Name from that day forward. And Saint Paul said unto thee that thou hadst suffered much tribulation because of his writings, and he promised thee that thou shouldst have as much grace thereagainst, for his love, as ever thou hadst

shame and reproof for his love. He told thee also of many joys of Heaven, and of the great love that I had for thee.

"And, daughter, I have oftentimes said to thee that there is no saint in Heaven, but, if thou wilt speak with him, he is ready to comfort thee and speak with thee in My Name. My angels are ready to offer thy holy thoughts and thy prayers to Me, and the tears of thine eyes; also because thy tears are angels' drink, and are very wine and honey to them.

"Therefore, My dearworthy daughter, be not irked of Me on earth, to sit alone by thyself and think of My love, for I am not irked of thee and My merciful eye is ever upon thee.

"Daughter, thou mayest boldly say to Me:—'Jesus est amor meus'; that is to say, 'Jesus is my love.'

"Therefore, daughter, let Me be all thy love and all the joy of thy heart.

"Daughter, if thou wilt be-think thee well, thou hast right good cause to love Me above all things, for the great gifts I have given thee beforetime. And yet thou hast another great cause to love Me, for thou hast thy will of chastity as if thou wert a widow, thy husband living in good health.

"Daughter, I have drawn the love of thy heart from all men's hearts into My heart. At one time, daughter, thou thoughtest it had been in a manner impossible to be so, and at that time sufferedest thou full great pain in thy heart with fleshly affections. And then couldst thou well cry to Me, saying:—'Lord, for all Thy wounds' smart, draw all the love of my heart into Thy heart.'

"Daughter, for all these causes, and many other causes and benefits which I have shewn for thee on this half the sea, and on yon half the sea, thou hast great cause to love Me."

Juliana of Norwich

(1343-1413)

LITTLE is known of Juliana except that she was a Benedictine nun living a reclusive life in Norwich. At thirty years of age she wrote *Sixteen Revelations of Divine Love*, called "the most perfect fruit of later medieval mysticism in England." Although not a woman of formal education, she is aware of other writers on mysticism, and in particular does she reflect knowledge of Rolle and Hilton. Her devotional pattern, however, is singularly her own. While her earlier experiences were filled with visions and auditions, her later devotional insights were sanely balanced. This first section of her book is typical of the tone throughout.

[REVELATIONS AND GIFTS]

From *Sixteen Revelations of Divine Love*

HERE BEGINNETH THE FIRST CHAPTER

This is a Revelation of Love, that Jesu Christ our endless blisse made in xvi. shewings: of which,

The *first* is of his precious crowning of thornes, and therein was conteined and specified the blessed Trinity, with the incarnation and the uniting between God and mans soul, with manie faire shewings and teachings of endless wisdom and love: in which all the shewings that follow be grounded and joyned.

The *second* is, of the discolouring of his haire face, in tokening of his dear worthie passion.

The *third* is, that our Lord God Almighty, all wisdom and all love, right also verilie as he hath made all thinges that are right, also verilie he doth and worketh all things that are done.

The *fourth* is, scourging of his tender bodie with plenteous shedding of his precious blood.

The *fifth* is, that the fiend is overcome by the precious passion of Christ.

The *sixth* is, the worshipfull thanking of our Lord God, in which he rewardeth all his blessed servants in heaven.

The *seventh* is, oftentimes feeling of weale and woe. Feeling of weale is gracious touching and lightning, with true sikernes of endless joy: the feeling of woe is of temptation by heavines, and wearines of our fleshlie living with ghostelie understanding, that we be kept also verelie in love, in woe as in weal, by the goodnes of God.

The *eighth* is, the last paines of Christ and his cruell dying.

The *ninth* is, of the liking which is in the blessed Trinity of the hard passion of Christ after his rufull and sorrowful dying: in which joy and liking he will that we be in solace and mirth with him, till that we come to the glorie in heaven.

The *tenth* is, our Lord Jesu Christ by love his blessed heart even cloven in two.

The *eleventh* is, an high ghostlie shewing of his deare worthie Mother.

The *twelfth* is, that our Lord God is all sovoraign being.

The *thirteenth* is, that our Lord God will that we have great regard to all the deedes which he hath done in the great nobletie of all things making, and of the excellency of mans making, the which is above all his works; and of the precious *amends* that he hath made for mans sin, turning all our blame into endeles worship. Than meaneth he thus, "*Beholde and see, for by the same might, wisdome and goodness that I have done all this, by the same might, wisdome and goodness I shall make well all that is not well, and thou shalt see it.*" And in this he will that we keep us in the faith and truth of Holie Church, not willing to wit his privities, not but as it longeth to us in this life.

The *fourteenth* is, that our Lord God is the ground of our beseekinge. Herein was seen *two* fair properties: that *one* is rightful praier: that *other* is verie trust, which he will both be one like large, and thus our praier liketh him, and he of his goodness fulfilleth it.

The *fifteenth* is, that we should soudeinlie be taken from all our paine, and from all our woe, and of his goodnes we shall come up above, where we shall have our Lord Jesu to our meed, and for to be fulfilled with joy and blisse in heaven.

The *sixteenth* is, that the blessed Trinitie, our maker in Christ Jesu our Saviour, eldleslie dwelleth in our soule, worshipfullie rewarding and commanding all things, us mightilie and wiselie saving and keeping for love, and we shall not be over-come of our enemy.

THE SECOND CHAPTER

This Revelation was made to a simple creature unlettered, living in deadlie flesh, the year of our Lord, a thousand three hundreth lxxiij, the xiiij*th* daie of Maie: which creature desired before *three* gifts by the grace of God.

The *first*, was mind of the passion.

The *second*, was bodilie sickness.

The *third*, was to have of Gods gift three woundes. For the first, me thought I had some deale feeling in the passion of Christ, but yet I desired to have more by the grace of God. Me thought I would have been that time with Magdalen, and with other that were Christs lovers, that I might have seen bodilie the passion that our Lord suffered for me, that I might have suffered with him as others did that loved him; and therefore I desired a bodilie sight, wherein I might have more knowledge of the bodilie paines of our Saviour, and of the compassion of our Lady, and of all his true lovers that were living that time, and saw his paines: for I would have bene one of them, and have suffered with them. Other sight nor shewing of God desired I never none,

till when the soule were departed from the body, for I believed to be saved by the mercy of God.

This was my meaning; for I would after because of that shewing have the more true mind in the passion of Christ. For the *second* came to my mind with contrition freelie, without anie seeking, a wilfull desire to have of Gods gift, a bodilie sicknes. I would that that sicknes were so hard as to the death, that I might in that sicknes have undertaken all the Rights of Holie Church, my self weening that I should have died, and that all creatures might suppose the same that saw me: for I would have no manner of comfort of fleshly, ne earthly life in that sicknes. I desired to have all manner of paines, bodilie and ghostlie, that I should have if I should have died: all the dreads and temptations of fiends, and all manner of other paines, saving the out-passing of the soule. And this meant I, for I would be purged by the mercy of God, and after live more to the worship of God because of that sicknes. For I hoped that it might have bene to my reward when I should have died, for I desired to have bene soone with my God and Maker.

These two desires of the passion, and of the sicknes that I desired of him, was with a condition: for me thought this was not the common use of praier. Therefore I said, "Lord thou knowest what I would, and if that it be thy will that I might have it; and if it be not thy will, good Lord, be not displeased, for I will not but as thou wilt."

This sicknes I desired in my youth, that I might have it when I were thirtie years old.

For the third, by the grace of God and teaching of Holie Church, I conceived a mightie desire to receive *three* wounds in my life, that is to say, the wound of verie *contrition*, the wound of kind *compassion*, and the wound of *willful longing* to God.

Right as I asked the other twaine with a condition, so asked I this third mightilie without any condition. These twaine desires before said, passed from my mind, and the third dwelled continuallie.

THE THIRD CHAPTER

And when I was thirtie yeares old and a halfe, God sent me a bodilie sickness, in which I lay three daies and three nights, and on the fourth night, I tooke all my Rights of Holie Church, and went not to have liven till daie. And after this I laie two daies and two nights, and on the third night I weened oftentimes to have passed, and so weened they that were with me, and yet in this I felt a great loathness to die, but for nothing that was in earth that me liketh to live for, ne for no paine that I was afraid of, for I trusted in God of his mercy: but it was, for I would have lived to have loved God better, and a longer time; that I might by the grace of that living have the more knowing and loving of God in the blisse of heaven. For methought all that time that I had lived here, so litle and so short in regarde of that endles blisse, I thought, "Good Lord, may my living be no longer to thy worshippe?"

And I understood in my reason, and by the feeling of my paines that I should die; and I assented fullie with all the will of myne heart to be at Gods will.

Thus I endured till daie, and by then was my bodie dead from the middes downwarde, as to my feeling.

Then was I holpen to be sett upright, undersett with help, for to have the more freedome of my heart to beat Gods will, and thinking on God while my life lasted.

My Curate was sent for to be at my ending, and before he came I had sett up my eien, and might not speak. He sett the crosse before my face, and said, "I have brought the image of our Saviour, looke thereupon and comfort thee therewith." Me thought I was well, for my eien were sett upright into heaven, where I trusted to come by the mercy of God. But neverthelesse I assented to sett my eien in the face of the crucifix, if I might, and so I did; for me thought I might longer dure to looke even forth than right up. After this my sight began to faile, it waxed as darke about me in the chamber as if it had bene night, save in the image of the crosse, wherein held a common light, and I wist not how; all that was besides the crosse was uglie and fearefull to me, as it had bene much occuped with fiendes.

After this the over-parte of my bodie began to die, so farre forth that unneath I had any feeling; my most paine was shortnes of breath, and failing of life.

Then went I verilie to have passed, and in this case sodenlie all my paine was taken from me, and I was as whole, and namely in the over-part of my bodie, as ever I was before. I marvailed of this sodaine change: for me thought that it was a privie working of God, and not of kind. And yet by feeling of this ease, I trusted never the more to have lived; ne the feeling of this ease was no full ease unto me: for me thought I had rather have bene delivered of this world, for my heart was wilfullie sett thereto.

Then came sodeinlie to my mind, that I should desire the seconde wound of our Lords gift, and of his grace, that my bodie might be fulfilled with mind and feeling of his blessed passion, as I had before praied. For I would that his paines were my paines with compassion, and afterwards longing to God.

Thus thought me, that I might with his grace have the wounds that I had before desired. But in this I desired never no bodilie sight; ne no manner shewing of God, but compassion, as me thought that a kind soule might have with our Lord Jesu, that for love would become a deadlie man with him. I desired to suffer living in my deadlie bodie, as God would give me grace.

Nicholas of Cusa

(1401-1464)

NICHOLAS, bishop of Brixen and later cardinal, was one of the profound philosophers and theologians of the fifteenth century. Out of his learning he was able to envision a synthesis of Eckhart's Neo-Platonic method with that of orthodox scholasticism. The warmth of his mystical devotion is portrayed in "The Gaze of God" where man can say, "Look [gaze] then on me in mercy, and my soul is healed!" As we feel ourselves under this sight, we discern ourselves as we truly are.

The following selection is from *The Vision of God*, translated by Emma Gurney Salter from the Latin and used by permission of the publisher, E. P. Dutton & Co.

[THE GAZE OF GOD]

From *The Vision of God*

*A*pproach thee now, brother contemplative, unto the icon of God, and place thyself first to the east thereof, then to the south, and finally to the west. Then, because its glance regardeth thee alike in each position, and leaveth thee not whithersoever thou goest, a questioning will arise in thee and thou wilt stir it up, saying: Lord, in this image of Thee I now behold Thy providence by a certain experience of sense. For if Thou leavest not me, who am the vilest of men, never and to none wilt Thou be lacking. For Thou art present to all and to each, even as to those same, all and each, is present the Being without whom they cannot exist. For Thou, the Absolute Being of all, art as entirely present to all as though Thou hadst no care for any other. And this befalleth because there is none that doth not prefer its own being to all others, and its own mode of being to that of all others, and so defendeth its own being as that it would rather allow the being of all others to go to perdition than its own. Even so, Thou, Lord, dost regard every living thing in such wise that none of them can conceive that Thou hast any other care but that it alone should exist, in the best mode possible to it, and that each thinketh all other existing things exist for the sole purpose of serving this end, namely, the best state of him whom Thou beholdest.

Thou dost not, Lord, permit me to conceive by any imagining whatsoever that Thou, Lord, lovest aught else more than me; since Thy regard leaveth not me, me only. And, since where the eye is, there is love, I prove by experience that Thou lovest me because Thine eyes are so attentively upon me, Thy poor little servant. Lord, Thy glance is love. And just as Thy gaze beholdeth me so attentively that it never turneth aside from me, even so is it with Thy love. And since 'tis deathless, it abideth ever with me, and Thy love, Lord, is naught else but Thy very Self, who lovest me. Hence Thou art ever with me, Lord; Thou desertest me not, Lord; on all sides Thou guardest me, for that Thou takest most diligent care for me. Thy Being, Lord, letteth not go of my being. I exist in that measure in which Thou art with me, and, since Thy look is Thy being, I am because Thou dost look at me, and if Thou didst turn Thy glance from me I should cease to be.

But I know that Thy glance is that supreme Goodness which cannot fail to communicate itself to all able to receive it. Thou, therefore, canst never let me go so long as I am able to receive Thee.

Wherefore it behoveth me to make myself, in so far as I can, ever more able to receive Thee. But I know that the capacity which maketh union possible is naught else save likeness. If, therefore, I have rendered myself by all possible means like unto Thy goodness, then, according to the degree of that likeness, I shall be capable of the truth.

Lord, Thou hast given me my being, of such a nature that it can make itself continuously more able to receive thy grace and goodness. And this power, which I have of Thee, wherein I possess a living image of Thine almighty power, is freewill. By this I can either enlarge or restrict my capacity for Thy grace. The enlarging is by conformity with Thee, when I strive to be good because Thou art good, to be just because Thou art just, to be merciful because Thou art merciful; when all my endeavour is turned toward Thee because all Thy endeavour is turned toward me; when I look unto Thee alone with all my attention, nor ever turn aside the eyes of my mind, because Thou dost enfold me with Thy constant regard; when I direct my love toward Thee alone because Thou, who art Love's self, hast turned Thee toward me alone. And what, Lord, is my life, save that embrace wherein Thy delightsome sweetness doth so lovingly enfold me? I love my life supremely because Thou art my life's sweetness.

Now I behold as in a mirror, in an icon, in a riddle, life eternal, for that is naught other than that blessed regard wherewith Thou never ceasest most lovingly to behold me, yea, even the secret places of my soul. With Thee, to behold is to give life; 'til unceasingly to impart sweetest love of Thee; 'til to inflame me to love of Thee by love's imparting, and to feed me by inflaming, and by feeding to kindle my yearnings, and by kindling to make me drink of the dew of gladness, and by drinking to infuse in me a fountain of life, and by infusing to make it increase and endure. 'Til to cause me to share Thine immortality, to endow me with the glory imperishable to Thy heavenly and most high and most mighty kingdom, 'til to make me partaker of that inheritance which is only of Thy Son, to stablish me in possession of eternal bliss. There is the source of all delights that can be desired; not only can naught better be thought out by men and angels, but naught better can exist in any mode of being! For it is the absolute maximum of every rational desire, than which a greater cannot be.

O how great and manifold is Thy sweetness which Thou hast hidden up for them that fear Thee! It is a treasure that may not be unfolded, in the joy of fullest gladness. For to taste that Thy sweetness is by the touch of experience to lay hold on the sweetness of all delights at its source, 'til in Thy wisdom to attain unto the reason of all things desirable. To behold Absolute Reason, which is the reason of all things, is naught else than in mind to taste Thee, O God, since Thou art very Sweetness, the Being of life, and intellect. What else, Lord, is Thy seeing, when Thou beholdest me with pitying eye, than that Thou art seen of me? In beholding me Thou givest Thyself to be seen of me, Thou who are a hidden God. None can see Thee save in so far as Thou grantest a sight of Thyself, nor is that sight aught else than Thy seeing him that seeth Thee.

I perceive, Lord, in this image of Thee how ready Thou art to show Thy face unto all that seek Thee, for never dost Thou close Thine eyes, never dost Thou turn them away. And albeit I turn me away from Thee when I turn me utterly to some other thing, yet for all this dost Thou never move Thine eyes nor Thy glance. If Thou beholdest me not with the eye of grace, the fault is mine, who have cut me off from Thee, by turning aside, and by turning round to some other thing which I prefer before Thee; yet even so dost Thou not turn Thee utterly away, but Thy mercy followeth me, that, should I at any time be fain to turn unto Thee again, I may be capable of grace. If Thou regardest me not, 'tis because I regard not Thee, but reject and despise Thee.

O infinite Pity! how unhappy is every

sinner who deserteth Thee, the channel of life, and seeketh Thee, not in Thyself, but in that which in itself is nothing, and would have remained nothing hadst Thou not called it out of nothingness! How demented is he who seeketh Thee, who art Goodness, and, while seeking Thee withdraweth from Thee, and turneth aside his eyes! All seekers seek only the good, and every seeker after the good who withdraweth from Thee withdraweth from that he seeketh.

Every sinner, then, strayeth from Thee and departeth afar off. Yet so soon as he return unto Thee Thou dost hasten to meet him, and before he perceiveth Thee, Thou dost cast Thine eyes of mercy on him, with fatherly love. For with Thee 'tis one to behold and to pity. Accordingly, Thy mercy followeth every man so long as he liveth, whithersoever he goeth, even as Thy glance never quitteth any. So long as a man liveth, Thou ceasest not to follow him, and with sweet and inward warning to stir him up to depart from error and to turn unto Thee that he may live in bliss.

Thou, Lord, art the companion of my pilgrimage; wheresoever I go Thine eyes are alway upon me. Now with Thee seeing is motion. Therefore Thou movest with me and never ceasest from motion so long as I move. If I am at rest, there Thou art with me also. If I ascend, Thou ascendest, if I descend, Thou descendest; whithersoever I turn me, there Thou art. Nor dost Thou desert me in the day of trouble; as often as I call upon Thee, Thou art near. For to call upon Thee is to turn unto Thee, and Thou canst not fail him that turneth unto Thee, nor could any turn unto Thee wert not Thou already at hand. Thou art present before I turn unto Thee. For, unless Thou were present and didst entreat me, I should know naught at all of Thee, and how could I turn unto Thee whom I knew not at all?

Thou, then, my God, art He who beholdeth all things. And with Thee to behold is to work. So Thou workest all things. Therefore not unto us, O Lord, not unto us, but unto Thy great Name, which is Θεός, I will sing glory for ever. For I have naught save that Thou givest, nor could I keep that Thou hast given didst not Thou Thyself preserve it. Thus Thou ministerest all things unto me. Thou art the Lord, powerful and pitiful, who givest all; Thou art the Minister who administerest all; Thou art the Provider, and He that taketh thought for us, and our Preserver. And all these things Thou workest with one implest glance of Thine, Thou who art blessed for evermore.

O Lord my God, the longer I look upon Thy face the more keenly dost Thou seem to turn the glance of Thine eyes upon me! Thy gaze causeth me to consider how this image of Thy face is thus perceptibly painted, since a face cannot be painted without colour, nor can colour exist without quantity. But I perceive, not with my fleshly eyes, which look on this icon of Thee, but with the eyes of my mind and understanding, the invisible truth of Thy face, which therein is signified, under a shadow and limitation. Thy true face is freed from any limitation, it hath neither quantity nor quality, nor is it of time or place, for it is the Absolute Form, the Face of faces.

When, therefore, I meditate on how that face is truth, and the most adequate measure of all faces, I am brought into a state of great wonder. For that face which is the true type of all faces hath not quantity. Wherefore, it is neither greater nor less than others, and yet 'tis not equal to any other; since it hath not quantity, but 'tis absolute, and exalted above all. It is, therefore, the Truth, which is equality, freed from all quantity. Thus, then Lord, I comprehend Thy face to precede every face that may be formed, and to be the pattern and true type of all faces, and all faces to be images of Thy face, which may not be limited or shared. Each face, then, that can look upon Thy face beholdeth naught other or differing from itself, because it beholdeth its own true type. And the pattern truth cannot be other or differing, but those attributes are found in the image just by reason that it is not the very pattern.

Thus, then, while I look on this pictured face, whether from the west or south, it seemeth in like manner itself to look on me, and, after the same fashion, according as I move my face, that face seemeth turned toward me. Even so is Thy face turned toward all faces that look upon Thee. Thy glance, Lord, is Thy face. He, then, who looketh on Thee with loving face will find Thy face looking on himself with love, and the more he shall study to look on Thee with greater love, by so much shall he find Thy face more loving. He who looketh on Thee in wrath shall in like manner find Thy face wrathful. He who looketh on Thee with joy shall find Thy face joyful, after the same sort as is his own who looketh on Thee. 'Tis as when the eye of flesh, looking through a red glass, thinketh that it seeth all things red, or, looking through a green glass, all things green. Even so the eye of the mind, muffled up in limitation and passivity, judgeth Thee, the mind's object, according unto the nature of its limitation and passivity.

Man can only judge with human judgment. When a man attributeth a face unto Thee, he doth not seek it beyond the human species, because his judgment, bound up with human nature, in judging transcendeth not its limitation and passivity. In like manner, if a lion were to attribute a face unto Thee, he would think of it as a lion's; an ox, as an ox's; and an eagle, as an eagle's.

O Lord, how marvellous is Thy face, which a young man, if he strove to imagine it, would conceive as a youth's; a full-grown man, as manly; an aged man, as an aged man's! Who could imagine this sole pattern, most true and most adequate, of all faces—of all even as of each —this pattern so very perfectly of each as if it were of none other? He would need to go beyond all forms of faces that may be formed, and all figures. And how could he imagine a face when he must go beyond all faces, and all likenesses and figures of all faces, and all concepts which can be formed of a face, and all colour, adornment, and beauty of all faces? Wherefore he that goeth forward to behold Thy face, so long as he formeth any concept thereof, is far from Thy face. For all concept of a face falleth short, Lord, of Thy face, and all beauty which can be conceived is less than the beauty of Thy face; every face hath beauty yet none is beauty's self, but Thy face, Lord, hath beauty and this having is being. 'Tis therefore Absolute Beauty itself, which is the form that giveth being to every beautiful form. O face exceeding comely, whose beauty all things to whom it is granted to behold it, suffice not to admire!

In all faces is seen the Face of faces, veiled, and in a riddle; howbeit unveiled it is not seen, until above all faces a man enter into a certain secret and mystic silence where there is no knowledge or concept of a face. This mist, cloud, darkness or ignorance into which he that seeketh Thy face entereth when he goeth beyond all knowledge or concept, is the state below which Thy face cannot be found except veiled; but that very darkness revealeth Thy face to be there, beyond all veils. 'Tis as when our eye seeketh to look on the light of the sun which is its face, first it beholdeth it veiled in the stars, and in colours and in all things that share its light. But when it striveth to behold the light unveiled, it goeth beyond all visible light, because all this is less than that which it seeketh. A man seeking to see a light beyond his seeing knoweth that, so long as he seeth aught, it is not that which he seeketh. Wherefore it behoveth him to go beyond all visible light. For him, then, who must go beyond all light, the place he entereth must needs lack visible light, and is thus, so to speak, darkness to the eye. And while he is in that darkness which is a mist, if he then know himself to be in a mist, he knoweth that he hath drawn nigh the face of the sun; for that mist in his eye proceedeth from the exceeding bright shining of the sun. Wherefore, the denser he knoweth the mist to be, by so much the more truly doth he attain in

NICHOLAS OF CUSA   231

the mist unto the light invisible. I perceive that 'tis thus and not otherwise, Lord, that the light inaccessible, the beauty and radiance of Thy face, may, unveiled be approached.

My heart is not at rest, Lord, because Thy love hath inflamed it with so great desire that it can only rest in Thee. I began to pray the Lord's Prayer, and Thou didst inspire me to consider in what manner thou art our Father. For Thy love is Thy regard, Thy fatherhood is Thy regard, which embraceth us all in fatherly wise: for we say: Our Father. For Thou art the Father of the whole world, and of each individual. Each saith Our Father, and because of it Thy fatherly love comprehendeth each and all of Thy sons. For a father so loveth all his sons as he doth each one, because he is as much the father of all as he is of each one. He so loveth each of his sons that each may imagine himself to be favoured beyond all.

If, then, Thou art a Father, and our Father, we are Thy sons. But paternal love precedeth filial. As long as we Thy sons look upon Thee as do sons, Thou ceasest not to look upon us as doth a father. Therefore Thou wilt be our fatherly Providence, having fatherly care for us. Thy regard is providence. But if we Thy sons reject Thee our Father, we cease to be Thy sons, nor are we thenceforth free sons nor our own masters; but, separating ourselves from Thee, we go into a far country, and then endure grievous slavery under a prince that is Thine adversary, O God. But Thou our Father, who hast granted us freedom because we are Thy sons and Thou art very Liberty, dost permit us to depart, and to squander our liberty and our noblest substance, after the corrupt desires of our senses. Yet for all that Thou dost not leave us utterly, but art ever at our side beseeching us, and Thou speakest within us, calling us back to return unto Thee, ever ready to behold us again with Thy fatherly eye as aforetime, if we return, if we turn again unto Thee. O pitiful God, look on me, who, remorseful, now return from my wretched slavery, from the slime and filth of the swine, where I perished with hunger, and in Thy house would seek to be fed after any wise. Feed me with Thy gaze, O Lord, and teach me how Thy gaze regardeth every sight that seeth, and all that may be seen, and each act of seeing, and every power of seeing, or of being seen, and all the seeing which thence resulteth. For with Thee to see is to cause; Thou seest all things who causest all things.

Teach me, O Lord, how at one glance Thou discernest both all together and each in particular. When I open a book to read, I see the whole page confusedly, and, if I wish to distinguish separate letters, syllables, and words, I must needs turn my particular attention to each individual thing in succession. I can only read one letter in turn after another, and one word after another, and one passage after another. But Thou, Lord, dost see and read the whole page together, in an instant. If two of us read the same thing, one more quickly, the other more slowly, Thou readest with us both, and dost appear to read in time, since Thou readest with them that read; yet dost Thou see and read it all together, above and beyond time. For with Thee to see is to read. Thou from eternity hast seen and read, together and once and for all, all written books, and those that can be written, regardless of time; and, in addition, Thou dost read those same books one after another with all who read them. Nor dost Thou read one thing in eternity and another with them that read in time, but the same; Thou behavest Thyself in the same way, since Thou changest not, being a fixed eternity. Yet eternity, because it is bound up with time, seemeth to be moved with time, albeit motion in eternity is rest.

Lord, Thou seest and hast eyes. Thou art an Eye, since with Thee having is being, wherefore in Thyself Thou dost observe all things. If in me my seeing were an eye, as 'tis in Thee, my God, then in myself I should see all things, since the eye is like a mirror. And a mirror, however small it be, beholdeth in itself the image of a great mountain, and of all that existeth on the surface of that mountain, and so the species of all things are contained in the mirror of the eye. Notwithstanding this, our sight, through the mirror of the eye, can only see that particular object toward which it is turned, because its power can only be determined in a particular object toward which it is turned, because its power can only be determined in a particular manner by the object, so that it seeth not all things contained in the mirror of the eye. But Thy sight, being an eye or living mirror, seeth all things in itself. Nay more, because it is the cause of all things visible, it embraceth and seeth all things in the cause and reason of all, that is, in itself.

Thine eye, Lord, reacheth to all things without turning. When our eye turneth itself toward an object 'tis because our sight seeth but through a finite angle. But the angle of Thine eye, O God, is not limited, but is infinite, being the angle of a circle, nay, of an infinite sphere also, since Thy sight is an eye of sphericity and of infinite perfection. Wherefore it seeth at one and the same time all things around and above and below.

O how marvellous is Thy glance, my God, which is Θεός unto all that examine it! How fair and lovely is it unto all that love Thee! How dread is it unto all them that have abandoned Thee, O Lord my God! For 'tis every spirit, and makest glad every saint, and puttest to flight every sorrow. Look then on me in mercy, and my soul is healed!

Gerhard Groot
(1340-1384)
Thomas a Kempis
(1380-1471)

A STUDENT of Ruysbroeck, Gerhard Groot became the founder of the "Brothers of the Common Life," and the Netherlands' most popular preacher. Although given to extreme asceticism in his early years, he became a mystic of sane, practical, balanced devotional living. He never gave way to an exaggerated kind of ecstasy; instead he wanted religion to grip the whole of man's experience. His greatest contribution to posterity was his part in *The Imitation of Christ.*

Thomas à Kempis was admitted to the Augustinian convent of Mount St. Agnes in 1399. He spent the rest of his life in this convent, where in 1429 he was made subprior. His life in its outward activity was not eventful, but few have understood as did he the inner world of mystical devotion to Christ. He is best known for his work, in 1441, on this diary of Groot.

Scholars are of the opinion that Thomas à Kempis is not the author of *The Imitation of Christ,* but the editor of Groot's spiritual diary. It has passed through more than three thousand editions, and in the eyes of many critics ranks next to the Bible as devotional literature.

[SOME GUIDES TO A CHRISTLIKE LIFE]
From *The Imitation of Christ*

FROM BOOK I. ADMONITIONS, USEFUL
FOR A SPIRITUAL LIFE

*H*e that followeth Me, walketh not in darkness," saith the Lord. These are the words of Christ, by which we are taught to imitate His life and manners if we would be truly enlightened, and be de-

livered from all blindness of heart. Let therefore our chief endeavor be to meditate upon the life of Jesus Christ. . . .

But it falleth out that many, albeit they often hear the Gospel of Christ, are yet but little affected, because they have not the Spirit of Christ.

Whosoever then would fully and feelingly understand the words of Christ, must endeavor to conform his life wholly to the life of Christ.

3. What will it avail thee to be engaged in profound reasonings concerning the Trinity, if thou be void of humility, and art thereby displeasing to the Trinity?

Surely great words do not make a man holy and just; but a virtuous life maketh him dear to God.

I had rather FEEL compunction, than know the definition thereof.

If thou knewest the whole Bible by heart, and the sayings of all the philosophers, what would it profit thee without the love of God and without grace?

Vanity of vanities, all is vanity, except to love God, and Him only to serve.

This is the highest wisdom, by contempt of the world to tend towards the kingdom of Heaven.

4. It is therefore vanity to seek after perishing riches, and to trust in them.

It is also vanity to strive after honors, and to climb to high degree.

It is vanity to follow the desires of the flesh, and to labor for that for which thou must afterwards suffer grievous punishment.

It is vanity to desire to live long, and not to care to live well.

It is vanity to mind only this present life, and not to make provision for those things which are to come.

It is vanity to love that which speedily passeth away, and not to hasten thither where everlasting joy awaiteth thee.

5. Call often to mind that proverb, "The eye is not satisfied with seeing, nor the ear filled with hearing."

Endeavor therefore to withdraw thy heart from the love of visible things, and to turn thyself to the invisible. . . .

II. All men naturally desire knowledge; but what availeth knowledge without the fear of God?

Surely, an humble husbandman that serveth God, is better than a proud philosopher who, neglecting himself, is occupied in studying the course of the heavens.

Whoso knoweth himself, is lowly in his own eyes, and delighteth not in the praises of men.

If I understood all things in the world, and had not charity, what would it avail me in the sight of God, who will judge me according to my deeds?

2. Cease from an inordinate desire of knowledge, for therein is much distraction and deceit.

Learned men are anxious to seem learned to others, and to be called wise.

There be many things to know which doth little or nothing profit the soul: And he is very unwise who minds other things more than those that tend to his salvation.

Many words do not satisfy the soul; but a good life comforteth the mind, and a pure conscience giveth great confidence toward God.

3. The more thou knowest, and the better thou understandest, the more strictly shalt thou be judged, unless thy life be also the more holy.

Be not therefore elated in thine own mind because of any art or science, but rather let the knowledge given thee make thee afraid.

If thou thinkest that thou understandest and knowest much; yet know that there be many more things which thou knowest not.

Affect not to be overwise, but rather acknowledge thine own ignorance.

Why wilt thou prefer thyself before others, seeing there be many more learned, and more skilful in the Scripture than thou?

If thou wilt know or learn anything profitably, desire to be unknown, and to be little esteemed.

4. The highest and most profitable lesson is the true knowledge and lowly esteem of ourselves.

It is great wisdom and perfection to think nothing of ourselves, and to think always well and highly of others.

If thou shouldest see another openly sin, or commit some heinous offence, yet oughtest thou not to think the better of thyself; for thou knowest not how long thou shalt be able to stand.

We are all frail, but do thou esteem none more frail than thyself.

III. . . . It is a great folly to neglect the things that are profitable and necessary, and to choose to dwell upon that which is curious and hurtful. . . .

He to whom all things are one, he who reduceth all things to one, and seeth all things in one; may enjoy a quiet mind, and remain at peace in God.

O God, who art the truth, make me one with thee in everlasting love. . . .

The more a man is at one within himself, and becometh of single heart, so much the more and higher things doth he understand without labor; for that he receiveth the light of wisdom from above.

A pure, single, and stable spirit is not distracted, though it be employed in many works; for that it doeth all to the honor of God, and being at rest within, seeketh not itself in anything it doth. . . .

A good and devout man arrangeth within himself beforehand those things which he ought to do. . . .

Who hath a greater combat than he that laboreth to overcome himself?

This ought to be our endeavor, to conquer ourselves, and daily to wax stronger, and to grow in holiness. . . .

A humble knowledge of thyself is a surer way to God than a deep search after learning.

Yet learning is not to be blamed, nor the mere knowledge of any thing whatsoever, for that is good in itself, and ordained by God; but a good conscience and a virtuous life are always to be preferred before it.

But because many endeavor rather to get knowledge than to live well; therefore they are often deceived, and reap either none or but little fruit. . . .

6. O, how quickly doth the glory of the world pass away! . . .

How many perish by reason of vain learning of this world, who take little care of the serving of God.

And because they rather choose to be great than humble, therefore they become vain in their imaginations.

He is truly great who hath great love.

He is truly great that is little in himself, and that maketh no account of any height of honor.

He is truly wise that accounteth all earthly things as dung, that he may win Christ.

And he is truly learned, that doeth the will of God, and forsaketh his own will.

IV. . . . Alas, such is our weakness, that we often rather believe and speak evil of others than good. . . .

2. It is great wisdom not to be rash in thy doings, nor to stand stiffly in thine own conceits;

As also not to believe everything which thou hearest, nor immediately to relate again to others what thou hast heard or dost believe. . . .

The more humble a man is in himself, and the more subject unto God, the more wise and peaceful shall he be in all things.

VI. . . . The proud and covetous can never rest. The poor and humble in spirit dwell in the multitude of peace.

The man that is not yet perfectly dead to himself, is quickly tempted and overcome in small and trifling things. . . .

There is then no peace in the heart of a carnal man, nor in him that is given to outward things, but in the spiritual and devout man.

VII. He is vain that putteth his trust in man, or in creatures.

Be not ashamed to serve others for the love of Jesus Christ; nor to be esteemed poor in this world. . . .

Trust not in thine own knowledge, nor in the skill of any living creature; but rather in the grace of God, who helpeth the humble, and humbleth those that are proud.

2. Glory not in wealth if thou have it, nor in friends because they are powerful; but in God who giveth all things, and who desireth to give thee Himself above all things.

Esteem not thyself for the height of thy stature nor for the beauty of thy person, which may be disfigured and destroyed by a little sickness.

Please not thyself in thy natural gifts or wit, lest thereby thou displease God, to whom appertaineth all the good what-soever thou hast by nature.

3. Esteem not thyself better than others, lest perhaps in the sight of God, who knoweth what is in man, thou be accounted worse than they.

Be not proud of well-doing; for the judgment of God is far different from the judgment of men, and that often offendeth Him which pleaseth them.

If there be any good in thee, believe that there is much more in others, that so thou mayest preserve humility.

It hurteth thee not to submit to all men: but it hurteth thee most of all to prefer thyself even to one.

The humble enjoy continual peace, but in the heart of the proud is envy, and frequent indignation. . . .

X. Fly the tumult of the world as much as thou canst; for the treating of worldly affairs is a great hindrance, although it be done with sincere intention. . . .

If it be lawful and expedient for thee to speak, speak those things that may edify. . . .

Yet discourse of spiritual things doth greatly further our spiritual growth, especially when persons of one mind and spirit associate together in God.

XI. We might enjoy much peace, if we would not busy ourselves with the words and deeds of other men, and things which appertain nothing with to our charge.

How can he abide long in peace, who thrusteth himself into the cares of others, who seeketh occasions abroad, who little or seldom cometh to himself? . . .

When but a small adversity befalleth us, we are too quickly dejected, and turn ourselves to human consolations.

4. If we would endeavor like brave men to stand in the battle, surely we should feel the assistance of God from Heaven.

For he who giveth us occasion to fight, to the end we may get the victory, is ready to succor those that fight, and that trust in His grace.

If we esteem our progress in religious life to consist only in some outward ob-servances, our devotion will quickly be at an end.

But let us lay the axe to the root, that being freed from passions, we may find rest to our souls.

5. If every year we would root out one vice, we should sooner become perfect men.

But now oftentimes we perceive, on the contrary, that we were better and purer at the beginning of our conversion, than after many years of our profession.

Our fervor and profiting should increase daily: but now it is accounted a great matter, if a man can retain but some part of his first zeal.

If we do but a little violence to ourselves at the beginning, then should we be able to perform all things afterwards with ease and delight. . . .

But if thou dost not overcome small and easy things, when wilt thou overcome harder things? . . .

O if thou didst but consider how much inward peace unto thyself, and joy unto others, thou wouldest procure by demeaning thyself well, I think that thou wouldest be more careful of thy spiritual progress.

XII. It is good that we have sometimes some troubles and crosses; for they often make a man enter into himself, and consider that he is here in banishment, and ought not to place his trust in any worldly thing.

It is good that we be sometimes contradicted, and that men think ill or inadequately; and this, although we do and intend well.

These things help often to the attaining of humility, and defend us from vainglory: for then we are more inclined to seek God for our inward witness, when outwardly we be contemned by men, and when there is no credit given unto us.

2. And therefore a man should settle himself so fully in God, that he need not to seek many comforts of men.

When a good man is afflicted, tempted, or troubled with evil thoughts; then he understandeth better the great need he hath of God, without whom he perceiveth he can do nothing that is good. . . .

XIII. . . . All the Saints passed through man's tribulations and temptations, and profited thereby. . . .

5. The beginning of all evil temptations is inconstancy of mind, and small confidence in God.

For as a ship without a helm is tossed to and fro by the waves, so the man who is careless and forsaketh his purpose, is many ways tempted.

Fire trieth iron, and temptation a just man. . . .

7. We ought not therefore to despair when we are tempted, but so much the more fervently to pray unto God, that He will vouchsafe to help us in all tribulations; for He will surely, according to the words of St. Paul, make with the temptation a way to escape, that we may be able to bear it.

Let us therefore humble our souls under the hand of God in all temptations and tribulations; for He will save and exalt the humble in spirit. . . .

XVIII. Consider the lively examples of the holy Fathers in whom true perfection and religion shone; and thou shalt see how little it is, and almost nothing, which we do now in these days. . . .

The Saints and friends of Christ served the Lord in hunger and thirst, in cold and nakedness, in labor and weariness, in watchings and fastings, in prayer and holy meditations, in many persecutions and reproaches. . . .

They renounced all riches, dignities, honors, friends, and kinsfolk; they desired to have nothing which appertained to the world; they scarce took the necessaries of life; they grudged even the necessary care of the body.

Therefore they were poor in earthly things, but very rich in grace and virtues.

Outwardly they were destitute, but inwardly they were refreshed with grace and divine consolation. . . .

They were grounded in true humility, they lived in simple obedience. . . .

XIX. The life of a good Religious person ought to excel in all virtues; that he may inwardly be such as outwardly he seemeth to men. . . .

From festival to festival we should purpose, as though we were then to depart out of this world, and to come to the everlasting festival.

Therefore ought we carefully to prepare ourselves at holy times, and to live more devoutly, and to keep more exactly all things that we are to observe, as though we were shortly at God's hands to receive the reward of our labors. . . .

XX. Seek a convenient time of leisure for thyself, and meditate often upon God's loving-kindness. . . .

If thou wilt withdraw thyself from speaking vainly, and from gadding idly, as also from hearkening after novelties and rumors, thou shalt find leisure enough and suitable for meditation on good things. . . .

And this we find true, when we talk long together. It is easier not to speak at all, than not to exceed in speech. . . .

He therefore that intends to attain to the more inward and spiritual things of religion, must with Jesus depart from the multitude and press of people! . . .

O what great peace and quietness would he possess, that would cut off all vain anxiety, and think only upon divine things, and such as are profitable for his soul, and would place all his confidence in God! . . .

In thy chamber thou shalt find what abroad thou shalt too often lose.

The more thou visitest thy chamber, the more thou wilt enjoy it; the less thou comest thereunto, the more thou wilt loathe it. . . .

6. In silence and in stillness a religious soul advantageth itself, and learneth the mysteries of Holy Scripture.

There it findeth rivers of tears, wherein it may every night wash and cleanse itself; that it may be so much the more familiar with its Creator, by how so much the farther off it liveth from all worldly disquiet.

It is better for a man to live privately, and to have regard to himself, than to neglect his soul, though he could work wonders in the world. . . .

XXI. . . . Busy not thyself in matters which appertain to others; neither do thou entangle thyself with the affairs of thy betters.

Still have an eye to thyself first, and be sure more especially to admonish thyself before all thy friends.

If thou hast not the favor of men, be not grieved at it; but take this to heart, that thou dost not behave thyself so warily and circumspectly as it becometh the servant of God, and a devout, religious man.

XXII. Miserable thou art, wheresoever thou be, or whithersoever thou turnest, unless thou turn thyself unto God.

5. O my brother, cast not away thy confidence of making progress in godliness; there is yet time, the hour is not yet past. . . .

XXIII. Very quickly there will be an end of thee here; see therefore to thy state: to-day man is; tomorrow he is gone. . . .

O the stupidity and hardness of man's heart, which thinketh only upon the present, and doth not rather care for what is to come!

Thou oughtest so to order thyself in all thy thoughts and actions, as if to-day thou wert to die. . . .

2. What availeth it to live long, when there is so small amendment in us?

Alas! length of days doth not always better us, but often rather increaseth our sin.

O that we had spent but one day in this world thoroughly well! . . .

Be thou therefore always in readiness, and so lead thy life that death may never take thee unprepared. . . .

When that last hour shall come, thou wilt begin to have a far different opinion of thy whole life that is past, and be exceeding sorry that thou hast been so careless and remiss.

4. O how wise and happy is he that now laboreth to be such an one in his life, as he will desire to be found at the hour of death! . . .

Labor now so to live, that at the hour of death thou mayest rather rejoice than fear.

Learn now to die to the world, that thou mayest then begin to live with Christ. . . .

Now, whilst thou hast time, heap unto thyself everlasting riches. . . .

XXIV. In all things look to the end, and see how thou wilt be able to stand before that severe Judge from whom nothing is hid, who is not pacified with gifts, nor admitteth any excuses, but will judge according to right. . . .

XXV. Be watchful and diligent in the service of God; and often bethink thyself wherefore thou camest hither, and why thou hast left the world. . . .

If thou continuest faithful and fervent in thy work, no doubt but that God will be faithful and liberal in rewarding thee. . . .

One thing there is that draweth many back from a spiritual progress, and the diligent amendment of their lives: the fear of the difficulty, or the labor of the combat.

But they especially exceed others in all virtue, who make the greatest effort to overcome those things which are most grievous and contrary unto them. . . .

Be careful also to avoid with great diligence those things in thyself, which do commonly displease thee in others.

5. Gather some profit to thy soul wheresoever thou art; so that if thou seest or hearest of any good examples, thou stir up thyself to the imitation thereof. . . .

6. Be mindful of the profession which thou hast made, and have always before the eyes of thy soul the remembrance of thy Saviour crucified.

Thou hast good cause to be ashamed in looking upon the life of JESUS Christ, seeing thou hast not as yet endeavored to conform thyself more unto Him, though thou hast been a long time in the way of God.

A Religious person that exerciseth himself seriously and devoutly in the most holy life and passion of our Lord, shall there abundantly find whatsoever is necessary and profitable for him; neither shall he need to seek any better thing *out* of JESUS.

O if JESUS crucified would come into our hearts, how quickly and fully should we be taught! . . .

FROM BOOK TWO. ADMONITIONS CONCERNING INWARD THINGS

I. . . . Learn to despise outward things, and to give thyself to things inward, and thou shalt perceive the kingdom of God to be come in thee. . . .

2. O faithful soul, make ready thy heart for this Bridegroom, that He may vouchsafe to come unto thee, and to dwell within thee.

For thus saith He, "If any man love me, he will keep my words, and we will come unto him, and will make our abode with him."

Give therefore admittance unto Christ, and deny entrance to all others.

When thou hast Christ, thou art rich, and hast enough. . . .

3. There is no great trust to be put in a frail and mortal man, even though he be profitable and dear unto us: neither ought we to be much grieved, if sometimes he cross and contradict us.

They that to-day take thy part, to-morrow may be against thee; and often do men turn like the wind.

Put all thy trust in God, let Him be thy fear and thy love. . . .

6. If thou hadst but once perfectly entered into the secrets of the Lord JESUS, and tasted a little of His ardent love; then wouldst thou not regard thine own convenience or inconvenience, but rather wouldst thou rejoice in reproaches, if they should be cast upon thee; for the love of JESUS maketh a man to despise himself.

He that knoweth how to live inwardly, and to make small reckoning of things without, neither requireth places, nor awaiteth times for performing of religious exercises.

A spiritual man quickly recollecteth himself, because he never poureth out himself wholly to outward things. . . .

III. First keep thyself in peace, and then shalt thou be able to make peace among others.

A peaceable man doth more good than he that is well learned. . . .

A good and peaceable man turneth all things to good.

He that is in peace, is not suspicious of any. . . .

It is no great matter to associate with the good and gentle; for this is naturally pleasing to all, and every one willingly enjoyeth peace, and loveth those best that agree with him.

But to be able to live peaceably with hard and perverse persons, or with the disorderly, or with such as go contrary to us, is a great grace, and a most commendable and manly thing. . . .

He that knoweth best how to suffer, will best keep himself in peace. That man is conqueror of himself, and lord of the world, the friend of Christ, and an heir of heaven.

IV. . . . If thou intend and seek nothing else but the will of God and the good of thy neighbor, thou shalt thoroughly enjoy inward liberty. . . .

If there be joy in the world, surely a man of a pure heart possesseth it. . . .

As iron put into the fire loseth its rust, and becometh clearly red-hot, so he that wholly turneth himself unto God, putteth off all slothfulness, and is transformed into a new man. . . .

V. . . . And he that diligently attendeth unto himself, can easily keep silence concerning others.

Thou wilt never be thus in heart religious, unless thou pass over other men's matters with silence, and look especially to thyself. . . .

Let nothing be great unto thee, nothing high, nothing pleasing, nothing acceptable, but only God Himself, or that which is of God. . . .

God alone is everlasting, and of infinite greatness, filling all creatures; the comfort of the soul, and the true joy of the heart.

VI. . . . Have a good conscience, and thou shalt ever have joy.

A good conscience is able to bear very much, and is very cheerful in adversities.

An evil conscience is always fearful and unquiet. . . .

The glory of the good is in their consciences, and not in the tongues of men. The gladness of the just is of God, and in God; and their joy is of the truth.

He that desireth true and everlasting glory, careth not for that which is temporal. . . .

He enjoyeth great tranquillity of heart, that careth neither for the praise, nor dispraise of men. . . .

Thou art not the more holy for being praised; nor the more worthless for being dispraised.

What thou art, that thou art; neither by words canst thou be made greater than what thou art in the sight of God.

If thou consider what thou art in thyself, thou wilt not care what men say of thee.

Man looketh on the countenance, but God on the heart. Man considereth the deeds, but God weigheth the intentions. . . .

To walk in the heart with God, and not to be held in bondage by any outward affection, is the state of a spiritual man. . . .

Thou oughtest to be naked and open before God, ever carrying thy heart pure towards Him, if thou wouldst be free to consider and see how sweet the Lord is. . . .

For when the grace of God cometh unto a man, then he is made able for all things. And when it goeth away, then is he poor and weak, and as it were left only for affliction.

In this case thou oughtest not to be cast down, nor to despair; but to resign thyself calmly to the will of God, and whatever comes upon thee, to endure it for the glory of JESUS Christ; for after winter followeth summer, after night the day returneth, and after a tempest a great calm.

IX. . . . A man must strive long and mightily within himself before he can learn fully to master himself, and to draw his whole heart unto God.

When a man trusteth in himself, he easily slideth unto human comforts.

But a true lover of Christ, and a diligent follower of all virtue, does not fall back on comforts, nor seek such sensible sweetnesses; but rather prefers hard exercises, and to sustain severe labors for Christ. . . .

When consolation is taken from thee, do not immediately despair; but with humility and patience wait for the heavenly visitation; for God is able to give thee back again more ample consolation.

There is nothing new nor strange unto them that have experience in the way of God; for the great saints and ancient prophets had oftentimes experience of such kind of vicissitudes. . . .

6. Whereupon then can I hope, or wherein ought I to trust, save in the great mercy of God alone, and in the only hope of heavenly grace?

For whether I have with me good men, either religious brethren, or faithful friends; whether holy books, or beautiful treatises, or sweet psalms and hymns; all these help but little, and have but little savor, when grace forsaketh me, and I am left in mine own poverty. . . .

7. I never found any so religious and devout, that he had not sometimes a withdrawing of grace, or felt not some decrease of zeal. . . .

God doeth well for us in giving the grace of comfort; but man doeth evil in not returning all again unto God with thanksgiving. . . .

He that desireth to keep the grace of God, let him be thankful for grace given, and patient for the taking away thereof: let him pray that it may return; let him be cautious and humble, lest he lose it.

XI. . . . Jesus hath now many lovers of His heavenly kingdom, but few bearers of His cross.

He hath many desirous of consolation, but few of tribulation. . . .

Many follow JESUS unto the breaking of bread; but few to the drinking of the cup of His passion. . . .

3. O how powerful is the pure love of JESUS, which is mixed with no self-interest, nor self-love!

Are not all those to be called mercenary, who are ever seeking consolations? Do they not show themselves to be rather lovers of themselves than of Christ, who are always thinking of their own profit and advantage? . . .

XII. . . . In the cross is salvation, in the cross is life, in the cross is protection against our enemies, in the cross is infusion of heavenly sweetness, in the cross is strength of mind, in the cross joy of spirit, in the cross the height of virtue, in the cross the perfection of sanctity. . . .

3. Behold! in the cross all doth consist, and all lieth in our dying thereon; for there is no other way unto life, and unto true inward peace, but the way of the holy cross, and of daily mortification. . . .

9. It is not according to man's inclination to bear the cross, to love the cross, to chastise the body and bring it into subjection, to flee honors, willingly to suffer contumelies, to despise one's self and to wish to be despised, to endure all adversities and losses, and to desire no prosperity in this world.

If thou look to thyself, thou shalt be able of thyself to accomplish nothing of this kind.

But if thou trust in the Lord, strength shall be given thee from heaven, and the world and the flesh shall be made subject to thy command. . . .

And the more any man dieth to himself, so much the more doth he begin to live unto God.

From Book Three. Of Internal Consolation

I. . . . Blessed is the soul which heareth the Lord speaking within her, and receiveth from His mouth the word of consolation.

Blessed are the ears that gladly receive the pulses of the Divine whisper, and give no heed to the many whisperings of this world. . . .

Blessed are the eyes which are shut to outward things, but intent on things within.

2. Consider these things, O my soul, and shut up the door of thy sensual desires, that thou mayest hear what the Lord thy God shall speak in thee. . . .

II. . . . Let not Moses speak unto me, nor any of the prophets, but rather do thou speak, O Lord God, the inspirer and enlightener of all the prophets; for thou alone without them canst perfectly instruct me, but they without thee can profit nothing.

2. They indeed may utter words, but they cannot give the Spirit.

Most beautifully do they speak, but if thou be silent, they inflame not the heart.

They teach the letter, but thou openest the sense: they bring forth mysteries, but thou unlockest the meaning of sealed things.

They declare thy commandments, but thou helpest us to fulfill them.

They point out the way, but thou givest strength to walk in it.

They work only outwardly, but thou instructest and enlightenest the heart.

They water, but thou givest the increase.

They cry aloud in words, but thou impartest understanding to the hearing.

Speak therefore, Lord, for thy servant heareth; for thou hast the words of eternal life.

Speak thou unto me, to the comfort, however imperfect, of my soul, and to the amendment of my whole life, and to thy praise and glory and honor everlasting.

III. . . . I taught the prophets from the beginning (saith the Lord), and cease not, even to this day, to speak to all; but many are hardened, and deaf to my voice.

Most men do more willingly listen to the world than to God; they sooner follow the desires of their own flesh, than God's good pleasure.

The world promiseth things temporal and mean, and is served with great eagerness: I promise things most high and eternal; and yet the hearts of men remain torpid and insensible. . . .

5. *A Prayer to implore the Grace of Devotion.*

O Lord my God! Thou art to me whatsoever is good. . . .

Yet do thou remember, O Lord, that

I am nothing, have nothing, and can do nothing.

Thou alone art good, just, and holy; thou canst do all things, thou accomplishest all things, thou fillest all things, only the sinner thou leavest empty.

Remember thy mercies, and fill my heart with thy grace, thou who wilt not that thy works should be void and in vain. . . .

Teach me, O Lord, to do thy will; teach me to live worthily and humbly in thy sight; for thou art my wisdom, thou dost truly know me, and didst know me before the world was made, and before I was born into the world.

IV. My son, walk thou before me in truth, and ever seek me in simplicity of thy heart. . . .

If the truth shall have made thee free, thou shalt be free indeed, and shalt not care for the vain words of men. . . .

Let nothing seem great, nothing precious and wonderful, nothing worthy of estimation, nothing high, nothing truly commendable, and to be desired, but that alone which is eternal.

Let the eternal truth be above all things pleasing to thee: Let thine own extreme unworthiness be always displeasing to thee.

V. . . . Love is a great thing, yea, a great and thorough good; by itself it makes everything that is heavy, light: and it bears evenly all that is uneven.

For it carries a burden which is no burden, and makes everything that is bitter, sweet and savory.

The noble love of JESUS impels a man to do great things, and stirs him up to be always longing for what is more perfect. . . .

Love desires to be free, and estranged from all worldly affections, that so its inward sight may not be hindered; that it may not be entangled by any temporal prosperity, or subdued by any adversity.

Nothing is sweeter than love, nothing more courageous, nothing higher, nothing wider, nothing more pleasant, nothing fuller nor better in heaven and earth; because love is born of God, and cannot rest out in God, above all created things.

4. He that loveth, flieth, runneth and rejoiceth; he is free and is not bound. . . .

Love feels no burden, thinks nothing of trouble, attempts what is above its strength, pleads no excuse of impossibility; for it thinks all things lawful for itself and all things possible.

It is therefore able to undertake all things, and it completes many things, and brings them to a conclusion, where he who does not love, faints and lies down.

5. Love watcheth, and, sleeping, slumbereth not.

Though weary, love is not tired; though pressed, it is not straitened; though alarmed, it is not confounded: but as a lively flame and burning torch, it forces its way upwards, and securely passes through all. . . .

7. Love is active, sincere, affectionate, pleasant, and amiable; courageous, patient, faithful, prudent, long-suffering, manly, and never seeking itself.

For in whatever instance a person seeketh himself, there he falleth from love.

VI. . . . A courageous lover standeth firm in temptations, and giveth no credit to the crafty persuasions of the enemy. . . .

2. A wise lover regardeth not so much the gift of him who loves him, as the love of the giver.

He esteems the good will rather than the value of the gift, and sets all gifts below him whom he loves.

VII. My son, it is more profitable for thee and more safe, to conceal the grace of devotion, not to lift thyself on high, nor to speak much thereof, nor to dwell much thereon; but rather to despise thyself, and to fear lest the grace have been given to one unworthy of it. . . .

Think when thou art in grace, how miserable and needy thou art wont to be without grace. . . .

Better is it to have a small portion of good sense, with humility and a slender understanding, than great treasures of science with vain self-complacency. . . .

If thou couldest always continue humble and moderate within thyself, and also couldest thoroughly moderate and govern thy spirit, thou wouldst not so quickly fall into danger and offence.

It is good counsel, that when fervor of spirit is kindled within thee, thou shouldst consider how it will be, when that light shall leave thee.

And when this happeneth, then remember that the light may return again, which, as a warning to thyself, and for mine own glory, I have withdrawn for a time.

5. Such trials are oftentimes more profitable, than if thou shouldst always have things prosper according to thy will. . . .

IX. . . . From me, as from a living fountain, the small and the great, the poor and the rich, do draw the water of life; and they that willingly and freely serve me shall receive grace for grace.

But he who desires to glory in things out of me, or to take pleasure in some private good, shall not be grounded in true joy, nor be enlarged in his heart, but shall many ways be encumbered and straitened. . . .

I have given thee all, and my will is to have thee all again; and with great strictness do I exact from thee a return of thanks.

3. This is the truth whereby vainglory is put to flight. . . .

XI. . . . Various longings and desires oftentimes inflame thee, and drive thee forwards with vehemence: but do thou consider whether thou be not moved rather for thine own advantage, than for my honor.

If I be the cause, thou wilt be well content, howsoever I shall ordain; but if there lurk in thee any self-seeking, behold, this it is that hindereth thee and weigheth thee down.

2. Beware therefore thou lean not too much upon any desire, conceived without asking my counsel, lest perhaps afterwards it repent thee, or thou be displeased with that which at first pleased thee, and which thou desiredst earnestly, as the best.

XVI. Whatsoever I can desire or imagine for my comfort, I look for it not here but hereafter.

For if I alone should possess all the comforts of the world, and might enjoy all the delights thereof, it is certain that they could not long endure.

Wherefore, O my soul, thou canst not be fully comforted, nor have perfect refreshment, except in God, the comforter of the poor, and the helper of the humble.

Wait a little while, O my soul, wait for the divine promise, and thou shalt have abundance of all good things in heaven.

If thou desire beyond measure the things that are present, thou shalt lose those which are heavenly and eternal.

Use temporal things, and desire eternal. . . .

XVIII. . . . It is but little which thou sufferest, in comparison of those who suffered so much, who were so strongly tempted, so grievously afflicted, so many ways tried and exercised.

Thou oughtest therefore to call to mind the more heavy sufferings of others, that so thou mayest the more easily bear thine own very small troubles. . . .

However, whether they be small or whether they be great, endeavor patiently to undergo them all. . . .

4. Be thou therefore prepared for the fight, if thou wilt win the victory.

Without a combat thou canst not attain unto the crown of patience. . . .

XXII. . . . Witnesses are thine apostles themselves, whom thou hast made princes over all the earth.

And yet they lived in the world without complaint; so humble and simple, without all malice and deceit, that they even rejoiced to suffer reproach for thy name; and what the world abhorreth, they embraced with great affection. . . .

XXIII. . . . Be desirous, my son, to do the will of another rather than thine own.

Choose always to have less rather than more.

Seek always the lowest place, and to be beneath every one.

Wish always, and pray, that the will of God may be wholly fulfilled in thee. . . .

XXV. . . . My peace is with the humble and gentle of heart; in much patience shall thy peace be. . . .

2. But never to feel any disturbance at all, nor to suffer any trouble of mind or body, belongs not to this life, but to the state of eternal rest.

Think not therefore that thou hast found true peace, if thou feel no heaviness; nor that all is well, when thou art vexed with no adversary; nor that all is perfect, if all things be done according to thy desire.

Neither do thou think at all highly of thyself, nor account thyself to be specially beloved, if thou be in a state of great devotion and sweetness; for it is not by these things that a true lover of virtue is known, nor doth the spiritual progress and perfection of a man consist in these things. . . .

XXVII. . . . Know thou that the love of thyself doth hurt thee more than any thing in the world. . . .

If thy love be pure, simple, and well-ordered, thou shalt be free from bondage.

Do not covet that which it is not lawful for thee to have. Do not have that which may hinder thee, and may deprive thee of inward liberty.

Strange it is that thou committest not thyself wholly unto me from the bottom of thy heart, together with all things thou canst have or desire.

2. Why dost thou consume thyself with vain grief? why dost thou weary thyself with needless cares? . . .

XXVIII. My son, take it not grievously if some think ill of thee, and speak that which thou wouldest not willingly hear.

Thou oughtest to be the hardest judge of thyself, and to think no man weaker than thyself.

If thou dost walk spiritually, thou wilt not much weigh fleeting words. . . .

2. Let not thy peace depend on the tongues of men; for, whether they judge well of thee or ill, thou art not on that account other than thyself. Where are

true peace and true glory? are they not in me?

And he that careth not to please men, nor feareth to displease them, shall enjoy much peace. . . .

XXIX. . . . And hence it cometh to pass that all doth little profit thee, until thou well consider that I am he who doth rescue them that trust in him; and that out of me there is neither powerful help, nor profitable counsel, nor lasting remedy.

But do thou, having now recovered breath after the tempest, gather strength again in the light of my mercies; for I am at hand (saith the Lord) to repair all, not only entirely, but also abundantly and in most plentiful measure. . . .

XXXII. My son, thou canst not possess perfect liberty unless thou wholly renounce thyself. . . .

For all that is not of God shall perish. . . .

XXXIII. . . . My son, trust not to thy feelings, for whatever they be now, they will quickly be changed towards some other thing.

As long as thou livest, thou art subject to change, even against thy will; so that thou art at one time merry, at another sad; at one time quiet, at another troubled; now devout, now undevout; now diligent, now listless; now grave, and now light.

But he that is wise and well instructed in the Spirit standeth fast upon these changing things; not heeding what he feeleth in himself, or which way the wind of instability bloweth; but that the whole intent of his mind may be to the right and the best end.

For thus he will be able to continue one and the same and unshaken, in the midst of so many various events directing continually the single eye of his intent unto me. . . .

The eye of our intent therefore is to be purified, that it may be single and right, and is to be directed unto me, beyond all the various earthly objects which come between.

XXXIV. "Behold! My God, and my

All." What would I more, and what greater happiness can I desire?

O sweet and delightful word! but to him only that loveth the word, not the world nor the things that are in the world. . . .

For when thou art present, all things do yield delight; but when thou art absent, everything becometh irksome.

Thou givest quietness of heart, and much peace, and pleasant joy. . . .

XXXV. . . . My son, thou art never secure in this life, but, as long as thou livest, thou shalt always need spiritual armor.

Thou dwellest among enemies, and art assaulted on the right hand and on the left.

If therefore thou defend not thyself on every side with the shield of patience, thou canst not be long without a wound.

Moreover, if thou fix not thy heart on me with sincere willingness to suffer all things for me, thou wilt not be able to bear the heat of this combat, nor to attain to the palm of the blessed. . . .

2. If thou seek rest in this life, how wilt thou then attain to the everlasting rest?

Dispose not thyself for much rest, but for great patience. . . .

3. Thinkest thou that thou shalt always have spiritual consolations at will?

My saints had not such always, but they had many afflictions, and sundry temptations, and great discomforts.

But in all these they did bear up themselves patiently, and trusted rather in God than in themselves, knowing that the sufferings of this time are not worthy to be compared to the future glory. . . .

Wait for the Lord, behave thyself manfully, and be of good courage; be not faithless, do not leave thy place, but steadily expose both body and soul for the glory of God. . . .

3. Who art thou that fearest a mortal man? to-day he is, and to-morrow he is not seen.

Fear God, and thou shalt not need to shrink from the terrors of men. . . .

And if for the present thou seem to be worsted and to suffer shame undeserv-edly, do not therefore repine, neither do thou by impatience lessen thy crown.

But rather lift thou up thine eyes to me in heaven, who am able to deliver thee from all shame and wrong, and to render to every man according to his works.

XL. . . . Mere empty glory is in truth an evil pest, a very great vanity; because it draweth a man from true glory, and robbeth him of heavenly grace.

For whilst he pleaseth himself, he displeaseth thee; whilst he gapeth after the praise of men, he is deprived of true virtues.

5. But the true glory and holy exultation is for a man to glory in thee, and not in himself; to rejoice in thy name, not in his own strength, and not to delight in any creature but for thy sake.

Praised be thy Name, not mine; magnified be thy work, not mine. Let thy holy Name be blessed, but to me let no part of men's praises be given.

Thou art my glory, thou art the joy of my heart.

In thee will I glory and rejoice all the day, but as for myself, I will not glory, but in my infirmities. . . .

For all human glory, all temporal honor, all worldly height, compared to thy eternal glory, is vanity and folly. . . .

XLII. . . . My son, if thou rest thy peace on any because of the opinion which thou hast of him, or because of thine intimate acquaintance with him, thou shalt ever be inconstant and enthralled.

But if thou have recourse unto the ever-living and abiding Truth, the departure or death of a friend shall not grieve thee.

Thy regard for thy friend ought to be grounded in me; and for my sake is he to be beloved, whosoever he be that thou thinkest well of, and who is very dear unto thee in this life.

Without me friendship hath no strength, and no continuance; neither is that love true and pure, which is not knit by me.

Thou oughtest to be so dead to such affections towards thy friends, that (as much as appertaineth unto thee) thou shouldst be willing to be without all human friendship.

Man approacheth so much the nearer unto God, the farther he departeth from all earthly comfort.

And the lower he descendeth in himself, and the meaner he becometh in his own sight, the higher he ascendeth towards God.

But he that attributeth any good unto himself, hindereth the entry of God's grace; for the grace of the Holy Spirit ever seeketh an humble heart.

If thou knewest perfectly to annihilate thyself, and to empty thyself of all created love, then should I be constrained to flow into thee with great abundance of grace. . . .

XLIII. . . . I am he who instructeth men to despise earthly things, to loathe things present, to seek things heavenly, to relish things eternal, to flee honors, to endure offences, to place all hope in me, out of me to desire nothing, and above all things ardently to love me. . . .

XLV. . . . How often have I been deceived, finding want of faithfulness where I thought myself sure!

And how often have I found it, where beforehand I least expected it.

It is in vain therefore to trust in men, but the salvation of the righteous is of thee, O God!

Blessed be thou, O Lord my God, in all things that befall us.

We are weak and unstable; we are quickly deceived, and soon changed.

2. Who is he, that is able in all things so warily and circumspectly to keep himself, as never to fall into any deceit or perplexity?

But he that trusteth in thee, O Lord, and seeketh thee with a single heart, doth not so easily fall.

And if he do fall into any tribulation, be he never so much entangled, yet he shall quickly either through thee be delivered, or by thee be comforted; for thou wilt not forsake him that trusteth in thee, even to the end.

A friend is rarely to be found that continueth faithful in all his friend's distresses.

Thou, O Lord, even thou alone art most faithful at all times, and there is none like unto thee.

3. O how wise was that holy soul that said, "My mind is firmly settled and grounded in Christ."

If it were so with me, then would not human fear easily vex me, nor the darts of words move me.

Who can foresee all things? who is able to beware beforehand of evils to come? If things even foreseen do oftentimes hurt us, how can things unlooked for do otherwise than wound us grievously?

But wretched that I am, why did I not provide better for myself? why also have I so easily trusted others?

But we are men, nothing else but frail men, although by many we may be reputed and called angels.

To whom shall I give credit, O Lord? to whom but to thee? thou art the truth, which neither doth deceive, nor can be deceived. . . .

5. O how good is it, and how it tendeth to peace, to be silent about other men, and not to believe at random all that is said, nor eagerly to report what we have heard.

How good it is to lay one's self open to few, and always to be seeking after thee who art the searcher of the heart.

Nor should we be carried about with every wind of words, but we should desire that all things, both within and without, be accomplished according to the pleasure of thy will. . . .

XLVI. My son, stand steadily, and put thy trust in me; for what are words, but words?

They fly through the air, but hurt not the rock.

If thou be guilty, see that thou be willing to amend thyself; if conscience reproach thee not, resolve to suffer willingly for God's sake.

It is but a small matter to suffer sometimes a few words, if thou hast not yet the courage to endure hard stripes.

And why do such small matters go to

thy heart, but because thou art yet carnal, and regardest men more than thou oughtest?

For because thou art afraid to be despised, therefore thou art not willing to be reproved for thy faults, but seekest the shelter of excuses.

2. But look better into thyself, and thou shalt acknowledge that the world is yet alive in thee, and a vain desire to please men.

For when thou shunnest to be abased and reproved for thy faults, it is evident that thou are neither truly humble, nor truly dead to the world, nor the world crucified to thee.

But give diligent ear to my words, and thou shalt not regard ten thousand words spoken by men.

Behold, if all should be spoken against thee that could be most maliciously invented, what would it hurt thee, if thou sufferedst it to pass entirely away, and madest no more reckoning of it than of a mote? . . .

Whereas he that trusteth in me, and hath no wish to trust in his own judgment, shall be free from the fear of men. . . .

XLVII. My son, be not dismayed by the painful labors which thou hast undertaken for me, neither be thou utterly cast down because of any tribulations which befall thee; but let my promise strengthen and comfort thee in all events.

I am able to reward thee above all measure and degree.

Thou shalt not long toil here, and shalt not always be oppressed with grief.

Wait a little while, and thou shalt see a speedy end of thine evils.

There will come an hour when all labor and trouble shall cease.

Poor and brief is all that which passeth away with time.

2. Do with thy might what thou doest; labor faithfully in my vineyard; I will be thy reward.

Write, read, mourn, keep silence, pray, suffer crosses manfully; life everlasting is worthy of all these, yea, and of greater combats.

Peace shall come in the day which is known unto the Lord, and it shall be neither day nor night, such as now is, but everlasting light, infinite brightness, steadfast peace, and secure rest. . . .

3. O if thou hadst seen the everlasting crowns of the saints in heaven, and with how great glory they now rejoice, who in times past were contemptible to this world, and esteemed unworthy of life itself; truly thou wouldst presently humble thyself even unto the dust, and wouldst rather seek to be under the feet of all, than to have command so much as over one.

Neither wouldst thou desire the pleasant days of this life, but rather wouldst rejoice to suffer affliction for God, and esteem it thy greatest gain to be reputed as nothing amongst men. . . .

Are not all painful labors to be endured for the sake of life eternal? . . .

LIII. My son, my grace is precious, it suffereth not itself to be mingled with outward things, nor with earthly consolations.

Thou oughtest therefore to cast away all hindrances to grace, if thou desire to receive the inpouring thereof.

Choose therefore a secret place to thyself, love to live alone with thyself, desire the conversation of none; but rather pour out devout prayer unto God, that thou mayest keep thy soul contrite, and thy conscience pure.

Esteem thou the whole world as nothing, prefer attendance upon God before all outward things.

For thou wilt not be able to attend upon me, and at the same time to take delight in things transitory.

Thou oughtest to remove thyself away from thine acquaintance and friends, and not to depend on any temporal comfort. . . .

LIV. . . . Nature willingly receiveth honor and reverence.

Grace faithfully attributeth all honor and glory unto God.

3. Nature feareth shame and contempt.

Grace rejoiceth to suffer reproach for the name of JESUS.

Nature loveth leisure and bodily ease.

Grace cannot be unemployed, but cheerfully embraceth labor.

Nature seeketh to have things that are curious and beautiful, and abhorreth those which are cheap and coarse.

Grace delighteth in what is plain and humble, despiseth not rough things, and refuseth not to be clothed in that which is old and worn. . . .

5. Nature turneth every thing to her own gain and profit, she cannot bear to do any thing without reward, but for every kindness she hopeth to obtain either what is equal, or what is better, or at least praise or favor; and is very earnest to have her works and gifts much valued.

Grace seeketh no temporal thing, nor desireth any other reward save God alone. . . .

Girolamo Savonarola

(1452-1498)

BECAUSE of his forceful oratory and his life of purity, Savonarola held great influence in Florence. He was orthodox in theology, but his moral sensitivities led him to denunciation of political and papal corruption. In 1498 he and two of his disciples, Fra Domenico and Fra Silvestro, were hanged on the false charge of heresy. Their bodies were burned and thrown into the Arno. "Miserere," an exposition of the fifty-first psalm, was written during the imprisonment which preceded Savonarola's martyrdom. The closing sentence of *Miserere* gives a deep insight into the great soul of this Italian monk: "Establish me with Thy free Spirit, that I may be able to persevere in Thy obedience, and to give my life for Thee." The translation from the Latin is by F. C. Cowper.

MISERERE

I

Have mercy upon me, O God, according to Thy great mercy."

O God! Who dwellest in the inaccessible light! O God! Who hidest Thyself, who canst not be seen with the carnal eye, nor comprehended by the mind of the creature, nor described in the language of men (or of angels); O, my God! Thee, the incomprehensible, I seek; Thee, the unspeakable, I invoke, whatever Thou art, who art in every place.

I know, indeed, that Thou art the Supreme Being. If, then, Thou art Being Itself, and not exclusively the cause of all being, and yet withal the Cause—somewhere I shall find the Name by which I seek to address Thy unspeakable Majesty.

Thou art God, say I, who art whatsoever is in Thee. For Thou art Thy wisdom itself, Thine Excellency, Thy Power, Thy Supreme Felicity.

Since, then, Thou art merciful, what art Thou but Mercy itself? And what am I but Misery itself?

Behold, therefore, O Mercy, O God! behold Misery standing before Thy face. What wilt Thou do, O Mercy? Surely Thou wilt perform Thy work. It is not possible, is it, for Thee to act against Thy attributes?

And what is Thy work? To do away with misery, to lift up men sunken in wretchedness. Then have mercy upon me, O God! O God! nay, O Mercy! take away my wretchedness, take away my sins, which are now my sum of wretchedness. Lift me up who am in misery. Show forth in me Thy work. Exercise upon me Thy virtue.

Deep calleth unto deep. The deep of misery calleth unto the deep of mercy. The deep of transgressions calleth unto the deep of grace. Greater is the deep of mercy than the deep of misery. Therefore let deep swallow deep. Let the deep of mercy swallow up the deep of misery.

Have mercy upon me, O God, according to Thy great mercy, not according to man's mercy, which is small; but according to Thine, which is great, which is immeasurable, which is incomprehensible, which exceedeth the measure of all transgressions; according to that Thy great mercy, by which Thou so lovedst the world, that Thou gavest Thine only-begotten Son.

What greater mercy can there be? What greater love? Who can yield to despair? Who can refuse to have confidence? God was made Man; and for men was crucified. Have mercy upon me, therefore, O God, according to this Thy mercy. By which Thy Son gave Himself for us. By which, through the same, Thou hast taken away the sins of the world. By which through His cross, Thou hast illumined all men. By which, through the Same, Thou has renewed the things which are in heaven, and the things which are in earth. Wash me, O Lord, in His blood. Enlighten me in His humility. Renew me by His resurrection.

Have mercy upon me, O God. Not according to a small measure of Thy mercy. For this is the small measure of Thy mercy, when Thou deliverest men from their bodily woes.

But thy mercy is great when Thou dost take away their sins, and when through Thy grace, Thou liftest men above the heights of earth. Therefore, O Lord have mercy upon me according to this Thy great mercy, and turn me unto Thee, that Thou mayest make an end of my sins, that Thou mayest justify me through Thy grace.

III

"Wash me thoroughly from my iniquity: and cleanse me from my sins."

I confess, O Lord, that once Thou hast put away mine iniquity. A second time hast Thou put it away. Thou hast washed me a thousand times.

Wash me again from mine iniquity, because again have I fallen. Shalt Thou place on erring man a definite number to his sins? Thou, who, to Peter's question— How oft shall my brother sin against me

and I forgive him? till seven times?—repliedst, I say not unto thee till seven times, but unto seventy times seven, using a limited number to denote an unlimited. Shalt Thou, then, be surpassed in forgiveness by a man? Is not God greater than a man? Is He not better than a man? Rather, is not God the Mighty Lord, and the Upholder of the universe?

Every man living is feeble. God alone is good. But every man is deceitful.

Hast Thou not said, Whensoever a sinner shall repent, I will remember the sum of his iniquities no more?

Behold! I am a sinner. I repent in anguish. For my wounds are corrupt by reason of my foolishness. I am troubled. I am bowed down even to extremity. All the day long I go mourning unto Thee. I am afflicted and I am humbled; yea I have roared through the anguish of my heart.

O Lord, all my longing is before Thee, and my groaning is not hid from Thee. My heart is disquieted within me; my strength hath left me, and the very light of mine eyes is gone from me.

Why therefore, O Lord, dost Thou not do away mine iniquity? And if Thou hast already put it away, according to the multitude of Thy compassions wash me thoroughly from my sin; for hitherto I have been cleansed imperfectly. Complete Thy work. Take away the whole body of sin. Take away the guilt. Increase the light. Inflame my heart with Thy love. Drive away fear; for perfect love casteth out fear. Let the love of the world, the love of the flesh, the love of glory, and self-love, wholly depart from me.

Thoroughly (and more and more), shalt Thou wash me from mine iniquity wherein I have sinned against my neighbor; and from my sin wherewith I have offended against God.

Wash me, that Thou mayest take away, not the crime and the guilt alone, but likewise the fuel of sins.

Thou shalt wash me, verily, with the water of Thy manifold grace; with the water thereof whosoever shall drink, shall never thirst; but it shall be in him a well of water springing up into everlasting life.

Wash me with the water of my tears.

Wash me with the water of Thy Scriptures, that I may be worthy to be numbered among those to whom Thou hast already said, Ye are clean according to My word.

XI

"Create in me a clean heart, O God, and renew a right spirit in my inward parts."

For my heart hath forsaken me. It never thinketh upon me, being altogether forgetful of its own safety. It wandereth through crooked paths. It has taken its departure away from home. It followeth after vanities, and its eyes are cast into the extremities of the earth. I have called unto it, and it hath not answered me. It hath departed. It hath perished. It hath been sold unto sins.

What then, O Lord, what shall I say? Create a clean heart in me, O God. An humble heart. A meek heart. A peaceful heart. A benevolent heart. A devout heart. Which doeth evil to no man. Which repayeth not evil for evil; but, for evil, good. Which loveth Thee above all things; thinketh always upon Thee; speaketh concerning Thee; giveth Thee thanks; taketh delight in hymns and spiritual songs; hath its conversation in Heaven.

Create such a heart in me, O God. Evolve it out of nothing; that, such as it cannot be by nature, such it may become through grace. For this cometh into the soul from Thee alone, by creation. This is the form of a clean heart, bringing with it all virtues, at the same time it driveth out all vices. Therefore create in me a clean heart, O God, through Thy grace.

And renew a right spirit in my inward parts. For Thy Spirit shall lead me into the right way; because it will purge me from worldly affections, and shall uplift me toward the heavenly. For the loving and the beloved are one. Who therefore, loveth carnal things is carnal. But whoso loveth the Spirit is spirit.

Grant unto me a spirit loving Thee, and worshipping Thee, the Supreme Spirit. For God is a Spirit; and they who worship Him must worship Him in spirit and in truth.

Give a right spirit, not one which seeketh its own things, but the things which are Thine. Renew a right spirit in my inward parts. Renew it, because the first which Thou gavest to me, my sins have destroyed. Give a fresh spirit which reneweth, which becometh established.

For my soul is spirit; and by Thee was so created, that in itself it was just. For by its own nature it loveth Thee more than itself, and for Thy sake desireth all things. For natural love is just, in so far as it is from Thee. But through its depraved will it hath become established in sins, and maketh natural love to pine away.

Renew, therefore, this spirit, and this love, through Thy grace, that it may press on justly, in accordance with its nature.

Renew it in my inward parts, that it may so make fast its roots in Thine, that it never more can be plucked out.

Renew it, I say, in my inward parts, that it may always inflame me with divine love; may always make me to pant after Thee; to hold Thee fast and never to forsake Thee.

"Restore unto me the joy of Thy salvation; and establish me with Thy free Spirit."

XIII

I ask a great favour, O Lord. For Thou art God the mighty Lord, and the great King above all gods. He doeth Thee wrong who asketh a small thing of Thee.

All things are small which are transitory. All carnal things are small. The spiritual are great and precious. Take away the spirit, take away the soul from the body, what remaineth but excrement? what but dust and a shadow? Therefore there is as wide a difference between the spirit and the body as between the body and its shadow. Who, therefore, asketh of Thee carnal things asketh small things. But whoso demandeth spiritual things, verily demandeth great things. But he who asketh the joy of Thy salvation asketh the greatest of all.

For what is Thy salvation but Jesus, Thy Son? This is the true God and eternal life.

Why, then, may I not ask of Thee, O infinite and most bountiful Father, this salvation which Thou didst yield up for me upon the cross? Thou didst offer Him to me. Wherefore should I blush to ask Him?

He is the greatest and infinite Gift, and I am not worthy of a Gift so great. Nevertheless it becometh Thee to give such great things. Hence, by reason of this ineffable tenderness, I dare to approach Thee trustingly and to ask the joy of Thy salvation.

For if any son should ask a fish from the father of his flesh, will he offer him a serpent? And if he should ask an egg, would he give him a scorpion? And if he should ask bread, will he give him a stone?

If, therefore, earthly fathers, being evil and sinners, know how to give to their children the good things which have been bestowed on them by Thee, how much more wilt Thou, O heavenly Father, Who art good in Thy very essence, give the Holy Spirit to them that ask Thee.

Behold! Thy son returned from a far country, grieving and repentant, asketh of Thee a fish of faith; (for, just as a fish lurketh beneath the waters, so is faith concerning those things which are not seen.) He asketh, I say, a true faith, that he may rejoice in Thy salvation. Wilt Thou offer unto him a serpent? Wilt Thou give to him the poisons of unbelief which proceed from the tortuous and old serpent, the Devil?

I ask of Thee, O Lord, an egg of Hope. That just as a chicken is hoped for from the egg, so Thou mayest grant unto me to come out of hope unto the actual vision of Thy salvation; that out of hope itself the vision may come forth, like as the chicken from the egg.

I ask an egg of hope, that my soul may be sustained by very hope in this vale of tears, and may rejoice in Thy salvation.

Wilt Thou give to me a scorpion of despair, that just as a scorpion hath poison in the end of his tail, so also I may reserve sin in the extremity of my life? and may flatter myself in the allurements of the world, just as a scorpion outwardly seemeth to flatter?

I ask also of Thee the bread of Christ's charity, by which He communicateth Himself to all as bread, that I may always rejoice in Thy salvation. Wilt Thou give me a stone, which is hardness of heart? God forbid.

Why therefore shall I hesitate to ask and to demand great things of Thee, O Lord, who reassurest me and invitest me to the asking and the knocking, even to importunity? But what can I ask, more pleasing to Thee and more wholesome for me, than that Thou shouldest restore to me the joy of Thy salvation?

I have already tasted how good the Lord is, how easy and how light is His burden.

I recall how great peace, how great tranquillity of soul I did enjoy, when I rejoiced in the Lord and exulted in God my Jesus. Yea, now I grieve the more, because I know what I have lost. I know what very great benefits I have lost. Yea, I clamor importunately—Restore to me the joy of Thy salvation: restore what Thou hast taken away from me on account of my sins: restore what I have lost through my own fault: restore, I beseech Thee, through His merits, who ever standeth at Thy right hand and maketh intercession for us. That through Him I may feel that Thou art reconciled to me; that the seal is set upon my heart; that I may say with the Apostle—I am nailed to the Cross with Christ: nevertheless I live; yet not I, but Christ liveth in me.

Verily, because my frailty is great, establish me with Thy free Spirit that I may, through no disquietudes, be capable of separation from Christ; through no terrors, of departing from Thee; through no tortures of becoming weak. For my strength is not such that it can do battle with the old serpent and prevail against him.

Peter hath instructed me how great is our infirmity. He beheld Thee, Lord Jesus! He conversed with Thee on most familiar terms. He was partaker of Thy glory in the Mount, when Thou wast transfigured. He heard the voice of the Father. He saw with his own eyes Thy wonderful works. He himself, in like manner, through Thy power, performed many miracles. He walked over the waters on his feet. He heard daily Thy words, so great in power, so great in gentleness. He appeared most fervent of faith. And he declared that he was ready to go with Thee both to prison and to death. And when Thou foretoldest to him his denial, he did not believe Thee. He trusted in his own strength. He directed his faith more toward himself, a man, than toward Thee, God.

But when a maiden said to him—Thou art one of them—immediately, being terrified, he denied it. Another maiden came, and said—Surely thou art one of them. A second time he denied it. He could not stand before a mere woman. How could he have stood before kings and tyrants?

And when again he was questioned and accused by them that stood by, he began to swear, and to call to witness that he knew Thee not. What thinkest Thou he said? I believe he sware by God, and by the Law of Moses, that he knew Thee not; and that he uttered an imprecation, saying—Think ye that I am a disciple of this Samaritan, seducer, and demoniac, who hath destroyed our Law? I am a disciple of Moses. As for this Fellow, I know not whence He is.

Thanks be to God that the questioning ceased. For if the questioning had not ceased, neither would the denying have ceased. For a thousand questions there had been a thousand denials; and as a consequence, a thousand perjuries and imprecations.

Moreover, these questions were but words. How had it been if the Jews had resorted to scourges? Verily, Peter would have left nothing undone, by means of which, through denials, and perjuries, imprecations and blasphemies, he might extricate himself from their hands. But Thou, tender Lord, didst look back upon him and straightway he knew his sin. But not yet did he dare to spring forth in the midst, and confess Thee to be the Son of God; because not yet was he established with power from on high. For I am far from doubting that he would again have made denial, if he had seen the scourges made ready for him. Indeed, on maturer thought, he went forth and wept bitterly. And Thou, verily, after Thy resurrection, appearedst unto him and re-assuredst him.

Nevertheless he remained hidden for fear of the Jews. He saw Thee so gloriously ascending into heaven. And he was comforted by a vision of angels. And yet he dared not even now to appear in public. Experience, in fact had taught him his frailty, and proved his weakness. He earnestly awaited the promise of the Holy Ghost. He came and replenished his bosom with grace. Then he issued forth. Then he began to speak. Then he bore the testimony of Thy resurrection with great power. Then he feared not chief priests and kings, but gloried in tribulations, and embraced the cross as the sum of delights.

Therefore, O Lord, establish me in Thy free Spirit, that I may continue fast in the joy of Thy salvation. Otherwise I am unable to persevere against so many warfares. The flesh lusteth against the spirit. The world presseth me on every side. The devil sleepeth not. Give to me the power of Thy Spirit, that a thousand may fall beside me, and ten thousand at my right hand, that I may be a faithful and strong witness of thy faith.

For if Peter, whom Thou endowedst with so many gifts and graces, fell so miserably, what could I do, O Lord, who have never beheld Thee in the flesh, nor have partaken of Thy glory in the Mount, nor have been eye-witness of Thy miracles? Nay rather, I have with difficulty comprehended Thy wonderful works from afar: and I have never heard Thy voice, but have always abode in sins. Therefore establish me with Thy free Spirit, that I may be able to persevere in Thy obedience, and to give my life for Thee.

Catherine of Genoa

(1447-1510)

NAMED after Catherine of Siena, Catherine of Genoa was born into one of the most illustrious of all the Guelph families. Two from her father's family had been popes. Her father was viceroy of Naples, and a cousin was a member of the College of Cardinals. In 1463 she was married to Giuliano Adorno, a wealthy but worldly individual, with whom she had little in common. After ten years of standing the social vanities of the world, she was converted to the contemplative life, and in the same year her husband found his fortune largely squandered. With their remaining income they sought simple quarters among the poor in Genoa. Giuliano became a member of the Third Order of St. Francis, and both of them worked among the poor and the ill. In 1479 they left their home to live in two rooms of a hospital where they gave all their time in service. A year later Giuliano died, and in 1490 Catherine became matron.

Catherine of Genoa was a mystic who was able to tie her profound love of man and God to the world of practical philanthropy. Ecstatic in feeling, original in thought, she is perhaps best remembered by her deeds of mercy. *Life and Teachings*, which ranks with her *Dialogues* as her most important literary contribution, is the work quoted here. The material is reprinted from Friedrich von Hügel's *The Mystical Element of Religion As Studied in Saint Catherine of Genoa and Her Friends*, Vol. I, by permission of E. P. Dutton & Co.

SIN, PURIFICATION, ILLUMINATION

From *Life and Teachings*

The creature is incapable of knowing anything but what God gives it from day to day. If it could know (beforehand) the successive degrees that God intends to give it, it would never be quieted. . . . When from time to time I would advert to the matter, it seemed to me that my love was complete; but later, as time went on and as my sight grew clearer, I became aware that I had had many imperfections. . . I did not recognize them at first, because God-Love was determined to achieve the whole only little by little, for the sake of preserving my physical life, and so as to keep my behaviour tolerable for those with whom I lived. For otherwise, with such other insight, so many excessive acts would ensue, as to make one insupportable to oneself and to others. . . . Every day I feel that the motes are being removed, which this Pure Love casts out (*cava fuori*). Man

cannot see these imperfections; indeed, since, if he saw these motes, he could not bear the sight, God ever lets him see the work he has achieved, as though no imperfections remained in it. But all the time God does not cease from continuing to remove them. . . . From time to time, I feel that many instincts are being consumed within me, which before had appeared to be good and perfect; but when once they have been consumed, I understand that they were bad and imperfect. . . . These things are clearly visible in the mirror of truth, that is of Pure Love, where everything is seen crooked which before appeared straight. . . .

This our self-will is so subtle and so deeply rooted within our own selves, and defends itself with so many reasons, that, when we cannot manage to carry it out in one way, we carry it out in another.

We do our own wills under many covers (pretexts),—of charity, of necessity, of justice, of perfection. . . . I saw this love to have so open and so pure an eye, its sight to be so subtle and its seeing so far-reaching, that I stood astounded. . . . True love wills to stand naked, without any kind of cover, in heaven and on earth, since it has not anything shameful to conceal. . . . This naked love ever sees the truth; whilst self-love can neither see it nor believe in it. . . . Pure love loves God without any *for* (any further motive). . . .

I see every one to be capable of my tender Love. . . . Truth being, by its very nature, communicable to all, cannot be the exclusive property of any one.
. . .

Pure Love loves God without why or wherefore (*perchè*). . . . Since Love took over the care of everything, I have not taken care of anything, nor have I been able to work with my intellect, memory and will, any more than if I had never had them. Indeed every day I feel myself more occupied in Him, and with greater fire. . . . I had given the keys of the house to Love, with ample permission to do all that was necessary, and determined to have no consideration for soul or body, but to see that, of all that the law of pure love required, there should not be wanting the slightest particle (*minimo chè*). And I stood so occupied in contemplating this work of Love, that if He had cast me, body and soul, into hell, hell itself would have appeared to me all love and consolation. . . .

I find myself every day more restricted, as if a man were (first) confined within the walls of a city, then in a house with an ample garden, then in a house without a garden, then in a hall, then in a room, then in an ante-room, then in the cellar of the house with but little light, then in a prison without any light at all; and then his hands were tied and his feet were in the stocks, and then his eyes were bandaged, and then he would not be given anything to eat, and then no one would be able to speak to him; and then, to crown all, every hope were taken from

him of issuing thence as long as life lasted. Nor would any other comfort remain to such a one, than the knowledge that it was God who was doing all this, through love with great mercy; an insight which would give him great contentment. And yet this contentment does not diminish the pain or the oppression.
. . .

God and Sin, however slight, cannot live peaceably side by side (*stare insieme*). Since some little thing that you may have in your eye does not let you see the sun, we can make a comparison between God and the sun, and then between intellectual vision and that of the bodily eye. . . . After considering things as they truly are, I find myself constrained to live without self. . . . Since the time when God has given the light to the soul, it can no more desire to operate by means of that part of itself which is ever staining all things and rendering turbid the clear water of God's grace. The soul then offers and remits itself entirely to Him, so that it can no more operate except to the degree and in the manner willed by tender Love Himself; and henceforth it does not produce works except such as are pure, full and sincere; and these are the works that please God-Love. . . .

I will not name myself either for good or for evil, lest this my (selfish) part should esteem itself to be something. . . . Being determined to join myself unto God, I am in every manner bound to be the enemy of His enemies; and since I find nothing that is more His enemy than is self in me, I am constrained to hate this part of me more than any other thing; indeed, because of the contrariety that subsists between it and the spirit, I am determined to separate it from all the goods of this world and of the next, and to esteem it no more than if it were not.
. . .

When she saw others bewailing their evil inclinations, and forcing themselves greatly to resist them, and yet the more they struggled to produce a remedy for their defects, the more did they commit them, she would say to them: "You have subjects for lamentation (*tu hai li guai*) and bewail them, and I too would be having and bewailing them; you do evil and bewail it, and I should be doing and be bewailing it as you do, if God Almighty were not holding me. You cannot defend yourself, nor can I defend myself. Hence it is necessary that we renounce the care of ourselves unto Him, Who can defend this our true self; and He will then do that which we cannot do. . . .

As to the annihilating of man, which has to be made in God, she spoke thus: "Take a bread, and eat it. When you have eaten it, its substance goes to nourish the body, and the rest is eliminated, because nature cannot use it at all, and indeed, if nature were to retain it, the body would die. Now, if that bread were to say to you: 'Why dost thou remove me from my being? if I could, I would defend myself to conserve myself, an action natural to every creature': you would answer: 'Bread, thy being was ordained for a support for my body, a body which is of more worth than thou; and hence thou oughtest to be more contented with thine end than with thy being. Live for thine end, and thou wilt not care about thy being, but thou wilt exclaim (to the body): "Swiftly, swiftly draw me forth from my being, and put me within the operation of the end of mine, for which I was created." ' . . . And, when the soul has consumed all the evil inclinations of the body, God consumes all the imperfections of the soul." . . .

The soul is made to know in an instant, by means of a new light above itself, all that God desires it to know, and this with so much certainty that it would be impossible to make the soul believe otherwise. Nor is more shown it than is necessary for leading it to greater perfection. . . . This light is not sought by man, but God gives it unto man when He chooses; neither does the man himself know how he knows the thing that he is made to know. And if perchance man were determined to seek to know a little further than he has been made to know, he would achieve nothing, but would remain like unto a stone, without any capacity. . . .

Be Thou my understanding; (thus) shall I know that which it may please Thee that I should know. Nor will I henceforth weary myself with seeking; but I will abide in peace with Thine understanding, which shall wholly occupy my mind. . . . If a man would see properly in spiritual matters, let him pluck out the eyes of his own presumption. . . . He who gazes too much upon the sun's orb, makes himself blind; even thus, I think, does pride blind many, who want to know too much. . . . When God finds a soul that does not move, He operates within it in His own manner, and puts His hand to greater things. He takes from this soul the key of His treasures which He had given to it, so that it might be able to enjoy them; and gives to this same soul the care of His presence, which entirely absorbs it. . . .

The selfishness of man is so contrary to God and rebellious against Him, that God Himself cannot induce the soul to do His will, except by certain stratagems (*lusinghe*): promising it things greater than those left, and giving it, even in this life, a certain consoling relish (*gusto*). And this He does, because He perceives the soul to love things visible so much, that it would never leave one, unless it saw four. . . .

If a man were to see that which, in return for his good deeds, he will have in the life to come, he would cease to occupy himself with anything but heavenly things. But God, desiring that faith should have its merit, and that man should not do good from the motive of selfishness, gives him that knowledge little by little, though always sufficiently for the degree of faith of which the man is then capable. And God ends by leading him to so great a light as to things that are above, that faith seems to have no further place.—On the other hand, if man knew that which hereafter he will have to suffer if he die in the miserable state of sin, I feel sure that, for fear of it, he would let himself be killed rather than commit one single sin. But God, unwilling as He is that man should avoid doing evil from the motive of fear, does not allow him to see so terrifying a spectacle, although He shows it in part to such souls as are so clothed and occupied by His pure love that fear can no more enter in. . . .

God let her hear interiorly: "I do not want thee henceforward to turn thine eyes except towards Love; and here I would have thee stay and not to move, whatever happens to thee or to others, within or without"; "he who trusts in Me, should not doubt about himself." . . .

I see this tender Love to be so courteously attentive to these my spiritual children, that I cannot ask of It anything for them, but can only present them before His face.

Thomas More

(1478-1535)

BETTER known as an English statesman, philosopher, and author of *Utopia*, Thomas More also deserves high rank for his spiritual writings. His education at Oxford, where he came under Erasmus' humanistic influence, found constant expression in his work for man's rights. In *Utopia* he not only denounces the abuses of power, but also argues for religious toleration. In his criticism of the marriage of Henry VIII to Anne Boleyn and his refusal to recognize the king as the temporal head of the English church, he incurred the sovereign's wrath. More was put to death for refusing to take the oath of supremacy to the king. While in the Tower awaiting trial he wrote "A Godly Meditation." Several days before he was beheaded he wrote "A Devout Prayer." Both writings focus his spiritual courage. They appear in *English Prayers and Treatise on the Holy Eucharist by Thomas More* edited by P. E. Hallett.

A GODLY MEDITATION

Give me thy grace, good Lord,
To set the world at nought,
To set my mind fast upon thee.
And not to hang upon the blast of men's mouths.
To be content to be solitary,
Not to long for worldly company,
Little and little utterly to cast off the world,
And rid my mind of all the business thereof.
Not to long to hear of any worldly things,
But that the hearing of worldly phantasies may be to me displeasant.
Gladly to be thinking of God,
Piteously to call for his help,
To lean unto the comfort of God,
Busily to labour to love him:
To know mine own vility and wretchedness,
To humble and meeken myself under the mighty hand of God,
To bewail my sins passed,

For the purging of them, patiently to suffer adversity.
Gladly to bear my purgatory here,
To be joyful of tribulations,
To walk the narrow way that leadeth to life.
To bear the cross with Christ,
To have the last thing in remembrance,
To have ever afore mine eye my death that is ever at hand,
To make death no stranger to me,
To foresee and consider the everlasting fire of hell,
To pray for pardon before the judge come.
To have continually in mind the passion that
Christ suffered for me,
For his benefits uncessantly to give him thanks.
To buy the time again that I before have lost.
To abstain from vain confabulations,

To eschew light foolish mirth and gladness,

Recreations not necessary to cut off.

Of worldly substance, friends, liberty, life and all, to set the loss at right nought, for the winning of Christ.

To think my most enemies my best friends,

For the brethren of Joseph could never have done him so much good with their love and favour as they did him with their malice and hatred.

These minds are more to be desired of every man, than all the treasure of all the princes and kings, Christian and heathen, were it gathered and laid together all upon one heap.

A DEVOUT PRAYER

O Holy Trinity, the Father, the Son, and the Holy Ghost, three equal and co-eternal Persons, and one Almighty God, have mercy on me, vile, abject, abominable, sinful wretch: meekly knowledging before thine High Majesty my long-continued sinful life, even from my very childhood hitherto.

In my childhood, in this point and that point, etc. After my childhood in this point and that point, and so forth by every age, etc.

Now, good gracious Lord, as thou givest me thy grace to knowledge them, so give me thy grace, not in only word but in heart also with very sorrowful contrition to repent them and utterly to forsake them. And forgive me those sins also, in which by mine own default, through evil affections and evil custom, my reason is with sensuality so blinded that I cannot discern them for sin. And illumine, good Lord, mine heart, and give me thy grace to know them, and forgive me my sins negligently forgotten, and bring them to my mind with grace to be purely confessed of them.

Glorious God, give me from henceforth thy grace, with little respect unto the world, so to set and fix firmly mine heart upon thee, that I may say with thy blessed apostle St. Paul: *"The world is crucified to me and I to the world." "To me to live is Christ, and to die is gain." "I desire to be dissolved and to be with Christ."*

Give me thy grace to amend my life, and to have an eye to mine end without grudge of death, which to them that die in thee, good Lord, is the gate of a wealthy life.

Almighty God, *"Teach me to do thy will." "Make me to run after thee to the odour of thy ointments." "Take thou my right hand and guide me in the straight path because of my enemies." "Draw me after thee." "With bit and bridle bind fast my jaws when I come not near unto thee."*

O glorious God, all sinful fear, all sinful sorrow and pensiveness, all sinful hope, all sinful mirth, and gladness take from me. And on the other side concerning such fear, such sorrow, such heaviness, such comfort, consolation and gladness as shall be profitable for my soul: *"Deal with me according to thy great goodness, O Lord."*

Good Lord, give me the grace, in all my fear and agony, to have recourse to that great fear and wonderful agony that thou, my sweet Saviour, hadst at the Mount of Olivet before thy most bitter passion, and in the meditation thereof, to conceive ghostly comfort and consolation profitable for my soul.

Almighty God, take from me all vainglorious minds, all appetites of mine own praise, all envy, covetise, gluttony, sloth, and lechery, all wrathful affections, all appetite of revenging, all desire or delight of other folks' harm, all pleasure in provoking any person to wrath and anger, all delight of exprobation or insultation against any person in their affliction and calamity.

And give me, good Lord, an humble, lowly, quiet, peaceable, patient, charitable, kind, tender, and pitiful mind, with all my works, and all my words, and all my thoughts, to have a taste of thy Holy, Blessed Spirit.

Give me, good Lord, a full faith, a firm hope, and a fervent charity, a love to the good Lord incomparable above the love to myself; and that I love nothing to thy displeasure, but everything in an order to thee.

Give me, good Lord, a longing to be with thee, not for the avoiding of the calamities of this wretched world, nor so much for the avoiding of the pains of purgatory, nor of the pains of hell neither, nor so much for the attaining of the joys of heaven, in respect of mine own commodity, as even for a very love to thee.

And bear me, good Lord, thy love and favour, which thing my love to thee-ward (were it never so great) could not but of thy great goodness deserve.

And pardon me, good Lord, that I am so bold to ask so high petitions, being so vile a sinful wretch, and so unworthy to attain the lowest. But yet, good Lord, such they be, as I am bounden to wish and should be nearer the effectual desire of them, if my manifold sins were not the let. From which, O glorious Trinity, vouchsafe of thy goodness to wash me, with that blessed blood that issued out of thy tender body, O sweet Saviour Christ, in the divers torments of thy most bitter passion.

Take from me, good Lord, this lukewarm fashion, or rather keycold manner of meditation, and this dullness in praying unto thee. And give me warmth, delight and quickness in thinking upon thee. And give me thy grace to long for thine holy sacraments, and specially to rejoice in the presence of thy very blessed body, Sweet Saviour Christ, in the holy sacrament of the altar, and duly to thank thee for thy gracious visitation therewith, and at that high memorial, with tender compassion, to remember and consider thy most bitter passion.

Make us all, good Lord, virtually participant of that holy sacrament this day, and every day make us all lively members, sweet Saviour Christ, of thine holy mystical body, thy Catholic Church.

"*Deign, O Lord, to keep us on that day without sin. Have mercy on us, O Lord, have mercy on us. Let thy mercy, O Lord, be upon us, as we have hoped in thee. In thee, O Lord, have I hoped, let me not be confounded for ever.*"

"*Pray for us, O holy mother of God, that we may be made worthy of the promises of Christ.*"

THE SIXTEENTH CENTURY
PROTESTANT SAINTS JOIN THE FELLOWSHIP

Martin Luther
(1483-1546)

No man has done more to shift the tide of the Christian tradition than Martin Luther. Although not a profound scholar, organizer, or politician, he influenced men by the depth of his religious experience. Born in Eisleben of a peasant mining family, he was inspired by his father to pursue the study of law and went to the University of Erfurt. However, in deep anxiety for the salvation of his soul, he entered the monastery of Augustinian hermits in July, 1505. Here he came into an understanding of Augustine and Bernard of Clairvaux. Later his hunger for piety was fed by Tauler, the Bible—especially Romans—and *Theologia Germanica*. In 1518 he edited *Theologia Germanica*.

Ordained to the priesthood in 1507, he was professor of biblical literature at Wittenberg by 1512, and in 1515 he was made district vicar of eleven monasteries. His lectures at Wittenberg on the Epistle to the Romans did much to form his theological viewpoint. When in 1517 he nailed the ninety-five theses on the castle church at Wittenberg, he formally started the Protestant Reformation.

Luther was not only a man of zeal and leadership, but a man of deep piety. The selections on "Prayer" and "Worship" reflect his devotional spirit. They are from *A Compend of Luther's Theology*, edited by H. T. Kerr and used by permission of The Westminster Press. Acknowledgements are also made to the following copyright owners for sections of their works which are incorporated in these selections: The Luther Press: *The J. N. Lenker Edition of Luther's Works;* The United Lutheran Publication House: *The Table-Talk of Martin Luther*, tr. William Hazlitt, and *Works of Martin Luther;* The Pilgrim Press: *Conversations with Luther*, tr. and ed. P. Smith and H. P. Gallinger.

[PRAYER]

By "prayer" we understand simply formal words or expressions—as, for instance, the Lord's Prayer and the psalms—which sometimes express more than our request. In "supplication" we strengthen prayer and make it effective by a certain form of persuasion; for instance, we may entreat one to grant a request for the sake of a father, or of something dearly loved or highly prized. We entreat God by his Son, his saints, his promises, his name. Thus Solomon says, "Jehovah, remember for David all his affliction." And Paul urges, "I beseech you therefore, brethren, by the mercies of God"; and again, "I . . . entreat you by the meekness and gentleness of Christ." "Petitioning" is stating what we have at heart, naming the desire we express in prayer and supplication. In the Lord's Prayer are seven petitions, beside prayer proper. Christ says: "Ask, and it shall be given you; seek, and ye shall find; knock, and it shall be opened unto you: for every one that asketh receiveth; and he that seeketh findeth; and to him that knocketh it shall be opened." In "thanksgiving" we recount blessings received and thus strengthen our confidence and enable ourselves to wait trustingly for what we pray.

Prayer is made vigorous by petitioning; urgent by supplication; by thanksgiving, pleasing and acceptable. Strength

258

and acceptability combine to prevail and secure the petition. This, we see, is the manner of prayer practiced by the Church; and the holy fathers in the Old Testament always offered supplication and thanks in their prayers. The Lord's Prayer opens with praise and thanksgiving and the acknowledgment of God as a Father; it earnestly presses toward him through filial love and a recognition of fatherly tenderness. For supplication, this prayer is unequaled. Hence it is the sublimest and the noblest prayer ever uttered.

—*"Epistle Sermon, Fourth Sunday in Advent"* (*Lenker Edition,* Vol. VII, #31-32).

We should pray, not as the custom is, counting many pages or beads, but fixing our mind upon some pressing need, desire it with all earnestness, and exercise faith and confidence toward God in the matter, in such wise that we do not doubt that we shall be heard. So St. Bernard instructs his brethren and says: "Dear brethren, you shall by no means despise your prayer, as if it were in vain, for I tell you of a truth that, before you have uttered the words, the prayer is already recorded in heaven; and you shall confidently expect from God one of two things: either that your prayer will be granted, or that, if it will not be granted, the granting of it would not be good for you."

Prayer is, therefore, a special exercise of faith, and faith makes the prayer so acceptable that either it will surely be granted, or something better than we ask will be given in its stead. So also says St. James: "Let him who asketh of God not waver in faith; for if he wavers, let not that man think that he shall receive anything of the Lord." This is a clear statement, which says directly: he who does not trust, receives nothing, neither that which he asks, nor anything better.

And to call forth such faith, Christ Himself has said, Mark xi: "Therefore I say unto you, What things soever ye desire, when ye pray, believe that ye receive them, and ye shall surely have them." And Luke xi: "Ask, and it shall be given you; seek, and ye shall find; knock, and it shall be opened unto you; for every one that asketh receiveth; and he that seeketh findeth; and to him that knocketh it shall be opened. Or what father is there of you, who, if his son shall ask bread, will he give him a stone? or if he ask a fish, will he give him a serpent? or if he ask an egg, will he give him a scorpion? But if you know how to give good gifts to your children, and you yourselves are not naturally good, how much more shall your Father which is in heaven give a good spirit to all them that ask Him!"

Who is so hard and stone-like, that such mighty words ought not to move him to pray with all confidence joyfully and gladly? But how many prayers must be reformed, if we are to pray aright according to these words! Now, indeed, all churches and monastic houses are full of praying and singing, but how does it happen that so little improvement and benefit result from it, and things daily grow worse? The reason is none other than that which St. James indicates when he says: "You ask much and receive not, because ye ask amiss." For where this faith and confidence is not in the prayer, the prayer is dead, and nothing more than a grievous labor and work. If anything is given for it, it is none the less only temporal benefit without any blessing and help for the soul; nay, to the great injury and blinding of souls, so that they go their way, babbling much with their mouths, regardless of whether they receive, or desire, or trust; and in this unbelief, the state of mind most opposed to the exercise of faith and to the nature of prayer, they remain hardened.

From this it follows that one who prays aright never doubts that his prayer is surely acceptable and heard, although the very thing for which he prays be not given him. For we are to lay our need before God in prayer, but not prescribe to Him a measure, manner, time or place; but if He wills to give it to us better or in another way than we think, we are to leave it to Him; for frequently we do not know what we pray, as St. Paul says, Romans viii; and God works and gives above all that we understand, as he says, Ephesians iii, so that there be no doubt that the prayer is acceptable and heard, and we yet leave to God the time, place, measure and limit; He will surely do what is right. They are the true worshipers, who worship God in spirit and in truth. For they who believe not that they will be heard, sin upon the left hand against this Commandment, and go far astray with their unbelief. But they who set a limit for Him, sin upon the other side, and come too close with their tempting of God. So He has forbidden both, that we should err from His Commandment neither to the left nor to the right, that is, neither with unbelief nor with tempting, but with simple faith remain on the straight road, trusting Him, and yet setting Him no bounds. . . .

There is no Christian who does not have time to pray without ceasing. But I mean the spiritual praying, that is: no one is so heavily burdened with his labor, but that if he will he can, while working, speak with God in his heart, lay before Him his need and that of other men, ask for help, make petition, and in all this exercise and strengthen his faith.

This is what the Lord means, Luke xviii, when He says, "Men ought always to pray, and never cease," although in Matthew vi. He forbids the use of much speaking and long prayers, because of which he rebukes the hypocrites; not because the lengthy prayer of the lips is evil, but because it is not that true prayer which can be made at all times, and without the inner prayer of faith is nothing. . . .

But what are the things which we must bring before Almighty God in prayer and lamentation, to exercise faith thereby? Answer: First, every man's own besetting need and trouble, of which David says, Psalm xxxii: "Thou art my refuge in all trouble which compasseth me about; Thou art my comfort, to preserve me from all evil which surrounds me." Likewise, Psalm cxlii: "I cried unto the Lord with my voice; with my voice unto the Lord did I make my supplication. I poured out my complaint before Him;

I showed before Him my trouble." In the mass a Christian shall keep in mind the short-comings or excesses he feels, and pour out all these freely before God with weeping and groaning, as woefully as he can, as to his faithful Father, who is ready to help him. And if you do not know or recognise your need, or have no trouble, then you shall know that you are in the worst possible plight. For this is the greatest trouble, that you find yourself so hardened, hard-hearted and insensible that no trouble moves you.

There is no better mirror in which to see your need than simply the Ten Commandments, in which you will find what you lack and what you should seek. If, therefore, you find in yourself a weak faith, small hope and little love toward God; and that you do not praise and honor God, but love your own honor and fame, think much of the favor of men, do not gladly hear mass and sermon, are indolent in prayer, in which things every one has faults, then you shall think more of these faults than of all bodily harm to goods, honor and life, and believe that they are worse than death and all mortal sickness. These you shall earnestly lay before God, lament and ask for help, and with all confidence expect help, and believe that you are heard and shall obtain help and mercy.

—"Treatise on Good Works," *Works of Martin Luther,* Vol. I, pp. 225-231.

None can believe how powerful prayer is, and what it is able to effect, but those who have learned it by experience.

It is a great matter when in extreme need, to take hold on prayer. I know, whenever I have earnestly prayed, I have been amply heard, and have obtained more than I prayed for; God, indeed, sometimes delayed, but at last he came.

Ecclesiasticus says: "The prayer of a good and godly Christian availeth more to health, than the physician's physic."

O how great a thing, how marvellous, a godly Christian's prayer is! how powerful with God; that a poor human creature should speak with God's high Majesty in heaven, and not be affrighted, but, on the contrary, know that God smiles upon him for Christ's sake, his dearly beloved Son. The heart and conscience, in this act of praying, must not fly and recoil backwards by reason of our sins and unworthiness, or stand in doubt, or be scared away. We must not do as the Bavarian did, who, with great devotion, called upon St. Leonard, an idol set up in a church in Bavaria, behind which idol stood one who answered the Bavarian, and said: Fie on thee, Bavarian; and in that sort often repulsed and would not hear him, till at last, the Bavarian went away, and said: Fie on thee, Leonard.

When we pray, we must not let it come to: Fie upon thee; but certainly hold and believe, that we are already heard in that for which we pray, with faith in Christ. Therefore the ancients ably defined prayer an *Ascensus mentis ad Deum*, a climbing up of the heart unto God.

—*Table-Talk*, #CCCXXVIII.

Under the papacy it is taught that the saints in heaven do pray for us, though we cannot know this, since the Scriptures tell us no such thing. Not only so, but the saints have been made gods, so that they have to be our patrons, on whom we call, even though some of them have never existed. To each of these saints some special power and might have been ascribed. One has power over fire, another over water, another over pestilence, fever and all kinds of disease. Indeed it seems that God has to be idle and let the saints work and act in His stead. . . .

There is not a single word of God commanding us to call on either angels or saints to intercede for us, and we have no example of it in the Scriptures. There we find that the angels spoke with the fathers and the prophets but none of these angels was asked to intercede for them. So Jacob, the father of them all, did not ask the angel, with whom he fought, for any intercession, but only took a blessing from him. On the contrary, we find, in the Apocalypse, that the angel would not allow himself to be worshiped by John. Thus the worship of saints shows itself to be a mere trumpery of men and an invention of their own, outside the Word of God and the Scriptures.

It is not proper, however, for us to undertake anything in the way of worship without God's Word, and one who does so is tempting God. Therefore it is not to be advised or endured that one should call upon the departed saints to intercede for him or should teach others to do it; but it is rather to be condemned and others are to be taught to avoid it. For this reason I, too, shall not advise it and so burden my conscience with other people's iniquities. It was exceedingly bitter for me to tear myself away from the worship of the saints, for I was steeped and fairly drowned in it. But the light of the Gospel is now so clear that henceforth no one has any excuse to remain in darkness. We all know very well what we ought to do.

Moreover, this is, in itself, a dangerous and offense-giving service, because people are easily accustomed to turning from Christ and quickly learn to put more confidence in the saints than in Christ Himself. Our nature is, in any case, all too prone to flee from God and Christ, and to trust in men; nay, it is exceedingly hard for one to learn to trust in God and Christ, though we have vowed and are in duty bound to do so. Therefore this offense is not to be endured, so that weak and fleshly people may not begin an idolatry, against the First Commandment and against our baptism. Be satisfied to turn confidence and trust away from the saints, to Christ, both by teaching and practice. Even then there are difficulties and hindrances enough. There is no need to paint the devil on the door; he will be on hand.

—"On Translating: An Open Letter," *Works of Martin Luther*, Vol. V, pp. 23 f.

[WORSHIP]

The word, to worship, means to stoop and bow down the body with external gestures; to serve in the work. But to worship God in spirit is the service and

honor of the heart; it comprehends faith and fear in God. The worshipping of God is two-fold, outward and inward—that is, to acknowledge God's benefits, and to be thankful unto him.
—*Table-Talk,* #DCCVIII.

To praise the Lord with gladness is not a work of man; it is rather a joyful suffering, and the work of God alone. It cannot be taught in words, but must be learned in one's own experience. Even as David says, in Psalm xxxiv, "O taste and see that the Lord is sweet: blessed is the man that trusteth in Him." He puts tasting before seeing, because this sweetness cannot be known unless one has experienced and felt it for oneself; and no one can attain to such experience unless he trusts in God with his whole heart, when he is in the depths and in sore straits. Therefore David makes haste to add, "Blessed is the man that trusteth in God." Such a one will experience the work of God within himself, and will thus come to feel His sweetness, and thereby attain to all knowledge and understanding.
—"The Magnificat," *Works of Martin Luther,* Vol. III, pp. 131 f.

Even if different people make use of different rites, let no one either judge or despise the other; but let each one abound in his own opinion, and let them understand and know even if they do differently; and let each one's rite be agreeable to the other, lest diverse opinions and sects yield diverse uses, just as happened in the Roman Church. For external rites, even if we are not able to do without them,—just as we cannot do without food and drink,—nevertheless, do not commend us to God, just as food does not commend us to God. But faith and love commend us to God. Wherefore let this word of Paul govern here: The kingdom of God is not food and drink, but righteousness, peace and joy in the Holy Spirit. Thus no rite is the Kingdom of God, but faith within you, etc.
—"Formula of Mass and Communion for the Church at Wittenberg," *Works of Martin Luther,* Vol. VI, pp. 92 f.

It would also be a good thing if there were fewer saint's days, since in our times the works done on them are for the greater part worse than those of the work days, what with loafing, gluttony, and drunkenness, gambling and other evil deeds; and then, the mass and the sermon are listened to without edification, the prayer is spoken without faith. It almost happens that men think it is sufficient that we look on at the mass with our eyes, hear the preaching with our ears, and say the prayers with our mouths. It is all so formal and superficial! We do not think that we might receive something out of the mass into our hearts, learn and remember something out of the preaching, seek, desire and expect something in our prayer.
—"Treatise on Good Works," *Works of Martin Luther,* Vol. I, p. 222.

Ceremonies are to be given the same place in the life of a Christian as models and plans have among builders and artisans. They are prepared not as permanent structures, but because without them nothing could be built or made. When the structure is completed they are laid aside. You see, they are not despised, rather, they are greatly sought after; but what we despise is the false estimate of them, since no one holds them to be the real and permanent structure. If any man were so egregiously foolish as to care for nothing all his life long except the most costly, careful and persistent preparation of plans and models, and never to think of the structure itself, and were satisfied with his work in producing such plans and mere aids to work, and boasted of it, would not all men pity his insanity, and estimate that with what he has wasted something great might have been built?
—"A Treatise on Christian Liberty," *Works of Martin Luther,* Vol. II, p. 347.

It is not now, nor has it ever been, in our mind to abolish entirely the whole formal cultus of God, but to cleanse that which is in use, which has been vitiated by most abominable additions, and to point out a pious use. For this cannot be denied, that masses and the communion of bread and wine are a rite divinely instituted by Christ, which was observed, first under Christ Himself, then under the apostles, most simply and piously and without any additions. But so many human inventions have been added to it in course of time, that nothing of the mass and communion has come down to our age except the name.

—"Formula of Mass and Communion for the Church at Wittenberg," *Works of Martin Luther,* Vol. VI, pp. 84 f.

Christ . . . teaches us, in Matthew vi, not to speak much when we pray, as the Gentiles do, for they think that they shall be heard for their much speaking. Even so there is to-day in the churches a great ringing of bells, blowing of trumpets, singing, shouting, and intoning, yet I fear precious little worship of God, Who would be worshiped in spirit and in truth, as He says in John iv.

Solomon says, in Proverbs xxvii, "He that blesseth his friend with a loud voice, rising early in the morning, it shall be counted a curse to him." For such a one awakens the suspicion that he is endeavoring to adorn an evil cause; he protests too much and only defeats his own end. On the other hand, he that curses his neighbor with a loud voice, rising up early in the morning (that is, not indifferently, but with great zeal and urgency), is to be regarded as a praiser of him. For men do not believe him, but deem him impelled by hatred and a wicked heart; he hurts his own cause and helps his neighbor's. In the same way, to think to worship God with many words and a great noise, is to count Him either deaf or ignorant, and to suppose we must waken or instruct Him. Such an opinion of God tends to His shame and dishonor rather than to His worship.

—"Magnificat," *Works of Martin Luther,* Vol. III, p. 160.

Common prayer is precious and the most powerful, and it is for its sake that we come together. For this reason also the Church is called a House of Prayer, because in it we are as a congregation with one accord to consider our need and the needs of all men, present them before God, and call upon Him for mercy. But this must be done with heart-felt emotion and sincerity, so that we feel in our hearts the need of all men, and that we pray with true sympathy for them, in true faith and confidence. Where such prayers are not made in the mass, it were better to omit the mass. For what sense is there in our coming together into a House of Prayer, which coming together shows that we should make common prayer and petition for the entire congregation, if we scatter these prayers, and so distribute them that everyone prays only for himself, and no one has regard for the other, nor concerns himself for another's need? How can that prayer be of help, good, acceptable and a common prayer, or a work of the Holy Day and of the assembled congregation, which they make who make their own petty prayers, one for this, the other for that, and have nothing but self-seeking, selfish prayers, which God hates? . . .

The Christian Church on earth has no greater power or work than such common prayer against everything that may oppose it. This the evil spirit knows well, and therefore he does all that he can to prevent such prayer. Gleefully he lets us go on building churches, endowing many monastic houses, making music, reading, singing, observing many masses, and multiplying ceremonies beyond all measure. This does not grieve him, nay, he helps us do it, that we may consider such things the very best, and think that thereby we have done our whole duty. But in that meanwhile this common, effectual and fruitful prayer perishes and its omission is unnoticed because of such display, in this he has what he seeks. For when prayer languishes, no one will take anything from him, and no one will withstand him. But if he noticed that we wished to practise this prayer, even if it were under a straw roof or in a pig-sty, he would indeed not endure it, but would fear such a pig-sty far more than all the high, big and beautiful churches, towers and bells in existence, if such prayer be not in them. It is indeed not a question of the places and buildings in which we assemble, but only of this unconquerable prayer, that we pray it and bring it before God as a truly common prayer. . . .

We should do as they do who wish to ask a favor of great princes. These do not plan merely to babble a certain number of words, for the prince would think they mocked him, or were insane; but they put their request very plainly, and present their need earnestly, and then leave it to his mercy, in good confidence that he will grant it. So we must deal with God of definite things, namely, mention some present need, commend it to His mercy and goodwill, and not doubt that it is heard; for He has promised to hear such prayer, which no earthly lord has done.
—"Treatise on Good Works," *Works of Martin Luther*, Vol. I, pp. 233-237.

I am not of the opinion that arts are to be cast down and destroyed on account of the Gospel, as some fanatics protest; on the other hand I would gladly see all arts, especially music, in the service of Him who has given and created them.
—"Spiritual Hymn Booklet," *Works of Martin Luther*, Vol. VI, p. 284.

That the singing of spiritual hymns is a goodly thing and pleasing to God, I do not think is hidden from any Christian, since everyone is aware not only of the example of the kings and prophets in the Old Testament, (who praised God with singing and playing, with poesy and all manner of string music), but also of the universality of this custom in Christendom from the beginning, especially psalm singing. Indeed, St. Paul also instituted this in I Corinthians 14:15, and exhorted the Colossians (3:16) to sing spiritual songs and psalms heartily unto the Lord in order that God's Word and Christian teaching might be propagated by this means and practiced in every way.
—"Spiritual Hymn Booklet," *Works of Martin Luther*, Vol. VI, p. 283.

I always loved music; whoso has skill in this art, is of a good temperament, fitted for all things. We must teach music in schools; a schoolmaster ought to have skill in music, or I would not regard him; neither should we ordain young men as preachers, unless they have been well exercised in music.
—*Table-Talk*, #DCCXCIV.

Music is a noble gift of God, next to theology. I would not change my little knowledge of music for a great deal.
—*Conversations with Luther*, p. 99.

Ignatius of Loyola
(1491-1556)

BORN of a noble family in northern Spain and serving as a page in the court of Ferdinand, Ignatius became a soldier and was wounded at the battle of Pampeluna. While bedridden he read devotional literature, being particularly impressed by the lives of Christ, Dominic, and Francis of Assisi. On March 25, 1522 he transferred his zeal from the military life to religion, and spent a year in penitence and solitude in a cave near Manresa. Later he began the study of educational rudiments at Barcelona. After study at the University of Alcala and the University of Salamanca he entered the University of Paris in 1528, where he studied literature and theology for seven years.

In 1534 he founded the Society of Jesus at Montmartre, Paris. The members of this society purposed to love God and the church, and to put themselves at the disposal of the pope. In 1536 Ignatius envisioned his society as the military company of Jesus, bound by a military strictness of obedience and a careful, though spiritual, use of arms to fight infidels and heretics.

"Three Methods of Prayer" is taken from *Spiritual Exercises*, which lays down rules by which man's soul can be spiritually disciplined. The translation is by Elder Mullan.

THREE METHODS OF PRAYER

From *Spiritual Exercises*

FIRST METHOD OF PRAYER

The first Method of Prayer is on the Ten Commandments, and on the Seven Deadly Sins, on the Three Powers of the Soul and on the Five Bodily Senses. This method of prayer is meant more to give form, method and exercises, how the soul may prepare itself and benefit in them, and that the prayer may be acceptable, rather than to give any form or way of praying.

I. The Ten Commandments

First let the equivalent of the second Addition of the Second Week be made; that is, before entering on the prayer, let the spirit rest a little, the person being seated or walking about, as may seem best to him, considering where he is going and to what. And this same addition will be made at the beginning of all Methods of Prayer.

Prayer. A Preparatory Prayer, as, for example, to ask grace of God our Lord that I may be able to know in what I have failed as to the Ten Commandments; and likewise to beg grace and help to amend in future, asking for perfect understanding of them, to keep them better and for the greater glory and praise of His Divine Majesty.

For the first Method of Prayer, it is well to consider and think on the First Commandment, how I have kept it and in what I have failed, keeping to the rule of spending the space of time one says the *Our Father* and the *Hail Mary* three times; and if in this time I find faults of mine, to ask pardon and forgiveness for them, and say an *Our Father*. Let this same method be followed on each one of the Ten Commandments.

First Note. It is to be noted that when one comes to think on a Commandment on which he finds he has no habit of sinning, it is not necessary for him to delay so much time, but according as one finds in himself that he stumbles more or less on that Commandment so he ought to keep himself more or less on the consideration and examination of it. And the same is to be observed on the Deadly Sins.

Second Note. After having finished the discussion already mentioned on all the Commandments, accusing myself on them and asking grace and help to amend hereafter, I am to finish with a Colloquy to God our Lord, according to the subject matter.

II. On Deadly Sins

About the Seven Deadly Sins, after the Addition, let the Preparatory Prayer be made in the way already mentioned, only with the difference that the matter here is of sins that have to be avoided, and before of Commandments that have to be kept: and likewise let the order and rule already mentioned be kept, and the Colloquy.

In order to know better the faults committed in the Deadly Sins, let their contraries be looked at: and so, to avoid them better, let the person purpose and with holy exercises see to acquiring and keeping the seven virtues contrary to them.

III. On the Powers of the Soul

Way. On the three powers of the soul let the same order and rule be kept as on the Commandments, making its Addition, Preparatory Prayer and Colloquy.

IV. On the Bodily Senses

Way. About the five bodily senses the same order always will be kept, but changing their matter.

Note. Whoever wants to imitate Christ our Lord in the use of his senses, let him in the Preparatory Prayer recommend himself to His Divine Majesty, and after considering on each sense, say a *Hail Mary* or an *Our Father*.

And whoever wants to imitate Our Lady in the use of the senses, let him in the Preparatory Prayer recommend himself to her, that she may get him grace from Her Son and Lord for it; and after considering on each sense, say a *Hail Mary*.

SECOND METHOD OF PRAYER

It is by contemplating the meaning of each word of the Prayer.

Addition. The same Addition which was in the First Method of Prayer will be in this second.

Prayer. The Preparatory Prayer will be made according to the person to whom the prayer is addressed.

Second Method of Prayer. The Second Method of Prayer is that the person, kneeling or seated, according to the greater disposition in which he finds himself and as more devotion accompanies him, keeping the eyes closed or fixed on one place, without going wandering with them, says *Father*, and is on the consideration of this word as long as he finds meanings, comparisons, relish and consolation in considerations pertaining to such word. And let him do in the same way on each word of the *Our Father*, or of any other prayer which he wants to say in this way.

First Rule. The first Rule is that he will be an hour on the whole *Our Father* in the manner already mentioned. Which finished, he will say a *Hail Mary, Creed, Soul of Christ*, and *Hail, Holy Queen*, vocally or mentally, according to the usual way.

Second Rule. The Second Rule is that, should the person who is contemplating the *Our Father* find in one word, or in two, matter so good to think over, and relish and consolation, let him not care to pass on, although the hour ends on what he finds. The hour finished, he will say the rest of the *Our Father* in the usual way.

Third Rule. The third is that if on one word or two of the *Our Father* one has lingered for a whole hour, when he will want to come back another day to the prayer, let him say the above-mentioned word, or the two, as he is accustomed; and on the word which immediately follows let him commence to contemplate, according as was said in the second Rule.

First Note. It is to be noted that, the *Our Father* finished, in one or in many days, the same has to be done with the *Hail Mary* and then with the other prayers, so that for some time one is always exercising himself in one of them.

Second Note. The second note is that, the prayer finished, turning, in few words, to the person to whom he has prayed, let him ask for the virtues or graces of which he feels he has most need.

THIRD METHOD OF PRAYER

It will be by rhythm.

Addition. The Addition will be the same as in the First and Second Methods of Prayer.

Prayer. The Preparatory Prayer will be as in the Second Method of Prayer.

Third Method of Prayer. The Third Method of Prayer is that with each breath in or out, one has to pray mentally, saying one word of the *Our Father*, or of another prayer which is being recited: so that only one word be said between one breath and another, and while the time from one breath to another lasts, let attention be given chiefly to the meaning of such word, or to the person to whom he recites it, or to his own baseness, or to the difference from such great height to his own so great lowness. And in the same form and rule he will proceed on the other words of the *Our Father;* and the other prayers, that is to say, the *Hail Mary*, the *Soul of Christ*, the *Creed*, and the *Hail, Holy Queen*, he will make as he is accustomed.

First Rule. The First Rule is, on the other day, or at another hour, that he wants to pray, let him say the *Hail Mary* in rhythm, and the other prayers as he is accustomed; and so on, going through the others.

Second Rule. The second is that whoever wants to dwell more on the prayer by rhythm, can say all the above-mentioned prayers or part of them, keeping the same order of the breath by rhythm, as has been explained.

John Calvin

(1509-1564)

BORN at Noyon and educated at the University of Paris, John Calvin was reared in the atmosphere of high society and nobility. Although his father wished him to study theology, Calvin was by uncontrollable circumstances shifted to law. This he studied at the University of Orleans. Although he was never ordained, Calvin became the curate of St. Martin de Marteville in 1527. In 1534 he was converted to Protestantism which caused him two short imprisonments.

In 1536 he wrote his *Institutes of the Christian Religion*. By 1541 his influence in Geneva, Switzerland, began to grow in spite of opposition, and through his efforts that city became famed for its moral tone, material prosperity, and educational standing.

Augustine and Luther influenced Calvin's thinking, especially Augustine with his doctrines of grace and predestination. Less mystical than Augustine, more stern in temper, Calvin's concept of prayer is interestingly portrayed in "How Men Should Pray," which is one of his sermons. The anonymous translation is from an old edition of Calvin's sermons (New York, 1830).

HOW MEN SHOULD PRAY

After St. Paul hath informed us that our Lord Jesus Christ came into the world, and gave himself a ransom for all, and that the message of salvation is carried in his name to all people, both small and great, he exhorteth everyone to call upon God. For this is the true fruit of faith, to know that God is our Father, and to be moved by his love. The way is open for us to run to him, and it is easy to pray to him when we are convinced that his eyes are upon us, and that he is ready to help us in all our necessities.

Until God hath called us, we cannot come to him without too much impudent boldness. Is it not rashness for mortal man to presume to address himself to God? Therefore we must wait till God calleth us, which he also doth by his word. He promiseth to be our Saviour, and showeth that he will always be ready to receive us. He doth not tarry till we come to seek him, but he offereth himself, and exhorteth us to pray to him; yea, and therein proveth our faith.

St. Paul saith, Romans x. 14. "How shall they call on him in whom they have not believed? and how shall they believe in him of whom they have not heard? and how shall they hear without a preacher?" Thus it may be understood, that God is ready to receive us, although we be not worthy: when we once know his will, we may come to him with boldness, because he maketh himself familiar to us. The apostle addeth, Romans xv. "Praise the Lord, all ye Gentiles; and laud him, all ye people:" giving us to understand thereby, that the gospel belongeth to the Gentiles as well as the Jews, and that every mouth ought to be open to call upon God for help.

We must call upon God in all places, seeing we are received into his flock. The Gentiles were strangers to all the promises which God had made to his people Israel. But the apostle saith, behold, God hath gathered you into his flock: he hath sent you his only begotten Son, even for the fatherly love which he bare you: you may therefore boldly call upon him, for it is to this end, and for this purpose, that he hath given you this witness of his good will.

As often as the goodness of God is witnessed by us, and his grace promised, (although we be wretched sinners,) as oft also as we hear that our sins were forgiven us by the death and suffering of our Lord Jesus Christ, and that atonement was made for our transgressions and the obligations which were against us, and that God is at peace with us, the way is opened for us to pray to him and implore his blessings.

It is said in Hosea ii. "I will say to them which were not my people, Thou art my people, and they shall say, Thou art my God." Therefore, as soon as our Lord God maketh us taste his goodness, and promiseth that even as he sent his only begotten Son into the world, he will accept us in his name, let us doubt not, but come immediately to him in prayer and supplication. If we have faith, we must show it by calling upon God. If we make no account of prayer, it is a sure sign that we are infidels; notwithstanding we may make great pretence to a belief in the gospel. Thus we see what great blessings God bestoweth upon us, when we can have the privilege of prayer.

God informeth us that if we call upon him, it shall not be in vain; we shall not be deceived in our expectations if we come to him aright; we shall never be cast off, if we keep in the way which St. Paul hath marked out; namely, if we have Jesus Christ for our mediator, and trust in the merits of his death and passion, knowing that it is his office to keep us. And as he hath made reconciliation between God and us, he will keep us through his grace and mercy, if we put our trust in him.

When we are made sensible of the blessings which God hath bestowed upon us, in granting us the privilege of calling upon him by prayer, we must exercise ourselves in this duty faithfully: we must be careful both morning and evening to call upon God, for we have need of his assistance every hour. Again; we cannot pray to God unless we have the spirit of adoption; that is, unless we be assured that he taketh us for his children, and giveth us witness thereof by his gospel. As oft therefore as we read in holy writ, *pray to God, praise him,* &c. we must

know that the fruit of our faith is set forth by these words; because God hath revealed himself to us, and hath made the way easy whereby we may come to him.

I will therefore that men pray everywhere: we see also in the first epistle to the Corinthians, that the apostle saluteth all the faithful who call upon God, *both theirs and ours*: chap. i. 2. Here he joineth the Gentiles with the Jews; as if he had said, I will not confine the church of God to one particular people. It was so under the law, but after the wall was broken down, and the enmity between the Jews and Gentiles taken away, there was liberty among all nations and people, of calling upon God; because his grace is common to both Jew and Gentile.

Moreover, St. Paul meant to show that the ceremonies of the law were not to be continued after Jesus Christ was made manifest to the world. For in the time of the law, men were constrained to come together at the temple, to call upon God. It is true that the Jews prayed, every man at his own house, but it was not lawful to offer a solemn sacrifice except in the temple; for that was the place that God had chosen. According to the grossness of the people, it was requisite to have sacrifices, until the truth should be declared more plainly. The temple was a sign, which represents that we must come to God in one way only; and what is that? through our Lord Jesus Christ.

We cannot come nigh to God, unless we have one to lead us; we must therefore trust in him through the merits of Jesus Christ. The Jews had this in a figure; we have it in substance and in truth. Again; God thought proper to hold them as little children in the unity of faith, by means which were suitable for their rudeness; but at present we have such a clearness in the gospel, that we need those old shadows no more. Seeing that the order which God had established under the law is now abolished, that is to say, the order of the temple of Jerusalem, and all the rest of the ceremonies; we must stay ourselves no more upon them.

Our Lord Jesus Christ said to the woman of Samaria, John iv. 21. 23. "The hour cometh, when ye shall neither in this mountain, nor yet at Jerusalem, worship the Father. But the hour cometh, and now is, when the true worshippers shall worship the Father in spirit and in truth." In those days there was a great controversy between the Jews and the Samaritans; the temple of Samaria being built in despite of the Jews. Those that worshipped at the temple of Samaria, claimed the example of Abraham, of Isaac, and of Jacob. The Jews had the word of God. Christ saith, that in times past, the Jews knew what they worshipped, for they were ruled by a doctrine which was certain; but that the Samaritans were idolaters. But now, (saith he,) you must strive no more for the temple of Jerusalem, or for the temple of Samaria: and why so? because God shall be called upon in spirit and in truth throughout all the world.

Jesus Christ having made his appearance, the old shadows of the law are taken away; let us content ourselves therefore, seeing we have a temple which is not material, nor visible: yea, all the fulness of the Godhead dwelleth in our Lord Jesus Christ. It is sufficient for us, that he reacheth out his hand, being ready to present us before God: and that through his means we have an entrance into the true spiritual sanctuary, that God receiveth us, that the veil of the temple is rent, that we may no more worship afar off in the court of the temple, but may come and cry with open mouth, *Abba, Father*.

Abba, was a customary word, used in the Hebrew tongue; that is, in the Syrian tongue. St. Paul putteth two words, *Abba, Father*, in Hebrew and Greek, to show us that every man in his own tongue hath now liberty to call upon God. Yea, there is no more a particular place where we must come to worship: but as the gospel hath been preached throughout all the world, we must show that at this day every man may call upon God, and *pray everywhere, lifting up holy hands, without wrath and doubting*.

It is true, we may now have temples for our convenience, but not in such a manner as the Jews had them: that is, we are not under the necessity of coming to some particular place in order to be heard of God. If there were other places as convenient for us as this, there would be no difference between them. Let us therefore learn that all ceremonies ended at the coming of Christ. This is very necessary to be understood, in order to draw us from the superstitious notions of the papists, which only darken prayer.

The Jews had their lights, perfumes, incense, &c; and they had their priests of the law; by which we may understand, that we have need of a mediator between God and man. The papists keep all those things still; and in so doing, it is as much as if they renounced Jesus Christ. It pleased God to be served in shadows, (as St. Paul showeth, Col. ii.) before the coming of Jesus Christ, who is the true body; that is, the substance of all. Do not those that seek such ceremonies, estrange themselves from Christ? Do they not know that when Christ was here in the world, and took our flesh upon him, and suffered and died, that it was for this purpose, that we might put our trust in him, and have no more of these childish figures, which served only for a season? Thus, the papists, with all the fooleries which they use, not only darken the glory of our Lord Jesus Christ, but utterly deface it.

Let us therefore learn to worship God, and call upon him out of a pure heart; without all these mixtures, and things devised by our own brains; yea, and without borrowing that from the old law, which is no longer proper for us. We now have a full revelation in the gospel: let us not, therefore, do this injury to God, to put away the brightness which he hath caused to shine before our eyes; seeing the Son of justice, that is to say, our Lord Jesus Christ, is now made manifest to us. Why should we talk any more of walking in dark shadows, which were only of use when we were far from that great brightness which afterwards appeared?

We must pray to God as he hath commanded us in the gospel. The papists make pilgrimages, and go trotting up and down, this way and that, to find God: but in so doing they forsake him, and withdraw themselves wholly from him. Let us not follow these examples, but be confirmed in the doctrine of the gospel, wherein we are exhorted to pray daily, not doubting but God will hear us in all our requests. When we make our prayers to God, we must not bring thither our melancholy or fretful passions, as though we would be at defiance with him, as one that prayeth when he is angry, or murmuring, being disquieted by reason of affliction which God sendeth, for in so doing we dishonour him.

There are some who make a show, as though they prayed to God, by protesting against him, because they are not dealt with according to their own fancy. Thus, they will come to God, but it is to be at defiance with him, as if a woman should ask something of her husband, and at the same time say, *Oh, you care not for me!* This is the manner of prayer which some use, but it would be better for them not to pray at all, than to come to God with a heart so envenomed with wrath. Let us learn therefore to pray to God with a peaceable heart. St. Paul showeth us, that besides diligence in our prayers, we must also join thanksgiving: and if we do not immediately receive what we desire, wait patiently, and be content until God be pleased to grant our requests.

So, then, we must pray to God without murmuring, without fretting or foaming, yea, without using any reply, to ask him why he suffereth us to languish. It appears that St. Paul had another meaning in this place; for he regarded the circumstance which we have mentioned before; to wit, that the Jews would gladly have shut out the Gentiles. For, say they, we are the children of God, he hath chosen us; and shall not the stock of Abraham have more privileges than the uncircumcised nations? The Gentiles, on the other side, mocked the Jews, and considered them as children, not knowing that the ceremonies of the law were at an end.

Thus, the Jews despised the Gentiles, and disdained them, and would not receive them into their company. The Gentiles, on the other hand, mocked the Jews for their rudeness, because they continued to hold fast the rudiments of the law. Here arose many schisms; one party setting themselves against the other; and the church was, as it were, torn in pieces; yet above all things, God commendeth unity and brotherly love. Let us examine the form of prayer given us by our Lord Jesus Christ: *Our Father which art in heaven,* &c. He doth not say, *my Father!* therefore, when I say, *our,* I speak in the name of all; and every man must say the same.

We shall not have access to God by prayer, unless we be joined together; for he that separateth himself from his neighbours, shutteth his own mouth, so that he cannot pray to God as our Lord Jesus Christ hath commanded. To be short, we must agree together, and be bound in a bond of peace, before we can come nigh, and present ourselves to God. These discords and debates of which we have spoken, existed between the Jews and Gentiles. St. Paul showeth that they cannot call upon God, without being refused and cast back, until they be at peace one with another. This is the reason why he requesteth them here, to *lift up holy hands, without wrath and doubting.*

Thus the apostle advised them, not to enter into debates and contentions one with another. The Jews must not advance themselves above the Gentiles, because they were called first; nor the Gentiles condemn the Jews for the grossness of their understanding: all these contentions must cease, and a perfect reconciliation must be made, to show that they all have the spirit of adoption; that is to say, that they are governed by the spirit of God, even that spirit which bringeth peace and unity. Let us understand this doctrine: that before we can dispose ourselves to pray aright, we must have this brotherly love which God commandeth, and this unity and nearness.

He would not have each one to remain

by himself, but would have us unite in peace and concord: although every one speak, though every one be apart in his own place, and pray to God in secret, yet must our consent come to heaven, and we must all say with one affection, and in truth, *Our Father.* This word *our*, must bind us together, and so make us in fellowship one with another, that there will be, as it were, but one voice, one heart, and one spirit. Moreover, when we pray, let the churches be joined together. If we wish to pray aright, we must not do like those who endeavour to divide that which God hath joined together, under colour of some little ceremony which is not worthy of our notice, separating ourselves one from another, and dismembering the body; for those that conduct themselves in this manner, show plainly that they are possessed with the spirit of Satan, and are endeavouring to destroy the union that exists among the children of God.

Therefore let all controversy be laid aside, and trodden under foot; and let us in liberty and with freedom pray to God, being assured that our Lord Jesus Christ hath manifested himself to us, and that through his merits we shall obtain favour in the sight of God the Father. Truly, we cannot join with those that separate themselves from us: for example, the papists call themselves Christians; and cannot we communicate with them in prayer? No; because they have forsaken Christ Jesus. We know that if we swerve from him the least jot, we get out of the way: therefore, seeing the papists have separated themselves from Jesus Christ, the distance is too great between them and us, to be joined together. But we must give our hand to all those that will submit themselves to Jesus Christ; and with mutual accord come and render ourselves up to God.

Our Lord Jesus Christ saith, Mat. v. 23 and 24, "If thou bring thy gift to the altar, and there rememberest that thy brother hath aught against thee, leave there thy gift before the altar, and go thy way: first be reconciled to thy brother, and then come and offer thy gift." Do we wish God to be merciful to us? If we do, we must lay aside all enmity one against another: for if we be divided among ourselves, God will cast us off; for he will receive none but those that are members of his Son. We cannot be members of Jesus Christ, unless we be governed by his spirit: which is the spirit of peace and unity, as we have already shown. Let us therefore learn to live in friendship and brotherly love, if we wish to be received when we come to God.

When we see anything that may hinder our prayers, we must remember that the devil goeth about to put stumbling-blocks in our way; let us therefore shun them as most deadly plagues. There are many who seek nothing else, but to raise difficulties and disputations; as though the word of God was made to separate us one from another. We have already mentioned that the true intent of the gospel is, to call us to God; that we may be joined together, and made one in our prayers and requests to him. Those that indulge in contentious debates, and endeavour to advance themselves one above another, pervert good doctrine, and fight against it; and endeavour to bring the glory of God to nought. Therefore, they must not think that God will hear them when they pray to him, seeing they have not this unity and concord to go to him in the name of our Lord Jesus Christ.

St. Paul saith, *lifting up holy hands.* By this he would have us understand, that we must not abuse God's name, by coming to him in our filthiness; but that we must be purged and made clean: for prayer is called a sacrifice; and we know that in the time of the law, when they sacrificed, they first washed themselves. And why so? Our Lord meant thereby to show us that we are full of filthiness, unclean, and not worthy to come to him, until we have been cleansed. But the figures of the law are now at an end; we must therefore come to Christ, for he is our true washing. Yet notwithstanding, we must not continue in filthiness, for Christ Jesus was given that he might renew us by his holy spirit, and that we might forsake our wicked lusts.

God doth not command us to bring our filthiness and infections before him, but we must pray to him, acknowledging ourselves utterly confounded and ashamed, full of uncleanness and filthiness, ready to be cast off, unless cleansed through the merits of the Lord Jesus Christ. Thus, by acknowledging our faults and blemishes, we must run to this fountain, where we may be washed: that is, Christ having shed his blood to wash away our sins, we shall be accounted pure before God, and wholly clean. When Jesus Christ gave us the spirit of sanctification, although there was nothing but infection in us, he cleansed us from our faults, and gave us free access to God. Therefore, the apostle saith we must pray, *lifting up holy hands*.

In the time of the law and the Old Testament, God entertained the people with this ceremony, that he would have them purified before they offered sacrifice; yea, before they made solemn profession of their faith in the temple. These things are not in use at present, among the Christians, but we must keep the substance. And what is the substance? It is this; although we have no visible water for cleansing, yet we must come to the blood of our Lord Jesus Christ, which is our spiritual washing. Sometimes the Holy Ghost is represented as *clean water*: as it is said in Ezekiel xxxvi. 25. "Then will I sprinkle clean water upon you, and ye shall be clean; from all your filthiness, and from all your idols, I will cleanse you." This promise referreth to the coming of Jesus Christ. So then, God showeth us that instead of the old figures which he gave to the Jews, and instead of material and corruptible water, we shall be purified and made clean by the Holy Spirit.

David saith, Psalm xxiv. 6. "I will wash mine hands in innocency: so will I compass thine altar, O Lord." When David speaketh thus, he hath respect to the figures of the law. We shall understand this more easily, by noticing the passage where God reproacheth the Jews by his prophet Isaiah, because they came into the temple with filthy hands. It is said,

Isa. i. "When ye come to appear before me, who hath required this at your hand, to tread my courts? Bring no more vain oblations: incense is an abomination unto me; the new moons and sabbaths, the calling of assemblies, I cannot away with: it is iniquity, even the solemn meeting. Your new moons, and your appointed feasts, my soul hateth: they are a trouble unto me; I am weary to bear them. And when ye spread forth your hands, I will hide mine eyes from you; yea, when we make many prayers, I will not hear: your hands are full of blood. Wash you, make you clean; put away the evil of your doings from before mine eyes: cease to do evil."

As our Lord God reproved the Jews for coming before him with filthy or bloody hands, so he commandeth us by the mouth of St. Paul, to *lift up holy hands*: that is, not to be inwrapped in our evil affections. Thus we see what St. Paul meant; seeing we have this privilege, that we may pray to God, and draw near to him as our Father, we must not think that he will hear us, if we come to him in our natural state of filthiness; for he will not hold those guiltless that take his name in vain. On the contrary, seeing Jesus Christ hath come to purge us, and make us partakers of the Holy Ghost, we must endeavour to become pure; and as we cannot do it ourselves, we must have recourse to our Lord Jesus Christ, who is the fountain of all pureness, and the source of perfection.

We must not pray to God, as though he were an idol, and required to be served in a worldly manner; but our minds must be raised above our earthly affections: and as we lift up our hands, so must our hearts be lifted on high by faith. As oft then as we have our hands lifted up toward heaven, so oft should our minds be led to God in consideration of our weakness: knowing that we cannot have access to him, unless we lift ourselves above the world: that is, unless we withdraw ourselves from unruly passions, and vain affections. When we say, *Our Father which art in heaven*, we are reminded that we must seek him there, and must climb up thither by faith, though we still dwell on earth.

Let us learn therefore to renounce every thing which God doth not allow, knowing that our salvation is in him alone. Let us put our whole trust in him, believing that he will aid and assist us in all our troubles and afflictions: for if we do not pray in faith, although the ceremony may be good of itself, yet shall it be vain and superfluous. Those who lift up their hands to heaven, and at the same time remain fastened to things on earth, condemn themselves; yea, as much as though they should set down their condemnation in writing, and ratify it by their own hand and seal; condemning themselves as hypocrites, liars, and forsworn persons. For they come before God, protesting that they seek him, and at the same time remain attached to things below. They say they put their trust in him, and at the same time trust themselves or some other creature: they pretend to be lifted up to heaven by faith, and at the same time are drowned in earthly pleasures.

Let us therefore learn, when we pray to God, to be void of all earthly cares and wicked affections; knowing that there are many things which hinder us from coming to God. When we lift up our hands to heaven, it must be for the purpose of seeking God by faith; which we cannot do, unless we withdraw ourselves from the cares and wicked affections of the flesh.

Now let us fall down before the face of our good God, confessing our faults, and praying him to put them out of his remembrance, that we may be received by him; and in the meantime, that he would strengthen us, and sanctify us from day to day by his holy spirit, until we wholly cast off all our imperfections and sins: but as this cannot be done so long as we live in this mortal life, that he would bear with our infirmities, until he hath utterly put them away. And thus let us all say: Almighty God our heavenly Father, &c.

John Knox

(1505?-1572)

THE early years of John Knox are obscure. Probably born near Haddington, he was ordained to the priesthood by 1540, but within a few years joined the Protestant faith under the influence of George Wishart. Shortly after he accepted a call to the ministry at St. Andrews, that castle was taken by the French, and Knox was transported to France and worked in the galleys for nineteen months. When he returned to England in 1549, he was appointed a royal chaplain by Edward VI, and in 1552 declined an offer to become bishop of Rochester. During these years he helped to lay the foundations for English Puritanism.

In 1554 Mary Tudor ascended the throne, and Knox fled abroad. He later returned to Scotland where he preached for six months. In 1559 he again established himself in Scotland, where his *Book of Common Order* was approved by the General Assembly in 1564. Four years earlier a creed prepared by Knox, largely Calvinistic in spirit, had been adopted by the Church of Scotland. He did more than anyone else to bring the spirit of independent Protestantism into Scotland.

A man of stern reforming zeal rather than of mystical tendencies, he was nevertheless devout. This selection from *A Declaration of the True Nature and Object of Prayer* gives one an aperture into his interpretation of the devotional life. It is reprinted from *Selections from the World's Classics of Devotion* by permission of Funk & Wagnalls Co.

[AN INSIGHT INTO PRAYER]

From *A Declaration of the True Nature and Object of Prayer*

WHAT IS TO BE OBSERVED IN PRAYER

That this be most reverently done, should provoke us the consideration in whose presence we stand, to whom we speak, and what we desire; standing in the presence of the omnipotent Creator of heaven and earth, and of all the contents thereof; to whom assist and serve a thousand thousand of angels, giving obedience to his eternal majesty; and speaking unto him who knoweth the secrets of our hearts, before whom dissimulation and lies are always odious and hateful, and asking that thing which may be most to his glory and to the comfort of our conscience. But diligently should we attend, that such things as may offend his godly presence, to the uttermost of our power, may be removed. And first, that worldly cares and fleshly cogitations (such as draw us from contemplation of our God) be expelled from us, that we may freely without interruption call upon God. But, how difficult and hard is this one thing in prayer to perform knoweth none better than such as in their prayers are not content to remain within the bonds of their own vanity, but, as it were ravished, do intend to a purity allowed of God; asking not such things as the foolish reason of man desireth, but which may be pleasant and acceptable in God's presence. Our adversary, Satan, at all times compassing us about, is never more busy than when we address and bend ourselves to prayer. O! how secretly and subtly creepeth he into our breasts, and calling us back from God, causeth us to forget what we have to do; so that frequently when we (with all reverence) should speak to God, we find our hearts talking with the vanities of the world, or with the foolish imaginations of our own conceit. . . .

WHY WE SHOULD PRAY, AND ALSO UNDERSTAND WHAT WE DO PRAY

But men will object and say, Albeit we understand not what we pray, yet God understandeth, who knoweth the secrets of our hearts; he knoweth also what we need, altho we expone not, or declare not, our necessities unto him. Such men verily declare themselves never to have understanding what perfect prayer meant, nor to what end Jesus Christ commandeth us to pray; which is, first, that our hearts may be inflamed with continual fear, honor, and a love of God, to whom we run for support and help whensoever danger or necessity requireth; that we so learning to notify our desires in his presence, he may teach us what is to be desired and what not. Secondly, that we knowing our petitions to be granted by God alone, to him only we must render and give laud and praise, and that we ever having his infinite goodness fixt in our minds, may constantly abide to receive that which with fervent prayer we desire. . . .

TROUBLES ARE THE SPURS TO STIR US TO PRAY

Trouble and fear are very spurs to prayer; for when man, compassed about with vehement calamities and vexed with continual solicitude, having by help of man no hope for deliverance, with sore opprest and punished heart fearing also greater punishment to follow, from the deep pit of tribulation doth call to God for comfort and support; such prayer ascendeth into God's presence and returneth not in vain.

WHERE CONSTANT PRAYER IS, THERE THE PETITION IS GRANTED

Let no man think himself unworthy to call and pray to God because he hath grievously offended his majesty in times past; but let him bring to God a sorrowful and repenting heart, saying with David, "Heal my soul, O Lord, for I have offended against thee. Before I was afflicted, I transgressed, but now let me observe thy commandments." To mitigate or ease the sorrows of our wounded conscience two plasters hath our most prudent Physician provided to give us encouragement to pray (notwithstanding the knowledge of offenses committed), that is, a precept and a promise. The precept or commandment to pray is universal, frequently inculcated and repeated in God's Scriptures: "ask, and it shall be given unto you" (Matt. 7); "Call upon me in the day of trouble" (Ps. 40); "Watch and pray that ye fall not into temptation" (Matt. 26); "I command that ye pray ever without ceasing" (Tim. 2); "Make deprecations incessible (unceasing), and give thanks in all things" (I Thess. 5). Which commandments whoso contemneth or despiseth doth equally sin with him that doth steal; for in this commandment "thou shalt not steal" is a precept negative; so "thou shalt pray" is a commandment affirmative. And God requireth equal obedience of and to all his commandments. Yet more boldly will I say, he who, when necessity constraineth, desireth not support and help of God, Doth provoke his wrath no less than such as make false gods or openly deny God. . . .

What Should Be Prayed For

And if this we do truly acknowledge and confess, let us boldly ask of him whatsoever is necessary for us—as sustentation of this body; health thereof; defense from misery; deliverance from trouble; tranquility and peace to our common weal; prosperous success in our vocations, labors, and affairs, whatsoever they be, which God will, we ask of all of him, to certify us that all things stand in his regimen and disposition. And also by asking and receiving these corporal commodities, we have tast of his sweetness, and be inflamed with his love, that thereby our faith of reconciliation and remission of our sins may be exercised and take increase. . . .

The Petition of the Spirit

It is to be noted that God sometime doth grant the petition of the spirit, while he yet differeth the desire of the flesh. As who doubteth but God did mitigate the heaviness of Joseph, altho he sent not hasty deliverance in his long imprisonment; and that as he gave him favor in the sight of his jailor, so inwardly also gave he unto him consolation in spirit. And moreover God sometimes granteth the petition of the spirit, where all utterly he repelleth the desire of the flesh; for the petition always of the spirit is that we may attain to the true felicity, whereunto we must needs enter by tribulation and the final death, which both the nature of man doth ever abhor, and therefor the flesh, under the cross and at the sight of death, calleth and thirsts for hasty deliverance. But God, who alone knoweth what is expedient for us, sometime prolongeth the deliverance of his chosen, and sometime permitteth them to drink before the maturity of age the bitter cup of corporal death, that thereby they may receive medicine and cure from all infirmity. For who doubteth that John the Baptist desired to have seen more the days of Jesus Christ, and to have been longer with him in conversation? Or that Stephen would not have labored more days in preaching Christ's gospel, whom, nevertheless, he suffered hastily to taste of this general sentence? And, albeit we see therefore no apparent help to ourselves nor yet to others afflicted, let us not cease to call, thinking our prayers to be vain. For, whatsoever come of our bodies, God shall give unspeakable comfort to the spirit, and shall turn all to our commodities beyond our own expectation. . . .

Private Prayer

Private prayer, such as men secretly offer unto God by themselves, requires no special place; altho that Jesus Christ commandeth when we pray to enter into our chamber, and to close the door, and so to pray secretly unto our Father. Whereby he would that we should choose to our prayers such places as might offer least occasion to call us back from prayer; and also, that we should expel forth of our minds in time of our prayer all vain cogitations. For otherwise Jesus Christ himself doth observe no special place of prayer; for we find him sometime pray in Mount Olivet, sometime in the desert, sometime in the Temple, and in the garden. And Peter coveteth to pray upon the top of the house. Paul prayed in prison, and was heard of God. Who also commandeth men to pray in all places, lifting up unto God pure and clean hands; as we find that the prophets and most holy men did, whensoever danger or necessity required.

Appointed Places to Pray in, May Not Be Neglected

But public and common prayers should be used in place appointed for the assembly, from whence whosoever negligently extracted themselves is in no wise excusable. I mean not that to absent from that place is sin, because that place is more holy than another; for the whole earth created by God is equally holy. But the promise made that, "Wheresoever two or three be gathered together in my name, there shall I be in the midst of them," condemneth all such as contemneth the congregation gathered in his name. But mark well the word "gathered"; I mean not to hear piping, singing, or playing; nor to patter upon beads, or books whereof they have no understanding; nor to commit idolatry, honoring that for God which is no God indeed. For with such will I neither join myself in common prayer nor in receiving external sacraments; for in so doing I should affirm their superstitions and abominable idolatry, which I, by God's grace, never will do, neither counsel others to do, to the end. . . .

For Whom, and at What Time We Should Pray

Now there remaineth, for whom, and at what time, we should pray. For all men, and at all times, doth Paul command that we should pray. And principally for such of the household of faith as suffer persecution; and for commonwealths tyrannously opprest incessantly should we call, that God of his mercy and power will withstand the violence of such tyrants. . . .

God's Sentence May Be Changed

And when we see the plagues of God, as hunger, pestilence, or weir coming or appearing to ring then should we, with lamentable voices and repenting hearts, call unto God, that it would please his infinite mercy to withdraw his hand; which thing, if we do unfeignedly, he will without doubt revoke his wrath, and in the midst of his fury think upon mercy; as we are taught in the Scripture by his infallible and external verities. As in Exodus God saith, "I shall destroy this nation from the face of the earth"; and when Moses addrest himself to pray for them, the Lord proceedeth, saying, "Suffer me that I may utterly destroy them." And then Moses falleth down upon his face, and forty days continueth in prayer for the safety of the people; for whom at the last he obtained forgiveness. David, in the vehement plague, lamentable called unto God. And the king of Nineveh said, "Who can tell? God may turn and repent, and cease from his fierce wrath, that we perish not." Which examples and scriptures are not written in vain, but to certify us that God of his own native goodness will mitigate his plagues (by our prayers offered by Jesus Christ), altho he hath threatened to punish or presently doth punish. Which he doth testify by his own words saying, "If I have prophesied against any nation or people, that they shall be destroyed, if they repent of their iniquity, it shall repent me of the evil which I have spoken against them." (Jer. 18). This I write, lamenting the great coldness of men, which under so long scourges of God is nothing kindled to pray by repentance, but carelessly sleepeth in a wicked life; even as tho the continual wars, urgent famine, and quotidian plagues of pestilence, and other contagious, insolent, and strange maladies were not the present signs of God's wrath, provoked by our iniquities.

Teresa of Avila

(1515-1582)

TERESA joined a convent of the Carmelites in her eighteenth year. With John of the Cross, her writings are the best source books for knowledge of Spanish Carmelite mysticism. While Ignatius Loyola organized his body of "spiritual soldiers" to combat heresy, Teresa revitalized her religious order from within by stressing man's communion with the transcendental world. Through her own self-analysis and observation of the different stages of mystical experience she discovered, and left for others to study, valuable data for understanding the devotional life. She suffered much from illness, and experienced religious ecstasies during these periods. Once she was convinced that she had seen the real body of Christ.

The selections from *The Way of Perfection* are from William J. Doheny's translation.

[ON COMMUNION WITH GOD]

From *The Way of Perfection*

NEED OF HUMILITY AND OBEDIENCE FOR MENTAL PRAYER

I shall now explain mental prayer, since some of you may not clearly understand what it is. . . . Believe me, the King of Glory will never come into our souls, so as to unite to them, unless we earnestly strive to acquire solid virtues. . . .

Importance of Humility for Mental Prayer

As I have said, it is needful for us to understand how to grow constantly in humility. This is an indispensable virtue for all persons who devote themselves to prayer. . . . Humility, mortification, detachment, and the other virtues always offer the greatest security and do not expose one to dangers. . . . Realize that genuine humility consists largely in the prompt and joyful acceptance of whatever it pleases our Lord to order us to do, and in considering ourselves unworthy to be called His servants. . . .

. . . We ought to devote ourselves to mental prayer. Those who cannot apply themselves to mental prayer, can devote themselves to vocal prayer, to reading and to colloquies with our Lord. But we must never neglect the designated hours of prayer. . . .

Humility of Contemplatives

Contemplatives, like standard-bearers, must carry the banner of humility and bear all the blows received without returning any. Their duty is to suffer like Christ, always to bear aloft the cross, without abandoning it, no matter what dangers may threaten them. Neither may they show the least weakness in the midst of sufferings. . . .

Humility, Mortification, and Obedience

Our real treasure consists in profound humility, sincere mortification and obedience so perfect that it will never waver in the slightest degree from the command of the Superior, who holds the place of God. And it is truly God, as you know, who commands us by means of His representative.

Above all, I would recommend obedience. Without this virtue, in my opinion, a person is really not a Religious at all. . . . Why would a Sister ever dwell in a monastery except to fulfill conscientiously the vow of obedience? I do not know. At least, I can assure her that as long as she fails to observe this vow, she will never become a contemplative, nor even fulfill well the duties of the active life. This appears absolutely certain to me. . . .

THE UNIVERSAL NEED OF PRAYER
Prayer a Duty of Religious Persons

. . . Do not be deceived by anyone. Prayer is the only way that leads us to the Fountain. At present, I am not discussing whether this prayer should be mental or vocal for all. But I do say that you have need of both the one and the other. Prayer is the duty of religious persons. If someone warns you that danger lurks in prayer, look upon him as a source of evil to you and avoid him. Do not forget this counsel, for it may be helpful to you.

It would assuredly be dangerous to be devoid of humility and all the other virtues, but may God never permit the way of prayer to be dangerous. Satan seems to have invented this pretext to frighten souls; and by his wiles he has caused the fall of some who appeared to be devoted to prayer.

False Notion of World About Prayer

Notice how blind the world is. It disregards the thousands of unfortunate persons who have fallen into heresy and frightful crimes because of neglect of prayer and of right thinking. Yet should it so happen that, among the vast multitudes previously devoted to prayer, Satan for his own ends had succeeded in seducing only a few persons, the result is that people then begin to spread terrifying rumors concerning the danger of much praying, in order to deter certain souls from the practice of prayer.

Let those be on their guard who resort to this pretext in order to avert dangers, for they are neglecting good in an effort to protect themselves from the risks of evil. I have never heard of anything more basely false. It is clear that this is an invention of Satan. O my God, protect Thy own cause! See how people misinterpret Thy own work. Do not permit Thy servants to fall into such errors. . . .

Courageous Lovers of Truth

. . . O how great God is! At times, one or two men who speak the truth are more influential in pointing out the true way than a host of others, since God animates the truth lovers with courage. Is someone avers that prayer is filled with dangers, they simply strive to prove how beneficial it is by their deeds even more than by their words. To those who allege that it is not fitting to communicate often, courageous lovers of the truth merely reply by receiving Holy Communion even more frequently. And thus, with the aid of one or two men who fearlessly follow the way of more exalted perfection, our Lord gradually regains all that He had lost.

Futility of Vain Fears

Put aside then all vain fears. Do not give heed to popular notions in matters of this nature. This is not the time to place confidence in every type of person; it is rather a time to follow those who faithfully imitate the life of Christ. Carefully protect your purity of conscience, your humility, and your disdain of worldly things. Firmly believe the teachings of our holy Mother the Church and be certain that you follow the true way. I repeat, put aside all vain and groundless fears.

Need of Vocal and Mental Prayer

If anyone tries to frighten you, humbly explain to him the way you follow. Inform him that your Rule prescribes that you pray without ceasing. This is the fact, and you are obliged to be faithful to it. If he should reply that this obviously refers to vocal prayer, ask him if your spirit and heart should not concentrate on what you recite. If he answers in the affirmative (and he really cannot answer otherwise) you will understand from this admission that you must of necessity practice mental prayer, and even attain to contemplation, if God grants you the grace.

MENTAL PRAYER
Nature of Prayer

. . . Realize that the mere opening or closing of the mouth does not determine whether prayer is vocal or mental. If while praying vocally, I am entirely absorbed in God to whom I speak, and if I concentrate my attention more on Him than on the words I utter, I combine therein both mental and vocal prayer. . . . Since you ought to speak to God with all the respectful attention due to such a Master, it is only fitting that you consider who He is. And thus likewise realizing who you are, you shall be enabled to speak in a befitting way. . . .

Necessity of Mental Prayer

O Lord, never permit persons who pray to Thee to think that it is perfect to address Thee merely with the lips. O Christian souls, do you mean to say that mental prayer is not necessary? Do you really understand it yourselves? I believe that you do not. And this is why you would wish us to go astray on this point. You do not know what mental prayer is, nor how vocal prayer should be said, nor what is understood by contemplation. If you really did, you would not condemn on the one hand what you approve on the other. . . .

Contemplation of Innumerable Perfections of God

O Absolute Sovereign of the world! Thou art Supreme Omnipotence, Sovereign Goodness, Wisdom itself! Thou art without beginning and without end. Thy works are limitless, Thy perfections infinite, and Thy intelligence is supreme! Thou art a fathomless abyss of marvels! O Beauty, containing all other beauty! O great God, Thou art Strength itself! Would that I possessed at this moment all the combined eloquence and wisdom of men! Then, in as far as it is possible here below, where knowledge is so limited, I could strive to make known one of Thy innumerable perfections. The contemplation of these reveals ·to some extent the nature of Him who is our Lord and our only Good.

Practice of Mental Prayer

Draw close to Him; but realize and understand to whom you are about to speak or whom you are already to address. Even after a thousand lives like our own, you would never understand how to act with this Lord, before whom the angels tremble. He rules the entire universe. He can do all. For Him, to will is to accomplish. . . .

To understand these truths well, is to practise mental prayer. If you wish to combine vocal prayer with this, that is perfectly suitable. But when you speak to God, do not direct your attention to other things. To do so would be to fail to understand mental prayer. . . . If one wished to pray perfectly, one must strive wholeheartedly to be recollected.

Resolute Determination in Prayer

. . . I reiterate that it is very important to enter upon this way of prayer with the resolute determination to persevere in it. . . . Since we wish to devote to God certain times of prayer, let us give these to Him with a spirit that is generous and untrammeled with earthly thoughts. Let us give this time with the firm resolution never to take it back, no matter what trials, contradictions, or aridities may come. Reckon this time as something no longer belonging to us, but time for which we shall be held accountable on the score of justice, if we do not dedicate ourselves entirely to it. . . . God is ever attentive in order to repay us for our services to Him. Do not fear that He will ever permit the least action to go unrewarded, even one so insignificant as the lifting of your eyes to heaven, in remembrance of Him.

Satan's Fear of Valiant Souls

The second reason why we should resolutely devote ourselves to prayer is that Satan thereby has less chance to tempt us. He is most fearful of valiant souls. He knows from experience what harm they cause him. Everything Satan does to injure valiant souls, profits them and their neighbor, and he comes from the combat as the loser. Nevertheless, we ought not to be negligent nor to become less cautious. We must strive against traitors. If we are vigilant, they will not have the courage to attack us, because they are cowards. But if they notice that we are no longer alert, they can inflict great harm on us. As soon as they detect that a soul is vacillating, inconstant, and not resolutely determined to persevere, they will torment it day and night without ceasing. They will suggest a thousand fears and conjure up endless difficulties. Experience has taught me this at great cost, and that is why I speak of it to you. And I add that no one can possibly appreciate fully how important this counsel is.

Heroic Courage of Resolute Persons

The third very important reason for determined devotedness to prayer is that a resolute person fights with greater courage. He then realizes that he must never retreat, no matter what the odds may be. Notice the soldier on the battlefield. He knows that if he loses, his life is at stake, and that if he does not die in the thick of the battle, he will be executed afterward. And thus he fights more unflinchingly, and is determined to sell his life dearly, as the saying it. He has no fear of wounds because he is intent upon gaining the victory, and he realizes that victory is the only means of saving his life.

Assurance of Success in Prayer

Furthermore, it is necessary to begin with the assurance that we shall succeed, unless we deliberately permit ourselves to be vanquished. Success is absolutely certain. No matter how insignificant our gain may be, it will enrich us immeasurably. As I have previously stated, and would like to repeat a thousand times, do not fear that our Lord will permit you to die of thirst after having invited you to drink of this Fountain. Fear paralyzes to a great extent the ardor of those persons who have never had personal experience of our Lord's goodness, even though their faith assures them of it. I assure you that it is a great advantage to have known His friendship and to have experienced the tender care He bestows upon those who follow this way of prayer. . . .

VOCAL PRAYER

Importance of Vocal Prayer

Again I address myself to those souls who can neither recollect themselves nor concentrate their minds in mental prayer, nor can they make a meditation. We must avoid the very mention of these words, for persons of that type are not interested in such things. In fact, there are many who seem to be frightened by the very term mental prayer or contemplation. . . .

I shall teach you how you ought to pray vocally. It is only right that you should understand what you say. Perhaps those who are incapable of centering their thoughts on God will likewise become wearied by long prayers. I shall not treat of long prayers, but only of those every Christian is obliged to recite, namely, the Pater Noster, and the Ave Maria.

Proper Recitation of Vocal Prayers

When I recite the Credo, it seems only reasonable that I should advert to and understand what I believe. Likewise, when I recite the Pater Noster, it would be a mark of love to recall who this Father is, and who the Master is who taught us this prayer. If you should reply that it suffices to reflect upon this Master once and for all, you might as well argue that it is sufficient to recite this prayer once in a lifetime. . . . May God grant that we should be not unmindful of Him when we recite this prayer. However, it sometimes happens that we do forget Him, because of our frailty. . . .

I have already stated that one cannot speak to God and to the world at the same time. Still, this is exactly what those do who recite their prayers while listening to the conversation of others, or who dwell on other thoughts without any effort to banish distractions . . .

Solitude During Prayer

We should strive to seek solitude during prayer, in so far as we are able. And God grant that this may suffice to make us realize both the presence of Him who is with us and the answer that our Lord makes to our petitions. Do you think that He is silent, even though we cannot hear Him? Assuredly not! He speaks to the heart when the heart entreats Him.

Close Union with Jesus

It would be well for us to consider that our Lord has taught this prayer to each one of us, individually, and that He still teaches it to us at this very moment. The Master is never so distant that His disciple need raise his voice to be heard. On the contrary, He is very near. To enable you to recite the Pater Noster well, I should like to see you perfectly convinced of this truth, namely, that you must remain close to the Master who teaches it to you.

Relationship Between Vocal and Mental Prayer

You may again object that to pray thus would be meditation, and that you cannot, and consequently will not, pray except vocally. . . . I admit that you are right in calling this method mental prayer. But at the same time I assure you that I do not understand how vocal prayer, when well recited, can possibly be separated from mental prayer. We ought to realize to whom we are speaking. In fact, it is a duty to devote oneself with attention to prayer. God grant that all these means may aid us in reciting the Pater Noster well, and that we do not finish it amidst distracting thoughts! From experience, I have discovered that the best remedy against distractions is to strive to concentrate my thoughts on Him to whom I address my prayers. Be patient, then, and strive to become habituated to this method which is so necessary. It is indispensable for the formation of real Religious and, if I am not mistaken, even for the proper recitation of the prayers of true Christians. . . .

DISTINCTION BETWEEN VOCAL PRAYER, MENTAL PRAYER, AND CONTEMPLATION

Contemplation

Do not mistakenly believe that one draws only little profit from vocal prayer when it is well made. I assure you that it is quite possible for our Lord to raise you to perfect contemplation while you are reciting the Pater Noster or some other vocal prayer. And thus His Majesty shows that He hears one who prays in such a manner. This Sovereign Master speaks to the soul in return, suspends its understanding, checks its thoughts and, as it were, forms the very words before they are pronounced. And thus of oneself one cannot utter a single word without the greatest effort. The soul then realizes that the Master teaches it without any sound of words. He suspends the activity of the faculties which, instead of gaining benefits, would only cause harm if they tried to act.

In this state the faculties are filled with delight without knowing how they rejoice. The soul is inflamed with an increasing flow of love without perceiving how it loves. It knows that it enjoys the object of its love, but does not comprehend the nature of this enjoyment. Nevertheless, it realizes that the understanding of itself could never yearn for so ineffable a good. It realizes, too, that the will embraces the good without the soul's knowing how the will does this. If the soul can comprehend anything at all, its comprehension consists in the realization of the fact that nothing in the world could possibly merit this benefit. It is a gift of the Master of heaven and earth who in the end bestows this boon in a manner worthy of Him, This is contemplation. You can now understand wherein it differs from mental prayer.

Simplicity of Mental Prayer

Mental prayer, I repeat, consists in pondering over and seeking to understand what we say, in realizing to whom we speak, and who we are that we presume to address His Sovereign Majesty. To be preoccupied with these and similar considerations, such as the realization of the little we do for the service of God and of the obligation we are under to serve Him, is to make mental prayer. Therefore, don't imagine that it involves some very hidden mystery and do not be frightened by the term, mental prayer.

To recite the Pater Noster, the Ave Maria, or any other prayer of your choice is vocal prayer. But realize how discordant it would be without mental prayer. The very words do not otherwise follow in proper sequence. In contemplation, which I just described, we can do nothing of ourselves. His Majesty does everything therein. It is His work, and it transcends the powers of our nature. . . . He alone can bestow upon you the gift of contemplation. He will not refuse it if you do not loiter on the way, and if you do not neglect anything necessary to reach your destination.

THE NEED OF RECOLLECTION

Proper Preparation for Prayer

Let us return now to the consideration of vocal prayer. We should recite vocal prayers in such a way that we may receive all the other kinds from God. But to pray properly, you know that you must at the outset examine your conscience, recite the Confiteor and make the Sign of the Cross. Immediately after, seek companionship, and how could you possibly do better than to seek the company of the Master Himself, who taught you the prayer you are to recite?

Method During Prayer

Picture our Lord near you. Consider the love and the humility with which He instructs you. Believe me, you ought to strive always to be ever near so faithful a Friend. If you accustom yourselves to consider Him near you, and He sees you doing this with love, and striving to please Him, you will be unable, so to speak, to dismiss Him. He will never fail you. He will aid you in all your trials and you will constantly be in His company. Do you think it an unimportant thing to have such a Friend near you?

Need of Recollection

You who cannot develop thoughts with the understanding, nor fix your attention on a sacred mystery without distractions, accustom yourselves to this practise which I point out to you. I know that you can do it. During many years I myself suffered from my inability to concentrate on any subject during prayer. And this is a terrible trial. Nevertheless, I know that our Lord never abandons us so completely as to refuse us His company if we humbly entreat Him. If we do not acquire this favor within a year, let us strive several years for it. Do not begrudge time so well spent. And who is there to hurry us? You can, I repeat, accustom yourselves to this practice. Strive to remain in the company of this true Master.

Simple Gazing on Jesus

I am not asking you at this time to fix your attention on Him, nor to engage in discursive reasonings, nor to make subtle and learned considerations. All that I request is that you direct the glance of your soul to Him. Who is there who can prevent the turning of your gaze toward our Lord, even though it be only for a moment? Is it conceivable that you can look upon the most hideous objects and still you have not the power to behold the most ineffable sight that can be imagined? If you do not find Him beautiful, you need never look upon Him again. He, however, watches you constantly. Although you have offended Him by a thousand insults and indignities, He has been patient with you. Despite your faults, He has never ceased to fix His gaze upon you. Is it too much, then, to ask that you withdraw your gaze from exterior things to contemplate Him sometimes? . . . He values your glance so highly that He will neglect no means to ingratiate Himself with you.

Loving Study of Jesus

. . . Our Lord condescends to be subject to you, and wishes you to act as sovereign. He submits Himself to your will. Are you joyful? Contemplate Him then in His Resurrection. You have nothing else to do but to think of the glory with which He rose from the sepulcher, and you will be filled with joy. What splendor, what beauty, what majesty, what glory, and what exultation in His triumph! How gloriously He comes forth from the field of battle where He won so great a Kingdom, which is destined entirely for you. And at the same time, He gives Himself to you with this Kingdom. Is it, then, too much for you to raise your eyes occasionally toward this Master who has bestowed such bountiful gifts upon you?

Jesus in His Person

Are you pensive or sad? Behold your Lord then as He goes to the Garden of Olives. What overwhelming affliction fills His soul! He who is patience itself manifests and avows His sufferings! Or look upon Him bound to the column, covered with wounds and His flesh torn to shreds. And this is the measure of His great love for you! In the midst of His anguish, see how He is cruelly treated by some, spat upon by others, denied and deserted by His friends, without a single person to plead His cause. He is stiff from the cold and so extremely lonely that He and you may well console each other.

Jesus the Divine Model

Or, behold Him bearing the Cross, and not even given time to breathe. He will then turn to you with His beautiful and compassionate eyes filled with tears. He will even forget His sufferings to console you in yours, solely because you sought consolation from Him and turned your gaze upon Him. . . .

Observe the insupportable weariness that weighs upon Him and realize how His sufferings surpass yours. No matter how great you may imagine your trials to be, and however painful they may appear, you will gain confidence in reflecting that they are but trifles compared with the sufferings of our Lord.

Perhaps you will say: If we had seen His Majesty with our bodily eyes when He lived on earth, we would follow your advice wholeheartedly, and we would fix our gaze upon Him constantly. But I say: Do not be deluded. Whoever does not make an effort now to behold our Lord within his soul, when this entails no great danger or sacrifice, he assuredly would not have been at the foot of the Cross with Magdalen when the risk of death was involved. Who can describe the sufferings of the glorious Virgin and this holy Saint? . . . Indeed, their ordeal of suffering must have been terrible. Nevertheless, they were insensible to their own sufferings because they personally beheld a spectacle of suffering more poignant by far than their own. So then, do not deceive yourselves into believing that you could have borne such trials if you cannot conquer the slight difficulties I mentioned. Perfect yourselves first of all in the small things so as to become capable of greater deeds.

Helpfulness of Sacred Images and Holy Pictures

A helpful means to keep you in the presence of our Lord would be to have with you a favorite image or picture of Him. Do not be content merely to carry it without looking at it. Use it as a means of inspiring you to speak to Him. He will suggest what you are to say to Him. You know well how to converse with creatures. Why can you not then find words to speak to God? Do not imagine that this is beyond you. It most certainly is not; but you must form the habit of speaking to Him. . . .

Excellence of Spiritual Reading

Another excellent aid to recollection and vocal prayer is the reading of a good book, in the vernacular. And thus, either by means of coaxing the soul or by strategies, you can gradually accustom it to meditation without frightening it. Keep in mind the case of a wife long separated from her husband. Gentle tact is required to persuade her to return home. The case is similar with us, miserable sinners that we are. Our soul and thoughts are so habitually intent on pleasurable things, that the poor soul does not really understand itself. Hence, recourse must be had to many strategies before the soul will find happiness in dwelling in the abode of its heavenly Master. And one will not succeed in this unless gentle tact and skillful patience are employed.

Union with God

Again, I assure you that if you resolutely practise this method, you will reap benefits so great that it is really impossible for me to describe them. Therefore, remain close to this good Master. Keep the firm resolution to learn all that He teaches you. His Majesty will then see to it that you become His faithful disciples. This great God will never leave you unless you first abandon Him. Meditate on the words that come from the divine lips. At the very outset you will understand the love He has for you. And it is no small favor nor negligible joy for a disciple to see that he is loved by his Master.

John of the Cross
(1542-1591)

CARMELITE mystic and friend of Teresa of Avila, John of the Cross vitalized the Spanish mystic tradition, and from Spain his influence radiated to France. He was born at Hontiveros, Old Castile, of poor silk weavers, and given elementary education in the poor school at Medina del Campo. For seven years he worked in a hospital, waiting on the poor, and simultaneously attended a Jesuit school. In 1567 he was ordained, after higher education at Salamanca. The following year, with Teresa of Avila, he organized the Discalced Carmelites. This venture caused him persecution and a nine-months imprisonment. But his viewpoint finally was recognized.

John's chief work is *The Dark Night of the Soul*. Georgia Harkness speaks of this writing in her own book by that title as one which "deals with an experience which is not that of a remote time or place, or special degree of saintliness, but which besets the path of the earnest in every age. Its theme is the sense of spiritual desolation, loneliness, frustration, and despair which grips the soul of one who, having seen the vision of God and been lifted by it, finds the vision fade and the presence of God recede."

John of the Cross is not to be thought of as one who was merely austere and over-serious. He was serious, but he was also a man imbued with Christian mercy, a sensitive spirit deeply influenced by all that was lovely and attractive. The following selection from Thomas Baker's edition is used by his permission.

[CONDITIONS OF THE SPIRITUAL NATURE]
From *The Dark Night of the Soul*

VIII. EXPLANATION OF THE FIRST LINE OF THE FIRST STANZA. BEGINNING OF THE EXPLANATION OF THE DARK NIGHT.

In a dark night." This night—it is contemplation—produces in spiritual men two sorts of darkness or purgations conformable to the two divisions of man's nature into sensual and spiritual. Thus the first night or sensual purgation, wherein the soul is purified or detached, will be of the senses, subjecting them to the spirit. The other is that night or spiritual purgation wherein the soul is purified and detached in the spirit, and which subdues and disposes it for union with God in love. The night of sense is common, and the lot of many: these are the beginners, of whom I shall first speak. The spiritual night is the portion of very few; and they are those who have made some progress, exercised therein, of whom I shall speak hereafter.

2. The first night, or purgation, is bitter and terrible to sense. The second is not to be compared with it, for it is much more awful to the spirit, as I shall soon show. But as the night of sense is

the first in order and the first to be entered, I shall speak of it briefly—for being of ordinary occurrence, it is the matter of many treatises—that I may pass on to treat more at large of spiritual night; for of that very little has been said, either by word of mouth or in writing, and little is known of it even by experience.

3. But the behaviour of these beginners on the way of God is not noble, and very much according to their own liking and self-love, as I have said before. Meanwhile, God seeks to raise them higher, to draw them out of this miserable manner of loving to a higher state of the love of God, to deliver them from the low usage of the senses and meditation whereby they seek after God, as I said before, in ways so miserable and so unworthy of Him. He seeks to place them in the way of the spirit wherein they may the more abundantly, and more free from imperfections, commune with God now that they have been for some time tried in the way of goodness, persevering in meditation and prayer, and because of the sweetness they found therein have withdrawn their affections from the things of this world, and gained a certain spiritual strength in God, whereby they in some measure curb their love of the creature, and are able, for the love of God, to carry a slight burden of dryness, without going back to that more pleasant time when their spiritual exercises abounded in delights, and when the sun of the divine graces shone, as they think, more clearly upon them. God is now changing that light into darkness, and sealing up the door of the fountain of the sweet spiritual waters, which they tasted in God as often and as long as they wished. For when they were weak and tender, this door was then not shut, as it is written, "Behold, I have given before thee an opened door, which no man can shut; because thou hast a little strength, and hast kept My word, and hast not denied My name."

4. God thus leaves them in darkness so great that they know not whither to betake themselves with their imaginations and reflections of sense. They cannot advance a single step in meditation, as before, the inward sense now being overwhelmed in this night, and abandoned to dryness so great that they have no more any joy or sweetness in their spiritual exercises, as they had before; and in their place they find nothing but insipidity and bitterness. For, as I said before, God now, looking upon them as somewhat grown in grace, weans them from the breasts that they may become strong, and cast their swaddling-clothes aside: He carries them in His arms no longer, and shows them how to walk alone. All this is strange to them, for all things seem to go against them.

5. Recollected persons enter the dark night sooner than others, after they have begun their spiritual course; because they are kept at a greater distance from the occasions of falling away, and because they correct more quickly their worldly desires, which is necessary in order to begin to enter the blessed night of sense. In general, there elapses no great length of time after they have begun before they enter the night of sense, and most of them do enter it, for they generally suffer aridities. The Holy Scriptures throughout, but especially the Psalms and the prophetical books, furnish many illustrations of the night of sense, for it is so common; but, to avoid prolixity, I omit them for the present, for those who do not see them there must content themselves with the general experience.

IX. OF THE SIGNS BY WHICH IT MAY BE KNOWN THAT THE SPIRITUAL MAN IS WALKING IN THE WAY OF THIS NIGHT OR PURGATION OF SENSE.

But as these aridities frequently proceed, not from this night and purgation of the sensitive appetite, but from sins or imperfections, from weakness or lukewarmness, from some physical derangement or bodily indisposition, we shall here propose certain tests by which we may ascertain whether a particular aridity proceeds from the purgation of sense, or from any one of the vices I have just enumerated. There are three chief tests for this purpose:

2. The first is this: when we find no comfort in the things of God, and none also in created things. For when God brings the soul into the dark night in order to wean it from sweetness and to purge the desire of sense, He does not allow it to find sweetness or comfort anywhere. It is then probable, in such a case, that this dryness is not the result of sins or of imperfections recently committed; for if it were, we should feel some inclination or desire for other things than those of God. Whenever we give the reins to our desires in the way of any imperfection, our desires are instantly attracted to it, much or little, in proportion to the affection for it. But still, inasmuch as this absence of pleasure in the things of heaven and of earth may proceed from bodily indisposition or a melancholy temperament, which frequently cause dissatisfaction with all things, the second test and condition become necessary.

3. The second test and condition of this purgation are that the memory dwells ordinarily upon God with a painful anxiety and carefulness, the soul thinks it is not serving God, but going backwards, because it is no longer conscious of any sweetness in the things of God. In that case it is clear that this weariness of spirit and aridity are not the results of weakness and lukewarmness; for the peculiarity of lukewarmness is the want of earnestness in, and of interior solicitude for, the things of God.

4. There is, therefore, a great difference between dryness and lukewarmness, for the latter consists in great remissness and weakness of will and spirit, in the want of all solicitude about serving God. The true purgative aridity is accompanied in general by a painful anxiety, because the soul thinks that it is not serving God. Though this be occasionally increased by melancholy or other infirmity—so it sometimes happens—yet it is not for that reason without its purgative effects on the desires, because the soul is deprived of all sweetness, and its sole anxieties are referred to God. For when mere bodily indisposition is the cause, all that it does is to produce disgust and the ruin of bodily health, without the desire of serving God which belongs to the purgative aridity. In this aridity, though the sensual part of man be greatly depressed, weak and sluggish in good works, by reason of the little satisfaction they furnish, the spirit is, nevertheless, ready and strong.

5. The cause of this dryness is that God is transferring to the spirit the goods and energies of the senses, which, having no natural fitness for them, become dry, parched up, and empty; for the sensual nature of man is helpless in those things which belong to the spirit simply. Thus the spirit having tasted, the flesh becomes weak and remiss; but the spirit, having received its proper nourishment, becomes strong, more vigilant and careful than before, lest there should be any negligence in serving God. At first it is not conscious of any spiritual sweetness and delight, but rather of aridities and distaste, because of the novelty of the change. The palate accustomed to sensible sweetness looks for it still. And because the spiritual palate is not prepared and purified for so delicious a taste until it shall have been for some time disposed for it in this arid and dark night, it cannot taste of the spiritual good, but rather of aridity and distaste, because it misses that which it enjoyed so easily before.

6. These, whom God begins to lead through the solitudes of the wilderness, are like the children of Israel, who, though God began to feed them, as soon as they were in the wilderness, with the manna of heaven, which was so sweet that, as it is written, it turned to what every man liked, were more sensible to the loss of the onions and flesh of Egypt —for they liked them and had revelled in them—than to the delicious sweetness of the angelical food. So they wept and bewailed the flesh-pots of Egypt, saying, "We remember the fish that we ate in Egypt free-cost; the cucumbers come into our mind, and the melons, and the leeks, and the onions, and the garlic." Our appetite becomes so depraved that

we long for miserable trifles, and loathe the priceless gifts of heaven.

7. But when these aridities arise in the purgative way of the sensual appetite, the spirit, though at first without any sweetness, for the reasons I have given, is conscious of strength and energy to act because of the substantial nature of its interior food, which is the commencement of contemplation, dim and dry to the senses. This contemplation is in general secret, and unknown to him who is admitted into it, and with the aridity and emptiness which it produces in the senses, it makes the soul long for solitude and quiet, without the power of reflecting on anything distinctly, or even desiring to do so.

8. Now, if they who are in this state knew how to be quiet, to disregard every interior and exterior work,—"for the accomplishment of which they labour,"—to be without solicitude about everything, "and resign themselves into the hands of God, with a loving interior obedience to His voice," they would have, in this tranquillity, a most delicious sense of this interior food. This food is so delicate that, in general, it eludes our perceptions if we make any special effort to feel it, for, as I am saying, it does its work when the soul is most tranquil and free; it is like the air which vanishes when we shut our hands to grasp it.

9. The words of the bridegroom which, addressed to the bride, in the Canticles, are applicable to this matter: "Turn away thine eyes from me, for they have made me flee away." For this is God's way of bringing the soul into this state; the road by which He leads it is so different from the first, that if it will do anything in its own strength, it will hinder rather than aid His work. It was far otherwise once.

10. The reason is this: God is now working in the soul, in the state of contemplation, that is, when it advances from meditation to the state of proficients, in such a way as to seem to have bound up all the interior faculties, leaving no help in the understanding, no sweetness in the will, no reflections in the memory. Therefore, at this time, all that the soul can do of itself ends, as I have said, in disturbing the peace and the work of God in the spirit amid the dryness of sense. This peace, being spiritual and delicate, effects a work that is quiet and delicate, unobtrusive and satisfactory, pacific and utterly alien from the former delights, which were most gross and sensual. This is that peace, according to the Psalmist, which God speaks in the soul to make it spiritual. "He will speak peace unto His people." This brings us to the third test.

11. The third sign we have for ascertaining whether this dryness be the purgation of sense, is inability to meditate and make reflections, and to excite the imagination, as before, notwithstanding all the efforts we may make; for God begins now to communicate Himself, no longer through the channel of sense, as formerly, in consecutive reflections, by which we arranged and divided our knowledge, but in pure spirit, which admits not of successive reflections, and in the act of pure contemplation, to which neither the interior nor the exterior senses of our lower nature can ascend. Hence it is that the fancy and the imagination cannot help or suggest any reflections, nor use them ever afterwards.

12. It is understood here that this embarrassment and dissatisfaction of the senses do not arise out of any bodily ailment. When they arise from this, the indisposition, which is always changeable, having ceased, the powers of the soul recover their former energies, and find their previous satisfactions at once. It is otherwise in the purgation of the appetite, for as soon as we enter upon this, the inability to make our meditations continually grows. It is true that this purgation at first is not continuous in some persons, for they are not altogether without sensible sweetness and comfort —their weakness renders their rapid weaning inexpedient—nevertheless, it grows upon them more and more, and the operations of sense diminish, if they are going on to perfection. They, how-

ever, who are not walking in the way of contemplation, meet with a very different treatment, for the night of aridities is not continuous with them, they are sometimes in it, and sometimes not; they are at one time unable to meditate, and at another able as before.

13. God leads these persons into this night only to try them and to humble them, and to correct their desires, that they may not grow up spiritual gluttons, and not for the purpose of leading them into the way of the spirit, which is contemplation. God does not raise to perfect contemplation every one that is tried in the way of the spirit, nor even half of them, and He alone knoweth why. Hence it is that these persons are never wholly weaned from the breasts of meditations and reflections, but only, as I have said, at intervals and at certain seasons.

X. How THEY ARE TO CONDUCT THEMSELVES WHO HAVE ENTERED THE DARK NIGHT.

During the aridities, then, of the night of sense—when God effects the change of which I have spoken, drawing the soul out of the way of sense into that of the spirit, from meditation to contemplation, where it is helpless in the things of God, so far as its own powers are concerned, as I have said—spiritual persons have to endure great afflictions, not so much because of aridity, but because they are afraid that they will be lost on this road; thinking that they are spiritually ruined, and that God has forsaken them, because they find no help or consolation in holy things. Under these circumstances, they weary themselves, and strive, as they were wont, to fix the powers of the soul with some satisfaction upon some matter of meditation, imagining when they cannot do this, and are conscious of the effort, that they are doing nothing. This they do not without great dislike and inward unwillingness on the part of the soul, which enjoys its state of quietness and rest, the faculties not being at work.

2. In thus turning away from this state they make no progress in the other, because, by exerting their own spirit, they lose that spirit which they had, that of tranquillity and peace. They are like a man who does his work over again; or who goes out of a city that he may enter it once more; or who lets go what he has caught in hunting that he may hunt it again. Their labour is in vain; for they will find nothing, and that because they are turning back to their former ways, as I have said already.

3. Under these circumstances, if they meet with no one who understands the matter, these persons fall away, and abandon the right road; or become weak, or at least put hindrances in the way of their further advancement, because of the great efforts they make to proceed in their former way of meditation, fatiguing their natural powers beyond measure. They think that their state is the result of negligence or of sin. All their own efforts are now in vain, because God is leading them by another and a very different road, that of contemplation. Their first road was that of discursive reflection, but the second knows no imagination or reasoning.

4. It behoves those who find themselves in this condition to take courage, and persevere in patience. Let them not afflict themselves, but put their confidence in God, who never forsakes those who seek Him with a pure and upright heart. Neither will He withhold from them all that is necessary for them on this road until He brings them to the clear and pure light of love, which He will show them in that other dark night of the spirit, if they shall merit an entrance into it.

5. The conduct to be observed in the night of sense is this: in nowise have recourse to meditations, for, as I have said, the time is now past, let the soul be quiet and at rest, though they may think they are doing nothing, that they are losing time, and that their lukewarmness is the reason of their unwillingness to employ their thoughts. They will do enough if they keep patience, and persevere in prayer; all they have to do is to keep their soul free, unembarrassed, and at rest from all thoughts and all knowledge,

not anxious about their meditation, contenting themselves simply with directing their attention lovingly and calmly toward God; and all this without anxiety or effort, or desire to feel and taste His presence. For all such efforts disquiet the soul, and distract it from the calm repose and sweet tranquillity of contemplation to which they are now admitted.

6. And though they may have many scruples that they are wasting time, and that it may be better for them to betake themselves to some other good work, seeing that in prayer and meditation they are become helpless; yet let them be patient with themselves, and remain quiet, for that which they are uneasy about is their own satisfaction and liberty of spirit. If they were now to exert their inferior faculties, they would simply hinder and ruin the good which, in that repose, God is working in the soul; for if a man while sitting for his portrait cannot be still, but moves about, the painter will never depict his face, and even the work already done will be spoiled.

7. In the same way when the soul interiorly rests, every action and passion, or consideration at that time, will distract and disturb it, and make it feel the dryness and emptiness of sense. The more it strives to find help in affections and knowledge, the more will it feel the deficiency which cannot now be supplied in that way. It is therefore expedient for the soul which is in this condition not to be troubled because its faculties have become useless, yea, rather it should desire that they may become so quickly; for by not hindering the operation of infused contemplation, to which God is now admitting it, the soul is refreshed in peaceful abundance, and set on fire with the spirit of love, which this contemplation, dim and secret, induces and establishes within it.

8. Still, I do not mean to lay down a general rule for the cessation from meditation; that should occur when meditation is no longer feasible, and only then, when our Lord, either in the way of purgation and affliction, or of the most perfect contemplation, shall make it impossible. At other times, and on other occasions, this help must be had recourse to, namely, meditation on the life and passion of Christ, which is the best means of purification and of patience and of security on the road, and an admirable aid to the highest contemplation. Contemplation is nothing else but a secret, peaceful, and loving infusion of God, which, if admitted, will set the soul on fire with the spirit of love.

Lorenzo Scupoli

(1529-1610)

At forty years of age this nobleman joined the Order of the Theatines, at Naples, and eight years later was ordained a priest. As a man of oratory he was sent to preach in Piacenza, Genoa, Milan, Naples, and Venice. His fame caused his colleagues to grow jealous of him. They maligned his name, and caused him to be lowered to the rank of a lay brother. He retired to his cell, not embittered but spiritually deepened by this enmity. In retirement he wrote *The Spiritual Combat*, published in 1589. Before he died, this work had gone through fifty editions. It was translated into all the principal European languages, and into Latin and Armenian. "Of Prayer" is from the translation of *The Spiritual Combat* by Thomas Barns.

OF PRAYER

From *The Spiritual Combat*

*I*f distrust of ourselves, trust in God, and practice are as necessary in this combat as has been so far shown, above all prayer is necessary, for by it we are able to obtain not only those but all other good things from our Lord God.

For prayer is an instrument for obtaining all the graces which are showered down on us from that divine source of goodness and of love.

By prayer (if you use it aright) you will place a sword in the hand of God, so that He will fight and conquer for you.

And to make use of it aright there is need that you should be skilled, or that you should strive to be skilled in the following points.

First, That there should always be alive in you a true desire to serve His divine Majesty in all things, and in the way which is most pleasing to Him.

To kindle this desire in you consider:

That God by His most marvellous excellences, His goodness, His majesty, His wisdom, His beauty, and His other infinite perfections, is above all else most worthy of being served and honoured.

That to serve you He has suffered and endured thirty-three years; and has healed and cured your festering wounds which were poisoned by the malignity of sin, not with oil, and wine, and pieces of lint, but with the precious drops which flowed from His most sacred veins, and with His flesh, torn in its purity by the scourges, the thorns, and the nails.

And besides this, think what this service means, since by it we become masters of ourselves, superior to the devil, and sons of God Himself.

Secondly, There must be in you a living faith and trust that the Lord wishes to give you all that you need for His service and for your good.

This holy trust is the vessel that the divine mercy fills with the treasures of His gifts, and the larger and the more ample it is the richer will prayer return to our own bosom.

And how can the Lord, who is unchangeable and almighty, fail to make us partakers of His gifts, when He Himself has commanded us to ask them of Him, and promises us also His Spirit if we ask It with faith and perseverance?

Thirdly, That you should draw near in prayer with the intention of being willing to do God's will alone, and not your own will, as well in asking as in obtaining what you ask; that is, that you should be moved to pray because God wishes it, and that you should desire to be heard only so far as He wills. In short, your intention ought to be to unite your will to the divine will, and not to draw God's will to your own.

And this because your will, since it is infected and spoiled by self-love, is frequently in error, and does not know what it asks; but the divine will is always united with ineffable goodness and can never err. And therefore it is the rule and the queen of all other wills, and deserves and wishes to be followed and obeyed by all.

And therefore such things as are in harmony with the good pleasure of God must always be asked. And if you are in doubt as to what such a thing is, you will ask it with the condition of wishing for it if the Lord wills that you should have it.

And those things which you know for certain are pleasing to Him, such as the virtues, you will ask more for the purpose of giving Him satisfaction and rendering service to Him than for any other end or purpose, however spiritual it may be.

Fourthly, That you should enter upon your prayer adorned with works corresponding to your requests, and that after prayer you should strive more than ever to make yourself fit for the grace and virtue you desire.

For the practice of prayer must be so accompanied by the practice of mastering ourselves that the one may follow circling round the other; for otherwise, to ask for any virtue and not to make an effort to have it would be nothing else than rather to tempt God.

Fifthly, That for the most part thanksgivings for benefits received should go before your requests, in this or in a similar way: "My Lord, who hast created and redeemed me by Thy goodness, and on occasions so innumerable that I myself do not know them, hast freed me from the hands of my enemies, help me now, and do not deny me what I ask of Thee, even though I have always been rebellious against Thee and ungrateful to Thee."

And if you are about to ask any particular virtue, and have at hand something which is trying you, with the view of practising that virtue do not forget to give Him thanks for the opportunity He has given you by it; for this is indeed no small benefit from Him.

Sixthly, Because prayer takes its force and power from inclining God to our desires by the goodness and mercy which are natural to Him, from the merits of the life and Passion of His only-begotten Son, and from the promise He has given us that He will hear us, you will conclude your requests with one or more of the following petitions: "Grant me this grace, O Lord, for Thine infinite pity's sake. May the merits of Thy Son obtain for me in Thy presence that which I ask of Thee. Remember Thy promises, O my God, and incline Thyself unto my prayer."

And sometimes you will also ask for gifts by the merits of the Blessed Virgin Mary and other saints, who have much power in the presence of God, and are much honoured by Him, because in this life they showed honour to His divine Majesty.

Seventhly, It is needful that you should persevere in prayer, because humble perseverance conquers the Invincible; for if the assiduity and importunity of the widow in the Gospel inclined the judge, who was full of all wickedness, to her requests (St. Luke xviii.), will it not have force to draw to our prayers the very fulness of all that is good?

And therefore, although after prayer the Lord may delay to come and hear us, and even may show signs that are unfavourable to us, yet go on praying and having a firm and living trust in His help, since there never lack in Him, indeed there abound in Him in more than infinite measure, all those things which are necessary to bring about other gifts.

And if the fault is not on your side, be assured indeed that you will always obtain all that you ask, or else what will be more useful to you, or indeed both these together.

And the more you seem to be repulsed, the more you should humble yourself in your own eyes, and considering your own unworthiness, with a steadfast thought of the mercy of God, you will always increase your trust in Him, and this being kept living and constant the more it is attacked, so much the more will it be pleasing to our Lord.

Render then thanks to Him always, recognising Him as good and wise and loving, no less when some things are denied you than if they are granted to you; remaining steadfast whatever happens, and joyful in an humble submission to His divine providence.

Francis of Sales

(1567-1622)

In the seventeenth century the quietistic trend in mysticism came to the fore, with Francis of Sales as its chief exponent in France. Born of noble parents at the castle of Sales near Annecy, Savoy, he entered a Jesuit school in Paris. There he studied the classics, Hebrew, and philosophy, and led a life of severe self-discipline. Later he studied law at Padua, the humanities at Paris. After a severe illness, he was ordained a priest in 1591, against the wishes of his father. In 1602 he became bishop of Geneva.

Active against the Reformation around Geneva where Calvin's influence was strong, prolific in his writing, he is considered one of the doctors of the Western Church. His writings show a mystical depth wedded to an ethical participation in everyday affairs. Through men like Francis of Sales the devotion to the inner life became fashionable for well-to-do and educated people of France.

His best-known work, *Introduction to the Devout Life*, written in 1618, is based largely on Scupoli's *Spiritual Combat*. The first selection below is from W. W. Hutchings edition of this work. The second selection is from Book III of H. B. Mackey's edition of *On the Love of God* and is used by permission of the Newman Bookshop, Westminster, Maryland.

[AIDS TO THE DEVOUT LIFE]

From *Introduction to the Devout Life*

The Necessity of Prayer

Prayer opens the understanding to the brightness of Divine Light, and the will to the warmth of Heavenly Love; nothing can so effectually purify the mind from its many ignorances, or the will from its perverse affections. It is as a healing water which causes the roots of our good desires to send forth fresh shoots, which washes away the soul's imperfections, and allays the thirst of passion. . . . Give some time every day to meditation before dinner; if you can, let it be early in the morning, when your mind will be less cumbered, and fresh after the night's rest. Do not spend more than an hour thus, unless specially advised to do so by some spiritual guide. If you can make your meditation quietly in church, it will be well, and no one, father or mother, husband or wife, can object to some time spent there, and very probably you could not secure a time so free from interruption at home. Begin all prayer, whether mental or vocal, by an act of the Presence of God.

. . . Forms of devotion to our Lord's Life, Passion and Resurrection are helpful when rightly used, and there are various little books which contain these. . . . If, while saying vocal prayers, your heart feels drawn to mental prayer, do not resist it, but calmly let your mind fall into that channel, without troubling because you have not finished your appointed vocal prayers. The mental prayer you have substituted for them is more acceptable to God, and more profitable to your soul. . . .

Of the Worth of Souls

Consider how noble and excellent a thing your soul is, endowed with understanding, capable of knowing, not merely this visible world around us, but Angels and Paradise, of knowing that there is an All-Mighty, All-Merciful, Ineffable God; of knowing what is necessary in order so to live in this visible world as to attain to fellowship with those Angels in Heaven, and the eternal fruition of God. Yet more; your soul is possessed of a noble will, capable of loving God, and of being drawn to that love; your heart is full of generous enthusiasm, and can no more find rest in any earthly creation, or in aught save God, than the bee can find honey on a dunghill, or in aught save flowers. Let your mind boldly review the wild earthly pleasures which once filled your heart, and see whether they did not abound in uneasiness and doubts, in painful thoughts and uncomfortable cares, amid which your troubled heart was miserable. When the heart of man seeks the creature, it goes to work eagerly, expecting to satisfy its cravings; but directly it obtains what it sought, it finds a blank, and dissatisfied, begins to seek anew; for God will not suffer our hearts to find any rest, like the dove going forth from Noah's ark, until it returns to God, whence it came. Surely this is a most striking natural beauty in our heart; why should we constrain it against its will to seek creatures' love? . . .

ANXIETY OF MIND

Anxiety arises from an unregulated desire to be delivered from any pressing evil, or to obtain some hoped-for good. Nevertheless nothing tends so greatly to enhance the one or retard the other as over-eagerness and anxiety. Birds that are captured in nets and snares become inextricably entangled therein, because they flutter and struggle so much. Therefore, whensoever you urgently desire to be delivered from any evil, or to attain some good thing, strive above all else to keep a calm, restful spirit, steady your judgment and will, and then go quietly and easily after your object, taking all fitting means to attain thereto. By easily I do not mean carelessly, but without eagerness, disquietude, or anxiety; otherwise, so far from bringing about what you wish, you will hinder it, and add more and more to your perplexities. . . . Do not allow any wishes to disturb your mind under the pretext of their being trifling and unimportant; for if they gain the day, greater and weightier matters will find your heart more accessible to disturbance. When you are conscious that you are growing anxious, commend yourself to God, and resolve steadfastly not to take any steps whatever to obtain the result you desire, until your disturbed state of mind is altogether quieted; unless indeed it should be necessary to do something without delay, in which case you must restrain the rush of inclination, moderating it, as far as possible, so as to act rather from reason than impulse. If you choose to lay your anxiety before some spiritual guide, or at least before some trusty and devout friend, you may be sure that you will find great solace. . . .

A SHORT METHOD OF MEDITATION

It may be, my friend, that you do not know how to practice mental prayer. I will therefore give you a short and easy method for using it. And first of all, the Preparation, which consists of two points: first, placing yourself in the Presence of God; and second, asking His Aid. And in order to place yourself in the Presence of God, I will suggest four chief considerations which you can use at the beginning. First, a lively earnest realisation that His Presence is universal; that is to say, that He is everywhere, and in all, and that there is no place, nothing in the world, devoid of His Most Holy Presence, so that, even as birds on the wing meet the air continually, we, let us go where we will, meet with that Presence always and everywhere. . . . The second way of placing yourself in this Sacred Presence is to call to mind that God is not only present in the place where you are, but that He is very specially present in your heart and mind, which He kindles and inspires with His Holy Presence, abiding there as Heart of your heart, Spirit of your spirit. . . . The third way is to dwell upon the thought of our Lord, who in His Ascended Humanity looks down upon all men, but most particularly on all Christians, because they are His children: above all, on those who pray, over whose doings He keeps watch. . . . The fourth way is simply to exercise your ordinary imagination, picturing your Saviour to yourself in His Sacred Humanity as if He were beside you just as we are wont to think of our friends, and fancy that we see or hear them at our side. . . .

EVENING PRAYER AND EXAMINATION OF CONSCIENCE

As I have counselled you before your material dinner to make a spiritual repast in meditation, so before your evening meal you should make at least a devout spiritual collation. Make sure of some brief leisure before supper-time, and then prostrating yourself before God, and recollecting yourself in the Presence of Christ Crucified, setting Him before your mind with a steadfast inward glance, renew the warmth of your morning's meditation by some hearty aspirations and humble upliftings of your soul to your Blessed Saviour, either repeating those points of your meditation which helped you most, or kindling your heart with anything else you will. As to the examination of conscience, which we all should make before going to bed, you know the rules:

1. Thank God for having preserved you through the day past.

2. Examine yourself as to the way you have conducted yourself through the day, in order to which recall where and with whom you have been, and what you have done.

3. If you have done anything good, give thanks to God: if you have done amiss in thought, word, or deed, ask forgiveness of His Divine Majesty, confessing the fault with real sorrow, and full determination to do better for the future.

4. Then commend your body and soul, the Church, your relations and friends, to God. Ask God that His holy Angels may keep watch over you, and with God's Blessing go to the rest He has appointed for you. Neither this practice nor that of the morning should ever be omitted; by your morning prayer you open your soul's windows to the sunshine of Righteousness, and by your evening devotions you close them against the shades of hell. . . .

ON OBEDIENCE

Love alone leads to perfection, but an excellent way of acquiring it is through obedience, chastity, and poverty. Obedience is a consecration of the heart, chastity of the body, and poverty of all worldly goods to the Love and Service of God. These are the three members of the Spiritual Cross, and all three must be raised upon the fourth, which is humility. I am not going here to speak of these three virtues as solemn vows, nor even as vows at all, although such obligations are helpful to some persons in acquiring grace and virtue. But it is not necessary for perfection that they should be undertaken as vows so long as they are practised diligently. The three vows devoutly taken may be only the entrance into a state of perfection, whereas a diligent observance thereof brings a man to perfection itself. For, observe, there is a great difference between the state of perfection and perfection itself, inasmuch as all religious persons are in the former; although unfortunately it is too obvious that by no means all attain to the latter. Let us then endeavour to practise these three virtues, according to our several vocations, for although we are not all called to the religious life, we may attain through them to perfection itself, and of a truth we are all bound to practise them, although not all after the same manner. . . . If you would acquire a ready obedience to superiors, accustom yourself to yield to your equals, giving way to their opinions where nothing wrong is involved, without arguing or peevishness; and adapt yourself easily to the wishes of your inferiors as far as you reasonably can, and forbear the exercise of stern authority so long as they do well. . . .

OF SPIRITUAL BARRENNESS

Humble yourself profoundly before God, acknowledging your nothingness and misery. Alas what am I when left to myself! no better, Lord, than a parched ground, whose cracks and crevices on every side testify its need of the gracious rain of Heaven, while, nevertheless, the world's blasts wither it more and more to dust. Call upon God, and ask for his Gladness. "O give me the comfort of Thy help again! My Father, if it be possible, let this cúp pass from me." "Depart, O ye unfruitful wind, which parcheth up my soul, and come, O gracious south wind, blow upon my garden." Such loving desires will fill you with the perfume of holiness. You may too consult some spiritual adviser, and opening your heart thoroughly, let him see every corner of your soul, and take all his advice with the utmost simplicity and humility, for God loves obedience, and He often makes the counsel we take specially that of the guides of souls, to be more useful than would seem likely. . . . In every sort of affliction, then, whether bodily or spiritual, in every manner of distraction or loss of sensible devotion, let us say with our whole heart, and in the deepest submission, "The Lord gave me all my blessings, the Lord taketh them away, blessed be the Name of the Lord." If we persevere in this humility, He will restore to us His mercies as He did to Job, who ever spake thus amid all his troubles. And lastly, beloved, amid all our dryness let us never grow discouraged, but go steadily on patiently waiting the return of better things; let us never be misled to give up any devout practices because of it, but rather, if possible, ! t us increase our good works. . . .

On Conversation

Let your words be kindly, frank, sincere, straightforward, simple, and true; avoid all artifice, duplicity, and pretence, remembering that, although it is not always well to publish abroad everything that may be true, yet it is never allowable to oppose the truth. Make it your rule never knowingly to say what is not strictly true, either accusing or excusing, always remembering that God is the God of Truth. If you have unintentionally said what is not true, and it is possible to correct yourself at once by means of explanation or reparation, do so. A straightforward excuse has far greater weight than any falsehood. It may be lawful occasionally to conceal or disguise the truth, but this should never be done save in such special cases as make this reserve obviously a necessity for the service and glory of God. . . . Worldly prudence and artifice belong to the children of this world; but the children of God go straight on with a single heart and in all confidence; falsehood, deceit, and duplicity are sure signs of a mean, weak mind. . . . The silence, so much commended by wise men of old, does not refer so much to a literal use of few words, as to not using many useless words. On this score, we must look less to the quantity than the quality, and, as it seems to me, our aim should be to avoid both extremes. An excessive reserve and stiffness, which stands aloof from familiar friendly conversation, is untrusting, and implies a certain sort of contemptuous pride; while an incessant chatter and babble, leaving no opportunity for others to put in their word, is frivolous and troublesome. . . .

Of Creation

Place yourself in the Presence of God. Ask Him to inspire your heart. Consider that but a few years since, you were not born into the world, and your soul had as yet no existence. . . . God brought you out of this nothingness, in order to make you what you are, not because He had any need of you, but solely out of His Goodness. Consider the being which God has given you; for it is the highest being of this visible world, adapted to live eternally, and to be perfectly united to God's Divine Majesty. Humble yourself utterly before God, saying with the Psalmist, O Lord, I am nothing in respect of Thee; what am I, that Thou shouldst remember me? . . . Give God thanks. O Great and Good Creator, what do I not owe Thee, Who didst take me from out that nothingness, by Thy Mercy to make me what I am? . . . Confess your own shame. . . . Prostrate thyself before God. . . . Thank God. Bless the Lord, O my soul, and praise His Holy Name with all thy being, because His Goodness called me forth from nothingness, and His Mercy created me. Offer yourself. O my God, I offer Thee with all my heart the being Thou hast given me, I dedicate and consecrate it to Thee. Pray. O God, strengthen me in these affections and resolutions. Dear Lord, I commend myself, and all those I love, to Thy neverfailing Mercy. Our Father. At the end of your meditation linger a while, and gather, so to say, a little spiritual bouquet from the thoughts you have dwelt upon, the sweet perfume whereof may refresh you through the day. . . .

MORNING PRAYER

Thank God, and adore Him for His Grace which has kept you safely through the night, and if in anything you have offended against Him, ask His forgiveness. Call to mind that the day now beginning is given you in order that you may work for Eternity, and make a stedfast resolution to use this day for that end. Consider beforehand what occupations, duties and occasions, are likely this day to enable you to serve God; what temptations to offend Him, either by vanity, anger, etc., may arise; and make a fervent resolution to use all means of serving Him and strengthening your spiritual life; as also to avoid and resist whatever might hinder your salvation and God's Glory. Nor is it enough to make such a resolution, you must also prepare to carry it into effect. Thus, if you foresee having to meet some one who is hot-tempered and irritable, you must not merely resolve to guard your own temper, but you must consider by what gentle words to conciliate him. If you know you will see some sick person, consider how best to minister comfort to him, and so on. Next, humble yourself before God, confessing that of yourself you could carry out nothing that you have planned either in avoiding evil or seeking good. Then, so to say, take your heart in your hands, and offer it and all your good intentions to God's Gracious Majesty, entreating Him to accept them, and strengthen you in His Service. . . . All these acts should be made briefly and heartily, before you leave your room, if possible, so that all the coming work of the day may be prospered with God's blessing; but anyhow, beloved friend, I entreat you never to omit them. . . .

ON SPIRITUAL PREPARATION

Begin your preparation overnight, by sundry aspirations and loving ejaculations. Go to bed somewhat earlier than usual, so that you may get up earlier the next morning; and if you should wake during the night, fill your heart and lips at once with sacred words wherewith to make your soul ready to receive the Bridegroom, who watches while you sleep, and who intends to give you countless gifts and graces, if you on your part are prepared to accept them. In the morning rise with joyful expectation of the Blessing you hope for, and renewing your sorrows for your sins, go with the fullest trust, but at the same time with the fullest humility, to receive that Heavenly Food which will sustain your immortal life. And after having said the sacred words, "Lord, I am not worthy," do not make any further movement whatever, either in prayer or otherwise, but remaining in stillness, in the fulness of faith, hope, and love, receive Him in whom, by whom and through whom, you believe, hope, and love. O my friend, bethink you that just as the bee, having gathered heaven's dew and earth's sweetest juices from amid the flowers, carries it to her hive; so the Priest, having taken our Saviour, God's Own Son, who came down from Heaven, the Son of Mary, who sprang up as earth's choicest flower from the Altar, feeds you with that Bread of Sweetness and of all delight. When you have received it kindle your heart to adore the King of our Salvation, tell Him of all your own personal matters, and realise that He is within you, seeking your best happiness. In short, give Him the very best reception you possibly can, and act so that in all you do it may be evident that God is with you. . . .

OF SELF-EXAMINATION

How do you love yourself? Is it a love which concerns this life chiefly? If so, you will desire to abide here for ever, and you will diligently seek your worldly prosperity; but if the love you bear yourself has a heavenward tendency, you will long, or at all events, you will be ready to go hence whensoever it may please your Lord. Is your love of yourself well regulated? for nothing is more ruinous than an inordinate love of self. A well-regulated love implies greater care for the soul than for the body; more eagerness in seeking after holiness than aught else; a greater value for heavenly glory than for any mean earthly honour. . . . What manner of love do you bear to your own heart? Are you willing to minister to it in its maladies? for indeed you are bound to succour it, and seek help for it when harassed by passion, and to leave all else till that is done. What do you imagine yourself worth in God's Sight? Nothing, doubtless, nor is there any great humility in the fly which confesses it is nought, as compared with a mountain; or a drop of water, which knows itself to be nothing compared with the sea; or a cornflower, or a spark, as compared with the sun. But humility consists in not esteeming ourselves above other men, and in not seeking to be esteemed above them. How is it with you in this respect? In speech, do you never boast in any way? Do you never indulge in self-flattery when speaking of yourself? In deed, do you indulge in anything prejudicial to your health, I mean useless idle pleasures, unprofitable nightwatches, and the like? . . .

OF CONVERSATION; AND FIRST, HOW TO SPEAK OF GOD

If you love God heartily, my friend, you will often speak of Him among your relations, household and familiar friends, and that because "the mouth of the righteous speaketh wisdom, and his tongue talketh of judgment." Even as the bee touches nought save honey with his tongue, so should your lips be ever sweetened with your God, knowing nothing more pleasant than to praise and bless His Holy Name; as we are told that when S. Francis uttered the Name of the Lord, he seemed to feel the sweetness lingering on his lips, and could not let it go. But always remember, when you speak of God, that He is God; and speak reverently and with devotion, not affectedly, or as if you were preaching, but with a spirit of meekness, love, and humility; dropping honey from your lips in devout and pious words, as you speak to one or another around; in your secret heart the while asking God to let this soft heavenly dew sink into their minds as they hearken. And remember very specially always to fulfil this angelic task meekly and lovingly, not as though you were reproving others, but rather winning them. It is wonderful how attractive a gentle, pleasant manner is, and how much it wins hearts. Take care, then, never to speak of God, or those things which concern Him, in a merely formal, conventional manner; but with earnestness and devotion, avoiding the affected way in which some professedly religious people are perpetually interlarding their conversation with pious words and sayings, after a most unseasonable and unthinking manner. Too often they imagine that they really are themselves as pious as their words, which probably is not the case. . . .

ON GENTLENESS TOWARD OURSELVES

One important direction in which to exercise gentleness is with respect to ourselves, never growing irritated with one's self or one's imperfections; for although it is but reasonable that we should be displeased and grieved at our own faults, yet ought we to guard against a bitter, angry, or peevish feeling about them. . . . What we want is a quiet, steady, firm displeasure at our own faults. A judge gives sentence more effectually speaking deliberately and calmly than if he be impetuous and passionate. . . . Believe me, beloved, as a parent's tender affectionate remonstrance has far more weight with his child than anger and sternness; so, when we judge our own heart guilty, if we treat it gently, rather in a spirit of pity than anger, encouraging it to amendment, its repentance will be much deeper and more lasting than if stirred up in vehemence and wrath. . . . If any one does not find this gentle dealing sufficient, let him use sterner self-rebuke and admonition, provided only, that whatever indignation he may rouse against himself, he finally works it all up to a tender loving trust in God, treading in the footsteps of that great penitent who cried out to his troubled soul: "Why art thou so vexed, O my soul, and why art thou so disquieted within me? O put thy trust in God, for I will yet thank Him, Which is the help of my countenance, and my God." So then, when you have fallen, lift up your heart in quietness, humbling yourself deeply before God by reason of your frailty, without marvelling that you fell; there is no cause to marvel because weakness is weak, or infirmity infirm. Heartily lament that you should have offended God, and begin anew to cultivate the lacking grace, with a very deep trust in His Mercy, and with a bold, brave heart. . . .

What True Devotion Is

Devotion is simply a spiritual activity and liveliness by means of which Divine Love works in us, and causes us to work briskly and lovingly; and just as charity leads us to a general practice of all God's Commandments, so devotion leads us to practise them readily and diligently. And therefore we cannot call him who neglects to observe all God's Commandments either good or devout, because in order to be good, a man must be filled with love, and to be devout, he must further be very ready and apt to perform the deeds of love. And forasmuch as devotion consists in a high degree of real love, it not only makes us ready, active, and diligent in following all God's Commands, but it also excites us to be ready and loving in performing as many good

works as possible, even such as are not enjoined upon us, but are only matters of counsel or inspiration. Even as a man just recovering from illness, walks only so far as he is obliged to go, with a slow and weary step, so the converted sinner journeys along as far as God commands him, but slowly and wearily, until he attains a true spirit of devotion, and then, like a sound man, he not only gets along, but he runs and leaps in the way of God's Commandments, and hastens gladly along the paths of heavenly counsels and inspirations. The difference between love and devotion is just that which exists between fire and flame; love being a spiritual fire which becomes devotion when it is fanned into a flame; and what devotion adds to the fire of love is that flame which makes it eager, energetic and diligent, not merely in obeying God's Commandments, but in fulfilling His Divine Counsels and inspirations. . . .

The Nature and Excellence of Devotion

The world, looking on, sees that devout persons fast, watch and pray, endure injury patiently, minister to the sick and poor, restrain their temper, check and subdue their passions, deny themselves in all sensual indulgence, and do many other things which in themselves are hard and difficult. But the world sees nothing of that inward, heartfelt devotion which makes all these actions pleasant and easy. Watch a bee hovering over the mountain thyme; the juices it gathers are bitter, but the bee turns them all to honey, and so tells the worldling, that though the devout soul finds bitter herbs along its path of devotion, they are all turned to sweetness and pleasantness as it treads; and the martyrs have counted fire, sword, and rack but as perfumed flowers by reason of their devotion. And if devotion can sweeten such cruel torments, and even death itself, how much more will it give a charm to ordinary good deeds? We sweeten unripe fruit with sugar, and it is useful in correcting the crudity even of that which is good. So devotion is the real spiritual sweetness which takes away all bitterness from mortifications; and prevents consolations from disagreeing with the soul: it cures the poor of sadness, and the rich of presumption; it keeps the oppressed from feeling desolate, and the prosperous from insolence; it averts sadness from the lonely, and dissipation from social life; it is as warmth in winter and refreshing dew in summer; it knows how to abound and how to suffer want; how to profit alike by honour and contempt; it accepts gladness, and sadness with an even mind, and fills men's hearts with a wondrous sweetness. . . .

THE END OF CREATION

Place yourself before God. Ask Him to inspire your heart. God did not bring you into the world because He had any need of you, useless as you are; but solely that He might show forth His Goodness in you, giving you His Grace and Glory. And to this end He gave you understanding that you might know Him, memory that you might think of Him, a will that you might love Him, imagination that you might realise His mercies, sight that you might behold the marvels of His works, speech that you might praise Him, and so on with all your other faculties. Being created and placed in the world for this intent, all contrary actions should be shunned and rejected, as also you should avoid as idle and superfluous whatever does not promote it. Consider how unhappy they are who do not think of all this, who live as though they were created only to build and plant, to heap up riches and amuse themselves with trifles. Humble yourself in that hitherto you have so little thought upon all this. . . . Abhor your past life. Turn to God. Thou, my God and Saviour, shalt henceforth be the sole object of my thoughts. . . . Thank God, who has made you for so gracious an end. . . . Offer yourself. O Dearest Lord, I offer Thee all my affections and resolutions, with my whole heart and soul. Pray. I entreat Thee, O God, that Thou wouldest accept my desires and longings, and give Thy Blessing to my soul, to en-able me to fulfil them. . . . Gather your little spiritual bouquet. . . .

OF THE GIFTS OF GOD

Consider the material gifts God has given you, your body, and the means for its preservation; your health, and all that maintains it; your friends and many helps. Consider too how many persons more deserving than you are without these gifts; some suffering in health or limb, others exposed to injury, contempt and trouble, or sunk in poverty, while God has willed you to be better off. Consider the mental gifts He has given you. Why are you not stupid, idiotic, insane like many you wot of? Again, God has favoured you with a decent and suitable education, while many have grown up in utter ignorance. Further, consider His spiritual gifts. You are a child of His Church, God has taught you to know Himself from your youth. What grace has He given you in His Sacraments? what inspirations and interior lights, what reproofs, He has given to lead you aright; how often He has forgiven you, how often delivered you from occasions of falling; what opportunities He has granted for your soul's progress! Dwell somewhat on the detail, see how Loving and Gracious God has been to you. Marvel at God's Goodness. . . . Marvel at your own ingratitude. . . . Kindle your gratitude. . . . Go on, beloved, to refrain from this or that material indulgence. . . . Thank God for the clearer knowledge He has given you of His benefits and your own duty. Offer your heart and all its resolutions to Him. Ask Him to strengthen you to fulfil them faithfully by the Merits of the Death of His Son. . . .

ON DEATH

Place yourself in the Presence of God. Pray for His Grace. Suppose yourself to be on your deathbed, in the last extremity, without the smallest hope of recovery. Consider the uncertainty as to the day of your death. One day your soul will quit this body, will it be in summer or winter? in town or in country? by day or by night? will it be suddenly or with warning? will it be owing to sickness or an accident? will you have time to confess your sins? will God's Minister be at hand or will he not? Alas! of all these things we know absolutely nothing: all that we do know is that die we shall and for the most part sooner than we expect. Consider that then the world is at an end as far as you are concerned, there will be no more of it for you, it will be altogether overthrown for you, since all pleasures, vanities, worldly joys, empty delights will be as a mere fantastic vision to you. . . . Consider the universal farewell which your soul will take of this world. It will say farewell to riches, pleasures, and idle companions; to amusements and pastimes, to friends and neighbours, to husband, wife and child, in short to all creation. And lastly it will say farewell to its own body, which it will leave pale and cold, to become repulsive in decay. Consider how the survivors will hasten to put that body away, and hide it beneath the earth, and then the world will scarce give you another thought, or remember you, any more than you have done to those already gone. . . . Consider that when it quits the body the soul must go at once to the right hand or the left. To which will your soul go? what side will it take? none other, be sure, than that to which it had voluntarily drawn while yet in this world. . . .

Some Useful Hints as to Meditation

Above all things, beloved, strive when your meditation is ended to retain the thoughts and resolutions you have made as your earnest practice throughout the day. This is the real fruit of meditation, without which it is apt to be unprofitable, if not actually harmful, inasmuch as to dwell upon virtues without practising them tends to puff us up with unrealities, until we begin to fancy ourselves all that we have meditated upon and resolved to be; which is all very well if our resolutions are earnest and substantial, but on the contrary hollow and dangerous if they are not put in practice. You must

then diligently endeavour to carry out your resolutions, and seek for all opportunities, great or small. For instance, if your resolution was to win over those who oppose you by gentleness, seek through the day any occasion of meeting such persons kindly, and if none offers, strive to speak well of them, and pray for them. When you leave off this interior prayer, you must be careful to keep your heart in an even balance, lest the balm it has received in meditation be scattered. . . . Just so, after meditation, do not allow yourself forthwith to be distracted, but look straight before you. . . . You should strive, too, to accustom yourself to go easily from prayer to all such occupations as your calling or position lawfully require of you, even although such occupations may seem uncongenial to the affections and thoughts just before forming part of your prayer. . . . It may be that sometimes, immediately after your preparation, your affections will be wholly drawn to God, and then, my beloved, you must let go the reins, and not attempt to follow any given method. . . . In short, whenever such affections are kindled in your heart, accept them, and give them place in preference to all other considerations. . . .

"Ye have need of patience, that, after ye have done the Will of God, ye might receive the promise," says S. Paul; and our Saviour said, "In your patience possess ye your souls." The greatest happiness of any one is "to possess his soul;" and the more perfect our patience, the more fully we do so possess our souls. . . . Do not limit your patience to this or that kind of trial, but extend it universally to whatever God may send, or allow to befall you. Some people will only bear patiently with trials which carry their own salve of dignity, such as being wounded in battle, becoming a prisoner of war, being ill-used for the sake of their religion, being impoverished by some strife out of which they came triumphant. Now these persons do not love tribulation, but only the honour which attends it. A really patient servant of God is as ready to bear inglorious troubles as those which are honourable. A brave man can easily bear with contempt, slander, and false accusation from an evil world; but to bear such injustice at the hands of good men, of friends and relations, is a great test of patience. . . . Complain as little as possible of your wrongs, for as a general rule you may be sure that complaining is sin; the rather because self-love always magnifies our injuries; above all, do not complain to people who are easily angered and excited. If it is needful to complain to some one, either as seeking a remedy for your injury, or in order to soothe your mind, let it be to some calm, gentle spirit, greatly filled with the Love of God; for otherwise, instead of relieving your heart, your confidants will only provoke it to still greater disturbance; instead of taking out the thorn which pricks you, they will drive it further into your foot. . . .

ON EXTERIOR HUMILITY

You may test real worth as we test balm, which is tried by being distilled in water, and if it is precipitated to the bottom, it is known to be pure and precious. So if you want to know whether a man is really wise, learned, generous, or noble, see if his life is moulded by humility, modesty, and submission. If so, his gifts are genuine; but if they are only surface and showy, you may be sure that in proportion to their demonstrativeness so is their unreality. Those pearls which are formed amid tempest and storm have only an outward shell, and are hollow within; and so when a man's good qualities are fed by pride, vanity, and boasting, they will soon have nothing save empty show, without sap, marrow, or substance. . . . Those who are punctilious about rank, title, or precedence, both lay themselves open to criticism and degradation, and also throw contempt on all things; because an honour which is valuable when freely paid is worthless when sought for or exacted. When the peacock opens his showy tail, he exhibits the ugliness of his body beneath; and many flowers which are beautiful while growing, wither directly we gather them.

And just as men who inhale mandragora from afar as they pass find it sweet, while those who breathe it closely are made faint and ill by the same, so honour may be pleasant to those who merely taste it as they pass, without seeking or craving for it, but it will become very dangerous and hurtful to such as take delight in and feed upon it. An active effort to acquire virtue is the first step towards goodness; but an active effort to acquire honour is the first step towards contempt and shame. A well-conditioned mind will not throw away its powers upon such sorry trifles as rank, position, or outward forms; it has other things to do. . . .

OF A GOOD REPUTATION

An excessive fear of losing reputation indicates mistrust as to its foundations, which are to be found in a good and true life. Those towns where the bridges are built of wood are very uneasy whenever a sign of flood appears, but they who possess stone bridges are not anxious unless some very unusual storm appears. And so a soul built upon solid Christian foundations can afford to despise the pouring out of slanderous tongues, but those who know themselves to be weak are for ever disturbed and uneasy. Be sure, my friend, that he who seeks to be well thought of by everybody will be esteemed by nobody, and those people deserve to be despised who are anxious to be highly esteemed by ungodly, unworthy men. . . . If your good name suffers from some empty pursuit, some useless habit, some unworthy friendship, they must be renounced, for a good name is worth more than any such idle indulgence; but if you are blamed or slandered for pious practices, earnestness in devotion, or whatever tends to win eternal life, then let your slanderers have their way, like dogs that bay at the moon! Be sure that, if they should succeed in rousing any evil impression against you (clipping the beard of your reputation, as it were), your good name will soon revive, and the razor of slander will strengthen your honour, just as the pruning-knife strengthens the vine and causes it to bring forth more abundant fruit. . . . If we are unjustly blamed, let us quietly meet calumny with truth; if calumny perseveres, let us persevere in humility; there is no surer shelter for our reputation or our soul than the Hand of God. . . .

OF GENTLENESS AND ANGER

Humility makes our lives acceptable to God, meekness makes us acceptable to men. . . . Depend upon it, it is better to learn how to live without being angry than to imagine one can moderate and control anger lawfully; and if through weakness and frailty one is overtaken by it, it is far better to put it away forcibly than to parley with it; for give anger ever so little way, and it will become your master, like the serpent, who easily works in its body wherever it can once introduce its head. You will ask how to put away anger. My child, when you feel its first movements, collect yourself gently and seriously, not hastily or with impetuosity. Sometimes in a law court the officials who enforce quiet make more noise than those they affect to hush; and so, if you are impetuous in restraining your temper, you will throw your heart into worse confusion than before, and, amid the excitement, it will lose all self-control. . . . Moreover, when there is nothing to stir your wrath, lay up a store of meekness and kindliness, speaking and acting in things great and small as gently as possible. Remember that the Bride of the Canticles is described as not merely dropping honey, and milk also, from her lips, but as having it "under her tongue"; that is to say, in her heart. So we must not only speak gently to our neighbour, but we must be filled, heart and soul, with gentleness; and we must not merely seek the sweetness of aromatic honey in courtesy and suavity with strangers, but also the sweetness of milk among those of our own household and our neighbours; a sweetness terribly lacking to some who are as angels abroad and devils at home. . . .

HOW TO STRENGTHEN THE HEART AGAINST TEMPTATION

Examine from time to time what are the dominant passions of your soul, and having ascertained this, mould your life, so that in thought, word, and deed you may as far as possible counteract them. For instance, if you know that you are disposed to be vain, reflect often upon the emptiness of this earthly life, call to mind how burdensome all mere earthly vanities will be to the conscience at the hour of death, how unworthy of a generous heart, how puerile and childish, and the like. . . . Do as many lowly, humble deeds as lie in your power, even if you perform them unwillingly at first; for by this means you will form a habit of humility, and you will weaken your vanity, so that when temptation arises, you will be less predisposed to yield, and stronger to resist. Or if you are given to avarice, think often of the folly of this sin, which makes us the slave of what was made only to serve us; remember how when we die we must leave all we possess to those who come after us, who may squander it, ruin their own souls by misusing it, and so forth. Speak against covetousness, commend the abhorrence in which it is held by the world; and constrain yourself to abundant almsgiving, as also to not always using opportunities of accumulation. If you have a tendency to trifle with the affections, often call to mind what a dangerous amusement it is for yourself and others; how unworthy a thing it is to use the noblest feelings of the heart as a mere pastime; and how readily such trifling becomes mere levity. Let your conversation turn on purity and simplicity of heart, and strive to frame your actions accordingly, avoiding all that savours of affectation or flirting. . . .

OF A WELL-BALANCED REASONABLE MIND

We are strict in exacting our own rights, but expect others to be yielding as to theirs; we complain freely of our neighbours, but we do not like them to make any complaints of us. Whatever we do for them appears very great in our sight, but what they do for us counts as nothing. In a word, we are like the Paphlagonian partridge, which has two hearts; for we have a very tender, pitiful, easy heart towards ourselves, and one which is hard, harsh, and strict towards our neighbour. We have two scales, one wherein to measure our own goods to the best advantage, and the other to weigh our neighbours' to the worst. Holy Scripture tells us that lying lips are an abomination unto the Lord, and the double heart, with one measure whereby to receive and another to give, is also abominable in His Sight. Be just and fair in all you do. Always put yourself in your neighbour's place, and put him into yours, and then you will judge fairly. Sell as you would buy, and buy as you would sell, and your buying and selling will alike be honest. These little acts of dishonesty seem unimportant, because we are not obliged to make restitution, and we have, after all, only taken that which we might demand according to the strict letter of the law; but, nevertheless, they are sins against right and charity, and are mere trickery, greatly needing correction, nor does any one ever lose by being generous, noble-hearted, and courteous. Be sure then often to examine your dealings with your neighbour, whether your heart is right towards him, as you would have his towards you, were things reversed; this is the true test of reason. . . .

ON SLANDER

From rash judgments proceed mistrust, contempt for others, pride, and self-sufficiency, and numberless other pernicious results, among which stands forth prominently the sin of slander, which is a veritable pest of society. Oh, wherefore can I not take a live coal from God's Altar, and touch the lips of men, so that their iniquity may be taken away and their sin purged, even as the Seraphim purged the lips of Isaiah. He who could purge the world of slander would cleanse it from a great part of its sinfulness! He who unjustly takes away his neighbour's good name is guilty of sin, and is bound to make reparation, according to the nature of his evil speaking; since no man can enter into Heaven cumbered with stolen goods, and of all worldly possessions the most precious is a good name. Slander is a kind of murder; for we all have three lives: a spiritual life, which depends upon the Grace of God; a bodily life, depending on the soul; and a civil life, consisting in a good reputation. Sin deprives us of the first, death of the second, and slander of the third. But the slanderer commits three several murders with his idle tongue: he destroys his own soul and that of him who hearkens, as well as causing civil death to the object of his slander. . . . My friend, I entreat you never speak evil of any, either directly or indirectly; beware of ever unjustly imputing sins or faults to your neighbour, of needlessly disclosing his real faults, of exaggerating such as are overt, of attributing wrong motives to good actions, of denying the good that you know to exist in another, of maliciously concealing it, or depreciating it in conversation. . . .

OF REAL FRIENDSHIP

Do you, my child, love every one with the pure love of charity, but have no friendship save with those whose intercourse is good and true, and the purer the bond which unites you so much higher will your friendship be. If your intercourse is based on science it is praiseworthy, still more if it arises from a participation in goodness, prudence, justice, and the like; but if the bond of your mutual liking be charity, devotion, and Christian perfection, God knows how very precious a friendship it is! Precious because it comes from God, because it tends to God, because God is the link that binds you, because it will last for ever in Him. Truly it is a blessed thing to love on' earth as we hope to love in Heaven, and to begin that friendship here which is to endure for ever there. I am not now speaking of simple charity, a love due to all mankind, but of that spiritual friendship which binds souls together, leading them to share devotions and spiritual interests, so as to have but one mind between them. Such as these may well cry out, "Behold, how good and joyful a thing it is, brethren, to dwell together in unity!" Even so, for the "precious ointment" of devotion trickles continually from one heart to the other, so that truly we may say that to such friendship the Lord promises His Blessing and life for evermore. To my mind all other friendship is but as a shadow with respect to this, its links mere fragile glass compared to the golden bond of true devotion. Do you form no other friendships. I say "form" because you have no right to cast aside or neglect the natural bonds which draw you to relations, connections, benefactors, or neighbours.

OF THE PROGRESS AND PERFECTION OF LOVE

From *On the Love of God*

I. That Holy Love May Be Augmented Still More and More in Every One of Us

*T*he sacred Council of Trent assures us, that the friends of God, proceeding from virtue to virtue, are day by day renewed, that is, they increase by good works in the justice which they have received by God's grace, and are more and more justified, according to those heavenly admonitions; *He that is just, let him be justified still: and he that is holy, let him be sanctified still.* And: *Be not afraid to be justified even to death. The path of the just, as a shining light, goeth forwards and increaseth even to perfect day. Doing the truth in charity, let us in all things grow up in him who is the head, even Christ.* And finally: *This I pray, that your charity may more and more abound in knowledge and in all understanding.* All these are sacred words out of David, S. John, Ecclesiasticus, and S. Paul.

I never heard of any living creature whose growth was not bounded and limited, except the crocodile, who from an extremely little beginning never ceases to grow till it comes to its end, representing equally in this the good and the wicked: *For the pride of them that hate thee ascendeth continually,* says the great king David; and the good increase as the break of day, from brightness to brightness. And to remain at a standstill is impossible; he that gains not, loses in this traffic; he that ascends not, descends upon this ladder; he that vanquishes not in this battle is vanquished: we live amidst the dangers of the wars which our enemies wage against us, if we resist not we perish; and we cannot resist unless we overcome, nor overcome without triumph. For as the glorious S. Bernard says: "It is written in particular of man that *he never continueth in the same state;* he necessarily either goes forward or returns backward. *All run indeed but one obtains the prize, so run that you may obtain.* Who is the prize but Jesus Christ? And how can you take hold on him if you follow him not? But if you follow him you will march and run continually, for he never stayed, but continued his course of love and obedience until death and the death of the cross."

Go then, says S. Bernard; go, I say with him; go, my dear Theotimus, and admit no other bounds than those of life, and as long as it remains run after this Saviour. But run ardently and swiftly: for what better will you be for following him, if you be not so happy as to take hold of him! Let us hear the Prophet: *I have inclined my heart to do thy justifications for ever*: he does not say that he will do them for a time only, but for ever, and because he desires eternally to do well, he shall have an eternal reward. *Blessed are the undefiled in the way, who walk in the law of the Lord.* Accursed are they who are defiled, who walk not in the law of the Lord: it is only for the devil to say that he will *sit in the sides of the north.* Detestable one, wilt thou sit? Ah! knowest thou not that thou art upon the way, and that the way is not made to sit down but to go in, and it is so made to go in, that going is called making way. And God speaking to one of his greatest friends says: *Walk before me and be perfect.*

True virtue has no limits, it goes even further; but especially holy charity, which is the virtue of virtues, and which, having an infinite object, would be capable of becoming infinite if it could meet with a heart capable of infinity. Nothing hinders this love from being infinite except the condition of the will which receives it, and which is to act by it: a condition which prevents any one loving God as much as God is amiable, as it prevents them from seeing him as much as he is visible. The heart which could love God with a love equal to the divine goodness would have a will infinitely good, which cannot be but in God. Charity then in us may be perfected up to the infinite, but exclusively; that is, charity may become more and more, and ever more, excellent, yet never infinite. The Holy Ghost may elevate our hearts, and apply them to what supernatural actions it may please him, so they be not infinite. Between little and great things, though the one exceed the other never so much, there is still some proportion, provided always that the excess of the thing which exceeds be not an infinite excess: but between finite and infinite there is no proportion, and to make any, it would be necessary, either to raise the finite and make it infinite, or to lower the infinite and make it finite, which is impossible.

So that even the charity which is in our Redeemer, as he is man, though greater than Angels or men can comprehend, yet is not infinite of itself and in its own being, but only in regard to its value and merit, as being the charity of a divine Person, who is the eternal Son of the omnipotent Father.

Meanwhile it is an extreme honour to our souls that they may still grow more and more in the love of their God, as long as they shall live in this failing life: *Ascending by steps from virtue to virtue.*

IV. Of Holy Perseverance in Sacred Love

Even as a tender mother, leading with her her little babe, assists and supports him as need requires, letting him now and then venture a step by himself in less dangerous and very smooth places, now taking him by the hand and steadying him, now taking him up in her arms and bearing him, so Our Lord has a continual care to conduct his children, that is such as are in charity; making them walk before him, reaching them his hand in difficulties, and bearing them himself in such travails, as he sees otherwise insupportable unto them. This he declared by Isaias saying: *I am the Lord thy God, who take thee by the hand, and say to thee: fear not, I have helped thee.* So that with a good heart we must have a firm confidence in God, and his assistance, for if we fail not to second his grace, he will accomplish in us the good work of our salvation, which he also began, working in us *both to will and to accomplish,* as the holy Council of Trent assures us.

In this conduct which the heavenly sweetness makes of our souls, from their entry into charity until their final perfection, which is not finished but in the hour of death, consists the great gift of perseverance, to which our Saviour attaches the greatest gift of eternal glory, according to his saying: *He that shall persevere unto the end, he shall be saved:* for this gift is no other thing than the combination and sequence of the various helps, solaces and succours, whereby we continue in the love of God to the end: as the education, bringing up and supporting of a child is no other thing, than the many cares, aids, succours, and other offices necessary to a child, exercised and continued towards him till he grow to years in which he no longer needs them.

But the continuance of succours and helps is not equal in all those that persevere. In some it is short; as in such as were converted a little before their death: so it happened to the Good Thief; so to that officer, who seeing the constancy of S. James made forthwith profession of faith, and became a companion of the martyrdom of this great Apostle; so to the blessed gaoler who guarded the forty martyrs at Sebaste, who seeing one of them lose courage, and forsake the crown of martyrdom, put himself in his place and became Christian, martyr and glorious all at once; so to the notary of whom mention is made in the life of S. Antony of Padua, who having all his life been a false villain yet died a martyr: and so it happened to a thousand others of whom we have seen and read that they died well, after an ill-spent life. As for these, they stand not in need of a great variety of succours, but unless some great temptation cross their way, they can make this short perseverance solely by the charity given them, and by the aids by which they were converted. For they arrive at the port without voyaging, and finish their pilgrimage in a single leap, which the powerful mercy of God makes them take so opportunely that their enemies see them triumph before seeing them fight: so that their conversion and perseverance are almost the same thing. And if we would speak with exact propriety, the grace which they received of God whereby they attained as soon as the issue, as the beginning of their course, cannot well be termed perseverance, though all the same, because actually it holds the place of perseverance in giving salvation, we comprehend it under the name of perseverance. In others, on the contrary, perseverance is longer, as in S. Anne the prophetess, in S. John the Evangelist, S. Paul the first hermit, S. Hilarion, S. Romuald, S. Francis of Paula; —and they stood in need of a thousand sorts of different assistances, according to the variety of the adventures of their pilgrimage and the length of it.

But in any case, perseverance is the most desirable gift we can hope for in this life, and the one which, as the Council of Trent says, we cannot have but from the hand of God, who alone can assure him that stands, and help him up that falls: wherefore we must incessantly demand it, making use of the means which Our Saviour has taught us to the obtaining of it; prayer, fasting, alms-deeds, frequenting the sacraments, intercourse with the good, the hearing and reading of holy words.

Now since the gift of prayer and devotion is liberally granted to all those who sincerely will to consent to divine inspiration, it is consequently in our power to persevere. Not of course that I mean to say that our perseverance has its origin from our power, for on the contrary I know it springs from God's mercy, whose most precious gift it is, but I mean that though it does not come from our power, yet it comes within our power, by means of our will, which we cannot deny to be in our power: for though God's grace is necessary for us, to will to persevere, yet is this will in our power, because heavenly grace is never wanting to our will, and our will is not wanting to our power. And indeed according to the great S. Bernard's opinion, we may all truly say with the Apostle that: *Neither death, nor life, nor Angels, nor principalities, nor powers, nor things present, nor things to come, nor might, nor height, nor depth, nor any other creature, shall be able to separate us from the love of God, which is in Christ Jesus Our Lord.* Yes, indeed, for no creature can take us away by force from this holy love; we only can forsake and abandon it by our own will, except for which there is nothing to be feared in this matter.

So, Theotimus, following the advice of the holy Council, we ought to place our whole hope in God, who will perfect the work of our salvation which he has begun in us, if we be not wanting to his grace: for we are not to think that he who said to the paralytic: *Go, and do not will to sin again*: gave him not also power to avoid that willing which he forbade him: and surely he would never exhort the faithful to persevere, if he were not ready to furnish them with the power. *Be thou faithful until death*, said he to the bishop of Smyrna, *and I will give thee the crown of life. Watch ye, stand fast in the faith, do manfully, and be strengthened. Let all your actions be done in charity. So run that you may obtain.* We must often then with the great King demand of God the heavenly gift of perseverance, and hope that he will grant it us. *Cast me not off in the time of old age; when my strength shall fail, do not thou forsake me.*

Jakob Böhme

(1575-1624)

BÖHME, the "inspired shoemaker," was born near Görlitz of German Protestant peasants. Not formally educated, he found his training through prayer, the Bible, and the reading of books on mysticism. He was indirectly influenced by Hildegarde of Bingen. In 1589 he settled as a shoemaker at Görlitz and remained there all his life. At the basis of his mystical teaching is the stress on rebirth, sometimes difficult to understand because it is clothed in allegorical symbolism.

When his first book, *Aurora*, was published, it was condemned as heretical by the authorities. Called before the municipal council, Böhme was warned to cease such writings. However, he continued to write voluminously. His works deeply influenced Schlegel, Hegel, Schelling, William Law, William Blake, and Saint-Martin. He remains one of those imponderable immortals who must be rediscovered and reunderstood by the interpreters of every era.

[THE WAY TO GOD'S LOVE]

From *Of the Supersensual Life*

*T*he disciple being very earnest to be more fully instructed how he might arrive at the supersensual life; and how, having found all things, he might come to be a king over all God's words; came again to his master the next morning, having watched the night in prayer, that he might be disposed to receive and apprehend the instructions that should be given him by a divine irradiation upon his mind. And the disciple after a little space of silence, bowed himself, and thus brake forth:

Disciple: O my master! O my master! I have now endeavoured to recollect my soul in the presence of God, and to cast myself into that deep where no creature doth nor can dwell; that I might hear the voice of my Lord speaking in me; and be initiated into that high life, whereof I heard yesterday such great and amazing things pronounced. But, alas! I neither hear nor see as I should: There is still such a partition wall in me which beats back the heavenly sounds in their passage, and obstructs the entrance of that light by which alone divine objects are discoverable, as till this be broken down, I can have but small hopes, yea, even none at all, of arriving at those glorious attainments which you pressed me to, or of entering into that where no creature dwells, and which you call nothing and all things. Wherefore be so kind as to inform me what is required on my part, that this partition which hinders may be broken or removed.

Master: This partition is the creaturely will in thee: And this can be broken by nothing but by the grace of self-denial, which is the entrance into the true following of Christ; and totally removed by nothing but a perfect conformity with the divine will.

Disciple: But how shall I be able to break this creaturely will which is in me, and is at enmity with the divine will? Or, what shall I do to follow Christ in so difficult a path, and not to faint in a continual course of self-denial and resignation to the will of God?

Master: This is not to be done by thyself; but by the light and grace of God received into thy soul, which will, if thou gainsay not, break the darkness that is in thee, and melt down thine own will, which worketh in the darkness and corruption of nature, and bring it into the obedience of Christ, whereby the partition of the creaturely self is removed from betwixt God and thee.

Disciple: I know that I cannot do it of myself: But I would fain learn, how I must receive this divine light and grace into me, which is to do it for me, if I hinder it not my own self. What is then required of me in order to admit this breaker of the partition, and to promote the attainment of the ends of such admission?.

Master: There is nothing more required of thee at first, than not to resist this grace, which is manifested in thee; and nothing in the whole process of thy work, but to be obedient and passive to the light of God shining through the darkness of thy creaturely being, which comprehendeth it not, as reaching no higher than the light of nature.

Disciple: But is it not for me to attain, if I can, both the light of God, and the light of the outward nature too: And to make use of them both for the ordering my life wisely and prudently?

Master: It is right, I confess, so to do. And it is indeed a treasure above all earthly treasures, to be possessed of the light of God and nature, operating in their spheres; and to have both the eye of time and eternity at once open together, and yet not to interfere with each other.

Disciple: This is a great satisfaction to me to hear; having been very uneasy about it for some time. But how this can be without interfering with each other, there is the difficulty: Wherefore fain would I know, if it were lawful, the boundaries of the one and the other; and how both the divine and the natural light may in their several spheres respectively act and operate, for the manifestation of the mysteries of God and nature, and for the conduct of my outward and inward life?

Master: That each of these may be preserved distinct in their several spheres, without confounding things heavenly and things earthly, or breaking the golden chain of wisdom, it will be necessary, my child, in the first place to wait for and attend the supernatural and divine light, as that superior light appointed to govern the day, rising in the true east, which is the centre of paradise; and in great might breaking forth as out of the darkness within thee, through a pillar of fire and thunder-clouds, and thereby also reflecting upon the inferiour light of nature a sort of image of itself, whereby only it can be kept in its due subordination; that which is below being made subservient to that which is above; and that which is without to that which is within. Thus there will be no danger of interfering; but all will go right, and everything abide in its proper sphere.

Disciple: Therefore without reason or the light of nature be sanctified in my soul, and illuminated by this superior light, as from the central east of the holy light-world, by the eternal and intellectual sun; I perceive there will be always some confusion, and I shall never be able to manage aright either what concerneth time or eternity: But I must always be at a loss, or break links of wisdom's chain.

Master: It is even so as thou hast said. All is confusion, if thou hast no more but the dim light of nature, or unsanctified and unregenerated reason to guide thee by; and if only the eye of time be opened in thee, which cannot pierce beyond its own limit. Wherefore seek the fountain of light waiting in the deep ground of thy soul for the rising there of the sun of righteousness, whereby the light of nature in thee, with the properties thereof, will be made to shine seven times brighter than ordinary. For it shall receive the stamp, image, and impression of the supersensual and supernatural; so that the sensual and rational life will hence be brought into the most perfect order and harmony.

Disciple: But how am I to wait for the rising of this glorious sun, and how am

I to seek in the centre, this fountain of light, which may enlighten me throughout, and bring all my properties into perfect harmony? I am in nature, as I said before; and which way shall I pass through nature, and the light thereof, so that I may come into that supernatural and supersensual ground, whence this true light, which is the light of minds, doth arise; and this, without the destruction of my nature, or quenching the light of it, which is my—reason?

Master: Cease but from thine own activity, steadfastly fixing thine eye upon one point, and with a strong purpose relying upon the promised grace of God in Christ, to bring thee out of thy darkness into his marvellous light. For this end gather in all thy thoughts, and by faith press into the centre, laying hold upon the word of God, which is infallible, and which hath called thee. Be thou then obedient to this call; and be silent before the Lord, sitting alone with him in thy inmost and most hidden cell, thy mind being centrally united in itself, and attending his will in the patience of hope. So shall thy light break forth as the morning; and after the redness thereof is passed, the sun himself, which thou waitest for, shall arise unto thee, and under his most healing wings thou shalt greatly rejoice; ascending and descending in his bright and salutiferous beams. Behold this is the true supersensual ground of life.

Disciple: I believe it indeed to be even so. But will not this destroy nature? Will not the light of nature in me be extinguished by this greater light? Or, must not the outward life hence perish, with the earthly body which I carry?

Master: By no means at all. It is true, the evil nature will be destroyed by it; but by the destruction thereof you can be no loser, but very much a gainer. The eternal band of nature is the same afterward as before; and the properties are the same. So that nature hereby is only advanced and meliorated; and the light thereof, or human reason, by being kept within its due bounds, and regulated by a superiour light, is only made useful.

Disciple: Pray therefore let me know how this inferiour light ought to be used by me; how it is to be kept within its due bounds; and after what manner the superiour light doth regulate it and ennoble it.

Master: Know then, my beloved son, that if thou wilt keep the light of nature within its own proper bounds, and make use thereof in just subordination to the light of God; thou must consider that there are in thy soul two wills, an inferiour will, which is for driving thee to things without and below; and a superiour will, which is for drawing to things within and above. These two wills are now set together, as it were back to back, and in a direct contrariety to each other; but in the beginning it was not so. For this contraposition of the soul in these two is no more than the effect of the fallen state; since before that they were placed one under the other, that is, the superiour will above, as the lord, and the inferiour below, as the subject. And thus it ought to have continued. Thou must also further consider, that answering to these two wills there are likewise two eyes in the soul, whereby they are severally directed; forasmuch as these eyes are not united in one single view, but look quite contrary ways at once. They are in a like manner set one against the other, without a common medium to join them. And hence, so long as this double-sightedness doth remain, it is impossible there should be any agreement in the determination of this or that will. This is very plain: And it sheweth the necessity that this malady, arising from the disunion of the rays of vision, be some way remedied and redressed, in order to a true discernment in the mind. Both these eyes therefore must be made to unite by a concentration of rays; there being nothing more dangerous than for the mind to abide thus in the duplicity, and not to seek to arrive at the unity. Thou perceivest, I know, that thou hast two wills in thee, one set against the other, the superiour and the inferiour; and that thou hast also two eyes within, one against another; whereof the one eye may be called the right eye, and the other the left eye. Thou perceivest, too, doubtless, that it is according to the right eye that the wheel of the superiour will is moved; and that it is according to the motion of the left eye that the contrary wheel in the lower is turned about.

Disciple: I perceive this, sir, to be very true; and this it is which causeth a continual combat in me, and createth to me greater anxiety than I am able to express. Nor am I unacquainted with the disease of my own soul, which you have so clearly declared. Alas! I perceive and lament this malady, which so miserably disturbeth my sight; whence I feel such irregular and convulsive motions drawing me on this side and that side. The spirit seeth not as the flesh seeth; neither doth, or can the flesh see, as the spirit seeth. Hence the spirit willeth against the flesh; and the flesh willeth against the spirit in me. This hath been my hard case. And how shall it be remedied? O how may I arrive at the unity of will, and how come into the unity of vision!

Master: Mark now what I say: The right eye looketh forward in thee into eternity. The left eye looketh backward in thee into time. If now thou sufferest thyself to be always looking into nature, and the things of time, and to be leading the will, and to be seeking somewhat for itself in the desire, it will be impossible for thee ever to arrive at the unity, which thou wishest for. Remember this; and be upon thy watch. Give not thy mind leave to enter into, nor to fill itself with, that which is without thee; neither look thou backward upon thyself; but quit thyself, and look forward upon Christ. Let not thy left eye deceive thee, by making continually one representation after another, and stirring up thereby an earnest longing in the self-propriety; but let thy right eye command back this left, and attract it to thee, so that it may not gad abroad into the wonders and delights of nature. Yea, it is better to pluck it quite out, and to cast it from thee, than to suffer it to proceed forth without restraint into nature, and to follow its own lusts: However, there is for this no necessity, since both eyes may become very useful, if ordered aright; and both the divine and natural light may in the soul subsist together, and be of mutual service to each other. But never shalt thou arrive at the unity of vision or uniformity of will, but by entering fully into the will of our Saviour Christ, and therein bringing the eye of time into the eye of eternity; and then descending by means of this united through the light of God into the light of nature.

Disciple: So then if I can but enter into the will of my Lord, and abide therein, I am safe, and may both attain to the light of God in the spirit of my soul, and see with the eye of God, that is, the eye of eternity in the eternal ground of my will; and may also at the same time enjoy the light of this world nevertheless; not degrading, but adorning the light of nature; and beholding as with the eye of eternity things eternal, so with the eye of nature things natural, and both contemplating therein the wonders of God, and sustaining also thereby the life of my outward vehicle or body.

Master: It is very right. Thou hast well understood; and thou desirest now to enter into the will of God, and to abide therein as in the supersensual ground of light and life, where thou mayest in his light behold both time and eternity, and bring all the wonders created of God for the exteriour into the interiour life, and so eternally rejoice in them to the glory of Christ; the partition of thy creaturely will being broken down, and the eye of thy spirit simplified in and through the eye of God manifesting itself in the centre of thy life. Let this be so now; for it is God's will.

Disciple: But it is very hard to be always looking forwards into eternity; and consequently to attain to this single eye, and simplicity of divine vision. The entrance of a soul naked into the will of God, shutting out all imaginations and desires, and breaking down the strong partition which you mention, is indeed somewhat very terrible and shocking to human nature, as in its present state. O what shall I do, that I may reach this which I so much long for?

Master: My son, let not the eye of nature with the will of the wonders depart from that eye which is introverted into the divine liberty, and into the eternal light of the holy majesty: But let it draw to thee those wonders by union with that heavenly internal eye, which are externally wrought out and manifested in visible nature. For while thou art in the world, and hast an honest employment, thou art certainly by the order of providence obliged to labour in it, and to finish the work given thee, according to thy best ability, without repining in the least; seeking out and manifesting for God's glory, the wonders of nature and art. Since let the nature be what it will, it is all the work and art of God: And let the art also be what it will, it is still God's work; and his art, rather than any art or cunning of man. And all both in art and nature serveth but abundantly to manifest the wonderful works of God; that he for all, and in all, may be glorified. Yea, all serveth, if thou knowest rightly how to use them, but to recollect thee more inwards, and to draw thy spirit into that majestic light, wherein the original patterns and forms of things visible are to be seen. Keep therefore in the centre, and stir not out from the presence of God revealed within thy soul; let the world and the devil make never so great a noise and bustle to draw thee out, mind them not; they cannot hurt thee. It is permitted to the eye of thy reason to seek food, and to thy hands, by their labour, to get food for the terrestrial body: But then this eye ought not with its desire to enter into the food prepared, which would be covetousness; but must in resignation simply bring it before the eye of God in thy spirit, and then thou must seek to place it close to this very eye, without letting it go. Mark this lesson well.

Let the hands or the head be at labour, thy heart ought nevertheless to rest in God. God is a Spirit; dwell in the Spirit, work in the Spirit, pray in the Spirit, and do everything in the Spirit; for remember thou also art a spirit, and thereby created in the image of God: Therefore see thou attract not in thy desire matter unto thee, but as much as possible abstract thyself from all matter whatever; and so, standing in the centre, present thyself as a naked spirit before God, in simplicity and purity; and be sure thy spirit draw in nothing but spirit.

Thou wilt yet be greatly enticed to draw matter, and to gather that which the world calls substance, thereby to have somewhat visible to trust to: But by no means consent to the tempter, nor yield to the lustings of thy flesh against the spirit. For in so doing thou wilt infallibly obscure the divine light in thee; thy spirit will stick in the dark covetous root, and from the fiery source of thy soul will it blaze out in pride and anger; thy will shall be chained in earthliness, and shall sink through the anguish into darkness and materiality; and never shalt thou be able to reach the still liberty, or to stand before the majesty of God. Since this is opening a door for him who reigneth in the corruption of matter, possibly the devil may roar at thee for this refusal; because nothing can vex him worse than such a silent abstraction of the soul, and introversion thereof to the point of rest from all that is worldly and circumferential: But regard him not; neither admit the least dust of that matter into thee which he may pretend any claim to. It will be all darkness to thee, as much matter as is drawn in by the desire of thy will: It will darken God's majesty to thee; and will close the seeing eye, by hiding from thee the light of his beloved countenance. This the serpent longeth to do; but in vain, except thou permittest thy imagination, upon his suggestion, to receive in the alluring matter; else he can never get in. Behold then, if thou desirest to see God's light in thy soul, and be divinely illuminated and conducted, this is the short way that thou art to take; not to let the eye of thy spirit enter into matter, or fill itself with anything whatever, either in heaven or earth; but to let it enter by a naked faith into the light of the majesty; and so receive by pure love the light of God, and attract the divine power into itself, putting on the divine body, and growing up in it to the full maturity of the humanity of Christ.

Disciple: As I said before, so I say again, this is very hard. I conceive indeed well enough that my spirit ought to be free from the contagion of matter, and wholly empty, that it may admit into it the Spirit of God. Also, that this Spirit will not enter, but where the will entereth into nothing, and resigneth itself up in the nakedness of faith, and in the purity of love, to its conduct; feeding magically upon the word of God, and clothing itself thereby with a divine substantialty. But, alas, how hard is it for the will to sink into nothing, to attract nothing, to imagine nothing!

Master: Let it be granted that it is so. Is it not surely worth thy while, and all that thou canst ever do?

Disciple: It is so, I must needs confess.

Master: But perhaps it may not be so hard as at first it appeareth to be; make but the trial, and be in earnest. What is there required of thee but to stand still, and see the salvation of thy God? And couldst thou desire anything less? Where is the hardship in this? Thou hast nothing to care for, nothing to desire in this life, nothing to imagine or attract: Thou needest only cast thy care upon God, who careth for thee, and leave him to dispose of thee according to his good will and pleasure, even as if thou hadst no will at all in thee. For he knoweth what is best; and if thou canst but trust him, he will most certainly do better for thee, than if thou wert left to thine own choice.

Disciple: This I most firmly believe.

Master: If thou believest, then go and do accordingly. All is in the will, as I have shewn thee. When the will imagineth after somewhat, then entereth it into that somewhat, and this somewhat taketh presently the will into itself, and overcloudeth it, so as it can have no light, but must dwell in darkness, unless it return back out of that somewhat into nothing. But when the will imagineth or lusteth after nothing, then it entereth into nothing, where it receiveth the will of God into itself, and so dwelleth in light, and worketh all its works in it.

Disciple: I am now satisfied that the main cause of any one's spiritual blindness, is his letting his will into somewhat, or into that which he hath wrought, of what nature soever it be, good or evil, and his setting his heart and affections upon the work of his own hands or brain; and that when the earthly body perisheth, then the soul must be imprisoned in that very thing which it shall have received and let in; and if the light of God be not in it, being deprived of the light of this world, it cannot but be found in a dark prison.

Master: This is a very precious gate of knowledge; I am glad thou takest it into such consideration. The understanding of the whole Scripture is contained in it; and all that hath been written from the beginning of the world to this day, may be found herein, by him that having entered with his will into nothing, hath there found all things, by finding God; from whom, and to whom, and in whom are all things. By this means thou shalt come to hear and see God; and after this earthly life is ended, to see with the eye of eternity all the wonders of God and of nature, and more particularly those which shall be wrought by thee in the flesh, or all that the Spirit of God shall have given thee to labour out for thyself and thy neighbour, or all that the eye of reason enlightened from above, may at any time have manifested to thee. Delay not therefore to enter in by this gate, which if thou seest in the spirit, as some highly favoured souls have seen it, thou seest in the supersensual ground all that God is, and can do; thou seest also therewith, as one hath said who was taken thereinto, through heaven, hell, and earth; and through the essence of all essences. Whosoever findeth it, hath found all that he can desire. Here is the virtue and power of the love of God displayed. Here is the height and depth; here is the breadth and length thereof manifested, as fully as ever the capacity of thy soul can contain. By this thou shalt come into that

ground out of which all things are originated, and in which they subsist; and in
it thou shalt reign over all God's works,
as a prince of God.

Disciple: Pray tell me, dear master,
where dwelleth it in man?

Master: Where man dwelleth not;
there hath it its seat in man.

Disciple: Where is that in a man,
where man dwelleth not in himself?

Master: It is the resigned ground of a
soul, to which nothing cleaveth.

Disciple: Where is the ground in any
soul, to which there will nothing stick?
Or, where is that which abideth and
dwelleth not in something?

Master: It is the centre of rest and
motion in the resigned will of a truly
contrite spirit, which is crucified to the
world. This centre of the will is impenetrable consequently to the world,
the devil, and hell: Nothing in all the
world can enter into it, or adhere to it,
though never so many devils should be
in the confederacy against it; because the
will is dead with Christ unto the world,
but quickened with him in the centre
thereof, after his blessed image. Here it
is where man dwelleth not; and where
no self abideth, or can abide.

Disciple: O where is this naked ground
of the soul void of all self? And how shall
I come at the hidden centre where God
dwelleth, and not man? Tell me plainly,
loving sir, where it is, and how it is to
be found of me, and entered into?

Master: There where the soul hath
slain its own will, and willeth no more
anything as from itself, but only as God
willeth, and as his Spirit moveth upon
the soul, shall this appear: Where the
love of self is banished, there dwelleth the
love of God. For so much of the soul's
own will as is dead unto itself, even so
much room hath the will of God, which
is his love, taken up in that soul. The
reason whereof is this: Where its own
will did before sit, there is now nothing,
and where nothing is, there it is that the
love of God worketh alone.

Disciple: But how shall I comprehend it?

Master: If thou goest about to compre-

hend it, then it will fly away from thee;
but if thou dost surrender thyself wholly
up to it, then it will abide with thee, and
become the life of thy life, and be natural
to thee.

Disciple: And how can this be without dying, or the whole destruction of
my will?

Master: Upon this entire surrender and
yielding up of thy will, the love of God
in thee becometh the life of thy nature;
it killeth thee not, but quickeneth thee,
who art now dead to thyself in thine own
will, according to its proper life, even
the life of God. And then thou livest, yet
not to thy own will; but thou livest to
its will; forasmuch as thy will is henceforth become its will. So then it is no
longer thy will, but the will of God; no
longer the love of thyself, but the love of
God, which moveth and operateth in
thee; and then, being thus comprehended
in it, thou art dead indeed as to thyself,
but art alive unto God. So being dead
thou livest, or rather God liveth in thee
by his Spirit; and his love is made to thee
life from the dead. Never couldst thou,
with all thy seeking, have comprehended
it; but it hath apprehended thee. Much
less couldst thou have comprehended it:
But now it hath comprehended thee;
and so the treasure of treasures is found.

Disciple: How is it that so few souls
do find it, when yet all would be glad
enough to have it?

Master: They all seek it in somewhat,
and so they find it not: For where there
is somewhat for the soul to adhere to,
there the soul findeth but that somewhat
only, and taketh up its rest therein, until
she seeth that it is to be found in nothing,
and goeth out of the somewhat into
nothing, even into that nothing out of
which all things may be made. The soul
here saith, "I have nothing, for I am
utterly naked and stripped of everything:
I can do nothing; for I have no manner
of power, but am as water poured out:
I am nothing; for all that I am is no
more than an image of being, and only
God is to me I am; and so sitting down in
my own nothingness, I give glory to the
Eternal Being, and will nothing of my-

self, that so God may will all in me, being unto me my God and all things." Herein now it is that so very few find this most precious treasure in the soul, though every one would so fain have it; and might also have it, were it not for this somewhat in every one which letteth.

Disciple: But if the love should proffer itself to a soul, could not that soul find it, nor lay hold on it, without going for it into nothing?

Master: No verily. Men seek and find not, because they seek it not in the naked ground where it lieth; but in something or other where it never will be, neither can be. They seek it in their own will, and they find it not. They seek it in their self-desire, and they meet not with it. They look for it in an image, or in an opinion, or in affection, or a natural devotion and fervour, and they lose the substance by thus hunting after a shadow. They search for it in something sensible or imaginary, in somewhat which they may have a more peculiar natural inclination for, and adhesion to; and so they miss of what they seek, for want of diving into the supersensual and supernatural ground where the treasure is hid. Now, should the love graciously condescend to proffer itself to such as these, and even to present itself evidently before the eye of their spirit, yet would it find no place in them at all, neither could it be held by them, or remain with them.

Disciple: Why not, if the love should be willing and ready to offer itself, and to stay with them.

Master: Because the imaginariness which is in their own will hath set up itself in the place thereof: And so this imaginariness would have the love in it; but the love fleeth away, for it is in prison. The love may offer itself; but it cannot abide where the self-desire attracteth or imagineth. That will which attracteth nothing, and to which nothing adhereth, is only capable of receiving it; for it swelleth only in nothing, as I said, and therefore they find it not.

Disciple: If it swell only in nothing, what is now the office of it in nothing?

Master: The office of the love here is to penetrate incessantly into something; and if it penetrate into, and find a place in something which is standing still and at rest, then its business is to take possession thereof. And when it hath there taken possession, then it rejoiceth therein with its flaming love-fire, even as the sun doth in the visible world. And then the office of it is without intermission to enkindle a fire in this something, which may burn it up; and then with the flames thereof exceedingly to enflame itself, and raise the heat of the love-fire by it, even seven degrees higher.

Disciple: O loving master, how shall I understand this?

Master: If it but once kindle a fire within thee, my son, thou shalt then certainly feel how it consumeth all that which it toucheth; thou shalt feel it in the burning up thyself, and swiftly devouring all egoity, or that which thou callest I and Me, as standing in a separate root, and divided from the Deity, the fountain of thy being. And when this enkindling is made in thee, then the love doth so exceedingly rejoice in thy fire, as thou wouldst not for all the world be out of it; yea, wouldst rather suffer thyself to be killed, than to enter into thy something again. This fire now must grow hotter and hotter, till it shall have perfected its office with respect to thee, and therefore wilt not give over, till it come to the seventh degree. Its flame hence also will be so very great, that it will never leave thee, though it should even cost thee thy temporal life; but it would go with thee in its sweet loving fire into death; and if thou wentest also into hell, it would break hell in pieces also for thy sake. Nothing is more certain than this; for it is stronger than death and hell.

Disciple: Enough, my dearest master, I can no longer endure that anything should divert me from it. But how shall I find the nearest way to it?

Master: Where the way is hardest, there go thou; and what the world casteth away, that take thou up. What the world doth, that do thou not; but in all things walk thou contrary to the world. So thou comest the nearest way to that which thou art seeking.

Disciple: If I should in all things walk contrary to other people, I must needs be in a very unquiet and sad state; and the world would not fail to account me for a madman.

Master: I bid thee not, child, to do harm to any one, thereby to create to thyself any misery or unquietness. This is not what I mean by walking contrary in everything to the world. But because the world, as the world, loveth only deceit and vanity, and walketh in false and treacherous ways; thence, if thou hast a mind to act a clean contrary part to the ways thereof, without any exception or reserve whatsoever, walk thou only in the right way, which is called the way of light, as that of the world is properly the way of darkness. For the right way, even the path of light, is contrary to all the ways of the world.

But whereas thou art afraid of creating to thyself hereby trouble and inquietude, that indeed will be so according to the flesh. In the world thou must have trouble; and thy flesh will not fail to be unquiet, and to give thee occasion of continual repentance. Nevertheless in this very anxiety of soul, arising either from the world or the flesh, the love doth most willingly enkindle itself, and its cheering and conquering fire is but made to blaze forth with greater strength for the destruction of that evil. And whereas thou dost also say, that the world will for this esteem thee mad; it is true the world will be apt enough to censure thee for a madman in walking contrary to it: And thou art not to be surprised if the children thereof laugh at thee, calling thee silly fool. For the way to the love of God is folly to the world, but is wisdom to the children of God. Hence, whenever the world perceiveth this holy fire of love in God's children, it concludeth immediately that they are turned fools, and are besides themselves. But to the children of God, that which is despised of the world is the greatest treasure; yea, so great a treasure it is, as no life can express, nor tongue so much as name what this enflaming, all-conquering love of God is. It is brighter than the sun; it is sweeter than anything that is called sweet; it is stronger than all strength; it is more nutrimental than food; more cheering to the heart than wine, and more pleasant than all the joy and pleasantness of this world. Whosoever obtaineth it, is richer than any monarch on earth; and he who getteth it, is nobler than any emperor can be, and more potent and absolute than all power and authority.

Lancelot Andrewes

(1555-1626)

FELLOW of Pembroke Hall, Cambridge, one of the scholars appointed in 1607 to prepare the King James Version of the Bible, bishop of Ely, Winchester, and Chichester, chaplain to Queen Elizabeth—such titles depict the magnitude of Andrewes. Not widely known until recently when he was the subject of a book by T. S. Eliot, Andrewes surely ranks as one of the intellectual giants of English churchmen. *Private Devotions*, written out of the complexities of court problems in England, is one of the most rewarding devotional classics by English divines. "The First Day" is from a series of morning prayers for the seven days of the week. "An Horologue" is a prayer based on the hours of the day. These selections are reprinted from Alexander Whyte's edition, *Lancelot Andrewes and His Private Devotions*.

THE FIRST DAY

From *Private Devotions*

1. MEDITATION AND ADORATION

Through the tender mercy of our God
   the dayspring from on high hath
   visited us.
Glory be to Thee, O Lord, glory to
   Thee,
   Creator of the light, Enlightener of
   the world.
God is the Lord, who hath shewed us
   light:
   bind the sacrifice with cords,
   even unto the horns of the altar.
Glory be to Thee for the visible light:
   the sun's radiance, the flame of fire;
   day and night, evening and morning;
   for the light invisible and intellectual:
   that which may be known of God,
   that which is written in the law,
   oracles of prophets,
   melody of psalms,
   instruction of proverbs,
   experience of histories—
   a light which never sets.

By Thy resurrection raise us up unto
   newness of life,
   supplying to us frames of repentance,
The God of peace, that brought again
   from the dead our Lord Jesus,
   that great Shepherd of the sheep,
   through the blood of the everlasting
   covenant,
make us perfect in every good work to
   do His will,
working in us that which is well pleasing
   in His sight,
   through Jesus Christ;
   to whom be glory for ever and ever.

Thou who didst send down on Thy disciples
   Thy Thrice-Holy Spirit on this day,
   take not Thou the gift, O Lord,
   from us,
but renew it, day by day, in us, who ask
   Thee for it.

2. CONFESSION OF SIN

Merciful and pitiful Lord,
   longsuffering and full of compassion,
I have sinned, Lord, I have sinned against
   Thee;
   O wretched man that I am,
   I have sinned, Lord against Thee
   much and grievously,
   in observing lying vanities.

I conceal nothing: I make no excuses.
I give Thee glory, O Lord, this day.
I denounce against my self my sins.
Indeed I have sinned against the
   Lord, and thus and thus have I
   done.
I have sinned and perverted that which
   was right,
   and it profited me not.

And what shall I now say?
   or with what shall I open my mouth?
What shall I answer, seeing I have
   done it?
Without plea, without excuse, self-con-
   demned am I.
   I have destroyed myself.
O Lord, righteousness belongeth unto
   Thee,
   but unto me confusion of face.
And Thou art just in all that is brought
   upon me for Thou hast done right,
   but I have done wickedly.
And now, Lord, what is my hope?
Art not Thou, Lord?
Truly my hope is even in Thee,
   if hope of salvation remaineth to me,
   if Thy loving kindness vanquisheth
   the multitude of my iniquities.

O remember what my substance is,
   the work of Thy hands,
   the likeness of Thy countenance,
   the reward of Thy blood,
   a name from Thy name,
   a sheep of Thy Pasture,
   a son of Thy covenant.
Forsake not Thou the work of Thine
   own hands.

Hast Thou made in vain
Thine own image and likeness?
In vain, if thou destroy it.
And what profit is there in my
blood?
Thine enemies will rejoice.
May they never rejoice, O Lord.
Grant not to them my destruction.

Look upon the face of Thine Anointed,
and in the blood of Thy covenant,
in the propitiation for the sins of the
whole world.
Lord, be merciful to me a sinner,
even to me, O Lord, of sinners
the first, the chief, and the greatest.
For Thy name's sake, O Lord, pardon
mine iniquity,
for it is great; greater cannot be.
For Thy name's sake, that name beside which none other under
heaven is given among men,
whereby we must be saved,
the Spirit Himself helping our infirmities,
and making intercession for us with
groanings that cannot be uttered.
For the fatherly yearnings of the
Father,
the bloody wounds of the Son,
the unutterable groanings of the
Spirit,
O Lord, hear; O Lord, forgive;
O Lord, hearken and do;
defer not, for Thine own sake,
O My God.

For I acknowledge my transgressions;
and my sin is ever before me;
I remember my sins in the bitterness of
my soul,
I am sorry for them;
I turn back with groans,
I have indignation and revenge and
wrath against myself.
I abhor and bruise myself
that my penitence, Lord, O Lord,
is not deeper, is not fuller;
Lord, I repent,
help Thou mine impenitence;
and more, and still more,
pierce Thou, rend, crush my heart.

And remit, pardon, forgive
all things that are grief unto me and
offence of heart.
Cleanse Thou me for secret faults,
keep back Thy servant also from presumptuous sins.
Magnify Thy mercies towards the utter
sinner;
and in season, Lord, say to me,
Be of good cheer; thy sins are forgiven
thee;
My grace is sufficient for thee.
Say unto my soul, I am thy salvation.
Why art thou cast down, O my
soul?
and why art thou disquieted in me?
Return unto thy rest, O my soul;
for the Lord hath dealt bountifully with
thee.

O Lord, rebuke me not in Thine
anger,
neither chasten me in Thy hot displeasure.
I said, I will confess my transgressions
unto the Lord;
and Thou forgavest the iniquity of
my sin.
Lord, all my desire is before Thee;
and my groaning is not hid from
Thee.
Have mercy upon me, O God,
according to Thy lovingkindness:
according unto the multitude of Thy tender mercies blot out my transgressions.
Thou shalt arise, and have mercy on me,
O Lord,
for the time to favour me, yea, the set
time, is come.
If Thou, Lord, shouldest mark iniquities,
O Lord, who shall stand?
Enter not into judgment with Thy
servant:
for in Thy sight shall no man living
be justified.

3. PRAYER FOR GRACE

My hands will I lift up unto Thy
commandments, which I have
loved.
Open Thou mine eyes and I shall see,

incline my heart and I shall desire,
order my steps and I shall walk in
the way of Thy commandments.
O Lord God, be Thou to me a God,
and besides Thee let there be none
else,
no other, nought else with Thee.

Vouchsafe to me, to worship Thee and
serve Thee according to Thy commandments:
in truth of spirit, in reverence of
body,
in blessing of lips,
both in private and in public;
to pay honour to them that have the rule
over me,
by obedience and submission;
to shew affection to my own, by care and
providence;
to overcome evil with good;
to possess my vessel in sanctification and
honour;
to be free from the love of money,
content with such things as I have;
to speak the truth in love;
to be desirous not to lust, not to lust
passionately,
not to walk after lusts.

The Hedge of the Law

To bruise the serpent's head.
To consider my latter end.
To cut off occasions of sin.
To be sober.
Not to sit idle.
To shun the wicked.
To cleave to the good.
To make a covenant with the eyes.
To bring the body into subjection.
To give myself unto prayer.
To come to repentance.
Hedge up my way with thorns,
that I find not the path for following
vanity.
Hold Thou me in with bit and bri-
dle,
lest I come not near to Thee.
O Lord, compel me to come in to
Thee.

4. Confession of Faith

I believe, O Lord, in Thee,
Father, Word, Spirit, One God;

that by Thy fatherly love and power all
things were created;
that by Thy goodness and love to man
all things have been gathered together into one in Thy Word,
who, for us men and for our salvation,
became flesh,
was conceived, was born,
suffered, was crucified,
died, was buried,
descended, rose again,
ascended, sat down,
will return, will repay;
that by the forth-shining and operation
of Thy Holy Spirit
hath been called out of the whole
world
a peculiar people, into a common-
wealth
of faith in the truth
and holiness of life,
in which we are partakers
of the communion of saints
and forgiveness of sins in this world,
and in which we look for the resurrection of the flesh and the life everlasting in the world to come.
This most holy faith once delivered to
the saints
I believe, O Lord;
help Thou mine unbelief,
increase Thou my little faith.
And vouchsafe to me
to love the Father for His love,
to reverence the Almighty for His
power,
to Him, as unto a faithful Creator, to
commit my soul in well doing.
Vouchsafe to me to partake
from Jesus of salvation,
from Christ of anointing,
from the only begotten Son of adoption;
to serve the Lord
for His conception, in faith,
for His birth, in humility,
for His sufferings, in patience and in
impatience of sin;
for His cross, to crucify occasions
of sin,
for His death, to mortify the flesh,
for His burial, to bury evil thoughts
in good works,

for His descent, to meditate upon
hell,
for His resurrection, upon newness
of life,
for His ascension, to set my mind on
things above,
for His sitting on high, to set my
mind on the better things on His
right hand,
for His return, to fear His second
appearing,
for His judgment, to judge myself
ere I be judged.
From the Spirit
vouchsafe to me to receive the breath
of saving grace,
in the holy Catholic Church
to have my own calling, sanctification,
and portion,
and fellowship of her holy things,
prayers, fastings, groanings,
watchings, tears, sufferings,
for assurance of the remission of sins,
for hope of resurrection and translation to eternal life.

5. INTERCESSION

O Thou that art the confidence of all
the ends of the earth,
and of them that are afar off upon the
sea:
O Thou in whom our fathers trusted,
and Thou didst deliver them:
in whom they trusted,
and were not confounded:
Thou who art my trust from my
youth,
from my mother's breasts:
upon whom I was cast from the womb,
be Thou my hope now and evermore,
and my portion in the land of the living.

In Thy nature,
in Thy names,
in Thy types,
in Thy word,
in Thy deed,
my Hope,
disappoint me not of this my hope.

O Hope of all the ends of the earth,

remember Thy whole creation for
good,
visit the world in Thy compassion.
O Guardian of Men, O sovereign Lord,
Lover of men,
remember all our race;
Thou who hast concluded all in unbelief,
have mercy upon all, O Lord.

O Thou who to this end didst die and
live again,
to be Lord both of the dead and living,
live we or die we,
Thou art our Lord;
have mercy upon all, O Lord.
O Helper of the helpless,
refuge in times of trouble,
remember all who are in necessity
and need Thy succour.

O God of grace and truth,
establish all who stand in truth and
grace;
restore all who are sick with heresies
and sins.
O saving Strength of Thine anointed,
remember Thy congregation which
Thou hast purchased and redeemed of old;
O grant to all that believe
to be of one heart and one soul.
Thou who walkest in the midst of the
golden candlesticks,
remove not our candlestick out of its
place;
set in order the things that are wanting,
strengthen the things which remain,
which are ready to die.

O Lord of the harvest,
send forth labourers, made sufficient by
Thee,
into Thy harvest.
O Portion of those who wait in Thy temple,
grant to our clergy rightly to divide
the word of truth,
and to walk uprightly according
thereto; grant to thy people who
love Thee to obey and submit
themselves to them.

O King of nations unto the ends of the
earth,
  strengthen all the states of the in-
  habited world,
  as being Thine ordinance,
  though a creation of man;
  scatter Thou the peoples that delight
  in war;
  make wars to cease unto the end of the
  earth.
O Expectation of the isles, and their
Hope,
  Lord, save this island,
  and all the country in which we sojourn,
  from all affliction, peril, and need.

Lord of lords, Ruler of rulers, remember
  all rulers to whom Thou hast giv-
  en rule in the earth;
and O remember specially our divinely
  guarded king,
  and work with him more and more,
  and prosper his way in all things;
  speak good things unto his heart for
  Thy Church and all Thy people;
  grant to him profound and perpetual
  peace,
  that in his tranquillity we may lead
  a quiet and peaceable life in all
  godliness and honesty.

O Thou by whom the powers that be
  are ordained,
  grant to those who are chief in court
  to be chief in virtue and Thy fear;
  grant to the council Thy holy wisdom;
  to our mighty men, to have no might
  against but for the truth;
  to the courts of law Thy judgments,
  to judge all in all things without
  preference, without partiality.
O God of hosts,
  give a prosperous course and strength
  to all the Christian army against
  the enemies of our most holy faith.
Grant to our population to be subject
  unto the higher powers not only
  because of the wrath, but also for
  conscience sake.
Grant to farmers and graziers good seasons;

  to the fleet and fishers fair weather;
  to tradesmen, not to overreach one another;
  to mechanics, to pursue their business
  lawfully,
  down to the humblest workman, down
  to the poor.

O God, not of us only but of our seed,
  bless our children within us,
  that they may grow in wisdom as in
  stature,
  and in favour with Thee and with
  men.
Thou who wouldest have us provide for
  our own,
  and hatest those without natural affection,
remember Lord, my kinsmen according
  to the flesh;
  grant me to speak peace concerning
  them,
  and to seek their good.
Thou who wouldest have us make return
  to our benefactors,
  remember, Lord, for good
  all from whom I have received good;
keep them alive and bless them upon the
  earth,
  and deliver them not unto the will
  of their enemies.
Thou who hast noted the man who neglects his own as worse than an infidel,
  remember in Thy good pleasure
  all those in my household;
  peace be to my house,
  children of peace be all who dwell
  in it.
Thou who wouldest that our righteousness exceed the righteousness of
  sinners,
  grant me, Lord, to love those who love
  me;
  my own friends, and my father's
  friends,
  and my friends' children, never to forsake.

Thou who wouldest that we overcome
  evil with good,
  and pray for those who persecute us,

have pity on mine enemies, Lord, as
on me;
and lead them together with me to
Thy heavenly kingdom.
Thou who grantest the prayers thy servants make one for another,
remember, Lord, for good, and pity
all those who remember me in
their prayers,
or whom I have promised to remember
in mine.

Thou who acceptest the willing mind in
every good work,
remember, Lord, as if they prayed to
Thee,
those who for any sufficient cause
have not time for prayer.
Arise, and have mercy on those who are
in the last necessity;
for the time to favour them, yea, the set
time, is come.
Thou shalt have mercy on them, O
Lord,
as on me also, when in extremities.

Remember, Lord,
infants, children, the growing youth, the
young men,
the middle-aged, the old, the decayed,
hungry, thirsty, naked, sick,
captives, friendless strangers,
possessed with devils and tempted to
suicide,
troubled by unclean spirits,
the sick in soul or body, the faint-
hearted, the despairing,
all in prison and chains, all under sentence of death,
orphans, widows, foreigners, travellers,
voyagers,
women with child, women who give
suck,
all in bitter servitude, or mines, or galleys,
or in loneliness.

O Lord, Thou preservest man and
beast.
How excellent is Thy lovingkindness, O
God!
Therefore the children of men put their
trust

under the shadow of Thy wings.
The Lord bless us, and keep us:
the Lord make His face shine upon us,
and be gracious unto us:
the Lord lift up His countenance upon
us,
and give us peace.

I commend to Thee, O Lord,
my soul, and my body,
my mind, and my thoughts,
my prayers, and my vows,
my senses, and my members,
my words, and my works,
my life, and my death;
my brothers, my sisters, and their children;
my friends, my benefactors, my well-
wishers,
those who have a claim on me,
my kindred, my neighbours,
my country, and all Christian people.

I commend to Thee, Lord,
my impulses, and my occasions,
my resolves, and my attempts,
my going out, and my coming in,
my sitting down, and my rising up.

6. THANKSGIVING

How truly meet, and right, and comely,
and due,
in all, and for all things,
in all times, places, manners,
in every season, every spot,
everywhere, always, altogether,
to remember Thee, to worship Thee,
to confess to Thee, to praise Thee,
to bless Thee, to hymn Thee,
to give thanks to Thee,
Maker, Nourisher, Guardian, Governor,
Healer, Benefactor, Perfecter of all,
Lord and Father, King and God,
Fountain of life, and immortality,
Treasure of everlasting goods,
whom the heavens hymn,
and the heaven of heavens,
the angels and all the heavenly powers,
one to other crying continually,—
and we the while, weak and unworthy,

under their feet,—
Holy, holy, holy, Lord God of
Hosts:
full is the whole heaven, and the whole
earth,
of the majesty of Thy glory.

Blessed be the glory of the Lord out of
His place,

for His Godhead, His mysterious-
ness,
His height, His sovereignty, His almightiness,
His eternity, His providence.

The Lord is my strength, my strong
rock, my defence,
my deliverer, my succour, my buckler,
the horn of my salvation, my refuge.

AN HOROLOGUE

From *Private Devotions*

O Thou, who hast put in Thine own
power the times and the seasons:
give us grace that in a fitting and acceptable time we may pray unto
Thee;
and deliver us.
Thou, who for us men and for our salvation
wast born in the depth of night;
grant us to be born again daily by renewing of the Holy Ghost,
until Christ Himself be formed in us,
to a perfect man;
and deliver us.
Thou, who very early in the morning,
at the rising of the sun,
didst rise again from the dead:
raise us also daily to newness of life,
suggesting to us, for Thou knowest
them,
frames of repentance;
and deliver us.
Thou, who at the third hour didst send
down Thy Holy Spirit on the
apostles:
take not the same Holy Spirit from
us,
but renew Him daily in our hearts;
and deliver us.
Thou, who at the sixth hour of the sixth
day
didst nail together with Thyself upon
the cross the sins of the world:
blot out the handwriting of our sins
that is against us;
and, taking it away, deliver us.
Thou, who at the sixth hour didst let
down

a great sheet from heaven to earth,
the symbol of Thy Church:
receive into it us sinners of the Gentiles,
and with it receive us up into heaven;
and deliver us.
Thou, who at the seventh hour didst
command
the fever to leave the nobleman's
son:
if there be any fever in our hearts,
if any sickness, remove it from us
also;
and deliver us.
Thou, who at the ninth hour for us sinners and for our sins didst taste of
death:
mortify in us our members which are
upon the earth,
and whatsoever is contrary to Thy
will;
and deliver us.
Thou, who didst will the ninth hour to
be the hour of prayer:
hear us while we pray at the hour of
prayer,
and grant unto us that which we pray
for and desire and deliver us.
Thou, who at the tenth hour didst grant
unto Thine apostle to discover
Thy Son,
and to cry out with great gladness,
We have found the Messiah:
grant unto us also, in like manner,
to find the same Messiah,
and, having found Him, to rejoice in
like manner;
and deliver us.

Thou, who didst, even at the eleventh
  hour of the day,
  of Thy goodness send into Thy vine-
    yard those that had stood all the
    day idle,
    promising them a reward:
    grant unto us the like grace,
    and, though it be late,
    even as it were about the eleventh hour,
    favourably receive us who return unto
      Thee;
    and deliver us.
Thou, who at the sacred hour of the sup-
    per wast pleased to institute the
    mysteries of Thy body and blood:
    render us mindful and partakers of the
      same,
    yet never to condemnation, but to the
      remission of sin,
    and to obtaining of the promises of the
      new testament;
    and deliver us.
Thou, who at eventide wast pleased to be
    taken down from the cross,
    and laid in the grave:
    take away from us, and bury in Thy
      sepulchre,
    our sins,
    covering whatever evil we have com-
      mitted with good works;
    and deliver us.
Thou, who late in the night, by breathing
    on Thine apostles,
    didst bestow on them the power of
      the remission and retention of sins:
    grant unto us to experience that power
      for their remission, O Lord,
    not for their retention;
    and deliver us.
Thou, who at midnight didst raise David
    Thy prophet,
  and Paul Thine apostle, that they should
    praise Thee;
    give us also songs in the night,
    and to remember Thee upon our
      beds;
    and deliver us.
Thou, who with Thine own mouth hast
    declared,
  at midnight the Bridegroom shall
    come:
  grant that the cry may ever sound in
    our ears,

Behold, the Bridegroom cometh,
  that we may never be unprepared to go
    forth to meet Him;
  and deliver us.
Thou, who by the crowing of the clock,
    didst admonish Thine apostle,
  and didst cause him to return to re-
    pentance:
  grant that we, at the same warning, may
    follow his example,
  may go forth and weep bitterly for the
    things in which we have sinned
    against Thee;
  and deliver us.
Thou, who hast foretold Thy coming to
    judgment
  in a day when we think not, and in an
    hour when we are not aware:
  grant that every day and every hour
    we may be prepared, and waiting
    Thy advent; and deliver us.

Thou, who sendest forth the light,
  and createst the morning,
  and makest Thy sun to rise on the evil
    and on the good:
  enlighten the blindness of our minds by
    the knowledge of the truth,
  lift Thou up the light of Thy counte-
    nance upon us,
  that in Thy light we may see light,
  and at length in the light of grace the
    light of glory.
Thou, who givest food to all flesh,
  who feedest the young ravens which cry
    unto Thee,
  and hast held us up from our youth until
    now,
  fill our hearts with food and gladness,
  and stablish our hearts with Thy grace.

Thou, who hast made the evening the
    end of the day,
  so that Thou mightest bring the evening
    of life to our minds:
  grant us always to consider that our
    life passeth away like a day;
  to remember the days of darkness
    that they are many,
  That the night cometh wherein no man
    can work;
  by good works to prevent the darkness,
  lest we be cast out into outer darkness;

and continually to cry unto Thee,
    Abide with us, Lord,
for it is toward evening, and the day of
    our life is far spent.
The work of the Creator is justice;
    of the Redeemer, mercy;

of the Holy Ghost, inspiration,
who is the other Comforter,
    the Anointing,
    the Seal,
    the Earnest.

John Donne

(1573-1631)

DONNE is known chiefly as an Elizabethan poet through *Holy Sonnets*, although this book was not published until three years after his death. As dean of St. Paul's, London, Donne won reputation as a forceful preacher. His poems and sermons have a realistic tone showing how man's soul faces the constant tension between the enticements of the temporal world and the allurements of the divine love. The following excerpts on death portray the soul of man in spiritual struggle. They are selections from various sermons assembled by Logan Pearsall Smith in *Donne's Sermons: Selected Passages* (Oxford, 1919) and are reprinted by permission of The Clarendon Press.

Donne's reputation almost disappeared in the eighteenth century, but is now established again.

[THOUGHTS ON DEATH]

THE GATE OF DEATH

As he that travails weary, and late towards a great City, is glad when he comes to a place of execution, becaus he knows that is neer the town; so when thou comest to the gate of death, glad cf that, for it is but one step from that to thy *Jerusalem.* Christ hath brought us in some neerness to Salvation, as he is *vere Salvator mundi,* in that we *know, that this is indeed the Christ, the Saviour of the world*: and he hath brought it neerer than that, as he is *Salvator corporis sui,* in that we know, *That Christ is the head of the Church, and the Saviour of that body*: And neerer than that, as he is *Salvator tuus sanctus,* In that we know, *He is the Lord our God, the holy One of Israel, our Saviour*: But neerest of all, in the *Ecce Salvator tuus venit,* Behold thy Salvation commeth. It is not only promised in the Prophets, nor only writ in the Gospel, nor only seal'd in the Sacraments, nor only prepared in the visitations of the holy Ghost, but *Ecce,* behold it, now, when thou canst behold nothing else:

The sun is setting to thee, and that for ever; thy houses and furnitures, thy gardens and orchards, thy titles and offices, thy wife and children are departing from thee, and that for ever; a cloud of faintnesse is come over thine eyes, and a cloud of sorrow over all theirs; when his hand that loves thee best hangs tremblingly over thee to close thine eyes, *Ecce Salvator tuus venit,* behold then a new light, thy Saviours hand shall open thine eyes, and in his light thou shalt see light; and thus shalt see, that though in the eyes of men thou lye upon that bed, as a Statue on a Tomb, yet in the eyes of God, thou standest as a *Colossus,* one foot in one, another in another land; one foot in the grave, but the other in heaven; one hand in the womb of the earth, and the other in *Abrahams* bosome: And then *vere prope,* Salvation is truly neer thee, and neerer than when thou believedst, which is our last word.

OUR PRISON

We are all conceived in close Prison; in our Mothers wombes, we are close Prisoners all; when we are borne, we are borne but to the liberty of the house; Prisoners still, though within larger walls; and then all our life is but a going out to the place of Execution, to death. Now was there ever any man seen to sleep in the Cart, between New-gate, and Ty-borne? between the Prison, and the place of Execution, does any man sleep? And we sleep all the way; from the womb to the grave we are never thoroughly awake; but passe on with such dreames, and imaginations as these, I may live as well, as another, and why should I dye, rather then another? but awake, and tell me, sayes this Text, *Quis homo?* who is that other that thou talkest of? *What man is he that liveth, and shall not see death?*

ALL MUST DIE

Doth not man die even in his birth? The breaking of prison is death, and what is our birth, but a breaking of prison? Assoon as we were clothed by God, our very apparrell was an Embleme of death. In the skins of dead beasts, he covered the skins of dying men. Assoon as God set us on work, our very occupation was an Embleme of death; It was to digge the earth; not to digge pitfals for other men, but graves for our selves. Hath any man here forgot to day, that yesterday is dead? And the Bell tolls for to day, and will ring out anon; and for as much of every one of us, as appertaines to this day. *Quotidiè morimur, & tamen nos esse æternos putamus,* sayes S. *Hierome;* We die every day, and we die all the day long; and because we are not absolutely dead, we call that an eternity, an eternity of dying: And is there comfort in that state? why, that is the state of hell it self, Eternall dying, and not dead.

But for this there is enough said, by the Morall man; (that we may respite divine proofes, for divine points anon, for our severall Resurrections) for this death is meerly naturall, and it is enough that the morall man sayes, *Mors lex, tributum, officium mortalium.* First it is *lex*, you were born under that law, upon that condition to die: so it is a rebellious thing not to be content to die, it opposes the Law. Then it is *Tributum,* an imposition which nature the Queen of this world layes upon us, and which she will take, when and where she list; here a yong man, there an old man, here a happy, there a miserable man; And so it is a seditious thing not to be content to die, it opposes the prerogative. And lastly, it is *Officium,* men are to have their turnes, to take their time, and then to give way to death to successors; and so it is *Incivile, inofficiosum,* not to be content to die, it opposes the frame and form of government. It comes equally to us all, and makes us all equall when it comes. The ashes of an Oak in the Chimney, are no Epitaph of that Oak, to tell me how high or how large that was; It tels me not what flocks it sheltered while it stood, nor what men it hurt when it fell. The dust of great persons graves is speechlesse too, it sayes nothing, it distinguishes nothing: As soon the dust of a wretch whom thou wouldest not, as of a Prince whom thou couldest not look upon, will trouble thine eyes, if the winde blow it thither; and when a whirle-winde hath blowne the dust of the Church-yard into the Church, and the man sweeps out the dust of the Church into the Church-yard, who will undertake to sift those dusts again, and to pronounce, This is the Patrician, this is the noble flowre, and this the yeomanly, this the Plebeian bran. . . .

Death is the last, and in that respect the worst enemy. In an enemy, that appeares at first, when we are or may be provided against him, there is some of that, which we call Honour: but in the enemie that reserves himselfe unto the last, and attends our weake estate, there is more danger. Keepe it, where I intend it, in that which is my spheare, the Conscience: If mine enemie meet me betimes in my youth, in an object of tentation, (so *Joseph's* enemie met him in *Putifar's* Wife) yet if I doe not adhere to this enemy, dwell upon a delightfull meditation of that sin, if I doe not fuell, and foment that sin, assist and encourage that sin, by high diet, wanton discourse, other provocation, I shall have reason on my side, and I shall have grace on my side, and I shall have the History of a thousand that have perished by that sin, on my side; Even Spittles will give me souldiers to fight for me, by their miserable example against that sin; nay perchance sometimes the verture of that woman, whom I sollicite, will assist me. But when I lye under the hands of that enemie, that hath reserved himselfe to the last, to my last bed, then when I shall be able to stir no limbe in any other measure then a Feaver or a Palsie shall shake them, when everlasting darknesse shall have an inchoation in the present dimnesse of mine eyes, and the everlasting gnashing in the present chattering of my teeth, and the everlasting worme in the present gnawing of the Agonies of my body, and anguishes of my minde, when the last enemie shall watch my remedilesse body, and my disconsolate soule there, there, where not the Physitian, in his way, perchance not the Priest in his, shall be able to give any assistance, And when he hath sported himselfe with my misery upon that stage, my death-bed, shall shift the Scene, and throw me from that bed, into the grave, and there triumph over me, God knowes, how many generations, till the Redeemer, my Redeemer, the Redeemer of all me, body, as well as soule, come againe; As death is *Novissimus hostis*, the enemy which watches me, at my last weaknesse, and shall hold me, when I shall be no more, till that Angel come, *Who shall say, and sweare that time shall be no more*, in that consideration, in that apprehension, he is the powerfullest, the fearefulest enemy: and yet even there this enemy *Abolebitur*, he shall be destroyed.

Death Inevitable

Adam might have liv'd, if he would, but *I cannot*. God hath placed an *Ecce*, a marke of my death, upon every thing living, that I can set mine eye upon; every thing is a remembrancer, every thing is a Judge upon me, and pronounces, I *must* dye. The whole frame of the world is mortall, *Heaven and Earth passe away*: and upon us all, there is an irrecoverable Decree past, *statutum est*, It *is appointed*

to all men, that they shall once dye. But when? quickly; If thou looke up into the aire, *remember that thy life is but a winde*, If thou see a cloud in the aire, aske St. *James* his question, what is your life? and give St. *James* his answer, *It is a vapour that appeareth and vanisheth away*. If thou behold a *Tree*, the *Job* gives thee a comparison of thy selfe; A *Tree* is an *embleme* of thy selfe; nay a Tree is the *originall*, thou art but the *copy*, thou art not so good as it: for, *There is hope of a tree* (as you reade there) *if the roote wax old*, if *the* stock be dead, if it be cut down, yet by *the sent of the waters*, it will *bud*, but *man is sick*, and *dyeth*, and *where is he?* he shall not wake againe, till heaven be no more. Looke upon the *water*, and we are as that, and as that spilt upon the ground: Looke to the *earth*, and we are not like that, but we are earth it self: At our Tables we feed upon the dead, and in the Temple we tread upon the dead: and when we meet in a Church, God hath made many *echoes*, many testimonics of our death, in the walls, and in the windowes, and he onely knowes, whether he will not make another testimony of our mortality, of the youngest amongst us, before we part, and make the very *place of our buriall*, our *deathbed*.

The Expectation of Death

Now the general condemnation, which is upon all mankind, that they must dye, this alone scarce frights any man, scarce averts any man from his purposes. He that should first put to Sea in a tempest, he might easily think, it were in the nature of the Sea to be rough always. He that sees every Church-yard swell with the waves and billows of graves, can think it no extraordinary thing to dye; when he knows he set out in a storm, and he was born into the world upon that condition, to go out of it again.

The Death-Bed

Et in finem, he loved them to the end. It is much that he should love them *in fine*, at their end; that he should look graciously at last; that when their sunne sets, their eyes faint, his sunne of grace should arise, and his East should be brought to their West; that then, in the shadow of death, the Lord of life should quicken and inanimate their hearts; that when their last bell tolls, and calls them to their first and last judgment, which to this purpose is all one; for the passing bell and the Angels trump sound all but one note: *Surgite qui dormitis in pulvere, Arise ye that sleep in the dust,* which is the voice of the Angels; and, *Surgite qui vigilatis in plumis, Arise ye that cannot sleep in feathers,* for the pangs of death, which is the voice of the bell, is in effect but one voice: for God at the generall judgement, shall never reverse any particular judgement, formerly given: that God should then come to thy bed side *Ad sibilandum populum suum,* as the Prophet Ezechiel saith, to hisse softly for his childe, to speak comfortably in his eare, to whisper gently to his departing soul, and to drown and overcome with this soft musick of his all the clangour of the Angels trumpets, all the horrour of the ringing bell, all the cries, and vociferations of a distressed, and distracted, and scattering family; yea all the accusations of his own conscience, and all the triumphant acclamations of the devil himself: that God should love a man thus *in fine,* at his end, and return to him then, though he had suffered him to go astray before, is a great testimonie of an inexpressible love. Butt this love is not *in fine, in the end;* but *in finem, to the end.*

The Death of Ecstasy

Death and life are in the power of the tongue, sayes *Solomon,* in another sense; and in this sense too, If my tongue, suggested by my heart, and by my heart rooted in faith, can say, *Non moriar, non moriar;* If I can say, (and my conscience doe not tell me, that I belye mine owne state) if I can say, That the blood of my Saviour runs in my veines, That the breath of his Spirit quickens all my purposes, that all my deaths have their Resurrection, all my sins their remorses, all my rebellions their reconciliations, I will hearken no more after this question, as it

is intended *de morte naturali,* of a naturall death, I know I must die that death, what care I? nor *de morte spirituali,* the death of sin, I know I doe, and shall die so; why despaire I? but I will finde out another death, *mortem raptus,* a death of rapture, and of extasie, that death which S. *Paul* died more than once, The death which S. *Gregory* speaks of, *Divina contemplatio quoddam sepulchrum animæ,* The contemplation of God, and heaven, is a kinde of buriall, and Sepulchre, and rest of the soule; and in this death of rapture, and extasie, in this death of the Contemplation of my interest in my Saviour, I shall finde my self, and all my sins enterred, and entombed in his wounds, and like a Lily in Paradise, out of red earth, I shall see my soule rise out of his blade, in a candor, and in an innocence, contracted there, acceptable in the sight of his Father.

The Dead with Us

Little know we, how little a way a soule hath to goe to heaven, when it departs from the body; Whether it must passe locally, through Moone, and Sun, and Firmament, (and if all that must be done, all that may be done, in lesse time then I have proposed the doubt in) or whether that soule finde new light in the same roome, and be not carried into any other, but that the glory of heaven be diffused over all, I know not, I dispute not, I inquire not. Without disputing, or inquiring, I know, that when Christ sayes, *That God is not the God of the dead,* he saies that to assure me, that those whom I call dead, are alive. And when the Apostle tels me, *That God is not ashamed to be called the God of the dead,* he tels me that to assure me, That Gods servants lose nothing by dying.

He was but a Heathen that said, If God love a man, *Iuvenis tollitur,* He takes him young out of this world; And they were but Heathens, that observed that custome, To put on mourning when their sons were born, and to feast and triumph when they dyed. But thus much we may learne from these Heathens, That if the dead, and we, be not upon one floore, nor under one story, yet we are under one roofe. We think not a friend lost, because he is gone into another roome, nor because he is gone into another Land; And into another world, no man is gone; for that Heaven, which God created, and this world, is all one world. If I had fixt a Son in Court, or married a daughter into a plentifull Fortune, I were satisfied for that son and that daughter. Shall I not be so, when the King of Heaven hath taken that son to himselfe, and maried himselfe to that daughter, for ever? I spend none of my Faith, I exercise none of my Hope, in this, that I shall have my dead raised to life againe.

This is the faith that sustaines me, when I lose by the death of others, or when I suffer by living in misery my selfe, That the dead, and we, are now all in one Church, and at the resurrection, shall be all in one Quire.

THE SEVENTEENTH CENTURY
THE QUIETISTIC TREND LEAVES ITS
IMPRESS ON THE SAINTS

Augustine Baker
(1575-1641)

BORN of Protestant parents, educated at Oxford, a prosecutor of law in London, Baker embraced Roman Catholicism at the hands of Italian Benedictine fathers when he was thirty-two years of age. In 1619 he was ordained a priest, and appointed chaplain to the family of Philip Fursden in Devonshire. His duties left him much time for study and prayer—frequently he would spend eleven hours a day in devotional exercises. In 1623 he was ordered to assist in training a community of Benedictine nuns at Cambrai. Two of the most noted nuns were Catharine Gascoigne and Gertrude More. During his nine years at Cambrai he drew up a number of ascetic treatises. Fifteen years after Baker's death, Father Serenus Cressy compiled his writings in *Sancta Sophia* (Holy Wisdom). These selections are from Abbot Sweeney's edition (London, 1876) of that spiritual masterpiece.

[RESIGNATION TO THE WILL OF GOD]
From *Holy Wisdom*

ACTS OF GENERAL RESIGNATION

*M*y God, whatsoever I have, whatsoever I can do, all this Thou hast freely bestowed on me. Behold I offer myself and all that belongs to me to Thy heavenly will. Receive, O Lord, my entire will and liberty; possess my understanding, memory, and all my affections; only vouchsafe to bestow upon me Thy love, and I shall be rich enough; nothing more do I desire; Thou alone, O my God, sufficest me.

2. O my God and all my good, I have and do consecrate to Thy love and honour both my body and soul. Conserve them as it shall please Thee, and employ them according to Thine own will in Thy service.

3. My Lord, I here prostrate myself before Thee, to do Thee homage for what I am and may be by Thy grace.

4. My God, I beseech Thee to glorify Thyself by me, according to whatsoever manner Thou shalt please.

5. My God, hereafter I will never search any object of my affections out of Thee, since I see that all good is to be found in Thee.

6. *Ecce Domine, ecce cor meum quod offero Tibi, et quid volo nisi ut sit holocaustum charitatis ad aeternam gloriam Tuam?*

7. O most desireable goodness of my God, let it be to me even as Thou wilt, O eternal, most holy, and well-pleasing will of my Saviour; do Thou reign in and over all my wills and desires from this moment for ever.

8. My God and all my good, for that infinite love of Thine own self, grant that as I live in and by Thee, so may I live only to and for Thee.

9. *Deus meus et omne bonum meum, in voluntate Tua vita est; in mea mors: non mea voluntas fiat, sed Tua Domine in terra sicut in coelo.* Amen. Jesus.

10. O my soul, let us live to Him, and for Him only, that died for us; let us

disengage ourselves from this base world; let us pass from sense to reason, and from reason to grace; let us enter into commerce with the angels, that our conversation may be with Jesus, that so by all manner of ways we may be His, both in life and death, in time and eternity.

11. O my soul, let us freely submit ourselves to our Lord's judgments, renouncing our own judgment; let us adore them, though we be ignorant of them. Let us most assuredly believe that He doth nothing but for our greater good. Whatsoever befalls us, let us take it willingly and thankfully from His hands, which are always full of blessings for us.

12. Let Jesus only live and reign in my heart, and let the world and all its vain desires perish.

FORMS OF PARTICULAR ACTS OF RESIGNATION

1. *About External Goods*

For the love of God, and in conformity to His will, I resign myself: 1. To be deprived of any of the clothes that I have, or may have, though never so necessary; 2. or of books; 3. or of convenient lodgings; 4. and to have those things bestowed on me from which my nature is most averted. 5. To be driven to wear clothes that seem base, unfit, or inconvenient for the season. 6. To be ill accommodated in lodging, bedding, &c. 7. To want even necessary clothes. 8. To be forced to wear such clothes as will make me appear ridiculous. 9. To want meat or drink; 10. or to have only such as is ungrateful to nature. 11. To endure crosses that in any sort, spiritually or corporally, may fall on my friends or kindred, as loss of state, infirmity, death, &c.; 12. and, on the other side, to restrain all inordinate complacency in their prosperity. 13. To endure that my friends should neglect, forget, yea, hate and persecute me. 14. To be abandoned of all creatures, so that I may have no man or thing to cleave unto, save only Thee my God, who wilt abundantly suffice me. 15. To be indifferent in what place, company, &c., I shall live; 16. yea, to live with those from whom my nature is most averted. 17. To

live in all sorts of afflictions, as long as shall please Thee my God; 18. and not to yield to the motion of nature, which perhaps out of wearisomeness would fain have life at an end. But wholly to conform my will to Thy good will and pleasure; 19. yea, to take pleasure that Thy will may be fulfilled in me any way.

2. *Acts of Resignation about our Good Name*

For the love of Thee my God, and in conformity to Thy will, I resign myself: 1. To suffer all manner of disgraces, contempts, affronts, infamies, slanders &c., be they done to my face or behind my back; 2. though I have given no cause or provocations; 3. yea, after I have done the greatest kindnesses to my defamers; 4. if I have deserved them by my fault I am sorry for it and beg pardon, but am glad of this good effect of it, that it is an occasion of procuring this mortification and humiliation. 5. To suffer injuries either from superiors, equals, or inferiors. 6. To be in life or manner of my death shameful and odious to others; 7. and after death to be evil thought and evil spoken of by others; 8. yea, not to have any that will vouchsafe to pray for me; 9. yea, to be esteemed to have died in the state of eternal damnation; 10. yea, moreover, to have it expressed so to the world in a chronicle, to the shame of all that have relation to me; 11. in this life to be held for the scum of mankind, forsaken by all both in their doings and affections. 12. To be mortally persecuted by professed enemies (though I will account none such); 13. yea, by such as have had great proofs of my charity to them; 14. in sickness and other necessities to be driven to be chargeable and troublesome to others; 15. whereas I in the meantime am profitable to none at all; 16. so that all men do grow weary of me, and long to be rid of me; 17. and in this case to remain several years, yea, all my life long; 18. dying a natural death (so it be in Thy grace), to be esteemed by others to have destroyed myself; 19. and thereupon to have my body ignominiously used, buried in the highway or under the gallows, to the eternal loss of my fame and unspeakable confusion of my kindred, friends, &c.

3. Acts of Resignation about the Body

For the love of Thee, O my God, and in conformity to Thy will, I resign myself: 1. to suffer weaknesses, sickness; 2. pains; 3. deformity; 4. horror in the sight of others, as was the case of Job and Lazarus. 5. To suffer extremity of heat or cold; 6. want of necessary sleep, and hunger or thirst; 7. indigestion; 8. torments and defects about my five senses. 9. To be affrighted with horrible and hideous sights of devils, &c. 10. To be afflicted with fearful noises. 11. To suffer scourgings, beatings, &c. 12. To be spit upon, as Thou my Saviour wast. 13. To suffer incisions, torments, &c., external and internal. 14. To suffer loss of eyes, hearing, &c.; to be overtoiled with all sorts of labours; 15. and this being in feebleness of body. 16. To lose all pleasure and gust in meats and drinks. 17. To suffer any disfiguring in my face, or distortions in other parts of my body. 18. To suffer the loss of any of my members. 19. To receive harm in my imagination, and thereby to lose my perfect judgment, so as to become a fool or mad. 20. That my body should by little and little putrefy and rot away. 21. To die suddenly, or after long sickness and tokens of death. 22. To die without senses or memory, and distracted or mad. 23. To endure the agony of death, and the long torments that do accompany it. 24. To suffer the unwillingness and terror that nature feels in the separation of the soul from the body. 25. To die a natural death, or else a violent and painful one, procured by others. 26. To die at what time, in what place and manner it shall please Thee my God. 27. To die without the help of any of the Sacraments, being not able to come by them. 28. In the agony of death to endure such terror, afflictions, and temptations as the devil doth then usually procure. 29. Being dead, to want not only all decent or honourable, but even Christian burial, so as that my body may be made a prey to beasts and fowls.

4. Particular Acts of Resignation about the Soul

For the love of God, and in conformity to His will, I do resign myself: 1. To undergo all sorts of temptations that shall please Thee my God to lay on me or permit to befall me; 2. and to suffer them to the end of my life, ever adhering to Thee. 3. To endure all manner of desolations, aridities, and indevotions. 4. To suffer all obscurity and darkness in my understanding; all coldness and dulness of affection in my will to Thee, so far as I am not able to help it; 5. in all which I renounce the seeking any solace in creatures. 6. To want all manner of gifts and graces not necessary to my salvation; 7. nor to desire inordinately nor rest with affection in supernatural contemplations, sweetnesses, or other extraordinary visits or favours. 8. To resign myself to all things, be they never so contrary to sensuality. 9. To bear with the repugnance that I find in sensuality, till with Thy grace (sooner, or later, or never) it may be brought to perfect subjection to my spirit; in the meantime suffering patiently the difficulty that is in fighting against it, or resisting the desires of it. 10. To endure all the difficulties, tediousnesses, and expectations that are in a spiritual life; also such various changes, chances, and perplexities as are in it; notwithstanding all which my purpose is (through Thy grace) to persevere and go through them all. 11. To bear with my own defectuousness, frailty, and proneness to sin; yet using my best industry, and bearing with what I cannot amend. 12. To die before I can reach to perfection. 13. To live and die in that degree of a spiritual life as shall seem good to Thee, and not according to my own will; 14. yet ever desiring and endeavouring that I may not be wanting in cooperating with Thy calls and graces. 15. To be contented to serve Thee according to that manner Thou hast provided and appointed; that is, with regard to my natural talents, complexion, &c., as likewise such supernatural helps and graces as Thou shalt afford me, and not according to the talents and gifts bestowed on others. 16.

To be contented that Thou has bestowed greater gifts on other men than on me. 17. To understand and know no more nor no otherwise than Thy will is, and to remain ignorant in what Thou wilt have me be ignorant of. 18. To give up and offer to Thee my God whatsoever honour and contentment may come by such knowledge; for all is Thine. 19. To want all knowledges but such as are necessary to my salvation. 20. To follow Thee by all the ways whatsoever that Thou shalt call me, externally or internally, though I cannot understand how they can lead to a good issue; so walking, as it were, blindfold. 21. To be contented that others excel me in virtues, and that they be better esteemed; yet ever desiring that I may not be wanting in my industries. 22. To be content not to know in what case I am as to my soul; nor in what degree of perfection, nor whether I go backward or forward; 23. nor to know whether I be in the state of grace; only beseeching Thee that I be industrious to please Thee. 24. To be content that another should receive the fruit of all my endeavours and actions, though never so perfect, so purely do I desire to serve Thee. 25. To endure with patience all manner of injuries; 26. and yet to be esteemed by others that I endure them against my will, without humility, with murmuring, revengefulness, and pride, and that the fear of danger or discredit only hinders me from executing such revenge. 27. To serve Thee purely for Thine own sake, so as that I would serve Thee though there had been no reward or punishment. 28. To suffer the pains of Purgatory, though never so bitter, that Thou shalt ordain; 29. and this for as long a time as Thou shalt please. 30. To do and suffer in this life both in soul and body what, and in what manner, and for how long as it shall please Thee my God. 31. To be content to enjoy the lowest place in heaven; 32. and this, although Thou shouldst enable me to merit as much as any or all Thy Saints in heaven have done.

OTHER MIXED RESIGNATIONS

1. *O, how good art Thou, O my God, to those that trust in Thee, to the soul that truly seeks Thee! What art Thou, then, to those that find Thee!*

1. Whatsoever I shall suffer, O my God, by Thy ordinance, either in body or soul, and how long soever I shall suffer, I renounce all consolation but what comes from Thee.

2. My God, though Thou shouldst always hide Thy face from me, and never afford me any consolation, yet will I never cease to love, praise, and pray unto Thee.

3. For Thy sake I renounce all pleasure in eating and drinking, being resolved to make use of Thy creatures only in obedience to Thy will, and to the end thereby to be enabled to serve Thee.

4. I resign myself to abide all my lifetime among strangers; yea, or among such as have an aversion towards me, and which will never cease to molest me.

5. My God, casting myself wholly on Thy Fatherly providence, I renounce all care and solicitude for tomorrow concerning anything belonging to this life.

6. I offer unto Thee, O my God, this desire and resolution of my heart, that notwithstanding my continual indevotion, my infinite distractions and defects, &c., I will never give over the exercises of any internal life.

7. My desire is always to be in the lowest place, beneath all creatures, according to my demerit.

8. For Thy love, O my God, I renounce all inordinate affections to my particular friends or kindred.

9. I resign myself to suffer any lameness or distortedness in any of my members.

10. I resign myself to abide all my life among those that are enemies to Thy Catholic Church, and there to be in continual fears, dangers, and persecutions.

2. *Draw me, O God, we will run after Thee, because of the odour of Thy precious ointments.*

1. For Thy love, O my God, I resign myself to want necessary clothing, or

to be deprived of those which I have.

2. I resign myself patiently to bear with the repugnance I find in my corrupt nature, and the difficulty in resisting the unruly passions of it. Yes, through Thy grace, my purpose is to use my best industry and vigilance against it.

3. For Thy love I renounce the seeking after all curious impertinent knowledge.

4. I renounce all sensual contentment in sleep or other corporal refreshments, being desirous to admit no more of them than shall be necessary, and in obedience to Thy will.

5. My God, through Thy grace, neither hard usage from others, nor any mere outward corporal extremity or want, shall force me to seek a change of my present condition.

6. My God, I do consecrate myself to Thee alone, for the whole remnant of my life to pursue the exercises of an internal life, leaving the fruit and success of my endeavors to Thy holy will.

7. For Thy love, and in conformity to Thy blessed will, I resign myself to be abandoned of all creatures, so as to have none to have recourse unto but Thee only.

8. I offer myself unto Thee, with patience to suffer whatsoever Thou shalt inflict on me, and never to yield to the inclination and feebleness of nature, which perhaps out of wearisomeness would have life at an end. ·

9. When obedience or charity shall require it, I resign myself to go and abide in a place haunted with evil spirits, being assured that as long as I adhere to Thee they cannot hurt my soul.

10. I renounce rashness, readiness, and forwardness to judge the actions of others, employing all my severity in censuring against myself only.

3. *My God and all my good, in Thy heavenly will is life; but death is mine. Not my will, therefore, but Thine be done in earth as it is in heaven.*

1. For Thy love, O my God, I do resign myself to be deprived of all the gifts and privileges which in my nature

I do most affect, and to see them conferred on the person for whom I have the greatest aversion.

2. I resign myself not only to want the esteem or favour of my superiors, but also to be despised, and hardly, yea, injuriously treated by them.

3. When through my own demerit I do deserve such ill usage from them, I will be sorry and humbled for my fault, and bless Thee for punishing it so easily in this life.

4. O tepidity, I do detest thee.

5. I do resign myself, and am even desirous to find such usage in this world, that I may know and feel it to be only a place of exile.

6. My God, whatsoever affliction or desertion Thou shalt suffer to befall me, through Thy grace I will neither omit, neglect, nor shorten my daily appointed recollections.

7. I offer myself to Thee, O my God, entirely to be disposed of by Thee, both for life and death. Only let me love Thee, and that is sufficient for me.

8. Whatsoever natural or other defectuousness shall be in me, either for mind or body, by which I may incur disesteem from others, I do willingly embrace such occasions of humiliation.

9. I renounce all forwardness to give counsel to others, being much rather desirous to receive it from any other.

10. I do utterly renounce all familiarity and all unnecessary conversation or correspondence with persons of a different sex.

4. *My Lord Jesus, Thou who art Truth hast said, My yoke is easy and My burden light.*

1. I have received from Thy hands a cross of religious penitential discipline; through Thy grace I will continue to bear it till my death, never forsaking any ways to ease it by external employments, or to escape from it, and shake it off by missions, &c.

2. For Thy love, O my God, and in conformity to Thy will, I resign myself to die when, where, and in what manner Thou shalt ordain.

3. I am content to see others make a

great progress in spirit, and to do more good in Thy Church than myself.

4. I renounce all satisfaction and false peace which is got by yielding to my inordinate passions, and not by resisting and mortifying them.

5. My God, till Thou hast humbled that great pride which is in me, do not spare to send me daily yet more and greater humiliations and mortifications.

6. I offer myself unto Thee, to suffer with patience and quietness whatsoever desolations, obscurity of mind, or deadness of affections that shall befall in a spiritual course; notwithstanding all which, through Thy grace, I will never neglect a serious tendency to Thee.

7. I am content to serve Thee with those mean talents that Thou has given me.

8. I yield myself to endure all manner of injuries and contempts, and yet to be esteemed by others to be impatient and revengeful.

9. I do renounce all solicitude to please others, or to gain the affections of any one to myself.

10. I do resign myself to such painful and withal base offices as my proud and slothful nature doth abhor, whensoever obedience, charity, or Thy will shall impose them on me.

5. *My God, Thou art faithful, and will not suffer us to be tempted above that we are able; but wilt with the temptation give an issue that we may be able to bear it.*

1. My God, my desire is to serve Thee gratis, like a son, and not as a mercenary.

2. I came into religion to suffer and to serve; I renounce, therefore, all desires of procuring ease, plenty, or superiority.

3. In love of Thee, O my God, I resign myself to follow Thee, by whatsoever ways, external or internal, that Thou shalt conduct me, although I be not able to understand them, nor can see how there can be any good issues of them.

4. I am content to see all become weary and desirous to be rid of me.

5. I am resigned to want whatsoever

gift and graces are not necessary to my salvation.

6. In love to Thee, O my God, and in submission to Thy will, I do renounce all inordinate love and correspondence with the world, that I may attend to Thee only.

7. I resign myself to become a spectacle horrible and loathsome to men's eyes, as was Job or Lazarus.

8. I do adore and most humbly submit myself to Thy most wise and secret judgments concerning my death or future state.

9. I resign myself to suffer those most bitter pains of the stone, gout, colic, &c., if Thou shalt ordain them to fall on me.

10. I renounce all obstinacy in defending mine own opinions, and all desire of victory in discourse.

6. *My God, who is like unto Thee, who hast Thy dwelling most high, yet humblest Thyself to regard the things which are [done] in heaven and earth!*

1. I resign myself to abide in this place and in this present state of life wherein Thou hast put me; neither will I seek or ever procure a change for any outward sufferings till Thou shalt appoint.

2. Let all creatures scorn, abandon, and persecute me, so that Thou, O my God, wilt accompany and assist me; Thou alone sufficest me.

3. Through Thy grace I will never cease to approach nearer and nearer to Thee by prayer and abstraction from creatures.

4. I do resign myself, whensoever necessity, obedience, or charity shall require it, to visit and assist any one lying sick, though of the plague, or any other infectious or horrible disease.

5. I am contented that those who are nearest to me in blood or friendship should be so averted from me as to abhor my name.

6. I resign myself to die a natural or violent death, and as soon as it shall please Thee.

7. I offer unto Thee this desire and purpose of my heart, that I will esteem

no employment to be necessary but the aspiring to a perfect union with Thee, and that I will not undertake any other business but in order to this.

8. I do heartily renounce all affection to all, even venial imperfections and occasions of them.

9. I renounce all propriety in any dignity or office that I have or may have hereafter.

10. I desire to have no more to do with the world than if I were already dead and buried.

7. *My God, it is my only good to adhere unto Thee, who art the God of my heart and portion for ever.*

1. I offer myself unto Thee to be afflicted with whatsoever temptation, external or internal, Thou shalt permit to befall me; and though I should fall never so oft, yet will I not yield to dejection of mind or despair, but will rise up as soon as by Thy grace I shall be enabled.

2. I resign myself to follow Thee, O my Lord Jesus, in the same poverty of which Thou hast given me an example, renouncing all propriety in anything, and being contented and pleased to enjoy only what shall be necessary in all kinds.

3. I resign myself not only to be disfavoured by my superiors, but also to see those most favoured that are most averted from me.

4. My God, although Thou shouldst kill me, yet will I never cease to hope and trust in Thee.

5. I am content not to learn or know any more than Thou wouldst have me to know.

6. I do offer myself to all manner of contradictions and injuries to be sustained from my superiors or brethren, in patience, silence, and without complaining.

7. I renounce all impatience and unquietness for my many defects and hourly imperfections.

8. I do offer unto Thee my desire and resolution never to relinquish an internal spiritual course, notwithstanding any difficulties whatsoever that shall occur in it.

9. My God, I do not desire a removal of all temptations, which show me: how impossible it is to enjoy a perfect peace in this life; and how necessary unto me Thy grace and assistance is. I embrace the pain of them. Only let me not offend Thee by yielding to them.

10. For Thy love I resign myself to be deprived of all proper and certain habitation.

8. *Holy, Holy, Holy, Lord God of Sabaoth! All the earth is full of Thy glory. Glory be to Thee most High.*

1. For Thy love, O my God, and in conformity to Thy holy will, I resign myself unto Thee, with all that I am, have, can do, or suffer, in soul, body, goods, fame, friends, &c., both for time and eternity.

2. For Thy love I do renounce all desire of authority, especially all charge over the souls of others.

3. I am content not to learn or know more than Thou wouldst have me know.

4. I resign myself, whensoever Thou shalt call me to it, to sacrifice my life, in what manner soever Thou shalt ordain, for the defence of Thy Catholic truth, trusting in Thy merciful promise that Thou wilt assist me in such trials.

5. My God, I am content to be blotted out of the memory of all (except those that would afflict me).

6. My God, let me be the universal object of the contempt and hatred of all creatures, so that I may love Thee and enjoy Thy presence and grace.

7. Jesus, who art the Prince of peace, and whose habitation is in peace, I offer my heart unto Thee, that Thou mayest establish a firm peace in it, calming the tempestuous passions that so oft rage in it.

8. I renounce all affection to speaking.

9. I resign myself in sickness to be burdensome and chargeable to others, so as that all should become weary and desirous to be rid of me.

10. I renounce all facility in hearkening to or believing any ill that is reported concerning others, and much more to be a disperser of such report.

9. *I adore Thee, O my God, the blessed and only Potentate, King of kings and Lord of lords, who dwellest in unapproachable light: to Thee be glory and eternal dominion. Amen.*

1. I resign and offer myself unto Thee, to follow the conduct of Thy Holy Spirit in an internal life, through bitter and sweet, light and darkness, in life and death.

2. I do renounce all solicitous designs to gain the affections of superiors or of any others, with any intention thereby to procure ease or contentment to nature.

3. I do renounce all propriety in any endowments that Thou hast or shalt give me.

4. I am contented with whatsoever Thou shalt provide for my sustenance, how mean, how little, and how disgustful soever it be.

5. I resign myself in the agony of death to endure whatsoever pains, frights, or temptations Thou shalt permit to befall me, only let my spirit always adhere to Thee.

6. My God, I do here again renew and ratify my vows of religious profession, consecrating myself and all that I have or can do to Thy glory and service only.

7. I resolve, through Thy grace, that my great and daily defects shall not destroy my peace of mind nor confidence in Thy goodness.

8. I resign myself, for the humiliation and good of my soul, to be deprived of my endowments and gifts that may any way make me be esteemed by others.

9. I resign myself in sickness to want the assistance and comfort of friends, yea, even the use of Sacraments.

10. I resign myself (yea, would be glad) to lose all sensual pleasure in meats and drinks, if such were Thy will.

10. *Blessed is the man whose hope is only in the name of Thee my God, and that regardeth not vanities and deceitful frenzies.*

1. Though Thou shouldst always hide Thy face from me, yea, my God, although Thou shouldst kill me, yet will I never cease to approach to Thee, and to put my whole trust in Thee only.

2. I consecrate my whole life to Thee, to be spent in a continual tendency in soul to Thee; not presuming to expect any elevated contemplations or extraordinary graces, but referring to Thy holy pleasure whether I shall ever be raised above my present mean exercises.

3. I resign myself to be esteemed fit and capable only of the basest and most toilsome offices; the which if they shall be imposed upon me, I will not avoid them.

4. I resign myself to be guided only by Thee and Thy holy inspirations.

5. I resign myself to be continually tormented, and to have my sleeps broken with any kind of troublesome noises or frights, &c.

6. My God, I resign myself to Thee alone, to live and die in that state and degree of a spiritual life to which it shall seem good to Thee to bring me; only I beseech Thee, that I may not be negligent in coöperating with Thy grace and holy inspirations.

7. I resign myself to suffer the straits and tediousness of a prison, and there to be deprived of books, or any thing that may divert my mind.

8. I resign myself to suffer the extremity of heat and cold, and to want the comfort of all refreshments against heat, and of necessary clothes against cold.

9. I resign myself to be obliged to take meats and drinks loathsome to my nature.

10. I resign myself to see others, my inferiors, provided of all things, and myself only neglected.

11. *Our Lord is my light and salvation: whom then, should I fear?*

1. There is not any spiritual exercise so displeasing or painful to my nature which I would not embrace, if I knew or did believe Thy will to be such.

2. My God, so I may die in Thy grace and holy love, I resign myself to the infamy of being reputed to have procured my own death; and that therefore my

body should be ignominiously cast out, and none to have the charity to pray for my soul.

3. I resign myself to be affrighted with horrible noises, hideous apparitions, &c.

4. Through Thy grace, my God, I will not rest with affection in any of Thy gifts how sublime soever; but will only make use of them to pass by their means in to Thee, who art my only increated, universal, and infinite good.

5. I esteem this life to be a mere prison or place of exile.

6. My God, I offer my soul unto Thee, that Thou mayest establish a firm peace in it, not to be interrupted as now it is by every contradiction and cross.

7. I resign myself to have my superiors, and all others whom my nature would wish to be most friendly, to be in all things a continual contradiction and cross to me.

8. For Thy love I would be content rather to have no use of my tongue at all, than thus continually to offend Thee with it.

9. Let all creatures be silent before Thee, and do Thou, O my God, alone speak unto me; in Thee alone is all that I desire to know or love.

10. My God, I know that to fly Thy cross is to fly Thee that diedst on it; welcome, therefore, be (these) Thy crosses and trials.

12. *My God, with Thee is the fountain of life, and in Thy light we shall see light.*

1. My God, to Thee only do I consecrate the remainder of my life, purposing to account no business to be necessary, but only tendency to Thee by prayer and abnegation.

2. I resign myself, if such be Thy pleasure, even to be deprived of all use of these eyes, that are still so much delighted with vanity, curiosity, and all distracting objects.

3. O that I were nothing, that so Thou, my God, mayest be all in all!

4. I resign myself to be deprived of all certain habitation, and to live a vaga-

bond in the world, so that none should take care of me or own me.

5. My God, my desire is to serve Thee in a state wherein I may be deprived of all propriety and election in all things, as well internal as external: do Thou, my Lord, choose for me.

6. In conformity to Thy heavenly will, O my God, I do accept the pain and trouble that I feel from my continual indevotion, my unruly passions, and (almost) unremediable imperfections; and I will with patience expect Thy good time, when I shall be enabled with Thy grace to rectify them.

7. For Thy love I renounce all conversations and correspondences, which I do find to be occasions to me of falling into defects, by nourishing inordinate affection or unquietness.

8. I renounce the folly of being disquieted with seeing that others are not such as I would have them to be, since I cannot make myself such an one as I fain would.

9. I offer myself to become a fool unto all for Thee, my God.

10. So that thereby my pride may be humbled, I even beg of Thee, my God, that Thou wouldst not spare to send me crosses and contradictions.

13. *I know, my God, that Thou art the God that triest hearts and lovest simplicity, therefore in the simplicity of my heart I offer myself unto Thee.*

1. O my God, when will the time come that Thou wilt lead my soul into Thy solitude?

2. For Thy love I renounce all complacency in any kind of endowment or skill in any arts (as far as any of these are in me), consecrating all that by Thy free gift is in me to Thy glory and service only.

3. I do utterly renounce all familiarity and unnecessary conversations or correspondences with persons of a different sex.

4. My God, it is Thou that hast placed me in this present condition; and Thou only shalt displace me.

5. O tepidity, I abhor thee. My God,

teach me an effectual cure and remedy against it; let not my latter end be worse than my beginning.

6. My God, I offer unto Thee my heart, that whatsoever yet unknown inordinate desires are in it, Thou mayest teach me to mortify them by any ways Thou shalt please.

7. I resign myself, in case that obedience shall unavoidably oblige me thereto, to undertake that most fearful employment of the charge of souls (in the mission, &c.).

8. For Thy love and for the mortification of sensuality, I could content to be freed from all necessity of eating and drinking, if such were Thy pleasure.

9. I offer unto Thee, my God, this desire of my heart, that at last, this day, I may begin perfectly to serve Thee, having spent so much time unprofitably.

10. Feed me, O Lord, with the bread of tears, and give me drink in tears, according to the measure that Thou shalt think fit.

14. *My Lord and my God, from Thee are all things, by Thee are all things, to Thee are all things: to Thee only be glory, love, and obedience for ever.*

1. My God, if Thou wilt that I be in light, be Thou blessed for it; and if Thou wilt that I be in darkness, still be Thou blessed for it. Let both light and darkness, life and death, praise Thee.

2. Blessed be Thy holy name that my heart doth not (and never may it) find rest or peace in anything that I seek or love inordinately, whilst I do not love it in Thee and for Thee only.

3. I offer unto Thee this resolution of mine, that by all lawful and fitting ways I will endeavour to avoid any office of authority.

4. I resign myself to live and abide in any state or place where I shall daily have my health or life endangered.

5. I resign myself to suffer in Purgatory whatsoever pains, and as for as long a time, as shall seem good to Thee.

6. Through Thy grace and assistance, O my God, no hard usage from others, nor any desire of finding any ease or contentment to my nature, shall force me to change my present condition.

7. My God, if Thou shalt so ordain or permit, I resign my body to be possessed or tormented by evil spirits, so that my spirit may always adhere by love to Thee.

8. I resign myself to take part in any calamity, disgrace, &c., that Thy Divine Providence shall permit to befall the country or community in which I live.

9. I renounce all resting affection to sensible gusts in my recollections, resolving to adhere firmly to Thee, as well in aridities as consolations.

10. My God, I am nothing, I have nothing, I desire nothing, but Jesus, and to see Him in peace in Jerusalem.

15. *Blessed art Thou, O my God, in all Thy gifts, and holy in all Thy ways.*

1. I offer unto Thee the desire and resolution of my heart, that no employment which cannot without sin be avoided, nor much less any complacency in conversation with others, nor any unwillingness to break off conversation through impertinent civility, shall cause me to omit or shorten my daily appointed recollections.

2. Far be it from me that my peace should depend on the favour or affection of any creature, and not in subjection to Thy will only.

3. I renounce all knowledge that may hinder or distract me from the knowledge of my own defects and nothingness.

4. My God, I have neither devotion nor attention, and indeed do not deserve either; only I beseech Thee that Thou wilt accept of my sufferings.

5. My God, so that I may die in Thy holy fear and love, I resign myself to want all comforts and assistance from others, both in death and after it, if such be Thy will.

6. My God, through Thy grace I will never voluntarily undertake any employment or study, but such as shall serve to advance my principal and most necessary business of seeking Thee by prayer, to which all other designs shall give way.

7. My God, I beseech Thee not only to forgive, but to crown with some spe-

cial blessing all those that despise, depress, or persecute me, as being good instruments of Thy grace to abate pride and self-love in me.

8. Whatsoever dignity or privilege I enjoy, I am content to relinquish it whensoever it shall be Thy will; and if I were wrongfully deprived of it, I will not for the recovering endanger the loss of mine own peace or that of others.

9. I resign myself not only to suffer for mine own faults, but also the faults of my brethren.

10. My God, my desire is to live to Thee only. Place me, therefore, where Thou wilt; give me or take from me what Thou wilt. Only let me live to Thee and with Thee; that suffices me.

Gertrude More

(1606-1633)

GERTRUDE MORE's father was a great-grandson of Sir Thomas More. When she was nineteen, she took the vows of a Benedictine nun at Cambrai. After much struggle with the spiritual life she found the effective use of prayer through the guidance of Augustine Baker. She died suddenly of smallpox, and after her death Baker found some of her letters and edited them. Gertrude More transmits the mystical communion of love which flows from Augustine through Bernard and Thomas à Kempis. It is the core of Roman Catholic mysticism. The following brief passage beautifully expresses this "communion of love." It is reprinted from *The Soul Afire* by H. A. Reinhold, by permission of the publisher, Pantheon Books.

BE THOU MY CHOOSER FOR ME

O my God, let me walk in the way of love which knoweth not how to seek self in anything whatsoever. Let this love wholly possess my soul and heart, which I beseech Thee, may live and move only in, and out of, a pure and sincere love to Thee. Oh! that thy pure love were so grounded and established in my heart that I might sigh and pant without ceasing after Thee, and be able in strength of this Thy love to live without all comfort and consolation, human or divine. O sight to be wished, desired, and longed for, because once to have seen Thee is to have learned all things! Nothing can bring us to this sight but love. But what love must it be? Not a sensible love only, a childish love, a love which seeketh itself more than the Beloved. No, it must be an ardent love, a pure love, a courageous love, a love of charity, a humble love, and a constant love, not worn out with labours, nor daunted with any difficulties. O Lord, give this love into my soul, that I may never more live nor breathe but out of a most pure love of Thee, my All and only Good. Let me love Thee for Thyself, and nothing else but in and for Thee. Let me love nothing instead of Thee, for to give all for love is a most sweet bargain. . . . Let Thy love work in me and by men, and let me love Thee as Thou wouldst be loved by me. I cannot tell how much love I would have of Thee, because I would love Thee beyond all that can be imagined or desired by me. Be Thou in this, as in all other things, my chooser for me, for Thou art my only choice, most dear to me. The more I shall love Thee, the more will my soul desire Thee, and desire to suffer for Thee.

Joseph Hall
(1574-1656)

HALL, contemporary of the Cambridge Platonists, taught a philosophy touched with a Greek mystical tone. Hall's sermons as bishop of Exeter and later Norwich rank him among the most forceful of English preachers. He also achieved fame as a satirist, being called the "English Seneca." *Meditations and Vows* shows both spiritual depth and unusual common sense. Its popularity is evidenced by the large number of editions through which it has passed. The selected paragraphs reprinted here are from an edition by Charles Sayle.

[THE GOOD AND THE EVIL MAN]
From *Meditations and Vows*

In Meditation, those which begin Heavenly thoughts, and prosecute them not, are like those which kindle a fire vnder greene Wood, and leaue it so soone as it but begins to flame; leesing the hope of a good beginning; for want of seconding it with a sutable proceeding: When I set my selfe to meditate, I will not giue ouer, till I come to an Issue. It hath beene said by some, that the beginning is as much as the midst; yea, more then all: but I say, the ending is more then the beginning.

Expectation, in a weake mind, makes an euill, greater; and a good, lesse: but in a resolued minde, it digests an euill, before it come; and makes a future good, long before present. I will expect the worst, because it may come; the best, because I know it will come.

An ambitious man is the greatest Enemy to himselfe of any in the World besides. For he still torments himselfe with Hopes and Desires, and Cares: which hee might auoid, if hee would remit of the height of his thoughts, and liue quietly. My onely ambition shall be, to rest in Gods fauour on Earth, and to be a Saint in Heauen.

If I die, the World shall misse me but a little: I shall misse it lesse. Not it me; because it hath such store of better men: Not I it because it hath so much ill, and I shall haue so much happinesse.

Every man hath an Heauen, and an Hell: Earth is the wicked mans Heauen; his Hell is to come: on the contrarie, the godly haue their Hell vpon Earth; where they are vexed with Tentations, and Afflictions, by Satan and his Complices; their Heauen is aboue in endlesse happinesse: If it be ill with me on Earth, it is well my Torment is so short, and so easie; I will not be so couetous to hope for two Heauens.

Pride is the most dangerous of all sinnes: For, both it is most insinuatiue (hauing crept into Heauen, and Paradise) and most dangerous where it is. For, where all other Tentations are about euill, this alone is conuersant onely about good things; and one dram of it poysons many measures of grace. I will not be more afraid of doing good things amisse, then of being proud, when I haue well performed them.

When the Mouth prayeth, Man heareth; when the Heart, God heareth. Euery good Prayer knocketh at Heauen, for a Blessing; but an importunate Prayer pierceth it (though as hard as Brasse) and makes way for it selfe into the Eares of the Almightie. And as it ascends lightly vp, carried with the wings of Faith; so it comes euer laden downe againe, vpon our heads. In my Prayers, my Thoughts shall not bee guided by my Words; but my Words shall follow my Thoughts.

An euill Man is Clay to God: Waxe to the Deuill: God may stampe him into powder, or temper him anew; but none of his meanes can melt him. Contrariwise, a good Man is Gods Waxe, and Satans Clay: hee relents at euery Looke of God, but it is not stirred at any Temptation. I had rather bow then break, to God: but for Satan, or the World, I had rather be broken in pieces with their violence, than suffer my selfe to be bowed vnto their Obedience.

I find that all worldly things require a long labour in getting, and afford a short pleasure, in enjoying them. I will not care much, for what I haue; nothing, for what I haue not.

The eldest of our forefathers liued not so much as a day to God; to whom a thousand yeeres is as no more; wee liue but as an houre to the day of our forefathers; for if none hundreth and sixtie were but their day, fourescore is but as the twelfth part of it: and yet of this our houre wee liue scarce a minute to God: For, take away all that time that is consumed in sleeping, dressing, feeding, talking, sporting; of that little time there can remaine not much more than nothing: yet the most seeke pastimes to hasten it.

Those which seek to mend the pase of Time, spurre a running horse. I had more need to redeeme it with double care and labour, than to seeke how to sell it for nothing.

Each day is a new life, and an abridgement of the whole. I will so liue as if I accounted euery day my first, and my last: as if I began to liue but then, and should liue no more afterwards.

Hee that taketh his owne cares vpon himselfe, loades him selfe in vaine with an vneasie burden. The feare of what may come, expectation of what will come, desire of what will not come, and inabilitie of redressing all these, must needs breede him continuall torment. I will cast my cares vpon God, he hath bidden me: they cannot hurt him; he can redresse them.

The proud man hath no God; the enuious man hath no Neighbour; the angrie man hath not himselfe. What can that man haue, that wants himselfe? What is a man better, if he haue himselfe, want all others? What is he the neerer, if he haue himselfe, and others, and yet want God? What good is it then to be a man, if he be either wrathfull, proud, or enuious?

Blaise Pascal

(1623-1662)

Although not a trained theologian, Pascal may be called a literary philosopher and mathematician who sought a mystical rather than a rational basis for his faith. He believed that the heart had reasons for believing in God which the mind did not possess. When thirty-one years of age he visited his sister at Port Royal. There he heard a sermon which brought about a profound religious experience. He wrote this down on a piece of paper and thereafter wore it as a sort of amulet. He lived at Port Royal, though not a member of the community, and concentrated his studies on the Bible and the Church Fathers.

When he was thirty-seven he began to write the defense of his faith which death did not allow him to finish. After he died his scattered writings were edited as Pensées (thoughts) They reveal an erudite though torn genius attempting to climb through psychic torments to a final vision of the Absolute. The selections here are from the translation by W. F. Trotter.

[CONSIDERATIONS OF THE SPIRITUAL MIND]

From *Thoughts*

THE MISERY OF MAN WITHOUT GOD

Let man then contemplate the whole of nature in her full and grand majesty, and turn his vision from the low objects which surround him. Let him gaze on that brilliant light, set like an eternal lamp to illumine the universe; let the earth appear to him a point in comparison with the vast circle described by the sun; and let him wonder at the fact that this vast circle is itself but a very fine point in comparison with that described by the stars in their revolution round the firmament. But if our view be arrested there, let our imagination pass beyond; it will sooner exhaust the power of conception than nature that of supplying material for conception. The whole visible world is only an imperceptible atom in the ample bosom of nature. No idea approaches it. We may enlarge our conceptions beyond all imaginable space; we only produce atoms in comparison with the reality of things. It is an infinite sphere, the centre of which is everywhere, the circumference nowhere. In short it is the greatest sensible mark of the almighty power of God, that imagination loses itself in that thought.

Returning to himself, let man consider what he is in comparison with all existence; let him regard himself as lost in this remote corner of nature; and from the little cell in which he finds himself lodged, I mean the universe, let him estimate at their true value the earth, kingdoms, cities, and himself. What is a man in the Infinite?

But to show him another prodigy equally astonishing, let him examine the most delicate things he knows. Let a mite be given him, with its minute body and parts incomparable more minute, limbs with their joints, veins in the limbs, blood in the veins, humours in the blood, drops in the humours, vapours in the drops. Dividing these last things again, let him exhaust his powers of conception, and let

the last object at which he can arrive be now that of our discourse. Perhaps he will think that here is the smallest point in nature. I will let him see therein a new abyss. I will paint for him not only the visible universe, but all that he can conceive of nature's immensity in the womb of this abridged atom. Let him see therein an infinity of universes, each of which has its firmament, its planets, its earth, in the same proportion as in the visible world; in each earth animals, and in the last mites, in which he will find again all that the first had, finding still in these others the same thing without end and without cessation. Let him lose himself in wonders as amazing in their littleness as the others in their vastness. For who will not be astounded at the fact that our body, which a little ago was imperceptible in the universe, itself imperceptible in the bosom of the whole, is now a colossus, a world, or rather a whole, in respect of the nothingness which we cannot reach? He who regards himself in this light will be afraid of himself, and observing himself sustained in the body given him by nature between those two abysses of the Infinite and Nothing, will tremble at the sight of these marvels; and I think that, as his curiosity changes into admiration, he will be more disposed to contemplate them in silence than to examine them with presumption.

For in fact what is man in nature? A Nothing in comparison with the Infinite, an All in comparison with the Nothing, a mean between nothing and everything. Since he is infinitely removed from comprehending the extremes, the end of things and their beginning are hopelessly hidden from him in an impenetrable secret; he is equally incapable of seeing the Nothing from which he was made, and the Infinite in which he is swallowed up.

What will he do then, but perceive the appearance of the middle of things, in an eternal despair of knowing either their beginning or their end. All things proceed from the Nothing, and are borne towards the Infinite. Who will follow these marvellous processes? The Author of these wonders understands them. None other can do so.

Through failure to contemplate these Infinites, men have rashly rushed into the examination of nature, as though they bore some proportion to her. It is strange that they have wished to understand the beginnings of things, and thence to arrive at the knowledge of the whole, with a presumption as infinite as their object. For surely this design cannot be formed without presumption or without a capacity infinite like nature.

If we are well-informed, we understand that, as nature has graven her image and that of her Author on all things, they almost all partake of her double infinity. Thus we see that all the sciences are infinite in the extent of their researches. For who doubts that geometry, for instance, has an infinite infinity of problems to solve? They are also infinite in the multitude and fineness of their premises; for it is clear that those which are put forward as ultimate are not self-supporting, but are based on others which, again having others for their support, do not permit of finality. But we represent some as ultimate for reason, in the same way as in regard to material objects we call that an indivisible point beyond which our sense can no longer perceive anything, although by its nature it is infinitely divisible.

Of these two Infinites of science, that of greatness is the most palpable, and hence a few persons have pretended to know all things. "I will speak of the whole," said Democritus.

But the infinitely little is the least obvious. Philosophers have much oftener claimed to have reached it, and it is here they have all stumbled. This has given rise to such common titles as *First Principles*, *Principles of Philosophy*, and the like, as ostentatious in fact, though not in appearance, as that one which blinds us, *De omni scibili*.

We naturally believe ourselves far more capable of reaching the centre of things than of embracing their circumference. The visible extent of the world visibly exceeds us, but as we exceed little things, we think ourselves more capable of knowing them. And yet we need no less capacity for attaining the Nothing than the All. Infinite capacity is required for both, and it seems to me that whoever shall have understood the ultimate principles of being might also attain to the knowledge of the Infinite. The one depends on the other, and one leads to the other. These extremes meet and reunite by force of distance, and find each other in God, and in God alone.

Let us then take our compass; we are something, and we are not everything. The nature of our existence hides from us the knowledge of first beginnings which are born of the Nothing; and the littleness of our being conceals from us the sight of the Infinite. . . .

100. *Self-love.*—The nature of self-love and of this human Ego is to love self only and consider self only. But what will man do? He cannot prevent this object that he loves from being full of faults and wants. He wants to be great, and he sees himself small. He wants to be happy, and he sees himself miserable. He wants to be perfect, and he sees himself full of imperfections. He wants to be the object of love and esteem among men, and he sees that his faults merit only their hatred and contempt. This embarrassment in which he finds himself produces in him the most unrighteous and criminal passion that can be imagined; for he conceives a mortal enmity against that truth which reproves him, and which convinces him of his faults. He would annihilate it, but, unable to destroy it in its essence, he destroys it as far as possible in his own knowledge and in that of others; that is to say, he devotes all his attention to hiding his faults both from others and from himself, and he cannot endure either that others should point them out to him, or that they should see them.

Truly it is an evil to be full of faults; but it is a still greater evil to be full of them, and to be unwilling to recognise them, since that is to add the further fault of a voluntary illusion. We do not like others to deceive us; we do not think it fair that they should be held in higher esteem by us than they deserve; it is not then fair that we should deceive them, and should wish them to esteem us more highly than we deserve. . . .

131. *Weariness.*—Nothing is so insufferable to man as to be completely at rest, without passions, without business, without diversion, without study. He then feels his nothingness, his forlornness, his insufficiency, his dependence, his weakness, his emptiness. There will immediately arise from the depth of his heart weariness, gloom, sadness, fretfulness, vexation, despair.

132. Methinks Caesar was too old to set about amusing himself with conquering the world. Such sport was good for Augustus or Alexander. They were still young men, and thus difficult to restrain. But Caesar should have been more mature.

135. The struggle alone pleases us, not the victory. We love to see animals fighting, not the victor infuriated over the vanquished. We would only see the victorious end; and, as soon as it comes, we are satiated. It is the same in play and the same in the search for truth. In disputes we like to see the clash of opinions, but not at all to contemplate truth when found. To observe it with pleasure, we have to see it emerge out of strife. So in the passions, there is pleasure in seeing the collision of two contraries; but when one acquires the mastery, it becomes only brutality. We never seek things for themselves, but for the search. Likewise in plays, scenes which do not rouse the emotion of fear are worthless, so are extreme and hopeless misery, brutal lust, and extreme cruelty.

139. *Diversion.*—When I have occasionally set myself to consider the different distractions of men, the pains and perils to which they expose themselves at court or in war, whence arise so many quarrels, passions, bold and often bad ventures, &c., I have discovered that all the unhappiness of men arises from one single fact, that they cannot stay quietly in their own chamber. A man who has enough to live on, if he knew how to stay with pleasure at home, would not leave it to go to sea or to besiege a town. A commission in the army would not be bought so dearly, but that it is found insufferable not to budge from the town; and men only seek conversation and entertaining games, because they cannot remain with pleasure at home. . . .

Whatever condition we picture to ourselves, if we muster all the good things which it is possible to possess, royalty is the finest position in the world. Yet, when we imagine a king attended with every pleasure he can feel, if he be without diversion, he be left to consider and reflect on what he is, this feeble happiness will not sustain him; he will necessarily fall into forebodings of dangers, of revolutions which may happen, and, finally, of death and inevitable disease; so that if he be without what is called diversion, he is unhappy, and more unhappy than the least of his subjects who plays and diverts himself. . . .

The king is surrounded by persons whose only thought is to divert the king, and to prevent his thinking of self. For he is unhappy, king though he be, if he think of himself.

147. We do not content ourselves with the life we have in ourselves and in our own being; we desire to live an imaginary life in the mind of others, and for this purpose we endeavour to shine. We labour unceasingly to adorn and preserve this imaginary existence, and neglect the real. And if we possess calmness, or generosity, or truthfulness, we are eager to make it known, so as to attach these virtues to that imaginary existence. We would rather separate them from ourselves to join them to it; and we would willingly be cowards in order to acquire the reputation of being brave. A great proof of the nothingness of our being, not to be satisfied with the one without the other, and to renounce the one for the other! For he would be infamous who would not die to preserve his honour.

148. We are so presumptuous that we would wish to be known by all the world, even by people who shall come after, when we shall be no more; and we are so vain that the esteem of five or six neighbours delights and contents us.

149. We do not trouble ourselves about being esteemed in the towns through which we pass. But if we are to remain a little while there, we are so concerned. How long is necessary? A time commensurate with our vain and paltry life.

150. Vanity is so anchored in the heart of man that a soldier, a soldier's servant, a cook, a porter brags, and wishes to have his admirers. Even philosophers wish for them. Those who write against it want to have the glory of having written well; and those who read it desire the glory of having read it. I who write this have perhaps this desire, and perhaps those who will read it. . . .

OF THE NECESSITY OF THE WAGER

203. *Fascinatio nugacitatis.*—That passion may not harm us, let us act as if we had only eight hours to live.

204. If we ought to devote eight hours of life, we ought to devote a hundred years.

205. When I consider the short duration of my life, swallowed up in the eternity before and after, the little space which I fill, and even can see, engulfed in the infinite immensity of spaces of which I am ignorant, and which know me not, I am frightened, and am astonished at being here rather than there; for there is no reason why here rather than there, why now rather than then. Who has put me here? By whose order and direction have this place and time been allotted to me?

206. The eternal silence of these infinite spaces frightens me.

208. Why is my knowledge limited? Why my stature? Why my life to one hundred years rather than to a thousand? What reason has nature had for giving me such, and for choosing this number rather than another in the infinity of those from which there is no more reason to choose one than another, trying nothing else?

210. The last act is tragic, however happy all the rest of the play is; at the last a little earth is thrown upon our head, and that is the end for ever.

211. We are fools to depend upon the society of our fellowmen. Wretched as we are, powerless as we are, they will not aid us; we shall die alone. We should therefore act as if we were alone, and in that case should we build fine houses, &c.? We should seek the truth without hesitation; and, if we refuse it, we show that we value the esteem of men more than the search for truth.

OF THE MEANS OF BELIEF

257. There are only three kinds of persons: those who serve God, having found Him; others who are occupied in seeking Him, not having found Him; while the remainder live without seeking Him, and without having found Him. The first are reasonable and happy, the last are foolish and unhappy; those between are unhappy and reasonable.

273. If we submit everything to reason, our religion will have no mysterious and supernatural element. If we offend the principles of reason, our religion will be absurd and ridiculous.

275. Men often take their imagination for their heart; and they believe they are converted as soon as they think of being converted.

277. The heart has its reasons, which reason does not know. We feel it in a thousand things. I say that the heart naturally loves the Universal Being, and also itself naturally, according as it gives itself to them; and it hardens itself against one or the other at its will. You have rejected the one, and kept the other. Is it by reason that you love yourself?

278. It is the heart which experiences God, and not the reason. This, then, is faith: God felt by the heart, not by the reason.

279. Faith is a gift of God; do not believe that we said it was a gift of reasoning. Other religions do not say this of their faith. They only gave reasoning in

order to arrive at it, and yet it does not bring them to it.

280. The knowledge of God is very far from the love of Him.

281. Heart, instinct, principles.

The Philosophers

339. I can well conceive a man without hands, feet, head (for it is only experience which teaches us that the head is more necessary than feet). But I cannot conceive man without thought; he would be a stone or a brute.

345. Reason commands us far more imperiously than a master; for in disobeying the one we are unfortunate, and in disobeying the other we are fools.

346. Thought constitutes the greatness of man.

347. Man is but a reed, the most feeble thing in nature, but he is a thinking reed. The entire universe need not arm itself to crush him. A vapour, a drop of water suffices to kill him. But, if the universe were to crush him, man would still be more noble than that which killed him, because he knows that he dies and the advantage which the universe has over him; the universe knows nothing of this.

All our dignity consists then in thought. By it we must elevate ourselves, and not by space and time which we cannot fill. Let us endeavour then to think well; this is the principle of morality.

348. *A thinking reed.*—It is not from space that I must seek my dignity, but from the government of my thought. I shall have no more if I possess worlds. By space the universe encompasses and swallows me up like an atom; by thought I comprehend the world.

349. *Immateriality of the soul.*—Philosophers who have mastered their passions. What matter could do that?

Morality and Doctrine

474. *Members. To commence with that.*—To regulate the love which we owe to ourselves, we must imagine a body full of thinking members, for we are members of the whole, and must see how each member should love itself, &c. . . .

475. If the feet and the hands had a will of their own, they could only be in their order in submitting this particular will to the primary will which governs the whole body. Apart from that, they are in disorder and mischief; but in willing only the good of the body, they accomplish their own good.

476. We must love God only and hate self only.

If the foot had always been ignorant that it belonged to the body, and that there was a body on which it depended, if it had only had the knowledge and love of self, and if it came to know that it belonged to a body on which it depended, what regret, what shame for its past life, for having been useless to the body which inspired its life, which would have annihilated it if it had rejected it and separated it from itself, as it kept itself apart from the body! What prayers for its preservation in it! And with what submission would it allow itself to be governed by the will which rules the body, even to consenting, if necessary, to be cut off, or it would lose its character as member! For every member must be quite willing to perish for the body, for which alone the whole is.

480. To make the members happy, they must have one will, and submit it to the body.

525. The philosophers did not prescribe feelings suitable to the two states.

They inspired feelings of pure greatness, and that is not man's state.

They inspired feelings of pure littleness, and that is not man's state. There must be feelings of humility, not from nature, but from penitence, not to rest in them, but to go on to greatness. There must be feelings of greatness, not from merit, but from grace, and after having passed through humiliation.

527. The knowledge of God without that of man's misery causes pride. The knowledge of man's misery without that of God causes despair. The knowledge of Jesus Christ constitutes the middle

course, because in Him we find both God and our misery.

528. Jesus Christ is a God whom we approach without pride, and before whom we humble ourselves without despair.

530. A person told me one day that on coming from confession he felt great joy and confidence. Another told me that he remained in fear. Whereupon I thought that these two together would make one good man, and that each was wanting in that he had not the feeling of the other. The same often happens in other things.

534. There are only two kinds of men: the righteous, who believe themselves sinners; the rest, sinners, who believe themselves righteous.

535. We owe a great debt to those who point out faults. For they mortify us. They teach us that we have been despised. They do not prevent our being so in the future; for we have many other faults for which we may be despised. They prepare for us the exercise of correction and freedom from fault.

537. Christianity is strange. It bids man recognise that he is vile, even abominable, and bids him desire to be like God. Without such a counterpoise, this dignity would make him horribly vain, or this humiliation would make him terribly abject.

538. With how little pride does a Christian believe himself united to God! With how little humiliation does he place himself on a level with the worms of earth!

A glorious manner to welcome life and death, good and evil!

539. What difference in point of obedience is there between a soldier and a Carthusian monk? For both are equally under obedience and dependent, both engage in equally painful exercises. But the soldier always hopes to command, and never attains this, for even captains and princes are ever slaves and dependents; still he ever hopes and ever works to attain this. Whereas the Carthusian monk makes a vow to be always dependent. So they do not differ in their perpetual thral-dom, in which both of them always exist, but in the hope, which one always has, and the other never.

540. The hope which Christians have of possessing an infinite good is mingled with real enjoyment as well as with fear; for it is not as with those who should hope for a kingdom, of which they, being subjects, would have nothing; but they hope for holiness, for freedom from injustice, and they have something of this.

541. None is so happy as a true Christian, nor so reasonable, virtuous, or amiable.

542. The Christian religion alone makes man altogether *lovable and happy*. In honesty, we cannot perhaps be altogether lovable and happy.

545. Jesus Christ did nothing but teach men that they loved themselves, that they were slaves, blind, sick, wretched, and sinners; that He must deliver them, enlighten, bless, and heal them; that this would be effected by hating self, and by following Him through suffering and the death on the cross.

548. Not only do we know God by Jesus Christ alone, but we know ourselves only by Jesus Christ. We know life and death only through Jesus Christ. Apart from Jesus Christ, we do not know what is our life, nor our death, nor God, nor ourselves.

Thus without the Scripture, which has Jesus Christ alone for its object, we know nothing, and see only darkness and confusion in the nature of God, and in our own nature.

550. I love poverty because He loved it. I love riches because they afford me the means of helping the very poor. I keep faith with everybody; I do not render evil to those who wrong me, but I wish them a lot like mine, in which I receive neither evil nor good from men. I try to be just, true, sincere, and faithful to all men; I have a tender heart for those to whom God has more closely united me; and whether I am alone, or seen of men, I do all my actions in the sight of God, who must judge of them, and to whom I have consecrated them all.

These are my sentiments; and every day of my life I bless my Redeemer, who has implanted them in me, and who, of a man full of weaknesses, of miseries, of lust, of pride, and of ambition, has made a man free from all these evils by the power of His grace, to which all the glory of it is due, as of myself I have only misery and error.

THE FUNDAMENTALS OF THE CHRISTIAN RELIGION

556. . . . The Christian religion then teaches men these two truths; that there is a God whom men can know, and that there is a corruption in their nature which renders them unworthy of Him. It is equally important to men to know both these points; and it is equally dangerous for man to know God without knowing his own wretchedness, and to know his own wretchedness without knowing the Redeemer who can free him from it. The knowledge of only one of these points gives rise either to the pride of philosophers, who have known God, and not their own wretchedness, or to the despair of atheists, who know their own wretchedness, but not the Redeemer.

And, as it is alike necessary to man to know these two points, so is it alike merciful of God to have made us know them. The Christian religion does this; it is in this that it consists.

Let us herein examine the order of the world, and see if all things do not tend to establish these two chief points of this religion: Jesus Christ is the end of all, and the centre to which all tends. Whoever knows Him knows the reason of everything.

Those who fall into error err only through failure to see one of these two things. We can then have an excellent knowledge of God without that of our own wretchedness, and of our own wretchedness without that of God. But we cannot know Jesus Christ without knowing at the same time both God and our own wretchedness.

Therefore I shall not undertake here to prove by natural reasons either the existence of God, or the Trinity, or the immortality of the soul, or anything of that nature; not only because I should not feel myself sufficiently able to find in nature arguments to convince hardened atheists, but also because such knowledge without Jesus Christ is useless and barren. Though a man should be convinced that numerical proportions are immaterial truths, eternal and dependent on a first truth, in which they subsist, and which is called God, I should not think him far advanced towards his own salvation.

The God of Christians is not a God who is simply the author of mathematical truths, or of the order of the elements; that is the view of heathens and Epicureans. He is not merely a God who exercises His providence over the life and fortunes of men, to bestow on those who worship Him a long and happy life. That was the portion of the Jews. But the God of Abraham, the God of Isaac, the God of Jacob, the God of Christians, is a God of love and of comfort, a God who fills the soul and heart of those whom He possesses, a God who makes them conscious of their inward wretchedness, and His infinite mercy, who unites Himself to their inmost soul, who fills it with humility and joy, with confidence and love, who renders them incapable of any other end than Himself.

All who seek God without Jesus Christ, and who rest in nature, either find no light to satisfy them, or come to form for themselves a means of knowing God and serving Him without a mediator. Thereby they fall either into atheism, or into deism, two things which the Christian religion abhors almost equally.

Without Jesus Christ the world would not exist; for it should needs be either that it would be destroyed or be a hell.

If the world existed to instruct man of God, His divinity would shine through every part in it in an indisputable manner; but as it exists only by Jesus Christ, and for Jesus Christ, and to teach men both their corruption and their redemption, all displays the proofs of these two truths.

All appearance indicates neither a total

exclusion nor a manifest presence of divinity, but the presence of a God who hides Himself. Everything bears this character.

. . . Shall he alone who knows his nature know it only to be miserable? Shall he alone who knows it be alone unhappy?

. . . He must not see nothing at all, nor must he see sufficient for him to believe he possesses it; but he must see enough to know that he has lost it. For to know of his loss, he must see and not see; and that is exactly the state in which he naturally is.

. . . Whatever part he takes, I shall not leave him at rest . . .

561. There are two ways of proving the truths of our religion; one by the power of reason, the other by the authority of him who speaks.

We do not make use of the latter, but of the former. We do not say, "This must be believed, for Scripture, which says it, is divine." But we say that it must be believed for such and such a reason, which are feeble arguments, as reason may be bent to everything.

562. There is nothing on earth that does not show either the wretchedness of man, or the mercy of God; either the weakness of man without God, or the strength of man with God.

563. It will be one of the confusions of the damned to see that they are condemned by their own reason, by which they claimed to condemn the Christian religion.

564. The prophecies, the very miracles and proofs of our religion, are not of such a nature that they can be said to be absolutely convincing. But they are also of such a kind that it cannot be said that it is unreasonable to believe them. Thus there is both evidence and obscurity to enlighten some and confuse others. But the evidence is such that it surpasses, or at least equals, the evidence to the contrary; so that it is not reason which can determine men not to follow it, and thus it can only be lust or malice of heart. And by this means there is sufficient evidence to condemn, and insufficient to convince; so that it appears in those who follow it, that it is grace, and not reason, which makes them follow it; and in those who shun it, that it is lust, not reason, which makes them shun it.

Vere discipuli, vere Israëlita, vere liberi, vere cibus.

565. Recognise, then, the truth of religion in the very obscurity of religion, in the little light we have of it, and in the indifference which we have to knowing it.

566. We understand nothing of the works of God, if we do not take as a principle that He has willed to blind some, and enlighten others.

567. The two contrary reasons. We must begin with that; without that we understand nothing, and all is heretical; and we must even add at the end of each truth that the opposite truth is to be remembered.

580. Nature has some perfections to show that she is the image of God, and some defects to show that she is only His image.

581. God prefers rather to incline the will than the intellect. Perfect clearness would be of use to the intellect, and would harm the will. To humble pride.

582. We make an idol of truth itself; for truth apart from charity is not God, but His image and idol, which we must neither love nor worship; and still less must we love or worship its opposite, namely, falsehood.

I can easily love total darkness; but if God keeps me in a state of semi-darkness, such partial darkness displeases me, and, because I do not see therein the advantage of total darkness, it is unpleasant to me. This is a fault, and a sign that I make for myself an idol of darkness, apart from the order of God. Now only His order must be worshipped.

583. The feeble-minded are people who know the truth, but only affirm it so far as consistent with their own interest. But, apart from that, they renounce it.

584. The world exists for the exercise of mercy and judgment, not as if men were placed in it out of the hands of God,

but as hostile to God; and to them He grants by grace sufficient light, that they may return to Him, if they desire to seek and follow Him; and also that they may be punished, if they refuse to seek or follow Him.

585. *That God has willed to hide Himself.*—If there were only one religion, God would indeed be manifest. The same would be the case, if there were no martyrs but in our religion.

God being thus hidden, every religion which does not affirm that God is hidden, is not true; and every religion which does not give the reason of it, is not instructive. Our religion does all this: *Vere tu es Deus absconditus.*

586. If there were no obscurity, man would not be sensible of his corruption; if there were no light, man would not hope for a remedy. Thus, it is not only fair, but advantageous to us, that God be partly hidden and partly revealed; since it is equally dangerous to man to know God without knowing his own wretchedness, and to know his own wretchedness without knowing God.

587. This religion, so great in miracles, saints, blameless Fathers, learned and great witnesses, martyrs, established kings as David, and Isaiah, a prince of the blood, and so great in science, after having displayed all her miracles and all her wisdom, rejects all this, and declares that she has neither wisdom nor signs, but only the cross and foolishness.

For those, who, by these signs and that wisdom, have deserved your belief, and who have proved to you their character, declare to you that nothing of all this can change you, and render you capable of knowing and loving God, but the power of the foolishness of the cross without wisdom and signs, and not the signs without this power. Thus our religion is foolish in respect to the effective cause, and wise in respect to the wisdom which prepares it.

588. Our religion is wise and foolish. Wise, because it is the most learned, and the most founded on miracles, prophecies, &c. Foolish, because it is not all this which makes us belong to it. This makes us indeed condemn those who do not belong to it; but it does not cause belief in those who do belong to it. It is the cross that makes them believe, *ne evacuata sit crux.* And so Saint Paul, who came with wisdom and signs, says that he has come neither with wisdom or with signs; for he came to convert. But those who come only to convince, can say that they come with wisdom and with signs.

THE PROPHECIES

693. When I see the blindness and the wretchedness of man, when I regard the whole silent universe, and man without light, left to himself, and, as it were, lost in this corner of the universe, without knowing who has put him there, what he has come to do, what will become of him at death, and incapable of all knowledge, I become terrified, like a man who should be carried in his sleep to a dreadful desert island, and should awake without knowing where he is, and without means of escape. And thereupon I wonder how people in a condition so wretched do not fall into despair. I see other persons around me of a like nature. I ask them if they are better informed than I am. They tell me that they are not. And thereupon these wretched and lost beings, having looked around them, and seen some pleasing objects, have given and attached themselves to them. For my own part, I have not been able to attach myself to them, and, considering how strongly it appears that there is something else than what I see, I have examined whether this God has not left some sign of Himself.

Jeremy Taylor

(1613-1667)

BORN at Cambridge, England, son of a barber, winner of scholarly fame at Cambridge, chaplain to the king, and bishop of Down and Connar, Taylor is best known for his *Holy Living* and *Holy Dying*. As a vivid, illustrative, scholarly writer he left works which fill fifteen octavo volumes. A nineteenth-century writer compared the sermons of his day with Taylor's homilies in these words: "We have no modern sermons in the English language that can be considered as very eloquent. . . . For eloquence we must ascend as high as the days of Jeremy Taylor." The selections from *Holy Living* and *Holy Dying* show remarkable insight into the psychological aspect of religion. Of his many writings these two are the deepest in their devotional spirit.

OF HUMILITY

From *The Rule and Exercises of Holy Living*

Humility is the great ornament and jewel of Christian religion; that, whereby it is distinguished from all the wisdom of the world: it not having been taught by the wise men of the Gentiles, but first put into a discipline, and made part of a religion, by our Lord Jesus Christ, who propounded himself imitable by his disciples so signally in nothing as in the twin-sisters of meekness and humility. Learn of me, for I am meek and humble; and ye shall find rest unto your souls.

For all the world, all that we are, and all that we have, our bodies and our souls, our actions and our sufferings, our conditions at home, our accidents abroad, our many sins and our seldom virtues, are as so many arguments to make our souls dwell low in the deep valleys of humility.

ARGUMENTS AGAINST PRIDE BY WAY OF CONSIDERATION

1. Our body is weak and impure, sending out more uncleannesses from its several sinks than could be endured, if they were not necessary and natural: and we are forced to pass that through our mouths, which as soon as we see upon the ground, we loathe like rottenness and vomiting.

2. Our strength is inferior to that of many beasts, and our infirmities so many, that we are forced to dress and tend horses and asses, that they may help our needs, and relieve our wants.

3. Our beauty is in colour inferior to many flowers, and in proportion of parts it is no better than nothing; for even a dog hath parts as well proportioned and fitted to his purposes, and the designs of his nature, as we have; and when it is most florid and gay, three fits of an ague can change it into yellowness and leanness, and the hollowness and wrinkles of deformity.

4. Our learning is then best, when it teaches most humility; but to be proud of learning is the greatest ignorance in the world. For our learning is so long in getting, and so very imperfect, that the greatest clerk knows not the thousandth part of what he is ignorant; and knows so uncertainly what he seems to know, and knows no otherwise than a fool or a child, even what is told him or what he guesses at, that except those things which concern his duty, and which God hath revealed to him, which also, every woman knows so far as is necessary, the most learned man hath nothing to be proud of, unless this be a sufficient argument to exalt him, that he uncertainly guesses at some more unnecessary

thing than many others, who yet know all that concerns them, and mind other things more necessary for the needs of life and commonwealths.

5. He that is proud of riches is a fool. For if he be exalted above his neighbours, because he hath more gold, how much inferior is he to a gold mine? How much is he to give place to a chain of pearl, or a knot of diamonds? For certainly that hath the greatest excellence, from whence he derives all his gallantry and pre-eminence over his neighbours.

6. If a man be exalted by reason of any excellence in his soul, he may please to remember, that all souls are equal; and their differing operations are because their instrument is in better tune, their body is more healthful, or better tempered: which is no more praise to him, than it is that he was born in Italy.

7. He that is proud of his birth, is proud of the blessings of others, not of himself: for if his parents were more eminent in any circumstance than their neighbours, he is to thank God, and to rejoice in them; but still he may be a fool, or unfortunate, or deformed; and when himself was born, it was indifferent to him, whether his father were a king or a peasant, for he knew not any thing, nor chose any thing; and most commonly it is true, that he that boasts of his ancestors, who were the founders and raisers of a noble family, doth confess that he hath in himself a less virtue and a less honour, and therefore that he is degenerated.

8. Whatsoever other difference there is between thee and thy neighbour, if it be bad, it is thine own, but thou hast no reason to boast of thy misery and shame; if it be good, thou hast received it from God; and then thou art more obliged to pay duty and tribute, use and principal to him; and it were a strange folly for a man to be proud of being more in debt than another.

9. Remember what thou wert, before thou wert begotten. Nothing. What wert thou in the first regions of thy dwelling, before thy birth? Uncleanness. What wert thou for many years after? Weak-ness. What in all thy life? A great sinner. What in all thy excellences? A mere debtor to God, to thy parents, to the earth, to all the creatures. But we may, if we please, use the method of the Platonists, who reduce all the causes and arguments for humility, which we can take from ourselves, to these seven heads. 1. The spirit of man is light and troublesome. 2. His body is brutish and sickly. 3. He is constant in his folly and error, and inconstant in his manners and good purposes. 4. His labours are vain, intricate, and endless. 5. His fortune is changeable, but seldom pleasing, never perfect. 6. His wisdom comes not, till he be ready to die, that is, till he be past using it. 7. His death is certain, always ready at the door, but never far off. Upon these or the like meditations if we dwell, or frequently retire to them, we shall see nothing more reasonable than to be humble, and nothing more foolish than to be proud.

ACTS OR OFFICES OF HUMILITY

The grace of humility is exercised by these following rules.

1. Think not thyself better for any-thing, that happens to thee from without. For although thou mayest, by gifts bestowed upon thee, be better than another, as one horse is better than another, that is of more use to others; yet as thou art a man, thou hast nothing to commend thee to thyself but that only, by which thou art a man, that is, by what thou choosest and refusest.

2. Humility consists not in railing against thyself, or wearing mean clothes, or going softly and submissively: but in hearty and real evil or mean opinion of thyself. Believe thyself an unworthy person, heartily, as thou believest thyself to be hungry, or poor, or sick, when thou art so.

3. Whatsoever evil thou sayest of thyself, be content that others should think to be true: and if thou callest thyself fool, be not angry if another say so of thee. For if thou thinkest so truly, all men in the world desire other men to be of their opinion; and he is an hypocrite, that

accuses himself before others, with an intent not to be believed. But he that calls himself intemperate, foolish, lustful, and is angry when his neighbours call him so, is both a false and a proud person.

4. Love to be concealed, and little esteemed: be content to want praise, never being troubled when thou art slighted or undervalued; for thou canst not undervalue thyself, and if thou thinkest so meanly, as there is reason, no contempt will seem unreasonable, and therefore it will be very tolerable.

5. Never be ashamed of thy birth, or thy parents, or thy trade, or thy present employment, for the meanness or poverty of any of them; and when there is an occasion to speak of them, such an occasion as would invite you to speak of any thing that pleases you, omit it not, but speak as readily and indifferently of thy meanness as of thy greatness. Primislaus, the first king of Bohemia, kept his country-shoes always by him, to remember from whence he was raised: and Agathocles, by the furniture of his table, confessed, that, from a potter, he was raised to be the king of Sicily.

6. Never speak anything directly tending to thy praise or glory; that is, with a purpose to be commended, and for no other end. If other ends be mingled with thy honour, as if the glory of God, or charity, or necessity, or anything of prudence be thy end, you are not tied to omit your discourse or your design, that you may avoid praise, but pursue your end, though praise come along in the company. Only let not praise be the design.

7. When thou hast said or done anything, for which thou receivest praise or estimation, take it indifferently, and return it to God; reflecting upon him as the giver of the gift, or the blesser of the action, or the aid of the design: and give God thanks for making thee an instrument of his glory, or the benefit of others.

8. Secure a good name to thyself by living virtuously and humbly; but let this good name be nursed abroad, and never be brought home to look upon it: let others use it for their own advantage; let them speak of it if they please, but do not thou at all use it, but as an instrument to do God glory, and thy neighbour more advantage. Let thy face, like Moses's, shine to others but make no looking-glass for thyself.

9. Take no content in praise, when it is offered thee: but let thy rejoicing in God's gift be allayed with fear, lest this good bring thee to evil. Use the praise, as you use your pleasure in eating and drinking: if it comes, make it do drudgery, let it serve other ends, and minister to necessities, and to caution, lest, by pride, you lose your just praise, which you have deserved; or else, by being praised unjustly, you receive shame into yourself with God and wise men.

10. Use no stratagems and devices to get praise. Some use to inquire into the faults of their own actions or discourses, on purpose to hear, that it was well done or spoken, and without fault: others bring the matter into talk, or thrust themselves into company, and intimate and give occasion to be thought or spoke of. These men make a bait to persuade themselves to swallow the hook, till by drinking the waters of vanity they swell up and burst.

11. Make no suppletories to thyself, when thou art disgraced or slighted, by pleasing thyself with supposing thou didst deserve praise, though they understood thee not, or enviously detracted from thee: neither do thou get to thyself a private theatre and flatterers, in whose vain noises and fantastic praises thou mayest keep up thine own good opinion of thyself.

12. Entertain no fancies of vanity and private whispers of this devil of pride: such as was that of Nebuchadnezzar; "Is not this great Babylon, which I have built for the honour of my name, and the might of my majesty, and the power of my kingdom?" Some fantastic spirits will walk alone, and dream waking of greatnesses, of palaces, of excellent orations, full theatres, loud applauses, sudden advancement, great fortunes, and so will spend an hour with imaginative pleasure;

all their employment being nothing but fumes of pride, and secret indefinite desires and significations of what their heart wishes. In this, although there is nothing of its own nature directly vicious, yet it is either an ill mother or an ill daughter, an ill sign or an ill effect; and therefore at no hand consisting with the safety and interests of humility.

13. Suffer others to be praised in thy presence, and entertain their good and glory with delight; but at no hand disparage them, or lessen the report, or make objection; and think not the advancement of thy brother is a lessening of thy worth. But this act is also to extend further.

14. Be content that he should be employed, and thou laid by as unprofitable; his sentence approved, thine rejected, he be preferred, and thou fixed in a low employment.

15. Never compare thyself with others, unless it be to advance them and to depress thyself. To which purpose, we must be sure in some sense or other to think ourselves the worst in every company, where we come: one is more learned than I am, another is more prudent, a third more honourable, a fourth more chaste, or he is more charitable, or less proud. For the humble man observes their good, and reflects only upon his own vileness; or considers the many evils of himself certainly known to himself, and the ill of others but by uncertain report; or he considers, that the evils, done by another, are out of much infirmity or ignorance, but his own sins are against a clearer light; and if the other had so great helps, he would have done more good and less evil: or he remembers, that his old sins before his conversion were greater in the nature of the thing, or in certain circumstances, than the sins of other men. So St. Paul reckoned himself the chiefest of sinners, because formerly he had acted the chiefest sin of persecuting the church of God. But this rule is to be used with this caution: that though it be good always to think meanest of ourselves, yet it is not ever safe to speak it; because those circumstances and considerations which determine thy thoughts, are not known to others as to thyself; and it may concern others, that they hear thee give God thanks for the graces he hath given thee. But if thou preservest thy thoughts and opinions of thyself truly humble, you may with more safety give God thanks in public for that good which cannot, or ought not to be concealed.

16. Be not always ready to excuse every oversight, or indiscretion, or ill action: but if thou beest guilty of it, confess it plainly; for virtue scorns a lie for its cover: but to hide a sin with it, is like a crust of leprosy drawn upon an ulcer. If thou beest not guilty (unless it be scandalous), be not over earnest to remove it, but rather use it as an argument to chastise all greatness of fancy and opinion in thyself; and accustom thyself to bear reproof patiently and contentedly, and the harsh words of thy enemies, as knowing that the anger of an enemy is a better monitor, and represents our faults, or admonishes us of our duty with more heartiness, than the kindness does, or precious balms of a friend.

17. Give God thanks for every weakness, deformity, and imperfection, and accept it as a favour and grace of God, and an instrument to resist pride, and nurse humility; ever remembering, that when God, by giving thee a crooked back, hath also made thy spirit stoop, or less vain, thou art more ready to enter the narrow gate of heaven, than by being straight, and standing upright, and thinking highly. Thus the apostles rejoiced in their infirmities, not moral, but natural and accidental, in their being beaten and whipt like slaves, in their nakedness and poverty.

18. Upbraid no man's weakness to him to discomfort him, neither report it to disparage him, neither delight to remember it to lessen him, or to set thyself above him. Be sure never to praise thyself, or to dispraise any man else, unless God's glory or some holy end do hallow it. And it was noted to the praise of Cyrus, that among his equals in age, he would never play at any sport, or use any

exercise, in which he knew himself more excellent than they: but in such, in which he was unskillful, he would make his challenges, lest he should shame them by his victory, and that himself might learn something of their skill, and do them civilities.

19. Besides the foregoing parts and actions, humility teaches us to submit ourselves and all our faculties to God, "to believe all things, to do all things, to suffer all things," which his will enjoins us; to be content in every estate or change, knowing we have deserved worse than the worst we feel; and . . . he hath taken but half, when He might have taken all: to adore his goodness, to fear His greatness, to worship his eternal and infinite excellences, and to submit ourselves to all our superiors, in all things, according to godliness, and to be meek and gentle in our conversation towards others.

Now although, according to the nature of every grace, this begins as a gift, and is increased like a habit, that is, best by its own acts; yet besides the former acts and offices of humility, there are certain other exercises and considerations, which are good helps and instruments for the procuring and increasing this grace, and the curing of pride.

MEANS AND EXERCISES FOR OBTAINING AND INCREASING THE GRACE OF HUMILITY

1. Make confession of thy sins often to God; and consider what all that evil amounts to, which you then charge upon yourself. Look not upon them as scattered in the course of a long life; now, an intemperate anger, then, too full a meal; now idle talking, and another time, impatience; but unite them into one continued representation, and remember, that he whose life seems fair, by reason that his faults are scattered at large distances in the several parts of his life, yet, if all his errors and follies were articled against him, the man would seem vicious and miserable: and possibly this exercise, really applied upon thy spirit, may be useful.

2. Remember that we usually disparage others upon slight grounds and little instances; and towards them one fly is enough to spoil a whole box of ointment: and if a man be highly commended, we think him sufficiently lessened, if we clap one sin of folly or infirmity into his account. Let us, therefore, be just to ourselves, since we are so severe to others, and consider, that whatsoever good any one can think or say of us, we can tell him of hundreds of base, and unworthy, and foolish actions, any one of which were enough (we hope) to destroy another's reputation: therefore, let so many be sufficient to destroy our over-high thoughts of ourselves.

3. When our neighbour is cried up by public fame and popular noises, that we may disparage and lessen him, we cry out that the people is a herd of unlearned and ignorant persons, ill judges, loud trumpets, but which never give certain sound: let us use the same art to humble ourselves, and never take delight and pleasure in public reports, and acclamations of assemblies, and please ourselves with their judgment, of whom, in other the like cases, we affirm that they are mad.

4. We change our opinion of others, by their kindness or unkindness towards us. If he be my patron, and bounteous, he is wise, he is noble, his faults are but warts, his virtues are mountainous; but if he proves unkind, or rejects our importunate suit, then he is ill-natured, covetous, and his free meal is called gluttony: that which before we called civility, is now very drunkenness; and all he speaks is flat and dull, and ignorant as a swine. This, indeed, is unjust towards others; but a good instrument, if we turn the edge of it upon ourselves. We use ourselves ill, abusing ourselves with false principles, cheating ourselves with lies and pretences, stealing the choice and election from our wills, placing voluntary ignorance in our understandings, denying the desires of the spirit, setting up a faction against every noble and just desire; the least of which, because we should resent up to reviling the injurious person, it is but reason we should at

least not flatter ourselves with fond and too kind opinions.

5. Every day call to mind some one of thy foulest sins, or the most shameful of thy disgraces, or the indiscreetest of thy actions, or any thing that did then most trouble thee, and apply it to the present swelling of thy spirit and opinion, and it may help to allay it.

6. Pray often for his grace, with all humility of gesture and passion of desire; and in thy devotion interpose many acts of humility, by way of confession and address to God, and reflection upon thyself.

7. Avoid great offices and employments, and the noises of worldly honour. For in those states, many times so many ceremonies and circumstances will seem necessary, as will destroy the sobriety of thy thoughts. If the number of thy servants be fewer, and their observances less, and their reverences less solemn, possibly they will seem less than thy dignity; and if they be so much and so many, it is likely they will be too big for thy spirit. And here be thou very careful, lest thou be abused by a pretence, that thou wouldst use thy great dignity as an opportunity of doing great good. For supposing it might be good for others, yet it is not good for thee; they may have encouragement in noble things from thee, and, by the same instrument, thou mayest thyself be tempted to pride and vanity. And certain it is, God is as much glorified by thy example of humility in a low or temperate condition, as by thy bounty in a great and dangerous.

8. Make no reflex acts upon thy own humility, nor upon any other grace, with which God hath enriched thy soul. For since God oftentimes hides from his saints and servants the sight of those excellent things, by which they shine to others (though the dark side of the lantern be towards themselves,) that he may secure the grace of humility; it is good that thou do so thyself: and if thou beholdest a grace of God in thee, remember to give him thanks for it, that thou mayest not boast in that, which is none of thy own: and consider how thou hast sullied it, by handling it with dirty fingers, with thy own imperfections, and with mixture of unhandsome circumstances. Spiritual pride is very dangerous, not only by reason it spoils so many graces, by which we drew nigh unto the kingdom of God, but also because it so frequently creeps upon the spirit of holy persons. For it is no wonder for a beggar to call himself poor, or a drunkard to confess that he is no sober person; but for a holy person to be humble, for one whom all men esteem a saint, to fear lest himself become a devil, and to observe his own danger, and to discern his own infirmities, and make discovery of his bad adherences, is as hard as for a prince to submit himself to be guided by tutors, and make himself subject to discipline, like the meanest of his servants.

9. Often meditate upon the effects of pride, on one side, and humility on the other. First, That pride is like a canker, and destroys the beauty of the fairest flowers, the most excellent gifts and graces; but humility crowns them all. Secondly, That pride is a great hindrance to the perceiving the things of God; and humility is an excellent preparative and instrument of spiritual wisdom. Thirdly, That pride hinders the acceptation of our prayers; but "humility pierceth the clouds, and will not depart till the Most High shall regard." Fourthly, That humility is but a speaking truth, and all pride is a lie. Fifthly, That humility is the most certain way to real honour, and pride is ever affronted or despised. Sixthly, That pride turned Lucifer into a devil, and humility exalted the Son of God above every name, and placed him eternally at the right hand of his Father. Seventhly, That "God resisteth the proud," professing open defiance and hostility against such persons; but "giveth grace to the humble:" grace and pardon, remedy and relief against misery and oppression, content in all conditions, tranquillity of spirit, patience in afflictions, love abroad, peace at home, and utter freedom from contention, and the sin of censuring others, and the trouble of being censured themselves. For the humble man

will not "judge his brother for the mote in his eye," being more troubled at "the beam in his own eye;" and is patient and glad to be reproved, because himself hath cast the first stone at himself, and therefore wonders not, that others are of his mind.

10. Remember that the blessed Saviour of the world hath done more to prescribe, and transmit, and secure this grace, than any other; his whole life being a great continued example of humility, a vast descent from the glorious bosom of his Father to the womb of a poor maiden, to the form of a servant, to the miseries of a sinner, to a life of labour, to a state of poverty, to a death of malefactors, to the grave of death, and the intolerable calamities which we deserved; and it were a good design, and yet but reasonable, that we should be as humble, in the midst of our greatest imperfections and basest sins, as Christ was in the midst of his fulness of the Spirit, great wisdom, perfect life, and most admirable virtues.

11. Drive away all flatterers from thy company, and at no hand endure them; for he that endures himself so to be abused by another, is not only a fool for entertaining the mockery, but loves to have his own opinion of himself to be heightened and cherished.

12. Never change thy employment for the sudden coming of another to thee; but if modesty permits, or discretion, appear to him that visits thee, the same that thou wert to God and thyself in thy privacy. But if thou wert walking or sleeping, or in any other innocent employment or retirement, snatch not up a book to seem studious, nor fall on thy knees to seem devout, nor alter any thing to make him believe thee better employed than thou wert.

13. To the same purpose it is of great use, that he who would preserve his humility, should choose some spiritual person to whom he shall oblige himself to discover his very thoughts and fancies, every act of his and all his intercourse with others, in which there may be danger; that by such an openness of spirit he may expose every blast of vain-glory, every idle thought, to be chastened and lessened by the rod of spiritual discipline: and he that shall find himself tied to confess every proud thought, every vanity of his spirit, will also perceive they must not dwell with him, nor find any kindness from him: and besides this, the nature of pride is so shameful and unhandsome, that the very discovery of it is a huge mortification and means of suppressing it. A man would be ashamed to be told, that he inquires after the faults of his last oration or action on purpose to be commended: and therefore, when the man shall tell his spiritual guide the same shameful story of himself, it is very likely he will be humbled, and heartily ashamed of it.

14. Let every man suppose what opinion he should have of one that should spend his time in playing with drumsticks and cockle-shells, and that would wrangle all day long with a little boy for pins, or should study hard, and labour to cozen a child of his gauds; and, who would run into a river, deep and dangerous, with a great burden upon his back, even then when he were told of the danger, and earnestly importuned not to do it? and let him but change the instances and the person, and he shall find that he hath the same reason to think as bad of himself, who pursues trifles with earnestness, spending his time in vanity, and his "labour for that which profits not;" who knowing the laws of God, the rewards of virtue, the cursed consequents of sin, that it is an evil spirit that tempts him to it; a devil, one that hates him, that longs extremely to ruin him; that it is his own destruction that he is then working; that the pleasures of his sin are base and brutish, unsatisfying in the enjoyment, soon over, shameful in their story, bitter in the memory, painful in the effect here, and intolerable hereafter, and for ever; yet in despite of all this, he runs foolishly into his sin and his ruin, merely because he is a fool, and winks hard, and rushes violently like a horse into the battle, or like a madman to his death. He that can think great and

good things of such a person, the next step may court the rack for an instrument of pleasure, and admire a swine for wisdom, and go for counsel to the prodigal and trifling grasshopper.

After the use of these and such-like instruments and considerations, if you would try, how your soul is grown, you shall know that humility, like the root of a goodly tree, is thrust very far into the ground, by these goodly fruits, which appear above ground.

SIGNS OF HUMILITY

1. The humble man trusts not to his own discretion, but in matter of concernment relies rather upon the judgment of his friends, counsellors, or spiritual guides. 2. He does not pertinaciously pursue the choice of his own will, but in all things lets God choose for him, and his superiors, in those things which concern them. 3. He does not murmur against commands. 4. He is not inquisitive into the reasonableness of indifferent and innocent commands, but believes their command to be reason enough in such cases to exact his obedience. 5. He lives according to a rule, and with compliance to public customs, without any affectation or singularity. 6. He is meek and indifferent in all accidents and chances. 7. He patiently bears injuries. 8. He is always unsatisfied in his own conduct, resolutions, and counsels. 9. He is a great lover of good men, and a praiser of wise men, and a censurer of no man. 10. He is modest in his speech, and reserved in his laughter. 11. He fears, when he hears himself commended, lest God make another judgment concerning his actions than men do. 12. He gives no pert or saucy answers, when he is reproved, whether justly or unjustly. 13. He loves to sit down in private, and, if he may, he refuses the temptations of offices and new honours. 14. He is ingenuous, free, and open, in his actions and discourses. 15. He mends his fault, and gives thanks, when he is admonished. 16. He is ready to do good offices to the murderers of his fame, to his slanderers, backbiters, and detracters, as Christ washed the feet of Judas. 17. And is contented to be suspected of indiscretion, so before God he may be really innocent, and not offensive to his neighbour, nor wanting to his just and prudent interest.

THE VANITY AND SHORTNESS OF MAN'S LIFE

From *The Rule and Exercises of Holy Dying*

A man is a bubble (said the Greek proverb,) which Lucian represents with advantages and its proper circumstances to this purpose: saying, All the world is a storm, and men rise up in their several generations, like bubbles descending *à Jove pluvio*, from God and the dew of heaven, from a tear and drop of rain, from nature and Providence; and some of these instantly sink into the deluge of their first parent, and are hidden in a sheet of water, having had no other business in the world, but to be born, that they might be able to die: others float up and down two or three turns, and suddenly disappear, and give their place to others: and they that live longest upon the face of the waters, are in perpetual motion, restless and uneasy; and, being crushed with the great drop of a cloud, sink into flatness and a froth; the change not being great, it being hardly possible it should be more a nothing than it was before. So is every man; he is born in vanity and sin; he comes into the world like morning mushrooms, soon thrusting up their heads into the air, and conversing with their kindred of the same production, and as soon they turn into dust and forgetfulness: some of them without any other interest in the affairs of the world, but that they make their parents a little glad, and very sorrowful; others ride longer in the storm; it may be until seven years of vanity be expired, and then peradventure the sun shines hot upon their heads, and they fall into the shades below, into the cover of death and darkness of the grave to hide them. But if the bubble stands the shock of a bigger drop, and outlives the chances of a child, of a careless nurse, of drowning in a pail of water, of being overlaid by a sleepy servant, or such little accidents, then the young man dances like a bubble, empty and gay, and shines like a dove's neck, or the image of a rainbow, which hath no substance, and whose very imagery and colours are fantastical; and so he dances out the gaiety of his youth, and is all the while in a storm, and endures, only because he is not knocked on the head by a drop of bigger rain, or crushed by the pressure of a load of indigested meat, or quenched by the disorder of an ill-placed humour: and to preserve a man alive in the midst of so many chances and hostilities, is as great a miracle as to create him; to preserve him from rushing into nothing, and at first to draw him up from nothing, were equally the issues of an almighty power. And therefore the wise men of the world have contended, who shall best fit man's condition with words signifying his vanity and short abode. Homer calls a man "a leaf," the smallest, the weakest piece of a short-lived, unsteady plant. Pindar calls him "the dream of a shadow:" Another, "the dream of the shadow of smoke." But St. James spake by a more excellent Spirit, saying, "Our life is but a vapour," viz., drawn from the earth by a celestial influence; made of smoke, or the lighter parts of water tossed with every wind, moved by the motion of a superior body, without virtue in itself, lifted up on high, or left below, according as it pleases the sun, its foster-father. But it is lighter yet. It is but appearing; a fantastic vapour, an apparition, nothing real: it is not so much as a mist, not the matter of a shower, nor substantial enough to make a cloud; but it is like Cassiopeia's chair, or Pelops' shoulder, or the circles of heaven, φαινομενα, for which you cannot have a word that can signify a verier nothing.

And yet the expression is one degree more made diminutive; a *vapour* and *fantastical*, or a *mere appearance*, and this but for a little while neither; the very dream, the fantasm disappears in a small time, "like the shadow that departeth; or like a tale that is told; or as a dream when one awaketh." A man is so vain, so unfixed, so perishing a creature, that he cannot long last in the scene of fancy: a man goes off, and is forgotten, like the dream of a distracted person. The sum of all is this: that thou art a man, than whom there is not in the world any greater instance of heights and declensions, of lights and shadows, of misery and folly, of laughter and tears, of groans and death.

And because this consideration is of great usefulness and great necessity to many purposes of wisdom and the spirit; all the succession of time, all the changes in nature, all the varieties of light and darkness, the thousand thousands of accidents in the world, and every contingency to every man, and to every creature, doth preach our funeral sermon, and calls us to look and see, how the old sexton Time, throws up the earth, and digs a grave, where we must lay our sins or sorrows, and sow our bodies, till they rise again in a fair or an intolerable eternity. Every revolution which the sun makes about the world, divides between life and death; and death possesses both those portions by the next morrow; and we are dead to all those months which we have already lived, and we shall never live them over again: and still God makes little periods of our age. First we change our world, when we come from the womb to feel the warmth of the sun. Then we sleep and enter into the image of death, in which state we are unconcerned in all the changes of the world: and if our mothers or our nurses die, or a wild boar destroy our vineyards, or our king be sick, we regard it not, but during that state, are as disinterested, as if our eyes were closed with the clay that weeps in the bowels of the earth. At the end of seven years our teeth fall and die before us, representing a formal prologue to the tragedy; and still every seven years, it is odds, but we shall finish the last scene: and when nature, or chance, or vice, takes our body in pieces, weakening some parts and losing others, we taste the grave and the solemnities of our own funerals, first, in those parts that ministered to vice; and next, in them that served for ornament; and in a short time, even they that served for necessity become useless and entangled like the wheels of a broken clock. Baldness is but a dressing to our funerals, the proper ornament of mourning, and of a person entered very far into the regions and possession of death: and we have many more of the same signification: gray hairs, rotten teeth, dim eyes, trembling joints, short breath, stiff limbs, wrinkled skin, short memory, decayed appetite. Every day's necessity calls for a reparation of that portion, which death fed on all night, when we lay in his lap, and slept in his outer chambers. The very spirits of a man prey upon the daily portion of bread and flesh, and every meal is a rescue from one death, and lays up for another; and while we think a thought, we die; and the clock strikes and reckons on our portion of eternity; we form our words with the breath of our nostrils, we have the less to live upon for every word we speak.

Thus nature calls us to meditate of death by those things which are the instruments of acting it: and God, by all the variety of his providence, makes us see death every where, in all variety of circumstances, and dressed up for all the fancies, and the expectation of every single person. Nature hath given us one harvest every year, but death hath two: and the spring and the autumn send throngs of men and women to charnel-houses; and all the summer long, men are recovering from their evils of the spring, till the dog-days come, and then the Sirian star makes the summer deadly; and the fruits of autumn are laid up for all the year's provision, and the man that gathers them, eats and surfeits, and dies, and needs them not, and himself is laid up for eternity; and he that escapes till winter, only stays for another opportunity, which the distempers of that quarter minister to him with great variety. Thus death reigns in all the portions of our time. The autumn with its fruits provides disorders for us, and the winter's cold turns them into sharp diseases, and the spring brings flowers to strew our hearse, and the summer gives green turf and brambles to bind upon our graves. Calentures and surfeit, cold and agues, are the four quarters of the year, and all minister to death; and you can go no whither, but you tread upon a dead man's bones.

The wild fellow in Petronius, that escaped upon a broken table from the furies of a shipwreck, as he was sunning himself upon the rocky shore, espied a man rolled upon his floating bed of waves, ballasted with sand in the folds of his garment, and carried by his civil enemy, the sea, towards the shore to find a grave: and it cast him into some sad thoughts: that peradventure this man's wife, in some part of the continent, safe and warm, looks next month for the good man's return; or, it may be, his son knows nothing of the tempest; or his father thinks of that affectionate kiss, which still is warm upon the good old man's cheek, ever since he took a kind farewell; and he weeps with joy to think, how blessed he shall be, when his beloved boy returns into the circle of his father's arms. These are the thoughts of mortals, this is the end and sum of all their designs: a dark night and an ill guide, a boisterous sea and a broken cable, a hard rock and a rough wind, dashed in pieces the fortune of a whole family, and they that shall weep loudest for the accident, are not yet entered into the storm, and yet have suffered shipwreck. Then looking upon the carcass, he knew it, and found it to be the master of the ship, who, the day before, cast up the accounts of his patrimony and his trade, and named the day when he thought to be at home. See how the man swims, who was so angry two days since; his passions are becalmed with the storm, his accounts cast up, his cares at an end, his voyage done, and his gains are the strange events of death, which whether they be good or evil, the men, that are alive, seldom trouble themselves concerning the interest of the dead.

But seas alone do not break our vessel in pieces: every where we may be shipwrecked. A valiant general, when he is to reap the harvest of his crowns and triumphs, fights unprosperously, or falls into a fever with joy and wine, and changes his laurel into cypress, his triumphal chariot to a hearse; dying the night before he was appointed to perish, in the drunkenness of his festival joys. It was a sad arrest of the looseness and wilder feasts of the French court, when their king (Henry II.) was killed really by the sportive image of a fight. And many brides have died under the hands of paranymphs and maidens, dressing them for uneasy joy, the new and undiscerned chains of marriage, according to the saying of Bensirah, the wise Jew, "The bride went into her chamber, and knew not what should befal her there." Some have been paying their vows, and giving thanks for a prosperous return to their own house, and the roof hath descended upon their heads, and turned their loud religion into the deeper silence of a grave. And how many teeming mothers have rejoiced over their swelling wombs, and pleased themselves in becoming the channels of blessing to a family; and the midwife hath quickly bound their heads and feet, and carried them forth to burial! Or else the birthday of an heir hath seen the coffin of the father brought into the house, and the divided mother hath been forced to travail twice, with a painful birth, and a sadder death.

There is no state, no accident, no circumstance of our life, but it hath been soured by some sad instance of a dying friend: a friendly meeting often ends in some sad mischance, and makes an eternal parting; and when the poet Æschylus was sitting under the walls of his house, an eagle hovering over his bald head, mistook it for a stone, and let fall his oyster, hoping there to break the shell, but pierced the poor man's skull.

Death meets us every where, and is procured by every instrument, and in all chances, and enters in at many doors; by violence and secret influence, by the aspect of a star and the stink of a mist, by the emissions of a cloud and the meeting of a vapour, by the fall of a chariot and the stumbling at a stone, by a full meal or an empty stomach, by watching at the wine or by watching at prayers, by the sun or the moon; by a heat or a cold, by sleepless nights or sleeping days; by water frozen into the hardness and sharpness of a dagger; or water thawed into the floods of a river; by a hair or a raisin; by violent motion or sitting still; by severity or dissolution; by God's mercy or God's anger; by every thing in providence and every thing in manners; by every thing in nature and every thing in chance. *Eripitur persona, manet res;* we take pains to heap up things useful to our life, and get our death in the purchase; and the person is snatched away, and the goods remain. And all this is the law and constitution of nature; it is a punishment to our sins, the unalterable event of Providence, and the decree of Heaven. The chains that confine us to this condition are strong as destiny, and immutable as the eternal laws of God.

I have conversed with some men who rejoiced in the death or calamity of others, and accounted it as a judgment upon them for being on the other side, and against them in the contention; but within the revolution of a few months, the same man met with a more uneasy and unhandsome death: which when I saw, I wept, and was afraid; for I knew it must be so with all men; for we also shall die, and end our quarrels and contentions by passing to a final sentence.

REMEDIES AGAINST FEAR OF DEATH

From The Rule and Exercises of Holy Dying

He that would willingly be fearless of death, must learn to despise the world; he must neither love any thing passionately, nor be proud of any circumstance of his life. "O death, how bitter is the remembrance of thee to a man that liveth at rest in his possessions, to a man that hath nothing to vex him, and that hath prosperity in all things, yea, unto him that is yet able to receive meat!" said the son of Sirach. But the parts of this exercise help each other. If a man be not incorporated in all his passions to the things of this world, he will less fear to be divorced from them by a supervening death; and yet because he must part with them all in death, it is but reasonable, he should not be passionate for so fugitive and transient interest. But if any man thinks well of himself for being a handsome person, or if he be stronger and wiser than his neighbour, he must remember, that what he boasts of will decline into weakness and dishonour; but that very boasting and complacency will make death keener and more unwelcome, because it comes to take him from his confidences and pleasures, making his beauty equal to those ladies that have slept some years in charnel-houses, and their strength not so stubborn as the breath of an infant, and their wisdom such as can be looked for in the land, where all things are forgotten.

2. He that would not fear death, must strengthen his spirits with the proper instruments of Christian fortitude. All men are resolved upon this, that to bear grief honestly and temperately, and to die willingly and nobly, is the duty of a good and valiant man; and they that are not so, are vicious, and fools, and cowards. All men praise the valiant and honest; and that, which the very heathen admired in their noblest examples, is especially patience and contempt of death. . . . The religion of a Christian does more command fortitude, than ever did any institution; for we are commanded to be willing to die for Christ, to die for the brethren, to die rather than to give offence or scandal: the effect of which is this, that he, that is instructed to do the necessary parts of his duty, is, by the same instrument, fortified against death: as he that does his duty, need not fear death, so neither shall he; the parts of his duty are parts of his security. It is certainly a great baseness and pusillanimity of spirit that makes death terrible, and extremely to be avoided.

3. Christian prudence is a great security against the fear of death. For if we be afraid of death, it is but reasonable to use all spiritual arts to take off the apprehension of the evil: but therefore we ought to remove our fear, because fear gives to death wings, and spurs, and darts. Death hastens to a fearful man: if therefore you would make death harmless and slow, to throw off fear is the way to do it; and prayer is the way to do that. If therefore you be afraid of death, consider you will have less need to fear it, by how much the less you do fear it: and so cure your direct fear by a reflex act of prudence and consideration. . . . I remember a story of the wrestler Polydamas, that, running into a cave to avoid the storm, the water at last swelled so high, that it began to press that hollowness to a ruin: which when his fellows espied, they chose to enter into the common fate of all men, and went abroad: but Polydamas thought by his strength to support the earth, till its intolerable weight crushed him into flatness and a grave. Many men run for a shelter to a place, and they only find a remedy for their fears by feeling the worst of evils. Fear itself finds no sanctuary but the worst of sufferance: and they that fly from a battle, are exposed to the mercy and fury of the pursuers, who, if they faced about, were as well disposed to give laws of life and death as to take them, and at worst can but die nobly; but now, even at the very best, they live shamefully, or die timorously. Courage is the greatest security; for it

does most commonly safeguard the man, but always rescues the condition from an intolerable evil.

4. If thou wilt be fearless of death, endeavour to be in love with the felicities of saints and angels, and be once persuaded to believe, that there is a condition of living better than this; that there are creatures more noble than we; that above there is a country better than ours; that the inhabitants know more and know better, and are in places of rest and desire; and first learn to value it, and then learn to purchase it, and death cannot be a formidable thing, which lets us into so much joy and so much felicity. And indeed who would not think his condition mended, if he passed from conversing with dull mortals, with ignorant and foolish persons, with tyrants and enemies of learning, to converse with Homer and Plato, with Socrates and Cicero, with Plutarch and Fabricius? So the heathens speculated; but we consider higher. "The dead that die in the Lord," shall converse with St. Paul, and all the college of the apostles, and all the saints and martyrs, with all the good men, whose memory we preserve in honour, with excellent kings and holy bishops, and with the great shepherd and bishop of our souls Christ Jesus, and with God himself. For "Christ died for us, that, whether we wake or sleep, we might live together with him." Then we shall be free from lust and envy, from fear and rage, from covetousness and sorrow, from tears and cowardice: and these indeed, properly are the only evils that are contrary to felicity and wisdom. Then we shall see strange things, and know new propositions, and all things in another manner and to higher purposes. . . .

5. If God should say to us, Cast thyself into the sea, (as Christ did to St. Peter, or as God concerning Jonas,) I have provided for thee a dolphin, or a whale, or a port, a safety or a deliverance, security or a reward, were we not incredulous and pusillanimous persons, if we should tremble to put such a felicity into act, and ourselves into possession? The very duty of resignation and the love of our own interest are good antidotes against fear. In forty or fifty years we find evils enough, and arguments enough to make us weary of this life: and to a good man there are very many more reasons to be afraid of life than death, this having in it less of evil and more of advantage. And it was a rare wish of that Roman, that death might come only to wise and excellent persons, and not to fools and cowards; that it might not be a sanctuary for the timorous, but the reward of the virtuous; and indeed they only can make advantage of it.

6. Make no excuses to make thy desires of life seem reasonable; neither cover thy fear with pretences, but suppress it rather with arts of severity and ingenuity. Some are not willing to submit to God's sentence and arrest of death, till they have finished such a design, or made an end of the last paragraph of their book, or raised such portions for their children, or preached so many sermons, or built their house, or planted their orchard, or ordered their estate with such advantages. It is well for the modesty of these men, that the excuse is ready; but if it were not, it is certain they would search one out: for an idle man is never ready to die, and is glad of any excuse; and a busied man hath always something unfinished, and he is ready for every thing but death. And I remember that Petronius brings in Eumolpus composing verses in a desperate storm: and being called upon to shift for himself when the ship dashed upon the rock, crying out, to let him alone, until he had trimmed and finished his verse, which was lame in the hinder leg: the man either had too strong a desire to end his verse, or too great a desire not to end his life. But we must know, God's times are not to be measured by our circumstances; and what I value, God regards not: or if it be valuable in the accounts of men, yet God will supply it with other contingencies of his providence: and if Epaphroditus had died, when he had his great sickness St. Paul speaks of, God would have secured the

work of the gospel without him; and he could have spared Epaphroditus as well as St. Stephen, and St. Peter as well as St. James. Say no more; but, when God calls, lay aside thy papers; and first dress thy soul, and then dress thy hearse.

Blindness is odious, and widowhood is sad, and destitution is without comfort, and persecution is full of trouble, and famine is intolerable, and tears are the sad ease of a sadder heart: but these are evils of our life, not of our death. For the dead that die in the Lord, are so far from wanting the commodities of this life, that they do not want life itself.

After all this, I do not say it is a sin to be afraid of death: we find the boldest spirit, that discourses of it with confidence, and dares undertake a danger as big as death, yet doth shrink at the horror of it, when it comes dressed in its proper circumstances. And Brutus, who was as bold a Roman to undertake a noble action as any was since they first reckoned by consuls, yet when Furius came to cut his throat, after his defeat by Anthony, he ran from it like a girl: and being admonished to die constantly, he swore by his life, that he would shortly endure death. But what do I speak of such imperfect persons? Our blessed Lord was pleased to legitimate fear to us by his agony and prayers in the garden. It is not a sin to be afraid, but it is a great felicity to be without fear; which felicity our dearest Saviour refused to have, because it was agreeable to his purposes to suffer any thing that was contrary to felicity, every thing but sin. But when men will by all means avoid death, they are like those, who at any hand resolve to be rich. The case may happen, in which they will blaspheme, and dishonour Providence, or do a base action, or curse God and die: but, in all cases, they die miserable and insnared, and in no case do they die the less for it. Nature hath left us the key of the churchyard, and custom hath brought cemeteries and charnel-houses into cities and churches, places most frequented, that we might not carry ourselves strangely in so certain, so expected, so ordinary, so unavoidable an accident. All reluctancy or unwillingness, to obey the Divine decree is but a snare to ourselves, and a load to our spirits, and is either an entire cause, or a great aggravation of the calamity. Who did not scorn to look upon Xerxes when he caused three hundred stripes to be given to the sea, and sent a chartel of defiance against the mountain Athos? Who did not scorn the proud vanity of Cyrus, when he took so goodly a revenge upon the river Cydnus for his hard passage over it? or did not deride or pity the Thracians for shooting arrows against heaven when it thunders? To be angry with God, to quarrel with the Divine providence, by repining against an unalterable, a natural, an easy sentence, is an argument of a huge folly, and the parent of a great trouble; a man is base and foolish to no purpose, he throws away a vice to his own misery, and to no advantages of ease and pleasure. Fear keeps men in bondage all their life, saith St. Paul: and patience makes him his own man, and lord of his own interest and person. Therefore possess yourselves in patience, with reason and religion, and you shall die with ease.

If all the parts of this discourse be true, if they be better than dreams, and unless virtue be nothing but words, as a grove is a heap of trees; if they be not the fantasms of hypochondriacal persons, and designs upon the interest of men, and their persuasions to evil purposes; then there is no reason, but that we should really desire death, and account it among the good things of God, and the sour and labourious felicities of man. St. Paul understood it well, when he desired to be dissolved; he well enough knew his own advantages, and pursued them accordingly. But it is certain, that he, that is afraid of death, I mean, with a violent and transporting fear, with a fear apt to discompose his duty or his patience, that man either loves this world too much, or dares not trust God for the next.

John A. Comenius
(1592-1670)

No seventeenth-century religious leader had a clearer view of a universal society than Comenius. He felt that this common brotherhood could be established by universal education through a universal language, a world congress of religion, and the translation of the Bible into all languages. Comenius was ordained into the United Brethren Church in 1616. In 1621 he lost his wife and child in a plague. For three years following 1624 he and other evangelical ministers were exiled to the mountains of his native Moravia. His influence spread throughout Poland, England, Sweden, and Transylvania. In 1656 the Poles banished him to Amsterdam, where he gave himself to writing. The selections from *The Labyrinth of the World* illustrate the finest qualities of Christian sainthood, where "the saints have an abundance of everything." The work has been translated by Matthew Spinka (Chicago, 1942), who has given permission for the use of the section included here.

[THE GLORIES OF THE SAINTLY LIFE]
From *The Labyrinth of the World*

THE LIBERTY OF HEARTS DEVOTED TO GOD

Thence they derive what the wisest of the world vainly seek in their affairs—namely, perfect freedom of mind, so that they are subjected to or bound by nothing but God, nor are they constrained to do anything contrary to their will. While in the world I saw nothing done but by compulsion, all things going contrary to every one's desires, each binding himself or others more than was proper and then was compelled to do it either by the force of his or someone else's will, so that he was ever struggling either with himself or with others. Here all was serene. For all having given themselves to God so completely that they cared for nothing else, they acknowledged no one above themselves but God. Therefore, they did not obey the commands of the world, but spurned its promises, laughing at its threats, and regarding as inferior all external things, because of their certainty of the value of their inward riches.

The result is that a Christian, otherwise quite approachable, yielding, willing, and obliging, in the privilege of his heart is adamant. Hence he is attached neither to friends nor foes, nor to lord or king, nor to wife or children, nor finally even to himself to such an extent that he would feel obliged, for their sake, to recede in any way from his purpose, namely, from the fear of God, but proceeds unflinchingly forward. Whatever the world may do, say, threaten, promise, command, beg, advise, or order, he does not permit himself to be moved.

The world, ever perverse, grasping a shadow in place of the truth, imagines that liberty consists in being free, in serving no one, but in surrendering oneself to idleness, pride, and passions. Contrariwise, a Christian acts far differently: for he, after fortifying well his own heart that it may preserve its freedom in God, employs all else in ministering to the needs of his fellows. For I have seen and learned that no greater servitude exists anywhere, and none is more enslaved than the man devoted to God, for he performs willingly and gladly even the lowest menial services which one intoxicated with the world would loath. Whenever he sees an opportunity to be of benefit to his fellows, he hesitates not a moment, dallies not, spares not himself, exaggerates not the services rendered, does not continually remind the other of them, never fails, but whether treated with gratitude or not, quietly and joyfully keeps on serving.

Oh, the blessed servitude of the sons of God than which nothing freer could be imagined, in which man submits himself to God in order to be free everywhere else! Oh, the unhappy liberty of the world than which no greater slavery can be imagined, in which many not heeding God, permit themselves to become miserable slaves of things! Particularly when they serve creatures over whom they should rule, and resist God whom they should obey. Oh, mortals, would that we might understand that there is but one and only one who is higher than we, the Lord, our maker and our future judge! Who having the power to command us, does not constrain us as slaves, but invites us as children to His obedience; desiring that even when we obey we do so freely and unconstrained. Truly, to serve Christ is to reign over a kingdom: and to be a slave of God is a greater glory than to be the monarch of all the earth. What then shall it be to be a friend and a child of God!

The Rule of the Spiritual Christians

God indeed desires to have His children free, but not self-willed. Therefore, He surrounded them with certain rules more perfectly than anything similar I could find anywhere else in the world. There, indeed, everything was topsy-turvy; partly because it had no definite order, and partly because people did not observe what there was of it. But those who dwell within the partition, possess a most excellent rule and observe it. For they have rules given them by God himself, replete with justice, which decree that everyone devoted to God must profess and know none but Himself as God, and serve Him in spirit and in truth, without devising any carnal additions. He must employ his tongue not in offending but in honoring His revered name; he must spend the times and seasons appointed for the service in none but His outward and inward worship; to be subject to parents and others appointed by God over him; to cause no injury to the life of his neighbor; to preserve his body in purity; to respect the property of others; to eschew falsehood and trickery; and to restrain his mind within the bounds and limits prescribed.

In brief, he must love God above all which can be named and must sincerely desire as great a good for his neighbor as for himself. Which sum of God's laws, comprised in these two sentences, I have heard praised very highly, and myself have found and tested that it is worth all the innumerable laws, enactments, and decrees, yea, is a thousand times better than they.

For he who loves God with all his heart, needs no prescriptions as to when, where, and how much to serve, worship, and adore Him. For that sincere union with God in itself, as well as his readiness to obey, is the most acceptable worship to God and leads man to praise God through his very being and to glorify Him through all his deeds. Similarly, he who loves his neighbor as himself needs no elaborate directions where, when, and wherein he should have regard for him, wherein he should not injure him, and wherein to return the debt which is due; love will fully instruct and show him how to conduct himself. It is the sign of a wicked man to demand everywhere his rights and to guide himself in his conduct toward others strictly in accordance with written rules; for as the finger of God points out to our hearts that which we desire for ourselves, we are in duty bound to deal similarly with our neighbors. But because the world ignores the inner witness of its own conscience and observes only the external regulations, it follows that there is no rightful order in the world, but only suspicion, mistrust, misunderstanding, jealousies, quarrels, envy, hatred, theft, murder, and what not. But those who are truly devoted to God, guard their conscience above all, and whatever it forbids, they do not do; whatever it commands them as proper, they do, irrespective of gain, favor, or any such thing.

Thence follows a certain unanimity or similarity of one to another, for they are as if cast in the same mould: all think alike, believe alike, like and dislike the same, because all have been taught by one and the same Spirit. And it is remarkable (a thing I observed with gladness) that men who have never seen or heard of each other and have been separated by the breadth of the world, yet are so much alike as two peas: they speak the same things, see and feel the same, as if they were one. Nevertheless, there is a great diversity of their talents among them, just as among musical instruments the strings and pipes give out a different quality of tones, either softer or louder, yet their symphony is pleasing. This is the great secret of Christian unity, in fact a proof of the divine unity and the foreshadowing of eternity, where all things shall be dominated by one spirit.

From this unanimity arises their sympathy, so that they rejoice with those who rejoice and mourn with those who mourn. For I have remarked a most iniquitous thing in the world, which saddened me many a time: that whenever anyone fared ill, others were glad of it; whenever he strayed, they laughed at him; whenever he suffered loss, others tried to profit by it and for their profit, entertainment, and sport they themselves caused their neighbor's downfall and misfortune. Among these Christians I found no such thing; for each tried to ward off misfortune and calamity from his neighbor as earnestly and diligently as from himself; and if he could not ward it off, he was as genuinely grieved as if it had touched himself; as a matter of fact, it did touch him, for they were all but one heart and one soul. Just as all compass-needles, when magnetized, point in the same direction, so the hearts of these people, touched by the spirit of love, turn all in the same direction: in happiness to joy, in misfortune to grief. Here I learned that those are but false Christians who attend diligently only to their own affairs and care not for their neighbors, but evading adroitly the hand of God, protect only their own nests, leaving others out in the wind and the rain. Far different order have I observed here: when one suffered, the rest did not rejoice; when one was hungry, the rest did not feast; when one was fighting, the rest did not sleep; but all things were done in common, so that it was a joy to look at it.

Concerning possessions, I observed that although the majority of them were poor, not possessing or caring for much of what the world calls riches, nevertheless almost every one owned some; but he did not conceal it, and (as it happened in the world) hide it from the rest, but held it as if in common, ready and willing to aid anyone and to loan it to anyone in need of it. All used their property in such a way that it was no less than as if they all were around a common table and used the service with equal right. Seeing this, I was ashamed to think that with us it often happens contrariwise, some filling and cluttering their houses with furnishings, clothes, food, gold, and silver as much as they can, while at the same time others, who are no less God's servants, have scarcely enough to eat and to put on. Then I understood, I repeat, that it was by no means the will of God but the usage of this perverse world that some should go about in finery while others are naked; some belching with over-gorging while others yawn with hunger; some earning laboriously, others squandering profligately; some spending their time in amusements, others in weeping. From this follow pride and contempt of others on the part of the former, and envy, jealousy, and other passions on the part of the latter. But no such thing was found among these Christians; for everything was common to all, even to their very souls.

This resulted in their mutual intimacy, openness, and holy companionship, so that they regarded and dealt with one another as brethren in spite of their differences of talents and occupations. They declared that we all are of the same blood, are all redeemed and washed by the same blood, are children of one common Father, use the same common table, await the same inheritance in heaven, and so forth. With the exception of non-essential matters, one had no superiority over another. Therefore, I observed each to hold the other in higher estimation and honor, and to serve him willingly, employing his own circumstances to further the advancement of others; whoever had counsel, advised others; whoever learning, taught others; whoever strength, defended others; whoever power, maintained order among them. If anyone erred in anything, others admonished him; if he sinned, they punished him. Moreover each gladly submitted himself both to admonition and to punishment, being ready to make amends for anything if shown to have been wrong, even to give up his body if he were shown that it did not belong to him.

Hearts Devoted to God Find All Things Light and Easy

Nor do they find it difficult to conform to such a rule, but on the contrary it is their pleasure and delight, while in the world men conformed but unwillingly, only as they were constrained to do so. For God had changed the stony heart of His servants and gave them hearts of flesh, pliable and perfectly yielding to His will. And although the devil placed many obstacles in their way by his crafty suggestions, as well as the world with its corrupting examples, and the flesh by its natural disinclination toward the good, yet they care not for any of these things and drive the devil away by the bombardment of their prayers, guard themselves against the world by the shield of their unswerving determination, and compel their body to obedience by the scourge of discipline. Thus they joyfully continue to perform their duties, and the spirit of Christ, dwelling in them, restores their strength so that they lack neither in willingness nor in the actual performance of their duties (within the limits of their present possibility). Thus I found that in reality to serve God with one's whole heart is not a drudgery but a delight: and realized that those who too

frequently excused themselves on the score of human frailty, did not appreciate the power and validity of the new birth, and perhaps had never experienced it; that was, however, their own affair. But among the Christians I found none to defend his sins by alleging the weakness of the flesh, or to excuse the perpetration of a vile deed by the frailty of his human nature. But here I observed that whoever had surrendered his entire heart to Him who had created it, redeemed it, and sanctified it for His temple, found his other members freely and by degrees to follow the heart, and to incline where God directed. Oh, Christian, whoever you are, free yourself from the fetters of the flesh, discover, try, and learn that the obstacles which your mind imagines are not able to impede your will, provided only that you are in earnest!

But not only is it easy to do what God desires, but even to bear what He imposes. For not a few of those here present were buffeted, spat upon, and beaten by the world, but wept with joy and lifted their hands to God in praise that He had deemed them worthy to suffer for His name. So that they not only believed in the Crucified, but were also, in His honor, themselves crucified. Others, who had been spared the persecutions, envied them with a holy envy, fearing God's wrath for the lack of correction, and an alienation from Christ for the lack of the cross. Consequently, they kissed the scourge and the rod of God whenever they were scourged by Him and embraced every kind of cross.

All this was the result of the complete consecration of their will to God, so that they might do nothing else or desire to become nothing else than as God willed. Therefore, whatever befell them, they felt confident that it had come from God's providential decree. Nothing unexpected could overcome such men, for they counted stripes, prisons, tortures, and death among God's benefits. Whether they lived in abundance or in want was indifferent to them, save that the former they regarded as the more suspicious, the latter the safer. Consequently, they took pride and delight in their trials, wounds, and scars. In brief, they were so seasoned in God that unless they suffered, they regarded themselves as idling and wasting time. Nevertheless, it were better not to lay hands on them rashly: for the more eagerly they expose their backs, the more difficult it is to strike them; and the more like fools they seem, the more dangerous it is to ridicule them. For they belong no longer to themselves but to God, and what is done to them is regarded by God as done to Himself.

The Saints Have an Abundance of Everything

The world is full of Marthas, hustling and bustling, breathlessly gathering from all directions and yet never having enough. These Christians, on the contrary, have a different temper: for each desires only to sit quietly at the feet of the Lord, satisfied with whatever befalls him there. They regard as their truest riches the grace of God which dwells in them and comfort themselves with that alone. The external possessions which the world calls riches, they regard as more of a burden than of benefit, but use them for the necessities of life—the necessities, I say. Therefore, whatever God grants them whether it be much or little, they profess to be enough. They believe in and fully rely upon God's protection, and thus regard it as improper to desire anything beyond what God has granted them.

I observed a very puzzling phenomenon here: some had plenty of wealth, silver, gold, crowns, and sceptres (for God has even such among His own), others almost nothing save their ill-clad body, emaciated with hunger and thirst. Yet the former professed to have nothing, while the latter to have everything, and were of equally cheerful spirit. Then I understood that he alone is truly wealthy and lacks nothing who knows how to be content with what he has, whether it be much, little, or no money; a large, small or no house; expensive or cheap clothing, or position, office, honor, fame, or none; in brief, to be something

or nothing is equally indifferent to them, in the conviction that whatever God desires for them or leads them to, or lifts them up to, or seats them to, thus should they go, stand, or sit; all that being better than they understand.

Oh, the blessed and most desirable abundance! How happy are those who are wealthy in such a fashion! For even though in the eyes of the world some of them should appear wretched and miserable, yet in reality they are a thousand times better provided for, even from the temporal point of view, than many worldly rich. For the latter must protect themselves, being subject, along with their riches, to a thousand accidents, in danger of losing it by fire, water, rust, thieves, and other exigencies. The former have God for their guardian and ever find in Him a source of living supply of all their needs; for He feeds them daily from His stores, clothes them from His supply, gives them for their expenditures out of His treasury—if not beyond their needs, at least always what is properly needful. And if His grants are not in accordance with their desires, they are according to His providence in which they trust a thousand times more readily than in their own reason.

The Safety of Men Devoted to God

Although nothing seems so vulnerable and subjected to every kind of danger as the company of the devout—they being menaced, buffeted, and beaten both by the devil and the world—nevertheless I saw that they were well guarded. For their group was visibly surrounded by a fiery wall which—when I approached it —I perceived to be moving. For it was nothing less than a line of many thousand of thousands angels who prevented all enemies even from approaching their charges. Besides, every Christian had an angel ordained and sent by God to be his guardian, whose duty it was to watch over him and protect and defend him against dangers and snares, pits and ambush, traps and all manner of entanglements. They are indeed (as I myself learned and observed) lovers of men, being their own fellow-servants, when they see them observe the duties for which God created them; such they serve willingly, guarding them against the devil, wicked men, and unfortunate accidents, even carrying them in their arms, to protect them from harm. Then I realized how much depends upon piety, for these beautiful and pure spirits dwelt only where they perceived the fragrance of virtue, but were repelled by the stench of sins and impurity.

I likewise observed (a thing not proper to conceal) another benefit derived from this invisible holy company: namely, that they not only served as guardians, but also as teachers of the elect, to whom they often transmitted secret hints and whom they taught the deep hidden mysteries of God. For since they ever look upon the face of the omniscient God, none of those things which a pious man desires to know can remain hidden from them. They, in turn, reveal what they know, with God's permission, to men, if such knowledge is needed by the elect. Consequently, the heart of the devout often has a presentiment of what happens elsewhere, and finds itself sorrowful in untoward and joyful in auspicious circumstances. It follows then that through dreams and other visions or through inward inspiration they can picture in their minds either what has happened in the past, is taking place now, or shall come to pass in the future. From this source come increase of the gifts of God within us, penetrating, useful meditations, various astounding inventions with which a man often surpasses himself, not knowing where they originated. Oh, the blessed school of the sons of God! This is what often brings all the wisdom of the world to utter amazement, when it sees some plain person to proclaim deep mysteries and to foretell future changes in the world and the church as if he saw them before his eyes, and names then yet unborn Kings and heads of states, and predicts and announces other matters which could not possibly

be learned from any study of the stars nor from any exercise of human ingenuity. All these things are of such great benefit that we can never sufficiently thank our protector, God, for them, or ever to love those heavenly teachers enough. But let us return to the safety of the devout.

I saw that each one of them was surrounded not only by the angelic protection, but also by God's own august presence, so that they inspired terror in those who attempted to attack them without God's permission. I saw miracles performed by some who had been thrown into water, or fire, or to lions and wild beasts, but suffered no harm whatever. Some had been fiercely attacked by human ferocity, having been surrounded by a horde of tyrants and hangmen with their henchmen, so that sometimes powerful kings and whole kingdoms have labored assiduously for their destruction; but they remained unhurt and withstood it, cheerfully walking about their business. Then I realized what it was to have God for one's shield; for when He commands His servants to accomplish certain tasks in the world, and they go about their duty courageously, He, dwelling in and about them, guards them as the apple of His eye so that they do not succumb until their allotted task is finished.

They are well aware of this God's protection and cheerfully rely upon it. I heard some of them boast that they fear not even if the shadow of death be before them, or if thousands should fall beside them, or the whole world be risen up and the earth cast itself into the middle of the sea, or the world be full of devils, and so forth. Oh, the thrice happy security, unheard of in the world, when a man is held and protected so securely in the hand of God that he is safe from the power of all other things! Let us understand, ye true servants of Christ, that we have a most watchful guardian and protector—the almighty God Himself. Blessed are we!

Henry Scougal

(1650-1678)

IN the Scottish tradition no devotional writer ranks higher than Scougal, best known through his classic *The Life of God in the Soul of Man*. He was ordained in 1672, became precentor in the Aberdeen cathedral, was later appointed professor of divinity in King's College. He is reputed to be the first professor in Scotland to teach the philosophy of Francis Bacon. Scholarly in disposition, he nevertheless with mystical depth sees the heart of religious experience as "hid with Christ in God." *The Life of God in the Soul of Man* is portrayed through that medium. From that writing the selections below are taken.

[ON ATTAINING CHRISTIAN EXCELLENCE]

From *The Life of God in the Soul of Man*

WE MUST DO WHAT WE CAN, AND DEPEND ON THE DIVINE ASSISTANCE

Away then with all perplexing fears and desponding thoughts: to undertake vigorously, and rely confidently on the divine assistance, is more than half the conquest (I Chron. 22:16): "Let us arise and be doing, and the Lord will be with us." It is true, religion in the souls of men is the immediate work of God, and all our natural endeavors can neither produce it alone nor merit those supernatural aids by which it must be wrought: the Holy Ghost must come upon us, and the power of the Highest must overshadow us, before that holy thing can be begotten, and Christ be formed in us. But yet we must not expect that this whole work should be done without any concurring endeavors of our own: we must not lie loitering in the ditch, and wait till Omnipotence pull us from thence. No, no, we must bestir ourselves, and exert those powers which we have already received: we must put forth ourselves to our utmost capacities, and then we may hope that (I Cor. 15:58) "our labor shall not be in vain in the Lord." All the art and industry of man can not form the smallest herb, or make a stalk of corn to grow in the field, it is the energy of nature, and the influences of heaven, which produce this effect: it is God who (Ps. 104:14) "causes the grass to grow, and herb for the service of man"; and yet nobody will say, that the labors of the husbandman are useless or unnecessary. So, likewise, the human soul is immediately created by God: it is he who both formeth and enliveneth the child; and yet he hath appointed the marriagebed as the ordinary means for the propagation of mankind. Tho there must intervene a stroke of Omnipotence to effect this mighty change in our souls, yet ought we to do what we can to fit and prepare ourselves (Jer. 4:3); "for we must break up our fallow ground, and root out the weeds, and pull up the thorns, that so we may be more ready to receive the seeds of grace, and the dew of heaven." It is true, God hath been found of some who sought him not; he hath cast himself in their way, who were quite out of his; he hath laid hold upon them, and stopt their course of a sudden; for so was St. Paul converted in his journey to Damascus. But certainly this is not God's ordinary method of dealing with men: tho he hath not tied himself to means, yet he hath tied us to the use of them; and we have never more reason to expect the divine assistance, than when we are doing our utmost endeavors. It shall therefore be my next work, to show what course we ought to take for attaining that blessed temper I have hitherto described. But here, if in delivering my own thoughts, I shall chance to differ from what is or may be said by others in this matter, I would not be thought to contradict and oppose them, more than physicians do when they prescribe several remedies for the same disease, which perhaps are all useful and good. Every one may propose the method he judges most proper and convenient; but he doth not thereby pretend that the cure can never be effected unless that be exactly observed. I doubt it hath occasioned much unnecessary disquietude to some holy persons that they have not found such a regular and orderly transaction in their souls as they have seen described in books; that they have not passed through all those steps and stages of conversion, which some (who perhaps have felt them in themselves) have too peremptorily prescribed unto others. God hath several ways of dealing with the souls of men, and it sufficeth if the work be accomplished, whatever the methods have been.

Again, tho in proposing directions, I must follow that order which the nature of things shall lead to; yet I do not mean that the same method should be so punctually observed in the practise, as if the latter rules were never to be heeded till some considerable time have been spent in practising the former. The directions I intend are mutually conducive one to another, and are all to be performed as occasion shall serve, and we find ourselves enabled to perform them.

We Must Shun All Manner of Sin

But now, that I may detain you no longer, if we desire to have our souls molded to this holy frame, to become partakers of the divine nature, and have Christ formed in our hearts, we must seriously resolve, and carefully endeavor, to avoid and abandon all vicious and sinful practises. There can be no treaty of peace till once we lay down these weapons of rebellion wherewith we fight against heaven; nor can we expect to have our distempers cured, if we be daily feeding on poison. Every wilful sin gives a mortal wound to the soul, and puts it at a greater distance from God and goodness; and we can never hope to have our hearts purified from corrupt affections, unless we cleanse our hands from vicious actions. Now in this case, we can not excuse ourselves by the pretense of impossibility; for sure our outward man is some way in our power: we have some command of our feet, and hands, and tongue, nay, and of our thoughts and fancies too, at least so far as to divert them from impure and sinful objects and to turn our mind another way; and we should find this power and authority much strengthened and advanced, if we were careful to manage and exercise it. In the meanwhile, I acknowledge our corruptions are so strong, and our temptations so many, that it will require a great deal of stedfastness and resolution, of watchfulness and care, to preserve ourselves even in this degree of innocence and purity.

We Must Know What Things Are Sinful

And first, let us inform ourselves well what those sins are from which we ought to abstain. And here we must not take our measures from the maxims of the world, or the practises of those whom in charity we account good men. Most people have very light apprehension of these things, and are not sensible of any fault, unless it be gross and flagitious, and scarce reckon any so great as that which they call preciseness: and those who are more serious do many times allow themselves too great latitude and freedom. Alas! how much pride and vanity and passion and humor, how much weakness and folly and sin, doth every day show itself in their converse and behavior? It may be they are humbled for it, and striving against it, and are daily gaining some ground; but then the progress is so small, and their failings so many, that we have need to choose an exacter pattern. Every one of us must answer for himself, and the practises of others will never warrant and secure us. It is the highest of folly to regulate our actions by any other standard than that by which they must be judged. If ever we would "cleanse our way," it must be "by taking heed thereto according to the word of God" (Ps. 119:9); and that "word which is quick and powerful, and sharper than any two-edged sword, piercing even to the dividing asunder of soul and spirit, and of the joints and marrow, and is a discerner of the thoughts and intents of the heart" (Heb. 4:12), will certainly discover many things to be sinful and heinous, which pass for very innocent in the eyes of the world: let us therefore imitate the Psalmist, who saith, "Concerning the works of men, by the words of thy lips, I have kept myself from the paths of the destroyer" (Ps. 17:4). Let us acquaint ourselves with the strict and holy laws of our religion: let us consider the discourses of our blessed Savior (especially the divine sermon on the mount), and the writings of his holy apostles, where an ingenuous and unbiased mind may clearly discern those limits and bounds by which our actions ought to be confined: and then let us never look upon any sin as light and inconsiderable; but be fully persuaded that the smallest is infinitely heinous in the sight of God and prejudicial to the souls of men; and that if we had the right sense of things, we should be as deeply affected with the least irregularities as now we are with the highest crimes.

WE MUST KEEP A CONSTANT WATCH OVER OURSELVES

But it will not suffice to consider these things once and again, nor to form some resolutions of abandoning our sins unless we maintain a constant guard and be continually watching against them. Sometimes the mind is awakened to see the dismal consequences of a vicious life, and straight we are resolved to reform; but, alas! it presently falleth asleep, and we lose that prospect which we had of things, and then temptations take the advantage; they solicit and importune as continually, and so do frequently engage our consent before we are aware. It is the folly and ruin of most people to live at adventure, and take part in every thing that comes in their way seldom considering what they are about to say or do. If we would have our resolutions take effect, we must take heed unto our ways and set a watch before the door of our lips, and examine the motions that arise in our hearts, and cause them to tell us whence they come, and whither they go; whether it be pride or passion, or any corrupt and vicious humor, that prompteth us to any design, and whether God will be offended, or anybody harmed by it. And if we have no time for long reasonings, let us, at least, turn our eyes toward God, and place ourselves in his presence to ask his leave and approbation for what we do; let us consider ourselves under the all-seeing eye of that divine majesty, as in the midst of an infinite globe of light, which compasseth us about both behind and before, and pierceth to the innermost corners of our soul. The sense and remembrance of the divine presence is the most ready and effectual means, both to discover what is unlawful, and to restrain us from it. There are some things a person could make shift to palliate or defend, and yet he dares not look the Almighty God in the Face and adventure upon them.

If we look unto him, we shall be lightened; if we "set him always before us," he will "guide us by his eye, and instruct us in the way wherein we ought to walk."

WE MUST OFTEN EXAMINE OUR ACTIONS

This care and watchfulness over our actions must be seconded by frequent and serious reflections upon them, not only that we may obtain the divine mercy and pardon for our sins, by an humble and sorrowful acknowledgment of them; but also that we may re-enforce and strengthen our resolutions, and learn to decline or resist the temptations by which we have been formerly foiled. It is an advice worthy of a Christian, tho it did first drop from a heathen pen, that before we betake ourselves to rest, we renew and examine all the passages of the day, that we may have the comfort of what we have done aright, and may redress what we find to have been amiss, and make the shipwrecks of one day be as marks to direct our course in another. This may be called the very art of virtuous living, and would contribute wonderfully to advance our reformation, and preserve our innocence. But, withal, we must not forget to implore the divine assistance, especially against those sins that do most easily beset us; and tho it be supposed that our hearts are not yet molded into that spiritual frame, which should render our devotions acceptable, yet, methinks, such considerations as have been proposed to deter us from sin may also stir us up to some natural seriousness, and make our prayers against it as earnest, at least, as they are wont to be against other calamities: and I doubt not but God, who heareth the cry of the ravens, will have some regard even to such petitions as proceed from those natural passions which himself hath implanted in us. Beside, that those prayers against sin will be powerful engagements on ourselves to excite us to watchfulness and care; and common ingenuity will make us ashamed to relapse into those faults which we have lately bewailed before God, and against which we have begged his assistance.

We Must Restrain Ourselves in Many Lawful Things

Thus are we to make the first essay for recovering the divine life, by restraining the natural inclinations, that they break not out into sinful practises. But not I must add, that Christian prudence will teach us to abstain from gratifications that are not simply unlawful, and that, not only that we may secure our innocence, which would be in continual hazard, if we should strain our liberty to the utmost point; but also, that hereby we may weaken the forces of nature, and teach our appetites to obey. We must do with ourselves as prudent parents with their children, who cross their wills in many little indifferent things to make them manageable and submissive in more considerable instances. He who would mortify the pride and vanity of his spirit should stop his ears to the most deserved praises, and sometimes forbear his just vindication from the censures and aspersions of others, especially if they reflect only upon his prudence and conduct, and not on his virtue and innocence. He who would check a revengeful humor, would do well to deny himself the satisfaction of representing unto others the injuries which he hath sustained; and if we would so take heed to our ways that we sin not with our tongue, we must accustom ourselves much to solitude and silence, and sometimes, with the psalmist, "hold our peace even from good," till once we have gotten some command over that unruly member. Thus, I say, we may bind up our natural inclinations, and make our appetites more moderate in their cravings, by accustoming them to frequent refusals; but it is not enough to have them under violence and restraint.

We Must Strive To Put Ourselves Out of Love With the World

Our next essay must be, to wean our affections from created things, and all the delights and entertainments of the lower life, which sink and depress the souls of men, and retard their motions toward God and heaven; and this we must do by possessing our minds with a deep persuasion of the vanity and emptiness of worldly enjoyments. This is an ordinary theme, and everybody can make declamations upon it; but, alas! how few understand and believe what they say! These notions float in our brains, and come sliding off our tongues, but we have no deep impression of them on our spirits; we feel not the truth which we pretend to believe. We can tell, that all the glory and splendor, all the pleasures and enjoyments of the world are vanity and nothing; and yet these nothings take up all our thought, and engross all our affections; they stifle the better inclinations of our soul, and inveigle us into many a sin. It may be, in a sober mood we give them the slight, and resolve to be no longer deluded with them; but these thoughts seldom outlive the next temptation! the vanities which we have shut out at the door get in at the postern: there are still some pretensions, some hopes that flatter us! and after we have been frustrated a thousand times, we must continually be repeating the experiment: the least difference of circumstances is enough to delude us, and make us expect that satisfaction in one thing which we have missed in another; but could we once get clearly off, and come to a real and serious contempt of worldly things, this were a very considerable advancement in our way. The soul of man is a vigorous and active nature, and hath in it a raging and unextinguishable thirst, an immaterial kind of fire, always catching at some object or other, in conjunction wherewith it thinks to be happy; and were it once rent from the world, and all the bewitching enjoyments under the sun, it would quickly search after some higher and more excellent objects to satisfy its ardent and importunate cravings; and being no longer dazzled with glittering vanities, would fix on that supreme and all-sufficient Good, where it would discover such beauty and sweetness as would charm and overpower all its affections. The love of the world and the love of God are like the scales of a balance! as the one falleth, the other doth rise: when our natural inclinations prosper, and the creature is exalted in our soul, religion is faint, and doth languish; but when earthly objects wither away, and lose their beauty, and the soul begins to cool and flag in its prosecution of them, then the seeds of grace take root, and the divine life begins to flourish and prevail. It doth, therefore, nearly concern us, to convince ourselves of the emptiness and vanity of creature-enjoyments, and reason our heart out of love with them: let us seriously consider all that our reason, or our faith, our own experience, or the observation of others, can suggest to this effect! let us ponder the matter over and over, and fix our thoughts on this truth, till we become really persuaded of it.

Amid all our pursuits and designs, let us stop and ask ourselves, For what end is all this? at what do I aim? can the gross and muddy pleasures of sense, or a heap of white and yellow earth, or the esteem and affection of silly creatures, like myself, satisfy a rational and immortal soul? have I not tried these things already? will they have a higher relish and yield me more contentment to-morrow than yesterday, or the next year than they did the last? There may be some little difference betwixt for which I am now pursuing, and that which I enjoyed before; but sure, my former enjoyments did show as pleasant, and promise as fair, before I attained them; like the rainbow, they looked very glorious at a distance, but when I approached I found nothing but emptiness and vapor. O what a poor thing would the life of man be, if it were capable of no higher enjoyments! . . .

WE MUST DO THOSE OUTWARD ACTIONS THAT ARE COMMANDED

When we have got our corruptions restrained, and our natural appetites and inclinations toward worldly things in some measure subdued, we must proceed to such exercises as have a more immediate tendency to excite and awaken the divine life: and, first, let us endeavor conscientiously to perform those duties which religion doth require, and whereunto it would incline us, if it did prevail in our souls. If we can not get our inward disposition presently changed, let us study, at least, to regulate our outward deportment: if our hearts be not yet inflamed with divine love, let us, however, own our allegiance to that Infinite Majesty, by attending his service, and listening to his word, by speaking reverently of his name, and praising his goodness, and exhorting others to serve and obey him. If we want that charity and those bowels of compassion which we ought to have toward our neighbors, yet must we not omit any occasion of doing them good: if our hearts be haughty and proud, we must, nevertheless, study a modest and humble deportment. These external performances are of little value in themselves, yet they may help us forward to better things. The apostle indeed telleth us, that "bodily exercise profiteth little": but he seems not to affirm that it is altogether useless; it is always good to be doing what we can for then God is wont to pity our weakness, and assist our feeble endeavors; and when true charity and humility, and other graces of the divine Spirit, come to take root in our souls, they will exert themselves more freely, and with less difficulty, if we have before been accustomed to express them in our outward conversations. Nor need we fear the imputation of hypocrisy, tho our actions do thus somewhat outrun our affections, seeing they do still proceed from a sense of our duty; and our design is not to appear better than we are, but that we may really become so.

We Must Endeavor To Form Internal Acts of Devotion, Charity, Etc.

But as inward acts have a more immediate influence on the soul to mold it to a right temper and frame, so ought we to be most frequent and sedulous in the exercise of them. Let us be often lifting up our hearts toward God; and if we do not say that we love him above all things, let us, at least, acknowledge that it is our duty, and would be our happiness, so to do: let us lament the dishonor done unto him by foolish and sinful men, and applaud the praises and adorations that are given him by that blessed and glorious company above: let us resign and yield ourselves up unto him a thousand times, to be governed by his laws, and be disposed of at his pleasure: and tho our stubborn hearts should start back and refuse, yet let us tell him, we are convinced that his will is just and good; and, therefore, desire him to do with us whatsoever he pleaseth, whether he will or not. And so, for begetting in us a universal charity toward men, we must be frequently putting up wishes for their happiness, and blessing every person that we see; and when we have done any thing for the relief of the miserable, we may second it with earnest desires that God would take care of them, and deliver them out of all their distresses.

Thus should we exercise ourselves unto godliness, and when we are employing the powers that we have, the Spirit of God is wont to strike in, and elevate these acts of our soul beyond the pitch of nature, and give them a divine impression; and after the frequent reiteration of these, we shall find ourselves more inclined unto them, they flowing with greater freedom and ease.

We Should Meditate on God's Goodness and Love

Especially, if hereunto we add the consideration of God's favor and good will toward us; nothing is more powerful to engage our affection, than to find that we are beloved. Expressions of kindness are always pleasing and acceptable unto us, tho the person should be otherwise mean and contemptible: but, to have the love of one who is altogether lovely, to know that the glorious Majesty of heaven hath any regard unto us, how must it astonish and delight us, how must it overcome our spirits and melt our hearts, and put our whole soul into a flame! now, as the word of God is full of the expressions of his love toward man; so all his works do loudly proclaim it: he gave us our being, and, by preserving us in it, doth renew the donation every moment. He hath placed us in a rich and well-furnished world, and liberally provided for all our necessities; he raineth down blessings from heaven upon us, and causeth the earth to bring forth our provision; he giveth us our food and raiment, and while we are spending the productions of one year, he is preparing for us against another. He sweeteneth our lives with innumerable comforts, and gratifieth every faculty with suitable objects: the eye of his providence is always upon us, and he watcheth for our safety when we are asleep, neither minding him nor ourselves. But, lest we should think these testimonies of his kindness less considerable, because they are the easy issues of his omnipotent power, and do not put him to any trouble or pain, he hath taken a more wonderful method to endear himself to us; he hath testified his affection to us, by suffering as well as by doing; and, because he could not suffer in his own nature, he assumed ours. The eternal Son of God did clothe himself with the infirmities of our flesh, and left the company of those innocent and blessed spirits who knew well how to love and adore him that he might dwell among men, and wrestle with the obstinacy of that rebellious race, to reduce them to their allegiance and fidelity, and then to offer himself up as a sacrifice and propitiation for them. I remember one of the poets hath an ingenious fancy to express the passion wherewith he found himself overcome after a long resistance; that the god of love had shot all his golden arrows at him, but could never pierce his heart, till at length he put himself into the bow, and darted himself straight into his breast. Methinks this doth someway adumbrate God's method of dealing with men: he hath long contended with a stubborn world, and thrown down many a blessing upon them; and when all his other gifts could not prevail, he at last made a gift of himself, to testify his affection and engage theirs. The account which we have of our Savior's life in the gospel doth all along present us with the story of his love; all the pains that he took, and the troubles that he endured, were the wonderful effects and uncontrollable evidences of it. But, O that last, that dismal scene! is it possible to remember it, and question his kindness, or deny him ours? Here, here it is, my dear friend, that we should fix our most serious and solemn thoughts, "That Christ may dwell in our hearts by faith; that we being rooted and grounded in love; may be able to comprehend with all saints, what is the breadth, and length, and depth, and height; and to know the love of Christ which passeth knowledge, that we may be filled with all the fulness of God" (Eph. 3:17, 18, 19).

We ought also frequently to reflect on those particular tokens of favor and love, which God hath bestowed on ourselves; how long he hath borne with our follies and sins, and waited to be gracious unto us, wrestling, as it were, with the stubbornness of our hearts, and essaying every method to reclaim us. We should keep a register in our minds of all the eminent blessings and deliverances we have met with, some whereof have been so conveyed, that we might clearly perceive they were not the issues of chance, but the gracious effects of the divine favor, and the signal returns of our prayers. Nor ought we to embitter the thoughts of these things with any harsh or unworthy suspicion, as if they were designed on purpose to enhance our guilt, and heighten our eternal damnation. No, no, my friend, God is love, and he hath no pleasure in the ruin of his creatures. If they abuse his goodness, and turn his grace into wantonness, and thereby plunge themselves into greater depth of guilt and misery, this is the effect of their obstinate wickedness, and not the design of those benefits which he bestows.

If these considerations had once begotten in our hearts a real love and affection toward Almighty God, that would easily lead us into the other branches of religion, and therefore I shall need say the less of them.

To Beget Charity, We Must Remember That All Men Are Nearly Related Unto God

We shall find our hearts enlarged in charity toward men, by considering the relation wherein they stand unto God, and the impresses of his image which are stamped upon them. They are not only his creatures, the workmanship of his hands, but such of whom he taketh special care, and for whom he hath a very dear and tender regard, having laid the designs of their happiness before the foundations of the world, and being willing to live and converse with them to all the ages of eternity. The meanest and most contemptible person whom we behold is the offspring of heaven, one of the children of the Most High; and however unworthy he might behave himself of that relation, so long as God hath not abdicated and disowned him by a final sentence, he will have us to acknowledge him as one of his, and as such to embrace him with a sincere and cordial affection. You know what a great concernment we are wont to have for those that do any ways belong to the person whom we love; how gladly we lay hold on every opportunity to gratify the child or servant of a friend; and, sure, our love toward God would as naturally spring forth in charity toward men, did we mind the interest that he is pleased to take in them, and consider that every soul is dearer unto him than all the material world; and that he did not account the blood of his Son too great a price for their redemption.

Isaac Penington
(1617-1680)

SON of a mayor of London, Penington joined the Society of Friends in 1658. So imbued was he with the meaning of his faith that he was jailed six times. Altogether he spent five years in jail as a result of his desire to worship in a manner other than that of the Established Church. He also lost his property when he and his wife refused to take an oath in court. From his own experience in finding the light of truth through his suffering, he was able to give himself with tenderness and depth to others who were in sorrow or despair. His letters beautifully show both this sympathy and profound understanding of the needs of others, and the answer his Christian faith was able to give them. The following are from the edition of John Barclay (1828).

[LETTERS ON SPIRITUAL VIRTUES]

1. ON THE PURE, LIVING, SPIRITUAL FOOD

To the Friends at Chalfont, in Buckinghamshire

O Friends! Feed on the tree of life; feed on the measure of life, and the pure power thereof, which God hath revealed, and manifesteth in you. Do ye know your food, do ye remember the taste and relish of it? Then keep to it, and do not meddle with that which seemeth very desirable to the other eye, and very able to make wise. O abide in the simplicity that is in Christ, in the naked truth that ye have felt there! and there, ye will be able to know and distinguish your food, which hath several names in Scripture, but is all one and the same thing:—the bread, the milk, the water, the wine, the flesh and blood of Him that came down from heaven, &c. John vi. 51, &c.—it is the same, only it is given forth weaker and stronger, according to the capacity of him that receiveth it; and so hath different names given to it accordingly.

O keep out of that wisdom, which knoweth not the thing; for that is it, which also stumbles about the names. But keep to the principle of life—keep to the seed of the kingdom—feed on that which was from the beginning. Is not this meat indeed, and drink indeed! flesh indeed, and blood indeed! The Lord hath advanced you to that ministration of life and power, wherein things are known above and beyond names; wherein the life is revealed and felt, beyond names; wherein the life is revealed and felt, beyond what words can utter. O dwell in your habitations; and feed on the food which God brings you into your habitations; which is pure, living, spiritual, and will cause your souls and spirits more and more to live in and to God, as ye eat and drink thereof. So, be not shaken or disquieted by the wisdom of the flesh;

but feel that which settleth and establisheth in the pure power.

And the Lord God preserve you, and give you to watch against, and to feel victory and dominion over, all that is contrary to Him in any of you; and which stands in the way of your fellowship with Him, and of your joy and peace in Him.

This sprang unto you in the good will of your Father, from the life and love of your brother in the Truth.

24. On Simplicity of Faith and Dedication

To John Mannock

Friend,—It is a wonderful thing, to witness the power of God reaching to the heart, and demonstrating to the soul the pure way to life, as in his sight, and presence. Surely, he that partakes of this, is therein favoured by the Lord, and ought diligently to wait, for the giving up to the leadings of his Holy Spirit in every thing; that so, he may travel through all that is contrary to the Lord, into that nature and spirit which is of Him. It is a wonderful thing, also, to witness God's preservation from backsliding, and from being entangled by the subtlety of the enemy; who hath many ways and taking devices to ensnare the simple mind, and draw it from the sense of Truth, into some notions and belief of things; wherein the soul may be lulled asleep with hopes and persuasions, but hath not the feeling or enjoyment of the true life and power.

O Friend! hast thou a sense of the way to the Father? then be careful that thy spirit daily bow before him, and wait for breathings to him from his pure Spirit, that he would continue his mercy to thee; keeping thee in the true sense, and making thy way more and more clear before thee every day;—yea, and bearing thee up in all the exercises and trials which may befall thee, in every kind; that by his secret working in thy spirit, and helping thee with a little help from time to time, thou mayest still be advancing nearer and nearer towards the kingdom; until thou find the Lord God administer an entrance

unto thee thereinto, and give thee an inheritance of life, joy, righteousness, and peace therein;—which is strength unto the soul against sin and death, and against the sorrow and trouble which ariseth in the mind, for want of God's presence and holy power revealed there.

And, be not careful after the flesh, but trust the Lord. What though thou art weak, and little; though thou meet with those that are wise and knowing; and almost every way able to reason thee down; what though thou has not wherewith to answer; yet, thou knowest and hast the feeling of God's pure Truth in spirit, with a desire to have the life of it brought forth in thee, and so, to witness the change and renewings which are by his power. O dear heart, herein thou art accepted of the Lord, and here his tender love and care will be over thee, and his mercy will daily reach to thee; and thou shalt have true satisfaction in thy heart, and hold the Truth there, where all the reasonings of men, and all the devices of the enemy of thy soul, shall not be able to reach;—yea, thou shalt so feel the Lord to help his babe against the strength of the mighty, in the seasons of his good pleasure, as shall exceedingly turn to his praise; and so, thou shalt experience, that whom God preserves, all the gates of hell shall not be able to prevail against. Therefore, look not out at men, or at the words and wisdom of men; but, keep where thou hast felt the Lord visit thee, that he may visit thee yet again and again, every day, and be teaching thee further and further the way to his dwellingplace, and be drawing thee thither, where is righteousness, life, rest, and peace, forever!

This arose in my heart this morning, in tender love towards thee. Look up to the Lord, who can make it useful to thee, to warm, quicken, and strengthen thy heart and mind towards the Lord, and his pure Truth, wherewith he has visited thee. And if thou feel any thing therein, suitable to the state and condition of thy soul, O bow before the Lord! that in the true humility thou mayest confess, and give the glory to him of what belongs to him.

From thy Friend in the Truth, which cleanseth the heart from iniquity, as it is embraced and dwelt in.

41. ENCOURAGEMENT UNDER TRIALS INCIDENT TO BEARING THE CROSS OF CHRIST

Who is able to undergo the crosses and afflictions, either inward or outward, which befall those, whom God draws out of the spirit of this world and path of destruction, into the way of eternal rest and peace? Yet, the Lord is able to uphold that which feels its weakness, and daily waits on him for support, under the heaviness of the cross.

I know, dear heart, thy outward trials cannot but be sharp and bitter; and I know also, that the Lord is able to sustain thee under them, and cause thee to stand thy ground; that thou give not advantage to that spirit, which hereby would draw from the Lord, and from the way of life and happiness. O that thou couldst dwell in the knowledge and sense of this! even, that the Lord beholds thy sufferings with an eye of pity; and is able, not only to uphold thee under them, but also to do thee good by them; and to bring forth that life and wisdom in thee by means thereof, to which he will give dominion over that spirit which grieves and afflicts thee, and in his due season. Therefore, grieve not at thy lot, be not discontented, look not out at the hardness of thy condition; but, when the storm and matters of vexation are sharp, look up to Him who can give meekness and patience, can lift up thy head over all, and cause thy life to grow, and be a gainer by all. If the Lord God did not help us by his mighty arm, how often should we fall and perish! and if the Lord God help thee proportionable to thy condition of affliction and distress, thou wilt have no cause to complain, but to bless his name. He is exceedingly good, and gracious, and tender-hearted, and doth not despise the afflictions of the afflicted, for his name's sake, in any kind.

This is in tender love towards thee, with breathings to my Father, that his pleasant plant may not be crushed in thee, by the foot of pride and violence; but may overgrow it, and flourish the more because of it.

From thy truly loving Friend in the Truth, and for the Truth's sake.

52. ON LOVE, MEEKNESS, AND WATCHING OVER EACH OTHER

To Friends in Amersham

Friends,—Our life is love, and peace, and tenderness; and bearing one with another, and forgiving for another, and not laying accusations one against another; but praying one for another, and helping one another up with a tender hand, if there has been any slip or fall; and waiting till the Lord gives sense and repentance, if sense and repentance in any be wanting. O! wait to feel this spirit, and to be guided to walk in this spirit, that ye may enjoy the Lord in sweetness, and walk sweetly, meekly, tenderly, peaceably, and lovingly one with another. And then, ye will be a praise to the Lord; and anything that is, or hath been, or may be amiss, ye will come over in the true dominion, even in the Lamb's dominion; and, that which is contrary shall be trampled upon, as life rises and rules in you. So, watch your hearts and ways; and watch one over another, in that which is gentle and tender, and knows it can neither preserve itself, nor help another out of the snare; but the Lord must be waited upon, to do this in and for us all. So, mind Truth, the service, enjoyment, and possession of it in your hearts; and so to walk, as ye may bring no disgrace upon it, but may be a good savour in the places where ye live—the meek, innocent, tender, righteous life reigning in you, governing over you, and shining through you, in the eyes of all with whom ye converse.

Your Friend in the Truth, and a desirer of your welfare and prosperity therein.

92. ON THE FEAR OF GOD

To Those Persons That Drink of the Waters at Astrop Wells

There is a great God, the Creator of all things, who gave man a being here in this world; to whom every man must give an account, when he goes out of this world.

This great God, who loves mankind, and would not have them perish, is nigh unto man, to teach him the fear, which is due from him to God. The man that learns this pure fear of God, is daily exercised by it in departing from evil, both in thought, word, and deed, and in doing that which is good in his sight.

There is likewise another teacher near man, who is also ready to teach such as do not know God, or fear God, that which is dishonourable to the great God, who made man a vessel of honour, and to be to his glory. They that learn of this teacher, learn not to fear God, or to do good, but to please themselves in doing evil, both in thought, word, and deed. O! what account will all such give, when they go out of this world, and come to be judged by the great God, (who is of pure eyes, and cannot behold iniquity,) when all their sins are set in order by him before them and just judgment proportioned by him thereunto! O! why do men forget God their Creator, days without number, hearkening to him who first deceived them, doing the will of the deceiver and destroyer of souls, and not the will of the blessed Creator and Saviour!

O! hearken to wisdom's counsel, when she cries in the secret of your hearts against that which is evil, and contrary to the nature, life, and will of God; lest a day of calamity from God come upon you, and then ye cry unto the pitiful and tender God, and his face be turned against you, and he refuse to show mercy to you! Read Prov. i. 20, to the end of the chapter; and the Lord give you the weighty consideration and true understanding of it for your soul's good, and for the reclaiming of you from anything that is evil, and destructive to your souls.

This is written in tender love unto you, from one who pities and loves you, and desires your prosperity in this world, and your everlasting happiness with God forever.

93. Some Doubts Answered Respecting Prayer

To Widow Hemmings

Friend,—Well may there doubts and scruples arise in the minds of persons concerning prayer, as they come to any sense or touch of Truth from God's Holy Spirit; that duty having been performed and practised so long from the fleshly mind and nature, and not in the leading will and compass of God's Holy Spirit and power. And those who doubt therein, cannot be satisfied, till the Lord open their spirits, and make the thing manifest to them! yet, this is most certain, that all prayer, all true prayer to God, is in and from his Holy Spirit; and whatsoever is otherwise, is not accepted of the Father. The promise, indeed, is to the prayer in faith and to the Holy Spirit; but not to the prayer of the fleshly birth, will, or wisdom. Therefore, the great care and concern in prayer is, that that which is of God pray unto the Father, in the quickenings and motions of his own Spirit. For, the dead cannot praise God, nor can the dead truly pray unto him. And truly, in the forbearing praying, there can be no peace, for we are to pray continually; nor in praying in a formal way without life, without God's Spirit, (who gives to pray, and who makes intercession,) can there be any peace within; rather accusation and anguish to that mind, which, desiring to pray aright, yet knows not how so to do. But it is manifest, prayer is not in the time, will, or power of the creature; for, it is a gift of God, and the ability lodges in his Spirit; it is not ours, but as given of his Spirit,—which, therefore, is to be waited upon, when it will move and breathe in us, and so give us the ability of calling upon the Father, and the power of prevailing with the Father, in the name and through the life of the Son.

Now, as to thy queries, I shall answer in plainness, as the Lord shall please to open my heart.

As to the first. Whenever the creature finds breathings to the Father from a sense of its wants, these are not to be stopped, but to be offered up in that, from which the breathings come. For, there is no true sense of one's condition, or of one's wants, but from the Spirit of the Lord; and the Lord gives this sense, that the soul might feel its need of him, and cry to him; and every sigh and groan, that is thus offered up to him, is accepted of him, and prevails with him for good towards that soul, which it shall certainly receive, as it comes to know the Lamb of God, and follow him in the leadings of his good and Holy Spirit. And, in particular, it ought to pray for the appearance of God's Spirit and power; and, if it do already taste somewhat of it, it ought to pray for more of the Spirit, and that it may distinguish the requests that rise up in the heart, whether they come from God's Holy Spirit and will, or from the fleshy nature and will. For, the wrong birth also desires the kingdom, and would have the kingdom, and prays for the kingdom, and strives for the kingdom; but it prays amiss, and it strives amiss, even so, as it never shall obtain, the kingdom being appointed for, and given to another.

To the second. Those that do not know, nor are sensible partakers of the Spirit, yet feeling their want thereof, and true desires after it, ought to offer up those desires to God; and keeping in that which begets those desires, they shall not long be ignorant of God's Spirit, but find that God is more willing to give it, than a parent to give necessary things to his children. But those that have prayed long for the Spirit, yet have not hitherto received it, have just cause to question the nature and ground of their prayers; since God is so ready to give the Spirit to his children. For, doth a child ask bread of his father for many years, and not receive it? O consider this thing! If the child ask the Spirit aright, it is impossible but he should receive some proportion of it from the Father, so much as is necessary to his present state. God doth require his children to perform everything to him in and with his Spirit, knowing they can do nothing right without it; and surely, he will not require duties of them, and withhold that from them without which, they cannot acceptably perform these duties to him.

To the third. A notion that all the soul's supplies are from the Father, is not a sufficient ground of prayer; for the false birth may, and often doth pray so; but, a true feeling of the thing, is a sufficient ground, if the heart and mind keep within the limits of the feeling, and offer up no more than what ariseth there; for, truly, that is from the Spirit, of the Spirit, and in the Spirit, wherever it is found. And, O! that every one who hath any true sense of God, might wait on him, to savour this little which ariseth from God, from (amidst) the multitude of his thoughts, words, and desires, which are from another root,—even from the flesh, and are of a fleshly nature, neither are of value, nor avail with the Lord: but, the birth of life, the sensible breathings of his own life, in the poorest and weakest babe, are always of esteem, and prevail with the Father.

To the fourth. The creature may misapprehend its duty, may have a wrong sense, apprehending that to be its duty which is not, and may not apprehend that to be its duty which is; and so, if the sense be wrong, then the act of obedience, (according to this wrong sense,) is wrong also, and is not accepted with the Father. It is true, prayer is of God, and is a duty; not all prayer, but prayer after that manner that the Lord requires, which is in the true sense, and within the limits of the true Spirit and power—praying always in the Holy Ghost. The pure prayer, the pure breathings of God's child, of the true birth, is always within the limit which God hath prescribed. Therefore, watch unto prayer, watch unto God's preparing the heart, by the motion and virtue of his good Spirit, and offer up the breathings that then arise; and wait to distinguish between the desires which arise from the fleshly part, and the desires which arise from the spiritual and heavenly part. For, the first nature is earthly; but the second nature, the nature which is from the second Adam, the quickening Spirit, is pure and heavenly; and such are all the desires and breathings, that spring from that nature in the vessel. And, as thou comest into that nature, and into that Spirit from which the nature proceeds, thou wilt truly distinguish concerning prayer, concerning faith, concerning love, and all other spiritual things; and wilt know Him who is Truth and no lie, who deceives not, but preserves that mind which is given up to him, and abides in him, out of all error and deceit.

Thou seemest, also, to be disturbed about some other duties, as well as prayer. If the Lord have begun to put a stop to the workings of flesh in thee, and thou be subject to him therein, and cease from thy own willings and workings, and wait on him to be taught to perform things aright,—this is his love to thee; and, if thou come to feel the leadings of his Spirit further, and follow him, thou wilt have cause to bless his name, as many others have, whom in this day he hath thus led. Indeed, flesh should be silent before him. Alas! what room is there for his Spirit and power when there is such a multitude of thoughts, and workings, and reasonings, such a noise of flesh in many hearts and spirits? Happy is he who feels flesh silent, who comes to an end of his own willing and running, though that is a time of great distress, when the full mind is emptied and brought low; but then, He that shows mercy is near, and the day of mercy is not far off to that soul.

The Lord raise up that in thee, which is of him; and so guide and order thy heart, that it may long and cry after him, and be heard and satisfied by him.

Walter Marshall

(1628-1680)

EDUCATED at Oxford and ordained in the Presbyterian ministry in England, Marshall was ousted from his Presbyterian relationships at Hursley by the Act of Uniformity. He then took an independent church at Gosport, where he remained until his death eighteen years later. In discussing how man can prevent the loss of salvation, which God has originally given to him, Marshall shows the influence of Calvinism in his thinking, a viewpoint found throughout his classic devotional writing, *The Gospel Mystery of Sanctification*. Among Nonconformist groups this writing enjoyed wide circulation.

ENDEAVOUR FOR A RIGHT BELIEF

From *The Gospel Mystery of Sanctification*

You must believe with a full persuasion that you are a child of wrath by nature, as well as others; fallen from God by the sin of the first Adam; dead in trespasses and sins; subject to the curse of the law of God, and to the power of Satan, and to insupportable misery to all eternity; and that you can not possibly procure your reconciliation with God, or any spiritual life and strength to do any good work, by any endeavoring to get salvation according to the terms of the legal covenant; and that you can not find any way to escape out of this sinful and miserable condition by your own reason and understanding without supernatural revelation, nor to be freed from it except by that infinite power that raiseth the dead. We must not be afraid, as some are, to know our own vileness and sinfulness, neither must we be willing to think ourselves better than we are; but must be heartily desirous and glad to know the worst of our own condition; yea, when we have found out the worst that we can of ourselves, we must be willing to believe that our hearts are deceitful and desperately wicked, beyond all that we can know and find out (Jer. 17:9). This is all necessary to work in us true humiliation, self-despair, and self-loathing, that we may highly esteem and earnestly seek the salvation of Christ as the one thing necessary. It maketh us sick of sin and sensible of our need of the great Physician, and willing to be ordered, according to any of his prescriptions, whatsoever we suffer, rather than to follow our own wisdom (Matt. 9:12). It was for want of this humiliation that the scribes and Pharisees were not so forward to enter into the kingdom of heaven as the publicans and harlots (Matt. 21:31).

2. You are to believe assuredly, that there is no way to be saved without receiving all the saving benefits of Christ, his Spirit as well as his merits, sanctification as well as remission of sins by faith. It is the ruin of many souls that they trust on Christ for remission of sins without any regard to holiness; whereas these two benefits are inseparably joined in him, so that none are freed from condemnation by Christ but those that are enabled to walk holily, *i.e.*, not after the flesh, but after the Spirit (Rom. 8:1). It is also the ruin of souls to seek only remission of sins by faith in Christ, and holiness by our endeavors, according to the terms of the law; whereas we can never live to God in holiness except we be dead to the law, and live only by Christ living in us by faith. That faith which receiveth not holiness as well as remission of sins from Christ will never sanctify us; and therefore it will never bring us to heavenly glory (Heb. 12:14).

3. You are to be fully persuaded of the "all-sufficiency of Christ for the salvation of yourself and of all that believe on him; that his blood cleanseth from all sin" (1 John 1:7). Tho our sins be never so great and horrible, and continued in never so long, yet he is able to deliver from the body of death, and mortify our corruptions be they ever so strong. We find in Scripture that abominable wicked persons have been saved by him,

idolaters, adulterers, effeminate, covetous, drunkards, extortioners, etc. (1 Cor. 6:9, 10). Such as have sinned against the light of nature, as the heathen, and the light of Scripture, as the Jews; such as have denied Christ, as Peter, and persecuted and blasphemed him as Paul. Many that have fallen into great sins are ruined forever, because they do not account the grace of Christ sufficient for their pardon and sanctification: when they think they are gone and past all hope of recovery, that their sins are upon them, and they pine away in them, how shall they live? (Ezek. 33:10). This despair works secretly in many souls, without such trouble and honor, and maketh them careless of their souls and true religion. The devil fills some with horrid, filthy, blasphemous thoughts, on purpose that they think their sins too great to be forgiven; tho commonly such thoughts are the least of the sins of those that are pestered with them, and rather the devil's sin than theirs, because they are hurried into them sore against their wills; but if their hearts be somewhat polluted within them, Christ testifieth "that all manner of sin and blasphemy shall be forgiven, except blasphemy against the Holy Ghost" (Matt. 12:31). And as for those that are guilty of blasphemy against the Holy Ghost, the reason why they are never forgiven is not because of any want of sufficiency in the blood of Christ, or in the pardoning mercy of God; but because they never repent of that sin, and never seek to God for mercy through him, but continue obstinate until death; for the Scripture testifieth, that it is impossible to renew them again unto repentance (Heb. 6:5, 6). So that the merits of Christ are sufficient for all that seek to him for mercy by believing. There are others that despair of ever getting any victory over their lusts, because they have formerly made many vows and resolutions and have used many vigorous endeavors against them in vain. Such are to persuade themselves that the grace of Christ is sufficient for them when all other means have failed; as the woman that had the issue of blood, and was nothing bettered but rather grew worse by any remedies that physicians could prescribe, yet persuaded herself that, if she might but touch the clothes of Christ, she should be whole (Mark 5:25-28). Those that despair, by reason of the greatness of their guilt and corruption, do greatly dishonor and undervalue the grace of God, his infinite mercy, and the infinite merits of Christ's blood, and the power of his Spirit, and deserve to perish with Cain and Judas. Abundance of people that give up themselves to all licentiousness in this wicked generation lie under secret despair; which maketh them so desperate in swearing, blaspheming, whoring, drunkenness, and all manner of wickedness. How horrid and heinous soever our sins and corruptions have been, we should learn to account them a small matter in comparison to the grace of Christ, who is God as well as man, and offered up himself, by the Eternal Spirit, as a sacrifice of infinite value, for our salvation: and can create us anew as easily as he created the world by a word speaking.

4. You are to be fully persuaded of the truth of the general free promise, in your own particular case, that if you believe on Christ sincerely, you shall have everlasting life as well as any other in the world, without performing any condition of works to procure an interest in him; for the promise is universal. "Whosoever believeth on him shall not be ashamed" (Rom. 9:33), without any exception. And if God exclude you not, you must not exclude yourselves, but rather conclude peremptorily, that how vile, wicked, and unworthy soever you be, yet, if you come, you shall be accepted as well as any other in the world. You are to believe that great article of the creed, the remission of sins, in your own case, when you are principally concerned, or else it will little profit you to believe it in the case of others. This is that which hinders many broken, wounded spirits from coming to the great Physician, when they are convinced of the abominable filthiness of their hearts, that they are dead in sin without the least

spark of true grace and holiness in them. They think that it is in vain for such as they are to trust on Christ for salvation, and that he will never save such as they are. Why so? they can be but lost creatures at worst; and Christ came to seek and save those that are lost. If they that are dead in sin can not be saved, then all must despair and perish; for none have any spiritual life until they receive it by believing on Christ. Some think themselves to be worse than any others, and that none have such wicked hearts as they: and tho others be accepted, yet they shall be rejected. But they should know that Christ came to save the chief of sinners (1 Tim. 1:15); and that the design of God is to show the exceeding riches of his grace in our salvation (Eph. 2:7), which is most glorified by pardoning the greatest sinners. And it is but our ignorance to think ourselves like nobody; for all others, as well as we, are naturally dead in trespasses and sins; their mind is enmity to God, and is not subject to his law, nor indeed can be (Rom. 8:7), and every imagination of the thoughts of their hearts are only evil, and continually so (Gen. 6:5); they have all the same corrupt fountain of all abominations in their hearts, tho we may have exceeded many others in several actual sins. Others think that they have outstaid their time, and therefore now they should find no place for repentance, tho they should seek it carefully with tears (Heb. 12:17). But, behold "now is the accepted time; behold, now is the day of salvation" (2 Cor. 6:2), even as God calleth upon you by the gospel. And altho Esau was rejected, who sought rather the earthly than the spiritual blessings of the birthright; yet they shall not be rejected that seek the enjoyment of Christ and his salvation as their only happiness. If you come unto Christ's vineyard at the eleventh hour of the day, you shall have your penny, as well as those that came early in the morning; because the reward is of grace, and not of merit (Matt. 10:9, 10). And here you must be sure to believe stedfastly that Christ and all his salvation is bestowed as a free gift upon those that do not work to procure any right or title to him, or meetness or unworthiness to receive him, but only believe on him that justifieth the ungodly (Rom. 4:5). If you put any condition of works or good qualifications between yourselves and Christ, it will be a partition wall which you can never climb over.

5. You are to believe assuredly that it is the will of God you should believe in Christ and have eternal life by him, as well as any other; that your believing is a duty very acceptable to God; and that he will help you, as well as any other, in this work, because he calleth and commandeth you, by the gospel, to believe on him. This maketh us to set cheerfully upon the work of believing; as when Jesus commanded the blind man to be called, they said unto him, "Be of good comfort, rise; he calleth thee" (Mark 10:49). A command of Christ made Peter to walk upon the water (Matt. 14:29). And here we are not to meddle with God's secret of predestination, or the purpose of his will to give the grace of faith to some rather than others; but only with his revealed will, in his gracious invitations and commands, by which we are required to believe on Christ. This will of God is confirmed by his oath, "As I live, saith the Lord God, I have no pleasure in the death of the wicked, but that the wicked turn from his way, and live: turn ye, turn ye, from your evil ways; for why will ye die, O house of Israel" (Ezek. 33:11). Christ testifieth that he "would often have gathered the children of Jerusalem, even as a hen gathereth her chickens under her wings, and they would not" (Matt 23:27). And the Apostle Paul testifieth that God "will have all men to be saved" (1 Tim. 2:4). You are to reject and abandon all thoughts that are contrary to this persuasion. What if few be saved? thy salvation will not make the number too great; for few will follow thee in the duty of believing. What if the wrath of God be revealed from heaven against thee in many terrible judgments, and the work and thine own conscience con-

demn thee, and Christ seem to reckon thee no better than a dog, as he did the woman of Canaan (Matt. 15:26)? Thou art to make a good interpretation of all these things, that the end of them is to drive thee to Christ, as this was the end of the curses of the law and all the terrible dispensations of them (Rom. 10:4). If a prophet or an angel from heaven were sent of God, on purpose to declare that the sentence of everlasting damnation is declared against thee, it would be thy duty to believe that God sent him to give thee timely warning for this very end, that thou mightest believe and turn to God by faith and repentance. Jeremiah prophesied against the Jews, that God would pluck them up, pull them down, and destroy them for their sins; yet he himself taught them, "if they turned from their evil ways, God would repent him of the evil" (Jer. 18:11). Jonah preached nothing but certain destruction to Nineveh to be executed upon them within forty days (chapter 3:4), yet the intent of that terrible message was that those heathenish people might escape destruction by repentance. The most absolute and peremptory denunciations of divine vengeance against us, while we are in this world, must always be understood with a secret reserve of salvation for us, upon our faith and repentance. And we are to account that the reason why God doth so terribly denounce his judgments against us by his word is that we may escape them, by flying for refuge to his free mercy in Christ. Take heed of fostering any thoughts that God hath absolutely decreed to show no saving mercy to you, or that you have already committed the unpardonable sin; or that it is in vain for you to attempt the work of believing because God will not help you in it. If such thoughts prevail in your hearts, they will do you more hurt than the most blasphemous thoughts that terrify you, or any of the grossest abominations that ever you were guilty of, because they obstruct your believing on Christ for salvation. "The spirit and the bride say, come." Christ saith, "Whosoever will let him take the water of life freely" (Rev. 22:17). Therefore we are to abandon all thoughts that hinder our coming to Christ as very sinful and pernicious, arising in us from our own corruptions and Satan's delusions, and utterly opposite to the mind of Christ and the teachings of the Spirit. And what ground can we have to entertain such unbelieving thoughts? Hath God made us of his privy council that we should be able to know that God hath decreed us to damnation, before it be manifest by our final unbelief and impenitence? As for the unpardonable sin, it consisteth in renouncing the way of salvation by Christ with the whole heart after we have attained to the knowledge of it and are convinced of the truth of it by that gospel. It is the sin that the Christian Hebrews would have been guilty of, if they had revolted from Christianity to the religion of the unbelieving Jews, that accounted Christ to be an imposter and were most rancorous persecutors of him and his ways (Heb. 6:4, 5). They that have committed that sin continue implacable, malicious enemies to Christ and his ways to the end, without any repentance. Therefore, if you can but find that you desire seriously to get an interest in Christ, and to be better Christians than you are; if you be troubled and grieved that your hearts and lives are so wicked, and that you want faith, love, and true obedience; yea, if your hearts be not maliciously bent to persecute the gospel and prefer atheism, licentiousness, or any false religion before it, you have no cause to suspect yourselves to be guilty of this unpardonable sin.

6. Add to all these "a full persuasion of the incomparable glorious excellency of Christ, and the way of salvation by him." You are to esteem the enjoyment of Christ as the only salvation and true happiness, and such an happiness as hath in it unsearchable riches of glory, and will make our cup to run over with exceeding abundance of peace and joy and glory to all eternity. We must account all things but loss for the excellency of the knowledge of Christ Jesus our Lord (Phil. 3:8). Such a persuasion as this will allure and incline your wills and affections to choose and embrace Christ as the chief good, and never to rest satisfied without the enjoyment of him, and to reject everything that stands in competition with him or the enjoyment of him. Christ is precious in the esteem of all true believers (1 Pet. 2:7). Their high esteem of his incomparable preciousness and excellency induceth them to sell all, that they may buy this pearl of great price (Matt. 13:46). This maketh them to say, "Lord, evermore give us this bread, that cometh down from heaven, and giveth life to the world. Lord, to whom shall we go? thou hast the words of eternal life" (John 6:32, 33, 34, 68). Because of the savour of his good ointments, his name is as ointment poured forth; therefore do the virgins love him (Song of Songs 1:3). They are sick of love to him, because he is, in their eyes, the chiefest among ten thousand (Song of Songs 5:8, 10). As the glory of God that appeared in the wonderful beauty of the Temple, and in the wisdom and glory of Solomon, drew worshipers to God from the utmost parts of the earth, so the unparalleled excellency of Christ, which was prefigured by the glory of Solomon and the Temple, doth more powerfully draw believers in these gospel days. The devil, who is the god of this world, knows how necessary it is for our salvation to discern all the glory and excellency of Christ. And therefore where the gospel is preached he maketh it his great work to eclipse the glory of Christ's ministry, and to blind the minds of the people, lest the light of his glorious gospel should shine unto them (2 Cor. 4:4). One that is convinced of the truth of the gospel may be averse to the embracing of it until he sees also the goodness of it, that Christ is altogether lovely and excellent.

Benjamin Whichcote

(1609-1683)

In the seventeenth century a group of English divines desired a union of Nonconformists with the Established Church. They hoped to unite the two factions through Low-Church doctrines. Among those active in this movement was Whichcote. He was for twenty years Sunday afternoon lecturer at Trinity Church, Cambridge, provost of King's College, Cambridge, and curate of several parishes. When the Act of Uniformity was passed, he remained loyal to the Established Church. "The Excellence of a Meek and Quiet Spirit," posthumously published, is one of his sermons.

THE EXCELLENCE OF A MEEK AND QUIET SPIRIT

The ornament of a meek and quiet spirit, which is in the sight of God of great price.
—1 Pet. 3:4

We find it is in vain for any one to attempt to purge the stream, unless he first cleanse the fountain. You must begin at the spring-head. The heart is the principle of action. Life begins there; and motion is from thence. It is that which first lives, and last dies. Our Savior tells us that what proceeds out of the mouth comes from the heart, and so defiles a man. For, from thence come evil thoughts, murders, blasphemies, etc. (Matt. 15:18), and (Matt. 5:28) our Savior tells us of the adultery of the heart. And (Matt. 12:34) "Out of the abundance of the heart," etc., and verse 35: "A good man out of the good treasury of his heart, bringeth forth good things," etc. Men show their spirits by their words and actions: and these are as they are meant and intended. The greatest performance in the life of man, is the government of his spirit. So (Prov. 25:28; comp. 16:32), "He that is slow to anger, is better than the mighty: and he that ruleth his own spirit, than he that taketh a city." He that doth subdue the motion of irregular passion, doth a greater matter than he who conquers nations, or beats down walls and bulwarks. Therefore give me the man, of whom I may say: this is the person, who in "the true use of reason (the perfection of human nature), who in the practise and exercise of virtue (its accomplishment),

hath brought himself into such a temper as is conatural to those principles, and warranted thereby." Of all other men I may say that they have neglected their chief business, and have forgot the great work that was in their hand, and what ought chiefly to be done in the world. For, the greatest thing that lies upon every one to do, is the regulating of his own mind and spirit. And he that hath not done this hath been in the world to little purpose. For, this is the business of life; to inform our understandings, to refine our spirits; and, then, to regulate the actions of our lives; to settle, I say, such a temper of mind as is agreeable to the dictates of sober reason and constituted by the graces of the divine Spirit.

Now that I may give you an account of this in the text, this meek and quiet spirit, I must do it by looking into the state and operation of it. Through meekness, a man hath always fair weather within. Through meekness, he gives no manner of offense, or disturbance any where abroad. And in particular, I may say these (following) several things of the meek and quiet spirit.

First: There is no ungrounded passion; no boisterous motion; no exorbitancy, nothing of fury. No perplexity of mind, nor over-thoughtfulness. Men that are thus disquieted know not what to do, can give no answer, nor can resolve on anything. No confusion of thought; for that is darkness within, and brings men into such disorder that they know not what is before them. No eagerness of desire; no impetuosity. They do not say with her in the Scripture, "Give me children, or else I die" (Gen. 30:1). No respect to God, or man will quiet or moderate such spirits, if they have not what they are bent upon. No inordinancy of appetite; but so as always to be governed according to the measures and rules of reason and virtue. No partiality or self-flattery. One of a meek spirit does not over-value himself. Those of the contrary temper are always putting themselves into a fool's paradise, conceiting above what there is sense or reason for. No impotent self-will. He that gives way to self-will is an enemy to his own peace, and is the great disturber of the world; he is an anti-God, imposeth upon God himself, and is within no law. And (in the last place) no fond self-love. All these are verities of this meek and quiet spirit. And these are great things and tend to happiness, are suitable to our state, becoming the relation we stand in to God and to one another. The meek in temper are freed from all those internal dispositions that cause a great deal of unquietness in the world. For, as mischievous as the world, either is, or is thought to be, our sufferings from abroad, all the injuries that we meet with from without are neither so great nor so frequent as the annoyances that arise from discomposure of our own minds and from inward malignity. I say, that they who complain so much of the times and of the world may learn this; that the sufferings from injurious dealings from any without us are nothing in comparison to those we find from within. For this inward malady doth altogether disable the senses and succors of reason. This is a constant malady; and by this self-enjoyment is made very uncertain. This is the first thing, that through meekness of spirit we are always in a calm, have fair weather within our own breasts, and do arrive to a good state of health and settlement.

Secondly: Through this meekness of spirit, there is good carriage and behavior toward others. The meek are never injurious or censorious, but are ready to take in good part, and make the best construction that the case will bear. They will account other men's faults rather their infirmity than their crime; and they look upon the harm done them by others to be rather inadvertency than design—rather contingent ill accidents than bad meaning. The meek man is a good neighbor, a good friend; a credit to religion, one that governs himself according to reason, makes no injury by any misconstruction, and, in case of any wrong done, sits down with easy satisfaction. How much do men differ upon account of moderation, meekness, and fairness? We find, upon our ordinary application to some persons, that they will admit any reasonable and fair proposal; be ready to hear and take in good part; are of easy access, fair conditioned, easy to be entreated: but others there are of so bad a condition that you may come twenty times to them, before you find them in a good mood, or fit to be dealt withal. They are seldom in so good a disposition that indifferent proposal may be made to them. But for those that are of meek and quiet spirits, I may say of such persons either that they are very ready to grant what is desired, or else, if they do deny, it shall be upon such grounds of reason as will satisfy.

But because things are best known by their contraries, I will show you who those persons are of whom it can not be said, that they are of meek and quiet spirits; to wit, the proud, the arrogant, insolent, haughty, presumptuous, self-confident, and assuming. For these are boisterous, stormy, tempestuous, clamorous. These persons will put themselves and others, as much as they can, into a flame. These are the disturbers of mankind; and their neighbors are rid of a burden, when they are removed. What storms and tempests are in the world natural, these are in the world moral. Earthquakes, storms, and tempest, do not lay more heavy upon the world natural than these men do upon the world of mankind. But meekness doth so qualify the soil where it is, that all the moral virtues will there thrive and prosper; such as humility, modesty, patience, ingenuity, candor. But malice and envy are the worst of vices, being the greatest degeneracy and participation of the devilish nature. These have no place in this meek and quiet spirit.

Lastly, I add that an ill-natured person is altogether uncapable of happiness. If, therefore, it hath been any one's lot either to have been born or bred to an ill-nature, I say in this case, he is more concerned to apply a remedy than he that hath received a deadly wound, or is bodily sick, hath to apply himself to the chirurgeon, or to the physician, lest his wound or disease should prove mortal. For these inward maladies will otherwise prove fatal to his soul; and the only remedy to be applied is self-reflection, due consideration, self-examination, and the exercise and practise of virtue.

Observe, now, the incompetency of the world's judgment. How fond and partial is the world, who do applaud the great disturbers of mankind, such as make havoc and desolation in the family of God, bring in confusion, and turn all into hurly-burly giving to such as these titles of honor; naming them conquerors and victorious persons! How fond (I say) and partial is the world; who do so magnify the fame of high-spirited turbulent, self-willed persons! thinking them men of courage and resolution: and, on the other hand, accounting the innocent and harmless to be persons of no spirit or activity. Whereas the greatest sign of power and bravest performance in the life of man is to govern his own spirit, and to subdue his passions. And, this, if the Scripture may give judgment, is the greatest ornament belonging to a man, and that which is the most valued by God, from whose judgment there is no appeal. "The ornament of a meek and quiet spirit which is in the sight of God of great price." And, good old Jacob, when leaving the world, when about to bless his posterity, he came to Simeon and

Levi; remembering their horrid cruelty, it puts him to a loss; "O my soul, come not thou into their secret, for instruments of cruelty are in their habitation," etc. (Gen. 49:5, 6). Things are very differently accounted above and below. And by this it appears that the guise of the world and the fancy of men are the most impotent and fond things imaginable.

And further yet, as to the judgment of Scripture in this case: This is the true temper of religion, and prophesied of the gospel-state (Isa. 11:6 and 65:25). Our Savior, in his beatitudes (Matt. 5), begins with this spirit. And, that this is the temper that shall rule and prevail in the gospel-state, consult these Scriptures (Eph. 4:2; 1 Tim. 6:11). A man can not speak a good thing, without meekness. If he speaks of God, of matters of reason and religion, he spills that which he meddles with, if he be not meek. For we must in meekness instruct those that oppose themselves (2 Tim. 2:25). No good notion will take place; no good seed can be sown, no plant will thrive; every thing that is divine and heavenly will vanish, if it be not settled by this temper. "Who is a wise man, and endued with knowledge among you; let him show, out of a good conversation, his works, with meekness of wisdom" (James 1:21; 3:13). Wisdom is not, but in conjunction with meekness (1 Pet. 3:15). There is no religious disposition, or good conversation, where it is not. Meekness must accompany all motions in religion, or else 'tis passion, or a man's own interest. Without this, we are out of God's way, and have not his blessing (Ps. 25:9). And this is that qualification that makes us capable of the promises of the gospel. Tho this temper be accounted by the incompetent world a kind of sheepishness, and such as these are thought to be persons of no mettle nor spirit; yet the Holy Spirit reckons otherwise. See how the Scripture reckons of Moses; of whom it is said, he was the meekest man upon earth (Num. 12:3), and yet a person of great courage and resolution. How doth he appear to Pharaoh, to his face, tho threatened by

Pharaoh, who was a man of the greatest power? How did he act in the greatest dangers? Yet, of this Moses, of whom the greatest performances are recorded, it is said that he was the meekest man upon earth. We read of the Messias, that the Spirit of the Lord shall rest upon him; the spirit of counsel and might. With righteousness he shall judge the poor; and reprove with equity, for the meek of the earth (Isa. 11:2; 61:1). These are acts of authority and power; and thus is the Messiah declared. Consider also that St. Paul useth the meekness of our Savior for an argument to persuade others to that temper. I beseech you by the meekness and gentleness of Christ (2 Cor. 10:1). And (Matt. 11:29) our Savior saith, "Learn of me; for I am meek and lowly in heart." From all that I have said, it doth appear very reasonable that we should appeal from the judgment and sentence of worldly spirited men, who applaud persons that are of venturous undertakings, of fierce resolutions, of impotent passions, and unreasonable affections.

Wherefore let every man, in the first place, look after his home work—what he hath to do at home—to establish in himself a due frame and temper of mind; for, till this be done, he is not fit to walk abroad, or to have to do with others. When this is done, then there will be patient forbearance and making allowance. This is that which the apostle adviseth (Gal. 6:1); "Brethren, if any man be overtaken in a fault; ye which are spiritual, restore such an one, in the spirit of meekness, considering thyself, lest thou also be tempted." If any one do us an injury, and transgress, let us make him that allowance that God makes us; let us make him an abatement for the weakness of his nature, and for the multiplicity of his principles; for that government that he is charged withal. It may be, he may be at odds with himself, and his inferior appetites in rebellion and confusion: and it must be some time before he can recover himself, and bring things into order again in his family. God allows for this; and we should allow for it, in one another.

'Tis necessary, when ever we have to do with one another, that there should be given fair allowance and consideration of men's infirmities, tempers, and constitutions. For, it is a very hard thing for a man to work off these. The choleric are of quick and hasty apprehension, and readily do resent. The phlegmatic are more dull and slow, and do not so readily consider, they must have leisure and time, and what is said must be often repeated: and you must represent what you have to say, with all advantage. Also they that are of sanguine and melancholy constitutions do not fit each other. That which is pleasing to one is grievous to the other. The pleasantness of the one is not suitable to the seriousness of the other. The melancholy temper must have time and leisure; the sanguine temper doth all presently. Therefore we must bear with one another in those things wherein we differ, if no moral evil be there. Take every man at the best, and you will find him good for some purposes. Therefore bear with him wherein he is weak. 'Tis unmanly to take any one at a disadvantage, and very unchristian to take any man at the worst. There are incident offenses. Sometimes things fall out so crossly that one could not have imagined. Tho the thing might be well intended, yet it may happen for the worse. There are ordinary mistakes; sometimes of the things (in taking one thing or another), sometimes of the agent's part, and sometimes of the patient's side. We ourselves are often mistaken; and we acknowledge it, and say we would not have done this or that, if we had once thought, or imagined, as things are fallen out. Therefore, we must give allowance, when men mistake. There are sudden apprehensions, which should be allowed for. Some are too quick, and conceit before they have duly weighed and considered; and 'tis a hard matter to rectify a misconceit. Job's friends failed at first. They were rash in their first apprehensions, and therefore they ran on, in their severity, censure, and harsh dealings, till God interposed. Therefore take heed of the first stumble, for 'tis ominous: or, at best, a good step is lost. He is a person very ingenious that, upon shewing, will vary from his first thoughts; for if once men have taken up an ill opinion, 'tis hard to satisfy them: by reason of which, many men run on in an error and pursue their first fault.

These are considerations that I offer for fair and equal consideration one of another, for mutual patience and fair allowance. And these things never were but in this fixt frame and temper of spirit, recommended in the text.

But now on the other hand: there are some persons that are always murmuring, complaining, and finding fault; never pleased themselves, nor pleasing others; that either are provoking or provoked; both which are to be condemned. I will not provoke, because I will leave nobody less himself than I found him; he shall not be so much the worse for my company and acquaintance. I will not be provoked, because I will not disorder myself, nor lose the composure of my own mind; than which nothing without me can be more valuable.

There seems to be an enmity to peace and quietness in some dispositions. These are malicious and turbulent spirits, whose pleasure is to make disturbance; who were never taken with the beauty of order, nor ever tasted the sweet of peace, nor framed themselves to duty and obedience. What should such do in heaven, where all is order and harmony? They are only fit for the infernal hurry; company for fiends and devils, whom they exactly resemble. In hell is darkness, perplexity, confusion. They lead a hellish life who always are quarreling, contradicting, traducing. Yet, some applaud themselves in this; and can they delight in the presence of a good and merciful God, of a Compassionate Savior in the harmony of a heavenly choir, who have not been acquainted with charity, nor exercised in love and good will? No. They will not relish such company nor endure their employment. They must first be discharged of their malignity,

altered in temper, reconciled to righteousness, naturalized to things of the heavenly state, before that place can make them happy. For place, condition, and employment, unsuitable to disposition, are burdensome, and can not afford content or satisfaction; since to heart's ease and settlement all things must be proportionable and accommodate. They flatter themselves greatly, they grossly cheat and abuse themselves, who think of admittance into God's blissful presence hereafter, or into the society of blessed angels and glorified souls, whose minds are not in this preparatory state, discharged of selfishness and partiality, which make men importune, troublesome, and very unpleasing company. For, the pleasures of eternity are mental and intellectual, delightsome, and satisfactory, without molestation or contest.

Man is, in a sort, *felo de se*, by harboring displeasure in his breast. He makes himself uneasy by evil surmises and discontents. If one designed to do a man the greatest mischief imaginable, one would contrive to raise in him jealousy and suspicion; to beget in him malice, ill-will, displeasure; provoke him to envy, and to malign others; he will, then, lead the life of a fiend of darkness. The malignity of his own breast will more corrode him than the sharpest humors than can infest the body.

It lies upon every one to study himself, to rectify his own temper, and where, by constitution, we are inclined to that which reason or religion can not approve, there care is to be taken to amend such inclination, and to govern it by rules of virtue: as one replied when a physiognomer reported him vicious in several instances: "Thus (said he) I am, by bodily constitution; but, by the power of my mind, these things are subject to my reason." 'Twere a reproach to a man, if a physiognomer, by viewing his countenance, or an astrologer, by casting his nativity, should tell what he is, in respect of the principles of his mind; or what he will do, upon a moral account. If so, what effect is there of principles of reason? of grounds of religion and conscience? of measures of virtue, and rules of prudence? If by study, exercise, and good use of himself, man be not better than when he came at first into the world; if there be neither improvement nor refinement; what effect is there of Christianity?

Now, I do purposely challenge, as enemies to Christianity, peevishness, frowardness, malcontentedness, which are the more dangerous evils because men warrant themselves in them; supposing there is cause for their discontent, and that they are justifiable in it. So Jonah (4:9): "I do well to be angry." This is the case of ungoverned minds and choleric constitutions.

Those who transgress in their rage and fury, when they return to themselves and to the use of sober reason, either find cause to be ashamed and to wish they had kept in better compass (which is the recovery of good nature, or virtue), or else lose themselves upon this occasion, and become more immodest and unreasonable, and more settled and confirmed in naughtiness. For good nature and the effects of it, in man, are the soil wherein the seeds of virtue being sown will grow and thrive. But let a man degenerate into hard-heartedness or cruelty; virtue becomes a stranger to such a constitution. We have woeful examples what monsters of rational agents on a moral account some men become, by unnatural use of themselves; wrought quite off from all ingenuity, candor, sweetness; like themselves, what they were formerly known to be. There are indeed many ways of miscarrying, for there are sails of vices; but if a man would at once spoil his nature, raze his very foundation, and absolutely indispose himself to all acts of virtue, let him allow himself in frowardness, peevishness, malcontent; let him conceive displeasure in his breast; let him bear ill-will, live in envy, malice, and out of charity (1 John 4:8); for, since God is love, this temper is most abhorrent to him. So as that he only can dwell in God, who dwells in love (verse 16).

By discomposure of mind a person is unfit to attend upon God and incapable of enjoying him. The mind that doth contemplate God must be God-like. 'Tis only the quiet and serene mind that can contemplate God, and enjoy him; for God will not dwell where violence and fury is. We read that God was not in the fire, nor in the whirlwind, nor in the earthquake, but in the still voice (I Kings 19:11). And, as we are not fit to attend upon God, nor to enjoy him, so likewise, not to enjoy ourselves. In such temper, we have not the free use of our reason, nor any true content. For what is all the world to a troubled and discomposed mind? Therefore give me serenity of mind, calmness of thought; for these are better enjoyments than any thing without us. Therefore for these things will I daily praise God; for upholding the foundation of reason and understanding, which are so much in danger by the distemper of the mind; for continuing me in the privilege of liberty and freedom (for hereby I can present God with a free-will-offering, and bring unto him the consent of my mind); and for giving me power of self-enjoyment, and of taking content in myself. One may have much in the world as to right and title, and yet have nothing as to power of self-enjoyment. For in the case of misgovernment by lust, passion, and self-will, we dispossess ourselves of ourselves, and all that we may call ours.

'Tis a sinful temper, to be hard to please and ready to take offense. It is grievous to those about us, and we shall soon suffer for it; for men will soon withdraw from unquiet and turbulent spirits. Solomon hath observed, that he that would have a friend must behave himself friendly (Prov. 18:24). But these men are unacceptable everywhere; especially to those that are under them (for, as for equals, and superiors, they will soon withdraw); but every good man will take care of those that are under him. And upon this head I shall observe three or four things.

First, that we ought to make the lives of all those that live with us as happy and comfortable as we can, and their burdens as easy as may be. Let our advantages be never so much above theirs, and our power over them never so great, yet we should equally consider things, and do as we would be done unto, if in their circumstances.

Consider also that things may as well be done with gentleness and by fair means as otherwise; and that things that are so done are done with pleasure and satisfaction, and will better hold; for, things that are done by force, and with offense, will no longer last than that force continues.

There is more care to please when men are not captious, peevish, froward, or easy to take offense. Men that are often angry, and for every trifle, in a little time will be little regarded, and so lose the advantage of giving grave reproof. They will say, 'tis the manner of the person; and no one can help it: and so these persons will be less considered when they reprove with reason. Displeasure (when there is weighty reason for it) may prove to the offender a principle of reformation and amendment; but hasty and passionate men are not considered. Their fury is looked upon as a clap of thunder, and no one will much regard it.

Take notice what care God hath taken for the welfare and happiness of those that are inferiors, and under the power of others. The parent must not provoke his children to wrath (Eph. 6:4). Parents that have all authority over their children, must take care how they use it. The husband must not be bitter against his wife. He must give her no harsh language, but give honor to her as the weaker vessel (I Pet. 3:7). Masters must render to their servants that which is just and equal, forbearing threatenings; knowing that they have a Master in heaven (Eph. 6:9). Then for those that labor for us, that are but for a day and are gone again, God hath required that their wages be paid them; otherwise their cry will come up into the ears of the Lord of Sabbaoth (James 5:4). Then for strangers, that are without friends, relations, or acquaintance, what care doth God take for them! Be not forgetful to entertain strangers (Heb. 13:2). Then for the widow, and the fatherless persons, that are most helpless—what care hath God taken for them? So great, that he will be revenged on those that wrong them (Ex. 22:22, 23, 24); and, on the contrary will reckon those to have pure religion and undefiled that shall visit the widows and fatherless in their affliction (James 1:27).

This is the rule: The lower any one's condition is in the world, by so much the more he is pitiable; and so much the greater care should we take to ease him; he having burden enough upon him, without any other addition to his misery.

I will conclude this discourse with three rules. Whosoever will do his work, with fair words; I would not have him chid into it. I would never blame any one for common incidences, such as might befall myself or any one else; nor ever blame any one for not doing that wherein he hath not particular direction. You will say, these are low things to be spoken in a pulpit. But let them be as low as they will, the disorder of our minds, many times, is occasioned for want of them; and great disquietness is occasioned in many families for want of that peaceable temper, which my text speaks of,

Robert Leighton

(1611-1684)

AT forty-one Leighton was made principal of Edinburgh University. At the time of the Restoration he reluctantly became one of the bishops of Scotland. He chose the diocese of Dunblane, and in 1670 he was translated to the archdiocese of Glasgow. A man reputed for his humility, he asked that his writings be destroyed at his death. His friends, however, edited his papers, among them being "Rules and Instructions for a Holy Life," of which the first half is reproduced here. It has been described as "perhaps the rarest flower that has grown out of Scotch theology." Leighton and Scougal rank as the foremost Scotch contributors to "the fellowship of the saints."

RULES AND INSTRUCTIONS FOR A HOLY LIFE

For disposing you the better to observe these rules, and profit by them, be pleased to take the following advise.—

1. Put all your trust in the special and singular mercy of God, that he for his mercy's sake, and of his only goodness, will help and bring you to perfection. Not that absolute perfection is attainable here, but the meaning is, to high degrees of that spiritual and divine life, which is always growing, and tending toward the absolute perfection above; but in some persons comes nearer to that and riseth higher, even here, than in the most. If you with hearty and fervent desires do continually wish and long for it, and with most humble devotion daily pray unto God and call for it, and with all diligence do busily labor and travail to come to it, undoubtedly it shall be given you. For you must not think it sufficient to use exercises, as though they had such virtues in them, that of themselves alone, they could make such as do use them perfect; for neither those nor any other, whatever they be, can of themselves (by their use only) bring unto perfection. But our merciful Lord God, of his own goodness, when you seek with hearty desires and fervent sighings, maketh you to find it. When you ask daily with devout prayer, then he giveth it to you; and when you continually, with unwearied labor and travail, knock perseveringly, then he doth mercifully open unto you. And because those exercises do teach you to seek, ask, and knock, yea, they are none other than very devout petitions, seekings, and spiritual pulsations for the merciful help of God; therefore they are very profitable means of coming to perfection by God's grace.

2. Let no particular exercise hinder your public and standing duties to God and your neighbors: but for these, rather intermit the other for a time, and then return to it as soon as you can.

3. If, in time of your spiritual exercise, you find yourself drawn to any better, or to as good a contemplation as that is, follow the traek of that good motion so long as it shall last.

4. Always take care to follow such exercises of devout thoughts, withal putting in practice such lessons as they contain and excite to.

5. Though at first ye feel no sweetness in such exercises, yet be not discouraged, nor induced to leave them, but continue in them faithfully, whatsoever pain or spiritual trouble ye feel; for, doing them for God and his honor, and finding none other present fruit, yet you shall have an excellent reward for your diligent labor and your pure intentions. And let not your falling short of these models and rules, nor your daily manifold imperfections and faults, dishearten you; but continue steadfast in your desires, purposes, and endeavors; and ever ask the best, aim at the best, and hope the best, being sorry that you can do no better;

and they shall be a most acceptable sacrifice in the sight of God, *and in due time you shall reap if you faint not.* And of all such instructions let your rule be, to follow them as much as you can; but not too scrupulously thinking your labor lost if you do not exactly and strictly answer them in everything. Purpose still better, and by God's grace all shall be well.

I

Rule 1. Exercise thyself in the knowledge and deep consideration of our Lord God, calling humbly to mind how excellent and incomprehensible he is; and this knowledge shalt thou rather endeavor to obtain by fervent desire and devout prayer, than by high study and outward labor. It is the singular gift of God, and certainly very precarious.

2. Pray, then, "Most gracious Lord, whom to know is the very bliss and felicity of man's soul, and yet none can know thee, unless thou wilt open and show thyself unto him; vouchsafe of thy infinite mercy now and ever, to enlighten my heart and mind to know thee, and thy most holy and perfect will, to the honor and glory of thy name. Amen."

3. Then lift up thy heart to consider (not with too great violence, but soberly) the eternal and infinite power of God, who has created all things by his excellent wisdom; his unmeasurable goodness, and incomprehensible love; for he is very and only God, most excellent, most high, most glorious, the everlasting and unchangeable goodness, an eternal substance, a charity infinite, so excellent and ineffable in himself, that all dignity, perfection, and goodness, that is possible to be spoken or thought of, can not sufficiently express the smallest part thereof.

4. Consider that he is the natural place, the centre, and rest of thy soul. If thou then think of the most blessed Trinity, muse not too much thereon, but with devout and obedient faith, meekly and lowly adore and worship.

5. Consider Jesus the Redeemer and Husband of thy soul, and walk with him as becomes a chaste spouse, with reverence and lowly shamefulness, obedience and submission.

6. Then turn to the deep, profound consideration of thyself, thine own nothingness, and thy extreme defilement and pollution, thy natural aversion from God, and that thou must, by conversion to him again, and union with him, be made happy.

7. Consider thyself and all creatures as nothing in comparison of thy Lord; that so thou mayest not only be content, but desirous to be unknown; or being known, to be contemned and despised of all men, yet without thy faults or deservings, as much as thou canst.

8. Pray: "O God, infuse into my heart thy heavenly light and blessed charity, that I may know and love thee above all things; and above all things loath and abhor myself. Grant that I may be so ravished in the wonder and love of thee, that I may forget myself and all things; feel neither prosperity nor adversity; may not fear to suffer all the pains of this world, rather than to be parted and pulled away from thee, whose perfections infinitely exceed all thought and understanding. O! let me find thee more inwardly and verily present with me, than I am with myself; and make me most circumspect how I do use myself in the presence of thee, my holy Lord.

"Cause me always to remember how everlasting and constant is the love thou bearest toward me, and such a charity and continual care, as though thou hadst no more creatures in heaven or earth beside me. What am I? A vile worm and filth."

9. Then aspire to great contrition for thy sins, and hatred of them, an abhorring thyself for them; then crave pardon in the blood of Jesus Christ; and then offer up thyself, soul and body, an oblation or sacrifice, in and through him: as they did of old, laying wood on the altar, and then burning up all: so this shall be a sacrifice of sweet savor, and very acceptable to God.

10. Offer all that thou hast, to be nothing, to use nothing of all that thou hast about thee and is called thine, but to his

honor and glory; and resolve through his grace to use all the powers of thy soul, and every member of thy body, to his service, as formerly thou hast done to sin.

11. Consider the passion of thy Lord, how he was buffeted, scourged, reviled, stretched with nails on the cross, and hung on it three long hours; suffered all the contempt and shame, and all the inconceivable pain of it, for thy sake.

12. Then turn thy heart to him, humbly saying, "Lord Jesus, whereas I daily fall, and am ready to sin, vouchsafe me grace as oft as I shall, to rise again; let me never presume, but always most meekly and humbly acknowledge my wretchedness and frailty, and repent, with a firm purpose to amend; and let me not despair because of my great frailty; but ever trust in thy most loving mercy and readiness to forgive."

II

1. Thou shalt have much to do in mortifying of thy five senses, which must be all shut up in the crucified humility of Jesus Christ, and be as if they were plainly dead.

2. Thou must now learn to have a continual eye inwardly to thy soul and spiritual life, as thou hast used heretofore to have all thy mind and regard to outward pleasure and worldly things.

3. Thou must submit and give thyself up to the discipline of Jesus, and become his scholar, resigning and compelling thyself altogether to obey him in all things; so that thy willing and nilling thou utterly and perfectly do cast away from thee, and do nothing without his license: at every word thou wilt speak, at every morsel thou wilt eat, at every stirring or moving of every article or member of thy body, thou must ask leave of him in thy heart, and ask thyself whether, having so done, that be according to his will and holy example, and with sincere intention of his glory. Hence,

4. Even the most necessary actions of thy life, though lawful, yet must thus be offered up with a true intention unto God, in the unison of the most holy works, and blessed merits of Christ; saying, "Lord Jesus, bind up in the merits of thy blessed senses, all my feeling and sensation, and all my wits and senses, that I never hereafter use them to any sensuality."

5. Thus labor to come to this union and knitting up of thy senses, in God and thy Lord Jesus, and remain so fast to the cross, that thou never part from it, and still behave thy body and all thy senses as in the presence of thy Lord God, and commit all things to the most trusty providence of thy loving Lord, who will then order all things delectably and sweetly for thee. Reckon all things besides for right naught; and thus mayest thou come unto wonderful illuminations and spiritual influence from the Lord thy God.

6. If, for his love, thou canst crucify, renounce, and forsake perfectly thyself and all things, thou must so crucify thyself to all things and love and desire God only, with thy care and whole heart, that in this most steadfast and strong knot and union unto the will of God, if he would create hell in thee here, thou mightest be ready to offer thyself, by his grace, for his eternal honor and glory, to suffer it, and that purely for his will and pleasure.

7. Thou must keep thy memory clean and pure, as it were a wedlock-chamber, from all strange thoughts, fancies, and imaginations; and it must be trimmed and adorned with holy meditations and virtues of Christ's life and passion, that God may continually and ever rest therein.

A Prayer

8. "Lord, instead of knowing thee, I have sought to know wickedness and sin; and, whereas my will and desire were created to love thee, I have lost that love, and declined to the creatures. While my memory ought to be filled with thee, I have painted it with the imagery of innumerable fancies, not only of all creatures, but of all sinful wickedness. Oh! blot out these by thy blood, and imprint thy own blessed image in my soul, blessed Jesus, by that blood that issued out from thy most loving heart, when thou

hangedst on the cross. So knit my will to thy most holy will, that I may have no other will but thine, and may be most heartily and fully content with whatsoever thou wouldst do to me in this world; yea, if thou wilt, so that I hate thee not, nor sin against thee, but retain thy love, make me suffer the greatest pains."

III

Rule 1. Exercise thyself to a perfect abnegation of all things which may let or impede this union. Mortify in thee everything that is not of God, nor for God, or which he willeth and loveth not. Resigning and yielding up to the high pleasure of God all love and affection for transitory things, desire neither to have nor hold them, nor bestow nor give them, but only for the pure love and honor of God. Put away superfluous and unnecessary things, and affect not even things necessary.

2. Mortify all affection to and seeking of thyself, which is so natural to men in all the good they desire, and in all the good they do, and in all the evil they suffer: yea, by the inordinate love of the gifts and graces of God, instead of himself, they fall into spiritual pride, gluttony, and greediness.

3. Mortify all affection to, and delectation in, meat and drink, and vain thoughts and fancies, which, though they proceed not to consent, yet defile the soul, and grieve the Holy Ghost, and do great damage to the spiritual life.

4. Imprint on thy heart the image of Jesus crucified, the impressions of his humility, poverty, mildness, and all his holy virtues: let thy thoughts of him turn into affection, and thy knowledge into love. For the love of God doth most purely work in the mortification of nature: the life of the spirit, purifying the higher powers of the soul, begets the solitariness and departure from all creatures, and the influence and flowing into God.

5. Solitude, silence, and the strict keeping of the heart, are the foundations and grounds of a spiritual life.

6. Do all thy necessary and outward works without any trouble or carefulness of mind, and bear thy mind amid all and always inwardly lifted up and elevated to God, following always more the inward exercise of love, than the outward acts of virtue.

7. To this can no man come, unless he be rid and delivered from all things under God, and be so swallowed up under God, that he can contemn and despise himself and all things; for the pure love of God maketh the spirit pure and simple, and so free, that, without pain or labor, it can at all times turn and recollect itself in God.

8. Mortify all bitterness of heart toward thy neighbors, and all vain complacency in thyself, all vain glory and desire of esteem, in words and deeds, in gifts and graces. To this thou shalt come by a more clear and perfect knowledge and consideration of thy own vileness, and by knowing God to be the fountain of all grace and goodness.

9. Mortify all affection to inward, sensible, spiritual delight in grace, and the following devotion with sensible sweetness in the lower faculties or powers of the soul, which are nowise real sanctity and holiness in themselves, but certain gifts of God to help our infirmity.

10. Mortify all curious investigation or search, all speculation and knowledge of unnecessary things, human or Divine; for the perfect life of a Christian consisteth not in a high knowledge, but profound meekness, in holy simplicity, and in ardent love of God; wherein we ought to desire to die to all affection to ourselves and all things below God; yea, to sustain pain and dereliction, that we may be perfectly knit and united to God, and be perfectly swallowed up in him.

11. Mortify all undue scrupulousness of conscience and trust in the goodness of God: for our doubting and scruples ofttimes arise from inordinate self-love, and therefore vex us; they do no good, neither work any real amendment in us; they cloud the soul, and darken faith, and cool love; and it is only the stronger beams of these that can dispel them. And the stronger that faith and Divine confi-

dence is in us, and the hotter Divine love is, the soul is so much the more excited and enabled to all the parts of holiness, to mortifications of passions and lusts, to more patience in adversity, and to more thankfulness in all estates.

12. Mortify all impatience in all pains and troubles, whether from the hands of God or men, all desire of revenge, all resentment of injuries; and by the pure love of God, love thy very persecutors as if they were thy dearest friends.

13. Finally, mortify thy own will in all things, with full resignation of thyself to suffer all dereliction, outward and inward, all pain, and pressures, and deso-

lations, and that for the pure love of God: for from self-love and self-will spring all sin and all pain.

A Prayer

14. "O Jesus, my Savior! thy blessed humility, impress it on my heart. Make me most sensible of thy infinite dignity, and of my own vileness, that I may hate myself as a thing of naught, and be willing to be despised and trodden upon by all as the vilest mire of the streets; that I may still retain these words—I am nothing, I have nothing, I can do nothing, and I desire nothing but one."

John Bunyan
(1628-1688)

BORN at Elstow, son of a tinker, Bunyan was drafted at sixteen into the army, where he took part in the civil war between Roundheads and Royalists. After joining the Gifford Christian Fellowship in 1653, he began preaching in various villages near Bedford. In 1655, a period of religious conflict being resolved, he joined a Baptist society. His preaching conflicted with George Fox, and he wrote against Quakers. At the Restoration he was imprisoned, and for twelve years he was in and out of jail at Bedford. During this interim he wrote *Grace Abounding*. Freed for three years, he was again jailed and spent his time writing *Pilgrim's Progress*. It passed through ten editions before his death. His earlier service in the Parliamentary army provided him with many of the figures found in his books.

Although Bunyan is known chiefly as the greatest allegorist of Christian writings, his work on prayer gives a clear picture of man's spirit in communion with God. The selections below were compiled in *The Riches of Bunyan* (New York, 1850) by Jeremiah Chaplin.

[PRAYER]

CHARACTERISTICS OF PRAYER

What is prayer? A sincere, sensible, affectionate pouring out of the soul to God, through Christ, in the strength and assistance of the Spirit, for such things as God hath promised.

The best prayers have often more groans than words.

Alas, how few there be in the world whose heart and mouth in prayer shall go together. Dost thou, when thou asketh for the Spirit, or faith, or love to God, to

holiness, to saints, to the word, and the like, ask for them with love to them, desire of them, hungering after them? Oh, this is a mighty thing; and yet prayer is no more before God than as it is seasoned with these blessed qualifications. Wherefore it is said, that while men are praying, God is searching the heart to see what is the meaning of the Spirit, or whether there be the Spirit and his meaning in all that the mouth hath uttered, either by words, sighs, or groans, because it is by him and through his help only that any make prayers according to the will of God. Rom. 8:26, 27.

PREPARATION FOR PRAYER

Before you enter into prayer, ask thy soul these questions: To what end, O my soul, art thou retired into this place? Art thou not come to discourse the Lord in prayer? Is he present, will he hear thee? Is he merciful, will he help thee? Is thy business slight, is it not concerning the welfare of thy soul? What words wilt thou use to move him to compassion?

THE THRONE OF GRACE

We know the throne of grace from other thrones by the glory that it always appears in when revealed to us of God: its glory outshines all; there is no such glory to be seen anywhere else, either in heaven or earth. But I say, this comes by the sight that God gives, not by any excellency that there is in my natural understanding, as such: my understanding and apprehension, simply as natural, are blind and foolish; wherefore, when I set to work in mine own spirit and in the power of mine own abilities, to reach to this throne of grace and to perceive somewhat of the glory thereof, then am I dark, rude, foolish; I see nothing, and my heart grows flat, dull, savorless, lifeless, and has no warmth in the duty; but it mounts up with wings like an eagle when the throne is truly apprehended.

This throne is the seat of grace and mercy, and therefore it is called the mercy-seat and throne of grace. This throne turns all into grace, all into mercy; this throne makes all things work together for good. It is said of Saul's sons, 2 Sam. 21:10-14, they were not buried after they were hanged until water dropped upon them out of heaven; and it may be said of us, there is nothing suffered to come near us until it is washed in that water that proceeds from the throne of grace. Hence afflictions flow from grace; persecutions flow from grace; poverty, sickness, yea, death itself is now made ours by the grace of God through Christ. Psa. 119:67-71; 1 Cor. 3:22; Rev. 3:19; Heb. 12:5-7. O grace, O happy church of God! all things that happen to thee are for Christ's sake turned into grace. They talk of the philosopher's stone, and how if one had it, it would turn all things into gold. Oh, but can it turn all things into grace—can it make all things work together for good? No, no; this quality, virtue, excellency—what shall I call it?—nothing has in it but the grace that reigns on the throne of grace, the river that proceeds from the throne of God. This, this turns majesty, authority, the highest authority, glory, wisdom, faithfulness, justice, and all into grace. Here is a throne; may God let us see it. John had the honor to see it, and to see the streams proceeding from it. O sweet sight, O heart-cherishing sight! "He showed me a pure river of water of life proceeding out of the throne of God."

Indeed, as was hinted before, in the days of the reign of antichrist there are not those visions of this throne, nor of the river that proceedeth therefrom; now he holdeth back the face of his throne, and spreadeth a cloud upon it; but the preserving, saving benefits thereof we have, as also have all the saints in the most cloudy and dark day. And since we can see so little, we must believe the more; and by believing, give glory to God. We must also labor for more clear scripture knowledge of this throne, for the holy word of God is the perspective-glass by which we may, and the magnifying-glass that will cause us to behold with open face the glory of this Lord. 2 Cor. 3:18.

"A throne was set in heaven, and one sat on the throne;" that is, God. And this intimates his desirable rest for ever; for to sit is to rest, and Christ is his rest for ever. Was it not therefore well worth the seeing—yea, if John had taken the pains to go up thither upon his hands and knees?

It is grace that chooses, it is grace that calleth, it is grace that preserveth, and it is grace that brings to glory, even the grace that, like a river of water of life, proceeds from this "throne of grace;" and hence it is, that from first to last, we must cry, Grace, grace, unto it.

Thus you see what a throne the Christian is invited to: it is a throne of grace whereon doth sit the God of all grace; it is a throne of grace before which the Lord Jesus ministers continually for us; it is a throne of grace sprinkled with the blood, and in the midst of which is a Lamb as it had been slain; it is a throne with a rainbow round about it, which is the token of the everlasting covenant, and out of which proceeds a river, a pure river of water of life, clear as crystal.

Look then for these signs of the throne of grace, all you that would come to it, and rest not until by some of them you know that you are even come to it: they are all to be seen, have you but eyes; and the sight of them is very delectable, and has a natural tendency to revive and quicken the soul.

Prayer in the Name of Christ

He that thinks to find grace at God's hand, and yet enters not into the holiest by the blood of Jesus, will find himself mistaken, and will find a dead instead of a living way. For if not any thing below or besides blood can yield remission on God's part, how should remission be received by us without our acting faith therein? We are justified by his blood, through faith in his blood.

Wherefore look, when thou approachest the throne of grace, that thou give diligence to seek for the "Lamb as it had been slain," that is in the midst of the throne of grace; and then thou wilt have not only a sign that thou presentest thy supplication to God where and as thou shouldst, but there also wilt thou meet with matter to break, to soften, to bend, to bow, and to make thy heart as thou wouldst have it. This sight shall dissolve and melt down the spirit of that man that is upon his knees before the throne of grace for mercy; especially when he shall see, that not his prayers, nor his tears, nor his wants, but the blood of the Lamb, has prevailed with a God of grace to give mercy and grace to an undeserving sinner.

God hath prepared a golden altar for thee to offer thy prayers and tears upon, coming sinner. A golden altar! It is called a *golden altar*, to show what worth it is of in God's account; for this golden altar is Jesus Christ—this altar sanctifies thy gift, and makes thy sacrifice acceptable.

This altar then makes thy groans golden groans, thy tears golden tears, and thy prayers golden prayers, in the eye of that God thou comest to.

Benefit of Prayer

Pray often; for prayer is a shield for the soul, a sacrifice to God, and a scourge for Satan.

Look yonder! Ah, methinks mine eyes do see
Clouds edged with silver, as fine garments be;
They look as if they saw the golden face
That makes black clouds most beautiful with grace.

Unto the saints' sweet incense of their prayer,
These smoky curled clouds I do compare;
For as these clouds seem edged or laced with gold,
Their prayers return with blessings manifold.

Prayer is as the pitcher that fetcheth water from the brook, therewith to water the herbs: break the pitcher and it will fetch no water, and for want of water the garden withers.

The godly have found all other places, the throne of grace excepted, empty, and places that hold no water. They have been at mount Sinai for help, but could find nothing there but fire and darkness, but thunder and lightning, but earthquakes and trembling, and a voice of killing words.

They have sought for grace by their own performances; but, alas, they have yielded them nothing but wind and confusion: not a performance, not a duty, not an act in any part of religious worship, but they, looking upon it in the glass of the Lord, do find it specked and defective.

They have sought for grace by their resolutions, their vows, their purposes, and the like; but alas, they all do as the other, discover that they have been very imperfectly managed, and so are such as can by no means help them to grace.

They have gone to their tears, their sorrow, and repentance, if perhaps they might find some help there, but all has fled away like the early dew.

They have gone to God as the great Creator, and have beheld how wonderful his works have been; they have looked to the heavens above, to the earth beneath, and to all their ornaments; but neither have these, nor what is of them, yielded grace to those that had sensible want thereof.

They have gone with these pitchers to their fountains, and have returned empty and ashamed; they found no water, no river of water of life.

Paul, not finding it in the law, despairs to find it in any thing else below, but presently betakes himself to look for it where he had not yet found it: he looked for it by Jesus Christ, who is the throne of grace, where he found it, and rejoiced in hope of the glory of God.

O, when a God of grace is upon a throne of grace, and a poor sinner stands by and begs for grace, and that in the name of a gracious Christ, in and by the help of the Spirit of grace, can it be otherwise but such a sinner must obtain mercy and grace to help in time of need?

All the sorrow that is mixed with our Christianity proceeds, as the procuring cause, from ourselves, not from the throne of grace; for that is the place where our tears are wiped away, and also where we hang up our crutches: the streams thereof are pure and clear, not muddy nor frozen, but warm and delightful, and they make glad the city of God.

DISCOURAGEMENTS IN PRAYER

There is an aptness in those that come to the throne of grace, to cast every degree of faith away that carries not in it self-evidence of its own being and nature, thinking that if it be faith, it must be known to the soul; yea, if it be faith, it will do so and so—even so as the highest degree of faith will do: when, alas, faith is sometimes in a calm, sometimes up, and sometimes down, and sometimes in conflict with sin, death, and the devil. Faith now has but little time to speak peace to the conscience; it is now struggling for life, it is now fighting with angels, with infernals; all it can do now, is to cry, groan, sweat, fear, fight, and gasp for life.

I know what it is to go to God for mercy, and stand all the while through fear afar off, being possessed with this, Will not God now smite me at once to the ground for my sins? David thought something so when he said as he prayed, "Cast me not away from thy presence, and take not thy Holy Spirit from me."

None know, but those that have them, what turns and returns, what coming on and going off, there are in the spirit of a man that indeed is awakened, and that stands awakened before the glorious Majesty in prayer.

It is a great matter, in praying to God, not to go too far, nor come too short; and a man is very apt to do one or the other. The Pharisee went so far, he was too bold; he came into the temple making such a ruffle with his own excellencies, there was in his thoughts no need of a Mediator.

It has been the custom of praying men to keep their distance, and not to be rudely bold in rushing into the presence of the holy and heavenly Majesty, especially if they have been sensible of their own vileness and sins, as the prodigal, the lepers, and the poor publican were. Yea, Peter himself, when upon a time he perceived more than commonly he did of the majesty of Jesus his Lord, what doth he do? "He fell down at Jesus' knees, saying, Depart from me, for I am a sinful man, O Lord."

Oh, when men see God and themselves, it fills them with holy fear of the greatness of the majesty of God, as well as with love to, and desire after, his mercy.

What is poor sorry man, poor dust and ashes, that he should crowd up, and go jostlingly into the presence of the great God?

For my part, I find it one of the hardest things that I can put my soul upon, even to come to God, when warmly sensible that I am a sinner, for a share in grace, in mercy. Oh, methinks it seems to me as if the whole face of the heavens were set against me. Yea, the very thought of God, strikes me through; I cannot bear up, I cannot stand before him; I cannot but with a thousand tears say, "God be merciful to me a sinner." Ezra 9:15.

At another time, when my heart is more hard and stupid, and when his terror doth not make me afraid, then I can come before him and ask mercy at his hand, and scarce be sensible of sin or grace, or that indeed I am before God. But above all, they are the rare times, when I can go to God as the publican, sensible of his glorious majesty, sensible of my misery, and bear up, and affectionately cry, "God be merciful to me a sinner."

At certain times the most godly man in the world may be hard put to it by the sin that dwelleth in him; yea, so hard put to it, that there can be no way to save himself from a fall, but by imploring heaven and the throne of grace for help. This is called the needy-time, the time when the wayfaring man that knocked at David's door shall knock at ours; or when we are got into the sieve into which Satan did get Peter; or when those fists are about our ears that were about Paul's; and when that thorn pricks us that Paul said was in his flesh. But why, or how comes it to pass, that the godly are so hard put to it at these times, but because there is in them—that is, in their flesh—no good thing, but consequently all aptness to close in with the devil and his suggestions, to the overthrow of the soul?

But now, here we are presented with a throne of grace, unto which, as David says, we must continually resort; and that is the way to obtain relief and to find help in time of need.

DISCOURAGEMENTS TO PRAYER REMOVED

Query. What would you have a poor creature do, that cannot tell how to pray?

Answer. Thou canst not, thou complainest, pray; canst thou see thy misery? Hath God showed thee that thou art by nature under the curse of his law? If so, do not mistake. I know thou dost groan, and that most bitterly; I am persuaded thou canst scarcely be found doing any thing in thy calling. But prayer breaks from thy heart. Have not thy groans gone up to heaven from every corner of thy house? I know it is thus: and so also doth thine own sorrowful heart witness thy tears and thy forgetfulness of thy calling. Is not thy heart so full of desires after the things of another world, that many times thou dost even forget the things of this world? Prithee, read this scripture: Job 23:12.

Query. Yea, but when I go in secret, and intend to pour out my soul before God, I can scarce say any thing at all.

Answer. Ah, sweet soul, it is not thy words that God so much regards, that he will not mind thee except thou comest before him with some eloquent oration. His eye is on the brokenness of thy heart; and that it is which makes the compassions of the Lord run over: "A broken and a contrite heart, O God, thou wilt not despise."

The stopping of thy words may arise from overmuch trouble in thy heart. David was so troubled sometimes that he could not speak. But this may comfort all such sorrowful hearts as thine, that though thou canst not through the anguish of thy spirit speak much, yet the Holy Spirit stirs up in thy heart groans and sighs so much the more vehement.

AFFECTIONATE CONFIDENCE IN PRAYER

God has given thee his Son's righteousness to justify thee; he has also, because thou art a son, sent forth the Spirit of his Son into thy heart to satisfy thee, and to help thee to cry unto him, Father, Father!

Wilt thou not cry? wilt thou not desire? Thy God has bidden thee open thy mouth; he has bid thee open it wide, and promised, saying, "and I will fill it;" and wilt thou not desire?

Oh, thou hast a license, a leave, a grant to desire; wherefore, be not afraid to desire great mercies of the God of heaven.

Objection. "But I am an unworthy creature."

Answer. That is true; but God gives to no man for his worthiness, nor rejects any for their sinfulness, that come to him sensible of the want and worth of mercy for them. Besides, the desires of a righteous man, and the desires of his God, agree. God has a desire to thee, thou hast a desire to him. God desires truth in the inward parts, and so dost thou with all thy heart. God desires mercy, and to show it to the needy; that is what thou also wantest, and what thy soul craves at his hand.

Seek, man; ask, knock, and do not be discouraged; the Lord will grant all thy desires. Thou sayest thou art unworthy to ask the greatest things, things spiritual and heavenly: well, will carnal things serve thee, and answer the desires of thy heart? Canst thou be content to be put off with a belly well filled and a back well clothed?

"Oh, better I never had been born."

See! thou wilt not ask the best, and yet canst not make shift without them.

"Shift? no; no shift without them; I am undone without them, undone for ever and ever," sayest thou.

Well then, desire.

"So I do," sayest thou.

Ah, but desire with more strong desires; desire with more large desires; desire spiritual gifts, covet them earnestly; thou hast a license too to do so. God bids thee do so, for he hath said, "The desire of the righteous shall be granted."

God's Method of Answering Prayer

"The desire of the righteous shall be granted." But I find it not so, says one; for though I have desired and desired a thousand times upon my knees, for something that I want, yet I have not my desire; and indeed, the consideration of this has made me question whether I am one of those to whom the promise of granting desires is made.

Answer. What are the things thou desirest; are they lawful or unlawful? for a Christian may desire unlawful things.

But we will suppose that the thing thou desirest is good, and that thy heart may be right in asking, as, suppose thou desirest more grace; yet there are several things for thy instruction may be applied to thy objection: as,

1. Thou, though thou desirest more of this, mayest not yet be so sensible of the worth of what thou askest, as perhaps God will have thee be before he granteth thy desire.

2. Hast thou well improved what thou hast received already?

3. When God gives to his people the grant of their desires, he doth it so as may be best for our advantage: as,

(1.) Just before a temptation comes; then if it rains grace on thee from heaven, it may be most for thy advantage. This is like God's sending plenty in Egypt just before the years of famine came.

(2.) Christians, even righteous men, are apt to lean too much to their own doings; and God, to wean them from them, ofttimes defers to do, what they be doing expect, until in doing their spirits are spent, and they, as to doing, can do no longer. When they that cried for water, had cried till their spirits failed, and their tongue did cleave to the roof of their mouth for thirst, then the Lord did hear, and then the God of Israel did give them their desire. The righteous would be too light in asking, and would too much overprize their works, if their God should not sometimes deal in this manner with them.

(3.) It is also to the advantage of the righteous, that they be kept and led in that way which will best improve grace already received, and that is, when they spin it out and use it to the utmost; when they do with it as the prophet did with that meal's meat that he ate under the juniper-tree, "go in the strength of it forty days and forty nights, even to the mount of God." Or when they do as the widow did—spend upon their handful of flour in the barrel, and upon that little oil in the cruse, till God shall send more plenty.

A little true grace will go a great way, yea, and do more wonders than we are aware of. If we have but grace enough to keep us groaning after God, it is not all the world that can destroy us.

4. Perhaps thou mayest be mistaken. The grace thou prayest for may in a great measure be come unto thee.

Thou hast been desiring of God, thou sayest, more grace, but hast it not.

But how, if while thou lookest for it to come to thee at one door, it come to thee at another? And that we may a little inquire into the truth of this, let us a little consider what are the effects of grace in its coming to the soul, and then see if it has not been coming unto thee almost ever since thou hast set upon this fresh desire after it.

(1.) Grace, in the general effect of it, is to mend the soul, and to make it better disposed. Hence, when it comes, it brings convincing light along with it, by which a man sees more of his baseness than at other times. If, then, thou seest thyself more vile than formerly, grace by its coming to thee has done this for thee.

(2.) Grace, when it comes, breaks and crumbles the heart in the sense and sight of its own vileness. A man stands amazed and confounded in himself; breaks and falls down on his face before God; is ashamed to lift up so much as his face to God, at the sight and apprehension of how wicked he is.

(3.) Grace, when it comes, shows to a man more of the holiness and patience of God; his holiness to make us wonder at his patience, and his patience to make us wonder at his mercy, that yet, even yet, such a vile one as I am should be admitted to breathe in the land of the living, yea more, suffered to come to the throne of grace.

(4.) Grace is of a heart-humbling nature; it will make a man account himself the most unworthy of any thing, of all saints. It will make a man put all others before him, and be glad too if he may be one beloved, though least beloved because more unworthy. It will make him with gladness accept of the lowest room, as counting all saints more worthy of exaltation than himself.

(5.) Grace will make a man prize other men's graces and gracious actions above his own; as he thinks every man's candle burns brighter than his, every man improves grace better than he, every good man does more sincerely his duty than he. And if these be not some of the effects of the renewings of grace, I will confess I have taken my mark amiss.

(6.) Renewings of grace beget renewed self-bemoanings, self-condemnations, self-abhorrences.

And say thou prayest for communion with, and the presence of God. God can have communion with thee and grant thee his presence, and all this shall, instead of comforting thee at present, more confound thee and make thee see thy wickedness.

Some people think they never have the presence and renewings of God's grace upon them, but when they are comforted and when they are cheered up —when, alas, God may be richly with them, while they cry out by these visions, My sorrows are multiplied; or, Because I have seen God, I shall die.

And tell me now, all these things considered, has not grace, even the grace of God which thou hast so much desired, been coming to thee and working in thee in all these hidden methods? Thus therefore thy desire is accomplishing, and when it is accomplished will be sweet to thy soul.

5. But we will follow thee a little in the way of thy heart. Thou sayest thou desirest, and desirest grace, yea, hast been a thousand times upon thy knees before God for more grace, and yet thou canst not attain.

I answer, (1.) It may be, the grace which thou prayest for is worth thy being upon thy knees yet a thousand times more. We find that usually they that go to king's courts for preferment, are there at great expenses, yea, and wait a great while, even until they have spent their whole estates, and worn out their patience too.

Yet they at last prevail, and the thing desired comes; yea, and when it is come, it sets them up anew and makes them better men, though they did spend all they had to obtain it, than ever they were before. Wait, therefore, wait, I say, on the Lord; bid thy soul cheer up and wait. "Blessed are all they that wait for him."

(2.) Thou must consider that great grace is reserved for great service. Thou desirest abundance of grace; thou doest well, and thou shalt have what shall qualify thee for the service that God has for thee to do for him, and for his name in the world. The apostles themselves were to stay for great grace until the time their work was come.

I will not allot thy service, but assure thyself, when thy desire cometh, thou wilt have occasion for it—new work, new trials, new sufferings, or something that will call for the power and virtue of all the grace thou shalt have to keep thy spirit even, and thy feet from slipping, while thou art exercised in new engagements.

Assure thyself thy God will not give thee straw, but he will expect brick. "For unto whomsoever much is given, of him much shall be required." Wherefore, as thou art busy in desiring more grace, be also desirous that wisdom to manage it with faithfulness may also be granted unto thee.

Thou wilt say, Grace, if I had it, will do all this for me.

It will, and will not. It will, if thou watch and be sober; it will not, if thou be foolish and remiss. Men of great grace may grow consumptive in grace, and idleness may turn him that wears a plush jacket into rags. David was once a man of great grace, but his sin made the grace which he had so to shrink up and dwindle away as to make him cry out, O take not thy Spirit utterly from me!

(3.) Or, perhaps God withholds what thou wouldst have, that it may be the more prized by thee when it comes. "Hope deferred maketh the heart sick; but when the desire cometh, it is a tree of life."

(4.) Lastly. But dost thou think that thy more grace will exempt thee from temptations? Alas, the more grace, the greater trials. Thou must be, for all that, like the ship of which thou readest: sometimes high, sometimes low; sometimes steady, sometimes staggering; and sometimes even at the end of thy very wits: "For so he brings us to our desired haven."

Yet grace is the gold and preciousness of the righteous man: yea, and herein appears the uprightness of his soul, in that, though all these things attend the grace of God in him, yet he chooseth grace here above all, for that it makes him the more like God and his Christ, and for that it seasons his heart best to his own content; and also for that it capacitates him to glorify God in the world.

RELIEF IN PRAYER

If from a sense of thy vileness thou do pour out thy heart to God, desiring to be saved from the guilt and cleansed from the filth with all thy heart, fear not; thy vileness will not cause the Lord to stop his ear from hearing thee. The value of the blood of Christ, which is sprinkled upon the mercy-seat, stops the course of justice, and opens a floodgate for the mercy of the Lord to be extended unto thee.

FAITH IN PRAYER

Of old, beggars did use to carry their bowls in their laps when they went to a door for alms; consequently, if their bowls were but little, they ofttimes came off with a loss, though the charity of the giver was large. Art thou a beggar, a beggar at God's door? be sure thou gettest a great bowl, for as thy bowl is, so will be thy mess. "According to thy faith be it unto thee."

WRESTLING PRAYER

A wrestling spirit of prayer is a demonstration of an Israel of God; this Jacob had, this he made use of, and by this he obtained the name of Israel. A wrestling spirit of prayer in straits, difficulties, and distresses—a wrestling spirit of prayer when alone, in private, in the night, when no eye seeth but God's, then to be at it, then to lay hold of God, then to wrestle, to hold fast, and not to give over until the blessing is obtained, is a sign of one that is an Israel of God.

As this word, "*Let* Israel hope in the Lord," is sometimes equivalent to a command, so it is expressed sometimes also to show a grant, leave, or license to do a thing; such are these that follow: "Let us come boldly to the throne of grace; let us draw near with a true heart; let us hold fast the profession of our faith without wavering."

Understand the word thus, and it shows you how muddy, how dark those of Israel are, and how little they are acquainted with the goodness of their God who stand shrinking at his door like beggars, and dare not in a godly sort be bold with his mercy. Wherefore standest thou thus with thy *ifs* and thy *O-buts*, O thou poor benighted Israelite? Wherefore puttest thou thy hand in thy bosom, as being afraid to touch the hem of the garment of thy Lord?

The Publican's Prayer

"God be merciful to me a sinner." Herein the publican showeth wonderful wisdom. For,

1. By this he thrusts himself under the shelter and blessing of the promise; and I am sure it is better and safer to do so than to rely upon the best excellencies that this world can afford. Hosea 14:1-4.

2. He takes the ready way to please God; for God takes more delight in showing mercy than in any thing that we can do. Hosea 6:6; Matt. 9:13; 12:7. Yea, and that also is the man that pleaseth him, even he that hopes in his mercy. Psalm 147:1. The publican, therefore, whatever the Pharisee might think, stood all this while upon sure ground, and had by far the start of him for heaven. Alas, his dull head could look no further than to the conceit of the pitiful beauty and splendor of his own righteousness; nor durst he leave that to trust wholly to the mercy of God. But the publican comes out, though in his sins, yet like an awakened, enlightened, resolved man; and first abases himself, then gives God the glory of his justice, and after that the glory of his mercy, by saying, "God be merciful to me a sinner." And thus in the ears of the angels he did ring the changes of heaven. And,

3. The publican, in his thus putting himself upon mercy, showeth that in his opinion there is more virtue in mercy to save, than there is in the law and sin to condemn. And although this is not counted a great matter to do, while men are far from the law and while their conscience is asleep within them, yet when the law comes near and conscience is awake, whoso tries it will find it a laborious work. Cain could not do thus for his heart, no, nor soul; nor Judas neither. This is another kind of thing than most men think it to be, or shall find it whenever they shall behold God's angry face, and when they shall hear the words of his law.

However, our publican did it, and ventured his body, soul, and future condition for ever in this bottom, with other the saints and servants of God; leaving the world to swim over the sea of God's wrath, if they will, in their weak and simple vessels of bulrushes, or to lean upon their cobweb-hold, when he shall arise to the judgment that he hath appointed.

"He would not lift up his eyes to heaven." Why? Surely because shame had covered his face. Shame will make a man blush and hang his head like a bulrush. Shame for sin is a virtue, a comely thing, yea, a beauty-spot in the face of a sinner that cometh to God for mercy.

Oh, to stand, or sit, or lie, or kneel, or walk before God in prayer, with blushing cheeks for sin, is one of the excellent sights that can be seen in the world.

Posture in Prayer

There is no stinted order presented for our behaving ourselves in prayer, whether kneeling, or standing, or walking, or lying, or sitting; for all these postures have been used by the godly. Paul kneeled down and prayed; Abraham and the publican stood and prayed; David prayed as he walked; Abraham prayed lying upon his face; Moses prayed sitting. And indeed prayer, effectual fervent prayer, may be and often is made unto God under all these circumstances. For God has not tied us up to any of them; and he that shall tie himself or his people to any of these, doeth more than he hath warrant for from God. And let such take care of innovating; it is the next way to make men hypocrites and dissemblers in those duties in which they should be sincere. Acts 20:36; 2 Sam. 15:30, 31; Gen. 17:17, 18; Exod. 17:12.

Closet-Iniquity

Let those that name the name of Christ depart from the iniquity of their closet —when men have a closet to talk of, not to pray in; a closet to look upon, not to bow before God in; a closet to lay up gold in, but not to mourn in for the sins of the life; a closet that, could it speak, would say, My owner is seldom here upon his knees before the God of heaven, seldom here humbling himself for the iniquity of his heart, or to thank God for the mercies of his life.

Then also a man is guilty of closet-iniquity when, though he doth not utterly live in the neglect of duty, he formally, carnally, and without reverence and godly fear, performs it. Also when he asketh God for that which he cannot abide should be given him; or when he prayeth for that in his closet, that he cannot abide in his house nor his life.

It is a great thing to be a closet-Christian, and to hold it; he must be a close-Christian that will be a closet-Christian. When I say a close-Christian, I mean one that is so in the hidden part, and that also walks with God. Many there be that profess Christ, who do oftener frequent the coffee-house than their closet; and that sooner in a morning run to make bargains, than to pray unto God and begin the day with him. But for thee, who professest the name of Christ, do thou depart from all these things; do thou make conscience of reading and practising; do thou follow after righteousness; do thou make conscience of beginning the day with God. For he that begins it not with him, will hardly end it with him; he that runs from God in the morning, will hardly find him at the close of the day; nor will he that begins with the world and the vanities thereof in the first place, be very capable of walking with God all the day after. It is he that finds God in his closet, that will carry the savor of him into his house, his shop, and his more open conversation. When Moses had been with God in the mount his face shone, he brought of that glory into the camp. Exod. 34.

Formal Prayer

"Thy kingdom come; thy will be done." Wouldst thou have the kingdom of God come indeed, and also his will to be done in earth as it is in heaven? Nay, notwithstanding thou sayest, "Thy kingdom come," yet would it not make thee ready to run mad, to hear the trumpet sound, to see the dead arise, and thyself just now to go and appear before God, to reckon for all the deeds thou hast done in the body? Nay, are not the very thoughts of it altogether displeasing to thee?

And if God's will should be done on earth as it is in heaven, must it not be thy ruin? There is never a rebel against God in heaven; and if he should so deal on earth, must he not whirl thee down to hell? And so of the rest of the petitions.

Ah, how sadly would even these men look, and with what terror would they walk up and down the world, if they did but know the lying and blaspheming that proceedeth out of their mouth, even in their most pretended sanctity!

The Prayerless

I tell thee who never prayest, the ravens shall rise up in judgment against thee; for they will, according to their kind, make signs and a noise for something to refresh them when they want it; but thou hast not the heart to ask for heaven, though thou must eternally perish in hell if thou hast it not.

George Fox

(1624-1691)

Son of a weaver in Fenny Drayton, England, Fox was to become one of the select religious geniuses of English history. When nineteen years of age he saw Christians at a drinking party, and decided that he would act as a Christian probe to the reality of religion. He was disgusted with those who confused theory and practice. He concluded that Christianity is "an inner light" rather than an outer confession, that God speaks directly to men and enlivens them for his service, that outward elements in the sacraments are unnecessary and misleading, that war is unlawful for a Christian, and that slavery is evil. He founded the Society of Friends in 1652 at Preston Patrick in northern England. Fox and his Friends were constantly persecuted and imprisoned. His *Journal*, in which he tells about "seeking spiritual help," ranks as an outstanding devotional classic. In many ways Fox radiates the mystical note of Böhme, who died the year Fox was born.

[SEEKING SPIRITUAL HELP]

From the *Journal*

After some time I went into my own country again, and was there about a year, in great sorrows and troubles, and walked many nights by myself.

Then the priest of Drayton, the town of my birth, whose name was Nathaniel Stevens, came often to me, and I went often to him; and another priest sometimes came with him; and they would give place to me to hear me, and I would ask them questions, and reason with them. And this priest Stevens asked me a question, viz. Why Christ cried out upon the cross, "My God, my God, why hast thou forsaken me?" and why he said "If it be possible, let this cup pass from me; yet not my will, but thine be done"? I told him that at that time the sins of all mankind were upon him, and their iniquities and transgressions with which he was wounded, which he was to bear, and to be an offering for, as he was man, but he died not, as he was God: and so, in that he died for all men, and tasted death for every man, he was an offering for the sins of the whole world. This I spake, being at that time in a measure sensible of Christ's sufferings, and what he went through. And the priest said, "It was a very good, full answer, and such a one as he had not heard." At that time he would applaud and speak highly of me to others; and what I said in discourse to him on the weekdays, he would preach on the first-days; for which I did not like him. This priest afterwards became my great persecutor.

After this I went to another ancient priest at Mancetter, in Warwickshire, and reasoned with him about the ground of despair and temptations; but he was ignorant of my condition: he bade me take tobacco and sing psalms. Tobacco was a thing I did not love, and psalms I was not in a state to sing; I could not sing. Then he bid me come again, and he would tell me many things; but when I came he was angry and pettish, for my former words had displeased him. He told my troubles, and sorrows, and griefs to his servants, so that it was got among the milk-lasses; which grieved me that I should open my mind to such a one. I saw they were all miserable comforters; and this brought my troubles more upon me. Then I heard of a priest living about Tamworth, who was accounted an experienced man, and I went seven miles to him; but I found him only like an empty, hollow cask. I heard also of one called Dr. Cradock, of Coventry, and went to him; I asked him the ground of temptations and despair, and how troubles came to be wrought in man? He asked me, Who was Christ's father and mother? I told him, Mary was his mother, and that he was supposed to be the son of Joseph, but he was the Son of God. Now as we were walking together in his garden, the alley being narrow, I chanced, in turning, to set my foot on the side of a bed; at which the man was in a rage as if his house had been on fire. Thus all our discourse was lost, and I went away in sorrow, worse than I was when I came. I thought them miserable comforters, and saw they were all as nothing to me; for they could not reach my condition. After this I went to another, one Macham, a priest in high account. He would needs give me some physic, and I was to have been let blood; but they could not get one drop of blood from me, either in arms or head, (though they endeavoured it,) my body being, as it were, dried up with sorrows, grief, and troubles, which were so great upon me that I could have wished I had never been born, or that I had been born blind, that I might never have seen wickedness or vanity; and deaf, that I might never have heard vain and wicked words, or the Lord's name blasphemed. When the time called Christmas came, while others were feasting and sporting themselves, I looked out poor widows from house to house, and gave them some money. When I was invited to marriages, (as I sometimes was,) I went to none at all, but the next day, or soon after, I would go and visit them; and if they were poor, I gave them some money, for I had

wherewith both to keep myself from being chargeable to others, and to administer something to the necessities of others.

About the beginning of the year 1646, as I was going to Coventry, and approaching towards the gate, a consideration arose in me, how it was said, that "all Christians are believers, both Protestants and Papists;" and the Lord opened to me that, if all were believers, then they were all born of God, and passed from death to life; and that none were true believers but such; and though others said they were believers, yet they were not. At another time, as I was walking in a field on a first-day morning, the Lord opened unto me, "that being bred at Oxford or Cambridge was not enough to fit and qualify men to be ministers of Christ. . . . But my relations were much troubled, that I would not go with them to hear the priest; for I would get into the orchard, or the fields, with my Bible, by myself. I asked them, did not the apostle say to believers, that "they needed no man to teach them, but as the anointing teacheth them"? And though they knew this was Scripture, and that it was true, yet they were grieved because I could not be subject in this matter, to go to hear the priest with them. I saw that to be a true believer was another thing than they looked upon it to be. . . . So neither them, nor any of the Dissenting people, could I join with, but was a stranger to all, relying wholly upon the Lord Jesus Christ.

At another time it was opened in me, "That God, who made the world, did not dwell in temples made with hands." This at first seemed a strange word, because both priests and people used to call their temples or churches, dreadful places, holy ground, and the temples of God. But the Lord showed me clearly, that he did not dwell in these temples which men had commanded and set up, but in people's hearts: for both Stephen and the apostle Paul bore testimony, that he did not dwell in temples made with hands, not even in that which he had once commanded to be built, since he put an end to it; but that his people were his temple, and he dwelt in them. This opened in me as I walked in the fields to my relations' house. When I came there, they told me that Nathaniel Stevens, the priest, had been there, and told them "he was afraid of me, for going after new lights." I smiled in myself, knowing what the Lord had opened in me concerning him and his brethren; but I told not my relations, who though they saw beyond the priests, yet they went to hear them, and were grieved because I would not go also. But I brought them Scriptures, and told them, there was an anointing within man to teach him, and that the Lord would teach his people himself. I had also great openings concerning the things written in the Revelations; and when I spoke of them, the priests and professors would say, that was a sealed book, and would have kept me out of it: but I told them, Christ could open the seals, and that they were the nearest things to us; for the Epistles were written to the saints that lived in former ages, but the Revelations were written of things to come.

After this, I met with a sort of people that held, women have no souls, (adding in a light manner,) no more than a goose. But I reproved them, and told them that was not right; for Mary said, "My soul doth magnify the Lord, and my spirit hath rejoiced in God my Saviour."

Removing to another place, I came among a people that relied much on dreams: and I told them, except they could distinguish between dream and dream, they would confound all together; for there were three sorts of dreams; multitude of business sometimes caused dreams; and there were whisperings of Satan in man in the night-season; and there were speakings of God to man in dreams. But these people came out of these things, and at last became Friends.

Now though I had great openings, yet great trouble and temptation came many times upon me; so that when it was day, I wished for night, and when it was night, I wished for day: and by reason of the openings I had in my troubles, I could say as David said, "Day unto day uttereth speech, and night unto night showeth knowledge." When I had openings, they answered one another, and answered the Scriptures; for I had great openings of the Scriptures: and when I was in troubles, one trouble also answered to another.

About the beginning of the year 1647, I was moved of the Lord to go into Derbyshire, where I met with some friendly people, and had many discourses with them. Then passing further into the Peak-country, I met with more friendly people, and with some in empty, high notions. Travelling on through some parts of Leicestershire and into Nottinghamshire, I met with a tender people, and a very tender woman, whose name was Elizabeth Hootton; and with these I had some meetings and discourses. But my troubles continued, and I was often under great temptations; I fasted much, and walked abroad in solitary places many days, and often took my Bible, and went and sat in hollow trees and lonesome places till night came on; and frequently, in the night, walked mournfully about by myself; for I was a man of sorrows in the times of the first workings of the Lord in me.

During all this time I was never joined in profession of religion with any, but gave up myself to the Lord, having forsaken all evil company, and taken leave of father and mother and all other relations, and travelled up and down as a stranger in the earth, which way the Lord inclined my heart; taking a chamber to myself in the town where I came, and tarrying sometimes a month, sometimes more, sometimes less in a place; for I durst not stay long in any place, being afraid both of professor and profane, lest, being a tender young man, I should be hurt by conversing much with either. For which reason I kept myself much as a stranger, seeking heavenly wisdom and getting knowledge from the Lord; and was brought off from outward things, to rely wholly on the Lord alone. Though my exercises and troubles were very great, yet were they not so continual but that I had some intermissions, and was sometimes brought into such a heavenly joy, that I thought I had been in Abraham's bosom. As I cannot declare the misery I was in, it was so great and heavy upon me; so neither can I set forth the mercies of God unto me in all my misery. Oh, the everlasting love of God to my soul, when I was in great distress! when my troubles and torments were great, then was his love exceeding great. . . .

Now after I had received that opening from the Lord, that "to be bred at Oxford or Cambridge, was not sufficient to fit a man to be a minister of Christ," I regarded the priests less, and looked more after the Dissenting people. Among them I saw there was some tenderness; and many of them came afterwards to be convinced, for they had some openings. But as I had forsaken the priests, so I left the separate preachers also, and those called the most experienced people; for I saw there was none among them all that could speak to my condition. When all my hopes in them and in all men, were gone, so that I had nothing outwardly to help me, nor could I tell what to do; then, O! then I heard a voice which said, "There is one, even Christ Jesus, that can speak to thy condition;" and when I heard it, my heart did leap for joy. Then the Lord let me see why there was none upon the earth, that could speak to my condition, namely, that I might give Him all the glory; for all are concluded under sin, and shut up in unbelief, as I had been, that Jesus Christ might have the preeminence, who enlightens, and gives grace, and faith, and power. Thus when God doth work, who shall let it? and this I knew experimentally. My desires after the Lord grew stronger, and zeal in the pure knowledge of God, and of Christ alone, without the help of any man, book, or writing. For though I read the Scriptures that spake of Christ and of God; yet I knew him not, but my revelation, as he who hath the key did open, and as the Father of Life drew me to his Son by his Spirit. Then the Lord gently led me along and let me see his love, which was endless and eternal, surpassing all the knowledge that men have in the natural state, or can get by history or books; and that love let me see myself as I was without him. I was afraid of all company, for I saw them perfectly where they were, through the love of God, which let me see myself. . . .

At another time, I saw the great love of God, and I was filled with admiration at the infiniteness of it; I saw what was cast out from God, and what entered into God's kingdom; and how by Jesus, the opener of the door, with his heavenly key, the entrance was given: and I saw death, how it had passed upon all men, and oppressed the seed of God in man, and in me; and how I in the seed came forth, and what the promise was to. Yet it was so with me, that there seemed to be two pleading in me; questionings arose in my mind about gifts and prophecies; and I was tempted again to despair, as if I had sinned against the Holy Ghost. I was in great perplexity and trouble for many days; yet I gave up myself to the Lord still. One day when I had been walking solitarily abroad, and was come home, I was taken up in the love of God, so that I could not but admire the greatness of his love. While I was in that condition, it was opened unto me by the eternal light and power, and I therein clearly saw, "that all was done, and to be done, in and by Christ; and how he conquers and destroys this tempter, the Devil, and all his works, and is a-top of him; and that all these troubles were good for me, and temptations for the trial of my faith, which Christ had given me." . . . When at any time my condition was veiled, my secret belief was stayed firm, and hope underneath held me, as an anchor in the bottom of the sea, and anchored my immortal soul to its Bishop, causing it to swim above the sea, the world, where all the raging waves, foul weather, tempests, and temptations are. But, oh! then did I see my troubles, trials, and temptations more clearly than ever I had done. As the light appeared, all appeared that is out of the light; darkness, death, temptations, the unrighteous, the ungodly; all was manifest and seen in the light. After this, a pure fire appeared in me; then I saw how he sat as a refiner's fire and as fullers' soap;—then the spiritual discerning came into me, by which I did discern my own thoughts, groans, and sighs; and what it was that veiled me, and what it was that opened me. That which could not abide in the patience, nor endure the fire, in the light I found it to be the groans of the flesh, that could not give up to the will of God; which had so veiled me, that I could not be patient in all trials, troubles, and anguishes, and perplexities;—could not give up self to die by the cross, the power of God, that the living and quickened might follow him, and that that which would cloud and veil from the presence of Christ,—that which the sword of the Spirit cuts down, and which must die, might not be kept alive. . . . Several things did I then see as the Lord opened them to me; for he showed me that which can live in his holy refining fire, and that can live to God under his law. He made me sensible how the law and the prophets were until John; and how the least in the everlasting kingdom of God, is greater than John. . . .

I saw also the mountains burning up; and the rubbish, the rough and crooked ways and places, made smooth and plain, that the Lord might come into his tabernacle. . . . I saw many talked of the law, who had never known the law to be their school-master; and many talked of the gospel of Christ, who had never known life and immortality brought to light in them by it. . . . Though the Lord in that day opened these things unto me in secret, they have since been published by his eternal Spirit, as on the house top. . . .

I heard of a woman in Lancashire, that had fasted two and twenty days, and I travelled to see her; but when I came to her I saw that she was under a temptation. When I had spoken to her what I had from the Lord, I left her, her father being one high in profession. Passing on, I went among the professors at Duckingfield and Manchester, where I stayed a while, and declared truth among them. There were some convinced, who received the Lord's teaching, by which they were confirmed and stood in the truth. But the professors were in a rage, all pleading for sin and imperfection, and could not endure to hear talk of perfection, and of a holy and sinless life. But the Lord's power was over all; though they were chained under darkness and sin, which they pleaded for, and quenched the tender thing in them.

About this time there was a great meeting of the Baptists, at Broughton, in Leicestershire, with some that had separated from them; and people of other notions went thither, and I went also. Not many of the Baptists came, but abundance of other people were there. The Lord opened my mouth, and the everlasting truth was declared amongst them, and the power of the Lord was over them all. For in that day the Lord's power began to spring, and I had great openings in the Scriptures. Several were convinced in those parts, and were turned from darkness to light, and from the power of Satan unto God; his power they did receive, and by it many were raised up to praise God. When I reasoned with professors and other people, some were convinced and did stand. I was still under great temptations sometimes, and my inward sufferings were heavy; but I could find none to open my condition to but the Lord alone, unto whom I cried night and day. I went back into Nottinghamshire, and there the Lord showed me that the natures of those things, which were hurtful without, were within, in the hearts and minds of wicked men. . . . I cried to the Lord, saying, "Why should I be thus, seeing I was never addicted to commit those evils?" and the Lord answered, "That it was needful I should have a sense of all conditions, how else should I speak to all conditions!" and in this I saw the infinite love of God. I saw also, that there was an ocean of darkness and death; but an infinite ocean of light and love, which flowed over the ocean of darkness. In that also I saw the infinite love of God, and I had great openings. And as I was walking by the steeple-house side, in the town of Mansfield, the Lord said unto me, "That which people trample upon, must be thy food." And as the Lord spoke he opened it to me, that people and professors trampled upon the life, even the life of Christ; they fed upon words, and fed one another with words; but they trampled upon the life; trampled under foot the blood of the Son of God, which blood was my life, and lived in their airy notions, talking of him. It seemed strange to me at the first, that I should feed on that which the high professors trampled upon; but the Lord opened it clearly to me by his eternal Spirit and Power.

Then came people from far and near to see me; but I was fearful of being drawn out by them; yet I was made to speak, and open things to them. There was one Brown, who had great prophecies and sights upon his death-bed of me. He spoke only of what I should be made instrumental by the Lord to bring forth. And of others he spoke, that they should come to nothing; which was fulfilled on some who then were something in show. When this man was buried, a great work of the Lord fell upon me, to the admiration of many, who thought I had been dead; and many came to see me for about fourteen days. I was very much altered in countenance and person, as if my body had been new moulded or changed. While I was in that condition, I had a sense and discerning given me by the Lord, through which I saw plainly, that when many people talked of God and of Christ, &c., the serpent spoke in them; but this was hard to be borne. Yet the work of the Lord went on in some, and my sorrows and troubles began to wear off, and tears of joy dropped from me, so that I could have wept night and day with tears of joy to the Lord, in humility and brokenness of heart. I saw into that which was without end, things which cannot be uttered, and of the greatness and infiniteness of the love of God, which cannot be expressed by words. For I had been brought through the very ocean of darkness and death, and through the power, and over the power of Satan, by the eternal, glorious power of Christ, even through that darkness was I brought, which covered over all the world, and which chained down all, and shut up all in the death. The same eternal power of God, which brought me through these things, was that which afterwards shook the nations, priests, professors, and people. . . . I saw the harvest white, and the seed of God lying thick in the ground, as ever did wheat that was sown outwardly, and none to gather it; for this I mourned with tears. A report went abroad of me, that I was young man that had a discerning spirit; whereupon many came to me, from far and near, professors, priests, and people. The Lord's power broke forth; and I had great openings and prophecies; and spoke unto them of the things of God, which they heard with attention and silence, and went away, and spread the fame thereof. Then came the tempter, and set upon me again, charging me, that I had sinned against the Holy Ghost; but I could not tell in what. Then Paul's condition came before me, how, after he had been taken up into the third heavens, and seen things not lawful to be uttered, a messenger of Satan was sent to buffet him. Thus by the power of Christ, I got over that temptation also.

In the year 1648, as I was sitting in a friend's house in Nottinghamshire, (for by this time the power of God had opened the hearts of some to receive the word of life and reconciliation,) I saw there was a great crack to go throughout the earth, and a great smoke to go as the crack went; and that after the crack there should be a great shaking: this was the earth in people's hearts, which was to be shaken, before the seed of God was raised out of the earth. And it was so; for the Lord's power began to shake them, and great meetings we began to have, and a mighty power and work of God there was amongst people, to the astonishment of both people and priests.

And there was a meeting of priests and professors at a justice's house, and I went among them. Here they discoursed how Paul said, "He had not known sin, but by the law, which said, Thou shalt not lust:" and they held that to be spoken of the outward law. But I told them, Paul spoke that after he was convinced; for he had the outward law before, and was bred up in it, when he was in the lust of persecution; but this was the law of God in his mind, which he served, and which the law in his members warred against; for that which he thought had been life to him, proved death. So the more sober of the priests and professors yielded, and consented that it was not the outward law, but the inward, which showed the inward lust which Paul spoke of after he was convinced: for the outward law took hold upon the outward action; but the inward law upon the inward lust.

After this I went again to Mansfield, where was a great meeting of professors and people; here I was moved to pray; and the Lord's power was so great, that the house seemed to be shaken. When I had done, some of the professors said, it was now as in the days of the apostles, when the house was shaken where they were. After I had prayed, one of the professors would pray, which brought deadness and a veil over them: and others of the professors were grieved at him, and told him, it was a temptation upon him. Then he came to me, and desired that I would pray again; but I could not pray in man's will.

Soon after there was another great meeting of professors, and a captain, whose name was Amor Stoddard, came in. They were discoursing of the blood of Christ; and as they were discoursing of it, I saw, through the immediate opening of the invisible Spirit, the blood of Christ. And I cried out among them, and said, "Do ye not see the blood of Christ? See it in your hearts, to sprinkle your hearts and consciences from dead works, to serve the living God:" for I saw it, the blood of the New Covenant, how it came into the heart. This startled the professors, who would have the blood only without them, and not in them. But Captain Stoddard was reached, and

said, "Let the youth speak; hear the youth speak;" when he saw, they endeavoured to bear me down with many words. . . .

Now, after I had had some service in these parts, I went through Derbyshire into my own county, Leicestershire again, and several tender people were convinced. Passing thence, I met with a great company of professors in Warwickshire, who were praying and expounding the Scriptures in the fields. They gave the Bible to me, and I opened it on the fifth of Matthew, where Christ expounded the law; and I opened the inward state to them, and the outward state; upon which they fell into a fierce contention, and so parted; but the Lord's power got ground.

Then I heard of a great meeting to be at Leicester, for a dispute, wherein Presbyterians, Independents, Baptists, and Common prayer-men were said to be all concerned. The meeting was in a steeple-house; and thither I was moved by the Lord God to go, and be amongst them. I heard their discourse and reasonings, some being in pews, and the priest in the pulpit; abundance of people being gathered together. At last one woman asked a question out of Peter, What that birth was, viz. a being born again of incorruptible seed, by the Word of God, that liveth and abideth for ever? And the priest said to her, "I permit not a woman to speak in the church;" though he had before given liberty for any to speak. Whereupon I was wrapped up, as in a rapture, in the Lord's power; and I stepped up and asked the priest, "Dost thou call this (the steeple-house) a church? Or dost thou call this mixed multitude a church?" For the woman asking a question, he ought to have answered it, having given liberty for any to speak. But, instead of answering me, he asked me What a church was? I told him, "The church was the pillar and ground of truth, made up of living stones, living members, a spiritual household, which Christ was the head of: but he was not the head of a mixed multitude, or of an old house made up of lime, stones, and wood." This set them all on fire: the priest came down out of his pulpit, and others out of their pews, and the dispute there was marred. But I went to a great inn, and there disputed the thing with the priests and professors of all sorts; and they were all on a fire. But I maintained the true church, and the true head thereof, over the heads of them all, till they all gave out and fled away. One man seemed loving, and appeared for a while to join with me; but he soon turned against me, and joined with a priest, in pleading for infants' baptism, though he himself had been a Baptist before; and so left me alone. Howbeit, there were several convinced that day; and the woman that asked the question was convinced, and her family; and the Lord's power and glory shined over all.

After this I returned into Nottinghamshire again, and went into the Vale of Beavor. As I went, I preached repentance to the people; and there were many convinced in the Vale of Beavor, in many towns; for I stayed some weeks amongst them. One morning, as I was sitting by the fire, a great cloud came over me, and a temptation beset me; but I sat still. And it was said, "All things come by nature;" and the elements and stars came over me, so that I was in a manner quite clouded with it. But as I sat still, and said nothing, the people of the house perceived nothing. And as I sat still under it, and let it alone, a living hope arose in me, and a true voice, which said, "There is a living God, who made all things." And immediately the cloud and temptation vanished away, and life rose over it all; my heart was glad, and I praised the living God. After some time, I met with some people who had a notion, that there was no God, but that all things came by nature. I had a great dispute with them, and overturned them, and made some of them confess that there is a living God. Then I saw that it was good that I had gone through that exercise. We had great meetings in those parts, for the power of the Lord broke through in that side of the country. Returning into Nottinghamshire, I found there a company of shattered Baptists, and others; and the Lord's power wrought mightily, and gathered many of them. Afterwards I went to Mansfield and thereaway, where the Lord's power was wonderfully manifested both at Mansfield, and other towns thereabouts. In Derbyshire the mighty power of God wrought in a wonderful manner. At Eton, a town near Derby, there was a meeting of Friends, where there was such a mighty power of God, that they were greatly shaken, and many mouths were opened in the power of the Lord God. Many were moved by the Lord to go to steeple-houses, to the priests and to the people, to declare the everlasting truth unto them.

At a certain time, when I was at Mansfield, there was a sitting of the justices about hiring of servants; and it was upon me from the Lord to go and speak to the justices, that they should not oppress the servants in their wages. So I walked towards the inn where they sat; but finding a company of fiddlers there, I did not go in, but thought to come in the morning, when I might have a more serious opportunity to discourse with them, not thinking that a seasonable time. But when I came again in the morning, they were gone, and I was struck even blind, that I could not see. I enquired of the innkeeper where the justices were to sit that day; and he told me, at a town eight miles off. My sight began to come to me again; and I went and ran thitherward as fast as I could. When I was come to the house where they were, and many servants with them, I exhorted the justices not to oppress the servants in their wages, but to do that which was right and just to them; and I exhorted the servants to do their duties, and serve honestly, &c. They all received my exhortation kindly; for I was moved of the Lord therein.

Moreover, I was moved to go to several courts, and steeple-houses at Mansfield, and other places, to warn them to leave off oppression and oaths, and to turn from deceit to the Lord, and do justly. Particularly at Mansfield, after I had been at a court there, I was moved to go and speak to one of the wicked men in the country, one who was a common drunkard, a noted whore-master, and a rhyme-maker; and I reproved him in the dread of the mighty God, for his evil courses. When I had done speaking, and left him, he came after me, and told me, that he was so smitten when I spoke to him, that he had scarce any strength left in him. So this man was convinced, and turned from his wickedness, and remained an honest, sober man, to the astonishment of the people who had known him before. Thus the work of the Lord went forward, and many were turned from the darkness to the light, within the compass of these three years, 1646, 1647, 1648. Divers meetings of Friends, in several places, were then gathered to God's teaching, by his light, Spirit, and power; for the Lord's power broke forth more and more wonderfully.

Now was I come up in Spirit through the flaming sword, into the paradise of God. All things were new; and all the creation gave another smell unto me than before, beyond what words can utter. I knew nothing but pureness, and innocency, and righteousness, being renewed up into the image of God by Christ Jesus; so that I say I was come up to the state of Adam, which he was in before he fell. The creation was opened to me; and it was showed me how all things had their names given them, according to their nature and virtue. I was at a stand in my mind, whether I should practice physic for the good of mankind, seeing the nature and virtues of the creatures were so opened to me by the Lord. But I was immediately taken up in Spirit, to see into another or more steadfast state than Adam's innocency, even into a state in Christ Jesus, that should never fall. And the Lord showed me, that such as were faithful to him, in the power and light of Christ, should come up into that state in which Adam was before he fell; in which the admirable works of the creation, and the virtues thereof may be known, through the openings of that divine Word of wisdom and power, by

which they were made. Great things did the Lord lead me into, and wonderful depths were opened unto me, beyond what can by words be declared; but as people come into subjection to the Spirit of God, and grow up in the image and power of the Almighty, they may receive the Word of Wisdom, that opens all things, and come to know the hidden unity in the Eternal Being.

Thus I travelled on in the Lord's service, as the Lord led me. And when I came to Nottingham, the mighty power of God was there among Friends. From thence I went to Clawson, in Leicestershire, in the Vale of Beavor, and the mighty power of God was there also, in several towns and villages where Friends were gathered. While I was there, the Lord opened to me three things, relating to those three great professions in the world, physic, divinity, (so called,) and law. He showed me, that the physicians were out of the wisdom of God, by which the creatures were made; and so knew not the virtues of the creatures, because they were out of the Word of Wisdom, by which they were made. He showed me that the priests were out of the true faith, which Christ is the author of; the faith which purifies and gives victory, and brings people to have access to God, by which they please God; which mystery of faith is held in a pure conscience. He showed me also, that the lawyers were out of the equity, and out of the true justice, and out of the law of God, which went over the first transgression, and over all sin, and answered the Spirit of God, that was grieved and transgressed in man. And that these three, the physicians, the priests, and the lawyers, ruled the world out of the wisdom, out of the faith, and out of the equity and law of God; the one pretending the cure of the body, the other the cure of the soul, and the third the property of the people. But I saw they were all out, out of the wisdom, out of the faith, out of the equity and perfect law of God. And as the Lord opened these things unto me, I felt his power went forth over all, by which all might be reformed, if they would receive and bow unto it. The priests might be reformed, and brought into the true faith, which was the gift of God. The lawyers might be reformed, and brought into the law of God, which answers that of God, which is transgressed, in every one, and brings to love one's neighbour as himself. This lets man see, if he wrongs his neighbour he wrongs himself; and this teaches him to do unto others as he would they should do unto him. The physicians might be reformed, and brought into the wisdom of God, by which all things were made and created; that they might receive a right knowledge of the creatures, and understand the virtues of them, which the Word of Wisdom, by which they were made and are upheld, hath given them. . . .

I saw also, how people read the Scriptures without a right sense of them, and without duly applying them to their own states. For when they read that death reigned from Adam to Moses; that the law and the prophets were until John; and that the least in the kingdom is greater than John; they read these things without them, and applied them to others . . . but they did not turn in to find the truth of these things in themselves. But as these things came to be opened in me, I saw death reigned over them from Adam to Moses, from the entrance into transgression, till they came to the ministration of condemnation, which restrains people from sin, that brings death. Then when the ministration of Moses is passed through, the ministry of the prophets comes to be read and understood, which reaches through the figures, types, and shadows unto John, the greatest prophet born of a woman; whose ministration prepares the way of the Lord, by bringing down the exalted mountains, and making straight paths. And as this ministration is passed through, an entrance comes to be known into the everlasting kingdom. Thus I saw plainly that none could read Moses aright, without Moses's spirit, by which Moses saw how man was in the image of God in Paradise, and how he fell, how

death came over him, and how all men have been under this death. I saw how Moses received the pure law, that went over all transgressors; and how the clean beasts, which were figures and types, were offered up, when the people were come into the righteous law that went over the first transgression. Both Moses and the prophets saw through the types and figures, and beyond them, and saw Christ the great prophet, that was to come and fulfil them. I saw that none could read John's words aright, and with a true understanding of them, but in and with the same divine Spirit, by which John spoke them; and by his burning, shining light, which is sent from God. . . . Thus I saw, it was an easy matter to say, death reigned from Adam to Moses; and, that the law and the prophets were until John; and, that the least in the kingdom is greater than John: but none could know *how* death reigned from Adam to Moses &c., but by the same Holy Spirit that Moses, the prophets, and John were in. They could not know the spiritual meaning of Moses's, the prophets', and John's words, nor see their path and travels, much less see through them, and to the end of them into the kingdom, unless they had the Spirit and light of Jesus; nor could they know the words of Christ and of his apostles, without his Spirit. But as man comes through, by the Spirit and power of God, to Christ, who fulfills the types, figures, shadows, promises, and prophecies that were of him, and is led by the Holy Ghost into the truth and substance of the Scriptures, sitting down in him who is the author and end of them; then are they read, and understood, with profit and great delight.

Moreover, the Lord God let me see (when I was brought up into his image in righteousness and holiness, and into the paradise of God) the state, how Adam was made a living soul; and also the stature of Christ, the mystery that had been hid from ages and generations; which things are hard to be uttered, and cannot be borne by many. For of all the sects in Christendom (so called) that I discoursed withal, I found none that could bear to be told that any should come to Adam's perfection, into that image of God, that righteousness and holiness that Adam was in before he fell; to be clear and pure without sin, as he was. Therefore, how should they be able to bear being told that any should grow up to the measure of the stature of the fulness of Christ, when they cannot bear to hear that any should come, whilst upon earth, into the same power and Spirit that the prophets and apostles were in? Though it is a certain truth, that none can understand their writings aright, without the same Spirit by which they were written. . . .

On a certain time, as I was walking in the fields, the Lord said unto me; "Thy name is written in the Lamb's book of life, which was before the foundation of the world;" and as the Lord spoke it, I believed, and saw it in the new birth. Then some time after, the Lord commanded me to go abroad in the world, which was like a briery, thorny wilderness; and when I came, in the Lord's mighty power, with the word of life into the world, the world swelled, and made a noise, like the great raging waves of the sea. Priests and professors, magistrates and people, were all like a sea, when I came to proclaim the day of the Lord amongst them, and to preach repentance to them.

I was sent to turn people from darkness to the light, that they might receive Christ Jesus: for to as many as should receive him in his light, I saw that he would give power to become the sons of God; which I had obtained by receiving Christ. I was to direct people to the Spirit, that gave forth the Scriptures, by which they might be led into all truth, and so up to Christ and God, as they had been who gave them forth. I was to turn them to the grace of God, and to the truth in the heart, which came by Jesus; that by this grace they might be taught, which would bring them salvation, that their hearts might be established by it, and their words might be seasoned, and all might come to know their salva-

tion nigh. I saw that Christ died for all men, and was a propitiation for all; and enlightened all men and women with his divine and saving light; and that none could be a true believer, but who believed in it. I saw that the grace of God, which bringeth salvation, had appeared to all men, and that the manifestation of the Spirit of God was given to every man, to profit withal. These things I did not see by the help of man, nor by the letter (though they are written in the letter), but I saw them in the light of the Lord Jesus Christ, and by his immediate spirit and power, as did the holy men of God, by whom the Holy Scriptures were written. Yet I had no slight esteem of the Holy Scriptures, but they were very precious to me, for I was in that Spirit by which they were given forth; and what the Lord opened in me, I afterwards found was agreeable to them. I could speak much of these things, and many volumes might be written, but all would prove too short to set forth the infinite love, wisdom, and power of God, in preparing, fitting, and furnishing me for the service he had appointed me to; letting me see the depths of Satan on the one hand, and opening to me, on the other hand, the divine mysteries of his own everlasting kingdom.

Now when the Lord God and his Son Jesus Christ sent me forth into the world, to preach his everlasting gospel and kingdom, I was glad that I was commanded to turn people to that inward light, Spirit, and grace, by which all might know their salvation, and their way to God; even that Divine Spirit which would lead them into all truth, and which I infallibly knew would never deceive any.

But with and by this divine power and Spirit of God, and the light of Jesus, I was to bring people off from all their own ways, to Christ the new and living way; and from their churches, which men had made and gathered, to the church of God, the general assembly written in heaven, which Christ is the head of; and off from the world's teachers, made by men, to learn of Christ, who is the way, the truth, and the life, of whom the Father said, "This is my beloved Son, hear ye him"; and off from all the world's worships, to know the Spirit of truth in the inward parts, and to be led thereby; that in it they might worship the Father of spirits, who seeks such to worship him; which Spirit they that worshipped not in, knew not what they worshipped. And I was to bring people off from all the world's religions, which are vain; that they might know the pure religion, might visit the fatherless, the widows, and the strangers, and keep themselves from the spots of the world; then there would not be so many beggars, the sight of whom often grieved my heart, as it denoted so much hardheartedness amongst them that professed the name of Christ. I was to bring them off from all the world's fellowships, and prayings, and singings, which stood in forms without power; that their fellowship might be in the Holy Ghost, and in the Eternal Spirit of God; that they might pray in the Holy Ghost, and sing in the Spirit and with the grace that comes by Jesus; making melody in their hearts to the Lord, who hath sent his beloved Son to be their Saviour, and caused his heavenly sun to shine upon all the world, and through them all, and his heavenly rain to fall upon the just and the unjust (as his outward rain doth fall, and his outward sun doth shine on all) which is God's unspeakable love to the world. I was to bring people off

from Jewish ceremonies, and from heathenish fables, and from men's inventions and worldly doctrines, by which they blowed the people about this way and the other way, from sect to sect; and all their beggarly rudiments, with their schools and colleges for making ministers of Christ, who are indeed ministers of their own making, but not of Christ's: and from all their images and crosses, and sprinkling of infants, with all their holy-days (so called) and all their vain traditions, which they had gotten up since the apostles' days, which the Lord's power was against; in the dread and authority of which, I was moved to declare against them all, and against all that preached and not freely, as being such as had not received freely from Christ.

Moreover, when the Lord sent me forth into the world, he forbade me to "put off my hat" to any, high or low; and I was required to Thee and Thou all men and women, without any respect to rich or poor, great or small. And as I travelled up and down, I was not to bid people Good morrow or Good evening; neither might I bow or scrape with my leg to any one; and this made the sects and professions to rage. But the Lord's power carried me over all to his glory, and many came to be turned to God in a little time; for the heavenly day of the Lord sprung from on high, and broke forth apace, by the light of which many came to see where they were.

Robert Barclay

(1648-1690)

THROUGH his training in Scotch Calvinistic thinking and Roman Catholic theology at the Scots College in Paris, Barclay was schooled to win Scotland back from its atmosphere of Calvinism. In his *Apology* he attempts to show that Quaker ideas are in line with the spirit of the Reformation. The aliveness of his mind is shown in his use of a Moslem book by Ibn Topfail—*Hai Ibn Yocdan*—to prove the Quaker idea of the inner light!

Influenced by his study of Calvin and Augustine, Barclay views the inner light as the means by which God touches man's soul lacking spiritual capacity within itself. His spirit radiated sweetness and tenderness. His whole life was marked by deep spirituality.

[KNOWLEDGE THROUGH REVELATION]

From *Apology for the True Christian Divinity*

THE TRUE FOUNDATION OF KNOWLEDGE

Seeing the height of all happiness is placed in the true knowledge of God; "This is life eternal, to know thee the only true God, and Jesus Christ whom thou hast sent;" the true and right understanding of this foundation and ground of knowledge is that which is most necessary to be known and believed in the first place.

He that desireth to acquire any art or science, seeketh first those means by which that art or science is obtained. If we ought to do so in things natural and earthly, how much more then in spiritual? In this affair then should our enquiry be the more diligent, because he that errs in the entrance is not so easily brought back again into the right way; he that misseth his road from the beginning of his journey, and is deceived in his first marks, at his first setting forth, the greater his mistake is, the more difficult will be his entrance into the right way.

Thus when a man first proposeth to himself the knowledge of God, from a sense of his own unworthiness, and from the great weariness of his mind, occasioned by the secret checks of his conscience, and the tender, yet real glances of God's light upon his heart; the earnest desires he has to be redeemed from his present trouble, and the fervent breathings he has to be eased of his disordered passions and lusts, and to find quietness and peace in the certain knowledge of God, and in the assurance of his love and good-will towards him, make his heart tender, and ready to receive any impression; and so—not having then a distinct discerning—through forwardness embraceth any thing that brings present ease. If, either through the reverence he bears to certain persons, or from the secret inclination to what doth comply with his natural disposition, he fall upon any principles or means, by which he ap-

prehends he may come to know God, and so doth centre himself, it will be hard to remove him thence again, how wrong so ever they may be: for the first anguish being over, he becomes more hardy; and the enemy being near, creates a false peace, and a certain confidence, which is strengthened by the mind's unwillingness to enter again into new doubtfulness, or the former anxiety of a search.

This is sufficiently verified in the example of the Pharisees and Jewish doctors, who most of all resisted Christ, disdaining to be esteemed ignorant; for this vain opinion they had of their knowledge hindered them from the true knowledge; and the mean people, who were not so much pre-occupied with former principles, nor conceited of their own knowledge, did easily believe. Wherefore the Pharisees upbraid them, saying, "Have any of the rulers or Pharisees believed on him? But this people, which know not the law, are accursed." This is also abundantly proved by the experience of all such, as being secretly touched with the call of God's grace unto them, do apply themselves to false teachers, where the remedy proves worse than the disease; because instead of knowing God, or the things relating to their salvation aright, they drink in wrong opinions of him; from which it is harder to be disentangled, than while the soul remains a blank, or *Tabula rasa*. For they that conceit themselves wise, are worse to deal with than they that are sensible of their ignorance. Nor hath it been less the device of the devil, the great enemy of mankind, to persuade men into wrong notions of God, than to keep them altogether from acknowledging him; the latter taking with few, because odious; but the other having been the constant ruin of the world: for there hath scarce been a nation found, but hath had some notions or other of religion; so that not from their denying any Deity, but from their mistakes and misapprehensions of it, hath proceeded all the idolatry and superstition of the world; yea, hence even atheism itself hath proceeded: for these many and various opinions of God and religion, being so much mixed with the guessings and uncertain judgments of men, have begotten in many the opinion, That there is no God at all. This, and much more that might be said, may show how dangerous it is to miss in this first step: "All that come not in by the door, are accounted as thieves and robbers."

Again, how needful and desirable that knowledge is, which brings life eternal, Epictetus showeth, saying excellently well, cap. 38. Know that the main foundation of piety is this, To have right opinions and apprehensions of God.

This therefore I judged necessary, as a first principle, in the first place to affirm; and I suppose will not need much farther explanation or defence, as being generally acknowledged by all—and in these things that are without controversy I love to be brief—as that which will easily commend itself to every man's reason and conscience; and therefore I shall proceed to the next proposition; which, though it be nothing less certain, yet by the malice of Satan, and the ignorance of many, comes far more under debate.

Of Immediate Revelation

Seeing "no man knoweth the Father but the Son, and he to whom the Son revealeth him;" and seeing the "revelation of the Son is in and by the Spirit:" therefore the testimony of the Spirit is that alone by which the true knowledge of God hath been, is, and can be only revealed; who as, by the moving of his own Spirit, he disposed the chaos of this world into that wonderful order in which it was in the beginning, and created man a living soul, to rule and govern it, so by the revelation of the same Spirit he hath manifested himself all along unto the sons of men, both patriarchs, prophets, and apostles; which revelations of God by the Spirit, whether by outward voices and appearances, dreams, or inward objective manifestations in the heart, were of old the formal object of their faith, and remain yet so to be; since the object of the saints' faith is the same in all ages, though held forth under divers administrations. Moreover, these divine inward revelations, which we make absolutely necessary for the building up of true faith, neither do nor can ever contradict the outward testimony of the scriptures, or right and sound reason. Yet from hence it will not follow, that these divine revelations are to be subjected to the test, either of the outward testimony of the scriptures, or of the natural reason of man, as to a more noble or certain rule and touchstone; for this divine revelation and inward illumination, is that which is evident and clear of itself, forcing, by its own evidence and clearness, the well-disposed understanding to assent, irresistibly moving the same thereunto, even as the common principles of natural truths do move and incline the mind to a natural assent: as, that the whole is greater than its part, that two contradictories can neither be both true, nor both false.

It is very probable, that many carnal and natural Christians will oppose this proposition; who being wholly unacquainted with the movings and actings of God's Spirit upon their hearts, judge the same nothing necessary; and some are apt to flout at it as ridiculous; yea, to that height are the generality of Christians apostatized and degenerated, that though there be not any thing more plainly asserted, more seriously recommended, or more certainly attested, in all the writings of the holy scriptures, yet nothing is less minded and more rejected by all sorts of Christians, than immediate and divine revelation; insomuch that once to lay claim to it is matter of reproach. Whereas of old none were ever judged Christians, but such as had the Spirit of Christ. But now many do boldly call themselves Christians, who make no difficulty of confessing they are without it, and laugh at such as say they have it. Of old they were accounted "the sons of God, who were led by the Spirit of God." But now many aver themselves sons of God, who know nothing of this leader; and he that affirms himself so led, is, by the pretended orthodox of this age, presently proclaimed an heretic. The reason hereof is very manifest, viz.: Because many in these days, under the name of Christians, do experimentally find, that they are not actuated nor led by God's Spirit; yea, many great doctors, divines, teachers, and bishops of Christianity, (commonly so called,) have wholly shut their ears from hearing and their eyes from seeing this inward guide, and are so become strangers unto it; whence they are, by their own experience, brought to this strait, either to confess that they are as yet ignorant of God, and have only the shadow of knowledge, and not the true knowledge of him, or that this knowledge is acquired without immediate revelation.

For the better understanding then of this proposition, we do distinguish betwixt the certain knowledge of God, and the uncertain; betwixt the spiritual knowledge, and the literal; the saving heart-knowledge, and the soaring airy head-knowledge. The last, we confess, may be divers ways obtained; but the first, by no other way than the inward immediate manifestation and revelation of God's Spirit, shining in and upon the heart, enlightening and opening the understanding. . . .

That this certain and undoubted method of the true knowledge of God hath been brought out of use, hath been none of the least devices of the devil, to secure mankind to his kingdom. For after the light and glory of the Christian religion had prevailed over a good part of the world, and dispelled the thick mists of the heathenish doctrine of the plurality of gods, he that knew there was no probability of deluding the world any longer that way, did then puff man up with a false knowledge of the true God; setting him on work to seek God the wrong way, and persuading him to be content with such a knowledge as was of his own acquiring, and not of God's teaching. And this device hath proved the more successful, because accommodated to the natural and corrupt spirit and temper of man, who above all things affects to exalt himself; in which self-exaltation, as

God is greatly dishonored, so therein the devil hath his end; who is not anxious how much God is acknowledged in words, provided himself be but always served; he matters not how great and high speculations the natural man entertains of God, so long as he serves his own lusts and passions, and is obedient to his evil suggestions and temptations. Thus Christianity is become as it were an art, acquired by human science and industry, like any other art or science; and men have not only assumed the name Christians, but even have procured themselves to be esteemed as masters of Christianity, by certain artificial tricks, though altogether strangers to the spirit and life of Jesus. But if we make a right definition of a Christian, according to the scriptures, That he is one that hath the spirit of Christ, and is led by it, how many Christians, yea, and of these great masters and doctors of Christianity, so accounted, shall we justly divest of that noble title?

If those therefore who have all the other means of knowledge, and are sufficiently learned therein, whether it be the letter of the scripture, the traditions of churches, or the works of creation and providence, whence they are able to deduce strong and undeniable arguments —which may be true in themselves—are not yet to be esteemed Christians according to the certain and infallible definition above mentioned; and if the inward and immediate revelation of God's Spirit in the heart, in such as have been altogether ignorant of some, and but very little skilled in others, of these means of attaining knowledge, hath brought them to salvation; then it will necessarily and evidently follow, that inward and immediate revelation is the only sure and certain way to attain the true and saving knowledge of God.

But the first is true: therefore the last.

Now as this argument doth very strongly conclude for this way of knowledge and against such as deny it, so in this respect it is the more to be regarded, as the propositions from which it is deduced are so clear, that our very adversaries cannot deny them. For as to the first it is acknowledged, that many learned men may be, and have been, damned. And as to the second, who will deny but many illiterate men may be, and are, saved? Nor dare any affirm, that none come to the knowledge of God and salvation by the inward revelation of the Spirit, without these other outward means, unless they be also so bold as to exclude Abel, Seth, Noah, Abraham, Job, and all the holy patriarchs from true knowledge and salvation.

I would however not be understood, as if hereby I excluded those other means of knowledge from any use or service to man; it is far from me so to judge, as concerning the scriptures, in the next proposition, will more plainly appear. The question is not, what may be profitable or helpful, but what is absolutely necessary. Many things may contribute to further a work, which yet are not the main thing that makes the work go on.

The sum then of what is said amounts to this: That where the true inward knowledge of God is, through the revelation of his Spirit, there is all; neither is there an absolute necessity of any other. But where the best, highest, and most profound knowledge is, without this there is nothing, as to the obtaining the great end of salvation. This truth is very effectually confirmed by the first part of the proposition itself, which in few words comprehendeth divers unquestionable arguments, which I shall in brief subsume.

First, That there is no knowledge of the Father but by the Son.

Secondly, That there is no knowledge of the Son but by the Spirit.

Thirdly, That by the Spirit God hath always revealed himself to his children.

Fourthly, That these revelations were the formal object of the saint's faith.

And Lastly, That the same continueth to be the object of the saint's faith to this day.

And because the Spirit of God is the fountain of all truth and sound reason, therefore we have well said, That it cannot contradict either the testimony of the scripture, or right reason: "Yet, as the proposition itself concludeth, to the last part of which I now come, it will not from thence follow, that these divine revelations are to be subjected to the examination either of the outward testimony of scripture, or of the human or natural reason of man, as to a more noble and certain rule or touchstone; for the divine revelation, and inward illumination, is that which is evident by itself, forcing the well-disposed understanding, and irresistibly moving it to assent by its own evidence and clearness, even the common principles of natural truths do bend the mind to a natural assent."

He that denies this part of the proposition must needs affirm, that the Spirit of God neither can, nor hath ever manifested itself to man without the scripture, or a distinct discussion of reason; or that the efficacy of this supernatural principle, working upon the souls of men, is less evident than natural principles in their common operations; both which are false.

For, First, Through all the scriptures we may observe, that the manifestation and revelation of God by his Spirit to the patriarchs, prophets, and apostles, was immediate and objective, as is above proved; which they did not examine by any other principle, but their own evidence and clearness.

Secondly, To say that the Spirit of God has less evidence upon the mind of man than natural principles have, is to have too mean and too low thoughts of it. How comes David to invite us to taste and see that God is good, if this cannot be felt and tasted? This were enough to overturn the faith and assurance of all the saints, both now and of old. How came Paul to be persuaded, that nothing could separate him from the love of God, but by the evidence and clearness which the Spirit of God gave him? The apostle John, who knew well wherein the certainty of faith consisted, judged it no ways absurd, without further argument, to ascribe his knowledge and assurance, and that of all the saints, hereunto in these words; "Hereby know we that we dwell in him, and he in us, because he hath given us of his Spirit," 1 John, iv. 13. And again, chap. v. ver. 6: "It is the Spirit that beareth witness, because the Spirit is truth."

Observe the reason brought by him, "Because the Spirit is truth;" of whose certainty and infallibility I have heretofore spoken. We then trust to and confide in this Spirit, because we know, and certainly believe, that it can only lead us aright, and never mislead us; and from this certain confidence it is that we affirm, that no revelation coming from it can ever contradict the scripture's testimony nor right reason: not as making this a more certain rule to ourselves, but as condescending to such, who not discerning the revelations of the Spirit, as they proceed purely from God, will try them by these mediums. Yet those that have their spiritual senses, and can savour the things of the Spirit, as it were in prima instantia, i.e., at the first blush, can discern them without, or before they apply them either to scripture or reason; just as a good astronomer can calculate an eclipse infallibly, by which he can conclude, if the order of nature continue, and some strange and unnatural revolution intervene not, there will be an eclipse of the sun or moon such a day, and such an hour; yet can he not persuade an ignorant rustic of this, until he visibly sees it. So also a mathematician can infallibly know, by the rules of art, that the three angles of a right triangle are equal to two right angles; yea, can know them more certainly than any man by measure. And some geometrical demonstrations are by all acknowledged to be infallible, which can be scarcely discerned or proved by the senses, yet if a geometer be at the pains to certify some ignorant man concerning the certainty of his art, by condescending to measure it, and make it obvious to his senses, it will not thence follow, that that measuring is so certain as the demonstration itself, or that the demonstration would be uncertain without it.

But to make an end, I shall add one argument to prove, that this inward, immediate, objective revelation, which we have pleaded for all along, is the only sure, certain, and unmovable foundation of all Christian faith; which argument, when well considered, I hope will have weight with all sorts of Christians, and it is this:

That which all professors of Christianity, of what kind soever, are forced ultimately to recur unto, when pressed to the last; that for and because of which all other foundations are recommended, and accounted worthy to be believed, and without which they are granted to be of no weight at all, must needs be the only most true, certain, and unmovable foundation of all Christian faith.

But inward, immediate, objective revelation by the Spirit, is that which all professors of Christianity, of what kind soever, are forced ultimately to recur unto, &c.

Therefore, &c.

The proposition is so evident, that it will not be denied; the assumption shall be proved by parts.

And first, As to the Papists, they place their foundation in the judgment of the church and tradition. If we press them to say, Why they believe as the church doth? Their answer is, Because the church is always led by the infallible Spirit. So here the leading of the Spirit is the utmost foundation. Again, if we ask them Why we ought to trust tradition? They answer, Because these traditions were delivered us by the doctors and fathers of the church; which doctors and fathers, by the revelation of the Holy Ghost, commanded the church to observe them. Here again all ends in the revelation of the Spirit.

And for the Protestants and Socinians, both which acknowledge the scriptures to be the foundation and rule of their faith; the one as subjectively influenced by the Spirit of God to use them, the other as managing them with and by their own reason; ask both, or either of them, Why they trust in the scriptures, and take them to be their rule? Their answer is, Because we have in them the mind of God delivered unto us by those to whom these things were inwardly, immediately, and objectively revealed by the Spirit of God; and not because this or that man wrote them, but because the Spirit of God dictated them.

It is strange then that men should render that so uncertain and dangerous to follow, upon which alone the certain ground and foundation of their own faith is built; and that they should shut themselves out from that holy fellowship with God, which only is enjoyed in the Spirit, in which we are commanded both to walk and live.

If any reading these things find themselves moved, by the strength of these scripture arguments, to assent and believe such revelations necessary, and yet find themselves strangers to them, which, as I observed in the beginning, is the cause that this is so much gainsaid and contradicted, let them know, that it is not because it is ceased to become the privilege of every true Christian that they do not feel it, but rather because they are not so much Christians by nature as by name; and let such know, that the secret light which shines in the heart, and reproves unrighteousness, is the small beginning of the revelation of God's Spirit, which was first sent into the world to reprove it of sin. And as by forsaking iniquity thou comest to be acquainted with that heavenly voice in thy heart, thou shalt feel, as the old man, or the natural man, that savoureth not the things of God's kingdom, is put off, with his evil and corrupt affections and lusts; I say, thou shalt feel the new man, or the spiritual birth and babe raised, which hath its spiritual senses, and can see, feel, taste, handle, and smell the things of the Spirit; but till then the knowledge of things spiritual is but as an historical faith. But as the description of the light of the sun, or of curious colours to a blind man, who, though of the largest capacity, cannot so well understand it by the most acute and lively description, as a child can by seeing them; so neither can the natural man, of the largest capacity, by the best words, even scripture words, so well understand the mysteries of God's kingdom, as the least and weakest child who tasteth them, by having them revealed inwardly and objectively by the Spirit.

Wait then for this in the small revelation of that pure light which first reveals things more known; and as thou becomest fitted for it, thou shalt receive more and more, and by a living experience easily refute their ignorance, who ask, How dost thou know that thou art actuated by the Spirit of God? Which will appear to thee a question no less ridiculous, than to ask one whose eyes are open, how he knows the sun shines at noonday? And though this be the surest and most certain way to answer all objections; yet by what is above written it may appear, that the mouths of all such opposers as deny this doctrine may be shut, by unquestionable and unanswerable reasons.

John Flavel

(1630-1691)

FLAVEL, educated at Oxford, was ordained a Presbyterian minister in 1650. After the Act of Uniformity, he continued to preach as a private minister in his parish at Dartmouth. He was a prolific writer, always portraying the pastoral note in his books. Among his many writings, *A Saint Indeed* is of profound devotional value. It is an exposition of the familiar verse from Proverbs: "Keep thy heart with all diligence; for out of it are the issues of life."

[IN PROSPERITY AND ADVERSITY]

From *A Saint Indeed*

[How to Keep the Heart in Time of Prosperity]

*T*he first season is the time of prosperity, when providence smiles upon us, and dandles us upon its knee. Now, Christian, keep thy heart with all diligence; for now it will be exceeding apt to grow secure, proud, and earthly, *Rara virtus est humilitas honorata*, (saith Bernard) to see a man humble under prosperity, is one of the greatest rarities in the world. Even a good Hezekiah could not hide a vainglorious temper under his temptation, and hence that caution to Israel, "And it shall be when the Lord thy God shall have brought thee into the land which he sware to thy fathers, to Abraham, Isaac, and Jacob, to give thee great and goodly cities which thou buildest not, and houses full of all good things which thou filledst not, &c. Then beware lest thou forget the Lord:" and indeed so it fell out, "for Jeshurun waxed fat, and kicked."

Case 1. *How a Christian may keep his heart from pride and carnal security, under the smiles of providence, and constancy of creature-comforts?* There are seven choice helps to secure the heart from the dangerous snares of prosperity; the first is this,

1. *To consider the dangerous ensnaring temptations attending a pleasant and prosperous condition; few, yea, very few of those that live in the pleasures and prosperity of this world, escape everlasting perdition.* "It is easier (saith Christ) for a camel to pass through the eye of a needle, than for a rich man to enter into the kingdom of heaven;" and "Not many mighty, not many noble are called." It might justly make us tremble when the scripture tells us in general, that few shall be saved; much more when it tells us, that of that rank and sort of which we are speaking, but few shall be saved. When Joshua called all the tribes of Israel to lot upon them for the discovery of Achan, doubtless Achan feared; when the tribe of Judah was taken, his fear increased; but when the family of the Zarhites was taken, it was time then to tremble. So when the scripture comes so near as to tell us that of such a sort of men very few shall escape, it is time to look about; *Miror si potest servari aliquis rectorum*, saith Chrysostom; I should wonder if any of the *rulers* be saved. O how many have been coached to hell in the chariots of earthly pleasures, while others have been whipped to heaven by the rod of affliction! how few, like the daughter of Tyre, come to Christ with a gift! how few among the rich entreat his favour!

2. *It may keep us yet more humble and watchful in prosperity, if we consider that among Christians many have been much the worse for it.* How good had it been for some of them, if they had never known prosperity! When they were in a low condition, how humble, spiritual, and heavenly, were they! but when advanced, what an apparent alteration hath been upon their spirits? It was so with Israel, when they were in a low condition in the wilderness; then Israel was *holiness to the Lord*, but when they came into Canaan, and were fed in a fat pasture, then, "we are lords, we will come no more unto thee." Outward gains are ordinarily attended with inward losses; as in a low condition their civil employments were wont to have a tang and savour of their duties, so in an exalted condition their duties commonly have a tang of the world. He indeed is rich in grace, whose graces are not hindered by his riches; there are but few Jehoshaphats in the world, of whom it is said, "He had silver and gold in abundance, and his heart was lifted up in the way of God's commands:" Will not this keep thy heart humble in prosperity, to think how dear many godly men have paid for their riches, that through them they have lost that which all the world cannot purchase? Then, in the next place,

3. Keep down thy vain heart by this

consideration, *that God values no man a jot the more for these things.* God values no man by outward excellencies, but by inward graces; they are the internal ornaments of the Spirit, which are of great price in God's eyes. He despises all worldly glory, and accepts no man's person; "but in every nation, he that feareth God, and worketh righteousness, is accepted of him." Indeed, if the judgment of God went by the same rule that man's doth, we might value ourselves by these things, and stand upon them: But as one said (when dying) I shall not appear before God as a doctor, but as a man; *tantus quisque est, quantus est apud Deum.* So much every man is, and no more, as he is in the judgment of God. Doth thy heart yet swell? And will neither of the former considerations keep it humble?

4. Then, *fourthly,* Consider, *how bitterly many persons have bewailed their folly when they came to die, that ever they set their hearts upon these things, and heartily wished that they had never known them.* What a sad story was that of Pius Quintus, who dying cried out despairingly, when I was in a low condition, I had some hopes of salvation; but when I was advanced to be cardinal, I greatly doubted it; but since I came to the Popedom, I have no hope at all. Mr. Spencer also tells us a real, but sad story, of a rich oppressor, who had scraped up a great estate for his only son; when he came to die, he called his son to him, and said, son; do you indeed love me? The son answered, that nature, besides his paternal indulgence, obliged him to that. Then said the father, express it by this; hold thy finger in the candle as long as I am saying a *pater noster:* The son attempted, but could not endure it. Upon that the father broke out into these expressions, thou canst not suffer the burning of thy finger for me, but to get this wealth, I have hazarded my soul for thee, and must burn body and soul in hell for thy sake: Thy pains would have been but for a moment, but mine will be unquenchable fire.

5. The heart may be kept humble, by considering *of what a clogging nature* earthly things are to a soul heartily engaged in the way to heaven; they shut out much of heaven from us at present, though they may not shut us out of heaven at last. If thou consider thyself under the notion of a stranger in this world, travelling for heaven, and seeking a better country, thou hast then as much reason to be taken, and delighted with these things, as a weary horse hath with a heavy clog-bag: There was a serious truth in that atheistical scoff of Julian when he took away the Christians' estate, and told them it was to make them fitter for the kingdom of heaven.

6. Is thy spirit, for all this, flatulent and lofty? Then urge upon it *the consideration of that awful day of reckoning, wherein, according to our receipts of mercies, shall be our accompts for them:* And methinks this should awe and humble the vainest heart that ever was in the breast of a saint. Know for certain, that the Lord records all the mercies that ever he gave thee, from the beginning to the end of thy life. "Remember, O my people, from Shittim unto Gilgal," &c. yea, they are exactly numbered, and recorded in order to an account; and thy account will be suitable. "To whomsoever much is given, of him much shall be required." You are but stewards, and your Lord will come to take an account of you; and what a great account have you to make, who have much of this world in your hands? What swift witnesses will your mercies be against you, if this be the best fruits of them?

7. It is a very humbling consideration, *that the mercies of God should work otherwise upon my spirit, than they use to do upon the spirits of others, to whom they come as sanctified mercies from the love of God.* Ah Lord what a sad consideration is this! enough to lay me in the dust; when I consider,

(1.) That their mercies have greatly humbled them; the higher God has raised them, the lower they have laid themselves before God. Thus did Jacob, when God had given him much substance. "And Jacob said, I am not worthy of the least of all thy mercies, and all the truth which thou hast shewed thy servant; for with my staff I passed over this Jordan, and now I am become two bands." And thus it was with holy David. When God had confirmed the promise to him, to build him a house, and not reject him as he did Saul, he goes in before the Lord, and saith, "Who am I? and what is my father's house, that thou hast brought me hitherto?" And so indeed God required, when Israel was to bring to God the first-fruits of Canaan, they were to say, "A Syrian ready to perish was my father," &c. Do others raise God the higher for the raising them? And the more God raises me, the more shall I abuse him, and exalt myself? O what a sad thing is this?

(2.) Others have freely ascribed the glory of all their enjoyments to God, and magnified not themselves, but him, for their mercies: So David, "Let thy name be magnified, and the house of thy servant be established." He doth not fly upon the mercy, and suck out the sweetness of it, looking no farther than his own comfort; no, he cares for no mercy except God be magnified in it. So when God had delivered him from all his enemies: "The Lord (saith he) is my strength, and my rock, he is become my salvation." They did not put the crown upon their own heads, as I do.

(3.) The mercies of God have been melting mercies unto ·others, melting their souls in love to the God of their mercies. So Hannah, when she received the mercy of a son, "My soul (saith she) rejoiceth in the Lord;" not in the mercy, but in the God of the mercy. And so Mary, "My soul doth magnify the Lord, my spirit rejoiceth in God my Saviour." The word signifies to make more room for God; their hearts were not contracted, but the more enlarged to God.

(4.) The mercies of God have been mighty restraints to keep others from sin. So Ezra "Seeing thou, our God, hast given us such a deliverance as this, should we again break thy commandments?" Ingenuous souls have felt the force of the obligations of love and mercy upon them.

(5.) To conclude, The mercies of God

to others have been as oil to the wheels of their obedience, and made them fitter for services. Now if mercies work contrarily upon my heart, what cause have I to be afraid that they come not to me in love? I tell you, this is enough to damp the spirit of any saint, to see what sweet effects they have had on others, and what sad effects on him.

[How to Keep the Heart in Time of Adversity]

The second special season in the life of a Christian requiring more than a common diligence to keep his heart, is *the time of adversity;* When providence frowns upon you, and blasts your outward comforts, then look to your hearts, keep them with all diligence from repining against God, or fainting under his hand; for troubles, though sanctified, are troubles still; even sweet-brier and holy thistles, have their prickles. Jonah was a good man, and yet how pettish was his heart under affliction? Job was the mirror of patience, yet how was his heart discomposed by troubles? You will find it as hard to get a composed spirit under great afflictions, as it is to fix quick-silver. O the hurries and tumults which they occasion even in the best hearts!

Case 2. *How a Christian under great afflictions may keep his heart from repining, or desponding under the hand of God?* Now there are nine special helps I shall here offer, to keep thy heart in this condition; and the first shall be this, to work upon your hearts this great truth,

1. *That by these cross providences, God is faithfully pursuing the great design of electing love upon the souls of his people, and orders all these afflictions as means sanctified to that end.*

Afflictions fall not out by casualty, but by counsel, by this counsel of God they are ordained as means of much spiritual good to saints. "By this shall the iniquity of Jacob be purged," &c. "But he for our profit," &c. "All things work together for good." They are God's workmen upon our hearts, to pull down the pride and carnal security of them; and being so, their nature is changed; they are turned into blessings and benefits. "It is good for me that I have been afflicted." And sure, then, thou hast no reason to quarrel with, but rather so admire that God should concern himself so much in thy good, to use any means for the accomplishing of it. "Paul could bless God, if by any means he might attain the resurrection of the dead." "My brethren, (saith James) count it all joy when you fall into divers temptations." My father is about a design of love upon my soul, and do I well to be angry with him? All that he doth is in pursuance of, and in reference to some eternal, glorious ends upon my soul. O it is my ignorance of God's design, that makes me quarrel with him! he saith to thee in this case, as to Peter, "What I do thou knowest not now, but hereafter thou shalt know it."

Help 2. *Though God hath reserved to himself a liberty of afflicting his people, yet he hath tied up his own hands by promise never to take away his loving-kindness from them.* Can I look that scripture in the face with a repining, discontented spirit. "I shall be his father, and he will be my son; if he commit iniquity, I will chasten him with the rod of men, and with the stripes of the children of men: Nevertheless, my mercy shall not depart away from him." O my heart! my haughty heart! dost thou well to be discontented, when God hath given thee the whole tree, with all the clusters of comfort growing on it, because he suffers the wind to blow down a few leaves; Christians have two sorts of goods, the goods of the throne, and the goods of the footstool; moveables, and immoveables: If God have secured these, never let my heart be troubled at the loss of those; indeed, if he had cut off his love, or discovenanted my soul, I had reason to be cast down; but this he hath not, nor can he do it.

Help 3. It is of marvellous efficacy to keep the heart from sinking under affliction, *to call to mind, that thine own father hath the ordering of them*: Not a creature moves hand or tongue against thee, but by his permission. Suppose the cup be a bitter cup, yet it is the cup which thy father hath given thee to drink; and canst thou suspect poison to be in that cup which he delivers thee? Foolish man, put home the case to thine own heart, consult with thine own bowels; canst thou find in thy heart to give thy child that which would hurt, or undo him? No, thou wouldest as soon hurt thyself as him: "If thou then being evil knowest how to give good gifts to thy children," how much more doth God? The very consideration of his nature, a God of love, pity, and tender mercies, or of his relation to thee as a Father, Husband, Friend, might be security enough, if he had not spoken a word, to quiet thee in this case; and yet you have his word too, *I will do you no hurt.* You lie too near his heart to hurt you; nothing grieves him more than your groundless and unworthy suspicions of his designs do; would it not grieve a faithful, tender-hearted physician when he hath studied the case of his patient, prepared the most excellent receipts to save his life, to hear him cry out, O he hath undone me! he hath poisoned me; because it gripes and pains him in the operation? O when will you be ingenious!

Help 4. *God respects you as much in a low, as in a high condition; and therefore it need not so much trouble you to be made low*: nay, to speak home, he manifests, more of his love, grace, and tenderness, in the time of affliction, than prosperity. As God did not at first choose you because you were high, so he will not forsake you because you are low: Men may look shy upon you, and alter their respects, as your condition is altered. When providence hath blasted your estates, your summer friends may grow strange, as fearing you may be troublesome to them; but will God do so? No, no! "I will never leave thee, nor forsake thee." Indeed if adversity and poverty could bar you from access to God, it were a sad condition; but you may go to God as freely as ever. "My God (saith the church) will hear me." Poor David, when stripped of all earthly comforts, could yet encourage himself in the Lord his God; and why cannot you? Suppose your husband or child had lost all at sea, and should come to you in rags; could you deny the relation, or refuse to entertain him? If you would not, much less would God: Why then are ye so troubled? Though your condition be changed, your Father's love and respects are not changed.

Help 5. *And what if by the loss of outward comforts, God will preserve your souls from the ruining power of temptation? Sure then, you have little cause to sink your hearts by such sad thoughts about them.* Are not these earthly enjoyments the things that make men shrink and warp in times of trial? For the love of these many have forsaken Christ in such an hour. "He went away sorrowful, for he had great possessions." And if this be God's design, what have I done in quarrelling with him about it? We see mariners in a storm can throw over-board rich bales of silk, and precious things, to preserve the vessel and their lives with it, and every one saith they act prudently; we know it is usual for soldiers in a city besieged, to batter down, or burn the fairest buildings without the walls, in which the enemy may shelter in the siege; and no man doubts but it is wisely done; Such as have gangrened legs or arms, can willingly stretch them out to be cut off, and not only thank, but pay the chirurgeon for his pains: And must God only be repined at, for casting over what will sink you in a storm? For pulling down that which would advantage your enemy in the siege of temptation? For cutting off what would endanger your everlasting life? O inconsiderate, ungrateful man! are not these things, for which thou grievest, the very things that have ruined thousands of souls? Well, what Christ doth in this, thou knowest not now, but hereafter thou mayest.

Help 6. It would much stay the heart under adversity, to consider *That God, by such humbling providences, may be accomplishing that for which you have long prayed and waited*: And should you be troubled at that? Say, Christian, hast thou not many prayers depending before God upon such accounts as these:

that he would keep thee from sin, discover to thee the emptiness and insufficiency of the creature; that he would kill and mortify thy lusts, that thy heart may never find rest in any enjoyment but Christ? Why now, by such humbling and impoverishing strokes, God may be fulfilling thy desire: Wouldst thou be kept from sin? Lo, *he hath hedged up thy way with thorns.* Wouldst thou see the creature's vanity? Thy affliction is a fair glass to discover it; for the vanity of the creature is never so effectually and sensibly discovered, as in our own experience of it. Wouldst thou have thy corruptions mortified? This is the way; now God takes away the food and fuel that maintained them; for as prosperity begat and fed them, so adversity, when sanctified, is a mean to kill them. Wouldst thou have thy heart to rest nowhere but in the bosom of God? What better way canst thou imagine providence should take to accomplish thy desire, than by pulling from under thy head, that soft pillow of creature delights on which thou restedst before? And yet you fret at this, peevish child! how dost thou exercise thy Father's patience? If he delay to answer thy prayers, thou art ready to say he regards thee not; if he do that which really answers the scope and main end of them, but not in the way thou expectedst, thou quarrellest with him for that: as if instead of answering, he were crossing all thy hopes and aims; is this ingenuous? Is it not enough that God is so gracious to do what thou desirest, but thou must be so imprudent to expect he should do it in the way which thou prescribest.

Help 7. Again, It may stay thy heart, if thou consider, *That in these troubles, God is about that work, which if thou didst see the design of, thy soul would rejoice.* We, poor creatures, are bemisted with much ignorance, and are not able to discern how particular providences work towards God's end; and therefore, like Israel in the wilderness, are often murmuring, because Providence leads us about in a howling desert, where we are exposed to straits; though yet, then he led them, and is now leading us, *by the right way, to a city of habitations.* If you could but see how God, in his secret counsel, hath exactly laid the whole plot and design of thy salvation, even to the smallest means and circumstances; this way, and by these means such a one shall be saved, and by no other; such a number of afflictions I appoint for this man, at this time, and in this order; they shall befal him thus, and thus they shall work for him: Could you, I say, but discern the admirable harmony of divine dispensations, their mutual relations to each other, together with the general respect and influence they all have unto the last end; of all the conditions in the world, you would chuse that you are now in, had you liberty to make your choice. Providence is like a curious piece of arras, made up of a thousand shreds, which single we know not what to make of, but put together, and stitched up orderly, they represent a beautiful history to the eye. As God works all things according to the counsel of his own will, so that the counsel of God hath ordained this as the best way to bring about thy salvation; Such a one hath a proud heart, so many humbling providences I appointed for him: such a one an earthly heart, so many impoverishing providences for him: Did you but see this, I need say no more to support the most dejected heart.

Help 8. Farther, It would much conduce to the settlement of your hearts, to consider, *That by fretting and discontent, you do yourself more injury than all the afflictions you lie under could do;* your own discontent is that which arms your troubles with a sting; it is you that make your burden heavy, by struggling under it. Could you but lie quiet under the hand of God, your condition would be much easier and sweeter than it is. *Impatiens ægrotus crudelem facit medicum.* This makes God lay on more strokes, as a father will upon a stubborn child that receives not correction.

Besides, it unfits the soul to pray over its troubles, or take in the sense of that good which God intends by them: Affliction is a pill, which being wrapt up in patience and quiet submission, may be easily swallowed; but discontent chews the pill and so embitters the soul: God throws away some comfort which he saw would hurt you, and you will throw away your peace after it; he shoots an arrow which sticks in your clothes, and was never intended to hurt, but only to fright you from sin: and you will thrust it onward to the piercing of your very hearts by despondency and discontent.

Help 9. Lastly, if all this will not do, but thy heart, like Rachel, still refuses to be comforted, or quieted, then consider one thing more, which, if seriously pondered, will doubtless do the work; and that is this, *Compare the condition thou art now in, and art so much dissatisfied with, with that condition others are, and thyself deservest to be in:* Others are roaring in flames, howling under the scourge of vengeance, and amongst them I deserve to be. O my soul! is this hell? Is my condition as bad as the damned? O what would thousands now in hell give to change conditions with me! It is a famous instance which Dr. Taylor gives us of the duke of Conde; "I have read (saith he) that when the duke of Conde had entered voluntarily into the incommodities of a religious poverty, he was one day espied and pitied by a lord of Italy, who out of tenderness wished him to be more careful and nutritive of his person. The good duke answered, Sir, be not troubled, and think not that I am ill provided for conveniences, for I send an harbinger before me, who makes ready my lodgings, and takes care that I be royally entertained. The lord asked him who was his harbinger? he answered, The knowledge of myself, and the consideration of what I deserve for my sins, which is eternal torments; and when with this knowledge I arrive at my lodging, how unprovided soever I find it, methinks it is even better than I deserve." *Why doth the living man complain?* And thus the heart may be kept from desponding, or repining under adversity.

Nicholas Herman

(1611-1691)

BORN into a meager home in Lorraine, France, prepared with no formal education, experienced as a soldier and a household servant, Herman, known as "Brother Lawrence," has left one of the classic memoirs of the devotional life. In 1666 he became a lay brother of the Discalced Carmelites in Paris, where he worked in the kitchen as "a servant of the servants of God" until his death. He was able to clothe the most menial tasks with a sacramental significance. Like Benedict and Bernard of Clairvaux, he wedded work with prayer. *The Practice of the Presence of God* contains conversations and letters of Herman, edited shortly after his death by the Grand Vicar to Cardinal de Noailles, M. Beaufort. It is a book of beautiful, simple religious insight. The unusual beauty of *The Practice of the Presence of God* is due to its swift translation of religious beliefs into action. The letters here are reprinted by permission from the edition of Fleming H. Revell Co.

[HOW TO PRACTICE GOD'S PRESENCE]

From *The Practice of the Presence of God*

FIRST LETTER

*S*ince you desire so earnestly that I should communicate to you the method by which I arrived at that *habitual sense of God's presence*, which our Lord, of His mercy, has been pleased to vouchsafe to me, I must tell you that it is with great difficulty that I am prevailed on by your importunities; and now I do it only upon the terms that you show my letter to nobody. If I knew that you would let it be seen, all the desire that I have for your advancement would not be able to determine me to it. The account I can give you is:

Having found in many books different methods of going to God, and divers practices of the spiritual life, I thought this would serve rather to puzzle me than facilitate what I sought after, which was nothing but how to become wholly God's. This made me resolve to give the all for the all; so after having given myself wholly to God, that He might take away my sin, *I renounced, for the love of Him, everything that was not He, and I began to live as if there was none but He and I in the world.* Sometimes I considered myself before Him as a poor criminal at the feet of his judge; at other times I beheld Him in my heart as my Father, as my God. I worshiped Him the oftenest that I could, keeping my mind in His holy presence, and recalling it as often as I found it wandered from Him. I found no small pain in this exercise, and yet I continued it, notwithstanding all the difficulties that occurred, without troubling or disquieting myself when my mind had wandered involuntarily. I made this my business as much all the day long as at the appointed times of prayer; for at all times, every hour, every minute, even in the height of my business, I drove away from my mind everything that was capable of interrupting my thought of God.

Such has been my common practice ever since I entered in religion; and though I have done it very imperfectly, yet I have found great advantages by it. These, I well know, are to be imputed to the mere mercy and goodness of God, because we can do nothing without Him; and *I* still less than any. But when we are faithful to keep ourselves in His holy presence, and set Him always before us, this not only hinders our offending Him and doing anything that may displease

Him, at least wilfully, but it also begets in us a holy freedom, and, if I may so speak, a familiarity with God, wherewith we ask, and that successfully, the graces we stand in need of. In fine, by often repeating these acts, they become *habitual,* and the presence of God is rendered as it were *natural* to us. Give Him thanks, if you please, with me, for His great goodness toward me, which I can never sufficiently admire, for the many favors He has done to so miserable a sinner as I am. May all things praise Him. Amen.

Second Letter

Not finding my manner of life in books, although I have no difficulty about it, yet, for greater security, I shall be glad to know your thoughts concerning it.

In a conversation some days since with a person of piety, he told me the spiritual life was a life of grace, which begins with servile fear, which is increased by hope of eternal life, and which is consummated by pure love; that each of these states had its different stages, by which one arrives at last at that blessed consummation.

I have not followed all these methods. On the contrary, from I know not what instincts, I found they discouraged me. This was the reason why, at my entrance into religion, I took a resolution to give myself up to God, as the best return I could make for His love, and, for the love of Him, to renounce all besides.

For the first year I commonly employed myself during the time set apart for devotion with the thought of death, judgment, heaven, hell, and my sins. Thus I continued some years, applying my mind carefully the rest of the day, and even in the midst of my business, *to the presence of God,* whom I considered always as *with* me, often as *in* me.

At length I came insensibly to do the same thing during my set time of prayer, which caused in me great delight and consolation. This practice produced in me so high an esteem for God that *faith* alone was capable to satisfy me in that point.

Such was my beginning, and yet I must tell you that for the first ten years I suffered much. The apprehension that I was not devoted to God as I wished to be, my past sins always present to my mind, and the great unmerited favors which God did me, were the matter and source of my sufferings. During this time I fell often, and rose again presently. It seemed to me that all creatures, reason, and God Himself were against me, and *faith* alone for me. I was troubled sometimes with thoughts that to believe I had received such favors, was an effect of my presumption, which pretended to be *at once* where others arrive with difficulty; at other times, that it was a wilful delusion, and that there was no salvation for me.

When I thought of nothing but to end my days in these troubles (which did not at all diminish the trust I had in God, and which served only to increase my faith), I found myself changed all at once; and my soul, which till that time was in trouble, felt a profound inward peace, as if she were in her center and place of rest.

Ever since that time I walk before God simply, in faith, with humility and with love, and I apply myself diligently to do nothing and think nothing which may displease Him. I hope that when I have done what I can, He will do with me what He pleases.

As for what passes in me at present, I cannot express it. I have no pain or difficulty about my state, because I have no will but that of God, which I endeavor to accomplish in all things, and to which I am so resigned that I would not take up a straw from the ground against His order, or from any other motive but purely that of love to Him.

I have quitted all forms of devotion and set prayers but those to which my state obliges me. And I make it my business only to persevere in His holy presence, wherein I keep myself by a simple attention, and a general fond regard to God, which I may call an *actual presence of God;* or, to speak better, an habitual, silent, and secret conversation of the soul with God, which often causes me joys and raptures inwardly, and sometimes also outwardly, so great that I am forced to use means to moderate them and prevent their appearance to others.

In short, I am assured beyond all doubt that my soul has been with God above these thirty years. I pass over many things that I may not be tedious to you, yet I think it proper to inform you after what manner I consider myself before God, whom I behold as my King.

I consider myself as the most wretched of men, full of sores and corruption, and who has committed all sorts of crimes against his King. Touched with a sensible regret, I confess to Him all my wickedness, I ask His forgiveness, I abandon myself in His hands that He may do what He pleases with me. This King, full of mercy and goodness, very far from chastising me, embraces me with love, makes me eat at His table, serves me with His own hands, gives me the key to His treasures; He converses and delights Himself with me incessantly, in a thousand and a thousand ways, and treats me in all respects as His favorite. It is thus I consider myself from time to time in His holy presence.

My most useful method is this simple attention, and such a general passionate regard to God, to whom I find myself often attached with greater sweetness and delight than that of an infant at the mother's breast; so that, if I dare use the expression, I should choose to call this state the bosom of God, for the inexpressible sweetness which I taste and experience there.

If sometimes my thoughts wander from it by necessity or infirmity, I am presently recalled by inward motions so charming and delicious that I am ashamed to mention them. I desire your Reverence to reflect rather upon my great wretchedness, of which you are fully informed, than upon the great favors which God does me, all unworthy and ungrateful as I am.

As for my set hours of prayer, they are only a continuation of the same exercise. Sometimes I consider myself there as a stone before a carver, whereof he is to makes a statue; presenting myself thus before God, I desire Him to form His perfect image in my soul, and make me entirely like Himself.

At other times, when I apply myself to prayer, I feel all my spirit and all my soul lift itself up without any care or effort of mine, and it continues as it were suspended and firmly fixed in God, as in its center and place of rest.

I know that some charge this state with inactivity, delusion, and self-love. I confess that it is a holy inactivity, and would be a happy self-love if the soul in that state were capable of it, because in effect, while she is in this repose, she cannot be disturbed by such acts as she was formerly accustomed to, and which were then her support, but which would now rather hinder than assist her.

Yet I cannot bear that this should be called delusion, because the soul which thus enjoys God desires herein nothing but Him. If this be delusion in me, it belongs to God to remedy it. Let Him do what He pleases with me; I desire only Him, and to be wholly devoted to Him. You will, however, oblige me in sending me your opinion, to which I always pay a great deference, for I have a singular esteem for your Reverence.

Richard Baxter

(1615-1691)

THROUGH a courageous self-discipline Baxter was able to overcome the handicaps of ill health and the lack of a university education to become one of the outstanding Nonconformist leaders of England. He was ordained in the Church of England, although his sympathies were always with the Puritans. At the time of Civil War, in 1642, he ministered to the soldiers, and at the Restoration he became chaplain to the king. He declined the bishopric of Hereford.

Shortly before the Act of Uniformity was passed, he left the Church of England and retired to Acton, Middlesex. There he did much of his theological writing. At the same time, he preached to large throngs of people, twice being imprisoned for his religious and political views. *The Saints' Everlasting Rest* is one of the best devotional insights to come out of this perplexing time in England. A chapter is here reproduced from Benjamin Fawcett's edition.

THE NATURE OF HEAVENLY CONTEMPLATION

From *The Saints' Everlasting Rest*

*O*nce more I entreat thee, reader, as thou makest conscience of a revealed duty, and darest not wilfully resist the Spirit; as thou valuest the high delights of a saint, and the soul-ravishing exercise of heavenly contemplation; that thou diligently study, and speedily and faithfully practise the following directions. If, by this means, thou dost not find an increase of all thy graces, and dost not grow beyond the stature of a common christian, and art not made more serviceable in thy place, and more precious in the eyes of all discerning persons; if thy soul enjoy not more communion with God, and thy life be not fuller of comfort, and thou hast not more support in a dying hour; then cast away these directions, and exclaim against me for ever as a deceiver.

The duty which I press upon thee so earnestly, and in the practice of which I am now to direct thee, is, "The set and solemn acting of all the powers of thy soul in meditation upon thy everlasting rest." . . .

It is not improper to illustrate a little the manner in which we have described this duty of meditation, or the considering and cotemplating of spiritual things.

It is *confessed to be a duty* by all, but practically denied by most. Many, that make conscience of other duties, easily neglect this. They are troubled if they omit a sermon, a fast, or a prayer, in public or private; yet were never troubled that they have omitted meditation perhaps all their lifetime to this very day; though it be that duty by which all other duties are improved, and by which the soul digests truth for its nourishment and comfort. It was God's command to Joshua, "This book of the law shall not depart out of thy mouth, but thou shalt meditate therein day and night, that thou mayest observe to do according to all that is written therein." As digestion turns food into chyle and blood for vigorous health, so meditation turns the truths received and remembered into warm affection, firm resolution, and holy conversation.

This meditation is the acting of *all the powers of the soul*. It is the work of the living, and not of the dead. It is a work the most spiritual and sublime, and therefore not to be well performed by a heart that is merely carnal and earthly. Men must necessarily have some relation to heaven before they can familiarly converse there. I suppose them to be such as have a title to rest, when I persuade them to rejoice in the meditations of rest. And supposing thee to be a christian, I am now exhorting thee to be an active christian. And it is the work of the soul I am setting thee to, for bodily exercise here profiteth little. And it must have all the powers of the soul to distinguish it from the common meditation of students; for the understanding is not the whole soul, and therefore cannot do the whole work. As in the body, the stomach must turn the food into chyle and prepare for the liver, the liver and spleen turn it into blood and prepare for the heart and brain; so in the soul, the understanding must take in truths, and prepare them for the will, and that for the affections. Christ and heaven have various excellencies, and therefore God hath formed the soul with different powers for apprehending these excellencies. What the better had we been for odoriferous flowers, if we had no smell? or what good would language or music have done us, if we could not hear? or what pleasure should we have found in meats and drinks, without the sense of taste? So what good could all the glory of heaven have done us, or what pleasure should we have had in the perfection of God himself, if we had been without the affections of love and joy? And what strength or sweetness canst thou possibly receive by thy meditations on eternity, while thou dost not exercise those affections of the soul by which thou must be sensible of this sweetness and strength? It is the mistake of christians to think that meditation is only the work of the understanding and memory, when every school-boy can do this, or persons that hate the things which they think on. So that you see there is more to be done than barely to remember and think of heaven. As some labors not only stir a hand or a foot, but exercise the whole body; so doth meditation the whole soul. As the affections of sinners are set on the world, are turned to idols and fallen from God as well as their understanding;

so must their affections be reduced to God as well as the understanding; and as their whole soul was filled with sin before, so the whole must be filled with God now. See David's description of the blessed man: "His delight is in the law of the Lord, and in his law doth he meditate day and night."

This meditation is *set and solemn.* As there is solemn prayer, when we set ourselves wholly to that duty; and ejaculatory prayer, when, in the midst of other business, we send up some short request to God; so also there is solemn meditation, when we apply ourselves wholly to that work; and transient meditation, when, in the midst of other business, we have some good thoughts of God in our minds. And as solemn prayer is either set in a constant course of duty, or occasional, at an extraordinary season; so also is meditation. Now, though I would persuade you to that meditation which is mixed with your common labors, and also that to which special occasions direct you; yet I would have you likewise make it a constant standing duty, as you do hearing, praying, and reading the Scriptures; and no more intermix other matters with it, than you would with prayer, or other stated solemnities.

This meditation is *upon thy everlasting rest.* I would not have you cast off your other meditations; but surely, as heaven hath the pre-eminence in perfection, it should have it also in our meditation. That which will make us most happy when we possess it, will make us most joyful when we meditate upon it. Other meditations are as numerous as there are lines in the Scripture, or creatures in the universe, or particular providences in the government of the world. But this is a walk to Mount Sion; from the kingdoms of this world to the kingdom of saints; from earth to heaven; from time to eternity: it is walking upon sun, moon and stars, in the garden and paradise of God. It may seem far off; but spirits are quick: whether in the body or out of the body, their motion is swift. You need not fear, like the men of the world, lest these thoughts should make you mad. It is in heaven, and not hell, that I persuade you to walk. It is joy, and not sorrow, that I persuade you to exercise. I urge you to look on no deformed objects, but only upon the ravishing glory of saints, and the unspeakable excellencies of the God of glory, and the beams that stream from the face of his Son. Will it distract a man to think of his only happiness? Will it distract the miserable to think of mercy, or the prisoner to foresee deliverance, or the poor to think of approaching riches and honor? Methinks it should rather make a man mad to think of living in a world of woe, and abiding in poverty and sickness, among the rage of wicked men, than to think of living with Christ in bliss. "But wisdom is justified of all her children." Knowledge hath no enemy but the ignorant. This heavenly course was never spoken against by any but those that never knew it, or never used it. I fear more the neglect of men that approve it, than the opposition or arguments of any against it.

First. As to *the fittest time* for this heavenly contemplation, let me only advise that it be stated—frequent—and seasonable.

1. Give it a *stated* time. If thou suit thy time to the advantage of the work, without placing any religion in the time itself, thou hast no need to fear superstition. Stated time is a hedge to duty, and defends it against many temptations to omission. Some have not their time at command, and therefore cannot set their hours; and many are so poor, that the necessities of their families deny them this freedom; such persons should be watchful to redeem time as much as they can, and take their vacant opportunities as they fall, and especially join meditation and prayer as much as they can with the labors of their calling. Yet those who have more time to spare from their worldly necessities, and are masters of their time, I still advise to keep this duty to a stated time. And indeed, if every work of the day had its appointed time, we should be better skilled both in redeeming time and performing duty.

2. Let it be *frequent* as well as stated. How oft it should be I cannot determine, because men's circumstances differ; but in general, Scripture requires it to be frequent, when it mentions meditating day and night. For those, therefore, who can conveniently omit other business, I advise that it be once a day at least.

Frequency in heavenly contemplation is particularly important, to prevent a shyness between God and thy soul. Frequent society breeds familiarity, and familiarity increases love and delight, and makes us bold in our addresses. The chief end of this duty is, to have acquaintance and fellowship with God; and therefore, if thou come but seldom to it, thou wilt still keep thyself a stranger. When a man feels his need of God, and must seek his help in a time of necessity, then it is great encouragement to go to a God we know and are acquainted with, "O," saith the heavenly christian, "I know both whither I go, and to whom. I have gone this way many a time before now. It is the same God that I daily converse with, and the way has been my daily walk. God knows me well enough, and I have some knowledge of him." On the other hand, what a horror and discouragement will it be to the soul, when it is forced to fly to God in straits, to think, "Alas! I know not whither to go. I never went the way before. I have no acquaintance at the court of heaven. My soul knows not that God that I must speak to, and I fear he will not know my soul." But especially when we come to die, and must immediately appear before this God, and expect to enter into his eternal rest, then the difference will plainly appear; then what a joy will it be to think, "I am going to the place that I daily conversed in; to the place from whence I tasted such frequent delights; to that God whom I have met in my meditation so often! My heart hath been in heaven before now, and hath often tasted its reviving sweetness; and if my eyes were so enlightened and my spirits so refreshed when I had but a taste, what will it be when I shall feed on it freely?" On the contrary, what a terror will it be to think, "I must die and go I know not whither; from a place where I am acquainted, to a place where I have no familiarity or knowledge!" It is an inexpressible horror to a dying man to have strange thoughts of God and heaven. I am persuaded that it is the neglect of this duty which so commonly makes death, even to godly men, unwelcome and uncomfortable. Therefore I persuade to frequency in this duty.

And as it will prevent shyness between thee and God, so also it will prevent unskilfulness in the duty itself. How awkwardly do men set their hands to a work in which they are seldom employed! Whereas frequency will habituate thy heart to the work, and make it more easy and delightful. The hill which made thee pant and blow at first going up, thou mayest easily run up when thou art once accustomed to it.

Thou wilt also prevent the loss of the heart and life thou hast obtained. If thou eat but once in two or three days, thou wilt lose thy strength as fast as it comes. If in holy meditation thou get near to Christ and warm thy heart with the fire of love, and then come but seldom, thy former coldness will soon return; especially as the work is so spiritual and against the bent of depraved nature. It is true, the intermixing of other duties, especially secret prayer, may do much to the keeping of thy heart above; but meditation is the life of most other duties, and the view of heaven is the life of meditation.

3. Choose also the most *seasonable* time. All things are beautiful and excellent in their season. Unseasonableness may lose the fruit of thy labor, may raise difficulties in the work, and may turn a duty to a sin. The same hour may be seasonable to one and unseasonable to another. Servants and laborers must take that season which their business can best afford; either while at work, or in travelling, or when they lie awake in the night. Such as can choose what time of the day they will, should observe when they find their spirits most active and fit for contemplation, and fix upon that as the stated time. I have always found that the fittest time for myself is the evening, from sun-setting to the twilight. I the rather mention this, because it was the experience of a better and wiser man; for it is expressly said, "Isaac went out to meditate in the field at the even-tide."

The Lord's Day is exceeding seasonable for this exercise. When should we more seasonably contemplate our rest than on that day of rest which typifies it to us? It being a day appropriated to spiritual duties, methinks we should never exclude this duty, which is so eminently spiritual. I verily think this is the chief work of a christian Sabbath, and most agreeable to the design of its positive institution. What fitter time to converse with our Lord than on the Lord's day? What fitter day to ascend to heaven than that on which he arose from earth, and fully triumphed over death and hell? The fittest temper for a true christian is, like John, to "be in the Spirit on the Lord's day." And what can bring us to this joy in the Spirit, but the spiritual beholding of our approaching glory? Take notice of this, you that spend the Lord's day only in public worship; your allowing no time to private duty, and therefore neglecting this spiritual duty of meditation, is very hurtful to your souls. You, also, that have time on the Lord's day for idleness and vain discourse, were you but acquainted with this duty of contemplation, you would need no other pastime; you would think the longest day short enough, and be sorry that the night had shortened your pleasure. Christians, let heaven have more share in your Sabbath, where you must shortly keep your everlasting Sabbaths. Use your Sabbaths as steps to glory, till you have passed them all, and are there arrived. Especially you that are poor, and cannot take time in the week as you desire, see that you well improve this day; as your bodies rest from their labors, let your spirits seek after rest from God.

Besides the constant seasonableness of every day, and particularly every Lord's day, there are also more peculiar seasons for heavenly contemplation. As for instance:

When God hath more abundantly warmed thy spirit with fire from above, then thou mayest soar with greater freedom. A little labor will set thy heart a going at such a time as this; whereas at another time thou mayst take pains to little purpose. Observe the gales of the Spirit, and how the Spirit of Christ doth move thy spirit. "Without Christ we can do nothing;" and therefore let us be doing while he is doing! and be sure not to be out of the way, nor asleep, when he comes. When the Spirit finds thy heart, like Peter, in prison and in irons, and smites thee, and says, "Arise up quickly, and follow me!" be sure thou then arise and follow; and thou shalt find thy chains fall off, and all doors will open, and thou wilt be at heaven before thou art aware.

Another peculiar season for this duty is, when thou art in a *suffering*, distressed, or tempted state. When should we take our cordials but in time of fainting? When is it more seasonable to walk to heaven than when we know not in what corner of earth to live with comfort? Or when should our thoughts converse more above than when we have nothing but grief below? Where should Noah's dove be but in the ark, when the waters cover all the earth, and she cannot find rest for the sole of her foot? What should we think on but our Father's house, when we have not even the husks of the world to feed upon? Surely God sends thy afflictions for this very purpose. Happy art thou, poor man, if thou make this use of thy poverty! and thou that art sick, if thou so improve thy sickness! It is seasonable to go to the promised land, when our burdens are increased in Egypt and our straits in the wilderness! Reader, if thou knewest what a cordial to thy griefs the serious views of glory are, thou wouldst less fear these harmless troubles, and more use that preserving, reviving remedy. "In the multitude of my" troubled "thoughts within me," saith David, "thy comforts delight my soul." "I reckon," saith Paul, "that the sufferings of this present time are not worthy to be compared with the glory which shall be revealed in us." "For which cause we faint not; but though our outward man perish, yet the inward man is renewed day by day. For our light affliction, which is but for a moment, worketh for us a far more exceeding and eternal weight of glory, while we look not at the things which are seen, but at the things which are not seen; for the things which are seen are temporal, but the things which are not seen are eternal."

And another season peculiarly fit for this heavenly duty is when the messengers of God summon us *to die*. When should we more frequently sweeten our souls with the believing thoughts of another life, than when we find that this is almost ended? No men have greater need of supporting joys than dying men; and these joys must be drawn from our eternal joy. As heavenly delights are sweetest when nothing earthly is joined with them, so the delights of dying christians are oftentimes the sweetest they ever had. What a prophetic blessing had dying Isaac and Jacob for their sons! With what a heavenly song and divine benediction did Moses conclude his life? What heavenly advice and prayer had the disciples from their Lord, when he was about to leave them! When Paul was "ready to be offered," what heavenly exhortation and advice did he give the Philippians, Timothy, and the elders of Ephesus! How near to heaven was John in Patmos, but a little before his translation thither! It is the general temper of the saints to be then most heavenly when they are nearest heaven. If it be thy case, reader, to perceive thy dying time draw on, O where should thy heart now be but with Christ? Methinks thou shouldst even behold him standing by thee, and shouldst bespeak him as thy father, thy husband, thy physician, thy friend. Methinks thou shouldst, as it were, see the angels about thee, waiting to perform their last office to thy soul; even those angels which disdained not to carry into Abraham's bosom the soul of Lazarus, nor will think much to conduct thee thither. Look upon thy pain and sickness as Jacob did on Joseph's chariots, and let thy spirit revive within thee, and say, "It is enough. Christ is yet alive; because he liveth, I shall live also." Dost thou need the choicest cordials? Here are choicer than the world can afford; here are all the joys of heaven, even the vision of God and Christ, and whatsoever the blessed here possess. These dainties are offered thee by the hand of Christ; he hath written the receipt in the promises of the Gospel; he hath prepared the ingredients in heaven; only put forth the hand of faith and feed upon them, and rejoice, and live. The Lord saith to thee, as to Elijah, "Arise and eat, because the journey is too great for thee." Though it be not long, yet the way is miry; therefore obey his voice, arise and eat, "and in the strength of that meat thou mayst go to the mount of God;" and, like Moses, "die in the mount whither thou goest up;" and say, as Simeon, "Lord, now lettest thou thy servant depart in peace, for mine eye" of faith "hath seen thy salvation."

Secondly. Concerning *the fittest place* for heavenly contemplation, it is sufficient to say that the most convenient is *some private retirement.* Our spirits need every help, and to be freed from every hindrance in the work. If, in private prayer, Christ directs us to "enter into our closet and shut the door, that our Father may see us in secret," so should we do this in meditation. How often did Christ himself retire to some mountain, or wilderness, or other solitary place! I give not this advice for occasional meditation, but for that which is set and solemn. Therefore withdraw thyself from all society, even that of godly men, that thou mayest awhile enjoy the society of thy Lord. If a student cannot study in a crowd, who exerciseth only his invention and memory, much less shouldst thou be in a crowd, who art to exercise all the powers of thy soul, and upon an object so far above nature. We are fled so far from superstitious solitude, that we have even cast off the solitude of contemplative devotion. We seldom

read of God's appearing by himself, or by his angels, to any of his prophets or saints, in a crowd: but frequently when they were alone.

But observe for thyself what place best agrees with thy spirit, within doors or without. Isaac's example, in "going out to meditate in the field," will, I am persuaded, best suit with most. Our Lord so much used a solitary garden, that even Judas, when he came to betray him, knew where to find him: and though he took his disciples thither with him, yet he "was withdrawn from them" for more secret devotions; and though his meditation be not directly named, but only his praying, yet it is very clearly implied; for his soul is first made sorrowful with bitter meditations on his sufferings and death, and then he poureth it out in prayer. So that Christ had his accustomed place, and consequently accustomed duty; and so must we: he hath a place that is solitary, whither he retireth, even from his own disciples; and so must we: his meditations go further than his thoughts; they affect and pierce his heart and soul; and so must ours. Only there is a wide difference in the object: Christ meditates on the sufferings that our sins had deserved, so that the wrath of his Father passed through all his soul; but we are to meditate on the glory he hath purchased, that the love of the Father and the joy of the Spirit may enter our thoughts, and revive our affections, and overflow our souls.

Thirdly. I am next to advise thee concerning *the preparation of thy heart* for this heavenly contemplation. The success of the work much depends on the frame of thy heart. When man's heart had nothing in it to grieve the Spirit, it was then the delightful habitation of his Maker. God did not quit his residence there till man expelled him by unworthy provocations. There was no shyness or reserve till the heart grew sinful, and too loathsome a dungeon for God to delight in. And were this soul reduced to its former innocency, God would quickly return to his former habitation; yea, so far as it is renewed and repaired by the Spirit, and purged from its lusts, and beautified with his image, the Lord will yet acknowledge it as his own: Christ will manifest himself unto it, and the Spirit will take it for his temple and residence. So far as the heart is qualified for conversing with God, so far it usually enjoys him. Therefore, "with all diligence keep thy heart, for out of it are the issues of life." More particularly,

1. Get thy heart as *clear from the world* as thou canst. Wholly lay by the thoughts of thy business, troubles, enjoyments, and every thing that may take up any room in thy soul. Get it as empty as thou possibly canst, that it may be the more capable of being filled with God. If thou couldst perform some outward duty with a part of thy heart while the remainder is absent, yet this duty, above all, I am sure thou canst not. When thou shalt go into the mount of contemplation, thou wilt be like the covetous man at the heap of gold, who, when he might take as much as he could, lamented that he was able to carry no more: thou wilt find as much of God and glory as thy narrow heart is able to contain, and almost nothing to hinder thy full possession but the incapacity of thy own spirit. Then thou wilt think, "O that this understanding and these affections could contain more! It is more my unfitness than any thing else that even this place is not my heaven. 'God is in this place, and I know it not.' This 'mount is full of chariots of fire;' but mine eyes are shut, and I cannot see them. O the words of love Christ hath to speak, and wonders of love he hath to show, but I cannot bear them yet! Heaven is ready for me, but my heart is unready for heaven." Therefore, reader, seeing thy enjoyment of God in this contemplation much depends on the capacity and disposition of thy heart, seek him here, if ever, with all thy soul. Thrust not Christ into the stable and the manger, as if thou hadst better guests for the chief rooms. Say to all thy worldly business and thoughts, as Christ to his disciples, "Sit ye here, while I go and pray yonder;" or as Abraham to his servants, when he went to offer Isaac, "Abide ye here, and I will go yonder and worship, and come again to you." Even as "the priests thrust king Uzziah out of the temple," where he presumed to burn incense, when they saw the leprosy upon him; so do thou thrust those thoughts from the temple of thy heart, which have the badge of God's prohibition upon them.

2. Be sure to enter upon this work with the *greatest solemnity of heart and mind*. There is no trifling in holy things. "God will be sanctified in them that come nigh him." These spiritual, excellent, soul-raising duties, are, if well used, most profitable; but, when used unfaithfully, most dangerous. Labor, therefore, to have the deepest apprehensions of the presence of God and his incomprehensible greatness. If queen Esther must not draw near "till the king hold out the sceptre," think, then, with what reverence thou shouldst approach Him who made the worlds with the word of his mouth, who upholds the earth as in the palm of his hand, who keeps the sun, moon and stars in their courses, and who sets bounds to the raging sea! Thou art going to converse with Him, before whom the earth will quake and devils do tremble, and at whose bar thou and all the world must shortly stand and be finally judged. O think! "I shall then have lively apprehensions of his majesty. My drowsy spirits will then be awakened, and my irreverence be laid aside: and why should I not now be roused with the sense of his greatness, and the dread of his name possess my soul?" Labor also to apprehend the greatness of the work which thou attemptest, and to be deeply sensible both of its importance and excellency. If thou wast pleading for thy life at the bar of an earthly judge, thou wouldst be serious, and yet that would be a trifle to this. If thou wast engaged in such a work as David against Goliath, on which the welfare of a kingdom depended; in itself considered, it were nothing to this. Suppose thou wast going to such a wrestling as Jacob's or to see the sight which the three disciples saw in the mount, how seriously, how reverently wouldst thou both approach and

behold! If but an angel from heaven should appoint to meet thee at the same time and place of thy contemplations, with what dread wouldst thou be filled! Consider, then, with what a spirit thou shouldst meet the Lord, and with what seriousness and awe thou shouldst daily converse with him. Consider, also, the blessed issue of the work, if it succeed; it will be thy admission into the presence of God, and the beginning of thy eternal glory on earth; a means to make thee live above the rate of other men, and fix thee in the next room to the angels themselves, that thou mayest both live and die joyfully. The prize being so great, thy preparations should be answerable. None on earth live such a life of joy and blessedness as those who are acquainted with this heavenly conversation. The joys of all other men are but like a child's plaything, a fool's laughter, or a sick man's dream of health. He that trades for heaven is the only gainer, and he that neglects it is the only loser. How seriously, therefore, should this work be done!

Miguel de Molinos

(1640-1697)

IN Spain quietism had the same influence as the Society of Friends had in England, and in both countries the leaders suffered persecutions from the traditionalists. The chief exponent of Spanish quietism was de Molinos, a man of piety and brilliance, with a doctorate from Coimbra. Although he was admired by many Spanish churchmen, church authorities had him arrested as a dangerous heretic because of his quietistic stress on the inward authority. He died in a prison at Rome. His *Spiritual Guide Which Disentangles the Soul and Brings It by the Inward Way to the Getting of Perfect Contemplation and Inward Peace* ranks among the finest Spanish devotional literature.

[INTERNAL PEACE]

From *The Spiritual Guide*

THE MEANS OF OBTAINING PEACE INTERNAL IS NOT THE DELIGHT OF SENSE; NOT SPIRITUAL CONSOLATION, BUT THE DENYING OF SELF-LOVE.

It is the saying of St. Bernard, that to serve God is nothing else but to do good and suffer evil. He that would go to perfection by the means of sweetness and consolation is mistaken. You must desire no other consolation from God than to end your life for his sake, in the state of true obedience and subjection. Christ our Lord's way was not that of sweetness and softness, nor did he invite us to any such, either by his words or example, when he said: "He that will come after me, let him deny himself, and let him take up his cross and follow me" (Mark 8:34). The soul that would be united to Christ must be conformable to him, and follow him in the way of suffering.

Thou wilt scarce begin to relish the sweetness of divine love in prayer before the enemy with his deceitful craftiness will be kindling in thy heart desires of the desert and solitude, that thou mayest without anybody's hindrance spread the sails to continual and delightful prayers. Open thine eyes, and consider that this counsel and desire is not conformable to the true counsel of Christ our Lord, who has not invited us to follow the sweetness and comfort of our own will, but the denying of ourselves, saying, "Let him deny himself." As if he should say, he that will follow me and come unto perfection, let him part with his own will wholly; and leaving all things, let him entirely submit to the yoke of obedience and subjection by means of self-denial, which is the truest cross.

There are many souls dedicated to God, which receive from his hand great thoughts, visions, and mental elevations, and yet for all that the Lord keeps from them the grace of working miracles, understanding hidden secrets, foretelling future contingencies, as he communicates these things to other souls which have constantly gone through tribulations, temptations, and the true cross, in the state of perfect humility, obedience, and subjections.

Oh, what a great happiness is it for a soul to be subdued and subject! what great riches is it to be poor! what a mighty honor to be despised! what a height is it to be beaten down! what a comfort is it to be afflicted! what a credit of knowledge is it to be reputed ignorant! and finally, what a happiness of happiness is it to be crucified with Christ! This is that lot which the apostle gloried in, "Far be it from me to glory, save in the cross of our Lord Jesus Christ" (Gal. 6:14). Let others boast in their riches, dignities, delights and honors; but to us there is no higher honor than to be denied, despised, and crucified with Christ.

But what a grief is this, that scarce is there one soul which prizes spiritual pleasures, and is willing to be denied for Christ, embracing his cross with love. "Many are called, few are chosen" (Matt. 22:14), says the Holy Ghost: many are they who are called to perfection, but few are they that arrive at it; because they are few who embrace the cross with patience, constancy, peace, and resignation.

To deny oneself in all things, to be subject to another's judgment, to mortify continually all inward passions, to annihilate oneself in all respects, to follow always that which is contrary to one's own will, appetite, and judgment, are things that few can do: many are those that teach them, but few are they that practise them.

Many souls have undertaken, and daily do undertake this way; and they persevere all the while they keep the sweet relish of their primitive fervor; but this sweetness and sensible delight is scarce done, but presently, upon the overtaking of a storm of trouble, temptation, and dryness (which are necessary things to help a man up the high mountain of perfection), they falter and turn back a clear sign that they sought themselves and not God or perfection.

May it please God that the souls which have had light and been called to an inward peace, and by not being constant in dryness and tribulation and temptation have started back may not be cast into outward darkness with him that had not on him a wedding garment; altho he was a servant, for not being acquiescent, giving himself up to self-love.

This monster must be vanquished, this seven-headed beast of self-love must be beheaded, in order to get up to the top of the high mountain of peace. This monster puts his head everywhere; sometimes it gets among relations which strangely hinder with their conversations, to which nature easily lets itself be led; sometimes it gets, with a good look of gratitude, into affection that is passionate and without restraint toward the confessor; sometimes into affection to most subtle spiritual vainglories and temporal ones and niceties of honor, which things stick very close; sometimes it cleaves to spiritual pleasures, staying even in the gifts of God and in his graces freely bestowed; sometimes it desires exceedingly the preservation of health with disguise to be used well—and its own profit and conveniences; sometimes it would seem well with very curious subtleties; and lastly, it cleaves with a notable propensity to its own proper judgment and opinion in all things, the roots of which are closely fixt in its own will. All these are effects of self-love, and if they be not denied, impossible it is that a man should ever get up to the height of perfect contemplation, to the highest happiness of the loving union, and the lofty throne of peace internal.

MAXIMS TO KNOW A SIMPLE, HUMBLE, AND
TRUE HEART.

Encourage thyself to be humble, embracing tribulations as instruments of thy good; rejoice in contempt, and desire that God may be thy holy refuge, comfort, and protector.

None, let him be never so great in this world, can be greater than he that is in the eye and favor of God; and therefore the truly humble man despises whatever there is in the world even to himself, and puts his only trust and repose in God. The truly humble man suffers quietly and patiently internal troubles; and he is the man that makes great way in a little time, like one that sails before the wind. The truly humble man finds God in all things; so that whatever contempt, injury, or affronts come to him by means of the creatures, he receives it with great peace and quiet internal, as sent from the divine hand, and loves greatly the instrument with which the Lord tries him.

He that is taken with praise is not yet arrived at profound humility, tho he does not desire praise, nor seek it, but rather avoids it; because, to an humble heart, praises are bitter crosses, altho it be wholly quiet and immovable.

He has no internal humility who doth not abhor himself, with a mortal but withal a peaceable and quiet hatred; but he will never come to possess this treasure who has not a low and profound knowledge of his own vileness and rottenness, and misery.

He that makes excuses and replies has not a simple and humble heart, especially if he does this with his superior; because replies grow from a secret pride that reigns in the soul, and from thence proceeds the total ruin of it.

Perfidiousness supposes little submission, and this less humility; and both together they are the fuel of inquietness, discord, and disturbance.

The humble heart is not disquieted by imperfections, tho these grieve it to the soul, because they are against its loving Lord. Nor is he concerned that he can not do great things, for he always stands in his own nothingness and misery; nay, he wonders at himself that he can do anything of virtue, and presently thanks the Lord for it, with a true knowledge that it is God that doth all, and remains dissatisfied with what he does himself.

The truly humble man, tho he sees all, yet he looks upon nothing to judge it, because he judges ill only of himself. The truly humble man doth always find an excuse to defend him that mortifies him, at least in a sound intention. Who therefore would be angry with a man of good intention?

So much (nay more) doth false humility displease God, as true pride does; because that is hypocrisy besides.

The truly humble man, tho everything falls out contrary to him, is neither disquieted nor afflicted by it; because he is prepared, and thinks he deserves no less. He is not disquieted under troublesome thoughts, wherewith the devil seeks to torment him, nor under temptations, tribulations, and desertions; but rather acknowledges his unworthiness, and is affected that the Lord chastises him by the devil's means, tho he be a vile instrument; all he suffers seems nothing to him, and he never doth a thing that he thinks worth any great matter.

He that is arrived at perfect and inward humility, altho he be disturbed at nothing, as one that abhors himself because he knows his imperfection in everything, his ingratitude and his misery, yet he suffers a great cross in enduring himself. This is the sign to know true humility of heart by. But the happy soul, which is gotten to this holy hatred of itself, lives overwhelmed, drowned, and swallowed up in the depths of its own nothingness, out of which the Lord raises him, by communicating divine wisdom to him, and filling him with light, peace, tranquillity, and love.

INWARD SOLITUDE IS THAT WHICH CHIEFLY
BRINGS A MAN TO THE PURCHASE OF
INTERNAL PEACE.

Know, that altho exterior solitude doth much assist for the obtaining internal peace yet the Lord did not mean this, when he spake by his prophet (Hos. 2:14)—"I will bring her into solitude, and speak privately to her"; but he meant the interior solitude, which jointly conduces to the obtaining the precious jewel of peace internal. Internal solitude consists in the forgetting of the creatures, in disengaging oneself from them, in a perfect nakedness of all the affections, desires, thoughts, and one's own will. This is the true solitude, where the soul reposes with a sweet and inward serenity in the arms of its chiefest good.

Oh, what infinite room is there in a soul that is arrived at this divine solitude! Oh, what inward, what retired, what secret, what spacious, what vast distances are there within a happy soul that is once come to be truly solitary! There the Lord converses and communicates himself inwardly with the soul; there he fills it with himself, because it is empty; clothes it with light and with his love, because it is naked; lifts it up, because it is low; and unites it with himself, and transforms it, because it is alone.

O delightful solitude and cipher of eternal blessings! O mirror, in which the Eternal Father is always beheld! There is great reason to call thee solitude; for thou art so much alone that there is scarce a soul that looks after thee, that loves and knows thee. O divine Lord! How is it that souls do not go from earth to this glory? How come they to lose so great a good, through the only love and desire of created things? Blessed soul, how happy wilt thou be, if thou dost but leave all for God! Seek him only, breathe after none but him; let him only have thy sighs. Desire nothing, and then nothing can trouble thee; and if thou dost desire any good, how spiritual soever it be, let it be in such a manner that thou mayest not be disquieted if thou miss it.

If, with this liberty, thou wilt give thy soul to God, taken off from the world, free and alone, thou wilt be the happiest creature upon earth, because the Most High has his secret habitation in this holy solitude. In this desert and paradise is enjoyed the conversation of God; and it is only in this internal retirement that that marvelous, powerful, and divine voice is heard. If thou wouldst enter into this heaven of earth, forget every care and every thought; get out of thyself, that the love of God may live in thy soul. Live as much as ever thou canst abstracted from the creatures, dedicate thyself wholly to thy Creator, and offer thyself in sacrifice with peace and quietness of spirit. Know that the more the soul disrobes itself, the more way it makes into this interior solitude, and becomes clothed with God; and the more lonesome and empty of itself the soul gets to be, the more the divine Spirit fills it.

There is not a more blessed life than a solitary one; because in this happy life God gives himself all to the creature and the creature all to God, by an intimate and sweet union and love. Oh, how few are there that come to relish this true solitude!

To make the soul truly solitary, it ought to forget all the creatures, and even itself; otherwise it will never be able to make any near approach to God. Many men leave and forsake all things, but they do not leave their own liking, their own will, and themselves; and therefore these truly solitary ones are so few. Wherefore, if the soul does not get off from its own appetite and desire, from its own will, from spiritual gifts, and from repose even in the spirit itself, it never can arrive at this high felicity of internal solitude.

Go on, blessed soul! Go on, without stop, toward this blessedness of internal solitude. See how God calls thee to enter into thy inward center, where he will renew thee, change thee, fill thee, clothe thee, and show thee a new and heavenly kingdom, full of joy, peace, content, and serenity.

In Which Is Shown What Infused and Passive Contemplation Is, and Its Wonderful Effects.

You must know that when once the soul is habituated to internal recollection and acquired contemplation that we have spoken of; when once it is mortified, and desires wholly to be denied its appetites;

when once it efficaciously embraces internal and external mortification, and is willing to die heartily to its passions and its own ways, then God uses to take it alone by itself, and raise it more than it knows to a complete repose, where he sweetly and inwardly infuses in it his light, his love, and his strength, enkindling and inflaming it with a true disposition to all manner of virtue.

There the divine spouse, suspending its powers, puts it to sleep in a most sweet and pleasant rest; there it sleeps, and quietly receives and enjoys (without knowing it) what it enjoys with a most lovely and charming calm. There the soul, raised and lifted up to this passive state, becomes united to its greatest good, without costing it any trouble or pains for this union. There, in that supreme region and sacred temple of the soul, that greatest good takes its complacency, manifests itself, and creates a relish from the creature in a way above sense and all human understanding. There also only the pure Spirit, who is God (the purity of the soul being incapable of sensible things), rules it, and gets the mastership of it, communicating to its illustrations and those sentiments which are necessary for the most pure and perfect union.

The soul, coming to itself again from these sweet and divine embracings, becomes rich in light and love, a mighty esteem of the divine greatness, and the knowledge of its own misery, finding itself all changed divinely, and disposed to embrace, suffer, and to practise a perfect virtue.

A simple, pure, infused, and perfect contemplation therefore is a known and inward manifestation, which God gives of himself, of his goodness, of his peace, of his sweetness, whose object is God, pure, unspeakable, abstracted from all particular thoughts, within an inward·silence. But it is God delightful, God that draws us, God that sweetly raises us in a spiritual and most pure manner; an admirable gift which the divine Majesty bestows to whom he will, tho the state of this life be rather a state of the cross, of patience, of humility, and of suffering than of enjoying.

Never wilt thou enjoy this divine nectar till thou art advanced in virtue and inward mortifications, till thou dost heartily endeavor to fix in thy soul a great peace, silence, forgetfulness, and internal solitude. How is it possible to hear the sweet, inward, and powerful voice of God in the midst of the noise and tumults of the creatures? And how can the pure spirit be heard in the midst of considerations and discourses of artifice? If the soul will not continually die in itself, denying itself to all these materialities and satisfactions, the contemplation can be no more but a mere vanity, a vain complacency and presumption.

God doth not always communicate himself with equal abundance in this sweetest and infused contemplation. Sometimes he grants this grace more than he doth at other times; and sometimes he expects not that the soul should be so dead and denied, because this gift being his mere grace, he gives it when he pleases and as he pleases; so that no general rule can be made of it, nor any rate set to his divine greatness; nay, by means of this very contemplation he comes to deny it, to annihilate and die.

Sometimes the Lord gives greater light to the understanding, sometimes greater love to the will. There is no need here for the soul to take any pains or trouble; it must receive what God gives it, and rest united, as he will have it: because his Majesty is Lord, and in the very time that he lays it asleep he possesses and fills it, and works in it powerfully and sweetly, without any industry or knowledge of its own; insomuch that before ever it is aware of this so great mercy, it is gained, convinced, and changed already.

The soul which is in this happy state hath two things to avoid—first, the activity of human spirit and interestedness. Our human spirit is unwilling to die in itself, but loveth to be doing and discoursing after its way, being in love with its own actions. A man had need to have a great fidelity, and divesting himself of selfishness, to get a perfect and passive capacity of the divine influences; the continual habits of operating freely which it has are a hindrance to its annihilation.

Second, interestedness in contemplation itself. Thou must therefore procure in thy soul a perfect divesting of all which is not God, without seeking any other end or interest, within or without, but the divine will.

In a word, the manner that thou must use on thy part to fit thyself for this pure, passive, and perfect prayer is a total and absolute consignment of thyself into the hands of God, with a perfect submission to his most holy will; to be busied according to his pleasure and disposition, receiving what he ordains thee with an even and perfect resignation.

Thou must know that few be the souls which arrive at this infused and passive prayer; because few of them are capable of these divine influences, with a total nakedness and death of their own activity and power. Those only who feel it know that this perfect nakedness is acquired (by the help of God's grace) by a continual and inward mortification, dying to all its own inclinations and desires.

At no time must thou look at the effects which are wrought in thy soul, but especially herein; because it would be a hindrance to the divine operations which enrich it so to do; all that thou hast to do is to pant after indifference, resignation, forgetfulness; then without thy being sensible of it, the greatest good will leave in thy soul a fit disposition for the practise of virtue, a true love of thy cross, of thy own contempt, of thy annihilation, and greater and stronger desires still of thy greater perfection and the most pure and affective union.

OF THE TWO MEANS WHEREBY THE SOUL ASCENDS UP TO INFUSED CONTEMPLATION, WITH THE EXPLICATION OF WHAT AND HOW MANY THE STEPS OF IT ARE.

The means whereby the soul ascends to the felicity of contemplation and affective love are two—the pleasure and the desires of it. God uses at first to fill the soul with sensible pleasures, because it is so frail and miserable that without this preventive consolation it can not take wing toward the fruition of heavenly things. In this first step it is disposed by contrition, and is exercised in repentance, meditating upon the Redeemer's passion, rooting out diligently all worldly desires and vicious courses of life; because the kingdom of heaven suffers violence, and the faint hearts and delicate never conquer it, but those that use violence and force with themselves.

The second is the desires. The more the things of heaven are delighted in, the more they are desired; and from thence there do ensue upon spiritual pleasures desires of enjoying heavenly and divine blessings and contempt of worldly ones. From these desires arises the inclination of following Christ our Lord, who said, "I am the way" (John 14:6). The steps of his imitation by which a man must go up are charity, humility, meekness, patience, poverty, self-contempt, the cross, prayer, and mortification.

The steps of infused contemplation are three. The first is satiety. When the soul is filled with God it conceives a hatred to all worldly things; then it is quiet and satisfied only with divine love. The second is intoxication. And this step is an excess of mind and an elevation of soul arising from divine love and satiety of it. The third is security. This step turns out all fear: The soul is so drenched with love divine, and resigned up in such a manner to the divine good pleasure, that it would go willingly to hell if it did but know it so to be the will of the Most High. In this step it feels such a certain bond of the divine union that it seems to it an impossible thing to be separated from its beloved and his infinite treasure.

There are six other steps of contemplation, which are these: fire, union, elevation, illumination, pleasure, and repose. With the first the soul is enkindled, and, being enkindled, is anointed; being anointed, is raised; being raised, contemplates; contemplating, it receives pleasure; and, receiving pleasure, it finds repose. By these steps the soul rises higher, being abstracted and experienced in the spiritual and internal way.

In the first step, which is fire, the soul is illustrated by the means of a divine and ardent ray, enkindling the affections divine and drying up those which are but human. The second is the unction, a sweet and spiritual liquor which, diffusing itself all the soul over, teaches it, strengthens it, and disposes it to receive and contemplate the divine truth; and sometimes it extends even to nature itself, corroborating it by patience with a sensible pleasure that seems celestial.

The third is the elevation of the inner man over itself, that it may get fittest to the clear fountain of pure love.

The fourth step, which is illumination, is an infused knowledge, whereby the soul contemplates sweetly the divine truth, rising still from one clearness to another, from one light to another, from knowledge to knowledge, being guided by the Spirit divine.

The fifth is a savory pleasure of the divine sweetness issuing forth from the plentiful and precious fountain of the Holy Ghost.

The sixth is a sweet and admirable tranquillity, arising from the conquest of fighting within and frequent prayer; and this very few have experience of. Here the abundance of joy and peace is so great that the soul seems to be in a sweet sleep, solacing and reposing itself in the divine breast of love.

SIGNS TO KNOW THE INNER MAN AND THE MIND THAT IS PURGED.

The signs to know the inner man by are four. The first, if the understanding produce no other thoughts than those which stir up to the light of faith; and the will is so habituated that it begets no other acts of love than of God, and in order to him. The second, if, when he ceases from an external work in which he was employed, the understanding and the will are presently and easily turned to God. The third, if, in entering upon prayer, he forgets all outward things as if he had not seen or used them. The fourth, if he carries himself orderly toward outward things as if he were entering into the world again, fearing to embroil himself in business and naturally abhorring it, unless when charity requires it of him.

Such a soul as this is free from the outward man, and easier enters into the interior solitude where it sees none but God, and itself in him, loving him with quiet and peace and true love. There, in that secret center, God is kindly speaking to it, teaching it a new kingdom, and true peace and joy.

This spiritual, abstracted, and retired soul hath its peace no more broken, tho outwardly it may meet with combats; because through the infinite distance tempests do never reach to that serenest heaven within, where pure and perfect love resides; and tho sometimes it may be naked, forsaken, fought against, and desolate, this is the only fury of the storm, which threatens and rages nowhere but without.

This secret love within hath four effects. The first is called enlightenment, which is a savory and experimental knowledge of the greatness of God and of its own nothingness. The second is enkindling, which is an ardent desire of being burned, like the salamander, in this kind and Divine fire. The third is sweetness, which is a peaceable, joyful, sweet, and intimate fruition. The fourth is a swallowing up of the powers in God, by which immersion the soul is so much drenched and filled with God that it cannot any longer seek, desire, or will anything but its greatest and infinite good.

From this fullest satiety two effects arise. The first is a great courage to suffer for God; the second is a certain hope or assurance that it can never lose him nor be separated from him.

Here in this internal retirement the beloved Jesus hath his paradise, to whom we may go up, standing and conversing on the earth. And if thou desirest to know who he is who is altogether drawn to this inward retirement, with enlightened exemplification in God, I tell thee it is he that in adversity, in discomfort of spirit, and in the want of necessities stands firm and unshaken. These constant and inward souls are outwardly naked and wholly infused in God, whom they continually do contemplate; they have no spot; they live in God and of himself; they shine brighter than a thousand suns; they are beloved by the Son of God; they are the darlings of God the Father; and elect spouses of the Holy Ghost.

By three signs is a mind that is purged to be known, as St. Thomas says in a treatise of his: The first sign is diligence, which is a strength of mind that banishes all neglect and sloth, that it may be disposed with earnestness and confidence to the pursuit of virtue. The second is severity, which likewise is a strength of mind against concupiscence, accompanied with an ardent love of deprivation, lack of comforts, and holy poverty. The third is benignity and sweetness of mind, which drives away all rancour, envy, aversion, and hatred against one's neighbor.

Till the mind be purged, the affection purified, the memory naked, the understanding brightened, the will denied and set afire, the soul can never arrive at the intimate and affective union with God; and, therefore, because the spirit of God is purity itself, and light and rest, the soul (where he intends to make his abode) must have great purity, peace, attention, and quiet. Finally, the precious gift of a purged mind those only have who with continual diligence seek, love, and retain it, and desire to be reputed the most vile in the world.

Simon Patrick

(1626-1707)

INFLUENCED by the Cambridge Platonists, especially John Smith, Patrick was first ordained as a Presbyterian minister, but accepted ordination in the Church of England in 1654. Chaplain to the king, bishop of Chichester and later of Ely, Patrick became one of the most voluminous writers of the Church of England. Altogether he wrote fifty-one books, the most weighty and popular being his ten-volume commentary—with William Lowth—on the Old Testament. For 150 years it was considered the classic commentary in the English language. He was also a founder of the Society for the Promotion of Christian Knowledge. His prayers show the deep saintly side of this erudite churchman.

[PRAYERS]

A PRAYER FOR PATIENCE

O Father of Mercies, and God of all comforts; who to all thy other benefits wherewith thou continually loadest us, hast bestowed upon us the gospel of thy grace: that we through patience and comfort of the holy Scriptures might have hope: accept of the humble and thankful acknowledgments which I make to thy divine goodness, for this riches of mercy in Christ Jesus: who was pleased for our sake to humble himself to death, even the death of the cross; and with great patience to suffer the sharpest pains and agonies, with many reproaches and contradictions of sinners. And when he was opprest, and afflicted, and blasphemed, yet silently endured: being brought as a lamb to the slaughter, and as a sheep before the shearer is dumb, so opened he not his mouth. I praise and magnify with all my soul his wonderful love to us, and his perfect subjection to thee: beseeching thee to fix in my heart such an ardent love to his blessed memory, and such an high admiration of his glorious example, that I may be inspired thereby with Christian resolution to follow after him in all the paths of humble, meek, and patient virtue. O that I may feel myself prest by the mighty poser of that love, not only to be a doer of thy will, but for conscience toward thee, my God, to endure grief, suffering wrongfully; and to run with patience the whole race that is set before us: looking unto Jesus, the author and finisher of our faith, who for the joy that was set before him, endured the cross, despising the shame, and is set down at the right hand of the throne of God. Preserve in me such a reverence toward thee, the Father of Spirits, that I may neither despise nor faint under thy corrections: But tho thou bringest me into great and sore troubles, I may still be in subjection to thee, and live in hope of that immortal glory. And not only so, but I may rejoice, and glory also in tribulations for Christ's sake, knowing that tribulation worketh patience; and patience, experience; and experience, hope; and hope maketh not ashamed.

And whatsoever the cross be, which lies in my way to heaven, O that I may never turn aside, in the least, from thee to avoid it: but take it up willingly, and bear it as long as thou pleasest; without murmuring or repining, and with some courage and cheerfulness of spirit. And as for the common miseries of this life, endue my spirit with such principles of wisdom, and help me to preserve it in such innocence, clearness and integrity, that it may be able to sustain my infirmity; and whatsoever sicknesses, or pains, or other bodily calamities befall me, I may receive them and bear them with an equal and constant mind: knowing that as we receive good from thy hand, we ought in reason to receive evil; and in every thing to give thanks, which is thy will concerning us in Christ Jesus.

O blessed Lord, lead me whither thou pleasest, I will follow thee without complaint. I submit to thy orders: I reverence thy wisdom: I trust myself with thy goodness; I depend upon thy almighty power: I rely on thy promises; beseeching thee to support me, till patience having its perfect working in me, I may be perfect, and entire, wanting nothing. I know the time is but short, and that thou hast prepared long joys to recompense our momentary sorrows; help me therefore always to possess my soul in patience at present (giving thanks for the hope we have as an anchor of the soul both sure and stedfast) that so I may at last, after I have done thy will, O God, inherit the promise. Amen.

A Prayer for Resignation to God's Will, and Perfect Contentment of Mind

O Lord, the Almighty Creator of the world, the most wise Governor of all things which thou hast made, and our most gracious and loving Father in the Lord Jesus; by whom thou hast abundantly declared thy good-will to sinners, being desirous not only to receive them again into thy favor, but to bestow greater blessing on them than they could have challenged from thee, if they had remained in innocence, and never offended thee. Thou designest us to no less happiness than eternal life; and hast laid the strongest obligations on us to mind our own welfare, having made our happiness so sure that if we love ourselves, and will attend at all to our own good and satisfaction, we can not be miserable. I acknowledge, O Lord, with all thankfulness this thy tender mercy, in ordering all things so by thy Son Jesus, that we can not without the greatest negligence and inconsideration, and without a manifest force and contradiction to our own understanding, ruin and undo our immortal souls. How much do I owe thee that thou hast been pleased to call me to the knowledge of thy grace; that thou hast invited me by such precious promises; drawn me so often and so powerfully by the motions of thy Holy Spirit; and marvelously disposed and provoked me by many happy providences, only to do myself good, and seek my own eternal felicity. I see, O Lord, the strangeness and unusualness of thy love: and am ashamed of my own backwardness and untowardness of spirit; that after all this I have so little mind to be happy, and am no more serious about that which so infinitely concerns me, and by thy grace is made so easy to me. Be still so gracious, I most humbly beseech thee, as to touch my heart with such a lively sense of thy wonderful goodness, as may perfectly subdue me to thy love and obedience; and make me absolutely surrender both soul and body to thee, of whose care and kindness I am so abundantly assured. O that I may know more feelingly what a satisfaction it is to be blessed of the Lord, which made heaven and earth; to wait for thy salvation in Christ Jesus; to have thy Holy Spirit for my guide and comforter; and to be secure of thy good providence here, and to live in hope of immortal glory hereafter. Strengthen me with might by thy Spirit in the inner man, that I may be able to comprehend what is the breadth, and length, and depth, and height, and to know the love of Christ which passeth knowledge, till I be filled with all the fulness of thee, my God. That being full of divine wisdom and knowledge, full of faith, and love, and hope, and all the fruits of righteousness, there may be no room for any trouble or disquiet in my heart: but with an equal mind and resigned will I may pass through all the changes and chances of this mortal life. I have frequently offered up and devoted myself unto thee; and here again I renew the surrender, delivering up soul and body entirely to do and suffer thy holy will and pleasure. O preserve in my mind such an high esteem of thy infinite wisdom and goodness that I may ever cheerfully commit myself and all I have into thy hands, to be disposed of as thou judgest most meet and convenient. And whatsoever thou art pleased to order for my portion, Lord, help me to be perfectly contented and well pleased with it, believing it to be the result of thine infinite understanding, and of thy fatherly care and tender mercy; and looking at those unseen enjoyments to which thou knowest best by what ways to conduct and lead me, all the time of my sojourning here in this world. Lift up my thoughts still higher and higher toward that holy place where the Lord Jesus is enthroned. Fix my mind stedfastly on that bliss, which he is gone to prepare for us; that I may feel it drawing my heart after him to follow his great example; and not only satisfying me in all conditions of life, but filling me with joy in believing, with joy unspeakable and full of glory. Unto thee, O Lord Jesus, I commend myself. I trust thee with my health, my estate, my friends, and all I have. Allot what thou pleasest for us. Let it be unto us according to thy will. Not our will, but thy will be done. Amen.

A PRAYER FOR COURAGE IN THE PROFESSION OF CHRISTIANITY

O Lord of heaven and earth, who art everywhere the rest and peace, the refuge and security, the strength, help and salvation of all those who repose an holy trust and confidence in thee; for nothing, not death itself, can separate them from thee. I adore thy infinite love, which hath assumed our nature to such a nearness to thy own, and raised the Lord Jesus from the dead, and given him glory at thy right hand; that all his faithful followers might rest assured of thy eternal care of them, and that they shall never perish, but have everlasting life. Blessed, blessed be thy name for this glad tidings of great joy which raises our spirits above this world, and places them in quietness and safety amidst all the troubles and dangers of this life. I stand infinitely indebted to thee for this revelation thou hast made of thy good will to us in Christ Jesus, and for the glorious example that he hath set us: who before Pontius Pilate witnessed a good confession, and sealed thy truth with his blood, knowing that his flesh should rest in hope, and that thou wouldst not suffer thy Holy One to see corruption. O that I may feel myself enlivened with the same spirit which was in our Head, the Captain of our Salvation, made perfect through sufferings, being faithful to him to the very death, and not doubting I shall receive a crown of life. It is but reason that I should part with all I have for him, and his righteousness; who hath made himself so freely a sacrifice of inestimable value and efficiency for us sinners. O that I could do that cheerfully, which I am bound to do in duty; being strengthened with all might according to his glorious power, unto all patience and long-suffering with joyfulness; giving thanks to thee who hast made us meet to be partakers of the inheritance of the saints in light. It is a faithful saying, I know, that if we be dead with him, we shall also live with him: if we suffer, we shall also reign with him: if we deny him, he will also deny us. Defend me, O God, from so foul a wickedness as the thought of denying my Lord and Master, and his holy truth: but keep me by thy power through faith unto salvation; that the trial of my faith, being much more precious than of gold that perisheth, tho it be tried with fire, may be found unto praise and honor and glory at the appearing of Jesus Christ. Settle, confirm and strengthen me in the Christian faith; that a stedfast belief of thy precious promises, a lively hope in thee through the resurrection of the Lord Jesus, may not only bear me up with constancy and patience, under shame, reproaches, loss of liberty and goods; but inspire me with courage and undaunted resolution in all dangers, even in death itself. Fill and greaten my mind with such a powerful sense of those immortal joys that nothing may appear so dreadful here as to terrify me from my duty, or turn me aside from the paths of righteousness, charity, truth and piety: but suffering according to thy will, O God, I may commit the keeping of my soul to thee in well doing as unto a faithful Creator. And endue me, I beseech thee, with such a perfect love to my Lord and Master Christ Jesus, as may cast out all base fear of suffering. Fortify my heart with such a zealous affection to his religion, that I may not be terrified by any adversaries, nor afraid of their threats, neither be troubled: but sanctify thee, the Lord God, in my heart, not fearing those that can kill the body, but thee who canst destroy both soul and body in hell.

Regard, O Lord, the supplications of thy servant, who here hath made an oblation of himself wholly unto thee. And endue me with Christian prudence as well as courage; that I may be both as wise as a serpent, and as innocent as a dove; and never dishonor my religion either by rashness or by cowardice: but with a discreet zeal cleave unto truth and righteousness, saying boldly, The Lord is my helper, and I will not fear what man shall do unto me. In God have I put my trust, therefore shall I never be confounded. Amen.

John Norris

(1657-1711)

NORRIS is representative of the type of clergyman in the Church of England in his era who possessed a sound philosophic basis for his theological thinking. He was a student and a fellow at Oxford, and for the last twenty years of his life rector of Bemerton, a parish once served by George Herbert, the poet. Influenced by Plato and Malebranche, Norris' writings show a blending of religion and philosophy. This appears in the excerpts below.

[CONTEMPLATIONS OF GOD AND MAN]

From *Reason and Religion*

PART I. INTRODUCTION

*B*y devotion here I do not meerly understand that special disposition or act of the soul, whereby we warmly and passionately address ourselves to God in prayer (which is what is commonly meant by devotion); but I use the word in a greater latitude, so as to comprehend under it faith, hope, love, fear, trust, humility, submission, honour, reverence, adoration, thanksgiving, in a word, all that duty which we owe to God. Nor by this acceptation do I stretch the word beyond what either from its rise it may or, by frequent use among the learned, it does signifie. Devotion is *a devovendo*, from devoting, or giving up one's self wholly to the service of another. And accordingly those among the heathens who deliver'd and consign'd themselves up to death, for the safety of their country, were called *devoti*. And so in like manner for a man to give up himself wholly and intirely to the service of God, and actually to demean himself towards him in the conduct of his life, as becomes a creature towards his Creator, is devotion.

To shew how much contemplation serves to the advantage of devotion, we need only consider that devotion is an act of the will, that the object of the will is good apparent, or good understood, and consequently that every act of the will is influenc'd and regulated by consideration. Devotion therefore is as much influenc'd by consideration as any other act of the will is.

I deny not but that knowledge and devotion often go assunder, and the wisest are not always the devoutest. But then this is not owing to the natural and direct influence of knowledge, but comes to pass only occasionally and accidentally, by reason of some other impediment: suppose pride, lust, covetousness, or some such disposition of mind, which is of more force and prevalency to let our devotion, than knowledge is to further it. And then no wonder that the heavier scale weighs down. But still knowledge has a natural aptness to excite devotion, and will infallibly do it if not hinder'd by some other cause. So that we may take this for a never-failing rule, That all other things being equal, the more knowing and considering, still the more devout. And in this sense also that of the psalmist will be verifi'd, while I was musing the fire kindled.

Contemplation I. Of the General Idea of God

O thou whose name is Jehovah, who art the very essence of being, who art being itself, how can I ever sufficiently love, fear, reverence and adore thee! Thou art above all the affections of my heart, all the motions of my will, yea and all the conceptions of my understanding. No sooner do I begin to think of thee, but I am plunged beyond my depth, my thoughts are all swallow'd up and overwhelm'd in their first approach to thy essence, and I shall sooner lose myself than find thee.

O dreadful Excellence, I tremble to think of thy essence, my soul turns herself from thee, she cannot look forward, she pants, she burns, she languishes, is beaten back with the light of thy glories, and returns to the familiarity of her own darkness, not because she chuses it, but because she is weary.

O soveraign Greatness, how am I impoverish'd, how am I contracted, how am I annihilated in thy presence. Thou only art, I am not, thou art all, I am nothing. But 'tis well, O my God, that I am nothing, so thou art all; 'tis well I am not in myself, so I am in thee.

O Being itself, 'tis in thee that I live, move, and have my being. Out of thee I am nothing. I have nothing, I can do nothing. I am but little and inconsiderable with thee, and what then should I be without thee? To thee therefore I devote and dedicate my whole self, for I am wholly thine. I will ever live to thee, since I must ever live in thee. And Oh let my beloved be ever mine, as I am, and ever will be his. Amen.

Contemplation II. That God Is a Being Absolutely Perfect Proved from the Preceding General Idea of God

My Lord and my God, with what awful apprehensions do I contemplate thy perfections! How am I struck, dazled, and confounded with the light of thy glories! Thy being standeth like the strong mountains, and thy perfections are like the great deep. How can I think of thee without wonder and astonishment, and how can I think of anything else but thee!

O thou circle of excellency, thou endless orb of perfection, where shall I begin to love thee? Thou art altogether lovely; oh that I were also altogether love. My God, I desire nothing but to love thee, and to be loved by thee. Thou art all fair, my love, there is no spot in thee. My beloved is light, and in him is no darkness at all; Let him therefore kiss me with the kisses of his mouth, for his love is better than wine.

My great God, how do I despise myself and the whole creation when I once think upon thee! Whom have I in heaven but thee, and there is none upon earth that I desire in comparison of thee. Thou alone dost so fill my thoughts so ravish my affections, that I can contemplate nothing but thee, I can admire nothing but thee, and I can love nothing but thee. Nor do I think my soul straiten'd in being confined to thee, for thou, O my God, art all.

O my God, I have lookt for thee in holiness, that I might behold this thy power and thy glory. I can now see it but in a glass darkly, but thou hast told us that those who are pure in heart shall hereafter see thee face to face. Grant therefore I may so love, fear, and serve thee here, that I may behold thee, and enjoy thee, as thou art in thy infinite self, for ever hereafter. Amen.

Contemplation III. That Therefore All the Perfections of Particular Beings Exist in God, and that After a More Excellent Manner Than They Do in Particular Beings Themselves

No, my fair Delight, I will never be drawn off from the love of thee by the charms of any of thy creatures. Thou art not only infinitely more excellent than they, but hast their very excellencies in a more perfect manner than they have or can have. What temptation then can I have to leave thee? No, O my fairest, I want temptation to recommend my love to thee. 'Tis too easie and too cheap a fidelity to adhere to thee, my first love, when by changing I can gain no more.

Thou, O Soveraign fair, hast adorn'd thy creation with a tincture of thy brightness, thou hast shin'd upon it with the light of thy divine glory, and hast pour'd forth thy beauty upon all thy works. But they are not fair as thou art fair, their beauty is not as thy beauty. Thou art fairer, O my God, than the children of men, or the orders of angels, and the arrows of thy love are sharper than theirs. They are indeed, my God, thy arrows are very sharp, and were we not too securely fenc'd about with our thick houses of clay, would wound us deeper than the keenest charms of any created beauties. But these every day wound us, while we stand proof against thy divine artillery, because these are sensible, and thine only intelligible; these are visible to our eyes, thine only to our minds, which we seldom convert to the contemplation of thy beauties.

But, O thou infinite fair, did we but once taste and see, did we but contemplate thy original beauty, as we do those faint images of it that are reflected up and down among our fellow creatures, as thy charms infinitely exceed theirs, so would our love to thee be wonderful, passing the love of women.

Contemplation IV. Of the Attributes of God in General; Particularly of the Unity of God: Which Is Proved from His Idea

O thou mighty One-all, who art too great to be multiplied, and yet too full not to be communicated, what a greatness, what a fulness is this of thine! O rich solitude, how unlike is all created excellence to thine! Other things are to be admired for their numbers, thou for thy oneness and singularity, they glory in their multitudes, but 'tis the prerogative of thy perfection to be alone.

In thee, my only centre, I rest, upon thee I wholly depend, for I have none in heaven but thee, and none upon earth in comparison of thee. I utterly renounce therefore all absolute power and supremacy besides thine, and I will fear none but thee, and obey none but thee. Thou only shalt have dominion over me, I am only thine, and thee only will I serve.

Many, O God, are the beauties which thou hast made, and thy whole creation is fill'd with thy glory. There are threescore queens, and fourscore concubines, and virgins without number; but my love, my undefiled, is but one. Take then to thyself the empire of my heart. For all that deserves the name of love there shall be thine. O that it were more inlarged for thy reception; but thou shalt have it all, and I will love thee with my whole heart, though that whole be but little.

O my only delight, other gods besides thee, and other lords besides thee, have often usurp'd a dominion over me. But my heart is now fix'd O God, my heart is fix'd. It is fix'd upon thee, and how can it ever wander out of the sphere of thy beauty! Or what beauty is there whose influence may vye with thine? Or how can I love any but one, when that one, and none but that one, is infinitely lovely.

Contemplation V. Of the Omniscience and Omnipresence of God

Do thou then, O my God, so imprint the sense of this thy omniscience and omnipresence upon every faculty and power of my soul, that I may ever think, speak, and act as in the light of thy all-seeing eye, and as immediately surrounded, and intimately possessed with the glory of thy presence. O fill me with the profoundest awe and reverence, compose my levities, confirm my doubtfulness, and fix my wandrings, and make me ever satisfied with the methods of thy wise providence.

And when by the meditation of this thy knowledge and presence, I shall learn to demean myself in any measure as I ought; grant that upon the same consideration I may content myself with thy divine approbation and allowance, whatever I am thought of in man's judgment. Finally, O my God, grant I may so set thee before me here, that I may not be afraid to appear before thee hereafter. Amen.

Contemplation VI. Of the Omnipotence of God

With thee, O my god, is power and strength, and with thee ought to be dominion and fear. My flesh trembles for fear of thee: and I am afraid of thy judgments. Thou art terrible, O my God, as well as lovely, but thou art also lovely in thy very terrour. Turn away thine eyes from me, for they have overcome me; they have overcome me with their dread, as well as with their beauty; for, as thou art beautiful, O my love, as Tirzah, comely, as Jerusalem; so art thou also terrible, as an army with banners.

O my Omnipotent Love, with what safety, as well as delight, do I sit under thy banquetting-house, and thy banner over me is power as well as love. Thy love is stronger than death; what need I fear, thy left hand is under my head, and thy right hand does imbrace me; and why then should any dread approach me? The Lord is my light and my salvation, whom then shall I fear? He is the strength of my life, of whom then should I be afraid.

O my God, why is not my faith like thy power? Thou canst do all things; and why is my faith limited? Let me imitate thee, O my God, in this thy infinity: and grant me such a victorious, such an omnipotent faith, that, as to thee nothing is too hard to do, so to me nothing may be too hard to believe. Amen.

Contemplation VII. Of the Divine Justice and Veracity

My God, my Judge, who art righteous in all thy ways, and holy in all thy works, I delight to think of thee, tho' I am too guilty to contemplate thee, in this thy attribute, without fear and trembling. For there is judgment as well as mercy with thee that thou shouldst be fear'd. O enter not into judgment with thy servant, for in thy sight shall no man living be justify'd.

My God, how strangely impious are they who dare say or think that the way of the Lord is not equal! My God, I am none of those, nor will I ever be of that profane number. I will ever acquiesce in the equity of thy dispensations, whether I am able to comprehend it or no. For I know tho' clouds and darkness may sometimes be round about thee, yet righteousness and judgment are always the habitation of thy seat.

I readily and firmly assent, O my God, to all the declarations thou hast made of thy mind and will. I believe all thy predictions, all thy promises, and all thy threatenings, that they shall be fulfill'd all in their season. I know that nothing but truth can proceed from thee who art truth itself; I know that, O God, can'st not deceive us, O Grant that we may not deceive ourselves. Amen.

Contemplation VIII. Of the Divine Goodness and Philanthropy

O my great and good God, who art good in all thy greatness, and whose chiefest greatness is to be good, how can I possibly think amiss of thee, distrust thee, or harbour any jealous apprehensions concerning thee? And how unworthy should I be of this thy goodness if I should!

But, O God, my love, 'tis my infirmity to be afraid of that excellence which I should rather love, for my love of thee is not yet perfect enough to cast out all fear; but blessed be thy goodness, who in the midst of my fears and doubtful surmises art pleased to remind me of thy nature, and to say to my soul, as thou didst once to the diffident disciples, It is I, be not afraid.

The voice of my beloved! I will therefore turn my fears to love, and love more than I ever yet feared or loved. I will also magnifie thee, O God, my King: and I will praise thy name for ever and ever. Every day will I give thanks unto thee: and praise thy name for ever and ever. For I have tasted and seen how gracious thou art, and I find it is a good thing to praise thee: and that 'tis a joyful and pleasant thing to be thankful. I know, O my God, that thy goodness is as much above my praise as thy greatness is above my comprehension. My praises can add nothing to thee, neither can I praise thee according to the goodness. But, O, my God, I will praise thee according to my strength, and I know that the same goodness of thine, which is too great to be praised worthily, is also too great not to accept our unworthy praises.

My God, I know thou requirest from me only the praises of a man, but I am troubled that I cannot praise thee as an angel. O that I were now in heaven, if 'twere only that I might praise thee as thy angels praise thee: this, O my God, I will do hereafter, my gratitude shall run then as high as theirs, and it shall be lasting too; it shall last as long as thy goodness and my being lasts; and as thy mercy, so my praise shall endure for ever.

PART II. WHEREIN THE GROUNDS AND MEASURES OF DEVOTION ARE CONSIDER'D FROM THE NATURE OF MAN

Contemplation I. Of Man, Consider'd as a Creature

My God, my Creator, how can I be ever sufficiently humble, when I consider that I once was not; when I consider that even thou with all thy omnipotence can'st not reduce me to a lower degree of nothing than that from whence thou took'st me! When I consider that I still so depend upon thee, that I cannot subsist one moment without thee! What a vanity, what a shadow, what a nothing then am I, who once was not, and now am only because thou art, and can no longer stand in being than supported by the arm of thy power!

O my God, I know not whether of the two I ought more to adore and magnifie, either that power that could raise me from nothing, to be what I am, or that goodness which could determine that power to so strange and wonderful a production. One deep, O my God, calleth upon another, and my thoughts are all lost, and swallow'd up in both.

Praise and adoration to be to thee, O my great and good God for 'twas from thy power and goodness that I receiv'd my being. Thou art he that took me out of my mother's womb, and thou also wast my hope when I hanged yet upon my mother's breast. I have been also left unto thee ever since I was born: thou art my God even from my mother's womb. My soul still hangeth upon thee: thy right hand does uphold me. Thou holdest my soul in life, and sufferest not my feet to slip.

To thee then, O Father of spirits, I give up and devote my whole self, for I am intirely from thee, intirely by thee, and therefore intirely thine. How then can I ever offend thee, or rebel against thee, with those powers which thou hast given me, and dost still uphold and maintain in me! My God, I will not, but as thou art he whose I am, so thou shalt be he whom I will ever serve. Free me therefore, O God, from my passions, and make me but once my own, and I will then ever be thine. Amen.

Contemplation II. Of Man, Consider'd as an Intelligent Creature

My God, my Light, what is man that thou art mindful of him, and the son of man that thou so regardest him? But much more, what is man that he should so regard himself? that he should regard himself for that which is least of all his own, his knowledge and wisdom? For, O God, we are not a light to ourselves, but 'tis thou, O God, art our light, and in thy light do we see light.

O my wonderful counsellour, with what humility and poverty of spirit ought I to reflect upon the richest endowments of my mind since I see only by thy light, and depend upon thee for what I know, as much as for what I am: and how unworthy should I be of thy divine light, should I be puffed up through the abundance of this thy revelation.

Not unto me therefore, O my God, my Light, not unto me, but to thy greatness and goodness be the praise and the glory. For 'tis thy word, thy eternal word, that is a lantern unto my feet, and a light unto my paths. The Lord is my light and my salvation, and it is he that teacheth man knowledge. I will therefore thank the Lord for giving me warning, my reins also chasten me in the night-season.

Lighten my darkness then, I beseech, O Father of lights, and shine upon me more and more with the brightness of thy glory. O send out thy light and thy truth, that they may lead me, and bring me unto thy holy hill, and to thy dwelling.

Shew the light of thy countenance upon thy servant, and teach me thy statutes. O let the angel of thy presence go always before me in this my pilgrimage, and grant that I may always attend and give heed to his counsel and direction, that so walking in thy light here, I may forever live and forever rejoyce in the full and open light of thy countenance hereafter. Amen.

Contemplation III. Of Man, Consider'd as an Amorous Creature

My God, my Love, how absurd a thing it is that an amorous creature should be a proud creature! My love is occasion'd by my indigence, and I cannot love but I am minded of that indigence; how ill then would pride become me, having so much reason to be humble, and that reason so continually set before me!

Divine Fountain of love, 'tis from thee I receive all my love, and upon whom should I place it but upon thee? The fire that descends from heaven, where should it be spent but upon the altar? Thou hast a right, O my God to all my love, for I cannot love thee with any love but what is thy own. O then do thou regulate this thy own divine impression, and grant I may never sin against thee by the abuse of that love which thou hast given me. I thank thee, O Father, Lord of heaven and earth, for doing so much towards the guidance and regulation of my love as to carry me directly only to universal good, thereby teaching me, that I ought to make thee the only direct and primary object of my love. My God, I will love as thou teachest me, the first and direct motion of love shall be towards thee, and whatever I love besides thee, I will love only in and for thee.

I thank thee also, my God, for that thou hast made it so necessary for me to love universal good. Thou, O God, art this universal good, and I ought to love thee with the very same love wherewith I love happiness itself. O that I were as necessarily inclined to love thee as I am to love happiness! I do not desire to be trusted with any liberty in the love of thee. But this, my God, I cannot hope for, till I shall see thee as thou art. O let me therefore love thee to the utmost capacity of a free creature. Thou, O God, hast set no bounds to my love of thee, O let not me set any. My God, I do not, I love thee with all my heart, soul, mind and strength. Lord thou knowest all things, thou knowest that I love thee.

Contemplation IV. Of Man, Consider'd as an Irregular Lover

To thee, O my God, belongs praise and adoration for endowing me with those excellent powers of understanding and love, but to me shame and confusion of face, for misapplying the one and not attending to the dictates of the other.

I blush, O my God, and am ashamed to think that my nature should stand so much inclined to irregular love, a thing so full of mischief and folly, but much more that I myself should bring myself into such a state of impotence and depravation. My heart sheweth me the great foulness and abominableness of sin, and yet I find myself over prone to commit it. So foolish am I and ignorant, and even as a beast before thee.

But I desire, O my God, to be yet more vile. I am not vile enough in my own eyes, thou too much so in thine. Nor can I ever be vile enough in my opinion, for being so vile in my nature. Strike me then I beseech thee with a deep and with a lively sense of my own wretchedness, and make me as humble as I am wicked.

And since, through the infirmity of my flesh, I am so apt to err in the conduct and application of my love, O hold thou up my goings in thy paths, that my footsteps slip not. Make me always to attend to that divine light of thine within my breast, and let the victorious sweetness of thy grace outcharm all the relishes of sensible good. But above all keep thy servant from presumptuous sins, lest they get the dominion over me. And let all these words of my mouth, and this whole meditation of my heart be always acceptable in thy sight, O Lord, my strength and my redeemer. Amen.

François Fénelon

(1651-1715)

THE quietistic movement in France developed into a "fashionable" experience for the well-to-do. Among those who kept the quietistic movement sincere was Madame Guyon, and among her most ardent followers was Fénelon. He was archbishop of Cambrai and upheld Madame Guyon's stress on mysticism in his own book *Maxims of the Saints*. Pope Innocent XII condemned it. Fénelon, however, remained an ardent churchman all his life. He bitterly opposed Jansenism, which was an attempt to revive the teaching of Augustine. He also fought Jacques Bossuet, who labored to reconcile Protestantism to Catholicism in France.

Pietistic in spirit, Fénelon shows in his writings the deep devotional side of his life. This aspect is well portrayed in the selections which follow.

ON PRAYER AND MEDITATION

You ask to be taught how to pray, and how to seek union with God, so as to be sustained against life's temptations, and I am sure you greatly desire to find the help you need in this holy practice. I think you cannot treat God with too much confidence. Tell Him all that is in your heart, as one unloads one's heart to a dear friend of all that gives it pain or pleasure. Tell Him your troubles, that He may comfort you; tell Him your joys, that He may sober them; tell Him your longings, that He may purify them; tell Him your mislikings, that He may help you to conquer them; talk to Him of your temptations, that He may shield you from them; show Him all the wounds of your heart, that He may heal them. Lay bare to Him your indifference to good, your depraved tastes for evil, your dissipation, your instability, your leanings to a corrupt world. Tell Him how self-love disposes you to be unjust to your neighbours, how vanity tempts you to be insincere, and to dazzle those with whom you are concerned; how your pride disguises you to yourself as well as to others. If you thus pour out to Him all your weakness, needs, and troubles, there will be no lack of what to say; you will never exhaust this subject, it is continually being renewed. People who have no secrets from each other never want subjects of conversation; they do not premeditate or weigh their words, because there is nothing to be kept back. Neither do they seek for something to say; they talk together out of the abundance of their heart—without consideration, just what they think. The heart of each speaks to the other; they pour out, so to say, one into another. Blessed are they who attain to such familiar, unreserved intercourse with God!

In proportion as you talk to Him He will talk to you; and often you should be silent and let Him speak, so that you may listen in the stillness of your heart. Say, "Speak, Lord, for Thy servant heareth;" and "I will hearken what the Lord will say concerning me." Add with a loving, dutiful mind, "Lord, think no scorn of me." The Spirit of Truth will teach you inwardly all that Jesus Christ teaches you outwardly in the Gospel. This is no extraordinary inspiration in which you need fear delusion; it will only inspire you with the virtues suited to your condition and the ways of dying to yourself that you may live to God. It is an inward voice, which teaches us as we have need from time to time.

God is the True Friend who always gives us the counsel and comfort we need. Our danger lies in resisting Him; so it is essential that we get a habit of hearkening to His Voice, of keeping silence within, and listening so as to lose nothing of what He says to us. We know well enough how to keep outward silence and to hush our spoken words; but we know little of interior silence. It lies in hushing our idle, restless, wandering imagination, in quieting the promptings of our worldly minds, and in suppressing the crowd of unprofitable thoughts which excite and disturb the soul. In prayer we should confine ourselves to simple affections and few points, on which it is better to dwell rather with love than argumentatively. Head-work tires, disgusts, exhausts us; but acquiescence of mind and union of the heart do not weary us in the same way. The spirit of faith and love never stanches so long as we do not forsake the source.

But, as you will say, I am not master over my own imagination, which wanders, gets excited, and disturbs me; my mind becomes distracted, and carries me away in spite of myself to ever so many dangerous, or at best unprofitable, subjects. I am accustomed to argue; my mental inquisitiveness predominates. I get worried directly that I try to resist it; this worry in itself is no less a distraction than the things which excite my curiosity. During all this my meditation slips away, and I spend the whole time in being conscious that I am not making way.

I answer that it is with the heart that we pray, and that a sincere and persevering will to pray is true prayer. Really involuntary distractions do not hinder the will from reaching forth to God. There is still always a certain element of prayer which the schoolmen call virtual intention. Every time one discovers one's distraction it is put aside and we return to God, resuming the subject of meditation; so that, beyond the original element of prayer, which exists even in seasons of distraction like fire hidden beneath ashes, a half unconscious search after God, one further excites in one's self, directly on perceiving the distraction, lively and clear affections on the truths which recur to one. So the time is not lost. If you will try it patiently, you will find that there are seasons of prayer which, though spent amid distractions and tediousness, are yet, owing to a good intention, fruitful to the heart, strengthening it against all temptation.

Dry prayer, provided it be perseveringly and faithfully kept up, accustoms the soul to carry its cross, hardens it against itself, humbles it, and practises it in the dark paths of faith. If we always enjoyed a bright, fervent, sensibly attractive prayer, we should feed all our lives on milk, instead of eating hard, dry bread we should only look for sensible enjoyment instead of abnegation and death; we should be like those of whom Jesus Christ said reproachfully that they followed Him, not for His doctrine, but for the loaves which He multiplied. So do not be discouraged though your prayer seems to you dry, lifeless, and hindered by distractions. Be patient, then, in prayer, for God's sake, and go on without stopping; you will be sure to make great way. But do not struggle directly with your distractions; the very struggle itself becomes a worse distraction. The best way is to let them drop, and quietly replace yourself mentally before God. The more agitated you get, the more you will excite your imagination, which will harass you persistently. On the contrary, the quieter you are, merely turning back to the subject of your meditation, the more you will attain to that inward occupation with heavenly things which is your aim. You might spend your whole time fighting the gnats which hum about you; let them buzz in your ears, but meanwhile accustom yourself to go on with your work as though they did not exist.

As to the subject of your meditations, take such passages of the Gospel or of the Imitation of Jesus Christ as move you most. Read slowly, and when a passage touches you, use it as you would a sweetmeat, which you hold in your mouth till it melts. Let the meaning sink slowly into your heart, and do not pass on to something else until you feel that to be exhausted. Thus you will spend a full quarter of an hour in meditation almost unconsciously; and if you manage your time so as to do this twice in the day, it will give you half an hour of meditation. You will do it easily if you do not try to do too much, or seek too much to see results. Trust God simply, like a child, in telling Him whatever comes into your mind. The thing is to open your heart to God, to make it familiar with Him, to strengthen it with love. Carefully fostered love enlightens, amends, corrects, encourages.

As to your occupations, they should be divided between duty and amusement. I count all attentions paid to your generals and chief officers to whom they are due among duties; those should be performed during the hours reserved for society. Beyond these you must have some private intercourse with a small number of real friends who feel with and serve God with you, or at all events do not lead you from Him. They should be suitable to you in position and worth. Besides religious reading, you should read history, and other books calculated to cultivate your mind, whether on military or other topics in which you are interested. I should say that one of your principal occupations ought to be to see all the workings of the army, and discuss them with clever and experienced men. You should seek out such, and treat them with deference, with a view to your own improvement. As to mere idle reading, which does not strengthen the mind, I should retrench it directly that you find it excites you. A wise man gives up wine if it intoxicates him. At most, I should only indulge in such amusement, which is unduly honoured with the name of study, as one might play a game of chess after dinner. The main thing is to nurture the spark of grace in your heart. Put aside whatever can extinguish it; seek all that will fan it. Be vigorous in your efforts. "The kingdom of heaven suffereth violence, and the violent take it by force." Dwell upon the Mercy of God, and His Patience towards you. "Knowest thou not that the Goodness of God leadeth to repentance?" There is no day that I do not pray for you. God knows how devoted I am to you for life.

HUMILITY

The Saints have all agreed that true humility is the groundwork of every virtue, and that because it is the offspring of pure love, and because humility is truth itself. There are but two real truths—the Almightiness of God and the nothingness of us His creatures; and if humility is real, it will make us pay continual homage to God through our lowliness, abiding in our proper place, content to be nought. Jesus Christ bids us be meek and lowly of heart; meekness is the child of humility, as anger of pride. Jesus Christ alone can give us this His Own true humility of heart. It comes from His Grace; it does not consist, as some imagine, in external deeds of humility, however excellent these may be in their proper season, but in simply abiding where God has placed us. He who imagines himself to be something is not truly humble; neither is he who seeks anything for himself. But he who so entirely forgets himself that his thoughts do not recur to self or self-seeking; who is lowly within, never offended at anything, though not affecting outward tokens of patience; who speaks of himself as he would of another; who does not pretend to ignore himself while really bursting with self-consciousness; who gives himself up for love's sake, without considering whether to do so looks like pride or humility; who is content to be thought deficient in humility—in short, he who is full of love, such an one is truly humble. He who does not seek his own interest, but solely God's interest in time and eternity, he is humble. The purer his love, the more perfect his humility. Do not test humility by external appearances, by this or the other action, but solely by love. Pure love strips self from off a man, and clothes him with Jesus Christ, so that "it is no more I that live, but Christ that liveth in me."

Men are always seeking to be some great thing, to be conspicuous in religion as of old in things of the world, which now they have forsaken. Why? Because they crave distinction under all circumstances. But the humble man seeks no distinction; praise or blame are alike to him. Wherever his lot is cast, therein he abides; it does not occur to him to seek for anything different. Many people study exterior humility who are a long way off this sort of heartfelt humbleness; yet exterior humility which does not flow from love is spurious. The more it stoops, the loftier it inwardly feels itself; but he who is conscious of stooping does not really feel himself to be so low that he can go no further. People who think much of their humility are very proud, and all such unreal stooping is a subtle search how to go up higher. There will be none of this sort of humility in Heaven. It must give place to simple love, which alone is worthy of God, and into which alone He deigns to pour Himself. They who are full of Him cannot consciously humble or lower themselves, for they feel beneath all possible abasement. They are not hurt or humbled by any contempt or blame of men, neither are they exalted by any praise they may receive. They believe that no one ever humbled himself below what he really is save the Word in His Incarnation; therefore Holy Scripture says of Him that He "emptied" Himself, which it says of no earthly creature.

Many men deceive themselves herein; seeking to be humble by an effort of will, and failing in perfect resignation and self-renunciation, they sin against Divine Love, without which there is no humility. Fuller light would enable them to see that they are exalting themselves by that which they mean for humility; their supposed setting aside of self is self-seeking; they are puffed up with the pride of humility, and glory in the humble acts they perform. But the really humble man does not do anything of the sort: he lets himself be carried hither and thither; he is satisfied that God should do as He will with him, as the wind with a straw; and there is more real humility in accepting even greatness in such a spirit, than in thwarting God's plans beneath a pretext of lowliness. He who chooses abasement rather than elevation is not necessarily humble, though he may wish to be; but he who lets himself go,—up or down,—heedless whether he be praised or blamed, unmindful of what is said of him, is really humble, whatever men may think, it is because he waits solely on God's Pleasure.

Such a man asks nothing, refuses nothing; not out of a deliberate principle, but from such entire self-forgetfulness that he does not consider the matter. A really humble man is one of those children of whom our Lord said, "Of such is the Kingdom of Heaven." A little child does not know what it wants; it can do nothing, foresee nothing, but let itself be carried about. So let us give ourselves up boldly; if God does not use us, it is but just, for we are good for nothing. If He uses us for great purposes, it is for His Own Glory, and we will say, like Mary, "He hath done great things for us, for He hath regarded our lowliness."

RIGHT USE OF TRIALS

People find it very hard to believe that God heaps crosses on those He loves out of loving-kindness. Why should He take pleasure in causing us to suffer? they ask. Could He not make us good without making us miserable? Yes, doubtless God could do so, for to Him all things are possible. His All-powerful Hands hold the hearts of men, and turn them as He pleases, as he who commands the source of a reservoir turns the stream whither he will. But though God could save us without crosses, He has not willed so to do, just as He has willed that men should grow up through the weakness and troubles of childhood, instead of being born fully developed men. He is the Master; we can only be silent, and adore His Infinite Wisdom without understanding it. The one thing we do see plainly is that we cannot become really good save in so far as we become humble, unselfish, in all things turning from self to God.

But the operation of grace in turning us thus from self cannot—save through a miracle of that same grace—be other than painful, and God does not perform continual miracles in the order of grace any more than in the order of nature. It would be as great a miracle in the first sense were we to see one full of himself die suddenly to self-consciousness and self-interest, as to see a child go to bed a mere child, and rise up the next morning a man of thirty! God hides His work beneath a series of imperceptible events, both in the order of grace and of nature, and thus He subjects us to the mysteries of the faith. Not only does He accomplish His work gradually, but He does it by the most simple and likely means, so that its success appears natural to men; otherwise all God does would be as a perpetual miracle, which would overthrow the life of faith by which He would have us exist.

Such a life of faith is necessary, not only to mould the good, by causing them to sacrifice their own reason amid a world of darkness, but also to blind those whose presumption misleads them. Such men behold God's works without comprehending them, and take them to be simply natural. They are without true intelligence, inasmuch as that is only given to those who mistrust their own judgment, and the proud wisdom of man is unworthy to enter into the counsels of God.

So it is in order that the operation of grace may abide a mystery of faith that God permits it to be slow and painful. He makes use of the inconstancy, the ingratitude of men, of the disappointments and failures which attend human prosperity, to detach us from the creature and its good things. He opens our eyes by letting us realise our own weakness and evil in endless falls. It all seems to go on in the natural course of events, and this series of apparently natural causes consumes us like a slow fire. We would fain be consumed at once by the flames of pure love, but so speedy a process would cost us nothing, and it is in very selfishness that we seek to attain perfection so cheaply and so fast.

Why do we rebel against our prolonged trials? Because of self-love; and it is that very self-love that God purposes to destroy, for so long as we cleave to self His work is not achieved. What right have we to complain? We suffer from an excessive attachment to the creature—above all, to self. God orders a series of events which detach us gradually from the first, and finally from the last also. The operation is painful, but our corruption makes it needful, and therefore it is we suffer so keenly. If the flesh were sound, the surgeon would not need to probe it; he uses his knife in proportion to the depth of the wound and the extent of proud flesh. If we feel his operation too keenly, it is because the disease is active. Is it cruelty which makes the surgeon probe us to the quick? No, far otherwise, it is skill and kindness; he would do the same by his only child.

Even so God treats us. He never puts us to any pain save unwillingly; His fatherly Heart does not desire to grieve us, but He cuts to the quick that He may heal the ulcers of our spiritual being. He must needs tear from us that which we love amiss, unreasonably and excessively, or to the hindrance of His Love. And so doing, He causes us to cry out like a child from whom one takes the knife with which it would maim or kill itself. We cry loudly in our despair, and murmur against God, as the petulant babe against its mother; but He lets us cry, and saves us nevertheless. He only afflicts us for our correction; even when He seems to overwhelm us, it is for our own good, and to spare us the greater evil we should do to ourselves. The things for which we weep would have caused us eternal woe; that which we count as lost was then most indeed when we fancied it our own. God has stored it up safely, to be returned to us in eternity, which is fast drawing near. He does not deprive us of the things we prize in order to teach us to love them purely, truly,

and highly; in order that we may enjoy them for ever in His Presence; in order to do a hundred-fold better for us than we can even desire for ourselves.

Nothing can happen in the world save what God wills. He does all, arranges all, makes all to be as it is. He counts the hairs of our head, the leaves of every tree, the sand on the seashore, the drops of water which form the mighty ocean. When He made the world, His Wisdom weighed and measured every atom. Every moment He renews and sustains the breath of life. He knows the number of our days; He holds the cords of life or death. What seems to us weightiest is as nothing in the eyes of God; a little longer or shorter life becomes an imperceptible difference before Him. What matters it whether this frail vessel, this poor clay, be thrown aside a little sooner or later? How short-sighted and erring we are! We are aghast at the death of one in the flower of his age. "What a sad loss!" men cry out. But to whom is the loss? What does he who dies lose? Some few years of vanity, delusion, and peril! God takes him away from the evil, and saves him from his own weakness and the world's wickedness. What do they lose who love him? The danger of earthly happiness, a treacherous delight, a snare which caused them to forget God and their own welfare; but, in truth, they gain the blessing of detachment through the cross. That same blow by which he who dies is saved fits those who are left to work out their salvation in hope. Surely, then, it is true that God is very good, very loving, very pitiful to our real needs, even when He seems to overwhelm us, and we are most tempted to call Him hard!

What difference is there now between two people who died during the last century, one some twenty years, say, before the other? Both are dead now; their departure seems to us now but as the same thing; and soon all that is separated will be reunited, and there will be no trace left of that brief separation. Men seem to think this life immortal, or at least likely to endure for ages! Yet every day the living are treading rapidly after the dead; and the man who is just about to start upon a journey need not feel so very far off him who went yesterday. Life rushes on like a torrent: already the past is but a dream; the present, even while we think we grasp it, slips from us and becomes the past, and it will be no otherwise with the future. Days, months, years hurry on like the surging waves of a flood; a few moments more, and all will be ended. Verily, what now seems long, by reason of weariness and sadness, will seem short enough when it is over.

It is owing to the sensitiveness of self-love that we are so alive to our own condition. The sick man who cannot sleep thinks the night endless, yet it is no longer than any other night. In our cowardice we exaggerate all we suffer; our pain may be severe, but we make it worse by shrinking under it. The real way to get relief is to give one's self up heartily to God; to accept suffering, because God sends it to purify us and make us worthier Him. The world smiled upon you, and was as a poison to your soul. Would you wish to go on in ease, pleasure, display, in the pride of life and soul-destroying luxury, clinging to the world, which is Christ's enemy, rejecting the cross, which alone can sanctify you up to the hour of death? The world will turn away, forget, despise, ignore you. Well, need you wonder that the world is worldly, unjust, deceitful, treacherous? Yet you are not ashamed to love this world, from which God snatches you to deliver you from its bondage and make you free, and you complain of your very deliverance. It is as your own enemy that you are so alive to the world's indifference, that you cannot endure what is for your real good, and so keenly regret what is fatal to you. This is the source of all your grief and pain.

O my God, who beholdest the depths of our misery, Thou alone canst heal us! Give us faith, love, hope, Christian courage. Help us to turn our eyes continually to Thee, O All-powerful Father, and to Thy Son, our Example in suffering. Thou didst nail Him, the Man of Sorrows, to the Cross, that we might learn the blessing of suffering. Let our ease-loving nature be silent when we gaze on Jesus steeped in shame and agony. Lift up our hearts, strengthen them against self; make us to fear nought save displeasing Thee, save eternal loss, instead of fearing what will be our infinite gain. Lord, Thou knowest the weakness and misery of Thy creature. I have nothing—but what matter, so long as I have Thee, so long as I can seek Thee with certainty of finding all that is not to be found in myself!

Madame Jeanne Guyon

(1648-1717)

MADAME GUYON was born at Montargis, France, and educated in convents. When but fifteen she married a wealthy invalid of thirty-eight. Unhappy in her marriage, she sought happiness and strength in the devotional life. She leaned toward asceticism, which drew her into the quietistic movement. Confined by royal order in a convent of the Visitation for a year, she was released, only to be imprisoned in Vincennes and the Bastille. Almost twenty-five years of her life were spent in these confinements due to the antagonism of the king to quietism. Not until 1702 was she released. Many of her writings, with a tendency toward "a passive orison," were written during these years. Her maxims are guides to her type of mystical living. They are reproduced from *Spiritual Progress*, a selection from the writings of Fénelon and Madame Guyon edited by James W. Metcalf (New York, 1853).

[SPIRITUAL MAXIMS]

To rob God of nothing; to refuse Him nothing; to require of Him nothing; this is great perfection.

2. In the commencement of the spiritual life, our hardest task is to bear with our neighbor; in its progress, with ourselves, and in its end, with God.

3. He that regards self only with horror, is beginning to be the delight of God.

4. The more we learn what humility is, the less we discover of it in ourselves.

5. When we suffer aridity and desolation with equanimity, we testify our love to God; but when He visits us with the sweetness of His presence, He testifies His love to us.

6. He that bears the privations of the gifts of God and the esteem of men, with an even soul, knows how to enjoy his Supreme Good beyond all time and above all means.

7. Let no one ask a stronger mark of an excellent love to God, than that we are insensible to our own reputation.

8. Would you exert all your powers to attain Divine Union? Use all your strength for the destruction of self.

9. Be so much the enemy of self as you desire to be the friend of God.

10. How are we directed in the law to love ourselves? In God and with the same love that we bear to God; because as our true selves are in Him, our love must be there also.

11. It is a rare gift to discover an indescribable something, which is above grace and nature; which is not God, but which suffers no intermediate between God and us. It is a pure and unmixed emanation of a created being who is immediately connected with the Uncreated Original, from whom he proceeds. It is a union of essence with essence, in which nothing that is neither can act the part of an intermediate.

12. The ray of the creature is derived from the Sun of the Divinity; it cannot, however, be separated from it; and if its dependence upon its divine principle is essential, its union is not less so. O wonder! The creature which can only be by the power of God, cannot exist without Him, and the root of its borrowed life clings so closely to the origin of all being, that nothing can come between or cause the slightest separation. This is the common condition of all creatures; but it is only perceived by those whose purified faculties can trace the grandeur of their centre, and whose interior, freed from the defilement that covered it, begins to return to its origin.

13. Faith and the cross are inseparable: the cross is the shrine of faith, and faith is the light of the cross.

14. It is only by the death of self that the soul can enter into Divine Truth, and understand in part what is the light that shineth in darkness.

15. The more the darkness of self-knowledge deepens about us, the more does the divine truth shine in the midst.

16. Nothing less than a divine operation can empty us of the creature and of self, for whatever is natural tends constantly to fill us with the creature, and occupy us with ourselves. This emptiness without anything distinct, is, then, an excellent sign, though it exist surrounded by the deepest and, I may say, the most importunate temptations.

17. God causes us to promise in time of peace what He exacts from us in time of war; He enables us to make our abandonments in joy, but He requires the fulfilment of them in the midst of much bitterness. It is well for thee, O Love! to exercise Thy rights; suffer as we may, we will not return to self, or if we suffer because we have done so, the remedy for the evil is to devote ourselves afresh with an enlarged abandonment. Strange malady, the cure of which is only to be found in a worse! O Lord, cause me to do whatever Thou wilt, provided I do only thy will!

18. How hidden is the theology of Love! O Love, Thou sulliest to excess what Thou wouldst raise to the heights of purity! Thou profanest thine own sanctuary; there is not left one stone

upon another that is not cast into the dirt. And what shall be the end? Thou knowest it from the beginning; it is worthy of so great a Workman that his work should be hidden, and that while He seems to destroy, He should accomplish it the most effectually.

19. Ah Lord! who seest the secrets of the heart, Thou knowest if I yet expect anything from myself, or if there be anything which I would refuse to Thee!

20. How rare is it to behold a soul in an absolute abandonment of selfish interests, that it may devote itself to the interests of God!

21. The creature would willingly cease to be creature if it could become God; but where shall we find one willing that God should resume everything He has bestowed without receiving anything in return? I say everything, and everything without reserve, even to our own righteousness, which is dearer to man than his existence, and to our rest, by which we may enjoy self and the gifts of God in self, and in which we place our happiness, without knowing it. Where shall we find an abandonment that is as comprehensive as the will of God, not only when accompanied by delights, illumination, and feeling, but under all circumstances and in fact? O it is a fruit of Paradise that can scarce be found upon the earth!

22. God is infinitely more honored by the sacrifices of death than by those of life; by the latter we honor Him as a great Sovereign, but by the former, as God, losing all things for his glory. This is the reason why Jesus Christ made many more sacrifices of death than of life; and I suspect no one will gain all without having lost all.

23. Reason should not undertake to comprehend the last destructions; they are ordained expressly to destroy our reason.

24. God has means more efficient, more conducive to his own glory, and more edifying for souls, but they are less sanctifying. These great and dazzling gifts are very gratifying to nature, even when it seems to give way beneath their weight, and thus nourish its secret life; but distresses, continual dyings, and unprofitableness for any good, crucify the most vital parts of the soul, which are those which prevent the coming of the kingdom of God.

25. In our solemn feasts, some strive to do something for Thee, O my God! and others, that Thou mayest do something for them; but neither of these is permitted to us. Love forbids the one and cannot suffer the other.

26. It is harder to die to our virtues than to our vices; but the one is just as necessary as the other for perfect union. Our attachments are the stronger as they are more spiritual.

27. What is a help to perfection at one time, is a hindrance at another; what formerly helped you in your way to God, will now prevent your reaching Him; the more wants we have, the further we are from God, and the nearer we approach him, the better can we dispense with everything that is not Himself. When we have come there, we use everything indifferently, and have no more need but of Him.

28. Who can say to what extent the divine abandonment will carry the poor soul that is given up to it? or rather, to whom can we describe the extremity of sacrifice which God exacts from his simple victim? He raises him by degrees, and then plunges him into the abyss; he discovers new points in him day by day, and never ceases until he has sacrificed everything God wills, putting no other bounds to his abandonment than God does to his decrees. He even goes further, submitting to everything that God could do, or his sovereign will ordain. Then every selfish interest is given up; all is surrendered to the Author of All, and God reigns supreme over his nothingness.

29. God gives us gifts, graces, and natural talents, not for our own use, but that we may render them to Him. He takes pleasure in giving and in taking them away, or in so disposing of us, that we cannot enjoy them; but their grand use is to be offered in a continual sacrifice to Him; and by this He is most glorified.

30. Naked faith keeps us in ignorance, uncertainty, and oblivion of everything, excepts nothing, neither grace nor nature, virtue nor vice; it is the darkness concealing us wholly from ourselves, but revealing so much the more of the Divinity and the greatness of his works; an obscurity that gives us an admirable discernment of spirits, and dislodges the esteem and love of self from its most secret recesses. Pure love reigns underneath, notwithstanding; for how can a soul go about to consider its own interest, when it cannot so much as look at itself? Or, how could it be pleased to look at what it cannot see? It either sees nothing, or nothing but God, who is All and in all, and the more it is blinded to self, the more it beholds of Him.

31. There are but few men who are led by their reason, most of them blindly following their senses and passions; they are fewer, indeed, who act from an illuminated faith, or from reason enlightened by faith; but shall we find a single one who admits no guide but a blind faith, which, though it leads him straight to God by the short road of abandonment, seems, nevertheless, to precipitate him into abysses from which he has no hope of ever escaping? There are, however, some such souls, who have noble trust enough to be blindfolded, and led they know not whither. Many are called but few are willing to enter, and they who have most fully surrendered themselves to the sway of their sense, their passions, their reason, and the distinct illuminations of faith, are they who have the greatest difficulty in plunging into the gulf of the blindest and most naked faith; whereas the simple souls enter with ease. It is the same as with the shipwrecked; those who know how to swim, or who have perhaps seized a plank of the ship, struggle and contend for a long while before they drown; but those who cannot swim, and who have nothing to sustain them, are instantly submerged, and, sinking without a struggle beneath the surface, die and are delivered from their suffering.

32. The spirituality of most spiritual persons is nothing but presumption. When the Divine Truth penetrates to their centre, it discovers many a theft from God in their course, and teaches them that the only way to secure themselves is by an abandonment without reserve to God, and submission to his guidance; for, whenever we endeavor to bring our own perfection about, or that of others, by our own efforts, the result is simply imperfection.

33. The soul that is destined to have no other support but God himself, must pass through the strangest trials. How much agony and how many deaths must it suffer before losing the life of self! It will encounter no purgatory in the other world, but it will feel a terrible hell in this; a hell not only of pain—that would be a small matter—but also of temptations, its own resistance to which it does not perceive; this is the cross of crosses, of all sufferings the most intolerable, of all deaths the most despairing.

34. All consolation that does not come from God is but desolation; when the soul has learned to receive no comfort but in God only, it has passed beyond the reach of desolation.

35. By the alternations of interior union and desertion, God sometimes makes us feel what He is, and sometimes gives us to perceive what we are. He does the latter to make us hate and die to ourselves, but the former to make us love Him, and to exalt us into union.

36. It is in vain for man to endeavor to instruct man in those things which the Holy Spirit alone can teach.

37. To take and receive all things not in ourselves, but in God, is the true and excellent way of dying to ourselves and living only to God. They who understand the practice of this, are beginning to live purely; but, outside of this, nature is always mingled with grace, and we rest in self instead of permitting ourselves no repose, except in the Supreme Good, who should be the center of every movement of the heart, as He is the final end of all the measures of love.

38. Why should we complain that we

have been stripped of the divine virtues, if we had not hidden them away as our own? Why should we complain of a loss, if we had no property in the thing lost? Or why does deprivation give us so much pain, except because of the appropriation we had made of that which was taken away?

39. When thou canst not find thyself, nor any good, then rejoice that all things are rendered unto God.

40. O monster justly abhorred of God and man! after being humiliated in so many ways, I cannot become humble, and I am so pampered with pride, that when I most endeavor to be humble. I set about my own praises!

41. Some saints have been sanctified by the easy and determined practice of all the virtues, but there are others who owe their sanctification to having endured with perfect resignation the privation of every virtue.

42. If we do not go so far as to be stopped by nothing short of the power of God, we are not entirely free from presumption; and if your abandonment is bounded by anything short of the possible will of God, we are not yet disengaged from appropriation; and presumption and appropriation are impurities.

43. I have never found any who prayed so well as those who had never been taught how. They who have no master in man, have one in the Holy Spirit.

44. He who has a pure heart will never cease to pray; and he who will be constant in prayer, shall know what it is to have a pure heart.

45. God is so great and so independent, that He can find means to glorify Himself even by sin.

46. While our abandonment blesses or spares us, we shall find many to advise it; but let it bring us into trouble, and the most spiritually-minded will exclaim against it.

47. It is easy enough to understand the course of such as go on from Virtue to virtue, but who can comprehend the decrees that send some dashing from one precipice to another, and from abyss to abyss? or who shall bring aid and comfort to these hidden favorites of God, whom He gradually deprives of every stay, and who are reduced to an inability to know or help themselves as utter as their ignorance of what sustains them?

48. Who can comprehend the extent of that supreme homage which is due to the will of God?

49. Those who are abandoned are cast from one precipice to another, and from one abyss to another, as if they were lost.

50. The harmlessness of the dove consists in not judging another; the wisdom of the serpent in distrusting ourselves.

51. Self-seeking is the gate by which a soul departs from peace; and total abandonment to the will of God, that by which it returns.

52. Alas! how hard it is to will only the will of God, and yet to believe that we do nothing but what is contrary to that will! to desire nothing so much as to do His will, and not even to know what it is! to be able to show it with great confidence to others, but not to find it for ourselves! When we are full of His will, and everywhere penetrated by it, we no longer know it. This is, indeed, a long and painful martyrdom, but one which will result in an unchangeable peace in this life, and an incomprehensible felicity in the next!

53. He who has learned to seek nothing but the will of God, shall always find what he seeks.

54. Which is the harder lot for a soul that has known and loved God, not to know whether it loves God, or whether God loves it?

55. Which of the two would the perfect soul choose, if the choice were presented, to love God, or to be loved by Him?

56. Tell me, what is that which is neither separated from God nor united to God, but which is inseparable from Him?

57. What is the state of a soul which has neither power nor will, and what can it do, and not do?

58. Who shall measure the extent of the abandonment of a soul that is no longer self-possessed in anything, and

which has an absorbing sense of the supremacy of the power and will of God?

59. Who can take in the extent of the interior sacrifices of Jesus Christ, except him to whom He shall manifest them?

60. How can they be delivered from the life of self, who are not willing to abandon all their possessions? How can they believe themselves despoiled of all, who possess the greatest treasure under heaven? Do not oblige me to name it, but judge, if you are enlightened; there is one of them which is less than the other, which is lost before it, but which those who must lose everything have the greatest trouble in parting with.

Elizabeth Rowe

(1674-1737)

ELIZABETH Rowe, poet, musician, and artist, was the daughter of a Nonconformist minister residing at Ilchester and Frome, England. At twelve years of age she began writing poetry. In her later years one of her friends described her as "the most amiable female then existing." When she was still young, her husband died of consumption, and she moved from London to Frome. She vowed for herself a life of widowhood. During these years, devoted in part to her writing, she led a semi-reclusive life. She was exemplary for her serenity, affability, and meekness. In every social virtue she seemed to radiate a sanctity.

When she died she left a note to her friend Dr. Isaac Watts to edit her papers, now entitled *Devout Exercises of the Heart*. Of these letters Watts remarks: "They are animated with such fire as seems to speak the language of holy passion."

A JOYFUL VIEW OF APPROACHING DEATH

From *Devout Exercises of the Heart*

O death, where is thy sting? where is thy boasted victory? The conquest is mine: I shall pass in triumph through thy dark dominions; and through the grace of the Son of God, my divine leader, I shall appear there, not a captive, but a conqueror.

O King of Terrors, where are thy formidable looks? I can see nothing dreadful in thy aspect: thou appearest with no tokens of defiance, nor dost thou come with a summons from a severe judge, but gentle invitations from my blessed Redeemer, who has passed gloriously through thy territories in his way to his throne.

Thrice welcome, thou kind messenger of my liberty and happiness! a thousand times more welcome than jubilee to the wretched slave, than pardon to a condemned malefactor. I am going from darkness and confinement, to immense light and perfect liberty; from these tempestuous regions to the soft and peaceful climes above; from pain and grief to everlasting ease and tranquillity. For the toils of virtue, I shall immediately receive its vast rewards; for the reproach of fools, the honour and applause of angels. In a few minutes I shall be higher than yonder stars, and brighter far than they. I shall range the boundless aether, and breathe the balmy airs of paradise. I shall presently behold my glorious Maker, and sing hallelujahs to my exalted Saviour.

And now come, ye bright guardians of the just, conduct me through the unknown and trackless aether, for you pass and repass the celestial road continually; you have commission not to leave me till I arrive at Mount Sion, the heavenly Jerusalem, the city of the living God; till I come to the innumerable company of angels, and spirits of just men made perfect.

Hold out, faith and patience; it is but a little while, and your work will be at an end; but a few moments, and these sighs and groans shall be converted into everlasting hallelujahs; but a few weary steps, and the journey of life will be finished. One effort more, and I shall have gained the top of the everlasting hills, and from yonder bright summit shall presently look back on the dangers I have escaped in my travels through the wilderness.

Roll faster on, ye lingering minutes: the nearer my joys, the more impatient I am to seize them: after these painful agonies, how greedily shall I drink in immortal ease and pleasure! Break away, ye thick clouds! begone, ye envious shades, and let me behold the glories ye conceal: let me see the promised land, and survey the happy regions I am immediately to possess. How long will ye interpose between me and my bright sun —between me and the unclouded face of God? Look up, my soul, see how sweetly those reviving beams break forth! how they dispel the gloom, and gild the shades of death.

O blessed eternity! with what a cheerful splendour dost thou dawn on my soul! With thee comes liberty, and peace, and love, and endless felicity: but pain, and sorrow, and tumult, and death, and darkness, vanish before thee for ever. I am just upon the shores of those happy realms where uninterrupted day and eternal spring reside; yonder are the delectable hills and harmonious vales which continually echo to the songs of angels. There the blissful fields extend their verdure, and there the immortal groves ascend. But how dazzling is thy prospect, O city of God, of whom such glorious things are spoken! In thee "there shall be no more night, nor need of the sun or moon, for the throne of God and of the Lamb is in the midst of thee; and the nations that are saved shall walk in thy light, and the kings of the earth shall bring their glory and honour into thee; and there the glorious Lord shall be to us a place of defence, a place of streams and broad rivers;" and the voice of joy, and the shout of triumph, shall be heard in thee for ever.

There holy souls perpetual sabbaths keep,
And never are concern'd for food or sleep:
There new-come saints with wreaths of light
    are crown'd,
While ivory harps and silver trumpets sound:
There flaming seraphs sacred hymns begin,
And raptur'd cherubs loud responses sing.

"My eyes shall there behold the King in his beauty;" and Oh! how ravishing will the aspects of his love be! What unutterable ecstasies shall I feel, when I meet those smiles which enlighten heaven, and exhilarate all the celestial regions; when I shall view the beatific glory, without one interposing cloud to eternity —when I shall drink my fill at the fountains of joy, and in those rivers of pleasure that flow from his right hand for ever.

IMPORTUNATE REQUESTS FOR THE RETURN OF GOD TO THE SOUL

From *Devout Exercises of the Heart*

Thou great and glorious, thou invisible and universal Being, art thou no nearer to be approached? or do I search thee amiss?—Is there a corner of the creation unvisited by thee, or any place exempt from thy presence?—I trace thy footsteps through heaven and earth, but I cannot overtake thee.

Why do I seek thee, if thou art not here? Or find thee not, if thou art every where?

Tell me, O my God, and my all! tell me where thou art to be found; for there is the place of my rest. What imaginable good can supply thy absence?—Deprived of thee, all that the world could offer would be like a jest to a dying man, and provoke my aversion and disdain. It is a God that I seek.

My wishes stoop not to a lower aim;
Thou, thou hast kindled this immortal flame,
    Which nothing could allay.

Adieu, adieu to all human things! Let me find my God, the end of all my wishes: why dost thou keep back the face of thy throne? why do the cloud and sacred darkness conceal thee?

Thy voice produced the seas and spheres,
    Bid the waves roll, and planets shine;
But nothing like thyself appears,
    Through all these various works of thine.

O thou fairer than all the works of thy hands! wilt thou ever hide thyself from a creature that loves and seeks thee with so intense desire?—I appeal to thee, O Lord! are not my breathings after thee most hearty and unfeigned? Does not my soul pant after thee with a fervour which cannot be extinguished, and a sincerity which cannot be disguised?

For thee I pine, and am for thee undone,
As drooping flowers that want their parent sun.

How so my spirits languish for thee! —No similitudes can express the vehemence of my desires: wealth and glory, friends and pleasure, lose their names compared to thee. To follow thee, I would leave them all behind: I would leave the whole creation, and bid the fields and sparkling skies adieu. Let the heavens and earth be no more, while thou endurest for ever, I can want no support; my being itself, with all its blessedness, depends entirely on thee.

Place me far from the bounds of all creation, remote from all existence but thy own; in that ineffable solitude let me be lost—let me expatiate there for ever— let me run the endless rounds of bliss; —but, alas! I flatter myself in vain with scenes of unattainable happiness. I will search thee, then, where I hope thou mayst be found. I cast my eyes to the bright regions above, and almost envy the happy beings that see thy face unveiled: I search thee in the flowery meadows, and listen for thee among the murmuring springs: then, silent and abstracted from

human things, I search thee in holy contemplation. It is all in vain: nor fields, nor floods, nor clouds, nor stars reveal thee.

Ye happy spirits, that meet his smiles, and hear his voice, direct a mournful wanderer, while I seek him whom my soul loves—while I sigh and complain, and cast my languishing eyes to yonder happy mansions; fain would I penetrate the starry pavilions, and look through the separating firmament: Oh! that thou wouldst divide the clouds, that thou wouldst rend the heavens, and give me one glimpse of thy glory! that thou wouldst display thy beauty, and, in the midst of these earthly scenes of amusing vanity, give me one moment's interval of celestial blessedness!

One look of mercy from thy eye,
    One whisper of thy voice,
Exceed a whole eternity
    Employ'd in carnal joys.
Could I the spacious earth command,
    Or the more boundless sea,
For one dear hour at thy right hand
    I'd give them both away.

If things were put into just balances, and computed aright, for the first moment of this satisfaction, I am ready to say the whole creation would be cheaply lost: how gladly would I resign all for such a bliss!—Adieu to human things! Let me find my God, the end of all my wishes: 'tis he whom I seek, 'tis he alone can satisfy my infinite desires. Oh! why dost thou withdraw? why thus long conceal thyself?—where dost thou retire?— Nor earth, nor heaven, reply to my repeated calls.

Let me invoke thee by every gracious title, my God, and the God of my fathers: from one generation to another thou hast been our dwelling place: the claim has descended from age to age; thy covenant has been established with us, and thy faithfulness remains unblemished. Oh! forget not thy covenant; forget not the blessings entailed on me: forget not the prayers and tears by which my pious ancestors have engaged thy mercy for me; forget not their vows and solemn dedication of me to thee: Oh! recall thy ancient favours, and renew thy former mercy to a family, which has been thine in a succession of ages.

Let me invoke thee now by a nearer propriety; my covenant God, my father, and my friend! If by all those tender names I have ever known thee, forget me not. By those sacred engagements, O Lord! I entreat thy return. If all thy past favours were real—if all was waking bliss, and not a gay delusion, Oh restore my heaven again!—Life of my soul, light of my eyes, return: come, and bring all thy sacred consolations; once again: let me experience those holy joys that thy presence imparts: once again let me hear thy voice, and once again be blessed with thy smiles.

> Oh! hear, and to my longing eyes
> Restore thy wonted light;
> And suddenly, or I shall sleep
> In everlasting night.

Blessed Saviour! in thee we behold the face of God, as a reconciled father; and dost thou withdraw thyself? Oh how welcome will thy returns be! how like the breakings of immortal day will thy presence cheer me! how dearly shall I prize my happiness! how fearful shall I be of every thing that would offend thee! how joyful in the blessed discovery and possession of thy love! I'd whisper my bliss to the listening streams and groves:

> I'd carve thy passion on the bark,
> And every wounded tree
> Shall droop, and bear some mystic mark
> That JESUS died for me.
> The swains shall wonder when they read,
> Inscrib'd on all the grove,
> That Heav'n itself came down and bled
> To win a mortal's love.

But why do I flatter myself with these delightful scenes? I find thee absent still: I mourn and complain as one unpitied. What is life while thou art absent? Oh! return and bless me with thy presence, thou who knowest my distresses, and art acquainted with my secret cares. Thou who art the witness of my midnight sighs, and dost hear when at the dawning day I call thee; but still thou answerest not, and seemest deaf to my prayers. I am, 'tis true, a worthless wretch; but vile as I am, thou hast, in thy immense compassion, brought me into covenant with

thee. My beloved is mine, and I am his.

> He is my sun, though he refuse to shine;
> Though for a moment he depart,
> I dwell for ever on his heart,
> For ever he on mine.

Nothing can break the sacred union: but for this confidence, I were undone; but for this beam of hope, I were lost in eternal darkness. "Why art thou disquieted, O my soul! and why art thou cast down within me? Hope in God, for I shall yet praise him for the light of his countenance;" I shall yet welcome his return—I shall yet hear his cheering voice, and meet his favourable smiles.

But why, O my God! this long suspense? Why do these intervals of night and darkness abide upon me, and torment my heart so long! Wilt thou deny a bliss so easily granted? I ask not more than is lawful for mortality to wish: I ask not the visions of angels here below, nor the beatitudes of perfected spirits; I ask but what thou hast bid me seek, and given me hopes to obtain; I ask that sacred fellowship, that ineffable communion, with which thou favourest thy saints.

Oh! let me hear those heavenly whispers, that give them the foretastes of immortal pleasure: let me be sensible of those divine approaches that kindle celestial ardour in their souls; let me meet those beams that darken all mortal beauty: let me enjoy, at this earthly distance, those smiles that are the bliss of angels in heaven. Though it is but darkly, and afar off, yet let me feel their influence; it will brighten the passage of life, it will direct me through its mazes, and gild its rough and gloomy paths; it will raise the flames of sacred love, it will awaken the divine principle within me, and set it glowing through all my powers. I abandon, I shall forget the vanities below, and the glories of the world will be no more: but while thou, O my God! hidest thy face, I lose my sun, I languish and die; yet to thee I will lift up my eyes to thee I lift up my soul.

> Come, Lord, and never from me go:
> This world's a darksome place:
> I find no pleasure here below,
> When thou dost veil thy face.

Philip Doddridge
(1702-1751)

DODDRIDGE is best known by his two hymns: "Awake, My Soul, Stretch Every Nerve" and "O Happy Day, That Fixed My Choice." A Nonconformist, stimulated by Presbyterian influence, he was not ordained and did not accede to the creed of any church. After six years in the pastorate he was called in 1729 to a parish at Northampton where eight ministers ordained him. His chief devotional writing is *The Rise and Progress of Religion in the Soul*. The following selection from this work is an illustration of how the book presents the man and the Christian in a great variety of circumstances—some that are hurtful to the spiritual life and others that assure its growth.

[CHERISH THE MERCY OF GOD]
From *The Rise and Progress of Religion in the Soul*

I would now suppose my reader to find, on an examination of his spiritual state, that he is growing in grace. And if you desire that this growth may at once be acknowledged and promoted, let me call your soul "to that more affectionate exercise of love to God and joy in him," which suits, and strengthens, and exalts the character of the advanced Christian; which I beseech you to regard, not only as your privilege, but as your duty too. Love is the most sublime, generous principle of all true and acceptable obedience; and with love, when so wisely and happily fixed, when so certainly returned, joy, proportionable joy, must naturally be connected. It may justly grieve a man that enters into the spirit of Christianity, to see how low a life even the generality of sincere Christians commonly live in this respect; "Rejoice then in the Lord, ye righteous, and give thanks at the remembrance of his holiness," and of all those other perfections and glories which are included in that majestic, that wonderful, that delightful name, the Lord thy God. Spend not your sacred moments merely in confession or in petition, though each must have their daily share; but give a part, a considerable part, to the celestial and angelic work of praise. Yea, labor to carry about with you continually a heart overflowing with such sentiments, warmed and inflamed with such affections.

2. Are there not continually rays enough diffused from the great Father of light and love to enkindle it in our bosom? Come, my Christian friend and brother, come and survey with me the goodness of our heavenly Father. And O that he would give me such a sense of it, that I might represent it in a suitable manner; that "while I am musing, the fire may burn" in my own heart, and be communicated to yours and O that it might pass, with the lines I write, from soul to soul, awakening in the breast of every Christian that reads them, sentiments more worthy the children of God and the heirs of glory, who are to spend an eternity in those sacred exercises to which I am now endeavoring to excite you.

3. Have you not reason to adopt the words of David, and say, "How many are thy gracious thoughts unto me, O Lord. How great is the sum of them. When I would count them, they are more in number than the sand." You indeed know where to begin the survey, for the favors of God to you began with your being. Commemorate it therefore with a grateful heart, that the eyes which "saw your substance, being yet imperfect," beheld you with a friendly care "when you were made in secret," and have watched over you ever since; and that the hand which "drew the plan of your members, when as yet there was none of them," not only fashioned them at first, but from that time has been concerned in "keeping all your bones, so that none of them is broken," and that, indeed, it is to this you owe it that you live. Look back upon the path you have trod, from the day that God brought you out of the womb, and say whether you do not, as it were, see all the road thick set with the marks and memorials of the divine goodness. Recollect the places where you have lived, and the persons with whom you have most intimately conversed, and call to mind the mercies you have received in those places, and from those persons, as the instruments of the divine care and goodness. Recollect the difficulties and dangers with which you have been surrounded, and reflect attentively on what God has done to defend you from them, or to carry you through them. Think how often there has been but a step between you and death, and how suddenly God has sometimes interposed to set you in safety, even before you apprehended your danger. Think of those chambers of illness in which you have been confined; and from which perhaps, you once thought you should go forth no more; but said, with Hezekiah, in the cutting off of your days, "I shall go to the gates of the grave: I am deprived of the residue of my years." God has, it may be, since that time, added many years to your life; and you know not how many are in reserve, or how much usefulness and happiness may attend each. Survey your circumstances in relative life; how many kind friends are surrounding you daily, and studying how they may contribute to your comfort. Reflect on those remarkable circumstances in providence which occasioned the knitting of some bonds of this kind, which next to those which join your soul to God, you number among the happiest. And forget not in how many instances, when these dear lives have been threatened, lives perhaps more sensibly dear than your own, God has given them back from the borders of the grave, and so added new endearments, arising from that tender circumstance, to all your after-converse with them. Nor forget in how gracious a manner he has supported some others in their last moments, and enabled them to leave behind a sweet odor of piety, which hath embalmed their memories, revived you when ready to faint under the sorrows of the last separation, and on the whole, made even the recollection of their death delightful.

4. But it is more than time that I lead on your thoughts to the many spiritual mercies which God has bestowed upon you. Look back, as it were, to "the rock from whence you were hewn, and to the hole of the pit from whence you were digged." Reflect seriously on the state wherein divine grace found you: under how much guilt, under how much pollution; in what danger, in what ruin. Think what was, and O think, with yet deeper reflection, what would have been the case. The eye of God, which penetrates into eternity, saw what your mind, amused with the trifles of present time and sensual gratification, was utterly ignorant and regardless of: it saw you on the borders of eternity, and pitied you; saw that you would in a little time have been such a helpless, wretched creature as the sinner that is just now dead, and has, to his infinite surprise and everlasting terror, met his unexpected doom; and would, like him, stand thunderstruck in astonishment and despair. This God saw, and he pitied you; and being merciful to you, he provided, in the counsel of his

eternal love and grace, a Redeemer for you, and purchased you to himself, through the blood of his Son—a price which, if you will pause upon it, and think seriously what it was, must surely affect you to such a degree as to make you fall down before God in wonder and shame, to think it should ever have been given for you. To accomplish these blessed purposes, he sent his grace into your heart; so that, though "you were once darkness, you are now light in the Lord." He made that happy change which you now feel in your soul, and "by his Holy Spirit, which is given to you," he shed abroad that principle of love, which is enkindled by this review, and now flames with greater ardor than before. Thus far he has supported you in your Christian course, and "having obtained help from him," it is that you continue even to this day. He hath not only blessed you, but "made you a blessing," and though you have not been so useful as that holy generosity of heart which he has excited would have engaged you to desire, yet some good you have done in the station in which he has fixed you. Some of your brethren of mankind have been relieved; perhaps, too, some thoughtless creature reclaimed to virtue and happiness by his blessing on your endeavors. Some in the way to heaven are praising God for you; and some perhaps, already there, are longing for your arrival, that they may thank you, in nobler and more expressive forms, for benefits, the importance of which they now sufficiently understand, though while here they could never conceive it.

5. Christian, look around on the numberless blessings of one kind and of another with which you are already encompassed, and advance your prospect still farther to what faith yet discovers within the veil. Think of those now unknown transports with which thou shalt drop every burden in the grave, and thine immortal spirit shall mount, light and joyful, holy and happy, to God, its original, its support, and its hope; to God, the source of being, of holiness, and of pleasure; to Jesus, through whom all these blessings are derived to thee, and who will appoint thee a throne near to his own, to be for ever a spectator and partaker of his glory. Think of the rapture with which thou shalt attend his triumph in the resurrection-day, and receive this poor mouldering, corruptible body, transformed into his glorious image; and then think, "These hopes are not mine alone, but the hopes of thousands and millions. Multitudes, whom I number among the dearest of my friends upon the earth, are rejoicing with me in these apprehensions and views; and God gives me sometimes to see the smiles on their cheeks, the sweet, humble hope that sparkles in their eyes, and shines through the tears of tender gratitude, and to hear that little of their inward complacency and joy which language can express. Yea, and multitudes more, who were once equally dear to me with these, though I have laid them in the grave, and wept over their dust, are living to God, living in the possession of inconceivable delights, and drinking large draughts of the water of life, which flows in perpetual streams at his right hand."

6. O Christian, thou art still intimately united and allied to them. Death cannot break a friendship thus cemented, and it ought not to render thee insensible of the happiness of those friends for whose memory thou retainest so just an honor. They live to God as his servants; they "serve him, and see his face," and they make but a small part of that glorious assembly. Millions, equally worthy of thine esteem and affections with themselves, inhabit those blissful regions; and wilt thou not rejoice in their joy? And wilt thou not adore that everlasting spring of holiness and happiness from whence each of their streams is derived? Yea, I will add, while the blessed angels are so kindly regarding us, while they are administering to thee, O Christian, and bearing thee in their arms, "as an heir of salvation," wilt thou not rejoice in their felicity too? And wilt thou not adore that God who gives them all the superior glory of their more exalted

nature, and gives them a heaven which fills them with blessedness even while they seem to withdraw from it that they may attend on thee?

7. This, and infinitely more than this, the blessed God is, and was, and shall ever be. The felicities of the blessed spirits that surround his throne, and thy felicities, O Christian, are immortal. These heavenly luminaries shall glow with an undecaying flame, and thou shalt shine and burn among them when the sun and the stars are gone out. Still shall the unchanging Father of lights pour forth his beams upon them; and the lustre they reflect from him, and their happiness in him, shall be everlasting, shall be ever growing. Bow down, O thou child of God, thou heir of glory—bow down, and let all that is within thee unite in one act of grateful love; and let all that is around thee, all that is before thee in the prospects of an unbounded eternity, concur to elevate and transport thy soul, that thou mayest, as far as possible, begin the work and blessedness of heaven, in falling down before the God of it, in opening thine heart to his gracious influences, and in breathing out before him that incense of praise which these warm beams of his presence and love have so great a tendency to produce, and to ennoble with a fragrancy resembling that of his paradise above.

Jean Pierre de Caussade

(1675?-1751)

A MEMBER of the Society of Jesus, a preacher and teacher at Perpignan and Toulouse in France, de Caussade shows in his writings the deep longing of the soul for refreshment from the grace of God. "State of Abandonment" clearly portrays this experience. He possessed a most sensitive soul, similar to that of Jeremiah, as evidenced in these words: "There is nothing more sublime than contemplation as we find it in books; nothing more beautiful or grander than passive prayer in theory. But in practice there is nothing more humiliating, more crucifying."

STATE OF ABANDONMENT

Offer a sacrifice of justice," says the Prophet, "and hope in the Lord." This means that the great and solid foundation of the spiritual life is to give oneself to God in order to be the subject of His good pleasure in everything internal and external, and afterwards to forget oneself so completely that one considers oneself as a thing sold and delivered to the purchaser to which one has no longer any right, in such a way that the good pleasure of God makes all our joy and His happiness, glory and being becomes our sole good.

This foundation being laid, the soul has nothing to do save to pass all her life in rejoicing that God is good, abandoning herself so completely to His good pleasure that she is equally content to do this or that, or the contrary, at the disposal of God, without reflecting on the use which His good pleasure makes of her.

To abandon oneself! This then is the great duty which remains to be fulfilled after we have acquitted ourselves faithfully of the duties of our state. The perfection with which this duty is accomplished will be the measure of our sanctity.

A holy soul is but a soul freely submitted to the Divine will with the help of grace. All that follows this simple acquiescence is the work of God and not of man. This soul should blindly resign herself in self-abandonment and universal indifference. This is the only disposition asked of her by God; the rest belongs to Him to choose and determine according to His designs, as an architect selects and marks the stones of the building he proposes to construct.

We should then love God and His order in everything, and we should love it as it presents itself, desiring nothing more. That these or those objects should be presented is no concern of the soul, but of God, and what He gives is best. The whole of spirituality can be expressed in abridged form in this maxim: we should abandon ourselves purely and entirely to the Order of God, and when we are in that Order we should with a complete self-forgetfulness be eternally busied with loving and obeying Him, without all these fears, reflections, returns on ourselves, and disquietudes which sometimes result from the care of our own salvation and perfection. Since God offers to manage our affairs for us, let us once for all hand them over to His infinite wisdom, in order to occupy ourselves only with Himself and what belongs to Him.

Come, my soul, let us pass with head erect over all that happens within us or outside us, remaining always content with God, content with what He does with us and with what He makes us do. Let us be very careful not to engage imprudently in that multitude of restless reflections which like so many paths leading nowhere present themselves to our mind to make it wander and stray endlessly to our sheer loss: let us pass this labyrinth of our own self-love by vaulting over it and not by following it out in all its interminable details.

Come, my soul, let us pass beyond our languors, our illnesses, our aridities, our inequalities of humor, our weaknesses of mind, the snares of the devil and of men with their suspicions, jealousies, sinister ideas and prejudices. Let us fly like the eagle above all these clouds, our gaze fixed on the sun and on its rays, which are our duties. We feel all these miseries, and it does not depend on us to be insensible to them, but let us remember that our life is not a life of feeling. Let us live in that higher region of the soul where the Will of God produces His eternal operation, ever equal, ever uniform, ever immutable. In that spiritual home where the Uncreated, the Formless, the Ineffable, keeps the soul infinitely removed from all the specific detail of created shadows and atoms, we remain calm even when our senses are the prey of the tempest. We have become independent of the senses; their agitations and disquietudes, their comings and goings and the hundreds of metamorphoses they pass through do not trouble us any more than the clouds that darken the sky for a moment and disappear. We know that everything happens in the senses as in the air where all is without connection or order, in a state of perpetual change. God and His will is the eternal object which charms the heart in the state of faith, as in the state of glory He will be its true felicity; and the state of the heart in glory will have its effect on the whole of our material being, at present the prey of monsters, owls and weird beasts. Under these appearances, however terrible they may be, the Divine action will give to our being a heavenly power and make it as shining as the sun; for the faculties of the sensitive soul and of the body are prepared here below like gold, iron, fine linen and precious stones. Like the material substratum of these various things, they will only enjoy the splendour and purity of their form after much manipulation and when much has been destroyed and cut away. All that souls endure here below under the hand of God has no other purpose than to prepare them for this.

Jonathan Edwards

(1703-1758)

THE greatest religious awakening of eighteenth-century America came from Edwards and his followers. Born in Connecticut and educated at Yale, for twenty-three years Edwards ministered in Northampton, Massachusetts. Upon his dismissal from that parish he became a missionary to the Indians at Stockbridge until he accepted the presidency of Princeton in 1758. He died after only a few weeks in office. Edwards was a Calvinist, an evangelist, and the keenest philosophic mind of his era. He saw religious experience as the gift of God to men, sin as selfishness, and virtue as "disinterested benevolence." *A Treatise on Religious Affections* emphasizes these aspects at the heart of Christian sainthood. Defining affections as "no other than the more vigorous and sensible exercises of the inclination and will of the soul," he includes the material here as a portion of the third part of his book.

DISTINGUISHING SIGNS OF TRULY GRACIOUS AND HOLY AFFECTIONS

From *A Treatise on Religious Affections*

SECTION I. AFFECTIONS THAT ARE TRULY SPIRITUAL AND GRACIOUS, ARISE FROM THOSE INFLUENCES AND OPERATIONS ON THE HEART, WHICH ARE SPIRITUAL, SUPERNATURAL, AND DIVINE.

We find that true saints, or those persons who are sanctified by the Spirit of God, are in the New Testament called *spiritual* persons. And their being *spiritual* is spoken of as their peculiar character, and that wherein they are distinguished from those who are not sanctified. . . . Christians are called spiritual persons, because they are born of the Spirit, and because of the indwelling and holy influences of the Spirit of God in them. And things are called spiritual as related to the Spirit of God. . . .

Natural men may be the subjects of many influences of the Spirit of God, as is evident by many scriptures, yet they are not in the sense of the scripture, spiritual persons; neither are any of those effects, common gifts, qualities, or affections, that are from the influence of the Spirit of God upon them, called spiritual things. The great difference lies in these two things.

1. The Spirit of God is given to the true saints to dwell in them, as his proper lasting abode; and to influence their hearts, as a principle of new nature, or as a divine supernatural spring of life and action. The scriptures represent the Holy Spirit, not only as moving, and occasionally influencing the saints, but as dwelling in them as his temple, his proper abode, and everlasting dwelling-place. And he is represented as being there so united to the faculties of the soul, that he becomes there a principle or spring of a new nature and life. . . . The Spirit of God being thus communicated and united to the saints, they are from thence properly denominated from it, and are called *spiritual*.

On the other hand, though the Spirit of God may many ways influence natural men, yet because it is not thus communicated to them, as an indwelling principle, they do not derive any denomination or character from it; for there being no *union*, it is not their *own*. . . .

2. Another reason why the saints and their virtues are called spiritual, (and which is the principal thing,) is, that the Spirit of God, dwelling as a vital principle in their souls, produces there those

effects wherein he exerts and communicates himself in his own *proper nature.* Holiness is the nature of the Spirit of God, therefore he is called in scripture the *Holy Ghost.* Holiness, which is as it were the beauty and sweetness of the divine nature, is as much the proper nature of the Holy Spirit, as heat is the nature of fire. . . . The Spirit of God so dwells in the hearts of the saints, that he there, as a seed or spring of life, exerts and communicates himself, in this his sweet and divine nature. He makes the soul a partaker of God's beauty and Christ's joy, so that the saint has truly fellowship *with* the Father, and *with* his Son Jesus Christ, in thus having the communion or participation *of* the Holy Ghost. . . .

But the Spirit of God never influences the minds of natural men after this manner. Though he may influence them many ways, yet he never, in any of his influences, communicates himself to them in his own proper nature. . . .

Thus, not only the manner of the Spirit's *relation* to the subject of his operations, is different; but the influence and *operation itself,* and the *effect wrought* exceeding different. . . . It is a spiritual work in this high sense; and therefore above all other works is peculiar to the Spirit of God. There is no work so high and excellent; for there is no work wherein God doth so much communicate himself, and wherein the mere creature hath, in so high a sense, a participation of God. . . . And this is what I mean by those influences that are *divine,* when I say, that *truly gracious affections arise from those influences that are spiritual and divine.* . . .

Those gracious influences of the saints, and the effects of God's Spirit which they experience, are entirely above nature, and altogether of a different kind from any thing that men find in themselves by the exercise of natural principles. No improvement of those principles that are natural, no advancing or exalting of them to higher degrees, and no kind of composition will ever bring men to them; because they not only differ from what is natural, and from everything that natural men experience, in degree and circumstances, but also in kind; and are of a nature vastly more excellent. And this is what I mean by *supernatural,* when I say, that *gracious affections are from those influences that are supernatural.*

From hence it follows, that in those gracious exercises and affections which are wrought in the saints, through the saving influences of the Spirit of God, there is a new inward *perception* or *sensation* of their minds, entirely different in its nature and kind, from any thing that ever their minds were the subjects of before they were sanctified. . . . Here is, as it were, a new *spiritual sense,* . . . which is in its whole nature different from any former kinds of sensation of the mind, as tasting is diverse from any of the other senses. And something is perceived by a true saint, in the exercise of this new sense of mind, in spiritual and divine things, as entirely diverse from anything that is perceived in them, by natural men, as the sweet taste of honey is diverse from the ideas men get of honey by only looking on and feeling it. So that the spiritual perceptions which a sanctified and spiritual person has, are not only diverse from all that natural men have as the perceptions of the same sense may differ one from another, but rather as the ideas and sensations of different senses differ. . . .

SECTION V. TRULY GRACIOUS AFFECTIONS ARE ATTENDED WITH A CONVICTION OF THE REALITY AND CERTAINTY OF DIVINE THINGS.

This seems to be implied in the text that was laid as the foundation of this discourse: *Whom having not seen, ye love; in whom though now ye see him not, yet believing, ye rejoice with joy unspeakable, and full of glory.* All gracious persons have a solid, full, thorough and effectual conviction of the truth of the great things of the gospel. They no longer halt between two opinions; the great doctrines of the gospel cease to be any longer doubtful things, or matters of opinion, which, though probable, are yet disputable; but with them, they are points settled and determined, as un-doubted and indisputable; so that they are not afraid to venture their all upon their truth. Their conviction is an *effectual* conviction; so that the great, spiritual, mysterious, and invisible things of the gospel, have the *influence* of real and certain things upon them; they have the *weight* and *power* of real things in their hearts; and accordingly rule in their affections, and govern them through the course of their lives. . . .

There are many religious affections, which are not attended with such a conviction of the judgment. Many apprehensions and ideas which some call *divine discoveries*, are *affecting*, but not *convincing*. Though for a little while, they may seem to be more persuaded of the truth of religion, than they used to be, and many yield a forward assent, like many of Christ's hearers, who believe for a while, yet they have no thorough and effectual conviction. . . . They do not live under the influence and power of a realizing conviction of the infinite and eternal things which the gospel reveals; if they were, it would be impossible for them to live as they do. . . .

Unless men may come to a reasonable solid persuasion and conviction of the truth of the gospel, by internal evidences. . . , by a sight of its glory, it is impossible that those who are illiterate, and unacquainted with history, should have any thorough and effectual conviction of it at all. . . . But the gospel was not given only for learned men. There are at least nineteen in twenty, if not ninety-nine in a hundred, of those for whom the scriptures were written, who are not capable of any certain or effectual conviction of the divine authority of the scriptures, by such arguments as learned men use. If men who have been brought up in heathenism, must wait for a clear and certain conviction of the truth of Christianity, until they have learning and acquaintance with the histories of politer nations, enough to see clearly the force of such kind of arguments, it will make the evidence of the gospel, to them, immensely cumbersome, and will render the propagation of the gospel among them infinitely difficult. . . .

If we come to fact and experience, there is not the least reason to suppose, that one in a hundred of those who have been sincere Christians, and have had a heart to sell all for Christ, have come by their conviction of the truth of the gospel this way. If we read over the histories of the many thousands that died martyrs for Christ, since the beginning of the reformation, and have cheerfully undergone extreme tortures, in a confidence of the truth of the gospel, and consider their circumstances and advantages; how few of them were there, that we can reasonably suppose, ever came by their assured persuasion, this way; or indeed for whom it was possible, reasonably to receive so full and strong an assurance, from such arguments! Many of them were weak women and children, and the greater part of them illiterate persons; many of whom had been brought up in popish ignorance and darkness, were but newly come out of it, and lived and died in times, wherein those arguments for the truth of Christianity from antiquity and history, had been but very imperfectly handled. And indeed, it is but very lately that these arguments have been set in a clear and convincing light, even by learned men themselves: and since it has been done, there never were fewer thorough believers, among those who have been educated in the true religion; infidelity never prevailed so much, in any age, as in this, wherein these arguments are handled to the greatest advantage.

The true martyrs of Jesus Christ, are not those who have only been strong in *opinion* that the gospel of Christ is true, but *those that have seen the truth of it;* as the very name of martyrs or witnesses (by which they are called in scripture) implies. Those are very improperly called witnesses of the truth of any thing, who only declare they are very much of opinion that such a thing is true. Those only are proper witnesses, who can, and do testify that they have seen the truth of the thing they assert. . . .

It must be noted, that among those

who have a spiritual sight of the divine glory of the gospel, there is a great variety in degrees of strength of faith, as there is a vast variety of the degrees of clearness of views of this glory: but there is no true and saving faith, or spiritual conviction of the judgment, of the truth of the gospel, that has nothing in it, of this manifestation of its internal evidence, in some degree. The gospel of the blessed God does not go abroad a begging for its evidence, so much as some think; it has its highest and most proper evidence in itself. Though [yet] great use may be made of external arguments; they are not to be neglected, but highly prized and valued; for they may be greatly serviceable to awaken unbelievers, and bring them to serious consideration, and to confirm the faith of true saints; yea, they may be in some respects subservient *to the begetting* of a saving faith in men. Though [yet] what was said before remains true, that there is no spiritual conviction of the judgment, but what arises from an apprehension of the spiritual beauty and glory of divine things. . . .

SECTION VI. GRACIOUS AFFECTIONS ARE AT-TENDED WITH EVANGELICAL HUMILIATION.

Evangelical humiliation is a sense that a Christian has of his own utter insufficiency, despicableness, and odiousness, with an answerable frame of heart. . . . They that are destitute of this, have not true religion, whatever profession they may make, and high soever their religious affections may be. . . . God has abundantly manifested in his word, that this is what he has a peculiar respect to in his saints, and that nothing is acceptable to him without it. . . . As we would therefore make the holy scriptures our rule, in judging of the nature of true religion, and judging of our own religious qualifications and state; it concerns us greatly to look at this humiliation, as one of the most essential things pertaining to real Christianity. . . .

Many hypocrites make great pretences to humility, as well as other graces. . . . We must believe that they are thus humble, and see themselves so vile, upon the credit of their *say so;* for nothing appears in them of any savour of humility, in the manner of their deportment and deeds. There are many full of expressions of their own vileness, who yet expect to be looked upon as eminent and bright saints by others, as their due; and it is dangerous for any, so much as to hint the contrary, or to carry it towards them any otherwise, than as if we looked upon them some of the chief of Christians. Many are much in exclaiming against their wicked hearts, their great shortcomings, and unprofitableness, and in speaking as though they looked on themselves as the meanest of the saints; who yet, if a minister should seriously tell them the same things in private, and should signify, that he feared they were very low and weak Christians—and thought they had reason solemnly to consider of their great barrenness and unprofitableness, and falling so much short of many others—it would be more than they could digest; they would think themselves highly injured; and there would be danger of a rooted prejudice in them against such a minister. . . .

There is a pretended great humiliation, being dead to the law, and emptied of self, which is one of the most elated things in the world. . . . Some, who think themselves quite emptied of themselves, confident that they are abased in the dust, are full as they can hold with the glory of their own humility, and lifted up to heaven with an high opinion of their abasement. Their humility is a swelling, self-conceited, confident, showy, noisy, assuming humility. . . .

It is astonishing how greatly many are deceived about themselves as to this matter, imagining themselves most humble, when they are most proud, and their behaviour is really the most haughty. The deceitfulness of the heart of man appears in no one thing so much, as this of spiritual pride and self-righteousness. . . .

He that is under the prevalence of this distemper, is apt to think highly of his attainments in religion, as comparing himself with others. It is natural for him to fall into that thought of himself, that he is an eminent saint, that he is very high amongst the saints, and has distinguishingly good and great experiences. . . . But he whose heart is under the power of Christian humility, is of a contrary disposition. If the scriptures are at all to be relied on, such an one is apt to think his attainments in religion to be comparatively mean, and to esteem himself low among the saints and one of the least of saints. . . .

Some persons' experiences naturally make them think highly of their experiences; and they often speak of them as very great and extraordinary; they freely speak of the *great things they have met with*. This *may* be spoken and meant in a *good* sense. In one sense, every degree of saving mercy is a *great thing*: it is indeed a thing *great*, yea, *infinitely great*, for God to bestow the least crumb of children's bread on such dogs as we are in ourselves; and the more humble a person is that hopes God has bestowed such mercy on him, the more apt will he be to call it a *great thing that he has met with*, in this sense. But if by *great things which they have experienced*, they mean comparatively great spiritual experiences, or beyond what is ordinary, which is evidently oftentimes the case; then for a person to say, *I have met with great things*, is the very same thing as to say, *I am an eminent saint*, and have more grace than ordinary. . . .

Such is the nature of grace, and of true spiritual light, that they naturally dispose the saints in the present state, to look upon their grace and goodness little, and their deformity great. And they that have most grace and spiritual light, of any in this world, have most of this disposition. This will appear most clear and evident to any one that soberly and thoroughly weighs the nature and reason of things, and considers the things following.

That grace and holiness is worthy to be called little, which is little in comparison of what it ought to be; and so it seems to one that is truly gracious. Such an one has his eye upon the rule of his duty; a conformity to that is what he aims at; it is what his soul reaches after; and it is by that he estimates and judges of what he does, and what he has. To a gracious soul, and especially to one eminently gracious, *that* holiness appears little, which is little compared with what it should be; little in comparison of that for which he sees infinite reason and obligation. If his holiness appears to him to be at a vast distance from this, it naturally appears despicable in his eyes, and not worthy to be mentioned as any beauty or amiableness in him. . . .

The nature of true grace and spiritual light, opens to a person's view the infinite reason there is that he should be holy in a high degree. The more grace he has, the greater sense he has of the infinite excellency and glory of the divine Being, the infinite dignity of the person of Christ, and the boundless length and breadth, and depth and height, of the love of Christ to sinners. . . . And so the more he apprehends, the more the smallness of his grace and love appears strange and wonderful: and therefore is more ready to think that others are beyond him. Wondering at the littleness of his own grace, he can scarcely believe that so strange a thing happens to other saints. It is amazing to him, that one who is really a child of God, and who has actually received the saving benefits of the unspeakable love of Christ, should love no more. He is apt to look upon it as a thing peculiar to himself, a strange instance; for he sees only the outside of other Christians, but he sees his own inside. . . .

The true love of God in the most eminent saints in this world, is truly very little in comparison of what it ought to be. Because the highest love that ever any attain to in this life, is poor, cold, exceeding low, and not worthy to be named in comparison of what our obligations appear to be, from the joint consideration of these two things; viz. 1. The reason

God has given us to love him, in the manifestations he has made of his infinite glory, in his word and works, and particularly in the gospel of his Son, and what he has done for sinful man by him. And, 2. The capacity there is in the soul of man, by those intellectual faculties which God has given it, of seeing and understanding these reasons, which God has given us to love him. . . . And therefore he that has much grace, apprehends much more than others, that great height to which his love ought to ascend; and he sees better than others, how little a way he has risen towards that height. And therefore, estimating his love by the whole height of his duty, hence it appears astonishingly little and low in his eyes. . . .

I would not be understood, that the saints on earth have, in all respects, the worst opinion of themselves, when they have most of the exercise of grace. In many respects it is otherwise. With respect to the *positive exercises* of corruption, they may appear to themselves freest and best when grace is most in exercise, and worst when the actings of grace are lowest. . . . But yet it is true, and demonstrable from the forementioned considerations, that the children of God never have such a *sensible* and *spiritual* conviction of their deformity, and so great, quick, and abasing sense of their present vileness and odiousness, as when they are highest in the exercise of true grace; and never are they so much disposed to set themselves low among Christians as then. . . .

SECTION VII. ANOTHER THING, WHEREIN GRACIOUS AFFECTIONS ARE DISTINGUISHED FROM OTHERS, IS, THAT THEY ARE ATTENDED WITH A CHANGE OF NATURE.

All gracious affections arise from a spiritual understanding, in which the soul has the excellency and glory of divine things discovered to it, as was shewn before. But all spiritual discoveries are also transforming. They not only make an alteration of the present exercise, sensation and frame of the soul, but such is their power and efficacy, that they alter its very nature. . . . Such power as this, is properly divine, and is peculiar to *the Spirit of the Lord*. Other power may make a great alteration in men's present frames and feelings, but it is the power of a Creator only that can change the nature. And no discoveries or illuminations, but those that are divine and supernatural, will have this supernatural effect. But this effect all those discoveries have, that are truly divine. The soul is deeply affected by these discoveries; so affected, as to be transformed. . . .

Therefore if there be no great and remarkable abiding change in persons, who think they have experienced a work of conversion, vain are all their imaginations and pretences, however they may have been affected. Conversion (if we may give any credit to the scripture) is a great and universal change of the man, turning him from sin to God. . . . If, therefore, after a person's high affections at his supposed first conversion, it happens that in a little time there is no very remarkable alteration in him, as to those bad qualities and evil habits which before were visible in him—and he is ordinarily under the prevalence of the same kind of dispositions as heretofore, and the same things seem to belong to his character, he appearing as selfish, carnal, stupid, and perverse, unchristian, and unsavoury as ever—it is greater evidence against him, than the brightest story of experiences that ever was told can be for him. . . .

Allowances, indeed, must be made for the natural temper, which conversion does not entirely eradicate: those sins which a man by his natural constitution was most inclined to before his conversion, he may be most apt to fall into still. But yet conversion will make a great alteration even with respect to these sins. . . . If a man before his conversion was, by his natural constitution, prone to lasciviousness, or drunkenness, or maliciousness, converting grace will make a great alteration in him, with respect to these evil dispositions; so that however he may be still most in danger of these sins, they shall no longer have dominion over him; nor will they any more be properly his character. . . .

SECTION VIII. TRULY GRACIOUS AFFECTIONS DIFFER FROM THOSE THAT ARE FALSE AND DELUSIVE, IN THAT THEY NATURALLY BEGET AND PROMOTE SUCH A SPIRIT OF LOVE, MEEKNESS, QUIETNESS, FORGIVENESS AND MERCY, AS APPEARED IN CHRIST.

The evidence of this in the scripture is very abundant. If we judge of the nature of Christianity, and the proper spirit of the gospel, by the word of God, this spirit is what may, by way of eminency, be called *the Christian spirit;* and may be looked upon as the true, and distinguishing disposition of the hearts of Christians, as such. When some of the disciples of Christ, said something, through inconsideration and infirmity, that was not agreeable to such a spirit, he told them that *they knew not what manner of spirit they were of,* implying, that this spirit of which I am speaking, is the proper spirit of his religion and kingdom. All real disciples of Christ, have this spirit in them; and not only so, but they *are of* this spirit; it is the spirit by which they are so possessed and governed, that it is their true and proper character. . . .

Every thing that appertains to holiness of heart, does indeed belong to the nature of true Christianity, and the character of Christians; but a spirit of holiness, as appearing in some particular graces, may more especially be called the Christian spirit or temper. Some amiable qualities and virtues more especially agree with the nature of the gospel constitution, and Christian profession; because there is a special agreeableness in them with those divine *attributes* which God has more remarkably manifested and glorified in the work of redemption by Jesus Christ, the grand subject of the Christian revelation. . . . And what are these virtues but such as humility, meekness, love, forgiveness, and mercy; which belong to the character of Christians, as such?

These things are spoken of as what are especially the character of Jesus Christ himself, the great head of the Christian church. . . . And as these things are especially the character of Christ; so they are all especially the character of Christians. Christians are *Christ-like;* none deserve the name who are not so in their prevailing character. . . .

Many persons seem to be quite mistaken concerning the nature of Christian fortitude. It is an exceeding diverse thing from a brutal fierceness, or the boldness of beasts of prey. True Christian fortitude consists in strength of mind, through grace, exerted in two things: in ruling and suppressing the *evil* passions and affections of the mind; and in stedfastly and freely exerting, and following *good* affections and dispositions, without being hindered by sinful fear, or the opposition of enemies. But the *passions restrained,* and kept under in the exercise of this Christian strength and fortitude, are those very passions that are vigorously and violently *exerted* in a false boldness for Christ. And those affections which are vigorously exerted in true fortitude, are those Christian holy affections, that are directly contrary to the others. Though Christian fortitude appears in withstanding and counteracting enemies without us, yet it much more appears in resisting and suppressing the enemies that are within us; because they are our worst and strongest enemies, and have greatest advantage against us. The strength of the good soldier of Jesus Christ appears in nothing more, than in stedfastly maintaining the holy calm, meekness, sweetness, and benevolence of his mind, amidst all the storms, injuries, strange behaviour, and surprising acts and events of this evil and unreasonable world. . . .

The surest way to make a right judgment of what is a holy fortitude in fighting with God's enemies, is to look to the Captain of all God's hosts, our great leader and example, and see wherein *his* fortitude and valour appeared, in his chief conflict. . . . How did he show his holy boldness and valour at that time? Not in the exercise of any fiery passions; not in fierce and violent speeches, vehemently declaiming against the intolerable wickedness of opposers, *giving them their own* in plain terms; but in not opening his mouth when afflicted and oppressed, in going as a lamb to the slaughter, and as a sheep before his shearers is dumb, not opening his mouth; praying that the Father would forgive his cruel enemies, because they knew not what they did; nor shedding others' blood, but with all-conquering patience and love shedding his own. . . . And never was the patience, meekness, love, and forgiveness of Christ, in so glorious a manifestation, as at that time. . . .

There is a pretended boldness for Christ that arises from no better principle than pride. A man may be forward to expose himself to the dislike of the world, and even to provoke their displeasure, out of pride. For it is the nature of spiritual pride to cause men to seek distinction and singularity; and so oftentimes to set themselves at war with those whom they call carnal, that they may be more highly exalted among their party. . . . And that duty which tries whether a man is willing to be despised by those of his own party, and thought the least worthy to be regarded by them, is a more proper trial of his boldness for Christ, than his being forward to expose himself to the reproach of opposers. . . . He is bold for Christ, who has Christian fortitude enough to confess his fault openly, when he has committed one that requires it, and as it were to come down upon his knees before opposers. Such things as these are much greater evidence of holy boldness, than resolutely and fiercely confronting opposers.

As some are much mistaken concerning the nature of true *boldness* for Christ, so they are concerning Christian *zeal*. It is indeed a flame, but a sweet one; or rather it is the heat and fervour of a sweet flame. For the flame of which it is the heat, is no other than that of divine love, or Christian charity; which is the sweetest and most benevolent thing that can be, in the heart of man or angel. Zeal is the fervour of this flame, as it ardently and vigorously goes out towards the

good that is its object; and so consequently in opposition to the evil that is contrary to, and impedes it. There is indeed opposition, vigorous opposition, that is an attendant of it; but it is against *things*, and not *persons*. Bitterness against the *persons* of men is no part of, but is contrary to it; insomuch that the warmer true zeal is, and the higher it is raised, so much the further are persons from such bitterness, and so much fuller of love both to the evil and to the good. . . . And as to what opposition there is in it to *things*, it is *firstly* and chiefly against the *evil things* in the person *himself* who has this zeal: against the enemies of God and holiness in his own heart; (as these are most in his view, and what he has most to do with;) and but *secondarily* against the sins of others. And therefore there is nothing in a true Christian zeal contrary to the spirit of meekness, gentleness, and love; the spirit of a little child, a lamb and dove, that has been spoken of; but is entirely agreeable to, and tends to promote it.

But I would say something particularly concerning this Christian spirit as exercised in these three things, *forgiveness*, *love* and *mercy*. The scripture is very clear and express concerning the absolute *necessity* of each of these, as belonging to the temper and character of every Christian. A *forgiving* spirit is necessary, or a disposition to overlook and forgive injuries. Christ gives it to us both as a negative and positive evidence; and is express in teaching us, that if we are of such a spirit, it is a sign we are in a state of forgiveness and favour ourselves; and that if we are not of such a spirit, we are not forgiven of God; and seems to take special care that we should always bear it on our minds. . . .

And that all true saints are of a *loving*, benevolent and beneficent temper, the scripture is very plain and abundant. . . . There is no one virtue, or disposition of mind, so often and so expressly insisted on, as marks laid down in the New Testament, whereby to know true Christians. It is often given as a sign peculiarly distinguishing, by which all may know

Christ's disciples, and by which they may know themselves; and is often laid down, both as a negative and positive evidence. . . .

And the scripture is as plain as possible, that none are true saints, but those who are of a disposition to *pity* and *relieve* their fellow-creatures, who are poor, indigent, and afflicted. . . . Christ in that description he gives us of the day of judgment . . . represents, that judgment will be passed at that day, according as men have been of a merciful spirit and practice, or otherwise. . . .

Thus we see . . . that those who are truly gracious, are under the government of that lamb-like, dove-like Spirit of Jesus Christ, and that this is essentially and eminently the nature of the saving grace of the gospel, and the proper spirit of true Christianity. We may therefore undoubtedly determine, that all truly Christian affections are attended with such a spirit; and that this is the natural tendency of the fear and hope, the sorrow and the joy, the confidence and the zeal of true Christians.

SECTION IX. GRACIOUS AFFECTIONS SOFTEN THE HEART, AND ARE ATTENDED WITH A CHRISTIAN TENDERNESS OF SPIRIT.

. . . False affections, with the delusion that attends them, finally tend to stupify the mind, and shut it up against those affections wherein tenderness of heart consists. The effect of them at least is, that persons in the settled frame of their minds, become less affected with their present and past sins, and less conscientious with respect to future sins; less moved with the warnings and cautions of God's word, or chastisements in his providence; more careless of the frame of their hearts, and the manner and tendency of their behaviour; less quick-sighted to discern what is sinful, and less afraid of the appearance of evil, than they were while under legal awakenings and fears of hell. Now they have been the subjects of impressions and affections, have a high opinion of themselves, and look on their state to be safe, they can be much more easy than before,

though living in the neglect of duties that are troublesome and inconvenient. They are much more slow and partial in complying with difficult commands: and are not alarmed at the appearance of their own defects and transgressions. . . .

Such persons as these, instead of embracing Christ as their *Saviour from sin,* trust in him as the *Saviour of their sins.* . . . They trust in Christ to preserve to them the quiet enjoyment of their sins, and to be their shield to defend them from God's displeasure; while they come close to him, even to his bosom, the place of his children, to fight against him, with their mortal weapons hid under their skirts. . . .

Gracious affections are of a quite contrary tendency; they turn a heart of stone more and more into a heart of flesh. Holy love and hope are principles vastly more efficacious upon the heart, to make it tender, and to fill it with a dread of sin, or whatever might displease and offend God; and to engage it to watchfulness, and care, and strictness, than a slavish fear of hell. . . . Holy fear is so much the nature of true godliness, that it is called in scripture by no other name more frequently, than the *fear of God.* Hence gracious affections do not tend to make men bold, forward, noisy and boisterous; but rather to *speak, trembling.* . . .

But, is there no such thing as a holy boldness in prayer, and the duties of divine worship? There is doubtless such a thing; and it is chiefly to be found in eminent saints, persons of great degrees of faith and love. But this holy boldness is not in the least opposite to *reverence;* though it be to *disunion* and *servility.* . . . No boldness in poor sinful worms of the dust, who have a right view of God and themselves, will prompt them to approach God with less fear and reverence, than spotless and glorious angels in heaven, who cover their faces before his throne. . . . It becomes such sinful creatures as we, to approach a holy God, (although with faith, and without terror) yet with contrition, penitent shame, and confusion of face. . . .

One reason why gracious affections are attended with this tenderness of spirit, is, that true grace tends to promote convictions of conscience. Persons are wont to have some convictions of conscience before they have any grace: and if afterwards they are truly converted, have true repentance, joy, and peace in believing; this has a tendency to put an end to *terrors*, but has no tendency to put an end to *convictions of sin;* it rather increases them. Grace does not stupify a man's conscience; but makes it more sensible, more easily and thoroughly to discern the sinfulness of that which is sinful, and to receive a greater conviction of the heinous and dreadful nature of sin. . . . Grace tends to give the soul a further and *better conviction* of the *same* things concerning sin, that it was convinced of under a legal work of the Spirit; viz. its great contrariety to the will, and law, and honour of God, the greatness of God's hatred of it, and displeasure against it, and the dreadful punishment it exposes to and deserves. . . .

All gracious affections have a tendency to promote this Christian tenderness of heart. Not only godly sorrow, but even a gracious joy does this. . . . Yea, the most confident and assured hope, that is truly gracious, has this tendency. The higher a holy hope is raised, the more there is of this Christian tenderness. The banishing of servile fear by a holy assurance, is attended with a proportionable increase of a reverential fear. The diminishing of the fear of God's displeasure in future punishment, is attended with a proportionable increase of fear of his displeasure *itself;* a diminished fear of hell, with an increase of the fear of sin. . . .

SECTION X. ANOTHER THING WHEREIN THOSE AFFECTIONS THAT ARE TRULY GRACIOUS AND HOLY, DIFFER FROM THOSE THAT ARE FALSE, IS BEAUTIFUL SYMMETRY AND PROPORTION.

Not that the symmetry of the virtues and gracious affections of the saints, in this life, is perfect: it oftentimes is in many things defective, through the imperfection of grace, want of proper instructions, errors in judgment, some particular unhappiness of natural temper, defects in education, and many other disadvantages that might be mentioned. But yet there is in no wise that monstrous disproportion in gracious affections, and the various parts of true religion in the saints, that is very commonly to be observed in the false religion and counterfeit graces of hypocrites.

In the truly holy affections of the saints is found that proportion, which is the natural consequence of the universality of their sanctification. They have the whole image of Christ upon them: they have *put off the old man,* and have *put on the new man* entire in all his parts and members. *It hath pleased the Father that in Christ all fulness should dwell*: there is in him every grace; *he is full of grace and truth*: and they that are Christ's *of his fulness receive, and grace for grace.* There is every grace in them which is in Christ, *grace for grace*: that is, grace answerable to grace: there is no grace in Christ, but there is its image in believers to answer it. The image is a *true* image; and there is something of the same beautiful proportion in the image, which is in the original; there is feature for feature, and member for member. . . .

It is with hypocrites, as it was with Ephraim of old, at a time when God greatly complains of their hypocrisy; *Ephraim is a cake not turned,* half roasted and half raw: there is commonly no manner of uniformity in their affections. There is in many of them a great partiality, with regard to the several kinds of religious affections; great affections in some things, and no proportion in others. A holy hope and holy fear go together in the saints. But in some of these there is the most confident hope, while they are void of reverence, self-jealousy and caution, and while they to a great degree cast off fear. . . .

Not only is there often in hypocrites, an essential deficiency, as to the various kinds of religious affections; but also a strange partiality and disproportion, in the same affections, with regard to different objects. Thus as to the affection of *love,* some make high pretences, and a great show of love to God and Christ, and it may have been greatly affected with what they have heard or thought concerning them: but they have not a spirit of love and benevolence towards men, but are disposed to contention, envy, revenge, and evil-speaking; and will, it may be, suffer an old grudge to rest in their bosoms towards a neighbour for seven years together, if not twice seven years; living in real ill-will and bitterness of spirit towards him. . . . On the other hand, there are others who appear as if they had a great deal of benevolence to men, who are very good-natured and generous in their way; but have no love to God.

And as to love to men, there are some who have flowing affections to some; but their love is far from being of so extensive and universal a nature, as a truly Christian love is. They are full of dear affections to some, and full of bitterness towards others. They are knit to their own party, those who approve, those who love, and admire them; but are fierce against those that oppose and dislike them. . . . Some show a great affection to their neighbours, and pretend to be ravished with the company of the children of God *abroad*: but at the same time are uncomfortable and churlish towards their near relations *at home,* and are very negligent of relative duties. And as to the great love to sinners and opposers of religion, and the great concern for their souls, that some express, even to extreme agony—singling out a particular person from among a multitude for its object—while at the same time there is no general compassion to sinners in equally miserable circumstances, but what is in a monstrous disproportion; this seems not to be of the nature of a gracious affection. . . .

And as there is a monstrous disproportion in the love of some, in its exercises towards *different* persons, so there is in their seeming exercises of love towards the *same* persons. Some men show a love to others as to their outward man, they are liberal of their worldly substance, and often give to the poor; but have no love to, or concern for the *souls* of men. Others pretend a great love to men's souls, but are not compassionate and charitable towards their *bodies.* To make a great show of love, pity, and distress for souls, costs them nothing; but in order to show mercy to men's bodies, they must part with money. But a true Christian love to our brethren, extends both to their souls and bodies; and herein is like the love and compassion of Jesus Christ. . . .

What has been observed of the affections of *love,* is applicable also to *other* religious affections. Those that are true, extend in some proportion to their due and proper objects: but the false, are commonly strangely disproportionate. So it is with religious *desires* and longings; these in the saints, are towards those things that are spiritual and excellent in general, and in some proportion to their excellency, importance, or necessity, or the near concern they have in them: but in false longings, it is often far otherwise. They will strangely run, with impatient vehemence, after something of less importance, when other things of greater importance are neglected. . . .

And so as to *hatred* and *zeal,* when these are from right principles, they are against sin in general, in some proportion to the degree of sinfulness. . . . But a false hatred and zeal against sin, is against some particular sin only. Thus some seem to be very zealous against profaneness, and pride in apparel, who themselves are notorious for covetousness, closeness, and it may be backbiting, envy towards superiors, turbulency of spirit towards rulers, and rooted ill-will to those who have injured them. False zeal is against the sins of others; while he that has true zeal, exercises it chiefly against his own sins; though he shews also a proper zeal against prevailing and dangerous iniquity in others.

SECTION XI. ANOTHER GREAT AND VERY DISTINGUISHING DIFFERENCE IS, THAT THE HIGHER GRACIOUS AFFECTIONS ARE RAISED, THE MORE IS A SPIRITUAL APPETITE AND LONGING OF SOUL AFTER SPIRITUAL ATTAINMENTS INCREASED: ON THE CONTRARY, FALSE AFFECTIONS REST SATISFIED IN THEMSELVES.

The more a true saint loves God with a gracious love, the more he desires to love him, and the more uneasy is he at his want of love to him: the more he hates sin, the more he desires to hate it, and laments that he has so much remaining love to it. . . . The kindling and raising of gracious affections is like kindling a flame; the higher it is raised, the more ardent it is; and the more it burns, the more vehemently does it tend and seek to burn. So that the spiritual appetite after holiness, and an increase of holy affections, is much more lively and keen in those that are eminent in holiness, than others; and more when grace and holy affections are in their most lively exercise, than at other times. . . .

But with those joys, and other religious affections, that are false and counterfeit, it is otherwise. If before there was a great desire, of some sort, after grace; as these affections rise, *that* desire ceases, or is abated. It may be before, while the man was under legal convictions, and much afraid of hell, he earnestly longed that he might obtain spiritual light in his understanding, faith in Christ, and love to God: but now, when these false affections deceive him, and make him confident that he is converted, and his state good, there are no more earnest longings after light and grace; for his end is answered; he is confident that his sins are forgiven him, and that he shall go to heaven; and so he is satisfied. . . .

William Law

(1686-1761)

ONE of the provocative voices which aroused eighteenth-century England from her coldness and lethargy of religion was that of Law. His influence was felt indirectly in the Wesleyan revival; it caused Samuel Johnson to begin an earnest inquiry into religion; and it stimulated John Henry Newman. Law was a man of mystical tendencies who saw the results of religious experience in humanitarian acts, as evidenced by his distribution of milk from four cows each day to his poor neighbors. Of his several remarkable religious writings, *A Serious Call to a Devout and Holy Life* ranks highest. It played a tremendous role in creating a new religious atmosphere in England after its publication in 1728. Its theme is the dominant idea in Law's life—that the devout man no longer lives by his own will or by the way of the world, but entirely by the will of God.

[FOR INNER PEACE AND HAPPINESS]

From *A Serious Call to a Devout and Holy Life*

Some people will perhaps object, that all these rules of holy living unto God in all that we do, are too great a restraint upon human life; that it will be made too anxious a state, by thus introducing a regard to God in all our actions; and that by depriving ourselves of so many seemingly innocent pleasures, we shall render our lives dull, uneasy, and melancholy.

To which it may be answered,

First, That these rules are prescribed for, and will certainly procure a quite contrary end. That instead of making our lives dull and melancholy, they will render them full of content and strong satisfactions. That by these rules, we only change the childish satisfactions of our vain and sickly passions, for the solid enjoyments and real happiness of a sound mind.

Secondly, That as there is no foundation for comfort in the enjoyments of this life, but in the assurance that a wise and good God governeth the world, so the more we find out God in every thing, the more we apply to Him in every place, the more we look up to Him in all our actions, the more we conform to His will, the more we act according to His wisdom, and imitate His goodness, by so much the more do we enjoy God, partake of the Divine nature, and heighten and increase all that is happy and comfortable in human life.

Thirdly, He that is endeavouring to subdue, and root out of his mind, all those passions of pride, envy, and ambition, which religion opposes, is doing more to make himself happy, even in this life, than he that is contriving means to indulge them. For these passions are the causes of all the disquiets and vexations of human life: they are the dropsies and fevers of our minds, vexing them with false appetites, and restless cravings after such things as we do not want, and spoiling our taste for those things which are our proper good.

Do but imagine that you somewhere or other saw a man that proposed reason as the rule of all his actions; that had no desires but after such things as nature wants, and religion approves; that was as pure from all the motions of pride, envy, and covetousness, as from thoughts of murder; that, in this freedom from worldly passions, he had a soul full of Divine love, wishing and praying that all men may have what they want of worldly things, and be partakers of eternal glory in the life to come. Do but fancy a man living in this manner, and your own conscience will immediately tell you, that he is the happiest man in the world, and that it is not in the power of the richest fancy to invent any higher happiness in the present state of life.

And, on the other hand, if you suppose him to be in any degree less perfect; if you suppose him but subject to one foolish fondness or vain passion, your own conscience will again tell you that he so far lessens his own happiness, and robs himself of the true enjoyment of his other virtues. So true is it, that the more we live by the rules of religion, the more peaceful and happy do we render our lives.

Again; as it thus appears that real happiness is only to be had from the greatest degrees of piety, the greatest denials of our passions, and the strictest rules of religion; so the same truth will appear from a consideration of human misery. If we look into the world, and view the disquiets and troubles of human life, we shall find that they are all owing to our violent and irreligious passions.

Now all trouble and uneasiness is founded in the want of something or other: would we, therefore, know the true cause of our troubles and disquiets, we must find out the cause of our wants; because that which creates and increaseth our wants, does, in the same degree, create and increase our troubles and disquiets.

God Almighty has sent us into the world with very few wants; meat, and drink, and clothing, are the only things necessary in life; and as these are only our present needs, so the present world is well furnished to supply these needs.

If a man had half the world in his power, he can make no more of it than this; as he wants it only to support an animal life, so is it unable to do any thing else for him, or to afford him any other happiness.

This is the state of man,—born with few wants, and into a large world very capable of supplying them. So that one would reasonably suppose that men should pass their lives in content and thankfulness to God; at least, that they should be free from violent disquiets and vexations, as being placed in a world that has more than enough to relieve all their wants.

But if to all this we add, that this short life, thus furnished with all that we want in it, is only a short passage to eternal glory, where we shall be clothed with the brightness of Angels, and enter into the joys of God, we might still more reasonably expect that human life should be a state of peace, and joy, and delight in God. Thus it would certainly be, if reason had its full power over us.

But, alas! though God, and nature, and reason, make human life thus free from wants and so full of happiness; yet our passions, in rebellion against God, against nature and reason, create a new world of evils, and fill human life with imaginary wants, and vain disquiets.

The man of pride has a thousand wants, which only his own pride has created; and these render him as full of trouble as if God had created him with a thousand appetites, without creating any thing that was proper to satisfy them. Envy and ambition have also their endless wants, which disquiet the souls of men, and by their contradictory motions, render them as foolishly miserable, as those that want to fly and creep at the same time.

Let but any complaining, disquieted man, tell you the ground of his uneasiness, and you will plainly see that he is the author of his own torment; that he is vexing himself at some imaginary evil, which will cease to torment him as soon as he is content to be that which God, and nature, and reason, require him to be.

If you should see a man passing his days in disquiet, because he could not walk upon the water, or catch birds as they fly by him, you would readily confess that such a one might thank himself for such uneasiness. But now if you look into all the most tormenting disquiets of life, you will find them all thus absurd: where people are only tormented by their own folly, and vexing themselves at such things as no more concern them, nor are any more their proper good, than walking upon the water, or catching birds.

What can you conceive more silly and extravagant, than to suppose a man racking his brains, and studying night and day how to fly?—wandering from his own house and home, wearying himself with climbing upon every ascent, cringing and courting everybody he meets to lift him up from the ground, bruising himself with continual falls, and at last breaking his neck?—and all this from an imagination that it would be glorious to have the eyes of people gazing up at him, and mighty happy to eat, and drink, and sleep, at the top of the highest trees in the kingdom: would you not readily own

that such a one was only disquieted by his own folly?

If you ask, what it signifies to suppose such silly creatures as these, as are nowhere to be found in human life?

It may be answered, that wherever you see an ambitious man, there you see this vain and senseless flyer.

Again: if you should see a man that had a large pond of water, yet living in continual thirst, not suffering himself to drink half a draught, for fear of lessening his pond; if you should see him wasting his time and strength, in fetching more water to his pond; always thirsty, yet always carrying a bucket of water in his hand, watching early and late to catch the drops of rain, gaping after every cloud, and running greedily into every mire and mud, in hopes of water, and always studying how to make every ditch empty itself into his pond: if you should see him grow grey and old in these anxious labours, and at last end a careful, thirsty life, by falling into his own pond; would you not say that such a one was not only the author of all his own disquiets, but was foolish enough to be reckoned amongst idiots and madmen? But yet foolish and absurd as this character is, it does not represent half the follies, and absurd disquiets, of the covetous man.

I could now easily proceed to show the same effects of all our other passions, and make it plainly appear that all our miseries, vexations, and complaints, are entirely of our own making, and that, in the same absurd manner, as in these instances of the covetous and ambitious man. Look where you will, you will see all worldly vexations, but like the vexation of him that was always in mire and mud in search of water to drink, when he had more at home than was sufficient for a hundred horses.

Cælia is always telling you how provoked she is, what intolerable, shocking things happen to her, what monstrous usage she suffers, and what vexations she meets with everywhere. She tells you that her patience is quite worn out, and there is no bearing the behaviour of people. Every assembly that she is at, sends her home provoked; something or other has been said, or done, that no reasonable, well-bred person ought to bear. Poor people that want her charity are sent away with hasty answers, not because she has not a heart to part with any money, but because she is too full of some trouble of her own to attend to the complaints of others. Cælia has no business upon her hands but to receive the income of a plentiful fortune; but yet, by the doleful turn of her mind, you would be apt to think that she had neither food nor lodging. If you see her look more pale than ordinary, if her lips tremble when she speaks to you, it is because she is just come from a visit, where Lupus took no notice at all of her, but talked all the time to Lucinda, who has not half her fortune. When cross accidents have so disordered her spirits, that she is forced to send for the doctor, to make her able to eat, she tells him, in great anger at Providence, that she never was well since she was born, and that she envies every beggar that she sees in health.

This is the disquiet life of Cælia, who has nothing to torment her but her own spirit.

If you could inspire her with Christian humility, you need do no more to make her as happy as any person in the world. This virtue would make her thankful to God for half so much health as she has had, and help her to enjoy more for the time to come. This virtue would keep off tremblings of the spirits, and loss of appetite, and her blood would need nothing else to sweeten it.

I have just touched upon these absurd characters, for no other end but to convince you, in the plainest manner, that the strictest rules of religion are so far from rendering a life dull, anxious, and uncomfortable (as is above objected), that, on the contrary, all the miseries, vexations, and complaints, that are in the world, are owing to the want of religion; being directly caused by those absurd passions which religion teaches us to deny.

For all the wants which disturb human life, which make us uneasy to ourselves, quarrelsome with others, and unthankful to God; which weary us in vain labours and foolish anxieties; which carry us from project to project, from place to place, in a poor pursuit of we know not what, are the wants which neither God, nor nature, nor reason, hath subjected us to, but are solely infused into us by pride, envy, ambition, and covetousness.

So far, therefore, as you reduce your desires to such things as nature and reason require; so far as you regulate all the motions of your heart by the strict rules of religion, so far you remove yourself from that infinity of wants and vexations, which torment every heart that is left to itself.

Most people, indeed, confess that religion preserves us from a great many evils, and helps us in many respects to a more happy enjoyment of ourselves; but then they imagine that this is only true of such a moderate share of religion, as only gently restrains us from the excesses of our passions. They suppose that the strict rules and restraints of an exalted piety are such contradictions to our nature, as much needs make our lives dull and uncomfortable.

Although the weakness of this objection sufficiently appears from what hath been already said, yet I shall add one word more to it.

This objection supposes that religion, moderately practised, adds much to the happiness of life; but that such heights of piety as the perfection of religion requireth, have a contrary effect.

It supposes, therefore, that it is happy to be kept from the excesses of envy, but unhappy to be kept from other degrees of envy. That it is happy to be delivered from a boundless ambition, but unhappy to be without a more moderate ambition. It supposes, also, that the happiness of life consists in a mixture of virtue and vice, a mixture of ambition and humility, charity and envy, heavenly affection and covetousness. All which is as absurd as to suppose that it is happy to be free from excessive pains, but unhappy to be without more moderate pains: or that the happiness of health consisted in being partly sick and partly well.

For if humility be the peace and rest of the soul, then no one has so much happiness from humility, as he that is the most humble. If excessive envy is a torment of the soul, he most perfectly delivers himself from torment, that most perfectly extinguishes every spark of envy. If there is any peace and joy in doing any action according to the will of God, he that brings the most of his actions to this rule, does most of all increase the peace and joy of his life.

And thus it is in every virtue; if you act up to every degree of it, the more happiness you have from it. And so of every vice: if you only abate its excesses, you do but little for yourself; but if you reject it in all degrees, then you feel the true ease and joy of a reformed mind.

As for example: If religion only restrains the excesses of revenge, but lets the spirit still live within you in lesser instances, your religion may have made your life a little more outwardly decent, but not made you at all happier, or easier in yourself. But if you have once sacrificed all thoughts of revenge, in obedience to God, and are resolved to return good for evil at all times, that you may render yourself more like to God, and fitter for His mercy in the kingdom of love and glory; this is a height of virtue that will make you feel its happiness.

Secondly, As to those satisfactions and enjoyments, which an exalted piety requireth us to deny ourselves, this deprives us of no real comfort of life.

For Piety requires us to renounce no ways of life, where we can act reasonably, and offer what we do to the glory of God. All ways of life, all satisfactions and enjoyments, that are within these bounds, are no way denied us by the strictest rules of piety. Whatever you can do, or enjoy, as in the presence of God, as His servant, as His rational creature that has received reason and knowledge from Him; all that you can perform conformably to a rational nature, and the will of God, all this is allowed by the laws of piety. And will you think that your life will be uncomfortable unless you may displease God, be a fool, and mad, and act contrary to that reason and wisdom which He has implanted in you?

And as for those satisfactions which we dare not offer to a holy God, which are only invented by the folly and corruption of the world, which inflame our passions, and sink our souls into grossness and sensuality, and render us incapable of the Divine favour, either here or hereafter; surely it can be no uncomfortable state of life to be rescued by religion from such self-murder, and to be rendered capable of eternal happiness.

Let us suppose a person destitute of that knowledge which we have from our senses, placed somewhere alone by himself, in the midst of a variety of things which he did not know how to use; that he has by him bread, wine, water, golden dust, iron chains, gravel, garments, fire, etc. Let it be supposed that he has no knowledge of the right use of these things, nor any direction from his senses how to quench his thirst, or satisfy his hunger, or make any use of the things about him. Let it be supposed, that in his drought he puts golden dust into his eyes; when his eyes smart, he puts wine into his ears; that in his hunger, he puts gravel into his mouth; that in pain, he loads himself with the iron chains; that feeling cold, he puts his feet in the water; that being frighted at the fire, he runs away from it; that being weary, he makes a seat of his bread. Let it be supposed, that through his ignorance of the right use of the things that are about him, he will vainly torment himself whilst he lives, and at last die, blinded with dust, choked with gravel, and loaded with chains. Let it be supposed that some good being came to him, and showed him the nature and use of all the things that were about him, and gave him such strict rules of using them, as would certainly, if observed, make him the happier for all that he had, and deliver him from the pains of hunger, and thirst, and cold.

Now could you with any reason affirm, that those strict rules of using those things that were about him, had rendered that poor man's life dull and uncomfortable?

Now this is in some measure a representation of the strict rules of religion; they only relieve our ignorance, save us from tormenting ourselves, and teach us to use everything about us to our proper advantage.

Man is placed in a world full of variety of things; his ignorance makes him use many of them as absurdly as the man that put dust in his eyes to relieve his thirst, or put on chains to remove pain.

Religion, therefore, here comes in to his relief, and gives him strict rules of using everything that is about him; that by so using them suitably to his own nature, and the nature of the things, he may have always the pleasure of receiving a right benefit from them. It shows him what is strictly right in meat, and drink, and clothes; and that he has nothing else to expect from the things of this world, but to satisfy such wants of his own; and then to extend his assistance to all his brethren, that, as far as he is able, he may help all his fellow-creatures to the same benefit from the world that he hath.

It tells him that this world is incapable of giving him any other happiness; and that all endeavours to be happy in heaps of money, or acres of land, in fine clothes, rich beds, stately equipage, and show and splendour, are only vain endeavours, ignorant attempts after impossibilities, these things being no more able to give the least degree of happiness, than dust in the eyes can cure thirst, or gravel in the mouth satisfy hunger; but like dust and gravel misapplied, will only serve to render him more unhappy by such an ignorant misuse of them.

It tells him that although this world can do no more for him than satisfy these wants of the body, yet that there is a much greater good prepared for man than eating, drinking, and dressing; that it is yet invisible to his eyes, being too glorious for the apprehension of flesh and blood; but reserved for him to enter upon, as soon as this short life is over; where, in a new body formed to an angelic likeness, he shall dwell in the light and glory of God to all eternity.

It tells him that this state of glory will be given to all those that make a right use of the things of this present world, who do not blind themselves with golden dust, or eat gravel, or groan under loads of iron of their own putting on; but use bread, water, wine, and garments, for such ends as are according to nature and reason; and who, with faith and thankfulness, worship the kind Giver of all that they enjoy here, and hope for hereafter.

Now can any one say that the strictest rules of such a religion as this debar us of any of the comforts of life? Might it not as justly be said of those rules that only hinder a man from choking himself with gravel? For the strictness of these rules only consists in the exactness of their rectitude.

Who would complain of the severe strictness of a law that, without any exception, forbad the putting of dust into our eyes? Who could think it too rigid, that there were no abatements? Now this is the strictness of religion; it requires nothing of us strictly, or without abatements, but where every degree of the thing is wrong, where every indulgence does us some hurt.

If religion forbids all instances of revenge, without any exception, it is because all revenge is of the nature of poison; and though we do not take so much as to put an end to life, yet if we take any at all, it corrupts the whole mass of blood, and makes it difficult to be restored to our former health.

If religion commands an universal charity, to love our neighbour as ourselves, to forgive and pray for all our enemies without any reserve; it is because all degrees of love are degrees of happiness, that strengthen and support the Divine life of the soul, and are as necessary to its health and happiness, as proper food is necessary to the health and happiness of the body.

If religion has laws against laying up treasures upon earth, and commands us to be content with food and raiment, it is because every other use of the world is abusing it to our own vexation, and turning all its conveniences into snares and traps to destroy us. It is because this plainness and simplicity of life secures us from the cares and pains of restless pride and envy, and makes it easier to keep that straight road that will carry us to eternal life.

If religion saith, "Sell that thou hast, and give to the poor," it is because there is no other natural or reasonable use of our riches, no other way of making ourselves happier for them; it is because it is as strictly right to give others that which we do not want ourselves, as it is right to use so much as our own wants require. For if a man has more food than his own nature requires, how base and unreasonable is it to invent foolish ways of wasting it, and make sport for his own full belly, rather than let his fellow-creatures have the same comfort from food which he hath had. It is so far, therefore, from being a hard law of religion, to make this use of our riches, that a reasonable man would rejoice in that religion which teaches him to be happier in that which he gives away, than in that which he keeps for himself; which teaches him to make spare food and raiment be greater blessings to him, than that which feeds and clothes his own body.

If religion requires us sometimes to fast, and deny our natural appetites, it is to lessen that struggle and war that is in our nature, it is to render our bodies fitter instruments of purity, and more obedient to the good motions of Divine grace; it is to dry up the springs of our passions that war against the soul, to cool the flame of our blood, and render the mind more capable of Divine meditations. So that although these abstinences give some pain to the body, yet they so lessen the power of bodily appetites and passions, and so increase our taste of spiritual joys, that even these severities of religion, when practised with discretion, add much to the comfortable enjoyment of our lives.

If religion calleth us to a life of watch-ing and prayer it is because we live amongst a crowd of enemies, and are always in need of the assistance of God. If we are to confess and bewail our sins, it is because such confessions relieve the mind, and restore it to ease; as burdens and weights taken off the shoulders, relieve the body, and make it easier to itself. If we are to be frequent and fervent in holy petitions, it is to keep us steady in the sight of our true good, and that we may never want the happiness of a lively faith, a joyful hope, and well-grounded trust in God. If we are to pray often, it is that we may be often happy in such secret joys as only prayer can give; in such communications of the Divine Presence, as will fill our minds with all the happiness that beings not in Heaven are capable of.

Was there anything in the world more worth our care, was there any exercise of the mind, or any conversation with men, that turned more to our advantage than this intercourse with God, we should not be called to such a continuance in prayer. But if a man considers what it is that he leaves when he retires to devotion, he will find it no small happiness to be so often relieved from doing nothing, or nothing to the purpose; from dull idleness, unprofitable labour, or vain conversation. If he considers that all that is in the world, and all that is doing in it, is only for the body, and bodily enjoyments, he will have reason to rejoice at those hours of prayer, which carry him to higher consolations, which raise him above these poor concerns, which open to his mind a scene of greater things, and accustom his soul to the hope and expectation of them.

If religion commands us to live wholly unto God, and to do all to His glory, it is because every other way is living wholly against ourselves, and will end in our own shame and confusion of face.

As everything is dark, that God does not enlighten; as everything is senseless, that has not its share of knowledge from Him; as nothing lives, but by partaking of life from Him; as nothing exists, but because He commands it to be; so there is no glory or greatness, but what is of the glory and greatness of God.

We indeed may talk of human glory as we talk of human life, or human knowledge: but as we are sure that human life implies nothing of our own but a dependent living in God, or enjoying so much life in God; so human glory, whenever we find it, must be only so much glory as we enjoy in the glory of God.

This is the state of all creatures, whether men or Angels; as they make not themselves, so they enjoy nothing from themselves: if they are great, it must be only as great receivers of the gifts of God; their power can only be so much of the Divine power acting in them; their wisdom can be only so much of the Divine wisdom shining within them; and their light and glory, only so much of the light and glory of God shining upon them.

As they are not men or Angels, because they had a mind to be so themselves, but because the will of God formed them to be what they are; so they cannot enjoy this or that happiness of men or Angels, because they have a mind to it, but because it is the will of God that such things be the happiness of men, and such things the happiness of Angels. But now if God be thus all in all; if His will is thus the measure of all things, and all natures; if nothing can be done, but by His power; if nothing can be seen, but by a light from Him; if we have nothing to fear, but from His justice; if we have nothing to hope for, but from His goodness; if this is the nature of man, thus helpless in himself; if this is the state of all creatures, as well those in Heaven as those on earth; if they are nothing, can do nothing, can suffer no pain, nor feel any happiness, but so far, and in such degrees, as the power of God does all this; if this be the state of things, then how can we have the least glimpse of joy or comfort, how can we have any peaceful enjoyment of ourselves, but by living wholly unto that God, using and doing everything conformably to His will? A life thus de-voted unto God, looking wholly unto Him in all our actions, and doing all things suitable to His glory, is so far from being dull and uncomfortable, that it creates new comforts in everything that we do.

On the contrary, would you see how happy they are who live according to their own wills, who cannot submit to the dull and melancholy business of a life devoted unto God; look at the man in the parable, to whom his Lord had given one talent.

He could not bear the thoughts of using his talent according to the will of Him from whom he had it, and therefore he chose to make himself happier in a way of his own. "Lord," says he, "I knew thee, that thou art an hard man, reaping where thou hadst not sown, and gathering where thou hadst not strawed: and I was afraid, and went and hid thy talent in the earth! lo, there thou hast that is thine."

His Lord, having convicted him out of his own mouth, despatches him with this sentence, "Cast the unprofitable servant into outer darkness: there shall be weeping and gnashing of teeth."

Here you see how happy this man made himself, by not acting wholly according to his Lord's will. It was, according to his own account, a happiness of murmuring and discontent; I knew thee, says he, that thou wast an hard man: it was a happiness of fears and apprehensions; I was, says he, afraid: it was a happiness of vain labours and fruitless travels; I went, says he, and hid thy talent; and after having been awhile the sport of foolish passions, tormenting fears, and fruitless labour, he is rewarded with darkness, eternal weeping, and gnashing of teeth.

Now this is the happiness of all those who look upon a strict and exalted piety, that is, a right use of their talent, to be a dull and melancholy state of life.

They may live a while free from the restraints and directions of religion; but, instead thereof, they must be under the absurd government of their passions: they must, like the man in the parable, live in murmurings and discontents, in fears and apprehensions. They may avoid the labour of doing good, of spending their time devoutly, of laying up treasures in Heaven, of clothing the naked, of visiting the sick; but then they must, like this man, have labours and pains in vain, that tend to no use or advantage, that do no good either to themselves or others; they must travel, and labour, and work, and dig, to hide their talent in the earth. They must, like him, at their Lord's coming, be convicted out of their own mouths, be accused by their own hearts, and have everything that they have said and thought of religion, be made to show the justice of their condemnation to eternal darkness, weeping, and gnashing of teeth.

This is the purchase that they make, who avoid the strictness and perfection of religion, in order to live happily.

On the other hand, would you see a short description of the happiness of a life rightly employed, wholly devoted to God, you must look at the man in the parable to whom his Lord had given five talents. "Lord," says he, "thou deliveredst unto me five talents; behold, I have gained beside them five talents more. His Lord said unto him, Well done, thou good and faithful servant; thou hast been faithful over a few things, I will make thee ruler over many things: enter thou into the joy of thy Lord."

Here you see a life that is wholly intent upon the improvement of the talents, that is devoted wholly unto God, is a state of happiness, prosperous labours, and glorious success. Here are not, as in the former case, any uneasy passions, murmurings, vain fears, and fruitless labours. The man is not toiling and digging in the earth for no end or advantage; but his pious labours prosper in his hands, his happiness increases upon him; the blessing of five becomes the blessing of ten talents; and he is received with a "Well done, good and faithful servant: enter thou into the joy of thy Lord."

Now as the case of these men in the parable left nothing else to their choice, but either to be happy in using their gifts to the glory of the Lord, or miserable by using them according to their own humours and fancies; so the state of Christianity leaves us no other choice.

All that we have, all that we are, all that we enjoy, are only so many talents from God: if we use them to the ends of a pious and holy life, our five talents will become ten, and our labours will carry us into the joy of our Lord; but if we abuse them to the gratifications of our own passions, sacrificing the gifts of God to our own pride and vanity, we shall live here in vain labours and foolish anxieties, shunning religion as a melancholy thing, accusing our Lord as a hard master, and then fall into everlasting misery.

We may for a while amuse ourselves with names and sounds, and shadows of happiness; we may talk of this or that greatness and dignity; but if we desire real happiness, we have no other possible way to it but by improving our talents, by so holily and piously using the powers and faculties of men in this present state, that we may be happy and glorious in the powers and faculties of Angels in the world to come.

How ignorant, therefore, are they of the nature of religion, of the nature of man, and the nature of God, who think a life of strict piety and devotion to God to be a dull uncomfortable state; when it is so plain and certain that there is neither comfort nor joy to be found in anything else!

John Woolman

(1720-1772)

BORN in a farming community in Burlington County, New Jersey, Woolman, through self-discipline, became an educated person. He was a farmer, store clerk, tailor, and schoolmaster. At thirty, he gave himself to the Society of Friends. In this ministry he traveled from Maine to South Carolina, and finally to England, where he died. He stressed simplicity of living, the necessity of a worthy trade—he turned to tailoring—a conscientious objection toward war and slavery. Of him Dean Willard L. Sperry says, "If I were asked to date the birth of social conscience in its present-day form, I think I should put it on the twenty-sixth day of the eighth month of the year 1758—the day John Woolman in a public meeting verbally denounced Negro slavery." His *Journal* is a portrait of a man who stands for the ideals of the Society of Friends.

[ON HUMILITY AND SIMPLICITY]

From the *Journal*

My Heart was replenished with Mirth and Wantonness, and pleasing Scenes of Vanity were presented to my Imagination, till I attained the Age of eighteen Years; near which Time I felt the Judgments of God, in my Soul, like a consuming Fire; and, looking over my past Life, the Prospect was moving.—I was often sad, and longed to be delivered from those Vanities; then again, my Heart was strongly inclined to them, and there was in me a sore Conflict: At Times I turned to Folly, and then again, Sorrow and Confusion took hold of me. In a while, I resolved totally to leave off some of my Vanities; but there was a secret Reserve, in my Heart, of the more refined Part of them, and I was not low enough to find true Peace. Thus, for some Months, I had great Troubles; there remaining in me an unsubjected Will, which rendered my Labours fruitless, till at length, through the merciful Continuance of heavenly Visitations, I was made to bow down in Spirit before the Lord. I remember one Evening I had spent some Time in reading a pious Author; and walking out alone, I humbly prayed to the Lord for his Help, that I might be delivered from all those Vanities which so ensnared me. Thus, being brought low, he helped me; and, as I learned to bear the Cross, I felt Refreshment to come from his Presence; but, not keeping in that Strength which gave Victory, I lost Ground again; the Sense of which greatly affected me; and I sought Desarts and lonely Places, and there, with Tears, did confess my Sins to God, and humbly craved Help of him. And I may say with Reverence, he was near to me in my Troubles, and in those Times of Humiliation opened my Ear to Discipline. . . .

As I lived under the Cross, and simply followed the Openings of Truth, my Mind, from Day to Day, was more enlightened; my former Acquaintance were left to judge of me as they would, for I found it safest for me to live in private, and keep these Things sealed up in my own Breast. While I silently ponder on that Change wrought in me, I find no Language equal to it, nor any Means to convey to another a clear Idea of it. I looked on the Works of God in this visible Creation, and an Awfulness covered me; my Heart was tender and often contrite, and universal Love to my Fellow-creatures increased in me: This will be understood by such as have trodden the same Path. Some Glances of real Beauty may be seen in their Faces, who dwell in true Meekness. There is a Harmony in the Sound of the Voice to which divine Love gives Utterance, and some Appearance of right Order in their Temper and Conduct, whose Passions are regulated; yet all these do not fully shew forth that inward Life to such as have not felt it: But this white Stone and new Name is known rightly to such only as have it.

Though I had been thus strengthened to bear the Cross, I still found myself in great Danger, having many Weaknesses attending me, and strong Temptations to wrestle with; in the feeling whereof I frequently withdrew into private Places, and often with Tears besought the Lord to help me, whose gracious Ear was open to my Cry. . . .

My Mind, through the Power of Truth, was in a good degree weaned from the Desire of outward Greatness, and I was learning to be content with real Conveniences, that were not costly; so that a Way of Life, free from much Entanglement, appeared best for me, though the Income might be small. I had several Offers of Business that appeared profitable, but did not see my Way clear to accept of them; as believing the Business proposed would be attended with more outward Care than was required of me to engage in.

I saw that a humble Man, with the blessing of the Lord, might live on a little; and that where the Heart was set on Greatness, Success in Business did not satisfy the craving; but that commonly, with an Increase of Wealth, the Desire of Wealth increased. There was a Care on my Mind so to pass my Time, that nothing might hinder me from the most steady Attention to the Voice of the true Shepherd. . . .

In my Youth I was used to hard Labour; and, though I was middling healthy, yet my Nature was not fitted to endure so much as many others: So that, being often weary, I was prepared to sympathize with those whose Circumstances in Life, as free Men, required constant Labour to answer the Demands of their Creditors, and with others under Oppression. In the Uneasiness of Body, which I have many Times felt by too much Labour, not as a forced but as a voluntary Oppression, I have often been excited to think on the original Cause of that Oppression, which is imposed on many in the World: And, the latter Part of the Time wherein I laboured on our Plantation, my Heart, through the fresh Visitations of heavenly Love, being often tender, and my leisure Time frequently spent in reading the Life and Doctrines of our blessed Redeemer, the Account of the Sufferings of Martyrs, and the History of the first Rise of our Society, a Belief was gradually settled in my Mind, that if such, as had great Estates, generally lived in that Humility and Plainness which belongs to a *Christian* Life, and laid much easier Rents and Interests on their Lands and Monies, and thus led the Way to a right Use of Things, so great a Number of People might be employed in Things useful, that Labour both for Men and other Creatures, would need to be no more than an agreeable Employ; and divers Branches of Business, which serve chiefly to please the natural Inclinations of our Minds, and which, at present, seem necessary to circulate that Wealth which some gather, might, in this Way of pure Wisdom, be discontinued.

[FROM A LETTER TO FRIENDS]

. . . First, my dear Friends, dwell in Humility, and take Heed that no Views of outward Gain get too deep hold of you, that so your Eyes being single to the Lord, you may be preserved in the Way of Safety. Where People let loose their Minds after the Love of outward Things, and are more engaged in pursuing the Profits, and seeking the Friendships, of this World, than to be inwardly acquainted with the Way of true Peace; such walk in a vain Shadow, while the true Comfort of Life is wanting: Their Examples are often hurtful to others; and their Treasures, thus collected, do many Times prove dangerous Snares to their Children.

But where People are sincerely devoted to follow Christ, and dwell under the Influence of his holy Spirit, their Stability and Firmness, through a divine Blessing, is at Times like Dew on the tender Plants round about them, and the Weightiness of their Spirits secretly works on the Minds of others; and in this Condition, through the spreading Influence of divine Love, they feel a Care over the Flock; and Way is opened for maintaining good Order in the Society: And though we meet with Opposition from another Spirit, yet, as there is a dwelling in Meekness, feeling our Spirits subject, and moving only in the gentle peaceable Wisdom, the inward Reward of Quietness will be greater than all our Difficulties. Where the pure Life is kept to, and Meetings of Discipline are held in the Authority of it, we find by Experience that they are comfortable, and tend to the Health of the Body.

[TESTIMONY AT A MEETING]

". . . I was led to mention the Integrity and Constancy of many Martyrs, who gave their Lives for the Testimony of Jesus; and yet, in some Points, held Doctrines distinguishable from some which we hold: And that, in all Ages, where People were faithful to the Light and Understanding which the Most High afforded them, they found Acceptance with him; and that now, though there are different Ways of Thinking amongst us in some Particulars, yet, if we mutually kept to that Spirit and Power which crucifies to the World, which teaches us to be content with Things really needful, and to avoid all Superfluities, giving up our Hearts to fear and serve the Lord, true Unity may still be preserved amongst us: And that if such, as were, at Times, under Sufferings on Account of some Scruples of Conscience, kept low and humble, and in their Conduct in Life manifested a Spirit of true Charity, it would be more likely to reach the Witness in others, and be of more Service in the Church, than if their Sufferings were attended with a contrary Spirit and Conduct." In which Exercise I was drawn into a sympathizing Tenderness with the Sheep of Christ, however distinguished one from another in this World; and the like Disposition appeared to spread over others in the Meeting. Great is the Goodness of the Lord toward his poor Creatures!

[ON SICKNESS]

From a letter in the *Journal*

In this thy late Affliction I have found a deep Fellow-feeling with thee; and had a secret Hope throughout, that it might please the Father of Mercies to raise thee up, and sanctify thy Troubles to thee; that thou, being more fully acquainted with that Way which the World esteems foolish, mayst feel the Clothing of divine Fortitude, and be strengthened to resist that Spirit which leads from the Simplicity of the everlasting Truth.

We may see ourselves crippled and halting, and, from a strong Bias to Things pleasant and easy, find an Impossibility to advance forward; but Things impossible with Men are possible to God; and, our Wills being made subject to his, all Temptations are surmountable.

This Work of subjecting the Will is compared to the Mineral in the Furnace; "He refines them as Silver is refined.— He shall sit as a Refiner and Purifier of Silver." By these Comparisons we are instructed in the Necessity of the Operation of the Hand of God upon us, to prepare our Hearts truly to adore him, and manifest that Adoration, by inwardly turning away from that Spirit, in all its Workings, which is not of him. To forward this Work, the all-wise God is sometimes pleased, through outward Distress, to bring us near the Gates of Death; that, Life being painful and afflicting, and the Prospect of Eternity open before us, all earthly Bonds may be loosened, and the Mind prepared for that deep and sacred Instruction, which otherwise would not be received. If Parents love their Children and delight in their Happiness, then he, who is perfect Goodness, in sending abroad mortal Contagions, doth assuredly direct their Use: Are the Righteous removed by it? Their Change is happy: Are the Wicked taken away in their Wickedness? The Almighty is clear: Do we pass through with Anguish and great Bitterness, and yet recover, he intends that we should be purged from Dross, and our Ears opened to Discipline.

And now that, on thy Part, after thy sore Affliction and Doubts of Recovery, thou art again restored, forget not him who hath helped thee; but in humble Gratitude hold fast his Instructions, thereby to shun those Bypaths which lead from the firm Foundation. I am sensible of that Variety of Company, to which one in thy Business must be exposed: I have painfully felt the Force of Conversation proceeding from Men deeply rooted in an earthly Mind, and can sympathize with others in such Conflicts, in that much Weakness still attends me.

I find that to be a Fool as to worldly Wisdom, and commit my Cause to God, not fearing to offend Men, who take Offence at the Simplicity of Truth, is the only Way to remain unmoved at the Sentiments of others.

The Fear of Man brings a Snare; by halting in our Duty, and giving back in the Time of Trial, our Hands grow weaker, our Spirits get mingled with the People, our Ears grow dull as to hearing the Language of the true Shepherd; that when we look at the Way of the Righteous, it seems as though it was not for us to follow them.

There is a Love clothes my Mind, while I write, which is superior to all Expressions; and I find my Heart open to encourage a holy Emulation, to advance forward in *Christian* Firmness. Deep Humility is a strong Bulwark; and, as we enter into it, we find Safety: The Foolishness of God is wiser than Man, and the Weakness of God is stronger than Man. Being unclothed of our own Wisdom, and knowing the Abasement of the Creature, therein we find that Power to arise, which gives Health and Vigour to us.

[ON THE REARING OF CHILDREN]

From a letter in the *Journal*

Do we feel an affectionate Regard to Posterity; and are we employed to promote their Happiness? Do our Minds, in Things outward, look beyond our own Dissolution; and are we contriving for the Prosperity of our Children after us? Let us then, like wise Builders, lay the Foundation deep; and, by our constant uniform Regard to an inward Piety and Virtue, let them see that we really value it: Let us labour, in the Fear of the Lord, that their innocent Minds, while young and tender, may be preserved from Corruptions; that, as they advance in Age, they might rightly understand their true Interest, may consider the Uncertainty of temporal Things, and, above all, have their Hope and Confidence firmly settled in the Blessing of that Almighty Being, who inhabits Eternity, and preserves and supports the World.

In all our Cares, about worldly Treasures, let us steadily bear in Mind, that Riches, possessed by Children who do not truly serve God, are likely to prove Snares that may more grievously entangle them in that Spirit of Selfishness and Exaltation, which stands in Opposition to real Peace and Happiness; and renders them Enemies to the Cross of Christ, who submit to the Influence of it.

To keep a watchful eye towards real Objects of Charity, to visit the Poor in their lonesome Dwelling-places, to comfort them who, through the Dispensations of divine Providence, are in strait and painful Circumstances in this Life, and steadily to endeavour to honour God with our Substance, from a real Sense of the Love of Christ influencing our Minds thereto, is more likely to bring a Blessing to our Children, and will afford more Satisfaction to a *Christian* favoured with Plenty, than an earnest Desire to collect much Wealth to leave behind us.

ON THE RIGHT USE OF THE LORD'S OUTWARD GIFTS

As our Understandings are opened by the pure Light, we experience that, through an inward approaching to God, the Mind is strengthened in Obedience; and that by gratifying those Desires which are not of his begetting, those Approaches to him are obstructed, and the deceivable Spirit gains Strength.

These Truths, being as it were engraven upon our Hearts, and our everlasting Interest in Christ evidently concerned herein, we become fervently engaged, that nothing may be nourished which tends to feed Pride or Self-love in us. Thus in pure Obedience, we are not only instructed in our Duty to God, but also in the Affairs which necessarily relate to this Life, and the Spirit of Truth which guides into all Truth, leavens the Mind with a pious Concern, that *whatsoever we do in Word or Deed, may be done in his Name.*

Hence such Buildings, Furniture, Food, and Raiment, as best answer our Necessities, and are the least likely to feed that selfish Spirit which is our Enemy, are the most acceptable to us.

In this State the Mind is tender, and inwardly watchful, that the Love of Gain draw us not into any Business, which may weaken our Love to our Heavenly Father, or bring unnecessary Trouble to any of his Creatures.

Thus the Way gradually opens to cease from that Spirit which craves Riches and Things fetched far, which so mixeth with the Customs of this World, and so intrudes upon the true Harmony of Life, that the right Medium of Labour is very much departed from. And as the Minds of People are settled in a steady Concern, not to hold nor possess any Thing but what may be held consistent with the Wisdom from above, they consider what they possess as the Gift of God, and are inwardly exercised, that in all Parts of their Conduct they may act agreeable to the Nature of the peaceable Government of Christ.

A little supports such a Life; and in a State truly resigned to the Lord, the Eye is single, to see what outward Employ he leads into, as a Means of our Subsistence, and a lively Care is maintained to hold to that without launching further.

There is a Harmony in the several Parts of this Divine Work in the Hearts of People; he who leads them to cease from those gainful Employments, carried on in that Wisdom which is from beneath, delivers also from the Desire after worldly Greatness, and reconciles the Mind to a Life so plain, that a little doth suffice.

Here the real Comforts of Life are not lessened. Moderate Exercise, in the Way of true Wisdom, is pleasant both to Mind and Body.

Food and Raiment sufficient, though in the greatest Simplicity, is accepted with Content and Gratitude.

The Mutual Love, subsisting between the faithful Followers of Christ, is more pure than that Friendship which is not seasoned with Humility, how specious soever the Appearance.

Where People depart from pure Wisdom in one Case, it is often an Introduction to depart from it in many more; and thus a Spirit which seeks for outward Greatness, and leads into worldly Wisdom to attain it, and support it, gets Possession of the Mind.

In beholding the customary Departure from the true Medium of Labour, and that unnecessary Toil which many go through, in supporting outward Greatness, and procuring Delicacies. . . .

When the Prophet *Isaiah* had uttered his Vision, and declared that a Time was coming wherein *Swords should be beat into Plowshares, and Spears into pruning Hooks, and that Nation shall not lift up Sword against Nation, nor learn War any more;* he immediately directs the Minds of People to the Divine Teacher, in this remarkable Language; *O House of* Jacob! *come ye, and let us walk in the Light of the Lord.*

To wait for the Direction of this light, in all temporal as well as spiritual Concerns, appears necessary; for if in any Case we enter lightly into temporal Affairs, without feeling this Spirit of Truth to open our Way therein, and through the Love of this World proceed on, and seek for Gain by that Business or Traffick, which *is not of the Father, but of the World,* we fail in our Testimony to the Purity and Peace of his Government, and get into that which is for Chastisement.

This Matter hath lain heavy on my Mind, it being evident, that a Life less humble, less simple and plain, than that which Christ leads his Sheep into, does necessarily require a Support, which pure Wisdom does not provide for; hence there is no Probability of our being *a peculiar People, so zealous of good Works, as to have no Fellowship with Works of Darkness,* while we have Wants to supply which have their Foundation in Custom, and do not come within the Meaning of those Expressions, *your Heavenly Father knoweth that ye have need of all these Things.*

These Things which he beholds necessary for his People, he fails not to give them in his own Way and Time; but as his Ways are above our Ways, and his Thoughts above our Thoughts, so imaginary Wants are different *from these Things which he knoweth that we have need of.*

As my Meditations have been on these Things, Compassion hath filled my Heart toward my Fellow Creatures, involved in Customs, grown up in *the Wisdom of this World, which is Foolishness with God.* And O that the Youth may be so thoroughly experienced in an humble Walking before the Lord, that they may be his Children, and know him to be their Refuge, their safe unfailing Refuge, through the various Dangers attending this uncertain State of Being!

If those whose Minds are redeemed from the Love of Wealth, and who are content with a plain, simple Way of living, do yet find that to conduct the Affairs of a Family, without giving Countenance to unrighteous Proceedings, or having Fellowship with Works of Darkness, the most diligent Care is necessary.

If Customs, distinguishable from universal Righteousness, and opposite to the true Self-denying Life, are now prevalent, and so mixed with Trade, and with almost every Employ, that it is only through humble waiting on the inward Guidance of Truth, that we may reasonably hope to walk safely, and support an uniform Testimony to the peaceable Government of Christ:

If this be the Case, how lamentably do they expose themselves to Temptations, who give way to the Love of Riches, conform to expensive Living, and reach forth for Gain, to support Customs, which our Holy Shepherd leads not into.

ON THE EXAMPLE OF CHRIST

From *Considerations on the True Harmony of Mankind*

As my Mind hath been brought into a Brotherly Feeling with the Poor, as to the Things of this Life, who are under Trials in regard to getting a Living in a Way answerable to the Purity of Truth; a Labour of Heart hath attended me, that their Way may not be made difficult through the Love of Money in those who are tried with plentiful Estates, but that they with Tenderness of Heart may sympathize with them.

It was the Saying of our blessed Redeemer, *Ye cannot serve God and Mammon.* There is a deep Feeling of the Way of Purity, a Way in which the Wisdom of the World hath no Part, but is opened by the Spirit of Truth, and is called *the Way of Holiness;* a Way in which the Traveller is employed in watching unto Prayer; and the outward Gain we get in this Journey is considered as a Trust committed to us, by him who formed and supports the World; and is the rightful Director of the Use and Application of the Product of it.

Now except the Mind be preserved chaste, there is no Safety for us; but in an Estrangement from true Resignation, the Spirit of the World casts up a Way, in which Gain is many Times principally attended to, and in which there is a selfish Application of outward Treasures.

How agreeable to the true Harmony of Society, is that Exhortation of the Apostle? *Look not every Man on his own Things, but every Man also on the Things of others. Let this Mind be in you which was also in Christ Jesus.*

A Person in outward Prosperity may have the Power of obtaining Riches, but the same Mind being in him which is in Christ Jesus, he may feel a Tenderness of Heart towards those of low Degree; and instead of setting himself above them, may look upon it as an unmerited Favour, that his Way through Life is more easy than the Way of many others; may improve every Opportunity of leading forth out of those Customs which have entangled the Family; employ his Time in looking into the Wants of the poor Members, and hold forth such a perfect Example of Humiliation, that the pure Witness may be reached in many Minds; and the Way opened for a harmonious walking together.

Jesus Christ, in promoting the Happiness of others, was not deficient in looking for the Helpless, who lay in Obscurity, nor did he save any Thing to render himself honourable amongst Men, which

might have been of more Use to the weak Members in his Father's Family; of whose Compassion towards us I may now speak a little. He who was perfectly happy in himself, moved with infinite Love, *took not upon him the Nature of Angels,* but our imperfect Natures, and therein wrestled with the Temptations which attend us in this Life; and being the Son of him who is greater than Earthly Princes, yet became a Companion to poor, sincere-hearted Men; and though he gave the clearest Evidence that Divine Power attended him, yet the most unfavourable Constructions were framed by a self-righteous People; those Miracles represented as the Effect of a diabolical Power, and Endeavours used to render him hateful, as having his Mission from the Prince of Darkness; nor did their Envy cease till they took him like a Criminal, and brought him to Trial. Though some may affect to carry the Appearance of being unmoved at the Apprehension of Distress, our dear Redeemer, who was perfectly sincere, having the same human Nature which we have, and feeling, a little before he was apprehended, the Weight of that Work upon him, for which he came into the World, was *sorrowful even unto Death;* here the human Nature struggled to be excused from a Cup so bitter; but his Prayers centered in Resignation, *Not my Will but thine be done.* In this Conflict, so great was his Agony that *Sweat like Drops of Blood fell from him to the Ground.*

Behold now, as foretold by the Prophet, he is in a Judicial Manner *numbered with the Transgressors!* Behold him as some poor Man of no Reputation, standing before the High Priest and Elders, and before *Herod* and *Pilate,* where Witnesses appear against him, and he mindful of the most gracious Design of his Coming, declineth to plead in his own Defence, *but as a Sheep that is dumb before the Shearer,* so under many Accusations, Revilings, and Buffetings, remained silent. And though he signified to *Peter,* that he had Access to Power sufficient to overthrow all their outward

Forces; yet retaining a Resignation to suffer for the Sins of Mankind, he exerted not that Power, but permitted them to go on in their malicious Designs, and pronounce him to be worthy of Death, even him who was perfect in Goodness; thus *in his Humiliation his Judgment was taken away*, and he, like some vile Criminal, *led as a Lamb to the Slaughter.* Under these heavy Trials (tho' poor unstable *Pilate* was convinced of his Innocence, yet) the People generally looked upon him as a Deceiver, a Blasphemer, and the approaching Punishment as a just Judgment upon him; *They esteemed him smitten of God and afflicted.* So great had been the Surprize of his Disciples, at his being taken by armed Men, that they *forsook him, and fled;* thus they hid their Faces from him, he was despised, and by their Conduct it appeared as though *they esteemed him not.*

But contrary to that Opinion, of his being smitten of God and afflicted, it was for our Sakes that *he was put to Grief; he was wounded for our Transgressions; he was bruised for our Iniquities;* and under the Weight of them manifesting the deepest Compassion for the Instruments of his Misery, laboured as their Advocate, and in the Deeps of Affliction, with an unconquerable Patience, cried out, Father, forgive them, they know not what they do!

Now this Mind being in us, which was in Christ Jesus, it removes from our Hearts the Desire of Superiority, Worldly Honour, or Greatness; a deep Attention is felt to the Divine Counsellor, and an ardent Engagement to promote, as far as we may be enabled, the Happiness of Mankind universally: This State, where every Motion from a selfish Spirit yieldeth to pure Love, I may, with Gratitude to the Father of Mercies acknowledge, is often opened before me as a Pearl to dig after; attended with a living Concern, that amongst the many Nations and Families on the Earth, those who believe in the Messiah, that *he was manifested to destroy the Works of the Devil,* and thus to *take away the Sins of the World,* may experience the Will of our Heavenly Father, *may be done on Earth as it is in Heaven.* Strong are the Desires I often feel, that this Holy Profession may remain unpolluted, and the Believers in Christ may so abide in the pure inward Feeling of his Spirit, that the Wisdom from above may shine forth in their Living, as a Light by which others may be instrumentally helped on their Way, in the true harmonious Walking.

ON DIVINE ADMONITIONS

From *Considerations on the True Harmony of Mankind*

Such are the Perfections of our Heavenly Father, that in all the Dispensations of his Providence, it is our Duty, *in every Thing, to give Thanks.* Though from the first Settlement of this Part of *America*, he hath not extended his Judgments to the Degree of Famine, yet Worms at Times have come forth beyond numbering, and laid waste Fields of Grain and Grass, where they have appeared; another Kind, in great Multitudes, working out of Sight, in Grass Ground, have so eat the Roots, that the Surface, being loosened from the Soil beneath, might be taken off in great Sheets.

These Kind of devouring Creatures appearing seldom, and coming in such Multitudes, their Generation appears different from most other Reptiles, and by the Prophet were called *God's Army sent amongst the People.*

There have been Tempests of Hail, which have very much destroyed the Grain where they extended. Through long Drought in Summer, Grain in some Places hath been less than half the usual Quantity; and in the Continuance thereof, I have beheld with Attention, from Week to Week, how Dryness from the Top of the Earth, hath extended deeper and deeper, while the Corn and Plants have languished; and with Reverence my

Mind hath been turned towards him, who being perfect in Goodness, in Wisdom and Power, doeth all Things right. And after long Drought, when the Sky hath grown dark with a Collection of Matter, and Clouds like Lakes of Water hung over our Heads, from whence the thirsty Land hath been soaked; I have at Times, with Awfulness, beheld the vehement Operation of Lightning, made sometimes to accompany these Blessings, as a Messenger from him who created all Things, to remind us of our Duty in a right Use of those Benefits, and give striking Admonitions, that we do not misapply those Gifts, in which an Almighty Power is exerted, in bestowing them upon us.

When I have considered that many of our Fellow Creatures suffer much in some Places, for want of the Necessaries of Life, whilst those who rule over them are too much given to Luxury, and divers Vanities; and behold the apparent Deviation from pure Wisdom amongst us, in the Use of the outward Gifts of God; those Marks of Famine have appeared like humbling Admonitions from him, that we might be instructed by gentle Chastisements, and might seriously consider our Ways; remembering that the outward Supply of Life is a Gift from our Heavenly Father, and no more venture to use, or apply his Gifts, in a Way contrary to pure Wisdom.

Should we continue to reject those merciful Admonitions, and use his Gifts at Home, contrary to the gracious Design of the Giver, or send them Abroad in a Way of Trade, which the Spirit of Truth doth not lead into; and should he whose Eyes are upon all our Ways, extend his Chastisements so far as to reduce us to much greater Distress than hath yet been felt by these Provinces; with what sorrow of Heart might we meditate on that Subject, *Hast thou not procured this unto thyself, in that thou hast forsaken the Lord thy God, when he led thee by the Way? Thine own Wickedness shall correct thee, and thy Backslidings shall reprove thee; know therefore, and see that it is an evil Thing and bitter, that thou hast forsaken the Lord thy God, and that my Fear is not in thee, saith the Lord of Hosts.*

My Mind hath often been affected with Sorrow, in beholding a wrong Application of the Gifts of our Heavenly Father; and those Expressions concerning the Defilement of the Earth have been opened to my Understanding; *The Earth was corrupt before God, and the Earth was filled with Violence.* Again, *The Earth also is defiled under the Inhabitants thereof.*

The Earth being the Work of a Divine Power, may not as such be accounted unclean; but when Violence is committed thereon, and the Channel of Righteousness so obstructed, that *in our Skirts are found the Blood of the Souls of poor Innocents; not by a secret Search, but upon all these.*

When Blood shed unrighteously remains unatoned for, and the Inhabitants are not effectually purged from it, when they do not wash their hands in Innocency, as was figured in the Law, in the Case of one being found slain; but seek for Gain arising from Scenes of Violence and Oppression, here the Land is polluted with Blood.

Moreover, when the Earth is planted and tilled, and the Fruits brought forth are applied to support unrighteous Purposes; here the gracious Design of infinite Goodness, in these his Gifts being perverted, the Earth is defiled; and the Complaint formerly uttered becomes applicable; *Thou hast made me to serve with thy Sins; thou hast wearied me with thine Iniquities.*

ON LOVING OUR NEIGHBORS AS OURSELVES

From *Remarks on Sundry Subjects*

When we love the Lord with all our Hearts, and his Creatures in his Love, we are then preserv'd in Tenderness both toward Mankind and the Animal Creation; but if another Spirit gets Room in our Minds, and we follow it in our Proceedings, we are then in the Way of disordering the Affairs of Society.

If a Man successful in Business expends Part of his Income in Things of no real Use, while the Poor employed by him pass through great Difficulties in getting the Necessaries of Life, this requires his serious Attention.

If several principal Men in Business unite in setting the Wages of those who work for Hire, and therein have Regard to a Profit to themselves answerable to unnecessary Expence in their Families, while the Wages of the other on a moderate Industry will not afford a comfortable Living for their Families, and a proper Education for their Children, this is like laying a Temptation in the Way of some to strive for a Place higher than they are in, when they have not Stock sufficient for it.

Now I feel a Concern in the Spring of pure Love, that all who have plenty of outward Substance, may Example others in the right Use of Things; may carefully look into the Condition of poor People, and beware of exacting on them with Regard to their Wages.

While hired Labourers, by moderate Industry, through the Divine Blessing, may live comfortably, raise up Families, and give them suitable Education, it appears reasonable for them to be content with their Wages.

If they who have Plenty love their Fellow Creatures in that Love which is Divine, and in all their Proceedings have an equal Regard to the Good of Mankind universally, their Place in Society is a Place of Care, an Office requiring Attention, and the more we possess, the greater is our Trust, and with an Increase of Treasure, an Increase of Care becomes necessary.

When our Will is subject to the Will of God, and in relation to the Things of this World, we have nothing in View, but a comfortable Living equally with the rest of our Fellow Creatures, then outward Treasures are no farther desirable than as we feel a Gift in our Minds

equal to the Trust, and Strength to act as dutiful Children in his Service, who hath formed all Mankind, and appointed a Subsistence for us in this World.

A Desire for Treasures on any other Motive, appears to be against that Command of our blessed Saviour, *Lay not up for yourselves Treasures here on Earth.*

He forbids not laying up in the Summer against the Wants of Winter; nor doth he teach us to be slothful in that which properly relates to our being in this World; but in this Prohibition he puts in *yourselves, Lay not up for* yourselves *Treasures here on Earth.*

Now in the pure Light, this Language is understood, for in the Love of Christ there is no Respect of Persons; and while we abide in his Love, we live not to *ourselves,* but to him who died for us. And as we are thus united in Spirit to Christ, we are engaged to labour in promoting that Work in the Earth for which he suffer'd.

In this State of Mind our Desires are, that every honest Member in Society may have a Portion of Treasure, and Share of Trust, answerable to that Gift, with which our Heavenly Father hath gifted us.

In great Treasure, there is a great Trust. A great Trust requireth great Care. But the laborious Mind wants Rest.

A pious Man is content to do a Share of Business in Society, answerable to the Gifts with which he is endowed, while the Channels of Business are free from Unrighteousness, but is careful lest at any Time his Heart be overcharg'd.

In the harmonious Spirit of Society *Christ is all in all.*

Here it is that *old Things are past away, all Things are new, all Things are of God,* and the Desire for Outward Riches is at an End.

They of low Degree who have small Gifts, enjoy their Help who have large Gifts; those with their small Gifts, have a small degree of Care, while these with their large Gifts, have a large degree of Care: And thus to abide in the Love of Christ, and enjoy a comfortable Living in this World is all that is aimed at by those Members in Society, to whom Christ is made Wisdom and Righteousness.

But when they who have much Treasure, are not faithful Stewards of the Gifts of God, great Difficulties attend it. Now this Matter hath deeply affected my Mind. The Lord, through merciful Chastisements, hath given me a Feeling of that Love, in which the Harmony of Society standeth, and a Sight of the Growth of that Seed which bringeth forth Wars and great Calamities in the World, and a Labour attends me to open it to others.

Now to act with Integrity, according to that Strength of Mind and Body with which our Creator hath endowed each of us, appears necessary for all, and he who thus stands in the lowest Station, appears to be entitled to as comfortable and convenient a Living, as he whose Gifts of Mind are greater, and whose Cares are more extensive.

If some endowed with strong Understandings as Men, abide not in the harmonious State, in which we *love our Neighbours as ourselves,* but walk in that Spirit in which the Children of this World are wise in their Generation; these by the Strength of Contrivance may sometimes gather great Treasure, but the Wisdom of this World is Foolishness with God; and if we gather Treasures in Worldly Wisdom, we lay up *Treasures for ourselves;* and great Treasures managed in any other Spirit, than the Spirit of Truth, disordereth the Affairs of Society, for hereby the good Gifts of God in this outward Creation are turned into the Channels of Worldly Honour, and frequently applied to support Luxury, while the Wages of poor Labourers are such, that with moderate Industry and Frugality they may not live comfortably, raise up Families, and give them suitable Education, but through the Streightness of their Condition, are often drawn on to labour under Weariness, to toil through Hardships themselves, and frequently to oppress those useful Animals with which we are intrusted.

From Age to Age, throughout all Ages, Divine Love is that alone, in which Dominion has been, is, and will be rightly conducted.

In this the Endowments of Men are so employed, that the Friend and the Governor are united in one, and oppressive Customs come to an End.

Riches in the Hands of Individuals in Society, is attended with some degree of Power; and so far as Power is put forth separate from pure Love, so far the Government of the Prince of Peace is interrupted; and as we know not that our Children after us will dwell in that State in which Power is rightly applied, to lay up Riches for them appears to be against the Nature of his Government.

The Earth, through the Labour of Men under the Blessing of him who formed it, yieldeth a Supply for the Inhabitants from Generation to Generation, and they who walk in the pure Light, their Minds are prepared to taste and relish not only those Blessings which are spiritual, but also feel a Sweetness and Satisfaction in a right Use of the Good Gifts of God in the visible Creation.

Here we see that Man's Happiness stands not in great Possessions, but in a Heart devoted to follow Christ, in that Use of Things, where Customs contrary to universal Love have no Power over us.

In this State our Hearts are prepared to trust in God, and our Desires for our Children and Posterity are, that they, with the rest of Mankind, in Ages to come, may be of that Number, of whom he hath said, *I will be a Father to them, and they shall be my Sons and Daughters.*

When Wages in a fruitful Land bear so small a Proportion to the Necessaries of Life, that poor honest People who have Families cannot by a moderate Industry attain to a comfortable Living, and give their Children sufficient Learning, but must either labour to a degree of Oppression, or else omit that which appears to be a Duty.

While this is the Case with the Poor, there is an Inclination in the Minds of most People, to prepare at least so much Treasure for their Children, that they with Care and moderate Industry may live free from these Hardships which the Poor pass through.

Now this Subject requireth our serious Consideration: To labour that our Children may be put in a Way to live comfortably, appears in itself to be a Duty, so long as these our Labours are consistent with universal Righteousness; but if in striving to shun Poverty, we do not walk in that State where *Christ is our Life*, then we wander; *He that hath the Son, hath Life. This Life is the Light of Men.* If we walk not in this Light, we walk in Darkness, and *he that walketh in Darkness, knoweth not whither he goeth.*

To keep to right Means in labouring to attain a right End is necessary: If in striving to shun Poverty, we strive only in that State where Christ is the Light of our Life, our Labours will stand in the true Harmony of Society; but if People are confident that the End aimed at is good, and in this Confidence pursue it so eagerly, as not to wait for the Spirit of Truth to lead them, then they come to Loss. *Christ is given to be a Leader and Commander of the People.* Again; *The Lord shall guide thee continually.* Again; *Lord, thou wilt ordain Peace for us, for thou also hast wrought all our Works in us.*

In the Lord have we Righteousness and Strength.

In this State our Minds are preserved watchful in following the Leadings of his Spirit in all our Proceedings in this World, and a Care is felt for a Reformation in general. That our own Posterity, with the rest of Mankind in succeeding Ages, may not be entangled by oppressive Customs, transmitted to them through our Hands; but if People in the Narrowness of natural Love, are afraid that their Children will be oppressed by the Rich, and through an eager Desire to get Treasures, depart from the pure Leadings of Truth in one Case, though it may seem to be a small Matter, yet the Mind even in that small Matter may be embolden'd to continue in a Way of Proceeding, without waiting for the Divine Leader.

Thus People may grow expert in Business, wise in the Wisdom of this World, retain a fair Reputation amongst Men, and yet being Strangers to the Voice of Christ, the safe Leader of his Flock, the Treasures thus gotten, may be like Snares to the Feet of their Posterity.

Now to keep faithful to the pure Counsellor, and under trying Circumstances suffer Adversity for Righteousness Sake, in this there is a Reward.

If we, being poor, are hardly dealt with by those who are rich, and under this Difficulty are frugal and industrious, and in true Humility open our Case to them who oppress us, this may reach the pure Witness in their Minds; and though we should remain under Difficulties as to the outward, yet if we abide in the Love of Christ, all will work for our Good.

When we feel what it is to suffer in the true suffering State, then we experience the Truth of those Expressions, that, *as the Sufferings of Christ abound in us, so our Consolation aboundeth by Christ.*

But if poor People who are hardly dealt with, do not attain to the true suffering State, do not labour in true Love with those who deal hardly with them, but envy their outward Greatness, murmur in their Hearts because of their own Poverty, and strive in the Wisdom of this World to get Riches for themselves and their Children; this is like wandering in the Dark.

If we who are of a middle Station between Riches and Poverty, are affected at Times with the Oppressions of the Poor, and feel a tender Regard for our Posterity after us, O how necessary is it that we wait for the pure Counsel of Truth!

Many have seen the Hardships of the Poor, felt an eager Desire that their Children may be put in a Way to escape these Hardships; but how few have continued in that pure Love which openeth our Understandings to proceed rightly under these Difficulties!

How few have faithfully followed that Holy Leader who prepares his People to labour for the Restoration of true Harmony amongst our Fellow Creatures!

In the pure Gospel Spirit we walk by Faith and not by Sight.

In the Obedience of Faith we die to the Narrowness of Self-love, and our Life being hid with Christ in God, our Hearts are enlarg'd toward Mankind universally; but in departing from the true Light of Life, many in striving to get Treasures have stumbled upon the dark Mountains.

Now that Purity of Life which proceeds from Faithfulness in following the Spirit of Truth, that State where our Minds are devoted to serve God, and all our Wants are bounded by his Wisdom, this Habitation has often been open'd before me as a Place of Retirement for the Children of the Light, where we may stand separated from that which disordereth and confuseth the Affairs of Society, and where we may have a Testimony of our Innocence in the Hearts of those who behold us.

ON SILENT WORSHIP

From *Remarks on Sundry Subjects*

Worship in Silence hath often been refreshing to my Mind, and a Care attends me that a young Generation may feel the Nature of this Worship. . . .

In pure silent Worship, we dwell under the Holy Anointing, and feel Christ to be our Shepherd.

Here the best of Teachers ministers to the several Conditions of his Flock, and the Soul receives immediately from the Divine Fountain, that with which it is nourished. . . .

I have felt tender Desires in my Heart that we who often sit silent in our Meetings, may live answerable to the Nature of an inward Fellowship with God, that no Stumbling-block through us, may be laid in their Way.

Such is the Load of unnecessary Expence which lieth on that which is called Divine Service in many Places, and so much are the Minds of many People employ'd in outward Forms and Ceremonies, that the opening of an inward silent Worship in this Nation to me hath appeared to be a precious Opening. . . .

My Mind is often affected with a Sense of the Condition of those People who in different Ages have been meek and patient, following Christ through great Afflictions; And while I behold the several Steps, of Reformation, and that Clearness, to which through Divine Goodness, it hath been brought by our Ancestors; I feel tender Desires that we who sometimes meet in Silence, may never by our Conduct lay Stumblingblocks in the Way of others, and hinder the Progress of the Reformation in the World. . . .

In real silent Worship the Soul feeds on that which is Divine. . . .

If Christ is our Shepherd, and feedeth us, and we are faithful in following him, our Lives will have an inviting Language, and the Table of the Lord will not be polluted.

John Wesley

(1703-1791)

LECKY remarks that Wesley, by evangelizing the common people of eighteenth-century England, saved that country from a revolution similar to that in France. Another historian says that the best record of English history in the eighteenth century is to be found in John Wesley's *Journal*. Wesley's conversion took place at a prayer meeting in an Aldersgate Street meetinghouse on May 24, 1738. Of this experience he remarks, "I felt my heart strangely warmed." This experience reached far out into the Methodist movement, from which *Christian Perfection* emerges as one of the classic treatises of the devotional life.

Wesley was one of nineteen children of a devoted mother and an Anglican minister. He was educated at Christ Church College, Oxford, ordained in the Anglican ministry, and was later made a fellow of Lincoln College. While at Oxford he and a group of friends were so devoted to their religious practices that they were called "Methodists."

His preaching in England and America was directed to the common man outside the church. He preached to thousands often before the work of the day had begun. He had no desire to form a movement separate from the Church of England. The first Methodist society was formed in 1739, and this was perhaps the formal beginning of the Methodist Church.

In *Christian Perfection* Wesley gives detailed advice to those who would embrace this doctrine of perfection, which he defines as loving God "with all our heart, mind, soul, and strength."

[CHRISTIAN BEHAVIOR]

From *Christian Perfection*

It is, therefore, to guard them who are saved from sin, from every occasion of stumbling, that I give the following advices. But first I shall speak plainly concerning the work itself.

I esteem this late work to be of God; probably the greatest now upon earth. Yet, like all others, this also is mixed with much human frailty. But these weaknesses are far less than might have been expected; and ought to have been joyfully borne by all that loved and followed after righteousness. That there have been a few weak, warm-headed men, is no reproach to the work itself, no just ground for accusing a multitude of sober-minded men, who are patterns of strict holiness. Yet—just the contrary to what ought to have been—the opposition is great; the helps few. Hereby many are hindered from seeking faith and holiness by the false zeal of others; and some

who at first began to run well are turned out of the way.

Q. 32. What is the first advice that you would give them?

A. Watch and pray continually against pride. If God has cast it out, see that it enter no more: it is full as dangerous as desire. And you may slide back into it unawares, especially if you think there is no danger of it. "Nay, but I ascribe all I have to God." So you may, and be proud nevertheless. For it is pride, not only to ascribe any thing we have to ourselves, but to think we have what we really have not. Mr. L., for instance, ascribed all the light he had to God, and so far he was humble; but then he thought he had more light than any man living; and this was palpable pride. So you ascribe all the knowledge you have to God, and in this respect you are humble. But if you think you have more than you really have, or if you think you are so taught of God, as no longer to need man's teaching, pride lieth at the door. Yes, you have need to be taught, not only by Mr. Morgan, by one another, by Mr. Maxfield, or me, but by the weakest preacher in London; yea, by all men. For God sendeth by whom he will send.

Do not, therefore, say to any who would advise or reprove you, "You are blind; you can not teach me." Do not say, "This is your wisdom, your carnal reason;" but calmly weigh the thing before God.

Always remember, much grace does not imply much light. These do not always go together. As there may be much light where there is but little love, so there may be much love where there is little light. The heart has more heat than the eye; yet it can not see. And God has wisely tempered the members of the body together, that none may say to another, "I have no need of thee."

To imagine none can teach you, but those who are themselves saved from sin, is a very great and dangerous mistake. Give not place to it for a moment; it would lead you into a thousand other mistakes, and that irrecoverably. No; dominion is not founded in grace, as the madmen of the last age talked. Obey and regard "them that are over you in the Lord," and do not think you know better than they. Know their place and your own; always remembering much love does not imply much light.

The not observing this has led some into many mistakes, and into the appearance, at least, of pride. O, beware of the appearance and the thing! Let there "be in you that lowly mind which was in Christ Jesus." And "be ye likewise clothed with humility." Let it not only fill, but cover you all over. Let modesty and self-diffidence appear in all your words and actions. Let all you speak and do show that you are little, and base, and mean, and vile in your own eyes.

As one instance of this, be always ready to own any fault you have been in. If you have at any time thought, spoken or acted wrong, be not backward to acknowledge it. Never dream that this will hurt the cause of God; no, it will farther it. Be therefore open and frank when you are taxed with any thing; do not seek either to evade or disguise it; but let it appear just as it is, and you will thereby not hinder, but adorn the Gospel.

Q. 33. What is the second advice which you would give them?

A. Beware of that daughter of pride, enthusiasm. O, keep at the utmost distance from it! Give no place to a heated imagination. Do not hastily ascribe things to God. Do not easily suppose dreams, voices, impressions, visions, or revelations, to be from God. They may be from him. They may be from nature. They may be from the devil. Therefore, "believe not every spirit, but try the spirits whether they be of God." Try all things by the written word, and let all bow down before it. You are in danger of enthusiasm every hour, if you depart ever so little from Scripture; yea, or from the plain, literal meaning of any text, taken in connection with the context. And so you are, if you despise or lightly esteem reason, knowledge, or human learning; every one of which is an excellent gift of God, and may serve the noblest purposes.

I advise you never to use the words wisdom, reason, or knowledge, by way of reproach. On the contrary, pray that you yourself may abound in them more and more. If you mean worldly wisdom, useless knowledge, false reasoning, say so; and throw away the chaff, but not the wheat.

One general inlet to enthusiasm is, expecting the end without the means; the expecting knowledge, for instance, without searching the Scriptures and consulting the children of God; the expecting spiritual strength without constant prayer and steady watchfulness; the expecting any blessing without hearing the word of God at every opportunity.

Some have been ignorant of this device of Satan. They have left off searching the Scriptures. They said, "God writes all the Scriptures on my heart.

Therefore I have no need to read it." Others thought they had not so much need of hearing, and so grew slack in attending the morning preaching. O, take warning, you who are concerned herein! You have listened to the voice of a stranger. Fly back to Christ, and keep in the good old way, which was "once delivered to the saints;" the way that even a heathen bore testimony of: "That the Christians rose early every day to sing hymns to Christ as God."

The very desire of "growing in grace" may sometimes be an inlet of enthusiasm. As it continually leads us to seek new grace, it may lead us unawares to seek something else new, beside new degrees of love to God and man. So it has led some to seek and fancy they had received gifts of a new kind, after a new heart, as, (1.) The loving God with all our mind: (2.) With all our soul: (3.) With all our strength: (4.) Oneness with God: (5.) Oneness with Christ: (6.) Having our life hid with Christ in God: (7.) Being dead with Christ: (8.) Rising with him: (9.) The sitting with him in heavenly places: (10.) The being taken up into his throne: (11.) The being in the New Jerusalem: (12.) The seeing the tabernacle of God come down among men: (13.) The being dead to all works: (14.) The not being liable to death, pain, or grief, or temptation.

One ground of many of these mistakes is the taking every fresh, strong application of any of these Scriptures to the heart, to be a gift of a new kind; not knowing that several of these Scriptures are not fulfilled yet; that most of the others are fulfilled when we are justified; the rest the moment we are sanctified. It remains only to experience them in higher degrees. This is all we have to expect.

Another ground of these and a thousand mistakes, is, the not considering deeply that love is the highest gift of God; humble, gentle, patient love; that all visions, revelations, manifestations whatever, are little things compared to love; and that all the gifts above mentioned are either the same with, or infinitely inferior to it.

It were well you should be thoroughly sensible of this—the heaven of heavens is love. There is nothing higher in religion; there is, in effect, nothing else; if you look for any thing but more love, you are looking wide of the mark, you are getting out of the royal way. And when you are asking others, "Have you received this or that blessing?" if you mean any thing but more love, you mean wrong; you are leading them out of the way, and putting them upon a false scent. Settle it then in your heart, that from the moment God has saved you from all sin, you are to aim at nothing more, but more of that love described in the thirteenth of the Corinthians. You can go no higher than this, till you are carried into Abraham's bosom.

I say yet again, beware of enthusiasm. Such is, the imagining you have the gift of prophesying, or of discerning of spirits, which I do not believe one of you has; no, nor ever had yet. Beware of judging people to be either right or wrong by your own feelings. This is no Scriptural way of judging. O, keep close to "the law and to the testimony!"

Q. 34. What is the third?

A. Beware of Antinomianism; "making void the law," or any part of it "through faith." Enthusiasm naturally leads to this; indeed, they can scarce be separated. This may steal upon you in a thousand forms, so that you can not be too watchful against it. Take heed of every thing, whether in principle or practice, which has any tendency thereto. Even that great truth, that "Christ is the end of the law," may betray us into it, if we do not consider that he has adopted every point of the moral law, and grafted it into the law of love. Beware of thinking, "Because I am filled with love, I need not have so much holiness. Because I pray always, therefore I need no set time for private prayer. Because I watch always, therefore I need no particular self-examination." Let us "magnify the law," the whole written Word, "and make it honorable." Let this be our voice: "I prize thy commandments above gold or precious stones. O, what love have I unto thy law! all the day long is my study in it." Beware of Antinomian books; particularly the works of Dr. Crisp and Mr. Saltmarsh. They contain many excellent things; and this makes them the more dangerous. O, be warned in time! Do not play with fire. Do not put your hand on the hole of a cockatrice' den. I entreat you, beware of bigotry. Let not your love or beneficence be confined to Methodists, so called, only; much less to that very small part of them who seem to be renewed in love; or to those who believe yours and their report. O, make not this your Shibboleth! Beware of stillness; ceasing in a wrong sense from your own works. To mention one instance out of many: "You have received," says one, "a great blessing. But you began to talk of it, and to do this and that; so you lost it. You should have been still."

Beware of self-indulgence; yea, and making a virtue of it, laughing at self-denial, and taking up the cross daily, at fasting or abstinence. Beware of censoriousness; thinking or calling them that any ways oppose you, whether in judgment or practice, blind, dead, fallen, or "enemies to the work." Once more, beware of Solifidianism; crying nothing but "Believe, believe!" and condemning those as ignorant or legal who speak in a more Scriptural way. At certain seasons, indeed, it may be right to treat of nothing but repentance, or merely of faith, or altogether of holiness; but, in general, our call is to declare the whole counsel of God, and to prophesy according to the analogy of faith. The written word treats of the whole and every particular branch of righteousness, descending to its minutest branches; as to be sober, courteous, diligent, patient, to honor all men. So, likewise, the Holy Spirit works the same in our hearts, not merely creating desires after holiness in general; but strongly inclining us to every particular grace, leading us to every individual part of "whatsoever is lovely." And this with the greatest propriety: for as "by works faith is made perfect," so the completing or destroying the work of faith, and enjoying the favor, or suffering the displeasure of God, greatly depends on every single act of obedience or disobedience.

Q. 35. What is the fourth?

A. Beware of sins of omission; lose no opportunity of doing good in any kind. Be zealous of good works; willingly omit no work, either of piety or mercy. Do all the good you possibly can to the bodies and souls of men. Particularly, "thou shalt in any wise reprove thy neighbor, and not suffer sin upon him." Be active. Give no place to indolence or sloth; give no occasion to say, "Ye are idle, ye are idle." Many will say so still; but let your whole spirit and behavior refute the slander. Be always employed; lose no shred of time; gather up the fragments, that nothing be lost. And whatsoever thy hand findeth to do, do it with thy might. Be "slow to speak," and wary in speaking. "In a multitude of words there wanteth not sin." Do not talk much; neither long at a time. Few can converse profitably above an hour. Keep at the utmost distance from pious chitchat, from religious gossiping.

Q. 36. What is the fifth?

A. Beware of desiring any thing but God. Now you desire nothing else; every other desire is driven out; see that none enter again. "Keep thyself pure;" let your "eye" remain "single, and your whole body shall be full of light." Admit no desire of pleasing food, or any other pleasure of sense; no desire of pleasing the eye or the imagination, by any thing grand, or new, or beautiful; no desire of money, of praise, or esteem; of happiness in any creature. You may bring these desires back; but you need not; you need feel them no more. O, stand fast in the liberty wherewith Christ has made you free!

Be patterns to all of denying yourselves, and taking up your cross daily. Let them see that you make no account of any pleasure which does not bring you nearer to God, nor regard any pain which does; that you simply aim at pleasing him, whether by doing or suffering; that the constant language of your heart, with regard to pleasure or pain, honor or dishonor, riches or poverty, is,

> All's alike to me, so I
> In my Lord may live and die!

Q. 37. What is the sixth?

A. Beware of schism, of making a rent in the Church of Christ. That inward disunion, the members ceasing to have a reciprocal love "one for another" (1 Cor. xii, 25,) is the very root of all contention, and every outward separation. Beware of every thing tending thereto. Beware of a dividing spirit; shun whatever has the least aspect that way. Therefore, say not, "I am of Paul or of Apollos," the very thing which occasioned the schism at Corinth. Say not, "This is my preacher; the best preacher in England. Give me him, and take all the rest." All this tends to breed or foment division, to disunite those whom God hath joined. Do not despise or run down any preacher; do not exalt any one above the rest, lest you hurt both him and the cause of God. On the other hand, do not bear hard upon any by reason of some incoherency or inaccuracy of expression; no, nor for some mistakes, were they really such.

Likewise, if you would avoid schism, observe every rule of the society, and of the bands, for conscience' sake. Never omit meeting your class or band; never absent yourself from any public meeting. These are the very sinews of our society, and whatever weakens, or tends to weaken, our regard for these, or our exactness in attending them, strikes at the very root of our community. As one saith, "That part of our economy, the private weekly meetings for prayer, examination, and particular exhortation, has been the greatest means of deepening and confirming every blessing that was received by the word preached, and of diffusing it to others, who could not attend the public ministry; whereas, without this religious connection and intercourse, the most ardent attempts, by mere preaching, have proved of no lasting use."

Suffer not one thought of separating from your brethren, whether their opinions agree with yours or not. Do not dream that any man sins in not believing you, in not taking your word; or that this or that opinion is essential to the work, and both must stand or fall together. Beware of impatience of contradiction. Do not condemn or think hardly of those who cannot see just as you see, or who judge it their duty to contradict you, whether in a great thing or a small. I fear some of us have thought hardly of others merely because they contradicted what we affirmed. All this tends to division; and, by every thing of this kind, we are teaching them an evil lesson against ourselves.

O, beware of touchiness, of testiness, not bearing to be spoken to; starting at the least word; and flying from those who do not implicitly receive mine or another's sayings!

Expect contradiction and opposition, together with crosses of various kinds. Consider the words of Saint Paul: "To you it is given, in the behalf of Christ, [for his sake, as a fruit of his death and intercession for you,] not only to believe, but also to suffer for his sake," Phil. i, 29. *It is given!* God gives you this opposition or reproach; it is a fresh token of his love. And will you disown the Giver; or spurn his gift, and count it a misfortune? Will you not rather say, "Father, the hour is come that thou shouldst be glorified: now thou givest thy child to suffer something for thee: do with me according to thy will?" Know that these things, far from being hindrances to the work of God, or to your soul, unless by your own fault, are not only unavoidable in the course of providence, but profitable, yea, necessary for you. Therefore receive them from God—not from chance—with willingness, with thankfulness. Receive them from men with humility, meekness, yieldingness, gentleness, sweetness. Why should not even your outward appearance and manner be soft? Remember the character of Lady Cutts: "It was said of the Roman Emperor, Titus, never any one came displeased from him. But it might be said of her, never any one went displeased to her: so secure were all of the kind and favorable reception which they would meet with from her."

Beware of tempting others to separate from you. Give no offense which can possibly be avoided; see that your practice be in all things suitable to your profession, adorning the doctrine of God our Savior. Be particularly careful in speaking of yourself: you may not, indeed, deny the work of God; but speak of it, when you are called thereto, in the most inoffensive manner possible. Avoid all magnificent, pompous words; indeed, you need give it no general name; neither perfection, sanctification, the second blessing, nor the having attained. Rather speak of the particulars which God has wrought for you. You may say, "At such a time I felt a change which I am not able to express; and since that time I have not felt pride, or self-will, or anger, or unbelief; nor any thing but a fullness of love to God and to all mankind." And answer any other plain question that is asked, with modesty and simplicity.

And if any of you should at any time fall from what you now are, if you should again feel pride or unbelief, or any temper from which you are now delivered, do not deny, do not hide, do not disguise it at all, at the peril of your soul. At all events go to one in whom you can confide, and speak just what you feel. God will enable him to speak a word in season, which shall be health to your soul. And surely he will again lift up your head, and cause the bones that have been broken to rejoice.

Q. 38. What is the last advice that you would give them?

A. Be exemplary in all things; particularly in outward things—as in dress—in little things, in the laying out of your money—avoiding every needless expense—in deep, steady seriousness, and in the solidity and usefulness of all your conversation. So you shall be "a light shining in a dark place." So shall you daily "grow in grace," till "an entrance be ministered unto you abundantly into the everlasting kingdom of our Lord Jesus Christ."

Most of the preceding advices are strongly enforced in the following reflections; which I recommend to your deep and frequent consideration, next to the holy Scriptures:

(1.) The sea is an excellent figure of the fullness of God, and that of the blessed Spirit. For as the rivers all return into the sea, so the bodies, the souls, and the good works of the righteous, return into God, to live there in his eternal repose.

Although all the graces of God depend on his mere bounty, yet is he pleased generally to attach them to the prayers, the instructions, and the holiness of those with whom we are. By strong though invisible attractions he draws some souls through their intercourse with others.

The sympathies formed by grace far surpass those formed by nature.

The truly devout show that passions as naturally flow from true as from false love; so deeply sensible are they of the goods and evils of those whom they love for God's sake. But this can only be comprehended by those who understand the language of love.

The bottom of the soul may be in repose, even while we are in many outward troubles; just as the bottom of the sea is calm while the surface is strongly agitated.

The best helps to growth in grace are the ill-usage, the affronts, and the losses which befall us. We should receive them with all thankfulness, as preferable to all others, were it only on this account—that our will has no part therein.

The readiest way to escape from our sufferings is to be willing they should endure as long as God pleases.

If we suffer persecution and affliction in a right manner, we attain a higher measure of conformity to Christ, by a due improvement of one of these occasions, than we could have done merely by imitating his mercy, in abundance of good works.

One of the greatest evidences of God's love to those that love him is, to send them afflictions, with grace to bear them.

Even in the greatest afflictions, we ought to testify to God that, in receiving them from his hand, we feel pleasure in the midst of the pain, from being afflicted by Him who loves us, and whom we love.

The readiest way which God takes to draw a man to himself is, to afflict him in that he loves most, and with good reason; and to cause this affliction to arise from some good action done with a single eye; because nothing can more clearly show him the emptiness of what is most lovely and desirable in the world.

(2.) True resignation consists in a thorough conformity to the whole will of God; who wills and does all—excepting sin—which comes to pass in the world. In order to this we have only to embrace all events, good and bad, as his will.

In the greatest afflictions which can befall the just, either from heaven or earth, they remain immovable in peace, and perfectly submissive to God, by an inward, loving regard to him, uniting in one all the powers of their souls.

We ought quietly to suffer whatever befalls us, to bear the defects of others and our own, to confess them to God in secret prayer, or with groans which can not be uttered; but never to speak a sharp or peevish word, nor to murmur or repine; but thoroughly willing that God should treat you in the manner that pleases him. We are his lambs, and therefore ought to be ready to suffer, even to the death, without complaining.

We are to bear with those we can not amend, and to be content with offering them to God. This is true resignation. And since he has borne our infirmities, we may well bear those of each other for his sake.

To abandon all, to strip one's self of all, in order to seek and to follow Jesus Christ naked to Bethlehem, where he was born, naked to the hall where he was scourged, and naked to Calvary, where he died on the cross, is so great a mercy, that neither the thing, nor the knowledge of it, is given to any, but through faith in the Son of God.

(3.) There is no love of God without patience, and no patience without lowliness and sweetness of spirit.

Humility and patience are the surest proofs of the increase of love.

Humility alone unites patience with love; without which it is impossible to draw profit from suffering; or, indeed, to avoid complaint, especially when we think we have given no occasion for what men make us suffer.

True humility is a kind of self-annihilation; and this is the center of all virtues.

A soul returnéd to God ought to be attentive to every thing which is said to him, on the head of salvation, with a desire to profit thereby.

Of the sins which God has pardoned, let nothing remain but a deeper humility in the heart, and a stricter regulation in our words, in our actions, and in our sufferings.

(4.) The bearing men, and suffering evils in meekness and silence, is the sum of a Christian life.

God is the first object of our love: its next office is to bear the defects of others. And we should begin the practice of this amid our own household.

We should chiefly exercise our love toward them who most shock either our way of thinking, or our temper, or our knowledge, or the desire we have that others should be as virtuous as we wish to be ourselves.

(5.) God hardly gives his Spirit even to those whom he has established in grace, if they do not pray for it on all occasions, not only once, but many times.

God does nothing but in answer to prayer: and even they who have been converted to God without praying for it themselves—which is exceedingly rare—were not without the prayers of others. Every new victory which a soul gains is the effect of a new prayer.

On every occasion of uneasiness we should retire to prayer, that we may give place to the grace and light of God, and then form our resolutions, without being in pain about what success they may have.

In the greatest temptations, a single

look to Christ, and the barely pronouncing his name, suffices to overcome the wicked one, so it be done with confidence and calmness of spirit.

God's command to "pray without ceasing," is founded on the necessity we have of his grace to preserve the life of God in the soul, which can no more subsist one moment without it, than the body can without air.

Whether we think of, or speak to, God, whether we act or suffer for him, all is prayer, when we have no other object than his love and the desire of pleasing him.

All that a Christian does, even in eating and sleeping, is prayer, when it is done in simplicity, according to the order of God, without either adding to or diminishing from it by his own choice.

Prayer continues in the desire of the heart, though the understanding be employed on outward things.

In souls filled with love, the desire to please God is a continual prayer.

As the furious hate which the devil bears us is termed the roaring of a lion, so our vehement love may be termed crying after God.

God only requires of his adult children that their hearts be truly purified, and that they offer him continually the wishes and vows that naturally spring from perfect love. For these desires, being the genuine fruits of love, are the most perfect prayers that can spring from it.

(6.) It is scarce conceivable how strait the way is wherein God leads them that follow him: and how dependent on him we must be, unless we are wanting in our faithfulness to him.

It is hardly credible of how great consequence before God the smallest things are; and what great inconveniences sometimes follow those which appear to be light faults.

As a very little dust will disorder a clock, and the least sand will obscure our sight, so the least grain of sin which is upon the heart will hinder its right motion toward God.

We ought to be in the Church as the saints are in heaven, and in the house as the holiest men are in the church; doing our work in the house as we pray in the church; worshipping God from the ground of the heart.

We should be continually laboring to cut off all the useless things that surround us; and God usually retrenches the superfluities of our souls in the same proportion as we do those of our bodies.

The best means of resisting the devil is to destroy whatever of the world remains in us, in order to raise for God, upon its ruins, a building all of love. Then shall we begin, in this fleeting life, to love God as we shall love him in eternity.

We scarce conceive how easy it is to rob God of his due, in our friendship with the most virtuous persons, until they are torn from us by death. But if this loss produce lasting sorrow, that is a clear proof that we had before two treasures, between which we divided our heart.

(7.) If, after having renounced all, we do not watch incessantly, and beseech God to accompany our vigilance with his, we shall be again entangled and overcome.

As the most dangerous winds may enter little openings, so the devil never enters more dangerously than by little, unobserved incidents, which seem to be nothing, yet insensibly open the heart to great temptations.

It is good to renew ourselves from time to time, by closely examining the state of our souls, as if we had never done it before: for nothing tends more to the full assurance of faith, than to keep ourselves by this means in humility, and the exercise of all good works.

To continual watchfulness and prayer ought to be added continual employment. For grace flies a vacuum as well as nature; and the devil fills whatever God does not fill.

There is no faithfulness like that which ought to be between a guide of souls and the person directed by him. They ought continually to regard each other in God, and closely to examine themselves, whether all their thoughts are pure, and all their words directed with Christian discretion. Other affairs are only the things of men; but these are peculiarly the things of God.

(8.) The words of St. Paul, "No man can call Jesus Lord, but by the Holy Ghost," show us the necessity of eyeing God in our good works, and even in our minutest thoughts; knowing that none are pleasing to him but those which he forms in us and with us. From hence we learn that we cannot serve him, unless he use our tongue, hands, and heart, to do by himself and his Spirit whatever he would have us to do.

If we were not utterly impotent, our good works would be our own property; whereas now they belong wholly to God, because they proceed from him and his grace: while raising our works, and making them all divine, he honors himself in us through them.

One of the principal rules of religion is, to lose no occasion of serving God. And since he is invisible to our eyes, we are to serve him in our neighbor; which he receives as if done to himself in person, standing visibly before us.

God does not love men that are inconstant, nor good works that are intermitted. Nothing is pleasing to him, but what has a resemblance of his own immutability.

A constant attention to the work which God intrusts us with is a mark of solid piety.

Love fasts when it can, and as much as it can. It leads to all the ordinances of God, and employs itself in all the outward works whereof it is capable. It flies, as it were, like Elijah over the plain, to find God upon his holy mountain.

God is so great, that he communicates greatness to the least thing that is done for his service.

Happy are they who are sick, yea, or lose their life, for having done a good work.

God frequently conceals the part which his children have in the conversion of other souls. Yet one may boldly say, that person who long groans before him for the conversion of another, whenever that soul is converted to God, is one of the chief causes of it.

Charity can not be practiced right, unless, first, we exercise it the moment God gives the occasion; and, secondly, retire the instant after to offer it to God by humble thanksgiving. And this for three reasons: first, to render him what we have received from him. The second, to avoid the dangerous temptation which springs from the very goodness of these works. And the third, to unite ourselves to God, in whom the soul expands itself in prayer, with all the graces we have received; and the good works we have done, to draw from him new strength against the bad effects which these very works may produce in us if we do not make use of the antidotes which God has ordained against these poisons. The true means to be filled anew with the riches of grace is thus to strip ourselves of it; and without this it is extremely difficult not to grow faint in the practice of good works.

Good works do not receive their last perfection, till they, as it were, lose themselves in God. This is a kind of death to them, resembling that of our bodies, which will not attain their highest life, their immortality, till they lose themselves in the glory of our souls, or rather of God, wherewith they shall be filled. And it is only what they had of earthly and mortal, which good works lose by this spiritual death.

Fire is the symbol of love; and the love of God is the principle and the end of all our good works. But truth surpasses figure; and the fire of divine love has this advantage over material fire, that it can reascend to its source, and raise thither with it all the good works which it produces. And by this means it prevents their being corrupted by pride, vanity, or any evil mixture. But this can not be done otherwise than by making these good works, in a spiritual manner, die in God, by a deep gratitude, which plunges the soul in him as in an abyss, with all that it is, and all the grace and works for which it is indebted to him;

a gratitude whereby the soul seems to empty itself of them, that they may return to their source, as rivers seem willing to empty themselves, when they pour themselves, with all their waters, into the sea.

When we have received any favor from God, we ought to retire, if not into our closets, into our hearts, and say, "I come, Lord, to restore to thee what thou hast given; and I freely relinquish it, to enter again into my own nothingness. For what is the most perfect creature in heaven or earth in thy presence, but a void capable of being filled with thee and by thee; as the air, which is void and dark, is capable of being filled with the light of the sun, who withdraws it every day to restore it the next, there being nothing in the air that either appropriates this light or resists it? O, give me the same facility of receiving and restoring thy grace and good works! I say, *thine;* for I acknowledge the root from which they spring is in thee, and not in me."

26. In the year 1764, upon a review of the whole subject, I wrote down the sum of what I had observed in the following short propositions:

(1.) There is such a thing as perfection; for it is again and again mentioned in Scripture.

(2.) It is not so early as justification; for justified persons are to "go on unto perfection," Heb. vi, 1.

(3.) It is not so late as death; for St. Paul speaks of living men that were perfect, (Phil. iii, 15.)

(4.) It is not absolute. Absolute perfection belongs not to man, nor to angels, but to God alone.

(5.) It does not make a man infallible; none is infallible while he remains in the body.

(6.) Is it sinless? It is not worth while to contend for a term. It is "salvation from sin."

(7.) It is "perfect love," 1 John iv, 18. This is the essence of it; its properties or inseparable fruits, are, rejoicing evermore, praying without ceasing, and in everything giving thanks, (1 Thess. v, 16,) etc.

(8.) It is improvable. It is so far from lying in an indivisible point, from being incapable of increase, that one perfected in love may grow in grace far swifter than he did before.

(9.) It is amissible, capable of being lost; of which we have numerous instances. But we were not thoroughly convinced of this till five or six years ago.

(10.) It is constantly both preceded and followed by a gradual work.

(11.) But is it in itself instantaneous or not? In examining this, let us go on step by step.

An instantaneous change has been wrought in some believers: none can deny this.

Since that change, they enjoy perfect love; they feel this, and this alone; they "rejoice evermore, pray without ceasing, and in every thing give thanks." Now, this is all I mean by perfection; therefore, these are witnesses of the perfection which I preach.

"But in some this change was not instantaneous." They did not perceive the instant when it was wrought. It is often difficult to perceive the instant when a man dies; yet there is an instant in which life ceases. And if even sin ceases, there must be a last moment of its existence, and a first moment of our deliverance from it.

"But if they have this love now, they will lose it." They may; but they need not. And whether they do or no, they have it now; they now experience what we teach. They now are all love; they now rejoice, pray, and praise without ceasing.

"However, sin is only suspended in them; it is not destroyed." Call it which you please. They are all love to-day; and they take no thought for the morrow.

"But this doctrine has been much abused." So has that of justification by faith. But that is no reason for giving up either this or any other Scriptural doctrine. "When you wash your child," as one speaks, "throw away the water; but do not throw away the child."

"But those who think they are saved from sin say they have no need of the merits of Christ." They say just the contrary. Their language is,

Every moment, Lord, I want the merit of thy death.

They never before had so deep, so unspeakable conviction of a need of Christ in all his offices as they have now.

Therefore, all our preachers should make a point of preaching perfection to believers constantly, strongly, and explicitly; and all believers should mind this one thing, and continually agonize for it.

James Fordyce

(1720-1796)

BORN in Aberdeen and educated at Marischal College in Scotland, Fordyce was ordained to the Presbyterian ministry in 1743 and served Presbyterian churches in his home country for the first seventeen years of his ministry. In 1762 he was called to a London church where he remained until his retirement in 1782. He wrote nine books, among which were some on moral problems, a book of poetry, and one primarily devotional—*Addresses to the Deity*.

ON CONTEMPLATION

From *Addresses to the Deity*

Delighted with the blessings and wonders of creation, transported by the yet higher wonders and blessing of redemption, my soul would ascend with fresh aspiration to thee, O God, the origin of both; to thee, the greatest and best of beings, the greatest because the best; from whom alone proceeds whatever is good and great; to whom, therefore, be all the glory from all thy reasonable offspring. To praise thee, thou sovereign Parent, is surely the most becoming exercise of reason; and they are the happiest who perform it most worthily— the bright assembly of saints and seraphim, who circle thy throne rejoicing and with unbroken harmony celebrate thy perfections. Fain would thy servant here below anticipate their joys. Fain would he learn their language, and join, however feebly, their elevated chorus, "the Lord God omnipotent reigneth, hallelujah!"

2. Compassionate Father, forgive the languor and unevenness with which my spirit, prest down by the weight of mortality, attempts so high a service. Ah, that my heart were in better tune, and more alive to gratitude, love and admiration, to the noblest affections of every mind in unison with the melody of nature, and of heaven! Almighty Maker, assist my weak endeavors. Let no jarring passion disturb my thoughts. Teach me to correct every irregular movement, and diligently to cherish that spirit of pious contemplation which soothes the breast into serenity, supplies devotion with its amplest strains, and lifts the faculties to him who gave them.

3. What shall I render, O Lord, for the exalted satisfaction of tracing thy attributes in this capacious universe, for the transcendent privilege of walking with thee, amidst the glory of thy works? Dispose me more attentively to study, tho I can never fully comprehend, them. Unable as I am in a survey so immense and so various, to discover the contrivance or the use of many parts, I have yet abundant cause to believe that they are worthy of their Author; such con-

sistency of design, such consummate wisdom, such boundless goodness are conspicuous in all the rest! I rejoice in the reflection that the farther inquiry is extended by the largest and most enlightened minds, they meet yet brighter marks of intelligence and benignity and are more fully convinced that those appearances which the ignorant and the discontented have censured as blemishes in the plan, or defects in the execution, are to be numbered among the strongest demonstrations of thy skill and care, Almighty Architect. But, O my God, if views which this limited state of humanity renders at the utmost imperfect yield so much delight, what will it be when every remaining cloud that now obscures thy workmanship shall vanish, and the light of eternity, breaking forth on our transported eyes, shall give us to behold it in all its magnitude and splendor?

4. The whole creation is full of thee. Forbid that the beauty, or diversity which it displays, should become a veil to hide thee from my sight, where, "by the things that are made, thy power and Godhead may be clearly seen." Where, for the trial of my faith, thou art pleased "to hold back the face of thy throne," may I still perceive the influence of the present divinity, and still adore the great supreme! When from that elevated throne I am favored with the radiations of light and mercy, may I lay myself open to them with thankfulness, humility and meekness!

5. "Where is the wise? where is the scribe? where is the disputer of this world?" Thou hast shown me, O Lord, that "professing to be wise, they become fools." Their confidence abuses their understanding. Beguiled by the glare of novelty, and fired by the ambition of fame for freedom of thought and discernment above others, in matters where docility and diffidence are chiefly required, they turn from the sober pursuit of truth, and are led away into pernicious errors. "The heavens declare thy glory; and the firmament showeth thy handiwork. Day unto day uttereth speech; and night unto night teacheth knowledge."

The eloquence of the creation, proclaiming thy greatness, and pleading for thy rights, is heard and understood by the honest but unpretending believer, by the self-denied and single-hearted worshiper. Neither the illiterate hind nor the untutored savage has been wholly insensible to the language of nature. But the ungodly man, who is spoiled by vain philosophy and perplexed "by the oppositions of science falsely so called, stoppeth his ear, like the deaf adder, and will not hear the voice of the charmer, though charming never so wisely." Misled by the cavils of infidelity, and lost in the maze of metaphysics, he wanders forever in a dark and crooked path, farther and yet farther from the straight and cheerful road that leads to everlasting day.

6. Save me, Heavenly Father, from the boasted benevolence of those who, while they promise liberty from the shackles of superstition and prejudice, are laboring to overthrow every principle which thou hast established among mankind as the foundation of their virtue and their happiness. Deliver me from the false pretexts of those whose "tender mercies are cruelty"; who would rob the fainting spirit of its richest cordial, tear from the children of sorrow their most powerful support, and leave without reward or expectation the generous toils of the true patriot, the useful and arduous researches of the devout philosopher, the patient conflicts and heroic sacrifices of the follower Jesus. May I ever regard with abhorrence their impious system, who would transform this beautiful and glorious universe into a scene of desolation, excluding thy creative energy, and banishing that sovereign presence which directs, enlivens, and adorns it! Defend, I beseech thee, every virtuous mind and every unwary youth from the deceitfulness of all that are wickedly striving to undermine and destroy "whatsoever things are just, and true, and venerable," and holy among men, whatsoever things can endear them to each other as members of thy family or recommend them to thee as subjects of thy government,

whatsoever things become their dignity and their hopes as immortal beings. Inspire them with an utter and unabating detestation of that depravity which, not contented to disturb the peace and order of human life, seeks with frigid argumentation, deliberate subtlety, or wanton mirth, to dump and degrade the heaven-born soul that was made after thine image, and at last to sink it with all its faculties and honors into the fearful abyss of nothing.

7. But, blessed Creator, is it indeed possible that such indignity to thee, such insensibility to the dearest interests of human kind, should be found in creatures called rational? Alas! who can tell to what strong delusions those may be abandoned in thy righteous judgment, who so profanely pervert the invaluable gift of reason, who turn it so audaciously against the Giver? Most truly hath thy word declared that "the fool hath said in his heart, there is no God." In his heart the malady begins. "Through the pride of his heart, he will not seek after thee." Thy justice is offended, and he is conscious of his danger. He secretly hates the power he dreads. His evil passions, whether more open or disguised, increase his aversion to thy laws. Thence he is eager to question thy existence. He wishes and strives to disbelieve it. He wishes and strives in vain. However he may argue, whatever he may boast, chilling apprehensions will arise: specters of horror will haunt him in the silent watches of the night; they will pursue him at noon-day; in the midst of society they will poison his pleasures, nor will the voice of laughter or the face of gaiety prove him to be free from inward anguish. His conscience takes part with thee. "Thy terrors make him afraid": thy thunder startles, thy lightning flashes conviction into his soul. Altho in his folly he "makes a mock of sin, and utters great swelling words of vanity"; when pain, and grief, and sickness, and decay come upon him, where shall he find refuge from thy displeasure? Whither shall he flee from himself? One resource, one dreadful resource, he hath

long endeavored to hope may yet remain; that when the last messenger arrives, he shall escape in a night eternal.

8. Merciful Deity, is there then no other resource for this man, no better refuge? Permit thy sinful servant, who hath "tasted and seen that thou art good," to implore thy pity for a fellow creature that little thought, when he entered on "the error of his way," how far it might entice him from truth and happiness! Spare him, O Lord, spare him to repent, if it be not yet too late. Change his heart by thy almighty Spirit, if consistent with the laws of thy righteous government. Would there not be "joy among the angels that are in heaven," if by an extraordinary contrition and a triumphant faith this very man were made a trophy of peculiar grace?

9. But however thy unerring will may determine in respect to him and offenders of his enormity, hear me, Parent of benevolence, oh! hear me, when with redoubled fervor I beseech thee to guard the young and the ingenuous from the snares of unbelief. Lead them forth into the lovely and instructive walks of nature. Dispose them to view, with the serious collected eye of contemplation, the spacious earth, the boundless sea, the awful rocks, the lofty hills, and the fruitful valleys; the fields, the flocks, and the herds; the springs and the rivers, with "the green pastures by the still waters"; the solemn woods and groves; the cheerful garden adorned with trees, and herbs, and flowers, "after their kind"; the smiling sky, and yonder refulgent sun. In these may they learn to admire thy perfections! And when from these they look upon themselves, and see how "wonderfully they are made," and feel that multiplied delights thou hast given them to know, may they reflect with gladness that they live, not in a forlorn and fatherless world, but in a creation over which the Creator presides; may they acknowledge with gratitude and devotion that "thou art in all, and through all, and over all, God blessed for ever," and ever inclined to bless thy children.

10. Heavenly Father, what satisfaction

is his, who often withdrawing from the tumult of business and the noise of folly, flies to the sanctuary of divine meditation, there recovers the composure of his mind, enjoys undisturbed tranquility, and tastes that peace of thine "which passeth all understanding!" What improvements, when in the silence of the passions he harkens with profound attention to thy voice within him, prompting each pious thought, each charitable deed, each ardent desire after immortality! What elevation, when conversant with the order and beneficence displayed on every side, he is taught to admire, and admiring to copy them, till he becomes like thee, "holy as thou art holy, and merciful as thou art merciful!"

11. But, alas, it grieves me to look upon the multitudes immersed in sensuality, enslaved to covetousness, or by constant dissipation become incapable of thought. "They regard not the operation of thy hands." Created by thy power, they say not, "where is God our maker?" Maintained by thy providence, and "loaded with thy benefits," they pay thee no tribute, "neither are they thankful." The beasts of the field and the fowls of the air have more feeling than they. "The ox knoweth his owner, and the ass his master's crib: but they do not know, they do not consider." The lark that mounts toward heaven, with implicit gratitude chanting thy praise, the birds that sing among the branches, straining in sweet emulation to warble forth the joy with which thou hast inspired them, upbraid those sons and daughters of men who neglect to join in the symphony. Father of spirits, awaken them to reason, and to duty. Show them the emptiness of sin, and the wisdom of religion. Oh, persuade them that those alone are in the path of happiness, who seek it in glorifying thee, in doing good, and retiring, when they may, from the vanities of life, to contemplate in sacred solitude and manifestations of divine perfection.

12. How truly delightful to break away from clamor, confusion, and discord, into a calm retreat, and there to harmonize with nature, and with thee her God! What relief to the burdened and pensive mind, there to drop its cares, to shake off for a while those anxious thoughts that too often entangle and depress it, and "as with the wings of an eagle to mount up" to the serene region of pious hope and self-enjoyment, from thence to look down upon the lessening world, to pity the distractions of its lovers, and triumph in the portion of the righteous!

13. From privileges like these, O Lord, thy servants return to the offices of social virtue with renewed activity and vigor, acquire a greater superiority to the temptations of their state, and are armed to meet its difficulties and dangers with firmer resolution. Thus I read in thy holy word, that when the pious and benevolent labors of the day were past, "Jesus went up into a mountain apart to pray." And thus it was, that by conversing with thee, remote from interruption, and nearer to thy seat of majesty in that sublime retirement, his soul derived new strength, lay open to the fullest emanations of thy paternal favor, and glowed with fresh ardor of zeal and charity to go about doing good, to teach, to suffer, and to die for mankind.

14. But, O my Father and my God, where shall I find language or conceptions adequate to thy inestimable love, in the redemption of the world by Jesus Christ, that last and brightest discovery of thy attributes, that divinest object of human or angelic study? Here, indeed, all my faculties are swallowed up in wonder, veneration, and joy. Here my heart is overwhelmed with speechless humility and thankfulness; and while I adore in silence this unequaled mystery, I would "behold in it, as in a glass, thy glory"; till by its transforming power I am "changed into the same image," prepared to "see thee as thou art," and, through the intercession of my Savior, received to the contemplations of heaven. Amen.

Jean Nicholas Grou

(1731-1803)

BORN in Calais, France, and educated by the Jesuits, Grou spent sixty years of his life as a Jesuit priest, during which study and devotion were his cardinal virtues. At the French Revolution he fled to Lulworth, England. Here he spent the last ten years of his life. Partaking of the last sacrament, he said, "My God, it is indeed sweet to die in thy arms." Grou once remarked that the greatest gift God gave to him was a childlike and trusting spirit. In *The Hidden Life of the Soul* this simplicity of spirit is shown. Of him one writer said, "Those who will adopt Père Grou as a spiritual teacher, and study his writings thoughtfully and sincerely, will find for themselves an intensely helpful guide to a life of steadfast devotion." The selection is from the edition of W. H. Hutchings (London, 1881).

[THE MEANS TO A HOLY LIFE]

From *The Hidden Life of the Soul*

TRUE HOLINESS

But few, even of those who have specially devoted their lives to God, have accurate ideas as to the character of true holiness. Most people are apt to believe that it consists in a routine of religious practices, and a diligent observance of certain externals. If, moreover, they occasionally experience some conscious religious emotions, they make no question but that they are really holy,—never stopping to ascertain whether these emotions are from God, or merely the action of their own hearts. Yet often such persons are liable to many faults unperceived by themselves, and which it would not be easy to make them see. They may be narrowminded, pharisaically precise in their devotions, full of self-esteem, touchy, self-conceited, obstinate, unyielding or affected in outward manner,—altogether deficient in truthfulness, simplicity, and reality, yet all the while they secretly esteem themselves more highly than other men, and they may even despise and condemn the true piety of others, which they are unable to perceive. This real, harsh judgment is sadly too common

among Christians; but surely it is the self-same spirit which crucified our Lord Jesus Christ; and in truth it crucifies Him in His servants even to this day; for whoever gives himself wholly to God, and seeks earnestly to lead an interior life, runs a risk of drawing down jealousy and criticism, perhaps calumny and persecution, upon himself.

If you would realise perfect holiness, seek it as set forth in Jesus Christ. He is our only Example, and it was to give us such an example that He took upon Him the form of man. All holiness which is not shaped and formed upon that model, is false and unacceptable to God, and if it deceives men, it can never deceive God, or win any entrance into Heaven. Be it yours to study holiness with Jesus for your Teacher, and be not slack in asking Him for light and grace, that you may learn His lesson perfectly.

Jesus "pleased not Himself" (Rom. 15:3). He never sought His own pleasure or gain;—no single deed of His was ever wrought with a view to the praise of man, or that He might shun man's wrath. God the Father, His Will, His Glory, were the objects of the Saviour's every movement. "I came not to do My own Will, but the Will of Him that sent Me." Our great Example has taught us that holiness is inward—it does not consist in excited evanescent feelings, but in a deep honest conviction, which finds vent in action;—in an entire sacrifice of self to God, a boundless love and charity towards men. Such was the spirit of the Saviour's Life. He fulfilled every title of the Law, but meanwhile He taught by word and deed that all such observance must spring from inward love, or it is no better than slavish obedience. He has taught us to esteem this life as a mere pilgrimage—a passage—a time of probation in which our love to God may be ripened. He "minded not earthly things;" —He taught us not to be anxious for the morrow but to rest wholly on His Father's good Providence. Jesus voluntarily embraced that life which men shrink from most, and which they seldom endure save from necessity. He did not condemn riches, but He gave the preference to poverty. He did not condemn the distinctions of rank and position, which are in truth God's own appointment, but He taught us that there is a choicer blessing, a greater nearness to Heaven, to be found in a lowly condition; and that self-esteem, founded on high birth, wealth, or power, is a fatal snare. All irregular pleasures He has condemned, and while permitting us the use of certain lawful enjoyments, He himself abstained even from these. Prayer and the exercise of His gracious Ministry, filled His earthly life—"Wist ye not that I must be about My Father's business"?

If we may say it reverently, nothing could be more simple, plain, or unaffected than the deeds and words of our Lord. He taught "as one having authority;" but it was lovingly, in a familiar way, without pomp or display; His miracles were often almost secret, and His apostles and evangelists were led by the Holy Spirit to record His earthly history with the same striking simplicity.

Remember too His tender compassion for all true penitents—"I came to call, not the righteous, but sinners to repentance." Think of His pitying goodness to the publican, to Mary Magdalene, to the Samaritan, to the woman taken in adultery; and compare it with His condemnation of the Pharisees' pride, their avarice and hypocrisy. Remember too how patiently He bore with the roughness and frailties of His own apostles. From our point of view, it seems as though it must have been a sore trial to His incomparable refinement to live with those ignorant men, full of imperfections and faults as they were. Even the holiest men find no small difficulty in sanctifying their intercourse with their fellow creatures;—the closer they are to God, the more gentleness, patience, and toleration they need in their dealings with those around—it is a perpetual struggle. But Jesus bore every persecution in patience, meeting every attack with truth and innocence; silent before His accusers, forgiving His murderers, shedding His blood for them. All who "seek to live a godly life must suffer persecution"—it may be through ridicule and slander, or it may be through more overt acts. Then is the time to take Jesus as an example—to bear all things in defence of the truth; to make no answer to calumny, save by a holy life; to be silent when words are not necessary; to leave our justification with God; to put aside all bitterness, all resentment; to render good for evil; to pray for those who injure us, and believe that they are but instruments working out God's Will upon us. Such conduct as this is worthy to be called holy, and God seldom sends such trials until a man has been long proved and moulded. Blessed are they who endure!

"If ye suffer with Him, ye shall also reign with Him." It can only be through an altogether extraordinary grace that any one is able to accept such trials gladly, still less to desire them. Let us rather be content with our "day of small things," seeking nothing lofty for our weak purposes, but daily imploring God that no human respect may ever make us unfaithful to the duty which we owe to Him.

How to Attain Real and Steadfast Virtue

1. The first means, which albeit seemingly the most ordinary, is in truth the hardest, is to will so to attain. But the will must be sincere, hearty, effectual, and persevering; and such a will is no common thing. We deceive ourselves into thinking we have it, while really we have only vague wishes and desires; which are widely different from a firm resolute will. People wish to be religious, but after their own fashion—to a certain point—they would not "go too far,"—or give up anything for it; and thus they stop short in wishes. Practical religion is quite another thing, and they lose heart directly that any effort is required, when faults must be overcome, natural inclinations or imperfections resisted. There may be a fervent beginning, but such persons soon grow slack, they give up what was scarcely begun, and shut their eyes to the fact that everything depends on perseverance. Do you ask God daily to confirm and strengthen your will and each day's perseverance will help forward the morrow.

2. The second means for attaining a steadfast progress in holiness, is to have a daily rule, and to observe it punctually. But it is not well to overload one's self with observances at first—it is better to increase spiritual exercises gradually. Due regard must be had to health, age, position, and the duties entailed thereby. Be sure that it is a mistaken devotion which interferes with the duties of your natural state of life.

3. A third means is the continual recollection of God's Presence; and to this end you must firmly believe that God dwells within our hearts, and that He is to be found there by those who seek Him; that He inspires us with holy thoughts, leading us from sin to seek righteousness. We often call conscience that which is in truth God's own Voice; warning, rebuking, enlightening, directing the soul;—our part is to be attentive in listening, and steadfast in obeying this Voice. Dissipation and excitement hinder us from hearing it; it is when we are calm and still—our passions and imagination at rest—that the Voice of God fills the heart; and there is no step towards perfection so great, as when we learn the habit of always watching for it. But for this we require a tranquil heart, avoiding whatever disturbs, engrosses, or distracts it;—and all this is the work of time, together with diligent self-examination and resolute efforts.

4. The fourth means is to give a fixed daily time to God, during which His Presence is our sole occupation, and in which we listen to Him and talk with Him, not with the lips, but in the heart. This is real mental prayer. Those who are beginners in this exercise cannot do better than use *The Imitation of Christ*, pausing on each sentence and meditating upon it. At first a quarter of an hour morning and evening is enough, but you should acquire, if possible, the habit of at least half an hour's morning meditation. When you learn to take delight in it, and can dispense with the help of books, it is well at times merely to lie passive before your Lord, asking Him to work His own good pleasure in your soul: it is a great mistake to fancy such time to be lost whether you are conscious of His Grace operating within you or not.

5. The fifth means of progress is diligently to use the means of grace which God has provided in His Church; if you use confession, guard against over-scrupulousness, but beware lest confession be a mere formal routine, a danger to some who use it frequently. Those who aim at perfection should chiefly accuse themselves of their resistance to grace—their indulgence of self-love—their voluntary and deliberate words or deeds contrary to that aim. That Communion is unquestionably good, from which you come filled with fresh courage, and a renewed purpose of hearty faithfulness to God. Do not fancy that it is necessary to a good preparation for Communion, to be fettered by the acts of devotion you find in books:—such acts are useful for young persons whose attention is wandering, for those who communicate but rarely,

and for all who have not the habit of recollection. But those who are accustomed to practise mental prayer, will often prepare for and receive the Holy Communion more devoutly without the help of books.

6. A sixth means of progress is spiritual reading, for which a wide field is open to you. It is well to select such books as touch your heart, and rouse it to fervour. Rodriquez on *Perfection* is a useful book for beginners, and for those more advanced the *Imitation*, the works of S. Francis de Sales, Surin, and *The Lives of the Saints*, to say nothing of Holy Scripture above all. Your spiritual reading should in some respects be like a meditation, that is to say, you should watch for God's action within you, and pause when you feel your heart touched by what you read. *Always read with a view to practise.* Spiritual books are not equally adapted to all minds; therefore confine yourself chiefly to those which profit you most, but avoid multiplying devotions or exercises so as to confine and hamper your mind.

7. The seventh means is mortification of the heart. All our instincts through the corruption of our nature are set against our supernatural progress, and would fain subject us to self-love and self-indulgence; so that we must keep up a perpetual warfare both against impressions from without and corruption within. You cannot be too watchful over your heart and all its movements; at first such watchfulness may be toilsome, but as you grow in recollection and in realisation of God's Presence, it will become easy.

8. An eighth means is frequent meditation on the virtues of humility and purity, taking the Blessed Virgin as an example, of whom Holy Scripture tells us that she is "blessed among women." A constant remembrance that God sends His angels to visit and protect us, will also be very profitable; for they are ministering spirits, sent forth to minister for them who shall be heirs of salvation.

9. Finally, it often may be very helpful to seek out some discreet spiritual adviser from whom you may receive counsel in matters which concern your soul: who being himself led by God's Holy Spirit, is therefore capable of leading you in the right way. You may be certain that those who heartily desire to advance in holiness, will find a suitable guide; God will not fail to supply their need, if they pray to Him to send them the help they require, and then receive that help with meekness and confidence. With a hearty will and wise guidance the soul can scarce fail to advance in the paths of holiness.

John Frederic Oberlin

(1740–1826)

BORN at Strasbourg, graduate of Strasbourg University in 1758, consecrated to God at the age of twenty, Oberlin spent over half a century in his Alsatian parish of Waldbach. This rocky, barren district, devastated by wars, was materially and spiritually transformed by his energy and mild Christian spirit. He not only prayed daily for his parishioners; he also put Christianity into practical action. He improved agricultural and mechanical arts; he introduced new industries, such as cotton ginning, weaving, straw-plaiting; he founded schools and employed competent teachers; he introduced infant schools; he rebuilt roads; he gave his people religious instruction. In an age of religious bigotry, Protestants and Roman Catholics worshiped together in his church, and he shielded Jews in his parish.

Although he received a gold medal from the French Royal Agricultural Society in 1818 and was decorated with the ribbon of the Legion of Honor in 1819, Oberlin's highest honor was the saintly esteem placed upon him by his parish. A contemporary writer calls him "a Protestant saint" whose "life is one of the best illustrations in human history of greatness achieved through fidelity to a despised and neglected field of work."

[A LETTER ON TITHING]

*M*y *dear friend,*

You ask me for some explanation respecting the different tithes which God has commanded me to pay. I will tell you how I manage. I endeavour to devote three tithes of all that I earn, of all that I receive, and of all my revenue, of whatever name or nature it may be, to his service or to useful objects.

For this purpose I keep three boxes; the first for the first tithe; the second for the second; and the third box for the third tithe.

When I cannot pay ready money all at once, I mark how much I owe upon a bit of paper, which I put into the box; and when, on the contrary, a demand occurs which ought to be defrayed by one of the three allotments, and there is not sufficient money deposited, I advance the sum, and make the box my debtor, by marking upon it how much it owes me.

By this means I am always able to assist in any public or charitable undertaking; and as God has himself declared that 'it is more blessed to give than to receive,' I look upon this regular disbursement of part of my property rather in the light of a privilege than a burden.

The first of the afore-mentioned boxes contains a deposit for the worship of God.

I put a paper, with the following verses from the Old Testament written upon it into the box:—

And all the tithe of the land, whether of the seed of the land or of the fruit of the tree, is the Lord's: it is holy unto the Lord. —Levit. xxvii. 30.

Bring ye all the tithes into the storehouse, that there may be meat in mine house, and prove me now herewith, saith the Lord of hosts, if I will not open you the windows of heaven, and pour you out a blessing, that there shall not be room enough to receive it.—Mat. iii. 10.

I devote the contents of this box to the building and repairing of churches and schoolrooms; the support of conductrices; and the purchase of Bibles and pious books; in short, to any thing connected with divine worship, or the extension of the knowledge of our Redeemer's kingdom.

My parishioners are at liberty to recall from this tithe any present that either generosity, or the supposition that I expected it, may have induced them to make me.

The second box contains tithes for useful purposes.

I have written the following passages in it:—

Thou shalt truly tithe all the increase of thy seed, that the field bringeth forth year by year. And thou shalt eat before the Lord thy God, in the place which he shall choose to place his name there, the tithe of thy corn, of thy wine, and of thine oil, and the firstlings of thy herds and of thy flocks; that thou mayest learn to fear the Lord thy God always. And if the way be too long for thee, so that thou art not able to carry it; or if the place be too far from thee, which the Lord thy God shall choose to set his name there, when the Lord thy God hath blessed thee: then shalt thou turn it into money, and bind up the money in thine hand, and shalt go unto the place which the Lord thy God shall choose: and thou shalt bestow that money for whatsoever thy soul lusteth after, for oxen, or for sheep, or for wine, or for strong drink, or for whatsoever thy soul desireth: and thou shalt eat there before the Lord thy God, and thou shalt rejoice, thou and thine household, and the Levite that is within thy gates; thou shalt not forsake him; for he hath no part nor inheritance with thee.—Deut. xiv. 22–27.

Three times in a year shall all thy males appear before the Lord thy God in the place which he shall choose; in the feast of unleavened bread, and in the feast of weeks, and in the feast of tabernacles; and they shall not appear before the Lord empty.—Deut. xvi. 16.

I employ this tithe for a variety of purposes:—

1. For the improvement of the roads to the churches and schools.

2. For the schoolmasters' salaries.

3. For all works of public utility.

4. For the little expenses incurred by my becoming godfather.

5. For Sunday dinners to my poor people of the other villages. (*My parishioners might add to this catalogue.*)

6. For the churchwardens. (*For whether they do their duty voluntarily from love to God, or make a claim upon me, I always pay them well.*)

7. For expenses incurred among the peasantry of Belmont, Foudai, and Zolbach.

8. For what the poor of Waldbach expend, by inviting the poor of the other villages to come and see them.

9. For the repairing of injuries.

The third box contains tithes for the poor. (That is, it contains the third tithe every three years, or the thirtieth every year.)

I have written there the following texts:—

At the end of three years thou shalt bring forth all the tithe of thine increase the same year, and shalt lay it up within thy gates. And the Levite (because he hath no part nor inheritance with thee), and the strangers and the fatherless, and the widow, which are within thy gates, shall come, and shall eat and be satisfied; that the Lord thy God may bless thee in all the work of thine hand which thou doest.—Deut. xiv. 28, 29.

And when ye reap the harvest of your land, thou shalt not wholly reap the corners of thy field, neither shalt thou gather the gleanings of thy harvest. And thou shalt not glean thy vineyard, neither shalt thou gather every grape of thy vineyard: thou shalt leave them for the poor and the stranger: I am the Lord your God.—Levit. xix. 9, 10.

I devote the contents of this box to the service of the poor; to the compensation of losses occasioned by fire; to wood, flannel, and bread, for those who stand in need, &c. &c.

[QUESTIONS ADDRESSED TO PARISHIONERS]

*D*o you, and your family, regularly attend places of religious instruction?

2. Do you never pass a Sunday without employing yourself in some charitable work?

3. Do neither you, nor your wife or

children, ever wander in the woods on a Sunday, in search of wild raspberries, strawberries, whortle-berries, mulberries, or hazel-nuts, instead of going to church? —and, if you have erred in this manner, will you solemnly promise to do so no more?

4. Are you careful to provide yourself with clean and suitable clothes for going to church in on the Sunday?

5. Do those who are provided with necessary clothes employ a regular part of their income to procure them for their destitute neighbours, or to relieve their other necessities?

6. Have your civil and ecclesiastical overseers reason to be satisfied with your conduct, and that of other members of your family?

7. Do you so love and reverence our Lord and Saviour, Jesus Christ, as to feel united in the bonds of Christian fellowship with that flock of which he is the pastor?

8. Do the animals which belong to you cause no injury or inconvenience to others?—(Guard against this, for it would be as fire in tow, and a source of mutual vexation.)

9. Do you give your creditors reason to be satisfied with your honesty and punctuality?—or can they say of you that you are more desirous of purchasing superfluous clothes than of discharging your debts?

10. Have you paid all that is due this quarter to the churchwarden, schoolmaster and shepherd?

11. Do you punctually contribute your share towards the repairing of the roads?

12. Have you, in order to contribute to the general good, planted upon the common at least twice as many trees as there are heads in your family?

13. Have you planted them properly, or only as idle and ignorant people would do, to save themselves trouble?

14. When the magistrate wishes to assemble the commonalty, do you always assist him as far as lies in your power; and if it be impossible for you to attend yourself, are you careful to inform him of your absence, and to assign a proper reason for it?

15. Do you send your children regularly to school?

16. Do you watch over them as God requires you should do? And is your conduct towards them, as well as your wife's, such as will ensure their affection, respect, and obedience?

17. Are you frugal in the use of wood? And do you contrive to make your fires in as economical a manner as possible?

18. Do you keep a dog unless there be absolute necessity?

19. Have you proper drains in your yard for carrying off the refuse water?

20. Are you, as well as your sons, acquainted with some little handicraft work to employ your spare moments, instead of letting them pass away in idleness?

[LETTER TO HIS SCHOLARS]

Waldbach; September 16th, 1810

My dear Scholars,

I am very sensible of the honour you have intended me, in sending your garlands as a token of your remembrance of my 70th birth-day, completed the 31st of last August. You seem, however, to have forgotten that an honour which one is conscious of not deserving, is in itself humiliating and abasing. If, by my feeble exertions, I have been enabled to be of some utility to you, all the honour belongs to God, who has kindled in my heart the love I bear you, and who has given and preserved my strength till this period to carry forward my heart's desire, which is good.

The beautiful flowers with which your great Creator adorned our country, gave you the means of presenting me with this testimony of your united love. These flowers will very soon fade, but the impression they have made on my heart will never die, and I earnestly pray that you may become unfading flowers in the Paradise of God.

May he bless you, and may he bless the persons who labor for your instruction, with perseverance and faithfulness, that you may prosper, and become useful in the service of our dear and beloved Saviour.

But I have still one wish:—a wish that though I am *old* in years is always fresh in my heart:—a wish that reigns predominant in my thoughts and never forsakes me. It is that my parish might make one solemn feast before God, a general and universal dedication, and one in which all persons without distinction might partake, every one according to his respective ability. That is, a dedication of the heart, in honour and remembrance of, and faith in Him, who shed his blood for us in Gethsemane, and permitted himself to be smitten, and nailed to the cross, that we might receive the heaven which our sins had forfeited.—This is the dedication that I so much desire every soul in my parish might join together to make,—even the surrender of himself to Jesus, each one as he is, with all his faults, with all his sins, in order to find in Him, pardon, righteousness, sanctification and redemption.

Your affectionate Papa,
John Frederic Oberlin

THE NINETEENTH CENTURY UNTIL THE CLOSE OF WORLD WAR I

THE FELLOWSHIP INCLUDES MEN OF EVERY HIGH RELIGIOUS INTEREST

William Ellery Channing

(1780-1842)

BORN in Newport, Rhode Island, educated at Harvard, ordained as a Congregational minister in 1803, Channing began his ministry with great effectiveness in the Federal Street Church, Boston. In his preaching he was a critic of Calvinism, an antagonist of Trinitarian beliefs, and a staunch advocate of the antislavery movement.

In 1819 he went to Baltimore, Maryland, to preach at the ordination of Jared Sparks. What he said then is considered the initiatory statement of the Unitarian movement in the United States. In 1825 the American Unitarian Association was formed with Channing as its recognized leader. Ralph Waldo Emerson and Theodore Parker were his close friends in this liberal movement.

A visitor at Arlington Street Church, Boston, can see the graceful pulpit used by Channing in his Federal Street Church. It stands as a shrine of simple beauty to a man who consecrated his life to reason, humanity, and the power of the spirit. The following brief tract shows the deep, sensitive spirit which emerged into liberal theological and social outlets.

DAILY PRAYER

The Scriptures of the Old and New Testaments agree in enjoining prayer. Let no man call himself a Christian who lives without giving a part of life to this duty. We are not taught how often we must pray; but our Lord, in teaching us to say, "Give us this day our daily bread," implies that we should pray daily. He has even said to us, "pray always"—an injunction to be explained, indeed, with that latitude which many of his precepts require, but which is not to be satisfied, we think, without regular and habitual devotion. As to the particular hours to be given to this duty, every Christian may choose them for himself. Our religion is too liberal and spiritual to bind us to any place or any hour of prayer. But there are parts of the day particularly favorable to this duty, and which, if possible, should be redeemed for it. On these we shall offer a few reflections.

The first of these periods is the morning, which even nature seems to have pointed out to men of different religions as a fit time for offering to the Divinity. In the morning our minds are not so much shaken by worldly cares and pleasures as in other parts of the day. Retirement and sleep have helped to allay the violence of our feelings, to calm the feverish excitement so often produced by intercourse with men. The hour is a still one. The hurry and tumults of life are not begun, and we naturally share in the tranquillity around us. Having for so many hours lost our hold on the world, we can banish it more easily from the mind, and worship with less divided attention. This, then, is a favorable time for approaching the invisible Author of our being, for strengthening the intimacy of our minds with him, for thinking upon a future life, and for seeking those

534

spiritual aids which we need in the labors and temptations of every day.

In the morning there is much to feed the spirit of devotion. It offers an abundance of thoughts friendly to pious feeling. When we look on creation, what a happy and touching change do we witness! A few hours past, the earth was wrapped in gloom and silence. There seemed "a pause in nature." But now a new flood of light has broken forth, and creation rises before us in fresher and brighter hues, and seems to rejoice as if it had just received birth from its Author. The sun never sheds more cheerful beams, and never proclaims more loudly God's glory and goodness, than when he returns after the coldness and dampness of night, and awakens man and inferior animals to the various purposes of their being. A spirit of joy seems breathed over the earth and through the sky. It requires little effort of imagination to read delight in the kindled clouds, or in the fields bright with dew. This is the time when we can best feel and bless the Power which said, "let there be light;" which "set a tabernacle for the sun in the heavens," and made him the dispenser of fruitfulness and enjoyment through all regions.

If we next look at ourselves, what materials does the morning furnish for devout thought! At the close of the past day, we were exhausted by our labors, and unable to move without wearisome effort. Our minds were sluggish, and cold not be held to the most interesting objects. From this state of exhaustion, we sunk gradually into entire insensibility. Our limbs became motionless; our senses were shut as in death. Our thoughts were suspended, or only wandered confusedly and without aim. Our friends, and the universe, and God himself were forgotten. And what a change does the morning bring with it! On waking, we find that sleep, the image of death, has silently infused into us a new life. The weary limbs are braced again. The dim eye has become bright and piercing. The mind is returned from the region of forgetfulness to its old posses-sions. Friends are met again with a new interest. We are again capable of devout sentiment, virtuous effort, and Christian hope. With what subjects of gratitude, then, does the morning furnish us! We can hardly recall the state of insensibility from which we have just emerged without a consciousness of our dependence, or think of the renovation of our powers and intellectual being without feeling our obligation to God. There is something very touching in the consideration, if we will fix our minds upon it, that God thought of us when we could not think; that he watched over us when we had no power to avert peril from ourselves; that he continued our vital motions, and in due time broke the chains of sleep, and set our imprisoned faculties free. How fit is it, at this hour, to raise to God the eyes which he has opened, and the arm which he has strengthened; to acknowledge his providence; and to consecrate to him the powers which he has renewed! How fit that he should be the first object of the thoughts and affections which he has restored! How fit to employ in his praise the tongue which he has loosed, and the breath which he has spared.

But the morning is a fit time for devotion, not only from its relation to the past night, but considered as the introduction of a new day. To a thinking mind, how natural at this hour are such reflections as the following:—I am now to enter on a new period of my life, to start afresh in my course. I am to return to that world where I have often gone astray; to receive impressions which may never be effaced; to perform actions which will never be forgotten; to strengthen a character which will fit me for heaven or hell. I am this day to meet temptations which have often subdued me; I am to be entrusted again with opportunities of usefulness which I have often neglected. I am to influence the minds of others, to help in moulding their characters, and in deciding the happiness of their present and future life. How uncertain is this day! What unseen dangers are before me! What unexpected changes may await me! It may be my last day! It will certainly bring me nearer to death and judgment! Now, when entering on a period of life so important yet so uncertain, how fit and natural is it, before we take the first step, to seek the favor of that Being on whom the lot of every day depends, to commit all our interests to his almighty and wise providence, to seek his blessing on our labors and his succor in temptation, and to consecrate to his service the day which he raises upon us! This morning devotion not only agrees with the sentiments of the heart, but tends to make the day happy, useful, and virtuous. Having cast ourselves on the mercy and protection of the Almighty, we shall go forth with new confidence to the labors and duties which he imposes. Our early prayer will help to shed an odor of piety through the whole life. God, having first occupied, will more easily recur to our mind. Our first step will be in the right path, and we may hope a happy issue.

So fit and useful is morning devotion, it ought not to be omitted without necessity. If our circumstances will allow the privilege, it is a bad sign when no part of the morning is spent in prayer. If God find no place in our minds at that early and peaceful hour, He will hardly recur to us in the tumults of life. If the benefits of the morning do not soften us, we can hardly expect the heart to melt with gratitude through the day. If the world then rush in and take possession of us, when we are at some distance and have had a respite from its cares, how can we hope to shake it off when we shall be in the midst of it, pressed and agitated by it on every side? Let a part of the morning, if possible, be set apart to devotion; and to this end we should fix the hour of rising, so that we may have an early hour at our own disposal. Our piety is suspicious if we can renounce, as too many do, the pleasures and benefits of early prayer, rather than forego the senseless indulgence of unnecessary sleep. What! we can rise early enough for business. We can even anticipate the dawn, if a favorite pleasure or an uncom-

mon gain requires the effort. But we cannot rise that we may bless our great Benefactor, that we may arm ourselves for the severe conflicts to which our principles are to be exposed! We are willing to rush into the world, without thanks offered, or a blessing sought! From a day thus begun, what ought we to expect but thoughtlessness and guilt?

Let us now consider another part of the day which is favorable to the duty of prayer,—we mean the evening. This season, like the morning, is calm and quiet. Our labors are ended. The bustle of life has gone by. The distracting glare of the day has vanished. The darkness which surrounds us favors seriousness, composure, and solemnity. At night the earth fades from our sight, and nothing of creation is left us but the starry heavens, so vast, so magnificent, so serene, as if to guide up our thoughts above all earthly things to God and immortality.

This period should in part be given to prayer, as it furnishes a variety of devotional topics and excitements. The evening is the close of an important division of time and is therefore a fit and natural season for stopping and looking back on the day. And can we ever look back on a day which bears no witness to God, and lays no claim to our gratitude? Who is it that strengthens us for daily labor, gives us daily bread, continues our friends and common pleasures, and grants us the privilege of retiring, after the cares of the day, to a quiet and beloved home? The review of the day will often suggest not only these ordinary benefits, but peculiar proofs of God's goodness, unlooked-for successes, singular concurrences of favorable events, signal blessings sent to our friends, or new and powerful aids to our own virtue, which call for peculiar thankfulness. And shall all these benefits pass away unnoticed? Shall we retire to repose as insensible as the wearied brute? How fit and natural is it to close with pious acknowledgment the day which has been filled with Divine beneficence!

But the evening is the time to review, not only our blessings, but our actions.

A reflecting mind will naturally remember at this hour that another day is gone, and gone to testify of us to our Judge. How natural and useful to inquire what report it has carried to heaven. Perhaps we have the satisfaction of looking back on a day which, in its general tenor, has been innocent and pure, which, having begun with God's praise, has been spent as in his presence; which has proved the reality of our principles in temptation; and shall such a day end without gratefully acknowledging him in whose strength we have been strong, and to whom we owe the powers and opportunities of Christian improvement? But no day will present to us recollections of purity unmixed with sin. Conscience, if suffered to inspect faithfully and speak plainly, will recount irregular desires and defective motives, talents wasted and time misspent; and shall we let the day pass from us without penitently confessing our offences to him who has witnessed them, and who has promised pardon to true repentance? Shall we retire to rest with a burden of unlamented and unforgiven guilt upon our consciences? Shall we leave these stains to spread over and sink into the soul? A religious recollection of our lives is one of the chief instruments of piety. If possible, no day should end without it. If we take no account of our sins on the day on which they are committed, can we hope that they will recur to us at a more distant period, that we shall watch against them to-morrow, or that we shall gain the strength to resist them, which we will not implore?

One observation more, and we have done. The evening is a fit time for prayer, not only as it ends the day, but as it immediately precedes the period of repose. The hours of activity having passed, we are soon to sink into insensibility and sleep. How fit that we resign ourselves to the care of that Being who never sleeps, to whom the darkness is as the light, and whose providence is our only safety! How fit to entreat him, that He would keep us to another day; or, if our bed should prove our grave, that He would give us a part in the resurrection of the just, and awake us to a purer and immortal life. The most important periods of prayer have now been pointed out. Let our prayers, like the ancient sacrifices, ascend morning and evening. Let our days begin and end with God.

Søren Kierkegaard

(1813-1855)

In the last thirty years Christian theology has been vitally affected and "corrected" by a movement known as Neo-supernaturalism. Its first virile stimulus was given in Europe by Karl Barth at the beginning of World War I. Since then it has radiated to all parts of the theological world. Back of this movement, and especially through the focus of Barth, lies the rediscovery of the Danish theologian Kierkegaard.

Kierkegaard was born in Copenhagen and graduated from its university. After two years in Germany he returned to Copenhagen where he remained the rest of his life. In 1843 his first book—and one of his most important writings—was published. It was *Either-Or*. His religious philosophy was a reaction against speculative systems of thought. Greatly dismayed by the postwar days of the Napoleonic era, Kierkegaard felt a great chasm between man and God, an "unlimited qualitative difference between time and eternity." During his later years he denounced the state church because he felt that religion concerned the individual soul.

No devotional theologian has done more to help modern man overcome his deep-seated pride than Kierkegaard, and no foreign theological writer has gone into such rapid English translation in the last decade as this gloomy, serious Danish thinker. The devotional excerpts are from *The Journals of Søren Kierkegaard*, translated by Alexander Dru, and are used by permission of Oxford University Press. His *Journals* were started while Kierkegaard was still at the university. They became "the accompanying meditation on his destiny."

[RELATIONSHIP TO GOD]

From the *Journals*

TRULY SOCRATIC

I said to God: I cannot any longer endure being so near to thee; allow me to withdraw myself. Thou art love; and when I perceive that a near relationship to thee (in the pain of that unlikeness of mine) will continue to be sheer suffering, thou wilt in "grace" permit me, yea, thou wilt aid me to slip away a little further from thee; for this I understand, that the nearer one comes to thee, the more suffering there is in this life. So thou wilt not be wrath, and in another way thou wilt watch over me, that now, when this pain is taken away which day by day bound me to thee and reminded me of thee, that now I may not forget thee and finally invert the whole relationship, and imagine that the fact that I now feel no pain is a sign of thy good pleasure, instead of being perhaps thy ill-pleasure with me, for as I have said, I well understand that nearer to thee, the more pain—Oh, but I cannot, thou loving one, thou must permit me to withdraw further from thee.

So I thought to myself. And yet it did not come to pass.

GOD IS LOVE

. . . If the lover does not talk the beloved's language then either he or she must learn it, however difficult they may find it; for otherwise they cannot be happy together, they cannot even talk together. So too with dying to the world, in order to be able to love God. God is spirit—only one who is dead can speak that language at all. If you do not desire to die then neither can you love God, you talk of quite different things from him.

Thus we see that in Christianity it is not even the law which commands you to die; it is love which says: do you not love me? And if the answer is yes, then it follows of itself that you must die. But the human race has egoistically turned Christianity completely topsy-turvy.

Christianity does not preach the law, on the contrary it preaches what God in his infinite love has done for man. To God that will appear so much that even stones must be moved. And so Christian preaching stops at that. There follows a pause, for God does not wish to command what follows, he waits for it, waits for it to move man in such a way that he determines to love God. But if man takes that decision he also decides, *eo ipso* to die to the world.

But as Christianity is now twisted we men have been humbugging God. . . .

Oh, just be a loving man: you will see how human egoism can make use of it—but since God made it known that he is love: what an opportunity for human egoism. . . .

And so in Christianity God has, as it were, to speak in human terms, proposed to us in order to win our love: all this he gave us, a gift of love and so he thought: now it is impossible that mankind should not love me. But we men both were and are devilishly clever: we accepted and we accept the presents—and we call it loving God, when we live according to our own ideas and then thank God. Imagine a father. There was something he wished the child to do—and the child knew what it was. So, thought the father, I will contrive something that will please the child immensely. So he presents it to him (indeed it is far too much I am doing for the child!) I am sure he will love me in return. "He will love me in return"—by that the father meant that the child would now do its father's will. But the child—a devilish shrewd child—accepted the present but did not do his father's will. On the other hand the child thanked and thanked again, said "Many, many thanks," and said, "What a dear, good father"—but had its own way.

The same is true of us men where God is concerned. When he became love: we profited by it and behave as though it were love to have our own way; but we clap our hands, blow trumpets and say with tears in our eyes: God is love, who shall not love a loving God?

SUFFERING, THE SIGN OF THE RELATION TO GOD, OR THE LOVE OF GOD

It is easy to see that this thought might be dangerous. If suffering is the characteristic of the relation to God then the individual might stoically wish, as it were, to challenge God to send him suffering in order to show that he can love God all the same. That is presumption and as unlike the fear of God as is well possible, since it is egoism which impertinently wishes to measure itself against God.—From another point of view: one might grow afraid at the thought that suffering is the characteristic of the relation to God, so that one dared not embark upon it at all, because it was like challenging God to continue the suffering. And one might grow so afraid as to fly away from this thought (which is nevertheless true Christianity), back to that which is not really Christianity, but only an approximation to Christianity. The following must therefore be noted. (1) One must never desire suffering. No, you have only to remain in the condition of praying for happiness on earth. If a man desire suffering then it is as though he were able, by himself, to solve this terror: that suffering is the characteristic of God's love. And that is precisely what he cannot do; it is "the spirit" which witnesses with him that it is so; and consequently he must not himself have desired suffering. In any case the desire for suffering would have to be understood as meaning that he begged at the same time for "the spirit," so that he did not beg for suffering in and for itself, but for suffering as the condition for receiving "the witness of the spirit." Yet this too is so high that care is necessary and there must be frequent rest in lower forms.

(2) You must certainly dare, for to dare (for the truth etc.) is Christianity. But for the time being you must not dare in such a way that there is no possibility, humanly speaking, of your coming out

on top, as one says. That is to say: there is the possibility of failure, and also the possibility of success.

But if suffering cannot be, humanly speaking and understood, avoided, and you nevertheless understand yourself before God in being obliged and willing to dare: yet suffering itself must never be the τέλος, you must not dare in order to suffer, for that is presumptuous, and is to tempt God. To expose yourself to suffering for the sake of suffering is a presumptuous personal impertinence and forwardness towards God, as though you were challenging God to a contest. But when it is for the cause—even though you see that the suffering is humanly speaking unavoidable, just go on and dare. You do not dare for the sake of suffering, but you dare in order not to betray the cause.

God's Guidance

Originally I was in possession of the outward requirements for the enjoyment of life; and within me, that is all too certain, there was desire enough to enjoy life —but there was given to me a thorn in the flesh, a cross: and I could not really succeed in enjoying life.

Then, as the conditions for enjoying life began to disappear, and financial worries came upon me, it occurred to me that it might be possible for the thorn in the flesh to be taken from me. I would then have been able to put the abilities and gifts granted me to my own use, and humanly speaking I should certainly have secured, by acquisition, the conditions for enjoying life, and so all the same have succeeded in enjoying life. . . .

And now things begin to happen as I expected. That thorn in the flesh will perhaps be taken from me; but by then I shall no longer be in possession of the requirements necessary for enjoying life, and I will be so tried in suffering and so far out, that I shall have cut myself off from all possibility of acquiring the conditions.

So perhaps there will be still one more course left for me to go through. The thorn in the flesh will be taken from me —and then suddenly all the requirements for enjoying life will be offered to me, almost forced upon me. And then the task will perhaps be for me to be so dead to the world, so mature a spirit, as to have the strength to say freely: no, I will not accept them.

And so in the end I shall never enjoy life. Oh, my God, that was certainly my qualification, you had something far better for me than that I should waste my life in enjoyment—and repent through all eternity.

But at first I could not understand that and could not do it, and so force had to be used, just as one puts splints on a broken leg. The education consisted in leading me to being able to do freely what at first I had to be compelled to do.

Works

Take a feeble analogy, imagine a girl in love; for a time she will be satisfied with expressing her love in words; but the time will come when that will no longer satisfy her, where she will long to be allowed to throw herself in the arms of her love. This means to say: she requires a stronger expression of her passions. So with the believer in relation to God: finally the time will come when he will have to say: I can no longer endure to express my thankfulness in words and perhaps even in carefully chosen words (and that is a completely wrong turn), that no longer satisfies my need, you must allow me, O God, a far stronger expression of my thankfulness: Works.

And so, even if this were not what was demanded it would have to become that which the better man himself desired— while the fact that it is required of us liberates him from every worry as to whether it is pleasing to God or not.

Which is it? Is God's meaning, in Christianity, simply to humble man through the model (that is to say by putting before us the ideal) and to console him with "Grace," but in such a way that through Christianity there is expressed the fact that between God and man there is no relationship, that man must express his thankfulness like dog to a man, so that the adoration becomes more and more true, and more and more pleasing to God, as it becomes less and less possible for man to imagine that he could be like the model? . . . Is that the meaning of Christianity?

Or is it the very reverse, that God's will is to express that he desires to be in relation with man, and therefore desires the thanks and the adoration which is in spirit and in truth: imitation.

The latter is certainly the meaning of Christianity. But the former is a cunning invention of us men (although it may have its better side) in order to escape from the real relation to God, because in its beginning it is really suffering.

How so? Let me take an illustration. Imagine a great king; all his love is given to a certain peasant, and the king's love is so great that it cannot be appeased unless the peasant is adopted as the king's son and successor. Now let us talk quite unreservedly. Would the peasant not say to himself: this is a real misfortune for me; if the king really loves me then let him express his love by doing what I want, let him give me a good farm so that I can marry Catherine, then I should thank him all my life long. But on the contrary, for me, a simple peasant, to be dragged into the great world where I do not belong at all, that is the greatest pain. That is more or less what he will think to himself. But to the king he would probably say (for hypocrisy and being a man are almost inseparable): you are doing much too much for me, I am both too humble and too modest to desire such things (though of course it is not he who ought to desire, it is the king who offers it to him, wishes him to have it); I should be inexpressibly happy if you would just give me a fully stocked farm. . . .

The Relation to God

The thought of doing this or that, of offering this or that, of risking this or that—in order to serve God's cause, has never moved me; for I always thought it rather silly that the Almighty, to whom a million worlds are as nothing, should have a cause for which it was important

that Tom, Dick and Harry should do this or that.

No, that is not my way. Things are easier for me if I think of God as an examiner who says: I desire this and this of you. I do not thereby mean that it is some entirely useless achievement, no, it is something profitable, but the thought that God has a cause in the sense that a man could help it on, seemed to me to have been an excusable childishness, once upon a time, but now mere galimatias; for to say that God has a cause in that sense comes to the same thing as saying that he is a part, he who is all.

No, it is not God who has a cause, but each man has a cause.

It cannot be denied that the idea, that God quite simply had a cause, that it was important that you or I should fight for his cause, that this idea has in its time moved very many and made it easy for them to give up everything. But that cannot be helped, it is in spite of everything imagination, and it would be frightful conceit if men, at that time, had so developed an idea of God's infinite elevation as can be had now. On the other hand it is certain that this infinite blessed peace in which we imagine God infinitely above the world can easily have a stupefying effect intellectually, so that we observe instead of acting; but that cannot be helped, we must break through to action, to the same infinite enthusiasm which the early centuries possessed under the illusion that they were almost coming to God's help when they fought for his cause.

Here once again there is a doubling or reduplication which makes it very difficult to break through, a reduplication which is found wherever enthusiasm is to be on the other side of or after the illusion. To look upon a man's endeavour as absolutely childish with one eye, indeed as the least important thing in the world (for the Almighty has millions of ways out, and is always infinitely victorious) and nevertheless to be able to strain every nerve to the utmost, quite as well as anyone whose enthusiasm seriously sprang from the idea that upon his powers of endurance and daring depended neither more nor less than the victory or defeat of God.

In a sense I am tempted to cry out: O fortunate ones! for what would a man not endure who once convinced himself that his efforts were so infinitely important, that it was God's cause. In another sense however I consider myself fortunate: for how fortunate to have an infinitely higher conception. . . .

No, no amount of effort can procure one eternal happiness. Therefore it is "grace." And here again is the danger of this (the fact that it is "grace"), having a paralysing effect. . . .

THE RELATION TO GOD
FATHER—SON—SPIRIT

Usually the relation is represented in this way; it is Christ who leads us to God, man needs a mediator in order to come to God.

But that is not how the relationship is represented in the New Testament, neither can this be so if it is true that progress in the relation to God can be recognised because one is degraded.

The relation to God begins with the Father, or the relation to God as Father, without a mediator. This is childlike; to the child nothing is too high, the child says "you" to the Emperor just as it does to its nurse, and finds it perfectly natural that God should be its father.

But when a man reaches a certain stage of maturity God becomes too infinitely exalted for him to call God Father simply and directly, if it is not to be merely a manner of speech. To a certain extent God is of the same opinion.

It is then that God refers man to the Son, to the mediator (John 6:45). To the man himself it appears almost presumptuous to call God Father, simply and directly; and to a certain extent God is of the same opinion. And therefore he seems to say: I can be your father in the mediator.

Then comes the mediator. At the same time the mediator is the model. Here we find a youthfulness which is characterised by an adorable simplicity which finds nothing too high. To him it seems perfectly natural to have so infinitely high a model and he is piously convinced, in his lovable illusion, that the two of them, the model and he, the one who strives, can, in a good sense, become sufficiently alike. . . .

But when a man reaches a certain degree of maturity the model seems so infinitely beyond him that he dare not simply and directly start trying to be like it in a brotherly sort of way, in a good sense.

To a certain extent the model is also of the opinion that it would really be presumptuous.

There is, however, another angle from which the model may be seen; the model is also "The Redeemer." This is the aspect of which youth is not really aware, for in its zeal it begins immediately to try and become like the model, because it discovers no difficulty in that infinite elevation, so that youth lacks the necessary category for the infinite elevation of the model (the fact of its being different in quality from the purely human) and also has an illusory conception of its own strength.

The "Redeemer" must not, however, supplant the "model"; the model remains, demanding to be striven after.

And so the model, once again, points away from itself to the "spirit" (just as the father pointed to the mediator), as though saying: you cannot simply start trying, that would, as you yourself feel, be presumptuous (which youth is too naïve to discover, and so it is not guilty of presumption in what it does). No, you require the Spirit to help you.

And consequently it is not the Spirit who leads one to the Son, and the Son who leads one to the Father, but the Father who points to the Son, the Son to the Spirit; and only then does the Spirit lead to the Son and the Son lead to the Father.

This is, if I may so express it, God's parsimony with his majesty which is nothing less than imperious, or elevated, and is inseparable from his being. Precisely by giving himself more, by entering into closer relation with mankind, or by his wishing to do so, man is degraded, although elevated. In truth he is lifted up, but he is lifted up by receiving an infinitely higher conception of God, and so he is degraded.

How ennobling! No human Sovereign can protect himself from importunity in that way. . . . "He must increase but I must decrease," that is the law for every approach to God. Even though separated by a million steps he would not be so secure against importunity, for after a time they could be surmounted. But to be protected against importunity by the law of reversal: infinite majesty!

"But then, in a sense, I lose God." How, because he increases! No, if I lose anything it is my egoism, myself, until I find perfect happiness in this prayer: He must increase, but I must decrease.

That is the law of all true love. If I desired things otherwise, if I desired to *increase at the same time* that God increased, then that would be self-love.

No, he must increase but I must decrease; only that he remains my father all the same, he becomes my father through the Spirit in the mediator.

ALL IS GRACE

But this does not mean that one should hide from self-denial, no, no. But only that it is not legally binding on all, which is what makes self-denial hard and makes the mind rebel; and that, on the contrary, it is moving when Christ says: all is given to thee in Grace—look upon me and my suffering, does that not move you to wish to mortify yourself?

I remember in my childhood and youth, what has so often occurred to me in this connection as something which helped me. It bored me much to copy father's letters, but he only had to say to me: all right then, I will do them myself. I was immediately willing. Oh, if he had scolded, alas, there would simply have been a row; but this was moving. In the same way many a self-denial may come difficult to a man and embitter him, if it is imposed by law, but the Saviour's look and his words: Everything is given

to thee, it is nothing but grace, only look upon me and upon my suffering which won this grace: yes, that is moving!

MELANCHOLY

It is quite certain that the more the individual has to do with God the more difficulties enter his life; at times it seems as though God let everything go wrong for him—and yet he can have the blessing of believing that God does so out of love. The melancholy thing is that others cannot understand it thus. And so he may desire as an alleviation that others should be ignorant of all his misfortunes and sufferings, because they do not share his understanding of them, whilst he does not, on the other hand, desire to be freed from the sufferings. It is seldom however that a man lives in such godly piety that he really lives thus in the confidence of God, so that misfortune and suffering really mean God's love to him.

MY PRAYER

There was a time—it came so naturally, it was childlike—when I believed that God's love also expressed itself by sending earthly "good gifts," happiness, prosperity. How foolhardy my soul was in desiring, and daring—for this is how I thought of it: one must not make the all-powerful petty; I prayed for everything, even the most foolhardy things, yet one thing excepted, exemption from the deep suffering beneath which I have suffered from my earliest days, but which I understood as belonging to my relation to God. But as for the rest, I should have dared anything. And when (for the suffering was simply the Exceptional), everything succeeded, how rich my soul was in thankfulness, so happy in giving thanks,—for I was convinced that God's love could express itself by sending the good gifts of the earth.

Now it is otherwise, How did that happen? Quite simply, but little by little. Little by little I noticed increasingly that all those whom God really loved, the examples etc. had all had to suffer in this world. Furthermore, that that is the teaching of Christianity: to be loved by God and to love God is to suffer.

But if that were so then I dared not pray for good fortune and success because it was as though I were to beg at the same time: will you not, O god, cease loving me and allow me to stop loving you. When a desire awoke in me —and I wished to pray, all my former burning inwardness was blown away; for it was as though God looked upon me and said: little child, think carefully what you are doing, do you wish me not to love you, and do you wish to be excused from loving me?

On the other hand, to pray directly for suffering appeared to me too exalted, and it also seemed to me that it might easily be presumptuous, and that God might grow angry at my perhaps wishing to defy him.

For a long time my prayer has therefore been different, it is really a silent surrendering of everything to God, because it is not quite plain to me how I should pray.

I am brought to a stop by that difficulty. And yet the question presents still another difficulty. For even if I were really frank enough to grasp that to be loved by God, and to love God, is to suffer, for which after all I was disposed by nature, I who from my earliest days believed I was marked out for suffering —what of other men? That is how I had understood my life from this point of view. Now, for better or for worse, I live in the isolated cabin of melancholy —though I may rejoice at the sight of other people's joy and may sanction it from a *Christian* point of view. To be loved by a woman, to live happily married, to enjoy life—well, that has been denied me; but when I step forth from my isolated cabin I may rejoice to see the good fortunes of others, may strengthen them in the conviction that God is pleased at their joy in life. To be strong and healthy, a complete man with the expectation of a long life—well, that was never granted me. But when I step forth from my lonely suffering I come out among happy people; I thought I might have the melancholy joy of confirming them in their enjoyment of life. Oh, but I have to preach mortification, and that to be loved by God and to love God is to suffer, then I have to disturb others in their happiness, I cannot have the melancholy joy of rejoicing in their joy, the melancholy love of thus being loved by them.

And consequently I am brought to a stop by that difficulty. If anyone can prove to me from Holy Scripture that to be loved by God and to love God is compatible with enjoying this life; I shall accept this interpretation from God's Hand with unspeakable thankfulness, happy on my own account but also on account of others, for I understand only too well what comes so naturally to man. If anyone can make that plain to me from the New Testament: then the position of my cause, if I may so express it, would be so brilliant at that moment that with a little worldly wisdom and confidence in God it would be sure to be victorious in this world. *Aber, aber,* my soul is suspicious of earthly enjoyment and worldly victories. That is why I dare not use worldly wisdom—I am almost afraid of winning a temporal victory; for, from a Christian point of view, to be loved by God and to love God is to suffer. In any case, in order to have confidence in God—for I cannot combine confidence in God and worldly wisdom in such a way as to use worldly wisdom with confidence in God—I must have the frankness not to use worldly wisdom, and if I am victorious temporally, I must be able to say honestly: it was God's will, I attribute it to him—by renouncing the use of worldly wisdom. . . .

However, as I have said, I am held up by this difficulty; as yet I dare not decide absolutely whether God might not wish me to be victorious in the world, whether it is not only true of the chosen ones that to be loved by God is to suffer, whereas like men in general I am excepted therefrom, but then too have not so close a relation to God; I am not yet strong enough to pray for suffering.

But I am brought to a standstill, and

resigning myself silently to God I await a nearer understanding. It is so infinitely high, this: to be loved by God and to love God is to suffer—oh, and nothing, nothing makes me so afraid as the thought of approaching too near to God uncalled. . . . And so with the models, the glorious ones, the chosen of God; but this is precisely the difficulty with "Christendom," that there, on a frightful scale, people have made it only too easy for themselves to rid themselves of the chosen ones, to manœuvre them out of the way, to presume that everything strict in the New Testament is said to the Apostles in *particular*. The question is whether the New Testament recognises any kind of Christian other than the "disciple." For the humility which does not desire to be an apostle or a disciple —oh, it can be such a swindle: to wish to be freed from the apostles' suffering and then, as usual in this human thieves' slang, lyingly call it humility and gain two advantages: to be freed from suffering and to be honoured as suffering. Not to desire the gifts of an apostle— yes, that may be all right, that is humility; but that it should be "humility" not to desire his sufferings, no, that ends in hypocrisy.

Friedrich A. G. Tholuck

(1799-1877)

AMONG nineteenth-century German devotional theologians, Tholuck ranks very high. After his theological training at Berlin University, he spent almost fifty years as professor of theology at Halle, the center of German rationalism. For two years—1827-29—he was chaplain of the Prussian embassy in Rome. Most of his writings, edited in eleven volumes in 1872, show a fine blending of the rational and the mystical. A number of his works are in English. Of these, *Hours of Christian Devotion* is of an unusual religious beauty. "God Is the Chief Good" explains how the soul is taught by heavenly wisdom to pray. It is one of the short devotional readings or sermonettes into which the book is divided. This translation is by Robert Menzies.

GOD IS THE CHIEF GOOD

From *Hours of Christian Devotion*

I

O Lord, I long to pray to Thee *aright*. Wilt not Thou Thyself instruct me how to do it?

Heavenly Wisdom: Tell me, my child, why thou desirest to pray to me? Is it for *my* sake or *thine own?*—is it to *laud* and *praise* me, or to *crave* some *boon* for *thyself?*

The Soul: Lord, Thy question perplexes and puts me to shame. But the purpose of it is to bring to light what is in man. Thou art my chief and eternal good, and well I know that I ought to pray, and give Thee thanks and praise, *solely for Thy sake*. And yet there is something for which I have a keen and perpetual desire, and which I passionately long to obtain from Thee by my prayers.

Heavenly Wisdom: And what is it on which thou hast thus set thy heart above all measure?

The Soul: Lord, it is to know for certain that, after this life in time, I shall enjoy a blessed eternity in Thy presence.

Heavenly Wisdom: And why, O soul, is thy desire for heavenly blessedness so keen?

The Soul: Lord, it is, as Thou knowest,

because this earth, with all its good things, cannot fully satisfy me.

Heavenly Wisdom: Well, then, thou shalt obtain the boon on which thy heart is so fondly set. I shall command the chief of my heavenly ministers to apportion to thee the treasures of Paradise, and shall rejoice to hear that my heaven can give what my little earth was too poor to supply.

The Soul: *Hear* this, dost Thou say? Methought that it was *in Thy presence* O Love Eternal, that I was to enjoy the delights of heaven: but how can even heaven be heaven to me, if I do not find Thee there?

Heavenly Wisdom: What good, O soul, can it do thee to have my presence at thy enjoyments? Have I not promised thee my gifts, and was it not for these that thou didst desire to pray to me? Surely thou art asking too much.

The Soul: O Lord, Thou knowest my inmost heart. It was *before Thy face, and only there*, that I thought of enjoying Thy good things; but if my joy be not also Thine, and thy joy mine, even Thy Paradise can not content me.

Heavenly Wisdom: Well, then, if thou canst not be happy without me, art thou willing to have me, even though I bring thee *no gifts* at all?

The Soul: Lord, Thou leadest me into temptation; but I reflect, and still I answer; "*Whom have I in heaven but Thee? and there is none upon earth that I desire beside Thee.*" Yet if I have found favour in Thy sight, permit me still further to ask a question.

Heavenly Wisdom: Say on, my son; I wish to know all that is in thy heart.

The Soul: Whilst Thou wert speaking, a blessed light arose within me, and now I know what Thou art. Art Thou not so transcendently great a good, that if I were only to possess Thee, I should possess all the other things which I wish to have—wisdom, and peace, and love, and beauty, and rest?

Heavenly Wisdom: Thou hast spoken well. I am indeed the shield of the righteous, and their exceeding great reward. And now I understand what it is which thou didst wish to obtain by thy prayers. Tell me, then, if in asking me to teach thee how to pray, thy purpose was to thank and praise me, or rather, to obtain me as a boon to thyself.

The Soul: Again Thou art pleased to lead me into temptation. Why dost Thou ask that question? Is not my love all that Thou carest for? What else but Thyself dost Thou give us in Thy gifts? and how can a creature laud and praise Thee more than by making Thee the boon for which he craves?

Heavenly Wisdom: My son, thou sayest what is right, but mark the delusion in which thou wert entangled. When intending, in thy prayers, to *laud* and *praise* me as the chief good, it yet was not *myself* but my *gifts* that were the object of thy desire.

II

The Soul: Lord, Thou art to me so high and precious a good, that henceforth I will no longer pray for any earthly good at all, but solely for Thyself.

The Lord: 'Tis well, my son. The portion thou needest of the good things of earth will be given to thee by Him into whose hand they are committed.

The Soul: How shall I understand Thee, Lord? Is there, then, any other hand but Thine own into which good things are committed?

The Lord: No, my son, *mine* is the hand from which all the good things both of earth and heaven are received. Why, then, wilt thou not ask from me the earthly ones, nor thank *me* for them? Methought I was so dear to thee that thou wouldst accept of no gift unless it came from a Father's hand. Methought that, on that account, all my gifts would seem to thee to be fraught with blessing. When I presented thee with an earthly good, did I not mean by it, no less than by my spiritual gifts, to attest to thee the continuance of my love? And dost thou value an attestation of my love at so low a rate?

The Soul: Lord, now that Thou showest it to me, I see how foolishly I spake. It was, however, only that my whole endeavor might be aimed with a more single eye at Thyself, that I wanted not to have my thoughts diverted by any perishable object, and therefore meant no longer to pray to Thee for earthly blessings.

The Lord: Dear soul, thou sayest thou didst not wish to distract thy mind by looking at transitory things, but observe how thou didst divide thy heart; for didst thou not intend to praise me for what my heaven bestows, but to be dumb for every boon that my earth confers?

The Soul: Lord, Thou puttest me to shame. In my desire to be *simple-minded* I have erred in my own wisdom, and become *double-minded*. As Thou art the Lord of heaven, and *no less also the Lord of earth*, I no doubt ought to ask, and likewise thank Thee, for earthly blessings. Forgive me for what I said in my folly; but, inasmuch as I have taken upon me to speak unto Thee, and fear that my heart may cleave to created things, I now entreat that Thou wouldst Thyself teach me the right way to pray for earthly blessings.

The Lord: My son, thou has said that there is none in heaven or earth whom thou desirest more than me, and that I am thy chief and eternal good. If, then, that be true, I will show thee the way to pray for earthly blessings, and yet to have thy heart wholly detached from them. Thou didst strive with ardent desire to reach *my* heart; *strive therefore after every blessing I bestow, as if it were a path by which my heart may be reached.*

The Soul: Full well I know that the spiritual influences emanating so blissfully from Thee are nothing but beams of light, intended to guide us back to the Sun from whence they came. But with Thy permission I would ask if this be also the case with earthly blessings?

The Lord: Didst thou ever, at the rising of the sun, observe how its image is reflected, as if it were a miniature sun, in every drop of dew? Such is the relation between my divinity and all this earthly creation. In none of the creatures oughtest thou to enjoy anything save what is gentle, and sweet, and lovely; and whatever is gentle, and sweet, and lovely in any created thing, is *my* signature and mark. On the contrary, all that is harsh, and hateful, and bitter, belongs to the creature itself. And so, my child, you see how, from every created thing upon the earth, there is a way to the heart of my Godhead.

The Soul: I do see it; but be not angry with me if I once again open my mouth, for there is still something which is strange in my eyes. If every created thing be a way to Thy heart, how comes it that Thy manner has always been to impoverish the most pious of Thy servants here below more than all others, although they are most accustomed to read Thy signature and mark; while, on the other hand, Thou lavishest the good things of *earth* on those who are far from Thee?

The Lord: For no other cause or reason, dear son, save that I am the Lord, and have ordered all things in weight, number, and measure. As the signature and mark which I impress upon terrestrial blessings are written in large letters, legible even to the simple, it is to the simple that in my wisdom I have allotted terrestrial blessings. But as my wisdom has inscribed a better signature, although in fainter lines, upon poverty and privation, these are the boons I have reserved for them who are the "children of the secret."

The Soul: "A word fitly spoken is like apples of gold in dishes of silver." Lord, this is a hard saying, but Thy Spirit will be to me a light within.

John Henry Newman

(1801-1890)

THREE Oriel College, Oxford, men were among those active in the Oxford Movement which began in England in 1833. They were Richard Froude, John Keble, and Newman. To Newman the Church of England was the "golden mean" between the Roman Catholic Church and the Protestant churches. But doubts about the catholicity of the Church of England assailed him, and in October, 1845, Newman made his submission to the Roman Catholic Church. In 1879 he was created a cardinal by Pope Leo XIII. In *Apologia pro Vita Sua*, one of the world's classic spiritual autobiographies, Newman defends the Roman Catholic faith against charges made by Charles Kingsley. In this book he discerns the authority of religious experience within·the confines of an infallible church.

[THE CATHOLIC CHURCH IS INFALLIBLE]

From *Apologia pro Vita Sua*

Starting then with the being of a God, (which, as I have said, is as certain to me as the certainty of my own existence, though when I try to put the grounds of that certainty into logical shape I find a difficulty in doing so in mood and figure to my satisfaction,) I look out of myself into the world of men, and there I see a sight which fills me with unspeakable distress. The world seems simply to give the lie to that great truth, of which my whole being is so full; and the effect upon me is, in consequence, as a matter of necessity, as confusing as if it denied that I am in existence myself. If I looked into a mirror, and did not see my face, I should have the sort of feeling which actually comes upon me, when I look into this living busy world, and see no reflexion of its Creator. This is, to me, one of those great difficulties of this absolute primary truth, to which I referred just now. Were it not for this voice, speaking so clearly in my conscience and my heart, I should be an atheist, or a pantheist, or a polytheist when I looked into the world. I am speaking for myself only; and I am far from denying the real force of the arguments in proof of a God, drawn from the general facts of human society and the course of history, but these do not warm me or enlighten me; they do not take away the winter of my desolation, or make the buds unfold and the leaves grow within me, and my moral being rejoice. The sight of the world is nothing else than the prophet's scroll, full of "lamentations, and mourning, and woe."

To consider the world in its length and breadth, its various history, the many races of man, their starts, their fortunes, their mutual alienation, their conflicts; and then their ways, habits, governments, forms of worship; their enterprises, their aimless courses, their random achievements and acquirements, the impotent conclusion of long-standing facts, the tokens so faint and broken of a superintending design, the blind evolution of what turn out to be great powers or truths, the progress of things, as if from unreasoning elements, not towards final causes, the greatness and littleness of man, his far-reaching aims, his short duration, the curtain hung over his futurity, the disappointments of life, the defeat of good, the success of evil, physical pain, mental anguish, the prevalence and intensity of sin, the pervading idolatries, the corruptions, the dreary hopeless irreligion, that condition of the whole race, so fearfully yet exactly described in the Apostle's words, "having no hope and without God in the world"—all this is a vision to dizzy and appal; and inflicts upon the mind the sense of a profound mystery, which is absolutely beyond human solution.

What shall be said to this heart-piercing, reason-bewildering fact? I can only answer, that either there is no Creator, or this living society of men is in a true sense discarded from His presence. Did I see a boy of good make and mind, with the tokens on him of a refined nature, cast upon the world without provision, unable to say whence he came, his birthplace or his family connexions, I should conclude that there was some mystery connected with his history, and that he was one, of whom, from one cause or other, his parents were ashamed. Thus only should I be able to account for the contrast between the promise and the condition of his being. And so I argue about the world;—*if* there be a God, *since* there is a God, the human race is implicated in some terrible aboriginal calamity. It is out of joint with the purposes of its Creator. This is a fact, a fact as true as the fact of its existence; and thus the doctrine of what is theologically called original sin becomes to me almost as certain as that the world exists, and as the existence of God.

And now, supposing it were the blessed and loving will of the Creator to interfere in this anarchical condition of things, what are we to suppose would be the methods which might be necessarily or naturally involved in His purpose of mercy? Since the world is in so abnormal a state, surely it would be no surprise to me, if the interposition were of necessity equally extraordinary—or what is called miraculous. But that subject does not directly come into the scope of my present remarks. Miracles as evidence, involve a process of reason, or an argument; and of course I am thinking of some mode of interference which does not immediately run into argument. I am rather asking what must be the face-to-face antagonist, by which to withstand and baffle the

fierce energy of passion and the all-corroding, all-dissolving scepticism of the intellect in religious inquiries? I have no intention at all of denying, that truth is the real object of our reason, and that, if it does not attain to truth, either the premiss or the process is in fault; but I am not speaking here of right reason, but of reason as it acts in fact and concretely in fallen man. I know that even the unaided reason, when correctly exercised, leads to a belief in God, in the immortality of the soul, and in a future retribution; but I am considering the faculty of reason actually and historically; and in this point of view, I do not think I am wrong in saying that its tendency is towards a simple unbelief in matters of religion. No truth, however sacred, can stand against it, in the long run; and hence it is that in the pagan world, when our Lord came, the last traces of the religious knowledge of former times were all but disappearing from those portions of the world in which the intellect had been active and had had a career.

And in these latter days, in like manner, outside the Catholic Church things are tending,—with far greater rapidity than in that old time from the circumstance of the age,—to atheism in one shape or other. What a scene, what a prospect, does the whole of Europe present at this day! and not only Europe, but every government and every civilization through the world, which is under the influence of the European mind! Especially, for it most concerns us, how sorrowful, in the view of religion, even taken in its most elementary, most attenuated form, is the spectacle presented to us by the educated intellect of England, France, and Germany! Lovers of their country and of their race, religious men, external to the Catholic Church, have attempted various expedients to arrest fierce wilful human nature in its onward course, and to bring it into subjection. The necessity of some form of religion for the interests of humanity, has been generally acknowledged: but where was the concrete representative of things invisible, which would have the force and toughness necessary to be a breakwater against the deluge? Three centuries ago the establishment of religion, material, legal, and social, was generally adopted as the best expedient for the purpose, in those countries which separated from the Catholic Church; and for a long time it was successful; but now the crevices of those establishments are admitting the enemy. Thirty years ago, education was relied upon: ten years ago there was a hope that wars would cease for ever, under the influence of commercial enterprise and the reign of the useful and fine arts; but will any one venture to say that there is any thing any where on this earth, which will afford a fulcrum for us, whereby to keep the earth from moving onwards?

The judgment, which experience passes whether on establishments or on education, as a means of maintaining religious truth in this anarchical world, must be extended even to Scripture, though Scripture be divine. Experience proves surely that the Bible does not answer a purpose for which it was never intended. It may be accidentally the means of the conversion of individuals; but a book, after all, cannot make a stand against the wild living intellect of man, and in this day it begins to testify, as regards its own structure and contents, to the power of that universal solvent, which is so successfully acting upon religious establishments.

Supposing then it to be the Will of the Creator to interfere in human affairs, and to make provisions for retaining in the world a knowledge of Himself, so definite and distinct as to be proof against the energy of human scepticism, in such a case,—I am far from saying that there was no other way,—but there is nothing to surprise the mind, if He should think fit to introduce a power into the world, invested with the prerogative of infallibility in religious matters. Such a provision would be a direct, immediate, active, and prompt means of withstanding the difficulty; it would be an instrument suited to the need; and, when I find that this is the very claim of the Catholic Church, not only do I feel no difficulty in admitting the idea, but there is a fitness in it, which recommends it to my mind. And thus I am brought to speak of the Church's infallibility, as a provision, adapted by the mercy of the Creator, to preserve religion in the world, and to restrain that freedom of thought, which of course in itself is one of the greatest of our natural gifts, and to rescue it from its own suicidal excesses. And let it be observed that, neither here nor in what follows, shall I have occasion to speak directly of Revelation in its subject-matter, but in reference to the sanction which it gives to truths which may be known independently of it,—as it bears upon the defence of natural religion. I say, that a power, possessed of infallibility in religious teaching, is happily adapted to be a working instrument, in the course of human affairs, for smiting hard and throwing back the immense energy of the aggressive, capricious, untrustworthy intellect:—and in saying this, as in the other things that I have to say, it must still be recollected that I am all along bearing in mind my main purpose, which is a defence of myself.

I am defending myself here from a plausible charge brought against Catholics, as will be seen better as I proceed. The charge is this:—that I, as a Catholic, not only make profession to hold doctrines which I cannot possibly believe in my heart, but that I also believe in the existence of a power on earth, which at its own will imposes upon men any new set of *credenda*, when it pleases, by a claim to infallibility; in consequence, that my own thoughts are not my own property; that I cannot tell that to-morrow I may not have to give up what I hold to-day, and that the necessary effect of such a condition of mind must be a degrading bondage, or a bitter inward rebellion relieving itself in secret infidelity, or the necessity of ignoring the whole subject of religion in a sort of disgust, and of mechanically saying everything that the Church says, and leaving to others the defence of it. As then I have above spoken of the relation of my mind towards the Catholic Creed, so now I shall speak of the attitude which it takes up in the view of the Church's infallibility.

And first, the initial doctrine of the infallible teacher must be an emphatic protest against the existing state of mankind. Man had rebelled against his Maker. It was this that caused the divine interposition: and to proclaim it must be the first act of the divinely-accredited messenger. The Church must denounce rebellion as of all possible evils the greatest. She must have no terms with it; if she would be true to her Master, she must ban and anathematize it. This is the meaning of a statement of mine which has furnished matter for one of those special accusations to which I am at present replying: I have, however, no fault at all to confess in regard to it; I have nothing to withdraw, and in consequence I here deliberately repeat it. I said, "The Catholic Church holds it better for the sun and moon to drop from heaven, for the earth to fail, and for all the many millions on it to die of starvation in extremest agony, as far as temporal affliction goes, than that one soul, I will not say, should be lost, but should commit one single venial sin, should tell one wilful untruth, or should steal one poor farthing without excuse." I think the principle here enunciated to be the mere preamble in the formal credentials of the Catholic Church, as an Act of Parliament might begin with a "*Whereas.*" It is because of the intensity of the evil which has possession of mankind, that a suitable antagonist has been provided against it; and the initial act of that divinely-commissioned power is of course to deliver her challenge and to defy the enemy. Such a preamble then gives a meaning to her position in the world, and an interpretation to her whole course of teaching and action.

In like manner she has ever put forth, with most energetic distinctness, those other great elementary truths, which either are an explanation of her mission or give a character to her work. She does not teach that human nature is irreclaimable, else wherefore should she be sent? not, that it is to be shattered and reversed, but to be extricated, purified, and restored; not, that it is a mere mass of hopeless evil, but that it has the promise upon it of great things, and even now, in its present state of disorder and excess, has a virtue and a praise proper to itself. But in the next place she knows and she preaches that such a restoration, as she aims at effecting in it, must be brought about, not simply through certain outward provisions of preaching and teaching, even though they be her own, but from an inward spiritual power or grace imparted directly from above, and of which she is the channel. She has it in charge to rescue human nature from its misery, but not simply by restoring it on its own level, but by lifting it up to a higher level than its own. She recognizes in it real moral excellence though degraded, but she cannot set it free from earth except by exalting it towards heaven. It was for this end that a renovating grace was put into her hands; and therefore from the nature of the gift, as well as from the reasonableness of the case, she goes on, as a further point, to insist, that all true conversion must begin with the first springs of thought, and to teach that each individual man must be in his own person one whole and perfect temple of God, while he is also one of the living stones which build up a visible religious community. And thus the distinctions between nature and grace, and between outward and inward religion, become two further articles in what I have called the preamble of her divine commission.

Such truths as these she vigorously reiterates, and pertinaciously inflicts upon mankind; as to such she observes no half-measures, no economical reserve, no delicacy or prudence. "Ye must be born again," is the simple, direct form of words which she uses after her Divine Master; "your whole nature must be reborn; your passions, and your affections, and your aims, and your conscience, and your will, must all be bathed in a new element, and reconsecrated to your Maker, —and, the last not the least, your intellect." It was for repeating these points of her teaching in my own way, that certain passages of one of my Volumes have been brought into the general accusation which has been made against my religious opinions. The writer has said that I was demented if I believed, and unprincipled if I did not believe, in my own statement, that a lazy, ragged, filthy, story-telling beggar-woman, if chaste, sober, cheerful, and religious, had a prospect of heaven, such as was absolutely closed to an accomplished statesman, or lawyer, or noble, be he ever so just, upright, generous, honourable, and conscientious, unless he had also some portion of the divine Christian graces; yet I should have thought myself defended from criticism by the words which our Lord used to the chief priests, "The publicans and harlots go into the kingdom of God before you." And I was subjected again to the same alternative in imputations, for having ventured to say that consent to an unchaste wish was indefinitely more heinous than any lie viewed apart from its causes, its motives, and its consequences: though a lie, viewed under the limitation of these conditions, is a random utterance, an almost outward act, not directly from the heart, however disgraceful and despicable it may be, however prejudicial to the social contract, however deserving of public reprobation; whereas we have the express words of our Lord to the doctrine that "whoso looketh on a woman to lust after her, hath committed adultery with her already in his heart." On the strength of these texts, I have surely as much right to believe in these doctrines which have caused so much surprise, as to believe in original sin, or that there is a supernatural revelation, or that a Divine Person suffered, or that punishment is eternal.

Passing now from what I have called the preamble of that grant of power, which is made to the Church, to that power itself, Infallibility, I premise two brief remarks:—1. on the one hand, I am not here determining any thing about the essential seat of that power, because that is a question doctrinal, not historical and practical; 2. nor, on the other hand, am I extending the direct subject-matter, over which that power of Infallibility has jurisdiction, beyond religious opinion:— and now as to the power itself.

This power, viewed in its fulness, is as tremendous as the giant evil which has called for it. It claims, when brought into exercise but in the legitimate manner, for otherwise of course it is but quiescent, to know for certain the very meaning of every portion of that Divine Message in detail, which was committed by our Lord to His Apostles. It claims to know its own limits, and to decide what it can determine absolutely and what it cannot. It claims, moreover, to have a hold upon statements not directly religious, so far as this,—to determine whether they indirectly relate to religion, and, according to its own definite judgment, to pronounce whether or not, in a particular case, they are simply consistent with revealed truth. It claims to decide magisterially, whether as within its own providence or not, that such and such statements are or are not prejudicial to the *Depositum* of faith, in their spirit or in their consequences, and to allow them, or condemn and forbid them, accordingly. It claims to impose silence at will on any matters, or controversies, of doctrine, which on its own *ipse dixit*, it pronounces to be dangerous, or inexpedient, or inopportune. It claims that, whatever may be the judgment of Catholics upon such acts, these acts should be received by them with those outward marks of reverence, submission, and loyalty, which Englishmen, for instance, pay to the presence of their sovereign, without expressing any criticism on them on the ground that in their matter they are inexpedient, or in their manner violent or harsh. And lastly, it claims to have the right of inflicting spiritual punishment, of cutting off from the ordinary channels of the divine life, and of simply excommunicating, those who refuse to submit themselves to its formal declarations. Such is the infallibility lodged in the Catholic Church, viewed in the concrete, as clothed and surrounded by the appendages of its high sovereignty: it is, to re-peat what I said above, a supereminent prodigious power sent upon earth to en-counter and master a giant evil.

Austin Phelps
(1820-1890)

PHELPS was born in Massachusetts, educated at the University of Pennsylvania, Andover Theological Seminary, and Union Theological Seminary. After serving the Pine Street Congregational Church, Boston, for several years, he became professor of sacred rhetoric at Andover Theological Seminary in 1848. This position he held until his retirement. He also served as chairman of the faculty for ten years.

Phelps is remembered as a saintly figure. From the records of his diary this beautiful story is taken: On the eve of his ordination he writes of dedicating his life to God, and on the last page, written with trembling fingers, these final words, "Led by His Spirit all the way." From this consecrated life came several devotional books, among them *The Still Hour*.

ABSENCE OF GOD IN PRAYER
From *The Still Hour*

*I*f God had not said, 'Blessed are those that hunger,' I know not what could keep weak Christians from sinking in despair. Many times, all I can do is to complain that I want Him, and wish to recover him."

Bishop Hall, in uttering this lament, two centuries and a half ago, only echoed the wail which had come down, through living hearts, from the patriarch, whose story is the oldest known literature in any language. A consciousness of the *absence of God* is one of the standing incidents of religious life. Even when the forms of devotion are observed conscientiously, the sense of the presence of God, as an invisible Friend whose society is a joy, is by no means unintermittent.

The truth of this will not be questioned by one who is familiar with those phases of religious experience which are so often the burden of Christian confession. In no single feature of "inner life," probably, is the experience of many minds less satisfactory to them than in this. They seem to themselves, in prayer, to have little, if any, effluent emotion. They can speak of little in their devotional life that seems to them *like* life; of little that appears like

the communion of a living soul with a living God. Are there not many "closet hours," in which the chief feeling of the worshipper is an oppressed consciousness of the absence of reality from his own exercises? He has no words which are, as George Herbert says, heart deep. He not only experiences no ecstacy, but no joy no peace, no repose. He has no sense of being at home with God. The stillness of the hour is the stillness of a dead calm at sea. The heart rocks monotonously on the surface of the great thoughts of God, of Christ, of Eternity, of Heaven—

> As idle as a painted ship
> Upon a painted ocean.

Such experiences in prayer are often startling in the contrast with those of certain Christians, whose communion with God, as the hints of it are recorded in their biographies, seems to realize, in actual being, the scriptural conception of a life which is hid with Christ in God.

We read of Payson, that his mind, at times, almost lost its sense of the external world, in the ineffable thoughts of God's glory, which rolled like a sea of light around him, at the throne of grace.

We read of Cowper, that, in one of the few lucid hours of his religious life, such was the experience of God's presence which he enjoyed in prayer, that, as he tells us, he thought he should have died with joy, if special strength had not been imparted to him to bear the disclosure.

We read of one of the Tennents, that on one occasion, when he was engaged in secret devotion, so overpowering was the revelation of God which opened upon his soul, and with augmenting intensity of effulgence as he prayed, that at length he recoiled from the intolerable joy as from a pain, and besought God to withhold from him further manifestations of his glory. He said, "Shall Thy servant *see* Thee and live?"

We read of the "sweet hours" which Edwards enjoyed "on the banks of Hudson's River, in secret converse with God," and hear his own description of the inward sense of Christ which at times came into his heart, and which he "knows not how to express otherwise than by a calm, sweet abstraction of soul from all the concerns of this world; and sometimes a kind of vision . . . of being alone in the mountains, or some solitary wilderness, far from all mankind, sweetly conversing with Christ, and rapt and swallowed up in God."

We read of such instances of the fruits of prayer, in the blessedness of the suppliant, and are we not reminded by them of the transfiguration of our Lord, of whom we read, "As he prayed, the fashion of his countenance was altered, and his raiment became white and glistening?" Who of us is not oppressed by the contrast between such an experience and his own? Does not the cry of the patriarch come unbidden to our lips, "Ah that I knew where *I* might find Him"?

Much of even the ordinary language of Christians, respecting the joy of communion with God,—language which is stereotyped in our dialect of prayer,—many cannot honestly apply to the history of their own minds. A calm, fearless self-examination finds no counterpart to it in anything they have ever known. In the view of an honest conscience, it is not the vernacular speech of their experience. As compared with the joy which such language indicates, prayer is, in all that they know of it, a dull duty. Perhaps the characteristic of the feelings of many about it is expressed in the single fact, that it *is* to them a duty as distinct from a privilege. It is a duty which, they cannot deny, is often uninviting, even irksome.

If some of us should attempt to define the advantage we derive from a performance of the duty, we might be surprised, perhaps shocked, as one after another of the folds of a deceived heart should be taken off, at the discovery of the littleness of the residuum, in an honest judgment of ourselves. Why did we pray this morning? Do we often derive *any* other profit from prayer, than that of satisfying convictions of conscience, of which we could not rid ourselves if we wished to do so, and which will not permit us to be at ease with ourselves, if all forms of prayer are abandoned? Perhaps even so slight a thing as the pain of resistance to the momentum of a habit, will be found to be the most distinct reason we can honestly give for having prayed yesterday or to-day.

There may be periods, also, when the experiences of the closet enable some of us to understand that maniacal cry of Cowper, when his friends requested him to prepare some hymns for the Olney Collection. "How can you ask of me such a service? I seem to myself to be banished to a remoteness from God's presence, in comparison with which the distance from East to West is vicinity, is cohesion."

If such language is too strong to be truthful to the common experience of the *class* of professing Christians to which those whom it represents belong, many will still discern in it, as an expression of joylessness in prayer, a sufficient approximation to their own experience, to awaken interest in some thoughts upon the causes of a want of enjoyment in prayer.

The evil of such an experience in prayer, is too obvious to need illustration. If any light can be thrown upon the causes of it, there is no man living, whatever may be his religious state, who has not an interest in making it the theme of inquiry. "Never any more wonder," says an old writer, "that men pray so seldom. For there are very few that feel the relish, and are enticed with the *deliciousness,* and refreshed with the *comforts,* and acquainted with the *secrets* of a holy prayer." Yet, who is it that has said, "I will make them *joyful* in my house of prayer"?

Anthony W. Thorold

(1825-1895)

BISHOP of Rochester (1877-90) and of Winchester (1890-95), special preacher at Oxford, and examining chaplain to the archbishop of York, Thorold is well known for a number of devotional-theological writings with a Christocentric view. The devotional stress on Christian life as qualitatively worthy of inheriting eternal life is basic to the discussion of the final verse in his lectures on the twenty-third psalm, *The Presence of Christ,* from which this excerpt is taken.

[HOW TO REMAIN DEVOUT]

From *The Presence of Christ*

*O*nce more: it is absolutely impossible to maintain the heart in a condition of real devoutness without a steady and frequent use of those means of grace ordained and provided for us by a higher wisdom than our own, and to neglect which is both presumption and folly.

PRAYER

First and foremost of these is prayer—secret, frequent, sustained, and fervent prayer—prayer not only for the supply of needs, or for the sense of pardon, but for close spiritual communion with the Lord of our spirit, in at least an effort after that adoring and holy praise which is the substance of the worship in heaven. I know how hard prayer is almost at all times; how glad we sometimes feel to be able to say anything; that our best prayers ever fall short of our true aspirations; that our worst prayers are often so cold, so feeble, so poor, so wandering, they hardly deserve to be called prayers at all. And it is the humbling personal knowledge of the inadequacy and shortcomings of his own prayers that may well make a Christian writer pause, before he raises a standard that he himself so very inadequately reaches unto, as well as shrink from making a heart sad, which God would not make sad, by inviting prayer, which to many would seem so distant and so impracticable as only to reduce them to despair. Yet prayer is a habit; and the more we pray, the better we shall pray; and the highest mountain can be climbed by steady, patient walking; and if we never set a mark before us, to aim at and try for, we may soon discover that nothing is so perilous to the soul's life as contentedly sitting still. Sometimes to go to be alone with God and Christ in the fellowship of the Spirit, just for the joy and blessedness of it; to open, with reverent yet eager hands, the door into the presence chamber of the great King, and then to fall down before him, it may be, in silent adoration; our very attitude an act of homage, our merely being there, through the motive that prompts it, being the testimony of our soul's love; to have our set day-hours of close communion, with which no other friends shall interfere, and which no other occupations may interrupt, to which we learn to look forward with a living gladness, on which we look back with satisfaction and peace; this, indeed, is prayer, for its own sake, for God's sake, for our friend's sake, for the Church's sake, and for our work's sake; prayer which we do not hurry through, to still the conscience, but which (other things permitting) we can even linger over to satisfy the heart. Oh, if we Christians, who talk so much about the privilege and blessedness of prayer, would try to avail ourselves of it more than we do, how we should reflect on the world all around us the glory, as it streams on us from the face of the Incarnate Mediator! What a power we should become to rebuke sin, and proclaim pardon, and promise liberty, and offer peace, through our continually laying hold on the hem of the garment of our glorified Lord!

STUDY OF THE BIBLE

There must also be a full and frequent study of God's holy Word. In holy Scripture, as Christ himself has said, we have eternal life. He is the living Word of God; the Bible is the written word. There are some persons who, without the special excuse of but little leisure, go so far as to say that the Bible is the only book that Christians ought to study, other books involving but a waste of time. It may be sufficient to reply, that to impose this as a duty on all men alike is certainly to go beyond the letter of Scripture itself; that it is hardly consistent with the reasonable and justifiable cultivation of the various mental gifts and faculties with which God has endowed us, meaning us to use them, and that we are not particularly encouraged to it by any special largeness of mental vision or Christian charity in the few individuals who observe this rule themselves. It does not, however, follow that because the Bible is not the only book for Christians to study, that they might not study it much more than they do, and with much more pains and diligence and prayer. When we open our Bibles, quite as much as when we fall on our knees, we place ourselves in God's immediate presence; and we should read his Word both in the sense of listening to his voice and with the object of discovering his will. It is quite impossible for any Christian whatever to grow in the love of God without growing in the knowledge of him. Let any one who is doubtful about it read the epistles of St. Paul's first imprisonment, and his doubts will soon disappear. But how can we grow in the knowledge of God without being much in the study of the Bible? For, first, it is the one object of the Bible to teach us the original and authoritative truth of God; and then we never appreciate truth so vividly, or receive it so gladly, or retain it so tenaciously, or impart it so intelligently, as when we have discovered it for ourselves by our own thought and effort. One hour's devotional study of Scripture will often do more than a dozen sermons to stir up in our hearts the love of God. There are many external proofs of the inspiration of the Bible. Christ's own teaching, the doctrine of his apostles, the tradition of the Jews, the universal consent of the Christian Church of all times, place the divine authority of both Old and New Testaments on a foundation which can not be moved. To let go the blessed truth of the plenary inspiration of holy Scripture, is to lose the sheet anchor of revelation, and to drift away toward the dark and restless sea of human speculation, and "science, falsely so called" (1 Tim. 6:20). But there is internal as well as external evidence of this inspiration: hundreds and thousands of simple Christians, who know nothing of argument or controversy, have discovered, through the witness of God's Spirit in their own hearts, that the Bible is the very voice of God; and there is no argument half so efficacious with the great majority of readers, for proving the divine authorship of Scripture, as the hallowing influence that the Bible itself seems to breathe over us when we bring ourselves into real contact with its contents.

CONTEMPLATION

Again, a great help to devoutness in this restless and distracting age is contemplation. It may be distinguished from meditation as being the attention of the mind and heart to a person rather than to a truth; and while meditation may be defined as the pondering of the spirit on some divine doctrine, with (so to speak) closed eyes and abstracted senses, contemplation is the adoring gaze of the believing and worshiping heart on the glory of its Lord and King. "Out of sight, out of mind" is a truth true in many ways. If we never set Christ himself preaching on the mountains of Galilee, dying on the cross, glorified at his Father's right hand, before our heart and imagination, we must expect only faintly to realize all that he has suffered, all that he is now doing for us; and the result will be our spiritual loss. To look on Jesus with the purified eye of faith and love, though it may be a rare, is, however, a truly blessed means of grace. There is a sense in which even now we may see, if we will, our King in his beauty; and if in the day of his return we are to be made like him in body as well as in soul through seeing him as he is, we may become spiritually like him now through contemplating his person, and meditating on his work, and pondering his character, and feeding on his words. For, even now, "we all, with open face beholding as in a glass the glory of the Lord, are changed into the same image, from glory to glory, even as by the spirit of the Lord" (2 Cor. 3:18).

FREQUENT RECEIVING OF THE LORD'S SUPPER

There is yet one other aid toward the stirring up within us of a living devoutness to Christ, and that is, a frequent receiving of the Lord's Supper. Even in the lowest and poorest interpretation of this sacrament, as nothing more than an act of commemoration of the Lord's sacrifice, one would think that nothing would be so likely to stir up our gratitude, and dispose our hearts to receive his mercy, as often to partake of the memorial of his passion; and that none of the Savior's words would be more tenderly cherished or more studiously obeyed than his dying injunction, "This do in remembrance of me" (Luke 22:19). . . .

Now if this indeed be so—if, whenever we partake of the Lord's table in a right spirit—we feed on the very Christ himself, given to us there by the operation of his Spirit to be our meat and drink, our strength and joy, must not that blessed means of grace be especially calculated to fill us with thankfulness and self-abasement, to stir up renewed self-surrender and more habitual self-denial? And as to the objection, so frequently, and not at all unreasonably, made to a frequent reception of it, on the ground of our losing blessing through a greater familiarity with it, may we not thereby be doubting, though quite unconsciously, God's wisdom in ordaining this privilege, and mistrusting his power to prevent his ordinance falling short of his purpose to bless? Of course, it must always be a matter for individual discretion how often it may be expedient to partake of this ordinance; and while we are careful to reserve to ourselves the free exercise of our own judgment, the same liberty must be granted to our brethren. Still, it is certain that from not fully appreciating the blessedness, and apprehending the meaning, and using the opportunities, and welcoming the grace of this sacrament, some of us fall short of God's offers of blessing; for while it strengthens faith and quickens love, it also animates hope. The memorial of the cross is also the promise of the glory; and they who at the Lord's table on earth love to "show forth their Lord's death till he come" (1 Cor. 11:26) are surely more likely than others to be looking forward to the glorious moment when they will be called to sit down to the marriage supper of the Lamb.

ETERNAL LIFE IN HEAVEN

Now, all this throws light on the eternal life in heaven, which we come to consider in the latter part of the verse, "I will dwell in the house of the Lord forever" (Ps. 23:6). Whether David himself actually meant to refer to it is open to reasonable doubt. Certain, however, it is that he had been divinely instructed about it, and some of the most beautiful of his psalms anticipate its blessedness in language which Christians, looking back at their Lord's resurrection, can gladly and consistently use. But it is one of the features of the inspired Word that it contains depth within depth of the divine doctrine, well beneath well of the living water; and it is hardly possible for a Christian to utter these words without declaring the "blessed hope of the glorious appearing" (Titus 2:13) to be his own.

Heaven is spoken of here under three points of view—as a home, as a permanent home, as a home in the presence of God. It is to be a house, not a tent; a home, not a lodging; the no longer seeing through a glass darkly, but the beholding as with open face the vision of God.

Now, eternal life in heaven is plainly but a continuation and a development of eternal life on earth. It will be the same in the essence of its character, in the motive of its service, in the substance of its joys, in the nature of its glory. It will be different, for there will be no mortal body to hamper its action, no sinful nature to interrupt its progress; in perfect liberty, and in entire security, with energies that will never be exhausted, with opportunities that will never be thrown away, it will expand in the glorified soul through the eternal ages, to the praise of God and the joy of men.

The character of heaven will be the perfect unalloyed love of sinless and glorified beings. Dwelling in love, we shall, in the full sense of the word, dwell in God, and God in us.

Coventry Patmore

(1823-1896)

ALTHOUGH known primarily as a mystical poet, Patmore has written a good deal in prose. His most important book is *The Rod, the Root, and the Flower*. This consists of essays of a mystical-aesthetic nature, and shows the influence of the Oxford Movement upon the writers of that time. At his marriage to his second wife, Patmore became a member of the Roman Catholic Church. "Knowledge and Science" from *The Rod, the Root, and the Flower* shows the dual interest which he held in his appreciation of the soul and God, and the world and God. These fusions are likened in an allegorical sense to "married love." Patmore regarded theology as "the mistress" of scientific thought. The passage is quoted here by permission of the publisher, George Bell, London.

KNOWLEDGE AND SCIENCE

From *The Rod, the Root, and the Flower*

I

If we would find in God that full satisfaction of all our desires which He promises, we must believe extravagantly, i.e., as the Church and the Saints do; and must not be afraid to follow the doctrine of the Incarnation into all its natural consequences. Those who fear to call Mary the "Mother of God" simply do not believe in the Incarnation at all; but we must go further, and believe His word when He rebuked the people for regarding her as exclusively His Mother, declaring that every soul who received Him with faith and love was also, in union with Her, His Mother, the Bride of the Holy Spirit. We must not be afraid to believe that this Bride and Mother, with whom we are identified, is "Regina Coeli," as well as "Regina Mundi"; and that this Queen of Heaven and Earth is simply a pure, natural woman; and that one of our own race, and each of us, in union with her, has been made "a little lower than the angels," in order to be "crowned with honour and glory" far beyond the honour and glory of the highest and His purely spiritual creatures. "It is not written that He has taken hold (or united Himself) with any of the angels"; but of the lowest of His spiritual creatures, who alone is also flesh, "He has taken hold"; and the Highest has found His ultimate and crowning felicity in a marriage of the flesh as well as the Spirit; and in this infinite contrast and intimacy of height with depth and spirit with flesh He, who is very Love, finds, just as ordinary human love does, its final rest and the full fruition of its own life; and the joy of angels is in contemplating, and sharing by perfect sympathy with humanity, that glory which humanity alone actually possesses. This, the literal doctrine of the Church and the Scriputres, sounds preposterous in the ears of nearly all "Christians" even; and yet its actual truth has been realised, even in this life, as something far more than a credible promise, by those who have received the message of their Angel with somewhat of the faith of Mary, and to each of whom it has been said: "Blessed art thou because thou hast believed; for there shall be a performance of the things which have been promised to thee." Let Christians leave off thinking of the Incarnation as a thing past, or figure of speech, and learn to know that it consists for them in their becoming the intimately and humanly beloved of a divine and yet human Lover; and His local paradise and heaven of heavens.

II

"My heart is enlarged, I see, I wonder, I abound; my sons come from afar, and my daughters rise up at my side." This is the knowledge, the personal knowledge of God, which immediately follows the first great and uncompromising sacrifice of the Soul to Him. The heart becomes an ocean of knowledge actually perceived. All that previously was confessed by faith is seen far more clearly than external objects are seen by the natural eye. Sons, that is, corroborative truths, come from afar; the most remote facts of past experience and of science are confirmations strong as proofs of Holy Writ; and daughters, all natural affections and desires, find suddenly their interpretation, justification, and satisfaction, and are henceforward as "the polished corners of the Temple."

III

When once God "has made known to us the Incarnation of His Son Jesus Christ by the message of an Angel," that is to say, when once it has become, not an article of abstract faith, but a fact discerned in our own bodies and souls, we are made sharers of the Church's infallibility; for our reasoning is thenceforward from discerned reality to discerned reality, and not from and to those poor and always partially fallacious and misleading signs of realities, thoughts which can be formulated in words. Though he may express himself erroneously, no man, so taught, can be otherwise than substantially orthodox, and he is always willing and glad to submit his expressions to the sole assessor of verbal truth, whose judgments have never been convicted of inconsistency, even by the most hostile and malevolent criticism.

IV

"Eternity," says Aquinas, "is the entire, simultaneous, and perfect possession of a life without end." God goes forth from simplicity into all particulars of reality; man returns from all his peculiar and partial apprehensions of reality to God, and his eternity is "the entire, simultaneous, and perfect possession of a life" which is the synthesis of all the real apprehensions, or perceptions of good, which he has acquired here. Hence the acquisition of knowledge is the first business of mortal life,—not knowledge of "facts," but of realities, which none can ever begin to know until he knows that all knowledge but the knowledge of God is vanity.

V

"God," writes a Persian Poet, "is at once the mirror and the mirrored, the Lover and the Beloved." Every Soul was created to be, if it chose, a participator of this felicity, i.e., of "the glory which the Son had with the Father before the beginning of the world." This is the sum total of "mysticism," or true "science"; and he who has not attained, through denial of himself, to some sensible knowledge of this felicity, in reality knows nothing; for all knowledge, worthy of the name, is nuptial knowledge.

VII

"No prophecy is of private interpretation." We must believe nothing in religion but what has been declared by the Church, but many things declared by the Church must be spoken by the Spirit in the Soul before she can hear them in the word of the Church. Her orthodoxy, then, consists in this, that she must try what she hears in herself by that word, in which all is contained, either explicitly or implicitly. This is not hard, for the one deep calls to the other, and the Spirit knows what the Spirit speaks. Flavour and palate, perfume and nostrils, are not closer correlatives than are revelation and human consciousness.

VIII

Plato's cave of shadows is the most profound and simple statement of the relation of the natural to the spiritual life ever made. Men stand with their backs to the Sun, and they take the shadows cast by it upon the walls of their cavern for realities. The shadows, even, of heavenly realities are so alluring as to provoke ardent desires, but they cannot satisfy us. They mock us with unattainable good, and our natural and legitimate passions and instincts, in the absence of their true and substantial satisfactions, break forth into frantic disorders. If we want fruition we must turn our backs on the shadows, and gaze on their realities in God.

It may be added that, when we have done this, and are weary of the splendours and felicities of immediate reality, we may turn again, from time to time, to the shadows, which, having thus become intelligible, and being attributed by us to their true origin, are immeasurably more satisfying than they were before, and may be delighted in without blame. This is the "evening joy," the joy of contemplating God in His creatures, of which the theologians write; and this purified and intelligible joy in the shadow —which has now obtained a core of substance—is not only the hundredfold "promise of this life also," but it is, as the Church teaches, a large part of the joy of the blest.

XII

After the main dogmas, which are of faith, the teaching of theologians is very largely derived from facts of psychology within the reach of every one who chooses to pay the cost. For example, one of the most important of these facts is that there are four states or aspects of the Soul towards God; states or aspect which rapidly and inevitably succeed each other, and recur almost daily in the life of every Soul which is doing its full duty. The theologians call these states by those times of the day to which they strikingly correspond: Morning, Noon, Evening, and Night. The Morning is the mood of glad, free, and hopeful worship, supplication, and thanksgiving; the Noon is the perfect state of contemplation, or spiritual fruition; this cannot be sustained, say the theologians, even by the Angels for very long, and it passes into the "Evening joy," in which the Soul turns, not from God, but to God in His creatures —to all natural delights, rendered natural indeed by supernatural insight. Lastly, Night is that condition of the Soul which, in this stage of being, occupies by far the greatest part of the lives even of the most holy, but which will have no existence when the remains of corruption which cause the darkness shall have passed away. "The wicked," however, "have no bonds in their death," and this terrible and daily recurring trail is as little known to them as that other after which the "Bride" sighed: "Show me where Thou pasturest Thy sheep in the noonday."

XIII

The "touch" of God is not a figure of speech. "Touch," says Aquinas, "applies to spiritual as well as to material things." The same authority says, "Touch is the sense of alimentation, taste that of savour." A perfect life ends, as it begins, in the simplicity of infancy: it knows nothing of God on whom it feeds otherwise than by touch and taste. The fullness of intelligence is the obliteration of intelligence. God is then our honey, and we, as St. Augustine says, are His; and who wants to understand honey or requires the rationale of a kiss? "The Beatific Vision," says St. Bernard, "is not seen by the eyes, but is a substance which is sucked as through a nipple."

XIV

To the living and affirmative mind, difficulties and unintelligibilities are as dross, which successively rises to the surface, and dims the splendour of ascertained and perceived truth, but which is cast away, time after time, until the molten silver remains unsullied; but the negative mind is lead, and, when all its formations of dross are skimmed away, nothing remains.

XV

I once asked a famous theologian why he did not preach the love and knowledge of God from his pulpit as he had been discoursing of them for a couple of hours with me, instead of setting forth

Doctrine hard
In which Truth shows herself as near a lie
As can comport with her divinity.

He answered that, if he were to do so, his whole congregation would be living in mortal sin before the end of the week. It is true. The work of the Church in the world is, not to teach the mysteries of life, so much as to persuade the soul to that arduous degree of purity at which God Himself becomes her teacher. The work of the Church ends when the knowledge of God begins.

George Matheson

(1842-1906)

Of best-loved poems, "O Love That Wilt Not Let Me Go" ranks high. It was composed by Matheson in five minutes when he was forty years old. By this hymn he is known and loved by hundreds of thousands. Although blind, he graduated with honors at Edinburgh University. Through determination he was able to be ordained when he was twenty-four. At Innellan, where he wrote his beloved hymn, he ministered for eighteen years, and at St. Bernard's, Edinburgh, he served the last thirteen years of his active ministry. His fine self-discipline in meeting his handicap, his innate saintly spirit, and his capacity for intellectual activity brought from his pen a large number of theological books. Matheson was at his best when stressing the devotional note. This deep feel of religious experience is well portrayed in *My Aspirations*.

[THE SOUL IN DESPAIR]

From *My Aspirations*

A THIRST FOR GOD

What a wonderful breadth of divine charity! He who is altogether righteous will accept from us even the thirst for righteousness. He will not reserve his blessing until I become actually pure; he will bless my very effort after purity. He will accept the mere desire for him; the mere wish of my heart to be like him; the mere throb of my pulse to be near him. Tho I have not reached him, if only I see in him a beauty that I long for, he will count it unto me for righteousness. Tho I claim not to be like him, and despair even to touch the hem of his garment, if only I can admire afar off the kingliness of his beauty, he will bless my very hunger and my very thirst for him. Yet, say not, Oh my soul, that thou hast salvation without goodness. Thou couldst not hunger after him, thou couldst not thirst for him, if he were not already in thee. Thou couldst not see in him any beauty to desire if thou thyself hadst not the germ of the same beauty. "We shall be like him, for we shall see him as he is"; thy vision of him is the proof of thy likeness to him. If thou were not like him, thou wouldst not see him as he is. If he were not in thee thou couldst not wish to imitate him—couldst not even feel thy despair of imitating him. Thou canst not admire what is out of thy nature, nor seek what is not kindred to thy being. Therefore, my soul, thy hunger pleads for thee, thy thirst intercedes for thee, thy longing advocates for thee, thy very sense of moral want predicts that the spirit is at the door. Thou canst cry for outward food before thou knowest the taste thereof, but thou canst not cry for righteousness until thou hast "tasted that the Lord is good." He who sees the King in his beauty has himself begun to be beautiful; he who hungers and thirsts after righteousness is already beginnning to be filled.

THE FIRE OF LOVE

The only thing which is not consumed by burning is my soul. Fire is the death of my body, but fire is the life of my soul. When my goods are burned they perish, but when my soul takes fire it for the first time begins to live. It is the want of fire that consumes my soul. It is because I have so little enthusiasm that I have so little life. The worm of worldly care gnaws at my heart just because there is no fire in my heart to destroy it. My force is wasted by its expenditure on myself. I want something to lift me out of myself in order that I may be strong. Nothing can lift me out of myself but fire, the fire of the heart—love. If I could only be kindled into love, the last enemy would be conquered—death. Love would consume all my cares, but it would give new strength to me. There might be a wilderness around me, but my bush would be glorious—luminous. It would be seen afar off by all the travelers in the desert. It would be a light to lighten the ages, untouched by passing clouds, undimmed by flying years. My heart would never be consumed if only it could burn.

In thee, O Lord, let my heart be kindled! Thy love alone can wake my love. Thy fire alone can impart fire to me. Thy light alone can illuminate and warm me with that ardor which consumes not. Thou divine love of Bethlehem, of Gethsemane, of Calvary, descend into my heart and kindle it! Fan it into thine own sacred flame. Wake it into the fervor of burning zeal. Stir it into the glow of warm aspiration. Stimulate it into the blaze of an high enthusiasm which shall people the very wilderness with interests innumerable. Then shall my heart be ever young. Every hour shall be morning, every season shall be spring, every year shall be the year of jubilee. They that are planted in the house of the Lord shall bring forth fruit even in old age. Their eye shall not be dim, nor their natural strength abated, for the fire that burns within them is a fire that does not consume.

THE POWER TO SEE GOD IN SORROW

A strange thought, surely; why should every eye see him when he cometh with clouds? Do not the clouds obscure the sight? Would we not have expected the words to be: "Behold he cometh without clouds, and every eye shall see him"? Yet bethink thee. It is not said that he cometh in clouds, but he cometh with clouds. The clouds are not to envelop him; they are to accompany him. All the mysteries of life are to follow in his train to prove that they have been all along the servants and ministers of his love. Why is it that to me the God of the universe often seems to hide his face? It is because the clouds of the universe are seen apart from him. They are looked at as blots in his handwriting. They are seen as accidents that have marred the plan of his providence. They are felt as influences that have disputed the reign of his empire. But I could be told that the clouds are with him, if I could be made to feel that they are parts of himself, modes of his being, features of his plan, workings of his love—if I could be brought to know that, so far from delaying his coming, they are the very chariots in which he comes—then, indeed, I should understand what the seer of Patmos meant. Every eye sees the clouds of life, therefore every eye shall see him when he is known to be coming with the clouds. All hearts have the revelation of sorrow, therefore all hearts shall have a revelation of him when sorrow is known to be a voice from him. O thou that hast made the cloud as well as the sunshine, help me to see that the cloud as well as the sunshine follows in thy train! Help me to learn that thou makest the very winds thy ministering spirits! Help me to know that the affliction of time is actually working out the weight of glory in eternity! Let my vision of thy faithfulness reach even unto the clouds of my earthly day! Show me thy love in the things I called loveless; show me thy face as it shines behind the veil!

ENLARGEMENT IN SORROW

This is one of the grandest testimonies ever given by man to the moral government of God. It is not a man's thanksgiving that he has been set free from suffering. It is a thanksgiving that he has been set free through suffering: "Thou hast enlarged me when I was in distress." He declares the sorrows of life to have been themselves the source of life's enlargement. And have not you and I a thousand times felt this to be true? It is written of Joseph in the dungeon that "The iron entered into his soul." We all feel that what Joseph needed for his soul was just the iron. He had seen only the glitter of the gold. He had been rejoicing in youthful dreams; and dreaming hardens the heart. He who sheds tears over a romance will not be most apt to help reality; a real sorrow will be too unpoetic for him. We need the iron to enlarge our nature. The gold is but a vision; the iron is an experience. The chain which unites me to humanity must be an iron chain. That touch of nature which makes the world akin is not joy, but sorrow; gold is partial, but iron is universal.

My soul, if thou wouldst be enlarged into human sympathy, thou must be narrowed into the limits of human suffering; Joseph's dungeon is the road to Joseph's throne. Thou canst not lift the iron load of thy brother if the iron hath not entered into thee. It is thy limit that is thine enlargement. It is the shadows of thy life that are the real fulfilment of thy dreams of glory. Murmur not at the shadows; they are better revelations than thy dreams. Say not that the shades of the prison-house have fettered thee; thy fetters are wings—wings of flight into the bosom of humanity. The door of thy prison-house is a door into the heart of the universe. God has enlarged thee by the binding of sorrow's chain.

George Tyrrell
(1861-1909)

WHEN eighteen years old, Tyrrell became a Roman Catholic. He entered the Society of Jesus in 1880, and was ordained a priest in 1891. Because he criticized some views of the Roman Catholic Church, especially regarding hell, he was virtually excommunicated when he answered in the London *Times* the Vatican's attack against modernism. Of his religious writings A. L. Lilley has said, "So long as men delight in beautiful sensitive English speech, and so long as they can recognize skilled guidance in probing the deepest mysteries of their own being, will the writings of George Tyrrell be read with . . . wonder and delight." The selections from *Lex Orandi* are representative samples of Tyrrell's works. They are used by permission of the publisher, Longmans, Green & Co.

[FRIENDSHIP WITH GOD]
From *Lex Orandi*

II. THE TWO WORLDS

All our conscious life and movement is swayed by our will—our likes and dislikes; our wants and aversions; by our affection for ourselves or for others; for things, or for persons. First, not in fact, but in order of dependence, come the necessities of our separate and individual life. To exist at all is pre-requisite to any higher sort of life. Our temporal or bodily life depends on our power over that physical world around us with which we are in ceaseless conflict, which claims back every particle of dust that we have wrested from it and built up into our animal organism. Sooner or later our enemy will be victorious: "earth to earth, ashes to ashes, dust to dust"—that is our doom; but to delay that victory as long as possible is the chief aim of our struggle for physical existence. Our success depends largely on the extent to which we understand the machinery of the physical world and can work it in our own interest. Hence the struggle to live and enjoy involves a struggle to know. We feel about tentatively, we taste this and that; try one method and then another; we remember our experiences, classify them, put them together

into a system; we frame a theory of the world, its nature and history. And the truer the theory is, the better does it serve as an instrument, a guide, a chart whereby to direct our action fruitfully and to control Nature to our service.

Our very self-interest, however, forces us to cling together, to co-operate, to give to others that we may gain from them. But this herding together occasions the manifestation of a higher and better sort of life, the life of social affection and self-forgetfulness. It reveals to us a new joy and happiness—that of friendship or will-union with others—which thereupon becomes the principal goal of our endeavour. This new life implies a new world, a new system of facts and laws with which we have set ourselves in correspondence. Here again, in order to learn we must first experiment, and from our experience build up some rude conception of the world of wills—the social world—its nature and its laws.

Compared with this invisible spiritual world, that of physical Nature is mere shadow. For nothing can be more real to me than myself. Self is the very test and measure of all reality. If I ascribe reality to things in Nature, it is only because to understand or deal with them at all I must assume that they are like me in some way, that they are to some degree separate, individual, active, if not actually sentient and conscious, as I am. Children and savages personify everything with Nature. It is only experience and reflection that make us modify this instinctive assumption in various degrees, and teach us how the reality of these things falls short of our own. Furthermore, it is in willing, acting, and originating that we recognize our selfhood or reality. Our dreams or dreamy states, in which we are to a great extent passive, are marked by a sense of unreality; we are not ourselves; we are not all there. We are most real only when we are most free, conscious and energetic.

What does all this imply except that the spirit which acts and wills is alone felt to be "real" in the full sense; and that the world given to our outward senses is shadowy and dreamy, except so far as we ascribe to it some of the characteristics of will and spirit?

Thus the life of friendship and social affection relates us to a system of spiritual realities like ourselves; whereas the solitary and selfish life relates us to a world of appearances and shadows, whose semblance of reality is but a broken reflex of our own.

What, after all, and apart from religion, do we feel to be the most solid and undeniable value that this wretched world can offer us; that without which neither health nor wealth nor fame nor strenuous work can save us from terrible moments of disillusionment and life-weariness; that with which we can bear the loss of all these as not even touching the substance of our heart's treasure; what, but the life of affection and friendship? When to our dying eyes and listless ears all these shall be as idle dreams, yet the failing energies which we shall then, perhaps, summon to return the clasp of some loving hand locked in ours will testify to our conviction that all has not been vanity and vexation of spirit; that the life of love binds us to reality for ever.

Now religion is the life of friendship with God and with His friends; it relates us to the most real of all realities—the Divine Will—that which lends all their reality to our created wills, and apart from which they are not even intelligible.

We see then, that in virtue of our twofold nature we live in two worlds—one bodily, the other spiritual; one the shadow and the sacrament; the other, the substance and the signified reality.

III. The Life of Religion

It is therefore the spirit-world, the will-world, that is real to us beyond every other. In it our soul lives its inmost life, and finds its deepest rest or unrest according as it succeeds or fails in adjusting itself to its laws.

It is in willing and acting that our reality is revealed to us; and we account other things real in so far as they seem to oppose a will to ours. We *are*, each of us, a single "willing," which, however we may analyse it into a sum-total of past and present "willings" from which it results, is, nevertheless, one simple act by which we adapt ourselves to the total situation in which we now find ourselves —the past, behind us; the present, around us; the future before us. Every instant of our life this "willing" modifies itself and dissolves into something different, in response to a similar transformation of our surroundings. Through that world to which our body belongs, and of which our senses, memory, and understanding take account, we are made aware of other wills, which express themselves therein, as we ourselves do, by the sensibly evident results of their action. It is in our *felt* relation to these other wills that our spiritual life and reality consists. That relation is, with regard to each several will, one of agreement and attraction, or of revolt and dislike, or rather of a complex blending of likes and dislikes, according to the innumerable elements into which each moral personality, each total will-attitude, may be virtually resolved. Like the motes in a sunbeam the whole world of wills is in ceaseless commotion; each changing its attitude with regard to all the rest, as moment by moment the shifting situation demands a new response. Wherever we find another will accordant with our own in any particular, we experience a sense of re-enforcement and expansion of our spiritual life and being; and this, in proportion to the nature and extent of the agreement, and the nature and number of wills in agreement. On the other hand, there is a sense of spiritual impoverishment and contraction wherever we recognise a will-force in opposition to our own—a sense as though we were losing hold of that community of souls whose being we share, and were dropping away into the void and nothingness of solitude. By their will-attitude in regard to certain personalities, certain deeds, certain aims, in a word, in regard to certain governing will-attitudes, men can be spiritually classified and brought into that system of relations which constitutes the will-world. A Christian, a republican, a Gladstonian, and such names by which men are grouped together, imply always a common end towards which their wills are set in agreement.

But if any sort of will-union with another is desirable in the abstract (*i.e.*, considered alone and apart from the infinity of other will-relations) yet in the concrete it always involves a relation of disagreement with contrary will-attitudes, and a mingling of pain with pleasure. "No man can serve two masters"; if he love the one, he must hate the other. Hence, while this chaos and contrariety prevails, and pending that process of sifting and settling-down through which the stars of this spiritual firmament tend, perhaps eternally, towards the equilibrium of some system of established constellations, we cannot take mere will-union as an end in itself, or as a decisive motive of action. We may not seek rest in agreement, without asking "Rest in what?" "Agreement with what?" Throughout the whole universe of will-attitudes the difference of evil and good, false and true, fair and foul, passes like a two-edged sword. "Right" is a rule of choice clearly higher than the blind and impotent rule of love which would pull

us in every direction at once, and lead us in none. Even if we *might* follow the impulse to be at one with all men, we could not. We may err and falter in our judgment as to what is true, fair, or right; we may turn away from our duty when we know it; but we can never falter in our conviction as to the absolute and imperative character of these will-attitudes; we can never doubt that we *ought* to be in sympathy with men of good-will and out of sympathy with the insincere, the selfish, the low-minded. Now this imperative character of the Absolute is simply the force of that supreme, eternal, eventually irresistible Will, which we call God—that Will to which the whole will-world must be subordinate, and in union or agreement with which each created will is saved and realised, even were it at variance with all the rest. This love of God, this dynamic union with the infinite will, is the very substance and reality of our spiritual living and being; other lovings and agreeings belong to the perfection, but not to the essence of our blessedness.

The true orientation of our will must, therefore, be towards that Supreme Will so far as it is manifested in the will-attitudes of those who live by it—of Christ and of all Christ-like men. We know nothing of that Will in its attitude towards extra-human affairs; we only feel it mingling and conflicting with our own in each concrete action that is submitted to our freedom of choice.

Love is, after all, the very substance of our spiritual life, the bond that binds personalities together, and is to the will-world what gravitation is to the physical. But above all wills there is the will of God; and above all loves there is the love of God; and in this, the life of religion consists. It is exercised in the same acts by which we conquer the chaos of our inward life, and transform it to the pattern of those absolute ideals which are the ends and aims of the Divine will.

Our religious character is something that *results from* this action of our will by which we overcome the chaos that is given us, as it were, a wilderness to till and cultivate. From the fact that our will takes this or that attitude in regard to matters of thought, or conduct, or feeling, it is brought into a relation of harmony or discord with every other will, and takes a new position in the will-world. This sense of our ever-changing relation to other wills, of loving and being loved, of hating and being hated, is, as has been seen, the very reality and substance of our spiritual life, it is the motive and the end of all that labour of transformation in which our will expresses itself. Our own mental, moral, and aesthetic formation, our external and social labour only furnishes a medium, an occasion whereby our relation of agreement or disagreement with other wills may be determined—much as their attitude towards the same performance might determine the relation of sympathy between two artists. St. Augustine notes how strangers in a theatre are for the moment drawn together when they see one another applauding the same thing. The pleasure of this sympathy is of quite another order to the artistic pleasure which is its occasion. The latter is from the agreement of the object with our artistic ideals; the former, from the sense of our solidarity with others. In like manner we cannot do what God wills without in that very act bringing our will closer to His; the ethical act entails the religious result, and if done in view of that result, puts on a religious character.

But, to will the same as another whom we do not know, or whose will we do not know, does not put us into that will-relationship with him in which love consists. It is only when the agreement is revealed that there is that rushing of soul to soul, that sense of reinforcement and enlargement, which is so utterly distinct from the ethical or artistic satisfaction which may be the occasion of the agreement. To know that God wills what we will, gives birth to that expression of will-union, that sense of friendship, which no merely ethical satisfaction in duty done can possibly yield.

Since every action we do is built into our spiritual substance as an eternal possession, and does not pass away like its temporal results in the outer world, it is plain that our union with God, our growth in grace and love, admits of an endless accumulative progress; that we can go on for ever determining our relation to Him (and our relation to others viewed as related to Him) more and more exactly as long as life lasts.

IV. THE LIFE OF PRAYER

Obviously then it is by conduct, but primarily, by prayer in its widest sense, that this union with the Divine Will is fostered and the soul established and strengthened by the sense of its solidarity with the entire will-world as systematised through Him, who is its indwelling source and end. Union with any part of it that is separated from Him must in the end lead to an absolute solitude of the soul, unloved and unloving, shut apart into that outer darkness which is spiritual death.

Prayer, as here taken, is not merely directed to conduct, but is itself directly effective of that will-sympathy with God which is the richest fruit, as it is also the highest motive, of conduct. The religious effort is directed explicitly to the adjustment of our will to God's: and this, not merely as to ourselves, but as to all things that come under His will, so that in all we shall seek to know and feel and act with Him. Here it is that prayer supplements the narrowness of our practical life and gives us as it were artificial occasions of will-union.

A great part of our spiritual discipline is indeed directed to the "religionising" of our general conduct by its explicit conformity and reference to the Divine Will. We prepare ourselves to do what has to be done, as perfectly as possible, not merely in the ethical interest, for the sake of the work done; not merely that our mind, our impulses, our tastes, our whole personality may be conformed to the absolute impersonal standards of the True, the Good, and the Fair; but in the religious interest; in order that in thus effecting *what* God wills, our will may come closer to His, that His will may be more fully in ours; in fact, that we may dwell in Him and He in us—for in no other way are persons united. Again, as every skill is acquired through self-criticism; so too, some kind of self-examination enters into the practice of religion; we need to stand aside and compare our attainments with our ideals more deliberately than is possible in the haste and pressure of action.

But plainly such spiritual exercises as these, are but the pauses for foresight and retrospection which mingle with every sort of production; differing only in this, that they are directed to the adjustment and criticism of the religious aspect of our life. They are directed to living religiously; they impart a religious quality or tinge to our moral life, but they are not strictly exercises of the life of religion. A man at his daily work is living for his family, but he returns from his labour to the enjoyment of family life. Our whole life must be *for* God, but only part of it can be *with* God. This latter involves a certain contemplative and mystical effort whereby we consciously bring ourselves and are brought into an affectionate sympathy with the Divine Will viewed personally; it means a continual growth in the love, not only of those things which God loves, but, through and in them, of the Divine Lover. For however closely connected, the two things are not only distinct, but even separable, and sometimes separated. One can rest in the work without passing on to its author; men can love justice, truth, and goodness, can feel the absolute and imperative character of their claims, and yet fail to recognise them as the expression of a personal will; they can love God's laws, but not the lawgiver. But the love of an abstract law is not the sort of love that binds us to the will-world and gives us our spiritual subsistence.

The love that binds us to other wills is not to be conceived statically, as a hard and fast iron band; it is a process of continual adjustment, which may at times seem to be stilled only because the two wills move parallel and at the same rate. But since no living will is ever at rest, but transforms itself ceaselessly into something new, love or the union of wills is essentially a "becoming." Relatively to us, to whom it is gradually disclosed in the measure that we correspond to it, the Divine Will is ever transforming and developing itself; and our union with it involves a like self-transforming on our part.

The mystical life consists in this process. It interfuses itself spontaneously in various degrees of frequency, continuity, and intensity, with the rest of our life, according to the measure of our graces and of our fidelity to better things, *i.e.*, dependently on the free exercise of the Divine Will and of our own, whose times and seasons need not necessarily coincide. "Spiritual exercises" in the proper sense —those that are not merely directed to the "religionising" of our conduct—are directed to this work of harmonising our wills with God's, *i.e.*, to the increase of personal love, or as is commonly said, to converse with God. Instead of waiting till we are moved, we seek to move ourselves; and by memory, reflection, consideration, and inquiry, we multiply the chances of our hearts being kindled by some new aspect of the Divine Goodness.

No otherwise are our human affections deepened. A certain leisureliness is the condition of any very firm and lasting bond between soul and soul. Nowhere are family ties of affection stronger than where the lives are somewhat narrow and vacant of conflicting interests, which, like thorns, spring up and choke the seed of love. The rush and multifariousness of a busy life are incompatible with the brooding habit by which love is fostered and matured. The treasuring and pondering of words spoken, of deeds done, of looks and smiles that open vistas into the inward self, fan the flame of affection as surely as spiritual absence and forgetfulness tend to extinguish it. The moral and spiritual significance of our so-called "idle" musings cannot be too highly estimated; especially when we acknowledge that our deepest life and reality is that of our affection, our will-action, whereof our outer action is but the contingent and ever imperfect expression. When our hands are still and our voice silent, our will pursues its ceaseless evolutions from form to form, and seeks new adjustments of its position relatively to all other wills. As the stream of our imaginings, memories, and reflections, flows past, our will is now drawn, now thrust away, never still for an instant. Hence the educative value of every sort of contemplation, artistic or religious. It is with the latter we are here concerned—that by which we muse upon God as revealed to us inwardly and outwardly.

This is the essence and end of the contemplative effort, and surely it is simple enough, looked at from this point of view. If, to some extent (to be defined later), the character of the Divine Will is revealed in the world of necessity, if the wisdom and power of God are written in the book of physical Nature for those who have eyes to see, yet it is only because their results resemble those of our own wisdom and power, and because we ascribe them to an agency like ourselves that they tell us anything of God at all. It is through self, through man, through the world of freedom and will, that we get to know God as a personality, as a possible object of personal love and affection. It is in the relative and unsatisfying goodness of the human will, that the absolute and satisfying goodness of the Divine Will is revealed to us; even as the light of the hidden sun might be revealed to us in the reflected brilliancy of the moon or the planets. He is the Will, from conformity to which every human character derives all its true lovableness, whether inborn or self-wrought. It is in men that He, the hidden God, is to be sought, studied, and loved—not in abstractions like Truth and Righteousness, but in concrete actions and will-attitudes, in "whatsoever things are true, honest, just, pure, lovely, and of good report." This is the proper field of contemplative search. We are not moved to love by the colourless universals and thought-frames, into which these living realities are forced for scientific purposes—by such divine attributes as Wisdom, Justice, Truth, and the like. What moves us is this or that concrete deed of goodness, which reveals the present attitude of the living wills, divine and human, that gave birth to it—this unique and never-to-be-repeated act of mercy, or of courage, or of self-sacrifice, or of truth and fidelity, in which a flash of God's infinite glory lightens on us through some momentary rift in the veil of the finite. These are real facts and events in the will-world in regard to which we have to determine our own attitude so as to come into relation with God, whose will is revealed and uttered in every good will. Hence, every act of right love that binds us to other wills by sympathy and conformity, binds us with a new bond to the Divine Will as soon as this is recognised as a personality, as the source of all goodness, as the centre and unitive principle of the will-world—indwelling, all-pervading, and all-transcending.

Leo Tolstoy

(1828-1910)

BORN of Russian nobility and given the finest opportunities for education, Tolstoy revolted in his teens against academic learning and the social caste of Russian nobility. After his parents' death he tried to raise the conditions of the serfs on his estates, resorted for a time to dissipation, joined the army, and at thirty-five rebelled against the Greek Orthodox Church. In 1880 he renounced a life of ease, and entered upon a life of toil in the fields and simplicity of living. In 1888 he wished to give his wealth to the poor and live a life of poverty, but instead he was persuaded to give his wealth to his wife. In 1901 he was excommunicated by the Greek Orthodox Church.

In *My Confession* and *My Religion* Tolstoy shows the deep urge of a noble heart to correct evil. He believed that love woven into social action was the heart of Christianity, that the social order would approach its ideal only to the degree that men learn to love and understand each other.

[THE STRUGGLE AND VICTORY OF THE SPIRIT]

From *My Confession*

X

These men, deprived of all that for us and for Solomon makes the only good in life, experience the highest happiness both in amount and kind. I looked more carefully and more widely around me, I studied the lives of the past and contemporary masses of humanity, and I saw that, not two or three, not ten or a hundred, but thousands and millions had so understood the meaning of life that they were able both to live and to die. All these men, infinitely divided by manners, powers of mind, education, and position, all alike in opposition to my ignorance, were well acquainted with the meaning of life and of death, quietly labored, endured privation and suffering, lived and died, and saw in all this, not a vain, but a good thing.

I began to grow attached to these men. The more I learned of their lives, the lives of the living and of the dead of whom I read and heard, the more I liked them, and the easier I felt it so to live. I lived in this way during two years, and then there came a change which had long been preparing in me, and the symptoms of which I had always dimly felt: the life of my own circle of rich and learned men, not only became repulsive, but lost all meaning whatever. All our actions, our reasoning, our science and art, all appeared to me in a new light. I understood that it was all child's play, that it was useless to seek a meaning in it. The life of the working classes, of the whole of mankind, of those that create life, appeared to me in its true significance. I understood that this was life itself, and that the meaning given to this life was a true one, and I accepted it.

XI

When I remembered how these very doctrines had repelled me, how senseless they had seemed when professed by men whose lives were spent in opposition to them, and how they had attracted me and seemed thoroughly reasonable when I saw men living in accordance with them, I understood why I had once rejected them and thought them unmeaning, why I now adopted them and thought them most reasonable. I understood that I had erred, and how I had erred. I had erred, not so much through having thought incorrectly, as through having lived ill. I understood that the truth had been hidden from me, not so much because I had erred in my reasoning, as because I had led the exceptional life of an epicure bent on satisfying the lusts of the flesh. I understood that my question as to what my life was, and the answer, an evil, were in accordance with the truth of things. The mistake lay in my having applied an answer which only concerned myself to life in general. I had asked what my own life was, and the answer was, an evil and a thing without meaning. Exactly so, my life was but a long indulgence of my passions; it was a thing without meaning, an evil; and such an answer therefore, referred only to my own life, and not to human life in general.

I understood the truth which I afterwards found in the Gospel; "That men loved darkness rather than light, because their deeds were evil. For every man that doeth evil hateth the light, neither cometh to the light, lest his deeds should be reproved." I understood that, for the meaning of life to be understood, it was first necessary that life should be something more than an evil and unmeaning thing discovered by the light of reason. I understood why I had so long been near to, without apprehending, this self-evident truth, and that if we would judge and speak of the life of mankind, we must take that life as a whole, and not merely certain parasitic adjuncts to it.

This truth was always a truth, as $2 \times 2 = 4$, but I had not accepted it, because, besides acknowledging $2 \times 2 = 4$, I should have acknowledged that I was evil. It was of more importance to me to feel that I was good, more binding on me, than to believe $2 \times 2 = 4$. I loved good men, I hated myself, and I accepted truth. Now it was all clear to me. What if the executioner, who passes his life in torturing and cutting off heads, or a confirmed drunkard, asked himself the question, What is life? he could but get the same answer as a madman would give, who had shut himself up for life in a darkened chamber, and who believed that he would perish if he left it; and that answer could but be—Life is a monstrous evil.

The answer would be a true one, but only for the man who gave it. Here, then, was I such a madman? Were all of us rich, clever, idle men, mad like this? I understood at last that we were; that I, at any rate, was. Look at the birds; they live but to fly, to pick up their food, to build their nests, and when I see them doing this their gladness rejoices me. The goat, the hare, the wolf live but to feed and multiply, and bring up their young; and when I see them doing this, I am well convinced of their happiness, and that their life is a reasonable one. What, then, should man do? He also must gain his living like the animals, but with this difference, that he will perish if he attempt it alone; he must labor, not for himself, but for all. And when he does so, I am firmly convinced he is happy, and his life is a reasonable one.

What had I done during my thirty years of conscious life? I had not only not helped the life of others, I had done nothing for my own. I had lived the life of a parasite, and contented myself with my ignorance of the reason why I lived at all. If the meaning of the life of man lies in his having to work out his life himself, how could I, who during thirty years had done my best to ruin my own life and that of others, expect to receive any other answer to my questioning of life but this, that my life was an evil and had no meaning in it? It was an evil; it was without meaning.

The life of the world goes on through the will of some one. Some one makes our own life and that of the universe his own inscrutable care. To have a hope of understanding what that will means, we must first carry it out, we must do what is required of us. Unless I do what is required of me, I can never know what that may be, and much less know what is required of us all and of the whole universe.

If a naked, hungry beggar be taken from the cross-roads into an enclosed space in a splendid establishment, to be well clothed and fed, and made to work a handle up and down, it is evident that the beggar, before seeking to know why he has been taken, why he must work the handle, whether the arrangements of the establishment are reasonable or not, must first do as he is directed. If he do so he will find that the handle works a pump, the pump draws up water, and the water flows into numerous channels for watering the earth. He will then be taken from the well and set to other work; he will gather fruits and enter into the joy of his lord. As he passes from less to more important labors, he will understand better and better the arrangements of the whole establishment; and he will take his share in them without once stopping to ask why he is there, nor will he ever think of reproaching the lord of that place.

And thus it is with those that do the will of their master; no reproaches come from simple and ignorant working-men, from those whom we look upon as brutes. But we the while, wise men that we are, devour the goods of the master, and do nothing of that which he wills us to do; but instead, seat ourselves in a circle to argue why we should move the handle, for that seems to us stupid. And when we have thought it all out, what is our conclusion? Why, that the master is stupid, or that there is none, while we ourselves are wise, only we feel that we are fit for nothing, and that we must somehow or other get rid of ourselves.

XII

My conviction of the error into which all knowledge based on reason must fall assisted me in freeing myself from the seductions of idle reasoning. The conviction that a knowledge of truth can only be gained by living, led me to doubt the justness of my own life, but I had only to get out of my own particular groove, and look around me to observe the simple life of the real working class, to understand that such a life was the only real one. I understood that, if I wished to understand life and its meaning, I must live, not the life of a parasite, but a real life; and, accepting the meaning given to it by the combined lives of those that really form the great human whole, submit it to a close examination.

At the time I am speaking of, the following was my position.

During the whole of that year, when I was constantly asking myself whether I should or should not put an end to it all with a cord or a pistol, during the time that my mind was occupied with the thoughts which I have described, my heart was oppressed by a tormenting feeling, which I cannot describe otherwise than as a searching after God.

This search after a God was not an act of my reason, but a feeling, and I say this advisedly, because it was opposed to my way of thinking; it came from the heart. It was a feeling of dread, or orphanhood, of isolation amid things all apart from me, and of hope in a help I knew not from whom. Though I was well convinced of the impossibility of proving the existence of God—Kant had shown me, and I had thoroughly grasped his reasoning, that this did not admit of proof—I still sought to find a God, still hoped to do so, and still, from the force of former habits, addressed myself to one in prayer. Him whom I sought, however, I did not find.

At times I went over in my mind the arguments of Kant and of Schopenhauer, showing the impossibility of proving the existence of the Deity; at times I began to refute their reasoning.

I would say to myself that causation is not in the same category as thought and space and time. If I am, there is a cause of my being, and that the cause of all causes. That cause of all things is what is called God; and I dwelt upon this idea, and strove with all the force that was in me to reach a consciousness of the presence of this cause.

No sooner was I conscious of a power over me than I felt a possibility of living. That I asked myself: "What is this cause, this power? How am I to think of it? What is my relation to what I call God?" And only the old familiar answer came into my mind, "He is the creator, the giver of all." This answer did not satisfy me, and I felt that the staff of life failed me, I fell into great fear, and began to pray to Him whom I sought, that He would help me. But the more I prayed, the clearer it became that I was not heard, that there was no one to whom to pray. With despair in my heart that there was no God, I cried: "Lord, have mercy on me, and save! O Lord, my God, teach me!" But no one had mercy on me, and I felt that life stood still within me.

Again and again, however, the conviction came back to me that I could not have appeared on earth without any motive or meaning—that I could not be such a fledgling dropped from a nest as I felt myself to be. What if I wail, as the fallen fledgling does on its back in the grass? It is because I know that a mother bore me, cared for me, fed me, and loved me. Where is that mother? If I have been thrown out, then who threw me? I cannot but see that some one who loved me brought me into being. Who is that some one? Again the same answer, God. He knows and sees my search, my despair, my struggle. "He is," I said to myself. I had only to admit that for an instant to feel that life re-arose in me, to feel the possibility of existing and the joy of it. Then, again, from the conviction of the existence of God, I passed to the consideration of our relation towards Him, and again I had before me the triune God, our Creator, who sent His Son, the Redeemer. Again, I felt this to be a thing apart from me and from the world. This God melted, as ice melts, from before my eyes; again there was nothing left, again the source of life dried up. I fell once more into despair, and felt that I had nothing to do but to kill myself, while, worst of all, I felt also that I should never do it.

I went through these changes of conviction and mood, not once, not twice, but hundreds of times—now joy and excitement, now despair from the knowledge of the impossibility of life.

I remember one day in the early spring-time I was listening to the sounds of a wood, and thinking only of one thing, the same of which I had constantly thought for two years—I was again seeking for a God.

I said to myself: "It is well, there is no God, there is none that has a reality apart from my own imaginings, none as real as my own life—there is none such. Nothing, no miracles can prove there is, for miracles only exist in my own unreasonable imagination."

And then I asked myself: "But my conception of the God whom I seek, whence comes it?" And again life flashed joyously through my veins. All around me seemed to revive, to have a new meaning. My joy, though, did not last long, for reason continued its work: "The conception of God is not God. Conception is what goes on within myself; the conception of God is an idea which I am able to rouse in my mind or not as I choose; it is not what I seek, something without which life could not be." Then again all seemed to die around and within me, and again I wished to kill myself.

After this I began to retrace the process which had gone on within myself, the hundred times repeated discouragement and revival. I remembered that I had lived only when I believed in a God. As it was before, so it was now; I had only to know God, and I lived; I had only to forget Him, not to believe in Him, and I died. What was this discouragement and revival? I do not live when I lose faith in the existence of a God; I should long ago have killed myself, if I had not had a dim hope of finding Him. I only really live when I feel and seek Him. "What more, then, do I seek?" A voice seemed to cry within me, "This is He, He without whom there is no life. To know God and to live are one. God is life."

Live to seek God, and life will not be without Him. And stronger than ever rose up life within and around me, and the light that then shone never left me again.

Thus I was saved from self-murder. When and how this change in me took place I could not say. As gradually, imperceptibly as life had decayed in me, till I reached the impossibility of living, till life stood still, and I longed to kill myself, so gradually and imperceptibly I felt the glow and strength of life return to me.

It was strange, but this feeling of the glow of life was no new sensation; it was old enough, for I had been led away by it in the earlier part of my life.

I returned, as it were, to the past, to childhood and my youth. I returned to faith in that Will which brought me into being and which required something of me; I returned to the belief that the one single aim of life should be to become better; that is, to live in accordance with that Will; I returned to the idea that the expression of that Will was to be found in what, in the dim obscurity of the past, the great human unity had fashioned for its own guidance; in other words, I returned to a belief in God, in moral perfectibility, and in the tradition which gives a meaning to life. The difference was that formerly I had unconsciously accepted this, whereas now I knew that without it I could not live.

The state of mind in which I then was may be likened to the following. It was as if I had suddenly found myself sitting in a boat which had been pushed off from some shore unknown to me, had been shown the direction of the opposite shore, had had oars given me, and had been left alone. I use the oars as best I can, and row on; but the farther I go towards the centre, the stronger becomes the current which carries me out of my course, and the oftener I meet other navigators, like myself, carried away by the stream. There were here and there solitary sailors who row hard, there are others who have thrown down their oars, there are large boats, and enormous ships crowded with men; some struggle against the stream, others glide on with it. The farther I get, the more, as I watch the long line floating down the current, I forget the course pointed out to me as my own. In the very middle of the stream, beset by the crowd of boats and vessels, and carried like them along, I forget altogether in what direction I started, and abandon my oars. From all sides the joyful and exulting navigators, as they row, or sail down stream, with one voice cry out to me that there can be no other direction. I believed them, and let myself go with them. I am carried far, so far that I hear the roar of the rapids in which I must perish, and I already saw boats that have been broken up within them. Then I come to myself. It is long before I clearly comprehend what has happened. I see before me nothing but destruction. I am hurrying towards it; what, then, must I do? On looking back, however, I perceive a countless multitude of boats engaged in a ceaseless struggle against the force of the torrent, and then I remember all about the shore, the oars, and the course, and at once I begin to row hard up the stream and again towards the shore.

The shore is God, the course tradition, the oars are the free-will given me to make for the shore to seek union with the Deity. And thus the vital force was renewed in me, and I began again to live.

Léon Bloy

(1846-1917)

BLOY is one of the misunderstood French "saints" of the twentieth century. His deep devotional life was the inspiration for Jacques and Raïssa Maritain to become Roman Catholic converts. Of Bloy, Jacques Maritain wrote, "Once the threshold of this [Bloy's] house was crossed all values were dislocated, as though by an invisible switch. One knew, or one guessed, that only one sorrow existed here—not to be of the saints. And all the rest receded into the twilight." Said Barbey d'Aurevilly of Bloy, "He is a cathedral gargoyle who pours down the waters of heaven on the good and on the wicked."

Like Francis of Assisi, Bloy was wedded to Lady Poverty. He lived humbly with his wife and two daughters, and from his writings tried to eke out a living. He wrote a book each year which brought him about five hundred francs. Out of this suffering through poverty his soul was refined by the spiritual depth of a genuine saint. *Mon Journal* especially reveals his spirit.

Two of Bloy's writings are translated into English—*La Femme Pauvre* ("The Woman Who Was Poor") and *Lettres à la Fiancée* ("Letters to His Fiancee"). Of the former writing Maurice Maeterlinck said, "If by genius one understands certain *flashes in the depths*, *La Femme Pauvre* is the only work of the present day in which there are evident marks of genius."

Bloy held great admiration for the Jewish race and wrote a scriptural exegesis on some of its biblical figures in *La Salut par les Juifs*. The following selections are from Raïssa Maritain, *We Have Been Friends Together*, translated by Julie Kernan, and are reprinted by permission of Longmans, Green & Co.

PROVIDENCE IS A PACTOLUS OF TEARS

From *Quatre Ans de Captivité à Cochons-sur-Marne*

*L*ord, I often weep. Is it from sorrow over my suffering? Is it from joy in thinking of You? How disentangle these things and how not weep while trying to disentangle them? . . .

For some time I have not dared speak of my awakenings. It must be a heartache for God and His saints to see a soul suffer so greatly from the very first hour of each day. . . .

One clings to hope as long as one can, but reason falters. One can no longer see. One is like the beasts groaning and crouching upon the earth. This torture is truly intolerable. If only one had a sign, a little help, a word of kindness. When I went out to get a syphon of Seltzer water in the neighbourhood, the old man who waited on me gave me a spray of lilies from a bunch he had just cut in the garden. The flowers were half faded, but what does that matter? It was hard for me to keep back my tears because I had the illusion or the evidence of an impulse of goodness. . . .

I remember having seen very clearly in my sleep what it is to help one's neighbour. I had the deep feeling—and I am distressed not to be able to express it—that there is only one help. It is the absolute gift of oneself, such as Jesus practiced it. One must allow oneself to be buffeted, spit upon, scourged, crucified. The commonplace expression *to cast oneself into the arms of someone*, singularly clarifies this. All the rest is vanity.

[LETTER TO RAÏSSA MARÏTAIN]

Paris, August 25, 1905

*O*ur dear friend Raïssa,
To begin, I can only write you what I wrote on June 29, 1903, to a poor musician who had also spoken to me with enthusiasm of *Le Salut par les Juifs*.

"Then you are truly my brother and truly the friend of God. *He who loves grandeur and who loves the abandoned man* will recognize grandeur, if grandeur is present." This remarkable sentence was written by Ernest Hello, who was a man abandoned.

Therefore, Raïssa, you must truly be my sister, in order to have done me this charity. When someone likes *Le Salut*, he is not only my friend, but perforce something more. For it is extremely obscure, this book which represents in surprising abridgement many years of work, of prayers and of sufferings which were, I believe, out of proportion, entirely out of proportion.

In an intellectual period it would have been considered, at least with reference to its literary form, the greatest artistic effort of my whole life.

I quite candidly admit that I hoped in '92 that some learned and profound Hebrews would see the importance of this Christian book—*a paraphrase of the sublime eleventh chapter of the Jew Saint Paul to the Romans*—the only one in over nineteen centuries, in which a Christian voice has been heard in behalf of Israel, affirming with the necessary learning and eloquence that there is no repentance for the divine Promises, and that everything shall belong, when all is said and done, to the Race which begot the Redeemer. I was mistaken. . . .

Now I want to try to answer the more serious part of your letter.

"I am not a Christian," you say, "I can only seek, and mourn." Why do you continue to seek, my friend, since *you have found*? How could you like what I write if you did not think and feel as I do? You are not only Christian, Raïssa, you are a fervent Christian, a well-beloved daughter of the Father, a spouse of Jesus Christ at the foot of the Cross, a loving servant of the Mother of God in her ante-room as the Queen of the world. . . .

Only you do not know, or rather you did not know, and you were sent to us to learn.

. . . The importance, the *dignity* of souls is beyond utterance, and your souls, Jacques and Raïssa, are so precious that it took no less than the Incarnation and the agony of God to ransom them—exactly as my own. . . . *Empti estis pretio magno*, you have been bought at a great price. That, my friends, is the key of everything, in the Absolute. We have been ransomed, like most precious slaves, by the ignominy and the willing torture of Him Who made heaven and earth. When we know this, when we see and feel it, we are like Gods, and we do not cease from weeping.

Your desire to see me less unhappy, my good Raïssa, was a thing which was in yourself, profoundly, in your substantial being, in your soul which prolongs God, long before the birth of Nachor who was the grandfather of Abraham. Strictly, it is the desire for the Redemption, accompanied by the presentiment or the intuition of what it cost Him Who alone could pay the price. That is Christianity, and there is no other way of being a Christian.

Kneel down at the edge of this well and pray for me thus:

My God Who hast bought me at a great price, I humbly ask Thee to put me in union of faith, hope and love with this poor man who suffered in Thy service and who perhaps is suffering mysteriously for me. Deliver him and deliver me for the eternal life which Thou didst promise to all those who would hunger after Thee.

My very dear and blessed Raïssa, here is all that a truly unhappy man can write you today, yet he is filled with the most sublime hope for himself and for all those whom he carries in his heart.

Yours,

Léon Bloy

Washington Gladden
(1836-1918)

ORDAINED as a Congregational minister, Gladden served from 1882 until 1914 as minister of the First Congregational Church, Columbus, Ohio. During part of this time he was on the editorial staff of the *Independent*. His many books cover a wide field of practical religious problems, but all are written from the pastoral viewpoint. "The Christian's Quiet Life" is a good index of the devotional side of his writings. As a man whose tolerance envisioned religion as a way of living rather than a set of dogmas to assure salvation, Gladden was sympathetic with all constructive faiths. A symbol of the way other churches appreciated his leadership is evidenced by the presentation to him of an honorary degree by Notre Dame University.

THE CHRISTIAN'S QUIET LIFE
From *The Christian Way*

Service and not sanctification is, as we have seen, the supreme object of the Christian's desire and endeavor. "To serve the present age," this is his high calling. The attainment of a perfect character is not neglected by him, but that is an object to be sought indirectly.

It may be said that character is the supreme thing; that a perfect soul is better than any or all the acts that issue from it; just as the mind of Shakespeare is greater than the sum of all his dramas. That is true. But Shakespeare's wonderful mind was not the result of constant labor expended directly upon his mind. If his mind had been a constant care to him, he would have been a noodle. It was not by nursing his mind but by using his mind, that he became paragon of poets, and the prince of modern interpreters of human life. The man who devotes his whole life to the study of his mental processes, and the curing of his mental ailments, and the discovery of the laws of mental hygiene and the practice of mental gymnastics, will probably develop a very pretty little model of a mind, but like the inventor's model engine, it is fitted to look at or to play with, not to use. It is the vigorous and productive use of the mind in the study of truth, in the business life, that makes the intellectual man.

Happiness like mental culture is missed by those who seek it directly.

"O Happiness, our being's end and aim," cries out the unphilosophical Pope. But they who make happiness their being's end and aim, who say to themselves "Go to! let us be happy," are always sure to make themselves miserable. Happiness always flies from those that pursue it; it is found only by those who forget to seek it, and devote their lives to some honest and beneficent labor.

What is true of mental development and of happiness is true also of moral and spiritual perfection. The highest religious culture is not attained by those who make religious culture the supreme object of their thought and their endeavors. Those Christians whose chief concern is their own spiritual condition, are a very poor sort of Christians. A self-conscious holiness is a contradiction in terms. It is through a self-forgetful service that the highest culture is gained; through a faithful following of Him who came not to minister to himself, not to be ministered unto, but to minister to others; who became King of kings and Lord of lords by his utter self-surrender; and whose highest praise is spoken in the scoffs of his murderers—"He saved others—himself he cannot save."

Nevertheless there are passive virtues as well as active virtues; and there are, or ought to be, many hours in the Christian's life when he is not employed directly in doing good to others, and when he must think of himself—of his own spiritual condition, of the gains and losses of his daily commerce in the heavenly treasures of wisdom and grace and power. There is a time to meditate as well as a time to act; and this quiet life of the Christian, in which his spirit is refreshed and his strength for labor is replenished, is a most essential part of the regimen under which his character is developed. Perhaps many of us do not know so much as we ought about the peace of the still hour, the fruitful growths of the quiet life. I would not say that there is too much service and too little culture. Too much genuine service there cannot be; but there may easily be too much parade of service; too much bustle and noise of doing too much public service as compared with those more private and unostentatious ministries in which some of the best traits of the Christian character are wholly developed. But while service is the principal thing, and while, if rightly divided and directed, there cannot be too much of it, there may easily be too little of meditation, too little dwelling apart in the secret silence of the mind. Our Lord himself went away more than once from those ministries of love in which his strength was consumed, and climbed the mountain side to spend the night in prayer. If he needed such seasons of repose and refreshment much more do we.

"But thou when thou prayest, enter into thy closet, and when thou hast shut thy door pray to thy Father which is in secret; and thy Father which seeth in secret shall reward thee openly." These words from the Sermon on the Mount are not a prohibition of public prayer or social prayer; they are only a reproof of those who performed their private devotions in public places; who said their prayers on the corners of the streets to be seen by men. It is this ostentatious abuse which our Lord condemns in the verse before the one I have quoted. But these words are the most explicit authority for that quiet life of prayer and meditation of which we have been speaking. The closet hours are to be sacredly set apart and sacredly observed. It is not well to leave this most important business to impulse or caprice. The volitions that lead to it ought to be fenced in with the force of habit. That which is habitual is easy of performance; and a good habit like this may come to rule the soul as firmly as those evil habits do that hold us in painful thrall.

I have spoken already of the uses of reading in preparing us to speak well; but reading is also a good help to those who would think well. There are many books that are not fit companions for the closet hour; but there are a few with which we may well sit down in the secret place, because they will aid us in calling in our thoughts from the noisy world outside and in fixing them upon the things that are unseen and eternal. It sometimes requires a strong effort of the will to wrench one's attention loose from the cares and interests of this present life: and if we begin the silent hour by simply trying to think good thoughts, the good thoughts may fail to come when we summon them, and thoughts that are unbidden and unprofitable guests may throng in and fill the space that ought to be sacred to devotion. But many whose mental discipline has not been sufficient to enable them to think consecutively and profitably in such a season, can yet fix their attention upon a book, and out of the truth which it contains may draw stimulus and refreshment. And though the book should not occupy all the time set apart from meditation, it may often serve as a bridge over which the Christian may pass from the busy life to the quiet life. Such books as Professor Phelps' *The Still Hour*, Miss Dora Greenwell's *The Patience of Hope*, and *A Present Heaven*, Dr. J. P. Thompson's *The Holy Comforter*, Dr. W. W. Patton's *Spiritual Victory*, Dr. E. H. Sears' *Sermons and Songs for the Christian Life*, the Sermons of Dr. Bushnell or President Woolsey or President Hopkins or Frederick Robertson or Robert Leighton or Jeremy Taylor; the Life and Letters of Robertson, Pascal's *Thoughts*, or Dean Goulburn's *Thoughts on Personal Religion*, may lead the studious disciple into that contemplative mood in which the great themes of the immortal life become realities. Novels, even those of most religious intent, are to be eschewed in the hour of meditation; what the soul needs is not excitement nor even exhilaration, but the clearing of its spiritual vision and the strengthening of its pinions for flights above the world of sense.

But while such books as I have named may often serve us well in our quiet hours, there is but one book, after all, that is fit to be the inseparable companion of the closet, and that is the Bible. For instruction, for inspiration, for stimulus, no other words are to be compared with those which we find upon its sacred pages. Not all parts of the Bible are equally adapted to the uses of the closet; the Psalms and the Book of Job, and the Prophecies of the Old Testament, with the whole of the New Testament, are the portions from which we shall derive most benefit. The Bible in the closet is not to be used as a text-book of theology; it is not by the microscopic method of interpretation that we get the most good from it; we must beware how we place too much stress on a literal rendering of certain texts; it is by large and free use of the book that its truth is unfolded to us; the letter killeth but the spirit giveth life. To put ourselves in the place of the sacred writer so far as we are able; to feel the impulse that moves him to write —the lift and sweep of his inspiration; to get into the current of the divine thought that is bearing him on; to catch his spirit and see the life that now is and the life that is to come with his eyes—this is the right method for him who uses the Bible as an aid to secret meditation and devotion. At other times and for other purposes it may be well to study the Book critically, grammatically, narrowly, but

that is not the way to use it in the closet. It is to our feelings rather than to our critical faculties that it ought to address itself there; the awakening of our desires for better life, the kindling of our hopes, the quickening of our consciences, the enlarging of our faith is the service we then demand of it. And this is obtained, not when we set ourselves up as inquisitors, and controversialists, to cross question the Bible, but when we drink in with reverent faith its holy inspirations, when without setting forth in quest of somewhat upon its pages, we quietly wait and let the truth discover us. We do not always need to seek God in the Bible, for in the Bible God is seeking us, and he will surely find us, if we are ready to be found of him.

To read, and think; to think while we are reading; to pause in our reading for more careful thought; to "mark, ponder, and inwardly digest" the word of truth as it is brought to us whether upon the inspired or uninspired page,—this is a means of grace that we cannot afford to neglect. Not all our thinking however, will be the product of our reading. Life as well as literature will furnish us with profitable themes; the events that happen within our knowledge, the passages in our daily experience will be fruitful of thought. If we are faithfully endeavoring to apply our religion to our lives, difficult questions will be arising continually, of which we shall need to think; questions of conduct, questions of service. Offhand decisions of problems of duty are often unwise; a fuller investigation of the subject in all its bearings would have resulted in a different judgment. For such careful examination of the doubtful cases arising in our every day practice time is wanted—and the hour of quiet study is the right time.

There is need also of some thorough probing of the inner life; some strict and stern self-judgment. All that I have said about the unwisdom of making one's own spiritual condition the uppermost concern is true. The religious life whose energies are consumed in self-questioning, whose one great concern is expressed in the hymn:

Do I love the Lord or no?
Am I his or am I not?

is always an unfruitful life. Yet there is a time for careful self-examination, for thorough inspection of the foundations of character. Old George Herbert's quaint counsel is to be duly heeded:

By all means use sometimes to be alone;
 Salute thyself; see what thy soul doth
  wear;
Dare to look in thy chest, for 'tis thine own,
 And tumble up and down what thou
  find'st there.

The comparison of our conduct with our ideals; the measurement of our daily practice by the perfect standard of Christ's law; the fair estimate of our attainments in the light of our opportunities—these are useful exercises. They are not to be too frequently resorted to; the staple of Christian devotion is not self-examination; but in due measure they are profitable. Ask yourself about the temper, whether that is growing less fractious and less sullen; about the will, whether that is growing firmer and steadier in its adherence to right principles and good purposes, and more pliable and gentle when honest opinions collide, and opposing interests are to be harmonized; about the thoughts, whether they are becoming purer, and holier; whether the flocks of evil fancies that were once continually darkening the mind, now return less frequently, and are more quickly driven away; about the disposition, whether that is growing more generous and loving; whether it is easier than once it was to practice self-denial in the small affairs of every day, as well as in the great sacrifices that now and then must be made; whether the foolish vanity that puts the externals of life above its realities, and the foolish pride that leads you to despise those less fortunate than you, and the mean envy and jealousy that sometimes disfigure your characters, and the petty ambitions that often domineer your better natures—whether all these degrading passions are being subdued;

ask yourself about the tongue, whether that is getting tamer, slower to censure, swifter to bless; about the appetites, whether they are learning to submit to the sway of the nobler affections and the reason; you will find questions enough doubtless to ask yourself, and if you urge them with thoroughness and answer them with honesty, the inquisition may be fruitful of good.

Such a candid survey of one's own character is pretty certain to discover weak points, easily besetting sins. There are faults of temperament, or faults of training, or faults of habit to which we are all addicted, and which such an inspection will make us conscious of. And the result ought to be the direction of our efforts at self-discipline toward these weak points. "Especially," says the apostle, (for this is the right reading) "especially" let us guard against "the sin which doth so easily beset us." The weakest point in the defenses is the point that the enemy will assail and it is there that the strongest force must be massed.

But study and reflection and self-examination are not the only occupations of the still hour. It is also, and more especially, the time for prayer. It is well to commune with wise men who have left for us in the books that they have written the record of their own experience; it is well to commune with those holy men of old who spake as they were moved by the Holy Ghost, and whose words, written for our learning, are profitable for doctrine, reproof and instruction in righteousness; it is well to commune with our own hearts in silence as we measure the poor achievements of our lives with the high calling of God in Christ Jesus; but to commune with God himself, to speak distinctly to him and know that he hears us; to open all our hearts to him in thanksgiving, in confession, in entreaty, in intercession, and be assured that he is more responsive, more sympathetic, more compassionate than the tenderest father, the most loving mother into whose ear the erring but trusting child pours the story of his penitence and his purpose of better living,—

this is at once the highest privilege, the greatest honor, and the noblest occupation permitted to mortal men. Public prayer, social prayer, and family prayer are all useful and even indispensable means of grace; but the prayer that most enriches the believer, that brings him into the closest fellowship with his Lord and Master, is that which is lifted up in the secret place. It is when none but God is near, that the heart most freely utters its need, and most strongly urges its petitions. In your closet you can pray for many things that you have no right to speak of in the prayer-meeting, or even at the family altar. The deepest needs of the human soul are often those which none but God can know; the deepest sorrows are those which we can tell none but him; the struggles that are most decisive in our spiritual warfare are those that are waged when we are left alone, as Jacob was, and wrestle with the Angel of the covenant sometimes even unto the breaking of the day. The Christian who lives without secret prayer, or who prays in secret perfunctorily and drily—just saying his prayers and letting that suffice, —is neither a growing Christian nor a working Christian. I doubt whether he is a Christian at all.

Let me offer a word or two of counsel concerning the manner in which this duty of private devotion may best be performed.

1. Be simple and direct in your secret prayer. The grace of simplicity is not to be despised in public prayer; but when we call on God in secret, any formality or elaborateness in our petitions is an offense.

2. Pray audibly. You need not lift your voice to be heard in the street, but it is vastly better to pray not merely in our thoughts but also with words. The utterance of our wants helps to define them. Wishes that merely drift through the mind and never find articulate expression are not apt to be influential in their effect upon our characters. And prayers on which we are not willing to put the emphasis of utterances are not likely to be effectual prayers. I do not deny that

a silent wish, a sincere desire of the soul, unexpressed as well as uttered, may be recognized as genuine prayer and may be answered; but I say that when one enters into his closet to pray to his Father in secret, it is far better that he should put his petition into plain words. "Beware," says Dr. James W. Alexander, "of confining yourself to mental prayer, but in your regular devotions employ audible utterance; for great is the reflex influence of the voice upon the feelings."

3. Be honest in your secret prayer. Do not express any want that you do not feel. Do not confess any fault that you do not mean to forsake. Do not keep anything back. Remember that it is He that searcheth the heart to whom you are speaking. Do we not sometimes while conscious of a fault or a sin ignore it in our devotions, praying all round it, but never mentioning it? We know that we are in the wrong, but we do not mean to forsake the wrong; therefore we choose to pass the matter by in silence. Such prayers as these must be arid and profitless for they are an abomination to the Lord. If there is a secret fault to which we deliberately cling we cannot expect the favor of him who demands of every worshipper the whole heart.

4. Pray earnestly. The words need not be loud, but the desire should be intense. "The fervent, energetic prayer of a righteous man availeth much." "The Kingdom of heaven suffereth violence, and the violent take it by force." No listless, drowsy petitioning will serve. The closet is a quiet place, but there are strenuous and mighty forces that do their work in silence.

5. Do not mock God in your prayers. Do not beg him to come to you. You know that he is never far from any soul that seeks him. That prayer is answered before you utter it. Do not ask God to do for you that which he has expressly bidden you to do. How grossly in such prayers as these we abuse his infinite patience. Ask him always to help you; in every strife, in every service, in every simplest act of devotion or obedience you need his help: but do not beseech him to

do your duties for you and to give you without labor those gifts which he has expressly declared shall not be enjoyed except as the fruit of labor.

6. Pray always with special reference to the needs of the day and the hour;—the warfare to be waged, the temptations to be resisted, the work to be done, the sorrow to be borne; put your life into your prayer; and let it be the most real and the most immediate business of your life.

No doubt these seasons of secret devotion will sometimes be seasons of conflict. It was when our Lord was alone in the wilderness that Satan tempted him; and every one who seeks the still hour will be sure to encounter the same adversary. Times of reflection are often times of doubt. While we are pondering the great themes of eternity the unexplained and inexplicable mysteries of the life that is to come will sometimes settle like a thick mist upon our minds and envelop us in bewildering uncertainties. Oftener still our own lapses into sin, our failures to keep the vows we have spoken, or to conquer the evils we have tried to overcome fill us with discouragement, and make us doubt whether there be indeed any truth in this Gospel we profess. For the solution of these doubts there are a few simple rules.

1. "Hold fast that which thou hast." In the midst of this uncertainty, some things will be certain. Adhere to these. You are perplexed about many duties but there are duties about which you have no misgivings. Set right about them with a resolute purpose and a thorough diligence.

2. Resolve that just as fast as truth is given you, you will accept it and live by it.

3. Remember that religious truth can never be ascertained by mere speculation. It is largely truth of experience and can only find entrance to the mind through the life. It is heat as well as light, and you must suffer it to warm the heart as well as with your reason. Take therefore the character of Christ as delineated in the Gospels, and the character of God as

Christ has unfolded it in his teachings, and reverently study them, asking yourself all the while what relation you sustain to these persons; and whether there is in your heart and life any room for such a friendship as that which Christ offers, any need of such a salvation as he has provided, any witness to the truth of which his life is the revelation. I think that when you come to study carefully first your own moral condition, and then the person and work of Jesus Christ, you will find a marvelous correlation between them, and that you will be convinced that he is indeed the very Friend you need. If you will then commit yourself to him as your Saviour and your Guide, you will soon find the way out of your bewilderment.

This topic is too large to be treated here with any fullness; let me commend to all whose lives are sometimes overcast by the haze of unbelief, a noble sermon of Dr. Bushnell's, printed in his last volume, and entitled *The Dissolving of Doubts*.

I have spoken now of the Christian's quiet hour in the closet, the hour that is sacred to study and thought and prayer, the hour which he sets apart for silent communings with things unseen and with Him whose presence fills all secret places. But the Christian lives a quiet life outside the closet. His communion with high truth, and with the Invisible God is not all enjoyed in secret places. In the clatter of the shop, in the din of the street, in the hum of busy voices he is often alone with God.

> Still with thee, O my God,
>   I would desire to be,
> By day, by night, at home, abroad,
>   I would be still with thee.
>
> With thee when dawn comes in
>   And calls me back to care;
> Each day returning to begin
>   With thee, my God, in prayer.
>
> With Thee amid the crowd
>   That throngs the busy mart;
> To hear thy voice, 'mid clamor loud,
>   Speak softly to my heart.

It is this consciousness of a presence always near, in the noise as well as in the silence, of a help that never fails in danger and extremity, that makes the Christian's life so blessed. The comfort of this assurance is very sweet. So long as he keeps it he is safe from temptation and strong for duty. The Friend that walks unseen beside Him is mighty to deliver. His thought, reaching out in the pauses of his toil, in the emergencies of his experience, always rests on the Almighty Helper. Quick as the volition can spring from the brain to the eyelid, the desire can fly to Immanuel and come back satisfied. "Let your thoughts," says Dr. Alexander, "during the employments of the day often go up in ejaculatory prayer, which is so called because such aspirations are like arrows shot up toward heaven; and blessed is he that hath his quiver full of them."

Walter Rauschenbusch

(1861-1918)

No American theologian can better claim the title "Modern Father of the Social Gospel" than Rauschenbusch. His writings, his living, and his devotional thoughts were all saturated with deep concern for the social aspects of the Christian religion. Like Francis of Assisi he loved men rather than humanity, and was concerned that the strong should help emancipate the weak of their burdens.

Born in Rochester, New York, his early education was received in Germany. In 1883 he graduated with first honors from the Classical Gymnasium, Gütersloh, Germany. He then returned to the United States, where he graduated from both the University of Rochester and Rochester Theological Seminary. He was ordained in the Baptist ministry.

He worked with German immigrants in New York City, 1886-97, helping them with social and religious problems. From 1897 to 1902 he concentrated his efforts in educational work for German ministers in this country, and from 1902 until his death he was professor of church history at Rochester Theological Seminary.

His chief books are: *Christianity and the Social Crisis, Christianizing the Social Order, Theology for the Social Gospel, Social Principles of Jesus*, and *Prayers of the Social Awakening*. From this last book the prayers printed here are selected. They are used by permission of The Pilgrim Press.

[PRAYERS]

From *Prayers of the Social Awakening*

At Eveningtime

*A*ccept the work of this day, O Lord, as we lay it at thy feet. Thou knowest its imperfections, and we know. Of the brave purposes of the morning only a few have found their fulfilment. We bless thee that thou art no hard taskmaster, watching grimly the stint of work we bring, but the father and teacher of men who rejoices with us as we learn to work. We have naught to boast before thee, but we do not fear thy face. Thou knowest all things and thou art love. Accept every right intention however brokenly fulfilled, but grant that ere our life is done we may under thy tuition become true master workmen, who know the art of a just and valiant life.

For Employers

We invoke thy grace and wisdom, O Lord, upon all men of good will who employ and control the labor of men. . . . When they are tempted to follow the ruthless ways of others, and to sacrifice human health and life for profit, do thou strengthen their will in the hour of need, and bring to naught the counsels of the heartless. . . . May they not sin against the Christ by using the bodies and souls of men as mere tools to make things, forgetting the human hearts and longings of these their brothers.

Raise up among us employers who shall be makers of men as well as of goods. . . . Give us men of faith who will see beyond the strife of the present and catch a vision of a nobler organization of our work, when all will still follow the leadership of the ablest, not in fear but by the glad will of all, and when none shall be master and none shall be man, but all shall stand side by side in a strong and righteous brotherhood of work.

For Workingmen

O God, thou mightiest worker of the universe, source of all strength and author of all unity, we pray thee for our brothers, the industrial workers of the nation. As their work binds them together in common toil and danger, may their hearts be knit together in a strong sense of their common interests and . . . to fulfil the law of Christ by bearing the common burdens.

Grant the organizations of labor quiet patience and prudence in all disputes. . . . Raise up for them still more leaders of able mind and large heart, and give them grace to follow the wiser counsel. . . . Bless all classes of our nation, and build up for the republic of the future a great body of workers, strong of limb, clear of mind, fair in temper, glad to labor, conscious of their worth, and striving together for the final brotherhood of all men.

For This World

O God, we thank thee for this universe, our great home; for its vastness and its riches, and for the manifoldness of the life which teems upon it and of which we are a part. We praise thee for the arching sky and the blessed winds, for the driving clouds and the constellations on high. We praise thee for the salt sea and the running water, for the everlasting hills, for the trees, and for the grass under our feet. We thank thee for our senses by which we can see the splendor of the morning, and hear the jubilant songs of love, and smell the breath of the springtime. Grant us, we pray thee, a heart wide open to all this joy and beauty, and save our souls from being so steeped in care or so darkened by passion that we pass heedless and unseeing when even the thorn-bush by the wayside is aflame with the glory of God.

For Those Who Labour at Night

Our Father, as we turn to the comfort of our rest, we remember those who must wake that we may sleep. Bless the guardians of peace who protect us against men of evil will, the watchers who save us from the terrors of fire, and all the many who carry on through the hours of the night the restless commerce of men on sea and land. We thank thee for their faithfulness and sense of duty. We pray for thy pardon if our covetousness or luxury makes their nightly toil necessary. Grant that we may realize how dependent the safety of our loved ones and the comforts of our life are on these our brothers, that so we may think of them with love and gratitude and help to make their burden lighter.

For World Peace

Break thou the spell of the enchantments that make the nations drunk with the lust of battle and draw them on as willing tools of death. Grant us a quiet and steadfast mind when our own nation clamors for vengeance or aggression. Strengthen our sense of justice and our regard for the equal worth of other peoples and races. Grant to the rulers of the nations faith in the possibility of peace through justice, and grant to the common people a new and stern enthusiasm for the cause of peace. Bless our soldiers and sailors for their swift obedience and their willingness to answer the call of duty, . . . and may they never for love of private glory or advancement provoke its coming. May our young men still rejoice to die for their country with the valor of their fathers, but teach our age nobler methods of matching our strength and more effective ways of giving our life for the flag.

O thou strong Father of all nations, draw all thy great family together with an increasing sense of our common blood and destiny, that peace may come on earth at last, and thy sun may shed its light rejoicing on a holy brotherhood of peoples.

For Grace to Make Amends

Grant us this boon, that for every harm we have done, we may do some brave act of salvation, and that for every soul that has stumbled or fallen through us, we may bring to thee some other weak or despairing one, whose strength has been renewed by our love, that so the face of thy Christ may smile upon us and the light within us may shine undimmed.

For the Indifferent

We pray thee for those who amid all the knowledge of our day are still without knowledge; for those who hear not the sighs of the children that toil, nor the sobs of such as are wounded because others have made haste to be rich; for those who have never felt the hot tears of the mothers of the poor that struggle vainly against poverty and vice. Arouse them, we beseech thee, from their selfish comfort and grant them the grace of social repentance. Smite us all with the conviction that for us ignorance is sin, and that we are indeed our brother's keeper if our own hand has helped to lay him low. Though increase of knowledge bring increase of sorrow, may we turn without flinching to the light and offer ourselves as instruments of thy spirit in bringing order and beauty out of disorder and darkness.

Augustine Poulain

(1836-1919)

A FRENCH theologian whose activities centered in Paris, and a member of the Society of Jesus, Poulain has given to the world of mystical appreciation one of the finest comprehensive works by a Roman Catholic writer—*The Graces of Interior Prayer*. Originally written in French, the book has been translated into a number of languages. Of this classic Daniel Considine says, "Père Poulain's book is much more than an examination of spiritual marvels. It is a survey of the Kingdom of Prayer in all its length and breadth, in its lowest as well as its most perfect forms." The selection is from the translation by Leonora L. Yorke Smith and is used by permission of B. Herder Book Co., St. Louis, Mo., and Kegan Paul, Trench, Trübner & Co., London.

[AFFECTIVE PRAYER]

From *The Graces of Interior Prayer*

In ordinary prayer there are four degrees: 1° vocal prayer, which is a recitation; 2° meditation, also called methodical or discursive prayer. This last term indicates a chain of quite distinct reflections or arguments. We can include in this degree meditated readings and the slow recitations of a vocal prayer, accompanied by some reflections which help us to penetrate its meaning; 3° affective prayer; 4° the prayer of simple regard or of simplicity.

I shall say nothing of the first two degrees. They are outside my subject, and are explained at great length in a number of excellent treatises with which the reader is familiar, so that he will not wish me to traverse the same ground again.

2. We call affective prayer that mental prayer in which the affections are numerous or occupy much more space than the considerations and the arguments.

Not that the considerations are absent (we must necessarily go on thinking), but they are less varied, less prolonged.

In this degree we generally find as a foundation some dominant idea which does not, however, exclude a host of other secondary and less perceptible ideas. It is accompanied by very ardent affections.

This degree differs from meditation, therefore, merely as from the greater to the less. It is a discourse, only less varied and less apparent and leaving more room for sentiments of love, praise, gratitude, respect, submission, contrition, etc., and also for practical resolutions. The deduction of truths is partly replaced by intuition. From the intellectual point of view the soul becomes simplified.

This simplification may be greater or less. In a word, the degree is more or less marked and elevated according to the individual case.

3. But the simplification can be carried farther still, and may extend, in a certain measure, to the will, which then becomes satisfied with very little variety in the affections. There is nothing to prevent them from being very ardent at times, but they are usually produced without many words. That is what we call the prayer of simplicity or of simple regard.

It can be defined thus: a mental prayer where 1° intuition in a great measure replaces reasoning; 2° the affections and resolutions show little variety and are expressed in a few words.

When this state has reached its full development, not only do certain acts, of which I have just spoken, become rare, but the attempt to produce them results in a feeling of impotence and distaste. And it is then the same also with those representations of the imagination which would aid other persons in their prayer.

4. The preceding definition is primarily negative, because it consists in saying what it is that has in part disappeared: the discursive act and the variety of words. It will be well to complete it by describing its positive side thus: in the prayer of simplicity there is a thought or a sentiment that returns incessantly and easily (although with little or no development) amongst many other thoughts, whether useful or no.

This dominant thought does not go as far as to be continuous. It merely returns frequently and of its own accord. We may compare it to the strands which thread the pearls of a necklace, or the beads of a Rosary, and which are only visible here and there. Or, again, it is like the fragment of cork, that, carried away by the torrent, plunges ceaselessly, appears and disappears. The prayer of simple regard is really only a slow sequence of single glances cast upon one and the same object.

This degree only differs from the preceding degrees as the greater differs from the less. The persistence of one principal idea, however, and the vivid impression that it produces, point as a rule to an increased action on God's part.

5. An exaggerated picture of the prayer of simplicity has been drawn at times. It has been so described as to lead us to suppose that the intellect and the will continue inactive before a single idea; one showing, that is to say, neither interruptions nor the least modifications. In this case the multiplicity of acts would have disappeared entirely and during the whole time that the prayer lasted; whereas it has only diminished notably and for a certain—long enough to draw attention to it. The simplicity is approximate only and liable to interruption.

We shall see that this is so even in the mystic states. In the prayer of quiet, the principal act is often accompanied by other acts, though on different levels of consciousness; a crowd of little thoughts pass and repass though but half perceived.

Those who appear to believe that the simplicity and the immobility are absolute, and last for a considerable time, forget to state whether they have ever met with such cases in practice, or if they have imagined them, a priori, in the study. For it would be a more extraordinary state than the mystic states themselves Suarez considers it unlikely that there should not be a certain renewal of ideas, and especially of sentiments (*De Orat.*, Book II, Ch. x, Nos. 12, 13). He concludes thus: "I think that it is in this sense only that contemplation can habitually be prolonged; but that it is very rare for the simple act to continue for long."

Scaramelli, on the other hand, seems to consider that the absence of consideration has reached an extreme degree when he says: "To know truths by a simple glance of the soul, is a mode of knowledge above our human intelligence, whose property is to seek after truth by reasoning . . . it is a superhuman mode." (Tr. 2, Nos. 156, 69, 143). We can begin by replying that it is less a question here of seeking truth than of enjoying it. And then we shall see by examples (No. 26) that this state, stripped of all exaggerations, and as it actually exists in real life, is very human.

Let us not invent chimerical states, and then substitute them for the real ones. Otherwise, in practice, our treatises will be useless. No one will be able to recognise his own state in our descriptions.

This exaggerated way of imagining the prayer of simple regard also leads to its being classed wrongly amongst the mystic states. For we are so struck by the exceptional character . with which it is endowed, that we feel obliged to find it a place far above the modest prayer of meditation.

6. Many writers, include the prayer of simplicity in affective prayer, which they thus regard as exhibiting two degrees of elevation. And in this case, between them and us, it is a mere question of words.

7. Before these two states could really constitute separate degrees of prayer, they may be capable of being prolonged for more than a few minutes at a time; they should continue, for instance, for an hour or more. For a very brief space, nothing is easier than for the mind to formulate ardent affections or to operate

in a simple manner. Everybody can do it.

It is on this account that these states, although requiring the co-operation of grace, are not called mystic (see the definition, ch. i, No. 1).

We can express this reason differently, by saying that the name "mystic" has never been given to an exercise having the appearance of a purely natural operation. Now, this is the case with these degrees of prayer.

8. Various names. The two states which we have just defined have sometimes been called the prayer of the heart, in order to indicate that the considerations do not predominate in them.

I believe that the term affective prayer was created by Alvarez de Paz (*Opera*, Vol. 111, *De Inquisitione pacis*, 1616). He devotes to this degree three hundred folio pages, full of pious aspirations. Some later writers have adopted this language. Others have employed different terms; others, again, include in their classifications neither the name nor the things. We see from this circumstance how slowly the science of prayer has come to distinguish the facts that it observes and to coin its own language.

The term, prayer of simplicity, which is very clear, seems to have been invented by Bossuet.

This state, again, has been called active recollection or active repose (as opposed to mystic or passive repose), active quietude (as opposed to true quietude, that which is understood in St. Teresa's sense, and which is quite different), active silence (as opposed to the passive prayer of silence), and most frequently, ordinary or acquired contemplation (see ch. iv, No. 6).

St. Francis of Sales called it the prayer of simple committal to God. This expression requires to be properly understood. It does not mean that we are to come to our prayer without preparation, doing nothing on our own side and committing to God the care of doing everything. But it supposes that God acts, and that we yield ourselves to this action, in spite of our natural tendency to prefer our own more restless action as being more pleasing to the natural faculties.

9. All these different names given to the prayer of simplicity have led to an error on the part of certain writers; for they have supposed them to correspond to different degrees. But if we look closely at their descriptions, making abstraction from the names we perceive that the differences which they point out bear upon insignificant shades only. At most, these might serve to distinguish variations in one and the same degree. The multitude of classifications merely embarrasses the mind instead of assisting it.

Besides, a priori, it is easy to prove that ordinary prayer cannot comprise any general degrees other than those enumerated. There are two cases only. Either we reason, and then it is meditation, or we do not reason, and then it is affective prayer or the prayer of simplicity. All must necessarily enter one or other of these categories.

10. Transitions. The preceding states may be linked one with another and, again, with meditation by a series of insensible transitions; whereas in the simplification of acts there may be either more or less.

It is a prejudice, then, to believe that there is a wall, as it were, erected between these simpler ways and the set methods of prayer. These last are not a prison from which we are forbidden to emerge. They are rather an open garden. We can remain in it if we like the regular walks, the ribbon-borders, where every plant has its own place. But these paths merge into woods, where those who are so inclined may wander in greater freedom, penetrating farther into the forest. St. Ignatius, at the conclusion of his stay at Manresa, wrote out a collection of methods; but he certainly meditated upon their subjects in a much simpler and higher manner than did those to whom he explained them later on. He kept to the spirit rather than to the letter.

11. In respect of the diminution of the reasonings, the prayer of simplicity leads on by a gentle ascent to the mystic states. And these latter are really prayers of simple regard, although we give them an-

other name in order to avoid confusion. And so we get evidence here of the law of continuity, a law that we must not take in too narrow a sense, and that we express in this way: Natura non facit saltus (Nature does not proceed by sudden bounds).

It is true that in the mystic state we have a new gift, but we still find an approximate continuity in this gift also. For it is usually granted only in a low degree to beginners. So that the transitions are gradual.

12. Analogies. In the natural order we find conditions of soul that are analogous to the prayer of simplicity.

The mother watching over her child's cradle thinks of him lovingly for hours together, but with interruptions, and she does this without any arguments.

Two friends have not always new ideas to interchange. And yet they can remain in each other's society for long periods of time, enjoying the happiness of being together in tranquillity and silence.

In the case of a child who is unhappy because he is separated from his family, the impression is intense and persistent, but without any reasonings; his grief is no less strong, however, so far from being so is it that he sometimes loses sleep and the health is affected.

So, too, when a man falls in love, he thinks day and night of the object of his passion; but this thought, this sentiment, often shows no variety. It is always the same confused image, the same thought, happy or sad, that reappears, and each time that it presents itself he finds satisfaction in it without experiencing any need of change.

Finally, the artist remains motionless before some beautiful spectacle in nature or wonderful Old Master.

13. To sum up: in all great preoccupations or in strong emotions of sorrow, joy, or admiration, we get personal proof of this double fact to which we have just called attention in the prayer of simplicity—namely, that the idea or the memory by which we are impressed is not absolutely continuous, but only very frequent, and that when it reappears it is

without any appreciable development.

14. The examples just given, not only serve to convey a clear idea of the nature of the prayer of simplicity, but they show, a priori, that it must exist.

This existence is clearly established by experience. . . . But it will be as well to offer a further proof to those who decline to recognise anything between ordinary meditation and the mystic state.

This is the argument. We have just proved the existence, in the natural order, of states of soul presenting exactly the same characteristics as those which we have taken as the definition of the prayer of simplicity. Only that the mind is occupied with earthly things instead of divine. Now, as grace works in accordance with the plan of nature, being content at first to elevate it secretly without changing its outward appearance, it follows that there should be quite similar states in the supernatural order.

15. General aspect of the spiritual life. When these simplifications of the soul make their appearance during prayer, the same thing occurs with the other exercises of the interior life. The examination of conscience, for instance, takes place more intuitively, more rapidly, and by a single glance.

16. Object of these prayers. They can be applied to all those subjects that used to offer themselves for meditation: God, Jesus, Christ, His mysteries or interior states, the Blessed Virgin, the saints, or such truths as man's last end, our own nothingness, the vanity of all things, etc. (Bossuet, loc. cit., 8, note).

17. The prayer of simplicity, however, has often a tendency to simplify itself even with regard to its object, which thus at times becomes to a certain extent unique. The soul is then drawn to content herself with thinking of God or of His presence in a confused and general manner. It is an affectionate remembrance of God. If this be consoling, the soul feels a sacred flame which burns on gently within her and takes the place of reasonings.

This very special state, the one approaching most nearly to the mystic states, is called the prayer of loving attention to God. It is important to note that, in this case, other subjects are not excluded; they are merely of a secondary importance. They are intertwined with another and a more persistent subject—the thought of God. This mingling will become still more evident in the prayer of quiet.

This prayer of loving attention to God is nothing else than the exercise of the presence of God, so much recommended by all ascetical writers, only it has this peculiarity, that it is confused and with few or no reasonings. It is not a meditation upon the presence of God.

The quietists exaggerated the simplicity of this state. They went too far also in supposing that all prayer of simple regard must have the confused thought of God for its object. This is one of its kinds only.

Some good writers, such as Courbon, have perpetuated the same error in their classifications. Without actually saying so, or being aware of it, they reduced all prayer of simplicity to this one special variety. Any Christian truth can, however, be considered in this simple way.

18. Use of the imagination. If we feel the need of employing it, nothing hinders our calling in its aid. But it will not then multiply imageries. The picture will usually be blurred and without details.

In the course of the day it may even do us a service in the following manner. If in my morning prayer I have thought of one of Our Lord's virtues, contemplating such or such a scene in His life, it will be sufficient to conjure up this picture amidst my various occupations, and I shall then not only remember Him, but also the virtue in question. This is a sweet and simple manner of prayer.

19. Distractions. Distractions may occur in these states as in discursive prayer. It is a labour to repulse them. Yet, notwithstanding, these states have been called the prayer of repose; but this is merely an allusion to the diminution of reasoning.

20. Efforts. The prayer of simplicity, then, requires efforts at times, especially

in order to curtail distractions, just as this is so with the prayer of quiet itself. Everything depends upon the force with which the wind of grace blows. It is the same with meditation. When the vessel's sails are not unfurled, the oars must take their place.

We see, therefore, that, compared with meditation, the prayer of simple regard is not what inertia and absence of effort are to labour, except occasionally and in appearance only; it is merely what uniformity is to variety. In both cases there is action, and energetic action at times. This is often present in intuition when it is well directed and rendered fruitful, just as it is in acts of reasoning.

21. Sufferings. These states are produced, sometimes with consolations, sometimes with aridity (for this last case, see ch. xv). If there is aridity and the soul is unable to meditate, this inaction may be extremely painful. But the soul often suffers even when the prayer of simplicity is partly consoling. For our own curiosity prefers a variety of ideas, our faculties feel the need of movement like children whom we cannot keep still. The imagination becomes irritated at not being called upon, and goes to seek its diversion elsewhere. And, finally there is the trial of having to fight against distractions.

In the prayer of quiet, similar sufferings often occur. I will explain them with greater detail when dealing with this state later on.

It is very important to realise that upon quitting the degree of meditation, we enter upon a path which is far from being strewn with roses, only, as many people suppose. Crosses abound. If we are ignorant of this main truth, we shall quickly fall into anxieties, and discouragement during our periods of aridity. And then we shall be tempted to abandon our prayer in virtue of such false principles as the following: "If God approved of my praying, or of my praying in any particular manner, He would give me proof of His approval by consolations." Or, "It is simply losing time to continue in such a purgatory, when I might de-

velop my activities so well in another direction" (see ch. xxiv, 58 bis).

We often constrain ourselves to continue in a friend's company, even when our subjects of conversation are exhausted. We ought not to depart from God because He seems to hide Himself.

22. Question. How can we say that a state of aridity belongs rather to the prayer of simplicity than to the way of meditation? In both cases there are distractions and incapacity for reasoning; is it not the same thing, therefore?

No. There is this difference, that in the prayer of simplicity there is one dominant thought which returns persistently (see No. 4).

23. Fatigue. This varies from one person to another. It is less in proportion as the action of grace is greater.

24. Various degrees of facility. All alike have not the same facility for affective prayer, and especially for the prayer of simple regard. For a few moments together, this latter is quite easy to any soul of good will. For after painfully amassing considerations, the soul is inclined to enjoy them tranquilly, for a few minutes at any rate, and to content herself with a general and confused view of things.

But it is especially important to inquire which are the persons who possess this facility for a longer time. The complexion of mind, the kind of occupations or of intellectual culture may dispose towards it, and then a merely ordinary supply of grace is sufficient. But at other times a stronger grace is required, on account of the obstacles presented by a certain type of mind, or of the great perfection to which it is approaching. Let us now come to the details.

25. Sooner or later many persons arrive at this manner of prayer, and by a natural process, so to speak. When anyone has made twenty meditations upon death, for instance, the considerations to which he might apply himself upon this subject and all that arises from it, do not interest him any more; he is almost weary of them; or, rather, these considerations would be useless to him. They are present

in his memory, and he embraces them at a glance. He comes at last to form general impressions. And if we take pleasure in these truths, they return easily to the mind; and this is one of the characteristics of the prayer of simplicity (No. 4).

It is the same also if we revert daily to two or three virtues, the need of which is more particularly felt.

Or, again, we have formed a habit of connecting all our thoughts with some one saying, or central idea, such as the Passion or the Blessed Sacrament, and we rest in this thought without any great developments. So that, unless we possess a nature over-flowing with activity, we come easily enough to the prayer of simple regard, provided that we lend ourselves to it.

St. J. B. de la Salle, who gives a very good description of this state in his Explication de la methode d'Oraison (Part ii, ch. i, & 1), alludes to this progressive simplification of the soul when, at the conclusion of his explanations upon the "three different ways of applying ourselves to prayer by dwelling upon a mystery, such as the holy presence of God," he says: "They can be brought approximately to the three states of the spiritual life. Conversations by discourse and multiplied reasonings, to that of the beginners; some few reflections, persisted in for a long time, to that of the proficients (or the more advanced); and simple attention to that of the perfect."

It is my conviction that many of those who practise mental prayer daily, come, at the end of several years, to the prayer of simplicity, although often without being aware of it.

26. Let us now see who they are that arrive there fairly rapidly: 1°. Those who, like St. Teresa, are endowed with but little memory or imagination. They must perforce be satisfied with small things, and they have no inclination to make any great efforts to acquire that with which nature has dowered them so sparingly.

The prayer of simple regard, on the other hand, is very difficult for those in whom these two faculties are highly de-

veloped or who have a restless temperament. A flood of memories, images, and sensible emotions come to them. They find more pleasure in this variety than in a state which is peaceful and monotonous as the desert.

27. 2°. It is the same with unlettered, simple souls when they wish to pray mentally, instead of being satisfied with vocal prayers. They have no taste for high considerations. Possessed of but few ideas, only to be nearer to God is happiness to them. It is sufficient for them to love Him. This is the prayer of Magdalen at Our Lord's feet.

On the other hand, St. Teresa reproaches certain of her confessors, who were great preachers or learned theologians, with their tendency to employ their hours of prayer in composing real sermons, full of texts from Holy Scripture (Life, ch. xv). This tendency in certain preachers can be explained. Having the art of developing a subject and the habit of expounding the truths of religion with many considerations and much imagery, they find it easy and pleasant to act in the same manner during prayer. They continue preaching, but to themselves.

Father Balthasar Alvarez knew this temptation to substitute study for prayer, and he dissuaded persons from it, saying: "If we do not emerge from this prayer with fresh thoughts, at least we possess more virtues and are on better terms with God" (Life, From the French of Louis du Pont, ch. xli).

28. 3°. Loving natures feel attracted towards all practices in which acts of love preponderate over acts of the understanding. And, moreover, the memory of the object loved returns frequently of itself.

29. 4°. Women are generally inclined to a very simple form of mental prayer. St. J. F. de Chantal writes: "Our blessed Father used to say that women had not much capacity for lofty considerations; but that we must, however, make all who enter religion begin with these considerations when they are not accustomed to this holy exercise, for that it is very

important to impress the truths of religion firmly on their minds at the beginning." (*Reponses sur le Coutumier*, art. 24, Migne ed., col. 233).

And, in fact, if we question women as to the subject of their prayer, we discover that everything is usually summed up in a few words. Instead of making long arguments, they have a happy facility for continuing for a long time under the impression of some one idea, and this is very profitable. It is true that in convents, the subject for the morning's meditation is read overnight. But when the hour of prayer comes, it often happens that the nuns do not succeed in developing it; at times, even, there is no inclination to make use of it at all.

30. 5°. In the Contemplative Orders, where much time is given to prayer, it very soon comes to be simplified. If a continued exercise of the understanding were necessary, the head would quickly become weary.

31. St. Francis of Sales, and St. J. F. de Chantal wished all their spiritual daughters to understand the prayer of simplicity and to practise it as far as possible. The results corresponded to this direction. St. J. F. de Chantal wrote: "The more I see, the more I am convinced that Our Lord leads nearly all the sisters of the Visitation to the prayer of simple union, a simple abiding in the presence of God" (*Reponses sur le Coutumier*, art. 24, translated in the *Life of St. J. F. de Chantal*, Bougaud, Vol. 1, p. 446). And elsewhere: "The almost universal attraction of the sisters of Visitation is a very simple attention to the presence of God, and I might well omit the almost, for I have remarked that all who apply themselves to prayer as they should, are drawn to it from the very first, and that all who perform their duty with regard to self-mortification and the exercise of the virtues, arrive there at last. Many are drawn to it from the outset, and it seems as if God made use of this sole means in order to make us reach the goal and our soul's perfect union with Him. Finally, I hold that this manner of prayer is essential to our little Congregation; and that

it is a great gift from God for which we should be infinitely grateful" (*Letter to a Superior*, ed. Plon, Vol. III, p. 337. *Life by Mgr. Bougaud*, ch. xviii).

32. If, on the other hand, which God forbid, the Directors of a Community were prejudiced and had an aversion for this kind of prayer, the result would probably be that they would make it less common. This would not be so, I admit, if the persons concerned merely resisted the attraction in good faith and through obedience. They would then escape with the loss only of their peace of soul during the prolonged struggle. But we go beyond this as a rule. Not knowing that we are receiving a gift at God's hands, we take no interest in it, and become careless over the removal of the obstacles that it encounters in our lives. It is this negligence that God punishes by diminishing His graces. The director has been the occasion only; the real fault lies with us.

32. 6°. The brevity of the power or other circumstances may have the effect of facilitating simple prayers—at certain moments, at any rate. Here are some examples: (a) Those who make a short visit to the Blessed Sacrament do not, as a rule, think of going through any set meditation or of reciting a vocal prayer. They continue tranquilly and lovingly in the thought that God or Our Blessed Lord is there present. This is already the prayer of simple regard, although of short duration. We have not here the more complicated case of a daily half-hour or hour prayer (see 52). (b) It is often the same during the thanksgiving after Communion, when the Mass has been preceded by mental prayer. For a certain fatigue has resulted, which tends to repose and justifies it. (c) Nuns who recite a Latin Office without understanding it can neither occupy their minds with what they are reading nor follow any other connected train of thought, but they often think of God in a confused way, and with love. This will be the prayer of simplicity.

33. We have now said enough to show that our natural dispositions and mode of life have an influence upon the nature of

our prayer. We shall not be surprised, therefore, to find that one person should have passed on at once to affective prayer, having had hardly any acquaintance with the prayer of meditation, and that another should have arrived at certain other degrees without having first gone through all those that were intermediary.

34. In order to facilitate the practice of affective prayer, it is as well to do as St. Ignatius did, and to take as subjects for prayer, not the abstract virtues, but the historic facts that teach these virtues. When we meditate on any Mystery of Our Lord's life, it is easy to make the affections predominate by testifying our respect, love, gratitude or compassion to Our Saviour or His Blessed Mother, and holding "colloquies" with them.

We can also establish a certain order in the sentiments that we try to excite. To produce affections is really to make interior acts of certain virtues; we shall therefore draw up a list of virtues appropriate to our needs. We begin, for instance, by acts of faith, hope, or charity towards God and our neighbour. We then go on to contempt of self, resignation, zeal, love of regularity, etc.; or the four ends of the holy sacrifice of the Mass: adoration, thanksgiving, petitions for pardon and for graces.

Emily Herman

(1876-1923)

EDUCATED in London, wife of a Presbyterian minister, Emily Herman became well known as a writer and journalist. She was editor of the *Presbyterian*, assistant editor of *Everyman* and the *Challenge*. As a writer whose chief interest was in religious experience, she wrote two books which have high rank: *Creative Prayer* and *The Meaning and Value of Mysticism*. "The Secret Garden of the Soul" and "The Altar Fire" from *The Secret Garden of the Soul and Other Devotional Studies* indicate both the depth and the sincerity of mystical religion. They are two of the simple yet profound studies compiled posthumously in this volume, which is called "the self-revelation of a saint." The selections appear here through permission of James Clarke & Co., Ltd., London.

THE SECRET GARDEN OF THE SOUL

From *The Secret Garden of the Soul*

Every soul that is truly alive has a garden of which no other holds the key; and in hours of weariness, when it is breathless with the hot race of life, and harassed by a babel of voices, it slips through the gate and walks at peace among the flowers. There is a garden of the soul also, of which that beyond the brook Kedron is the type, where Jesus walks with His disciples, and the clash of the world cannot drown the music of His voice. It was said of the garden on the farther side of Kedron that "Jesus ofttimes resorted thither with His disciples"; and when the High Priest's servants sought to convict Peter of his discipleship, they clinched their appeal with, "Did not I see thee in the garden with Him?" And still the true Christian disciple is a man of the garden. He carries with him a breath of the pure, invigorating, fragrant air that blows across the secret garden of communion. The sound of its crystal fountains is in his voice; the radiance of its sunlit flowers is mirrored in his eyes. He is not as other men are; he carries a garden in his heart, and his fellows take knowledge of him that he has been with Jesus.

In the garden of communion the clamour of the world and the contendings of the Church are alike unheard. No sound of controversy penetrates that enclosed sanctuary; no rivalries can live within its gates of peace. There the Twelve clamour no longer for the highest place in the Kingdom; there Peter steps out of the shallows of impetuosity into the clear depths of love, John unlearns on the bosom of his Lord the passion that would call down fire from heaven, and Philip's questionings are lost in a certainty deeper than that of the enquiring mind. Small wonder that the disciples loved the garden, and that disciples of all ages have been loth to exchange its sweet intimacies for the rough and irritating traffic of the open road! It belonged at once to the strength and to the weakness of mediæval sainthood that it lingered so persistently in the garden.

The Christian mind, whether mediæval or modern, has always tended to swing between two extremes—it has given to the garden either far more or far less than its true place. One might say, indeed, that the supreme test of a full-orbed and perfectly balanced Christian character is found in its attitude toward that secret garden of the soul's delight. It takes most of us a lifetime to learn how to use that hidden retreat. We are fascinated by the open road, and follow so long and eagerly that we can no longer find our way back to the garden; or else we enter into the garden and lock the gate, and breathe its flower-sweet air till our eyes are drowsy and the days pass over us like white clouds across a summer sky. Then we wake and find ourselves alone among withered flowers and dried-up fountains; for while we dreamed the time away, Jesus has gone forth upon the high-road, conquering and to conquer, and we are left with our faded emotions and sterile longings.

With religious and social activities multiplying around us, and the call of a world's need in our ears, we are at times tempted to neglect the quiet place. To walk with God in the garden in the cool of the day seems to us a misuse of time when so much remains to be done. There

is, indeed, no cool of day for us; it is always sweltering noon, and toil as we may, the evensong bell still tarries. We race and pant; we work feverishly and beyond our strength; yet our efforts seem doomed to ineffectiveness because we have forgotten the garden. Among the greatest saints have been men and women whose external activities have been of necessity few—men and women who lived in times when the contemplative rather than the active ideal of the Christian life prevailed, or who, living in modern times, spent their days on beds of suffering or under cramped and fettering conditions. They did few things, but they did them superlatively well, for they did them in the spirit and atmosphere of the garden. There was a "shapeliness" about their actions beside which our efforts appear crude, for they were the expression of Divine grace allowed to have its perfect work in the heart. Behind them was a supernatural momentum—that pure and fervent intention of soul that comes of living in communion with God. Our actions are numerous and precipitous rather than weighty. They tread on each other's heels, neutralize each other, become increasingly mechanical and futile. "Are there not twelve hours in the day?" asks Jesus. "He that believeth shall not make haste," and of all the hours of the day, that spent in the garden gives colour to the rest.

When a crisis finds us unready and inadequate to its demands, it is largely because, while we have jostled our brethren along the high-road of religious activity, and kept ourselves busy in the house of organized effort, we have neglected the garden. The glare of the road and the bustle of the house have deceived us. We thought ourselves sterling coin, and when the hand of our Maker rang our metal against the counter of hard fact we were dismayed at the hollow sound. Had we but submitted ourselves to the gentle testing of the garden, we would have escaped this shame. For the garden is a great touchstone. In its clear, quiet light, what passed as gold under the lime-light is seen to be tinsel; beside its delicate bloom the pageantry of the public highway appears as so much crude pretentiousness. No soul can remain utterly artificial in the garden of secret fellowship. Its sunshine kills the poison-germ of unreality; its deep quietude lays bare the hidden equivocation, the latent apostasy of our recalcitrant hearts.

But if many are tempted to ignore the garden, many tend to dwell in it so exclusively as to turn its refreshing quietude into an enervating narcotic. The garden has an irresistible attraction for peace-loving souls. It is so delightful to shut the gate and forget the struggles and contentions, the burning questions and searching issues, which meet the soul on life's highway. It is easy to be sweet and gentle in the garden, easy to cast controversy to the winds and give oneself up to spiritual consolations and raptures. It is possible for a sincerely devout soul to shine in the garden, but to prove itself ineffective on the high-road; to excel in the devotional life, but fail to translate its devotion into terms of social righteousness.

Our Lord often went into the garden with His disciples, but the greater part of His ministry was spent, not in the garden, but on the highway and in the market-place. There was much to fret and irritate the disciples in these busy centres, where rough controversy and blunt opposition met them at every turn, and they were often betrayed into ignoble tempers and fierce quarrels. But the Master did not see in this a reason for withdrawing them from the ordeal of publicity and keeping them at peace in the garden. The crowded streets, the clamorous synagogue, the storm-lashed sea, the grim wilderness—these were to be their class-room and training-ground; and so were but the prelude to Calvary and to the world-wide Apostolate that followed the Resurrection. The hours in the garden were ever cut short by the Master's "Arise, let us go hence"; and when the wearied disciples begged Him to send the thronging multitude away, His verdict was: "They need not depart." He chose, not to abide on the heights of contemplation, but to live and work among men. He did not intend His Gospel to be an esoteric possession, carefully guarded from every breath of opposition, but proclaimed it in the open air, where men were free to question and oppose, to sneer and revile. He has no use for a discipleship that is of the garden merely. In His eyes of flame, no fervour of cloistered devotion can atone for a refusal to bear the cross in the world of business and public duty.

To give the garden its true place, then, is our task, for without the garden we cannot live; and by the garden, rightly used, our work in the world is determined. And if in estimating our own condition we must take our garden hours into account, we need to do the same in judging others. Our judgments are often harsh and cruel because we only see the high-road and the house-frontage of our brother's life: we leave the garden behind the house out of our reckoning. How should we judge Bishop Andrewes, if we knew only of the infamy into which his servile partisanship betrayed him, and did not possess also those incomparable *Private Devotions*, steeped in the tears of his contrition, in which his deeper soul is revealed? What verdict should we pass on Samuel Rutherford, if only the story of his bitter tempers and fierce quarrels had been preserved, and not his seraphic *Letters?* Who would pronounce upon the spiritual quality of Bishop Butler, without placing side by side with his dry and judicial "Sermons" his dying confession of trust in his Saviour?

And what is true of leaders among men is true of the obscurest. Every day we meet and fail to recognize those who, behind an apparently mean and narrow house of life, can show a garden of flowers and singing birds. It belongs to the perfection of our Lord's Saviourhood that He can detect a garden where men see only a dead wall; and His disciples are known by their share in that Divine instinct. "You say you know a rogue at first sight," growls Carlyle; "tell me rather, what is more to the purpose, do you know a good man when you see him?" We need to learn the art of knowing a good man at sight, and the Christian soul is discerned only by him who knows how to discover the hidden garden, because he, too, carries a garden in his heart.

THE ALTAR FIRE

From *The Secret Garden of the Soul*

Our age has been called an age of "togetherness." We have discovered the sweetness and potency of corporate prayer and effort. We have come to see that the man who, under any pretext, cuts himself off from the community precludes his own best future; that the believer who thinks he can dwell alone, and serve God outside the fellowship and concerted activity of the Christian congregation, is not merely withholding good things from himself, but seriously imperilling the spiritual life which he is so greatly concerned to guard. Humble, patient, forbearing co-operation with even the most imperfect and unlovely company of Christians is infinitely better, and far less dangerous to the soul, than the most strenuous and lofty effort to live the Christian life in isolation. To dissociate oneself from the fellowship of the Church is to court, not merely a stunted spiritual development, but the graver peril of self-complacency and self-deception.

And with the sense of corporate unity there has come a passion for service. "To do one's bit" sums up the aspiration toward service for thousands whose ideals are dim and inarticulate. "Lord, use me," is the daily prayer of the twentieth-century Christian whose eyes have been unsealed to perceive his Lord in "the least of these little ones," and whose deepest soul is gathered up in the one absorbing, invincible desire to have a share, however humble, in a Kingdom which embraces all ministries of help and healing done in the name of Christ.

But alongside of the unique value of the community there lies the inalienable supremacy of the individual personality. In spite of the popular heresy that the individual exists for the sake of the community, we must insist that the community exists for the sake of the individual. Its function is to draw out and perfect the love and truth, the honour and chivalry and high striving, that lie latent in every heart. It is the individual who makes the community possible, for only free and high-souled men can combine into vital organizations; and to decry the individual is to belittle the community. Behind corporateness is individuality, and behind service character. We have those in plenty who are pathetically eager to serve their fellow-men: we need more who are able to stand alone with God in that awful singleness of relation which is the very foundation of a healthy society. A man is never so near to his fellow-men as when, in dread solitude, he lifts his heart to the Father of spirits.

"The fire shall ever be burning upon the altar; it shall never go out." What more eloquent picture could there be of life dead at the core, of life well-ordered on the circumference but empty and impotent at the center, than a sanctuary whose altar fire has been allowed to die? There is an altar in man—a deep and majestic place where the soul transacts with its God, and life is cleansed and kindled with unearthly flame. If the soul is orientated like a temple, it is because it enshrines an altar. Let the altar fire go out, and what was once a meeting place of earth and heaven, pulsing with angelic life, becomes a ruin, a pathetic survival, a landmark which may interest the historian and antiquarian, but makes no appeal to the life around it. When God wants to move men, He begins by moving one man here and another there; and always His dynamic word is spoken from amid the altar fire.

We wonder sometimes how ineffective and uninfluential our best efforts are, how much thought and energy and sheer good intention we spend upon activities which seem to acomplish very little. And still the cry is for more activity and more helpers. We are too few, we say. If only we could inspire our brethren who profess the same faith to help us translate it into service! Not a few in these crowded days quote with approval the remark of William Wilberforce, in reply to a lady who, in the midst of his anti-slavery crusade showed concern about his soul, that he had forgotten he had a soul. The retort was not unsuited to the occasion, but quoted out of its context, it only serves to obscure the issue. The choice does not lie between active service and spiritual self-culture; we all recognize that the Christian is pledged to the service of his fellow-men. The only question is how to make that service effectual by making our work the inevitable outcome of what we *are*. The answer is, Keep the altar fire burning. Be not more greatly concerned about the gold than about the temple; neither esteem the gift to be greater than the altar which sanctifies the gift. There is only one effectual dynamic for service—God, and the life that is lived in the realized presence of God. Everything else is delusion and moral drug-taking.

The great Christian men of action have always been men of prayer. We think of Livingstone on his knees, of General Gordon praying in his tent, of a great worker declaring that he had so much business he could not get on without spending three hours daily in prayer, and we stand convicted of neglect. But no outward imitation will suffice, nor have we mastered the secret of the saints when stern tasks and grave responsibilities drive us to our knees. The man with the altar fire burning at the centre of his soul is the man whose communion with God is his very life. Prayer to him is indeed "the motion of a hidden fire that trembles in the breast." To hold converse with God is in him a spontaneous and irrepressible impulse, the secret undercurrent which runs unceasingly beneath the stream of daily business, "the pulse of that life which is hid with Christ in God." Such a soul is a centre of energy, a storehouse of divine momentum that may set great human masses in motion. Men who light the altar fire in their rare, decisive moments often achieve much; but the holy flame that burns steadily and hiddenly day and night is the flame that sets the world on fire.

We may always suspect the activity that renders the soul distracted and unconcentrated, making it a weariness to dwell upon the thought of God. There is something radically wrong about work that unfits the soul for what is its supreme business. Arduous and trying duties may curtail our time for prayer and meditation; but the spiritual life does not depend upon our leisure, and he who cannot find God in the performance of humble and irksome duties will find Him nowhere else. It is not with such duties, however, that we are here concerned. It is with self-imposed tasks, with work undertaken impulsively and without enquiring if our eagerness arises from a sense of the Divine call, or merely from the promptings of self-will, or the fatal lust of being busy at any cost. St. Ambrose retails the quaint old belief that when eaglets arrive at a certain age, the parent bird takes them to the edge of the rock and holds their heads up to the sun. If they can stand its blaze without blinking, it knows they are true eagles; if they wince and close their eyes, it drops them over the edge of the abyss. Here is a test for the Christian worker. Does my work unfit me for that sustained gaze into the face of God which is my very life? Does it make impossible that quiet recollection—that gathering home of all the senses unto God—which is a primary condition of heavenly commerce? If so, it is not the work I am called to, however attractive it is, however effective it seems, however eagerly my friends press me to continue in it. I must exchange it, not, indeed, for idleness under the plea of gaining more time for communion with God, but for that service to which I am truly called. I must once more wait upon God, and in the silence of my soul listen for His unmistakable word, sending me forth to work of His appointing.

The altar is not the place of idle or sentimental piety. It offers no encouragement to those who, in the words of Thomas à Kempis, follow the Lord to the breaking of bread but refuse to drink of the cup of His passion—self-indulgent souls who enjoy the rapture of devotion but evade its stern consequences. The altar is the place of dedication to high tasks, the dread and awful spot where those who love not their lives unto death yield them up to God. It is the place where the knights of God receive the consecrated sword that must pierce the swordsman before it can hurt the foe; where the lips of the spokesman of God are purged with living coal, and the eager spirit of the reformer has to pass through the fire ere it can purify Churches and nations with its breath of flame. True, those who have kept the altar fire alive in their hearts are dowered with rare and radiant beauty and crowned with ineffable joy; but if their faces are illumined, it is as the faces of priests are illumined—by the sacrificial flame that leaps about them.

The watchword of the soul's altar ever is: "For their sakes I sanctify myself." That is not an easy thing to do, when the clamant cry of human need all but drowns the call to personal consecration. It was never an easy thing, for the world has always thought more highly of the man who distributes loaves than of the man who "merely" prays, and whose influence is primarily spiritual. There is no need, however, to dissociate the dealing of bread to the hungry from that drawing forth of a compassionate and God-filled soul which gives the action its real value. We must first sanctify ourselves, before we can give bread to the poor in such fashion as shall make the gift a blessing and not a curse. Are we troubled and distressed at the sin and the indifference of the crowd about our doors? Then, as the iron of it enters our hearts, let us first bring ourselves to the altar as we have never done before. The place of the world's healing is not a parliament of nations, but the Cross of Christ. It takes courage amid the charitable bustle of the day to seek the soul's sanctuary, and remain in stillness before its inmost shrine until we know what God means us to *be*, and therefore what He means us to *do*. Yet this, and not the spending of our goods or our skill, is the first and supreme debt we owe our fellow-men, the great fundamental charity out of which all charities spring.

> For this is Love's nobility—
> Not to scatter bread and gold,
> Goods and raiment bought and sold;
> But to hold fast his simple sense,
> And speak the speech of innocence,
> And with hand, and body, and blood,
> To make his bosom-counsel good.
> He that feeds men serveth few;
> He serveth all that dares be true.

Friedrich von Hügel

(1852-1925)

Son of an Austrian ambassador, von Hügel received his education in Florence and Brussels. He was born in Florence, but moved with his family in 1867 to Torquay. In 1914 he became a naturalized British subject.

He had sympathy for all seekers after religious truth, but felt that the Roman Catholic Church possessed the richest and fullest interpretation of religious experience. He held to the higher criticism of the Bible with other modernists, but could not follow modernists like Loisy and Duchesne when they revolted against Rome.

Few men have made so thorough a study of mysticism as von Hügel, and among the most profound interpretations of mysticism his *Mystical Element of Religion as Studied in Saint Catherine of Genoa and Her Friends* ranks high. "True Relation of the Soul to Its Fellows" is taken from Vol. II. of that classic work. The second selection is the final chapter of his book *Eternal Life*, "an analysis of more or less advanced states of soul—of considerable spiritual experience and of considerable articulation of such experience." Both selections are reprinted from *Readings from Friedrich von Hügel*, edited by Algar Thorold, by permission of E. P. Dutton & Co.

TRUE RELATION OF THE SOUL TO ITS FELLOWS

From *The Mystical Element of Religion as Studied in Saint Catherine of Genoa and Her Friends*

*L*et us take first the relation of the single human soul to its fellow-souls.

(1) Now Kierkegaard tells us: "the Absolute is cruel, for it demands *all*, whilst the Relative ever continues to demand *some* attention from us." And the Reverend George Tyrrell, in his stimulating paper, *Poet and Mystic*, shows us that, as regards the relations between man's love for man and man's love for God, there are two conceptions and answers in reply to the question as to the precise sense in which God is "a jealous God," and demands to be loved alone. In the first, easier, more popular conception, He is practically thought of as the First of Creatures, competing with the rest for Man's love, and is here placed alongside of them. Hence the inference that whatever love they win from us by reason of their inherent goodness, is taken from Him: He is not loved perfectly, till He is loved alone. But in the second, more difficult and rarer conception, God is placed, not alongside of creatures but behind them, as the light which shines through a crystal and lends it whatever lustre it may have. He is loved here, not apart from, but through and in them. Hence if only the affection be of the right kind as to mode and object, the more the better. The love of Him is the "form," the principle of order and harmony; our natural affections are the "matter" harmonized and set in order; it is the soul, they are the body, of that one Divine Love whose adequate object is God in, and not apart from, His creatures. Thus we have already found that even the immensely abstractive and austere St. John of the Cross tells us: "No one desires to be loved except for his goodness; and when we love in this way, our love is pleasing unto God and in great liberty; and if there be attachment in it, there is greater attachment to God." And this doctrine he continuously, deliberately practises, half-a-century after his Profession, for he writes to his penitent, Donna Juana de Pedrazas in 1589: "All that is wanting now, is that I should forget you; but consider how that

is to be forgotten which is ever present to the soul."

But Father Tyrrell rightly observes: "To square this view with the general ascetic tradition of the faithful at large is exceedingly difficult." Yet I cannot help thinking that a somewhat different reconciliation, than the one attempted by him, really meets all the substantial requirements of the case.

(2) I take it, then, that an all-important double law or twin fact, or rather a single law and fact whose unity is composed of two elements, is, to some extent, present throughout all characteristically human life, although its full and balanced realization, even in theory and still more in practice, is ever, necessarily, a more or less unfulfilled ideal: viz. that not only there exist certain objects, acts, and affections that are simply wrong, and others that are simply right or perfect, either for all men or for some men: but that there exist simply no acts and affections which, however right, however obligatory, however essential to the perfection of us all or of some of us, do not require, on our own part, a certain alternation of interior reserve and detachment away from, and of familiarity and attachment to, them and their objects. This general law applies as truly to Contemplation as it does to Marriage.

And next, the element of detachment which has to penetrate and purify simply all attachments,—even the attachment to detachment itself,—is the more difficult, the less obvious, the more profoundly spiritual and human element and movement, although only on condition that ever some amount of the other, of the outgoing element and movement, and of attachment, remains. For here, as everywhere, there is no good and operative yeast except with and in flour; there can be no purification and unity without a material and a multiplicity to purify and to unite.

And again, given the very limited power of attention and articulation possessed by individual man, and the importance to the human community of having impressive embodiments and examples of this, in various degrees and ways, universally ever all-but-forgotten, universally difficult, universally necessary, universally ennobling renunciation: we get the reason and justification for the setting apart of men specially drawn and devoted to a maximum, or to the most difficult kinds, of this renunciation. As the practically universal instinct, or rudimentary capacity, for Art, Science, and Philanthropy finds its full expression in artists, scientists, philanthropists, whose specific glory and ever necessary corrective it is that they but articulate clearly, embody massively and, as it were, precipitate what is dimly and intermittingly present, as it were in solution, throughout the consciousness and requirements of Mankind; and neither the inarticulate instinct, diffused among all, would completely suffice for any one of the majority, without the full articulation by a few, nor the full articulation by this minority could thrive, even for this minority itself, were it not environed by, and did it not voice, that dumb yearning of the race at large: so, and far more, does the general religiosity and sense of the Infinite, and even its ever-present element and requirement of Transcendence and Detachment, seek and call forth some typical, wholesomely provocative incorporation,—yet, here, with an even subtler and stronger interdependence, between the general demand and the particular supply.

And note that, if the minority will thus represent a maximum of "form," with a minimum of "matter," and the majority a maximum of "matter," with a minimum of "form": yet some form as well as some matter must be held by each; and the ideal to which, by their mutual supplementations, antagonisms, and corrections, they will have more and more to approximate our corporate humanity will be a maximum of "matter," permeated and spiritualized by a maximum of "form." If it is easy for the soul to let itself be invaded and choked by the wrong kind of "matter," or even simply by an excess of the right kind, so that it will be unable to stamp the "matter" with spiritual "form"; the opposite extreme also, where the spiritual forces have not left to them a sufficiency of material to penetrate or of life-giving friction to overcome, is ever a most real abuse.

[ETERNAL LIFE GIVEN IN EXPERIENCE]

From *Eternal Life*

As regards the development of the consciousness of Eternal Life, and a fully fruitful conviction concerning it, we find that the history of Religion, and the deepest experiences and revelations vouchsafed to us, indicate the true lines to be as follows. (We here adopt, not the historical or physical, but the logical order.)

1. Eternal Life, in its pregnant, concrete, ontological sense,—the operative conviction of its reality,—is not, primarily, a matter of Speculation and Philosophy, but reveals itself clearly only in the course of ages, and even then only to riper, deeper souls, as having been all along (in some manner and degree) experienced and postulated in all that men feel, will, do, and are of a characteristically human kind. It is only Religion that, in this matter, has furnished man with a vivid and concrete experience and conviction of permanent ethical and spiritual value. Philosophy, as such, has not been able to do more than analyse and clarify this religious conviction, and find, within its own domain and level, certain intimations and requirements converging towards such a conviction. It has not itself been able vividly to experience, or unshakably to affirm, a corresponding Reality as actually present and ever operative in the production of these very intimations and requirements.

2. Eternal Life, as thus operative in man's life and discovered for us there by Religion, is not an ultimate cause, a self-subsisting entity, which (accidentally or necessarily) evolves a living subject or subjects; but it is simply the effect, the action, of a living Reality, or the effect, the interaction, of several such realities. Hence Eternal Life is no substitute for either God or man; but it is the activity, the effect, of God, or of man, or of both.

3. Eternal Life, in the fullest thinkable sense, involves three things—the plenitude of all goods and of all energizings that abide; the entire self-consciousness of the Being Which constitutes, and Which is expressed by, all these goods and energizings; and the pure activity, the non-successiveness, the simultaneity, of this Being in all It has, all It is. Eternal Life, in this sense, precludes not only space, not only clock-time—that artificial chain of mutually exclusive, ever equal moments, but even *duration*, time as actually experienced by man, with its overlapping, interpenetrating successive stages. But Eternal Life precludes space and clock-time because of the very intensity of its life. The Simultaneity is here the fullest expression of the Supreme Richness, the unspeakable Concreteness, the overwhelming Aliveness of God; and is at the opposite pole from all empty unity, all mere being—any or all abstractions whatsoever.

4. Eternal Life, in a real, though not in the fullest sense, is attributable to man. This lesser eternal life appears to have its range between the pure Simultaneity of God, and mere Clock-Time, and to have its true form in *Duration*—an ever more or less overlapping succession, capable of being concentrated into quasi-simultaneities. And this lesser eternal life, although unending, is never boundless; nor does it (here below at least) ever become entirely actual.

5. Now, owing to this our likeness in unlikeness to It, the Eternal Living Spirit (though necessarily incomprehensible by our own) can be, and is, continuously apprehended by us—since that Spirit really penetrates us and all Its creatures.

And this our apprehension occurs, not separately, abstractively, clearly, statically; but ever more or less in, or contrasting with, finite, contingent, changing things; and it does so obscurely, yet with an immensely far-reaching dynamic operativeness. From hence alone can spring our unquenchable thirst after the Eternal and Abiding, the Objective, the Final; and our intolerable pain at the very idea of being entirely confined to the merely fleeting, subjective, momentary—a pain which persists even if we extend the validity and permanence of our life's experience to all humanity, taken simply as such. For this thirst and pain could not be so ineradicable and so profoundly operative, and could not constitute so decidedly the very flower and test of our fullest manhood, did it not proceed from a Reality or Realities deeper than any exclusively human projection or analysis whatsoever.

Nor will it suffice to refer this experience to the operation, within us, of Spirit in the making—to the gradual and painful coming to self-consciousness of the one concrete Universe (of which we form an integral part) precisely through our spirits and their growth. For we have no other instance of an unrealized perfection producing such pain and joy, such volitions, such endlessly varied and real results; and all by means of just this vivid and persistent impression that this Becoming is an already realized Perfection. Religion would thus deceive us precisely in the conviction and act which are central in all its higher forms and stages—Adoration. And the noblest root and flower of the Jewish-Christian religion and of European civilization,— the sense of *Givenness*, of grace, of dependence upon a Reality other and higher than ourselves, singly or collectively—would also have to go. For such a habit of mind requires (logically, and in the long run also practically) my belief in a Reality not less but more self-conscious than myself—a Living One Who lives first and lives perfectly, and Who, touching me, the inferior, deriva-

tive life, can cause me to live by His aid and for His sake.

6. Thus such a sense of the Divine Eternity or Simultaneity will be developed by man within, and in contrast to, *duration*. And it will be strengthened in proportion as man effects, in others and in himself, results spiritually real within this (for him) real duration; and as he collects his spirit (in alternation to such action) away from all particular strivings, and concentrates it, more exclusively, upon the Divine Living One— the ever-present Background and Support of his little life. *Time* then, in the sense of *duration* (with the spiritual intercourse and the growth in spiritual character which we develop and consolidate in such time), is, for us men, not a barrier against Eternal Life, but the very stuff and means in and by which we vitally experience and apprehend that Life. Man's temporal life is thus neither a theory nor even a vision; nor something that automatically unrolls itself. Nor, on the other hand, is it, even at its deepest, itself the Ultimate experienced by man. But man's life is one long, variously deep and wide, rich and close, tissue of (ever more or less volitional) acts and habits—instinctive, rational, emotive; of striving, shrinkings, friction, conflict, suffering, harmony and joy; and of variously corresponding permanent effectuations in and by the spirit thus active. And hence man's life is full of cost, tension, and drama. Yet such an individual life never experiences, indeed never is constituted by, itself alone; but it is ever endlessly affected by the environment and stimulation of other realities, organisms, spirits; and it ever itself correspondingly affects such other realities. And the whole of this interconnected realm of spirits is upheld, penetrated, stimulated, and articulated by the one Infinite Spirit, God. Thus a real succession, real efforts, and the continuous sense of limitation and inadequacy are the very means in and through which man apprehends increasingly (if only he thus loves and wills) the contrasting yet sustaining Simultaneity,

Spontaneity, Infinity, and pure Action of the Eternal Life of God.

7. But also spatial concepts and imagery play two important rôles in the full and normal consciousness of Eternal Life. For whether or no the spatial category abides with man in the Beyond, in this earthly life at least he cannot persistently and vividly apprehend even the most spiritual realities, as distinct and different from' each other, except by picturing them as disparate in space. Now a vivid consciousness of the deep distinction and difference (within all their real affinity and closeness of intercourse) between God and man, and the continuous, keen sense that all man has, does, and is of good is ever, in its very possibility, a free gift of God, constitutes the very core of religion. Hence the spatial imagery, which, by picturing God as *outside* the soul and Heaven as *above* the earth, helps to enforce this fundamental truth, is highly valuable—as valuable, indeed, as the imagery (spatial still) which helps to enforce the complementary truth of God's likeness to the soul and His penetration of it, by picturing God as *within* the soul and Heaven as *in* this room.

And again, the principles, ideals and picturings of Mathematics and Physics (with their insistence upon ruthless law, utter interchangeableness of all individual instances, and flawless determinism) have a very certain place and function in the full spiritual life of the soul. For they provide that *preliminary* Pantheism, that transition through fate and utter dehumanization, which will allow the soul to affirm, ultimately and as ultimate, a Libertarianism and Personalism free from all sentimentality or slovenliness, and immune against the attacks of *ultimate* Pantheism, which can *now* be vanquished as only the caricature of the poorer half of a far richer whole. Yet for the sufficient operativeness of that Mathematico-physical world and outlook, vivid pictures of space and of quasi-space—clock-time—are absolutely necessary.

8. Finally, *material* things (however dead or seemingly dead) and abstract propositions (however empty if taken alone) can, and do, continually thwart or stimulate human spirits—within this life at least. Because God is Spirit, and because man is spirit and is more and more to constitute himself a personality, it does not follow that man is to effect this solely by means of spirits and personalities, divine and human. Nor does man require material things only for the expression and communication of a personality already developed independently of such material things. But, as in all mental apprehension and conviction there is always, somewhere, the element of the stimulation of the senses, so also does the spirit awaken to its own life and powers, on occasion of contact and conflict with material things. Hence Eternal Life will (here below at least) not mean for man aloofness from matter and the bodily senses, nor even a restriction of their use to means of spiritual self-expression; but it will include also a rich and wise contact with, and an awakening by means of, matter and *things*.

9. All this costly acceptance and affirmation of Eternal Life will be found to form the sole self-consistent alternative to a (more or less obscure, but none the less real and immensely operative) refusal of man's true call, and the election of the (always easier) course of evading the soul's deepest longings and requirements. This evasion will strengthen the animal instincts and chaotic impulses of the man's complex being; and will weaken those higher claims of human reason and of spiritual organization and transfiguration. And the soul may at last arrive at an abiding disintegration and self-contradiction, and be alive only in a superficial, distracted degree and way. And this shrinkage and pain of self-contradiction and self-stultification, which the soul itself has (at least indirectly) willed, would be the soul's death.

In any case, it seems clear that, with regard to a self-stultifying soul, neither Total Annihilation nor a consciousness equal, though contrary, to that of the soul which practises and experiences Eternal Life, meets the various facts as well as does the doctrine that the effects of such full self-determinations indeed abide both for good and for evil, but that they differ not only in quality, but also in intensity. Thus, though no soul would ever cease completely, and none of its fullest spiritual and moral self-determinations would ever, in their effects upon such a soul itself, be as though they had not been, the contrast between the saved and the lost soul would be between two different quantities, as well as qualities, of life. And whereas the sense of Time, in the most fully *eternalized* of human spirits, would be so *Durational* as almost to lapse into Simultaneity, the sense of Time with *phenomenalized* human souls would lose almost all Duration and be quite close to Clock-Time—to the mechanical movement of soulless matter. This is certainly the case in this life; here we are merely assuming that what already *is*, as the deepest of our experiences, will continue to obtain as long as we last at all.

10. Eternal Life, conceived as above, will be found to include and to require a deep sense of human Weakness and of man's constant need of the Divine Prevenience, and again of the reality of Sin and of our various inclinations to it; but also to exclude all conceptions of the total corruption of human nature, of the essential impurity of the human body, or of the utter debilitation of the will. The Pauline, Augustinian, Lutheran, Calvinist, Jansenist trend, impressive though it is, will have to be explained, in part, as a good and necessary (or at least as an excusable, temporary) corrective of some contrary excess; and, for the rest, it will have to suffer incorporation within a larger whole, which, in appearance more commonplace, is yet in reality indefinitely richer—the doctrine and practice of Jesus Christ Himself. "In my flesh abideth no good thing," will have somehow to be integrated within "the spirit indeed is willing, but the flesh is weak."

11. And lastly, Eternal Life will not be simply a Moralism, with just the addition of a theoretical or practical reference to God, as the sanction and source of morality. Such a Religion has, fortunately, never existed except in the heads of some Philosophers. In its central consciousness and action, this Life will be indeed religious, hence Adoration, a Cultus—a deep, rich, spiritual Cultus, but a Cultus still. This for the ingoing, recollective movement. And the outgoing movement will not only discover God as hidden in the deepest ideals, necessities, and impulsions of Ethics, but also in the fullest strivings of Art and in the widest and most delicate attempts of the speculative and analytical reason. God is no less truly the ultimate Source, Sustainer and End of perfect Beauty and of utter Truth than of complete Goodness and of the purest Self-Donation.

12. The sense, then, of Eternal Life requires, for its normal, general, and deepest development, *Duration*, history; Space, institutions; Material Stimulations, and symbols, something sacramental; and Transcendence, a movement away from all and every culture and civilization, to the Cross, to asceticism, to interior nakedness and the Beyond. Thus our very sense of, and search for, Eternal Life will, apparently, re-enforce or re-instate all the exclusive ecclesiastical claims, the dread oppressions and persecutions of the past. The bitterest of all earthly hatreds would thus seem to be an essential condition of heavenly love. Yet Religion, taken as here supposed, would, in three ways, powerfully counteract these very certain and most grave dangers.

Religion is here assumed, on the evidence of undeniable history, to exist and to function in various stages and degrees of depth, purity, and articulation, and with variously intense and true revelations from God through prophets inspired by Himself. And men who are in the fuller, truer, purer stages and degrees may increasingly learn to recognize, in the positive and fruitful constituents and effects of other religions, something good and from God—fragments and preparations for such fuller truth as they themselves possess.

Again Religion, even in its totality, is here supposed to be indeed the deepest, yet not the only activity of man's spirit;

and each of these several activities is taken to possess its own immanental laws, duties, and rights. And Religion has the difficult, yet quite feasible and supremely fruitful, task of ever respecting, whilst ever more and more harmonizing, purifying, and utilizing, each and all of these various realms, under penalty of finding, otherwise, that itself is more and more bereft of necessary material and stimulation, and that all the other activities of man's many-levelled nature escape more and more into a wilderness of rank secularism.

And finally, in this scheme of life the first cause, and the ultimate unity, of all things is found in God, as the supremely rich, self-revealing, self-giving Eternal Life. This ultimate Living Unity is trusted, and, in the long run, is mysteriously found, to permeate all, and to bring fruitfulness to any one good activity, from the other levels and kinds of goodness, even though apparently most distant or most contrary. And it is just because of this fundamental, ineradicable interconnection, and of the soul's conviction of it, that man's spirit can drive home this or that research or interest, and can remain sure of contributing (in proportion to his selfless attention to the immanent necessities and prophetic hints of its subject-matter) something of abiding value to the other departments and levels of man's energizings, and, ultimately, to his further seeking and finding of Eternal Life.

13. The many requirements thus articulated cannot fail to appear intolerably complex both to those who attempt to stand aloof from all Religion, and to those who, with little or no analysis or theory, are directly absorbed in its practice. Like all living realities, living Religion possesses a sovereign spontaneity and rich simplicity which seem to render all attempts at analysis an insult. Indeed, Religion in particular possesses three essentials, which continually bring expansion and simplicity to its tension and complexity.

Religion is essentially Social *horizon-tally;* in the sense that each several soul is *therefore* unique because intended to realize just *this* post, function, joy, effect within the total organism of all souls. Hence no soul is expected to be a "jack-of-all-trades," but only to develop fully its own special gifts and *attraits,* within and through, and for, that larger organism of the human family, in which other souls are as fully to develop their own differing gifts and *attraits,* as so many supplements and compensations to the others. The striving of any one soul can thus be peaceful, since limited in its range to what this particular soul, at its best, most really wants and loves.

And Religion is essentially Social *vertically*—indeed here is its deepest root. It is unchangeably a faith in God, a love of God, an intercourse with God; and though the soul cannot abidingly abstract itself from its fellows, it can and ought frequently to recollect itself in a simple sense of God's presence. Such moments of direct preoccupation with God alone bring a deep refreshment and simplification to the soul.

And Religion, in its fullest development, essentially requires, not only this our little span of earthly years, but a life beyond. Neither an Eternal Life that is already fully achieved here below, nor an Eternal Life to be begun and known solely in the beyond, satisfies these requirements. But only an Eternal Life already begun and truly known in part here, though fully to be achieved and completely to be understood hereafter, corresponds to the deepest longings of man's spirit as touched by the prevenient Spirit, God. And hence, again, a peace and simplification. For that doubly Social life I try to lead here (though most real, and though itself already its own exceeding great reward) constitutes, after all, but the preliminary practice, the getting ready, for ampler, more expansive, more utterly blissful energizings in and for man, the essentially durational, quasi-eternal, and God, the utterly Abiding, the pure Eternal Life.

John Chapman

(1865-1933)

As a Benedictine monk of Downside Abbey, in England, Chapman is known as a scholar of the Vulgate, especially of the New Testament. His interest has also centered in studies of sainthood, and his *St. Benedict in the Sixth Century* is a worthy example of the work that issued from this study. "Contemplative Prayer" is an essay that has been included in the collection of his works, *The Spiritual Letters of Dom John Chapman*, edited by Dom Roger Hudleston. It is used by permission of Sheed and Ward.

CONTEMPLATIVE PRAYER

But many persons pass long years in this dark night, when they cannot meditate, and yet are afraid to contemplate; and the signs may be less easy to recognize. They have tried methods, one after another, they have tried reading and pondering, and then reading again (a good way of keeping off distractions); alas, perhaps they have almost given up mental prayer in despair. They find it hard to believe that they are in the mystical "obscure night." They do not feel urged by a frequent thought of God, nor do they dare to say that they have a disgust of creatures. On the contrary, they have found the spiritual life so dry that they have felt thrown upon creatures for consolation: they have often taken refuge in distractions which are not sinful, because recollectedness seems impossible. They have imagined themselves to be going back, because they have no devotion, no "feelings"; and perhaps they are really going back, since they have not learnt the right path forward.

But they have the essential marks of the "obscure night," for they cannot meditate—it is a physical impossibility. (When they attempt it, either they cannot even fix their thoughts on the subject at all, or else they fall into distractions at once, in spite of themselves.) Nor do they wish to meditate. They are as able to think out a subject, to work out a sermon, as anyone else is; but they feel that such considerations are not prayer.

They want to unite themselves with God, not to reason about what He has done for them or what they have to do for Him. This they can do at any time, and all day long. They can examine themselves and make good resolutions, they can think of the mysteries of Christ's Life and Death, of the words of Holy Scripture, or Heaven and Hell; but when they come to prayer, all this vanishes: they feel that if they think, they put themselves out of prayer; they do not want thoughts about God, but God.

The rules to be observed by those who find themselves in this state—and it is the ordinary state of most of those who belong to a contemplative order—are extremely simple. St. John of the Cross has explained them in the passages which immediately follow those to which I have referred above. But a few notes, founded on his teaching and also on the experience of a number of people, will possibly be useful.

(1) All those who find it impossible to meditate, not from laziness or lukewarmness, and find they cannot fix their thoughts on a subject, or understand the meaning of the words unless they cease to feel that they are praying, are meant to cease *all thinking*, and only make acts of the will.

(2) There is sometimes a period when meditation is sometimes possible, sometimes not. In this case use meditation

whenever it is possible. This state will not last long.

(3) Reading a little, or one minute's consideration of some fresh truth, or a few prayers, may be very useful to help recollection at the beginning of prayer. But they are not necessary.

(4) *Let the acts come.* Do not force them. They ought *not* to be *fervent*, excited, anxious, but calm, simple, unmeaning, unfelt. Otherwise there is danger of our sensitive nature and emotion getting mixed up with the prayer. There are to be no feelings. We are not to know what we mean. To some God may some day give more definite knowledge and love; but I speak to beginners. Let us be thankful if we are like this for no more than twenty years.

(5) The acts will tend to be *always the same.* The first stage is usually (I think), —"I am a miserable sinner: have mercy on me," or something to this effect. But the *principal* stage consists of this: "O God, I want Thee, and I do not want anything else."—This is *the essence of pure contemplative prayer,* until the presence of God becomes vivid. (Then it *may* change, and praise or exultation may be the chief or sole act. But I imagine there is no rule.)

(6) For those who are able to practise this prayer, and who feel this *want of God,* interior mortification becomes as easy as it was before difficult. Any wilful immortification or imperfection stops prayer at once, until it is repudiated.

(7) The time of prayer is passed in the act of wanting God. It is an idiotic state, and feels like the completest *waste of time,* until it gradually becomes more vivid. The strangest phenomenon is when we begin to wonder whether we mean anything at all, and if we are addressing anyone, or merely repeating mechanically a formula we do not mean. The word *God* seems to mean nothing. If we feel this curious and paradoxical condition, we are starting on the right road, and we must beware of trying to think what God is and what He has done for us, etc.; or what we are before Him, etc., because this takes us out of prayer and spoils God's work, as St. John of the Cross says. Probably this is what St. Anthony meant, when he said that *no one is praying really* if he knows what he is and what God is. The saying is often referred to ecstatic prayer; but this seems to rob the words of all interest. St. Anthony must have meant the lowest kind of contemplative prayer, for he cannot have excluded all forms but ecstasy from true prayer.

(8) Progress may perhaps be seen when the acts are less frequent, and we are conscious of one continued act rather than its repetition.

(9) Distractions are of two kinds: (a) the ordinary distractions, such as one has in meditation, which take one right away; and (b) the harmless wanderings of the *imagination alone,* while the intellect is (to all appearances) idle and empty, and the will is fixed on God. These are quite harmless.

(10) When these latter distractions remain all the time, the prayer is just as good, often much better. The will remains united; yet we feel utterly dissatisfied and humbled.

(11) But we come away *wanting nothing but God.*

(12) The real value of prayer can be securely estimated by its effect on the rest of the day. It ought to produce very definite results:—

(a) A desire for the *Will of God* exactly corresponding to the irrational and unmeaning craving for God which went on in prayer.

(b) The cessation of multiple resolutions. We used to make and remake our resolutions, never keeping them for long. Now we only make one, to do and suffer God's Will—and we keep all our old ones, or rather, they seem to keep themselves without any trouble on our part.

(c) Hence we have arrived at simplicity: all our spiritual life is unified into the one desire of union with God and His Will. It is for this union that we were made, and we have found a loadstone which draws us.

(13) As to progress in knowledge:—

(i) With some people there is *no*

knowledge of God or of His nearness, only a blind certainty that He knows our want. We cannot *think* of His being present, for thinking stops prayer.

(ii) But others have a vague undefinable knowledge that God is there. This should be preserved all day, as far as possible, by those who feel it. It grows more and more definite and yet remains just as indefinite: that is to say, the soul becomes more and more definitely conscious of being in the presence of Something undefinable, yet above all things desirable, without any the more arriving at being able to think about it or speak about it—more and more conscious of its own nothingness before God, without knowing how—more and more convinced of the nothingness of creatures, without reasoning on the subject.

(iii) Again, there are *flashes of the infinite*—(it is difficult to find an expression for this)—when for an instant a conception passes, like lightning, of reality, eternity, etc. These leave an impression that the world is dust and ashes. The effect must be carefully preserved outside the time of prayer. Some people are more liable to these perceptions than others are. In some people they are habitual, and the less valued for this, and they do not produce the fruit in conduct that they ought.

(iv) In the developed "prayer of quiet" the soul does know that God is there. The pleasurable feelings of which St. Theresa speaks do not seem to be essential to the prayer of quiet. But when they are there, the soul may either be urged by them to more vehement desire, or be satisfied, and rather praise than pray.

(14) It is worth noting that Praise is in itself more perfect than simply "wanting" God; for the latter is rather hope than charity. Praise is the occupation of heaven, when the desire is fully satisfied. Even on earth, to give glory to God is the whole duty of the creature. But to desire God is right, for man must desire in this world, where he cannot be satisfied with creatures, and where he cannot fully attain to God. This is the virtue of hope—the most practical of virtues in this world, the virtue which most obtains for us an increase of charity. And the "want of God" includes charity; for God is not only desired as our own good, but as being in Himself infinite goodness; and this desire of Him is in itself a praise of Him for being what He is.

(15) Outside the time of prayer:—

(a) Meditation must never be dropped. It need not be elaborate consideration, but a mere glance at the mysteries of our Lord, especially of the Passion. Most people will find it very easy and helpful to make the Stations of the Cross in private.

(b) Similarly, examination of conscience becomes automatic so long as contemplative prayer is kept up. Good resolutions make themselves.

(c) Imperfections and even sins are such a help to that humility which is the condition of prayer, that they seem almost a help rather than a hindrance. To feel utterly crushed and annihilated, incapable of any good, wholly dependent on God's undeserved and infinite mercy, is the best and only preparation for prayer. It means an entire confidence, an exultation in being nothing because God is all, which brings the only peace which is true peace.

(d) A little practice makes it possible to meditate a little (or at least to retain the thought of some mystery or some great truth) without losing prayer, i.e. the consciousness of God. But this should not be indulged in during prayer time, as it is a half-and-half state, which produces far less effect in the soul than pure prayer does, in which there is no thought.

(e) Every kind of self-indulgence, or fully wilful imperfection (that is, doing what God asks us not to do, or omitting what we know He wishes us to do), makes prayer impossible until it is disowned. For contemplative prayer implies a state of wanting God and wanting God's Will (which is the same thing) wholly and entirely.

(f) But it does not follow that the beginner is to be expected to show at all a high degree of perfection. God does not show the soul all its faults nor all it has eventually to give up. It gives up something, and in time He will ask more. Meanwhile it has faults which are obvious enough to others, though probably not to itself.

A few hints may be added about the prayer itself.

(i) Beginners want to be alone or in the dark. Practice makes this less necessary. But it is rare that a contemplative is independent of externals. It is easier to be recollected when there is no noise, no distraction. The imagination has to be kept quiet. It is generally easiest to pray before the Blessed Sacrament. The night is a good time. The early morning is perhaps the best of all.

(ii) The simplest way of making an act of attention to God, though without thinking of Him, is by an act of inattention to everything else. This is the same act that one makes when one tries to go to sleep.

(iii) As distractions, when involuntary, do not spoil our prayer, and when merely of the imagination scarcely even disturb it, we ought to be perfectly satisfied to have them. We are not to be resigned to them, but more—to *will* them; for a contemplative is never to be resigned to God's Will, but to will It. The result of this practice will be to decrease distractions by decreasing worry. If we only want God's Will, there is no room for worry.

(iv) One must accept joyfully and with the whole will exactly the state of prayer which God makes possible for us here and now; we will to have that, and no other. It is just what God wills for us. We should like to be rapt to the third heaven; but we will to be as we are, dry, or distracted, or consoled, as God wills. It is just the same out of prayer. We may *wish* for a great many things—for a good dinner, or for more suffering, or the prayer of quiet—without any imperfection, provided these are involuntary wishes. But we *will* only what we have, what God's providence has arranged for us—only no sin, we repeat, only no imperfection.

SAINTS IN THE TWENTIETH CENTURY: AFTER WORLD WAR I UNTIL NOW

UPON THE SHOULDERS OF THE SAINTS THE COMING OF THE KINGDOM DEPENDS

Sundar Singh

(1889-1933)

ONE of the most remarkable conversions of the twentieth century is that of Singh. Religiously trained in early years by a devout Hindu mother, he eagerly sought spiritual peace in the teachings of that faith. After publicly opposing Christianity he experienced a vision of Christ somewhat like Paul's. His conversion estranged him from his father, whom he was able to convert only after many years. As a sadhu (holy man) he went about preaching the gospel throughout India. Later his travels took him to Europe and Great Britain.

Canon Streeter, of Oxford, once paid the finest tribute which can be given to any man when he said of Singh, "He is the most spiritual person I have ever known." The following selection gives insights into how Singh developed the spiritual character about which Canon Streeter speaks. It is the final chapter of a book in which Singh tells of the religious experiences of various persons, including a vivid description of his own conversion. The chapter is reprinted by permission of Harper & Brothers. (Copyright 1929 by Harper & Brothers.)

THE INNER LIFE

From *With and Without Christ*

Life, in every creature, is an unseen and hidden reality; whatever of life is seen outwardly is but its working and partial manifestation. When the atheist fails to understand what life is, he attributes it to matter. But the source of life is life, and lifeless matter cannot produce life. Only those who have an intimate relation with the Source of Life can understand this mystery.

We cannot grasp the real inner life of any creature, because it is hidden under a partial manifestation of itself. The full manifestation of the spiritual life is possible only in the spiritual world, for this material world is insufficient for its full expression.

We know an animal, for instance, only from the outside, without understanding what it is in itself. The animal has warmth, movement, growth, and other signs of life. These only we see and not the life of which they are the outward signs. We can know a thing outwardly without knowing what the thing is in itself. But, by living in Him who is the Source of Life, we can know Him as He is in Himself according to our needs and capacities. By knowing Him thus we come to know ourselves who are created after His "image and likeness" and also the real nature of our inner life.

The spirit of egotism hinders us from attaining a knowledge of reality. We should not be like Carneades, who said to his teacher: "If I have reasoned rightly, you are wrong; if not, O Diogenes, return to me the mina I paid you for my lesson." Carneades was not willing to admit his mistake. In any case, he wanted to lay the blame on his teacher. If he was right, the teacher was wrong. But, if he was wrong, even then the teacher was wrong, because he had not taught him to argue correctly.

It is very difficult to explain the deep experience of the inner life. As Goethe has said: "The highest cannot be spoken." But it can be enjoyed and put into action. This is what I mean. One day, during my meditation and prayer, I felt His presence strongly. My heart overflowed with heavenly joy. I saw that in this world of sorrow and suffering there is a hidden and inexhaustible mine of great joy of which the world knows nothing, because even men who experience it are not able to speak of it adequately and convincingly. I was anxious to go down to the neighbouring village to share that joy with others. But, because of my physical illness, there arose a conflict between my soul and my body. The soul wanted to go, the body lagged behind. But finally I overcame and dragged my sick body and told the people in the village what Christ's presence had done for me and would do for them. They knew that I was ill and that there was some inner compulsion which urged me to speak to them. Thus, though I was unable to explain all that Christ's presence had meant to me, that deep experience had been translated into action and men had been helped. Where the tongue is lacking, life, through action, reveals the reality. As St. Paul says: "The letter killeth, but the spirit giveth life" (2 Cor. iii. 6).

As some insects with their antennæ feel their surroundings and distinguish between hurtful and useful things, so spiritual men, through their inner senses, avoid dangerous and destructive influences and enjoy God's sweet and life-giving presence; they are constrained by their blissful experience to bear witness to God. As Tertullian has said: "Whenever the soul comes to itself and attains something of its natural soundness, it speaks of God."

Almost every one has an inner capacity—some more, some less—to sense spiritual truths without knowing how they have attained them. As some one has said: "They know without knowing how." For instance, Colburn (1804-1840), when six years old, was asked how many seconds there are in eleven years. In four seconds he gave the correct answer. When questioned as to how he had arrived at the answer the boy said that he did not know; all he could say was that the answer came to his mind. Just so God reveals spiritual realities to those who seek to live according to His will.

The will to live, which is present in every man, is an impulse urging him to carry life to its perfection, that is, to that state in which the purpose of God for that life will be fulfilled, so that he will be eternally happy in Him. On the other hand, to those who are without the experience of the joyful inner life in God, life is a burden. Schopenhauer was one of these; he said: "Life is hell." There is nothing strange in such people wanting to commit suicide. As a result of the teaching of the Greek philosopher, Hegesias, many young men committed suicide. Also several philosophers, like Zeno, Empedocles and Seneca, put an end to their lives. But the strange thing is that their philosophy did not show them how to remove those things which made them unhappy, instead of destroying their lives. Such is the philosophy of the world (James iii. 15). Although some, who are tired of this life on account of its struggles and anxieties, may repress the will-to-live, they cannot get rid of the will-to-believe. Even if they have no belief in God or in any other spiritual reality, they have at least belief in their unbelief, though Pyrrho said: "We cannot even be sure that we are not sure."

The inner life or personality of man cannot be freed by changing the place or by killing the body, but only by putting off the "old man" and putting on the new man, thus passing from death to life. Those who go astray, instead of satisfying their inner craving in the Creator, try to satisfy it in their own crooked ways. The result is that, instead of being happy and satisfied, they become miserable. For instance, a thief who is stealing and hoarding things as a means of happiness is not only missing his happiness, but by his acts of theft destroying the very capacity for it. That capacity is deadened by his sinful conduct. And if he loses the sense of the sinfulness of theft, and his conscience does not feel remorse, he has already committed spiritual suicide. He has not only killed the capacity, but has killed the soul, which had the capacity.

Real joy and peace do not depend on power, kingly wealth, or other material possessions. If this were so, all men of wealth in the world would be happy and contented, and princes like Buddha, Mahavira, and Bhartari would not have renounced their kingdoms. But this real and permanent joy is found only in the Kingdom of God, which is established in the heart, when we are born again.

The secret and reality of this blissful life in God cannot be understood without receiving, living, and experiencing it. If anyone tries to understand it only with the intellect, he will find his effort useless. A scientist had a bird in his hand. He saw that it had life, and, wanting to find out in what part of the bird's body the life was, and what the life itself was, he began dissecting the bird. The result was that the very life of which he was in search disappeared mysteriously. Those who try to understand the inner life merely intellectually will meet with a similar failure. The life for which they are looking will vanish in the analysis.

In comparison with this big world, the human heart is only a small thing. Though the world is so large, it is utterly unable to satisfy this tiny heart. Man's ever growing soul and its capacities can be satisfied only in the infinite God. As water is restless until it reaches its level, so the soul has not peace until it rests in God.

The material body cannot keep company for ever with the spirit. After fulfilling its purpose for some time, as the instrument of the soul for its work in the world, the body begins to refuse, through weakness and old age, to go along with the spirit any further. This is because the body cannot keep pace with the eternally-growing soul.

Although the soul and the body cannot live together for ever, the fruits of the work which they have done together will remain for ever. So it is necessary to lay carefully the foundation of our eternal life. But the pity of it is that man, by the misuse of his freedom, loses it for ever. Freedom means the capacity to do either good or bad deeds. By constantly choosing to do bad deeds, he becomes a slave of sin and destroys his freedom and life (John viii. 21, 34).

By giving up his sins, on the other hand, and by following the truth, he is made free for ever (John viii. 32). The works of those who are thus made free and spend all their life in His service, that is, of those who die in the Lord, will follow them (Rev. xiv. 13). To die in the Lord does not mean death, for the Lord is "the Lord of the living and not of the dead," but to die in the Lord means losing oneself in His work. As the Lord said: "Whosoever will lose his life for my sake, the same shall save it" (Luke ix. 23). . . .

We ought to make the best possible use of God-given opportunities, and should not waste our precious time by our neglect or carelessness. Many people say: there is plenty of time to do this or that; don't worry. But they do not realise that, if they do not make good use of this short time, the habit formed now will be so ingrained that when more time is given to us this habit will become our second nature and we shall waste that time also. "He that is unjust in the least is unjust also in much" (Luke xvi. 10).

Now it is meet that everyone should fulfil in his life the purpose of his Creator and spend that life for the glory of God and the good of others. Every one should follow his calling and carry on his work according to his God-given gifts and capacities. "There are diversities of gifts but the same Spirit" (1 Cor. xii. 4, 11). The same breath is blown into flute, cornet, and bagpipe, but different music is produced according to the different instruments.

In the same way the one Spirit works in us, God's children, but different results are produced, and God is glorified through them according to each one's temperament and personality.

In this world there is very little harmony between the inner and the outer life. But, if we live according to the will of God, then the time will come when there will be perfect harmony between the inner and the outer life for ever. The outer will be exactly like the inner and the inner exactly like the outer. And by His grace we shall become perfect like our Father in Heaven.

Rudolf Otto

(1869-1938)

In an analysis of sainthood two qualities usually stand in opposition to each other—man's humility in contrast to God's majesty. No writer has shown keener insight into the analysis of these two polar factors in mystical experience than Otto in *The Idea of the Holy*, which is described as "an inquiry into the non-rational factor in the idea of the divine and its relation to the rational." In explanation of the "holy," Otto views the "numinous" as the irrational, indescribable aspect of God which man in his creature-like nature must *feel*.

Otto was born in Germany, educated at the universities of Erlangen and Göttingen, taught systematic theology at Göttingen and Breslau, 1897-1917. In 1917 he was called to teach the philosophy of religion at Marburg, retiring in 1929. Of recent German contributors to the understanding of the devotional life, Otto and Friedrich Heiler, both former teachers at Marburg, rank supreme. For a number of years preceding his death, Otto conducted liturgical services of worship in an ancient chapel on the outskirts of Marburg.

The following selection is from the appendix of *The Idea of the Holy*, translated by John W. Harvey, and is used by permission of Oxford University Press.

THE RESURRECTION AS A SPIRITUAL EXPERIENCE

From *The Idea of the Holy*

I know that my Redeemer liveth": "I *believe* in Jesus Christ, risen from the dead": such is the Christian's confession.

"I know" and "I believe" or "have faith"—these are not here mutually exclusive expressions. This "knowing" is not that with which scientific theory is concerned, based upon empirical sense-knowledge; it is rather *faith-knowledge*, and faith-knowledge does not rely on the evidence of the senses, but is, in the scriptural phrase, "the evidence of things not seen," that is, not presented to sense-perception; and it would lose its essential nature and be transformed into a mere sorry empirical knowledge, if it relied on any other evidence than "the witness of the Holy Spirit," which is not that of sense-experience. And so we cannot afford to account Christ's resurrection, and our own, known facts, in this lower "scientific" sense of knowledge. The simplest understanding feels this. To speak of "resurrection" is to utter a mystery, and mystery is a subject for faith, not science. And, for Christianity, how this faith itself comes to be is no less a mystery, indeed the greatest of all mysteries. But if "faith" were knowledge, directly attested by the senses or based upon the tradition of a former occurrence attested by the senses, this mystery would wholly disappear.

And so we hold that in endeavouring

to account for our assurance of the Risen Christ two sorts of interpretation must be excluded, the naïvely supernaturalistic and the rationalistic. The former is that which has recourse to the "Empty Tomb." It holds that Christ's tomb was proved to be empty by the evidence of the senses, that the Risen Christ was perceived by the senses, and that the truth of the facts so certified in sense-experience was then handed down by human testimony. On this view the conviction of the resurrection was from the first not *faith*, but a piece of empirical knowledge. This is the most serious objection that can be brought against the naïve "supernaturalist" interpretation, a more serious objection than the uncertain and legendary character of the "Empty Tomb" narrative or the fact that the earliest and most authentic witness to the resurrection of Christ—that of St. Paul in 1 Cor. xv—makes no mention of the empty tomb, although there the Apostle is at pains to assemble all possible reasons for assurance in the reality of the Resurrection.

But the ordinary rationalistic interpretation is equally inadmissible. A deep "impression" of the person of Jesus had remained, so it is said, with the disciples and especially with Peter, and from this impression grew their conviction after His death, "Such an one cannot have remained dead." And this conviction, thus born in their minds, took imaginative and figurative form in visions, which must therefore be regarded as purely subjective. But this explanation is patently forced and unsatisfactory, and seems to us to miss altogether the uniqueness and coherence of the experience centering in the Resurrection. The two lines of interpretation have this in common, however: they both entirely ignore the fundamental fact about the experience, that it was a *mystery;* both agree in disregarding altogether its mystery character.

We can only get beyond the opposition between supernaturalism and rationalism by frankly recognizing that the experiences concerned with the Resurrection were *mystical experiences* and

their source "the Spirit." It is only "of the Spirit" that the higher knowledge is born. It is the eye of Spirit, not the eye of sense that beholds the eternal things; but what it sees is not a mere insecure, half-woven fabric of "convictions," but the adamantine certainty of the eternal truth itself.

II

To understand the matter truly we need to make clear to ourselves by examples drawn from occurrences in the Bible record to what more general class of experience those that are concerned with the Resurrection belong, and then to grasp what the essential character of this wider class is. Isaiah tells (ch. vi) how in that mysterious experience in the Temple his inward eye was opened to behold Yahweh in His holiness and majesty, how he received His command and became thereby the messenger of Yahweh to His people. This supreme, mysterious vision becomes thus for Isaiah his summons and his ordination, and his whole subsequent activity as prophet in its wider significance is founded upon this experience. And the occurrence is not one without a parallel, but rather is typical of all the great men who received God's summons (compare Jer. i, Ezek. i and ii, Amos i, and Hosea i).

But what really took place in these mystical experiences? Has God a body? Is He really seated upon a throne, or has He any place in a physical sense? Do beings such as the Cherubim and Seraphim are described surround Him in visible form? Has He a voice audible to our actual sense of hearing? Even those who, so far as concerns the Resurrection of Christ, think to base their faith upon an actually perceived Empty Tomb and a Body which, however "transfigured," yet remained an object to see and touch—even they will answer these questions with a decided negative as regards the vision of Isaiah. Even they will admit that these forms of imagery, in which the experience of Isaiah clothes itself, are nothing more than forms of imagery, born of the ideas of the time and merely a vesture for something seen and apprehended by other means than by stimulation of the senses, with which it indeed has nothing to do.

On the other side, the naturalistic rationalist will set up some sort of plausible psychological "explanation," differing according to the empirical psychology that is at his disposal; or, resorting to a still simpler mode of explanation, he will be inclined to say that such occurrences never occurred at all. But whoever knows anything of the Spirit and its miraculous nature, whoever feels in himself the Spirit active in those mysterious experiences that build up the Christian's life, will reject such explanations. He alone has the key to the truth of the matter. Just as the Scriptures as a whole, as the Christian believes, require the Spirit if they are to be taught or understood, so too is it with these occurrences. Only a first-hand spiritual experience teaches a man to see and enables him to estimate a spiritual experience of a former day. Possession of the Spirit at first hand becomes here a faculty of "retrospective prophecy," which is recognition in the sense of re-cognition or knowing again for oneself. And so only on the basis of a first-hand religious experience, of and from the Spirit, is there any possibility of obtaining a real and genuine historical knowledge of these things, for only such an experience is acquainted with and can estimate the effect of *all* the factors of the explanation. What the Spirit gives is not a view that transcends the historical, but the genuine historical view. And the naturalistic view gives on the other hand a falsification of history, for it has ignored an essential part of the facts it seeks to explain.

III

Let us now turn to the New Testament. Once we have come to understand aright, that is, in the Spirit, the experiences of the great prophets, we can recognize plainly how similar they are to the narratives of the great visions of Jesus at the outset and at the full height of His ministry—the vision at His Baptism and the vision at His "Transfiguration." As with the prophets, so with Jesus: these, too, are manifestly spiritual and mystical experiences; but these, too, were objectively real occurrences. And they are also to be counted as belonging to the same class of experiences for the reason that they too are manifestly visions of Call and Ordination. As before, we do not doubt that all that is recounted in perceptual terms stands upon just the same footing as the perceptual imagery that invests the mystical experience of Isaiah, the essential and unshakable truth of which lies not in that vesture, but in the knowledge and assurance born "of the Spirit."

And if we pass on to the Resurrection-experience of Paul on the road to Damascus, do we not at once recognize the same characteristic features? Have we here sense-perception or spiritual experience? Paul nowhere describes how and in what form he beheld the Risen Christ. That does not in itself make it the less likely that he did see Him in some form, probably as a royal figure of radiant glory rather than merely as a dazzling light. The material of his vision was no doubt supplied him by the current ideas of his time concerning royal splendour and messianic kinghood, and then his faculty of vision gave this material an individual and special form. That is but to say that the vision would have a vesture of outward form just as that of Isaiah did; but this does not, for Paul any more than for Isaiah, touch the inmost import of the experience, which is here: "*He lives;* He lives as the accepted of God, the preserved of God, the exalted of God, the transfigured of God, as the conqueror of Judgment, of the Cross, and of Death." And at the same time that further point of resemblance with the occurrences already mentioned is manifest, which, strangely enough, is here not generally noticed. For this vision of Paul, like those others, is not merely a vision of the Risen Christ, but again precisely inaugural, a vision of Calling and Ordination.

At the same time this experience of Paul has its place among a second class of experiences, which in turn stand fully illumined in the Pauline writings. For it is but the first link in a whole chain of spiritual happenings which develop in him and in his congregations. These are the "charismata" or "gifts of the Spirit," and among them is included the gift of "horasis" or mystic vision which Paul himself possessed. And what took place on the road to Damascus is not only the first link in the chain, but more fundamental and potent than all that followed. There it was that the "pneuma" first broke through, the Spirit which man makes not nor can bestow upon himself, which blows whither it lists, and kindles what it wills, and whose "prick" was already felt in Paul's heart.

Paul puts his experience on a parity with those of Peter and others, an indication that these also were of the same class as his own. And we could ourselves recognize as much even without Paul's express testimony. According to Paul's statement Peter was the first to receive the new revelation of the Risen Christ, and what we know otherwise of Peter is in accord with this. He has the gift of "vision," as the story in Acts x shows, and it had been manifested more than once while his Master was still on earth, as at the time of the Transfiguration on Mount Tabor. And the Synoptic record gives other more general indications of his rare spiritual endowment. Further, for Peter and the others to whom the experience came, the vision of the Risen Christ is once again an inaugural experience of Call and Ordination, as is indicated in the words, "Go ye therefore and teach all nations," which we are to take as a spiritual realization of mission just in the same way as the command of Yahweh to Isaiah: "Go and tell his people," and which, no less than the experience of the prophets, attest themselves as having been really "heard" in spiritual perception at a definite place and time. And again in the case of these original witnesses to the Resurrection, the vision of the Risen Christ is no more an isolated experience than in the case of Paul. For Paul and his converts are not the first to receive

"the Spirit" and its sevenfold gifts. These gifts are the possession of the earliest Christian community from the first, and characterize it, as Paul himself avows, when he justifies his position as an apostle in showing that he and his converts *also possess* the same spiritual gifts which the Christians of Jerusalem had from the first.

And so the consciousness of the Risen Christ loses its isolated character and is already manifested as one of a class of spiritual experiences, a mystical and spiritual apprehension of truth, beyond the opposition of supernaturalism and rationalism.

IV

The apostles proclaim their Lord not only as "raised from the dead," but as "exalted" and "ascended" into heaven. That is in harmony with the picture of the universe which they shared with antiquity as a whole. But whoever thinks it necessary to retain the bodily, physical idea in "raised from the dead" ought to realize that he is bound to do the same with the expression "exalted." For that also conveys in its literal sense a *spatial* idea; it presupposes the old notion that "Heaven," God's eternal realm, is somewhere high above us in space. This notion was natural enough in antiquity; but for us heaven and the eternal world of God is no more in space or time than God Himself is: it is in God's eternity, which is apart from space and time. This does not at all mean that the expressions "resurrection," "raising from the dead," lose their meaning. In contrast to the idea of "immortality," which properly is the denial of any state of real death, they affirm the *restoration* from real death to real life, or rather the admittance for the first time into plenary and genuine life. Nor have they in the Biblical view reference solely to the body. It is not the body merely, but the *man* that dies; and it is as soul as well as body that he sinks into the state of death, the "dread night of death," from which he can only be delivered and raised up by the power of God. If he is to live, man needs to be thus *awakened*, brought up out of Hades and from the shadow of death, and raised again "from the dead." To be sure, according to Paul's idea, there is *combined* with this at the same time a bodily restoration. But, as is often noticed, this is for him *not* a raising up of the *old* body, a "resurrection of the flesh." Rather he would on his own presuppositions have emphatically rejected such a notion; for "the flesh"—which is for him the essence of antagonism to God—is to pass away like the seed of corn sown in the earth, and the "resurrection of the body" is for him rather the bestowal of a *new* and quite other "spiritual" body, provided and prepared of God. This is also the direction in which our thought must turn if we are to attempt to represent to ourselves the new life of the resurrection. We too are unable to think of the completed perfected life of the Spirit without ascribing to the Spirit some *instrument* or "organ" whereby it realizes itself in practice. Now "body" is the instrument of spirit, and the phrase "spiritual body" affirms in an unambiguous manner that this instrument is not a fleshly body, not even "transfigured flesh"—a contradiction in itself—but is itself spiritual in kind. And that implies that it is not bound up with any one point in space or time, and so is in no sense a *physical* body, which cannot be severed from material and spatial determination.

But whatever our thought may be upon this matter, one thing at any rate holds good: the meaning of the Christian knowledge that is by Faith lies in this, that Christ Himself who really died was brought again by God to real life and perfected unto the glory of the eternal life of God; and that we live in expectation of the same with Him. This is a "knowing" which, for us to-day no less than for the apostles, can be born of the Spirit, but only of the Spirit. Whether the body belongs to the being of this Christ and to our own completed being is a physiological not a religious question, and one which pertains not at all to our confession of faith. But to any one who

has to meet this issue we would say, the "Risen Christ" is to be "our comfort," not a source of trouble in our conscientious fidelity to truth; and for a true understanding of the experiences bearing on the Resurrection we would refer him to the nature of spiritual revelation as recounted in Isaiah vi.

As regards the narratives of the "Empty Tomb," we shall judge of these as of the narratives of a later date which gathered about the birth of Jesus, appraising them as a holy legend, in which the supra-rational relation of the eternal to the temporal is mirrored in the medium of contemporary thought. They have an enduring value to us from the incomparable beauty and power with which they symbolize the essence of the "mystery." We would not be without them in our Bible, nor yet in the pictorial art of the churches, nor in the hymns that express our devotion. And we can retain them thus without being false to the obligation of the most rigid honesty if we remain fully conscious of that other obligation, without fulfilling which we neither can nor indeed should have either Biblical instruction or Christian doctrine. And that is the obligation we are under to train ourselves and the mind of our time to a sincere and devout understanding of three things. In the first place we need to realize the fringe of legend that surrounds the entire narrative of Holy Scripture and recurs as a constant problem from the first page of the Bible to the last. Secondly, we need to appreciate the signal value and beauty and the profound import which distinguish the Biblical narrative, even where it is of the nature of legend; and, finally, the fact that even in the holy saga and legend, shaped and fashioned unconsciously by the spirit of a people or a fellowship, there is present the very same eternal Spirit of God, which Hebrew prophecy and poetry and history also manifest, that Spirit which, in every form of its expression, is the Spirit of revelation and truth.

Burnett H. Streeter

(1874-1939)

KNOWN as both a New Testament critic and a religious philosopher, Streeter was deeply concerned with the analysis and description of religious experience. An Englishman by birth, he was educated at King's College School, London, and Oxford. His professional career as teacher and fellow was spent at Oxford, during which he also served as canon of Hereford (1915-34). Many of his writings during this period dealt with the devotional life, among them being *Reality, The Spirit, The Sadhu,* and *On Prayer.*

Streeter's own devotional life is beautifully portrayed by the following incident: On one of his last visits to the United States he spent one entire Good Friday in his hotel room, fasting and reading Thomas à Kempis' *Imitation of Christ.*

"Auto-suggestion and Prayer" is from the chapter on "Religion and the New Psychology" in *Reality.* This evaluation of religious experience as tested for validity in its moral, social, and intellectual fruition is representative of Streeter's balanced Christian theistic viewpoint. It is used by permission of The Macmillan Co. (Copyright 1926 by The Macmillan Co.)

AUTO-SUGGESTION AND PRAYER

From *Reality*

Through the fame of M. Coué, auto-suggestion has become a household word. But his theoretical account of the process, most fully expounded by his disciple Baudouin, differs more in balance of emphasis than in fundamental conception from the theory of hypnotic suggestion previously maintained by Prof. M'Dougall and other authorities. These hold that in hypnotic suggestion there is no magic influence, there is no subtle fluid passing from the physician to the patient, there is no imposition of superior will-power. What happens is this. The physician presents an idea to the patient's mind at a time and under conditions when the patient will accept it without question and without reserve. The critical faculty, the resistive impulse, is temporally inhibited, with the result that the idea penetrates right down into the subconscious, and then *begins to work.* But the extent to which the idea "works" depends, not on any magic gift in the physician, but on the receptivity of the patient, that is, on the degree to which the suggestion has been accepted.

The Baudouin-Coué theory says that this means, in effect, that all suggestion is in the last resort auto-suggestion; for to say that a suggestion proceeding from the physician operates only as and when accepted by the patient is virtually to say that it operates as and when it becomes an auto-suggestion. Accordingly, in this view, all that is required is to teach the patient how to practise auto-suggestion, that is, how to present the right idea to his own mind under the conditions favourable to maximum receptivity. And it is claimed that, as a matter of experience, in cases where the patient has learnt the lesson, cures are effected more rapidly and more thoroughly by auto-suggestion than where the physician continues himself to employ hetero-suggestion.

The value of auto-suggestion as a therapeutic method, or the possible dangers attending its indiscriminate use, are matters on which I am not competent to pronounce. I have mentioned M. Coué solely because through him public interest has been excited in phenomena the existence of which was previously known only to specialists, and of which the real nature is still very imperfectly understood. But however obscure the nature of the phenomena, and however difficult the question of the right limits of the use of suggestion in medicine, it appears to be an established fact that human beings, though to a very variable degree, are "suggestible." They are capable of accepting an idea in the depths of the subconscious, and an *idea* once so accepted by the subconscious *works*—setting up, as it were, a kind of fermentation which may result, not merely in mental and nervous, but even in physical, changes.

A striking experiment is recorded in *The Lancet*. In the presence of two other medical men, the experimenter told a hypnotised subject that he was about to be touched by a red-hot iron; one of the other doctors, as previously arranged, then put his finger gently on the subject's arm. He cried out as if touched by a hot iron; the arm was bandaged and the bandage sealed. Next day the bandage was removed, and on the spot touched was found a small blister of the same size and nature as one subsequently produced on the same subject by an actual touch of hot iron. It would seem that during the night the subconscious mind of the patient, convinced that an actual burn had been inflicted, had set in motion the complicated train of operations in bloodvessels and tissues which would have been the natural reaction of the organism to an actual physical burn. Persons as susceptible to suggestion as this one are extremely rare; but I have quoted the case in order to put side by side with it the still more remarkable, but well attested, story of St. Francis of Assisi, who, after a long period of meditation on the Passion of Our Lord culminating in a vision of a crucified cherub, was found to have imprinted on his hands and feet dark blister-like protrusions corresponding to the wounds of Christ. This experience of St. Francis and other incidents of a similar character seem to bear out the contention that auto-suggestion may be as powerful as, if not even more powerful than, hetero-suggestion; it also fits in with the theory that the principal agent in suggestion is the patient's own acceptance of the idea suggested, not some mysterious influence proceeding from the physician. Indeed it would seem as if the main law governing the operation of auto-suggestion might be expressed in the formula: "according to thy faith be it done unto thee." This is a discovery which raises questions of a far-reaching character both for Philosophy and Religion: for if under certain circumstances an idea—an entity purely mental—can directly initiate changes in the material sphere, we seem to catch a fleeting glimpse of mind in the act of creating.

We may now proceed to ask, What is the exact relation between the method of auto-suggestion as recommended by M. Coué and the Christian practice of prayer? M. Baudouin lays stress on three empirical generalisations.

(1) The power of an idea to work is largely dependent on its emotional associations. A mere intellectual concept, unless there is connected with it some feeling like hope, fear, attraction or repulsion, will produce little or no effect. So the saints have always held that mere intellectual belief about God is of small value; the faith which makes prayer effective must be grounded in love.

(2) Coué holds that a general suggestion, such as "Day by day, in all respects, I am getting better and better," is more potent than particular suggestions which concentrate attention on the details of the patient's ailment. Care is taken, however, to give him a preliminary suggestion, mentioning in detail the main forms and conditions of physical and mental health, so that the "general suggestion" which follows is actually to the patient's mind a kind of summarising formula full of concrete content, not a mere abstract phrase. Similarly in prayer the saints have deprecated too great concentration on points of detail, and recommended concentration on comprehensive ideas such as the love of God or His saving power; but this will generally follow confession of particular sins and will include mention of particular needs.

(3) A preliminary quiescence of the whole mind is required, leading up to a concentration of attention on a single idea. But this concentration is effective in proportion as the patient becomes able to maintain it with a minimum of voluntary effort. Baudouin points out the resemblance between this state of mind and that arrived at by some of the Indian methods of Yoga. He does not point out its resemblance to a state of mind such as that recommended as a preliminary to devotion by some of the Christian mystics; but consider this by St. Peter of Alcantara.

In meditation let the person rouse himself from things temporal, and let him collect himself within himself—that is to say, within the very centre of his soul, where lies impressed the very image of God. Here let him hearken to the voice of God as though speaking to him from on high, yet present in his soul, as though there were no other in the world save God and himself.

We notice that the points of contact between prayer and auto-suggestion are at their maximum in meditation and the "prayer of quiet," that is, when prayer takes on its highest and most characteristically Christian form and has moved furthest from the primitive pagan conception of inducing the gods to do man's will.

Our theory of the relation of the Divine activity to the reign of law in Nature could hardly be submitted to a more crucial test. Clearly there is some relation between the laws of human Psychology such as those above described and that communion with God of which the saints speak—with its resultant enhancement of mental and spiritual energy, and often of physical endurance as well. Are we, then, to say that prayer is auto-suggestion—and nothing more?

Once again I must point out that the answer we give to this question will depend entirely upon the answer we give to the prior question. Does God exist? If there is no God, then, of course, prayer is based upon illusion. But if God does exist, does it matter what name we give to the psychological mechanism by means of which the belief that He exists —and all that it involves—comes to be accepted below the merely surface consciousness in the inmost depths of my being?.Suppose the belief to be true; then, once accepted into the subconscious, it will "work" and will produce results in thought and action; and the results will surely be good. When to the psychological mechanism of such acceptance the name "auto-suggestion" is given, the question of the truth or falsehood of the idea accepted is simply left unraised. But he who prays *has* raised that question, and has answered that the idea *is* true. Prayer is—or at least includes—the absolute surrender of the self, subconscious as well as conscious, to an idea—the idea of God as a present, personal, spiritual Being. But it is the truth of the idea, not the mechanism of its acceptance, that makes it to be prayer.

There is a further consideration. Suppose God to be an infinite, omnipresent, conscious Being likely to wish for some kind of personal converse with His little children according to the capacity of their powers of recognition. If God is "the Beyond that is also Within," it is only from within that we can know Him. How otherwise, then, should we expect Him to communicate with finite minds if not in accordance with the laws which govern the internal operations of those minds? A human friend I can know by sight and touch, but from the nature of the case I can never see or touch the Infinite, the All-Pervading. What must here correspond to the external vision of my friend is my *idea* of God, the thought of Him that I entertain. And if God should be properly conceived as Creative Love, then it is the qualitative aspect of my conception of Him that is most important; and that means that He can only communicate Himself to me if my "idea" of Him is such as to educe an appropriate emotional response. Again, only if I surrender myself completely to this idea, so that it possesses my subconscious as well as my conscious mind, can I really appropriate it. For only so does it cease to be *mere* idea and become part of my actual life. Life, we have seen, cannot be intellectually understood; but it can be appreciated by life of a similar quality. The Infinite Life, then, can reveal Himself to those within whom life similar in quality to His own has begun to be generated. This involves a submission of the mind to an idea of God; but it is an aspiring submission to a living idea.

The methods of auto-suggestion, considered from a purely psychological point of view, are very like those advocated by the Mystics as preliminary to the "prayer of quiet." But these are only *methods*. Between M. Coué and the Mystics there are two essential differences.

(1) In the system of M. Coué the idea selected for concentration is spontaneously chosen, whether by the patient himself or his physician; and it is selected without any special regard to its truth or falsehood. In prayer the idea of God is not chosen but given, and it is accepted because it is felt to stand for ultimate truth.

(2) Prayer is *ascensio mentis ad deum*, a flight upwards, an offering of the mind to that which is more real than the self; auto-suggestion is a swoop downwards, a submission of the mind to an idea which is a creature of its own. Prayer brings the inspiration which comes from contact with a personality greater than one's own; auto-suggestion in the last resort is of the nature of "dope."

If Life is a principle of individuation, the higher the life the richer will be its individuality. The ideal life, therefore, must not be thought of as an exact reproduction of a standard pattern; even the imitation of Christ will be bad, if conceived mechanically. Standardisation is for machinery, not for souls; and what would be perfection in a billiard ball is futility in a saint. This fact has a bearing, which I think has not been pointed out before, on the ideal and the methods of prayer. Desires vary with the individual; reason, so far as it functions correctly, is the same for all men. Character is individualised life, considered from the standpoint of its quality; but both the test and

expression of the quality of a personality are to be seen in its dominant desires. Now no desire is ever quite the same after it has been offered up before God in prayer; a desire which has found expression in prayer is inevitably purified and elevated. Prayer, therefore, is the training-ground for character; we make it difficult for God to purify our desires unless we submit them to Him. But to climb a ladder we must begin at the bottom rung; and we must pray for the things of which we really feel our need, as well as for the things which we think, or know, we ought to want—saying not only "Thy will be done," but also, "give us this day our daily bread." Morality, say the psychologists, is best achieved, not by crushing, but by "sublimating" natural instincts. Just so, if God's aim is to develop individuality, rather than to lop it down to a standard pattern, our actual desires are the material He needs to work upon.

This last consideration is obviously one of the first importance in regard to the much-discussed question of the *petitionary* element in prayer. But to work that point out here would entail too long a digression. I feel, however, impelled to utter a misgiving. There is, I suspect, something seriously at fault in much of the traditional teaching and practice in regard to methods of devotion. Only under exceptional circumstances can the human mind remain for any long time on the mountain-tops of aspiration, vision or endeavour. A danger lies here. Prayer too long continued, especially if mechanical repetitions and the drill of a devotional system be invoked to sustain it, may easily and insensibly slip down to the level of mere auto-suggestion. It may even become a "pious habit" of mental vacuity which may blunt the edge of understanding, quench initiative, dull the moral sense. That hypothesis, at least, would explain why it has so often happened that those who have been the first to stone the prophets have been among the most devout. It would explain, too, the intellectual and moral sterility of so many of the best-intentioned supporters of organised religion. True prayer must be that which *succeeds* in being (what all prayer *aspires* to be) a realised contact with Creative Spirit—the Spirit that makes all things new. If so, the test in one's own life whether prayer is really prayer, or merely pious auto-suggestion, will be the extent to which it inspires to bold and constructive action and to moral and intellectual initiative.

Charles F. Andrews

(1871-1940)

BORN and educated in England, Andrews spent his life in Christian service in India and South Africa. In 1913 he joined Tagore in India, and from 1925-27 he was in South Africa to help with the Indo-Indian agreement between India and South Africa. During his many years in India Andrews was a close friend of Mahatma Gandhi and Sadhu Sundar Singh, and has written biographies of both these Indian leaders.

In his last book, *The Good Shepherd*, Andrews wrote shortly before his death: "The only success that has been worth anything at all has followed closely on those morning hours, which were begun with quiet prayer and silence; when Christ was with me and I listened to His voice, leading me forth and giving me His boundless friendship." These words reflect the genius of this modern saint.

The following selection, which shows the effect of Eastern mysticism upon this Christ-centered interpreter, is reprinted from *The Inner Life* by permission of Harper & Brothers.

THE PLACE OF QUIET IN THE CHRISTIAN LIFE

From *The Inner Life*

When I was young, as you are, and lived in England, I was very active and used to spend the day in ceaseless activities. Indeed, I would almost grudge the time that I spent in quiet and prayer and meditation. At that time, I was working among the poor in South London, and the work itself was Christ's own work; so I said to myself, "This work is surely the work of Christ. Let me do it with all my heart and take up all my time in doing it."

With this thought in my mind I used to work night and day, with hardly any pause or time for rest. In doing so, I forgot that Christ Himself went into retreat and retirement when He was working actively among the poor. But I did not realise the need of this while I was in England. Yet it was a grievous blunder. For it was causing my own character to be much too restless.

But when I came out to India, at the age of thirty-four, I noticed a great difference here between India and England. In India, I had more time for leisure and rest and prayer. But that was not all. For, from the first, I had a great friendship with a very noble Indian Christian, named Susil Kumar Rudra, and my friendship showed me how different he was from myself. How quiet he was, how patient, how gentle! His whole life was more balanced than mine! Love can notice these things very quickly.

When I became at last his true friend, he used to tell me about this side of my character which he had noticed: and he would say that he was quite certain that Jesus meant us as His followers to have peace and calm, and not to be so hurried and restless and over-anxious to get things done.

Then we used to go together in the hot weather to the Himalaya Mountains and there I met Sadhu Sundar Singh. I saw his face, and it was so peaceful and full of joy. I also watched his life—how he spent long hours in prayer and meditation. He did not talk much, but he was wonderfully full of love for Christ, and I saw that he had something which I had not got and I used to question him also about it. He silently taught me in his own remarkable way—though he was very much younger than I was—how Christ brings to us this peace even in the midst of the troubled anxieties of the world around us.

Later on, I stayed at Santiniketan with Rabindranath Tagore, and even though Tagore was not a Christian he had this same calmness of spirit; and I used to watch him also and see how different he was from what I was myself. Sometimes when I got up in the night, before daybreak, I would see Tagore already seated in quiet meditation. He would remain there, silent, in the moonlight, very, very early—perhaps for two or three hours before the day's work began.

So I said to myself, "Here is something I must learn. I must come to Christ and ask Him to teach me." And then I found He was ready to teach me so kindly. He said to me, "Come unto me, all ye that labour and are heavy laden, and I will give you rest. Take my yoke upon you, and learn of me; for I am meek and lowly in heart: and ye shall find rest unto your souls. For my yoke is easy, and my burden is light" (Matt. xi. 28-30). So, little by little, those who were my dearest friends, such as Sadhu Sundar Singh, Rudra, and Tagore all taught me, in their own way, this lesson of quietness and peace.

But I think the greatest of all lessons, which I learnt, was through illness; because, while I was at Santiniketan, I was attacked by cholera and was so near to death that for many weeks I was lying at death's door. In that time, I had my own simple and tender teaching from God Himself.

Don't mistake me. I haven't learned those lessons even yet. There are times when I get very restless about little things that I ought not to be worried about; nevertheless, God has given me, time after time, that inward peace, which is the greatest blessing in my life. And so I wanted to hand on this one lesson to you, while you are young, so that you may not make the same mistake that I did, many years ago, but find Christ in quietness of spirit and love Him as I have tried to do, but with more perfectness. For to be with Him brings joy and peace in the heart, which is the greatest treasure in all life. It is the pearl of great price, which is worth all the rest of the treasures of life put together.

Believe me, now that I have reached old age, when I say that this love of Christ in the heart is the truest and best and greatest treasure that anyone can possibly find in this life of ours. Jesus Himself said, "What shall it profit a man, if he gain the whole world and lose his own soul? and what shall a man give in exchange for his soul?"

The meaning of that is really just what I have been trying to say this evening. It means that if we do not give our time and our earnest longing to find Christ in the silence of our inner lives, then we shall lose our *true* life altogether. We may gain other things, but we shall lose the best thing of all.

So let us, in this Ashram, be active in doing our work, in the hospital, in the day school, and in the night school—do not let us fail there. Let us find Christ there. But, more than this, let us remember to find Him in this time of silence at *Sandhya* each evening, while we sit together; and also in our solitude, in the inner chamber of our hearts, when we are praying and are all alone. And if we find Him thus, both in action and in rest, we shall indeed win the victory.

Evelyn Underhill

(1875-1941)

No book has done more to evaluate and analyze the meaning of the saints from the time of Philo (20 B.C.-40 A.D.) to the beginning of the twentieth century than *Mysticism: A Study in the Nature and Development of Man's Spiritual Consciousness* by Evelyn Underhill. It has gone through thirteen editions. Of twentieth-century women who have made a special study of the devotional life, she ranks among the highest. Other writings of hers on the devotional life are: *The Mystic Way, Practical Mysticism, The Essentials of Mysticism.*

Miss Underhill's contribution to religious thinking is identified with that of Western thought, which correlates the good, ethical life with that of deep and meaningful devotion. Educated at King's College for Women, London, she spent much of her time in writing and lecturing. She was Upton lecturer at Manchester College, Oxford, 1921-22.

The following selection is from *The Essentials of Mysticism* and is used by permission of E. P. Dutton & Co. (Copyright 1920 by E. P. Dutton & Co., Inc.)

THE PLACE OF WILL, INTELLECT, AND FEELING IN PRAYER

From *The Essentials of Mysticism*

The psychology of religious experience, as yet so little understood, has few more important problems proposed to it than that which concerns the true place and right use of will, intellect, and feeling of prayer. This question, which to some may appear merely academic, really involves the whole problem of the method and proportion in which the various powers and activities of our being may best be used, when they turn from the natural world of concrete things to attend to the so-called "supernatural" world of Spirit—in fact, to God, Who is the source and sum of the reality of that world. That problem must be of practical interest to every Christian— more, to every one who believes in the spiritual possibilities of man—for it concerns itself with all those responses which are made by human personality to the impact of Infinite Life. It deals, in Maeterlinck's words, with "the harshest and most uninhabitable headlands of the Divine 'know thyself,'" and includes in its span the whole region "where the psychology of man mingles with the psychology of God."

In the first place, what do we mean by prayer? Surely just this: that part of our active and conscious life which is deliberately orientated towards, and exclusively responds to, spiritual reality. The Being of God, Who is that spiritual reality, we believe to be immanent in all things: "He is not far from each one of us: for in Him we live, and move, and have our being." In fact, as Christians we must believe this. Therefore in attending to those visible and concrete things, we are in a way attending to that immanent God; and in this sense all honest work is indeed, as the old proverb says, a sort of prayer. But when we speak of prayer as a separate act or activity of the self, we mean more than this. We mean, in fact, as a rule the other aspect of spiritual experience and communion; in the language of theology, attention to transcendent rather than to immanent Reality. Prayer, says Walter Hilton, in terms of which the origin goes back to the Neoplatonists, "is nothing else but an ascending or getting up of the desire of the heart into God, by withdrawing it from all earthly thoughts"—an ascent, says Ruysbroeck, of the Ladder of Love. In the same spirit William Law defines it as "the rising of the soul out of the vanity of time into the riches of eternity." It entails, then, a going up or out from our ordinary circle of earthly interests; a cutting off, so far as we may, of the "torrent or use and wont," that we may attend to the changeless Reality which that flux too often hides. Prayer stretches out the tentacles of our consciousness not so much towards that Divine Life which is felt to be enshrined within the striving, changeful world of things; but rather to that "Eternal truth, true Love, and loved Eternity" wherein the world is felt to be enshrined; and in this act it brings to full circle the activities of the human soul—that

> Swinging-wicket set between
> The Unseen and the Seen.

The whole of man's life really consists in a series of balanced responses to this Transcendent-Immanent Reality; because man lives under two orders, is at once a citizen of Eternity and of Time. Like a pendulum, his consciousness moves perpetually—or should move if it be healthy—between God and his neighbour, between this world and that. The wholeness, sanity, and balance of his existence will entirely depend upon the perfection of his adjustment to this double situation; on the steady alternating beat of his outward swing of adoration, his homeward-turning swing of charity. Now, it is the outward swing which we are to consider: the powers that may be used in it, the best way in which these powers may be employed.

First, we observe that those three capacities or faculties which we have under consideration—the thinking faculty, the feeling faculty, the willing or acting faculty—practically cover all the ways in which the self can react to other selves and other things. From their combination come all the possibilities of self-expression which are open to man. In his natural life he needs and uses all of them. Shall he need and use all of them in his spiritual life too? Christians, I think, are bound to answer this question in the affirmative. According to Christianity, it is the whole self which is called to turn towards Divine Reality—to enter the Kingdom—not some supposed "spiritual" part thereof. "Thou hast made us for Thyself," said Augustine; not, as the Orphic initiate would have said, "Thou hast made one crumb out of our complex nature for Thyself, and the rest may go on to the rubbish heap." It is the *whole man* of intellect, of feeling, and of will, which finds its only true objective in the Christian God.

Surely, the real difference which marks out Christianity from all other religions lies just here; in this robust acceptance of humanity in its wholeness, and of life in its completeness, as something which is susceptible of the Divine. It demands, and deals with, the whole man, his Titanic energies and warring instincts; not, as did the antique mysteries, separating and cultivating some supposed transcendental principle in him, to the exclusion of all else. Christians believe in a God immanent and incarnate, Who transfuses the whole of the life which He has created, and calls that life in its wholeness to union with Him. If this be so, then *Lex credendi, lex orandi;* our belief should find its fullest expression in our prayer, and that prayer should take up, and turn towards the spiritual order all the powers of our mental, emotional, and volitional life. Prayers should be the highest exercise of these powers; for here they are directed to the only adequate object of thought, of love, and of desire. It should, as it were, lift us to the top of our condition, and represent the fullest flowering of our consciousness; for here we breathe the air of the supernal order, and attain according to our measure to that communion with Reality for which we were made.

Prayer so thought of will include, of course, many different kinds of spiritual work; and also—what is too often forgotten—the priceless gift of spiritual rest. It will include many kinds of intercourse with Reality—adoration, petition, meditation, contemplation—and all the shades and varieties of these which religious writers have named and classified. As in the natural order the living creature must feed *and* grow, must suffer *and* enjoy, must get energy from the external world *and* give it back again in creative acts, if he would live a whole and healthy life, so, too, in the spiritual order. All these things—the giving and the receiving, the work and the rest—should fall within the circle of prayer.

Now, when we do anything consciously and with purpose, the transition from inaction to action unfolds itself in a certain order. First we form a concept of that which we shall do; the idea of it looms up, dimly or distinctly, in the mind. Then, we feel that we want to do it, or must do it. Then we determine that we *will* do it. These phases may follow one another so swiftly that they seem to us to be fused into one; but when we analyze the process which lies behind each conscious act, we find that this is the normal sequence of development. First we think, then we feel, then we will. This little generalization must not be pressed too hard; but it is broadly true, and gives us a starting-point from which to trace out the way in which the three main powers of the self act in prayer. It is practically important, as well as psychologically interesting, to know how they act or should act; as it is practically important to know, at least in outline, the normal operation of our bodily powers. Self-knowledge, said Richard of St. Victor, is the beginning of the spiritual life; and knowledge of one's self—too often identified with knowledge of one's sins—ought to include some slight acquaintance with the machinery we all have at our disposal. This machinery, as we see, falls into three divisions; and the perfection of the work which it does will depend upon the observing of an order in their operation, a due balance between them, without excessive development of one power at the expense of the others.

On the side of spiritual experience and activity, such an excessive and one-sided development often takes place. Where this exaggeration is in the direction of intellect, the theological or philosophical mood dominates all other aspects of religion. Where the purely emotional and instinctive side of the relation of the soul to God is released from the critical action of the intelligence, it often degenerates into an objectionable sentimentality, and may lead to forms of self-indulgence which are only superficially religious. Where the volitional element takes command, unchecked by humble love, an arrogant reliance upon our own powers, a restless determination to do certain hard things, to attain certain results—a sort of supersensual ambition—mars the harmony of the inner life. Any of these exaggerations must mean loss of balance, loss of wholeness; and their presence in the active life reflects back to their presence in the prayerful life, of which outward religion is but the visible sign. I think, therefore, that we ought to regard it as a part of our religious education to study the order in which our faculties should be employed when we turn towards our spiritual inheritance.

Prayer, as a rule—save with those natural or highly trained contemplatives who live always in the prayerful state, tuned up to a perpetual consciousness of spiritual reality—begins, or should begin, with something which we can only call an intellectual act; with thinking of what we are going to do. In saying this, I am not expressing a merely personal opinion. All those great specialists of the spiritual life who have written on this subject are here in agreement. "When thou goest about to pray," says Walter Hilton, "first make and frame betwixt thee and God a full purpose and intention; then begin, and do as well as thou canst." "Prayer," says the writer of the Cloud of Unknowing, "may not goodly be gotten in beginners or proficients, without thinking coming before." All mediaeval writers on prayer take it as a matter of course that "meditation" comes before "orison"; and meditation is simply the art of thinking steadily and methodically about spiritual things. So, too, the most modern psychologists assure us that instinctive emotion does its best work when it acts in harmony with our reasoning powers.

St. Teresa, again, insists passionately on the primal need of thinking what we are doing when we begin to pray; on "recollecting the mind," calling in the scattered thoughts, and concentrating the intellect upon the business in hand. It is, in fact, obvious—once we consider the matter in a practical light—that we must form *some* conception of the supernal intercourse which we are going to attempt, and of the parties to it; though if our prayer be real, that conception will soon be transcended. The sword of the spirit is about to turn in a new direction; away from concrete actualities, towards eternal realities. This change —the greatest of which our consciousness is capable—must be realized as fully as possible by the self whose powers of will and love it will call into play. It seems necessary to insist on this point, because so much is said now, and no doubt rightly said, about the non-intellectual and supremely intuitional nature of the spiritual life; with the result that some people begin to think it their duty to cultivate a kind of pious imbecility. There is notion in the air that when man turns to God he ought to leave his brains behind him. True, they will soon be left behind of necessity if man goes far on the road towards that Reality which is above all reason and all knowledge; for spirit in the swiftness of its flight to God quickly overpasses these imperfect instruments. But those whose feet are still firmly planted upon earth gain nothing by anticipating this moment; they will not attain to spiritual intuition by the mere annihilation of their intelligence. We cannot hope to imitate the crystalline simplicity of the saints; a simplicity which is the result, not of any deliberate neglect of reason, but of clearest vision, of intensest trust, of most ardent love— that is, of Faith, Hope, and Charity in their most perfect expression, fused together to form a single state of enormous activity. But this is no reason why we should put imbecility, deliberate vagueness, or a silly want of logic in the place of their exquisite simpleness; any more

than we should dare to put an unctuous familiarity in the place of their wonderful intimacy, or a cringing demeanour in the place of their matchless humility.

In saying this—in insisting that the reason has a well-marked and necessary place in the mechanism of the soul's approach to God—I am not advocating a religious intellectualism. It is true that our perception of all things, even the most divine, is conditioned by the previous content of our minds: the "apperceiving mass." Hence, the more worthy our thoughts about God, the more worthy our apprehensions of Him are likely to be. Yet I know that there is in the most apparently foolish prayer of feeling something warmly human, and therefore effective; something which in its value for life far transcends the consecrated sawdust offered up by devout intellectualism. "By love," said the old mystic, "He may be gotten and holden; by thought never." A whole world of experience separates the simple little church mouse saying her rosary, perhaps without much intelligence, yet with a humble and a loving faith, from the bishop who preferred "Oh, Great First Cause" to "Our Father," because he thought that it was more in accordance with scientific truth; and few of us will feel much doubt as to the side on which the advantage lies. The advantage must always lie with those "full true sisters," humility and love; for these are the essential elements of all successful prayer. But surely it is a mistake to suppose that these qualities cannot exist side by side with an active and disciplined intelligence.

Prayer, then, begins by an intellectual adjustment. By thinking of God, or of Spiritual Reality, earnestly and humbly, and to the exclusion of other objects of thought; by deliberately surrendering the mind to spiritual things; by preparing the consciousness for the impact of a new order, the inflow of new life. But, having thought of God, the self, if it stop there, is no more in touch with Him than it was before. It may think as long as it likes, but nothing happens; thought unhelped by feeling ever remains exterior to its object. We are brought up short against the fact that the intellect is an essentially static thing: we cannot think our way along the royal road which leads to heaven.

Yet it is a commonplace of spiritual knowledge that, if the state of prayer be established, something does happen; consciousness does somehow travel along that road, the field of perception is shifted, new contacts are made. How is this done? A distinguished religious psychologist has answered, that it is done "by the synthesis of love and will"— that is to say, by the craving in action which conditions all our essential deeds —and I know no better answer to suggest.

Where the office of thought ends, there the office of will and feeling begins: "Where intellect must stay without," says Ruysbroeck, "these may enter in." Desire and intention are the most dynamic of our faculties; they do work. They are the true explorers of the Infinite, the instruments of our ascents to God. Reason comes to the foot of the mountain; it is the industrious will urged by the passionate heart which climbs the slope. It is the "blind intent stretching towards Him," says the *Cloud of Unknowing*, "the true lovely will of the heart," which succeeds at last; the tense determination, the effort, the hard work, the definite, eager, humble, outward thrust of the whole personality towards a Reality which is felt rather than known. "We are nothing else but wills," said St. Augustine. "The will," said William Law, "maketh the beginning, the middle, and the end of everything. It is the only workman in nature, and everything is its work." Experience endorses this emphasis on will and desire as the central facts of our personality, the part of us which is supremely our own. In turning that will and desire towards Spiritual Reality, we are doing all that we can of ourselves; are selecting and deliberately concentrating upon it our passion and our power. Also, we are giving consciously, wholeheartedly, with intention, that with which we are free to deal; and self-donation is, we know, an essential part of prayer, as of all true intercourse.

Now, intellect and feeling are not wholly ours to give. A rich mental or emotional life is not possessed of all men; some are naturally stupid, some temperamentally cold. Even those who are greatly endowed with the powers of understanding or of love have not got these powers entirely under their own control. Both feeling and intellect often insist on taking their own line with us. Moreover, they fluctuate from day to day, from hour to hour; they are dependent on many delicate adjustments. Sometimes we are mentally dull, sometimes we are emotionally flat: and this happens more often, perhaps, in regard to spiritual than in regard to merely human affairs. On such occasions it is notoriously useless to try to beat ourselves up to a froth: to make ourselves think more deeply or make ourselves care more intensely. Did the worth of man's prayerful life depend on the maintenance of a constant high level of feeling or understanding, he were in a parlous case. But, though these often seem to fail him— and with them all the joy of spiritual intercourse fails him too—the regnant will remains. Even when his heart is cold and his mind is dim, the "blind intent stretching to God" is still possible to him. "Our wills are ours, to make them Thine."

The Kingdom of Heaven, says the Gospel, is taken by violence—that is, by effort, by unfaltering courage—not by cleverness, nor by ecstatic spiritual feelings. The freedom of the City of God is never earned by a mere limp acquiescence in those great currents of the transcendent order which bear life towards its home. The determined fixing of the will upon Spiritual Reality, and pressing towards that Reality steadily and without deflection; this is the very centre of the art of prayer. This is why those splendid psychologists, the mediaeval writers on prayer, told their pupils to "mean only God," and not to trouble about anything else; since "He who has

Him has all." The most theological of thoughts soon becomes inadequate; the most spiritual of emotions is only a fair-weather breeze. Let the ship take advantage of it by all means, but not rely on it. She must be prepared to beat to windward if she would reach her goal.

In proportion to the strength and sincerity of the will, in fact, so shall be the measure of success in prayer. As the self pushes out towards Reality, so does Reality rush in on it. "Grace and the will," says one of the greatest of living writers on religion, "rise and fall together." "Grace" is, of course, the theological term for that inflow of spiritual vitality which is the response made by the divine order to the human motions of adoration, supplication, and love; and according to the energy and intensity with which our efforts are made—the degree in which we concentrate our attention upon this high and difficult business of prayer—will be the amount of new life that we receive. The efficacy of prayer, therefore, will be conditioned by the will of the praying self. "Though it be so, that prayer be not the cause of grace," says Hilton, "nevertheless it is a way or means by which grace freely given comes into the soul." Grace presses in upon life perpetually, and awaits our voluntary appropriation of it. It is accessible to sincere and loyal endeavour, to "the true lovely will of the heart," and to nothing else.

So much we have said of will. What place have we left for the operation of feeling in prayer? It is not easy to disentangle will and feeling; for in all intense will there is a strong element of emotion—every volitional act has somewhere at the back of it a desire—and in all great and energizing passions there is a pronounced volitional element. The "synthesis of love and will" is no mere fancy of the psychologist. It is a compound hard to break down in practice. But I think we can say generally that the business of feeling is to inflame the will, to give it intention, gladness, and vividness; to convert it from a dull determination into an eager, impassioned desire. It

links up thought with action; effect, in psychological language, the movement of the prayerful self from a mere state of cognition to a state of conation; converts the soul from attention to the Transcendent to first-hand adventure within it. "All thy life now behoveth altogether to stand in desire," says the author of the *Cloud of Unknowing* to the disciple who has accepted the principle of prayer; and here he is declaring a psychological necessity rather than a religious platitude, for all sucecssful action has its origin in emotion of some kind. Though we choose to imagine that "pure reason" directs our conduct, in the last resort we always do a thing because of the feeling that we have about it. Not necessarily because we like doing it; but because instinctive feeling of some sort—selfish or unselfish, personal, social, conventional, sacrificial; the disturbing emotion called the sense of duty, or the glorious emotion called the passion of love—is urging us to it. Instinctive emotions, more or less sublimated; Love, Hatred, Ambition, Fear, Anger, Hunger, Patriotism, Self-interest; these are the true names of our reasons for doing things.

If this be true of our reactions to the physical world, it is none the less true of our intercourse with the spiritual world. The will is moved to seek that intercourse by emotion, by feeling; never by a merely intellectual conviction. In the vigour and totality with which the heroes of religion give themselves to spiritual interests, and in the powers which they develop, we see the marks of instinctive feeling operating upon the highest levels. By "a leash of longing," says the *Cloud of Unknowing* again, man is led to be the servant of God; not by the faultless deductions of dialectic, but by the mysterious logic of the heart. He is moved most often, perhaps, by an innate unformulated craving for perfection, or by the complementary loathing of imperfection—a love of God, or a hatred of self—by the longing for peace, the miserable sensations of disillusion, of sin, and of unrest, the heart's deep conviction that it needs a changeless object for its love. Or, if by none of these, then by some other emotional stimulus.

A wide range of feeling states—some, it is true, merely self-seeking, but others high and pure—influence the prayerful consciousness; but those which are normal and healthy fall within two groups, one of subjective, the other of objective emotion. The dominant motive of the subjective group is the self's feeling of its own imperfection, helplessness, sinfulness, and need, over against the Perfect Reality towards which its prayer is set; a feeling which grows with the growth of the soul's spiritual perceptions, and includes all the shaded emotions of penitence and of humility. "For meekness in itself is naught else but a true knowing and feeling of a man's self as he is." The objective group of feelings is complementary to this, and is centred on the goodness, beauty, and perfection of that Infinite Reality towards which the soul is stretching itself. Its dominant notes are adoration and love. Of these two fundamental emotions—humility and love—the first lies at the back of all prayer of confession and petition, and is a necessary check upon the arrogant tendencies of the will. The second is the energizing cause of all adoration: adoration, the highest exercise of the spirit of man. Prayer, then, on its emotional side should begin in humble contrition and flower in loving adoration. Adoring love—not mere emotional excitement, religious sentimentality or "spiritual feelings"—but the strong, deep love, industrious, courageous and self-giving which fuses all the powers of the self into one single state of enormous intensity; this is the immortal element of prayer. Thought has done all that it may when it has set the scene, prepared the ground, adjusted the mind in the right direction. Will is wanted only whilst there are oppositions to be transcended, difficult things to be done. It represents the soul's effort and struggle to be where it ought to be. But there are levels of attainment in which the will does not seem to exist any more as a separate thing. It is caught in the mighty rhythms of the Divine will,

merged in it and surrendered to it. Instead of its small personal activity, it forms a part of the great deep action of the Whole. In the higher degrees of prayer, in fact, will is transmuted into love. We are reminded of the old story of the phoenix: the active busy will seems to be burned up and utterly destroyed, but living love, strong and immortal, springs from the ashes and the flame. When the reasonable hope and the deliberate wilful faith in which man's prayer began are both fulfilled, this heavenly charity goes on to lose itself upon the heights.

Within the normal experience of the ordinary Christian, love should give two things to prayer; ardour and beauty. In his prayer, as it were, man swings a censer before the altar of the Universe. He may put into the thurible all his thoughts and dreams, all his will and energy. But unless the fire of love is communicated to that incense, nothing will happen; there will be no fragrance and no ascending smoke. These qualities —ardour and beauty—represent two distinct types of feelings, which ought both to find a place in the complete spiritual life, balancing and completing one another. The first is in the highest degree intimate and personal; the second is disinterested and aesthetic.

The intimate and personal aspect of spiritual love has found supreme literary expression in the works of Richard of St. Victor, of St. Bernard, of Thomas à Kempis, of our own Richard Rolle, Hilton, and Julian of Norwich, and many others. We see it in our own day in its purest form in the living mystic who wrote *The Golden Fountain*. Those who discredit it as "mere religious emotionalism" do so because they utterly mistake its nature; regarding it, apparently, as the spiritual equivalent of the poorest and most foolish, rather than the noblest, most heroic, and least self-seeking, types of human love. "I find the lark the most wonderful of all birds," says the author of *The Golden Fountain*. "I cannot listen to his rhapsodies without being inspired (no matter what I may be in the midst of doing or saying) to throw up my own love to God. In the soaring insistence of his song and passion I find the only thing in Nature which so suggests the high soaring and rapturous flights of the soul. But I am glad that we surpass the lark in sustaining a far more lengthy and wonderful flight; and that we sing, not downwards to an earthly love, but upwards to a heavenly." Like real human love, this spiritual passion is poles asunder from every kind of sentimentality. It is profoundly creative, it is self-giving, it does not ask for anything in exchange. Although it is the source of the highest kind of joy—though, as à Kempis says, the true lover "flies, runs, and rejoices; is free, and cannot be restrained"—it has yet more kinship with suffering than with merely agreeable emotions. This is the feeling state, at once generous and desirous, which most of all enflames the will and makes it active; this it is which gives ardour and reality to man's prayers. "For love is born of God, and cannot rest save in God, above all created things."

But there is another form of objective emotion besides this intimate and personal passion of love, which ought to play an important part in the life of prayer. I mean that exalted and essentially disinterested type of feeling which expresses itself in pure adoration, and is closely connected with the sense of the Beautiful. Surely this, since it represents the fullest expression of one power in our nature—and that a power which is persistently stretched out in the direction of the Ideal—should have a part in our communion with the spiritual, as well as with the natural world. The Beautiful, says Hegel, is the spiritual making itself known sensuously. It represents, then, a direct message to us from the heart of Reality; ministers to us of more abundant life. Therefore the widening of our horizon which takes place when we turn in prayer to a greater world than that which the senses reveal to us, should bring with it a more poignant vision of loveliness, a more eager passion for Beauty as well as for Goodness and Truth. When St. Augustine strove to express the intensity of

his regret for wasted years, it was to his neglect of the Beauty of God that he went to show the poignancy of his feeling, the immensity of his loss. "Oh Beauty so old and so new! too late have I loved thee!"

It needs a special training, I think—a special and deliberate use of our faculties—if we are to avoid this deprivation; and learn, as an integral part of our communion with Reality, to lay hold of the loveliness of the First and Only Fair. "I was caught up to Thee by Thy beauty, but dragged back again by my own weight," says Augustine in another place; and the weight of the soul, he tells us, is its love—the pull of a misplaced desire. All prayer which is primarily the expression of our wants rather than our worship, which places the demand for daily bread before instead of after the hallowing of the Ineffable Name, will have this dragging-back effect.

Now, as the artist's passion for sensuous beauty finds expression in his work, and urges him to create beauty as well as he can, so too the soul's passion for spiritual beauty should find expression in its work; that is to say, in its prayer. A work of art, says Hegel again, is as much the work of the Spirit of God as is the beauty of Nature; but in art the Holy Spirit works through human consciousness. Therefore man's prayer ought to be as beautiful as he can make it; for thus it approaches more nearly to the mind of God. It should have dignity as well as intimacy, form as well as colour. More, all those little magic thoughts—those delicate winged fancies, which seem like birds rejoicing in God's sight—these, too, should have their place in it. We find many specimens of them, as it were stuffed and preserved under glass shades, in books of devotion. It is true that their charm and radiance cannot survive this process; the colour now seems crude, the sheen of the plumage is gone. But once these were the living, personal, spontaneous expressions of the love and faith—the inborn poetry—of those from whom they came. Many a liturgic prayer, which now seems to us impersonal and official—foreign to us, perhaps, in its language and thought—will show us, if we have but a little imaginative sympathy, the ardent mood, the exquisite tact, the unforced dignity, of the mind which first composed it; and form a standard by which we may measure our own efforts in this kind.

But the beauty which we seek to incorporate into our spiritual intercourse should not be the dead ceremonious beauty which comes of mere dependence on tradition. It should be the freely upspringing lyric beauty which is rooted in intense personal feeling; the living beauty of a living thing. Nor need we fear the reproach that here we confuse religion with poetry. Poetry ever goes like the royal banners before ascending life; therefore man may safely follow its leadership in his prayer, which is—or should be—life in its intensest form. Consider the lilies: those perfect examples of a measured, harmonious, natural and creative life, under a form of utmost loveliness. I cannot help thinking that it is the duty of all Christians to impart something of that flower-like beauty to their prayer; and only feeling of a special kind will do it—that humble yet passionate love of the beautiful, which finds the perfect object of its adoration in God and something of His fairness in all created things. St. Francis had it strongly, and certain other of the mystics had it too. In one of his rapturous meditations, Suso, for whom faith and poetry were—as they should be—fused in one, calls the Eternal Wisdom a "sweet and beautiful wild flower." He recognized that flowery charm which makes the Gospels fragrant, and is included in that pattern which Christians are called to imitate if they can. Now, if this quality is to be manifested in human life, it must first be sought and actualized, consciously or unconsciously, in prayer; because it is in the pure, sharp air of the spiritual order that it lives. It must spring up from within outwards, must be the reflection of the soul's communion with "that Supreme Beauty which containeth in itself all goodness"; which was revealed to Angela of Foligno, but which "she could in no wise describe." The intellect may, and should, conceive of this Absolute Beauty as well as it can; the will may—and must—be set on the attaining of it. But only by intuitive feeling can man hope to know it, and only by love can he make it his own. The springs of the truest prayer and of the deepest poetry —twin expressions of man's outward-going passion for that Eternity which is his home—rise very near together in the heart.

Thomas R. Kelly

(1893-1941)

Born of Quaker parents in Ohio and educated at Haverford and Harvard, Kelly was called to Haverford in 1936 to teach in the department of philosophy. In 1917-18 he worked with German prisoners in England; in 1924-25 he guided the activities of the Quaker community in Berlin, Germany. Between his work in Berlin and his return to Haverford in 1936, he taught at Earlham College and the University of Hawaii. In 1941, in the midst of an active life, he died of a heart attack.

Few men of his age in recent times have left such an impression of radiated sainthood as Kelly. After his death Gerald Heard wrote to a mutual friend: "I was filled with a kind of a joy when I read of Thomas Kelly. It was formerly the custom of the Winston-Salem community of Moravians, in North Carolina, to announce the passing of a member by the playing of three chorales by the church band from the top of the church tower. So I feel I want to sing when I hear of such men emerging."

Rufus Jones writes of *A Testament of Devotion*, "There are a few—a very few—great [devotional books] . . . and here is a book I can recommend along with the best of the ancient ones." The following selection is from one of the five devotional addresses contained in it and is used by permission of Harper & Brothers. (Copyright 1941 by Harper & Brothers.)

THE LIGHT WITHIN

From *A Testament of Devotion*

I

Meister Eckhart wrote, "As thou art in church or cell, that same frame of mind carry out into the world, into its turmoil and its fitfulness." Deep within us all there is an amazing inner sanctuary of the soul, a holy place, a Divine Center, a speaking Voice, to which we may continuously return. Eternity is at our hearts, pressing upon our time-torn lives, warming us with intimations of an astounding destiny, calling us home unto Itself. Yielding to these persuasions, gladly committing ourselves in body and soul, utterly and completely, to the Light Within, is the beginning of true life. It is a dynamic center, a creative Life that presses to birth within us. It is a Light Within which illumines the face of God and casts new shadows and new glories upon the face of men. It is a seed stirring to life if we do not choke it. It is the Shekinah of the soul, the Presence in the midst. Here is the Slumbering Christ, stirring to be awakened, to become the soul we clothe in earthly form and action. And He is within us all.

You who read these words already know this inner Life and Light. For by this very Light within you, is your recognition given. In this humanistic age we suppose man is the initiator and God is the responder. But the Living Christ within us is the initiator and we are the responders. God the Lover, the accuser, the revealer of light and darkness presses within us. "Behold I stand at the door and knock." And all our apparent initiative is already a response, a testimonial to His secret presence and working within us.

The basic response of the soul to the Light is internal adoration and joy, thanksgiving and worship, self-surrender and listening. The secret places of the heart cease to be our noisy workshop. They become a holy sanctuary of adoration and of self-oblation, where we are kept in perfect peace, if our minds be stayed on Him who has found us in the inward springs of our life. And in brief intervals of overpowering visitation we are able to carry the sanctuary frame of mind out into the world, into its turmoil and its fitfulness, and in a hyperaesthesia of the soul, we see all mankind tinged with deeper shadows, and touched with Galilean glories. Powerfully are the springs of our will moved to an abandon of singing love toward God; powerfully are we moved to a new and overcoming love toward time-blinded men and all creation. In this Center of Creation all things are ours, and we are Christ's and Christ is God's. We are owned men, ready to run and not be weary and to walk and not faint.

But the light fades, the will weakens, the humdrum returns. Can we stay this fading? No, nor should we try, for we must learn the disciples of His will, and pass beyond this first lesson of His Grace. But the Eternal Inward Light does not die when ecstasy dies, nor exist only intermittently, with the flickering of our psychic states. Continuously renewed immediacy, not receding memory of the Divine Touch, lies at the base of religious living. Let us explore together the secret of a deeper devotion, a more subterranean sanctuary of the soul, where the Light Within never fades, but burns, a perpetual Flame, where the wells of living water of divine revelation rise up continuously, day by day and hour by hour, steady and transfiguring. The "bright shoots of everlastingness" can become a steady light within, if we are deadly in earnest in our dedication to the Light, and are willing to pass out of first stages into maturer religious living. Only if this is possible can the light from the inner sanctuary of the soul be a workaday light for the marketplace, a guide for perplexed feet, a recreator of culture-patterns for the race of men.

What is here urged are internal practices and habits of the mind. What is here urged are secret habits of unceasing orientation of the deeps of our being about the Inward Light, ways of conducting our inward life so that we are perpetually bowed in worship, while we are also very busy in the world of daily affairs. What is here urged are inward practices of the mind at deepest levels, letting it swing like the needle, to the polestar of the soul. And like the needle, the Inward Light becomes the truest guide of life, showing us new and unsuspected defects in ourselves and our fellows, showing us new and unsuspected possibilities in the power and life of goodwill among men. But, more deeply, He who is within us urges, by secret persuasion, to such an amazing Inward Life with Him, so that, firmly cleaving to Him, we always look out upon all the world through the sheen of the Inward Light, and react toward men spontaneously and joyously from this Inward Center. Yield yourself to Him who is a far better teacher than these outward words, and you will have found the Instructor Himself, of whom these words are a faint and broken echo.

Such practice of inward orientation, of inward worship and listening, is no mere counsel for special religious groups, for small religious orders, for special "interior souls," for monks retired in cloisters. This practice is the heart of religion. It is the secret, I am persuaded, of the inner life of the Master of Galilee. He expected this secret to be freshly discovered in everyone who would be his follower. It creates an amazing fellowship, the church catholic and invisible, and institutes group living at a new level, a society grounded in reverence, history rooted in eternity, colonies of heaven.

It is the special property of no group or sect, but is a universal obligation and privilege. Roman Catholics have treasured this practice, but have overlaid the authority of the Light Within by a heavy weight of external ecclesiastical authority. Protestant emphasis, beginning so nobly in the early Luther, has grown externally rationalistic, humanistic, and service-minded. Dogmas and creed and the closed revelation of a completed canon have replaced the emphasis upon keeping close to the fresh upspringings of the Inner Life. The dearth of rich Protestant literature on the interior aspect of Christian living, except as it bears on the opening experience of conversion, bears testimony to its emphasis being elsewhere.

The Society of Friends arose as a rediscovery of the ever-open inward springs of immediacy and revelation. George Fox and the Quakers found a Principle within men, a Shekinah of the soul, a Light Within that lights every man coming into the world. Dedicating themselves utterly and completely to attendance upon this Inward Living Christ, they were quickened into a new and bold tenderness toward the blindness of the leaders of Christian living. Aflame with the Light of the inner sanctuary, they went out into the world, into its turmoil and its fitfulness, and called men to listen above all to that God speaking within them, to order all life by the Light of the Sanctuary. "Dear Friends," writes Fox to his groups, "keep close to that which is pure within you, which leads you up to God." John Woolman, the Quaker tailor of Mt. Holly, New Jersey, resolved so to order his outward affairs, so to adjust his business burdens, that nothing, absolutely nothing would crowd out his prime attendance upon the Inward Principle. And in this sensitizing before the inward altar of his soul, he was quickened to see and attack effectively the evils of. slave-holding, of money-loaning, of wars upon the Indians.

But the value of Woolman and Fox and the Quakers of today for the world does not lie merely in their outward deeds of service to suffering men, it lies in that call to all men to the practice of orienting their entire being in inward adoration about the springs of immediacy and ever fresh divine power within the secret silences of the soul. The Inner Light, the Inward Christ, is no mere doctrine, belonging peculiarly to a small religious fellowship, to be accepted or rejected as a mere belief. It is the living Center of Reference for all Christian souls and Christian groups—yes, and of non-Christian groups as well—who seriously mean to dwell in the secret place of the Most High. He is the center and source of action, not the end-point of thought. He is the locus of commitment, not a problem for debate. Practice comes first in religion, not theory or dogma. And Christian practice is not exhausted in outward deeds. These are the fruits, not the roots. A practicing Christian must above all be one who practices the perpetual return of the soul into the inner sanctuary, who brings the world into its Light and rejudges it, who brings the Light into the world with all its turmoil and its fitfulness and recreates it (after the pattern seen on the Mount). To the reverent exploration of this practice we now address ourselves.

II

There is a way of ordering our mental life on more than one level at once. On one level we may be thinking, discussing, seeing, calculating, meeting all the demands, of external affairs, but deep within, behind the scenes, at a profounder level, we may also be in prayer and adoration, song and worship and a gentle receptiveness to divine breathings.

The secular world of today values and cultivates only the first level, assured that *there* is where the real business of mankind is done, and scorns, or smiles in tolerant amusement, at the cultivation of the second level—a luxury enterprise, a vestige of superstition, an occupation for special temperaments. But in a deeply religious culture men know that the deep level of prayer and of divine attendance is the most important thing in the world. It is at this deep level that the real business of life is determined. The secular mind is an abbreviated, fragmentary mind, building only upon a part of man's nature and neglecting a part— the most glorious part—of man's nature, powers and resources. The religious mind involves the whole of man, embraces his relations with time within their true ground and setting in the Eternal Lover. It ever keeps close to the fountains of divine creativity. In lowliness it knows joys and stabilities, peace and assurances, that are utterly incomprehensible to the secular mind. It lives in resources and powers that make individuals radiant and triumphant, groups tolerant and bonded together in mutual concern, and is bestirred to an outward life of unremitting labor.

Between the two levels is fruitful interplay, but ever the accent must be upon the deeper level, where the soul ever dwells in the presence of the Holy One. For the religious man is forever bringing all affairs of the first level down into the Light, holding them there in the Presence, reseeing them and the whole of the world of men and things in a new and overturning way, and responding to them in spontaneous, incisive and simple ways of love and faith. Facts remain facts, when brought into the Presence in the deeper level, but their value, their significance, is wholly realigned. Much apparent wheat becomes utter chaff, and some chaff becomes wheat. Imposing powers? They are out of the Life, and must crumble. Lost causes? If God be for them, who can be against them? Rationally plausible futures? They are weakened or certified in the dynamic Life and Light. Tragic suffering? Already He is there, and we actively move, in His tenderness, toward the sufferers. Hopeless debauchees? These are children of God, His concern and ours. Inexorable laws of nature? The dependable framework for divine reconstruction. The fall of a sparrow? The Father's love, for faith and hope and love for all things are engendered in the soul, as we practice their submission and our own to the Light Within, as we humbly see all things, even darkly and as through a glass, yet through the eye of God.

But the upper level of our mind plays upon the deeper level of divine immediacy of internal communion and of prayer. It furnishes us with the objects of divine concern, "the sensualized material of our duty," as Fichte called it. It furnishes us with those culture-patterns of our group which are at one and the same time the medium and the material for their regeneration, our language, our symbols, our traditions, and our history. It provides for the mystic the suggestions for his metaphors, even the metaphor of the Light, the Seed, the Sanctuary, whereby he would suggest and communicate the wonder of God's immediacy and power. It supplies the present-day tools of reflection whereby the experience of Eternity is knit into the fabric of time and thought. But theologies and symbols and creeds, though inevitable, are transient and become obsolescent, while the Life of God sweeps on through the souls of men in continued revelation and creative newness. To that divine Life we must cling. In that Current we must bathe. In that abiding yet energizing Center we are all made one, behind and despite the surface differences of our forms and cultures. For the heart of the religious life is in commitment and worship, not in reflection and theory.

How, then, shall we lay hold of that Life and Power, and live the life of prayer without ceasing? By quiet, persistent practice in turning of all our being, day and night, in prayer and inward worship and surrender, toward Him who calls in the deeps of our souls. Mental habits of inward orientation must be established. An inner, secret turning to God can be made fairly steady, after weeks and months and years of practice and lapses and failures and returns. It is as simple an art as Brother Lawrence found it, but it may be long before we achieve any steadiness in the process. Begin now, as you read these words, as you sit in your chair, to offer your whole selves, utterly and in joyful abandon, in quiet, glad surrender to Him who is within. In secret ejaculations of praise, turn in humble wonder to the Light, faint though it may be. Keep contact with the outer world of sense and meanings. Here is no discipline in absent-mindedness. Walk and talk and work and laugh with your friends. But behind the scenes, keep up the life of simple prayer and inward worship. Keep it up throughout the day. Let inward prayer be your last act before you fall asleep and the first act when you awake. And in time you will find as did Brother Lawrence, that "those who have the gale of the Holy Spirit go forward even in sleep."

The first days and weeks and months are awkward and painful, but enormously rewarding. Awkward, because it takes constant vigilance and effort and reassertions of the will, at the first level. Painful, because our lapses are so frequent, the intervals when we forget Him so long. Rewarding, because we have begun to live. But these weeks and months and perhaps even years must be passed through before He gives us greater and easier stayedness upon Himself.

Lapses and forgettings are so frequent. Our surroundings grow so exciting. Our occupations are so exacting. But when you catch yourself again, lose no time in self-recriminations, but breathe a silent prayer for forgiveness and begin again, just where you are. Offer *this* broken worship up to Him and say: "This is what I am except Thou aid me." Admit no discouragement, but ever return quietly to Him and wait in His Presence.

At first the practice of inward prayer is a process of alternation of attention between outer things and the Inner Light. Preoccupation with either brings the loss of the other. Yet what is sought is not alternation but simultaneity, worship undergirding every moment, living prayer, the continuous current and background of all moments of life. Long practice indeed is needed before alternation yields to concurrent immersion in both levels at once. The "plateaus in the learning curve" are so long, and many falter and give up, assenting to alternation as the best that they can do. And no doubt in His graciousness God gives us His gifts, even in intermittent communion, and touches us into flame, far beyond our achievements and deserts. But the hunger of the committed one is for unbroken communion and adoration, and we may be sure He longs for us to find it and supplements our weakness. For our quest is of His initiation, and is carried forward in His tender power and completed by His grace.

The first signs of simultaneity are given when at the moment of recovery from a period of forgetting there is a certain sense that we have not completely forgotten Him. It is as though we are only coming back into a state of vividness which had endured in dim and tenuous form throughout. What takes place now is not reinstatement of a broken prayer but return to liveliness of that which had endured, but mildly. The currents of His love have been flowing, but whereas we had been drifting in Him, now we swim. It is like the background of a picture which extends all the way across behind a tree in the foreground. It is not that we merely know intellectually that the background of the picture has unbroken extension; we experience aesthetically that it *does* extend across. Again, it is like waking from sleep yet knowing, not by inference but by immediate awareness, that we have lived even while we were asleep. For sole preoccupation with the world is sleep, but immersion in Him is life.

But period of dawning simultaneity and steadfast prayer may come and go, lapsing into alternation for long periods and returning in glorious power. And we learn to submit to the inner discipline of withdrawing of His gifts. For if the least taint of spiritual pride in our prayer-growth has come, it is well that He humble us until we are worthy of greater trust. For though we begin the practice of secret prayer with a strong sense that we are the initiators and that by our wills we are establishing our habits, maturing experience brings awareness of being met, and tutored, purged and disciplined, simplified and made pliant in His holy will by a power waiting within us. For God Himself works in our souls, in their deepest depths, taking increasing control as we are progressively willing to be prepared for His wonder. We cease trying to make ourselves the dictators and God the listener, and become the joyful listeners to Him, the Master who does all things well.

There is then no need for fret when faithfully turning to Him, if He leads us but slowly into His secret chambers. If He gives us increasing steadiness in the deeper sense of His Presence, we can only quietly thank Him. If He holds us in the stage of alternation we can thank Him for His loving wisdom, and wait upon His guidance through the stages for which we are prepared. For we cannot take Him by storm. The strong man must become the little child, not understanding but trusting the Father.

But to some at least He gives an amazing stayedness in Him, a well-nigh unbroken life of humble quiet adoration in His Presence, in the depths of our being. Day and night, winter and summer, sunshine and shadow. He is here, the great Champion. And we are with Him, held in His Tenderness, quickened into quietness and peace, children in Paradise before the Fall, walking with Him in the garden in the heat as well as the cool of the day. Here is not ecstasy but serenity, unshakableness, firmness of life-orientation. We are become what Fox calls "established men."

Such men are not found merely among the canonized Saints of the Church. They are the John Woolmans of today. They are housewives and hand workers, plumbers and teachers, learned and unlettered, black and white, poor and perchance even rich. They exist, and happy is the church that contains them. They may not be known widely, nor serve on boards of trustees, or preach in pulpits. Where pride in one's learning is found, there they are not. For they do not confuse acquaintance with theology and church history with commitment and the life lived in the secret sanctuary. Cleaving simply through forms and externals, they dwell in immediacy with Him who is the abiding Light behind all changing forms, really nullifying much of the external trappings of religion. They have found the secret of the Nazarene, and, not content to assent to it intellectually, they have committed themselves to it in action, and walk in newness of life in the vast fellowship of unceasing prayer.

There is no new technique for entrance upon this stage where the soul in its deeper levels is continuously at Home in Him. The processes of inward prayer do not grow more complex, but more simple. In the early weeks we begin with simple, whispered words. Formulate them spontaneously, "Thine only. Thine only." Or seize upon a fragment of the Psalms: "so panteth my soul after Thee, O God." Repeat them inwardly, over and over again. For the conscious co-operation of the surface level is needed at first, before prayer sinks into the second level as habitual divine orientation. Change the phrases, as you feel led, from hour to hour or from forenoon to afternoon. If you wander, return and begin again. But the time will come when verbalization is not so imperative, and yields place to the attitudes of soul which you meant the words to express, attitudes of humble bowing before Him, attitudes of lifting high your whole being before Him that the Light may shine into the last crevice and drive away all darkness, attitudes of approach and nestling in the covert of His wings, attitudes of amazement and marvel at His transcendent glory, attitudes of self-abandonment, attitudes of feeding in an inward Holy Supper upon the Bread of Life. If you find, after a time, that these attitudes become diffused and vague, no longer firm-textured, then return to verbalizations and thus restore their solidity.

But longer discipline in this inward prayer will establish more enduring up-reachings of praise and submission and relaxed listening in the depths, unworded but habitual orientation of all one's self about Him who is the Focus. The process is much simpler now. Little glances, quiet breathings of submission and invitation suffice. Voluntary or stated times of prayer merely join into and enhance the steady undercurrent of quiet worship that underlies the hours. Behind the foreground of the words continues the background of heavenly orientation, as all the currents of our being set toward Him.

Through the shimmering light of divine Presence we look out upon the world, and in its turmoil and its fitfulness, we may be given to respond, in some increased measure, in ways dimly suggestive of the Son of Man.

We may suppose these depths of prayer are our achievement, the precipitate of our own habits at the surface level settled into subconscious regions. But this humanistic account misses the autonomy of the life of prayer. It misses the fact that this inner level has a life of its own, invigorated not by us but by a divine Source. There come times when prayer pours forth in volumes and originality such as we cannot create. It rolls through us like a mighty tide. Our prayers are mingled with a vaster Word, a Word that at one time was made flesh. We pray, and yet it is not we who pray, but a Greater who prays in us. Something of our punctiform selfhood is weakened, but never lost. All we can say is, Prayer is taking place, and I am given to be in the orbit. In holy hush we bow in Eternity, and know the Divine Concern tenderly enwrapping us and all things within His persuading love. Here all human initiative has passed into acquiescence, and He works and prays and seeks His own through us, in exquisite, energizing life. Here the autonomy of the inner life becomes complete and we are joyfully *prayed through*, by a Seeking Life that flows through us into the world of men. Sometimes this prayer is particularized, and we are impelled to pray for particular persons or particular situations with a quiet or turbulent energy that, subjectively considered, seems utterly irresistible. Sometimes the prayer and this Life that flows through us reaches out to all souls with kindred vision and upholds them in His tender care. Sometimes it flows out to the world of blinded struggle, and we become cosmic Saviors, seeking all those who are lost.

This "infused prayer" is not frequently given, in full intensity. But something of its autonomous character remains, not merely as a memory of a time when the fountains of creation were once revealed and we were swept along in their rising waters. It remains as an increasing awareness of a more-than-ourselves, working persuadingly and powerfully at the roots of our own soul, and in the depths of all men. It is an experimental assurance of Divine Labor and persuasion pervading the world, impelling men to their cross. In holy awe we are drawn anew to "keep close to the fresh up-springings of the Life," amazed at that which is revealed as at work, at the base of all being, all men and ourselves. And we have our firsthand assurance that He who began that good work in us, as in Timothy, can establish us in Him, can transform intermittency and alternation into simultaneity and continuity.

III

Guidance of life by the Light within is not exhausted as is too frequently supposed, in special leadings toward particular tasks. It begins first of all in a mass revision of our total reaction to the world. Worshipping in the light we become new creatures, making wholly new and astonishing responses to the entire outer setting of life. These responses are not reasoned out. They are, in large measure, spontaneous reactions of felt incompatibility between "the world's" judgments of value and the Supreme Value we adore deep in the Center. There is a total Instruction as well as specific instructions from the Light within. The dynamic illumination from the deeper level is shed upon the judgments of the surface level, and lo, the "former things are passed away, behold, they are become new."

Paradoxically, this total Instruction proceeds in two opposing directions at once. We are torn loose from earthly attachments and ambitions—*contemptus mundi*. And we are quickened to a divine but painful concern for the world —*amor mundi*. He plucks the world out of our hearts, loosening the chains of attachment. And He hurls the world into our hearts, where we and He together carry it in infinitely tender love.

The second half of the paradox is more

readily accepted today than the first. For we fear it means world-withdrawal, world-flight. We fear a life of wallowing in ecstasies of spiritual sensuality while cries of a needy world go unheeded. And some pages of history seem to fortify our fears.

But there is a sound and valid *contemptus mundi* which the Inner Light works within the utterly dedicated soul. Positions of prominence, eminences of social recognition which we once meant to attain—how puny and trifling they become! Our old ambitions and heroic dreams—what years we have wasted in feeding our own insatiable self-pride, when only His will truly matters! Our wealth and property, security now and in old age—upon what broken reeds have we leaned, when He is "the rock of our heart, and our portion forever!"

Again, we have quailed and been tormented in our obscurity, we have fretted and been anxious because of our limitations, set by our own nature and by our surroundings. The tasks are so great, and we have accomplished so little, and been assigned such lowly talents and occupations.

But instructed in one point of view of the paradox, we bestride the mountains or the valleys of earthly importance with a holy indifference, contempt, and detachment. Placed in coveted surroundings, recipients of honors, we count them as refuse, as nothing, utterly nothing. Placed in the shadows, we are happy to pick up a straw for the love of God. No task is so small as to distress us, no honor so great as to turn our heads.

Such loosening of the chains of attachment is easy, if we be given times of a sense of unutterable nearness to Himself. In those moments what would we not leave for Him? What mean honors or dishonors, comforts or wants, in Him? For such persons, in such moments, the work of detachment, *contemptus mundi*, exists chiefly as an intellectual obligation, ominously hovering over their heads as duty, but not known as experienced joy in the new freedom of utter poverty. Still others obstruct this detachment, reject it as absurd or unneeded, and cling to mammon while they seek to cling to God.

Double-mindedness in this matter is wholly destructive of the spiritual life. Totalitarian are the claims of Christ. No vestige of reservation of "our" rights can remain. Straddle arrangements and compromises between our allegiances to the surface level and the divine Center cannot endure. Unless the willingness is present to be stripped of our last earthly dignity and hope, and yet still praise Him, we have no message in this our day of refugees, bodily and spiritual. Nor have we yielded to the monitions of the Inner Instructor.

But actually completed detachment is vastly harder than intended detachment. Fugitive islands of secret reservations elude us. Rationalizations hide them. Intending absolute honesty, we can only bring ourselves steadfastly into His presence and pray, "Cleanse thou me from secret faults." And in the X-ray light of Eternity we may be given to see the dark spots of life, and divine grace may be given to reinforce our will to complete abandonment in Him. For the guidance of the Light is critical, acid, sharper than a two-edged sword. He asks all, but He gives all.

William Adams Brown

(1865-1943)

THROUGHOUT his teaching ministry, which began in 1892, Brown was at Union Theological Seminary, New York, where in 1936 he became professor emeritus of systematic theology. His education was received at Yale, Union, and Berlin. American, Scottish, and English universities conferred honorary degrees upon him. In 1893 he was ordained in the Presbyterian ministry. Throughout his career he was vitally interested in many practical aspects of Christianity: the Federal Council of the Churches of Christ in America, in which he was chairman of the department of research and education; the Religious Education Association, of which he was once president; the World Conference on Faith and Order, of which he was an executive member; the Near East College Association, of which he acted as president; the Institute for the Deaf and Dumb in New York, of which he served as director; the Board of Home Missions of the Presbyterian Church; and the Grenfell Association of America, of which he was a founder.

Brown wrote twenty-six books, two of them being published posthumously. His last book, *How to Think of Christ*, brings to a focus the view which he held throughout his career, a Christo-centric interpretation of religious experience. His books which particularly deal with Christian sainthood are: *How to Think of Christ, Finding God in a New World, God at Work, Beliefs That Matter, The Life of Prayer in a World of Science, The Quiet Hour, The Creative Experience*, and *Pathways to Certainty*. "Ways of Reaching Certainty," from the last-mentioned book, supplements the scientific method with revelation in finding religious truth. It is reprinted here by permission of Charles Scribner's Sons. (Copyright 1930 by William Adams Brown.)

WAYS OF REACHING CERTAINTY

From *Pathways to Certainty*

HOW THE SCIENTIST'S USE OF THE FOUR WAYS DIFFERS FROM THAT OF THE RELIGIOUS MAN

*I*n deciding what weight to give to each of the four ways we follow in our quest of certainty, therefore, we must first be clear which is most appropriate for the issue which we wish to decide. Where we are studying physical phenomena like gravitation or electricity, the mathematical methods of exact science are appropriate; where personality is the subject of our inquiry other methods are essential. Here the feelings and the will, as well as the mind, have their contribution to make. In our study of nature the personal equation must be eliminated so far as it is possible to do so. In our study of persons it has an indispensable contribution to make.

This reminder is more necessary in view of the tendency, more than once referred to, to limit trustworthy knowledge to judgments which are reached through the methods of the exact sciences. That method is determined by its subject matter, namely, the uniformities of nature which make prediction possible. In studying a subject of this kind the restrictions which science imposes upon itself are not only legitimate but inevitable. But when we are dealing with realities like personality or with ideals like beauty or goodness other methods are in place. Here judgments of value, far from being disturbing factors, become the instruments through which alone trustworthy knowledge can be had.

We may illustrate this difference of aim in connection with each one of the four ways of testing belief. All four of them are used by scientists as well as by ordinary people, but in ways that are appropriate to their special aim.

Thus the scientist uses the method of intuition. Like all independent thinkers, he relies in the last analysis upon the conviction of truth which comes to him through his own immediate insight. But in his use of intuition he concentrates his attention upon those aspects of the subject in which the personal equation is least in evidence. Where his personal likes or dislikes are involved, he distrusts his conclusions and claims certainty only for those findings on which the senses can give a trustworthy report.

In like manner he uses the method of authority, but the only authority that he recognizes is that of the experts who have studied the subject before him. He takes their consensus of opinion as the basis of his own hypothesis and if he does not himself repeat their experiments it is only because he thinks it needless to do over again what men in whose accuracy and impartiality he has confidence have already done.

Again, he uses the method of reasoning. He compares all possible alternatives in order to clear his hypothesis of ambiguity and he refuses to consider any hypothesis as proved while any single fact remains in his universe with which it appears to be inconsistent. Probability is not enough. He will be satisfied with nothing less than complete demonstration.

But it is in the use of experiment that the excellencies and the limitations of the scientific method most clearly appear. No feature of modern scientific procedure is more remarkable than the ingenuity which it has employed in devising methods by which alternative possibilities can be isolated and their relevancy or irrelevancy to the situation under investigation can be determined. But the nature of the proof that is sought limits the experiments used to those which produce results which are capable of mathematical tests. For the great insights which have come to man in his best moments—to a Socrates in his prison, to a Jesus in the Garden—no system of measurement has yet been devised.

Within the limits thus set science is able to secure for us a very high degree of certainty. It can tell us when the sun will rise and how fast it will move, when to expect an eclipse and how it has been brought about, what combinations of elements make up specific substances and how they can be modified by heat or strain. It can tell us what drugs produce healing effects and how different people will react to them under prescribed conditions. It can tell us how the condition of the nervous system affects our mental states and which brain centres control perception, and which, action. The catalog of all the different things it can tell us would fill many volumes, and within the range which it has set itself its answers are trustworthy. When we do what the scientists tell us to do within the fields where their conclusions agree, the results which they promise follow. Indeed the sequence has become so familiar to us that we often forget the complicated process by which man's mastery of nature has been brought about.

But there are other matters, and these no less important, to which this way of approach is not applicable. When we are dealing not with facts or with sequences of facts but with the meanings they suggest and the purposes they serve, other methods are essential. What these methods are we may learn by watching the procedure of those to whom the world has accorded the first place in the field of letters or of art.

Thus in his use of authority the poet or the artist will give chief weight to those witnesses whose experience has been characterized by the most vivid sense of beauty or of proportion, in other words to those aspects of reality in which judgments of value play the largest part.

So in his use of intuition, instead of discounting the significance of his personal satisfaction as expressed in his response to ideals of nobility or of beauty, the artist will make this satisfaction central among the grounds of his faith. But he will guard against the danger of subjectivity by subordinating his transient mood to his permanent attitude, and checking his own experience by comparing it with that of the artists who have found satisfaction in beauty before him.

Reasoning, too, will have its place in his test of certainty. And by reasoning he will mean what the scientist means by that term—the attempt to reach a conclusion which is consistent with all other knowledge. Indeed it is just because he respects the principle of consistency so highly that he is not willing to accept the scientist's account of the world as adequate. How can any view which, for however laudable a motive, excludes from consideration one great segment of the many-sided realm of reality claim to give a view of the world which is consistent with the facts. Even if the artist cannot see how the values in life, as he sees it, can be reconciled with the facts of error or pain or death, he is not willing on that account to discredit these values. Somehow they must find their place in the total picture of reality, and, even if he cannot as yet work out the reconciliation in detail, he will hold to his faith that a reconciliation will some day be possible. In the meantime he is grateful for all the light which science can shed upon the matters that fall within its own immediate province and, in so far as its conclusions have been established, will take them up into his own synthesis.

But it is in experiment that the likeness and the unlikeness of the two procedures most clearly appear. Like the scientist, the artist makes large use of experiment, but it is experiment of a different kind. The experiments of the exact sciences are concerned with parts, or aspects, of reality and achieve their end in the measure that, by analysis, they segregate the parts to be investigated from others which, in life, are intimately associated with them. The experiments of art, on the other hand, are concerned with the effects produced upon us by the world as a whole, or by the lesser wholes of which it is composed—mountains and sea and trees and flowers and men and women. The aim of the artist is to exhibit the true relation between these different wholes, as that relation is illuminated by comprehensive ideals, like beauty, or honor, or goodness, and life as it is actually lived by men and women in the laboratory in which the artist verifies by experiment the correctness of his original intuition of the ideal.

These considerations we must bear in mind in our approach to the object of religious certainty, which is God. God is not an isolated fact which can be separated from its environment and demonstrated, as we can demonstrate the weight of a man or the date of an eclipse. God is the ultimate reality in the universe, the moving spirit in all nature and in all history, and everything that happens, whether in us or apart from us, may contribute to our understanding of his nature and will. To know God in the sense in which religion understands knowledge is not simply to apprehend him with the mind. It is to reverence and to obey him. In validating a belief so comprehensive we should not expect to secure the desired result by any purely intellectual process. Rather should we hope to find our confidence justified by the converging evidence of all possible methods of approach.

IS REVELATION A FIFTH WAY?

But I am sure that long before this some of my readers will have been saying to themselves, why limit the paths to be followed in our quest of certainty to four? Surely there is a fifth way open to us, the most direct and dependable of all, namely, the broad highway of divine revelation. All the methods we have been studying are no doubt good methods as far as they go. But they are human methods. And where the final responsibility rests with man there is always the possibility of mistake. The certainty of which we are in search in religion, on the other hand, is divine certainty. How can we find God unless he himself comes to meet us; and when he speaks how can there be any doubt as to what he says?

There is the best of authority for such a reminder. Belief in a definite and easily accessible revelation has been one of the oldest and most persistent of human beliefs. The Catholic finds such a revelation in the church, the Protestant in the Bible, the mystic in the immediate witness of God's Spirit to the spirit of man. Bible and church bring God's message in explicit terms of universal validity. The mystic revelation on the other hand is private and personal. Yet in each case the one to whom the revelation comes is sure that it is God with whom he has to do, and in each case the communication received has an authentic quality which seems to the recipient to preclude the possibility of mistake.

Waiving for a moment the question whether even divine revelation can preclude the possibility of mistake in man's understanding of it, it is sufficient here to point out that God's revelation when it comes will be found not outside the four ways already distinguished but inside. The Catholic, as we have seen, hears God speaking to him through the church, the Protestant through the Bible. But these are the two outstanding examples of the method of authority. The mystic, for his part, tells us that he needs no external authority, for he has heard God's Spirit speaking directly to his own spirit. But the witness of the Spirit is only the religious man's way of describing what the psychologist calls intuition. Even reason, the way of all ways that is most often set over against revelation as man's way in contrast to God's, is recognized by theologians of all schools as a form, even though a lower form, of revelation.

Revelation then is not to be thought of as a fifth way of reaching certainty, to be added to the other four ways as supplying us with additional material. Rather is it our way of expressing our conviction that in each of the four ways God is speaking to us and that no account of his ways of revealing himself can be complete which does not take them all in. God does speak to us through authority in the testimony of his Bible and of his church. He does speak to us through his Spirit in the intuitions of our best moments. But it is one thing to recognize the existence of a real God who is really revealing himself to us, and another to contrast that revelation not only with some of our subjective imaginings about him but with every conceivable process through which we men acquire knowledge. This is easy to do in words, difficult to do in fact. And while the motive is a natural and, in many respects, a laudable one, namely, to lift us above the uncertainties of our human apprehension and plant our feet upon the firm rock of divine truth, it will be found that the short cut does not lead to the goal as speedily as we thought. On the contrary, we shall discover that the pathway of revelation will lead us before we are through into each one of the other four paths which are now to be the subject of our study: the path of authority, the path of intuition, the path of reasoning, and the path of experiment, and that it is only when we have traversed the territory covered by them all that we shall arrive at last at our goal.

Alexis Carrel

(1873-1944)

CARREL was born in France and educated at the University of Lyon and the University of Dijon, receiving the degree of Doctor of Medicine from both. From 1906-39 he was a member of the Rockefeller Institute for Medical Research. Among other prizes won for his research were the Nordhoff-Jung medal for cancer research and the Nobel prize for suturing blood vessels. He was a Roman Catholic.

Carrel's role as a philosopher-scientist emerged in *Man, the Unknown*. The following selection which sees man's physical well-being as largely dependent upon his spiritual health, was originally published in *Reader's Digest*, March, 1941, and was later included in *The Reader's Digest Twentieth Anniversary Anthology* in 1941 as one of the best of the eight thousand articles printed during two decades. Permission is granted by this magazine for the reprint below.

PRAYER IS POWER

Prayer is not only worship; it is also an invisible emanation of man's worshiping spirit—the most powerful form of energy that one can generate. The influence of prayer on the human mind and body is as demonstrable as that of secreting glands. Its results can be measured in terms of increased physical buoyancy, a greater intellectual vigor, moral stamina, and a deeper understanding of the realities underlying human relationships.

If you make a habit of sincere prayer, your life will be very noticeably and profoundly altered. Prayer stamps with its indelible mark our actions and demeanor. A tranquillity of bearing, a facial and bodily repose, are observed in those whose inner lives are thus enriched. Within the depths of consciousness a flame kindles. And man sees himself. He discovers his selfishness, his silly pride, his fears, his greeds, his blunders. He develops a sense of moral obligation, intellectual humility. Thus begins a journey of the soul toward the realm of grace.

Prayer is a force as real as terrestrial gravity. As a physician, I have seen men, after all other therapy had failed, lifted out of disease and melancholy by the serene effort of prayer. It is the only power in the world that seems to overcome the so-called "laws of nature"; the occasions on which prayer has dramatically done this have been termed "miracles." But a constant, quieter miracle takes place hourly in the hearts of men and women who have discovered that prayer supplies them with a steady flow of sustaining power in their daily lives.

Too many people regard prayer as a formalized routine of words, a refuge for weaklings, or a childish petition for material things. We sadly undervalue prayer when we conceive it in these terms, just as we should underestimate rain by describing it as something that fills the birdbath in our garden. Properly understood, prayer is a mature activity indispensable to the fullest development of personality—the ultimate integration of man's highest faculties. Only in prayer do we achieve that complete and harmonious assembly of body, mind and spirit which gives the frail human reed its unshakable strength.

The words, "Ask and it shall be given to you," have been verified by the experience of humanity. True, prayer may not restore the dead child to life or bring relief from physical pain. But prayer, like radium, is a source of luminous, self-generating energy.

How does prayer fortify us with so much dynamic power? To answer this question (admittedly outside the jurisdiction of science) I must point out that all prayers have one thing in common. The triumphant hosannas of a great oratorio, or the humble supplication of an Iroquois hunter begging for luck in the chase, demonstrate the same truth: that human beings seek to augment their finite energy by addressing themselves to the Infinite source of all energy. When we pray, we link ourselves with the inexhaustible motive power that spins the universe. We ask that a part of this power be apportioned to our needs. Even in asking, our human deficiencies are filled and we arise strengthened and repaired.

But we must never summon God merely for the gratification of our whims. We derive most power from prayer when we use it, not as a petition, but as a supplication that we may become more like Him. Prayer should be regarded as practice of the Presence of God. An old peasant was seated alone in the last pew of the village church. "What are you waiting for?" he was asked; and he answered, "I am looking at Him and He is looking at me." Man prays not only that God should remember him, but also that he should remember God.

How can prayer be defined? Prayer is the effort of man to reach God, to commune with an invisible being, creator of all things, supreme wisdom, truth, beauty, and strength, father and redeemer of each man. This goal of prayer always remains hidden to intelligence. For both language and thought fail when we attempt to describe God.

We do know, however, that whenever we address God in fervent prayer we change both soul and body for the better. It could not happen that any man or woman could pray for a single mo-

ment without some good result. "No man ever prayed," said Emerson, "without learning something."

One can pray everywhere. In the streets, the subway, the office, the shop, the school, as well as in the solitude of one's own room or among the crowd in a church. There is no prescribed posture, time or place.

"Think of God more often than you breathe," said Epictetus the Stoic. In order really to mold personality, prayer must become a habit. It is meaningless to pray in the morning and to live like a barbarian the remainder of the day. True prayer is a way of life; the truest life is literally a way of prayer.

The best prayers are like the improvisations of gifted lovers, always about the same thing yet never twice the same. We cannot all be as creative in prayer as Saint Theresa or Bernard of Clairvaux, both of whom poured their adoration into words of mystical beauty. Fortunately, we do not need their eloquence; our slightest impulse to prayer is recognized by God. Even if we are pitifully dumb, or if our tongues are overlaid with vanity or deceit, our meager syllables of praise are acceptable to Him, and He showers us with strengthening manifestations of His love.

Today, as never before, prayer is a binding necessity in the lives of men and nations. The lack of emphasis on the religious sense has brought the world to the edge of destruction. Our deepest source of power and perfection has been left miserably undeveloped. Prayer, the basic exercise of the spirit, must be actively practiced in our private lives. The neglected soul of man must be made strong enough to assert itself once more. For if the power of prayer is again released and used in the lives of common men and women; if the spirit declares its aims clearly and boldly, there is yet hope that our prayers for a better world will be answered.

William Temple

(1881-1944)

IN recent years many have considered Temple, an archbishop of Canterbury, as the outstanding leader of Protestantism. He was born in The Palace, Exeter, the son of Frederick Temple, who later became archbishop of Canterbury. His education was received at Rugby and at Balliol College, Oxford. He was fellow and lecturer in philosophy at Queen's College, Oxford, 1904-10; chaplain to the archbishop of Canterbury, 1910-21; chaplain to the king, 1915-21; bishop of Manchester, 1921-28; archbishop of York, 1928-42; and archbishop of Canterbury at his death.

Temple felt a fine synthesis of the Greek tradition and the Jewish-Christian viewpoint. Several years ago he said that the three thinkers who meant the most to him were Plato, the writer of the Gospel of John, and Robert Browning. His thinking was touched on the one hand by an intellectual profundity, and on the other by a deep concern for the social reformation of the world. He was president of the Workers' Educational Association, 1908-24, and was active in the ecumenical movement and with groups concerned with social evils which oppress men. In 1937 he was chairman of the World Conference on Faith and Order, held in Edinburgh, Scotland.

His many books include *Plato and Christianity; Personal Religion and the Life of Fellowship; Nature, Man, and God; Christianity and the State;* and *Readings in St. John's Gospel.*

"Christian Social Principles" is part of a chapter from *Christianity and Social Order,* used by permission of Penguin Books. (Copyright 1942 by Penguin Books, Inc.)

CHRISTIAN SOCIAL PRINCIPLES

From *Christianity and Social Order*

The method of the Church's impact upon society at large should be twofold. The Church must announce Christian principles and point out where the existing social order at any time is in conflict with them. It must then pass on to Christian citizens, acting in their civic capacity, the task of re-shaping the existing order in closer conformity to the principles. For at this point technical knowledge may be required and judgments of practical expediency are always required. If a bridge is to be built, the Church may remind the engineer that it is his obligation to provide a really safe bridge; but it is not entitled to tell him whether, in fact, his design meets this requirement; a particular theologian may also be a competent engineer, and, if he is, his judgment on this point is entitled to attention; but this is altogether because he is a competent engineer and his theological equipment has nothing whatever to do with it. In just the same way the Church may tell the politician what ends the social order should promote; but it must leave to the politician the devising of the precise means to those ends.

This is a point of first-rate importance, and is frequently misunderstood. If Christianity is true at all it is a truth of universal application; all things should be done in the Christian spirit and in accordance with Christian principles. "Then," say some, "produce your Christian solution for unemployment." But there neither is nor could be such a thing. Christian faith does not by itself enable its adherent to foresee how a vast multitude of people, each one partly selfish and partly generous, and an intricate economic mechanism, will in fact be affected by a particular economic or political innovation—"social credit," for example.

"In that case," says the reformer—or, quite equally, the upholder of the *status quo*—"keep off the turf. By your own confession you are out of place here." But this time the Church must say "No; I cannot tell you what is the remedy; but I can tell you that a society of which unemployment (in peace time) is a chronic feature is a diseased society, and that if you are not doing all you can to find and administer the remedy, you are guilty before God." Sometimes the Church can go further than this and point to features in the social structure itself which are bound to be sources of social evil because they contradict the principles of the Gospel.

So the Church is likely to be attacked from both sides if it does its duty. It will be told that it has become "political" when in fact it has been careful only to state principles and point to breaches of them; and it will be told by advocates of particular policies that it is futile because it does not support these. If it is faithful to its commission it will ignore both sets of complaints, and continue so far as it can to influence all citizens and permeate all parties.

Before going on to state in outline the chief principles of Christian social doctrine, it may be wise, in the prevailing temper of our age, to add a further word of caution. For it is sometimes supposed that what the Church has to do is to sketch a perfect social order and urge men to establish it. But it is very difficult to know what a "perfect social order" means. Is it the order that would work best if we were all perfect? Or is it the order that would work best in a world of men and women such as we actually are? If it is the former, it certainly ought not to be established; we should wreck it in a fortnight. If it is the latter, there is no reason for expecting the Church to know what it is.

Here we are dealing with what is at this moment the least popular part of traditional Christianity: the doctrine of Original Sin. No doubt this has often been put forward in ways which men to-day find peculiar difficulty in accept-ing. It would be quite out of place to deal with the whole topic here. Quite enough for our present purpose may be expressed as follows. When we open our eyes as babies we see the world stretching out around us; we are in the middle of it; all proportions and perspectives in what we see are determined by the relation—distance, height, and so forth— of the various visible objects to ourselves. This will remain true of our bodily vision as long as we live. I am the centre of the world I see; where the horizon is depends on where I stand. Now just the same thing is true at first of our mental and spiritual vision. Some things hurt us; we hope they will not happen again; we call them bad. Some things please us; we hope they will happen again; we call them good. Our standard of value is the way things affect ourselves. So each of us takes his place in the centre of his own world. But I am not the centre of the world, or the standard of reference as between good and bad; I am not, and God is. In other words, from the beginning I put myself in God's place. This is my original sin. I was doing it before I could speak, and everyone else has been doing it from early infancy. I am not "guilty" on this account because I could not help it. But I am in a state, from birth, in which I shall bring disaster on myself and everyone affected by my conduct unless I can escape from it. Education may make my self-centredness less disastrous by widening my horizon of interest; so far it is like the climbing of a tower, which widens the horizon for physical vision while leaving me still the centre and standard of reference. Education may do more than this if it succeeds in winning me into devotion to truth or to beauty; that devotion may effect a partial deliverance from self-centredness. But complete deliverance can be effected only by the winning of my whole heart's devotion, the total allegiance of my will—and this only the Divine Love disclosed by Christ in His Life and Death can do.

The political problem is concerned with men as they are, not with men as

WILLIAM TEMPLE

they ought to be. Part of the task is so to order life as to lead them nearer to what they ought to be; but to assume that they are already this will involve certain failure and disaster. It is not contended that men are utterly bad, or that they are more bad than good. What is contended is that they are not perfectly good, and that even their goodness is infected with a quality—self-centredness —which partly vitiates it, and exposes them to temptations so far as they achieve either freedom or power. This does not mean that freedom or power should be denied to them; on the contrary, it is fundamental to the Christian position that men should have freedom even though they abuse it; but it is also to be recognized that they certainly will abuse it except so far as they are won by devotion to truth or to beauty to that selfless outlook, which is only perfectly established in men by love which arises in them in answer to the redemptive love of God.

In any period worth considering, and probably to the end of earthly history, statesmen will themselves be men, and will be dealing with men, who abuse freedom and power. Now the most fundamental requirement of any political and economic system is not that it shall express love, though that is desirable, nor that it shall express justice, though that is the first ethical demand to be made upon it, but that it shall supply some reasonable measure of security against murder, robbery and starvation. If it can be said with real probability that a proposed scheme would in fact, men being what they are, fail to provide that security, that scheme is doomed. Christians have some clues to the understanding of human nature which may enable them to make a more accurate estimate than others of these points. But they will not, if they are true to their own tradition, approach the question with rosy-tinted spectacles. Its assertion of Original Sin should make the Church intensely realistic, and conspicuously free from Utopianism.

There is no such thing as a Christian social ideal, to which we should conform our actual society as closely as possible. We may notice, incidentally, about any such ideals from Plato's *Republic* onwards, that no one really wants to live in the ideal state as depicted by anyone else. Moreover, there is the desperate difficulty of getting there. When I read any description of an Ideal State and think how we are to begin transforming our own society into that, I am reminded of the Englishman in Ireland who asked the way to Roscommon. "Is it Roscommon you want to go to?" said the Irishman. "Yes," said the Englishman; "that's why I asked the way." "Well," said the Irishman, "if I wanted to go to Roscommon, I wouldn't be starting from here."

But though Christianity supplies no ideal in this sense, it supplies something of far more value—namely, principles on which we can begin to act in every possible situation. To the consideration of these we now turn.

1. GOD AND HIS PURPOSE

All Christian thinking, and Christian thinking about society no less than any other, must begin not with man but with God. The fundamental conviction is that God is the creator of the world which could not begin or continue except by His will. The world is not necessary to God in the sense in which God is necessary to the world; for if there were no God, there would be no world but if there were no world, God would be just what He is—only (presumably) about to make the world. For He is impelled to make the world by His love; as Plato saw, He is far removed from envy and wishes to share out His blessedness. The world is not necessary to God as the object of His love, for He has that within Himself in the relations of the Persons of the Blessed Trinity; but it results from His love; creation is a kind of overflow of the divine love. In making the world He brought into existence vast numbers of things which always have to obey His law for them, and do so; He did this in order and electrons; these have no choice but to obey. But He also made creatures—men and women—who could disobey His law for them, and do so; He did this in order that among His creatures there might be some who gave Him a free obedience and answered His love with theirs. This involved the risk, amounting to a moral certainty, that they would take the self-centred outlook upon life, and then, partly by imitation and partly in self-defence, become hardened in selfishness, till society was a welter of competing selfishness instead of being a fellowship of love. That is what happened. To win them out of this, He came on earth and lived out the divine love in a human life and death. He is increasingly drawing men to Himself by the love thus shown. Lord Acton, who knew more history than any other Englishman of the last generation, deliberately declared: "The action of Christ who is risen on mankind whom He redeemed fails not, but increases." But this task of drawing all men to Himself, the divine purpose to "sum up all things in Christ," will not be effected till the end of history; and the fellowship of love which it is the divine plan to establish cannot come into being in its completeness within history at all, for it must be more than a fellowship of contemporaries. The Kingdom of God is a reality here and now, but can be perfect only in the eternal order.

2. Man: His Dignity, Tragedy and Destiny

The fundamental facts about man are two: he is made "in the image of God"; and this image is, so to speak, stamped upon an animal nature. Between these two there is constant tension resulting in perpetual tragedy.

The dignity of man is that he is the child of God, capable of communion with God, the object of the Love of God —such love as is displayed on the Cross —and destined for eternal fellowship with God. His true value is not what he is worth in himself or to his earthly state, but what he is worth to God; and that worth is bestowed on him by the utterly gratuitous Love of God.

All his life should be conducted and ordered with this dignity in view. The State must not treat him as having value only so far as he serves its ends, as Totalitarian States do; The State exists for its citizens, not the citizen for the State. But neither must a man treat himself, or conduct his life, as if he were himself the centre of his own value; he is not his own end; his value is his worth to God and his end is "to glorify God and enjoy Him for ever."

As a child of God, man is a member of a family, the family of God. This in complete development and expression is nothing less than mankind. But the inherently social and indeed "familial" character of man finds its first expression in the human family. This is the initial form of man's social life, and its preservation and security is the first principle of social welfare. On one side the family is a biological fact; children are born utterly dependent and need the care of both parents. But it is far more than biological. Other animals care for their young; but when the young are mature, the family connexion ceases. Among human beings the family tie lasts through life; what begins as a biological necessity becomes a spiritual possession. To ignore the family, as much in the organization of contemporary life ignores it, is to injure both citizens and society.

There are wider social units which are also necessary; with some of these we shall be concerned later, but only one is natural in a way at all resembling that in which the family is natural—and then in markedly less degree. The nation as we know it is a product of long history; but its origins in the clan and tribe give it the same relation as the family to the individual. And it is a product of historical development, not a deliberately manufactured structure. Every civilized man or woman is born a member of a nation as well as of a family. These nations have developed various cultural types, and the world is the richer for that variety.

Each individual is born into a family and a nation. In his maturity he is very largely what these have made him. The family is so deeply grounded in nature and the nation in history that anyone who believes in God as Creator and as Providence is bound to regard both as part of the divine plan for human life. Their claims have to be adjusted to one another, and so have the claims of the several families within each nation and of the several nations in the family of mankind. But any ordering of society which impairs or destroys the stability of the family stands condemned on that account alone; and any ordering of international life which obliterates the freedom of the several nations to develop their own cultural traditions is also condemned. The aim within the nation must be to create a harmony of stable and economically secure family units; the aim in the world as a whole must be to create a harmony of spiritually independent nations which recognize one another as reciprocally supplementary parts of a richly harmonious fellowship.

Such a harmony would be the earthly counterpart and "first fruits" (as St. Paul might call it) of the perfected Kingdom of God. It would supply the school, training the citizens of that Kingdom— of which the full life cannot be known under earthly conditions, for it is a fellowship of the servants of God in all generations alike with Him and with one another.

It is the tragedy of man that he conceives such a state of affairs and knows it for the only satisfaction of his nature, yet so conducts his life as to frustrate all hope of attaining that satisfaction. It is not only that his spirit and reason have as yet established but little control over the animal part of his nature; it is his spirit which is depraved, his reason which is perverted. His self-centredness infects his idealism because it distorts all his perspectives. So far as his reason acts in purely intellectual ways it may be trustworthy: $2 + 2 = 4$; that really is true; it is not the best approximation that can be expected of sinful man; it is an exact apprehension of absolute truth. Within what is capable of mathematical treatment man has this grasp of truth. But it carries us only a little way. It helps

us to make and manipulate aeroplanes; it does not help us to use them always and only for the benefit of mankind. All science is morally neutral. When we come to human relationships, to friendship, to falling in love—and out of it again—to social organization or to political construction, we enter on a sphere of life where reason is very fallible. Self-interest is always exercising its disturbing influence, not less (though more nobly) when it is being forcibly repudiated than when it is accepted as the guide of conduct.

Anyhow, we all know that Politics is largely a contention between different groups of self-interest—e.g., the Haves and the Have-nots. It may be the function of the Church to lead people to a purely disinterested virtue (though this is at least debatable); a statesman who supposes that a mass of citizens can be governed without appeal to their self-interest is living in dreamland and is a public menace. The art of Government in fact is the art of so ordering life that self-interest prompts what justice demands. Thus it is enacted that thieves should be sent to prison; but the object of the law is not to imprison thieves, but to make men reflect that even if they are not honest it is still prudent to behave honestly.

Yet these expedients are not purely prudential, and though the cynic finds plenty of material for his malicious wit, the real truth about man eludes his grasp. Man is self-centred; but he always carries with him abundant proof that this is not the real truth of his nature. He has to his credit both capacities and achievements that could never be derived from self-interest. The image of God—the image of holiness and love—is still there, though defaced; it is the source of his aspirations; it is even—through its defacement—the occasion of his perversity. It is capable of response to the Divine Image in its perfection if ever this can be presented to it. This is the glory of the Gospel. It enables man to see "the light of the knowledge of the glory of God in the face of Jesus Christ," and so "with unveiled face, reflecting as a mirror the glory of the Lord," man may be "transformed into the same image from glory to glory."

That is man's destiny. And his social life, so far as it is deliberately planned, should be ordered with that destiny in view. He must be treated as what he actually is, but always with a view to what in God's purpose he is destined to become. For the law, and the social order, is our schoolmaster to bring us to Christ.

Rufus M. Jones

(1863———)

No contemporary scholar has done more in his writings to explain and evaluate the saints than Jones. Born of Quaker parents in Maine, and educated at Haverford, Heidelberg, Oxford, and Harvard, he taught philosophy at his alma mater, Haverford, from 1893 until he became professor emeritus in 1934. During this half century he wrote more than forty books, many of them dealing with mysticism. He stands as the leading American exponent of Christian mysticism, viewed from the angle of a Quaker philosopher.

Of Rufus Jones, Bernard Meland writes, "He may undoubtedly be considered the most eminent American mystic of recent times, if, in fact, he is not the American mystic *par excellence*." "The Immanence of God" is part of a chapter in *Pathways to the Reality of God*. This "immanence," which touches man always in the realm of the "subconscious," is brought to the plane of awareness in religious experiences, and is the basis of mystical devotion. (The selection is reprinted here by permission of The Macmillan Co. (Copyright 1931 by The Macmillan Co.)

THE IMMANENCE OF GOD

From *Pathways to the Reality of God*

*T*he direction of the quest for God has in our times turned emphatically from outside in space to the realm of the spirit within man. This change of direction is not a sudden and complete revolution in thought, for there have always been some persons who have had the conviction that God is to be found within rather than without, that He is here rather than in some remote realm. In all periods of man's intensive travail for truth there have been some seekers who have had at least a dim surmise that we have our dealings with a pervasive and deeply interfused Spirit rather than with an absentee Being. All the major religions of the world have borne some testimony, however feeble, to the fact and the presence of an indwelling and resident Life, with whom we are akin and who comes into communion with man's spirit. The Stoic movement often gave a crude and confused account of the indwelling *Pneuma*, or *Logos*, the Soul of the world, but the movement succeeded in carrying to all Western lands a confession of faith in an omnipresent Spirit, a faith which is nobly expressed in the 139th Psalm, "If I take the wings of the morning and dwell in the uttermost parts of the sea; even there shall thy hand lead me, and thy right hand shall hold me."

But the doctrine of the Spirit was raised by St. Paul to an entirely new level and to a new intensity, and it was, again, taken up by St. John and carried by him to its loftiest ancient expression. There is, no doubt, a Stoic influence apparent in both of these apostolic interpreters, but it was almost certainly an unconscious influence and that strand of Stoic thought is so completely outweighed by a mighty personal experience of spiritual energies that the interpretation becomes at once unique and original.

The famous words from St. Paul's sermon on the Areopagus: "In God we live and move and are," have a distinct Stoic quality and they are followed almost immediately by a quotation from a Stoic poet, but the moment we turn to the great passages in the Epistles that speak of the Work of the Spirit, the Life of the Spirit, the Power of the Spirit, we quickly discover that we have left Stoic levels of thought far behind. Who else would have dared to say: "In Him we are builded together into a holy temple for a habitation of God through the Spirit" (Eph. ii:21). St. John's outlook is at many points quite different from St. Paul's and the former writer expresses his faith in a unique form, though they have much in common. It is not an exaggeration to say that the Johannine conception of the Spirit of Truth is one of the most wonderful interpretations that anyone has proclaimed anywhere at any time, for it rises to the clear and positive insight that God Himself is essentially Spirit, and that all true worship must be *real and spiritual*—"in Spirit and in Truth."

But in spite of this exalted teaching at the headwaters of the Christian stream, the prevailing tendency in the history of Western Christianity has been in the direction of a distinctly transcendent conception of God. Wherever the influence of Aristotle was effective on Christian thought it was quite natural for God to be conceived of as remote and absentee, and the Jewish thought of God as Creator working from the outside also pointed in the same direction. A combination of powerful movements of thought during the first three centuries sharply emphasized the dualistic aspects of the universe. It became the fashion to think of an undivine world here below and a faraway God beyond the seven circles who could effect His purposes for this lower realm only by miraculous interposition and by interruption of the natural order of things. The great controlling systems of Christian thought were formed and built around that basic idea.

And yet there were all the way down the line of historical Christianity frequent outbursts of pentecostal faith and fervor. Something like the experience that occurred in the upper room fifty days after the Crucifixion has swept more than once over the lives of smaller or larger groups of believers, and whenever the experience occurred it gave the groups assurance that God was here as Spirit and not a remote Sovereign in the sky. St. Paul's personal testimony, and St. John's spiritual interpretation, have been quick and powerful influences in all centuries, however dark and medieval, and Pentecosts have been repeated with fresh outbursts of enthusiasm and kindled fire. A mystical writer in the twelfth century announced the beginning of the *eternal Gospel*, by which he meant the good news that God is Spirit and works as Spirit directly on men's lives, and not alone through ecclesiastical channels.

The modern emphasis on the immanence of God is therefore not something new and revolutionary. What has happened is that this view is no longer a rare exception, or an occasional sporadic outbreak of fervid experience. There has come through a fusion of many lines of thought a well-ordered interpretation of the universe that is essentially *immanentist*. That does not mean that God is swallowed up and lost in the vast congeries of things. It does not imply that He is a mighty Pan, or the Allness of the All. It does not blur His reality or thin it away to a mere energy or driving power or blind urge, for Mind, or Spirit, by its essential nature is transcendent as well as immanent. Whenever spirit appears, even in the finite form of our own personal minds, it always outreaches and goes beyond its given expression and embodiment. We always transcend ourselves. We always live beyond our margins. We leap beyond anything that *is*—the here and now—and we are by the necessity of our being concerned with a more yet that ought to be. A God who is immanent, if He is to be thought of as Spirit, is just as certainly transcendent. A God who is the foundational Life of our lives must be the eternal guarantor of all that can be or that ought to be as well as of all that is. He must be both within us and beyond us, within the world and beyond it, in the midst of time and yet beyond it.

Let us now endeavor to think out our connection with God as immanent Spirit.

Few religious problems in man's long history have received so much effort of thought as has the formulated doctrine of the Trinity. It is in its sphere as great an achievement of genius as was the creation of the Gothic cathedrals of Europe. The time and labor and genius bestowed upon its elucidation might, if turned in other channels, almost have rebuilt the social fabric of humanity. I am not inclined, however, to regret that so much pains was taken to clarify the essential nature of God. It was in the main, I humbly think, a problem worth all the effort it has taken. I only regret that so little clarity and such meager practical results have been achieved by all these ages of agonizing speculation. The creeds of the churches bear quiet witness to the long travail of thought, but the rank and file of those who compose the communions of Christendom can point to very little in their actual thought of God that has been contributed to their mental insight by these centuries of fierce debate. And of all the aspects of the endless trinitarian problem the one that has received the least measure of clarity and elucidation is the nature of the Spirit. The creeds are almost silent on this point, or go no farther than to say: "And I believe in the Holy Ghost." Individual interpreters of the Holy Spirit have added a little increment to the growing wisdom. Some excellent studies have been made by modern writers, but even so we have thus far hardly got beyond the fringes of what ought to be the central topic of religious thought. . . .

We need to learn how to think of God as a resident presence coöperating vitally with us and in us here and now as an Emmanuel God, and at the same time we need just as urgently to see how our human lives can and do open out into a Beyond within ourselves. Almost every person who has attained to a mature spiritual life has had experiences which convinced him, at least in high moments, that he was *more than himself*. Help comes from somewhere and enables us to do what we had always thought could not be done. We find somewhere power to stand the universe when its waterspouts are let loose and even when they have gone over us. We discover strength from beyond our own stock of resources in the midst of our crises.

We do not know how far our own margins of being reach. We cannot completely map the full area that properly belongs to *us*. No one can with certainty draw the boundary between himself and the beyond himself, any more than we can tell where the tidal river ends and the ocean begins, but we unmistakably feel on occasions that tides from beyond our own margins sweep into us and refresh us. . . .

We are only now, after four centuries, gradually becoming aware of the spiritual consequences of the revolutionary discoveries made by Copernicus and his scientific followers. For untold ages, before the Polish monk in 1543 upset the ancient theory of the celestial revolutions, the sky was believed to be a crystalline dome with many concentric layers, all of which turned around the central earth, carrying along in unvarying regularity the sun and moon and stars which were supposed to be set into one or the other of these rotating domes. The planets wandered about with considerable latitude and consequently gave the suggestion which led Copernicus to his startling conclusion. The occasional comets which swept the sky seemed to conform to no system at all and quite naturally produced fright and terror. They exhibited the very height of irrationality, something in the sky that did not obey the order and harmony of the heavenly realm. The falling meteors, too, suggested revolt and disobedience in the upper regions. The story of the fall of Lucifer and the war in heaven, told in the most vivid style and in faultless poetry in Milton's *Paradise Lost*, goes back in its original form to the imaginative reaction in the popular mind to the downward plunge of a falling meteor, which appeared to break away from the divine order and to leave its heavenly abode forever:

> From morn
> To noon he fell, from noon to dewy eve,
> A summer's day; and with the setting sun
> Dropped from the zenith like a falling star.

This ancient system of thought furnished a happy solution of many of the central problems of religion. The sky, with its perfect order and unvarying regularity, except in the above-mentioned instances of seeming variation or rebellion, appeared to the ancient world to be the vestibule of the spiritual realm. Above the beauty and the glory of the highest sky-dome was thought to be the pure region where God dwelt in supreme majesty. The empyrean beyond the revolving spheres was naturally conceived to be the eternal home of the saints of all ages, and all the imagery of heaven in hymns and poetry is a pictorial creation which conforms to this general scheme of thought. In short, the basic structure of religious conception throughout almost the entire history of the race has been built around this sky theory. A great many of the words in the spiritual vocabulary of the widespread Aryan family are words that originally had to do with the *sky*, and we still go on using the word "heavenly" as though it were synonymous with "divine."

Slowly these last four hundred years of astronomical research have forced us to realize that there is no crystal-dome above our heads. There is no localized dwelling place for God or for the saints above the sky. The "empyrean" is a creation of imagination. The region *up there* is no more pure or perfect than the region down here. Stars, planets, suns and moons are just as crudely material in construction as is the earth on which we tread, or as is the stuff of which our bodies are made.

> Twinkle, twinkle little star,
> I need not wonder what you are;
> For seen by spectroscopic ken
> You're helium and hydrogen.

While we are "looking up" for our sky the earth dwellers in the antipodes are looking in precisely the opposite direction for their sky. Their up is our down.

We have plainly enough outgrown the imagery of the sky for our spiritual realities, and yet we have formed no substitute for it. We know in theory that God is not to be found in any peculiar or essential way by an ascent into the sky. Most of us have an intellectual insight that the spiritual heaven of our aspirations is not a space-occupying place at the top of the crystal canopy over our heads, but we go on using the old terminology, because we have no substitute for it. We teach our children to think of God and of heaven in terms of the sky, and we make little progress toward working out a new system of thought or toward creating new imagery that will better fit the facts of life and experience as they actually are.

One reason for the breakdown of the faith of so many high-minded and serious-minded persons in the present time is the collapse of the *imagery* through which they had at an earlier stage of their lives done all their religious thinking. That imagery has lost its meaning for them and they have found no other form for their creative imagination to work through. It is almost impossible to overestimate the part which pictorial imagery plays in the early life of the child, as well as in the primitive stage of the race, and when the pictorial imagery that has been acquired ceases to correspond to *reality* there is always serious trouble to be expected. That situation has now arrived.

There is no harm in continuing to talk of "sunrise" and "sunset," for when we use those ancient terms we always subconsciously interpret the words to mean that the earth moves rather than the sun. But when we pass over into our religious vocabulary, we have not yet made the adjustment, and we have formed no deeper meanings by which to reinterpret to our minds the old words "sky" and "heaven" as the dwelling place of God and His family of saints. Too often we are left without any reality corresponding to the words.

Where are we to turn to find our clue that will lead us back to the reality of God? How shall we think of Him so that He has for us the warmth and intimacy of a real Being? We can probably never find any imagery in any other domain that will be as vivid and impressive as the sky-imagery has been. The blue dome itself seems to the child's mind as it did to the primitive man's to be a perfect paradise for God. The rainbow, rising from earth to heaven, is a glorious sign of loving promise, or a bridge of many colors which links earth and heaven. The lightning in primitive pictorial imagery easily seems to be His stern messenger and the thunder, quite naturally, becomes His warning voice. But all the time this imagery is carrying the mind over unconsciously to a *spatializing* of God. He is all too easily and naturally thought of as a great man sitting on a throne at the apex of the sky-dome and acting as a man of might would act. With this imagery one is almost forced to think of Him as an absentee God. If he ever wants to reach the earth with a message of His will He must send someone across to bring it to us from the sky yonder. He is up there; we are down here. One has only to run through the theological thinking of the past to see how child-minded its imagery is, and what a large rôle this spatial-concept of God has played.

Our new imagery, as I have said, will perhaps be less vivid, but perhaps also it may succeed in making God real to us without at the same time making Him to quite the same extent foreign to our world and so completely a space-occupying Being. Of course we shall never get altogether free from the relations and necessities of space and time, for if we succeeded in doing that it would carry with it the futility of all our imaginative and visualizing capacity. God would be relegated to an order of reality wholly unlike the one in which we feel at home. We need a spiritual order that means something real to us, and we must consequently succeed in finding some way of thinking of God that is not incommensurable with our own central forms and ideals of life.

Space and time are not unreal and untrue, they are only—particularly space—inadequate for any order of spiritual reality. A reality to be *spiritual* must be more than a space-time reality. It must transcend space-time and attain a unity in which the "parts" do not lie outside one another but form an integral whole, in which past, present and future are not sundered but form a single *living now*, rich with all the gains of the time-process. A spiritual being is a being that can expand itself in ideal directions and that lives essentially in the experience and the achievement of beauty, goodness, love and truth, all of them timeless realities, rather than in movements from place to place or in changes on a clock-dial.

That type of spiritual achievement is possible for all of us who have reached the level of personal life, for to be a person is to have an inner life which cannot be adequately spread out or expressed in parts or space forms, and which binds time—past, present and future—as only a unifying mind can bind it, into a super-temporal experience that is charged with the intrinsic values of a cumulative life. Those traits and characteristics of life, at the very least, we may be sure belong to the nature of God as Spirit. Whatever more may be real and true of Him in His fullness, He cannot be less than that. It would seem then that our own essential spiritual qualities offer the best point of departure for our consideration of God as Spirit. He is more truly like the deepest reality in us than like anything else in the universe and we are nearest Him when we rise to the fullest height of our spiritual possibilities as men. At the heart and center of our being we as beings capable of moral autonomy partake of Him and open out inwardly into His Life. In so far as we are ourselves spiritual we have come from Spirit and carry with us and in us "the image and superscription" of our Source and Origin, the badge and mark of conjunctness with Him. . . .

The French philosopher, Émile Boutroux, has supplied us with a valuable phrase which may help us to link up this underlying world of Spirit with our own interior life of consciousness. He maintains that the "Beyond" that we have always been seeking is not in the sky, or in space somewhere. It is a "Beyond within us." We are no doubt still using a space word, "within," for we cannot altogether shake off our space-goggles, but we are not using the word "within" crudely to describe a *locality*. We are only calling attention to the fact that our conscious experience all the time reveals or implies junction with a More yet. William James in his famous Gifford Lectures came up from his review of a multitude of personal experiences of God's Life within to the conclusion that man within himself "is conterminous and continuous with a More of the same quality [as the higher spiritual part of himself], which is operative in the universe outside of him and which he can keep in working touch with." In another passage James says that "the conscious person is continuous with a wider Self through which saving experiences come."

In his latest and maturest period of life James came back to this hypothesis of a More within us.

Every bit of us [he says in *A Pluralistic Universe*] at every moment is part and parcel of a wider self, it quivers along various radii like the wind-rose on a compass, and the actual in it is continuously one with possibilities not yet in our present sight. And just as we are co-conscious with our own momentary margin, may we not ourselves form the margin of some more really central self in things which is co-conscious with the whole of us? May not you and I be confluent in a higher consciousness, and confluently active there though we know it not?

And finally he draws his own positive conclusion in these words of affirmation: "I think it may be asserted that there *are* religious experiences of a specific nature . . . which point with reasonable probability to the continuity of our consciousness with a wider spiritual environment." I am not here endorsing James' well-known conception of God which I do not share, I am only borrowing some of his luminous phrases to help supply vivid imagery for making God as Spirit *real* to our minds.

The major mystics in their own experience have always borne their testimony to "that wider spiritual environment." The philosophical mystics of the Middle Ages, especially those who had come under the influence of Aristotle, held that *the ground of the soul* in man is essentially divine, and that it "never has gone out from God." Sometimes the point of conjunction is called the "apex of the soul," sometimes it is "the soul-center," and sometimes "the ground of the soul," but in each case the point insisted upon was that there is something in the deeps of man which makes him essentially linked up with God, or at least unsundered from Him so that "spirit with Spirit may meet."

St. Augustine, in a famous passage of his *Confessions*, has tried to give an account of his experience of the Beyond which opens out from within. This passage from the great Carthaginian saint became a model and a pattern for almost all of the later mystics of the Church. The saint and his mother, Monica, were sitting together in the twilight, at Ostia by the Tiber, meditating and communing in one spirit upon the nature of "that which does not change but remains eternally self-same." They were yearning and aspiring for the homing stairway between the finite and the infinite, when suddenly in a flash of insight they saw that the way home was not a Jacob's ladder in the sky, but only an ascent of the soul by the inward way. They were filled with a flame of passion for the Real and the True and the Beautiful, and straining forward in their thought and desire to rise above all that is visible and tangible, "we came," the Saint says, "to our own souls"—like the lost boy in the parable who *came to himself*. In short, they gave up expecting to find God in things or above things or behind things. They left the outward path upward for the interior one through the highway of the soul. "Thither, on the way to God, one journeys," St. Augustine says elsewhere, "not with feet, nor by ships, nor by chariots" (and we may add "nor by aëroplanes"), "but only by the momentous will, for to will completely to be there is already to have arrived." It is an affair not of distance but of spiritual attitude. And so, here at Ostia, St. Augustine says, "In one swift leap—in a sudden intuition—we soared out beyond our souls and arrived at *That which is*—the God who is our Home." In this "trembling flash" God was felt to be "closer than breathing, nearer than hands or feet."

He is, we may well conclude, not away somewhere in another sphere, or above the circle of the sky. He is where we are when we are attuned for His presence, as the music of another continent suddenly is where our radio set is, when that radio set is "keyed" rightly to report it. The mystery of this type of experience is no greater than the mystery of any other type of experience. At the last we always touch mystery at some point. It comes down, in the last resort, to a question of *fact*, as is true of everything in the sphere of experience. The taste of sweetness, or the color-vision of redness, are just as unanalyzable and just as mysterious as is this instantaneous flash of God into our souls. We see stars billions of miles away, only because something from the star is actually operating on the retina and in the visual center of the brain; and so, too, we find God, only because Something that is God—God as Spirit—is actually in contact with the spiritual center within us that is kindred to Him.

There is no good reason why we should shy away from such an evident fact as self-transcendence, or why we should be afraid to own it as a fact. Every case of sense-perception is a case of self-transcendence. If we could not leap forward and grasp an object from beyond us, and know it as beyond us, all our ex-

perience would be doomed to be shut up in an inner subjective mirage. We could never have dealings and commerce with a real world beyond our inward seemings. We should forever remain victims of the "egocentric predicament." In a trembling flash, when we perceive things, we manage to leap beyond ourselves and know a reality that is not of us, but of a world beyond us. Nobody knows *how* we do it. It is another mystery—like sweetness and redness—but it is none the less a fact. The moment we *know* anything whatsoever we prove to be self-transcending beings. It is no less obvious that we are self-transcending in all our deepest relations with other *persons*. The moment we reduce the reality of other persons to subjective states within ourselves we have lost our world and are wanderers in a dreamland. It is a poor, thin psychology that sees in pity, sympathy and love only a glorification of the ego and not the finding of a new and higher self in and through an *alter*— another person—that is just as real as the ego is. It seems to be impossible to go out into a real world of social values—in other words, to have a real life—unless a self can transcend itself and can actually deal with a beyond.

Why then, should we assume that the mystery of the spiritual Beyond within us is the only mystery of self-transcendence? We are never mere "empirical" selves, describable selves, shut up within the hollow circle of our own flighty seemings, which are born of the futile beatings of our own hearts. To feel that one has arrived at *That which is* is no more strange or improbable or miraculous than it is to feel that the person whom one loves is a real person and that love is a genuine revelation. Do the St. Augustines and the St. Monicas give any convincing evidence that they have arrived? The evidence seems to me pretty clear and fairly convincing that they find something that reshapes and rebuilds the interior world within them—and eventually the larger social worlds around them—as truly as our experience of sense-facts shapes and constructs for us our world in space and time. . . .

I find that I love the good and hate the evil. The more I try to explain this fact, and the inward operations of my moral judgment, by my biological ancestry, and the customs of the past, the more I am convinced that it cannot be done. Some of the facts can be explained that way. We do carry the biological past along with us, but again there is a nucleus of moral and spiritual realities that demands another type of ancestry for its explanation. I can understand why we should be imperfect and why we should have propensities for evil, if we have come up from a long line of historic development. But how does this slow evolution from below account for my devotion to ideals of goodness and for my consecration to *what ought to be but is not yet?* What is the origin of my love of truth and my passion for purity of heart and my readiness to give my life for a cause that ought to triumph? Somewhere along the line upward something has *emerged* and is operating that was not here before. In the face of obvious material conditions that surround us we have persistent confidence in spiritual realities, just because we are inwardly allied to the Spirit that works in us.

The monumental evidence of God is, I believe, the fact of spiritual personality through which divine traits of character are revealed. Stars and mountains and ordered processes of nature reveal law and mathematics and beauty, but they reveal and can reveal no traits of character, no qualities of personality, no warmth and intimacy of heart and mind. If we are ever to be convinced that self-giving love is a reality of God's nature, we shall be convinced by seeing this love break through some human organ of His Spirit. The supreme revelation of the ages was not in the thunder and fire of Sinai, but in the life of a Person who was born of a woman, who increased in wisdom and stature, who was tempted as we are, who struggled and suffered, who battled for truth, who gave His life out of love for the rest of us, and who felt through it all that He was the organ of the Life and Love of God. Here on the highest level that has been reached since the race began God as Spirit has broken through into visibility and has shown His true nature in life and action. But it is an unending revelation. Christianity, in the best sense of the word, is eternally revealed in time,

> The silence of eternity
> Interpreted by love.

As the sap flows through the branches of the vine and vitalizes the whole organism so that it bursts into the beauty and glory of foliage and blossom and finally into fruit, so through the lives of men and women, inwardly responsive and joyously receptive, the life of God as Spirit flows carrying vitality, awakening love, creating passion for goodness, kindling the fervor of consecration and producing that living body, that organism of the Spirit, that "blessed community," which continues through the centuries the revelation of God as love and tenderness and eternal goodness.

Nikolai A. Berdyaev

(1874———)

ONE of the most widely read contemporary Russian writers of religious philosophy is Berdyaev. A member of the Orthodox Church, he was exiled for his criticism of the governing synod of the Orthodox Church in Russia. After the Revolution he was professor of philosophy at the University of Moscow. Because he upheld religion, he was expelled from Russia in 1922. He went to France where he directed his intellectual interests to "the philosophy of the spirit." In 1834 he became director of the Academy of the Philosophy of Religion in Paris, and editor of *Putj* ("The Way").

Berdyaev was early influenced through his study of Schopenhauer, Fichte, and Kant. Dostoevski, however, became the greatest stimulus to his thinking as he discerned mechanical civilization endangering the spiritual fiber of humanity. He said that Dostoevski "has played a decisive part in my spiritual life."

The striking thing about Berdyaev is his aristocracy of the spirit. He ranks supreme among Orthodox Church members whose interests lie in the devotional aspects of religion.

Many of his writings have been translated into English: *Fate of Man in the Modern World, Solitude and Society, Freedom and the Spirit, Destiny of Man, Meaning of History,* and *Slavery and Freedom.* From this last, a philosophical book which presupposes spiritual reform, "The Spiritual Liberation of Man" is taken. R. M. French is the translator, and it is used here by permission of Charles Scribner's Sons. (Copyright 1944 by Charles Scribner's Sons.)

THE SPIRITUAL LIBERATION OF MAN

From *Slavery and Freedom*

Man is in a state of servitude. He frequently does not notice that he is a slave, and sometimes he loves it. But man also aspires to be set free. It would be a mistake to think that the average man loves freedom. A still greater mistake would be to suppose that freedom is an easy thing. Freedom is a difficult thing. It is easier to remain in slavery. Love of freedom and aspiration towards liberation are an indication that some upward progress has already been achieved by man. They witness to the fact that inwardly man is already ceasing to be a slave. There is a spiritual principle in man which is not dependent upon the world and is not determined by the world. The liberation of man is the demand, not of nature, nor of reason, nor of society, as is often supposed, but of spirit. Man is not only spirit, he is of a complex make-up, he is also an animal, he is also a phe-nomenon of the material world, but man is spirit as well. Spirit is freedom, and freedom is the victory of spirit.

But it would be a mistake to think that the slavery of man is always the outcome of the power of the animal and material side of man. On the spiritual side of man itself there may be grievous loss of health, division, exteriorization, there may be self-estrangement of spirit, loss of freedom, captivity of spirit. In this lies all the complexity of the problem of freedom and slavery in man. The spirit is exteriorized, thrown out into the external, and acts upon man as necessity, and it returns to itself within, i.e. to freedom. Hegel understood one side of this process of the spirit, but he did not understand it all; he did understand what is perhaps the most important point. A man who is free should feel himself to be not on the circumference of the objectivized world, but at the centre of the spiritual world. Liberation is being present at the centre and not at the circumference, in real subjectivity and not in ideal objectivity.

But spiritual concentration, to which all the precepts of the spiritual life summon us, may be twofold in its results. It gives spiritual strength, and independence of the manifold which is a torment to man. But it may effect a narrowing of consciousness, it may lead to possession by one single idea. In that case spiritual liberation is turned into the new form of seduction and slavery. Those who tread the spiritual path are aware of this. Liberation never provides a simple escape from reality or the rejection of reality. Spiritual liberation is conflict. Spirit is not an abstract idea, it does not belong to the category of universals. Not only every man, but a dog, a cat, or an insect is of greater existential value, than an abstract idea, or than a common universal.

Spiritual liberation is accompanied by transition not to the abstract but to the concrete. The Gospel is evidence of this. In that lies the personalism of the Gospel. Spiritual liberation is victory over the power of what is foreign. In this is the meaning of love. But man easily becomes a slave, without noticing it. He is set free, because there is in him a spiritual principle, a capacity which is not determined from without. But so complex is human nature and so entangled man's existence, that he may fall out of one form of slavery into another, he may fall into abstract spirituality, into the determining power of a common idea. Spirit is unique, integral, and is present in each one of its acts. But man is not spirit, he only possesses spirit and therefore in man's spiritual acts themselves, dismemberment, abstraction and rebirth of the spirit are possible. The final liberation is possible only through a bond between the human spirit and the Spirit of God. Spiritual liberation is always a turning to a profounder depth than the spiritual principle in man, it is a turning to God. But even the turning to God may be impaired by a malady of the spirit and be converted into idolatry. Therefore constant purification is necessary. God can act only upon freedom, in freedom and through freedom. He does not act upon necessity, in necessity and through necessity. He does not act in the laws of nature or in the laws of the state. Therefore, the doctrine of Providence and the doctrine of Grace require revision, the traditional doctrines are not admissible.

The spiritual liberation of man is the realization of personality in man. It is the attainment of wholeness. And at the same time it is unwearied conflict. The fundamental question of the realization of personality is not a question of victory over the determinism of matter, that is one side of the subject only. The fundamental question is the question of an entire victory over slavery. The world is evil, not because matter is in it, but because it is not free, because it is enslaved. The troubles of man's life in the material world are not due to the fact that matter is evil, they have arisen from a wrong tendency of spirit. The fundamental antithesis is not between spirit and matter, but between freedom and slavery. The spiritual victory is not only victory over the elementary dependence of man upon matter. Still more difficult is the victory over deceptive illusions which precipitate man into slavery in its least recognizable form. The evil in human existence appears not only in plain view, but also in deceptive forms of good. Antichrist can seduce through a deceptive likeness to the form of Christ. Thus indeed it happens within the Christian world. Many universal common abstract ideas are evil in an exalted form. I have written about this throughout this whole book.

It is not enough to say that one must be set free from sin. Sin not only wears a primitive aspect and entices us, it is possible to be possessed by the idea of sin, the lure of a false conflict with the sin which is to be seen on all sides in life is also possible. It is not only real sin which enslaves man, but also possession by the idea of sin which corrodes the whole life. This is one of the servile perversions of the spiritual life. The slavery which is felt by man as violence from without is to be hated less passionately than the slavery which seduces man and which he has come to love. A demoniacal character attaches to everything relative which is transformed into the absolute, to everything finite which is transformed into the infinite, to everything profane which is transformed into the sacred, to everything human which is transformed into the divine. Man's relation to the state, to civilization, and even to the church becomes demoniacal. There is a church in the existential sense, which is community and fellowship, and there are churches which are objectivizations and social institutions. When the church, as objectivization and a social institution is regarded as holy and impeccable, then the creation of an idol and the slavery of man begin. This is a perversion of the religious life and a demoniacal element within religious life. Human life is mutilated by imaginary, exaggerated, exalted passions, religious, national, social, and by degrading fears. In this soil the enslavement of man springs up. Man possesses the capacity for turning love for God and for the highest ideas, into the most terrible slavery.

The victory of spirit over slavery is in the first place a victory over fear, over the fear of life and the fear of death. In fear-anguish, Kirkegaard sees the fundamental religious phenomenon, and a token of the significance of the inward life. The Bible says that the fear of the Lord is the beginning of wisdom. And at the same time fear is slavery. How are these to be reconciled? In this world man experiences the fear of life and the fear of death. This fear is weakened and dulled in the realm of everyday life. The organization of ordinary day to day life aims at establishing security, although, of course, it cannot completely overcome the dangers of life and death. But submerged in the realm of everyday life, absorbed in its interests, man deserts the deeps, and the disquietude that belongs to the deeps. Heidegger says truly that *Das Mann* takes the edge off the tragic in life.

But everything is inconsistent and twofold. Everyday life dulls the fears which are linked with the deeps of life and death, but establishes other fears of its own under the power of which man lives the whole time, fears linked with the affairs of this world. In actual fact, fear determines the greater part of political movements, it determines also the socialized forms of religion. Anxious solicitude which Heidegger regards as belonging to the structure of existence, inevitably passes into fear, into everyday fear, which must be distinguished from transcendental fear.

Fear can be a more exalted condition than heedless submersion in everyday things. But fear, fear of all sorts, is all the same a form of human slavery. Perfect love casteth out fear. Fearlessness is the highest state. Slavish fear hinders the revelation of truth. Fear gives birth to lies. Man thinks to protect himself from danger by falsehood, it is upon lies, and not upon truth that he establishes the realm of everyday life. The world of objectivization is penetrated through and through by useful lies, while truth, on the other hand, is made plain to the fearless. Knowledge of truth demands a victory over fear, it requires the virtue of fearlessness, and courage in the face of danger. The highest degree of fear, which is experienced and overcome, may become a source of knowledge. But the knowledge of truth is bestowed not by fear, but by victory over fear. The fear of death is the limit of fear. It may be a base everyday fear, but it may be a lofty transcendental fear. But the fear of death denotes the slavery of man, a slavery well known to every man. Man is the slave of death and triumph over the fear of death is the greatest triumph over fear in general.

And here there is to be noted an astounding inconsistency in man in relation to the fear of death. Man fears not only his own death, but also the death of other people. And at the same time man fairly easily makes up his mind to murder, and it would appear fears least of all the death which comes to pass as the result of his committing murder. This is the problem of crime, which is always, if not actual, at least potential, murder. Crime is linked with murder, murder is linked with death. Murder is committed not only by gangsters; murder is committed in an organized way and upon a colossal scale by the state, by those who are in possession of power, or by those who have only just seized it. And, mark, in all these murders, the horror of death shows itself dulled and blunted, even almost entirely absent, although the horror of the death ought to be doubled—as being horror of death in general, and horror of the death which is the result of murder having been committed as well. Capital punishment is ceasing to be taken as murder, so is death in war, and especially, it is ceasing to be taken as a death which arouses horror. And this is a consequence of the objectivization of human existence.

In the objectivized world, all values are perverted. Man instead of being a resuscitator, a conqueror of death, has become a murderer, a sower of death. And he kills, in order to create a life in which there will be less fear. Man kills from fear; at the root of every murder, whether committed by an individual person or by the state, lies fear and slavery. Fear and slavery always have fateful results. If man were to succeed in triumphing over slavish fear, he would cease to murder. From fear of death man sows death, as a result of feeling a slave, he desires to dominate. Domination is always constrained to kill. The state is always subject to fear and therefore it is constrained to kill. It has no desire to wrestle against death. Men in authority are very much like gangsters.

I know of no more lofty moral consciousness in its attitude to death than that of Feodorov. Feodorov grieved over the death of every being and demanded that man should become a resuscitator. But grieving over death, since it has become active, is not the fear of death. A resuscitator conquers the fear of death. Personalism does not put the question of death and immortality in exactly the same way as Feodorov. Feodorov is right in saying that the fight against death is not only a personal matter, it is a "public undertaking." It is not only my death, but the death of all, which sets me a problem. Victory not only over the fear of death but over death itself, is the realization of personality. The realization of personality is impossible in the finite, it presupposes the infinite, not quantitative infinity but qualitative, i.e. eternity. The individual person dies, since he is born in the generic process, but personality does not die, since it is not born in the generic process. Victory over the fear of death is the victory of spiritual personality over the biological individual. But this does not mean the separation of the immortal spiritual principle, from the mortal human principle, but the transfiguration of the whole man. This is not evolution, or development in the naturalist sense. Development is the result of deficiency, of inability to attain to completeness, and it is subordinate to the power of time, it is a process of becoming within time, and not creativeness which conquers time.

Insufficiency, deficiency, dissatisfaction, aspiration towards something greater have a twofold character; there is a lower and a higher condition of man. Wealth may be a false fulfilment, and a false liberation from slavery. The passing from deficiency to completeness, from poverty to riches, may be evolution and show itself from without as evolution. But behind this there is concealed a deeper process, a process of creativeness, a process of freedom which breaks through determinism. Victory over death cannot be evolution, cannot be a result of necessity. Victory over death is creativeness, the united creativeness of man and God, it is a result of freedom. The tension and passion of life attract to death and are linked with death. In the turning wheel of the world of nature, life and death cannot be torn asunder, "And may young life play at the entrance of the tomb." The tension of life's passion in itself attracts to death because it is enclosed in the finite, it does not issue forth into the infinite eternal. Eternal life is attained not by mortifying and destroying the passionate tension of life, but by its spiritual transfiguration, by the control of its creative activity of spirit. The rejection of immortality is weariness, a refusal of activity.

Creativeness is liberation from slavery. Man is free when he finds himself in a state of creative activity. Creativeness leads to ecstasy of the moment. The products of creativeness are within time, but the creative act itself lies outside time. Thus also every heroic act leads outside time. It is possible for the heroic act not to be subordinate to any end and to be the ecstasy of the moment. But pure heroism may be a lure arising from pride and self-assertion. It was so that Nietzsche understood heroism. So also does Malraux understand it. Man can experience various forms of liberating ecstasy. There can be the ecstasy of conflict, erotic ecstasy, there can be the ecstasy of wrath, in which man feels himself capable of destroying the world. There is the ecstasy of sacrificial service taken upon oneself— the ecstasy of the Cross. This is the Christian ecstasy. Ecstasy is always an issuing from a state in which man is shackled and enslaved, an emergence into a moment of freedom. But ecstasy can bestow a fictitious liberation and once more lead to a still greater enslavement of man. There are ecstasies which remove the boundaries of personality and plunge personality into the formless cosmic element. Spiritual ecstasy is characterized by this, that in it personality is not destroyed but strengthened. In ecstasy personality must issue from itself, but in issuing from itself, remain itself. There is the same enslavement in being confined within itself and in being dissolved in the formless world element. Here are the temptation of individualism and the opposite temptation of cosmic and social collectivism.

In the spiritual liberation of man there is movement in the direction of freedom, truth and love. Freedom cannot be vain and lead to no result. "Ye shall know the truth and the truth shall make you free." But the knowledge of truth presupposes freedom. Knowledge of truth which is not free, is not only valueless, it is also impossible. But freedom also presupposes the existence of truth, of meaning, of God. Truth and meaning liberate, and again liberation leads to truth, and meaning. Freedom must be loving and love must be free. It is only the gathering together of freedom, truth and love which realizes personality, free and creative personality. The exclusive affirmation of one of these principles only always introduces distortion, and injures human personality. Each one of the principles can in and by itself be a source of seduction and slavery. Freedom which is given a wrong direction may be a source of slavery. In the objectivization of the spirit the higher is dragged downwards and adjusted; but in creative incarnation of spirit the lower matter of this world is raised, and a change takes place in world data.

Human consciousness is subject to a variety of illusions in understanding the relation between this world in which man feels himself to be in a state of servitude, and the other world in which he awaits his liberation. Man is the point of intersection of two worlds. One of the illusions consists in interpreting the difference between the two worlds as a difference of substance. In actual fact it is a difference in mode of existence. Man passes from slavery to freedom, from a state of disintegration to a condition of completeness, from impersonality to personality, from passivity to creativeness, that is to say he passes over to spirituality. This world is the world of objectivization, of determinism, of alienation, of hostility, of law. While the other world is the world of spirituality, of freedom, love, kinship.

Another illusion of consciousness lies in this that the relations between the two worlds are understood as absolute objectivized transcendence. In this case the transition from one world to the other is passively awaited and the activity of man has no part to play. In actual fact the other world, the world of spirituality, the Kingdom of God, is not only awaited, it is constructed also by the creativeness of man, it is the creative transfiguration of a world which is exposed to the malady of objectivization. It is spiritual revolution. That other world cannot be established by human strength only, but also it cannot be established without the creative activity of man. This brings me to the problem of eschatology, to the problem of the end of history, and it means the liberation of man from his slavery to history.

⸺Albert Schweitzer

(1875⸺)

AUTHORITY on Bach, skillful organist, medical missionary in the Lambaréné Forest, and New Testament critic, Schweitzer well deserves the title of "saint." One of the world's most brilliant men, he has dedicated his talents to the alleviation of human suffering. He was born in Kaysersberg, Alsace, educated at Berlin and Strasbourg, teaching at the latter university from 1901 to 1912. He was also organist of the Société J. S. Bach of Paris. In 1913 he became missionary surgeon and founder of a hospital at Lambaréné, Gabon, French Equatorial Africa, where he is still active.

Out of My Life and Thought is one of the most thrilling spiritual autobiographies written in the twentieth century. The following selection, taken from the chapter "First Activities in Africa" in that work, can well be labeled the theme of Schweitzer's life. The life of no other contemporary Christian better exemplifies the way by which redemptive love can be used to help the downtrodden and the unfortunate. C. T. Campion is the translator, and the material is used by permission of Henry Holt & Co. (Copyright 1933 by Henry Holt & Co.)

REVERENCE FOR LIFE
From Out of My Life and Thought

The idea of Reverence for Life offers itself as the realistic answer to the realistic question of how man and the world are related to each other. Of the world man knows only that everything which exists is, like himself, a manifestation of the Will-to-Live. With this world he stands in a relation of passivity and of activity. On the other hand he is subordinate to the course of events which is given in this totality of life; on the other hand he is capable of affecting the life which comes within his reach by hampering or promoting it, by destroying or maintaining it.

The one possible way of giving meaning to his existence is that of raising his natural relation to the world to a spiritual one. As a being in a passive relation to the world he comes into a spiritual relation to it by resignation. True resignation consists in this: that man, feeling his subordination to the course of world-happenings, wins his way to inward freedom from the fortunes which shape the outward side of his existence. Inward freedom means that he finds strength to deal with everything that is hard in his lot, in such a way that it all helps to make him a deeper and more inward person, to purify him, and to keep him calm and peaceful. Resignation, therefore, is the spiritual and ethical affirmation of one's own existence. Only he who has gone through the stage of resignation is capable of world-affirmation.

As a being in an active relation to the world he comes into a spiritual relation with it by not living for himself alone, but feeling himself one with all life that comes within his reach. He will feel all that life's experiences as his own, he will give it all the help that he possibly can, and will feel all the saving and promotion of life that he has been able to effect as the deepest happiness that can ever fall to his lot.

Let a man once begin to think about

the mystery of his life and the links which connect him with the life that fills the world, and he cannot but bring to bear upon his own life and all other life that comes within his reach the principle of Reverence for Life, and manifest this principle by ethical world- and life-affirmation expressed in action. Existence will thereby become harder for him in every respect than it would be if he lived for himself, but at the same time it will be richer, more beautiful, and happier. It will become, instead of mere living, a real experience of life.

Beginning to think about life and the world leads a man directly and almost irresistibly to Reverence for Life. Such thinking leads to no conclusions which could point in any other direction.

If the man who has once begun to think wishes to persist in his mere living he can do so only by surrendering himself, whenever this idea takes possession of him, to thoughtlessness, and stupefying himself therein. If he perseveres with thinking he can come to no other result than Reverence for Life.

Any thinking by which men assert that they are reaching scepticism or life without ethical ideals, is not thinking but thoughtlessness which poses as thinking, and it proves itself to be such by the fact that it is unconcerned about the mystery of life and the world.

Reverence for Life contains in itself Resignation, World- and Life-Affirmation, and the Ethical, the three essential elements in a world-view, as mutually interconnected results of thinking.

Up to now there have been world-views of Resignation, world-views of World- and Life-Affirmation, and world-views which sought to satisfy the claims of the Ethical. Not one has there been, however, which has been able to combine the three elements. That is possible only on condition that all three are conceived as essentially products of the universal conviction of Reverence for Life, and are recognized as being one and all contained in it. Resignation and World- and Life-Affirmation have no separate existence of their own by the side of the

Ethical; they are its lower octaves.

Having its origin in realistic thinking, the ethic of Reverence for Life is realistic, and brings man to a realistic and steady facing of reality.

It may seem, at first glance, as if Reverence for Life were something too general and too lifeless to provide the content of a living ethic. But thinking has no need to trouble as to whether its expressions sound living enough, so long as they hit the mark and have life in them. Anyone who comes under the influence of the ethic of Reverence for Life will very soon be able to detect, thanks to what that ethic demands from him, what fire glows in the lifeless expression. The ethic of Reverence for Life is the ethic of Love widened into universality. It is the ethic of Jesus, now recognized as a necessity of thought.

Objection is made to this ethic that it sets too high a value on natural life. To this it can retort that the mistake made by all previous systems of ethics has been the failure to recognize that life as such is the mysterious value with which they have to deal. All spiritual life meets us within natural life. Reverence for Life, therefore, is applied to natural life and spiritual life alike. In the parable of Jesus, the shepherd saves not merely the soul of the lost sheep but the whole animal. The stronger the reverence for natural life, the stronger grows also that for spiritual life.

The ethic of Reverence for Life is found particularly strange because it establishes no dividing-line between higher and lower, between more valuable and less valuable life. For this omission it has its reasons.

To undertake to lay down universally valid distinctions of value between different kinds of life will end in judging them by the greater or lesser distance at which they seem to stand from us human beings —as we ourselves judge. But that is a purely subjective criterion. Who among us knows what significance any other kind of life has in itself, and as a part of the universe?

Following on such a distinction there

comes next the view that there can be life which is worthless, injury to which or destruction of which does not matter. Then in the category of worthless life we come to include, according to circumstances, different kinds of insects, or primitive peoples.

To the man who is truly ethical all life is sacred, including that which from the human point of view seems lower in the scale. He makes distinctions only as each case comes before him, and under the pressure of necessity, as, for example, when it falls to him to decide which of two lives he must sacrifice in order to preserve the other. But all through this series of decisions he is conscious of acting on subjective grounds and arbitrarily, and knows that he bears the responsibility for the life which is sacrificed.

I rejoice over the new remedies for sleeping-sickness, which enable me to preserve life, whereas I had previously to watch a painful disease. But every time I have under the microscope the germs which cause the disease, I cannot but reflect that I have to sacrifice this life in order to save other life.

I buy from natives a young fish-eagle, which they have caught on a sand-bank, in order to rescue it from their cruel hands. But now I have to decide whether I shall let it starve, or kill every day a number of small fishes, in order to keep it alive. I decide on the latter course, but every day I feel it hard that this life must be sacrificed for the other on my responsibility.

Standing, as he does, with the whole body of living creatures under the law of this dilemma (*Selbstentzweiung*) in the will-to-live, man comes again and again into the position of being able to preserve his own life and life generally only at the cost of other life. If he has been touched by the ethic of Reverence for Life, he injures and destroys life only under a necessity which he cannot avoid, and never from thoughtlessness. So far as he is a free man he uses every opportunity of tasting the blessedness of being able to assist life and avert from it suffering and destruction.

Devoted as I was from boyhood to the cause of the protection of animal life, it is a special joy to me that the universal ethic of Reverence for Life shows the sympathy with animals which is so often represented as sentimentality, to be a duty which no thinking man can escape. Hitherto ethics have faced the problem of man and beast either uncomprehending or helpless. Even when sympathy with the animal creation was felt to be right, it could not be brought within the scope of ethics, because ethics were really focussed only on the behaviour of man to man.

When will the time come when public opinion will tolerate no longer any popular amusements which depend on the ill-treatment of animals!

The ethic, then, which originates in thinking is not "according to reason," but non-rational and enthusiastic. It marks off no skillfully defined circle of duties, but lays upon each individual the responsibility for all life within his reach, and compels him to devote himself to helping it.

Any profound world-view is mysticism, in that it brings men into a spiritual relation with the Infinite. The world-view of Reverence for Life is ethical mysticism. It allows union with the infinite to be realized by ethical action. This ethical mysticism originates in logical thinking. If our will-to-live begins to think about itself and the world, we come to experience the life of the world, so far as it comes within our reach, in our own life, and to devote our will-to-live to the infinite will-to-live through the deeds we do. Rational thinking, if it goes deep, ends of necessity in the non-rational of mysticism. It has, of course, to deal with life and the world, both of which are non-rational entities.

In the world the infinite will-to-live reveals itself to us as will-to-create, and this is full of dark and painful riddles for us; in ourselves it is revealed as will-to-love, which will through us remove the dilemma (*Selbstentzweiung*) of the will-to-live.

The world-view of Reverence for Life

has, therefore, a religious character. The man who avows his belief in it, and acts upon the belief, shows a piety which is elemental.

Through the active ethic of love with its religious character, and through its inwardness, the world-view of Reverence for Life is essentially related to that of Christianity. Hence there is a possibility that Christianity and thought may now meet in a new relation to each other which will do more than the present one to promote spiritual life.

Christianity has once already entered into a connexion with thought, namely during the period of Rationalism in the eighteenth century. It did so because thought met it with an enthusiastic ethic which was religious in character. As a matter of fact, however, thought had not produced this ethic itself, but had, without knowing it, taken it over from Christianity. When, later on, it had to depend solely upon its own ethic, this latter proved to have in it so little life and so little religion that it had not much in common with Christian ethics. Then the bonds between Christianity and active thought were loosened, and the situation to-day is that Christianity has completely withdrawn into itself, and is concerned only with the propagation of its own ideas, as such. It no longer sees any use in proving them to be in agreement with thought, but prefers that they be regarded as something altogether outside it, and occupying a superior position. It loses, however, thereby its connexion with the spiritual life of the time and the possibility of exercising any real influence upon it.

The emergence of the world-view of Reverence for Life now summons it to face once more the question whether it will or will not join hands with Thought which is ethical and religious in character.

Christianity has need of thought that it may come to the consciousness of its real self. For centuries it treasured the great commandment of love and mercy as traditional truth without recognizing it

as a reason for opposing slavery, witch-burning, torture, and all the other ancient and mediaeval forms of inhumanity. It was only when it experienced the influence of the thinking of the Age of Enlightenment (*Aufklärung*) that it was stirred into entering the struggle for humanity. The remembrance of this ought to preserve it for ever from assuming any air of superiority in comparison with Thought.

Many people find pleasure to-day in talking continually of how "shallow" Christianity became in the age of Rationalism. Justice surely demands that we should find out and admit how much compensation was made for that "shallowness" by the services rendered by that Christianity. To-day torture has been re-established. In many states the system of Justice acquiesces without protest in the most infamous tortures being applied, before and simultaneously with the regular proceedings of police and prison officials, in order to extract confessions from those accused. The sum-total of misery thus caused every hour passes imagination. But to this renewal of torture the Christianity of to-day offers no opposition even in words, much less in deeds, and similarly it makes hardly any effort to counter the superstitions of to-day. And even if it did resolve to venture on resisting these things and on undertaking other things such as the Christianity of the eighteenth century accomplished, it would be unable to carry out its intention because it has no power over the spirit of the age.

To make up to itself for the fact that it does so little to prove the reality of its spiritual and ethical nature, the Christianity of to-day cheats itself with the delusion that it is making its position as a Church stronger year by year. It is accommodating itself to the spirit of the age by adopting a kind of modern worldliness. Like other organized bodies it is at work to make good, by ever stronger and more uniform organization, its claim to be a body justified by history and practical success. But just in proportion as it gains in external power, it loses in spiritual.

Christianity cannot take the place of thinking, but it must be founded on it.

In and by itself it is not capable of mastering lack of thought and scepticism. The only age which can be receptive for the imperishable elements in its own thoughts is one animated by an elemental piety which springs from thinking.

Just as a stream is preserved from gradually leaking away, because it flows along above subsoil water, so does Christianity need the subsoil water of elemental piety which is the fruit of thinking. It can only attain to real spiritual power when men find the road from thought to religion no longer barred.

I know that I myself owe it to thinking that I was able to retain my faith in religion and Christianity.

The man who thinks stands up freer in the face of traditional religious truth than the man who does not, but the profound and imperishable elements contained in it he assimilates with much more effect than the latter.

The essential element in Christianity as it was preached by Jesus and as it is comprehended by thought, is this, that it is only through love that we can attain to communion with God. All living knowledge of God rests upon this foundation: that we experience Him in our lives as Will-to-Love.

Anyone who has recognized that the idea of Love is the spiritual beam of light which reaches us from the Infinite, ceases to demand from religion that it shall offer him complete knowledge of the supra-sensible. He ponders, indeed, on the great questions: what the meaning is of the evil in the world; how in God, the great First Cause, the will-to-create and the will-to-love are one; in what relation the spiritual and the material life stand to one another, and in what way our existence is transitory and yet eternal. But he is able to leave these questions on one side, however painful it may be to give up all hope of answers to them. In the knowledge of spiritual existence in God through love he possesses the one thing needful.

"Love never faileth: but . . . whether there be knowledge it shall be done away," says St. Paul.

The deeper piety is, the humbler are its claims with regard to knowledge of the supra-sensible. It is like a path which winds between the hills instead of going over them.

The fear that the Christianity which is favourably inclined to the piety originating in thought will step into pantheism is unreal. Every form of living Christianity is pantheistic in that it is bound to envisage everything that exists as having its being in the great First Cause of all being. But at the same time all ethical piety is higher than any pantheistic mysticism, in that it does not find the God of Love in Nature, but knows about Him only from the fact that He announces Himself in us as Will-to-Love. The First Cause of Being, as He manifests Himself in Nature, is to us always something impersonal. But to the First Cause of Being, who becomes revealed to us as Will-to-Love, we relate ourselves as to an ethical personality. Theism does not stand in opposition to pantheism, but emerges from it as the ethically determined out of what is natural and undetermined.

Unfounded, too, is the doubt whether the Christianity which has passed through a stage of thinking can still bring home his sinfulness to the consciousness of man with sufficient seriousness. It is not where sinfulness is most talked about that its seriousness is most forcibly taught. There is not much about it in the Sermon on the Mount. But thanks to the longing for freedom from sin and for purity of heart which Jesus has enshrined in the Beatitudes, these form the great call to repentance which is unceasingly working on man.

If Christianity, for the sake of any tradition or for any considerations whatever, refuses to have itself interpreted in terms of ethico-religious thinking, it will be a misfortune for itself and for mankind.

What Christianity needs is that it shall be filled to overflowing with the spirit of Jesus, and in the strength of that shall spiritualize itself into a living religion of inwardness and love, such as its destined purpose should make it. Only as such can it become the leaven in the spiritual life of mankind. What has been passing for Christianity during these nineteen centuries is merely a beginning, full of weaknesses and mistakes, not a full-grown Christianity springing from the spirit of Jesus.

Because I am devoted to Christianity in deep affection, I am trying to serve it with loyalty and sincerity. In no wise do I undertake to enter the lists on its behalf with the crooked and fragile thinking of Christian apologetic, but I call on it to set itself right in the spirit of sincerity with its past and with thought in order that it may thereby become conscious of its true nature.

My hope is that the emergence of an elemental mode of thought which must lead us to the ethico-religious idea of Reverence for Life, may contribute to the bringing of Christianity and thought closer to each other.

Harry Emerson Fosdick

(1878——)

CONSIDERED as one of America's great preachers and a leading exponent of constructive modernism, Fosdick became widely known in 1915 after publishing *The Meaning of Prayer*. This book, prepared as a guide for daily devotional reading, continues to have wide circulation.

Born in Buffalo, New York, and educated at Colgate, Columbia, and Union Theological Seminary, Fosdick was ordained in the Baptist ministry in 1903. He served as minister of the First Baptist Church, Montclair, New Jersey, 1904-15. From 1908-46 he taught homiletics and practical theology at Union Theological Seminary, and from 1926-46 he was minister of the Riverside Church, New York.

One of Fosdick's more recent books, *On Being a Real Person*, depicts the way to "sainthood" through the union of Christian insights with modern religious psychology.

The following selection from *The Meaning of Prayer* can well be called the theme of this classic on devotional living. It is used by permission of the Association Press.

THE NATURALNESS OF PRAYER

From *The Meaning of Prayer*

I

*W*hen any one undertakes to study the meaning and to cultivate the habit of prayer, it is well for him to understand from the beginning that he is dealing with a natural function of his life and not with an artificial addition. Raising palm trees in Greenland would be an unnatural proceeding. They never were intended to grow there, and never can grow there save under stress of artificial forcing. The culture of prayer would be just as strained a procedure, were it not true that the tendency to pray is native to us, that prayer is indigenous in us, that we *do* pray, one way or another, even though fitfully and without effect, and that men always have prayed and always will pray. The definition of man as a "praying animal," while not comprehensive, is certainly correct. *The culture of prayer, therefore, is not importing an alien, but is training a native citizen of the soul.* Professor William James of Harvard was thinking of this when he wrote: "We hear in these days of scientific enlightenment a great deal of discussion about the efficacy of prayer; and many reasons are given us why we should not pray, whilst others are given us why we should. But in all this very little is said of the reason why we do pray. . . . The reason why we do pray is simply that we cannot help praying."

Our justification for calling prayer natural may be found in part, in the *universality* of it. In some form or other, it is found everywhere, in all ages and among all peoples. The most discouraging circumstances do not crush it, and theories of the universe directly antagonistic do not prevent it. Buddhism, a religion theoretically without a God, ought logically to exclude prayer; but in countries where Buddhism is dominant, prayer is present. Confucius, a good deal of an agnostic, urged his disciples not to have much to do with the gods; and today Confucius is himself a god and millions worship him. *Before the tendency to pray all barriers go down.*

The traveler climbs the foothills of the Himalayas, and among the Khonds of North India hears the prayer: "O Lord, we know not what is good for us. Thou knowest what it is. For it we pray." The archeologist goes back among the Aztec ruins and reads their prayer in affliction: "O merciful Lord, let this chastisement with which thou hast visited us, give us freedom from evil and from folly." The historian finds the Greek world typical of all ancient civilizations at least in this, that prayer is everywhere. Xenophon begins each day's march with prayer; Pericles begins every address with prayer; the greatest of Greek orations, Demosthenes' "On the Crown," and the greatest of Greek poems, "The Iliad," are opened with prayer. When from the superstitious habits of the populace one turns to the most elevated and philosophic spirits to see what they will say, he hears Plato, "Every man of sense before beginning an important work will ask help of the gods." And turning from Plato's preaching to his practice, he reads this beautiful petition, "King Zeus, grant us the good whether we pray for it or not, but evil keep from us, though we pray for it."

If today one crosses the borders of Christianity into Mohammedanism, not only will he find formal prayer five times daily, when the muezzin calls, but he will read descriptions of prayer like this from a Sufi—"There are three degrees in prayer. The first is when it is only spoken by the lips. The second is when with difficulty, by a resolute effort, the soul succeeds in fixing its thought on divine things. The third is when the soul finds it hard to turn away from God." And if from all others, one looks to the Hebrew people, with what unanimous ascription do they say, "O thou that hearest prayer, unto thee shall all flesh come" (Psa. 65:2). A man is cutting himself off from one of the elemental functions of human life when he denies in himself the tendency to pray.

II

Moreover, justification for calling prayer natural is found in the fact that *mankind never outgrows prayer.* Both the practice and the theory of it have proved infinitely adaptable to all stages of culture. In its lowest forms, among the most savage peoples, prayer and magic were indistinguishable. To pray then was to use charms that compelled the assent of the gods. And from such pagan beginnings to Jesus in the Garden or a modern scientist upon his knees, prayer, like all other primary functions, has proved capable of unlimited development. It has not been crushed but has been lifted into finer forms by spiritual and intellectual advance. It has shaped its course like a river, to the banks of each generation's thought; but it has flowed on, fed from fountains that changing banks do not affect. Nowhere is this more plain than in the Bible. Compare the dying prayer of Samson, as he wound his arms around the sustaining pillars of the Philistine dining hall and cried: "O Lord Jehovah, remember me, I pray thee, and strengthen me, I pray thee, only this once, O God, that I may be at once avenged of the Philistines for my two eyes" (Judges 16:28); with the dying prayer of Stephen, as he was being stoned, "Lord, lay not this sin to their charge" (Acts 7:60). Both are prayers, but they come from two ages between which the revelation of God and the meaning of prayer had infinitely widened.

Both in the Scripture and out of it, the quality of prayer is suited to the breadth or narrowness of view, the generosity or bitterness of spirit, which the generation or the individual possesses. As Sabatier puts it, "*The history of prayer is the history of religion.*" At one end of the scale,

In even savage bosoms
There are longings, yearnings, strivings
For the good they comprehend not;
And their feeble hands and helpless,
Groping blindly in the darkness,
Touch God's right hand in that darkness
And are lifted up and strengthened.

At the other end of the scale, Coleridge says, "The act of praying is the very highest energy of which the human mind is capable"; and President Harper of the University of Chicago, on his death-bed prays: "May there be for me a life beyond this life; and in that life may there be work to do, tasks to accomplish. If in any way a soul has been injured or a friend hurt, may the harm be overcome, if it is possible." The human soul never outgrows prayer. At their lowest, men pray crudely, ignorantly, bitterly; at their best, men pray intelligently, spiritually, magnanimously. *Prayer is not only universal in extent; it is infinite in quality.* A man may well give himself to the deepening and purifying of his prayer, for it is as natural in human life as thought.

III

The naturalness of prayer is further seen in the fact that *prayer is latent in the life of every one of us.* At first the experience of some may seem to gainsay this. They have given up praying. They get on very well without it, and when they are entirely candid they confess that they disbelieve in it. But they must also confess that their disbelief lies in their *opinions* and not in their *impulses.* When some overwhelming need comes upon them, their impulse is still to pray.

Modern scepticism has done all that it could to make prayer unreasonable. It has viewed the world as a machine, regular as an automaton, uncontrollable as sunrise. It has made whatever God there is a prisoner in the laws of his own world, powerless to assist his children. It has denied everything that makes prayer possible; and yet men, having believed all that sceptical thought says, still have their times of prayer. Like water in an artesian well, walled up by modern concrete, prayer still seeps through, it breaks out; nature is stronger than artifice, and streams flowing underground in our lives insist on finding vent. Sometimes a crisis of personal danger lets loose this hidden impulse. "I hadn't prayed in ten years," the writer heard a railroad man exclaim when his train had just escaped a wreck; "but I prayed *then.*" Sometimes a crushing responsibility makes men pray almost in spite of themselves. General Kodoma, of the Japanese army during the Russian war, used to retire each morning for an hour of prayer. When asked the reason, he answered: "When a man has done everything in his power, there remains nothing but the help of the gods." Anything—peril, responsibility, anxiety, grief —that shakes us out of our mere opinions, down into our native impulses, is likely to make us pray.

This is true of whole populations as well as of individuals. Shall not a war like the appalling conflict in Europe make men doubt God and disbelieve all good news of him that they have heard? Only of far distant spectators is any such reaction true. In the midst of the crisis itself, where the burdens of sacrifice are being borne and super-human endurance, courage, and selflessness are required, the reaction of men, as all observers note, is accurately described in Cardinal Mercier's famous pastoral letter: "Men long unaccustomed to prayer are turning again to God. Within the army, within the civil world, in public, and within the individual conscience there is prayer. Nor is that prayer today a word learned by rote, uttered lightly by the lip; it surges from the troubled heart, it takes the form at the feet of God of the very sacrifice of life." Whether in the individual or in society, great shocks that loosen the foundations of human life and let the primal tendencies surge up, always set free the pent fountains of prayer. *In the most sceptical man or generation prayer is always underground, waiting.* Henry Ward Beecher was giving us something more than a whimsical smile when he said: "I pray on the principle that the wine knocks the cork out of a bottle. There is an inward fermentation and there must be a vent." Even Comte, with his system of religion that utterly banished God, soul, and immortality, prescribed for his disciples two hours of prayer daily, because he recognized the act itself as one of the elemental functions of human nature.

Whether, therefore, we consider the universality of prayer, or its infinite adaptability to all stages of culture and intelligence, or the fact that it is latent in every one of us, we come to the same conclusion: praying is a natural activity of human life. We may only note in passing the patent argument here for the truth of religion. *Can it be that all men, in all ages and all lands, have been engaged in "talking forever to a silent world from which no answer comes"?* If we can be sure of anything, is it not this —that wherever a human function has persisted, unwearied by time, uncrushed by disappointment, rising to noblest form and finest use in the noblest and finest souls, that function corresponds with some Reality? Hunger never could have persisted without food, nor breathing without air, nor intellectual life without truth, nor prayer without God. Burke said that it was difficult to press an indictment against a nation. It is far more difficult to sustain a charge against all mankind.

IV

From this argument which the naturalness of prayer suggests, we press on, however, to a matter more immediate to our purpose. The fact that prayer is one of our native tendencies accounts for one peril in our use of it. *We let prayer be merely a tendency, and therefore spasmodic, occasional, untrained.* A tragedy is always present in any fine function of human nature that is left undisciplined. The impulse to love is universal; but left to be merely an impulse, it is brutal and fleshly. The love that inspires our noblest poems and is celebrated in our greatest music, that builds Christian homes and makes family life beautiful, is a primal impulse trained and elevated, become intelligent, disciplined, and consecrated. The tendency to think is universal, but left as such, it is but the wayward and futile intellect of savages. Their powers of thinking are stagnant, called into activity by accident, not well understood, carefully trained, and intelligently exercised. So prayer left to spasmodic use is a futile thing. In the one-hundred and seventh Psalm, a marvelous description of a storm at sea ends with a verse which reveals the nature of impulsive prayer: "They . . . are at their wits' end. Then they cry unto Jehovah" (Psalm 107:27, 28). When prayer is left untrained, men pray only when they have reached their wits' end. In moments of extreme physical danger, men who never make a daily friend of God, cry to him in their need. "He that will learn to pray," says George Herbert, pithily, "let him go to sea"; and Shakespeare in the "Tempest," knowing human nature as the Psalmist knew it, has the sailors, when the storm breaks, cry: "All lost! To prayers! To prayers! All lost!" In extreme moral danger, also, where pleasant dalliance with evil has run out into the unbreakable habit of evil, men almost always pray. And in death how naturally men think of God! So Dame Quickly says of the dying Falstaff: "Now I, to comfort him, bid him a' should not think of God. I hoped there was no need to trouble himself with any such thoughts yet!"

Prayer, left as an undisciplined impulse, inevitably sinks into such a spasmodic and frantic use. "When my soul fainted within me, I remembered Jehovah" (Jonah 2:7). Like the old Greek dramatists, men hopelessly tangle the plot of their lives, until at the end, with a dilemma insoluble by human ingenuity and power, they swing a god from the wings by machinery to disentangle the desperate situation. They use prayer as a *deus-ex-machina*, a last resort when they are in extremity. In one way or another, how many of us must accuse ourselves of this fitful use of prayer! One of the supreme powers of our lives is left to the control of impulse and accident, its nature unstudied, and its exercise untrained.

V

The baneful effect of this spasmodic use of prayer is easily seen. *For one thing it utterly neglects all Christian conceptions of God and goes back to the pagan thought of him. God becomes nothing more than a power to be occasionally called in to our help.* This is the conception of an Indian woman bowing at an idol's shrine. Her god is power, mysterious and masterful, whose help she seeks in her emergencies. When, therefore, we pray as she does, fitfully running to God in occasional crises, we are going back in substance, if not in form, to paganism. We deserve Luther's rebuke in his sermon on praying to the saints: "We honor them and call upon them only when we have a pain in our legs or our heads, or when our pockets are empty." But the best of humanity have traveled a long way from such an idea of deity. The Christian God desires to be to every one an inward and abiding friend, a purifying presence in daily life, the One whose moral purpose continually restrains and whose love upholds. Above all advances made in human life none is so significant as this advance in the thought of God. We have moved from rumbling oxcarts to limited express trains, from mud huts to cathedrals, from tom-toms to orchestras. If we neglected these gains, we should rightly be regarded as strange anachronisms. Yet in our treatment of God how often are we ancient pagans born after our time! We are examples of religious reversal to type. We are misdated A.D. instead of B.C. when we use God as a power to be occasionally summoned to our aid.

Consider a new parable of a father and his two sons. One son looked upon his father as a last resort in critical need. He never came to him for friendly conference, never sought his advice, in little difficulties never was comforted by his help. He did not make his father his confidant. He went to college and wrote home only when he wanted money. He fell into disgrace, and called on his father only when he needed legal aid. He ran his life with utter disregard of his father's character or purpose, and turned to him only when in desperate straits. The other son saw in his father's love the supreme motive of his life. He was moved by daily gratitude so that to be well-pleasing to his father was his joy and his ideal. His father was his friend. He confided in him, was advised by him, kept close to him, and in *his* crises came to his father with a naturalness born of long habit, like Jesus, who having prayed without ceasing, now at last bows in Gethsemane. *Is there any doubt as to which is the nobler sonship? And is not the former type a true picture of our relationship with God when we leave prayer to be a merely instinctive and untrained cry of need?*

VI

For another thing, this use of prayer as merely a spasmodic cry out of an occasional crisis, makes it utterly selfish. We think of God solely with reference to our own emergencies. We never remember the Most High except when we wish him to run an errand for us. Our prayer does not concern itself with the fulfilment of his great purposes in us and in the world, and does not relate itself to a life devoted to his will. In utter selfishness we forget God until it occurs to us that we may get something from him.

Some men treat God in this respect as others treat their country. That regard for native land which in some has inspired heroic and sacrificial deeds, appears in others in the disguise of utter selfishness. Consider a man who does nothing whatever for his country; is not interested in her problems; is careless of the franchise, evades every public responsibility, and even dodges taxes. One would suppose that this man never thought of his country at all. Upon the contrary, there are occasions when he thinks of her at once. When his person or property is attacked and his rights invaded, this same man will appeal clamorously to the government for protection. He reserves every thought of his country for the hours of personal crisis. His relationship with his government is exhausted in spasmodic cries for help. *He furnishes a true parallel to that ignoble type of religion, in which prayer, left fitful and undisciplined, is nothing more than an occasional, selfish demand on God.*

VII

The shame of leaving thus uncultivated one of the noblest functions of man's spirit is emphasized when we face the testimony of the masters in prayer concerning its possibilities. What the power of thought can mean must be seen in the thinkers; what prayer can do must be seen in the pray-ers. Whenever *they* speak, language seems to them inadequate to describe the saving and empowering influences of habitual prayer. As in our Christian songs, where we leave the more superficial differences of opinion and go down into the essential spirit of worship, Catholics and Protestants, Jews and Gentiles, men of every shade of special belief and sectarian alliance are authors of the hymns we all sing, so in prayer men of opposite opinions agree as one. Luther, the Protestant, is alien at how many points from St. Bernard the Catholic, and yet says Luther —"In the faith wherein St. Bernard prays, do I pray also." Not only does a liberal philosopher, Sabatier, say, "Prayer is religion in act; that is, prayer is real religion"; and a conservative theologian, Hartman, say, "God has given to real prayer the power to shape the future for men and the world"; and a Catholic poet, Francis Thompson, say, "Prayer is the very sword of the saints"; even Professor Tyndall, the scientist, who was regarded by the Christians of his generation as the most aggressive antagonist of prayer, says: "It is not my habit of mind to think otherwise than solemnly of the feelings which prompt to prayer. Often unreasonable, even contemptible, in its purer forms prayer hints at disciplines which few of us can neglect without moral loss." If there is any element in human life to whose inestimable value we have abundant testimony, it is prayer; and to leave misunderstood and untrained a power capable of such high uses is a spiritual tragedy.

This, then, is the summary of the matter. Deep in every one of us lies the tendency to pray. If we allow it to remain merely a tendency, it becomes nothing but a selfish, unintelligent, occasional cry of need. But understood and disciplined, it reveals possibilities whose limits never have been found.

Von Ogden Vogt

(1879——)

Vogt was pastor of the First Unitarian Church, Chicago, Illinois, 1925-44. Born in Illinois, educated at Beloit College and Yale, he was ordained in the Congregational ministry in 1912. Before going to the First Unitarian Church, Chicago, he served Congregational churches in Cheshire and Chicago. During his ministry his special intellectual interest has centered in worship, especially as related to art and symbolism. *Modern Worship* and *Art and Religion* are two of his interpretive books on worship.

The following selection, part of the chapter "Symbols and Sacraments" from *Art and Religion,* is one the clearest statements to come from any writer of devotional literature who discerns the Protestant value of the Eucharist. It is used by permission of Yale University Press. (Copyright 1921 Yale University Press.)

[TRANSUBSTANTIATION OF PERSONS]

From *Art and Religion*

In the formal sense, a sacrament has an outward as well as an inward side: it includes physical elements. There is nothing especially mysterious about the nature of the elements, except in so far as the nature of matter in general is mysterious. Nor is there anything exceptionally mysterious about the nature of the influence or purpose of the material elements, except as the nature of all sensational influence is mysterious. The formulas that are spoken, the water that is poured, both physical act and material element, these call for, signify, and express the inner effort and act of the spirit. And if they do so successfully, then God is in the sacrament. If the outward acts, elements, or symbols do not serve to produce any motion of the spirit, either in the heart of the priest or of the people, then no sacrament has occurred, and no grace of God has been imparted.

It is only by long association that many have come to regard the material element as sacred. To the Protestant experience, the material element is essentially only a matter of artistry, a symbol, an idealization. The use made of the material element is not a matter of artistry, but a sacrament in which Divinity is present. In other words, the view of many Protestants that God is not in the sacrament is not the view here expressed. The conception here set forth is that Divinity is actually in the sacrament, as being in the spirits of persons performing the religious act which we call the sacrament. On the other hand, the view excludes the conception of any sense in which Divinity is extraordinarily resident in the material elements. Of course our conclusion comes from our definition. Otherwise define a sacrament and you must otherwise conceive the elements. Or begin with another conception of the outward form and it would be difficult to define the sacrament, in our manner, as a dedicatory religious act of persons.

The sacrament of the Eucharist is more complicated and so more mysterious than any other. Just as with some works of art it is difficult to decide whether we have the idea objectified or the object idealized, so here we halt between the symbolic and mystic conceptions. Both are involved. If even in Protestant feeling the strictly symbolical is minimized and merged into the sacramental or mystical, it is not difficult to see how the Romanist has confused the self-offering of the devotee with the formal offering of the elements, taking the elements out of the realm of symbolism into that of idealization and transubstantiation.

It is essentially the same point of view, often expressed by Protestants when they refer to the actual bread and wine as "the sacrament." In our view these elements are not the sacrament, but the symbols idealized to call forth and assist the inner and profound sacramental act. In whatever sense sanctity may be said to attach to the elements, according to the practice of some after they are set apart and thus consecrated, in actual usage amongst the reformed churches, the prayer of "consecration" expresses only a slight interest in the setting apart of the elements and a deep interest in the consecration of persons.

The abundant danger of this view is the danger of subjectivity and informality; the danger of placing a too slight value upon the external and formal administration, and the danger of a merely humanized experience. We do not sufficiently believe in or expect an actual visitation of Divinity in the sacrament, thinking rather of the experience as our own. And so, thinking of the experience as our own production, we have too little considered the powers of the church and of the formal administration.

There is an objective value in the historic sacraments. The nature of the spiritual life in a material world is ever a profound mystery. The nature of human salvation and sanctification is mysterious. . . . The sacrament bears the burden of initiation. It is not complete without the actual presence of God to give power to carry out the dedication that has occurred. But the power to make the dedication is lacking without the divine presence, and this visitation cannot come without humility. But even your humility you cannot produce of yourself. It is induced in you by your appreciation of something outside that makes you humble. This is the function of the material elements and the formal administration of the sacrament. They are symbols which bring near to you and represent the sacrifice of Christ. Through them you are helped to "be in contact with the real and living Christ." That contact begins in you a process of divinization which is partly your act of consecration and partly the action of the divine grace toward you and within you. "What we consecrate, God will sanctify." The transubstantiation which occurs is not that of the material elements, but a real transubstantiation of persons, a real change of human nature into divine nature. This is the essential miracle. . . .

Religion always offers more than ideas, and more than moral precepts; it supplies the energy to live by. It cannot be described in terms of truth or in programs of right conduct, but rather and chiefly in manifestations of power. . . . The world of the unknown is larger than the known. Known forces we can begin to understand and to manipulate; it is the vast unknown with which we must come to terms. . . .

Two things, therefore, I am trying to suggest: that religion must use symbols, definitive, concrete representations, to set forth what it knows or definitely believes; and that it must use sacraments as exercises of personal consecration to the highest reality, whatever that reality is, however much unknown, that the presence and power of Divinity may become more fully operative in human life. The first usage is merely artistic, the embodiment of ideas in objects, after the fashion of all Classic artists. Such embodiments may be in the form of pictures, or creeds, or more familiar concepts, or statues, or classic music, or the elements of a sacrament. By all these forms, fairly clear ideas are objectified and symbolized. The second usage quickly becomes more than artistry, more than the idealization of particular objects. The Romantic artist portrays objects so that we can see them in all the reaches of their relations, idealizing them. Religion takes hold on a man by a sacrament and not merely idealizes him but transforms him into the ideal. The process is carried out of the realm of artistic idealization into that of religious transubstantiation.

Albert W. Palmer

(1879———)

For many years Palmer was known chiefly as the president of a theological seminary. His interests in the field of practical theology have touched deeply the field of worship. Educated at the University of California and Yale, Palmer was ordained a Congregational minister in 1904. He served Congregational churches in the United States and Hawaii from 1904-30, when he became president of Chicago Theological Seminary. He is now president emeritus.

The following selection is taken from *Paths to the Presence of God*, a series of lectures first given as a Lenten series at Chicago Theological Seminary, and later before the National Council of Congregational and Christian Churches in Seattle, Washington. Besides worship, the "paths" to God discussed are nature, science, humanity, and Jesus. This selection is used by permission of The Pilgrim Press.

[THROUGH WORSHIP TO GOD]

From *Paths to the Presence of God*

The reawakening of the spirit of worship in our churches is one of the most heartening facts of contemporary life. Before those who have been troubled by the passing of the old-fashioned prayer meeting cry out, "They have taken away my Lord," they may well note the new emphasis on personal religion and the growing reverence for worship which is walking in the garden of the modern church and calling them by name. Worship is not only in a midweek meeting with a little group of mystic souls; it finds new life today in the hush of the sanctuary, as men and women on the full flood-tide of the Sunday morning service lift up their hearts to God and find a new light shining in their faces. There may have been days when worship was more or less a formal gesture of politeness to God, or when it descended to the depths of being regarded as only a set of preliminary exercises before the sermon; but those far-off unhappy days are gone forever, and the modern church increasingly looks upon worship as a creative experience through which we may come in tune with God and receive new strength and courage for our lives. Longfellow expressed it all most beautifully in his noble sonnet, "The Cathedral":

Oft have I seen at some cathedral door
  A laborer, pausing in the dust and heat,
  Lay down his burden, and with reverent feet
Enter, and cross himself, and on the floor
Kneel to repeat his paternoster o'er;
  Far off the noises of the world retreat;
  The loud vociferations of the street
Become an undistinguishable roar.
So, as I enter here from day to day,
  And leave my burden at this minster gate,
  Kneeling in prayer, and not ashamed to pray,
The tumult of the time disconsolate
  To inarticulate murmurs dies away.
  While the eternal ages watch and wait.

This age of ours peculiarly needs to worship. We are so driven by the various pressures of life that we need a time of refuge and of peace. We live so much in man-made cities where there are no hills to which we may lift up our eyes, that we need some spiritual sanctuary where our upward-questing vision may see a light shining on spiritual hills and mountains.

I attended recently, as an unknown worshipper in a pew assigned to strangers, a service of worship which was like a spiritual pilgrimage. It began with an organ prelude played by one who had passed beyond conscious technique to a high sense that he was preparing human spirits to lift up their hearts to God. This blended into a processional sung by an ample choir robed in purple gowns and white surplices, singing joyously in a way that set one's spirit free from all care and remembered trouble. Steadily, from step to step, the service moved forward without break or hesitation. There was no descent into the lesser gullies and quagmires of personal comment and announcement. It moved on like a spiritual pilgrimage and took me along, a willing follower, up upon the hills of praise, down into shadowed valleys of confession and humility, out over the highlands of assurance and renewal, until at last we all stood together on the mountain peak of dedication.

This service of worship was built upon a careful following of the sequence of ideas and emotions to be found in Isaiah's great worship experience as recorded in the Bible. "In the year that King Uzziah died I saw the Lord sitting upon a throne, high and lifted up; and his train filled the temple. Above him stood the seraphim; each one had six wings; with twain he covered his face, and with twain he covered his feet, and with twain he did fly. And one cried unto another, and said, Holy, holy, holy is the Lord of hosts: the whole earth is full of his glory. And the foundations of the thresholds shook at the voice of him that cried, and the house was filled with smoke. Then said I, Woe is me! for I am undone; because I am a man of unclean lips, and I dwell in the midst of a people of unclean lips: for mine eyes have seen the King, the Lord of hosts. Then flew one of the seraphim unto me, having a live coal in his hand, which he had taken with the tongs from off the altar: and he touched my mouth with it and said, Lo, this hath touched thy lips; and thine iniquity is taken away and thy sin forgiven. And I heard the voice of the Lord saying, Whom shall I send, and who will go for us? Then I said, Here am I; send me."

As Von Ogden Vogt and others have pointed out, this is a practically perfect account of what happens in a normal worship experience. First of all, it begins in vision. Some great experience with natural beauty—a mountain, a starry night, a flower—moves us greatly and we catch a new vision of perfect beauty. It may come through some life experience; love or heroism, or birth or death steals in upon us and we see the nobility of human life on a new level; or the vision may come through the reading of a great book or from the uplifting influence of noble music.

It is noteworthy that this sense of vision often comes, perhaps most often comes, not when all is well with us but when we are burdened and borne down with trouble. It was in the year that King Uzziah *died*, that Isaiah had his great experience, not in the years of his long prosperity but in the year when the King had died of leprosy and left a sense of dread and foreboding on the land. So it is that times of disillusionment, when outward and material success recedes, are, more often than not, conducive to spiritual vision.

Now this capacity for spiritual vision is one of the glories of humanity. There are some prosaic souls like the one of whom it is written that

A primrose by a river's brim
A yellow primrose was to him,
And it was nothing more.

But, for most of us, the power of spiritual aspiration links us to the divine; and common people, quite as much as their more sophisticated brethren, find life suffused with a spiritual glory and almost agonized by an upthrust of the soul in search of God.

It is not far, the life of adoration,
For all about the many symbols lie:
Each dawn has known the mystic elevation,
And twilight burns pale tapers in the sky.

After vision, the next step in worship is humility and confession. It was when Isaiah saw the vision that he realized the shortcomings of himself and of his people. It was when Peter gained a new insight into the meaning and power of Jesus that he cried out, "Depart from me, for I am a sinful man, O Lord!" It is part of the spiritual nobility of man that he has a sense of his own shortcomings. No fault can be conquered, no sin uprooted, until it is seen and recognized; but once seen and recognized, there is that within man which will give him no rest or peace until it is rooted out and cast away.

A well-known New York psychiatrist, speaking before the faculty of the Chicago Theological Seminary recently on the subject of forgiveness, said, "After all a man, in the end, must forgive himself." I went home and told that to the lady whose judgment largely guides my destinies, and she said: "Oh, that's too easy! The trouble with most men is that they are only too ready to forgive themselves!" But I think the psychiatrist was right. At last each man must forgive himself—must face the inward judge at the bar of his own conscience, without rationalization or any other subterfuge. Only when he has made peace with himself can he find himself at peace with God, and so forgiveness sounds the deepest note in worship. A man faces the realities of life, commits himself without equivocation to the ideal, and knows within his soul the inner peace that comes from being at harmony with God. Forgiveness merges into illumination. Strength and moral purpose, eagerness and courage, all come racing back into the soul. A man feels that he can face anything now! And then comes the final stage of worship—dedication. Isaiah heard a voice saying, "Whom shall I send, and who will go for us?" And he cried out, as every man must cry out to God if his worship has been profound and true, "Here am I; send me!"

Worship then means a release of energy. It puts into life something which steps it up to a higher voltage. Through worship man comes to God at first hand, has an immediate experience with God, and goes forth transformed and stimulated to new levels of endeavor.

From an Old Testament experience let us go to a New Testament experience of worship. Let us enter with Jesus and the little group of followers the upper room where they are to eat the last supper together. That upper room may well be for us a symbol of the church as a place of worship.

There are three things worth noting about that upper room. The first is that it was a place of peace and quiet. Jerusalem is a tumultuous city—was then, is now. I have been there and know its narrow streets, its jostling crowds, its strident cries. Especially crowded must it have been at that Passover season with many pilgrims. I can understand that, too, for I have seen the Arab crowds along the Jericho Road at the feast of Nebi Mousa. But the upper room was on a quiet courtyard, shut off from the noisy street; it looked beyond the city to the hills which are round about Jerusalem, and at night it opened out upon the stars. Even so, a church should be in this modern world. Set in the midst of a rushing, mechanical civilization, speeded up to a constant rush and roar, the church should provide that place of hush and quiet we so greatly need. It should be a place of wider horizons, from which we can see the encircling hills of truth; and when night settles down upon our mortal plans and projects, it should give us the far-off vision of the stars.

The second thing about this upper room was that, in spite of its peace and quiet, it was a place of tension and anxiety. Those twelve men there had brought their cares and troubles into it from the crowded street. Think who they were! Not a group of placid theorists. Judas, the sinner, was there; and Peter, the impulsive and unstable; and Philip, theologically puzzled, ready to ask "Show us the Father"; and Thomas was there with his doubts already forming. And tragic news broke upon them there. "One of you shall betray me!" What a turmoil in each heart as they ask, "Is it I? Is it I?" Even so the church today must be a place where the tensions and anxieties of life come in. There are those who would keep the services of the church remote from living issues—no politics but those of the ancient Hebrews, no social problems but those of Moses, no personal tragedies but those of the New Testament! I cannot see it that way. No, life must come in to the church's upper room of worship—life with all its tensions, life with all its problems, its hungers, defeats and disappointments. You cannot let men in and leave life out, or only their bodies will be there while their minds are far away. Worship cannot be an ethereal, exotic, esoteric thing, remote from present reality and too pale and esthetic to meet life's living issues. No, it must come to grips with the things that men must meet the moment they step outside into the rushing street.

But the third thing about that upper room is that Jesus was there! Into their troubled counsels he came, to resolve their difficulties, relieve their tensions and overcome their fears. And this he did in very significant ways. For one thing he brought to pass a spirit of humility. He girded himself with a towel and performed the office of the humblest servant as he washed their feet. He banished all their pride as he said to them, ". . . he that is greater among you, let him become as the younger; and he that is chief, as he that doth serve. . . . I am in the midst of you as he that serveth." And then he lifted their minds from their present troubles to the great and abiding realities of the spirit. He could not and did not tell them there was no danger, no betrayer, no Caiaphas, no cross. But he did tell them of the abiding things which these perils could not alter: "I am the vine," he said, "ye are the branches: . . . in the world ye shall have tribulation; be of good cheer, I have overcome the world. . . . I will not leave you comfortless, I will come unto you. . . . Let not your heart be troubled: ye believe in God, believe also in me." And then he put it all into something deeper and more elemental than words; he put it into a symbol, and taking the humblest, simplest articles of peasant fare, the unleavened bread and sour wine there upon the table, made them symbols of his love and his devotion so that the disciples could never again partake of the simplest meal without remembering him.

Isn't there in all this a glorious illustration of what the church can do in worship? It can level all our pride and outward distinction of class and wealth and create in each worshiper a humble and a contrite heart. It can remind us of the eternal verities, and bid us lift up our hearts to the abiding truths of spiritual living. Not only can it celebrate the Last Supper as a formal sacrament, it can do something even more precious than that: it can take the events of daily life and fill them with spiritual meaning, make them also to be sacraments of the eternal values, until we have not two sacraments or seven, but seventy times seven.

But isn't there a peril in worship? May it not be seized upon as an escape from reality? Isn't all this modern emphasis on worship a confession of failure to build the kingdom of heaven in the outer world, and, because of this external failure, is there not a blind compensatory urge to retreat to an easier inner world of illusion and emotional subjectivism? Reinhold Neibuhr, speaking at the University of Chicago recently, warned us that it was so much easier to build a beautiful cathedral than a beautiful civilization that the peril was that we might be content just to build the cathedral! Nor has this warning been uttered to this generation alone. Jeremiah has a scathing denunciation of those who are content to go about praising the house of worship, saying, "The temple of the Lord, the temple of the Lord, the temple of the Lord, are these," and neglecting their deeper ethical responsibilities. And George Adam Smith has a stern and searching chapter on "The False Peace of Ritual."

But worship need not be a false peace or mere escape. It may rather be a release of new energy to grapple with the very problems it is sometimes accused of running away from. Indeed some escapes are valuable; sleep, vacations, travel, recreation, all these are escapes from which we return to take up life with new vigor. Even National Councils may come under this category! The test of any escape is: What does it do to you? How does it send you back? With a dark-brown taste and weakened morale, or with a tanned skin and hardened muscles and a sense of wider horizons and deeper purposes?

Isaiah found in his worship experience a new dedication and commitment to his social message. It all depends on the worshiper's attitude of mind and the content of the worship experience. Isaiah had a social conscience, and his vision of the holiness of God only served to put new power into his social ideals. Perhaps what the social gospel needs just now is a liturgical interpretation to give it greater emotional drive. We have rationalized the social gospel, debated it, dramatized it, written books about it. Why not translate it into liturgy and undergird it with the beauty and emotional aspiration of worship?

The great antidote for the danger of worship's becoming a mere retreat from reality is found in Wieman's great creative idea of what he calls "worshipful problem-solving," as set forth in his little book, *Methods of Private Religious Living.* He seizes upon the Lord's Prayer as his pattern of the true worship experience especially when linked to the specific task of problem solving. Freely paraphrased, his thought is that we should take our problems with us into our experience of worship. Take any problem you please—it may be personal to you alone or it may be one of the great baffling problems of the social order. Then let your worship follow the pattern of the Lord's Prayer. Begin with "Our Father, who art in heaven," thus lifting your thought at once to the contemplation of the highest and noblest thing you know. And then go on further and share God's problems! With true courtesy, you do not start on your own requests but say, "Thy kingdom come, thy will be done on earth as it is in heaven." A certain largeness of soul and outlook comes to you as for a few moments you get away from your own little limited viewpoint and look out on life from the standpoint of God. Then, and only then, do you bring your own problems into the center of the picture. And the Lord's Prayer provides for almost all the classes of problems you are likely to bring. First of all there is "Give us this day our daily bread"—that is the basic economic problem of the race. Then there is "Forgive us our debts as we forgive our debtors"—and about all the problems of social and racial and international relations can be gathered there. And then there is "Lead us not into temptation but deliver us from evil" —all of a man's struggle for personal integrity and nobility of soul is summed up in that petition. And then there is the final "Amen," "so be it," and we have set the seal of definite determination and registered purpose upon the aspiration of our souls.

Such worship is no opiate, no retreat from reality, no escape from facing the ugly sordid facts of modern life. Rather it gathers up those facts and takes them into the sanctuary itself, there to pray over them and dedicate life anew to their transformation. It is not choosing between beautiful cathedrals and a beautiful civilization. If it cannot have both it will insist on a beautiful civilization and let the cathedrals go. But it will not be content until at last it has them both.

What the world and the church and the religious life of man need just now is more passion, more mystical devotion, more sense of inner fellowship with the eternal verities of God. We are thinking our way through pretty clearly to a finer, higher social ethics, more truly Christ-like than the world has ever seen before. A new and ideal code on race relations, civic and industrial life, international problems, is growing up apace. We shall not fail in the intellectual formulation of these things.

But there is a hard long struggle ahead of us, before we shall have made these clear and beautiful ideals regnant in the world; and for the accomplishment of that task no mere intellectual assent or clarity of thought is sufficient. We shall need emotion touched with fire. We shall require the driving power of overwhelming spiritual devotion. Our sword will have to be bathed in heaven. We shall need to hear again a majestic "Thus saith the Lord." And these things can come only through worship. We must be lifted out of our petty selves and made one with the mighty purposes of God, willing to suffer and to sacrifice to make the dream come true. Lord, teach thy church how to worship in sincerity and in truth!

A little while ago I was sitting in a hotel lobby listening to some exquisite music by a string quartette. I think they were playing the "Londonderry Air." And I said to myself: What is music and what is it that it does to you? Oh, I know it can all be explained in terms of mathematics. Every note has a certain number of vibrations and there is a definite mathematical measurement for every melody and harmony; and if these basic mathematical conditions are violated or disregarded, the beauty of the music at once is broken into discord. And yet what is it that music does to our emotions? How it lifts us and comforts us and inspires us! It holds the secret of building a bridge from scientific truth to emotional truth and spiritual experience. And exactly that is the function of worship: it is the music of religion.

Willard L. Sperry

(1882———)

EDUCATED at Olivet College, Yale, and Oxford, where he was a Rhodes scholar, Sperry held Congregational pastorates in New England from 1908-22. During part of this time he also taught at Andover Theological Seminary. Since 1922 he has been dean of Harvard Divinity School. As a religious educator he has exerted a wide influence upon American religious life through his interpretation of literature, his insight into liturgy, and his prophetic voice.

Of his various books, two are particularly related to the saints and worship: *Strangers and Pilgrims* and *Reality in Worship*. This selection, the title chapter in the latter book, penetrates into the heart of that which is sincere in the act of devotion. It is used here by permission of The Macmillan Co. (Copyright 1925 by The Macmillan Co.)

REALITY IN WORSHIP

From *Reality in Worship*

In the present divided condition of the church we cannot hope for a single service of worship conveying final truthfulness in any one order of public worship. But we have the right to expect of others, as we have the duty to require of ourselves, sincerity in the application of science and art to our own experience and to the body of our belief. One does not have to be a Romanist to get the suggestion of reality conveyed by the high altar. And one does not have to be a Quaker to get the suggestion of reality conveyed by silence. We know that for the good Catholic the Mass is real. And we know that for the good Quaker the silence is real. What would wreck the whole affair would be the suspicion that the Mass was merely a pageant to the Catholic, and that silence was simply inertia with the Quaker. In either case we require faith in "The Real Presence."

So long as a form of public worship is substantially real to those who worship through its help, it is for them a valid form. The moment it raises questions that will not down, kindles suspicions that refuse to die out, and leaves the worshiper in doubt as to its objective truth or his sincerity in participating in it, it has become a defenceless form of wor-

ship, unprofitable to those in whom it wakens such reactions and even dangerous to the whole cause of religion. . . . What is in question is rather the suggestion of something only half real, a playing at religion, the suspicion that here life has not come to terms with itself, let alone its universe.

The implications of this major premise are many and by no means always clear. The minor premise will be the actual order of worship to which a man finds himself committed. No single individual will find a service of worship equally real to him in all parts. But every individual has a right to require of his church that in a service of public worship it shall provide him with a vehicle for communion with God and man which imparts a strong suggestion of reality from the transaction as a whole. If his church cannot provide such a service, because as artist or scientist he is at loggerheads with the science and art of his own communion, he is probably under the necessity of seeking another church, or of gathering persons like minded with himself and founding a new church. . . .

A man must be clear when he passes adverse criticism upon a service of worship that he understands the true intention and implication of the service and that in his own spirit he measures up to that which the service may rightly require of him. There is no service of worship in existence which would not profit by the thorough-going attempt of those who habitually use it to come nearer to exhausting its possibilities. Such an effort to measure up to the service should certainly precede all hasty and careless revision. Only personal religion can give sure instinct and insight into the strength or weakness of a particular order of worship. Liturgical knowledge and theological learning do not suffice. A sentimental feeling for æsthetic values is a very fallible guide. What every service asks of us is an honest effort to test its form by its inspiring idea.

The first thing to be discovered regarding the setting and substance of an act of worship is its history. If a treatment of building stone, a symbol, a ceremony, a prayer or creed has its roots deep in church history there was originally a religious idea behind it. Our first task is to recover that idea which was the inspiration of the usage. If it still stands for credible truth the usage has significance and is valid. If the idea is at variance with our conception of the truth the usage is misleading and perplexing. We do not question the central place of the altar in a Catholic church. We have a right to question the implication of a similar piece of furniture, similarly placed, in a church which is frankly nonsacramentarian.

But only a fraction of our present difficulties can be defined and solved by this historical inquiry. By far the larger number of our difficulties arise from another source. The half-real character of the average church and its transactions is due in a far greater measure to the prevalence of patterns which plainly have no religious ideas behind them and represent the vagaries of some decorator who had a blank wall space to cover with designs, a window space to fill with colored glass, or forty minutes to fill with words and music. Two thirds of the patterns which have crept into church

art in the last half century have no precedent in Christian history and no occasion in any contemporary religious idea. The serpent swallowing its own tail, which winds all through early Celtic design, meant something once—eternal life—and still has interest for us as a symbol of that idea. The formal tree which appears in the Jesse windows meant something once, and may still mean something. The symbols of the four evangelists never cease to stir the imagination. All these patterns are intelligible.

But the chill and numbing sense of unreality which we get when we enter so many churches springs from the riot of meaningless patterns which have neither historic warrant nor symbolic worth. Few of us who have ever spent idle hours during interminable church services studying the monotonous vagaries of dull mechanical patterns stenciled on a wall or set in glass will assert that here is beauty authentic and altogether lovely and here is a religious idea adequately intimated in art. Polygons of red and blue glass seem to say, "I believe in Euclid," and a wearisome stencil along the border of a wall seems to say, "I believe in the plenary inspiration of the local decorator." The plain truth is that half the decoration in American churches means nothing and never can mean anything. . . .

Once you become conscious of the utter meaninglessness of most of these patterns which you find in the ecclesiastical decoration of the last fifty years, your life is made miserable for you as you go from church to church. Even if you are not conscious of a lack of meaning, the total suggestion must often be uncertain, confusing, and distracting. We may be grateful that the best church architects to-day will have nothing to do with adventitious decoration which has no warrant either in history or symbolism.

On the contrary, symbols which plainly have a religious idea behind them are powerfully effective, even though they may be poorly executed as works of art. There is, for example, painted on the wall behind the pulpit in a little Baptist church in a fishing village down on the coast of Maine, a ship's anchor. It is the only attempt at religious symbolism in an otherwise bare meeting house. The anchor itself is not perfect as a work of art. The painter has wrestled rather ineffectually with the problem of perspective and the three dimensions. But for all its queer flat angularity it is one of the best pieces of chancel art I know, simply because it suggests what the Christian religion means to those who go down to the sea in ships. . . .

But what is far more important, as one of my friends once pointed out in talking of these things, there is an element of illusion in the drama which is not compatible with the conception of worship. A service of worship is a deliberate and disciplined adventure in reality. In church if anywhere, we are under moral bonds to be real. Assuming the rôle of Esther, David, an angel, Charity, the League of Nations, is one thing. All these may be useful parts to play in the inculcation of historical and ethical lessons. But worshiping God is a more intimate and first hand transaction. In the worship of God you may if you choose deck yourself out in vestments, surround yourself with light and color, and express yourself in ceremony. But you remain yourself, you do not play at being some one you are not. Drama demands that the actor play many rôles, and depends upon the convention of an illusion, accepted by both player and spectator. Things are not what they seem. Worship requires us to put off the playing of rôles and to be ourselves. It has no interest in creating illusions. It requires authentic sincerity. . . .

I have only hinted at a problem, which is capable of statement in a hundred ways other than those immediately cited. A church service must have reality. It must not compare unfavorably in its setting and transactions with the "real world" of every day. . . . Most of us in our effort to "beautify" our services only complicate a problem already very serious, because we add decorative features to our fabric and our procedure which have no history behind them and no clear religious idea sustaining them. We do not need "beautiful" services, in this decorative sense of the word, half as much as we need real services. And real services have no place for decorative pattern apart from Christian conviction.

Jacques Maritain

(1882——)

MARITAIN is considered the foremost contemporary interpreter of Neo-Thomism. He has lectured in many countries, and in the United States at a number of universities. He was educated at Paris, Heidelberg, and in Rome. In 1906 he was converted to Roman Catholicism and in 1908 began his study of Scholasticism. Besides lecturing widely and writing profusely, he has been professor of philosophy at the Catholic Institute in Paris and at the Institute of Mediaeval Studies at Toronto. In 1945 he became French ambassador to the Vatican.

Among his many writings which relate Scholasticism to the various sectors of life are: *Art and Scholasticism, Art and Poetry, Education at the Crossroads, Scholasticism and Politics, Religion and Culture. True Humanism* is considered by some as the best general book on Neo-Thomism.

Raïssa Maritain collaborated with her husband in the writing of *Prayer and Intelligence,* and the translation is by Algar Thorold. The following selection from that book is used by permission of Sheed & Ward.

OF SACRED DOCTRINE

From *Prayer and Intelligence*

1. Verbum Spirans Amorem

In us as well as in God, love must proceed from the Word, that is from the spiritual possession of the truth, in Faith.

And just as everything which is in the Word is found once more in the Holy Spirit, so must all that we know pass into our power of affection by love, there only finding its resting-place.

Love must proceed from Truth, and Knowledge must bear fruit in love.

Our prayer is not what it ought to be, if either of these conditions is wanting.

And by prayer we understand no other thing than that supreme prayer which is made in the secret depth of the heart—in so far as it is directed to contemplation and union with God.

2. Et Pax Dei, Quae Exsuperat Omnem Sensum, Custodiat Intelligentias Vestras

The soul in order to arrive at her last end must act, whether she make use of her own activity aided by Grace, or whether God reserve to himself the initiative of moving her, of placing her in the state which we call passive because the activity of the soul when placed in it, although in reality raised above itself, is characterised by its complete dependence on the Divine Action, and the suspension of its human method of production. Until God shall introduce us into his repose, we should ourselves make use of all our faculties with a view to our sanctification and that of our neighbour. "O Love, O God!" cries S. Gertrude, "he who is courageous and alert in the labour of thy love, will keep himself continually before thy Royal Face."

We must therefore consecrate the whole effort of our intelligence, as of our will, to know and love God, to make him known and loved.

But the intelligence itself can only develop its highest powers in so far as it is protected and fortified by the peace given by prayer. The closer a soul approaches God by love, the simpler grows the gaze of her intelligence and the clearer her vision.

"None," says Tauler, "understand better the nature of real distinction than those who have entered into Unity." But no one enters into Unity save by Love.

There is, further, a special relation between the intellectual life and the life of prayer in this sense, that prayer demands of the soul that she should leave the region of sensory images for the sphere of the Pure Intelligible and what lies beyond, while the operation of the intelligence grows more perfect in proportion to its emancipation from sensory images.

The life of prayer, also, alone enables us to unite to a never-waning, never-failing, absolute fidelity to truth, a great charity—in particular a great intellectual charity—towards our neighbour. Finally, the life of prayer, alone by supernaturally rectifying our faculties of desire enables us to convert the truth into practice.

3. Sint Lucernae Ardentes in Manibus Vestris

Prayer, particularly in the case of intellectuals, can only preserve a perfectly right direction and escape the dangers which threaten it, on condition of being supported and fed by Theology.

Knowledge of the Sacred Doctrine has a peculiar tendency of its own to shorten and render safer the spiritual journey. It saves the soul from a number of errors, illusions and blind alleys. In relation to the purgative life, it possesses an ascetic virtue which succeeds in detaching the soul from the degradations and trivialities of self-love. As for those living the illuminative life, the purification that it brings simplifies the gaze of the soul and turns it from the human self to God alone. And finally, in relation to the unitive life, a knowledge of Theology plants the roots of the soul deep in Faith and the divine Truth, a predisposition essentially required for the life of union with God.

No doubt, Charity comes before everything. It is better, here below, to love God than to know him. It is his pleasure sometimes to raise the most ignorant to the sublimest contemplation, and on account of our perversity and vanity, knowledge is often an obstacle to the Holy Spirit. It would, however, be imprudent and rash to expect a gratuitous infusion of the doctrinal light which it is in our power to acquire by study—apart from the fact that the in-tellectually vitiated atmosphere of the modern world needs a general recourse to theological science. In conclusion we may say that the normal method for those who have the grace to lead these two lives together is to unite the life of the intelligence to that of Charity on a basis of mutual inter-aid, on condition, however, that they thoroughly understand that the latter is worth infinitely more than the former, and that they always hold themselves ready to abandon all for the sake of divine love.

Muriel Lester

(1883———)

KNOWN as the "Jane Addams of London," Muriel Lester has woven the devotional strength of Christianity into her work for the betterment of the underprivileged. This she has done especially at Kingsley Hall, a London settlement house. Indicative of her desire to help every man in his urge for finer living, *Dare You Face Facts?* is inscribed: "Dedicated to the common people by whose sweat our grain is produced, our livestock tended, our houses built, our clothes made, our furnaces stoked, our factories manned, and who keep the world sane." From this book, the following selection, a practical pattern for daily devotional living, is suggestive of the way by which all men can find poise and power to "keep the world sane." It is used here by permission of Harper & Brothers. (Copyright 1940 by Harper & Brothers.)

LET YOUR SOUL CATCH UP WITH YOUR BODY

From *Dare You Face Facts?*

Some hillsmen of a primitive race in South America were carrying the baggage and scientific instruments for a party of men who had been doing research in the interior. They had got on very well, the intellectuals and the primitives, but on the long trek back to the coast time ran short and boats don't wait. The porters were told the facts and did some extra miles for several days. Then they began to lag behind. Their employers appealed to them, then strode ahead, trusting to their friendliness and sympathy. When they looked back no porter was visible. They retraced their steps and found them all serenely sitting on the baggage. They did not move as the scientists approached, just sat there looking particularly restful and receptive. Seeing the white men's look of anxious enquiry, one of them quietly explained: "We are only waiting until our souls catch up with our bodies."

Perhaps this is what we have to do. What method shall we follow?

A PROGRAM

Here is a suggestion for a prayer program for one day.

In the Small Hours. Without forcing oneself to it, it is a blessed habit to awake sometime between two and six. One can turn over with a word of thankfulness and a sense of serenity and immediately return to unconsciousness. Or one can sit up and face the blackness of night. This may be actually a frightening experience to some. Perhaps that shows how important it is. A strange aloofness seems to pervade the room. Your ego is dwarfed. Complacency gone, it shrinks until it seems a thing of shreds and patches, a fish out of water, a branch torn from the parent stem, unrooted, unwanted, withering. You look out of the window. Surely the familiar outline of friendly trees and fields and hills will reassure you! But dawn is on its way. Everything is pale, devastatingly clear. The scene is no longer intimate, but hard, almost inimical, scornful of your petty enthusiasms, your little poses, your sentimental ideas. A sense of nothingness engulfs you. The very thought of God seems an absurdity. Senseless blind existence batters at your head, your eyes, your ears.

You have to outlast all this. Don't try to escape it. That's what we've all so often done, escaping into sleep, into good works, into gaiety, into smoke or drink or drugs. It must all be faced eventually. And it's much better to face it now while we're still in the body and in time. Here comes the experience of the wise to rescue us: "Be still and know that I am God. God breathed into man's spirit the breath of life and he became a living soul. God is a spirit and they that worship Him must worship Him in spirit and in truth. Lo, I am with you always even unto the end of the age."

Soon you learn to ponder on the reassuring dependability of the creative Spirit, the certainty and satisfying rhythm that are the sign of His presence, and when you have come to absorb a tiny fragment thereof you are content.

Dawn. Anytime between six and seven-thirty A.M. it may begin with a single note or two. Then comes a theme; other voices join, the harmony becomes richer, the music swells to symphonic splendor. The birds have started their day well. How can a pray-er but be gay in such a jocund company? Your first waking thought is equally joyful.

You can get up, go out and walk. The rhythm of walking is a help to prayer. But perhaps I should not say so to you Americans who have abjured it. You may pace to and fro in your room, or sit up in bed, or kneel. Some are careful to pray before they are distracted with bathing and dressing and doing their exercises.

Make this morning prayer quite objective. Forget yourself, forget the day's program, restrict yourself to praise, adoration and thanksgiving. As you become newly conscious of the things that ordinarily you have taken for granted, you realize that it's actually true that earth is crammed with heaven and that every common bush is aflame with God. Of course it is. As your thanksgiving inevitably narrows down from the sunrise and the fiery clouds, the blend of blue, purple and rose, to trees and good earthy smells, birds and music, poetry and friends, you at last consider yourself. You see yourself in God's presence. Yourself, bounded by time, yet aware of the Eternal, limited to three dimensions but in touch with infinity: your bodily mechanism, the miraculous affair which enables you to breathe this atmosphere and feel after God, is what makes it possible for you to learn about and to apprehend Reality. This is why you're on earth to learn a lesson. The coming day, like a day at school, will show whether or not you've learned your lesson. If you have, you'll find a lot more to learn.

With the day spread out before you, you can give thanks for whatever it may bring. You have already acquired a measure of that confidence which always emerges after entirely forgetting yourself in prayer. You can now hand the day over to God, remaining carefree yourself. You can go to breakfast. The coffee tastes better than usual.

Midday. At eleven or twelve, or sometime before lunch, break off from your figure adding, your dishwashing, your letter writing; if you're driving a machine or an engine you can manage to find some moment of relaxation. Now do some intercession. Enjoy the few moment's rest from strain of mind and body; and enjoy the fact of God. Let your breathing lengthen, then grow deeper to match the prayer "Breathe on me, breath of God; fill me with life anew." Then bring into this serene presence of God whomever you want to help—a patient awaiting an operation; a harassed friend who is wearing himself out with anxiety to keep up appearances when he could find bliss if he would stop bothering about other people's opinion of him; a sister in the tremendous peril of despair; a neighbor drenched and ready to drown in complacency; a fellow church member blinded with pride; a pitiable dictator of any of the three colors; a leader of any of the democracies. Any or all of these people can be held for a moment in the presence of God Who alone knows their deepest need. Such intercession need take no longer than thirty seconds. Your work is better afterwards, more fully integrated, and you are a more whole person, when you have breathed for two or three seconds the air "That blows in the unmeasured spaces which link star to star."

After Work. The after work prayer is essential. It is immensely important and demands a period leisurely enough to enable one to forget time. After the day's work is over, before or just after dinner, walking, sitting, standing or kneeling, take time to give yourself the deep content of enjoying God's presence. Remember you are His and that He understands you better than anyone else does. He sees something good in you that you don't see yourself. He knows your nature. He made you Himself. You will be ever restless until you find your rest in Him. Let your breathing follow its own rhythm. Notice that it becomes deeper and deeper, more and more regular as you abandon your unconscious tension. Now you are ready for spiritual cleansing. Here is a good exercise.

During the day various impressions have been made upon you, some rather surprising ones, some a little frightening perhaps, some depressing, some delight-ful. You lost your temper or lied. You spread a scandal or a smutty story. You were callous or cruel. You discovered a new fact or theory which if it proved true would knock the bottom out of one of your most precious principles. You heard that an interview you'd been dreading and therefore postponing must take place during the current week. Each of these impressions was followed by an immediate next thing you had to do. You could not stop to rectify or analyze any of them. You had to forget them. You were perhaps very glad to forget them. But loose, purposely forgotten ideas floating about in the dark unconscious are as dangerous as enemy mines sown on the high seas. They break into your sleep in the guise of unpleasant dreams. They wake you up in the night and keep you worrying. They color your outlook with a vague feeling of guilt. They destroy your confidence. Without confidence, which is another word for faith, it is impossible to do the work God is waiting for you to do.

Now that you have made an outlet for these thoughts, a place where they can be examined in the clearest possible light, they come up in orderly fashion, one by one. Here comes the cowardly lie you told, or the horrid thing you did. How foul it looks now that you face it in God's presence! It stinks to heaven. You deeply repent. "God forgive me," you groan. "What can I do to make some inadequate amends?" When your resolution is made the next impression follows. You don't have to search for it. There's no need to rack your memory. That new theory which shook one of your lifelong convictions can now be examined without fear, because God is with you and it cannot be truer than God. It is welcome if there is any truth in it. Take your time, pondering on it. You may not be able to gauge its importance or analyze its implications all at once, but it can no longer perturb you. Perhaps what you thought was a precious principle was actually only a petty prejudice. When your mind is ready, the next impression introduces itself. That dreaded interview—it must take place sometime this week, possibly tomorrow. You heave a sigh of dismay as you foresee the insalubrious details that may come to light, possibly be bandied about between you and many other persons. Then you suddenly begin to laugh. How ridiculous! Fancy fussing about a talk with anybody when God will be the third person present at the conversation! If you remember Him you will be able to honor and respect the other person. You may even be able to love him. The exact words you say won't matter much if you feel quiet and friendly and confident. You can't remain "strung up" when you are conscious of God.

The prayer is ended with thanksgiving. You may now read aloud to yourself the Psalms for the day, or chant them to yourself, in however raucous a voice, making up the tune as you go along. Or you may feel like making up a new psalm. That is how the old ones were made, isn't it? Thanksgiving and joy following a time of prayer. When the cleansing process has induced a state of well-being, the natural response is to put the feeling of relief and confidence into words, perhaps into music.

Evening. Evening prayer may contain praise, adoration, thanksgiving and intercession, but must always contain the great act of acceptance. Whatever your handicap be, riches or poverty, deficient strength or deficient imagination, loneliness or overcrowdedness, unpopularity, failure, mediocrity or the sort of success which gives you no rest, you accept that handicap. You accept your station in life because it is supremely honorable. There is nothing higher than sonship to the Eternal.

After the lights are out and when you are ready to sleep, let your last waking thought be "Father, into Thy hands I commit my spirit."

Recollection. During each day your energy is dissipated by work into many channels, streams, rills and creeks, some of them so shallow that you feel jaded, frayed at the edges. You have to take

time to turn often to consider the source of all energy and joy—God Himself.

It is good to let certain regularly repeated routine happenings be special reminders of God. The clock striking the hour, the staircase you go up or down, the elevator you enter, the red traffic light holding you up at the crossing, the tap you turn on at the kitchen sink.

On Meeting People. One wayside pulpit displayed a rather startling sentence: "Remember everyone you meet is fighting for his life." Can it be true? Most people are like ourselves. What meticulously hidden struggles are we engaged in? Why is Dopey the most beloved of all the seven dwarfs? Is it because we see ourselves in his clumsiness, his eagerness to do the right thing, his stupidity? He makes more mistakes than we do. How comforting to see that such as he can be attractive, lovable!

Let us learn to look on the people we meet, not as the efficient, successful people they pretend to be, but as secret and often defeated strugglers like ourselves. Let us allow God's spirit in us to go out silently to greet God's spirit in them. Let's make a short formula to use when entering a crowded bus or subway, remembering "how much each person there needs God and how much God loves each. How near He is to them, how dear they are to Him."

Grace before Meat. Many of the arguments that caused the last generation to react from the custom of asking God's blessing on their food have now proved to be fallacies. It was argued, why should one say a special prayer just because one's going to eat, as if food were the most important thing in the day? It sounded sensible and was a good escape anyhow.

The habit discarded, food speedily becomes an absorbing topic for conversation, the dullest spell of which is likely to be lively when someone starts describing a new diet: what not to eat and what new method of chasing sun-loaded vitamins is the firmest anchorage to health; where to obtain the cleanest milk of the most contented cows, fed on the most lush grass and the greenest clover in the sunniest month of the year; where this highly vitalized liquid can be found, concentrated, tested, put into capsules, exported over the ocean, and swallowed triumphantly. It is sad that the swallower seems still so much less vital than the grass and the cow and the clover field. Vitality might come less expensively, perhaps more spontaneously, if the health seeker prayed before he ate. Not that one wants to hold on to the habit of gabbling over a prayer and saying, "Pass the grapenuts, please," all in one breath. Now should I care to help reintroduce that strangely insulting sentence that was in vogue for so long: an impersonal assertion of a very grudging sort of gratitude. Surely it is an insult to one's hostess to have to ask help from above before one can be spontaneously thankful for the food "we are about to receive."

Grace before meat, at any rate, reminds one to do something definite about the hunger of others. For a cent a meal one can keep alive a Chinese person who is as dear to God as we are. Grace reminds us that the bread of life is still being broken for humanity by Christ. Some use this form of words: "Jesus said, 'Do this in remembrance of Me.' Lord Jesus, we would remember Thee always." It turns our thoughts from preoccupation with work to say: "It is a comely fashion to be glad. Let joy be the grace we say to God."

A definitely practical grace comes down from the old slave days in the South:

> Christ in the Kitchen
> White folk in the Hall
> For God's sake, gentlemen,
> Don't eat it all.

Silence is to many the best introduction to the social and gustatory pleasure of a common meal. Some keep the custom of joining hands in silence, encircling the table as they want to encircle the globe, with a sense of kinship in God. A young couple about to start a home may find this habit useful when neighbors drop in to test their calibre. When children come to enlarge the circle, they

have the advantage of finding already in operation a natural means of bringing God and their friends, the world and themselves into communion. In some homes it is customary for each in turn to say aloud in a sentence or two whatever is uppermost in his mind. This has proved of great physical as well as spiritual value; the youngest begins and then whoever sits next him continues till the circle is complete.

Vigilance. "Who will give us a background, a large framework of meaning?" enquired G. K. Chesterton in the first decade of the century. He went on to explain that we must have some such framework into which all happenings and efforts, hopes and ideas can be fitted, some background against which pain and pleasure can take their place instead of being meaningless. Without it he prophesied that people would become devil worshippers, opportunists, defeatists. Soon afterwards he joined the Roman Catholic Church. Some have failed to get a sense of order into their lives anywhere else. It is imperative that we discipline ourselves, as drastically as the Communists and Nazis. Our human traits of lazymindedness and of sloth, our habit of taking the line of least resistance economically and internationally, will beguile us to our destruction unless we cry halt. I know it is fearfully difficult suddenly to stop when one is rushing headlong down a steep slope. It wrenches all our muscles. To turn round and begin slowly to climb up again is a wearying job. But common sense demands it of us, this moment, this very instant, at whatever cost.

Perhaps only for the next few days, hours or weeks will you still have the opportunity to do the thing that must be done, for God, for the world, for the proper development of your spirit.

From where I am sitting on this olive-covered hill, two thickly planted rows of California poppies stretch their dainty gaiety almost out of sight. Beside me is a pond overspread with weed. Its hue is the rather sombre green usual in water plants but it happens at this moment that five or six of the leaves have just caught a ray of the sinking sun, which has colored them bright peacock blue, very excellent to behold. Each looks transparent, like a dragonfly's wing. Each is showing me a thing that I've never seen before. It can be seen only for a few minutes and only from the exact spot where I am sitting.

Let us be alert, on our guard. Let us watch. Let us remember the five bridesmaids. They were not nearly as silly as we are. Our job is to cooperate consciously with that unseen Power which is ever molding men and things to higher uses. In the evolutionary stream we have to keep adjusting ourselves to changing environment. We have to be often disturbed, made uncomfortable: otherwise we should be content with the second best. Unless we are to retrogress, we must keep aware, sensitive. To be purely passive beneficiaries is to be pauperized, however rich we happen to be. The middle-aged man who thinks he is still progressive because he once was, when he was at college, is to be found everywhere. The three, grim, prosperous, thin-lipped daughters of Revolution in Grant Wood's picture shows us how atrophy of the spirit affects our good looks.

We strut about on the surface of the globe, our body, a brilliantly contrived machine. What is the law of our being?

Does the fish soar to find the ocean?
The eagle plunge to find the air?

The ant fulfills its destiny. The lion, the squirrel and all dumb creatures follow the law of their being with precision with tireless vigilance.

How different are my vague comings and goings, my lazy downsittings, my purposeless uprisings! Until I find direction, I am the prey of my sick and errant will. But when I say "Yes" to God, I am taking the first step along that road which is as direct as the air path of the migratory bird; I am starting a work as precise and all-engrossing as that of the hive.

My every moment, my every fiber and sinew must be coordinated to the purposes of God. Words aren't enough; they often darken knowledge. Deeds aren't enough; they often hide God. My whole nature must be His, to use as He will. Results are not my concern. No wonder we keep trying to escape from such a discipline.

Escaping Escapism. "I fled Him down the nights and down the days. . . . I fled Him down the labyrinthine ways of my own mind." Francis Thompson's account of the soul of man trying to escape from the Hound of Heaven is now accepted as classic in East and West. He continues:

And in the mist of tears
I hid from Him, and under running laughter.

We are even naïve enough to hide behind the fact of our own unworthiness. As if God didn't know all about that! He even ignored Moses' excellent alibi, his stuttering tongue. When Moses made it his excuse, God said: "Who made man's mouth?" and sent him off to Egypt.

The most obvious sort of alibi is the binding program of the pleasure seekers who are haunted by the furies of inanity. Anyone can watch their feverish struggle to be always in company, to escape from solitariness, from thought. Then one day suddenly they stop short. They can't run any farther. They're sick of gaiety, of prettiness, sick of their own tricks, sick of their nooks and crannies and of all the other hiding places. They turn to face the thing that's chasing them.

Come Death, Hell or Torture. Nothing can be worse than the long-drawn-out retreat, the hag-ridden flight.

Nerved to expect the worst, they wait. And nothing happens, only a sense of immense relief at being able at last to accept the fact of their bankruptcy, their utter weariness. The blessed quietness persists. A sense of leisure permeates everything. There's no fuss; yet something immense is certainly happening. They don't know what. The divine Lover has arrived, the Friend of the soul of man. Henceforth they know themselves to be glad children of God.

Frank C. Laubach

(1884———)

In 1915 Laubach went with his wife to the Philippine Islands as a missionary. After founding churches on the island of Mindanao, he established and became dean of Union College in Manila. In 1930 he returned to Mindanao to work with the Mohammedan Moros, who regarded the Christian Filipinos as their enemies. It is estimated that through his educational efforts he has been able to teach one half of the ninety thousand people in that area to read and write. But more than that, he has been able to bring them a richer experience of God. The letters quoted below were written during his Mindanao days. They are taken from *Letters by a Modern Mystic*, and are used by permission of the Student Volunteer Movement. (Copyright 1937 by the Student Volunteer Movement.)

[LETTERS]

From *Letters by a Modern Mystic*

OPEN TOWARD GOD AND WIDE AWAKE

April 22, 1930

The "experiment" is interesting, although I am not very successful, thus far. The idea of God slips out of my sight for I suppose two thirds of every day, thus far. This morning I started out fresh, by finding a rich experience of God in the sunrise. Then I tried to let Him control my hands while I was shaving and dressing and eating breakfast. Now I am trying to let God control my hands as I pound the typewriter keys. If I could keep this morning up I should have a far higher average today than I have had for some time.

This afternoon as I look at the people teeming about me, and then think of God's point of view, I feel that this mighty stretch of time in which He has been pushing men upward is to continue for many more millions of years. We are yet to become what the spiritual giants have been and more than many of them were. Here the selection favors those who keep themselves wide open toward God and wide awake. Our possibilities are perhaps not limitless, but they are at least infinitely above our present possibilities of imagination.

There is nothing that we can do excepting to throw ourselves open to God. There is, there must be, so much more in Him than He can give us, because we are so sleepy and because our capacity is so pitifully small. It ought to be tremendously helpful to be able to acquire the habit of reaching out strongly after God's thoughts, and to ask, "God what have you to put into my mind now if only I can be large enough?" That waiting, eager attitude ought to give God the chance he needs. I am finding every day that the best of the five or six ways in which I try to keep contact with God is for me to *wait for his thoughts, to ask him to speak.*

IT IS WORKING

May 14, 1930

Oh, this thing of keeping in constant touch with God, of making him the object of my thought and the companion of my conversations, is the most amazing thing I ever ran across. *It is working.* I cannot do it even half of a day—not yet, but I believe I shall be doing it some day for the entire day. It is a matter of acquiring a new habit of thought. Now I *like* God's presence so much that when for a half hour or so he slips out of mind

—as he does many times a day—I feel as though I had deserted him, and as though I had lost something very precious in my life.

Souls Dead to God Look Sadly out of Hungry Eyes

May 24, 1930

This has been a week of wonders. God is at work *everywhere* preparing the way for his work in Lanao. I shall tell you some of the wonders presently. But just at this moment you must hear more of this sacred evening. The day had been rich but strenuous, so I climbed "Signal Hill" back of my house talking and listening to God all the way up, all the way back, all the lovely half hour on the top. And God talked back! I let my tongue go loose and from it there flowed poetry far more beautiful than any I ever composed. It flowed without pausing and without ever a failing syllable for a half hour. I listened astonished and full of joy and gratitude. I wanted a dictaphone for I knew that I should not be able to remember it—and now I cannot. "Why," someone may ask, "did God waste his poetry on you alone, when you could not carry it home." You will have to ask God that question. I only know He did and I am happy in the memory.

Below me lay the rice fields and as I looked across them I heard my tongue saying aloud, "child, just as the rice needs the sunshine every day, and could not grow if it had sun only once a week or one hour a day, so you need me all day of every day. People over all the world are withering because they are open toward God only rarely. Every waking minute is not too much."

A few months ago I was trying to write a chapter on the "discovering of God." Now that I have discovered Him I find that it is a continuous discovery. Every day is rich with new aspects of Him and His working. As one makes new discoveries about his friends by being with them, so one discovers the "individuality" of God if one entertains him continuously. One thing I have seen this week is that God loves beauty. Every-

thing he makes is lovely. The clouds, the tumbling river, the waving lake, the soaring eagle, the slender blade of grass, the whispering of the wind, the fluttering butterfly, this graceful transparent nameless child of the lake which clings to my window for an hour and vanishes for ever. Beautiful craft of God! And I know that He makes my thought-life beautiful when I am open all the day to Him. If I throw these mind-windows apart and say "God, what shall we think of now?" he answers always in some graceful, tender dream. And I know that God is love hungry, for he is constantly pointing me to some dull, dead soul which he has never reached and wistfully urges me to help Him reach that stolid, tight shut mind. Oh God, how I long to help you with these Moros. And with these Americans! And with these Filipinos! All day I see souls dead to God look sadly out of hungry eyes. I want them to know my discovery! That any minute can be paradise, that any place can be heaven! That any man can have God! That every man *does have God* the moment he speaks to God, or listens for him!

As I analyze myself I find several things happening to me as a result of these two months of strenuous effort to keep God in mind every minute. This concentration upon God is *strenuous*, but everything else has ceased to be so. I think more clearly, I forget less frequently. Things which I did with a strain before, I now do easily and with no effort whatever. I worry about nothing, and lose no sleep. I walk on air a good part of the time. Even the mirror reveals a new light in my eyes and face. I no longer feel in a hurry about anything. Everything goes right. Each minute I meet calmly as though it were not important. Nothing can go wrong excepting one thing. That is that God *may slip from my mind* if I do not keep on my guard. If He is there, the universe is with me. My task is simple and clear.

And I witness to the way in which the world reacts. Take Lanao and the Moros for illustration. Their responsiveness is to me a continuous source of amazement. I do nothing that I can see excepting to pray for them, and to walk among them thinking of God. They know I am a Protestant. Yet two of the leading Moslem priests have gone around the province telling everybody that I would help the people to know God.

ONE NEW LESSON

June 1, 1930

Inwardly this has been a very uneven week. As a whole my end of the experiment has been failure for most of the week. My physical condition and too many distractions have proven too much for me, and God has not been in the center of my mind for one-fifth of the time, or perhaps one-tenth. But today has been a wonderful day, and some of yesterday was wonderful. The week with its failures and successes has taught me one new lesson. It is this: "I must talk about God, or I cannot keep him in my mind. I must give Him away in order to have Him." That is the law of the spirit world. What one gives one has, what one keeps to oneself one loses.

Do you suppose that through all eternity the price we will need to pay for keeping God will be that we must endlessly be giving him away?

BEGIN TO BUILD HEAVEN

June 3, 1930

This experiment which I am trying is the most strenuous discipline which any man ever attempted. I am not succeeding in keeping God in my mind very many hours of the day, and from the point of view of experiment number one I should have to record a pretty high percentage of failure. But the other experiment—what happens when I do succeed—is so successful that it makes up for the failure of number one. God does work a change. The moment I turn to Him it is like turning on an electric current which I feel through my whole being. I find also that the effort to keep God in my mind does something to my mind which every mind needs to have done to it. I am given something difficult

enough to keep my mind with a keen edge. The constant temptation of every man is to allow his mind to grow old and lose its edge. I feel that I am perhaps more lazy mentally than the average person, and I require the very mental discipline which this constant effort affords.

So my answer to my two questions to date would be

1. "Can it be done all the time?" Hardly.

2. "Does the effort help?" Tremendously. Nothing I have ever found proves such a tonic to mind and body.

Are you building sacred palaces for yourself? I meant to write "places" to be sure, but I think I shall leave the word "palaces" for that is what any house becomes when it is sacred. The most important discovery of my whole life is that one can take a little rough cabin and transform it into a palace just by flooding it with thoughts of God. When one has spent many months in a little house like this in daily thoughts about God, the very entering of the house, the very sight of it as one approaches, starts associations which set the heart tingling and the mind flowing. I have come to the point where I must have my house, in order to write the best letters or think the richest thoughts.

So in this sense one man after the other builds his own heaven or his hell. It does not matter where one is, one can at once *begin to build heaven*, by thoughts which one thinks while in that place. . . . I have learned the secret of heaven building—anywhere.

This morning I read awhile about the tremendous consecration with which the scientists are studying the finest details about the sun, in an effort to find how to predict the weather, and to know how to use its power. And I feel that not yet have I thrown myself into the crucible of this experiment of mind with all the abandon of the successful scientist. We have heard the saying "All a man's failures are inside himself." And I am willing to confess that as yet I have not "striven unto blood" to win this battle. What I want to prove is that the thing *can be done* by all people under all conditions, but I have not proven it yet. This much I do see—what an incredibly high thing Jesus did.

A great lonesome hunger comes over me at this moment for someone who has passed through the same long, long channels of hope, and aspiration, and despair, and failure, to whom I can talk tonight. And yet—there is no such person. As we grow older all our paths diverge, and in all the world I suppose I could find nobody who could wholly understand me excepting God—and neither can you! Ah, God, what a new nearness this brings for Thee and me, to realize that Thou alone canst understand me, for Thou alone knowest all! Thou art no longer a stranger, God! Thou art the only being in the universe who is not partly a stranger! I invite others inside but they cannot come all the way. Thou art all the way inside with me—*here*—and every time I forget and push Thee out, Thou art eager to return! Ah, God, I mean to struggle tonight and tomorrow as never before, *not once* to dismiss Thee. For when I lose Thee for an hour I lose and the world loses more than we can know. The thing Thou wouldst do can only be done when Thou hast full swing *all the time.*

E. Stanley Jones
(1884———)

FEW men have spoken to more people in the last twenty-five years about the meaning of Christian experience than Jones. Nor have any writings about devotional living circulated to a wider group of readers than his *Abundant Living*. This excellent book of devotions, with a balanced psychological approach, sold nearly 600,000 copies in the six years following its publication in 1942.

Born in Baltimore, Maryland, and educated at Asbury College, Kentucky, Jones went to India in 1907 and became a missionary to the high castes. In 1928 he was elected a bishop of the Methodist Episcopal Church, but declined the office in order to continue his missionary work. For many years he has conducted ashrams where he has brought people of various religious faiths together for the purpose of discussing their experiences of God. In more recent years he has done evangelistic work in North and South America.

Jones first became widely known by his book *The Christ of the Indian Road*. Since its publication in 1925 it has been translated into eighteen languages and has sold over 400,000 copies. *How to Pray*, first printed as an article in *The Christian Advocate* and now available in pamphlet form, gives his pattern for finding God, set in a Christological framework. It is reprinted here by permission of *The Christian Advocate*.

HOW TO PRAY

WHAT PRAYER REALLY IS

When the disciples asked Jesus, "Lord, teach us to pray," they uttered one of the deepest and most universal cries of the human heart. For men of all ages have instinctively felt that prayer is the distilled essence of religion. If we know how to pray, we know how to be religious; if not, then religion is a closed book. Where there is no effective prayer life, the heart of religion has ceased to beat and religion becomes a dead body of forms and customs and dogmas.

And yet how few Christians have an effective prayer life! (And this includes many ministers.) If I were to put my finger on the greatest lack in American Christianity, I would unhesitantly point to the need for an effective prayer life among laity and ministers. Kagawa once said to second-generation Japanese Christians on the West Coast: "Your greatest lack is that you do not know how to pray." He saw that their Christianity was anemic and ineffective, because they had not learned the discipline of prayer.

If I had one gift, and only one gift, to make to the Christian Church, I would offer the gift of prayer. For everything follows from prayer.

Prayer tones up the total life. I find by actual experience I am better or worse as I pray more or less. If my prayer life sags, my whole life sags with it; if my prayer life goes up, my life as a whole goes up with it. To fail here is to fail all down the line; to succeed here is to succeed everywhere.

In the prayer time the battle of the spiritual life is lost or won. Prayer is not an optional subject in the curriculum of living. It is a required subject; it is *the* required subject. And there is no graduation into adequate human living without prayer.

Perhaps we are all more or less convinced of this viewpoint, but the "how" of prayer is the crux of the difficulty. To try to answer that word "how" is the burden of these articles. I propose to begin at the lowest rung of the ladder so that no one will feel I begin beyond him.

1. Breathe the prayer, "Lord, teach me to pray," as you begin the quest for a prayer life. Bathe your very quest in prayer. It may be dim, shadowy, unreal, but this may be the first, tottering step toward spiritual maturity.

2. As you begin your quest, you must hold in mind this background of thought about prayer: *The universe is an open universe.* . . .

3. Another thought that may serve as a background: *Prayer is not only the refuge of the weak; it is the reinforcement of the strong.* . . .

4. A still further thought we must hold: *Prayer is not bending God to my will, but it is a bringing of my will into conformity with God's will, so that his will may work in and through me.* . . .

5. Another consideration must be held in mind: *Prayer is not an occasional exercise to which you turn now and then;*

it is a life attitude. It is the will to co-operate with God in your total life. It is an attitude rather than an act. . . .

6. *Prayer, then, is primarily and fundamentally surrender.* . . .

7. *Prayer is secondarily assertion.* After you have surrendered to the will of God, you can assert your will within that will. . . .

Two attitudes combine—surrender and assertion. The two have to be together: if you only surrender you are weak; if you only assert you are weak. But if you are surrendered and then assertive, you are really strong. You are going to be a positive creative person because surrendered to the will of God.

You are beginning the adventure of co-operation with God. Prayer is just that—co-operation with God.

II. THE TIME AND PLACE FOR PRAYER

Now that we have put a background behind prayer we are probably in a position to take the first positive steps in the art of making the prayer life effective.

1. Begin with the environment, the surroundings in which we are to learn to pray. They should be as favorable as possible. In every home there should be a shrine, perhaps a place curtained off, into which you can enter to keep your tryst with God. In that little shrine there should be the kind of symbols that will help you achieve the prayer mood. If that shrine cannot be arranged, then go into some place corresponding to "the closet" of which Jesus spoke, where you will be alone without disturbance.

2. Perhaps neither plan is possible. Then make your own shrine by your power of inward withdrawal. Learn to "shut the door" even when amid conditions that would otherwise bring disturbance.

That would mean physical and mental relaxation. It is a psychological fact that you cannot engrave anything on a tense conscious mind. Relaxation is necessary to receptivity. This means that your body should be in a condition in which it is least obtrusive.

Be comfortable, but not slouchy. As you enter the prayer period say to your body: "O body of mine, you may be the vehicle through which God may come to me. Be receptive." And then to each organ: "My brain, you are now in the presence of God. Let go, and listen. He speaks; he penetrates; he heals. Receive, receive." And to the eyes: "My eyes, weary with looking at a distracting world, close, and inwardly see nothing except him into whose presence you have now come. He touches my eyes and they are rested and calm and single and healed." And to the nerves: "O nerves, intelligence department of my being, strained and torn by living in a world of chaos, I now set you to work on the job of reporting better news. Your God comes—comes with the good news of calm, of poise, of resources, of redemption. Open every cell to that healing, to that calm, to that restoration. Receive, receive, receive."

To your sex life say: "O creative part of me, I surrender you to the creator God. When denied your normal expression in procreation, I know that I can sublimate your power into other forms —art, poetry, music, creating new hopes, new souls, new life; I can become creative on another level. So I put you at God's disposal. He cleanses; he redirects." And to the whole body: "He is now in every part, untying knotty nerves in his gentleness, bathing every brain cell with his presence, reinforcing every weak place with his strength, healing all your diseases, co-ordinating all parts and making them into a co-operating whole. Open every door! Give him all the keys."

3. Then say to your soul: "O soul of mine, you are now in the audience chamber of God. You will meet him. He will come. He is coming. Let down all the barriers of your inmost being and welcome him. For he is here—now."

4. Remember that the essence of prayer is found in right relationships with God—not the getting of this thing or that thing. Don't hasten to put things before him for God to grant. Let that go for the moment. As he comes let him put his finger on anything in your life not fully surrendered to his will. If anything is sensitive and not fully frank in his presence bring it up honestly and frankly and look at it. If you see the lines of disapproval in his face, let it go. Otherwise that thing will become a barrier and will block your communion.

5. But if nothing comes up don't conjure up false guilts. Very often we think this conjuring up of false guilts is humility. It is not. God is not petty. He is not going around mote-picking. He wants to see if you are essentially sound and set in the right direction. Don't become condemned over imaginary guilts.

6. For instance, suppose that, while you are praying, your mind wanders. Don't become worried over that. Simply take the wandering thought and make it lead you back to him.

Just then I looked up in the midst of my meditation and saw that the clock had stopped. The thought came: "It needs winding and so do I. God, wind the spring of my life and set the hands to thy timing and thy purposes." I made the wandering thought lead me finally to him.

7. But suppose the wandering thought is not quite so innocent; it may be actually impure—some sex thought, for instance. That can be serious, of course, and can block your communion with him, but only if you harbor and hold the thought. If it is dismissed at once, there is no sin in its coming. Thoughts of sin become sinful thoughts only if entertained and given a seat.

We cannot repeat too much the old statement: "You cannot help the birds flying over your head, but you can help them building nests in your hair." The fleeting thought is not sin; the harbored thought is. I have a little technique of my own in dismissing wrong thoughts: I bat my eyes rapidly. That breaks up the thought, for the batting of the eyes demands attention, calling off the attention from the evil thought and then in the midst of it I pray, "O God, help me." That lets me gain my mental equilibrium and control. You may have to work out your own peculiar technique for controlling thoughts.

8. Suppose the interruption of your meditation is not from within by straying thoughts, but from without by disturbing events or persons. Don't let that upset you. Use the interruption. When Jesus went across the lake to get away from the multitudes in order to pray, the people ran around, and when he arrived for his prayer hour there were the crowds again. Instead of being angered and upset, "out of pity for them he proceeded to teach them at length." (Mark 6:34, after Moffatt.) After feeding them, "he dismissed the crowd, and after saying goodby to them, he went up into the hills to pray" (46). An interruption became an interpretation.

If you are interrupted, let the interruption be not an irritation, but an interpretation. But at the end come back to the prayer period as Jesus did. Don't let the interruption keep you permanently from the prayer time. The season of prayer will be richer for the mastery of the interruption, and the interruption will be richer because of the prayer period.

Almost the whole of Jesus' life was one interruption after another, but he didn't muddle those interruptions. He mastered them and made them contribute to the central purposes of his life. The spirit of his interrupted prayer went into the interruption and made it illustrate his essential spirit.

It may be that you can glory in interruptions as giving opportunity to "evangelize the inevitable." The mosaic of happenings is made into a Christian pattern by the prayer spirit. For prayer is not only an act; it is an attitude. The interrupted prayer act can be perpetuated in the prayer attitude during the interruption.

9. Suppose the prayer period is not interrupted from without or from within, but is simply dull and dry and unreal. That, too, should not upset you. There come such dry, dead emotional periods in every married life, but that needn't disturb the fundamental joy of marriage. The fact is still there intact, although the glow of it may be absent. Hold steady, the glow will return to your prayer hour. Don't give it up because there is no glow.

Pray by the clock if you cannot pray by the heartbeat. In doing so you will be fixing a prayer habit, even if you don't feel a prayer glow. The habit is getting into your nerve cells and is becoming a fixed attitude. That fact is more important than the glow. For, once the habit is fixed, the person is inwardly set for prayer as a life attitude.

Something is happening to you even amid the lack of the sense of reality, for you are being fashioned into a person who lives by principles rather than pulsebeats, by decisions rather than by delights. Prayer is always right, with or without an emotional content. If you cannot pray by an inward click then pray by the outward clock.

Admit of no exceptions in the prayer schedule for the exception will break down the habit. The habit is the important thing.

III. The Steps of Prayer

We are now ready to take the actual steps of prayer, and there are about nine of them.

First, decide what you really want. The "you" is important. It must not be a vagrant part of you wandering into the prayer hour with no intention of committing yourself to your prayer request. You cannot pray with a part of yourself and expect God to answer, for he hears what the whole of you is saying. "In the day that Thou seekest me with the whole heart, thou shalt be found of me." God can only give a whole response to a whole request from a whole person.

Note that Jesus often asked of a supplicant, "What do you want that I should do unto you?" This is vital, for often a sick person asks to be well, when down underneath he wants no such thing. He is using that illness or complaint as a life strategy to gain attention and attendance.

At a family gathering held periodically an aunt used to come regularly, but she always came ill. The rest of the family buzzed around her in sympathy and service. Although ill, she always managed to eat her portion of the big family dinner. There was no doubt that she made the illness her device for drawing attention to herself.

The same thing can happen in the realm of our moral and spiritual life. We pray with a portion of our beings for moral and spiritual victory. St. Agustine, before he became a saint, used to pray, "O God, make me pure, but not now." Before I was converted, very often I would pray for God to make me good, really afraid that he would take me at my word. Actually, I didn't want to be good. So my prayers were never answered, until in a crisis moment, I really wanted to be different! Then God heard and delivered me, and only then.

Perhaps you are willing that you pray with the whole "you," but the other "you" is not co-operative. Then tell God you are willing to be made willing. Offer your unwillingness to God and with your consent, he will make it into willingness.

Longing I sought Thy presence, Lord,
With my whole heart did I call and pray,
And going out toward Thee, I found Thee,
Coming to me on the way.

When you see him coming to you on the way you will find that he is more than half way to you.

Here is the experience of a woman who said in the beginning of our conversation, "We have everything in our home—everything and nothing." Now she has something. She says: "My day pivots around or radiates from the quiet hour. I had a miserable time establishing it. I could not control my thoughts and pray. Why, I couldn't offer a sane prayer. I even felt for a time that I was doing myself an injustice to keep trying. Then I confined that time to reading my Bible and writing God a letter. In these letters I am stripped of my self-will, and his will prevails. It is so satisfying. I am trying to catch up on back correspondence. I tell this to you, but if I intimated this to some of my associates, I doubtless

would be judged insane. But, if this is insanity, I readily confess I love it."

But there is a beautiful sanity in the procedure, for that woman is used to expressing herself clearly in letters. She transferred the habit to her dealings with God. Note that she says: "In them I am stripped of self-will and his will prevails." The whole person is beginning to talk to God in those letters.

Second, decide whether the thing you want is a Christian thing. God has shown us in Christ what the divine character is like. God is Christ-like. He can only act in a Christ-like way. He cannot answer a prayer that would not fit in with his character.

A woman who was having some illicit relationships with a married man said: "I thought God was going to answer my prayers and give him to me." But how could God do that? She had merely read her desires into the heavens, and the answer was only the echo of her own desires. Her whole wrong moral universe fell to pieces, and she emerged out of it chastened and disillusioned. God cannot reverse the moral universe which is an expression of his moral nature to answer a selfish or immoral whim.

Let us sit down and ask about all our prayers: "Is the thing I want a Christian thing?" And remember that, if it is not a Christian thing, it would do us no good if we got it, for only the Christian thing is the thing that is good for us. Ask God to cleanse your prayers as well as you. For prayer is the naked intent stretching out to God.

Jesus said, "If ye shall ask anything in my name" that is, in my character, according to my spirit—"that will I do." Within the limits of the character of Christ, which means within the limits of the moral universe, you are free to ask anything and God is free to give you anything.

Third, write it down. The writing of the prayer will probably help you in self-committal. For, if you write it, you will probably mean it. Committing a thing to writing is almost destiny to me; I can hardly change it afterward. The writing of it will also save you from hazy indefiniteness. You will be praying for this and not something else. There will come a time, of course, when you may not need to write things down, for they will have written themselves in you. You can then trust yourself to pray the Christian thing, but at the start it is well to use all the outer helps you can.

There are some who practice the method of writing down their sins and their failures, and then solemnly burning them in a fire as a symbol that the old self and its ways are burned up in the fire of God's love.

Whether it is the motive of getting rid of something, or the motive of getting something, it is well to write it down to clarify it.

Fourth, still the mind. The stilling of the mind is a step in receptivity. Prayer is pure receptivity in the first stage. "As many as *received* him, to them gave he power." If you come to God all tense, you can get little. Let down the bars. They are all on your side; there are none on his.

Receptivity is the first law of the spiritual life. It is the first law of all life. An organism can give out as much as it takes in and no more. If it hasn't learned to receive, it hasn't learned to live. The radiant soul mentioned above says: "God has done more for me in this one year that I have been receptive than I have done for myself in all the years of my life. The stupidity of people who live in a shell!"

In that period of stilling the mind I find myself saying over and over: "Oh, God, you've got me." And again and again the answer comes back: "I know it, my son." Then there is quiet absorptive rest in which you breathe into every fibre of your being the healing grace of the Father himself.

The first thing is to get God. If you get him, everything else follows. I seldom ask for things, for if I have him, I know I'll get all I need in addition. The stilling of the mind is to allow God to get at you, to invade you, to take possession of you. He then pours his very prayers

through you. They are his prayers—God-inspired, and hence God-answered.

Whenever I am about to speak I ask the audience to bow their heads in silent prayer. In that silence I always repeat my verse, "Ye have not chosen me, but I have chosen you and ordained you that you should go and bear fruit and that your fruit should remain; that whatsoever ye ask of the Father in my name, he may give it you." The stilling of the mind by the repetition of that verse makes it receptive. I am living in the passive voice. Preaching then is not eager straining; it is receptivity ending in release. The speaker is no longer a reservoir with just so much to give; he is a channel attached to unlimited resources.

The stilling of the mind reminds you not of your pitiful little store, but of the fact that you are now harnessing yourself to God's illimitable fullness.

Prayer is like the fastening of the cup to the wounded side of a pine tree to allow the rosin to pour into it. You are now nestling up into the side of God—the wounded side, if you will—and you allow his grace to fill your cup. You are taking in the very life of God.

"Be still and know," and you will be full. Be unstill and you will not know; you will remain empty.

IV. Using the Prayer Ladder

In our use of a prayer ladder we came in our last article to the step—Still the Mind. The stilling of the mind creates receptivity, and receptivity is the first law of life. Learn that and you know how to live; fail to learn that and you have failed to live.

Now you are ready for the fifth step: *Talk with God about it.* Note I say, "Talk with God," not "Talk to God," for it is a two-way conversation. And the most vital part may be, not what you will say to God, but what God will say to you. For God wants not merely to answer your prayer. He wants to *make* you—to make you into the kind of person through whom he can habitually answer prayer. So this prayer episode is part of a process of God-training. God will answer the prayer provided it will contribute in the long run to the making of you.

When you talk with God about it, set the prayer in the light of that general purpose of God to make you the best instrument of his purpose he can make of you. He may have to say a lesser "no," in order to a higher "yes." On the other hand, this prayer may be a part of that higher purpose. If so, then you can talk it over with him with confidence. A boldness will take hold of your spirit as you wait in his presence.

A few mornings ago I awoke at four o'clock coughing my lungs out. I had tried to stagger through an impossible schedule while just skirting pneumonia. That morning hour seemed decisive one way or the other. I grew desperate and bold and clutched the garment of God and held on and said, "O God, I don't ask for many things. I've wanted you more than things, but I am asking for this. If you don't help me I'm done for. I can't go on. Help me."

I knew that prayer moment had registered. The tide turned. As was said in many a Scripture episode, "He began to amend from that very hour."

Talk with God about it and talk with him in the confidence that he is aching to answer that prayer for you, if it is in line with his general purposes for you.

There is a sixth step: *Promise God what you will do to make this prayer come true*. Since the conversation is a two-way affair, the accomplishment is also two-way. You and God answer it together.

At this point be silent to hear God again, and see if he makes any suggestions to you about your part in answering the prayer. If definite suggestions come to you, then promise that you will carry them out.

For instance, this morning I prayed that Gandhi might not be allowed to die —to die pleading the freedom of his country. Immediately, as I became quiet, I saw that I could send a wire to the President urging him to intervene and

mediate. This article was laid aside for a moment to send that wire.

The impulses that come out of the prayer hour are usually true impulses of the Spirit. Some would say these impulses are of the spirit, but those of us who try this two-way living know that you cannot tell where your spirit ends and his Spirit begins. They are now flowing back and forth into each other.

The Spirit stimulates our spirit into Spirit-led activities. "Who caused his glorious arm to go to the right hand of Moses." When Moses lifted his arm God lifted his—their arms worked together —and what a working together!

Therefore, in the silence tell God what you will do to make the prayer come true.

Seventh: *Do everything loving that comes to your mind about it!* This step is important, for it is a cleansing and clarifying step. The word "loving" is important. It is the password to find the source of the suggestions that come to your mind. If the suggestion is not loving, it is probably from your subconscious mind, and not from the Spirit. The first fruit of the Spirit is "love," and if the suggestion does not fit in with love then don't do it. Wait for the suggestion that does fit in.

If the word "loving" is important, so is the word "do." If you only will to do something and never actually do it, then you will find that God cannot "do." He can only will, awaiting your doing. Your doing looses the floodgates of God's doing.

Eighth: *Thank God for answering in his own way*. God will answer that prayer. No prayers are unanswered. But he may answer "no," as well as "yes." "No" is an answer, and it may really be next in order leading on to a higher "yes."

Moreover, the answer may be delayed in order to toughen your fibre. The very persistence in asking for something over a long period may be one of the most character-toughening processes imaginable. The prayer becomes fixed in a life attitude, and it may be the organizing principle around which life revolves. God may be more concerned that the prayer be there than that the answer be forthcoming. He often holds us off to deepen our characters, so that we will not be spiritual "cry babies," if we do not get everything we want and get it at once.

There is a ninth step: *Release the whole prayer from your conscious thinking.* Don't keep the prayer at the center of your conscious thinking. It may become an anxiety-center. Let it drop down into the subconscious mind and let it work at that greater depth. Then there will be an undertone of prayer in all you do, but there will be no tense anxiety. Dismissing it from the conscious mind is an act of faith that, having committed it to God you leave it in his hands, believing he will do the best thing possible.

One or two thoughts may be helpful in closing this series of brief studies on the practice of prayer:

Prayer is not so much an act as an attitude. The first Beatitude says: "Blessed are the renounced in spirit for theirs is the kingdom of God." The renounced, the surrendered in spirit have what? The kingdom of God! They do not merely belong to the kingdom of God, but the kingdom of God belongs to them! All of its resources are behind them, they work with almighty power. Therefore, they go beyond themselves in thinking, in acting, in accomplishment. They are ordinary men doing extraordinary things.

"The Acts of the Apostles" could be called "The Acts of the Holy Spirit," for the Holy Spirit was taking ordinary human nature and heightening powers and insights until ordinary human nature was quite extraordinary. "My powers are heightened by my God," exclaims Miriam in her song. And that is literally true. There are no limits to what a man will do who does not limit God in his life.

Prayer is opening the channels from our emptiness to God's fullness, from our defeat to his victory.

Therefore, pray or be a prey—a prey to your impulses, to the last happening, to your surroundings. The man who prays overcomes everything, for he is overcome by the most redemptive fact of the universe, the will of God. To find that will and live by it is to find yourself. Prayer then makes the most absolutely free man this universe knows. The man who does the will of God actually does his own deepest will.

Henry N. Wieman

(1884——)

FROM 1927 to 1947 Wieman taught the philosophy of religion in the divinity school at the University of Chicago. He calls himself a naturalistic theist who sees God as a process of growth in the universe, immediately conceived and perceived. God works for good in every event to the degree that men co-operate with such a creative activity. This spirit of growth is superpersonal.

Wieman was born in Missouri, educated at Park, Harvard, Jena, and Heidelberg. Before going to Chicago he taught philosophy at Occidental College, 1917-27.

Of his many books, which cover a wide field of religion interest, *Methods of Private Religious Living* analyzes and gives practical suggestions for devotional living. This selection comes from that book and is used by permission of The Macmillan Co. (Copyright 1929 by The Macmillan Co.)

FINDING JOY IN LIFE

From *Methods of Private Religious Living*

The personal problem before us in this chapter is twofold: How can we increase our capacity for enjoyment? How can we preserve our critical moral judgment and our religious aspiration in the midst of these joys? The second part of this dual problem is much more complicated and difficult than the first. It arises out of the fact that joy in things as they are is likely to assume the form of complacency; and complacency is death to aspiration. How can we enjoy what is, without impairing our aspiration toward that better world which must be made out of this one? We shall not treat this second part of our problem until we have made answer to the first question: How increase our capacity for enjoyment. Some may scorn this problem, but they are hypocritical if they do, for they seek joy in some form.

1. How To Enjoy the World

Every one has something he should be able to enjoy. Very simple things we have in mind as well as great things, such as good food when hungry, rest when weary, trees, sky, friends, happy faces, and the like. Nobody has all of these things and some far fewer than others, but everybody has some. The list of things to enjoy is endless. One may be sick and not able to enjoy food, but he has something else. Another may not have the kind ministration of affectionate hands when he is ill, but there is another source of joy for him. Our problem is to enter into full appreciation and enjoyment of these good things. Our happiness might be many times greater than it is if we had the mental attitudes which enable one to appreciate to the full all the good things round about. Let us mention some of the wrong mental attitudes which must be corrected if we are to enter into the fullness of that joy which should be ours.

First is the feeling some people have that they are failing to meet some moral or religious requirements when they freely and fully enjoy such simple things as food and clothes and play. This feeling is correct only when the lesser good blinds us to the greater. How to avoid such blindness will engage our attention later. But when such blindness is not incurred there is nothing wrong in the greatest possible enjoyment of simple things. Some people have this mental habit of condemning simple joys so fixed that even when they know it is wrong to condemn them they cannot enter into them with freedom, and so their happiness is marred. This old habit must be rooted out like any other bad habit. There are many methods for overcoming a bad habit, one of which is worshipful autosuggestion.

A much more common hindrance to enjoyment of that which is good and pleasant is worry and anxiety. We are so anxious about the future that we cannot enjoy the present. We are so fearful lest we lose our health or comfort or friends or security or other good thing that we cannot enjoy these good things while we have them. Or we are like Martha, so cumbered about many things that the one thing needful we miss. The one thing needful is to enjoy the visitor when he is present with us, whether he come in the form of a sunset, or tall tree, or a singing bird, or a child tugging at our hand, or a pleasant fire on a winter evening, or what not.

The most common hindrance of our enjoyment of good things, however, especially here in America, is our restless striving after something not yet attained. There are times when we must be preoccupied with striving. A surgeon engaged in a delicate operation cannot at the same time enjoy the sunset. A man struggling to save another from drowning cannot listen to the sweet music of birds. Life must have its seasons of stern struggle when the eyes are turned away from all the sweet and lovely things around us to the end of achieving something which is not yet attained.

But our absorption in that which is not yet attained must not make us permanently unappreciative of what is already given to us. We must not be so absorbed in making the child into a good man that we cannot appreciate and rejoice in the child for what he already is. We must not be so intent on getting to the end of the picture gallery that we cannot enjoy the pictures that we pass. We must not be so preoccupied in making money for a better home that we cannot enjoy the home we already have. We must not be so strenuous in our efforts to bring the tour to a successful end that we cannot enjoy it as we go along. We must not try so hard to achieve some ultimate and unattained success that we destroy the value of every success that we ever do attain.

The only way to solve this problem is be the method of alternation. Seasons of striving and aspiration after the unattained must alternate with seasons of enjoying the good things already here. After the surgeon has completed the operation he must take some time when he can enjoy the sunset. After the terrible struggle over the drowning man there must be some time when one can listen to the birds.

This relaxation and enjoyment of the present moment, this quieting of the rush and striving after something which is still beyond us, this joy in the life which is already ours, must be cultivated. Perhaps most Americans need this side of life cultivated more than any other. A good method for cultivating it is to go out for a walk in park or open country some pleasant evening, either alone or with some very dear and intimate friend with whom you do not need to talk except as mood may require. Loitering thus together or alone in the quiet dusk of evening is the best time for cultivating the attitude of relaxation. One can give himself regular doses of this kind of treatment. For many of this age it is just as needful as medical treatment in time of physical illness.

A fourth great hindrance to joy is envy. We cannot enjoy our own clothes because they are not as good as another's. We cannot enjoy our work because it does not seem so honorable as another's. Our success seems not as great as another's, hence it is bitterness in the mouth rather than sweetness. We want what another has, and so cannot enjoy our own. Naboth's vineyard, because it belongs to him and not to us, destroys all the joy we might have in our own acres. So we turn away our face and will eat no bread.

Men have found joy in every kind of condition. If we cannot rejoice in the things which every man has to enjoy, then we are suffering from some perversion of mental attitude. Why do we not get more joy out of life? Why do we not enter into that fullness of joy which Jesus said he wished all men to have? The fault is our own. We destroy our own happiness. How? By a mistaken Puritanic habit which will not let us surrender to the joy of the passing hour. Or by some goading anxiety and worry that has got us in its clutches and will not let us go. Or by a habit of strenuous striving which has become so fixed as a mental attitude that we cannot throw it off in periods of relaxation that should alternate with periods of striving. Or by envy of what other people have. No doubt there are many other attitudes which cut us off from the joy of the world, but these serve to illustrate what we mean. Each individual by self-examination in worship must discover for himself the peculiar joy-killing attitudes which afflict him. Then he must treat them to a cure.

2. How To Cure the Joy-Killing Attitude

We have already suggested some measures for curing mistaken Puritanism and that strenuosity which has become a disease. But we can now lay down the principle for the cure of all four of these ills. The method of cure is to ascertain what is the right attitude which is the exact opposite of your wrong attitude, and suggesting it to oneself persistently and regularly day by day until it grows. If the wrong attitude is a mistaken Puritanism, the right and opposing attitude would be one of joyous acceptance and appreciation of every good thing. If the wrong attitude is worry, the right would be peaceful adaptation to every changing condition as it arises, with flexible readiness to use and enjoy to the utmost whatever may befall. If the wrong attitude is habitual strenuosity which cannot relax, the right would be restfulness and self-abandon to the hour of relaxation. If the wrong attitude is envy, the right is identifying yourself with the joy and success of the other so that his good becomes yours also.

3. How to Preserve Critical Moral Judgment and Christian Aspiration in the Midst of Our Joys

A life overflowing with joy in the good things of this world, such as we have suggested, will dull the keenness of our moral judgment and drag down the highest aspiration unless in the midst of our enjoyment we meet four requirements.

The first of these four is to keep ourselves intensely conscious of the unfathomable possibilities for good which are inherent in this present world despite all its evil. The second is to be deeply sensitive to the fact that this present actual world is immeasurably degraded and evil as compared to these possibilities for good which are inherent in it. The third requirement is that we use this present world as material out of which to construct the other better world. This means that we must enter into the fullest and richest experience of this world, entering into all its joys as well as its sorrows; for only as we learn to experience it, know it, master it, and use it can we make it better. If we do not enter into full appreciation of the joys of this present world, as well as of its pains and evils, we cut ourselves off from the materials, the standing-ground, the leverage, and the nourishment by which alone that better world can ever be brought into existence.

The fourth and last and greatest requirement of all which must be met if we are to enjoy the world in a Christian way is to hold ourselves constantly in readiness to make any sacrifice whatsoever when such sacrifice seems to be the best thing we can do to bring forth that other better world. But we must understand what sacrifice means. It does not consist in being miserable. It consists in just the opposite. It consists in taking pain, sorrow, loss and death and transmuting these into joy and goodness by making them contributory to the attainment of a better world.

Any sacrifice which is not made as a contribution to the high end of attaining a better world, and sacrifice which is made merely to demonstrate our own righteousness or to express our condemnation of evil, is not only mistaken, useless and foolish; it is positively evil. The sacrifice which Jesus recommended, for example, was not that we lose our lives, but that we lose them in order to save them. The sacrifice he recommended was never morbid. Never refuse a joy unless the refusing of it will yield a greater joy. That is what is meant by losing one's life to save it.

With this understanding of sacrifice we can say that readiness for such sacrifice on all occasions is needed if we are to enjoy the world in a Christian way. Without readiness for such sacrifice the joys of the world will distort our moral judgment, pervert our Christian aspiration, and blind us to those vast possibilities which constitute the kingdom of God. With this sacrifice, and with this only, can we enter into that full measure of joy which should be ours. We cut ourselves off from joy in so far as we are selfish. We find the joy of living in so far as we share deeply and widely the interests of our fellow men, providing we preserve our own integrity in doing so.

Ways of entering into the joy which the world has in store for us are innumerable and inexhaustible. First and most manifest to all is the way of preserving and cultivating good health. This is not the only way to joy. It may be blocked and other ways opened. But it is one, and a very important one. Economic security is something every man should seek for his own family and others. This is one component of a fully satisfying life. Then there are the joys of music to be found by cultivating capacity for its appreciation; the deep undercurrent of joy running like a stream under all our thoughts and moods when we have absorbed the rhythm and imagery and insight of poetry; there are scenes of beauty to behold and to cherish in memory through all the life-day long; there is the noble and joy-giving art of conversation; there is humor and there is the glorious thrill of aspiration. All these joys and many others require constant cultivation and discipline of all our habits and capacities. There is no other way of having the great joys of life save by discipline, cultivation and reconstruction of personality. These can be attained through the high art of worship.

Edgar S. Brightman

(1884———)

ONE of the American schools of thought which has succeeded in wedding philosophy and theology is that of personalism, whose founder was Borden P. Bowne of Boston University. Personalism sees personality as the key to reality, and particularly stresses the personality of Jesus as the norm for all men. As a sort of "Protestant Scholasticism," it unites the rational, the volitional, and the mystical in a coherent approach to God.

Since 1919 Brightman has held the Borden P. Bowne chair of philosophy at Boston University Graduate School, and has been a leading exponent of personalism. Born in Massachusetts, educated at Brown, Boston, Berlin, and Marburg, Brightman taught at Brown, Nebraska Wesleyan, and Wesleyan University before his present position. He is an ordained minister of The Methodist Church.

Of his many books, *Religious Values* most keenly shows the pattern by which man appreciates the devotional life: creative worship brings perspective, a spiritual ideal, power, and fruition in a community of love. The following selection is taken from this book by permission of Abingdon-Cokesbury Press. (Copyright 1925 by Edgar S. Brightman.)

THE FOUR STAGES OF WORSHIP

From *Religious Values*

What, then, is the nature of worship? Of what attitudes does it consist? Attitudes we say, not attitude; for worship is no fixed or single point of consciousness. It is a stream which becomes deeper and often stiller as it flows, a life which begets life. From observation of its historic and present forms we find it to consist of reverent contemplation, revelation, communion, and fruition. If we thus single out its stages, it is not intended to give the impression that they are all separate and distinct from each other or that the order given represents the constant or usual order of psychological development. Sometimes the stages seem to occur almost simultaneously. The point of importance is that each higher stage includes and presupposes those that precede it on the list, and that all four attitudes are present in all fully developed worship. Contemplation, revelation, communion, and fruition are all essential.

Contemplation is the first stage of worship. It is worship in its lowest terms; yet it involves more than belief in God. By contemplation is meant the fullest possible concentration of reverent attention on him. Man meditates on the mystery of a Creator who is also a Redeemer. As Richard Baxter quaintly puts it in the *Saints' Everlasting Rest*, there is "the set and solemn acting of all the powers of thy soul in meditation upon thy everlasting rest." The soul may be silent before Jehovah in contemplation, or may break forth into praise and thanksgiving.

But, however contemplation expresses itself, this stage of worship is incomplete without a higher. He who patiently waits upon the Lord finds that the Lord inclines unto him. Contemplation is followed by revelation. In contemplation man is seeking; in revelation God is giving. In contemplation man's attitude is active; in revelation it is passive. Each is necessary for the normal fulfillment of the other. First, "I saw the Lord"; then, "flew one of the seraphims unto me." First, meditation under the bo tree; then, the illumination of Nirvana.

> Who in heart not ever kneels
> Neither sinne nor Saviour feels.

Reverent contemplation fits us to receive God's judgment of our character and of his.

Yet it would be an error to regard this revelation as the end of worship. The saint who aims only at illumination is not the perfected saint. The passive recipient of revelation should become active again; yet now he does not return to mere contemplation, for he can enter into a mutual relation with the God who has revealed himself. This is most often expressed in prayer; but the practice of the presence of God may take many forms. Communion with God, then, differs from contemplation as fellowship with a present friend differs from thought about an absent one; for, although God is truly present to the mere contemplater, a God whose presence is not revealed is as good as absent. And a God revealed but unresponsive to our spirit's need is as though he were not. The literature of devotion is full of expressions of the intimacy of communion with God and warnings against its possible loss. To quote Richard Baxter again,

"Frequency in heavenly contemplation is particularly important to prevent a shyness between God and thy soul."

Sometimes this shyness is so successfully broken down as to destroy reverent contemplation and to produce an undue familiarity, akin to that which in the end breeds contempt. The extremes of so-called gospel songs may be matched in the Pietistic movement of the seventeenth and eighteenth centuries. Such "hymns" as the following were produced:

> Call me, Oh call me, thy bride,
>   Call me, I pray thee, thy dove;
> Bring me to thy dear side,
>   Fill me with trusting love.

A production of twenty-three stanzas gave attributes of Jesus in the following style:

> "Little Easter Lamb, how sweet,
>   How sweet thy taste to me.
> Honey flowing from thy wounds
>   Brings felicity.
> Of thy grace my soul has boasted.
> Life sprang up when thou wert roasted!"

Twenty-three stanzas of this would suffice to prevent shyness.

It was such excesses in the Pietistic movement that led Ritschl to denounce all mysticism. Nevertheless, it was Ritschl who said that "the fellowship which sinners may have with God is as close as that between the head and the members of a family," and that "in the personal sanctuary of this peculiar knowledge of God, of the world, and of oneself, which consists more of states of feeling than of intellectual reflections, one is absolutely independent over against men; or, if not, one has not yet attained the enjoyment of reconciliation." Communion with God thus gives man a sense of membership in an eternal spiritual whole that cannot fail; yet it is not the final stage of worship.

God is too overwhelming for man to endure long the intense feeling of direct communion with him. Conscious life is rhythmic, and attention must alternate, as Hocking has pointed out, between the whole and the part. This thought is allegorically expressed in a well-known passage in the *Theologia Germanica* (Chapter VII):

"Now the created soul of man hath also two eyes. The one is the power of seeing into eternity, the other of seeing into time and the creatures, of perceiving how they differ from each other as aforesaid, of giving life and needful things to the body, and ordering and governing it for the best. But these two eyes of the soul of man cannot both perform their work at once; but if the soul shall see with the right eye into eternity, then the left eye must close itself and refrain from working, and be as though it were dead. For if the left eye be fulfilling its office toward outward things, that is, holding converse with time and the creatures, then must the right eye be hindered in its working; that is, in its contemplation. Therefore whosoever will have the one must let the other go, for 'no man can serve two masters.'"

But the mystic writer has gone to extremes in the separation of the functions. God and his world are not two utterly distinct universes. When the worshiping mind turns from its moments of direct communion with "the center and soul of every sphere" to a concern with our fragmentary human experiences, it carries to them the power of the Whole which draws them to itself. God is the magnetic pole of our spiritual universe; and, contrary to the old mystic, he gives meaning to our life in the world.

Just as the mariner should not leave the lanes of navigation and flee to the pole, so the soul should not leave the world and flee to God. To be in the world yet not of it is the worshiper's portion. He steers toward port through tempest and sunshine, his compass held steady by a power beyond the clouds and the very sun. Then at last within his soul there dawns the final stage of worship, which is fruition. Not the ecstasy of mystic communion but the fruit of the Spirit— love, joy, peace, long-suffering, gentleness, faith, meekness, temperance—is the true goal or worship. These virtues when they grow out of a life of worship have a very different inner aspect than when they are cultivated for their own sakes. Fruits grow out of the life of the organism; so the fruit of the Spirit. As is the love of human person and human person, so is the love of human person and divine person: first, contemplation of the Loved One; then revelation of the mysteries of the true nature of the Loved One; then, a communion of life; and, finally, creation of new life, "birth in beauty," as Plato calls it. This should not be taken to mean that the worship of God is merely a means to an end, a mere instrument to personal character or social sentiments or conduct; it means, rather, that, unless the end sought is one of which worship is both root and integral part, the human personality will never find its maturest fruition.

John Baillie

(1886——)

BAILLIE was born in Gairloch, Scotland and educated at Inverness Royal Academy, Edinburgh, the University of Jena, and Marburg. He has taught at Edinburgh, Toronto, Union Theological Seminary, and Auburn Theological Seminary. In 1943 he was Moderator of the General Assembly of the Church of Scotland.

As a teacher of systematic theology, few men have better combined the devotional with the Christian theological structure than Baillie. A number of his writings have been directly related to the problems of worship and prayer. The devotional help he has found in the Christian tradition he beautifully expresses in these words: "For myself I will add this, and I will say it in full remembrance of the many puzzles and perplexities which the study of the New Testament still continues to present to me—that the light of Christian truth which has illumined for me the dark and difficult road of life nowhere shines with so clear and pure a radiance as just in the Synoptic story."

This selection is part of the closing chapter of *The Interpretation of Religion,* and is used by permission of Charles Scribner's Sons. (Copyright 1928 by Charles Scribner's Sons.)

THE IDEA OF REVELATION

From *The Interpretation of Religion*

What we have learned, then, is that human discovery and divine revelation, instead of dividing the field of religious knowledge between them, hold the whole field of it in common and are but complementary sides of the self-same fact of experience. The entire process by which men become aware of God may be described in terms of human seeking and finding, and we have done our best so to describe it. But it can be described in terms of divine self-disclosure too, and indeed must be so described if the full truth about it is to be told; although, as has been said, our human power to describe it from this end must ever be of the most limited kind.

What is here asserted is that every human discovery of God or of religious truth may be regarded under the correlative aspect of a divine revelation. Some recent writers have seemed to go further and to assert that *all* human knowledge, no matter in what field, may equally be regarded in this double way. "Discovery and revelation," we are told, "are two aspects of the same process," so that "all

truth is both discovered and revealed." This way of speaking, however, runs the risk of taking all meaning out of the idea of revelation. To say that God reveals Himself cannot mean merely that He exists to be known or that He is always there for men to discover if they can. His self-disclosure must mean something more active than this. Moreover, from this view of the matter it would follow that the greater part of revelation is not concerned with God at all, but with such things as human history, the ways of nature, and the properties of number and of geometrical figure; for it cannot properly be claimed that all knowledge is knowledge of God. What might, possibly, be claimed to be true is that in all knowledge there is present, at least potentially, an element of something like religious insight and therefore of divine revelation, or, as Plato would put it, that nothing is worthy to be called *epistēmē* which does not in some degree participate in the Form of the Good. But from this it does not follow that in so far as our knowledge is of the nature of discovery, to that extent it is also of the nature of revelation, and hence that all knowledge is equally of the nature of revelation; the truth being rather that while none of our knowledge stands wholly unrelated to God's self-disclosure of Himself to our souls, yet that knowledge which we regard as being specifically religious possesses the character of revelation in an altogether different degree from the rest.

What then is the logical basis of this distinction? In what sense can our conviction that (let us say) our souls will survive death be said to possess the character of revelation in an altogether different degree from our conviction that (let us say) a total eclipse of the sun will, if the sky be clear, be visible from Greenwich on such and such a day in the far-distant future?

If we are to have any light on this question, we must first address ourselves to the wider and prior question as to where in our human experience we do actually find God revealed.

In what ways does God reveal Himself to us? Through what media, in what signs, by what manifestations, does He make known to man His nature and His will? That God has left Himself entirely without witness in His world mankind has (as we saw) never been able to believe, and every religious system has accordingly taken it for granted that divination of some kind is possible. Serious difference of opinion arises only in regard to the nature of this witness and the authentic methods of this divination, and it is here that a real progress of thought can be traced. The line of advance may be said to be twofold. In the first place, we notice a progress from the outward to the inward. In the earlier stages of religious development men look for God mainly in external nature, and think to find some declaration of His will in the flight of birds or in the disposition of the stars. . . . But as such 'artificial' divination recedes more and more into the background and the main reliance comes to be placed on 'natural' divination by way of dream or trance or frenzy

or cataleptic fit, a real advance is registered; for now God is held to reveal His nature and His will, not by external omens and portents, but through the spirit of man. Nevertheless, another stadium of progress still remains to be traversed—the progress from the abnormal to the normal. The tendency to look to the abnormalities and anomalies of human experience for the traces of the Divine is common to both forms of divination in their earlier stages. In the case of 'artificial' divination it comes out in the attention paid to strange and unusual phenomena like comets and eclipses and unexplained events and coincidences of every kind, while in the case of 'natural' divination it comes out in almost exclusive concentration upon such experiences and conditions of the soul as are now generally held to be psychopathic in character. What we have now learned is to look for manifestations of the Divine, not in the occasional disturbances and obscurations of our human nature, but rather in the fullest daylight of its reasonable and healthy exercise.

Our conclusion accordingly is that it is in *man* that God reveals Himself most fully and that the most veridical clue to His mind and will are to be found; in man, moreover, when he is at his manliest and best. "He made man in his own image"—there, if they had only realised it, lay the secret which the diviners and the augurs and the soothsayers made the object of their ancient quest.

Yet we must try to give our meaning something of a sharper definition than this. For it might well be asked: "Is not this the maddest and most groundless of all megalomanias, that a particular animal species inhabiting a comparatively insignificant planet should find in its own specific nature the key to the nature of the Eternal Being?" And our answer to that question can only be that it is not in our own specific animal nature (not in our nature as vertebrates or as mammals or as bipeds, nor yet in the particular bundle of instincts which mark us off from our nearest brutish relatives, nor in what the old moralists called "the particular constitution of human nature") that we find the footprints of Divinity, but only in our nature as moral personalities. So once again we find ourselves led to our old conclusion, that it is in our human values that we find God revealed. Not in the procession of the stars, not in the flight of birds, not in the guttural frenzy of the Delphic maid, but in "the milk of human kindness" is the character of God made plain and His will made known. Not in the sound of thunder but in the voice of conscience do we hear Him speak most plainly. Not in hepatoscopic markings, nor yet on tables of stone, but on the tables of the human heart, are His words most plainly to be deciphered. As it has been finely put, "God speaks to us through ourselves. It is through our values and obedience to them that we attain to knowledge of Him" and "He is to be seen in the light of a cottage window as well as in the sun or the stars."

But the question may still be pressed why, instead of resting content with the ordinary language of discovery, we should, in speaking of this insight that comes to us through our values, feel it necessary to resort to the new category of revelation. The answer must begin from the consideration that our values are felt by us from the very beginning to be not really *ours* at all, but to belong to a wider order of reality of which (as Plato would say) we are privileged to "partake." Goodness is not in the first place something that exists in us, but rather something to which we feel ourselves called, something which makes an active claim upon us. Many efforts have indeed been made to put us off with a purely 'naturalistic' theory of value—a theory, that is to say, which would entirely explain our moral consciousness in terms of our animal ancestry or as a product of its antecedents in our own animal nature. But such explanations have always seemed to succeed only in proportion as they have lost sight of the deepest and most characteristic elements in the thing to be explained. It is of course undeniable that our consciousness

of moral obligation and of the Good to which we are obliged to conform has an evolutionary history behind it, and there may even be a carefully guarded sense in which it is allowable to speak of it as having been "developed from prior elements that are themselves of a non-moral kind." Yet to speak of evolution and development in such a case as this is in no sense to offer an explanation, but only to set a problem; and it is a problem which, as has been widely felt by earnest students of the subject, can never hope to find its real solution in any reference to antecedent and simpler elements. Our human experience of value, in short, cannot be understood in the light of anything that lies behind us, secured in the storehouse of the past; but only by a forward reference to something that lies ahead of us and beckons to us from above. We have here to do, fundamentally, not with an edifice built up from earthy foundations by human skill and creativity, but much rather with the progressive disclosure to our obedient minds of a higher order of reality. In the experience of moral obligation there is contained and given the knowledge, not only of a Beyond, but of a Beyond that is in some sort actively striving to make itself known to us and to claim us for its own. This conclusion is not a mere guess, nor a leap in the dark, nor a poetic hyperbole, but an honest drawing-out of what we find to be implied in the felt imperativeness of duty.

The general contention that our awareness of value cannot be explained in terms of its more earthy antecedents but only as a progressive participation in a higher world of being whose organising principle is the Good, goes back to the teaching of Plato, and forms indeed the central thought of his Theory of Ideas as well as the esoteric meaning of his famous Myth of Recollection. In our own day it has had few more notable champions than Rudolf Eucken, who throughout his long life and voluminous writings seemed always to be saying only one thing—that we do not make our values but they make us, that in our gradually developing awareness of them we are not building from below but rather grasping at something that is suspended from above, and that consequently we have here to do with nothing less than "the invasion of our life by a new Order of reality." We may quote at random:

"The movement to spirituality cannot be considered as a work of any separate individual faculties of the mere man; but it is a movement of the All, which certainly in our position needs our co-operation, but which, at the same time, takes us unto itself and makes of us something quite different from what we were at the first view of things."

"The True and the Good are not mere means and instruments of our welfare: to treat them thus is to destroy them at their root. They are rather the revealers of a new and nobler life, or a new world, participation in which is the crucial mark of distinction between man and animal, or rather between the spiritual and the animal in our own nature—our unique position being, in fact, due to our participation as spiritual beings in this higher life. . . . It [i.e., this life] cannot possibly be a mere product of human reflection. Its forms and powers are far too unique to be in any way derivable from us."

We can now understand why the world's great men of faith should always have represented their acquisition of religious insight as having its deepest origin, not in any activity of their own spirits, but rather in the activity of that greater Spirit Who was seeking to make Himself known. The real initiative in the whole matter lies not with man but with God, and before there is faith on our part there is grace on His. We may indeed go so far as to say, with St. Augustine, that faith itself is not an act but a gift; yet here it is necessary to speak very carefully and with delicate discrimination of the different factors involved. On the one hand it is certain that faith in God cannot be attained without an eager activity of search on the part of our own minds, but on the other hand it appears to be no less true that this eagerness must be largely of the nature of an eagerness

to *receive*, and that a spirit too restlessly striving may easily overreach itself; nor is this the only walk of life in which men may fail in their quest by trying too hard. It is all put admirably by Baron von Hügel when he writes that "man attains in religion, as truly as elsewhere—once given his whole-hearted striving—in proportion as he seeks not too directly, not feverishly and strainingly, but in a largely subconscious, waiting, genial, expansive, endlessly patient sunny manner. This is indeed the 'gütliche nicht grimmige Ernst' of the great German mediæval mystics."

But now there is a last point to which attention must be drawn. Our initial conclusion was that it is in man that God most truly reveals Himself. Then we went on to argue that it is not in man as a particular animal species that this revelation appears, but rather in those values which themselves belong to a higher world, yet of which man is privileged in some measure to partake. We must now, however, return from this further and more abstract analysis to the concreteness of our former statement. For value is in its very nature a concrete and personal thing which cannot exist in the emptiness of mere thought or conception at all, but only as it is incarnate in living spirits. No point has been more stressed in the thinking of our own age concerning divine revelation than that it is God Himself who is revealed to us and not mere truths or doctrines about Him—the divine self-disclosure always taking the form not of communication but of communion; and from this it may be taken to follow that the disclosure is made, at least in the first instance, not through books but through men. There is no doubt a sense in which the men here in question must be our individual selves, for no man can have any knowledge of God and the invisible world save as he hears God's voice speaking directly to him in his own conscience. At the same time, we shall all be ready to acknowledge that those manifestations of value which have done most to lighten our darkness are such as have been found, not in ourselves, but in other and better men, and that it is through our spiritual contacts with these others that our highest revelations of the Divine have always been mediated to us. As John Scotus Erigena so nobly has it, *"quanta fuerit sanctarum animarum multiplicatio, tanta erit divinarum theophaniarum possessio"*—"there are as many theophanies as there are saintly souls." In none of us, perhaps, is the image of God wholly defaced or His voice wholly silenced, yet there is not one of us who does not of his own experience know how the presence of a saintlier character in our midst may lead us both to a more steadfast assurance of God's reality and to a fuller understanding of His mind and will. Many of us would say that we know of no argument for the reality of the spiritual world that can compare for persuasive power with the remembrance of this and that saint of God whom we have been privileged to know. Such men put our scepticism to shame. In their presence doubt becomes a disloyalty and unbelief a betrayal. "A character can never be refuted." It is very noteworthy that even a philosophy like Bergson's finds its culmination in this conception of revelation through personality. In his Huxley Lecture on "Life and Consciousness" there are the following very remarkable words:

"The men of moral grandeur, particularly those whose inventive and simple heroism has opened new paths to virtue, are revealers of meta-physical truth. Although they are the culminating point of evolution, yet they are nearest the source and they enable us to perceive the impulsion which comes from the deep. It is in studying these great lives, in striving to experience sympathetically what they experience, that we may penetrate by an act of intuition to the life-principle itself. To pierce the mystery of the deep it is sometimes necessary to regard the heights. It is earth's hidden fire which appears at the summit of the volcano."

From the countless particular testimonies which might be drawn upon in illustration of this principle we must here make a single random choice. Of Fred-

erick Denison Maurice it has been said:

"He lived as few men have ever lived in the Divine. He was, as Mr. Gladstone has said of him, applying words from Dante, 'a spiritual splendour.' The Divine embraced him. He did not need to strive after it like most men. It was the Alpha and Omega of all his being—the only reality, in comparison with which all other things were shadowy. It is this more than anything that made him the spiritual power that he was. In the presence of Maurice it was hardly possible to doubt of a Divine sphere,—of a spiritual life. While the commercial world by its selfishness was denying God, and the religious world by its slanders degrading Him, and the scientific world by its theories hiding Him from view, or proclaiming Him unknown, there was a reality in Maurice's faith that left no room for doubt. I know of no life, with all the intellectual puzzles which it presents, so intensely and powerfully Divine."

It is assuredly in the light of such familiar experiences as these that the ancient history of revelation is to be understood by us. The Hebrew people, looking back upon their marvellous past, could not but see in it a progressive activity of self-disclosure on the part of the divine known to the nation as a whole rather than to any particular class within it, had yet used the nation's great men as His particular instruments or vessels. The successive stages in this self-disclosure were marked in the people's minds by the memory of certain great men of faith —Abraham, Moses, Joshua, Elijah, Isaiah, Jeremiah, and the rest. When they thought of these men, they did not boast of what their nation had produced; but rather gave thanks for what their nation had received. To their believing eyes the whole story was even more a record of divine love and guidance than it was a record of human achievement. They deeply felt that behind it all was the hand of God.

And the culminating chapter in this history cannot be better summed up than in the words of an old writer whose name we do not know: "God, who at sundry times and in divers manners spake in time past unto the fathers by the prophets, hath in these last days spoken unto us by a Son." What men had felt about Moses and the Prophets they felt in a still more compelling and definitive way about Jesus Christ. They felt that He had revealed to them the very face of the Most High. Here at length, they said, was the very "portrait of the invisible God." As they looked into the soul of this Man, they felt that they knew at last what God was like. From time immemorial men had been seeking a clue; the diviners and augers and soothsayers had made many a fruitless guess, followed many a false trail; yet the clue, when now at last it is discovered, turns out to be of a strange simplicity and homeliness—it is the soul of a Man. This great climax of a world's seeking is perfectly symbolized in the story of the Magi, wherein the Wise Men of the East who have nightly scanned the heavens and daily read the auspices for a sign or hint of Heaven's meaning, are guided at last by a star to a village stable wherein a peasant woman is giving birth to a peasant child—and there their long quest ends. They no longer look to the stars or to the auspices for a revelation of God, nor to any of the old omens or oracles. They know now that He is manifest in human flesh. Divination is still possible, but by a different sign.

Here then lies the deep meaning of the Christian doctrine of the Incarnation. If we would know what God is like, it is to a *Man* that we must turn—"the man Christ Jesus." If we would know where in our experience the divine Spirit most unmistakably manifests His presence, this is the answer: 'In the voice of conscience wherein His law is written in our hearts, in His Spirit bearing witness with our spirits that we are His Children, in deeds of love and mercy and heroic self-sacrifice, in the souls of good men wherein such things as these are most manifest to our eyes, and supremely and finally in the soul of Jesus Christ wherein they all shine with a new matchless radiance.' It

is the witness of all who have come under the spell of His spiritual presence that God was in Christ, reconciling the world unto Himself, and that he who hath seen Him hath seen the Father.

The truth we have here to grasp is that the highest human goodness, since it is the real meeting-point of earth and heaven, may be regarded from either of two points of view; it may be thought of as man reaching upwards or as God bending downwards. It is noteworthy that the New Testament writers, though making use of the widest variety of thought-forms and modes of expression, are nevertheless all agreed in regarding their Master from *both* points of view. To them all He is the greatest and the best of men, marking the summit of human attainment and of human insight into the things of God; but to them all, also, He is God's greatest gift to man, marking the climax of the divine self-disclosure. In Him our human aspiration joins hands with God's condescension. And so, for all their joy in Him as One perfectly obedient to His Heavenly Father's will, the prevailing note in all their speech concerning Him is not pride in something accomplished, but gratitude for something received. In the life and death of the Man of Nazareth St. Paul indeed sees "one man's obedience," but he sees also the seal and proof of the love of the Most High God. "God proves his love for us by this, that Christ died for us." "In Christ God reconciled the world to himself, instead of counting men's trespasses against them." And the response aroused in the hearts of the New Testament writers as a whole finds perfect expression in the words of the Johannine author. "In this was manifested the love of God toward us . . ." "Herein is love, not that we loved God but that he loved us and sent his son . . ." "God so loved the world that he gave his only begotten Son . . ." The Cross, this writer would tell us, is indeed the crowning incident in the history of our fitful human quest of the Divine, but it is also, and even more significantly, the crowning incident in the history of God's age-long quest of the human heart.

Thus it is that Jesus Christ has always seemed to stand in a twofold relation to His Church's life. He is the greatest of her saints, but He is also her Lord. In Him man was made perfect: in Him God was made manifest. To the Church He has always been at once the Son of Man and the Son of God; not indeed as though He had a dual personality, and was sometimes God and sometimes man, but rather in the sense in which a modern poet addresses Him:

Jesus, divinest when Thou most art man!

To some indeed it has in all good faith appeared that the Christian Church, in insisting (as it has always done so firmly) on the divinity of Christ, has been following a wholly false scent; and they would urge us to content ourselves with regarding our Master as the incarnation not of divine but of human perfection. That there is much in the barren and artificial logomachies of ecclesiastical Christology to excuse such a revolt we very readily allow; but after all *securus iudicat orbis terrarum*. It is not likely that on so cardinal an issue as this the instinct of nineteen centuries will turn out to have been wholly wrong. Nor is it difficult to see where it has been profoundly right and wise. The doctrine of our Lord's divinity is based on the perception which came long ago to the Galilean villagers and fisherfolk that, while Jesus was in one regard but a man like themselves seeking God, yet somehow also in His words to them and His deeds and presence among them God was seeking man; a perception which after His death on the Cross deepened itself into the realisation that not merely had one man triumphed, but high Heaven had spoken.

Regarded in this light, and as the culmination of the long history of divination, the doctrine of our Lord's divinity is surely expressive of the profoundest religious truth. It alienates us only when it is interpreted in such a manner as to obscure its organic connection with the history of revelation as a whole. The true Christian teaching has never been that God is incarnate in Jesus alone, but that in Him He was incarnate supremely. Revelation and incarnation are no unique historical prodigies but are, by God's grace, of the very warp and woof of our human experience. The God who speaks to us in Jesus Christ is the same God Who already has spoken, and Who still continues to speak, "at sundry times and in divers manners." "The Christian doctrine of the Divinity of Jesus," says von Hügel, ". . . is undoubtedly true and deeply enriching. Yet it can be wisely maintained by us only if we simultaneously remember that, however truly God revealed Himself with supreme fulness and in a unique manner in Jesus Christ, yet this same God had not left Himself, still does not leave Himself, without *some* witness to Himself throughout the ages before Christ, and throughout the countries, groups, and even individual souls whom the message, the fact, of the historic Jesus has never reached, or who, in sheer good faith, cannot understand, cannot see Him as He really is."

"Where love is, there God is." Where there is any love at all, He is not wholly absent; but where love is perfected, there He is altogether revealed. In moments of little faith, we may be haunted with the feeling that our religion is but a one-sided trafficking with an unresponsive God Who makes no sign to show He hears or cares, and Who is never directly present to our experience at all. "No man," we say, "hath seen God at any time." And then, perhaps, we remember how the sacred text continues: "God is love, and he that dwelleth in love dwelleth in God, and God in him." For it is not merely that through our values we reach God or that from them we infer Him, but rather that in them we find Him. Love is not merely an outward mark and symbol of His presence, but is His very self in action in our world. And in the soul of the Man of Nazareth, and in His life and death, wherein our world's highest values are embodied and love for us made perfect, it was no mere dim-descried shadow of an otherwise masked and inscrutable Deity that we saw and knew but, as His Church has always believed, very God of very God.

Karl Barth
(1886————)

BARTH has been one of the most provocative theological voices in the last thirty years. Some have evaluated him as the most stimulating voice in Protestantism since Luther. Formerly a Christian Socialist who believed that the Kingdom of God would gradually arrive by humanity's following the religion of Jesus, he changed his view before World War I, and became a pessimist, despairing of humanity's ability to create the Kingdom on earth. He became an exponent of crisis theology, in which only men of faith are seen as those to whom God *gives* the Kingdom.

He was born in Switzerland, educated at the universities of Bern, Berlin, Tübingen, and Marburg. He taught theology at Göttingen, Münster, Bonn, and Basel, and was editor of *Zwischen den Seiten.* His thinking was much stimulated by Søren Kierkegaard, the Danish theologian, and due to Barth's interest Kierkegaard's writings have been translated for the English-speaking world in recent years.

Barth's viewpoint, which is Neosupernaturalism, has found some followers in Great Britain and the United States. But his greatest influence has been in "correcting" many religious thinkers from their too man-centered concern for religious values.

The following selection is from a letter to American Christians appearing in the second chapter of *The Church and the War,* translated by Antonia H. Froendt and used by permission of The Macmillan Co. (Copyright 1942 by the Council on Foreign Relations, Inc. Copyright 1944 by The Macmillan Co.)

[THE CHURCH AND THE WORD OF GOD]
From *The Church and the War*

Your third question:

What is the true function of the Church and its ministers in relation to this war? Should church bodies and pastors actively support the prosecution of the war by preaching about the issues involved, by urging the membership of the churches to serve in the armed forces, to buy war bonds, etc.? Or should they confine their activities to the timeless "spiritual" ministries? What are the limits beyond which the Church should not go in identifying itself with any political cause? In what sense is it true that the Church is not at war?

If I understand correctly, you are asking me first of all what the churches, i.e., the church bodies and their ministers, should or should not say and do in the present situation. I should not like to evade the question, but I should like to point out that the first consideration is an entirely inward task of the Church. Is the Church clearly aware that its mission in every, and therefore also in this time, is solely (and this in the fullest sense of the concept!) *to preach the word of God to the mankind of today, according to the Holy Writ?* Has it accepted the events and problems of our time as an admonition to renew its awareness of the breadth of this mission in all its aspects? In other words, has the Church realized that the world catastrophe which has befallen us has a connection with a catastrophe of the Church, and that to face this fact is far more important and urgent than all the "yeas" and "nays" which the Church must preach to the outside, and that to face it is the prerequisite for every vigorous "yea" and "nay" directed to the outer world?

I should here like to take the liberty of

proposing a counter-question: what is being done today in the church bodies, ministerial conferences, theological faculties, but above all in the studies of the individual pastors of all denominations in the United States, to the end that the Church shall again be the Church, understand itself as such and act accordingly? Did not the manifest unsureness of the churches on both sides of the Atlantic in recent years, in the light of the events of our time, stem to some degree from the fact that nothing (or too little), had been done for the inward regeneration of the churches? You cannot gather grapes from thistles. It could not be expected that a club for the furtherance of religious humanism would have the discernment to recognize the National Socialist menace and find the correct warning voice to lift against it. And today we cannot expect that it would give the nations clear guidance in the great difficulties of their wartime problems and sufferings; that it would represent the Kingdom of Christ, and not enter the service of some earthly sovereignty. The narrow way of clean-cut decision and complete freedom is trod only by the Church that *is* the Church or is about to become the Church once more.

I do not know whether, and to what extent, such a Church again exists in America—we in Europe have scarcely taken more than the first steps in that direction—but if there is something comparable in the United States, I shall be all the better understood if I say that the true function of the Church consists first of all in its own regeneration: in a regeneration no less thorough than the Reformation through which Protestantism began in the sixteenth century. How do matters stand in your country in this respect? In sending this counter-question, I should like to reply as follows to your third question:

1. If the Church is really preaching the *Word of God*, then this will mean active support of the war effort in so far as it testifies, with a clarity consistent with the Word of God, that the carrying through of this stern police action against Hitler's Nihilism is a necessary task of the righteous state; that therefore the United States has rightly embarked upon this task and that the American Christian is obligated to help his country, within the framework of his vocation and his abilities, in the accomplishment of this task.

Recently we read here in Switzerland a pronouncement by ninety-three leading American Protestants and we were informed that this was a statement characteristic of the majority of the American churches. In this statement is the sentence: "We abhor war, but upon the outcome of this war depends the realization of Christian principles to which no Christian can be indifferent." I venture to doubt that this is the unequivocal language, appropriate to God's word, which should be employed today. If the realization of Christian principles depends upon the outcome of this war, then there is no point in the assurance that war is abhorrent: for it is surely only unnecessary and unjust wars which are condemned as abhorrent, and among this number the present one is not to be classed. If, conversely, war as such is really condemned, then the realization of Christian principles must definitely not be made dependent on its outcome: that would mean the determination to do evil in violation of conscience, in order that good may result. I give this as an example of what I do *not* consider to be the true exercise of the pastoral function and true preaching in the present situation. The Word of God cannot be rightly preached in such equivocal sentences, and an adequate "active undergirding of the war effort" can likewise not be attained by such phrases.

2. If the Church really proclaims the Word of God according to Holy Writ, then there can be no reason for its making the war, its causes, problems, tasks and outlook, the theme of its preaching and for its making the obligation to military service and to buy war bonds and the like the contents of its exhortation. Holy Writ does not demand of the preachers of the Gospel (nor is it needed by the people of today any more

than in all other ages) that they proclaim from the pulpit again what is already being sufficiently stated by the newspapers and the propaganda agencies of the State far better than the preachers could state it. Unhappy preachers, and above all, unhappy parishes, where that is the case.

What then, shall they preach? The Word of the reconciliation of the world with God through Jesus Christ (2 Cor. 5:17-21) and nothing else. But this in its full scope! When they preach about the sole sovereignty of Jesus Christ, His human origin among the people of Israel, His triumph over powers and dominations, about God's mercy and patience revealed in Him, the dual benefaction of Church and State realized in Him; about the impossibility of serving two masters, about freedom, and the service of the children of God conceived in the Holy Spirit, they are inevitably preaching, through a simple, strict interpretation of the biblical texts, (and as a rule without naming persons and things specifically) against Hitler, Mussolini and Japan; against anti-Semitism, idolization of the State, oppressive and intimidating methods, militarism, against all the lies and the injustice of National Socialism and Fascism in its European and its Asiatic forms, and thus they will naturally (and without "dragging politics into the pulpit") speak on behalf of the righteous state and also for an honestly determined conduct of the war. And this procedure will also admirably take care of the necessary practical exhortation—usually without the need to refer to military service, war loans, and the like. Just at this time the message of Holy Writ is in itself strong and unequivocal enough to be comprehensible in a very pointed way, even to a child. We must simply make ourselves once more obedient to it, whole-heartedly, and rule out all secondary purposes.

3. When the Church is truly preaching the Word of God to the *man of today*, there can be no question of confining itself to a "timeless" spiritual service. What exactly is that, anyway? There is a "time-less" religion, a "timeless" standard of morals. The Word of God, however, is never "timeless." The time in which we live is the time accorded to us, through God's patience, between the resurrection of Jesus Christ and His second coming. Therefore it is God's time. Therefore He and His Word have a necessary, innate relation to everything that transpires within this time, and thus to the American man of today who sees himself in one way or another involved in the war against Germany, Italy and Japan.

What kind of sermon and what sort of ministry would it be whose consolation and admonition guided mankind to some timeless vacuum remote from the real conditions of this world with its anxieties and problems, or which led men to a sort of religious-moral "private" life? I wonder if the people in America, who are now, it appears, sponsoring that type of preaching and ministry, are quite aware that they are thereby moving in the wake of a certain type of German Lutheranism which has been preaching for centuries that the Gospel and the Law, the transcendent and the terrestrial, the Church and the State, Christian and political living, may be regarded and treated as two neatly separated realms. Do they realize the extent to which this evil doctrine furthered the German nationalism, *étatisme* and militarism of the nineteenth century and finally the National Socialism of today? If the Church in America has a craving for smoothing the road in that country for the rise of a similar secularistic monster, a diligent regimen of "timeless" spiritual ministry is highly to be recommended: no slogan is more pleasing to the devil than this one! If such is not their desire, churchmen must bear in mind that for some reason it pleased the Word of God to become finite and therefore also law-bound, imminent and political in the person of Jesus Christ, not only without detracting from His character as Gospel, as hope of resurrection, as the utterance of the Church, but rather in confirmation and fulfillment thereof.

Leave to the Word its whole independence and dignity by preaching it according to Holy Writ! But leave to it also, on the other hand, its full strength and scope, by not forgetting for a moment to preach it to the man today as such and therefore also in its whole finite and political clarity and categorical firmness.

4. Identification of the Church with a political cause? No! Under no circumstances and not even within the most modest limits! That is not the idea at all, that the Church identify itself—even remotely—with any political cause, that of the Allies, for instance, and so provide the religious accompaniment to the terrible sounds which must now travel round the world. By doing so it would betray its Lord and surrender itself without rendering the cause of the Allies the least assistance. A single true man with an ordinary gun in his hand would be more useful to the Allies' cause than the bells and organs of all the churches in the world if they, having betrayed their Master and thereby surrendered themselves, were no longer "true" churches. In complete independence (of the Allied cause as well) they can and should be a light to their members and to the entire world, a light making visible the fact that the terrible calamity of our day is no blind accident, no mere expression of general human benightedness, no senseless free-for-all between different imperialistic systems; that it would not do any good to turn away from it in indignation and divert one's thoughts because it is so "horrible" and to escape from it and leave to others the responsibility for seeing it through.

The churches can and should make it plain that Jesus Christ is now, as always, Lord of the world and all its dominations and that today's world-rending struggle also is being fought (whether mankind realizes and admits it or not) for His sake and in honor of Him, and has His Promise, so that those who know and love Him must, before all others, take this war seriously. Or is there not some danger that the meaning of this war may be misconstrued, and become simply futile, insane, and abhorrent? How could it be otherwise? Human life is always threat-ened by this possibility. The noblest cause is not immune from becoming an evil one in our hands, and if this war is a good cause, it is nevertheless a dangerous one, a temptation for all the participating nations, governments, and armies.

Woe betide, if the Church should desecrate itself in this cause instead of seeing to it, on the contrary, that this cause be consecrated through the Church, that the righteousness and necessity of this war for the defense of the righteous state be preserved to the nations, to their governments and armies *consciously*, thus giving them a clear conscience in the conduct of it but also preserving the moderation necessary to its proper conclusion. This mission, by virtue of which it preaches a righteous peace in the midst of war and thus approves the war only for the sake of the righteous peace (but for its sake does so in wholehearted earnest), is the prophetic mission of the Church in this war. And if it is only Church, and remains Church, it cannot be estimated to what extent it may impose limitation on itself in its realization of this mission. Its spiritual mission in this respect is illimitable. Let the Church take care, however, that it be and remain strictly true to it as its spiritual mission!

5. The sentence, that the Church is not at war, is *true to the extent* that it may mean: the Church is in no sense one of the instruments of the warring state. In war as in peace it serves its own Lord, pursues its own cause and speaks its own language: the cause and message of the Gospel, which is directed to friend and foe alike and is not dependent on the outcome of the war, whatever it may be. It prays, while admonishing the friendly powers to remain absolutely steadfast, for the Church and for the enemy. It always remains determined and ready to intercede, if necessary, for the rights of the enemy also.

The same sentence is *in part not true*, in so far as it can mean: the Church is neutral, it looks on and takes care not to compromise itself. It preaches a Gospel which is indifferent to the question of a righteous state, motivated by no clear political decisions and objectives. It might even disseminate the lie that recognition between left and right, between good and evil in this war is not required. It confines its activities to that timeless spiritual service, etc., etc.

That same sentence is *wholly true* in so far as it means: the Church in wartime lives and works—to the very degree that it takes the war seriously—in the deepest peace of the knowledge that He, who makes all things new, is already seated victoriously at the right hand of God; the King, whose sovereignty has no end, who needs no service from us but who has not scorned the enlistment on His behalf of our earnest, determined, persistent service in Church and State.

Toyohiko Kagawa

(1888——)

AMONG contemporary Christians who practice redemptive love in the unfortunate areas of society, Kagawa stands among the foremost. Born in Japan, he was educated at Meijii Gakun College, Kobe Theological Seminary, and Princeton. From 1908 to 1923 he lived in the slums of Kobe, helping the downtrodden. In Japan he has worked with the Labor Federation, Farmer's Co-operative, Industrial Young Men's Association, Imperial Economic Conference. He has headed the Social Bureau of Tokyo.

Kagawa's work in the Kobe slums, his labor for co-operative societies in Japan, his role as a world evangelist, his loyalty to Christian ideals amid a Shinto civilization, mark him as one of the great saints of the twentieth century. He can readily be called the Francis of Assisi of modern times. Defective in sight and frail in body, yet understanding the power of the Christian gospel, he is worthy to write *Meditations on the Cross*. The following selection is from the English translation by Helen F. Topping and Marion R. Draper and is used by permission of Willett, Clark & Co.

THE CROSS AND DAILY LIFE

From *Meditations on the Cross*

*I*t is easy for the Japanese people to understand the conception of God, but it is hard for them to grasp the Cross. They may speak glibly of the Cross, but there are few who really understand it, and fewer still who practice it. It is particularly true of men of this modern age that they do not grasp the meaning of the Cross, nor do they live the life of the Cross in any thorough-going fashion. The civilization of this present day is in exact opposition to the Cross, for it makes self the center, and puts its claims first. Because the people of the present day take the position that if one's own class or one's own nation is getting along well, that is quite enough, we find widespread unrest among the oppressed, and the right to live, the right to labor, the rights of personality are defended with bitterness and desperation. Such movements as communism and socialism, which are not founded upon the Cross, take the attitude that it makes no difference what happens to others if only a man has work for himself. It is of no importance what happens to the rich—let him be out of work, let the landowner be out of employment; who cares? Let the proletarians work to establish the position of their own class, no matter what happens to the landlords! The fate of those who live on land rents is quite unimportant! Of course, the Cross is unintelligible to such people.

There are at least five points of significance in the Cross. In the first place, the Cross teaches us that whatever suffering may come is sent by God. If we feel that suffering comes through other men, it becomes intolerable; but we can accept it gladly if it is from God. Our modern thought does not agree with this at all. There is a general feeling that it is ridiculous to think of God as sending suffering. It has no meaning, it is suffering, and nothing more; as such it is to be avoided. Let us spend each day as it comes in pleasure and enjoyment of life.

We have the habit in Japan of running away from suffering. We have degenerated since the days of Hojo when the Zen sect taught self-discipline and an austere mode of life. When some great catastrophe, like the earthquake, happens, our lack of vigor and spirit comes to light. I have been told that there are a million or more Koreans who have emigrated to northeastern Manchuria because they have been dispossessed of their country. They are enduring the trials of the cold climate with courage; although the summer is short, still they manage to cultivate many acres of land, and even to grow some rice. But the Japanese are always looking for an easy mode of life, and they have lost the desire to persevere in enduring hardships. They are attempting to flee from the Cross. (Philippians 3:18.)

If you complain that Japan is limited in extent, there is the northern island of the Hokkaido with over one million acres of uncultivated land; there is still plenty of room for people to immigrate there. The Hokkaido can take care of five times the population of the main island. There is Southern Saghalin (Karafuto) with its three hundred thousand acres of land, if one has the spirit to go as a colonist, to live simply and to work hard. The reason that the Japanese do not go in and occupy such lands is because they lack the willingness to endure privations, the spirit of bearing a cross. We must lay more stress upon this spirit.

When the disciples of Christ begged him to become their king, he deliberately chose instead the suffering of the Cross. In the thirteenth century during the Hojo period of Japanese history, there was a man called Eizai who taught Japan

this way of suffering. He was a priest in the temple of Fudasan, belonging to the Zen sect, and he was a man of simple sincerity of spirit and vigor of character. It was this same spirit of simple frugality which occasioned many of the stories told of the heroes of that period, of Matsushita Zeni, and of Fujitsuna Aoto, who dragged the river to recover a copper coin—though it cost him more than the value of the coin—in order to restore it to circulation. It is told of Aoto that he took only the simplest fare, and the only relish he would take with his wine was *yake-miso*, a sort of toasted bean cake. Many other tales are told of him, which reveal a simple frugality of life almost religious in its atmosphere.

We moderns lack this atmosphere. The Hojo family had more of this tone than the Ashikaga or Tokugawa families, who succeeded them. Take, for example, Tokiyori Hojo, who when he was still a young man retired to the seclusion of a small temple, called Saimyoji, north of Yokohama, and built himself a hut and took up the simple and strictly ordered life of the Zen sect. In order to discipline himself and to develop courage, he would rise early in the morning for meditation; he lived on the simplest food, taking only a bowl of bean soup with his rice; and he wore the gloomy black robes of the priests. Tokiyori was succeeded by Tokimasa, and it was during the latter's rule that Kublai Khan invaded Japan. It is truly remarkable that Japan was able to resist this invasion, and in my opinion it is due to the influence of the Zen sect, with its system of self-discipline and its emphasis on a simple, austere mode of life.

According to Mrs. E. A. Gordon, who visited Japan, the Daruma, or famous Buddhist saint of Japan, was a foreigner. Mrs. Gordon felt that there was so much of the element of the early Christian teaching in the training and discipline of the Zen sect that she claimed that Daruma must have been either St. Thomas, the disciple of Christ, or one of his followers. The virility of the Kamakura period of Japanese history was due to the spiritual discipline practised at that time. The reason that the disciples of Christ conquered Europe was because they had the will to trample suffering under their feet. Unless the Japanese people have more of this spirit, Japan cannot make progress. Instead of trying to imitate the West, and doing it badly, it would be much better for us to study and understand clearly the way of Christ, whose origin was in Asia.

We who are followers of Christ must guard his secret. We must have the secret skill of turning every pain into joy. The only thing which brought the country through the crisis of the Hojo period was spiritual force. In our modern times, however, the individualistic religion of the Zen sect is inadequate. Many of the characteristic teachings of the Zen sect are to be found in Christianity, as well, but there must be group activity, too.

THE CONQUEST OF SORROW

In the second place, the Cross is a way of conquering sorrow. Not suffering alone but sorrow also is the lot of man. Suffering and sorrow may seem to be closely related, but there is a slight difference between them. Though a man may have a secure livelihood, he may be sad. Though he may have a lovely home and a good wife, and everything he needs, still that man may be sad. Some men are saddened by their lack of education; others are dissatisfied with life. Some meet with business failure. Shaka was born in a king's palace but he grieved over his environment which to others seemed so fortunate. Suffering is negative and sorrow is positive. The Cross is the way of conquest over sorrow. When one loses a child, one may not suffer in his own body, but as a parent he experiences sorrow. Although he tries to give up his child and resign himself to his loss, yet he cannot do it. Madame S—— was a countess, whose family belonged to the Nichiren sect. When she was in deep distress because of the loss of her child, she came to know the Way of Christ, which conquers sorrow. She suddenly awakened to the new truth and accepted Christian teaching. The teachings of Christianity make it possible to endure sorrow with a heart at peace.

When Jesus was being led away to the cross, a crowd of women followed him weeping. The road along which Christ was taken is called the Via Dolorosa today and many stories have gathered around it. Christ told the weeping women to mourn rather over the day of destruction which would come to them. (Luke 23:27-31.) I am much impressed by the way in which Christ forgot his own suffering and thought only of the suffering of others. We must discover the secret of this composure which can forget its own sufferings and suffer for others. Although the Japanese people should be strong in meeting suffering, still there are few who meet its blows with self-possession.

Tom Sawyer, the hero of Mark Twain's famous novel, was a mischievous youngster, but for all his mischief, he was not a bad boy. The story is laid in the years when the basin of the Mississippi River was being reclaimed, and this ragged little rascal wanders about from one place to another, meeting with all sorts of adventures. He is without a friend, but he has learned to endure the sorrow of loneliness with composure. He is an ultra-modern boy. In Japan if a boy is mischievous, he is sure to be bad, but we still find this spirit of boyish innocent mischief in America today. The Americans are disorderly; I was amazed to see students in a university putting their feet up on their desks while listening to a lecture. But this spirit of nonchalance has its value, for it enables one to pass through suffering triumphantly. It seems to me that these people who have subjugated the immense continent of America are the world's prize lovers of fun. The Japanese are too fond of formality and ceremony and are too much inclined to put on airs of elegance. We must go back to the real spirit of the tea-ceremony, and find joy in even a sip of tea. I wish we might grasp and hold fast the spirit which is able to surmount every sorrow.

Livingstone had this spirit; he met suffering triumphantly. He trampled it under foot. Livingstone was not clever at preaching sermons. He chose the most difficult place in the world for his work, darkest Africa. He endured all sorts of suffering during the thirty years of his work; his friends said he was insane; he was separated by death from the wife he loved, but he kept on, pressing forward all the time. He was truly an incarnation of the spirit of Christ. He was thoroughly versed in geology, zoology, botany, and natural science and yet, with all his learning, he was so tender-hearted that he even loved the slaves. I like his virility, and his unflinching persistence during these thirty years. Young men in these modern times do not have the spirit even to bore a hole with an awl. I wish we might stir one another up to undertake the most difficult or disagreeable tasks; though others may dislike and avoid them, let us undertake them joyfully.

The Conquest of Death

The third significance of the Cross is the conquest of death. There are two meanings in death; the death of the body, physical death, and the death of the self. When we speak of death, we immediately think of physical death. Everyone is averse to death, but Christ sought out death and went his way to the Cross. When Jesus was on his second journey he said, "I will die in a short time," showing that he had included death in the program of his life. He also said that he would come to life again. When one can be as thorough-going as this, the sorrow of death evaporates. When we feel as though we would like to live forever, death becomes a sorrow, but when we put it in our program right from the start, it becomes a joy. Death becomes part of one's mission, one's allotted task.

Why did God create death? Death has first the meaning of elimination, and second, it provides a way that the self may prolong its existence and continue to grow. We look forward to death as the immigrants to Brazil look forward to life in the new country. In order that we might find in death the significance of a migration, Christ said that in his Father's

house there were many dwelling places. Again he spoke of death as entrusting his soul to God. When we meditate on this meaning of death, we are not saddened by the fact of it.

The Conquest of Self

The second meaning of death is the death of the self. We may understand the meaning of physical death very clearly but the death of self is much more difficult to grasp. We find these words, "having slain the enmity," in the sixteenth verse of the second chapter of Ephesians. Besides our physical selves we have certain instincts. Although from the standpoint of our conscious selves we desire to do those things which are good, yet we are also inclined to follow our instincts blindly, and the self is divided into two selves. One self wants to do the good, the other self, the self of instinct, which clings to the physical, longs to do evil. When we study Christ's prayer in Gethsemane, we find him abandoning himself utterly to God until his will is conformed exactly to the will of God. We find the two selves struggling in conflict in Paul, but in Christ the self of instinct had been put to death, and the self which consciously willed to suffer had conquered. The willingness to suffer shines out bright and clear. The prayer of Gethsemane reveals that although Christ felt an instinctive desire to live, still he would not selfishly ask for life. Christ prayed this prayer three times, and in the end he joyfully and resolutely cast aside the instinctive self, for the self of instinct has missed its way. It carries a load of sin, of lust, of dishonesty, of falsehood, of physical heredity and social heredity, which from God's viewpoint is enmity to him. All this Christ resolutely flung aside. This is the Cross. . . .

The Conquest of Sin

The fifth significance of the Cross is the forgiveness of sin. Up to this point we have been looking at the cross from the standpoint of mankind, but here we are looking at it from God's standpoint. Christ completed the burial of his self and then entered into the realm of God. Mankind, let us say, can progress to a certain point. In order that man may reach yet higher to another stage, it is necessary that God should say, "I will forgive everything which has gone before." This willingness on God's part is revealed in the Cross. Those who have come to Christ are saved by virtue of Christ's deeds and conquer death—the self, sorrow, suffering, all—in him. This is the forgiveness of sin. While it is a wonderful thing to feel that one is pardoned if one believes in Christ, it is not enough only to be saved oneself. It is not enough to repeat some such prayer as "Namu, Amida Butsu!" (Save us, O Buddha!)

Christianity is to believe in the Cross of Christ, and then suffering and sorrow, death, and even selfishness, are conquered. The race has been saved through this revelation of God-like love. Christ hung on the Cross, moreover, because as he said the sin of the human race was an offense to God. In this sense Christ's Cross is a Cross of victory. It is a Cross which causes man in death to be resurrected to God. The Cross is the crystallization of the love of God. If a character such as Christ's appears, man's failures can be forgiven. Looking at the Cross we can discern the great love of God to man. Though we dwell in prison, in some lonely colony of emigrants or in a world of sorrow through being misunderstood, we can trample under foot every difficulty, for we live in the conviction that God forgives. This is the acme of religion. This is the secret of Christianity.

PRAYER

O God of Heaven and Earth: We thank Thee that nineteen hundred years ago Thou didst reveal the perfect figure for mankind in the person of a carpenter. Through his courage, through his pity, his love of his fellowmen and his victory over suffering, sorrow, selfishness and sin, and death, Thou didst manifest to us the perfect man. Teach us that our own pathways of life must lead on into the Way of Christ who hung upon a Cross. Wavering, unwilling to make the choice, we hesitate. We humbly confess it. Cause the spirit of Christ to dwell in us, that we may kill selfishness, and be children of God who love our fellowmen. This we pray in the name of Christ. Amen.

Gerald Heard

(1889——)

BORN in England, Heard was educated at Sherborne and Cambridge. In 1929 he became editor of the *Realist*. His B.B.C. broadcasts on "This Surprising World" and "Science in the Making" received much attention in England.

Heard came to the United States in 1937, and in recent years has lived at Laguna Beach, California, where he is a participant in a "college of prayer," in which the devotional life is studied practically and theoretically. It is a modern experiment in the art of sainthood.

Of his recent books which discuss the meaning and value of prayer, *A Preface to Prayer* is one of the most stimulating. The following selection from that book is used by permission of Harper & Brothers. (Copyright 1944 by Harper & Brothers.)

WHAT IS PRAYER ACTUALLY DOING TO US?

From *A Preface to Prayer*

We can now trace the steps whereby man resolves the ego, the paralyzing awareness of himself, the illusion that he is the only real consciousness, and extends that free detached consciousness, which has become aware that it is not merely an integral part of its environment but is distinct even from its body—until it recognizes the Consciousness with Whom it must and can find its integration and to whom it indeed belongs.

The ego is a morbid hypertrophy. Man had to attain to that intensity of consciousness, the detached analytic awareness which is the distinctive mark of human consciousness. Then, having been freed from racial instinct and being able to distinguish between himself and his race life, his body, his fellows and his environment, he should have gone on. He should then have asked: Who is this self that stands back, disengaged, but with a wider range of interest than any animal can feel? What is this vast scene which interests, intrigues, awakes wonder, fear and admiration? It seems external and even alien to the individual but even the analytic reason finds strange "tallies" between rational thought and the material structure and movements of the universe. Mathematics, physics, aesthetics and a number of other studies of the outer world show that the mind, even when individualistic, is not a wholly detached onlooker at a universe with which it has no tie. The mind is a key fitting into and opening many of the locks of our environment.

Had men then pursued analytic thought undistractedly, it would have brought him round and up to a more penetrating and more embracing understanding. It was not reason, or even a too limited rationalism that brought him to the edge of the precipice. Had he followed pure intellectual analysis it would have brought him on to integral thought. So he would have discovered the SELF, standing behind the self, the universal consciousness embracing the individualized consciousness as the brain embraces the eye. What prevented that was not mental limitation but selfish willfullness—the determination to be separate and (as he falsely imagined) with his freedom from instinct and his power to cheat tradition, to see and shape things for him-

self alone. Here may lie the Fall, the basic "faulting" in man's nature when he chose to attempt to use the new freedom given him, not to help to create a higher order than nature's but to pursue a purely aberrant way of life for his personal interests and gain.

Mystics say that the wish to be an independent self is the primary and root sin. If this is so then we cannot, just by correcting our intellectual ignorance, reverse the fatal process and set human life again upon the tracks of the upward spiral. Human life went off and over the edge at the sharp curve, by an act, not of misapprehension but of intention; by a choice, a determination to be "on its own," and not to be "for others." The primary mistake was not ignorance but greed and the strangulated consciousness which we know as the ego must always increase its alienation from true life by adding to greed. Then the only way of reversing this fatal process is by starting where it begins and where it still has its growing point—at greed. The frame of reference in which the process of hatching can be seen, is then one in which liberation and enlightenment are recognized as the goals, which consciousness attains as it sloughs off the ego. Further, even when detached consciousness has become completely egoistic and self-engrossed, when the self has become a mirror and not a window, even then we need not despair. Redemption and contrition are the curative psychological conditions under which the evolutionary process, which has been delayed and perhaps even arrested and has partly miscarried, can be restored and carried on to the point which it should originally have attained. That, as we have seen, is the hopeful difference between physiological and psychological evolution. But the price is clear. Recovery is possible provided the psyche thinks it worth while to unravel all it has woven, to leave all that it has built up as its defense and meaning, and, after having been dismantled, to build up again from the point where the wrong departure was begun. This is as painful as rubbing back the circulation into a frostbitten limb. Forgiveness is a fact and it is re-creation, but the re-creative absolution cannot work until there has been confession (frank owning of the mistake), a complete willingness to make reparation and a complete humbleness to accept forgiveness.

If these postulates are accepted then it is possible to view schematically the evolutionary direction of consciousness, and how, even when the free and detached consciousness of man has become completely self-centred, the real process of life may be restored and the creative power once more permitted to fulfill its design in and for the individual.

The first thing we have to realize is that the ego is not a stable state of consciousness. It is a degenerative process. If it is not corrected, if this strangulated aspect of consciousness is not reassimilated into the entire consciousness, it will and must continue its departure, become completely alienated, and, cut off, finally, from all reality, must perish. So the first step toward convincing ourselves that the ego is a degenerating form of consciousness, is to trace its descent when left to itself. Most people, unless they see that the ego is a degeneracy and see where that degeneracy must end, cannot feel sufficient repugnance to attempt to reverse that process. Most of us feel our first desire to reform ourselves through catching a glimpse of what we shall become if we don't, rather than through a vision of what we may become if we do.

Egotism when it gets an opportunity to grow unchecked by inner or outer controls (as is seen in criminals and tyrants) goes through the three phases of greed, fear and ignorance, which three phases make the single process which we include under the one term—egotism. In these acute stages, where the man has no power to repress his own ego—for he has no vision, he develops overmastering greed, and society, instead of checking him, becomes his prey. The greed manifests itself in rapacity which ends in complete ruthlessness i.e., with the complete sundering of that sense of compassion which is the intuitive sense of kinship and union with life. But, as we see with tyrants and criminals, this stage of the condition of isolation—when the ego is enjoying itself—cannot be sustained, for the man is, in reality, psychically dying and beginning to mortify. So the pleasurable state turns into a painful one. The sense of separation has to degenerate into further separateness. Greed turns into fear, for fear is always fossilized greed. Then the place of rapacity and ruthlessness is taken by suspicion degenerating in turn into complete paranoia. Finally as fear creates an ultimate condition of complete ignorance—for fear whenever it is present cuts off detached knowledge and finally all sensation of anything outside its own distress—mania and hallucination intervene. Then in fully developed madness the splintered-off fragment of consciousness reaches an extremity of alienation where nothing can contact it and it is sundered from man and from nature. As we shall see later, then nothing can reach it but a state of consciousness as much plus as it is minus, and, we may add, it is not likely to meet that restorer in this life. Yet we must remember that this is the state into which nearly all tyrants degenerate because neither their fellows nor they themselves can check the ego which is strangling them. Most studies of fully developed criminality would seem to show that this may take place in the private lawbreaker as well, if he has enough energy and sufficient opportunity.

We can now consider these three phases of the ego—greed, fear and ignorance—as they appear in our less fully developed selves. As Bernard Hart has pointed out, the value of studying abnormal mental conditions is that in the insane we may see magnified the states which are latent or in embryo in ourselves.

It may, of course, be debated as to whether the vicious spiral starts with ignorance or with greed. As has been said above, if the will is the basic thing in life then greed came first and led to fear and so to ignorance. If understanding came first then the process would be the other way round. But this is after all a "hen and egg" discussion. What is clear is that this process of greed, fear, ignorance does repeat itself in coil after coil of descent and constriction and that, with ourselves and where we find ourselves, we can say that greed is the growing point leading to more fear and that in turn to more ignorance. For us, surely, the uncoiling of the spiral must start with greed, for we are conscious of greed and it is increased by a voluntary act on our part; it is the spear-point of the ego. We are helpless with fear and are generally unaware of our ignorance. We enjoy being greedy, we don't like being frightened, and we are indifferent to our ignorance.

As we shall see when looking through the chart of the process, there is another reason why we should and must start with the reduction of greed if we would tackle the ego. We cannot start straight away with fear—still less with ignorance —for far greater *vitality* is needed to transcend fear than to discard greed. To have found that life has a meaning, a complete co-ordinative purpose, that is enough to check greed, for greed is really a *pis aller*. We are pretentious because there is no one sufficiently noble to draw out our worship: bloated with means, because no adequate end has drawn them off: self-indulgent, because there seemed nothing more interesting, or indeed possible to do with the body. But to get rid of fear we have to have our vitality stepped up until we actually know that there is no chance or accident, anywhere, anyhow. It takes great vitality so to live, for no event can be let slide. If there are to be no unhappy accidents then neither must there be any happy accidents. If every event is to be taken fearlessly, because it is "meant" then I must never excuse a lack of unselfish awareness, with the defense, "it will be all the same in a few years." It won't. Everything that happens has to be treated as a plus or minus in the "score" of creative living.

It will be seen that if this is so, then a still further increase of vitality is needed if ignorance is to be dissolved. Greed exists mainly in the conscious mind, fear in the subconscious, but ignorance in the senses themselves. The body itself must be more than half redeemed by the new, nonegoistic spirit, before the ignorance begins to lift. We cannot have the knowledge that disproves fear until we have unhooded the "eye" which we hoodwink with greed. It will be seen, of course, that these three ethical steps are correlatable with the three steps of the spiritual life. In purgation the soul must fight greed. This is what it must do and what it dislikes doing, but until it has done so, the other states and graces must wait. Then, in proficiency, fear begins to disappear under a process which the self-consciousness knows is greater than itself. Here we have the dawn of what theologians call later Grace—in distinction from the "prevenient Grace" which makes possible the soul's start on recovery. In the "unitive life" ignorance is transcended and the process of deliverance is completed.

We must repeat, the entire process is a spiral: as one cycle of greed, fear and ignorance is completed, the next is begun. We have seen the descent. But the ascent also is a fact. Right knowledge (of the meaning of life) gives us the impetus to cast out greed: right devotion casts out fear and right apprehension casts out ignorance. There is of course always some faint realization of ignorance (if only the surprised disgust at the inadequacy of greed to satisfy) before greed will be attacked. Then when the freedom from the obvious ego has been attained the process continues on a higher level. Greed for spiritual gain is abandoned. This freedom from spiritual greed, we know from the lives of the saints, frees from fear of spiritual loss and in turn, this state of freedom from fear leads to the transcendence of spiritual ignorance. With the above introductory explanation the accompanying chart should be clear.

THE SOLUTION OF THE EGO

Greed is the growing point of the Ego and leads to more Fear, and that, in turn, leads to 'increasing Ignorance. The pattern is therefore a vicious spiral. The uncoiling of the spiral starts with Greed, because Ignorance is unconscious—we don't know that we don't see.

Night of Senses — PURGATION

The Act of Faith-knowledge:
There is no Doubt

Greed, in its three aspects, is resolved by what you Do.

1.	Pretentiousness—love of fame	—is cancelled by its negative, Anonymity.	(The mind is a lens not a mirror.)	Result: we have a Goal.
2.	Possessiveness —love of gain	—is cancelled by its negative, Frugality.	(The event is a step not a nest.)	Result: we find a Way.
3.	Addictiveness —love of pleasure	—is cancelled by its negative, Continence.	(The body is a vehicle not a bed.)	Result: we have a Vessel.

This stage is within our power, therefore we have to do it ourselves, to give earnest of our wish to be freed. We must voluntarily yield the pleasure-seeking side of the ego before we can be brought where we can be rid of the involuntary unpleasant side.

The vitality needed for this stage is greater than that needed for the life of indulgence but less than the next stage because here only atrophy is required—only giving up. It is painful to give up, but it does not require creative action. In the succeeding stage an attack has to be made on what the ego has built into itself, its involuntary nature.

Night of Faith — PROFICIENCY

The Act of Faith-knowledge:
There is no Chance or Accident

Fear, in its three aspects, is resolved by what you Know.

1.	Dread of Blame and Shame	is cancelled by its positive, Anonymity.	(We do not reflect ourselves but see beyond.)	Result: Guidance. **
2.	Dread of Lack and Loss	is cancelled by its positive, Frugality.	(In living more for God and less for self we find supply.)	Result: Providence.
3.	Dread of Weakness and Pain*	is cancelled by its positive, Continence.	(We become aware that once emptied we are filled.)	Result: Possessed.

Night of Spirit — UNION

The Act of Faith-knowledge:
There is no Time: There is no self

Ignorance, in its three aspects, is resolved by what you directly Experience and Assimilate.

1.	Unawareness of what the "I" is	is cancelled by awareness of the consciousness of the All ("The Atman is Brahman").
2.	Unawareness of what the environment is	is cancelled by awareness that the temporal is the eternal.
3.	Unawareness of what the body is	is cancelled by awareness that the body is the projection and shell of the spirit.

---

* When the attention to God can be entire then pain need not be experienced: cf. the total anaesthesia but complete consciousness experienced in hypnosis, which is simply total attention to something other than the pain.

** It is only at this second stage, when Fear is being dissolved, that Guidance, Providence and the real immediate awareness of God's indwelling Presence is possible. In stage one there is only a general sense of direction.

Christopher Dawson

(1889——)

Of contemporary Neo-Thomist thinkers, Dawson ranks high. Few interpreters of history seem to probe more deeply into the meaning of present world conditions. Educated at Winchester and Oxford, he joined the Roman Catholic Church in 1914. He was lecturer in the history of culture at University College, Exeter, 1930-36, and was the Forwood lecturer in the philosophy of religion at Liverpool in 1934. Since 1940 he has been editor of the *Dublin Review*.

His main interest as a student of history and sociology has been to interpret the relationship between religion and culture. He is a historian and a philosopher of history who attempts to analyze the problems of the modern world and to suggest some panaceas. This selection, which is the concluding chapter of *Religion and the Modern State*, is both an analysis of, and a remedy for, the contemporary dilemma of civilization. It is used by permission of Sheed & Ward.

[THE FUNCTION OF THE CHURCH]

From *Religion and the Modern State*

To the present age this conception of civilization as the social expression of Divine Law appears no more than a fantastic dream. Nevertheless a similar conception lies at the base of all the great historic civilizations of the world; and without it no civilization has ever maintained its stability and permanence. It was the ideal of Sumer and Egypt, of Confucian China and Vedic India and Zoroastrian Persia, of Greece and of Israel. But above all it found expression in the traditional culture of Christendom which more than any other civilization seemed capable of realizing the ideal which Plato had adumbrated in *The Laws*. The fundamental primacy of the soul, the subordination of the State and the whole temporal order to spiritual ends, and the conception of humanity as, in the words of St. Thomas, a great community or republic under the rule of God were formerly accepted as the unquestioned principles of the European social order.

After the Reformation, however, this was no longer the case. Not only was Christendom divided, but its energies were so absorbed in religious controversy that it was powerless to check the progressive secularization of culture. The sectarianizing of the Church led to the secularizing of the State and to the increasing subordination of human life to economic ends. By the eighteenth century the most active minds had turned away in disgust from orthodox Christianity to the new philosophy of liberal humanitarianism which seemed to offer a rational alternative to the religious faith on which Western civilization had been founded.

But this philosophy has proved incapable of providing an enduring basis for culture, and to-day its ideals are being swallowed up by the subversive forces which it has itself liberated. The idealism of the great Liberal thinkers ended in the materialism of the acquisitive capitalist society against which the conscience of the modern world is in revolt. What we are suffering from is the morbid growth of a selfish civilization which has no end beyond itself—a monstrous cancer that destroys the face of nature and eats into the heart of humanity. As in the days of ancient Rome, but on a far larger scale, men have made themselves the masters of this world, and find themselves left with nothing but their own sterile lusts. For this "leisure civilization" in which the people sit down to eat and to drink and rise up to play is the dark world which has turned its face from God and from which God's face is hidden. It is terrible not only on account of its emptiness but because there is a positive power of evil waiting to fill the void, like the unclean spirit in the parable that came out of the waste places into the empty soul. . . .

At the present day we feel this slavery in its economic rather than in its sensual aspect. Nevertheless the Kingdom of Mammon and the Kingdom of Belial are one, and it matters little which of them is the nominal master, so long as the world is theirs.

It is the horror of this empty and sterile world far more than any economic hardship or political injustice that is driving men to revolutionary action. Nevertheless the economic materialism of the Communist State is but the same thing in a different form. It may relieve the tension on the individual by merging his consciousness in that of the mass, but at the same time it shuts out all hope of escape and thus completes his imprisonment.

The only true solution must be a religious one which will restore man's spiritual freedom and liberate him from the world of darkness and the kingdom of death. And it is in this that the real answer of Christianity to the social needs of the modern world is to be found. It is often objected that Christianity fails to find a remedy for our modern difficulties and that it has no clear-cut solutions for the political and economic problems of the present age. And this is in a sense true, inasmuch as it is not the business of Christianity to solve political and social problems except in so far as these problems become moral or religious. There is no Christian economic system that can be compared with the Capitalist system or with Communist economics. There is not even a Christian State in the absolute sense, there are only States that are more or less Christian and all more or less different from one another.

This is not to say, as Protestants used to say, that religion is a matter for the individual conscience and not a social matter at all. Christianity is anti-individualist—as anti-individualist as Communism itself. It is not merely a social religion, it is in its very essence a society, and it is only in the life of this One Body that the individual human being can attain his true end. But this society is not a State or an economic organization. It is the society of the world to come, the Bride of God, and the mystical body of Christ. Consequently Christian sociology is also theology. It is the theory of this divine society through which and through which alone the true destiny of the human race can be realized. All other societies are partial and relative ones— they exist to serve the temporary needs of humanity and to organize and protect the natural foundations on which the supernatural structure of the one absolute society is built up. As soon as they make themselves the absolute ends of human life they become *counter-churches*, representative of that City of Man which to the end of time makes war upon the City of God.

Thus the essence of Christian sociology is its political relativity. A Christian State is not marked by any particular political institutions, it is a State that recognizes Christian ends, and consequently recognizes its own limitations. And it is the same with Christian economics. The characteristic Christian view of economics, that we find in the Gospels and in the lives and teachings of the saints, is that economics are of very little importance. Live from hand to mouth, don't bother about the future, leave these things to the Gentiles, who have nothing better to do. These are the strange paradoxical teachings of Jesus, which were strange enough in the days when they were spoken, but are doubly strange to us who live in a society and an age entirely dominated by "Gentile" standards. To-day the world outside—the Gentile world—is so convinced that economics are the only thing in the world that matter that it is difficult for Christians not to be affected by this prevalent mentality; so to-day we often find Christians, both Protestant and Catholic, who believe the evangelical maxims are inapplicable to our present circumstances and that we must first transform our economic system before we can begin to live a Christian life.

But this view seems to me to rest on a serious misunderstanding of Christian ethics and a fundamental misinterpretation of history. . . . The Church does not wait until she finds a sound foundation of natural truth and natural virtue and then proceed to cultivate supernatural faith and virtue. She sows her seed broadcast among publicans and harlots, in the corruption of the great Roman and Hellenistic cities, in the welter of barbarism and violence of the Dark Ages, in the slums of Manchester and New York. If there has ever been a class entirely deprived of the necessary economic foundations of a good life it was the refugees of the great Irish famine, who were forced to escape from the physical death of starvation into the living death of the awful nineteenth-century slums of Northern England and Eastern America. They were forced to live as animals are not allowed to live nowadays. Yet it is to these men that the Catholic Church in England and America owes its strength to-day: they, even more than the survivors of the age of persecution and the converts of the Oxford Movement, are the true heroes of the faith and the creators of modern English and American Catholicism.

Now, the Communist objects that this indifference to economics is responsible for the evils of Capitalism and that the passivity of Christianity makes the Church the accomplice of social injustice. But as a matter of historic fact, Capitalism did not grow up by accident out of Christian society and in an atmosphere of Christian ideas. It was the result of a new social initiative and a new economic theory of life which had revolted against the Catholic tradition. First came the new faith of Liberalism, and secondly the new works of Capitalism. Communists are ready enough to recognize that the Catholic attitude to economics is fatal to their economic view of life, but they do not see what is equally true, that Catholicism is also fatal to the capitalist attitude and that Capitalism could never have arisen if the revolt against Catholicism had not first occurred.

Both Communism and Capitalism agree in putting economic things first and in ordering society to an economic end, and consequently they are both far more opposed to Catholicism than they are to one another.

Moreover, they help one another by their very opposition, for it is difficult to revolt against Capitalism without becoming the ally of Communism, or to revolt against Communism without becoming the ally of Capitalism. The fact is that European civilization has been on the wrong road for so long that it is impossible to set it right by any obvious kind of political or economic reform. Protestantism, Liberalism and Communism are the three successive stages by which our civilization has passed from Catholicism to complete secularism. The first eliminated the Church, the second eliminated Christianity, and the third eliminates the human soul. We cannot have a Christian society or a Christian economic life until our civilization has recovered its moral conscience, its faith in God and its membership of the Church. That may well be as slow and painful a process as the conversion of the Roman Empire. Indeed, it may never come at all, for the more secular a society becomes the lower becomes its vitality, and a civilization that has completely lost its soul is dead and damned. . . .

This secularization of culture is seen in its most striking form in the Communist State, where alone as yet the elimination of religion has been carried to its logical conclusion. Nevertheless, the same tendency exists elsewhere; in fact, it permeates the whole outlook of modern civilization. The average man lives more "totally" in the State than in the past, and even when he is not consciously hostile to religion, he no longer conceives it as a vital activity which must hold the central place in human life and society. He regards it rather as a moral and emotional stimulus which is all very well for those who like that sort of thing, but which has nothing to do with the real business of life.

This attitude is so deeply rooted in modern culture that it is by no means easy for Christians to escape from its influence. It is not only among the indifferent that we find the idea that religion is a private matter: that for six days a week men should join together in the real business of secular life, and that on Sundays the religious-minded should go off each to his own church or chapel for their spiritual recreation in the same way as the non-religious go off to their golf course or their country cottage.

Such ideas are natural enough to those who believe that the State is the only and ultimate society and that the Church is simply a limited organization for religious worship and moral instruction. But for a Christian who believes in the existence of a divine and universal society all such ideas are blasphemy against Christ the King. The Church is the true world society, the goal of humanity, the only society that answers the universal needs of the human soul, and the one order that is destined to incorporate everything that is of permanent value in human history. It differs from all other societies in that it transcends the limitations of time and the barriers of race and secular culture. It unites the past in living communion with the present, so that we still draw our life from the undying spiritual activity of the faithful of every age. Moreover, it enters into every human culture without identifying itself with them. It inherits all the riches of the Gentiles, Greek philosophy and Roman law, Oriental mysticism and Western humanism, and incorporates them in its own tradition while preserving its spiritual identity and the transcendent authority of this supernatural mission. But while the Church is the bearer of life to humanity it depends on the individual members of the Church whether they will be merely the passive recipients of the gift or whether they will be the agents of its diffusion in the world. All the tragedies of Christendom arose from the failure of individual Christians to rise to their opportunities and to permeate their life and their social and intellectual culture by their faith. Wherever Christians cease to be active, when they rest in a passive acquiescence in what they have received, Christianity tends to lose contact with contemporary culture and the world drifts away from the Church.

The Christian tradition contains an infinite depth of spiritual resources, but these possibilities can only be realized and actualized in a Christian culture by the dynamic activity of individual Christians. The supreme example of this vital religious action is to be seen in the saints, in whom alone the potentialities of Christianity are fully realized. And their action is not limited, as we sometimes suppose, to the sphere of their supernatural virtues; it flows out into the world and shows itself in social activity and intellectual culture. Whenever there has been a great outburst of spiritual activity it has been followed by a fresh development of Catholic thought and culture. Thus, after the age of the Martyrs came the age of the Fathers, after the monks of the Desert came St. Basil and St. Augustine, after St. Bernard and St. Francis came St. Bonaventure and St. Thomas.

Now, it is not possible for all men to be saints, or thinkers, or social leaders, but all can try to live as Christians and to think as Christians. . . .

Never, perhaps, in the whole of its history has the People of God seemed weaker and more scattered, and more at the mercy of its enemies than it is to-day. Yet this is no reason for us to despair. The Christian law of progress is the very reverse of that of the world. When the Church possesses all the marks of external power and success, then is its hour of danger; and when it seems that no human power can save it, the time of its deliverance is at hand. Christianity began with a startling failure, and the sign in which it conquered was the Cross on which its Founder was executed. The more persecution and unpopularity strip off the coating of human prestige that has gathered round the Church in the days of its temporal prosperity, the more room will there be for the development of its inherent spiritual vitality.

And while the City of God is stronger than it appears to be, the city of man is weaker. The forces that appear to make human civilization so irresistible—its wealth, its economic organization, and its military power—are essentially hollow, and crumble to dust as soon as the human purpose that animates them loses its strength. The real forces that rule the world are spiritual ones, and every empire and civilization waits for the hour when the sentence of the watchers goes forth and its kingdom is numbered and finished. The spirit of life goes out of its social traditions and institutions and a new age is begun. Thus from age to age the divine purpose towards the human race is carried on, and even the civilization which appears to resist that purpose is the unwilling servant of a power that it does not recognize.

To-day the world is ripe for renewal. The liberal and humanitarian ideals that inspired the civilization of the last two centuries are dead or dying and there is nothing left to take their place. The process of secularization has worked itself out to its logical conclusions in Communism and it can go no further. But this process of secularization in Western culture is but a moment in the general movement of history and not its goal, as Marxism believes. It is a negation that ultimately annuls itself, and gives place by the dialectic of history to a principle of a new order. On the other hand, it is of the very nature of Christianity to provide new solutions for new situations. It is not bounded like Marxism by the narrow horizon of historical materialism, but is open to the breath of the spirit that renews the face of the world.

Thus we may expect not merely the passing of the Liberal-capitalist order of the nineteenth century, but the End of the Age; a turning-point in world history which will alter the whole character of civilization by a change in its fundamental direction: a turning of the human mind from the circumference to the centre, from the emptiness of modern civilization and progress to the vision of spiritual reality which stands all the time looking down on our ephemeral activities like the snow mountains above the jazz and gigolos of a jerry-built hotel.

If this is so, it is clear that the real social mission of Christians is to be the pioneers in this true movement of world revolution: The spiritual order transcends the order of culture, and it has its own organs and instruments in the world which are not necessarily the ones that are highest in the scale of culture, or the most important from a human point of view. For in the words of St. Paul: "God has chosen the foolish things of the world that He may confound the wise, and He has chosen the weak things of the world that He may confound the strong. And the base things of the world and the things that are despised has God chosen, and the things that are not, that He might bring to nought the things that are; that no flesh should glory in His presence."

"For the foolishness of God is wiser than men, and the weakness of God is stronger than men."

Georgia Harkness

(1891——)

RECOGNIZED as one of the leading women theologians of this generation—and also gifted as a poet—Georgia Harkness has covered a wide gamut of religious themes in her writing. In recent years four of her books have been particularly related to religious experience: *Holy Flame, The Glory of God, Religious Living,* and *The Dark Night of the Soul.* This last deals carefully with the experiences of the saints, especially with the type of mystical devotion which wanes occasionally into despair, frustration, and spiritual desolation. Although this book takes its theme from John of the Cross, it radiates to many other saints who have shared this common experience.

Georgia Harkness was educated at Cornell, Boston, Yale, Harvard, and Union Theological Seminary. After teaching at Boston, Elmira, and Mount Holyoke, she became professor of applied theology at Garrett Biblical Institute in 1939. She has been active in the ecumenical movement, and has been a delegate to several interfaith conferences.

This selection from *Religious Living,* one of the Hazen books on religion, is used here by permission of the Association Press.

HOW TO PRAY

From *Religious Living*

*A*ll sincere Christians at times feel like saying as the disciples did to Jesus, Lord teach us to pray. It is so difficult, yet so vital, an art that one feels baffled before it.

Like any other art, it is impossible to reduce it to rules. To do so would make it a technique and not an art. But there are certain principles to observe.

First, *prayer must be centered upon God.* The Lord's prayer begins with an act of adoration. The psalmist wrote, "I have set the Lord always before me." Anyone who does not do this is not praying—he is simply rearranging his own thoughts. But it is not enough to begin with some formula of adoration or thanksgiving. You must feel your own littleness before God's greatness: you must genuinely feel grateful and receptive. To induce this mood, it is helpful to think over your blessings and your own shortcomings. Then self-searching and petition fall into their rightful places, and you can ask God to help you in anything of importance to you. It does not matter greatly about the sequence or

form in which the words shape themselves. The less you think about that, the better. But it matters much that God be put foremost in your attitudes.

Second, *prayer must be natural.* This means that some people pray best in forms familiar through long experience and others through petitions framed anew on each occasion. You have to discover in which way you can do it most readily. Variation is helpful—pray sometimes by using memorized prayers, sometimes thoughtfully read a prayer from some good collection, sometimes shape your own. No prayer made up by another will touch your life in everything, for no one else has exactly your experience and your needs. Yet the experience of others—particularly in the great prayers used by the Church for centuries —will help you as your own grows. You need especially to be on guard lest prayer become merely a mechanical repetition of words. The moment you find this happening, change to some other form.

Third, *prayer must be unhurried.* This does not mean that it must be long drawn out. Most of the great Christians I know are very busy people. There is danger of being so busy even about good works that God gets pushed out. To keep God at the center of one's life requires frequent renewal of power through prayer. But such renewal is not measured by the amount of time it takes, rather by the degree to which one is able even for a short time to have relaxed and unhurried communion with God. One can pray inwardly at any time and anywhere—in a subway or on an athletic field. But one prays best either alone or with understanding friends. To avoid neglecting to pray, it is best to have a time-habit and a place-habit. This is so important that it is worth great effort, in spite of the hurry of life and our lack of privacy.

Fourth, *prayer must be intellectually sincere*. It is a mistake to try to pray to a God you think does not exist, or to pray for something you think cannot possibly happen. This does not mean you should stop praying if you have some doubts. Often, to pray is the best way to get the personal depth of religious insight before which your doubts will flee away. But if prayer seems a "hollow mockery," do not go on letting it mock you. Get a book and read what some philosopher of religion whom you trust says about it. Decide whether you agree with him. Then pray according to whatever framework of belief seems to you intellectually satisfying. Do *not* try to philosophize while you are praying, for you cannot have a spiritually receptive and an intellectually analytical attitude at the same time. There is need for analysis before and after, but to try to analyze while you are praying is ruinous. Stop praying infantile prayers addressed to an elderly gentleman in the sky if you have been doing so, and pray with emotional and intellectual maturity.

Fifth, *prayer must combine alertness with passivity*. While you are praying, you ought not to work too hard at it. To do so is to screw yourself into a tension which prevents being receptive—and receptivity is of the essence of prayer. But neither ought you to relax so much that you fall asleep, or into a daydream. Praying is not *strenuous*, but it is *serious* business.

Sixth, *prayer must be accompanied by active effort*. It is a very irreligious attitude to pray and expect God to do all the work. There may be situations, as in serious illness, when there is nothing more you can do. As such times, to pray and then in calmness to leave the outcome to God is the best procedure. But almost always you can do something. In illness, to pray and not to give adequate medical care would be unwise and unethical. The same holds everywhere else. You need to pray for wisdom and strength for your own remaking, and then set yourself to it. You need to pray for others and set yourself to helping them. Some people do not believe in praying for other people, but I think it is required of us both for what it may lead to in itself and as a stimulus to our service.

Finally, *prayer must be based on intelligent trust*. This means that you ought not to pray for things which God cannot give you without upsetting his laws or doing contradictory things. This does not forbid you to pray for essential material things, for "daily bread" is an important part of life. But it will not come to you miraculously, and you should not expect it to. It is far more important to pray for strength and courage to accept deprivation with spirit undaunted than to pray for the specific things you want. The greatest prayer ever uttered was one spoken in a garden, "nevertheless not my will, but Thine, be done." Every petition should be made in this spirit. What matters supremely in prayer is that God be exalted and that you be brought to a life-transforming willingness to follow his way.

Reinhold Niebuhr

(1892——)

SINCE 1928 Niebuhr has been a professor at Union Theological Seminary. Few voices in the contemporary theological world have been more stimulating. As a right-wing theologian—a Neosupernaturalist—and a left-wing advocate of social-ethical theories, he has commanded attention from students of many theological viewpoints. Before coming to Union he was a pastor in Detroit, Michigan, 1915-28. His ordination is in the Evangelical Synod of North America. He was educated at Elmhurst College, Eden Theological Seminary, and Yale Divinity School. He gave the "Gifford Lectures," published as *The Nature and Destiny of Man.*

The selection from *Beyond Tragedy*, a book of sermonic essays, is used by permission of Charles Scribner's Sons. (Copyright 1937 by Charles Scribner's Sons.)

THE KINGDOM NOT OF THIS WORLD

From *Beyond Tragedy*

The Fourth Evangelist is not an historian but an interpreter of history. His record of the scene of Jesus before Pilate may therefore not be literal history. It is nevertheless a profoundly true drama. It is, in fact, an ageless drama, to which belong as individual acts the records of prophets standing before kings, and appealing to a higher judgment than that by which the king judges them. Jesus before Pilate is the climax of this drama. Here the incarnation of the Judge of the world is judged by the world—and judges it.

We may imagine Pilate the typical wielder of political power. Toward Jesus he had the attitude of mingled admiration and contempt which the man of power usually displays toward the power of pure goodness. It represents a majesty beyond his comprehension and yet a weakness in the domain in which he is master. Pilate's chief interest in Jesus was to determine whether his type of kingship represented a real threat to the Roman imperium. The chief priests had insisted that it did. In their indictments of Jesus before the Jewish court they had emphasised the religious implications of the Messianic idea and had accused him of blasphemy. Before the Roman court they emphasised the political implications of the Messianic idea (which Jesus had, incidentally, specifically disavowed) and accused him of treason. What Pilate wanted to know was whether this man before him was really a harmless religious dreamer and prophet or a dangerous insurrectionist. It may be observed in passing that the judgments of worldly courts are always weighted by that consideration. The most dangerous criminal is always the person who threatens the system which maintains the court itself. No court is ever impartial when questions of its own existence are involved, not even when, as in modern government, the judicial function is separated from executive power. This was the significance of his question: "Art thou the king of the Jews?"

I

Jesus' answer must have quieted Pilate's fears immediately: "My Kingdom is not of this world." With that assurance Pilate relaxed. All the Pilates and Cæsars of the world have been relieved by similar assurances. The Kingdom of God, the kingdom of truth, is not of this world.

Therefore the kingdoms of the world need not fear it. Its servants do not fight. They do not set power against power. The kingdoms of the world fear only power. Religion is, after all, a very innocuous vagary. It prompts men to dream of another world in which the injustices of this world will be righted and the sorrows of this world will be turned into joy. Why should not such dreams and such hopes persuade men to suffer present pains with patience? That question has suggested itself to every man of power through the ages. By it he is tempted to offer the prophet and priest of religion a position of auxiliary ruler in his kingdom. We know from history how frequently the offer is accepted.

Even when the prophet or priest is not consciously drawn into partnership with the ruler, the kingdom of which he is the messenger may support the kingdoms of the world. The sanctuary which the priest builds may be a thing of beauty to which men periodically escape from an ugly world, securing just enough relief from oppression to be beguiled from their rebellion against evil. The kingdom of righteousness of which the prophet speaks tempts men to feed on hopes when they are starved by realities. How could the Negroes of the days of slavery have borne their oppression, if they had not been able to sing:

When I go to heaven, I'll put on my shoes
And I'll walk all over God's heaven?

Oswald Spengler, the most brilliant apostle of political reaction in the modern day, has lifted this possible use of religion into a perfect system. A good priest, in his view, is one who persuades men that their hopes and dreams of perfection are not for this world. A bad priest is one who transmutes religious hopes into political discontent. Communism and every other political protest against injustice is thus, in his view, the illegitimate offspring of Christian perfectionism. Let Pilate be assured. Let the fears of Cæsar be dispelled. The Lord has said "My Kingdom is not of this world." Furthermore he has instructed his disciples to "Render unto Cæsar the things that are Cæsar's." Upon that assurance Pilate is able to report, "I find no fault in him"; and all who believe that religion is relevant to the world must be a little embarrassed by Pilate's acquittal. If Jesus' Kingdom does not threaten Pilate's kingdom any more than Pilate assumes, how can it overcome the injustice of Pilate's kingdom? How can it speak a word of legitimate hope to the victims of oppressive power?

II

Before we accept Pilate's complacency as justified it would be well to inquire further into the nature of this kingdom which is not of this world. Jesus defined it as a kingdom of truth: "To this end was I born, and for this cause came I into the world that I should bear witness unto the truth." The Johannine Gospel, speaking particulraly to the Greek world, makes much of the idea of truth and of light as the meaning of the Incarnation. It does not, however, regard the truth as some simple proposition which the natural reason of man can grasp. The truth is rather a revelation of the fundamental pattern of life which sin has obscured and which Christ restores. The Logos is the very pattern of the world. "All things were made by him; and without him was not anything made that was made." The world is in darkness of sin and does not comprehend this light. The pattern of life comes unto his own but his own receive him not. Yet as many as receive him may become sons of God.

The world is, in other words, alienated from its true character. Men do not know their true relation to God. Therefore they make themselves God and their minds are darkened by the confusion caused by this self-glorification. The kingdom of truth is consequently not the kingdom of some other world. It is the picture of what this world ought to be. This kingdom is thus not of this world, inasfar as the world is constantly denying the fundamental laws of human existence. Yet it is of this world. It is not some realm of eternal perfection which has nothing to do with historical existence. It constantly impinges upon man's every decision and is involved in every action.

It is important to recognise that the Kingdom of God, according to the biblical conception, is never purely an other-worldly perfection, not even when it is interpreted in a gospel which is directed primarily to the Greek world. The Christian is taught to pray constantly "Thy Kingdom come." The hope of this prayer, when vital, is a constant pressure upon the conscience of man in every action.

The kingdom which is not of this world is thus in this world, through man and in man, who is in this world and yet not altogether of this world. Man is not of this world in the sense that he can never rest complacently in the sinful standards which are normative in the world. He may be selfish but he cannot accept selfishness as the standard of conduct. He may be greedy but he knows that greed is wrong. Even when his actions do not conform to his ideals he cannot dismiss his ideals as irrelevant. Modern as well as ancient theologies which emphasise the total depravity of man fail to do justice to the difference between human ideals and human actions. The action may always be sinful and it stands under the criticism of the ideal. Every ideal of justice may be coloured by interest when it is applied to situations in which men are themselves involved; but they cannot consciously construct ideals of justice to conform to their interests. Every corruption of justice can exist only by borrowing from, and pretending to be, a more disinterested justice than it is. This vision of perfection is really what is intended in the stoic conception of the golden age and the Christian idea of perfection before the Fall. To relegate it to an historical period before an historical Fall is to take religious myths too literally and become confused by their historical symbols.

The kingdom which is not of this world is always in this world in man's uneasy conscience. Even in Plato, who is more inclined than biblical thought to relegate perfection to another world, the kingdom which is not of this world is never wholly irrelevant to human actions. At the close of the fourth book of his *Republic* Plato describes the perfect justice to which the wise man will devote himself, and discusses its relation to historical actualities in a dialogue between Socrates and Glaucon:

"To this nobler purpose the man of understanding will devote the energies of his life. He will not allow himself to be dazzled by the foolish applause of this world and heap up riches to his own harm. He will look to the city that is within him and see that no disorder occur there. . . ."

"Then if that is his motive," said Glaucon, "he will not be a statesman. By the dog of Egypt he will. In the city which is his own he certainly will, though in the land of his birth perhaps not.

"I understand," said Glaucon, "you mean that he will be a statesman in the city of which we are the founders and which exists in idea only, for I do not believe that there is such a one anywhere on earth."

"In heaven," I replied, "there is laid up a pattern of it methinks which he who so desires may behold and, beholding, may set his house in order. But whether such a one exists or ever will exist is no matter. For he will live after the manner of that city and have nothing to do with any other."

One is reminded, by this dialogue, of Jesus' words to his disciples when they joyfully reported that "even the devils are subject unto us through thy name." He answered: "Rejoice not, that the devils are subject unto you; but rather rejoice, because your names are written in heaven." There is, in other words, a particular power in the kingdom not of this world over this world, precisely because it does not ask to have its standards validated by worldly success. Its servants may not fight Pilate but they are able to defy Pilate wtih a cool courage which is not derived from this world.

There is this difference, however, between Plato's and the gospel's conception of the relation of the kingdom not of this world to the world: Plato's is a very individualistic conception. "Whether such a one exists *or ever will exist* is no matter," he declares. He is content to let the individual conscience defy the world without reference to the possible triumph of righteousness in the world. The biblical conception of the Kingdom of God is of an ultimate triumph in, or at least at the end of, history. For the Greek, perfection remains in heaven, because history is by its very character of temporality a corruption of it. In the biblical conception the sin of the world is not due to its temporal character but to man's rebellion against God. Christianity is therefore less confident than Plato that the wise man will obey the vision of perfection which intrigues him; but it is more confident that God will be able to overrule the sinfulness of man.

III

Even though we recognise the relevance of the Kingdom of God to every thought and action in the world, we have not yet faced the significance of Pilate's contemptuous sneer, "What is truth?" What indeed is truth or justice, no matter how high our conceptions may be in the abstract, when each man and nation is able to interpret and to corrupt the truth for its and for his purposes? That sneer comes significantly from a man of power and has particular significance in our own day. For we are living in a day in which new national religions are explicitly disavowing the universal validity of truth. Each nation fashions truth unashamedly in its own interest. Modern fascism thus explicitly affirms the relativity of truth which is implicitly involved in all human actions. If we mean by "the world" only the realm of actuality, the Kingdom of God is quite obviously not in it. It may be in the conscience of man but not in his action. The same man who dreams of an ideal justice or a perfect love acts according to his own interests when he ceases to contemplate and engages in action.

No deed is all its thought had been,
No will but feels the fleshly screen,

in the words of Robert Browning.

It is this fact which persuades certain types of Continental theology to regard the Kingdom of God as revealed in the Gospels as only a principle of judgment upon the world and not as a criterion of judgment in the world. In their view the world continues to live by purely egotistic standards and in the inevitable conflict of interests which results from such behaviour. Even the Christian must submit to these standards. If he succeeds in forgiving an enemy or loving a neighbour he must not expect such actions to change the quality of the world's life. Actions inspired by the truth of the Kingdom of God are merely symbols of judgment and hope set in a world which is destroying itself by its sin.

Perverse as such conceptions are, they have, at least, the merit of calling attention to the fact that the sinful world is not as easily transmuted into the Kingdom of God as modern theology had supposed. In one sense the Kingdom of God remains outside the world. The same Pilate who found no fault in Jesus became nevertheless his executioner. The power of Rome felt itself for the moment secure against the threat of this kingdom. But the power of the priests was not secure and they therefore insisted on his destruction. The fact that Pilate, the symbol of power, became the unwilling tool of the priests, is an instructive bit of history. The ambitions of the powerful are never quite as inimical to the Kingdom as the confusion of priests and prophets who are less cynical and more fanatical than Pilate, having mixed truth with sin in a more confusing mixture. Whether it is the state or the church through which we act, the Lord is crucified afresh in every human action.

Nevertheless the kingdom of truth constantly enters the world. And its entrance descends beyond conscience into action. The word is made flesh. The spiritual descendants of Pilate in Germany today are facing a determined band of spiritual sons of the Christ, and the former have found no way of quieting the defiance of the latter by their use of power. No threats of coercion and imprisonment have been able to change the actions of men whose primary loyalty is to God and not to some prince of the world. Their slogan, "We must obey God rather than man," has become a word of nemesis for those who sought to make power the sole source of truth.

The fact that it is the church in modern Germany which defies the state, while many apostles of a universal culture and a universal science have capitulated, is most instructive in regard to the relation of the kingdom not of this world to this world. The university was the pride of Germany; and the German church was more or less moribund. Yet the former has allowed its universal culture to be corrupted by the state while the latter has fought valiantly against such corruption. The culture of the university sought universal truth through the genius of the wise man; and forgot that the wise man is also a sinner, whose interest, passion and cowardice may corrupt the truth. The kingdom of truth which rests upon human wisdom is obviously of this world; so much so that the world may conquer it and reduce its pride to humiliation.

The only kingdom which can defy and conquer the world is one which is not of this world. This conquest is not only an ultimate possibility but a constant and immediate one. In every moment of existence those "who are of the truth" hear the Christ's voice, warning, admonishing and guiding them in their actions. The real truth condemns their lies; pure justice indicts their injustice; the law of love reveals their selfishness; and the vision of God reveals their true centre and source of existence. They may continue to be disobedient to the heavenly vision; but they can never be as they have been.

The kingdom which is not of this world is thus a more dangerous peril to the kingdoms of the world than any competing worldly kingdom. One nation may be destroyed by another more powerful nation. But civilisations and cultures in their larger historical development are never destroyed by external enemies without first having destroyed themselves. The force of their destruction is not only their own violation of the law of life but the loss of their moral authority under the challenge of those who speak against their power in the name of the Kingdom of God. Pure power cannot maintain itself. It must have some measure of moral respect. It must be admitted that pure conscience seldom defeats an unjust social system. Those who speak against its injustice are primarily its victims. Yet slavery would have persisted if only the slaves had recognised its oppression. A moral element thus enters into every successful challenge of Cæsar's authority.

It is hardly necessary to draw the conclusion from this fact that those who draw their inspiration from Christ's Kingdom must limit themselves to purely moral weapons in contending against historic injustice. Conscience may prompt the challenge of power by power, though it must recognise that the new justice, which emerges from the resulting conflict, will be less than the perfect justice in the name of which it initiated the conflict. The Kingdom of God is relevant to every moment of history as an ideal possibility and as a principle of judgment upon present realities. Sometimes it must be obeyed in defiance of the world, though such obedience means crucifixion and martyrdom. Sometimes courageous obedience forces the evil of the world to yield, thus making a new and higher justice in history possible. Sometimes the law of the Kingdom must be mixed with the forces of nature which operate in the world, to effect at least a partial mitigation of oppression. Martyrs, prophets and statesmen may each in his own way be servants of the Kingdom. Without the martyr we might live under the illusion that the kingdom of

Cæsar is the Kingdom of Christ in embryo and forget that there is a fundamental contradiction between the two kingdoms. Without the successful prophet, whose moral indictments effect actual changes in the world, we might forget that each moment of human history faces actual and realisable higher possibilities.

Without the statesman, who uses power to correct the injustices of power, we might allow the vision of the Kingdom of Christ to become a luxury of those who can afford to acquiesce in present injustice because they do not suffer from it.

Friedrich Heiler

(1892——)

REARED as a Roman Catholic, and by temperament a person of deep piety, Heiler became an advocate of the Church Universal. He was educated at Munich University, where he taught the history and philosophy of religion until his call to Marburg University in 1920. For years in Marburg he conducted worship services Saturday evenings in an ancient chapel, where he put into effect his liturgical patterns.

His writings are many. His chief contribution, *Prayer (Das Gebet)*, is the only one translated into English. One of the most profound and comprehensive of modern books on the meaning of sainthood, it has keen insight into the psychology and history of religion. The following selection from this work, which is translated by Samuel McComb and J. Edgar Park, is used by permission of Oxford University Press.

THE ESSENCE OF PRAYER

From *Prayer*

Prayer appears in history in an astonishing multiplicity of forms; as the calm collectedness of a devout individual soul, and as the ceremonial liturgy of a great congregation; as an original creation of a religious genius, and as an imitation on the part of a simple, average religious person; as the spontaneous expression of upspringing religious experiences, and as the mechanical recitation of an incomprehensible formula; as bliss and ecstasy of heart, and as painful fulfilment of the law; as the involuntary discharge of an overwhelming emotion, and as the voluntary concentration on a religious object; as loud shouting and crying, and as still, silent absorption; as artistic poetry, and as stammering speech; as the flight of the spirit to the supreme Light, and as a cry out of the deep distress of the heart; as joyous thanksgiving and ecstatic praise, and as humble supplication for forgiveness and compassion; as a childlike entreaty for life, health, and happiness, and as an earnest desire for power in the moral struggle of existence; as a simple petition for daily bread, and as an all-consuming yearning for God Himself; as a selfish wish, and as an unselfish solicitude for a brother; as wild cursing and vengeful thirst, and as heroic intercession for personal enemies and persecutors; as a stormy clamour and demand, and as joyful renunciation and holy serenity; as a desire to change God's will and make it chime with our petty wishes, and as a self-forgetting vision of and surrender to the Highest Good; as the timid entreaty of the sinner before a stern judge, and as the trustful talk of a child with a kind father; as swelling phrases of politeness and flattery before an unapproachable King, and as a free outpouring in the presence of a friend who cares; as the humble petition of a servant to a powerful master, and as the ecstatic converse of the bride with the heavenly Bridegroom.

In considering these varied contrasts and in the survey of the different leading types of prayer, the problem emerges: what is common to all these diverse kinds of prayer, what underlies all these phenomenal forms, in a word, what is the essence of prayer? The answer to this question is not easy. There is the danger of fundamentally misinterpreting prayer by making its essence an empty abstraction. If we would understand the essence of prayer we must look attentively at those types in which we see it as the naïve, spontaneous utterance of the soul; we must, therefore, separate the primary types from the secondary. This separation is easily effected. The primary types which cannot be confounded with the others are these:—the naïve prayer of primitive man, the devotional life of men of religious genius, the prayers of great men, the common prayer of public worship in so far as it has not hardened into a stiff, sacrosanct institution. In all these instances prayer appears as a purely psychical fact, the immediate expression of an original and profound experience of the soul. It bursts forth with innate energy. Very different are the secondary types. They are no longer an original, personal experience, but an imitation or a congealment of such a living experience. The personal prayer of the average religious man is a more or less true reflection of the original experience of another; it remains inferior to the ideal model in power, depth, and vitality. The philosophical idea of prayer is a cold abstraction built up in harmony with metaphysical and ethical standards; by it living prayer is subjected to an alien law, to the principles of philosophy, and is transformed and revised in accordance with this law. The product of this amendment is no longer real prayer, but its shadow, an artificial, dead simulacrum of it. The ritual forms of prayer, the cultual hymn, liturgical common prayer as an institution of the cultus, all these types are phenomena of congelation in which the upspringing personal life has been transmuted into objective, impersonal forms and rules. The penetration into their inner meaning may indeed give rise in devout, susceptible souls to new experiences of prayer, their recitation in public or private worship may take place in a devotional mood, but they themselves are not the direct expression of a personal experience. The essential features of prayer are never visible in these disintegrated, dead, secondary forms, but only in unadulterated, simple prayer as it lives in unsophisticated, primitive human beings and in outstanding men of creative genius. In determining the essence of prayer, therefore, we must fix our attention exclusively on prayer in its primitive simplicity. Only then can we take into consideration the secondary types and inquire how far the essence of prayer is expressed by them.

To answer our question, we must first of all discover the essential motive of prayer, its common psychological root. What moves men to pray? What do men seek when they pray? Da Costa Guimaraens, a French psychologist, defined it thus: "To pray means to satisfy a psychical need." The definition is superficial and is, moreover, insipidly formulated, but it is on the track of a correct psychological motivation. Prayer is the expression of a primitive impulsion to a higher, richer, intenser life. Whatever may be the burden of the prayer, to whatever realm of values it may belong, whether to the eudaemonistic, the ethical, or the purely religious realm—it is always a great longing for life, for a more potent, a purer, a more blessed life. "When I seek Thee, my God," prays Augustine, "I seek a blessed life." His words uncover the psychical root of all prayer. The hungry pygmy who begs for food, the entranced mystic, absorbed in the greatness and beauty of the infinite God, the guilt-oppressed Christian who prays for forgiveness of sins and assurance of salvation —all are seeking life; they seek a confirmation and an enrichment of their realization of life. Even the Buddhist beggar-monk, who by meditation works himself up into a state of perfect indifference, seeks in the denial of life to attain a higher and purer life.

The effort to fortify, to reinforce, to enhance one's life is the motive of all prayer. But the discovery of the deepest root of prayer does not disclose its peculiar essence. In order to get to the bottom of this, we should not ask for the psychological motive of prayer; we must rather make clear the religious ideas of him who prays in simplicity, we must grasp his inner attitude and spiritual aim, the intellectual presuppositions which underlie prayer as a psychical experience. What does the simple, devout person, undisturbed by reflection, think when he prays? He believes that he speaks with a God, immediately present and personal, has intercourse with Him, that there is between them a vital and spiritual commerce. There are three elements which form the inner structure of the prayer-experience; faith in a living personal God, faith in His real, immediate presence, and a realistic fellowship into which man enters with a God conceived as present.

Every prayer is a turning of man to another Being to whom he inwardly opens his heart; it is the speech of an "I" to a "Thou." This "Thou," this other with whom the devout person comes into relation, in whose presence he stands as he prays, is no human being but a supersensuous, superhuman Being on whom he feels himself dependent, yet a being who plainly wears the features of a human personality, with thought, will, feeling, self-consciousness. "Prayer," says Tylor, "is the address of a personal spirit to a personal spirit." Belief in the personality of God is the necessary presupposition, the fundamental condition of all prayer. The anthropomorphism which is always found in primitive prayer and which often appears in the prayer of outstanding religious personalities, the prophets among them, is a coarsening and materializing of this belief in God's personality; it does not, however, belong to the essence of prayer as faith does. But wherever the vital conception of the divine personality grows dim, where, as in the philosophical ideal or in pantheistic mysticism, it passes over into the "One and All," genuine prayer dissolves and becomes purely contemplative absorption and adoration.

The man who prays feels himself very close to this personal God. Primitive man believes that God dwells in a visible place; to this place he hastens when he would pray, or he turns his eyes and hands towards it. The religious genius experiences the divine presence in the stillness of his own heart, in the deepest recesses of his soul. But it is always the reverential and trustful consciousness of the living presence of God, which is the keynote of the genuine prayer-experience. It is true that the God to whom the worshipper cries transcends all material things—and yet the pious man feels His nearness with an assurance as undoubted as though a living man stood before him.

Belief in God's personality and the assurance of His presence are the two presuppositions of prayer. But prayer itself is no mere belief in the reality of a personal God—such a belief underlies even a theistic metaphysic;—nor is it a mere experience of His presence—for this is the accompaniment of the entire life and thought of the great men of religion. Prayer is rather a living relation of man to God, a direct and inner contact, a refuge, a mutual intercourse, a conversation, spiritual commerce, an association, a fellowship, a communion, a converse, a one-ness, a union of an "I" and a "Thou." Only an accumulation of these synonyms which human speech employs to make clear the innermost relations of man to man, can give an appropriate picture of the realistic power and vitality of that relation into which the praying man enters with God. Since prayer displays a communion, a conversation between an "I" and a "Thou," it is a social phenomenon. The relation to God of him who prays always reflects an earthly social relation: that of servant or child or friend or bride. In the praying of primitive man, as in the devoutness of creative religious personalities, the religious bond is conceived after the analogy of human society. It is just this earthly social element that lends to natural prayer its dramatic vivacity. Wherever, as with many mystics, the religious relation no longer exhibits an analogy to social relations, prayer passes over from a real relation of communion to mere contemplation and adoration.

As anthropomorphism is only a crude form of belief in the personality of God, so belief in the real influence of prayer on the divine will, in the winning over of God to our side as it appears most clearly in primitive and prophetic prayer, is only a crude form of immediate, vital, and dynamic intercourse with God. It does not belong to the essence of prayer. The miracle of prayer does not lie in the accomplishment of the prayer, in the influence of man on God, but in the mysterious contact which comes to pass between the finite and the infinite Spirits. It is by this very fact that prayer is a genuine fellowship of man with God, that it is something not merely psychological, but transcendental and metaphysical, or as Tholuck has expressed it, "no mere earthly power but a power which reaches to the heavens." In the words of Söderblom: "in the depths of our inner life we have not a mere echo of our own voice, of our own being, resounding from the dark depths of personality, but a reality higher and greater than our own, which we can adore and in which we can trust."

Prayer is, therefore, a living communion of the religious man with God, conceived as personal and present in experience, a communion which reflects the forms of the social relations of humanity. This is prayer in essence. It is only imperfectly realized in the subordinate types of prayer. In ritual prayer, cultual hymn, in liturgical prayer, as in prayer regulated by law and deemed a thing in itself meritorious, the experience of the Divine presence is, for the most part, weak and shadowy. Here we have prayer as a more or less external action, not as an inner contact of the heart with God. But also in the philosophical ideal of prayer and in certain forms of mystical communion, we can discern but faintly the essence of prayer. If we are to distinguish clearly between the religious experiences and states of mind related to prayer, which play an important part in the religion of philosophers and mystics, and prayer itself considered simply from the point of view which makes it to be prayer, some elucidation of what we mean by "adoration" and "devotion" is necessary.

Adoration (or reverent contemplation) and devotion are absolutely necessary elements in religious experience. Both terms stand for conceptions much wider than that of prayer; both denote religious experiences and states, the nature of which is obviously different from that of prayer; nay, we may go further and say that they comprehend psychical events and experiences which belong to the "secular," not to the strictly religious realm, or are on the borderland of both.

Adoration is the solemn contemplation of the "Holy One" as the highest Good, unreserved surrender to Him, a mingling of one's being with His. We see this even in the religious life of primitive peoples. The awe which primitive man evinces by speech and gesture as he stands in the presence of a "holy object," that is, an object filled with supernatural and magical power, is "adoration," although in a crude and imperfect fashion. The "holy" object has for him ideal worth: yes, even supreme value in the moment when, overcome by awe and wonder, he sinks in the dust before it. But it is in the personal experience of the poet and the mystic that we find adoration in its absolute purity and perfection. It is the soul-satisfying contemplation of the highest good, the very climax of mystical prayer: it is the unreserved losing of one's self in the glory of Nature as seen in the sacred poetry of ancient peoples and in the aesthetic mysticism of modern poets. Compared with it primitive ceremonial adoration is but a preliminary form. Now, a personal God can be the object of this adoration, just as He is the object of prayer. The God whom primitive man worships is an anthropomorphic being; the *summum bonum* of a mysticism centering in a personal God shows the traits of a spiritual personality. But the note of personality is by no means essential to the object of adoration. Primitive cults knew not only spiritual being made after man's image, but also lifeless objects which being "holy," that is, as *mana* and *tabu*, lay claim to worship. Moreover, the object in which the poetic spirit sinks in an ecstasy of adoration, is not personal: it is the life-giving sun, creative and nurturing Mother Nature, the Alone and the Infinite as revealed in the beautiful. There is, nevertheless, something that is beyond experience, something which shines through Nature as through a translucent medium. Just as the God whom the worshipper invokes, is felt to be palpably near and immediately present, so also the object of adoration which the pious spirit regards with awe is felt to be equally near and present. The relation to God into which he who prays enters, resembles in its intimacy the relation which subsists between the adoring person and the object of his adoration.

Subsidiary to religious adoration is the "secular." Ordinarily we indicate by the word "adoration" the state of being laid hold of by a supreme good, the complete surrender to it, whether this good be religious (*numinous*) or "secular," natural or supernatural, earthly or heavenly. Everything which man experiences as a supreme good, whatever is the object of "love"—a person, an association of persons, an abstract idea—can also in the wider sense of the word be an object of adoration. The young lover adores his beloved, the patriotic citizen his fatherland, the loyal working man his class, the creative artist his muse, the high-minded philosopher the idea of the true and the good. If love means the belief of a man in his supreme good, adoration is this belief at its highest point of intensity, the culmination of love. The adoring person steadily contemplates his ideal object; he is filled with inspiration, admiration, rapture, yearning; all other thoughts and wishes have vanished; he belongs only to the one object, loses himself in it, and in it dissolves away. *Adoration is the con-templative surrender to a supreme good.*

Devotion (*Andacht*) is a necessary presupposition and foundation alike of prayer and adoration. The praying man who converses with God, the adoring man who is absorbed in his highest ideal —both are devout, self-collected, concentrated. But the state of a soul in contemplation can just as well dispense with every reference to God or a supreme good. Devotion is, to begin with, concentration of the mind on a definite point, a wide-awake state of consciousness whose field is greatly circumscribed. But the mathematician who solves a geometrical problem also experiences this state of concentration, or the designer who constructs a model. Devotion, as distinct from mere mental concentration, from intensity of attention, is a solemn, still, exalted, consecrated mood of the soul. The philosopher experiences devotion when the mystery of the human spirit rises up before him in its autonomy and freedom: the scholar when he deciphers ancient documents and recalls to life long-forgotten men and peoples; the lover of nature when he stands before some lofty mountain peak or when he delights in the contemplation of some modest wild flower; the artist when suddenly a new idea forces itself upon him; the lover of art when he admires Raphael's Madonna or listens to a Symphony of Beethoven; the man engaged in a moral struggle when he searches his conscience, judges himself, and sets before himself lofty aims and tasks; the pious man when he participates in a holy act of worship or ponders on a religious mystery; even the irreligious man when he enters into the still dimness of a majestic cathedral or witnesses the solemn high mass in a Roman Catholic church. Devotion may rise into complete absorption; the field of consciousness is narrowed, the intensity of the experience grows; the concrete perceptions and ideas which aroused the experience of devotion wave themselves in a mood that is at once deep and agreeable. The states of absorption appear in the religious as in the "secular" experience. They meet us just as much in the mystical devotional life as in scientific investigation and artistic creation. In absorption the mystic experiences perfect stillness and serenity, holy joy and equanimity—all of them experiences which may be clearly distinguished from contemplative adoration. Yet in them there lives in some manner the thought of an ultimate and highest state, though not so vividly as in adoration. Even in Buddhist absorption the idea of an ultimate and a highest—Nirvana—is operative.

Devotion is, therefore, the quiet, solemn mood of the soul which is caused by the contemplation of ethical and intellectual, but especially of aesthetic and religious values, whether of external objects or of imaginative conceptions dominated by feeling. Whilst adoration is concerned inwardly with an ideal object and holds it fast with convulsive energy, the objective presupposition of the experience of devotion acts purely as a stimulus. Devotion itself tends to depart from its objective presupposition, and to become wholly subjective, concentrated, and absorbed. In short, adoration has an objective, devotion a subjective character.

The analysis of adoration and devotion enables us to set the essence of prayer in the clearest light. Prayer is no mere feeling of exaltation, no mere hallowed mood, no mere prostration before a supreme good. It is rather a real intercourse of God with man, a living fellowship of the finite spirit with the Infinite. And just because the modern has no correct conception of the immediacy and tenderness of the relation effected by prayer in which the simple and devout soul stands to God, he is constantly confusing with genuine prayer these more general religious phenomena—adoration and devotion—which have their analogies even outside the religious sphere. Because the man of to-day, entangled in the prejudices of a rationalistic philosophy, struggles against the primitive realism of frank and free prayer, he is inclined to see the ideal and essence of prayer in a vague, devotional mood and in aesthetic con-

templation. But the essence of prayer is revealed with unquestionable clearness to penetrating psychological study, and it may be put thus: *to pray means to speak to and have intercourse with God,* as suppliant with judge, servant with master, child with father, bride with bridegroom. The severely non-rational character of religion nowhere makes so overwhelming an impression as in prayer. For modern thought, dominated by Copernicus and Kant, prayer is as great a stone of stumbling as it was for the enlightened philosophy of the Greeks. But a compromise between unsophisticated piety and a rational world-view obliterates the essential features of prayer, and the most living manifestation of religion withers into a lifeless abstraction. There are only two possibilities: either decisively to affirm prayer "in its entirely non-rational character and with all its difficulties," as Ménégoz says, or to surrender genuine prayer and substitute for it adoration and devotion which resemble prayer. Every attempt to mingle the two conceptions violates psychological veracity.

Religious persons and students of religion agree in testifying that prayer is the centre of religion, the soul of all piety. The definition of the essence of prayer explains this testimony; prayer is a living communion of man with God. Prayer brings man into direct touch with God, into a personal relation with Him. Without prayer faith remains a theoretical conviction; worship is only an external and formal act; moral action is without spiritual depth; man remains at a distance from God; an abyss yawns between the finite and the Infinite. "God is in heaven and thou art on the earth." "We cannot come to God," says Luther, "except through prayer alone, for He is too high above us." In prayer man rises to heaven, heaven sinks to earth, the veil between the visible and the invisible is torn asunder, man comes before God to speak with Him about his soul's welfare and salvation. "Prayer," says Mechthild of Magdeburg, "draws the great God down into a small heart; it drives the hungry soul up to God in His fullness." Similarly Johann Arndt says: "In prayer the highest and the lowest come together, the lowliest heart and the most exalted God."

As the mysterious linking of man with the Eternal, prayer is an incomprehensible wonder, a miracle of miracles which is daily brought to pass in the devout soul. The historian and psychologist of religion can only be a spectator and interpreter of that deep and powerful life which is unveiled in prayer: only the religious man can penetrate the mystery. But in the final analysis scientific inquiry stands under the same overwhelming impression as living religion. It is compelled to agree with the confession of Chrysostom: "There is nothing more powerful than prayer and there is nothing to be compared with it."

George A. Buttrick

(1892——)

AFTER receiving his education at Lancaster Independent College, Manchester, England, and Victoria University, Buttrick came to the United States where he was ordained in the Congregational ministry in 1915. In 1920 he entered the Presbyterian ministry, and since 1927 he has been minister of the Madison Avenue Presbyterian Church, New York. He is a former president of the Federal Council of the Churches of Christ in America. During his ministry he has given a number of lecture series at American colleges and universities.

Of books by American authors which deal with prayer, Buttrick's book *Prayer* is one of the most comprehensive. The following chapter from that volume is used by permission of Abingdon-Cokesbury Press. (Copyright 1942 by Whitmore & Stone.)

A WAY OF PRIVATE PRAYER

From *Prayer*

*W*e now attempt some clear and detailed guidance in private prayer. There can be no rules, certainly no binding rules, but only hints. Yet no man need travel an unmarked path. The saints are our teachers; and other men, versed in prayer, who would be aghast to be called saints. Jesus himself is *the* Teacher. Prayer is friendship with God. Friendship is not formal, but it is not formless: it has its cultivation, its behavior, its obligations, even its disciplines; and the casual mind kills it. So we here offer, as guide-map not as chain, a simple regimen of private prayer.

I

Where shall we pray? In a *quiet and private place.* That was the bidding of Jesus: "But thou, when thy prayest, enter into thy inner chamber, and when thou hast shut thy door, pray to thy Father which is in secret." The counsel is specific: the room should be remote from distractions, the door shut against noise, and the prayer so free from posturing that it is "secret." Jesus himself, intent on quietness and sincerity, sometimes prayed on a mountainside, far into the night, or "rising up a great while before day . . . departed into a solitary place, and there prayed." Our age is restless and noisy: it is harder to find stillness now than in pioneer or rural days. City congestion and distraction war against the soul. A wiser civilization will disperse our teeming masses into friendly communities open to the fields and sky. As for sincerity, it is perhaps both more difficult in our age and more important than quietness; for it is our modern fashion to posture in the glare of publicity. Amid tumult and glare we must do the best we can: in some quiet corner of home or church, free from prying or approving eyes, we must make sanctuary. "Be still, and know that I am God." In the din of traffic we may be deaf to steeple bells, but in the quiet night we hear. It is wise to seek both stillness and privacy.

Prayer should be offered in *an accustomed place.* We are creatures of place and habit, and worthy habits fashion worthy life. Anything we learn returns more easily in the place where we learned it. If we should master Chinese in China, come home to speak our own tongue, and then return to China, the very setting would be our cue for the recovery of the foreign words, even before we heard people speak. Rousseau "wrote" best when walking, Sheridan composed best at night with a profusion of lights, and Vacano for his creative work sought the "hubbub of peasant life near an old mill." In each instance the environment was accustomed. There was no distraction of newness. The place not only suggested the task, but held in store the encouragement of past experience. These facts pertain also to a familiar place of prayer. That setting gives prompting and remembrance. A kneeling bench may be found helpful, with a few treasured books of devotion: Thomas à Kempis *Imitation of Christ,* Pascal's *Pensées,* Amiel's *Journal Intime,* the *Theologica Germanica;* or more modern books such as John Baillie's *A Diary of Private Prayer;* and always a Bible. Protestants might well adopt a Roman Catholic practice, and pray privately in church. Infinity has its center everywhere, and men can find God in any place, even in the roar of traffic; but the habit of prayer is best established in a quiet and accustomed place.

II

When shall we pray? At any time: God is not bound by occasions and seasons, and prayer is spontaneous like any friendship. But, for us, there is value in allotted and customary periods of prayer. Three times during the day have especial purpose. One is in the morning. "Well begun is half done," but, "Things bad begun make strong themselves by ill." The first moments of the day are an arena in which the revived worries or joys of yesterday, the responsible tasks of the coming hours, desires and hopes and fears, compete for our reinvigorated thought. Those moments are crucial. They often determine the day: they may make it an autopsy of past failures, an overleaping ambition, or an anxiety. There is great gain in pausing to realize that the day is a unity: a kindly Providence each night draws a line on one day soiled and marred, and each morning grants a new day fresh from time's loom. There is much greater gain in setting the tone and standard for the day by quiet prayer. After that worship the day will not be a distraction or a jumble: it will have integration like a poem or a picture. We shall be saved from the drab doom of "practical" people to whom "everything matters except everything." This prayer before or after breakfast may wisely be brief: the day's labor summons us. For the same reason it may wisely have a set form, to be changed only when its reality is threatened by rote. . . .

The second time for daily prayer is determined, not by the clock, but by the day's happenings. That is to say, our waking hours should be punctuated by ejaculatory prayers. The word *jacula* means spear. These prayers are thrown spears of resolve or thanksgiving or trust. The sense of gratitude for the sight of ocean, for great music, or for a friend's loyalty should become an instant prayer: "My Father, I thank thee for this blessing, from whom cometh every good and perfect gift." Sympathy for a neighbor when news comes of his misfortune should find expression in a prayer: "Do Thou defend him as he walks through shadow. Show me what I can do to help. May his pain not be wasted, but lead him to light." A journey should prompt a prayer for journeying mercies. Each new task, each sudden responsibility, should have its undelayed dedication: "I am able unto all things through Christ who makes me strong." Success and failure, joy and sorrow, are thus made consecrate. There have been people, among them the Celts and the Scandinavians, who had brief forms of prayers for each task of the day. The bread-baking, the feeding of the cattle, the lamplighting, each had its reverent ritual. It was a gracious custom. Even the scanty records of the Gospels show clearly that Jesus prayed at every juncture of his ministry. Ejaculatory prayers should be a part of the day's order of prayer. Added treasure is given by a few moments of noonday prayer in church.

But the most solving time to pray is at night. A wise mother offers her counsel and comfort when day is done, and sends her children to sleep with her blessing: so God deals tenderly and wisely with His children of earth. Facts gather to underscore the peculiarly creative grace of evening prayer: the day's clamor is done, and there is chance for meditation; the sunset glory is an open gate of vision; fading light gives retrospection; and the encroaching dark, in which we must lie unconscious, reminds us of our helplessness. There is a further fact which has incalculable issues: the nightly prayer lays under fee our hours of sleep. We say, "I'd better sleep on it before making a decision." The name which we cannot remember when we go to bed is on our lips of itself when we awake. Why? Because the mind is not inactive during sleep: its subconscious processes continue, carrying on the business—especially the urgent business or the last business—that has engaged the waking thought. Paul was a good psychologist when he advised, "Let not the sun go down upon your wrath." Anger churning in the mind at nightfall churns on during sleep: the next morning is turned sour. By the same token the night prayer works radiantly in our nature while we sleep: the subconscious becomes prayer's ally, doubling prayer's power. While we rest we gain a deeper rest: God visits us by a secret stair. Problems are solved and questions answered, ready for our waking. Perhaps a better translation of

"he giveth his beloved sleep" is, "giveth unto his beloved *in their sleep.*" At any rate that blessing *is* given through evening worship. What form should be impressed on this creative center of prayer? We now seek answer.

III

Evening prayer begins, not in a clamant asking, but in *a silent self-preparation.* We should not rush into the Presence, with a jostling crowd of fears, sins, and desires, like a mob breaking through a chancel door on pretense of worship. The church of nightly devotion should be entered through the vestibule in an orderly quietness. The psychologist speaks of "relaxation." Sometimes, when we are too tired to sleep, we realize that all our muscles are tense. Then we persuade each limb in turn to forgo its straining. So with the mind: we must calm each hungry desire—the psychologist advises—each vexing remorse, each bitter grudge or clamorous resolve. It is good counsel—if we can follow it. But can we? Man's self-tinkering has never been successful. The "relaxation" commended by psychology comes best as a by-product of a mind focused on God. This concentration is under no rule of thumb. Christian prayer will call upon Christ in reverent imagination. Almost any word of his is sufficient prompting: "I am the light of the world." We say to ourselves: "His light fills the world. It fills this room. His light pains a sickened eye. But it heals, guides, illumines. It cheers, as daybreak after the night watch. 'God is light, and in him is no darkness at all.' " Thus we meditate. Then, in specific act of devotion, we say: "Before this God, in all His holy love, in all His wisdom and delivering grace, I now kneel." Clearly the reading of a few verses from the Gospels is often the best prelude to our nightly prayer. In any event, the prelude of prayer is this preparation of ourself and realization of God: "I have set the Lord always before me." Jesus entered prayer through that vestibule: we can see him quietly realizing the Presence: "Our Father which art in heaven, Hallowed be thy name." Sometimes the prayer may go no further: it may remain in adoration. Perhaps that is the explanation of the prayer of St. Francis, which the eavesdropper heard him repeat all night: "My God and my All." The focusing of the mind on God is the proper beginning of prayer.

The next step is an *act of faith*, on which Jesus laid constant stress: "All things, whatsoever ye shall ask in prayer, believing, ye shall receive." The word "believing" is there a radiantly qualifying word: true prayer believes that God is like Christ, and asks what may be asked "in his Name and Nature." Therefore, in this initial silence of prayer we say to ourselves that whatever we ask in the "nature of Christ" is ours, granted only our earnestness in prayer and life. Sometimes this act of faith is an instant freedom: we know through Christ that God does not wish us to live in carking fear or unforgiven sin; and our prayer then is not in an importunity, but a joyous acceptance of a promised grace. Sometimes faith waits with confidence on fuller light: "If it is God's will for me to help So-and-so, or to discharge such-and-such a task, I can do it." Sometimes faith moves in the dark, believing in the ultimate good of untoward circumstance:

Out of my stony griefs
Bethel I'll raise.

But always prayer is prefaced by an act of faith. We take counsel with our certitudes, not with our doubts and fears: "For he that cometh to God must believe that he is, and that he is a rewarder of them that diligently seek him."

IV

For the prayer itself there is no fixed order, but both a primary impulse and the experience of praying men show that the first stage may be *thanksgiving*. A lecturer to a group of businessmen displayed a sheet of white paper on which was one blot. He asked what they saw. All answered, "A blot." They overlooked the white expanse, and saw only the blot. The test was unfair: it invited the wrong

answer. Nevertheless, there is an ingratitude in human nature by which we notice the black disfigurement and forget the widespread mercy. We need deliberately to call to mind the joys of our journey. Perhaps we should try to write down the blessings of one day. We might begin: we could never end: there are not pens or paper enough in all the world. The attempt would remind us of our "vast treasure of content." Therefore the prayer of thanksgiving should be quite specific: "I thank thee for *this* friendship, *this* threat overpassed, *this* signal grace." "For all thy mercies" is a proper phrase for a general collect, but not for a private gratitude. If we are thankful "for everything," we may end by being thankful for nothing. The thanksgiving should also probe deep, asking, "What are life's *abiding* mercies?" Thus gratitude would be saved from earthiness and circumstance, and rooted in Life beyond life. "Count your many blessings," says the old hymn, "and it will surprise you what the Lord hath done." This prayer should end in glad and solemn resolve: "Lord, seal this gratitude upon my face, my words, my generous concern for my neighbors, my every outward thought and act."

Prayer may next become *confession*. A rebound of nature hints that this is a wise order: "God has been passing kind, and I have given Him selfishness for love." True confession is neither self-excoriation—"To be merciless with anyone, even ourselves, is no virtue"—nor casual evasion. Overconscientiousness becomes morbid: underconscientiousness becomes indifference and decay. Confession to those we have wronged is sometimes, not always, wise: there are circumstances in which such confession would spread and aggravate the hurt. But confession to God, whom we have more deeply wronged, is always wise: He has understanding and love. Our sin is sin against the Living Order, and we have neither inward peace nor inward power until we have offered prayers of penitence. Confession, like thanksgiving, should be specific. It should not be ruthless, but it should not excuse: it should set hooks into the facts. "I confess *this* sharp judgment, *this* jealousy, *this* cowardice, *this* bondage of dark habit, *this* part in the world's evil." Contrition is not easy work: it is surgery. But, like surgery, it is not an end in itself: the wise prayer of confession always leads to an acceptance of God's pardon. . . . God does not wish us to remember, save as admonition and reminder of our dependence, anything He is willing to forget. It might be wise to rise from kneeling at this point in the prayer as token of our acceptance of God's pardon, our sure faith in His absolution, and our new freedom in His grace. That standing erect might also symbolize both our resolve to make wise restoration insofar as we have power to mend our blunders, and our sincere renunciation of our sins. Confession is incomplete without that resolve. Our will, however feeble it may be, must descend squarely on the side of a new life. Otherwise even our penitence may become a self-deceit and an abuse of God's goodness. But true confession is a very cleansing of the soul.

Then may follow a prayer of *intercession*, without which the most earnest prayer might sink into selfishness. *The Lord's Prayer* in almost every phrase keeps us mindful of our neighbors: "*Our* Father" . . . "*our* daily bread" . . . "*our* trespasses." Private intercession should be specific. "We humbly beseech Thee for all sorts and conditions of men," is an appropriate phrase in a collect—which, as the very word indicates, draws all worshipers into one act of devotion, and provides a form into which each worshiper may pour his secret prayer—but it is out of place in individual petition. Genuine love sees faces, not a mass: the good shepherd "calleth his own sheep by name." Intercession is more than specific: it is pondered: it requires us to bear on our heart the burden of those for whom we pray. Whose name should come first? Perhaps the name of our enemies. The injunction of Jesus is plain: "Pray for them which despitefully use you." He told us that worship is vain if

we are embittered; that we would be wise to leave our gift before the altar, go to make peace with our neighbor, and then worship. Only then can we truly worship. So the first intercession is: "Bless So-and-so whom I foolishly regard as foe. Bless So-and-so whom I have wronged. Keep them in Thy favor. Banish our bitterness." Intercession names also the leaders of mankind in statecraft, medicine, learning, art, and religion; the needy of the world; our comrades in work and play, and our loved ones. A sense of responsibility may prompt us to prepare a chart of intercession, so that night by night we may enter earnestly into the need of the world, and not forget nor fail anyone who closely depends upon our prayers. So true intercession is specific and pondered. It is also daring: it carries on its heart-entreaty the crisis of the world. Like thanksgiving, it is not complete without our vow. Sincere prayer-in-love is never in vain.

The fourth order in our prayer may be *petition*. It comes last, not because it is most important, but because it needs the safeguard of earlier prayer. We should not fear to lift our earthly needs before Eternal Eyes, for we are held in Eternal Love; but we should fear the encroachment of a selfish mind. Petition is defended against that threat if first we give thanks, confess our sins, and pray for our neighbors. Then the petition may have free course. Sometimes, in sorrow, dread, or helplessness, it will be a crisis cry of creaturehood—a beating on Heaven's door with bruised knuckles in the dark. Sometimes it will be friendship-talk with God about the affairs of everyday. Surely both prayers would be approved by Christ: his disciples cried in their extremity, "Save, Lord"; and day by day they spoke with him about the besetments, enigmas, and joys of the journey. To try to thwart the prayer of petition is to deny human nature. The New Testament has better wisdom: "Be overanxious for nothing; but in everything by prayer and supplication with thanksgiving let your requests be made known unto God." Yet petition should grow in grace so as to "covert earnestly the best gifts"; and it should always acknowledge that our sight is dim and that our purposes are mixed in motive. It should always conclude with, "Nevertheless not my will, but thine, be done."

The intervals of these four prayers should be filled by *meditation*. After thanksgiving we should contemplate God's abounding goodness, and await His word concerning His own gifts. After confession we should adore the pardoning Love made known in Christ, and listen for His guidance. After intercession we should pause to try to see the whole world's need as Christ saw it from his cross. After petition we should wait again to meditate upon the Will. Prayer is listening as well as speaking, receiving as well as asking; and its deepest mood is friendship held in reverence. So the nightly prayer should end as it begins—in adoration. The best conclusion is, "In the name of Jesus Christ: Amen." For in the name or nature of Jesus is our best understanding of God, and the best corrective of our blundering prayers. The word "Amen" is not idle: it means "So let it be." It is our resolve to live faithfully in the direction of our prayers, and our act of faith in God's power. It is the proper ending to our evening prayer.

V

Certain practical questions remain, and merit an answer. *Should private prayer be spoken or silent?* There is no binding rule, but there are certain guiding facts. Silence is the proper language of awe and adoration. The abyss of the night sky and the heartbreak of the Cross are literally beyond words: the tongue is helpless. So the beginning and ending of private prayer are an instinctive stillness. Silence is the language also of contemplation and receptiveness: we cannot hear if we always speak. So the intervals of meditation just described may all be silent. But silence has its dangers, especially in the waywardness of thought; and speech has its virtues. Any teacher knows that a lesson spoken is clearer than a lesson merely pondered. Words fashion our prayers to a spear point, and give them an action thrust. "Take with you words, and turn to the Lord." Words clarify thought, focus desire, and translate resolves into deeds. Therefore our prayers of thanksgiving, confession, intercession, and petition may wisely be spoken *aloud*. The words need not be wrought and polished. They may rush in intolerable craving, halt in ignorance, or break in sorrow. God regards the heart, not the word. Yes, in ordinary times, we are helped if we try to give clear, simple, and sincere expression to our prayer. By that effort the prayer itself becomes clear, simple, and sincere.

How shall we find time to pray? The very question shows the disproportion of our life. "First things" are not "first." Three-hundredth things, the make of an automobile, the fashion of a coiffure, are now first; and "first things" have dropped out of sight. St. Ignatius required of initiates in his order an initial thirty days of silence. Luther habitually prayed for three hours each day. Jesus often prayed all night, and said that "men ought always to pray, and not to grow weary in praying." If prayer is friendship with God, that friendship should rule all our time. Work or play should wait on prayer, not prayer on work or play. But since our age is frenzied, since with all the time gained from time-saving devices we have ever less time to live, this fact is worth stress: prayer saves time, and the saving is genuine. . . . Five minutes in the morning, arrow flights of prayer during the day, and fifteen minutes at night do not seem too large a demand for life's highest Friendship. That time spent in prayer can conquer time.

There is a sharper question. *How can we overcome an arid mind in private prayer?* The mind's periods of dryness are hard to explain. Any artist knows times when his imagination is like the dust and darkness of a forsaken church, and other times when it is like a church with banner hung, organ music rolling through high arches, and candles burning bright on every altar. The children of Israel wandered forty years in a desert before they reached their Promised Land. The wanderings were not loss: they taught Israel to trust God's leadings, purged them of a slave mind, and welded them into nationhood. In their history we can trace the reason for desert and disappointment: "O give thanks unto the Lord . . . to him which led his people through the wilderness: for his mercy endureth for ever." A realization that the arid stretches have a purpose will help us to journey through them in resolute faith. We must walk through darkness in memory of the light, and in confidence that light will return. There is some drudgery in every high art: in music there are weary hours of practice. The drudgery is not only the test of courage and patience, and therefore a bestowal of manhood, but it is promise of mastery. Prayer has its drudgery: if we shrink from the discipline we shall never gain the joy. In any art the period of irksomeness yields finally to an "opening," and the "openings" multiply to become freedom. When the mind is dry we should still persist in prayer, offering God the dryness in lack of better gift—telling Him about our journey of dust until he gives springs in the desert.

How can we overcome a wandering and moody mind? Dr. George S. Stewart suggests wisely that waywardness in prayer would be conquered if our prayers were more adventurous, and if expectantly we traced their answer. Jesus challenged men to daring prayer: he bade them "remove mountains" by their faith. He himself marked God's way in the world, and gave thanks for answers to prayer. Even more searchingly Dr. Stewart suggests that failure in prayer's disciplines may reflect a failure in life's disciplines, and that therefore moody distraction may itself reveal the prayer we most need to offer. If baleful humors come of secret unworthiness, the "line" of our prayer is clear; we must bring our secret sins into the light of God's countenance. Then prayer itself is the road of victory. Not every dark mood, of course, comes of unworthiness. The saints also have been overtaken by "the black night of the soul." Our wrestling is not against "flesh and blood" only, but against the "darkness of this world"; not only against the ebb and flow of human moods, but against the sudden unseen antagonism of unaccountable depressions. But we must endure the balefulness as we endure the drudgery. If there is nothing else we can do, we can tell God about the evil mood, making it our strange oblation to Him who gives His treasure for our need. There will come other hours so radiant that they atone for every untoward cloud. . . . In the very midst of prayer's barrenness, or when prayer is vexed by dark moods, the man on his knees may suddenly see Jesus plain. Then he can well "forget the rest."

Allan A. Hunter

(1893——)

ALTHOUGH active since 1926 as pastor of Mount Hollywood Congregational Church, Los Angeles, California, Hunter has given a great deal of attention to the study of the saints. Three of his most recent books have dealt explicitly with the meaning of sainthood: *Three Trumpets Sound, White Corpuscles in Europe,* and *Say Yes to the Light.*

Born in Toronto and brought to the United States in 1901, Hunter was educated at Princeton, Columbia, and Union Theological Seminary. In 1923 he was ordained in the Presbyterian ministry but later entered the Congregational Church. Besides serving Presbyterian and Congregational churches he has taught in China and Egypt, and has been active in movements concerned with world fellowship.

This selection from *Say Yes to the Light* is used by permission of Harper & Brothers. (Copyright 1944 by Harper & Brothers.)

TRAINING NOW

From *Say Yes to the Light*

In a special course of twenty-one days, a respectable citizen can be made over into a fighting fury, a commando unfailingly "bloody-minded." The day you arrive, after preliminary months of toughening, you take a six-mile run in full equipment. But that is only to warm up. Then you make a charge over and through obstacles. You climb a cliff pulling yourself up sixty feet of rope. You mount a platform fourteen feet high and jump to the ground to find yourself literally under fire. You wriggle through the grass on your stomach. These hornet noises overhead will not hurt you unless you are careless. But they are real bullets. Next, a reservoir of cold water, calculated to take the spirit out of you. Upon emerging on the other side you have to shoot some rounds of your own and get the adrenalin back into your blood. The instructor sees to that in language the reverse of prayer. The day's work is not over yet. He makes you travel back in double quick time. When the three weeks are up, you polish off your schooling with a sixty-mile march in twenty-four hours. All this is aimed to make you fighting mad and to keep you fighting-mad, and it works. The test is beyond human endurance? Almost. "But in some extraordinary way," Science Digest concludes, "it charges a man up like a battery with a will to go out and fight."

Can men be charged up with an equally dynamic will, to practice openness to what is most real and alive?

We have seen that they can be so trained. "To look in one direction and live in one way" may become a man's second nature. A Brother Lawrence, barefoot and active in the kitchen, can do virtually everything demanded of him simply and solely "for the love of God." A Quaker in prison for conscience writes to his wife, "Driving the milk truck within the grounds, I find I can do 'a Brother Lawrence' on wheels." Four days before he crashed at sea off Ellice Islands, Stuart Hunter, undergoing change, was able to write his father: "Every night I go off alone and have a few prayers for you and my friends. It makes me feel keener and stronger inside." Even in an insane asylum a young trainee can work with a clear sense of Presence. This is not a lost art. Nor do our temperament and social responsibilities have to exclude us from its practice. The discipline of becoming persons of integrity and good will is available for us, beginning now. Our progress may be less speedy than our egos demand. That does not mean that we ourselves cannot be gradually reconditioned.

Many a person, after an hour of the most intense effort to pay attention and to give allegiance to what he is trying to bet his life upon, has been shocked to see his ego five minutes later feverishly and violently colliding with the ego of child or wife or best friend. Our reflexes are in no hurry to be redirected. Our subconscious or unconscious mind is a wild animal that will not quickly be broken in to the decorum of the house in which our spirits intend to live.

A friend from Texas had made his decision. He would treat Negroes as he would Caucasians. One day he opened a door in the post office and stepped aside for the person behind him. He looked back. It was a Negro. Horrified and off guard, my friend slammed the door in his face. Quite soon the absurdity of what he had done struck him. But it was too late. He could not find the man he had insulted and ask his pardon. But that friend, after more than two years of hard work, is now on his way to becoming a more open-minded man. Our reflexes, however stubborn, are not the issue. The issue is "the naked intent of the will." Desire, as William Law used to say, is everything and does everything. We have enough freedom to commence training our desire now, without further delay. It will take a different kind of pressure on our wills from that to which commandos are taught to respond. Our problem may look less simple. Actually it may be, in the long run, less complicated though more difficult.

The commando is sprinting against time; our task is to catch up with eternity. It is not simply for the duration; it is for the whole of our lives. We are not dealing with a certain group of people or an all too vivid outpost that has to be wiped out. We are dealing with the invisible welfare of all men and that goodness which is always and everywhere. The desire to carry through a constructive, redemptive mission in contrast to that which commandos have to perform, seems hopelessly feeble. But is it? To be sure, the pressure upon the commando is "to kill or be killed," whereas ours is the unseen urgency of the Kingdom of God. The commando has an instructor competent to drill the necessary reflexes into his nervous system; the spiritual director we need is hard to find. The commando has blueprints, specific hard-and-fast orders about how to silence this battery or that radio station. All we have, at first, is a sense of general direction and an intuition perhaps of Presence that sometimes gets blurred.

As we face our own obstacles and possibilities, we may be tempted to think of ourselves as different and separate from those who risk their lives in war. Such self-righteousness would be a deadly mistake. Apparently the sin that Jesus considered among the most fatal was the complacency that considers itself good and others bad. The men who hazard everything in physical battle are always putting us to shame. In a sense they are absolutists. They obey without reservations. They are not preoccupied, as we are inclined to be, with whether the coffee is hot, whether the bedsprings hurt, whether security is guaranteed. Moreover, they suffer as we do where it really hurts, in the conscience.

A letter from a young flying friend who takes part in bombings throws light on a tragedy we must never forget. What holds his attention is not his chance of being killed or mutilated at any moment. "It's the thought of what I am doing with these bombs. I cannot do that and go to religious meetings. I read in my Testament, 'Ask and ye shall receive.' But no light comes." He is in darkness and the darkness torments him. About all he can say is, "It takes more courage not to get on the bandwagon." In the presence of such a spirit no man can be smug.

If he has turned away from the bandwagon, he also has perplexities. He is, let us say, trying to be a peacemaker in war time. That means that an interviewer from the F.B.I. will be asking his friends about his motives. Is he going to a civilian public service camp or to jail because he is a coward, a parasite, an individualist, an escapist? That same wonder burns into the man who would serve his country with the best integrity he can rally. He has heard the dictum of Schweitzer, "An easy conscience is the invention of the devil." But that dictum is little comfort to him now. He may break under his own self-analysis. Many a man joins the armed forces not because he believes in the method but because he wants to prove to himself that he is not afraid or unwilling to do his share of the hard dirty work. Unless this particular person now diagnosing the secret places of his heart has drilled himself to refer everything to the Center, his self-disgust may drive him into giving up his commitment. To maintain his stand, he will have to turn attention away from his own goodness—or, rather, lack of it—to the goodness of God.

That is what James Nayler found in his ordeal. The same insight we may also find as we set out to be trainees of the truth and good will we hope to reflect. At the last, apparently, he became imbued in the spirit that delights not in evil or revenge whose hope is

. . . to outlive all wrath and contention and to weary out all exaltation and cruelty or whatever is of a nature opposite to itself . . . for its ground and principle is the mercies and forgiveness of God.

Earlier, as an associate of George Fox and at a less mature stage, he made a serious mistake, due quite possibly to overconfidence. The authorities sentenced him to the pillory to be ridiculed, and to several months in prison where the rats could gnaw at him. A red-hot poker was to be stuck through his tongue; his body was to be whipped as he walked from one public humiliation to another. Upon hearing the sentence, the Quaker simply replied, "God gave me this body. God, I hope [he did not even venture the word 'trust'], will give me courage to endure." What matters is not so much our adequacy as what God is and does and what we are training to be. The first essential of training, says Gandhi, is to believe in God.

This means that we have more and more to recognize and to reply to relationships, not limiting ourselves to the human but going on toward the total Friendship that has no frontiers. A mustard seed of such determination is enough if from then on we try to commit ourselves to the Light surrounding us and to the nourishment our roots supply, as a young plant commits itself to growth. To live intentionally, we learn from those who are rungs above us, three things are necessary. We ourselves have to meditate and pray and practice doing the will. We have to feed our minds on what the saints and candidates for sainthood say. We have to associate ourselves with those who also want to live one-pointed lives.

What are the skills we need to be open and responsive to the best? The Sermon on the Mount provides adequate intelligence-character tests. Acting as best we can on that principle, we shall find our schedule and possibly our way of meeting people and making money being reordered. The mutation may come quite undramatically: going without a cigarette before breakfast and putting the penny thus saved into the Chinese rice bowl; putting in three minutes on the morning paper instead of eight and using the extra five minutes to ask the Congressman how he is voting on

reconstruction in Europe; outwitting the usual "will to be sorry for oneself" at 4:00 P.M. with "I will fly in the greatness of God as the marsh hen flies." Such little deaths and resurrections are often indications of sincerity. A young mother is ruthless with herself. "If it's a choice between eating and not meditating, I don't eat." Kagawa, when the bedbugs became too distracting, made a brilliant response: "This is God testing me."

We can undertake a routine of meditation and prayer for ourselves, remembering with von Hügel to see "not feverishly but in largely subconscious waiting, genial, expansive, endlessly patient, sunny manner." Ten or twenty minutes is a good start. Later, one will want to increase the time. It is probably better to sit erect in silence on the same chair in the same place regularly, though Muriel Lester sometimes walks outside and others kneel and repeat written prayers aloud. Stillness of the body is worth attempting no matter how agonizing the effort at first is. If we seriously work at this, we may soon discover that the real reason we have not been received more regularly into God's presence is fear lest we find how little we have believed and loved, and how distracted and childish we are. The experience has been described as like unto facing a firing squad once a day. One trainee confesses that he laughs when he looks in the mirror. Most of us, when we see ourselves as we are, feel that this is a preliminary experience of hell. We can excuse ourselves from this pain and effort and joy by piously declaring, "One has no right to withdraw so much energy from social service," but the actual practice of meditation may soon expose that as an excuse of the ego to go on masquerading as altruism.

To tell anyone else how to meditate is presumptuous. Each of us has to work out his own pattern of energy, as George Buttrick says, and not just of thought; and any pattern unless changed from time to time will go dead. The point in offering suggestions is to make it clear that a beginner can relax his mind. He does not have to strain and screw up his surface will, saying, "Go to now, I'm going to make my mind a blank." He could not if he tried. Moreover, the devil adores a vacuum, especially a mental one. Part of the job in meditation is to wash off as much ego as one can; but that does not oblige one to empty out the total significance, along with bath water. Meditation, at first, is like sitting before an organ. There are bewilderingly many keys. Not all have to be touched. Eventually, when the trainee is farther advanced, perhaps one single consideration will be enough. At the start, such concentration and freedom are impossible. It may help, therefore, to let the imagination play upon some such possibilities as these.

First, we can turn toward the wonder of the Presence that is above and inside, able to charge the whole earth with His grandeur and make a thousand times ten thousand times a million stars, able also to answer even our own feeblest effort toward Him and keep every person's need simultaneously in mind. The phrase "Our Father" could take an hour of reflection without going further. This body, this marvelous slowed-down streak of lightning, belongs to Him; so does this will that can point to the center instead of defying it; this capacity to share another's pain and to feel overflowing joy; this peephole into eternity called "now"; and this strange power to tie up time and space into little packages called "experience" and offer them all up to the Owner. These abilities have been rented to us. We are now trying to pay the rent, remembering that to whom much has been given, from him much will be required. Who are we, Lord, to have more comfort and opportunity than most of Thy other children on this earth? How shall we pay back for being overprivileged?

The sense of responsibility and awe can sting and vow the will. But there is also gratitude. We are glad, thinking of the gold network of friends who communicate to us the sense of what can be done with all these gifts. There is Frank Laubach, for example. He aims to teach a billion illiterates to read and write with his simplified method, but he does not ignore the people adjoining him. When he enters a restaurant, he sets out to speak directly to people from his center to theirs, saying silently, "You are my friends." There is Muriel Lester, now back home in the east end of London. She is athletic, integrated, and gay. Upon awaking, she turns her first thought away from self to God, repeating, "Thou are shining beauty, radiant joy, creative power, all-pervading love, perfect understanding, purity, and peace." There is Philippe Vernier in Belgium. He loves to sing and laugh with the boys he takes to summer camps. It is probable that his two children and wife have not yet been starved by the blockade. Under almost incredible pressure he has won this insight: "If you look at Jesus, his assurance will pass into you. You do not know exactly what is ahead. You do know that as you go forward, your Master will be there." The gold network includes many others, some of whom the world considers ordinary. At its head is Jesus who is more alive than anyone else today. As we put ourselves into the hands of his spirit, we find ourselves tossed up into the wind of reality until, as the Arabs say, "the chaff is blown away" and the wheat with the potentialities is cleansed.

The darkness in us is not often worth prolonged consideration (we must never stop with that), but it has always to be faced—not only the lack of love and of faith, the lust, the parasitism and pretentiousness, but also the fear of pain and the fear of losing security and face. We have to realize that it is not we who are good. Compared with the music we want to become a part of, we are but ugly discords. Held up against the light, we are nasty-looking black spiders. But the beautiful holiness, the splendor, wisdom, and courtesy of God—these are the notes that can most vibrantly wing their way through our spirit. Since we neglect God, if we neglect our neighbor, we now hold this and that person in the light, not asking anything, simply holding them there.

He knows the need of those Polish Jews still surviving, that Chinese child now being bombed, the soldiers we have promised to think of every day, the woman down the street in agony, that man about to break emotionally, our closest friends and family circle. We need not be frantic. God suffers with each one of us but not anxiously or with torn nerves, as we suffer with one another. His hand does not flutter. That thought is worth many seconds of quiet realization. There have been minor notes enough. Like Bach, let us now end with a major chord from Boehm: "We are all strings in the concert of His joy. Amen."

Going now to breakfast, we can sing with at least a few breaths our praise of God. There should be other reminders during the day; a spell at noon and another before supper, one trainer recommends; and as we enter the door from ordinary consciousness into sleep, it is well to repeat, "Into Thy hands I commend my spirit." The Lord's Prayer will prove to be worth at least fifteen minutes a day. It has the advantage of being universal and of having been tested for centuries. The danger is that we so easily parrot instead of meaning it. Whatever our pattern, we are to begin and gradually reduce the words, keeping ourselves reminded during the day. One friend on the way to work is recalled to the sense of Presence by the house finches that fling their lively song into the passing car. Another, before eating lunch, thinks of the undernourished over the world.

This effort to pay attention is not an escape from ethical obligations. It is a facing of them in the light that alone will make us fit to fulfill them. Seeking God, Toynbee, the historian, is convinced, "is itself a social act." It irradiates into the world a power of cohesion, the lack of which tends to disintegrate the world. The wrong kind of meditation does not have good effects. "The mistake of our civilization has been in thinking of self-consciousness as the highest form of consciousness." But if the emphasis is to turn as much attention as possible toward God during meditation and as much as possible toward fellow men during the rest of our waking time, facing the darkness of our egos but seeing the light beyond, the process can be trusted to serve society and to turn the world from a jungle into more of a home.

Just as there is no automatic progress in evolution, there is no automatic and easy access to the Reality we call God. The person who begins seriously to find his orientation by a conscious spiritual mastery of his interior life will discover that the road grows steeper and narrower. Just as an artist entering a room sees masses and color and line in arrangements too subtle for the average person to grasp, so the saint sees the selfishness and laziness which block his path to God, with an accuracy and clarity we cannot muster, certainly not right away. There are many rungs up the ladder toward the light. One of the great saints says that as you climb you have to pass through three dark nights before you reach the top. The first four rungs have been called "purgation"; the next four, "liberation and illumination"; the last set of steps up, "union."

Our task, to repeat, is to start where we are, and most of us will have to "keep a-inching along, lak a po' inchworm." It will take far more effort than the four years of drilling necessary to produce a perfect soldier. It will take everything we have and more—"the abandonment of all fear of bodily injury, of disease or death, of the loss of possessions, of family, or of reputation. "The reliance," Gandhi continues, "is not on self but on God alone." As trainees we may have to change our job or lose our income. Our lives are no longer our own. We shall have to keep close to the center of our spiritual life, as Vernier does, much of the misery of the world without becoming solemn or unelastic. But is not the effort worth it? Will anything else more dynamically recondition the world?

The force that prayer sends out into life to set into motion the powers of recovery sleeping there has to come from the center to the center. A friend and I were strolling up a trail in the California hills in the late autumn. On our path lay an alligator lizard, the body six or seven inches and the tail that long again. It had been a warm afternoon. The sun had lured him out from his winter hole in the rocks. We saw that he was still breathing. But if he remained long in that stupor, the oncoming cold or the coyotes might mean his death. To arouse the sleeper I tossed small stones around him. They had no effect. Then my friend did exactly what was needed. He got down on his knees and stayed there, breathing the heat of his own body into the heart of the lizard, again and again. Warmed and awakened, the benumbed creature suddenly came to life and scurried between our legs back to his place of safety.

The recharging of the will to save instead of destroying life requires reading as well as praying, though the reading can be a form of praying. A single word from *The Cloud of Unknowing* written in the fourteenth century is so basic that it could well be memorized:

God may well be loved, but not thought. By love may he be gotten and holden; but by thought never.

George Fox out of the seventeenth century offers tools that still have edge:

Your strength is to stand still, after ye see yourselves. Whatsoever ye see yourselves addicted to, Temptations, Corruptions, Uncleanness, . . . then ye think, ye shall never Overcome. And Earthly Reason will tell you, what ye shall lose; hearken not to that but stand still in the Light, that shews them to you, and then Strength comes from the Lord, and Help contrary to your Expectation.

The *Imitation of Christ* and *The Practice of the Presence of God* supply vitamins to many. The audacity of Saint Paul is indispensable; for him to live was Christ, that is, the will to lift life up and save it. The words of Jesus are inexhaustible daily bread. Coming down to contemporary books, there are *Preface to Prayer* and *Training for the Life of the*

Spirit, by Gerald Heard, and the recent writings of Evelyn Underhill. These are disconcertingly alive. A stiff and humbling exploration into the possibilities is Poulain's *Graces of Interior Prayer*. *With the Master*, by Philippe Vernier, is a small book of meditations written in prison; here are the findings of an authentic—simple, radioactive and profound. There is also Thomas R. Kelly's *A Testament of Devotion*. A glimpse into the difficulties and responsibilities opened up by these books will leave us not quite so casual as we were about our place in evolution. (Hobbes, however, wisely warns us: "If I read as many books as you do, I'd be as ignorant as you are.")

There is another condition of which we should take advantage if we possibly can: association with some person who believes in the unseen more intensively than we ourselves do, and membership in a small training group. When we meet a man who can say to us, "This next rung of the ladder that scares you I myself slipped from but finally was able to get back on and keep climbing," we are given a bracing breath of faith that few books can impart. Moreover, such energizing persons are often in our neighborhood waiting to be sought out. Participation in a team is also an aid. Most of us need reinforcement that comes of being bound together with others also trying to say Yes. That is what churches are for. Unfortunately, the intimacy has become so spread out that often it is necessary to pour into the stale pool a jet of freshness that only the very small group can release.

Perhaps fifteen is the maximum size. Two can begin, but before long there will probably be more. Each group works out its own specific ways of proceeding. Something is lost if the meetings are not regular. The first group I joined was at seminary. We only had eighteen or twenty minutes twice a week, but we found that all possible promptness and faithfulness were necessary; and we found, too, that what was thus given was worth more than many lectures.

The small group's magnetic field cannot be measured. Its influence carries farther than its members often suspect. Among the by-products are an increase of reverence for personality, the sense of being drawn by a purpose instead of being pushed around by miscellaneous pressures, and the encouragement that everybody needs. Otherwise, you are in danger of "seeing the price of everything and the value of nothing." If half a dozen others are with you on the climb, it is not likely that you will all be manically depressive at the same time. Somebody is sure to whistle out of sheer excess of vitality at the very moment when you feel most like quitting. Another thing. It is improbable that you will ever have a group experience without being led through that contact into the discovery of possibilities that you would not have come upon alone. The other night a training group of young people meeting in a home heard a fourteen-year-old in a matter-of-fact manner describe how she had been trying an experiment. She had read about it in a novel. The trick was to imagine before doing anything how Jesus would do it if he were analyzing, reacting, or making decisions through one's own personality. "It's so much fun," she went on, "that if you try it one day, you'll want to keep it up."

Two or three weeks later, asked how she was making out, she answered, "I find it's a little harder than I thought," but she had not yet forgotten her new project.

At another meeting a twenty-six-year-old, facing the chance of soon going to jail in the interests of his conscience, brought in his contribution of ozone. He had given up a job paying seventy-two cents an hour, making cheap furniture, for a cabinet job at fifty cents an hour. The choices he was making were touching off the creative powers that all his life had been cooped up. "When I was on the street car coming home from work," he told the group, "I didn't hear any voice or anything like that. But something inside seemed to be telling me this: 'See those eucalyptus branches waving. You didn't? All right, look at that pine tree. No? Will you look at the light green cactus? O well, then, here's another chance, this cherry tree with the blossoms. Surely you will pay attention now.' "

The magnetic field set up by such "cells" is the opposite of what is associated with that "immoral society" about which we have been so eloquently told, whose impersonal unrepentant collectives offer no hope. Instead, these huge entities are always, as Niebuhr reminds us, "losing their souls trying to save their skins." It is even claimed that when the devil captures such an institution, he is too clever to change the flag. He simply lets the old crowd carry on under their accustomed slogans. The cross under which Constantine's legions marched was thus a triumph for the dark power they were supposed to be fighting. Over against totalitarianism and bigness, which so often are but mass escapes from the urgency of each conscience to make right choices of its own, the small group stands, quietly inserting into the darkness the sparks of integrity and good will that are invaluable to the world. The group generates light and energy according as each member practices, at least in some degree, openness to what is more than beauty and truth and goodness. While absent from the group, he is under obligation to school himself in skills that might include these. Before meeting another person, he recalls the privilege of willing as Saint Paul willed, "May you be filled with the entire fullness of God." That other person he tries to see against no ordinary background. Behind him is the Grand Canyon with its depth and ever-changing glory as the slowly marching cloud shadows bring out the violets and reds of the cliffs ten miles away.

At the start, the trainee, undertaking to see people in terms of such dimensions, will constantly fail. Before the group, he will admit that during the past week he functioned only twice. The honesty will encourage him and them to do better the following week. The group will double-check each other with regard to perhaps another new habit; at least once a day each member will think of every other member as sincerely living up to the spirit and presence which the whole group is together seeking. The minimum of time agreed upon for meditation may be fifteen minutes every day. During that time each one pays attention to this Being through methods he or the group shapes as they go along. It is like learning to play tennis. There are false, ridiculous motions. The ball sails over the fence or drops into the net. The beginner hardly ever places it where he wants it. The failures do not deflect him. He is out to master this art of loving God, not for His gifts but for Himself. As a result of this individual practice something mysterious but unmistakable is multiplied in and not merely added to the group. One could almost call it "coordinating power." Without it, the institution, however imposing and "religious," might become a shell.

During its first vigorous unspoiled centuries Christianity's little groups developed a love and joy and peace that turned an empire upside down. This revolutionary fervor can be restored. Nothing less will be of much use to the world. But if the church is to function again as it once did, it will have to train at least some of its members to meet not alone in "good fellowship" with picnics and the usual club solidarity, or alone in extrovert efforts to get a better mayor and food to the children in Europe, important as these activities are. Nor will it be enough to encourage the growth of the sacramental relationship of sex in homes which are themselves small groups pouring a healthy spirit into social life. There will have to be comradeship even deeper than all these other expressions of the desire to be together, and that is the binding that comes only through intensive group and solitary meditation and prayer, and redemptive effort inspired by such discipline, redemptive effort that dares to demand the co-operative organization of the planet.

The church is meant to become a fellowship over the world, integrating and reconciling men. If it betrays Jesus by acquiescing to their standards, it will be betraying them. They will not say this out loud, but their eyes will show their disappointment. The time is coming when it will be hard for men to believe anything. There will be broken nerves, disillusionment, bitterness, and the darkness that has to come because we have broken God's law. What will be needed more than anything else will be faith and forgiveness. This is the church's opportunity. Beginning now, it can intensively train persons to become so full of integrity and good will that they can outmatch at least some of the negativism of a disenchanted world with the grace of God. The church will then have the right and the power to speak from its center and men will listen. Even now they will pay attention if with the authority of inward experience the church will clearly say:

"God is. We are in His presence now. He is nearer to us than we are to ourselves, and He is at least truth and love. He has given each one of us the appalling power to turn away from Him. He has also given us the marvelous power at any moment to turn toward him. The consequences of the harm we all have done will for a time continue. But we ourselves can move in a new direction and become less unlike Christ. We can begin this instant by ourselves forgiving. We can depend upon it: the resources will be given if we try to say Yes."

The encouraging thing today is the quality of commitment to this witness shown by thousands of people who have no intention of giving it up and who know they would be betraying even the men who fight if they did. They are not "moral parasites on the sins of soldiers." On the contrary, the faith which they seek to gain and share is the most valuable contribution they can make. Moreover, many a man in uniform recognizes the fact. There are combatants who would rather have their minister renounce the chance to be with them in danger where the minister would like to be, rather than forsake his commitment to what he believes to be the love and truth of God as exhibited in the life and death of Jesus. I have personal letters indicating how deep is the hope, secretly entertained by men in action, that someone will prove to be light in the midst of the present confusion that no hurricane of hate can blow out. The men who suffer and speak lightly of their suffering do not want those who represent Jesus to run away from Jesus just because there are panic and pressure. The method they are using to organize the world puzzles and sometimes sickens them. What they want is to have the disintegration "over with." If our conviction gives us no other choice but to rely on a different method, they are not likely to feel we are letting them down, so long as we are sincerely disciplining ourselves and becoming less flabby.

The training that alone will bring coherence into the world has to be drastic, and it has to start with the effort to win coherence within. Teamwork is imperative, in small units as well as big ones. But it has to be in terms of each man's own integrity and not in terms of what the herd, whether ecclesiastic or national, dictates. A man will not show reverence to his neighbor . . . unless he, first of all, is loyal to "that of God" which is in himself. It is up our own "secret stairway" that each of us, making his own unique response, has to climb toward the Light.

Walter M. Horton

(1895——)

WALTER HORTON has been one of America's most constructive Christian theistic writers. Out of a background of education in America, Germany, and France, and teaching experience in the Oberlin Graduate School of Theology for the past twenty years, his thinking has related Christian worship values to life in a comprehensive manner. Several of his books have described contemporary Christian thinking in countries other than the United States; all of his writings have related Christian theology in a deeply devotional fashion to the entirety of human experience. As an ecumenical leader he has given particular stress to the Church as the Living Body through which the Spirit integrates human beings with God.

The following selection clearly depicts his view of Christ's relationship to the devotional spirit which abides in the Church. Especially does it suggest how the terms "Holy Spirit" and "Christ" have relationship to the immanence of God in a Christian theistic pattern of thought. It is reprinted from *Our Eternal Contemporary* by permission of Harper & Brothers. (Copyright 1942 by Harper & Brothers.)

JESUS AS THE ONE WHO BECAME THE LIVING CHRIST

From *Our Eternal Contemporary*

Jesus might be described as the "head" and "founder" of a new humanity if he had merely furnished the Church with its "chief cornerstone," and determined the general lines on which the rest of the structure was to be built. This much he surely did. But actually, the relationship between the Church and her head has been more vital than any metaphor from the mechanic arts or the building trades can suggest. The Church has been the living, growing body of which he has been the animating soul, or, changing the figure, she has been the bride and he the husband. Nothing did more to create the Church in the first place than the conviction that Jesus had survived his Crucifixion and become, by his Spirit, *a living Presence at the heart of the Church,* "even unto the end of the world"; nothing has done more to keep the Church alive than the conviction that her Lord still lives, still guides, still intercedes, still works and fights in and through her for the enlargement of humanity.

It is not necessary to distinguish too sharply between the idea of the living Christ and the idea of the Holy Spirit. The Holy Spirit was felt by the Early Church to be both the abiding presence of the Risen Lord, and the abiding presence of that divine power which had raised him from the dead. God sent Jesus, Jesus sent the Spirit, God sent the Spirit. In distinction from that *coming-forth to meet us* which is the special characteristic of God the Word (whether in "parts and portions" in the prophets or in its fullness in Jesus) the special characteristic of God the Holy Spirit is a kind of *bubbling-up within us (or among us)*. The Spirit, or the Living Christ, is the most *immediate* and *inward* form in which we experience God. When we think of the inwardness of this experience, the way in which it fans to flame the spark of God that is at the depth of our own being, we speak of the Holy Spirit; when we connect it with its source, and the whole movement of redemption, we may properly refer to the Living Christ, for the flame in us is a flame kindled by Jesus, and constantly replenished by the grace that comes to us from the Word of Wisdom and Power that was incarnate in him. The Living Christ is the Yea to which the Spirit says Amen; the Yea and the Amen both testify to the same unshakable promises of God.

Whether we describe this inward Presence of God in the Church as the Holy Spirit, or as the Living Christ, it proceeds from Jesus, and is an extension of his life. Canon Quick has shown how disastrous are the effects upon Christian thought of the tendency to isolate the figure of the historic Jesus from the spiritual development of the Church in succeeding centuries. When thought concentrates (as in the Ritschlian school) upon the isolated figure of the historic Jesus, it ends either in a Unitarianism which minimizes the unique revelation of God in him, or in a "Jesuolatry" which loads every conceivable divine attribute upon his human shoulders. When thought concentrates (as in the Hegelian school) upon the development of the Christian movement, it ends either in an idolatrous worship of the Church as she is, or in a reduction of the Incarnation to a general embodiment of the divine Idea in man and nature. To avoid these and other grave deformations of the Christian Gospel, we need to think, when we say "Christ," both of the historic life of Jesus and of its continuation, through his Mind or Spirit, in the Church. The Christ who saves is this Christ, who once walked our human way amid all the difficulties we have to face, but triumphed over them all by God's power, and is "alive forevermore" in the midst of the Church.

In an earlier study, I have underlined the danger of baptizing conventional morals and average churchmanship into the name of "Christ." I still think the danger a real one, but it is serious only when the idea of the Living Christ is allowed to drift out of connection with the actual life of the historic Jesus. Then, indeed, the name of Christ becomes a blank check for all our favorite clichés and prejudices. But if the real historic Jesus, or his real Spirit, is anywhere about the premises, he does not tolerate such forgery of his name! There is something in the very heart of the Church that is properly called the Mind of Christ, and this Mind acts as a sharp criterion of much that is called "Christian." John on Patmos saw the Living Christ standing in the midst of the Seven Churches of Asia with a two-edged sword of judgment proceeding out of his mouth, while at the same time he held the stars of their divine destiny in his hand. So it is still. Christ's Spirit is not only our Comforter, but our Judge and our Vindicator. This it is that is divine in the Church, that sifts and purges the poor human materials of which the Church is composed, and uses the faithful "remnant" that remains for God's own purposes, so that the gates of hell cannot prevail against her. Churches can fall, but the Church of the Remnant never, for she is the chosen Body of the Living Christ, who is "God with us" still.

Douglas V. Steere
(1901——)

OF contemporary religious books which deal with the significance of sainthood in the modern world, Steere's *On Beginning from Within* is one of the best. A freshness of interpretation, a beauty of style, and an apt use of illustration make it deeply appealing to those interested in the devotional life.

Steere was educated at Michigan State College, Harvard, and Oxford, where he was a Rhodes scholar. Since 1928 he has taught philosophy at Haverford College. He is a member of the Society of Friends. His religious position is that of a critical realist who apprehends an "Other" as of basic value in religious experience.

"A New Set of Devotional Exercises" was given as one of four lectures in the William Belden Noble series at Harvard in March and April, 1943. It is reprinted from *On Beginning from Within* by permission of Harper & Brothers. (Copyright 1943 by Harper & Brothers.)

A NEW SET OF DEVOTIONAL EXERCISES
From *On Beginning from Within*

Now I am concerned that the *Spiritual Exercises* be written anew in our time. I am concerned that they be written out of as basic an insight into the sensual and bodily and psychological mechanisms of man as Ignatius possessed, but that they be devised in order to produce another type of obedience: an obedience which is neither military, as is the Jesuit obedience, nor even feudalistically paternal, as is Catholic piety generally, but which is a type of obedience that becomes a son, not of a feudal authoritarian Father for all of His love, but of a wise and mature Father, a type of obedience that becomes a human friend of "the friend behind phenomena," or that becomes a group of friends of God who are working together in His service.

TOWARD CREATIVE OBEDIENCE

I have glimpsed the nature of this obedience. I once travelled with two Friends through the Scandinavian countries. We were together for five weeks. We knew each other intimately before we began. Each of us knew that the purpose of our journey was not a matter of private employment but of corporate service in the ministry. No one in the group made decisions by right of even delegated priority, although often we divided tasks in order to execute them. Again and again in meetings we found one of us thrust back and another lifted up in the service. Again and again we found our plans remolded, and as we sat loose, things opened, or if we sat stubbornly tight and refused to yield, the result was not enduring. As we came near the end of our journey, we seemed to wear down individual resistance and to be able increasingly to know each other from within, and we became more and more free with each other. Obedience was there. We lived and travelled and dealt with our work and with each other under obedience.

William Penn once wrote of George Fox:

He was of an innocent life; no busybody, nor self-seeker, neither touchy nor critical . . . so meek, contented, modest, easy, steady, tender, it was a pleasure to be in his company.

He exercised no authority but over evil, and that everywhere and in all; but with love, compassion, and long-suffering.

There is the record of the fruit of this kind of obedience in a life. I have seen groups, in which individuals had made bitter accusations against each other, come under that authority, and in the midst of corporate, silent prayer first one and then the other of the assailants would ask pardon, and a creative solution of the dispute would emerge. That is a faint hint of the kind of obedience I would have these spiritual exercises encourage.

My wife and I once visited the little Dutch city of Deventer in Holland, where Gerard Groote lived some 550 years ago and where the Brethren of the Common Life were born. One Sunday afternoon we were walking near a great church that had a high flight of stone steps, perhaps thirty-five or forty of them leading up from the street to the entry way. A child of perhaps three had slowly climbed these steps and was now at the top. His parents were strolling about in the street below. Having reached the top, the child shouted and boasted of his accomplishment and they acknowledged it. Then he called to his father to come and get him. The father beckoned to him to come down. In succession the child shouted, screamed, stamped his little feet and went into a rage. But the father only beckoned to him to come down. Finally, he put down one foot cautiously to the first step, then another and another, and slowly and carefully he dismounted the steps. My wife and I watched him anxiously. A fall down those stone steps would have had serious consequences. At last, he reached the bottom safely and ran at top speed to the father and mother, who took him warmly by the hands, and they went off together. The costly act of that father and mother revealed creative love to me and that child learned creative obedience. After that they could go hand in hand together.

It is a costly business to draw forth an appropriate obedience to that kind of creative love, and yet it is to draw men and women to respond obediently to a God who offers that kind of love that I would like to see the *Spiritual Exercises* rewritten in our time. And all that follows here might be considered as *preliminary notes* for such a set of exercises, which I hope some reader, if that is his task, after he, like St. Ignatius, has practiced them on himself, has lived enough, has suffered enough, has yielded enough, and has known the needs of others intimately enough, may set down for our use.

Asceticism in the New Spiritual Exercises

I personally have little or nothing to say about the use of ascetic practices—of fasting, of keeping long periods of silence, of the simplifying of life, of celibacy—perhaps because my experience of them is more bookish than real. Yet I would not exclude a serious consideration of them from the new spiritual exercises. For none of the saints have ever gotten on without them. In all asceticism the principle of abstaining from things that are precious and good (from food, from speech, from physical comforts, from marriage) for the sake of accentuating something more good in itself is a sound principle and is sound practice, so long as it is done voluntarily and joyously and not grimly, and so long as it can be regarded as a matter of private vocation and is not universally pressed on others. Like Berdyaev I feel that "there is nothing more repulsive than petrified lifeless virtues, or than an ascetic turned mummy and become an enemy of all human impulses."

The older monastic orders have long ago learned that a man who is "an enemy of all human impulses" makes a poor monk. I once asked the prior of a Benedictine abbey some of the qualities which they looked for in a man who was being considered as a possible novice. Among other traits he emphasized that any man who was a confirmed misogynist, who had a hatred or contempt for, or a fear of, women or for the married state, was automatically disqualified. The principle seemed to be that one must possess and prize what one offers up in the monastic vows of chastity, if the sacrifice is to be creative. In the long introduction to his *The Flashing Stream*, Charles Morgan relates a similar case of a woman whose loquacity was so great that it became almost unbearable, even to herself, and so she resolved to enter one of the strictest of women's contemplative orders where perpetual silence was kept. On visiting the convent the wise mother superior promptly sent her away telling her that she must first learn the preciousness of speech by self-control before she came to offer it as a gift to God. To those whose special calling draws them to give up these precious and good things either temporarily or permanently, there has often come a particular holiness and preciousness about just these things, which the very abstention from them for God's sake has seemed to help accentuate.

The device of these ascetic practices which often reopen men and women to the presence of God and keep them humbly close to the suffering that is the lot of so considerable a part of the world may be replaced in many by their vocations, where they already share intimately in the daily sufferings of others in their own communities. But we are men and women of short memories, and some daily or periodical ascetic practice may be necessary to break the vegetative cycle and to make us "remember," as Theresa of Avila says, "the guest we have within us."

THE CASE FOR "ISLANDS" OF SILENCE

Next, in this new manual of training for the life of devotion, there should be a presentation of the necessity for taking time for retirement, for going apart, time to be alone and to enter into directed silence. When Professor Spragg, my teacher of plant breeding at the Michigan Agricultural College, wanted to increase a new strain of Rosen rye which he had gotten from Russia and had then bred until it yielded three times what common rye would yield on the same land, he took it out to several farmers who lived on an isolated little island called Manitou Island in Lake Michigan. There, with no other strain of rye being grown on the island, and with the lake a protection from alien pollen, the new Rosen rye might be grown and the strain kept free from cross-fertilization. In this way Professor Spragg was able to increase the pure Rosen rye until he had enough seed to send out to selected growers throughout the state. By this process of year after year putting uncrossed pure seed into the hands of the rye growers of the state, he almost tripled their rye yield on a given acreage. There is no increasing of the pure seed of the spiritual life that does not call for both initial and frequent returns to an island of silence.

The realization of the necessity of such "islands" is not new. Pythagoras required each applicant to his community of scholars to spend a year in complete silence in order to get back to first principles before he would begin to instruct him in mathematics. Francis de Sales would never think of preaching a course of Lenten Sermons without making a personal retreat of several days into directed silence. Sir Thomas More during the years of his heavy obligations as Lord High Chancellor and King's Counsellor took the Friday of each week for retirement into a little building on his estate in Chelsea, where he devoted himself to prayer and spiritual reading.

The psychological population, which is the number of people we are aware of, is estimated by sociologists to have been increased two hundred times by means of the vast network of communications which the past century has brought. In the urban life of the western world we live in a veritable hail of stimuli that solicit our continual response. The tempo of our lives has increased until we feel continually "driven" by life. Our very architecture shuns privacy. A Swedish architect described to me a new office building in Stockholm where transparent glass brick was used for all office partitions. He went on to tell how one occupant was so unhappy that he painted the inside walls of his glass brick in a desperate attempt to recover at least a skim of privacy. Lewis Mumform in his *Culture of Cities* says of this same architectural tendency in very modern dwelling houses:

In throwing open our buildings to the daylight and the outdoors, we will forget at our peril the coordinate need for quiet, for darkness, for inner privacy, for retreat. The home without such cells is but a barracks, the city that does not possess them is but a camp.

Living as we do in this kind of climate of dispersion, withdrawal, going apart, retirement, and being alone become no longer an option but an imperative to anyone who would enter and grow in the Christian life. George Herbert's counsel must, then, be central:

By all means use sometimes to be alone.
Salute thyself; see what thy soul doth wear.
Dare to look in thy chest; for 'tis thine own;
And tumble up and down what thou find'st there.
Who cannot rest till he good fellows find,
He breaks up house, turns out of doors his mind.

The new spiritual exercises should, therefore, both counsel the daily withdrawal and give more than vague instructions for the longer periodic times of retreat. This is not the place for such detailed suggestions in regard to the nature of these longer periods of retreat. But a new pattern, including a sustained period of silence which would, however, include spiritual instruction, devotional reading, private and corporate devotions, and manual work something after the fashion of the Iona Community in Scotland, has much to commend it for a fresh approach to this type of exercise. Experiments in this country with precisely this type of exercise have brought great inward refreshment to many of those participating.

This new set of spiritual exercises must not stop, however, at counselling a time of daily or periodic withdrawal. They must also teach an undisciplined mind and will the proper use of such a period. If it is to achieve its deepest goal, it must become more than a period of general

relaxation or even of relaxation to the surrounding world of nature. I like to read Thoreau's *Walden Pond* from time to time and I find that it cleanses me from some of the fevers of modern complexity. But it is of little help to me for that deeper fever known as multiplicity of heart. For that disease more penetrating remedies must be sought than those the Cosmic Yankee could provide. Therefore, the exercises should provide for more than relaxation in the presence of nature. They must direct the seeker to meditation and to prayer and they should give specific instruction in each, at the same time that it made clear that the diversity of ways that men approach God or that God approaches men may recast all of these instructions for any given man.

MEDITATION IN THE NEW SPIRITUAL EXERCISES

Meditation should be explained as a voluntary act of the mind, in which the mind out of the infinite subjects for thought at its disposal deliberately chooses to concentrate and continually to re-present to itself for consideration these particular scenes, these particular questions, these particular ideas which are the subjects of its meditation. It resolves to cease to flit over the world at large and to *think of these things*.

Is this not auto-suggestion? Yes, it is precisely that, and we ought to drive away all fear of the nickname which a decade ago so terrified religious people. For what is auto-suggestion anyway? Instead of the mind submitting itself to the objective tyranny of hetero-suggestion, in which the external stimuli determine the content and direction of its thought, in auto-suggestion it exercises a wise asceticism, pulls up the drawbridge, and as far as possible becomes inaccessible to new stimuli or outer suggestions. Then it chooses out of the vast riches available to it one or more specific areas and focuses its attention upon it. The meditator now determines the suggestion that shall be considered. It is auto-determined; it is auto-suggestion. And the fact that auto-suggestion is possible is one of the most remarkable evidences of the freedom of the human mind.

Meditation need not, and should not, enlist only the ideational mind, but should make wide use of the whole sensory imaginative powers. And it is here that these exercises have much to learn from Ignatius of Loyola, who knew, better than we seem to know, the truth of Marcus Aurelius' saying that "our lives are dyed the color of our imaginations." The use of the scenes from the life and death and reappearance of Christ should be central in the new exercises as they were in Loyola's. The value of hanging the picture gallery of the mind with these scenes and of keeping them freshly before us by frequent, prolonged revisitation, as in meditation, can scarcely be exaggerated. The drawing out of the senses in each of these scenes should be encouraged.

Listen to Ignatius' instructions for meditating on the Nativity scene:

It will be here with the sight of the imagination to see the way from Nazareth to Bethlehem, considering length, width, and whether such way be flat or whether through Valleys, or hills; likewise looking at the place or cave of the Nativity, how large, how tiny, how low, how high and how it was furnished . . . see the persons . . . our Lady, and Joseph, and the handmaid, and the infant Jesus after He was born, making myself a poor bit of a body and an unworthy little servant, looking at them, studying them and serving them in their needs, as if I were there present, with all possible readiness to serve with all possible reverence.

In the next two separate hours of meditation this exercise and a previous one on the Annunciation are repeated, "noting always some more striking portions in which the seeker has felt some enlightenment, consolation or desolation." And in a further hour of meditation the five senses of the imagination are passed over these two objects of meditation, first sight, then hearing, noting the things they say or may say, then smell and taste, and finally "to touch with the touch, as

for instance to embrace and kiss the place where such persons tread and sit."

Even in this brief extract from Ignatius on the enlistment of the sensory imagination we are made aware that this is no leisurely promenade through the Louvre. This is an *exercise*. And the seeker is stirred to participate in the action, to help at the birth scene, and in later meditation to join Jesus on his tramps through Palestine, to kneel with the weary disciples at Gethsemane, to bear His cross on his shoulders on the way up to Calvary, to gather in desperation in the throng at the cross and to walk with Him to Emmaus and sit at bread with Him. Beyond this, in each meditation there is the consideration of what this scene means for your life. In the light of it, what must you do to serve him this day? And in the colloquy, or what Francis de Sales calls "the little nosegay," with which each meditation is to end, the seeker is instructed to talk to Christ "just as one friend speaks to another," as one asks oneself, "What have I done for Christ? What am I doing for Christ? What ought I to do for Christ?" And having talked out these questions carry away some specific flower of insight or plan of action from each hour of meditation. These little plans of action may even be written out and returned to again and again through the day in the swift little prayers, the ejaculations, that do so much to restore us to obedience. The *Spiritual Exercises* furnish us with a whole library of such suggestions on the use of sensory imagery in the early stages of meditation.

In a modern set of spiritual exercises, however, there is equally the need for specific meditation or another feature of the Ignatian meditation, namely, upon the end and purpose of life, so that again and again we are brought to re-examine what we are here for and in the light of this to re-evaluate what we are uniquely commissioned to do. "There is no more desolate or Ismaelitish creature in nature than a man who has broken away from his true genius," wrote Nietzsche. "There is no reason to attack such a man, for he is a mere husk without a kernel, a painted cloth, tattered, sagging, a scarecrow, ghost, that can rouse no fear and certainly no pity." This can always best be done in the presence of some one, and once again we see that it is not by accident that Ignatius suggests that when we are beginning to learn to meditate on what we are here for, on the *Foundation*, or on our sins, we do so best by imagining ourselves in the presence of God or in the presence of Christ. Let this examination be made in Their company. Once again the military image of Christ, the Captain, supplied by Ignatius may well be replaced by a Friend or Father with creative love, by a love that draws and burns in the same stroke.

Of the soul in the presence of Jesus, John Henry Newman writes: "There is a pleading in His pensive eyes—Will pierce thee to the quick and trouble thee." This image of wounded love transforms the Ignatian military figure into a Presence that calls for an obedience that is neither militaristic nor feudalistically filial, but is an obedience that binds free men to that which can alone receive their complete devotion without exploiting them. It is in this Presence that the meditation should consciously enter.

These meditations should also include a contemplation of sin and of its consequences, and of our own sins. Here again the sense of doing it in the presence of another, of confessing at the foot of the cross, of facing sin in the presence of a departed one is of great assistance, and the sense of wounded love rather than of an oriental potentate's wrath or the terrors of a shrieking, stinking, sizzling pit will mark the setting of the modern exercises.

This sense of wounded love, that strikes at the sinful obsession with self, is uppermost in the *Theologia Germanica* where its unknown author wrote: "Nothing burneth in Hell but self-will." William Law puts it in extreme form when he declares in his *Spirit of Prayer* that "from eternity to eternity no spark of wrath ever was or ever will be in the holy triune of God." George Tyrrell,

although he is speaking of preaching, puts the basis of the revision of such a meditation with great precision in a posthumously published book of his:

Hence instead of Hell-fire, I should preach the hollowness of the self-life in and out, up and down, till men loathed it and cried 'Quis me liberabit?' And then I should turn men to the Christ-life, not only of Christ, but of all Christlike men, and make its reality, solidity, eternity stand out stereoscopically.

These modern meditations must not stop with personal sin but must go on to social sin and to its results, to the responsibility we bear for each other, perhaps even to the arousing of the spirit of an Origen who cannot believe that the whole travailing creation will ever stop until every soul has been redeemed, and even to Tyrrell's sense of corporate affection which he expresses in a letter to von Hügel written in 1902:

I don't think you understand how absolutely, and indeed culpably little I ever cared about my own soul, my present and future peace, except as a condition of helpfulness to others . . . Like Moses, I had rather be damned with the mass of humanity than saved alone or even with the minority.

There must be no saccharine piety about the counsel which these new spiritual exercises give on the use of meditation. "From silly devotions, God, deliver us," pleads Theresa of Avila with her blunt realism. These meditations are work, strenuous, voluntary work, and the learning to concentrate and hold the mind on them is for many far harder than most discursive reading and writing. A sailor boy was once taking an abbreviated Ignatian Meditation and was meditating on the *Foundation* that man is made to praise his Creator and is made for salvation. He was found pacing up and down the room stamping his foot from time to time and saying, "Damn it, it's true; damn it, it's true." I am not suggesting this as a pattern for your meditations, but quite likely education of the will was in progress here. Even when undertaken in repose and quiet these meditations are, as has been said earlier, acts of voluntary and directed intensity by which we loosen ourselves from the secular and vegetative and self-absorbed cycle and open the way for another order to enter.

MEDITATION YIELDS TO PRAYER

Helpful as such meditations may be, they are and can never be other than an exercise to open and prepare the person for prayer. And while the new spiritual exercises can never do more than incite to prayer, they must contain a deep enough notion of prayer to make all those who do not practice it have an acute sense of their poverty. Even Ignatius at the close of his manual insists that all the exercises are nothing but preparation for the prayer of affection and should drop away if and when it comes, just as we turn off the lamp when the sun comes up. For while there are elements of conscious guidance in prayer, in its deeper levels it becomes a simple, loving response to the creative love of God, and the pray-er may be taken far beyond where he has guided the prayer when he gives over the reins freely. In the new manual, therefore, all should lead up to prayer where not will or intellect or emotion is central but where the root or ground or principle in a man's nature that is beneath all of these is joyously exposed to this cooperation with God.

Augustine calls this underlying principle "desire," but he does not mean by it an emotional affair.

For thy desire is thy prayer; and if thy desire is without ceasing, thy prayer will also be without ceasing . . . There is interior prayer without ceasing, and this is your desire. Whatever else you do, if you do but long for that sabbath, you do not cease to pray. If you would never cease to pray, never cease to long after it. The continuance of your longing is the continuance of your prayer. You will be ceasing to speak if you cease to love. The chilling of charity is the silence of the heart. If love is without ceasing, you are always lifting up your voice; if you are ever lifting up your voice, you are ever longing for something; if you are longing, the rest you long for is in your mind.

This making of prayer as the deep, creative longing of the ground, Augustine once more expresses in a burst of aspiration:

My whole heart I lay upon the altar of thy praise, a holocaust of praise I offer to Thee. Let the flame of Thy love set on fire my whole heart; may I wholly burn toward Thee, wholly on fire towards Thee, wholly love Thee as though set aflame by Thee.

This emphasis upon prayer being the soul's deepest desire, however, is a linking of the life of the pray-er with the prayer. It means that the prayer means as much or as little as the man behind it, and if he remain brittle and cross and stiff-necked his prayer will be infected. Martin Buber in his book of ancient Jewish legends has drawn a vivid picture of a man who went into a synagogue to pray, but who found that the synagogue stifled him. From floor to ceiling it was full of dead prayers, prayers that had been said by worshipers only with their lips, but that had behind them no buoyant intent of deep desire to lift them to God. Inward prayer assumes that the whole man is behind the prayer and that his life is being ordered in accord with his inward yearning, which the prayer expresses.

Isaac Pennington puts it very simply when he says:

By prayer I do not mean any bodily exercise of the outward man; but the going forth of the spirit of life toward the foundation of life for fulness and satisfaction; the natural tendency of the poor, rent, derived spirit towards the foundation of spirits. . . Remember, oh my soul, the quietude of those in whom Christ governs, and in all thy proceedings feel after it.

In Cologne, early in 1940, a much-beloved professor of philosophy, Peter Wust, lay dying after a long illness. His pupils sent in word to him and asked him to give them a parting message of counsel from his deepest experience of life. He sent back to them the following message:

The magic key is not reflection, as you might expect from philosopher, but it is prayer. Prayer as the most complete act of devotion makes us quiet, makes us objective. A man grows in true humanity in prayer. Prayer is the final humility of the spirit. The greatest things in existence will only be given to those who pray. In suffering one learns to pray best of all.

This "final humility of the spirit," prayer, may be expressed so simply that it would seem almost a violation of its nature to elaborate the aspects of it. The Curé of Ars found one of his peasant parishioners often spending hours kneeling before the altar, utterly motionless, and obviously bent on speaking with God. One day the Curé asked him what he said to God. "Oh," replied the peasant, "He looks at me and I look at Him." That was all there was to it. Francis of Assisi prayed through the night, "My God and my All, what art Thou and what am I."

That utter and complete loving back with the longing and concern to bring every area of your own life, and to bring other persons or institutions or situations that stand outside of creative obedience into an agile response to this source of love is, of course, the heart of prayer. All confession, petition, intercession, waiting prayers and adoration are only aspects of this.

These exercises must give counsel in the use of the prayer of confession where a soul comes under the gaze of God and where in His silent and loving Presence this soul is pierced to the quick and becomes conscious of the things that must be forgiven and put right before it can continue to love One whose care has been so constant. It is one thing to be ordered from the table like a naughty boy to go and wash your hands. George Buttrick once told me of how he had sent his son David away from the table on such an errand one time, and as the boy left the room he said, "I'll go, Dad, but my heart isn't in it." It is another thing, however, to discover your own unclean hands when you sit down with someone for whom you care deeply and whose own cleanness arouses in you the awareness of your deficiency. When a child makes this discovery, quietly excuses itself, retires and returns with clean hands, even a parent forgives the delay and rejoices at the initiative. For he knows this time that the child had his heart in this creative act of obedience. Confession in prayer should be depicted like that in the new spiritual exercises.

The new spiritual exercises would recognize the universal tendency of men to carry their longings and desires into prayer in the form of either conscious or unconscious petition. This is not a thing to be encouraged or discouraged. It is a *given*. What is to be encouraged is that in prayer men should hold these desires sensitively enough and open enough and keep them there long enough to sense their congruity or incongruity with creative obedience to God's love. If this is made clear, then a man in prayer, as in free association, can begin anywhere. What matters is what he comes to. "Did thee yield?" the old Quaker asked. "Was thee faithful?" That is what matters about petitionary prayer.

INTERCESSION IS COOPERATION WITH GOD'S REDEMPTIVE POWER

The new exercises should encourage the all too seldom practice of intercessory prayer, what someone has called "unselfishness in prayer," or "loving your neighbor on your knees." Intercessory prayer may have to be called something else, for it does not mean interceding before a magistrate to ask a special privilege for another. It is rather a cooperating with God's already active redemptive powers to let them work in a given person, institution, or situation. It is a loving fellowship with them in the life of God which undergirds you both. There is no other way that friendship can be brought to its deepest fruit.

In 1901 von Hügel wrote his dear friend, Tyrrell, "I can most truthfully declare that no day passes but you are at least thrice definitely in my prayers; as you are one of the little band scattered throughout space, but united, I feel happily confident, in its struggles, prayers and ideals which ever cheers me on to try and do better, to give more, really all, gratefully, and to accept the *something* that comes of it."

Pastor John Frederic Oberlin in his parsonage at Ban de la Roche, on his knees at a given hour each morning to pray for each separate member of his congregation, and the people hushing each other in the street as they passed his house, knowing the time of day it was and what was going on; a New England pastor that I have corresponded with, dropping in at his church late in the afternoon, and sitting in the pew, now of this family and now of that one, holding them up before God that they might be released to let God work in and through them; the little band of friends who dined with the statesman Wilberforce before he went to Parliament to deliver his great address on the abolition of slavery in the British Empire, questioning whether to go with him to hear the speech in the gallery of the Commons or go home and pray that God might work in that situation, and deciding each to go to his own home and to pray; a Japanese girl praying that God might work in her drunken father and that he might respond with the full life she knew was in him, and the father yielding and becoming a member of the little religious community in which a friend of mine is counsellor—the new spiritual exercises will encourage this kind of prayer of cooperation with God, this prayer in which we have fellowship with others in that which is eternal.

Little need be said of the highest form of intentional, directed prayer, namely, that of adoration, of thankfulness to God. To pause in prayer and to thank Him for Himself, for His being what He is, to tilt the heart upward to the Lover and be glad, this has a natural place in all silent prayer. An old man was asked how he prayed, and he replied that he just sat for half an hour a day in a mood of profound thankfulness to God. His prayer was that, and that was his prayer.

THE PRAYER OF ATTENTIVE OPENNESS

But there is a further aspect of prayer which these devotional exercises must encourage if they are to penetrate beyond the anteroom of prayer. That is the simple prayer of attentive openness. George Fox has expressed it with great simplicity:

Be still and cool in thy own mind and spirit from thy own thoughts, and then thou wilt feel the principle of God, to turn thy mind to the Lord, from whom strength comes, whereby thou mayest receive His strength and power to allay all blusterings, storms and tempests. That is it which works up into patience, into innocency, into soberness, into stillness, into staidness. into quietness, up to God with His power . . . Therefore, be still awhile from thy own thoughts, searching, seeking, desires, and imaginations, and be staid in the principle of God in thee, that it may raise thy mind up to God; . . . and thou wilt find strength from Him, and find Him to be a God at hand, a present help in time of trouble and in need.

I remember a brilliant professor who was expressing his impatience with the use of this attentive openness in the meditation periods we try to cultivate in the planned day of our Quaker work camps. "When I sit down in silence I can only think of ways to mend the cistern, of concrete things, and I have to be thinking of concrete solutions or I can't abide it." In all mature prayer this immensely busy, discursive activity of the mind in our professor friend must be wearied out, must be left behind. "Be still and cool in thy own mind, from thy own thoughts." This mood of prayer is not thinking. It is a pausing from the harnessed activity of thought and in a mood of unhurried calm; it is an opening of the mind in all its oneness to its Source.

Here it is that the refreshment, that the renewal, that the healing may come, and here it is, too, that intimations and concerns may develop that no forced, intense, directed thinking would have aroused. If these specific concerns involve a serious change in life, they require testing by further waiting, by subsequent prayer, and at times by exposing them to others. These spontaneous insights may be of crucial importance to the life of the practicing Christian. Theresa of

Avila was about to taper off her activity in the founding of new reformed Carmelite Houses, and in a prayer of waiting it became clear to her that "this is not the time to rest." Dozens of Quaker social enterprises have grown out of such concerns.

But this mood of attentive openness need not always be directed as a specific exercise in prayer. Often it steals on involuntarily from one of the other aspects of prayer. Now and then it comes on so gently that we almost waken, startled to realize that we are no longer praying but are being prayed in, that we are no longer seeking but that we are being found. This is the best of all, and when it occurs, all other aspects of prayer are to be left behind and an inner holiday declared; for this is no longer intentional prayer but communion.

PRAYER AS WORKING COLLECTEDLY

These devotional exercises, however, must not be content to encourage a practice of prayer that is cut off from the rest of life. Professor William Ernest Hocking and Charles Bennett have presented most impressively the conception of alternation, where we work and wear our spirits down and then pray and build them up. Francis de Sales has likewise given us an image of our filling up a vessel full to the brimming in prayer and then trying to carry it so delicately through the day that it shall not be spilled. There is a certain provisional truth about both of these notions. Yet neither of these images exhausts the deepest conception of prayer which these new devotional exercises must encourage. Professor Hocking's notion of alternation, while it expresses a mood we all know too well, still tends to depict prayer and life as too mechanically detached from each other. Francis de Sales' image of the brimming cup is a temporary aspiration, but it is soon discovered as too vulnerable for use in this world. For the world that you and I know is too rough, too unsteady, to keep any such brimming cup from spilling before the first few moments of the day are passed, and if

this truly expresses the relation of prayer and life, discouragement is bound to overtake us. We must present a hardier image of the role of prayer in these spiritual exercises.

The new exercises, then, must seek to prepare the life of the pray-er to make it able to live, not simply in the times of prayer, but continually close to the center. "Though my head and my hand be at labor, yet doth my heart dwell in God," says Jacob Boehme. Dom Chapman says of the real goal of prayer:

Remember that the proper result of contemplative prayer is simplicity in the whole life; so that a contemplative is always doing the same thing all day and all night. He is praying, or having breakfast, or talking, or working, or amusing himself; but he is principally conscious that he is *doing God's will.* The different external activities seem to him a sort of varied outcome of one continuous internal intention as if in a long walk: one goes up hill and down, in rain or sun or wind, but the act of walking remains the same all the time, the same movement of the legs, but sometimes easy, sometimes hard, sometimes pleasant, sometimes unpleasant.

Here is practice *in* the presence of God that is beyond feeling and temperament and easy inclination. It makes prayer become less an alternation to ordinary life, less a brimming cup held out above life, than life's constant companion. Meister Eckhart has put all this with his customary deftness:

One should learn to work with this contemplation in him, with him, and emerging from him, so that one allows his inner life to break into his activity and his activity into his inner life so that one becomes accustomed to *working collectedly.* If they can both happen in him, that is best of all, for then he becomes a fellow workman with God.

This is the goal of these new spiritual exercises and the norm of the devotional life by which they are to be checked. The norm is not whether they make stiff Christian soldiers, or whether they produce feudal Christian liegemen, but whether they draw men and women in the thick of life to live as creative apostles, to *work collectedly* in His service.

If they can help accomplish this end, this generation can no longer afford to neglect this fresh concern with Christian nurture. And one of my readers may have laid upon him the concern to refashion Ignatius' service for our time and to give to the western Christian world the sharply realistic devotional manual that it so desperately needs.

Clarence Seidenspinner

(1904———)

In 1940-41 two books written by Seidenspinner were published. *Our Dwelling Place*, in which he collaborated with the photographer Gilbert Larsen, relates worship patterns to photographs of various life situations. This was a new and successful venture in devotional books. *Form and Freedom in Worship* deals with "the worship of yesterday" and "Christian worship for the new day." It relates the idiom of worship to the mood of contemporary life.

Seidenspinner was reared in Wisconsin, educated at Northwestern University and Garrett Biblical Institute, and was ordained in the Methodist ministry. In 1940 he wrote the worship patterns for the first General Conference of The Methodist Church. He has served Methodist churches in Wisconsin, and at present is pastor of the First Methodist Church, Racine, Wisconsin, and also teaches at Garrett. He has written many articles on various phases of the devotional life.

The selection below shows how the liturgical year ties into the devotional pattern for each individual worshiper. It is reprinted from *Form and Freedom in Worship* by permission of Willett, Clark & Co.

THE LITURGICAL YEAR

From *Form and Freedom in Worship*

Anyone who wishes to understand the deep psychology of the liturgical year would do well to read Thomas Mann's essay on "Freud and the Future." In this essay Mann discusses the power of the myth in human life. Through the myth men discover self-awareness and consecration. In the memoried formulas, in the never-to-be forgotten patterns of the past, which half-unconsciously men seek even now to fulfill, human life is brought to felicitous self-expression. "For the myth is the foundation of life; it is the timeless schema, the pious formula into which life flows when it reproduces its traits out of the unconscious."

Mann goes on to say that life in the myth tends to become religious in its forms. It becomes feast and celebration in which the storied past is changed into the present and living reality. "For a feast is an anniversary, a renewal of the past in the present. Every Christmas the world-saving Babe is born again on earth, to suffer, to die, and to rise. The feast is the abrogation of time, an event, a solemn narrative being played out conformably to an immemorial pattern, the events in it take place not for the first time, but ceremonially according to the prototype."

Undoubtedly, this occurs for the multitudes of people who worship according to the cycle of the historic church year. Christ and his church with its company of saints and martyrs are reclothed in radiant garments. During Advent the old messianic hope is rekindled; at Christmas the new-born babe is worshiped; at Epiphany the magi come with gifts and adorations; on Ash Wednesday Jesus goes into retreat; Holy Week renews his passion; Good Friday witnesses his crucifixion; Easter joyously tells of his resurrection and Ascension Day takes him into glory everlasting. These things did not occur nineteen hundred years ago; they take place now, at the moment of celebration, for the feast is a new incarnation. Real also are the lives of sainthood and martyrdom and the motherhood of the blessed Virgin whose reincarnations occur in their respective places in the patterns of the church year. These feasts and celebrations move beyond the point of mere commemoration. They are by no means only memorial services. They are the celebrations of life in the myth, the "ever becoming present" of the memoried past. They are moments when the worshiper enters into eternal life with God the Father Almighty and Jesus Christ his only Son, with the Holy Spirit and the communion of saints who constitute the church. All the blessed times when these great realities appeared in human history in blinding revelation, now occur again for the worshiper. Life in the church becomes an endless "here and now." Eternity replaces time; the incarnation is a continuous experience.

Surely a modern worship that chose to disregard this deep psychology would be unusually stupid. Protestantism tried it for a while and lost its sense of the communion of saints. This sense of the enveloping presence of the communion of saints, this feeling of eternity which comes upon one in the fellowship of great liturgical traditions, is one of the marvelous realities of life in the church. There is no need in the name of modernity to disregard this psychology and forget the historic festivals. The problem, rather, is that of selection. Because of content and emphasis, what phases of the historic calendar are impossible for Protestant Christians today? What festivals are useful still—yes, more than useful: what festivals have the power to let the light shine out of darkness and into our hearts, "to give the light of the knowledge of the glory of God in the face of Jesus Christ"?

The problem is more than one of selection, however. We live in a world which has its own contemporary problems and its own peculiar needs. It is not enough to bring the great revelations of the past into the here and now; they must be related to the contemporary situation. We cannot spend all our time celebrating the memorable events of yesterday while so much of importance is happening today. The new needs and the new experience and the new emerging life form must be sanctified and clarified by the liturgical cycle and be lifted up to God in the ordered prayer of the church.

With these two problems in mind, what can be said concerning the liturgical cycle for the new worship of the Protestant church? How can this old material be related to the new situation with its new materials and be changed into a church year that has unity and homogeneity? Many of the present Protestant experiments toward a yearly calendar are heterogeneous. They lack a unifying reference. Services are planned on the basis of expediency, tradition, sentiment, as the case may be. Mothers' Day and Bible Sunday, Brotherhood Day and Stewardship Day, Labor Sunday and Rural Life Sunday are pulled out one by one to form the yearly cycle. The resultant calendar has that casual appearance possessed by the patchwork quilt into which every woman of the guild has embroidered her own fancies and idiosyncrasies.

II

Let us now consider a unifying principle upon which the annual cycle of worship can be formulated for the church in the world today. There, we have it already. That is the simple situation in which, as churchmen, we find ourselves, and that is our liturgical pattern: *the church and the world.* On the one hand is the church; on the other hand is the world, human society organized apart from the imperative will of God, to use the New Testament interpretation of this word. Between the church and the world there is ceaseless interaction as one constantly impinges upon the other. It is the divine mission of the church to make the world identical with itself. In its worship, therefore, the church must regularly and dramatically include the various aspects of this mission. Its religious expression in leading the soul into affirmation and adoration of God and recognition of his imperative will must cover the various areas of religious experience in which the soul may be active. In organizing its liturgical year it will secure vitality and meaning by taking into consideration this comprehensive mission.

Such a principle would relate the past and the present in a living, organic liturgy. It would naturally include the celebration of Jesus as a contemporary reality who penetrates every fissure of human relations. He is the Head of the church which confronts the world. Therefore his advent upon this earth, his birth and manhood, his minstry of reconciliation, his passion, death and resurrection, his teaching and healing are all brought up from the well of the past into the living present. Without this Head whose living presence is the life blood of the body, the church would disintegrate. Something of the history and tradition of the church is also to overflow into the liturgy. We are part of an organism that has continuity with its own past, a past that has given us the Gospels and the Epistles, heroes, saints and churchmen, hymns, prayers and creeds. Surely the crisis moments, at least, are worth liturgical expression.

Such a principle would also include those points at which the church meets the individual and the world. The individual has his own interests, needs, problems and desires which may well find expression in the liturgy. Since the individual lives in a thoroughly modern world, these areas of interest will in their form be peculiar to his own day. These interests and problems are manifold and a generous portion of the yearly cycle must be devoted to them. The corporate group, the world, has its problems and needs also. The church brings its gospel to bear upon these areas in corporate life just as it brings the gospel to individual life, and this meeting of church and world is worthy of liturgical expression.

Another portion of the yearly cycle must be devoted to it.

Here, then, is a pattern which can give vitality to Protestant worship. It is no mere historical recapitulation of events long over and done. It is a continuous celebration of the church meeting the world with a redemptive gospel, an immediate and contemporary transaction. Such an ordered arrangement of the yearly calendar has a threefold value. Variety is secured in what otherwise might be a monotonous liturgical year. Particularly where the structure of the service remains the same from one Sunday to the next, the introduction of new and changing materials provides a much needed variety. It also makes possible an ordered emphasis in worship. Each season has its particular spirit which enables the church regularly to emphasize the various aspects of its faith and order, its life and work. Furthermore, the use of the liturgical year is a means of dramatizing the total religious experience. Lessons, prayers, anthems and ceremonial change with the seasons. Even the sanctuary appointments vary, as altar hangings are changed, altars are stripped or decorated and the chancel otherwise rearranged. The whole year takes on the dynamic nature of drama as the soul moves forward in its worship of God.

Here also is a pattern which can be set within the frame of the historic church year. Since a large portion of the calendar would be devoted to the celebration of Jesus Christ, such liturgical emphasis can be synchronized with the historic cycle. How obvious it is that the birth, passion, death and resurrection of Jesus should be observed at Christmas, Holy Week, Good Friday and Easter. A good Catholic would feel at home in the liturgical pattern of the church and the world. He would miss many of the familiar details, to be sure—the saints, martyrs, Mariology and other medieval emphases. He would likewise be astonished to discover a modern note, not only in the sermon but also in the service and calendar. But he would recognize the bold outline of the church year and in its familiar, comforting structure he would make himself at home.

The form of the liturgical year, together with the fundamental themes for sermons and other liturgical materials, would be as follows:

THE CHURCH AND THE WORLD

Advent—The world's need of a Savior.

Christmastide—The coming of Jesus Christ, the Savior.

Epiphanytide—The manifestation of the Savior to the world. Through the church he works for the new world, the City of God, which must be built.

Lent—The soul's retreat for the renewal of faith and will.

Holy Week—The passion of the Savior.

Easter—The triumph of the Savior.

Eastertide—The history, traditions, theology and Scriptures of the church.

Whitsunday—The great fellowship of the church.

Trinitytide—Through the church, God helps the individual.

Philippe Vernier

(1909———)

VERNIER was born of French Protestant missionary parents in Madagascar, and was educated for the ministry in France. Because he held a pacifistic position and would not bear arms, he was refused ordination. Because of his pacifism he spent twenty-nine months in prison, all but five in solitary confinement. By his ministry to a Belgian mission church, helping underprivileged children, and serving coal miners in Quaregnon, Vernier has lived the life of a saint in true Franciscan style. Of the devotional selections in *With the Master* Rufus Jones says, "These meditations need no praise from me. Unaided they will carry their rare quality to all readers who are eager for reality. They have the childlike simplicity of one who has found his way into the Kingdom." The translation is by Edith Lovejoy Pierce, and the portion appearing here is used by permission of Fellowship Publications.

[MEDITATIONS]

From *With the Master*

I AM NOT ALONE
John 16:32

Only the evildoer is alone," wrote Diderot. Why then did your Master know such bitter solitude? For that was his life: desertion ever more complete. Moreover he prophesied it: "Ye shall be scattered every man to his own, and shall leave me alone." A certain amiability may attract men, but holiness embarrasses and irritates them.

When Jesus said, "I am not alone," it was not of human company that he spoke, but of Him who manifests himself in solitude, in the absence of earthly associates. In the desert: "the Father is with me."

This companion of solitary individuals is unknown to the man who lives in crowds. The noisy group around him, chattering and seeking amusement, may delude him. But when he wakes up he is desperately alone; alone before life, before death, before himself, alone before the void.

To escape this terrible awakening and supreme solitude seek isolation from material goods, reserve for yourself hours far from the clamor, and flee the company of the superficially minded. There will your Master teach you to listen to the voice from the deeps. He who sees in secret will read in you confidences which no human eye had been able to guess. He who speaks in silence will abide with you when all others have left.

Your Master has promised: "I will not

leave your orphans." He wants to send to you the Spirit that dwelt in his solitude, that it may also inhabit your own.

Lovest Thou Me?
John 21:17

The principal thing is not to think right, but to love; or at any rate it is in loving that one thinks straight, and not the other way around. The Master does not ask his disciple "Do you believe that?" but "Do you love me?"

When the dark hours come, remember through the fog of tottering certainties, that his love remains, to which you can cling.

You cannot escape these painful moments; you must pass through them when you apply personal study to the faith of childhood. You will have to face the classic questions about miracles, the resurrection, and the evil permitted by God. It is doubtful that the answers will satisfy you, and all the old edifice will seem to you to crumble beneath the shock.

Then listen to your Master and his simple question: "Lovest thou me?" By this he refuses to judge you as would a pope or a theologian. You are sure that *they* would condemn you. He does not impose on you the words of a catechism. We seem to see that gesture of his hand that sets aside our doubts and dissolves our qualms: "What I want to know is your love for me." He is like a friend who would push away great volumes of accumulated knowledge, and all the apparatus of an examination, and say to you: "Leave all that! If you come with me just as you are, I will receive you." There indeed is the rock of every Christian life: a presence, a friend, Himself.

You can reconstruct the rest later, bit by bit. Near him, by stages, you will once more ask yourself each question, you will resolve all problems. He laid the foundation of the edifice, and made it firm, on the day when he asked you simply: "My child, lovest thou me?" and when with all your heart you were able to answer: "Yea Lord, thou knowest that I love thee!"

Your Life Is Hid
Colossians 3:3

Only one-eighth of the mass bulk of icebergs is visible; all the rest is under water. This is what makes them so formidable to navigators, this is what makes their strength. In the same way the life of a Christian should in large part be hidden: it is from what one does not see that its force is drawn.

The stability of a house cannot be gauged from its outward appearance; it is secured by its invisible foundations. When a storm comes some humble dwelling may stand while palaces crumble. The same way with every spiritual edifice: it is not a question of shining and dazzling people, but of being firmly founded, of having a "life hid with Christ in God."

This hidden life is made up of what you bring each day to your Master: mostly your tears and your troubles, the defeats and the ruins of your outer structures. These are by no means first-rate materials and the hours that you spend alone with your God often are miserable. What counts is that you seek his presence, far from prying eyes; while you groan he builds patiently in you, secretly, the indispensable foundations.

Outwardly you may remain very much like the person you were before, or like those around you. You will appear to be a peaceful, honest man, with nothing to distinguish you from the crowd. It will need the blows of the storm, the clash against the obstacle, to reveal to others and to yourself your mysterious firmness —that hidden life which no one suspected.

Restore unto Me the Joy of Thy Salvation
Psalms 51:12

See, Lord, I am but the least of thy disciples: I have not much intelligence, I am not versed in the things of heaven, but I love thee.

No doubt I have been too busy attending to the affairs of my material life, and that is why it is so difficult for thy life to be born in me!

It seems that I am made of a heavier clay than other men. How does it happen that my soul so rarely knows joy, when others more unfortunate than myself I hear laugh and sing? Without joy, Lord, even the faith of thy saints would be an earth without a sun, and their charity would have no perfume. They are like the birds of the air, like the flowers of the field, counting on thee to feed and clothe them, but thou givest them besides that overflowing of the heart that is like the song of birds and the scent of flowers.

It is for lack of this that thou seest me every day dejected. It seems that thou respondest so rarely to my call! So rarely does there sound in my heart that bell of joy that peals in the carillon of the gospel!

And yet thou didst say: "Blessed are they that mourn." Do I not grieve enough? "Blessed are they which do hunger and thirst." Knowest thou how I hunger to share the joy of thine elect?

Lord, I am ready to bless thee in spite of thy silences, and in spite of loneliness, but at least rekindle my soul! Give me something, even if it be only the joyous heart of a vagabond whistling along the road, or the song of the nightingale!

I would love thee as one who rejoices, and not as one who carries a crushing burden!

The Kingdom of Heaven Is at Hand
Matthew 3:2

It is at hand if you go straight toward it, but if you take byways and indirect paths, you will never get there.

The Kingdom of God means replacing your will by his, leaving the ground where you are master for the element where he rules. As one throws himself into the water so also the Kingdom is entered by a leap into the void. It means repentance with faith; then one reaches it immediately, recognizing that it was indeed close by.

But men, holding eagerly to the earth and not wishing to relinquish until the last possible moment the conduct of their own affairs, have sought for oblique ways that would lead to the Kingdom of God by a longer journey but without a jolt, evading the dangerous leap into the void of faith. All the different aspects of what is called progress are some of these oblique ways. We try to draw near to God by busying ourselves with societies and with means of being fed, clothed and educated by science and ethics. It is as though a person who had to get into the sea, skirted it at length, walking along the beach. To penetrate into the new element we must come out of our own. What good is a useless journey? If it is for fear of getting wet that you hesitate to throw yourself into the water, the fear will be the same no matter where. In vain is the Kingdom at hand; if one does not go toward it without a detour, by the direct way of repentance, one will never enter it. Bypaths do not lead to the goal.

Your Body Is the Temple of the Holy Spirit
1 Corinthians 6:19

The body is the dwelling-place of the spirit, but you are free, after all, to open yours to the good or to the evil spirit. It is like a house whose key you hand over to the lodger of your choice: to prayer or to debauchery, to God or to the devil.

All the spirits, of course, do not offer your body the same kind of life. The spirit of the world promises it luxury and pleasure, wishing to make of it a comfortable palace where turbulent passions will live like great ladies in splendid attire.

The Spirit of the Master makes of it a temple.

A temple is not necessarily magnificent. "Your body," said Francis of Assisi, "should be your *cell*. The soul is the hermit enclosed in this cell to pray to God and meditate upon him."

Your body therefore will remain a very unpretentious dwelling. Neither a cell nor a real temple has need of ornaments or of comfort. On the contrary, the important thing is that nothing should be present that would turn the hermit or the disciple from the thought of the God he serves. And this is what you should expect of your body also: it should not bother you by occupying your time, your attention, your will. It ought to serve the Spirit, and serve it discreetly. Give it its place, neither too high nor too low; conquer it without hating it, and without ill treating it dominate it always.

But if your body is but a simple container, the Holy Spirit of your God can come to live in it; he can make his temple of your humble dwelling. One day, perhaps, you will say in vain "Lord, I am not worthy that thou shouldst enter under my roof"; your Master will be there, flooding you with his glory. It is that which creates the dignity of the temple.

The Power of God
1 Corinthians 1:24

The goal is not a philosophy or a creed, nor even, strictly speaking, a religion; it is "the power of God."

The essential thing for you is not to belong to a church, to repeat formulas or to assist at ceremonies; it is to let "the power of God" lay hold of your life.

It is precisely because this power is beyond their control that men have organized a Christian religion and a Church that at least depend upon them. But all this forms no more than a framework for the action of the Spirit, a dwelling-place for his "power."

You have your own little framework: the moments when you pray, your attendance at service, your reading of the Bible. All that—all your religious life—does not suffice to make you a child of God, a real disciple of your Master.

It is his power that makes the true disciples, and it is he who sends it. He says to you, as to Blaise Pascal: "Your conversion is my affair, fear not, and pray with confidence!"

You are the servant who awaits the arrival of his Master, sweeps and garnishes the house, and often sighs, while scanning the horizon: "O Lord, come soon!"

The servant knows well that it is the Master who decides; he will come at the hour he has set, when he thinks best.

Wait for him without anxiety, without the feverish impatience of those who forget that all rests upon "his power," and without the despair of those who do not know that he is good.

APPENDIX

SUGGESTED READINGS

DEVOTIONAL WRITERS AND WRITINGS

Atkins, G. G.: *Pilgrims of the Lonely Road.* New York: Fleming H. Revell Co., 1913.

Baker, Augustine: *Holy Wisdom.* London: Burnes & Oates, 1876.

Bevan, Frances: *Three Friends of God.* New York: Loizeaux Bros.

Bodington, Charles: *Books of Devotion.* London: Longmans, Green & Co., 1903.

Herman, Emily: *The Meaning and Value of Mysticism.* New York: George H. Doran Co., 1925.

Harkness, Georgia: *The Dark Night of the Soul.* New York and Nashville: Abingdon-Cokesbury Press, 1945.

Hügel, Friedrich von: *The Mystical Element of Religion.* New York: E. P. Dutton & Co., 1923.

Hunter, Allan: *Three Trumpets Sound.* New York: Association Press, 1939.

Inge, William R.: *Christian Mysticism.* 6th ed. New York: Charles Scribner's Sons, 1932.

James, William: *Varieties of Religious Experience.* New York: Longmans, Green & Co., 1917.

Jones, Rufus M.: *The Flowering of Mysticism.* New York: The Macmillan Co., 1939.

——: *New Studies in Mystical Religion.* New York: The Macmillan Co., 1927.

——: *The Radiant Life.* New York: The Macmillan Co., 1944.

——: *Spiritual Reformers in the Sixteenth and Seventeenth Centuries.* New York: The Macmillan Co., 1914.

——: *Studies in Mystical Religion.* New York: The Macmillan Co., 1909.

McGiffert, A. C.: *A History of Christian Thought.* New York: Charles Scribner's Sons, 1932.

Menzies, Lucy: *Mirrors of the Holy.* Milwaukee: Morehouse Publishing Co., 1928.

Peers, E. A.: *Studies of the Spanish Mystics.* New York: The Macmillan Co., 1927.

Poulain, Augustine: *The Graces of Interior Prayer.* St. Louis: B. Herder Book Co., 1910.

Reinhold, H. A., ed.: *The Soul Afire.* New York: Pantheon Books, 1944.

Saudreau, Auguste: *The Life of Union with God.* New York: Benziger Bros., 1927.

Scott, Robert, and Gilmore, G. W.: *Selections from the World's Classics of Devotion.* 10 vols. New York: Funk & Wagnalls Co., 1916.

Sperry, W. L.: *Strangers and Pilgrims.* Boston: Little, Brown & Co., 1939.

Steere, Douglas V.: *On Beginning from Within.* New York: Harper & Bros., 1943.

Taylor, H. O.: *The Medieval Mind.* 4th ed. New York: The Macmillan Co., 1938.

Underhill, Evelyn: *The Essentials of Mysticism.* New York: E. P. Dutton & Co., 1920.

——: *Mysticism.* New York: E. P. Dutton & Co., 1911.

——: *The Mystic Way.* New York: E. P. Dutton & Co., 1913.

Williams, Michael, ed.: *Anthology of Classic Christian Literature.* New York: Tudor Publishing Co., 1933.

PRAYER AND WORSHIP

Brightman, Edgar S.: *Religious Values.* New York: Abingdon-Cokesbury Press, 1925.

Brinton, H. H.: *Creative Worship.* London: George Allen & Unwin, 1931.

Brown, W. A.: *The Life of Prayer in a World of Science.* New York: Charles Scribner's Sons, 1927.

Buttrick, George A.: *Prayer.* New York and Nashville: Abingdon-Cokesbury Press, 1942.

Byington, E. H.: *Quest for Experience in Worship.* New York: Harper & Bros., 1929.

Fosdick, H. E.: *The Meaning of Prayer.* New York: Association Press, 1916.

Frost, Bede: *The Art of Mental Prayer.* London: George Allen & Unwin, 1935.

Georgia Harkness: *Prayer and the Common Life*. New York and Nashville: Abingdon-Cokesbury Press, 1948.

————: *Religious Living*. New York: Association Press, 1937.

Heard, Gerald: *A Preface to Prayer*. New York: Harper & Bros., 1944.

Heiler, Friedrich: *Prayer*. New York: Oxford University Press, 1932.

Herman, Emily: *Creative Prayer*. New York: George H. Doran Co., 1925.

Hügel, Friedrich von: *The Life of Prayer*. New York: E. P. Dutton & Co., 1929.

Inge, W. R.: *Personal Religion and the Life of Devotion*. New York: Longmans, Green & Co., 1924.

Maxwell, W. D.: *An Outline of Christian Worship*. New York: Oxford University Press, 1936.

Meland, B. E.: *Modern Man's Worship*. New York: Harper & Bros., 1934.

Otto, Rudolf: *The Idea of the Holy*. New York: Oxford University Press, 1925.

Paterson, W. P., and Russell, David, eds.: *The Power of Prayer*. New York: The Macmillan Co., 1920.

Seidenspinner, Clarence: *Form and Freedom in Worship*. Chicago: Willett, Clark & Co., 1941.

Sperry, W. L.: *Reality in Worship*. New York: The Macmillan Co., 1925.

Steere, Douglas V.: *Prayer and Worship*. New York: Association Press, 1938.

Streeter, B. H., ed.: *Concerning Prayer*. New York: The Macmillan Co., 1934.

Underhill, Evelyn: *The Life of the Spirit and the Life of Today*. New York: E. P. Dutton & Co., 1922.

————: *Worship*. New York: Harper & Bros., 1937.

Vogt, V. O.: *Art and Religion*. New Haven: Yale University Press, 1921.

Wieman, H. N.: *Methods of Private Religious Living*. New York: The Macmillan Co., 1929.

PSYCHOLOGY

Allport, G. W.: *Personality: A Psychological Interpretation*. New York: Henry Holt & Co., 1937.

Boisen, A. T.: *The Exploration of the Inner World*. Chicago: Willet, Clark & Co., 1937.

Burnham, W. H.: *The Normal Mind*. New York: D. Appleton-Century Co., 1924.

Dollard, John: *Victory over Fear*. New York: Reynal & Hitchcock, 1942.

Fosdick, H. E.: *On Being a Real Person*. New York: Harper & Bros., 1943.

Hadfield, J. A.: *The Psychology of Power*. New York: The Macmillan Co., 1923.

Hiltner, Seward: *Religion and Health*. New York: The Macmillan Co., 1943.

Holman, C. T.: *The Cure of Souls*. Chicago: University of Chicago Press, 1932.

Jackson, Josephine A., and Salisbury, Helen M.: *Outwitting Our Nerves*. New York: D. Appleton-Century Co., 1937.

Johnson, Paul E.: *Psychology of Religion*. New York and Nashville: Abingdon-Cokesbury Press, 1945.

Jung, Carl G.: *Modern Man in Search of a Soul*. New York: Harcourt, Brace & Co., 1933.

Künkel, Fritz: *In Search of Maturity*. New York: Charles Scribner's Sons, 1943.

Liebman, Joshua L.: *Peace of Mind*. New York: Simon & Schuster, 1946.

Link, Henry C.: *The Rediscovery of Man*. New York: The Macmillan Co., 1938.

————: *The Return to Religion*. New York: The Macmillan Co., 1936.

Menninger, Karl: *The Human Mind*. New York: Alfred A. Knopf, 1937.

Stolz, Karl R.: *The Psychology of Religious Living*. Nashville: Abingdon-Cokesbury Press, 1937.

Weatherhead, Leslie: *Psychology in the Service of the Soul*. New York: The Macmillan Co., 1930.

Wise, C. A.: *Religion in Illness and Health*. New York: Harper & Bros., 1942.

AIDS TO THE DEVOTIONAL LIFE

Barclay, W. C.: *Challenge and Power*. New York: Abingdon-Cokesbury Press, 1936.

A Book of Prayers for Students. London: Student Christian Movement Press, 1915.

Bro, Marguerite H.: *Every Day a Prayer*. Chicago: Willett, Clark & Co., 1943.

Dawson, George: *A Collection of Prayers*. 9th ed. London: Kegan Paul, Trench, Trubner & Co., 1885.

Fosdick, H. E.: *The Manhood of the Master*. New York: Association Press, 1913.
———: *The Meaning of Prayer*. New York: Association Press, 1916.
———: *The Meaning of Service*. New York: Association Press, 1921.
Fox, Selina F.: *A Chain of Prayer Across the Ages*. 6th ed. New York: E. P. Dutton & Co., 1941.
Harlow, S. R.: *Prayers for Times Like These*. New York: Association Press, 1942.
Hunter, John: *Devotional Services*. 9th ed. New York: E. P. Dutton & Co., 1915.
Jones, E. Stanley: *Abundant Living*. New York and Nashville: Abingdon-Cokesbury Press, 1942.
———: *Victorious Living*. New York: Abingdon-Cokesbury Press, 1936.
———: *The Way*. New York and Nashville: Abingdon-Cokesbury Press, 1947.
The Kingdom, the Power and the Glory. New York: Oxford University Press, 1925.
Martineau, James: *Home Prayers*. London: Longmans, Green & Co., 1891.
McComb, Samuel: *A Book of Prayer*. New York: Dodd, Mead & Co., 1917.
McKee, E. M.: *Communion with God*. New York: Harper & Bros., 1922.
Newton, J. F.: *Altar Stairs*. New York: The Macmillan Co., 1928.
Noyes, Morgan P.: *Prayers for Services*. New York: Charles Scribner's Sons, 1941.
Orchard, W. E.: *Temple: A Book of Prayers*. New York: E. P. Dutton & Co., 1918.
Page, Kirby: *Living Abundantly*. New York: Farrar & Rinehart, 1944.
———: *Living Courageously*. New York: Farrar & Rinehart, 1936.
———: *Living Creatively*. New York: Farrar & Rinehart, 1932.
———: *Living Prayerfully*. New York: Farrar & Rinehart, 1941.
———: *Living Triumphantly*. New York: Farrar & Rinehart, 1934.
———: *Religious Resources for Personal Living and Social Action*. New York: Farrar & Rinehart, 1939.
Peabody, F. G.: *Prayers for Various Occasions and Needs*. Boston: Houghton Mifflin Co., 1930.
Rauschenbusch, Walter: *Prayers of the Social Awakening*. Boston: Pilgrim Press, 1909.
Seidenspinner, Clarence, and Larsen, Gilbert: *Our Dwelling Place*. New York and Nashville: Abingdon-Cokesbury Press, 1941.
Shrigley, G. A. C.: *Daily Prayer Companion*. Buffalo: Foster & Stewart, 1947.
Simpson, Hubert L.: *Let Us Worship God*. New York: Doubleday, Doran & Co., 1929.
Speer, Robert E.: *Five Minutes a Day*. Philadelphia: Westminster Press, 1943.
Willett, H. L., and Morrison, C. C.: *The Daily Altar*. Chicago: Christian Century Press, 1924.

CHRONOLOGY OF DEVOTIONAL WRITINGS

WITH A PARALLEL CHRONOLOGY OF EVENTS IN CHURCH HISTORY

FIRST CENTURY

	35-62 Activities of Paul.
	46-47 Jerusalem Council. Christianity separates from Judaism.
Clement of Rome (40?-97?) *The First Epistle to the Corinthians*	70-100 The Four Gospels written.
	ca. 93 The Council of Jamnia. Old Testament formed.

SECOND CENTURY

Ignatius of Antioch (d. 117)
  Letters
Hermas of Rome (*ca.* 115)
  The Shepherd
Justin Martyr (110?-165?)
  Apology
  Dialogue with Trypho
Anonymous author (*ca.* 130-160)
  Teaching of the Twelve Apostles
Irenaeus (135-200)
  Against Heresies

140 Marcion forms the first New Testament composed of ten letters of Paul and the Gospel of Luke.

150 Tatian combines the Four Gospels into the Diatessaron.

156 Montanism anticipates the world's end with the Holy Spirit incarnate in Montanus.

160 Reverence for martyrdom stressed.

150-175 The Apostles' Creed created to combat Gnosticism.

THIRD CENTURY

Clement of Alexandria (150?-220?)
  Stromata or *Miscellanies*
Tertullian (160?-230?)
  Against Praexas
  Apology
  Patience
Origen (185?-254?)
  On the Fundamental Doctrines (*De Principiis*)
Cyprian (200?-258)
  Letters
  Unity of the Church

250 Cyprian stresses the foundation of the church in the unity of bishops.

270 Anthony, an Egyptian ascetic, begins monastic movement. Monasticism, instead of martyrdom, becomes the highest achievement for Christians.

FOURTH CENTURY

Ephraem Syrus (306?-373?)
Nisibene Hymns

313   Constantine grants toleration to Christians. In 325 he asks his subjects to embrace Christianity.

Gregory of Nyssa (331?-396?)
Great Catechism
Soul and the Resurrection

325   Council of Nicaea decides that Christ and God are of the same substance, that Christ is divine.

Chrysostom (345?-407)
Homilies

388   Jerome translates the New Testament into the Latin Vulgate. With the help of Jewish friends he begins translation of the Old Testament.

Augustine (354-430)
Confessions
The City of God

395   Augustine is made bishop of Hippo. His writings lay the intellectual structure of the Roman Catholic Church.

397   Council of Carthage. Twenty-seven books of the New Testament added to the Old Testament.

FIFTH CENTURY

Leo the Great (390?-461)
Sermons

445   Valentian III orders all Christendom to obey Leo I, bishop of Rome.

451   Council of Chalcedon. Christ decreed both human and divine. Constantinople placed on equality with Rome. Mary, the mother of Jesus, is called "Mother of God" (*Theotokos*). About this time Coptic Christianity, emphasizing Christ's divinity and humanity as of one unique nature, finds its growth in Egypt.

476   Fall of the Roman Empire.

Dionysius the Areopagite (*ca.* 500)
On the Heavenly Hierarchy
On the Ecclesiastical Hierarchy
On the Names of God
On Mystical Theology

SIXTH CENTURY

Benedict (480?-543?)
Rule

501-543   Benedict of Nursia reforms and develops Western monasticism by his new rules.

Gregory the Great (540?-604)
Dialogues
Moralia
Pastoral Rule

590   Gregory the Great made pope; popularizes Augustine's teachings.

SEVENTH CENTURY

Isaac of Nineveh (?)
Letter to the Holy Father Simon

680-681   Sixth General Council at Constantinople views Christ of two natural wills.

EIGHTH CENTURY

The Venerable Bede (673-735)
Ecclesiastical History of the English Nation

795-816   Pope Leo III.

800 Pope Leo crowns Charlemagne, thus uniting the church and state into the Holy Roman Empire.

NINTH CENTURY

Erigena (815?-877?)
De divisione naturae
De praedestinatione
Photius (820?-891)
Myriobiblon

801-900 Revival of interest in Dionysius the Areopagite and Augustine.
871-901? Alfred the Great encourages education of the clergy.
858-867 Nicholas I increases papal claims.

TENTH CENTURY

Symeon (?-1040?)
Metaphrastes

910 Monasticism revived at Cluny.

ELEVENTH CENTURY

Anselm of Canterbury (1033-1109)
Monologion
Prosologion
Meditations
Cur Deus Homo

1054 Separation of the Eastern Church from the Roman Catholic Church. The Eastern Church places its authority in the councils.

1073-1085 Gregory VII is pope. Absolute world supremacy vested in the papacy.

TWELFTH CENTURY

Hugh of St. Victor (1096?-1141)
Concerning Contemplation
On the Mysteries of Faith
Bernard of Clairvaux (1090-1153)
Sermons
De Consideratione
Richard of St. Victor (d. 1173)
Benjamin Minor
Benjamin Major
Hildegarde of Bingen (1098-1179)
Sacred Analects

1098-1270 The Crusades occur as an outward manifestation of the deep religious feeling of the era.

1115 Bernard of Clairvaux founds the Cistercian abbey of Clairvaux. He stresses a mystic love of Christ as the highest spiritual joy.

1198-1216 Innocent III is pope. He takes the title of "Vicar of Christ," claiming authority over all men.

THIRTEENTH CENTURY

Francis of Assisi (1182-1226)
The Little Flowers of St. Francis
The Mirror of Perfection [1]

1216 Rise of the Dominicans and Franciscans.

[1] Francis inspired these books. He did not write them.

THIRTEENTH CENTURY (*continued*)

Bonaventura (1221-1274)
The Soul's Progress in God
The Virtues of a Religious Superior

Thomas Aquinas (1225?-1274)
Summa Theologica

Angela of Foligno (1248-1309)
Divine Consolations

Anonymous author (*ca.* 1300)
The Mirror of Simple Souls

1265 Scholasticism, developed chiefly by Anselm of Canterbury, Abélard, Hugh of St. Victor, William of Champeaux, and Peter Lombard, reaches its height in Thomas Aquinas. Philosophy and theology are wedded; reason and faith join hands in the quest for truth.

FOURTEENTH CENTURY

1301- A century in which mysticism is
1400   widespread.

1309   Seat of the papacy removed to Avignon, France, remaining there until 1377.

Dante (1265-1321)
Divine Comedy

Meister Eckhart (1260?-1328?)
Sermons
Tractates

Richard Rolle de Hampole (1290?-1349)
The Fire of Love
The Mending of Life

1311- Dante in *On Monarchy* views the
1318   papacy and the empire as both founded by God, with neither superior in authority. The church, with its authority in the New Testament, has purely religious functions.

Johannes Tauler (1300?-1361)
Golden Thoughts on the Higher Life
The Inner Way
Conferences and Sermons

Heinrich Suso (1300?-1366)
Exemplar
Sermons

Jan van Ruysbroeck (1293-1381)
Flowers of a Mystic Garden
The Adornment of the Spiritual Marriage
The Seven Degrees of Love
The Book of the Spiritual Tabernacle

ca. 1325 William of Ockham ("the first Protestant"), a Franciscan, renounces scholasticism. Religion and philosophy once more separated. He also stresses separation of the state from ecclesiastical authority.

Rulman Merswin (1307-1382)
The Spiritual Stairway
The Spiritual Ladder
A Revelation
Instruction
The Book of the Five Men
The Book of the Nine Rocks

Gerhard Groot (1340-1384)
The Imitation of Christ [2]

Catherine of Siena (1347-1380)
Dialogues
Letters

1382- John Wycliffe translates the Vul-
1384   gate into English. He stresses the Bible as the only rule of the church.

Walter Hilton (d. 1396)
The Scale of Perfection
The Song of Angels

ca. 1384 The Lollards, "Bible Preachers," organized by Wycliffe, carry knowledge of the Bible to the common people. Their influence felt especially in Bohemia.

Juliana of Norwich (1343-1413)
Sixteen Revelations of Divine Love

[2] Thomas à Kempis' work is largely based on Groot's journal.

FOURTEENTH CENTURY (*continued*)

Anonymous authors
  Theologia Germanica [3]
  The Cloud of Unknowing
Margery Kempe (*ca.* 1400)
  Contemplations
  The Book of Margery Kempe

FIFTEENTH CENTURY

Gerlac Peterson (*ca.* 1410)
  The Fiery Soliloquy With God
Nicholas of Cusa (1401-1464)
  The Vision of God
Thomas à Kempis (1380-1471)
  The Imitation of Christ
Denis the Carthusian (1402-1471)
  Concerning Contemplation
Girolamo Savonarola (1452-1498)
  Miserere
  Triumph of the Cross
Catherine of Genoa (1447-1510)
  Dialogues
  The Treatise on Purgatory

1414-
1417   After long debate the Council of
       Constance elects a Roman cardinal,
       Ottone Colonna, as Pope Martin V,
       thus ending the papal schism begun
       in 1309.

1415   John Huss burned at the stake after
       carrying the spirit of the Reforma-
       tion to Bohemia.

1453   With the fall of Constantinople the
       Renaissance begins. Rise of indi-
       vidual freedom.

SIXTEENTH CENTURY

Thomas More (1478-1535)
  Dialogue of Comfort Against Tribulation
  Treatises on Christ's Passion

Martin Luther (1483-1546)
  On Good Works
  On Christian Liberty

Ignatius Loyola (1491-1556)
  Spiritual Exercises
  The Testament of St. Ignatius Loyola
John Calvin (1509-1564)
  Institutes
  Sermons

[3] Printed by Martin Luther 1516-18.

1516   Erasmus edits the Greek New Testa-
       ment. As a Christian humanist, he
       revives an interest in the Christian
       classics.

1517   Luther nails his ninety-five theses
       to the church door at Wittenberg.
       In 1521 he begins his translation of
       the New Testament into German.

1523   The seed of the Baptist movement
       is sown by Balthasar Hubmaier in
       Waldshut, Switzerland.

1526   Tyndale translates the New Testa-
       ment from Greek into English.

1530   The Augsburg Confession becomes
       the basis of Lutheranism.

1533   Calvin is "converted." Protestant-
       ism carried to Switzerland.

1534   The Act of Supremacy declares
       the king of England is "the only
       supreme head on earth of the
       Church of England."

1541   Ignatius Loyola made "General" of
       the Society of Jesus, an order
       founded to fight for the church
       against heretics and infidels.

1549   The Act of Uniformity requires

SIXTEENTH CENTURY (*continued*)

Aonio Paleario (1503-1570)
The Benefit of Christ's Death
Pro se ipso

John Knox (1505?-1572)
Book of Common Order

Teresa of Avila (1515-1582)
The Life of St. Teresa of Jesus
The Letters of St. Teresa
The Interior Castle
The Way of Perfection

John of the Cross (1542-1591)
The Dark Night of the Soul
A Spiritual Canticle of the Soul
The Ascent of Mount Carmel

Lorenzo Scupoli (1529-1610)
The Spiritual Combat
The Peace of the Soul

	use of the *Book of Common Prayer*. Second prayer book appears in 1552.
1553	Forty-two Articles of Religion authorized by Edward VI as "creed" of the Church of England.
1553	Michael Servetus burned at the stake in Geneva, Switzerland, for questioning the doctrines of the Trinity and infant baptism.
1557	John Knox becomes Scottish leader of Protestantism.
1545-1563	The Councils at Trent reaffirm the doctrines of the Roman Catholic Church.
1559	The Church of England's Forty-Two Articles reduced to thirty-nine.
1564	Puritans arise as a party in England to purge the Church of England of Roman Catholic practices.
1579	Faustus Socinus organizes Unitarianism in Poland.
1581	The separatists, under Robert Browne and Robert Harrison, found the Congregational Church at Norwich, England.

SEVENTEENTH CENTURY

Rose of Lima (1581-1617)
The Foundations of Mystical Knowledge

Francis of Sales (1567-1622)
Introduction to the Devout Life
On the Love of God
Spiritual Letters
Practical Piety

Jakob Böhme (1575-1624)
The Threefold Life of Man
The Three Principles of Divine Essence
The Way to Christ
Dialogues on the Supersensual Life
The Signatures of All Things
Forty Questions Concerning the Soul

Lancelot Andrewes (1555-1626)
Private Devotions
Seventeen Sermons on the Nativity

John Donne (1573-1631)
Sermons

Augustine Baker (1575-1641)
Holy Wisdom
Commentary on The Cloud of Unknowing

ca. 1600	Socinianism emphasizes the ideal humanity of Jesus. Arminianism stresses man's freedom to receive or reject the grace of God.
1611	King James Version of the Bible published.
1621	In *Novum Organum* Francis Bacon gives new stress to use of the inductive method.
1626	The Pilgrim Fathers (Congregationalists), led by Elder Brewster, cross the Atlantic in the "Mayflower."
1634	Roman Catholicism established by Leonard Calvert in Maryland.
1639	The first Baptist Church in America founded in Rhode Island.

SEVENTEENTH CENTURY (*continued*)

Gertrude More (1606-1633)
Spiritual Exercises
The Inner Life
The Holy Practices of a Divine Lover

John Smith (1618-1652)
Discourses

Joseph Hall (1574-1656)
Meditations and Vows

Blaise Pascal (1623-1662)
Thoughts (Penseés)

Jeremy Taylor (1613-1667)
The Rule and Exercises of Holy Living
The Rule and Exercises of Holy Dying

John A. Comenius (1592-1670)
The Labyrinth of the World

Henry Scougal (1650-1678)
The Life of God in the Soul of Man
Reflections and Meditations

Antoinette Bourignon (1616-1680)
Works

Isaac Pennington (1617-1680)
Letters

Walter Marshall (1628-1680)
The Gospel Mystery of Sanctification

Benjamin Whichcote (1609-1683)
A Treatise of Devotion
Select Sermons
Moral and Religious Aphorisms

Robert Leighton (1611-1684)
Rules and Instructions for a Holy Life
Sermons

John Bunyan (1628-1688)
Grace Abounding
Holy War
Pilgrim's Progress

George Fox (1624-1691)
Journal

Robert Barclay (1648-1690)
Apology for the True Christian Divinity

John Flavel (1630-1691)
A Saint Indeed
The Fountain of Life Opened

Nicholas Herman [Brother Lawrence] (1611-1691)
The Practice of the Presence of God

ca. 1640 In Germany, Johann Andrae attempts to form a union of science and Christianity in Rosicrucianism.

1640 Scotch-Irish Presbyterians organize on Long Island in Southold church.

1646 George Fox's conversion begins the Society of Friends in England.

1648 The Westminster Confession and catechisms adopted by the English Parliament and Scottish General Assembly.

1650-1700 The genesis of the period of modern science and philosophy has its stimulus from these men: Francis Bacon (1561-1626) introduces the scientific method; Galileo (1564-1642) in his *Dialogue* (1632) supports Nicolaus Copernicus (1473-1543) in his negation of the Ptolemaic astronomy, and also introduces the telescope to scan the heavens; Isaac Newton (1642-1727) writes *Principia* (1687), in which he explains the motions of the heavenly bodies as caused by gravitation; René Descartes (1596-1650) in *Discourse on Method* (1644) employs reason as the test of real knowledge; Gottfried Leibniz (1646-1716) in *Monadology* views the universe as organic, and seeks a reunion of Roman Catholicism and Protestantism.

1656 Quakers arrive in Massachusetts, Virginia, and New York. In 1672 George Fox visits America. In 1681 William Penn founds the colony of Pennsylvania as a "holy experiment."

1653 Jansenism in France, supported by Pascal and others, attempts to reform the Roman Catholic Church. It revives Augustine's doctrines of sin and grace. Jansen's followers flee to Holland where they form the Jansenite Catholic Church.

1673 Robert Barclay in his *Catechism* and the *Fifteen Theses in Apology*

SEVENTEENTH CENTURY (*continued*)

Richard Baxter (1615-1691)
The Saints' Everlasting Rest
Call to the Unconverted

Miguel de Molinos (1640-1697)
The Spiritual Guide

Jane Lead (1623-1704)
The Tree of Faith
The Ascent to the Mount of Vision

Simon Patrick (1626-1707)
Mensa Mystica
The Heart's Ease

John Norris (1657-1711)
Reason and Religion

François Fénelon (1651-1715)
Letters
Maxims of the Saints

Madame Jeanne Guyon (1648-1717)
Short and Easy Method of Prayer
Autobiography

Elizabeth Rowe (1674-1737)
Devout Exercises of the Heart

(1675) reduces Quaker views into systematic thought.

1687   Miguel de Molinos, leader of quietism in Spain, condemned.

1689   The Toleration Act and the Bill of Rights grant freedom of worship to all Protestant dissenters.

1690   Scotland ratifies the Westminster Confession and recognizes Presbyterianism as the Church of Scotland.

1695   John Locke, in *Essay Concerning Human Understanding* and *Reasonableness of Christianity*, shows that Christianity may be beyond reason, but not contrary to reason.

1699   Quietism in France, expounded by Madame Guyon and François Fénelon, archbishop of Cambrai, condemned.

EIGHTEENTH CENTURY

Philip Doddridge (1702-51)
The Rise and Progress of Religion in the Soul

Jean Pierre de Caussade (1675-1751)
Spiritual Instructions

Jonathan Edwards (1703-1758)
On the Work of the Spirit

William Law (1686-1761)
A Serious Call to a Devout and Holy Life
The Spirit of Prayer
A Practical Treatise on Christian Perfection

John Woolman (1720-1772)
Journal

John Wesley (1703-1791)
Journal
Christian Perfection
Sermons

James Fordyce (1720-1796)
Addresses to the Deity
A Discourse on Pain

Jean Nicholas Grou (1731-1803)
The Hidden Life of the Soul

C. Eckartshausen (1752-1803)
The Cloud Upon the Sanctuary
God Is Love Most Pure

1721   Peter the Great substitutes the Holy Synod for the patriarchates, thus bringing church and state closely together.

1727   The Moravian movement founded in Germany by Zinzendorf.

1738   John Wesley converted at an Aldersgate Street meeting. Beginning of the Wesleyan revival.

1748   Henry Mühlenberg organizes the first German Lutheran synod in America at Philadelphia.

1757   David Hume, in *Natural History of Religion* and *Philosophical Essays* (1748), attacks both Deism and traditional Christian thought. He stresses experience (empiricism) as the way to truth.

1759   Thomas Paine, in *Age of Reason*, strongly argues for Deism.

1773   Theophilus Lindsey and Joseph Priestley organize a Unitarian church in London.

EIGHTEENTH CENTURY (*continued*)

1781 Immanuel Kant, awakened by Hume, writes *Critique of Pure Reason*. In 1788 he follows with *Critique of Practical Reason*. He held that religious truth is found through moral experience rather than through reason.

Louis Claude de Saint-Martin (1743-1803)
Man: His True Nature
Theosophic Correspondence

1784 John Wesley appoints Thomas Coke and Francis Asbury as superintendents of American Methodism.

John Frederic Oberlin (1740-1826)
Letters

1787 Archbishop of Canterbury consecrates bishops for the American Episcopal Church. Church adopts constitution in 1789.

1799 Friedrich Schleiermacher, influenced by Spinoza, Leibniz, and Kant, publishes *Addresses on Religion*. In 1822 he writes *Christian Belief*, showing the growth of theology based on religious experience.

NINETEENTH CENTURY

William Ellery Channing (1780-1842)
Works

1814 Society of Jesus re-established by Pope Pius VII.

1825 Stimulated by William Ellery Channing, the American Unitarian Association is formed.

Søren Kierkegaard (1813-55)
Either—Or
Training in Christianity
Stages on Life's Way
The Works of Love
Purity of Heart
Journals

1829 The Catholic Emancipation Act gives Roman Catholics and Dissenters in England like privileges.

1833 The Oxford Movement in the Church of England begins, led by Edward Pusey, John Keble, Richard Froude, and John Henry Newman. Newman submits to the Roman Catholic Church in 1845.

Friedrich A. G. Tholuck (1799-1877)
Hours of Christian Devotion
Light From the Cross
Miscellaneous essays

John Henry Newman (1801-1890)
Apologia pro Vita Sua

1848 Christian Socialism, under the leadership of F. D. Maurice, Charles Kingsley, and John M. F. Ludlow, begins in England.

Austin Phelps (1820-1890)
The Still Hour
My Note Book
My Portfolio
My Study

1859 Charles Darwin publishes *Origin of the Species*.

1867 The German Reformed Church becomes the Reformed Church in America.

Anthony Thorold (1825-1895)
Eternal Life
The Presence of Christ

1879 Mary Baker Eddy charters first Christian Science church.

Coventry Patmore (1823-1896)
The Rod, the Root, and the Flower

George Matheson (1842-1906)
My Aspirations

1880 Russian students, acquainted with Karl Marx in their studies at German universities, start a social religion in their homeland. This viewpoint, in criticism of the Orthodox Church, wins approval of industrial workers.

NINETEENTH CENTURY (*continued*)

George Tyrrell (1861-1909)
Lex Orandi
Autobiography
Nova et Vetera: Informal Meditations
Hard Sayings: A Selection of Meditations
Leo Tolstoy (1828-1910)
My Confession
My Religion

TWENTIETH CENTURY

Léon Bloy (1846-1917)
The Woman Who Was Poor
Letters to his fiancée
Washington Gladden (1836-1918)
The Christian Way
Walter Rauschenbusch (1861-1918)
Christianity and the Social Crisis
Christianizing the Social Order
Theology for the Social Gospel
Social Principles of Jesus
Prayers of the Social Awakening
Augustine Poulain (1836-1919)
The Graces of Interior Prayer
Spiritual Journal of Lucie Christine

Emily Herman (1876-1923)
Creative Prayer
The Secret Garden of the Soul
The Meaning of the Cross
The Meaning and Value of Mysticism
Friedrich von Hügel (1852-1925)
Letters
The Mystical Element of Religion
Eternal Life
Essays and addresses on *The Philosophy of Religion*

John Chapman (1865-1933)
The Spiritual Letters
Sundar Singh (1889-1933)
With and Without Christ
Spiritual Life and the Spiritual World
Rudolf Otto (1869-1938)
The Idea of the Holy
Mysticism: East and West
The Kingdom of God and the Son of Man
Burnett H. Streeter (1874-1939)
The Spirit
Reality
The God Who Speaks
On Prayer

1907 Pope Pius X uses the term "modernism" in criticizing Loisy and Duchesne, calling it "the synthesis of all heresies."

1908 Organization of the Federal Council of the Churches of Christ in America.

1914-1918 World War I stimulates science and social reform.

1922 With Lenin all religious toleration in Russia ceases.

1920-1930 Higher criticism of the Bible generally accepted by a majority of Protestant biblical scholars. A new stress is given to the social gospel. American Protestantism is "corrected" by scientific humanism which uses the inductive method as the only way to obtain all truth. Crisis theology from Europe, developed chiefly by Karl Barth and Emil Brunner, leaves its impress on American Neo-supernaturalism. Neo-Thomism, among Roman Catholics, urges a return to the basic principles of religion as synthesized by Thomas Aquinas. There is a new stress upon the psychological value of religion, some churches adding psychiatrists to their staffs. New cults arise stressing emotionalism. Many adherents, drawn from the ordinary mass of people, find worship in "temples" and "tabernacles." American theologians, scientists, and men of affairs, attempt to show that science and religion do not conflict: science describes the laws and facts of nature; religion deals with values and ideals.

TWENTIETH CENTURY (*continued*)

Charles F. Andrews (1871-1940)
The Inner Life
Christ in the Silence
Christ and Prayer
What I Owe to Christ
Sadhu Sundar Singh
Mahatma Gandhi at Work

Evelyn Underhill (1875-1941)
The Mystic Way
Mysticism
Practical Mysticism
Concerning the Inner Way
The Life of the Spirit and the Life of Today

Thomas R. Kelly (1893-1941)
A Testament of Devotion
Holy Obedience

William Adams Brown (1865-1943)
How to Think of Christ
Finding God in a New World
God at Work
Beliefs That Matter
The Life of Prayer in a World of Science
Pathways to Certainty

Alexis Carrel (1873-1944)
Man, the Unknown
Prayer Is Power

William Temple (1881-1944)
Personal Religion and the Life of Fellowship
Nature, Man, and God
Plato and Christianity
Christianity and the State
Readings in St. John's Gospel

Rufus M. Jones (1863———)
The Inner Life
Studies in Mystical Religion
New Studies in Mystical Religion
The Flowering of Mysticism
The Radiant Life

Nikolai A. Berdyaev (1874———)
Fate of Man in the Modern World
Solitude and Society
Freedom and the Spirit
Destiny of Man
Meaning of History
Slavery and Freedom
Spirit and Reality

Albert Schweitzer (1875———)
Out of My Life and Thought

Harry Emerson Fosdick (1878———)
The Meaning of Prayer
As I See Religion
The Meaning of Faith
The Meaning of Service
On Being a Real Person

1932 The World Conference for the Reduction and Limitation of Armaments meets in Geneva, Switzerland.

1937 Ecumenical conferences are held in Oxford, England and Edinburgh, Scotland, on behalf of church unity.

1938 Madras meeting of International Missionary Council.

1939 The World Council of Churches prepares "A Christian International Code."

1930-1940 Some liberal scholars in the United States ally themselves with Neo-Orthodoxy. A renewed interest in all religions is evident. Round-table discussions attempt to better relations between Jews, Protestants, and Roman Catholics.

1939-1945 World War II. Japan, in its Shinto ideals, and Germany, in its Nazi ideology, reduce religion to two narrow nationalisms. Christians in Europe firmly oppose Nazism.

1941 The Malvern Conference held by English churchmen to plan a postwar society for Britain.

1942 At Delaware, Ohio, delegates from denominations holding membership in the Federal Council of the Churches of Christ in America discuss the basis for "a just and durable peace."

TWENTIETH CENTURY (*continued*)

Von Ogden Vogt (1879——)
Modern Worship
Art and Religion

Albert W. Palmer (1879——)
Paths to the Presence of God
The Art of Conducting Public Worship

Willard L. Sperry (1882——)
Reality in Worship
Strangers and Pilgrims

Jacques Maritain (1882——)
Art and Scholasticism
Art and Poetry
Education at the Crossroads
Religion and Culture
True Humanism

Muriel Lester (1883——)
Dare You Face Facts?
Why Worship?

Henry N. Wieman (1884——)
Religious Experience and the Scientific
Method
Methods of Private Religious Living

Edgar S. Brightman (1884——)
Religious Values
The Spiritual Life

E. Stanley Jones (1884——)
Abundant Living
How to Pray
Victorious Living
The Way

Frank C. Laubach (1884——)
Letters By a Modern Mystic
Prayer Hymn Devotions

Karl Barth (1886——)
The Knowledge of God and the Service
of God
The Doctrine of the Word of God
The Holy Ghost and the Christian Life
Come, Holy Ghost

John Baillie (1886——)
The Interpretation of Religion

Toyohiko Kagawa (1888——)
Meditations on the Cross
Love, the Law of Life
New Life Through God
Songs from the Slums

Gerald Heard (1889——)
A Preface to Prayer

Christopher Dawson (1889——)
Religion and the Modern State
Judgment of the Nations

1942 Proposals for Christian unity of Methodist, Congregational, and Presbyterian churches in Australia adopted. Evangelical and Reformed Church and Congregational Christian Churches in the United States initiate union.

1944 Organization of Canadian Council of Churches. Union of Reformed Church in America and United Presbyterian Church of North America initiated.

1945 Churches in United States organize relief for parts of the world devastated by war. Chaplains to labor and industry and psychiatrists on church staffs aid postwar adjustments.

1946 Evangelical Church and the Church of the United Brethren in Christ unite. Ministers meet with atomic scientists to discuss implications of atomic bomb. Commission of Churches on International Affairs formed at Cambridge, England. Ecumenical Institute opened near Geneva, Switzerland. Russian Church begins to have new liberties.

TWENTIETH CENTURY (*continued*)

Georgia Harkness (1891——)
  Religious Living
  The Glory of God
  The Dark Night of the Soul
  Prayer and the Common Life
George A. Buttrick (1892——)
  Prayer
Friedrich Heiler (1892——)
  Prayer
  Gospel of Sadhu Sundar Singh
Reinhold Niebuhr (1892——)
  The Nature and Destiny of Man
  Beyond Tragedy
Allan A. Hunter (1893——)
  Say Yes to the Light
  Three Trumpets Sound
  White Corpuscles in Europe
Walter M. Horton (1895——)
  Our Eternal Contemporary
  God
  Revelation
Douglas V. Steere (1901——)
  Prayer and Worship
  On Beginning from Within
Clarence Seidenspinner (1904——)
  Form and Freedom in Worship
  Our Dwelling Place
Philippe Vernier (1909——)
  Not as the World Giveth
  With the Master

1947   World Conference of Christian Youth in Oslo. Growing tension between Western civilization and Russian communism.

1948   Constituent Assembly of World Council of Churches at Amsterdam.

INDEX OF AUTHORS